W9-BTG-174

CRITICAL SURVEY OF
Poetry
Fourth Edition

Topical Essays

CRITICAL SURVEY OF
Poetry
Fourth Edition

Topical Essays

Volume 1
African American Poetry—Latino Poetry

Editor, Fourth Edition
Rosemary M. Canfield Reisman
Charleston Southern University

SALEM PRESS
Pasadena, California
Hackensack, New Jersey

RENFRO LIBRARY
MARS HILL UNIVERSITY
MARS HILL, NC 28754

Editor in Chief: Dawn P. Dawson

Editorial Director: Christina J. Moose

Development Editor: Tracy Irons-Georges

Project Editor: Rowena Wildin

Manuscript Editor: Desiree Dreeuws

Acquisitions Editor: Mark Rehn

Editorial Assistant: Brett S. Weisberg

Research Supervisor: Jeffry Jensen

Research Assistant: Keli Trousdale

Production Editor: Andrea E. Miller

Page Design: James Hutson

Layout: Mary Overell

Photo Editor: Cynthia Breslin Beres

Cover photo: Milton's *Paradise Lost* (The Granger Collection, New York)

Copyright ©1983, 1984, 1987, 1992, 2003, 2011, by SALEM PRESS

All rights in this book are reserved. No part of this work may be used or reproduced in any manner whatsoever or transmitted in any form or by any means, electronic or mechanical, including photocopy, recording, or any information storage and retrieval system, without written permission from the copyright owner except in the case of brief quotations embodied in critical articles and reviews or in the copying of images deemed to be freely licensed or in the public domain. For information, address the publisher, Salem Press, at csr@salemspress.com.

Some of the essays in this work, which have been updated, originally appeared in the following Salem Press publications, *Critical Survey of Poetry, English Language Series* (1983), *Critical Survey of Poetry: Foreign Language Series* (1984), *Critical Survey of Poetry, Supplement* (1987), *Critical Survey of Poetry, English Language Series, Revised Edition*, (1992; preceding volumes edited by Frank N. Magill), *Critical Survey of Poetry, Second Revised Edition* (2003; edited by Philip K. Jason).

∞ The paper used in these volumes conforms to the American National Standard for Permanence of Paper for Printed Library Materials, X39.48-1992 (R1997).

Library of Congress Cataloging-in-Publication Data

Critical survey of poetry. — 4th ed. / editor, Rosemary M. Canfield Reisman.

    v. cm.

Includes bibliographical references and index.

    ISBN 978-1-58765-582-1 (set : alk. paper) — ISBN 978-1-58765-763-4 (set : topical essays : alk. paper) — ISBN 978-1-58765-764-1 (v. 1 : topical essays : alk. paper) — ISBN 978-1-58765-765-8 (v. 2 : topical essays : alk. paper)

1. Poetry—History and criticism—Dictionaries. 2. Poetry—Bio-bibliography. 3. Poets—Biography—Dictionaries. I. Reisman, Rosemary M. Canfield.

    PN1021.C7 2011

    809.1'003—dc22

2010045095

First Printing

PRINTED IN THE UNITED STATES OF AMERICA

NOV 2 8 2017

R
809.1
C9348+
v.1

PUBLISHER'S NOTE

Topical Essays is part of Salem Press's greatly expanded and redesigned *Critical Survey of Poetry* Series. The *Critical Survey of Poetry, Fourth Edition*, presents profiles of major poets, with sections on other literary forms, achievements, biography, general analysis, and analysis of the poet's most important poems or collections. Although the profiled authors may have written in other genres as well, sometimes to great acclaim, the focus of this set is on their most important works of poetry.

The *Critical Survey of Poetry* was originally published in 1983 and 1984 in separate English- and foreign-language series, a supplement in 1987, a revised English-language series in 1992, and a combined revised series in 2003. The *Fourth Edition* includes all poets from the previous edition and adds 145 new ones, covering 843 writers in total. The poets covered in this set represent more than 40 countries and their poetry dates from the eighth century B.C.E. to the present. The set also offers 72 informative overviews; 20 of these essays were added for this edition, including all the literary movement essays. In addition, 7 resources are provided, 2 of them new. More than 500 photographs and portraits of poets have been included.

For the first time, the material in the *Critical Survey of Poetry* has been organized into five subsets by geography and essay type: a 4-volume subset on *American Poets*, a 3-volume subset on *British, Irish, and Commonwealth Poets*, a 3-volume subset on *European Poets*, a 1-volume subset on *World Poets*, and a 2-volume subset of *Topical Essays*. Each poet appears in only one subset. *Topical Essays* is organized under the categories "Poetry Around the World," "Literary Movements," and "Criticism and Theory." A *Cumulative Indexes* volume covering all five subsets is free with purchase of more than one subset.

TOPICAL ESSAYS

The 2-volume *Topical Essays* contains 72 overviews, 20 of which are new for this edition and 7 of which have been updated by the editor, Rosemary M.

Canfield Reisman. The editor updated the bibliographies on the remaining previously published essays, which were reedited by the editors at Salem Press, to make sure all information in the text was current and accurate.

Each volume begins with a list of Contents for that volume and a Complete List of Contents covering the entire subset. The essays are divided into "Poetry Around the World," "Literary Movements," and "Criticism and Theory," and are divided between the two volumes.

The second volume contains the Resources section, which features three tools for interpreting and understanding poetry: "Explicating Poetry," "Language and Linguistics," and "Glossary of Poetical Terms." The Bibliography, Guide to Online Resources, Time Line, and Major Awards provide guides for further research and additional information on poets and poetry and are comprehensive versions covering all poets profiled in *Critical Survey of Poetry*. The Guide to Online Resources and Time Line were created for this edition.

Topical Essays contains a Geographical Index of Essays, in which essays are grouped by geographical area, and a Subject Index. The *Critical Survey of Poetry* Series: Master List of Contents lists all poets profiled in the complete series. *Topical Essays* does not contain a categorized index, but all categorized essays in this subset are included in the Categorized Index of Poets and Essays in the *Cumulative Indexes*, which also contains a comprehensive version of the Subject Index.

ONLINE ACCESS

Salem Press provides access to its award-winning content both in traditional, printed form and online. Any school or library that purchases *Topical Essays* is entitled to free, complimentary access to Salem's fully supported online version of the content. Features include a simple intuitive interface, user profile areas for students and patrons, sophisticated search functionality, and complete context, including appendixes. Access is available through a code printed on the inside cover of the first volume, and that access is unlimited and immediate. Our online customer service representatives, at (800) 221-1592, are happy to help with any questions. E-books are also available.

ORGANIZATION OF TOPICAL ESSAYS

The overviews in *Topical Essays* vary in length, with none shorter than 2,000 words and most significantly longer. The essays are grouped into three sections, "Essays Around the World," "Literary Movements," and "Criticism and Theory." Each essay contains numerous subheads to aid comprehension and ease of finding information. A date of publication is provided for each title mentioned in the text. Foreign language titles are accompanied by their date of publication, first English publication and its date, or a literal translation of the title (lower case and in parentheses). A bibliography and bylines complete the essay.

- *Essays Around the World* covers geographical areas and cultural identities. Two new essays, "Australian and New Zealand Poetry" and "Canadian Poetry," were added to 45 essays from the previous edition. The overviews discuss poetry from cultures such as African Americans, Latino Americans, and Asian Americans, and from geographical areas such as China, Croatia, England, France, Hungary, Poland, Russia, and Scandinavia.
- *Literary Movements* contains 14 new overviews, arranged in approximate chronological order, describing literary movements and schools such as the Metaphysical poets, Restoration poetry, Fireside poets, French Symbolists, Modernists, Harlem Renaissance, New York School, and the Black Mountain School.
- *Criticism and Theory* contains 11 overviews that examine various methods and schools of criticism and poetic theory. This section features 4 new essays: "Cultural Criticism," "New Historicism," "Postcolonial Criticism," and "Queer Theory."
- *Bibliography* lists secondary print sources for further study, annotated to assist users in evaluating focus and usefulness.
- *Byline* notes the original contributor of the essay. If the essay was updated, the name of the most recent

updater appears in a separate line and previous updaters appear with the name of the original contributor.

APPENDIXES

The "Resources" section in volume 2 provides tools for further research and points of access to the wealth of information contained in *Critical Survey of Poetry*.

- *Explicating Poetry* identifies the basics of versification, from meter to rhyme, in an attempt to demonstrate how sound, rhythm, and image fuse to support meaning.
- *Language and Linguistics* looks at the origins of language and at linguistics as a discipline, as well as how the features of a particular language affect the type of poetry created.
- *Glossary of Poetical Terms* is a lexicon of more than 150 literary terms pertinent to the study of poetry.
- *Bibliography*, which combines the bibliographies from the poet subsets, identifies general reference works and other secondary sources that pertain to poets and poetry.
- *Guide to Online Resources*, which combines the guides from the poet subsets and is new to this edition, provides Web sites pertaining to poetry and poets.
- *Time Line*, which combines the time lines from the poet subsets and is new to this edition, lists major milestones and events in poetry and literature in the order in which they occurred.
- *Major Awards*, which combines the awards from the poet subsets, lists the recipients of major poetry-specific awards and general awards where applicable to poets or poetry, from inception of the award to the present day.

INDEXES

The Geographical Index of Essays lists the overviews by geographical region, including France, Japan, Russia, and the United States. The *Critical Survey of Poetry* Series: Master List of Contents lists all poets profiled in the complete series. The Subject Index lists all titles, authors, subgenres, and literary movements or terms that receive substantial discussion in *Topical Essays*.

ACKNOWLEDGMENTS

Salem Press is grateful for the efforts of the original contributors of these essays and those of the outstanding academicians who provided updates for previous editions or wrote new material for the set. Their names and affiliations are listed in the "Contributors" section that follows. Finally, we are indebted to our editor, Professor Rosemary M. Canfield Reisman of Charleston Southern University, for her development of the table of contents for the *Critical Survey of Poetry, Fourth Edition* and her advice on updating the original articles to make this comprehensive and thorough revised edition an indispensable tool for students, teachers, and general readers alike.

Contributors

L. Michelle Baker
The Catholic University of America

Stanisław Barańczak
Harvard University

David Barratt
Montreat College

Walton Beacham
Beacham Publishing Corp.

Elizabeth J. Bellamy
Winthrop College

Richard P. Benton
Trinity College

Eleanor von Auw Berry
Milwaukee, Wisconsin

Dorothy M. Betz
Georgetown University

Nicholas Birns
Eugene Lang College, The New School

Franz G. Blaha
University of Nebraska-Lincoln

Patricia J. Boehne
Eastern College

András Boros-Kazai
Beloit College

Mitzi M. Brunsdale
Mayville State College

Richard J. Calhoun
Clemson University

Carole A. Champagne
University of Maryland-Eastern Shore

Balance Chow
San Jose State University

Robert Colucci
Pittsburgh, Pennsylvania

Peter Constantine
New York, New York

Anita Price Davis
Converse College

Dennis R. Dean
University of Wisconsin-Parkside

Lillian Doherty
University of Maryland

Paul A. Draghi
Indiana University

Desiree Dreeuws
Sunland, California

Robert P. Ellis
Worcester State College

Ann Willardson Engar
University of Utah

David L. Erben
University of South Florida

John Miles Foley
University of Missouri

Thomas C. Foster
University of Michigan-Flint

Vincent F. A. Golphin
The Writing Company

Sarah Hilbert
Pasadena, California

John R. Holmes
Franciscan University of Steubenville

Donald D. Hook
Trinity College

Tracy Irons-Georges
Glendale, California

Maura Ives
Texas A&M University

Gerald Janecek
University of Kentucky

Helen Jaskoski
California State University, Fullerton

Irma M. Kashuba
Chestnut Hill College

Richard Keenan
University of Maryland-Eastern Shore

Rebecca Kuzins
Pasadena, California

John Richard Law
Auburn University

Robert W. Leutner
University of Iowa

Dieter P. Lotze
Allegheny College

R. C. Lutz
CII Group

Joseph McLaren
Hofstra University

Richard Peter Martin
Princeton University

Laurence W. Mazzeno
Alvernia College

Julia M. Meyers
Duquesne University

Vasa D. Mihailovich
University of North Carolina

Christina J. Moose
Pasadena, California

Charmaine Allmon Mosby
Western Kentucky University

Joseph Natoli
Irvine, California

Holly L. Norton
University of Northwestern Ohio

Arsenio Orteza
WORLD Magazine

Makarand Paranjape
Indian Institute of Technology

Ward Parks
Louisiana State University

David Peck
Laguna Beach, California

Peter Petro
University of British Columbia

Ralph Reckley, Sr.
Morgan State University

Rosemary M. Canfield Reisman
Charleston Southern University

J. Thomas Rimer
University of Pittsburgh

Dorothy Dodge Robbins
Louisiana Tech University

Nancy Weigel Rodman
Minneapolis, Minnesota

Carl Rollyson
*Baruch College, City University of
New York*

Joseph Rosenblum
Greensboro, North Carolina

Robert L. Ross
University of Texas-Austin

Sven H. Rossel
University of Vienna

Patrizio Rossi
*University of California,
Santa Barbara*

Joachim Scholz
Washington College

Jack Shreve
Allegany Community College

Thomas J. Sienkewicz
Monmouth College

Richard Spuler
Rice University

James Stone
Shaker Heights, Ohio

Michael L. Storey
Baltimore, Maryland

Karen Van Dyck
Columbia University

Albert Wachtel
Pitzer College

Catharine E. Wall
University of California, Riverside

Craig Werner
University of Wisconsin

Shawncey Webb
Taylor University

James Whitlark
Texas Tech University

Gary Zacharias
Palomar College

Gay Pitman Zieger
Santa Fe College

CONTENTS

COMPLETE LIST OF CONTENTS

VOLUME 1

VOLUME 2

POETRY AROUND THE WORLD

AFRICAN AMERICAN POETRY

The struggle for freedom—social, psychological, and aesthetic—is the distinguishing attribute of African American poetry from its origins during slavery through its pluralistic flowering in the twentieth century. Although the impact of the struggle has only intermittently been simple or direct, it has remained a constant presence, both for writers concentrating directly on the continuing oppression of the black community and for those forging highly individualistic poetic voices not primarily concerned with racial issues.

Generally, two basic "voices" characterize the African American poetic sensibility. First, black poets attempting to survive in a literary market dominated by white publishers and audiences have felt the need to demonstrate their ability to match the accomplishments of white poets in traditional forms. From the couplets of Phillis Wheatley through the sonnets of Claude McKay to the modernist montages of Robert Hayden to the rap and hip-hop stylings of Queen Latifah, Public Enemy, Ice-T, Mos Def, Tupac Shakur, and KRS-One, African American poets have mastered the full range of voices associated with the evolving poetic mainstream. Second, black poets have been equally concerned with forging distinctive voices reflecting both their individual sensibilities and the specifically African American cultural tradition.

This dual focus within the African American sensibility reflects the presence of what W. E. B. Du Bois identified as a "double-consciousness" that forces the black writer to perceive himself or herself as both an "American" and a "Negro." The greatest African American poets—Langston Hughes, Sterling A. Brown, Gwendolyn Brooks, Robert Hayden, Amiri Baraka, Maya Angelou, Rita Dove, Yusef Komunyakaa, and Kevin Powell—draw on this tension as a source of both formal and thematic power, helping them to construct a poetry that is at once unmistakably black and universally resonant.

CAGED EAGLES

From the beginning, African American poets have continually adjusted to and rebelled against the fact of double consciousness. To be sure, the rebellion and adjustment have varied in form with changing social circumstances. Nevertheless, Baraka's statement in his poetic drama *Bloodrites* (pr. 1970) that the aware black artist has always been concerned with helping his or her community attain "Identity, Purpose, Direction" seems accurate. Over a period of time, the precise emphasis has shifted among the terms, but the specific direction and purpose inevitably reflect the individual's or the era's conception of identity. To some extent, this raises the issue of whether the emphasis in "African American" belongs on "African" or on "American." Some poets, such as Baraka during his nationalist period, emphasize the African heritage and tend toward assertive and frequently separatist visions of purpose and direction. Others, such as Jean Toomer in his late period, emphasize some version of the "American" ideal and embrace a variety of strategies for the purpose of reaching a truly integrated society.

Wheatley, the first important African American poet, was forced to confront this tension between African and American identities. As an "American" poet of the eighteenth century—before the political entity known as the United States was formed—her writing imitated the styles and themes of British masters such as John Milton, John Dryden, and Alexander Pope. Brought to America at age six, she experienced only a mild form of slavery in Philadelphia, because her owners, Thomas and Susannah Wheatley, felt deep affection for her and respected her gifts as a writer. Unlike other Wheatley servants, Phillis, treated more as a stepdaughter than as a servant, was exempted from routine duties and had a private room, books, and writing materials. At the same time, her career was hobbled by the blatant discrimination heaped on all "African" people. For example, in 1772, Susannah Wheatley sought patrons to help publish the then eighteen-year-old Phillis's first collection of twenty-eight poems. Colonial whites rejected the proposal because Phillis was a slave, forcing her to seek a publisher in London.

Although her poem "On Being Brought from Africa to America" views slavery as a "mercy," because it led

Phillis Wheatley (Library of Congress)

her from "pagan" darkness to Christian light, she was never accepted as a poet on her own merits. However, in England, whose antislavery movement was stronger than that of the colonies, people of wealth and stature, such as the countess of Huntingdon and the earl of Dartmouth, embraced the poet. Lady Huntingdon, to whom Wheatley's first volume, *Poems on Various Subjects, Religious and Moral* (1773), was dedicated, financed the publication and put Phillis's picture on the frontispiece. Wheatley's work was advertised as the product of a "sable muse," and she was presented as a curiosity; the racism of the times made it impossible for her to be accepted as a poet who was as accomplished as her white contemporaries. That sentiment was made clear by Thomas Jefferson in his *Notes on the State of Virginia* (1777): "Religion indeed has produced a Phyllis Whately [sic] but it could not produce a poet. The compositions published under her name are below the dignity of criticism." Those sentiments are counterbalanced by a contemporary, Jupiter Hammon, also a slave poet, who in "An Address to Miss Phillis Whealy

[sic]" praised her talent and influence as part of God's providence:

> While thousands tossed by the sea,
> And others settled down,
> God's tender mercy set thee free,
> From dangers that come down.

Other early writers, such as George Moses Horton and Frances Watkins Harper, shared a common purpose in their antislavery poetry but rarely escaped the confines of religious and political themes acceptable to the abolitionist journals that published their work. The pressures on the African American poet became even more oppressive during the post-Reconstruction era as the South "reconquered" black people, in part by establishing control over the literary image of slavery. "Plantation Tradition" portrayed contented slaves and benevolent masters living in pastoral harmony. Paul Laurence Dunbar attained wide popularity in the late nineteenth and early twentieth centuries, but only by acquiescing partially in the white audience's stereotypical preconceptions concerning the proper style (slave dialect) and tones (humor or pathos) for poetry dealing with black characters.

A VOICE OF THEIR OWN

Spearheading the first open poetic rebellion against imposed stereotypes, James Weldon Johnson, a close friend of Dunbar, mildly rejected Dunbar's dialect poetry in his preface to *The Book of American Negro Poetry* (1922), which issued a call for "a form that will express the racial spirit by symbols from within rather than by symbols from without." He explained:

The newer Negro poets discard dialect; much of the subject matter which went into the making of traditional dialect poetry, 'possums, watermelons, etc., they have discarded altogether, at least, as poetical material. This tendency will, no doubt, be regretted by the majority of white readers; and indeed, it would be a distinct loss if the American Negro poets threw away this quaint and musical folk-speech as a medium of expression. And yet, after all, these poets are working through a problem not realized by the reader, and perhaps, by many of these poets themselves not realized consciously. They are trying to break away, not from the Negro dialect itself, but the limitations on the Negro dialect imposed by the fixing effects of long convention.

The Negro in the United States has achieved or been placed in a certain artistic niche. When he is thought of artistically, it is as a happy-go-lucky, singing, shuffling, banjo-picking being or as a more or less pathetic figure. The African American poet realizes that there are phases of Negro life in the United States which cannot be treated in the dialect either adequately or artistically. Take, for example, the phases rising out of life in Harlem, that most wonderful Negro city in the world. I do not deny that a Negro in a log cabin is more picturesque than a Negro in a Harlem flat, but the Negro is here, and he is part of a group growing everywhere in the country, a group whose ideals are becoming increasingly more vital than those of the traditionally artistic group, even if its members are less picturesque.

HARLEM RENAISSANCE

This call was heeded by the poets of the Harlem Renaissance, who took advantage of the development of large black population centers in the North during the Great Northern Migration of blacks from the rural South to the urban North during the 1910's and 1920's. Where earlier poets lived either among largely illiterate slave populations or in white communities, the New Negroes—as Alain Locke, one of the first major black critics, labeled the writers of the movement—seized the opportunity to establish a sense of identity for a sizable black audience. Locke viewed the work of poets such as Claude McKay, Countée Cullen, and Jean Toomer as a clear indication that blacks were preparing for a full entry into the American cultural mainstream.

The support given Harlem Renaissance writers by such white artists and patrons as Carl Van Vechten and Nancy Cunard, however, considerably complicated the era's achievement. On one hand, it appeared to herald the merging predicted by Locke. On the other, it pressured individual black writers to validate the exoticism frequently associated with black life by the white onlookers. Cullen's "Heritage," with its well-known refrain "What is Africa to me?," reflects the sometimes arbitrarily enforced consciousness of Africa that pervades the decade. African American artists confronted with white statements such as Eugene O'Neill's "All God's Chillun Got Wings" could not help remaining

acutely aware that they, like Wheatley 150 years earlier, were cast more as primitive curiosities than as sophisticated artists. However, an expansion in the American literary canon and evolution in African American literature could not be denied. It was celebrated in the March, 1925, issue of Van Vechten's literary journal, *Survey Graphic*, guest-edited by Locke, who was then a Howard University philosophy professor.

The first flowering of Harlem as an artistic center came to an end with the Great Depression of the 1930's, which redirected African American creative energies toward political concerns. The end of prosperity brought a return of hard times to the African American community and put an end to the relatively easy access to print for aspiring black writers.

THE 1930'S

If the Harlem Renaissance was largely concerned with questions of identity, the writing in Hughes's *A New Song* (1938) and Brown's *Southern Road* (1932) reflects a new concern with the purpose and direction of both black artists and black masses. Hughes had earlier addressed the caution in an essay, "The Negro Artist and the Racial Mountain," published in the June 23, 1926, issue of *The Nation*:

> The Negro artist works against an undertow of sharp criticism from his own group and unintentional bribes from the whites. But in spite of the Nordicized Negro intelligentsia and the desires of some white editors we have an honest American Negro literature already with us. . . . I am ashamed for the black poet who says, "I want to be a poet, not a Negro poet," as though his own racial world were not as interesting as any other world. An artist must be free to choose what he does, certainly, but he must also never be afraid to do what he might choose.

Whereas many of the Harlem Renaissance writers had accepted Du Bois's vision of a "talented tenth" who would lead the community out of cultural bondage, the 1930's writers revitalized the African American tradition that perceived the source of power—poetic and political—in traditions of the "folk" community. Margaret Walker's "For My People" expresses the ideal community "pulsing in our spirits and our blood." This emphasis sometimes coincided or overlapped with the proletarian and leftist orientation that dominated African American fiction of the period. Again external events, this time World War II and the "sell-out" of blacks by the American Communist Party, brought an end to an artistic era.

THE POSTWAR ERA

The post-World War II period of African American poetry is more difficult to define in clear-cut terms. Many new poets became active, especially during the 1960's and 1970's, while poets such as Hughes and Brown, who had begun their careers earlier, continued as active forces. Nevertheless, it is generally accurate to refer to the period from the late 1940's through the early 1960's as one of universalism and integration, and that of the mid-1960's through the mid-1970's as one of self-assertion and separatism.

The return of prosperity, landmark court decisions, and the decline of legal segregation in the face of nonviolent protest movements created the feeling during the early postwar period that African American culture might finally be admitted into the American mainstream on an equal footing. Poets such as Brooks, who became the first black person to win the Pulitzer Prize in poetry—for *Annie Allen* (1949)—and Hayden, who later became the first black Library of Congress poet, wrote poetry that was designed to communicate to all readers, regardless of their racial backgrounds and experiences. Neither poet abandoned black materials or traditions, but neither presented a surface texture that would present difficulties for an attentive white reader. Brooks's poem "Mentors" typifies the dominant style of the "universalist" period. It can be read with equal validity as a meditation on death, a comment on the influence of artistic predecessors, a commitment to remember the suffering of the slave community, and a character study of a soldier returning home from war.

The universalist period also marked the first major assertion of modernism in black poetry. Although both Hughes and Toomer had earlier used modernist devices, neither was perceived as part of the mainstream of experimental writing, another manifestation of the critical ignorance that has haunted black poets since Wheatley. Hayden and Melvin B. Tolson adopted the radical prosody of T. S. Eliot and Ezra Pound, while Baraka, Bob Kaufman, and Ted Joans joined white poets in New York and San Francisco in forging a multiplicity of postmodernist styles, many of them rooted in African American culture, especially jazz.

THE BLACK ARTS MOVEMENT

As in the 1920's, however, the association of black poets with their white counterparts during the 1950's and 1960's generated mixed results. Again, numerous black writers believed that they were accepted primarily as exotics and that the reception of their work was racially biased. With the development of a strong Black Nationalist political movement, exemplified by Malcolm X (who was to become the subject of more poems by African American writers than any other individual), many of the universalist poets turned their attention to a poetry that would directly address the African American community's concerns in a specifically black voice. LeRoi Jones changed his name to Amiri Baraka and placed the term "Black Arts" in the forefront as an indicator of a new cultural aesthetic in the poem "Black Dada Nihilismus." Brooks announced her conversion to a pan-Africanist philosophy, and community arts movements sprang up in cities throughout the United States.

A major movement of young black poets, variously referred to as the New Black Renaissance or the Black Arts movement, rejected involvement with Euro-American culture and sought to create a new black aesthetic that would provide a specifically black identity, purpose, and direction. Poets such as Haki R. Madhubuti (Don L. Lee), Sonia Sanchez, Nikki Giovanni, and Etheridge Knight perceived their work primarily in relation to a black audience, publishing with black houses such as Broadside Press of Detroit and Third World Press of Chicago. Most poets of the Black Arts movement remained active after the relative decline of the Black Nationalist impulse in the late 1970's and 1980's, but, with such notable exceptions as Madhubuti, their tone generally became more subdued. They have been joined in prominence by a group of poets, many of whom also began writing in the 1960's, who have strong affinities with the modernist wing of the universalist period. If Madhubuti, Knight, and

Giovanni are largely populist and political in sensibility, poets such as Michael S. Harper, Ai, and Jay Wright are more academic and aesthetic in orientation. Although their sensibilities differ markedly, all the poets asserted the strength of both the African American tradition and the individual voice.

A new pluralism began to emerge, testifying to the persistence of several basic values in the African American sensibility: survival, literacy, and freedom. The publication of the anthology *Black Fire* (1968), coedited by Baraka and Larry Neal, signaled the emergence of the new age. The shift in goals, simply put, was from the uplift of the black community to the transformation of American society. The collection made it clear that African American artists had moved beyond cultural navel gazing. The poets now defined themselves as a Third World people engaged in a global struggle. Neal's essay "The Black Arts Movement" became the period's manifesto:

Amiri Baraka (AP/Wide World Photos)

> National and international affairs demand that we appraise the world in terms of our own interests. It is clear that the question of human survival is at the core of contemporary experience. The black artist must address himself to this reality in the strongest terms possible. Consequently, the Black Arts Movement is an ethical movement. Ethical, that is, from the viewpoint of the oppressed. And much of the oppression confronting the Third World and black America is directly traceable to the Euro-American cultural sensibility. This sensibility, antihuman in nature, has, until recently, dominated the psyches of most black artists and intellectuals. It must be destroyed before the black creative artist can have a meaningful role in the transformation of society.

Even highly idiosyncratic poets, such as Toomer in "Blue Meridian" and Ishmael Reed in his "neo-hoo-doo" poems, endorsed those basic values, all of which originated in the experience of slavery. In his book *From Behind the Veil: A Study of Afro-American Narrative* (1979), Robert B. Stepto identifies the central heroic figure of the African American tradition as the "articulate survivor," who completes a symbolic ascent from slavery to a limited freedom, and the "articulate kinsman," who completes a symbolic immersion into his cultural roots. The articulate survivor must attain "literacy" as defined by the dominant white society; the articulate kinsman must attain "tribal literacy" as defined by the black community.

In the 1960's and 1970's, the American Civil Rights and subsequent Black Power movements breathed life into human rights struggles throughout the world. Poets in other parts of the African world began to be heard in the United States during the 1970's, which gave evidence that black bids for survival, literacy, and freedom were indeed universal. Derek Walcott of St. Lucia, South African Dennis Brutus, and Nigeria's Wole Soyinka were among the most important voices.

Walcott, like McKay a Jamaican, showed a reverence for the native Caribbean cultures. Another theme in his early work was outrage at the injustices of colonial rule. Beginning with *The Gulf, and Other Poems* (1969), the poet begins to grapple with ideological and political questions. The strength of the reflection grows in *Sea Grapes* (1976) and comes to full potency in *The Star-Apple Kingdom* (1979).

Brutus's first volume of poems, *Sirens, Knuckles, Boots* (1963), was published while he was doing an eighteen-month stretch on Robben Island, apartheid South Africa's most infamous jail. The equivalent of Alcatraz, it was considered escape-proof because of the water that separated its inmates from the mainland. After release in 1965, Brutus was exiled to London. The poet joined the Northwestern University English faculty in 1970. Three years later, *A Simple Lust* detailed for American audiences the horror of South African prisons and apartheid's injustices. The collection was also influenced by medieval European sensibilities and images. In the first poem of the collection, Brutus speaks in the voice of a troubadour who fights for his beloved against social injustice and betrayal. Even though outwardly European, the poem reverberates the sense of the heroic found in many American-born black writers' works.

Like these Caribbean and South African counterparts, American poets of African descent made reference to, but transformed, European influences. Maya Angelou's "Still I Rise" and Mari Evans's "Vive Noir!" convey the drama of knighthood's quests against an unjust society through plain language and images drawn from black environments. The works also toss aside traditional notions of grammar, spelling, and punctuation as a means to emphasize the rejection of conventional European sensibilities. Evans, for example, sick of the language of oppressors as much as the slums of inner cities, asserts she is

> weary
>> of exhausted lands
>> sagging privies
>> saying yessuh yessah
>> yesSIR
>> in an assortment
>> of geographical dialects

The Black Arts movement faded in the mid-1970's, without changing the world or stabilizing the growth it gave to African American consciousness. New Orleans poet Kalamu ya Salaam, in an essay in *The Oxford Companion to African American Literature* (1997), traced the beginning of the swan song to 1974:

> As the movement reeled from the combination of external and internal disruption, commercialization and capitalist co-option delivered the coup de grace. President

Richard Nixon's strategy of pushing Black capitalism as a response to Black Power epitomized mainstream co-option. As major film, record, book and magazine publishers identified the most salable artists, the Black Arts movement's already fragile independent economic base was totally undermined.

1970's-1990's

As in the 1930's, after the Harlem Renaissance subsided most of the independent publications, public forums, and other outlets for African American cultural expression had evaporated. Lotus Press and Broadside Press in Detroit and Third World Press in Chicago would continue to create outlets for excellent literature. White-owned book companies and magazines shifted focus to the movements for women's equality and against the Vietnam War. That set the stage for the emergence of Audre Lorde, Lucille Clifton, and Yusef Komunyakaa.

Lorde's *The Black Unicorn* (1978) used African symbols and myths to explore the dimensions within her existence. Adrienne Rich acknowledged the volume as a kind of declaration of independence: "Refusing to be circumscribed by any single identity, Audre Lorde writes as a Black woman, a mother, a daughter, a Lesbian, a feminist, a visionary." In an interview with editor Claudia Tate in *Black Women Writers at Work* (1983), Lorde averred the Black Arts movement's stress on representation of the global experience of blacks and the oppressed. Tossing aside previous notions that true African American art is political at its core, she sketched a vision of poetry as a reflection of the personal:

> Black men have come to believe to their detriment that you have no validity unless you're "global," as opposed to personal. Yet our *real power* comes from the personal; our real insights about living come from the deep knowledge within us that arises from our feelings. Our thoughts are shaped by our tutoring. We were tutored to function in a structure that already existed but that does not function for our good. Our feelings are our most genuine path to knowledge. Men have been taught to deal only with what they understand. This is what they respect. They know that somewhere feeling and knowledge are important, so they keep women around to do their feeling for them, like ants do aphids.

The African American poets who rose in prominence during the 1980's employed stylistic traditions that stretched back to Hughes and other Harlem Renaissance writers. The themes of survival and freedom remained pronounced in their works. The major difference was that, instead of grappling with outside forces, they confronted their nightmares.

Komunyakaa took on Vietnam. The Bogalusa, Louisiana, native won a Bronze Star for his service during the war as a writer and editor of the military newspaper *The Southern Cross*. His poem "Facing It," which reflects on a visit to the Vietnam Veterans Memorial in Washington, D.C., exposes the war as a personal bad dream: "My clouded reflection eyes me like a bird of prey, the profile of the night slanted against the morning." The poet becomes the black granite slab and the archetype of the tens of thousands of visitors. As the poem unfolds, it becomes clear that the conflict is a ghost that will haunt every American for generations.

In September, 1994, the largest gathering of black poets since the end of the Black Arts period was held in Harrisonburg, Virginia, at James Madison University. Thirty of the top black poets since the 1960's—old voices such as Baraka, Madhubuti, Sanchez, Giovanni, and Evans, and new voices such as E. Ethelbert Miller and Toi Derricotte—came together with more than 250 scholars, reporters, and critics. According to a report in *The Washington Post* (October 1), the one subject none of the writers wanted to discuss was what qualities set African American poetry apart from the mainstream. The reporter said that the poets "hate the question, because it reminds them of days when black poetry was relegated to the 'Negro' section of anthologies." However, each of these poets was living with the deep awareness that African American poets were still not equal members of an elitist literary establishment.

Literacy, frequently illegal under the slave codes, both increases the chance of survival and makes freedom meaningful. Tribal literacy protects the individual's racial identity against submersion in a society perceived as inhumane and corrupt. "The literature of an oppressed people is the conscience of man," wrote Lance Jeffers in an essay printed in the January, 1971, issue of the journal *Black Scholar*:

Audre Lorde (The Granger Collection, New York)

Nowhere is this seen with more intense clarity than the literature of Afroamerica. An essential element of Afroamerican literature is that the literature as a whole—not the work of occasional authors—is a movement against concrete wickedness. The cry for freedom and the protest against injustice are a cry for the birth of the New Man, a testament to the Unknown World (glory) to be discovered, to be created by man.

To a large extent, black poets writing in traditional forms established their literacy as part of a survival strategy in the white literary world. Those concerned with developing black forms demonstrate their respect for, and kinship with, the culturally literate African American community.

JUST PLAIN FOLKS

Against this complex of values and pressures, folk traditions have assumed a central importance in the development of the African American sensibility. Embodying the "tribal" wisdom concerning survival tactics and the meaning of freedom, they provide both formal and thematic inspiration for many black poets.

African American poets have become extremely adept at manipulating various masks. Originating with the trickster figures of African folklore and African American heroes such as Brer Rabbit, these masks provide survival strategies based on intellectual, rather than physical, strength.

Existing in a situation during slavery in which open rebellion could easily result in death, the slave community capitalized on the intimate knowledge of white psychology encouraged by the need to anticipate the master's wishes. The white community, conditioned not to see or take into account black needs and desires, possessed no equivalent knowledge of black psychology. Lacking knowledge, whites typically turned to comfortable stereotypes—the loyal mammy, the singing darkie, the tragic mulatto, the black beast—for their interpretation of black behavior. The observant slave found it both easy and rewarding to manipulate white perceptions of reality by appearing to correspond to a stereotypical role while quietly maneuvering for either personal or community gain. The nature of the mask, which exploits a phenomenon of double consciousness by controlling the discrepancy between black and white perspectives, is such that the true goal must always remain hidden from the white viewer, who must always feel that he is making the "real" decisions. Brer Rabbit asks not to be thrown in the briar patch; he will be allowed to escape, however, only if Brer Bear, the symbolic white man, believes that Brer Rabbit's mask is his true face.

This folk tradition of masking adds a specifically African American dimension to the standard poetic manipulation of persona. African American poets frequently adopt personas that, when viewed by white audiences, seem transparent incarnations of familiar stereotypes. Dunbar's dialect poetry and Hughes's Harlem street poems, for example, have been both accepted and dismissed by white readers as straightforward, realistic portraits of black life. An awareness of the complex ironies inherent in the African American folk traditions on which each drew, however, uncovers increasingly complex levels of awareness in their work. Dunbar's melodious dialect songs of plantation life contrast sharply with his complaint against a world that forced him to sing "a jingle in a broken tongue."

Similarly, his classic poem "We Wear the Mask" expresses the anguish of a people forced to adopt evasive presentations of self in a nation theoretically committed to pluralism and self-fulfillment. Less agonized than Dunbar, Hughes manipulates the surfaces of his poems, offering and refusing stereotypical images with dazzling speed. "Dream Boogie" first connects the image of the "dream deferred" with the marching feet of an army of the dispossessed, only to resume the mask of the smiling darkie in the sardonic concluding lines:

> What did I say?
> Sure,
> I'm happy!
> Take it away!
> Hey, pop!
> Re-bop!! Mop!
> Y-e-a-h!

The critical record gives strong evidence that Hughes is frequently taken at "face" value. His mask serves to affirm the existence of a black self in control of the rhythm of experience, as well as to satirize the limitations of the white perception.

Throughout the history of African American poetry, poets choosing to address the black political experience without intricate masks have been plagued by the assumption that their relevance was limited by their concentration on racial subject matter. Particularly in the twentieth century, a new stereotype—that of the "angry black" writer—has developed. The conditions of black life frequently do, in fact, generate anger and protest. African American poets, from Wheatley through Alberry Whitman in the late nineteenth century to Cullen and Giovanni, frequently protest against the oppression of blacks. McKay's sonnet "If We Must Die" embodies the basic impulse of this tradition, concluding with the exhortation, "Like men we'll face the murderous, cowardly pack,/ Pressed to the wall, dying, but fighting back!" Far from being limited by its origins in the African American experience, such poetry embraces a universal human drive for freedom. Winston Churchill quoted lines from the poem (ironically written partially in response to British exploitation of McKay's native Jamaica) during the early days of World

War II. The stereotype of the angry black, while based on a limited reality, becomes oppressive at precisely the point that it is confused with or substituted for the full human complexity of the individual poet. Giovanni, at times one of the angriest poets of the Black Arts movement, pinpoints the problem in her poem "Nikki-Rosa":

> I really hope no white person ever has cause to write about me because they never understand Black love is Black wealth and they'll probably talk about my hard childhood and never understand that all the while I was quite happy.

The drive for freedom transcends any single tone or mode. While frequently connected with the protest against specific conditions limiting social, psychological, or artistic freedom, the impulse modifies a wide range of poetic voices. At one extreme, explicitly political poems such as Baraka's "Black Art" call for "Poems that shoot/ guns." Even Baraka's less assertive poems, such as "For Hettie" or the more recent "Three Modes of History and Culture," seek to envision a world free from oppression. At another extreme, the drive for freedom lends emotional power to "apolitical" poems such as Dunbar's "Sympathy," with its refrain, "I know why the caged bird sings." Although the poem does not explicitly address racial issues, the intense feeling of entrapment certainly reflects Dunbar's position as a black poet subject to the stereotypes of white society. Similar in theme, but more direct in confronting racial pressures, Cullen's sonnet "Yet Do I Marvel," a masterpiece of irony, accepts the apparent injustices of creation, concluding: "Yet do I marvel at this curious thing/ To make a poet black, and bid him sing." Hughes's "Mother to Son" and "I, Too," with their determination to keep moving, reflect a more optimistic vision. Despite the hardships of life in a country that forces even the "beautiful" black man to "eat in the kitchen," Hughes's characters struggle successfully against despair. Significantly, many of Hughes's poems are very popular in the Third World. "I, Too," for example, has become a kind of anthem in Latin America, which honors Hughes as a major poet in the Walt Whitman tradition.

Whereas Hughes and Walker frequently treat freedom optimistically, Brown's "Memphis Blues" provides a stark warning of the ultimate destruction awaiting a society that fails to live up to its ideals. McKay's sonnet "America," with its echoes of Percy Bysshe Shelley's "Ozymandias," strikes a similar note, envisioning the nation's "priceless treasures sinking in the sand." Perhaps Hayden best embodies the basic impulse in his brilliant "Runagate Runagate," which employs a complex modernist voice to celebrate the mutually nourishing relationship between the anonymous fugitive slaves and the heroic figure of Harriet Tubman, who articulates and perpetuates their drive for freedom. Blending the voices of slavemasters, runaway slaves, the spirituals, and American mythology, Hayden weaves a tapestry that culminates in the insistent refrain, "Mean mean mean to be free."

Hayden's use of the anonymous voice of the runaway slave with the voice of the spirituals underscores both the drive for freedom and the nature of the individual hero who embodies the aspirations of the entire community. It exemplifies the importance of folk traditions as formal points of reference for the African American poetic sensibility.

MUSIC AND MESSAGE

Poets seeking to assert a specifically black voice within the context of the Euro-American mainstream repeatedly turn to the rhythms and imagery of folk forms such as spirituals and sermons. During the twentieth century, the blues and jazz assumed equal importance. As Stephen Henderson observes in *Understanding the New Black Poetry* (1973), these folk traditions provide both thematic and formal inspiration. Hayden's "Homage to the Empress of the Blues," Brown's "Ma Rainey," Brooks's "Queen of the Blues," and poems addressed to John Coltrane by Harper ("Dear John, Dear Coltrane," "A Love Supreme"), Madhubuti ("Don't Cry, Scream"), and Sanchez ("A Coltrane Poem") are only a few of countless African American poems invoking black musicians as cultural heroes. Bluesmen such as Robert Johnson (who wrote such haunting lyrics as "Crossroads," "Stones in My Passageway," and "If I Had Possession over Judgement Day") and singers such as Bessie Smith frequently assume the stature of folk heroes themselves. At their best they can legitimately be seen as true poets working with the vast reservoir of imagery inherent in African American folk life. Du Bois endorsed the idea by montaging passages of African American music with selections of Euro-American poetry at the start of each chapter of *The Souls of Black Folk* (1903). Similarly, Johnson's poem "O Black and Unknown Bards" credits the anonymous composers of the spirituals with a cultural achievement equivalent to that of Ludwig van Beethoven and Richard Wagner.

These folk and musical traditions have suggested a great range of poetic forms to African American poets. Johnson echoed the rhythms of black preaching in his powerful volume *God's Trombones: Seven Negro Sermons in Verse* (1927), which includes such classic "sermons" as "The Creation" and "Go Down Death—A Funeral Sermon." Hughes and Brown used their intricate knowledge of black musical forms in structuring their poetry. Early in his career, Hughes was content simply to imitate the structure of the blues stanza in poems such as "Suicide." As he matured, however, he developed more subtle strategies for capturing the blues impact in "The Weary Blues," which establishes a dramatic frame for several blues stanzas, and "Song for Billie." The latter mimics the subtle shifts in emphasis of the blues line by altering the order of prepositions in the stanza:

> What can purge my heart
> of the song
> and the sadness?
> What can purge my heart
> But the song
> of the sadness?
> What can purge my heart
> of the sadness
> of the song?

The persona moves from a stance of distance to one of identification and acceptance of the blues feeling. In merging emotionally with the singer, he provides a paradigm for the ideal relationship between artist and audience in the African American tradition.

Brown's blues poem "Ma Rainey" incorporates this call-and-response aspect of the blues experience into its frame story. Ma Rainey attains heroic stature be-cause her voice and vision echo those of the audience that gathers from throughout the Mississippi Delta to hear its experience authenticated. Brown's attempt to forge a voice that combines call and response points to what may be the central formal quest of African American poetry. Such an ideal voice seeks to inspire the community by providing a strong sense of identity, purpose, and direction. Simultaneously, it validates the individual experience of the poet by providing a sense of social connection in the face of what Ralph Ellison refers to as the "brutal experience" underlying the blues impulse. Both Ellison and Hughes, two of the most profound critics of the blues as a literary form, emphasize the mixture of tragic and comic worldviews in the blues. Hughes's definition of the blues attitude as "laughing to keep from crying" accurately reflects the emotional complexity of much blues poetry.

Like the blues, jazz plays a significant formal role in African American poetry. Poets frequently attempt to capture jazz rhythms in their prosody. Ambiguous stress patterns and intricate internal rhyme schemes make Brooks's "We Real Cool" and "The Blackstone Rangers" two of the most successful poems in this mode. Brown's "Cabaret" and Hughes's "Jazzonia" employ jazz rhythms to describe jazz performances. On occasion, poets such as Joans ("Jazz Must Be a Woman") and Baraka ("Africa Africa Africa") create "poems" that, like jazz charts, sketch a basic rhythmic or imagistic structure that provides a basis for improvisation during oral performance. Jazz may be most important to African American poetry, however, because of its implicit cultural pluralism. In his critical volume *Shadow and Act* (1964), Ellison suggests a profound affinity between the aesthetics of African American music and European American modernism: "At least as early as T. S. Eliot's creation of a new aesthetic for poetry through the artful juxtapositioning of earlier styles, Louis Armstrong, way down the river in New Orleans, was working out a similar technique for jazz." As Ellison suggests, jazz provides an indigenous source for an African American modernism incorporating voices from diverse cultural and intellectual sources. In effect, this enables the African American poet to transform the burden of double consciousness, as manifested in the traditions of masking and ironic voicing, into sources of aesthetic power.

Many of the masterworks of African American poetry, such as Hughes's "Montage for a Dream Deferred," Brooks's "In the Mecca," Hayden's "Middle Passage," and Jay Wright's "Dimensions of History," accomplish precisely this transformation. Choosing from the techniques and perceptions of both European American and African American traditions, these works incorporate the dreams and realities of the American tradition in all its diversity. Aware of the anguish resulting from external denial of self and heritage, the African American tradition recognizes the potential inherent in all fully lived experience. Hughes's vision of individuals living out a multiplicity of dreams within the American Dream testifies to his profound respect and love for the dispossessed.

The blend of the spoken word, politics, and music in the 1970's laid the foundations for rap music to become a major art form for social criticism. From Gil Scott-Heron's "The Revolution Will Not Be Televised" to Public Enemy's "Fight the Power," the rhymed critiques of life in America move beyond racial icons to indict anyone who turns away from the plight of the oppressed as the enemy. There is debate outside the community as to whether rappers are poets or song stylists. Even some successful African American writers look on the rap and hip-hop as clever wordplay, but lacking the discipline of traditional poetry. Nevertheless, anthologies edited by up-and-coming African American poets such as Kevin Powell and Clarence Gilyard suggest that the works of some of these artists deserve to be added to the American canon.

In 2008, when voters of all races chose an African American to be president of the United States, it could no longer be claimed that racism continued to block the achievement of the American democratic ideal. Though the people of the United States still had their flaws, and though economic and social injustices still existed, it was now evident that the dreams expressed more than sixty years before by one of America's greatest poets, the late Margaret Walker, could at last come true: A new world was being born, a world for the lovers of freedom, a world that would be large enough for everyone.

BIBLIOGRAPHY

Brown, Sterling. *Afro-Blue: Improvisations in African American Poetry and Culture*. Urbana: University of Illinois Press, 2003. A study of the influence of the blues tradition on African American speech, poetry, and thought, noting the three distinct types of blues poetics, as explained in chapters on Sterling A. Brown, Langston Hughes, and Jayne Cortez. Notes and index.

Chapman, Abraham, and Gwendolyn Brooks, eds. *Black Voices: Anthology of African-American Literature*. New York: Signet Classics, 2001. A reissue of a classic anthology. The book, first produced in two volumes in the late 1960's and early 1970's, was the first great collection of black writing. It pulls together poetry, fiction, autobiography and literary criticism, with informative, concise author biographies.

Harper, Michael S., and Anthony Walton, eds. *The Vintage Book of African American Poetry*. New York: Vintage, 2000. This anthology contains the works of fifty-two poets, presented chronologically, and includes not only those who are famous but also some who are undeservedly neglected. Brief but insightful introduction by the editors. Biographical headnotes.

Lee, Valerie, ed. *The Prentice Hall Anthology of African American Women's Literature*. Upper Saddle River, N.J.: Pearson Prentice Hall, 2006. A comprehensive collection, beginning with works written during the colonial and antebellum period and ending with the twenty-first century. A final section is devoted to feminist and womanist criticism. Map. Bibliography.

Liggins Hill, Patricia et al., eds. *The Riverside Anthology of the African American Literary Tradition*. New York: Houghton Mifflin, 1998. Contains 550 selections, ranging from African proverbs, folktales, and chants to works by contemporary authors such as Rita Dove.

Miller, E. Ethelbert. *Beyond the Frontier: African American Poetry for the Twenty-first Century*. Baltimore: Black Classic Press, 2002. An unusual collection of poems, relating the experiences of African Americans as people who are indeed pioneers, whether they are struggling for social justice or discovering that the secret of survival is the capacity to love. More than one hundred poets are included. Compact disc available.

Powell, Kevin, ed. *Step into a World: A Global Anthology of the New Black Literature*. New York: John Wiley & Sons, 2000. The broadest collection of hip-hop generation writers available. Includes fiction writers, poets, journalists, and commentators, as well as established authors such as Junot Diaz, Edwidge Danticat, Danyel Smith, and Paul Beatty.

Rampersad, Arnold, and Hilary Herbold, eds. *The Oxford Anthology of African-American Poetry*. New York: Oxford University Press, 2005. Poems from different time periods, written in a wide variety of styles, are grouped thematically, though alphabetized within each of the fifteen sections. The result is a unique vision of the African American poetic tradition. Biographies and index.

Schwarz, A. B. Christa. *Gay Voices of the Harlem Renaissance*. Bloomington: Indiana University Press, 2003. Schwarz examines the work of four leading writers from the Harlem Renaissance—Countée Cullen, Langston Hughes, Claude McKay, and Richard Bruce Nugent—and their sexually nonconformist or gay literary voices.

Thomas, Lorenzo. *Extraordinary Measures: Afrocentric Modernism and Twentieth-Century American Poetry*. Tuscaloosa: University of Alabama Press, 2000. A critical reappraisal of the development of African American poetry during the twentieth century, noting in particular the influence of literary movements such as modernism and the effects of radical changes in American society.

Craig Werner; Vincent F. A. Golphin
Updated by Rosemary M. Canfield Reisman

AFRICAN POETRY

African literature, including poetry, finds its roots in a long tradition of oral literature in native languages. With European colonial intrusions between the fourteenth and twentieth centuries, much literature from the continent was expressed in English, French, Portuguese, and other foreign languages, particularly Arabic in North Africa. Postcolonial literatures continue in a variety of languages and a combination of traditions.

ORAL TRADITIONS

Traditionally, oral poetry was produced by specialized, trained poets who were connected to kings, chiefs, spiritual figures, or secret societies. In addition, certain groups, such as hunters, farmers, cattle herders, and warriors, had designated poets. Oral poets were often descended from family lineages. A large body of oral poems from Africa has been recorded, translated, and published. Traditional oral poets recited in indigenous languages, such as Hausa, Yoruba, Ewe, Kongo, Igbo, Mandika, Fulani, Wolof, Zulu, Tswana, Gikuyu, and Swahili. Performance artistry—memorization, improvisation, and gesture—and audience response are part of the oral presentation, which has social and cultural significance. The oral poet who recites well-known pieces can introduce self-inspired innovations.

Used to honor and criticize, the most widely discussed form of oral poetry is the praise poem, generally associated with royal courts but also applicable to other social strata. Praise poetry is designated by such names as *oriki* (Yoruba), *maboko* (Tswana), *izibongo* (Zulu), and *ijala*, poetry of professional Yoruba hunters. Among the Akan, women are known for their proficiency in the funeral dirge. Usually, the praise poem of the court poet rendered historical lineage and stressed positive characteristics, but a poem of this nature could also remind the celebrated figure of responsibilities to the community. A "freelance" oral poet can offer praise and possibly criticism of individuals of lesser status. There are a number of names for oral poets: *griot* (Mandinka), *kwadwumfo* (Asante), *imbongi* (southern Africa), *azmaris* (Ethiopia), and *umusizi* (central Africa). The *umusizi* of Rwanda recited at ceremonial occasions such as births, initiations, and funerals. The spiritual role of certain oral poets is exemplified by the Yoruba *babalawo*, whose verse is distinctly musical. Yoruba *Ifa* divination, associated with the *Ifa* oracle, is expressed in verses. Among the forms of oral poetry, which can be accompanied by drums and stringed instruments, are elegies, lyrics, political pieces, and children's songs. In addition, such African epics as *Sundjata* (Gambia) and *The Epic of Liyongo* (Kenya) display oral influences. Though the authorship of older oral poetry is often unknown, certain individuals have been recognized, such as the eighteenth century Somali poet Ugaas Raage.

EARLY WRITTEN POETRY

The earliest written poetry can be represented by Egyptian hieroglyphs such as the obelisk inscriptions of Queen Hatshepsut, Eighteenth Dynasty. Other early written poetry by writers of African descent is in such languages as Arabic, Latin, Portuguese, Swahili, Amharic, and Hausa. Antar (sixth century) and Rukn al-Din Baibars (c. 1268-?) wrote in Arabic, suggesting the Islamic influence; Juan Latino (c. 1518-c. 1594) in Latin; and Domingos Caldas Barbosa (c. 1738-1800) in Portuguese. The Kenyan woman Mwana Kupona binti Msham (d. 1865), who wrote in Swahili, composed "Poem of Mwana Kupona" (1858), addressed to her daughter. Ethiopian Blatta Gäbrä Egzi'abehĕr (c. 1860-?), educated in Eritrea, is reputedly the first to have written Amharic poetry.

COLONIAL PERIOD

Paralleling the legacy of oral verse, modern African written poetry developed through a series of generations, each coming to prominence in successive eras encompassing the colonial, liberation, and independence periods. As a result of the political and cultural impact of European colonialism during the first half of the twentieth century, the path to poetic recognition involved writing in the dominant colonial languages, which influenced poetic style and form: English (anglophone), French (francophone), and Portuguese (lusophone). Some of the principal poets born between 1900 and 1930 were the Madagascan (francophone) Jean-Joseph Rabéarivelo; the Senegalese (francophone) Annette M'Baye d'Erneville; Ghanaians (anglophone) Gladys May Casely-Hayford, Michael Dei Anang, R. E. G. Armattoe, and Kwesi Brew; Nigerians (anglophone) Dennis Chukude Osadebay and Gabriel Okara; the Kenyan (anglophone) Marjorie Oludhe Macgoye; and South Africans (anglophone and indigenous language) H. I. E. Dhlomo, Benedict Wallet Vilakazi (who published poems in Zulu), and Dennis Brutus. Highly recognized, Rabéarivelo employed Madagascan song forms and techniques of the French Symbolists. In 1953, Okara's poem "The Call of the River Nun" earned for him the Nigerian Festival of Arts award. Banned under apartheid, Brutus's *Sirens, Knuckles, Boots* appeared in 1963. The lusophone poets of this period include Jorge Barbosa of Cape Verde, Antonio Agostinho Neto and Antonio Jacinto of Angola, Alda do Espírito Santo of São Tomé, and Noémia de Sousa of Mozambique, the first African woman poet to be internationally recognized. North Africa also produced a number of poets, such as imprisoned and tortured Algerian Anna Gréki (1931-1966), who published in Arabic and French.

NEGRITUDE

One of the most important developments was the negritude movement, at its height from the 1930's through the 1960's and influenced by America's Harlem Renaissance. The movement had Caribbean and African cadres. Decidedly francophone, negritude, a valorization of African racial identity and anticolonialism, was represented by such poets as Aimé Césaire of Martinique, Léon Damas of French Guiana, Jacques Roumain of Haiti, Édouard Maunick of Mauritius, Tchicaya U Tam'si of Congo, Birago Diop and Léopold Senghor of Senegal, and David Diop, born in France of Cameroonian and Senegalese parentage. Born in 1906, Sénghor, to become president of Senegal in 1960, emerged as one of the leading African poets writing in French. His advocacy of negritude is evident in his 1945 poem "Femme noire" ("Black Woman"): "And your beauty strikes me to the heart, like the flash of an eagle."

LIBERATION PERIOD

In the 1950's and 1960's, the period in which African countries gained liberation, there emerged a dynamic group of poets publishing in English, many of whom were born in the 1930's; some of them directly criticized negritude as romantic. This group included Ghanaian Kofi Awoonor; Ugandans Okot p'Bitek and Taban Lo Liyong; Nigerians Christopher Okigbo (influenced by T. S. Eliot and Ezra Pound), Wole Soyinka (a vocal critic of negritude), and John Pepper Clark-Bekederemo, who founded the poetry magazine *The Horn*; Malawian David Rubadiri; and Gambian Lenrie Peters. Okigbo's first collection, *Heavensgate* (1962), contributed to his legendary reputation as a committed liberation poet, and indeed he was killed in the Biafran War. P'Bitek's *Song of Lawino* (1966), translated into English from Acholi, was one of the most influential poems challenging Western cultural values. Awoonor authored many volumes of poetry, including *Night of My Blood* (1971). Among the South African writers were Mazisi Kunene (who wrote in both Zulu and English), Cosmo Pieterse, Keorapetse Kgositsile, Arthur Nortje, and Amelia Blossom Pegram. Titles such as Kgositsile's *Spirits Unchained* (1969) and Pegram's *Our Sun Will Rise: Poems for South Africa* (1989) exemplify the protest voice.

Many poets were published in such magazines as *Présence africaine*, *Transition*, and *Black Orpheus*. Certain poets have also been accomplished in other literary genres. Novelists Chinua Achebe, Ayi Kwei Armah, Ama Ata Aidoo, and Ben Okri, and dramatists Femi Osofisan and Nobel laureate Soyinka, author of *Idanre, and Other Poems* (1967), have published poetry of note. By the 1960's and 1970's, critical works and edited collections of African poetry began to appear, produced by such advocates as Janheinz Jahn, Gerald Moore, Ulli Beier, Donald Herdeck, Soyinka, and Langston Hughes. Among later editors of African poetry are Awoonor, Isidore Okpewho, Jack Mapanje, Frank and Stella Chipasula, Musaemura Zimunya, and Adewale Maja-Pearce.

POST-INDEPENDENCE POETRY

With independence, African poets accelerated their poetic production. By the 1980's numerous anthologies, representing various regions and scores of poets, had been published. Many of the poets born after World War II were especially concerned with political and social issues relating to their newly independent governments. Critical of the state, certain poets were imprisoned or forced into exile. Among those imprisoned for political reasons were Soyinka, Awoonor, Brutus, and, from the then "younger" generation, the highly acknowledged Mapanje of Malawi, who published, among other works, *Of Chameleons and Gods* (1981). South African poets such as Mongane Wally Serote and Frank Chipasula of Malawi chose exile. Serote's *Third World Express* (1992) is an extended poem with a global scope. Representing North Africa, Abdellatif Laâbi of Morocco published numerous collections in French. Political commitment to the "nation" and beyond is a distinguishing feature of post-independence poets.

A good number of postindependence poets have come from anglophone countries. Their poetic production has been furthered by the establishment of writers' organizations in such countries as Ghana, Nigeria, and Kenya. Among the most prolific and highly recognized poets are Niyi Osundare, Tanure Ojaide, Chimalum Nwankwo, Lemuel Johnson, Catherine Acholonu, and Ifi Amadiume of Nigeria; Atukwei Okai, Kofi Anyidoho, Kojo Laing, and Kobena Eyi Acquah of Ghana; Mapanje, Steve Chimombo, Lupenga Mphande, and Frank Chipasula of Malawi; Syl Cheney-Coker of Sierra Leone; Serote of South Africa; Tijan Sallah of Gambia; Jared Angira of Kenya; and Zimunya and Chenjerai Hove of Zimbabwe. Holding advanced degrees, many of these poets have written critically, have been editors, and have taught at academic institutions in the United States, Europe, or Africa. For a variety of personal and political reasons, a good number of the post-independence-generation poets reside in the West.

Anyidoho addresses the African diaspora in *AncestralLogic and CaribbeanBlues* (1993), and Ojaide, a well-published literary critic, was the recipient of the Alliance Africa Okigbo Prize for Poetry. Ojaide's *The Fate of Vultures, and Other Poems* (1990) contains the award-winning title poem "The Fate of Vultures," a striking critique of political materialism. Amadiume's

Dennis Brutus (AP/Wide World Photos)

Passion Waves (1986) was followed by her critical work *Male Daughters, Female Husbands* (1987). Commonwealth Poetry Prize recipient Osundare was recognized for such works as *The Eye of the Earth* (1986), concerned with the environment. The end of the twentieth century generated still-to-be-recognized poets such as Solomon Omo-Osagie II of Nigeria and Kwame Okoampa-Ahoofe, Jr., of Ghana.

Most important, the 1980's and 1990's were marked by the recognition of female poets, who address gender and patriarchy, themes generally overlooked by their male counterparts. Representative of this group are Pegram, Lindiwe Mabuza, and Zindzi Mandela of South Africa; Amina Saïd of Tunisia; Ama Ata Aidoo, Naana Banyiwa Horne, and Abena Busia of Ghana; Molara Ogundipe-Leslie, Rashidah Ismaili, Amadiume, and Catherine Acholonu of Nigeria; Kristina Rungano of Zimbabwe; Stella Chipasula of Malawi; and Micere Githae Mugo of Kenya. Micere Mugo's "Wife of the

Husband," from *Daughter of My People, Sing* (1976), questions traditional marriage symbolized by "His snores," and Busia's *Testimonies of Exile* (1990) voices African feminism, expressed in the poem "Liberation": "For we are not tortured/ anymore." Concerned with state injustices, Mabuza's "Death to the Gold Mine!" (1991) recalls the shooting of mine workers by South African police through such images as "the calcified bones in the ridges." The younger guard of women poets includes Iman Mirsal of Egypt and Mabel Tobrise of Nigeria.

At the beginning of the twenty-first century, however, though more women poets were finding their way into publication, they still suffered from the sexist attitudes that had long been basic in African culture. While women might be idealized as earth-mothers, they were still not considered the intellectual equals of men. As a result, the works of women poets received little attention from critics and were not widely known in Africa, much less globally. One of the first attempts to remedy this problem was made by Irene Assiba d'Almeida and her colleague and translator, Janis A. Mayes, whose anthology *A Rain of Words: A Bilingual Anthology of Women's Poetry in Francophone Africa* (2009) was the first book of its kind. By making the works of women poets widely available, d'Almeida and Mayes took an important step toward the revision of the literary canon, which still excluded most women poets.

FORMS AND THEMES

The form of oral poems is not limited to set patterns of lines or rhythms. A good number of them are literally songs containing poetic elements such as rhyme, assonance, and alliteration. However, when transcribed and printed in European languages, oral poetry resembles free verse. Repetition is a common device of the praise poem, whose rhythm can reflect the tonal qualities of certain African languages. Written poetry of the colonial era borrows from oral poetry and European style; there is a modernist quality to the body of twentieth century African poetry—most notably the absence of rhyme. The Hausa oral poem "Ali, Lion of the World!" uses repetition effectively, as does modernist Cheney-Coker in "The Hunger of the Suffering Man" (1980).

A functional art, African poetry in its oral and written forms has addressed a variety of themes, including worldview, mysticism, values, religion, nature, negritude, personal relationships, anticolonialism, pan-Africanism, neocolonialism, urbanism, migration, exile, the African diaspora, and patriarchy, as well as such universals as valor, birth, death, betrayal, and love. Religious poetry is exemplified by Islamic influences in such languages as Arabic, Hausa, and Swahili and in *Ifa* oral verses. A primary motif is the spiritual world, often reflected in a praise or evocation of ancestors.

Imagery in African poetry frequently evokes the natural environment, as in Brutus's "Robben Island Sequence," in which the poet alludes to "the blood on the light sand by the sea," ironically blending imprisonment and seascape. Neto implies the hardships of colonization in "The African Train" through the image of "the rigorous African hill," and another lusophone writer, Sousa, suggests pan-Africanism in "Let My People Go," with references to "Negro spirituals," Paul Robeson, and Marian Anderson. Negritude is observable in U Tam'si's "Brush Fire" (1957): "my race/ it flows here and there a river."

Furthermore, the sometimes problematic experience of westernization is echoed in Macgoye's "Mathenge" (1984), which juxtaposes cultural memory and Western modernity: "the neon light, the photo flash." Similarly, Zimunya contrasts the urban and rural in "Kisimiso," which describes a son "boastful of his experiences in the city of knives and crooks." African poets have also mined their experiences outside the continent, suggested in Anyidoho's "The Taino in 1992" (1993), which remembers "a hurricane of Arawak sounds" in the Caribbean.

Gender themes appear in a line from a Zulu woman's oral self-praise poem, "I am she who cuts across the game reserve," and in the straightforward poem "Abortion," by an Egyptian poet born in the 1960's, Iman Mirsal, who evokes the image "lots of foetuses." Acholonu's "Water Woman" blends orality with natural imagery evoking a "daughter of the river."

Although most of the poetry in European languages uses standard grammar, Nigerian Ezenwa-Ohaeto composed "I Wan Bi President" (1988) in pidgin; earlier poets Casely-Hayford and Nigerian Frank Aig-Imoukhuede also wrote in africanized English. For the most part, African poets writing after the independence era have remolded free-verse forms and have borrowed or incorporated elements of oral poetry, using folklore, songs, rhythms, words, or concepts from indigenous languages. Osundare uses animal imagery in *Waiting Laughters* (1989):

> Ah! *Aramonda* [wonder of wonders]
> The mouth has swallowed something
> Too hard for the mill of the stomach

Furthermore, certain poets, who valorize African languages, compose initially in indigenous languages, such as Kenyan Gitahi Gititi (Gikuyu) and Eritrean (Tigrinya) Reesom Haile.

Modern African poets have strived for a poetic voice that recognizes orality and evocative metaphors, demonstrating how the imposed colonial languages along with African mother tongues can be honed to express relevant social and cultural images. Because written poetry may also be performed, African poets have worked for a balance between abstract and accessible metaphors in order to continue the functional and communal art of their poetic forebears.

BIBLIOGRAPHY

Chipasula, Stella, and Frank Chipasula, eds. *The Heinemann Book of African Women's Poetry*. Oxford, England: Heinemann, 1995. Works by forty-two women poets from eighteen different African countries reflect their shared experience of oppression by men and their determination to express their sense of injustice through their poetry. An important collection, the first of its kind.

D'Almeida, Irène Assiba, ed. *A Rain of Words: A Bilingual Anthology of Women's Poetry in Francophone Africa*. Translated by Janis A. Mayes. Charlottesville: University of Virginia Press, 2009. Includes poems by forty-seven relatively unknown writers. In her introduction, the editor discusses the plight of African women poets. The translator's comments on "Reverberations of African Culture and Women's Creativity in Poetry" are also helpful.

Finnegan, Ruth. *Oral Literature in Africa*. New York: Oxford University Press, 1976. One of the first comprehensive treatments of African oral literature, containing a substantial section devoted to poetry.

Gikandi, Simon, and Evan Mwangi. *The Columbia Guide to East African Literature in English Since 1945*. New York: Columbia University Press, 2007. Emphasizes the ways in which the distinctive history of the region and even its educational institutions have affected the literature. Bibliography and index.

Hughes, Langston, ed. *An African Treasury: Articles, Essays, Stories, Poems*. New York: Pyramid Books, 1961. Perhaps the first collection by an African American to recognize the emergence of modern African writing. The section devoted to poetry includes such poets as Léopold Senghor, Wole Soyinka, Gabriel Okara, and Jean-Joseph Rabéarivelo.

Maja-Pearce, Adewale, ed. *The Heinemann Book of African Poetry in English*. New ed. Oxford, England: Heinemann, 1997. Arranged chronologically, this collection includes poets from the "first generation," beginning with Dennis Brutus and continuing through the 1980's.

Moore, Gerald, and Ulli Beier, eds. *The Penguin Book of Modern African Poetry*. 4th ed. New York: Penguin, 2007. First published in 1963, this extensive volume was one of the first to focus exclusively on "modern" African poets, who are presented by country.

Ojaide, Tanure. *Ordering the African Imagination: Essays on Culture and Literature*. Lagos, Nigeria: Malthouse Press, 2007. Among the topics discussed in this volume are "divine mentoring" in poetry, the creative process, and contemporary African poetry, as well as more general subjects, such as myth, language, and the relationship between writer and audience. Bibliography and index.

Ojaide, Tanure, and Tijan M. Sallah, eds. *The New African Poetry: An Anthology*. Boulder, Colo.: Lynne Rienner, 1999. Organized by region and country, this collection focuses on the "third generation" of African poets, who came to the fore after independence.

Olaniyan, Tejumola, and Ato Quayson, eds. *African Literature: An Anthology of Criticism and Theory*. Malden, Mass.: Blackwell, 2007. A collection of ninety-seven essays on major issues in African life and literature, including the theory and the practice of poetry.

Soyinka, Wole, ed. *Poems of Black Africa*. New York: Hill and Wang, 1975. Organized thematically, this is a comprehensive collection edited by a foremost African writer.

Joseph McLaren
Updated by Rosemary M. Canfield Reisman

ASIAN AMERICAN POETRY

The term "Asian American" encompasses diverse groups of people whose ethnicity cannot be pinned down by a single label. Because they are immigrants or descendants of immigrants from various regions of Asia and at different junctures in the history of the United States, Asian American poets bring with them heterogeneous cultural values, practices, and expressions that interact with the mainstream white culture in various ways. Asian American poetry, the product of such interactions for more than a century, is therefore inherently pluralistic and polyphonic.

CHINESE AMERICAN POETRY

Chinese American poetry can be traced back to the mid-nineteenth century. In the isolated cultures of Chinatowns, Chinese immigrants began to compose poetry in Chinese. The earliest volumes in English that can be tracked down are Hsi Tseng Tsiang's *Poems of the Chinese Revolution* (1929) and Moon Kwan's *A Chinese Mirror: Poems and Plays* (1932), both of which have an ostensibly Chinese component. A preliminary breakthrough came when two Chinese-born poets, Stephen Shu Ning Liu (born 1930) and David Raphael Wang (born 1931), began publishing in English and continued to do so for several decades. Both Wang and Liu naturalize Chinese formats, sensibilities, and stylistics into idiomatic English, demonstrating that Chinese Americans fluent in both languages can be versatile poets capable of imbuing their work with either an American or a Chinese flavor.

Wang and Liu also epitomize the inevitable movement between two cultures that would become characteristic of the younger generation of Chinese American poets, especially those who have been directly exposed to the cultures of both China and the United States. Diana Chang (born 1934), for example, was American-born but was reared in China until 1945; she had authored half a dozen novels before turning out two volumes of poetry. Chang is constantly reminded of her cultural duality: "To me, it occurs that Cézanne/ Is not a Sung painter." Like many people of multicultural upbringing, she enjoys an immense personal freedom ("I shuttle passportless within myself,/ My eyes slant around both hemispheres") yet acknowledges a deep longing to be "accustomed,/ At home here." Embedded in the poetry of Liu, Wang, and Chang there is an acute awareness of global tensions between East and West, First World and Third World, tradition and modernity.

Most Chinese American poetry collected in book form is an outgrowth of the immigration experience, which is not only a collective memory but also a collective reality of the struggle for survival in an uncongenial environment. Authors intent on delineating inexhaustible vignettes of the immigration experience include Nellie Wong, Fay Chiang, Alan Chong Lau, Kitty Tsui, Amy Ling, Marilyn Chin, and Genny Lim. In their books, the poems are arranged according to thematic concerns such as ancestors, family, childhood, adulthood, and marriage. At times helpless, bitter, and outraged, at others respectful, nostalgic, and humorous, they join their variegated voices into a sonorous chorus for the combined elegy and eulogy of an ethnic destiny that has taken more than a century to be reckoned with.

When Chinese American poets speak of themselves as U.S. citizens, the immigrant background heightens their sense of identity, as in Genny Lim's "Yellow Woman":

> I am the daughter of
> seafarers, gold miners, quartz miners
> railroad workers, farm workers
> garment workers, factory workers
> restaurant workers,
> laundrymen
> houseboys, maids, scholars
> rebels, gamblers, poets
> paper sons

The background may be a stigma, but it can also be a means of self-definition, as in Kitty Tsui's "A Celebration of Who I Am": "I am afraid only of forgetting/ the chinese exclusion act of 1882."

In any case, thanks to their self-awareness, the generation of native-born American Chinese who survived the immigration predicament of their forebears took pride in being living contradictions to the stereotypes perpetuated by racist Americans. Daryl Ngee Chin, for example, expresses this pride in "Skin Color from the Sun."

The world of Chinese American poetry is fast becoming more dazzling in its wide variety. Mei-mei Berssenbrugge (born 1947) and John Yau (born 1950), who have published voluminously, are virtuosos of poetic form. Li-Young Lee's *Rose* (1986) deals mainly with haunting memories of a deceased father and a tender, loving relationship between husband and wife, and is exemplary in its seamless amalgamation of the best in both Chinese and Western poetry. While others shuttle between dualities, Lee blends the two cultures subtly and organically into a mellow brew.

At the beginning of the twenty-first century, younger poets began to reflect an interdisciplinary trend toward combining poetry, drama, and performance art. Lim, for example, wrote in a number of genres, includ-

Beau Sia (Getty Images)

ing fiction and drama, and became a member of the performance group Unbound Feet. In an interview, she complained about the labels that have been applied to her and other artists: "I am what I am. Chinese, American, woman . . . labeling is a preoccupation of mass media, marketers, and politicians. . . . My priority has never been to fit in a box." Whereas Chinese Americans once were confined to literal ghettos in the United States, now, Lim notes, they and many other cultural and racial groups have graduated to academic and literary ghettos, as represented by labels such as "Asian American" and "African American." Lim, therefore, seeks to escape the box of labels. In poems such as "Ahmisa" and "Bardo," she addresses universal themes. On stage, her multimedia performance pieces have incorporated Butoh, sculpture, live music, poetry, and video.

Beau Sia (born 1977) gives further proof of the desire to encompass more than one art form. Author of edgy confessionals that touch on fame, money, sex, and Asian cultural stereotypes, Sia has released a spoken-word compact disc, *Attack Attack Go!* (1998), that makes references to popular culture—Nike shoes, time shares, the role-playing game Dungeons & Dragons, and the *Transformers* television show. Sia is known for brutally honest, aggressive, and humorous performances in a deadpan delivery reminiscent of comedian Stephen Wright. He befriended Beat poet Allen Ginsberg, who, echoing other poets, taught him the interconnectedness of all: "He taught me how to be positive and genuine and connect everything universally," said Sia. Like other poets, Sia credits a wide variety of sources for his inspiration—rap music as well as Frank O'Hara and William Carlos Williams.

JAPANESE AMERICAN POETRY

Writing in the early twentieth century, the first generation of Japanese American poets, Yone Noguchi (1875-1947), Carl Sadakichi Hartmann (1867-1944), and Jun Fujita (1888-1963), employed Japanese forms such as tanka and haiku in their often nostalgic works. Later generations of Japanese American poets continued to explore Japanese poetic forms. After the great divide of World War II, however, Japanese American poetry began to be marked by a decisive sense of identity and coherence.

The trauma of the internment of Japanese Americans during World War II served as the rallying point for their literary expression. Lawson Fusao Inada produced a seminal collection of poems revolving around the relocation experience, *Before the War* (1971). Similarly conceived collections include James Masao Mitsui's *Journal of the Sun* (1974), Mitsuye Yamada's *Camp Notes, and Other Poems* (1976), and Lonny Kaneko's *Return from the Camp* (1986). Although not all have drawn their inspiration explicitly from the internment experience, Japanese American poets have used it to consolidate a collective memory and established an ethnic identity for themselves. However, rather than simply musing upon the wrongs they suffered in their incarceration, they have moved on to explore its various ramifications.

The result of such explorations is epitomized by the phrase "breaking silence." In *Shedding Silence* (1987), Janice Mirikitani develops the idea that "the strongest prisons are built/ with walls of silence" ("Prisons of Silence"). In the widely anthologized poem "Breaking Silence," she articulates the mission for an entire generation of younger Japanese American poets. The poem could very well be regarded as a manifesto in verse. In the first place, to break silence is to come to terms with the turmoils of the incarceration that Japanese Americans before the 1970's had generally avoided discussing:

> We were made to believe our faces
> betrayed us.
> Our bodies were loud with yellow screaming flesh
> needing to be silenced
> behind barbed wire.
>
> .   .   .   .
> We must recognize ourselves at last.

As a corollary, to break silence is also to learn a lesson about the body politic of racist America. In "Block 18, Tule Relocation Camp," Mitsui describes "a quiet man," by day surrounded by Italians and Germans, who by night retreats to a boiler room. There he fashions a samurai sword from scrap metal: "A secret edge/ to hold against the dark mornings." Mitsui is well aware of the stereotypes perpetuated about his race:

> White voices
> claim the other side of the ocean
> is so crowded
> the people want to find death
> across the phantom river.

By extension, then, to break silence is to sympathize with other peoples of color. Many of these poets look beyond the United States to discover an alliance with the developing world; many of them also condemn the warlike mentality that led to the great devastations of World War II and the Vietnam War. (See, for example, Geraldine Kudaka's *Numerous Avalanches at the Point of Intersection* (1979), Mirikitani's "We the Dangerous," and David Mura's "The Hibakusha's Letter.")

Above all, to break silence is to dare to critique and dissent in a country that, through legal instruments of exclusion, antimiscegenation laws, segregation, and discrimination, stubbornly refused to practice what it taught. In order to establish this voice, Japanese American poets such as Mura in *After We Lost Our Way* (1989) began to memorialize the details of the family lives of generations past and present. Others aimed to establish a sense of origins and direction (Garrett Kaoru Hongo, *Yellow Light*, 1982, and *The River of Heaven*, 1988) or to assess the everyday life of Americans at large (Ai, *Cruelty*, 1973; *Killing Floor*, 1979; and *Sin*, 1986). Especially worthy of attention is the fact that Japanese American poets looked toward the past of their immigrant forebears (Mura, *After We Lost Our Way*) and proudly but judiciously retraced their cultural roots and heritage (Yamada, *Desert Run*, 1988; Hongo, *The River of Heaven*).

In the midst of these developments, an interesting discord can be detected among those who hold opposite views of "tradition," which must be broken for a Japanese American to be American (Mirikitani, "Breaking Tradition") but at the same time must be preserved so as to retain one's distinctive voice as an American of color. The resolution of this conflict will probably continue to be a major issue in Japanese American poetry.

KOREAN AMERICAN POETRY

Korean American poetry is a very young literature, coming to the fore mainly in the second half of the twentieth century. In the 1970's, when memories of the Korean War were still fresh and were in fact heightened by the ongoing Vietnam War, there emerged a distinct voice centering on the historical and psychological issue of Koreans as a "lost" people whose destiny has been unfulfilled. This voice was often a questioning one, singing of the inexplicable predicament of a strong-spirited but disempowered people under oppression or in exile. In Gail Whang Desmond's "Korean Declaration of Independence" (appended to her "Memories of My Grandfather: Rev. Whang Sa Sun"), she describes her attempt to understand her grandfather:

> Korean Declaration of Independence
> yellow from age
> brittle from usage
>
> . . . .
>
> How many times has he read it?
> Why does he read it?
>
> . . . . . .
>
> Who are Koreans?

She explains how her grandfather arrived in the United States in 1913, full of dreams for a "good life," for an "education," but he has endured "nothing but pain, struggle." She wonders about the tiny lapel pin of a flying goose that he never takes off: "Why?" Her poem is plaintive: "It's the end of our first generation./ Will anyone ever understand?"

The questioning voice at times becomes an indictment, as in Kim Tong Il's poems, which sing of dreams about an independent, unified "Morning Calm" (literal translation of *Korea*) turned into nightmares of "the land of oppressed calm":

> Tell me the silent hills,
> Isn't it time for us
> To break down the barbed wire
> and determine our own destiny?
> I hear only a roaring
> Of gunfire

To be American is often a tragic irony to a Korean, because Americans have caused much suffering to Korea. In "Your Name Is Chang-Mee," Kim Tong Il describes one visible form of such oppression:

> you're pretty being found
> among the thorny bush and helpless,
>
> . . . .
>
> your Yankee daddy
> abandoned you long ago, and
> your mother has to sell her body
> to another Yankee tonight

Myung Mi Kim's "A Rose of Sharon" is a more refined poem along similar lines. This tragic irony looms large in many poems that depict an American-born Korean yearning to understand and internalize a historical and political background with which he or she has little familiarity.

Reading these poems, one is led to participate in the poets' efforts to understand the destiny of the first generation and later generations. For example, in "Leaving Seoul: 1953" (appearing in Joseph Bruchac's anthology *Breaking Silence*, 1983), Walter Lew (born 1955) describes how he discovered a familial duty, or burden, that was never explained to him. A family of three is leaving Seoul on an airplane. The father has told the mother to leave behind a number of urns. Secretly and with much difficulty, however, the mother, who is a doctor, smuggles them along:

> We have to bury the urns,
> Mother and I. We tried to leave them in a back room,
> Decoyed by a gas lamp, and run out
> But they landed behind us here, at the front gate.

Decades later, "tapping the tall glowing jars," the speaker finds that "they contain all that has made/ The father have dominion over her." This poem powerfully encapsulates the conflict between the imperative to preserve traditional values (ancestral worship, male supremacy) and the necessity of surviving in a time of turmoil. However, this conflict could not have been understood at the time it took place. A conflict between two generations is also present: The son, though he knows about the mother's action, does not see the point of it at that time. The father, described as "waiting at the airfield in a discarded U.S. Army/ overcoat" and "smoking Luckys like crazy," also serves to epitomize the calamitous tragedy to which an entire people falls victim. The series of urn poems that follow "Leaving Seoul: 1953" suddenly take on epic proportions.

Cathy Song, a Chinese Korean born in Hawaii in 1955, has attracted attention since the 1980's. Her work is both a continuation of and a departure from her three-cultured Asian heritage. In *Picture Bride* (1983), she finds in her grandmother a matrilineal archetype. The archetype, above all, allows her to define her own being by weaving calmly recollected family memories and patiently mediated everyday observations together into a fabric of life. Her poems focusing on her own experience of womanhood and motherhood are not only lyrical but also, in the light of this archetype, mythical. However, as is clear from the multilayered design (memory, family, art, history, culture, geography, and botany, to name a few) in which the poems of *Picture Bride* are arranged, Song is moving ahead to explore a new world grounded in, but transcending, ethnicity. Her multifaceted background has facilitated this move, and her *Frameless Windows, Squares of Light* (1988) and *School Figures* (1994) are further attempts in this direction.

FILIPINO AMERICAN POETRY

Filipino American literature is a direct offshoot of a continuous modern Filipino literature, which features a number of mature writers already versatile in Spanish and English and familiar with the Western tradition. José García Villa (1914-1997), who came to the United States in 1930, was a prolific poet. Steeped in the Western tradition and making little reference to his ethnic background, his poetry won the acclaim of American and European critics. He was a favorite of Edith Sitwell and other British critics, who found his poetry dealing with the mysterious beauty of God to be Blakean ("Be Beautiful, Noble, Like the Antique Ant"; "Imagine God a Peacock"). In contrast to Villa, Carlos Bulosan, arriving in America in 1931, felt compelled to scrutinize in his poetry (*Letters from America*, 1942, and *American Is in the Heart*, 1943), as in his prose, his Filipino heritage and his American life.

Filipinos often suffer from a perpetual identity crisis resulting from their four-century experience of colonization. In the spirit of Bulosan, younger generations of Filipino poets have examined their backgrounds carefully. They are generally acutely aware of their ethnicity—or more precisely, their anonymity. As Alfred Robles (born 1944) hilariously dramatizes his marginality in "It Was a Warm Summer Day" (in *Asian American Authors*, edited by Kai Yu Hsu and Helen Palubinskas, 1972), he is asked about his identity in a long series of questions that becomes a "laundry list" of American ethnic minorities. Upon his return to the Philippines, however, his alienation evaporates and gives way to a rejuvenating excitement ("Manong Federico Delos Reyes and His Golden Banjo," in *Breaking Silence*). Virginia Cerenio captures, in "You Lovely People," the same marginality and the same nostalgia, but in a more poignant manner:

> like indios, we are
> lost
> not in india or middle america
> or the wrong side of a carabao nickel
> but on a boat
> between oceans
> between continents.

Still, she affirms her people's strength:

> your old brown hands
> hold life, many lives
> within each crack
> a story

The marginality delineated by Robles and Cerenio constitutes an important theme in Filipino American literature. It is further defined by Jeff Tagami, who suggests that Filipino Americans may be anonymous ("Without Names") but nevertheless can still be identified by their contributions to the development of Hawaii as menial laborers—an episode that he memorializes and celebrates in *October Light* (1987).

Meanwhile, in the continuing search for a positive ethnic identity against a background of anonymity, Filipino American poetry was blessed with the arrival of Jessica Hagedorn (born 1949) from Manila, a city where, as Hagedorn says in her poem "Souvenirs" in reference to the Marcos regime,

> the president's wife
> dictates martial law
> with her thighs
> sanctity n piety
> is her name
> as she sips tea

Jessica Hagedorn (©Christopher Felver/CORBIS)

In the United States, "the loneliest of countries," she is entangled, like Robles, in mixed-up identities, as in this passage from "Song for My Father":

> in new york
> they ask me if i'm puerto rican
> and do i live in queens?
> i listen to pop stations
> chant to iemaja
> convinced i'm really brazilian

She identifies closely with other peoples of color and particularly comes to value the indigenous music of Latin America ("Latin Music in New York"; "The Woman Who Thought She Was More than a Samba"). For Hagedorn, the sense of self is also built on the sense of insecurity: "there are rapists/ out there/ some of them don't like asian women" ("Solea"). Increasingly, identity is impossible without an awareness of the negative aspects of American life, such as cheapened love ("Seeing You Again Makes Me Wanna Wash the Dishes"),

televised sensationalism ("Justifiable Homicide"), pervasive violence ("The Song of Bullets"), and women's vulnerability to men's lust ("The Leopard"). On the whole, Hagedorn has developed most of the themes central to Filipino American poetry and has added new ideas and stylistic expressions of her own that are geared to the problematics and aesthetics of modernity.

Russell Gonzaga, born in the Philippines and raised in San Francisco, also reflects the interdisciplinary work being done by so many poets at the beginning of the twenty-first century. He is a spoken-word poet and community activist who mixes street life and the academic world. He grew up in a community rich in oral tradition and was interested in rap music as a teenager. He realized rap was just a structure, regular metered rhyming verse, so he freed it up. He sees the interconnectedness of rap music and the spoken word and cites his inspiration from widely divergent sources: hip-hop, the Qur'ān, science fiction, and *The Autobiography of Malcolm X* (1965). Like other Asian Americans of his generation, he expresses a distaste for labels and a belief in universality and blending:

> it's part of the western philosophical paradigm to chop everything up and put it into compartments . . . but I think people of color aren't like that. . . . we understand everything informs everything else.

Gonzaga is a three-time winner of the San Francisco Poetry Slam Championship, in which poets read their works to an enthusiastic audience and are evaluated by a panel of judges.

SOUTHEAST ASIAN AMERICAN POETRY

In the 1990's and at the beginning of the twenty-first century, what many Asian American poets of various ethnic backgrounds shared was an ability to blend their work and their ethnicities with other groups and methods of communication, capitalizing on the interest in multiculturalism in the United States. Such a tendency is evident among many young poets of the turn of the century, including Chinese Americans Lim and Sia, and Filipino American Gonzaga.

Le Thi Diem Thuy (born 1972), a Vietnamese American, shares this interest in blending her work with other forms of presentation. She grew up in South Vietnam during fierce fighting. She left the country in 1979 and settled in the United States. As a performance artist, she has become well known for *Red Fiery Summer* (pr. 1995), which covers the period of terrible attacks from North Vietnam. On stage, she attempts to embody her father, to "express his presence," as she puts it. The presentation combines prose, poems, and monologues that reflect on war and its aftermath, from the days of the French involvement in Vietnam. Her passionate, terrifying stories are understated. She says, "I go about things in an oblique way." She gets to the point, but she feels the approach can be just as satisfying. She was selected by the *Village Voice* as a Writer on the Verge. Her powerful look at the way Vietnam still haunts its victims can be seen in a passage from "Shrapnel Shards on Blue Water," in which she compares first-generation Vietnamese Americans who relocated to the United States in the 1970's with the "shards" of war and then denies that self-identity with war to transform it, embracing and defending the image of her homeland as not war but rather "a piece of us".

> we are fragmented shards
> blown here by a war no one wants to remember
> in a foreign land
> with an achingly familiar wound
> our survival is dependent upon
> never forgetting that vietnam is not
> a word
> a world
> a love
> a family
> a fear
> to bury
>
> . . . . . .
>
> let people know
> VIETNAM IS NOT A WAR
> but a piece
> of
> us

Li-Young Lee (born 1957), born in Jakarta, Indonesia, represents another culture that has added to the American experience. Lim says of Lee, "He is a won-

derful poet and his work deeply reflects his affinity for Chinese poetry, consistent with western expectations." Her comments show again the blending that occurs when two cultures meet. For example, Lee writes repeatedly of his father, who at one time was Chinese leader Mao Zedong's personal physician but in the United States became a Presbyterian minister. Lee explores the dramatic differences in these two extremes. The poet writes of love, family, ordinary experiences, and his specific past.

In "Persimmons," for example, Lee recalls childhood experiences typical of the immigrant child: his teacher punishing him for not knowing the difference between the words "persimmons" and "precision"; then the precise method for choosing and eating a persimmon ("This is precision"); early sexual experimentation with an Anglo neighbor girl whom he teaches a few words of Chinese; and the difficulty of pronouncing the language ("Other words/ that got me into trouble were/ *fight* and *fright*, *wren* and *yarn*"). Each stanza's recalled experience leads to and interweaves with that of the next, mimicking the process of memory and displaying the constant interplay of the poet's dual cultural and ethnic experiences. At the same time that these experiences are shaped by the poet's cultural and linguistic background, they are nevertheless familiar to all readers, inviting and binding readers in the common obstacles and challenges of growing up.

BIBLIOGRAPHY

Carbo, Nick, ed. *Returning a Borrowed Tongue: Poems by Filipino and Filipino American Writers*. Minneapolis, Minn.: Coffeehouse Press, 1995. Contains translations of established writers such as Gemino Abad, Eugene Gloria, Catalina Cariaga, and Jessica Hagedorn. Newer poets such as Jaime Jacinto are also represented.

Chang, Juliana, ed. *Quiet Fire: Asian American Poetry*. New York: Asian American Writers' Workshop, 1996. This first book published by the workshop has become a landmark because it is the first historical survey of Asian American poetry. It contains early works of Joy Kogawa, Jessica Hagedorn, Lawson Fusao Inada, and others, selected to reflect both the high quality and wide range of Asian American poetic discourse through the mid-1990's. Bibliography. An indispensable collection.

Chang, Victoria, ed. *Asian American Poetry: The Next Generation*. Urbana: University of Illinois Press, 2004. An impressive collection of works by young poets from various ethnic backgrounds. In addition to Timothy Liu, Adrienne Su, Sue Kwock Kim, Mong-Lan, Branda Shaughnessy, and Rick Barot, the writers include those whose poems are difficult to find and some who were previously unpublished.

Cheung, King-Kok, ed. *An Interethnic Companion to Asian American Literature*. New York: Cambridge University Press, 1996. Contains the work of North American writers of Asian descent and introduces readers to each Asian American group's distinctive literary history. Notes issues that connect or divide these different groups. Bibliography, index.

Hongo, Garrett, ed. *The Open Boat: Poems from Asian America*. New York: Anchor, 1993. Edited by one of the best-known poets of the Asian American experience, this major collection includes work by Maxine Hong Kingston, David Mura, Marilyn Chin, John You, and twenty-seven other contemporary poets representing a variety of perspectives on the Asian American experience.

Huang, Guiyou, ed. *Asian American Poets: A Bio-Bibliographical Critical Sourcebook*. Westport, Conn.: Greenwood Press, 2002. In addition to providing biographical information, this volume directs students to other sources. An invaluable reference book.

Lew, Walter, ed. *Premonitions: The Kaya Anthology of New Asian North American Poetry*. New York: Kaya Production, 1995. This major anthology (of six hundred pages) focuses on writers of the post-1970's era.

Lim, Shirley Geok-lin, et al. *Transnational Asian American Literature: Sites and Transits*. Philadelphia: Temple University Press, 2006. Urges a new, global emphasis in the study of writers who move from their native countries. Of the thirteen essays in this volume, four are devoted to poetry. Among the writers discussed are Kimiko Hahn, Robert Grotjohn, Myung Mi Kim, Josephine Hock-Hee Park,

Agha Shahid Ali, Maimuna Dali Islam, Ha Jin, and Zhou Xiaojing.

Mahony, Phillip, ed. *From Both Sides Now: The Poetry of the Vietnam War and Its Aftermath*. New York: Simon & Schuster, 1998. These are poems by Vietnamese and Americans, adults and children, combatants and protesters. Many are from Vietnamese Americans and Amerasian poets. The volume constitutes a moving oral history of the war and those who were involved.

Park, Josephine Nock-Hee. *Apparitions of Asia: Modernist Form and Asian American Poetics*. New York: Oxford University Press, 2008. Examines the complex relationships between Asian American poetry, American Orientalism, American poetry, and modernist poetics. Concludes by demonstrating how Lawson Fusao Inada, Theresa Hak Kyung Cha, and Myung Mi Kim turn to aesthetics to make statements about past history.

Rustomji-Kerns, Roshni, ed. *Living in America: Poetry and Fiction by South Asian American Writers*. Boulder, Colo.: Westview Press, 1995. A volume divided between poetry and short fiction. The editor has provided an excellent historical introduction to the subject, as well as an essay on South Asian literary traditions. Contains a personal comment by each of the writers, and biographical information.

Tabios, Eileen, ed. *Black Lightning: Poetry in Progress*. New York: Asian American Writers' Workshop, 1998. Follows the early drafts of poems through to their final forms. Presents works by Meena Alexander, Mei-mei Berssenbrugge, Marilyn Chin, Jessica Hagedorn, Garrett Hongo, Timothy Liu, David Mura, Arthur Sze (who wrote an introductory essay for the book), and John Yau.

Tran, Barbara, et al., eds. *Watermark: Vietnamese American Poetry and Prose*. Philadelphia: Temple University press, 1998. Tran and her three coeditors give voice to Vietnamese American writers in this anthology collecting fiction, prose, and poetry, both previously published and never before published. The poems cover more than the war. Includes work of both first-generation and second-generation Vietnamese Americans. Authors include Linh Dinh, Andrew Lam, and Christian Longworthy.

Yu, Timothy. *Race and the Avant-Garde: Experimental and Asian American Poetry Since 1965*. Stanford, Calif.: Stanford University Press, 2009. A new approach to the study of Asian American poetry, dealing with it as a form of Language poetry and thus itself an avant-garde phenomenon. Thus, Yu argues that race, politics, and aesthetics are interrelated.

Zhou, Xiaojing. *The Ethics and Poetics of Alterity in Asian American Poetry*. Iowa City: University of Iowa Press, 2006. Traces the history and the psychological effects of the concept of otherness and its influence on poetic language and form, as seen in the poetry of Li-Young Lee, Marilyn Chin, David Mura, Kimiko Hahn, Timothy Liu, John Yau, and Myung Mi Kim.

Balance Chow; Gary Zacharias
Updated by Christina J. Moose

Australian and New Zealand Poetry

When the first Europeans arrived in Australia, they found that the land was inhabited by people who had no written language. Because the Aborigines were preliterate, the settlers assumed that they were also prehistorical. What the new settlers did not realize is that the indigenous peoples did indeed have a rich history as well as a shared system of mythical beliefs, which had been transmitted orally from generation to generation. Though the Aboriginal narratives were poetic in form, they were performance poetry: The stories were sung, danced, or acted out. Because this format was so ephemeral and because the Aborigines were reluctant to admit outsiders to their rituals, many of which were deemed sacred, white Australians had almost no knowledge of Aboriginal writings for the first hundred years that the colony was in existence. Moreover, when collections such as Catherine Langloh Parker's *Australian Legendary Tales* (1896) began to appear, even though the stories they contained followed the plot lines of their Aboriginal sources, their form was that of the European folktale.

By the middle of the twentieth century, anthropologists were producing books in which complete Aboriginal narratives, such as song cycles, appeared along with English translations, which reproduced the verbal patterns of the original works as closely as possible. Meanwhile, some Aborigines had begun to write in English, often to protest the treatment of their people. The first of these writer-activists was Kath Walker (1920-1993), who, in her first book of poetry, *We Are Going* (1964), warned white Australians that her people did not intend simply to disappear. In 1988, as a protest against Australia's bicentennial activities, Walker returned to her tribal name, Oodgeroo Noonuccal, which she used for the stories and poems she wrote during her final years. Another writer who adopted a tribal name was Colin Johnson (born 1939), whose book *Wild Cat Falling* (1965) was reputed to be the first novel published by an Aboriginal writer. Among the many other publications of Johnson, known since 1988 as Mudrooroo Narogin, or just Mudrooroo, are three verse collections, *The Song Circle of Jacky* (1986), *Dalwurra* (1988), and *The Garden of Gethsemane* (1991). Though Mudrooroo was recognized as a leading activist and an authority on Australian Aboriginal literature, *The Australian Magazine* published an article questioning his claim of Aboriginal identity in 1996. Nevertheless, Mudrooroo continued to be considered one of Australia's most important Aboriginal writers. By the beginning of the twenty-first century, it was customary for anthologies of Australian verse to contain both translations of ancient Aboriginal poetry and poems by writers of Aboriginal ancestry, who used the English language to recall their traditions and to express the concerns of their people.

The colonial period

The first book of poetry published in the colony of Australia was *First Fruits of Australian Poetry* (1819), by Barron Field (1786-1846), a judicial appointee from England. Field's volume contained two poems, "Botany Bay Flowers" and "The Kangaroo." Field found Australia interesting, but after seven years there, he was evidently happy to return home. Two native-born poets, William Charles Wentworth (1790-1872) and Charles Tompson (1807-1883), were more enthusiastic about their country. In his epic poem "Astralasia" (1823), Wentworth envisioned the colony's becoming a new, more perfect England, and in *Wild Notes, from the Lyre of a Native Minstrel* (1826), the first book of poetry by a native Australian to be published in Australia, Tompson pointed out the beauties of the Australian landscape and stressed the importance of preserving the natural environment.

The anonymous bush ballads and convict songs of this period present a very different picture of life in the colony. With wry humor, the writers describe their struggles against oppressive heat and persistent mosquitoes; comment on the difference between the lives of those Australians who have money and those who have none; warn those at "home" to avoid crime, lest they be transported; and clearly regard themselves as exiles struggling desperately to survive.

By the 1830's, the colony was producing some poets of more than historical importance. Charles Harpur

(1813-1868) was driven by his desire to be Australia's first major poet. He was underrated for decades but has come to be regarded as the finest poet of the colonial period. Although Harpur relies on traditional forms, his poetic works are not conventional or imitative in their content. Whether they are philosophical discourses ("The World and the Soul") or narratives with an Australian setting ("The Creek of the Four Graves"), Harpur's poems are both unique and memorable.

One of colonial Australia's most popular poets was Adam Lindsay Gordon (1833-1870), who exemplified the masculine values that characterized the later colonial period. Gordon was admired both for his superb horsemanship and for his poems about life in the outback. One of his best-loved poetic works is "The Sick Stockrider," a tribute to mateship, or comradeship, and to the stoical acceptance of one's fate. It appeared in Gordon's second volume of poetry, *Bush Ballads and Galloping Rhymes* (1870). The day after the book was published, Gordon committed suicide.

William Charles Wentworth was one of the first native-born Anglo-Australian poets. (The Granger Collection, New York)

Another important nineteenth century Australian poet was Henry Kendall (1839-1882), whose works ranged from lyrics such as "Bell Birds" and "September in Australia" to satirical portraits of outback types. Kendall also wrote poignant love poems; narratives with biblical, classical, or local settings; and patriotic or occasional verse.

WOMEN POETS IN THE COLONIAL PERIOD

Even in this new country, women did not have the freedom of thought and expression that they would a century later. Whatever their private feelings, they were expected to display a ladylike sentimentality in public. Nevertheless, several women managed to publish some creditable works. One of them was Eliza Hamilton Dunlop (1796-1880), who came to Australia from Ireland with her second husband, who was assigned as protector of a group of Aborigines. She was one of the first Australians to make a serious study of the language and the culture of the Aborigines. Her sympathy for them is evident in her frequently anthologized poem "The Aboriginal Mother," which first appeared in the *Australian* in 1838.

Louisa Anne Meredith (1812-1895), an Englishwoman who settled in Tasmania, won honors for her illustrated books, several of which were collections of her descriptive, lyric poetry. Another native of England, Ada Cambridge (1844-1926), spent much of her life in rural Victoria with her clergyman husband. A prolific writer, she published short fiction, novels, essays, and autobiographical works, as well as five collections of verse. Though Cambridge's poems tend to be sentimental in tone and often have a moral, they do sometimes exhibit some intellectual complexity, as when she writes of the loss of sexual desire in "The Physical Conscience" and "Unstrung." One of her most moving poems is "By the Camp Fire." In that poem, while acknowledging that God is at his most magnificent in Australia, the speaker still yearns for the organ music of England, where her soul seemed so secure.

A NEW ERA

During the last twenty years of the nineteenth century, it became increasingly evident that the attitudes and the values of Australians were changing. Because most of the population had been born in Australia, the old nostalgia for England had largely disappeared, and as the fervor of the 1888 bicentennary celebration demonstrated, Australians were taking pride in their own hard-won land. In addition, they were rejecting many of the old ideals, notably individualism, while they exalted mateship or the collaborative efforts of working men—men, not women, for Australia remained dominated by masculine values. The *Sydney Bulletin*, which was founded in 1880 and soon began calling itself the Bushman's bible, reflected the new Australia: It was against imperialism, colonialism, and capitalism, as well as Aborigines and Asians, but strongly supported workers, unions, and republicanism.

One of the first poets to emerge in this new era was Henry Lawson (1867-1922), who was born in the goldfields and grew up in rural New South Wales but later joined his mother in Sydney, where she was active in the republican movement. His first poem, "A Song of the Republic," appeared in the *Bulletin*. Lawson, who called himself the people's poet, became known both for protest poetry and for poems about life in the bush. Surprisingly, during World War I, Lawson wrote patriotic poems in support of the war. Although in his later years Lawson wrote a great deal of verse, his reputation rests primarily on the short fiction he wrote in the first decade of the twentieth century.

Bernard O'Dowd (1866-1953) was an even more radical writer than Lawson. The son of Irish Roman Catholic immigrants, O'Dowd was a radical socialist who voiced his demands for social justice and his hopes for Australia both in prose and in poems such as those in *Downward?* (1903) and in the long poetic work *The Bush* (1912). Another radical writer, who wrote under the pen name Furnley Maurice (Frank Wilmot; 1881-1942), published his first verses in O'Dowd's journal *Tocsin*. Wilmot was one of the most vocal opponents of Australia's entering World War I; he not only opposed war in general, but also, as a nationalist, believed that his country should avoid becoming involved in the corrupt politics of Europe and devote itself to its own development. By contrast, some poets, among them Lawson, saw wartime service as an example of mateship. Two books of colloquial verse narratives by C. J. Dennis (1876-1938) exemplified the "digger" ideal, *The*

Songs of a Sentimental Bloke (1915) and *The Moods of Ginger Mick* (1916); both of them were as popular with soldiers at the front as they were with people at home.

In 1923, the magazine *Vision* was established to oppose the mateship ideal, as well as isolationist nationalism, and to support the publication of poems in the Romantic-Symbolist tradition, focusing on the themes of art, memory, time, and death. Though only four issues of the magazine were published, it was responsible for introducing promising new poets to the Australian public. One of them was Kenneth Slessor (1901-1971), who served on the staff of the magazine. Slessor, who is credited with introducing modernism into Australian poetry, notably through his reliance on imagery, remains one of Australia's most important poets. Another *Vision* poet, R. D. Fitzgerald (1902-1987), is admired for his prizewinning long narrative poem *Between Two Tides*, which is built on his two major themes, the need for resolute action and the inevitability of death.

JINDYWOROBAKS, ANGRY PENGUINS, AND LYRICISTS

In the 1930's, Australians were again moving toward isolationism and nationalism, which had their most extreme expression in the Jindyworobak movement. In 1938, the Jindyworobak Club was founded in Adelaide, and that same year, the first *Jindyworobak Anthology* of poetry appeared. Poets associated with the movement sought inspiration from Australian history, from the outback, and from Aboriginal art. They urged becoming more closely tied to the environment, and some sought spiritual enlightenment through the Aboriginal "dreamtime." The practice that many Australians found objectionable, however, was the use of Aboriginal words in English-language poems. Even though the final anthology appeared in 1953, the Jindyworobak movement continues to exert an influence on Australian writers through its recognition of Aboriginal art and its environmental emphasis.

The Angry Penguin movement of the 1940's was very different from the Jindyworobak movement. It began in Adelaide with a quarterly journal called *Angry Penguins*, which opposed nationalistic socialism and was devoted to the avant-garde in film, the visual arts, and literature. Max Harris (1921-1995), one of its editors and a major contributor, was a target of a hoax perpetrated in 1944 by the conservative writers James McAuley (1917-1976) and Harold Stewart (1916-1995). The two wrote some nonsensical poems that were supposedly by a poet named Ernest Lalor "Ern" Malley and had them sent to Harris, who was so captivated by his discovery that he featured Malley and his poetry in a special edition of *Angry Penguins*. After the truth came out, Harris and his modernist magazine became a laughingstock. *Angry Penguins* did not survive, and for some time, the modernist movement attracted fewer followers.

Among the new poets emerging during the 1950's and 1960's were A. D. Hope (1907-2000), who is still admired for his use of classical allusions and mythological references; Douglas Stewart (1913-1985), a native of New Zealand, who described the natural beauty of Australia and New Zealand in moving lyrics; and David Campbell (1915-1979), whose meditative lyrics are ranked as some of his best poems. Also gaining recognition during this period were a number of women poets. In 1946, Judith Wright (1915-2000) published her first volume of poetry, *The Moving Image*. Wright would become one of the most highly regarded Australian poets, as well as a prominent literary critic, editor, short-fiction writer, and activist in conservation and in support of Aboriginal rights. In 1992, Wright became the first Australian to be awarded the Queen's Gold Medal for poetry. Other award-winning women poets who came to prominence during the period were Rosemary Dobson (born 1920), Gwen Harwood (1920-1995), and the feminist Dorothy Hewitt (1923-2002).

INFINITE VARIETY AND INTERNATIONAL
RECOGNITION

During the 1960's, a number of Australian poets had voiced their conviction that Australian poetry needed to develop new themes and settings to reflect the urbanization of the nation or to experiment with forms as the American postmodern poets had. One of these would-be reformers, Thomas Shapcott (born 1935), chose an unusual subject, life in a provincial town, for his *Shabbytown Calendar* (1975). Another, John Tranter (born 1943), used fragmentary, disjointed forms in his early poems, thus illustrating the kinds of

changes he had advocated in his introduction to *The New Australian Poetry* (1979), though his later poetry was more traditional. As the editor of the magazine *New Poetry*, Robert Adamson (born 1943) was another influential force for change. In *The Clean Dark* (1989), Adamson demonstrates that postmodern forms can be just as effective as a more traditional format in the communication of profound feelings, such as his love of the Hawkesbury River area, where he made his home.

Among the many experimental poets who attained recognition in the final decades of the twentieth century are Anna Walwicz (born 1951), Dorothy Porter (born 1954), Ken Bolton (born 1948), and Ross Clark (born 1953). Jennifer Maiden (born 1949) combines fiction, fictional autobiography, and autobiography with family memories and references to current events in her poetic works, which, though often puzzling, richly reward intensive study.

Others pursued very different paths. Though in the twenty-first century they are still as highly regarded as they were thirty years before, both Bruce Dawe (born 1930) and Les A. Murray (born 1938) continue to eschew postmodernism, believing that poetry can be significant only when it is accessible to ordinary readers. Thus the poems in which Dawe takes up the cause of the ordinary person against tyranny are written in colloquial language, and the poems in which Murray urges a return to the values of the early settlers, to what he calls the true spirit of Australia, are as straightforward as the rural people about whom he writes. Both Dawe and Murray have won numerous awards. In 2000, Dawe received the Australian Council for the Arts Emeritus Writers Award for his lifelong contribution to Australian literature, and in 1998, Murray was awarded the Queen's Gold Medal for Poetry, leading many to call him Australia's leading poet. When he was given Germany's Petrarch Prize (Petrarca Preis) in 1995, it was evident how much Murray has contributed to the international recognition of Australian poets.

NEW ZEALAND POETRY

Like the Australian Aborigines, the Polynesian people of New Zealand had their own mythology and rituals expressed in poetic form, and many of them were recorded by European scholars late in the nineteenth century. However, the first Maori poet to produce high-quality poetry written in the English language did not appear until well into the twentieth century. Hone Tuwhare (1922-2008) published his first collection of poems, *No Ordinary Sun*, in 1964. A playwright and short-story writer as well as a poet, Tuwhare proceeded to win many honors, including being named New Zealand's Te Mata Poet Laureate in 1999. His poems are routinely included in anthologies of New Zealand poetry. Another frequently anthologized Maori writer is Keri Hulme (born 1947). Although she is best known for her prizewinning novel *The Bone People* (1984), Hulme also produced several volumes of very fine poetry. In 1990, another distinguished Maori poet, Robert Sullivan (born 1967), published his first collection, *Jazz Waiata*. His fifth volume of poetry, *Voice Carried My Family*, appeared in 2005.

The Maori term for New Zealanders of European descent is Pakeha. One of the few nineteenth century Pakeha poets who is still remembered is Alfred Domett

(1811-1887), a statesman and the fourth premier of New Zealand. Ironically, though he was known for his uncompromising attitude toward the Maori people, after he returned to his native England, Domett wrote a fourteen-thousand-line epic about the Maoris called *Ranolf and Amohia: A South-Sea Day-Dream* (1872). Colonial writers often expressed ambivalent feelings about their new home and even about their roles there. In "A Colonist in His Garden," William Pember Reeves (1857-1932) admits that although he still loves England, he takes pride in his role as a "tamer" of the wilderness, while in "The Passing of the Forest," he expresses concern over the destruction of New Zealand's natural beauty for the sake of progress. It is significant that Reeves spent his final years in London, where he was New Zealand's agent-general. Another well-known nineteenth century poet was John Barr of Craigilee (1809-1889), who wrote poems in the Scottish dialect, sometimes praising life far from tyrannical lords and sometimes expressing his yearning for his na-

Maori poet Hone Tuwhare, left, with his biographer, Jane Hunt. (Getty Images)

tive Scotland. However, the most famous nineteenth century poet was Thomas Bracken (1843-1898), who used his position as editor of the *Saturday Advertiser* to provide an outlet for New Zealand writers. Bracken's poem *God Defend New Zealand*, which appeared in the *Advertiser* in 1876, became one of New Zealand's two national anthems.

THE TWENTIETH CENTURY AND BEYOND

Some of the most gifted poets of the twentieth century were women. In *Shingle-Short, and Other Verses* (1908), Blanche Baughan (1870-1958) experimented with open forms and unusual imagery, innovations that would not be seen again until the advent of modernism. The traditional lyrics of Eileen Duggan (1894-1972) brought her international acclaim. The serene poems that Mary Ursula Bethell (1874-1945) wrote during her years at Christchurch, many of which appeared in *From a Garden in the Antipodes* (1929), reflect her religious faith and her appreciation of natural beauty. Another important poet was Iris Guiver Wilkinson (1906-1939), who wrote striking poems under the pen name Robin Hyde. Though her present reputation rests primarily on her short fiction, Katherine Mansfield (1888-1923) was also a gifted poet.

The publication of *Kowhai Gold* (1930), an anthology edited by Quentin Pope, damaged the reputation of women writers. Although it contained poems by such fine poets as Duggan, Mansfield, and Hyde, the anthology was criticized as a collection of mere "magazine verse," resembling the effusions produced in the previous century by sentimental ladies and altered only by the addition of verbal decorations, or "kowhai gold." In a country still dominated by masculine values, it was tempting to apply these strictures to women writers who used traditional forms and themes.

With the publication in 1945 of *A Book of New Zealand Verse, 1923-1945*, Allen Curnow, the editor, became one of New Zealand's most influential literary critics. Curnow had established himself as a poet with the appearance of his first published collection, *Valley of Decision* (1933). Shortly thereafter, he had begun contributing to the publications of Caxton Press in Christchurch. By the end of the decade, Curnow's poetry was showing the influence of modernists such as

the American-born English poet T. S. Eliot. In his selection of poets to be included in the anthology, Curnow demonstrated his approval of poetic innovations, and in his lengthy introduction to the volume, Curnow called for exploration of the national identity, arguing that the poems in the collection reflected the imaginative problems of people confined to an isolated island nation.

In the 1950's and 1960's, Curnow's preeminent position in New Zealand letters was challenged by a group of poets operating out of Wellington, led by James K. Baxter (1926-1972). The young poets of the Wellington School resented Curnow's power and rejected his ideas, which they interpreted as nationalistic. They even managed to protest so effectively that the publication of Curnow's new anthology was delayed for two years. During the 1960's, the charismatic Baxter not only took Curnow's place as literary arbiter but also produced an immense quantity of fine poetry. After Baxter's death, Curnow began publishing again, this time poetry that was simpler and more colloquial in style and more personal in subject matter than what he had written earlier. Curnow's achievements were recognized in 1989, when he was awarded the Queen's Gold Medal for Poetry.

Just as in Australia, during the final decades of the twentieth century, New Zealand saw an explosion of poetic talent and the publication of poems written in a variety of styles. Among the many poets who came to prominence during the 1970's and 1980's were C. K. Stead (born 1932), Fleur Adcock (born 1934), Ian Wedde (born 1946), Bill Manhire (born 1946), Elizabeth Smither (born 1941), Tony Beyer (born 1948), Murray Edmond (born 1949), and Cilla McQueen (born 1949). Anthologies published during the 1990's and the first decade of the twenty-first century included poetry by the poet-painter Gregory O'Brien (born 1961), Andrew Johnston (born 1963), Virginia Were (born 1960), Jenny Bornholt (born 1960), and Michele Leggott (born 1956). If New Zealand writers had not yet agreed on a national identity, at least they had come to terms with themselves and with their situation in the wider world. In addition, the international community was learning where the real wealth of the island nation lay—in the rich imaginations of its people.

Bibliography

Bennett, Bruce, and Jennifer Strauss, eds. *The Oxford Literary History of Australia*. New York: Oxford University Press, 1998. Chris Wallace-Crabbe's discussion of "Poetry and Modernism" and Dennis Haskell's "Poetry Since 1965" provide an interesting perspective on modern Australian poetry. Bibliography, chronology, and index.

Bornholdt, Jenny, Gregory O'Brien, and Mark Williams, eds. *An Anthology of New Zealand Poetry in English*. New York: Oxford University Press, 1997. This extensive collection won the 1997 Montana New Zealand Book Award for Poetry. The editors' introduction provides an excellent overview of the subject. Bibliography and index.

Brins, Nicholas, and Rebecca McNeer, eds. *A Companion to Australian Literature Since 1900*. Rochester, N.Y.: Camden House, 2007. A collection of essays by various writers on a wide range of topics, including the history of Australian poetry, poets who have established international reputations, and issues connected with global and multicultural perspectives. Bibliography and index.

Brooks, David, ed. *The Best Australian Poetry, 2008*. Brisbane: University of Queensland Press, 2008. The sixth volume in a distinguished annual series, edited by Bronwyn Lea and Martin Duwell. The 2008 collection includes forty poems from print and online journals, selected by Brooks, a major poet and novelist and the editor of Australia's oldest literary journal. The foreword by Lea and Duwell and Brooks's introduction are both well worth reading. Biographical notes, along with contributors' comments on their poems.

Leonard, John, ed. *Australian Verse: An Oxford Anthology*. New York: Oxford University Press, 1998. A varied collection, including convict songs and bush ballads. Organized in reverse chronological order, beginning with contemporary poetry and ending with the early colonial period. Brief biographical notes. Indexed by first lines, titles, and writers.

Marsack, Robyn, and Andrew Johnstone, eds. *Twenty*

Contemporary New Zealand Poets: An Anthology. Manchester, England: Carcaret Press, 2009. Includes several generations of poets, writing in various styles, who together represent New Zealand's poetic voice.

Petrie, Barbara, ed. *Kiwi and Emu: An Anthology of Contemporary Poetry by Australian and New Zealand Women*. Springwood, N.S.W.: Butterfly Books, 1989. Petrie put together this volume in the hope of contributing to a closer connection between the women of Australia and New Zealand. The poems reflect similar experiences, including gender repression, and reveal the women's dedication to their craft. Indexes of titles, first lines, and new poems, and a glossary of Maori words.

Pierce, Peter, ed. *The Cambridge History of Australian Literature*. New York: Cambridge University Press, 2009. Traces Australian literary history from the colonial period to the early twenty-first century. Introduction by the editor. Two chapters focus on poetry, "Poetry, Popular Culture, and Modernity, 1890-1950," by Peter Fitzpatrick, and another covering poetry since 1950, by Dennis Haskell. Bibliography and index.

Rose, Peter, ed. *The Best Australian Poems, 2008*. Melbourne, Vic.: Black, 2008. A volume in a series that appears annually, featuring both established poets and promising newcomers. Among the poets included are Dorothy Porter, Les A. Murray, Chris Wallace-Crabbe, Rosemary Dobson, Tracy Ryan, and Laurie Duggan.

Wilde, William. *Australian Poets and Their Works: A Reader's Guide*. New York: Oxford University Press, 1996. An abridgement of the second edition of the *Oxford Companion to Australian Literature* (1995). However, some additional poets and publications have been added, as well as Wilde's introduction, which provides an excellent historical overview of Australian poetry. Alphabetized entries provide information about poets, major poems, publications, poetry societies, and other relevant topics.

Rosemary M. Canfield Reisman

Canadian Poetry

Long before the vast region that is now Canada was explored and settled by Europeans, it was home to a number of aboriginal peoples. Each group had its own culture and language, but the groups were similar in some ways. Like aboriginal tribes in other parts of the world, they had stories about the creation of the world and humanity, their natural surroundings, and animals that behaved like humans and, in some cases, actually became human beings. One of the common elements in these tribal stories was the inclusion of a trickster figure, whose function was to add suspense and humor to narratives.

How and when orally transmitted aboriginal stories became literature, which by definition means something that has been written down, is difficult to determine. Although the Canadian aboriginal peoples depended primarily on the oral transmission of their cultural heritage, contemporary observers reported that some tribes recorded texts on wampum or in hieroglyphic letters inscribed on birch bark. The first alphabetical transcriptions and translations of the poetry of the Canadian aboriginal peoples can be found in letters written by Jesuit missionaries and British and French military officers to their friends in Europe. The Jesuit missionaries taught their own writing system to aboriginal children.

In the late nineteenth century, Tekahionwake (1861-1913), a First Nations poet, became famous for English-language poems about her culture. The daughter of a Mohawk chief and his English wife, Emily Pauline Johnson, she was one of the most popular writers of the period. Between 1892 and 1910, she made several reading tours of Canada, the United States, and England, often wearing native dress. Her most famous book was the poetry collection *Flint and Feather* (1912).

More than half a century passed before poems by an aboriginal author about the heritage of the First Nations, the Inuit, or the Métis again became popular. The chapbook *Sweetgrass* (1971) contained poems by three Métis writers. It was followed by such works as *Okanagan Indian Poems and Short Stories* (1974) and *Wisdom of Indian Poetry* (1976). The Mi'kmaq-Canadian Rita Joe (1932-2007) published her first volume, *Poems of Rita Joe* (1978). Among the other poets to gain prominence during the following decades were Jeannette Armstrong (born 1948), Beth Cuthand (born 1949), and Daniel David Moses (born 1952). Although their works consistently reflect their dedication to preserving their cultural heritage, they also deal with contemporary issues, ranging from the status of Native women to social and political injustices both in Canada and elsewhere in the world.

Early francophone poetry

During the seventeenth and eighteenth centuries, the French established settlements in Nova Scotia and in Quebec. In 1713, most of the area in Nova Scotia, which was known as Acadia, was turned over to the British, but the French held onto the rest of their settlements in Canada until the fall of Quebec in 1759. With the Treaty of Paris in 1763, England took over New France. However, many of the people in the Maritime Provinces and most of the natives of Quebec continue to speak and write in French. The nationalistic fervor of the 1960's impelled those who lived there to insist on being called Québécois, leaving the label "French Canadian" for the French-speaking Canadians in Nova Scotia, New Brunswick, and the western provinces. In this essay, however, the authors of francophone works will be referred to by the more general term.

The earliest French Canadian works to appear were written by travelers and missionaries and published in France. However, after a printing press was established in Quebec in 1764, bilingual and French-language newspapers appeared. They published poems by such writers as the French dramatist Joseph Quesnel (1746-1809). In 1830, Michel Bibaud (1782-1857) published the first book of French Canadian poetry, *Épîtres, satire, chansons, épigrammes et autres pièces en vers* (epistles, satire, songs, epigrams, and other verses). In the 1840's, the École Patriotique de Quebec, a conservative, Roman Catholic literary group dedicated to the preservation of French Canadian traditions, formed around the poet and bookseller Octave Crémazie (1827-1879). In 1863, the Romantic poet Louis Fréchette (1839-1908) published a collection called *Mes loisirs* (my leisures), which was the first volume of lyric poetry to appear in Quebec. In 1880, a volume of his verses won for Fréchette the French Academy's Prix Montyon. Thereafter, he was thought of as the poet laureate of French Canada. His *La Légende d'un peuple* (1887; the legend of a people) is considered the most important francophone poetic work published during the nineteenth century.

FRANCOPHONE POETRY IN THE TWENTIETH CENTURY

At the turn of the century, Montreal was not only a thriving commercial center but also a city with a cosmopolitan culture, closely linked to intellectual developments in France and in Belgium. The Parnassian and Decadent movements in Europe provided the impetus for the founding of the École Littéraire de Montréal (the Montreal literary school), primarily to introduce the kind of poetry popularized by the French Symbolists and the Parnassians. Among the members of this group were Jean Charbonneau (1875-1960), Émile Nelligan (1879-1941), Charles Gill (1871-1918), and Charles Lozeau (1878-1924).

The poets associated with the periodical *Le Terroir* (the land), founded in 1909, were called the regionalists because their verse, although often neoclassical in form, tended to have patriotic themes; local, usually rural, subject matter; and sometimes religious content. Among the more distinguished regional poets were Nérée Beauchemin (1850-1931), Blanche Lamontagne-Beauregard (1889-1958), and Lionel Léveillé (1975-1955).

During the 1940's and the 1950's, the poets of Quebec turned inward, exploring their own psyches, feelings of alienation, and spiritual needs, as well as the meaning of mortality. Hector de Saint-Denys Garneau (1912-1943) was joined in these efforts by Alain Grandbois (1900-1975), Anne Hébert (1916-2000), and Rina Lasnier (1915-1997). Since the 1960's, under the influence of a more open, less repressive government, there has been not only an intensification of nationalism but also a proliferation of new writers. This trend was markedly influenced by the establishment of

small presses, among them L'Hexagone, founded in 1953, which published the works of such poets as Paul-Marie Lapointe (born 1929), Roland Giguère (1929-2003), Fernand Ouellette (born 1930), and Yves Préfontaine (born 1937). L'Hexagone stimulated the literary life of Quebec by sponsoring literary magazines and holding annual conferences of national and international writers.

The one characteristic that marks the francophone poetry that appeared during the final decades of the twentieth century is its diversity. Poet and novelist Nicole Brossard (born 1943) writes from a feminist-lesbian perspective. André Roy (born 1944) uses modernist modes, sometimes even filmlike forms, to create erotic poems about homosexuality and the ever-present threat of HIV-AIDS. François Charron (born 1952) is known for his lyrical works on a variety of themes, including the connection between his poetic expressions and his paintings. By contrast, the poems of Marie Uguay (1955-1981), written as she approached a death from cancer, are concise, personal, and introspective. Some writers have combined poetry with prose, as did Elise Turcotte (born 1957) in her poetic novel *Le Bruit des chose vivantes* (1991; *The Sound of Living Things*, 1993).

In the latter part of the twentieth century, francophone writing flourished in areas other than Quebec. For example, Patrice Desbiens (born 1948) is a Franco-Ontarian poet. Charles Le Blanc, born in 1950 in Montreal, made his home in Manitoba. Paul Savoie, who was born in Manitoba in 1946, settled in Toronto. Among the Acadian writers who have achieved fame are Dyane Léger (born 1954) of Moncton, New Brunswick, who is admired for her lyric poetry and poetic prose, and Herménégilde Chiasson (born 1946), also of New Brunswick. Although francophone literature will always remain the expression of a minority, it has proven to be a valuable element in the kaleidoscopic nation that Canada has become.

EARLY CANADIAN POETRY IN ENGLISH

Although most of the early anglophone Canadian writers turned out narrative and descriptive prose rather than poetry about the new country, Halifax, Nova Scotia, was becoming a cultural center as early as 1789, when it became the home of the first Canadian literary journal in English, *Nova-Scotia Magazine*. A native of New Brunswick, Oliver Goldsmith (1794-1861), wrote the epic poem *The Rising Village*, which was published in England in 1825. The poem, which celebrated pioneer life in Nova Scotia, was clearly meant as a response to *The Deserted Village* (1770), in which Goldsmith's granduncle, Oliver Goldsmith (1728 or 1730-1774), had deplored the fate of emigrants to the New World. Like *The Rising Village*, most of the poetry written during these early years was upbeat in tone and patriotic in theme, as can be seen in the first anthology of Canadian poetry, *Selections from Canadian Poets* (1864), edited by Edward H. Dewart (1828-1903). Not surprisingly, the poems in that volume are derivative, for Canadians had yet to develop a sense of who they were. In fact, that effort would dominate Canadian literature for the next hundred years.

When Canada became a self-governing dominion within the British Empire in 1867, Canadian writers were even more motivated to develop a distinctive national literature. In the next two decades, six of them founded a group that became known as the Confederation poets. Charles G. D. Roberts (1860-1943) and his cousin Bliss Carman (1861-1929) came from New Brunswick; Archibald Lampman (1861-1899), who was born in Ontario, made his home in Ottawa, as did Duncan Campbell Scott (1862-1947) and W. W. Campbell (1858-1918). Isabella Valency Crawford (1850-1887) eventually settled in Toronto. While the Confederation poets had a common goal, their modes of expression differed. Crawford is best known for her narrative poems, while Roberts and Carman both used descriptions of nature as they had experienced it in the Maritimes to dramatize their ideas about life. Neither of them was a Wordsworthian; the nature they knew was as temperamental as it was awe inspiring. Scott anticipated later western writers in choosing to write about the northern wilderness, thus showing nature at its most savage. Although at the time Carman was the most popular of the Confederation Poets, Lampman has come to be considered the finest. However, all of them were important in that they broke away from English models, both in form and in subject matter, thus inspiring the poets that were to follow them.

THE MODERNISTS

One of the most influential poets of the next generation was E. J. Pratt (1882-1964), a native of Newfoundland. Like his predecessors, Pratt excelled in natural description, as he demonstrated in his book *Newfoundland Verse* (1923), but he also wrote distinctive long narrative poems, such as *The Titanic* (1935) and *Dunkirk* (1941). Pratt also dramatized Canadian history in documentary narratives such as *Brébeuf and His Brethren* (1940). The fact that Pratt emphasized the heroic qualities of the Iroquois and those of the Jesuit missionaries whom they killed drew negative comments from some critics. However, the work won the Governor-General's Award for poetry. The independence Pratt displayed in his treatment of subject matter and in his willingness to experiment with new poetic forms links Pratt with the group who introduced modernism into Canadian poetry.

In the middle 1920's, A. J. M. Smith (1902-1980) began editing a literary supplement that soon became the *McGill Fortnightly Review*. His intent was to introduce the innovative spirit of modernism into Canadian poetry. What became known as the McGill movement and, later, the Montreal group included F. R. Scott (1899-1985), A. M. Klein (1909-1972), Leo Kennedy (1907-2000), and Leon Edel (1907-1997). In 1936, Smith and Scott brought out a collection called *New Provinces*, which contained poems by Smith, Scott, Klein, and Kennedy, as well as by Pratt and another Toronto poet, Robert Finch (1900-1995). This volume exemplified the tenets of modernism, notably by making poetry closer to everyday speech through the use of simple, colloquial language, concrete images, and free verse. The brilliant lyricist P. K. Page (1916-2010) also found inspiration through her association with this group.

Two other important poets of the period were Earle Birney (1904-1995), a socialist, and Dorothy Livesay (1909-1996). Birney, who was originally from Alberta, often used the imagery of western Canada in his poetry. As a longtime professor at the University of British Columbia, he established Canada's first department of creative writing. Livesay, too, was drawn to the West. In 1936, she moved to Vancouver, which was becoming a literary and cultural center. It was her home for the next twenty years.

By the 1940's, although Canadian writers were becoming better known in their own country, their works were still little read outside Canada. With the establishment in 1949 of the Royal Commission on National Development in the Arts, Letters, and Sciences (the Massey Commission), the Canadian government became committed to furthering cultural activities. Soon thereafter, the National Library was established. Another important step forward was the formation in 1957 of the Canada Council for the Encouragement of the Arts, Letters, Humanities, and Social Sciences, which provided financial aid for several projected literary magazines. (In 1978, this group was split into the Canadian Council for the Arts and the Social Sciences and Humanities Research Council of Canada.) The openness of these groups to experimentation made it possible for the modernists to flourish. Experimental poems consistently won the Governor-General's Award for poetry. For example, the 1958 award went to *A Suit of Nettles* (1958), by James Reaney, in which an Elizabethan form was used to describe events in Canadian history.

Margaret Atwood (AP/Wide World Photos)

CONTEMPORARY POETRY

In the late 1950's, Warren Tallman (1921-1994), an American-born poetry professor at the University of British Columbia, became interested in the theories of Robert Duncan, the San Francisco poet, and other Black Mountain poets, such as Robert Creeley, Denise Levertov, and Charles Olson. The British Columbians who met with Tallman and Duncan were especially interested in Olson's insistence that poetry is essentially oral, rather than written. This theory would eventually stimulate the growth of performance poetry.

In September, 1961, George Bowering (born 1935), Frank Davey (born 1940), David Dawson (born 1942), Jamie Reid (born 1941), and Fred Wah (born 1939) published the first issue of a magazine called *Tish*. Meanwhile, in Ontario, Al Purdy (1918-2000) began to write poems that derived their form from casual conversation. Thus, postmodernism came to Canada.

During the 1960's, Margaret Atwood (born 1939) began her long and distinguished career as a poet, novelist, short-story writer, and literary critic. In her poetry, Atwood explored such issues as love and death, human alienation, and social injustice. Another contemporary writer is Anne Carson (born 1950), a classics professor who merges past and present in poems that are noted for their timeless appeal.

Like Atwood, Michael Ondaatje (born 1943) has attained recognition in a number of different genres. His prizewinning novel *The English Patient* (1992) was a cowinner of the Booker Prize. However, his genius is best displayed in his most famous poetic work, *The Collected Works of Billy the Kid: Left Handed Poems* (1970), a mixture of lyrics, ballads, prose narratives, and even photographs that purport to tell the story of the famous American outlaw. Ondaatje, who was born in Sri Lanka and reared in England, sets his works in various locations throughout the world, thus exemplifying the cosmopolitan trend in Canadian literature that first emerged in the latter part of the twentieth century. By contrast, the poems of Ondaatje's friend B. P. Nichol (1944-1988)—including those in his multivolume work *The Martyrology* (1972-1987)—are closely tied to Toronto.

Canada's West did not lack for distinguished poets in the latter years of the century. Among them are Patrick Lane (born 1939), Lorna Crozier (born 1948), and Robert Bringhurst (born 1946). Bringhurst, a native Californian with Canadian parents who later settled in Vancouver, uses his studies of primitive cultures in his poetry. A dedicated postmodernist, originally influenced by the Tish group, Robert Kroetsch (born 1927) sees the western prairies as defining both life and poetic form.

Originally, the search for a Canadian identity was made more difficult because the country was so vast and varied and because its settlers were drawn from two different European cultures and spoke two different languages. As the value of the native heritage was recognized and as new immigrants poured into Canada, the identity issue became even more complicated. If there is one theme that dominates contemporary Canadian poetry, it is a plea for acceptance of people who are different, whether because of their race, their religion, their national background, their gender, or their sexual orientation. Clearly Canada's poets have come to the conclusion that there is no single Canadian identity. Indeed, the strength of the new country that is emerging in the twenty-first century will be its power to live in harmony with diversity.

BIBLIOGRAPHY

Atwood, Margaret, ed. *The New Oxford Book of Canadian Verse in English*. New York: Oxford University Press, 1982. A comprehensive collection, especially valuable for its inclusion of many early writers not represented elsewhere. Atwood's introductory essay is especially noteworthy. Index.

Blouin, Louise, Bernard Pozier, and D. G. Jones, eds. *Esprit de Corps: Québec Poetry of the Late Twentieth Century in Translation*. Winnipeg, Man.: Muses, 1997. Especially useful for anglophone readers.

Brandt, Di, and Barbara Godard, eds. *Wider Boundaries of Daring: The Modernist Impulse in Canadian Women's Poetry*. Waterloo, Ont.: Wilfrid Laurier University Press, 2009. Essays by various writers, emphasizing the contributions of women poets, critics, activists, and experimental prose writers to the development of literary modernism. Notes, bibliographies, and index.

Butling, Pauline, and Susan Rudy. *Writing in Our Time: Canada's Radical Poetries in English (1957-2003)*. Waterloo, Ont.: Wilfrid Laurier University Press, 2005. A guide to what the authors assert are the most significant events in Canadian literary history. Chronologies, extensive bibliographical references, and index.

Hammill, Faye. *Canadian Literature*. Edinburgh: Edinburgh University Press, 2007. A historical and thematic study of anglophone Canadian writers. Chronology, glossary, bibliographical references, and index.

Kroller, Eva-Marie, ed. *The Cambridge Companion to Canadian Literature*. New York: Cambridge University Press, 2004. Contains essays on major genres and on general topics, such as nature writing and writing by women. Plates and maps, chronology, bibliographical references, and index. An essential source.

Nischik, Reingard M., ed. *History of Literature in Canada: English-Canadian and French-Canadian*. Rochester, N.Y.: Camden House, 2008. Includes essays on both English Canadian and French Canadian poetry, as well as on traditional oral verse. Bibliographical references and index.

Quan, Andy, and Jim Wong-Chu, eds. *Swallowing Clouds: An Anthology of Chinese-Canadian Poetry*. Vancouver, B.C.: Arsenal Pulp Press, 1999. The first book-length collection of poems by Chinese Canadians. Some of the twenty-four writers included are well known; others are relatively new. Illustrated.

Starnino, Carmine, ed. *The New Canon: An Anthology of Canadian Poetry*. Montreal: Véhicule Press, 2006. Nearly two hundred poems by fifty Canadian poets, all born between 1955 and 1975, who reject traditional modes in favor of innovative forms. Includes an essay by the editor explaining the aims of this group.

Toye, William, ed. *The Concise Oxford Companion to Canadian Literature*. New York: Oxford University Press, 2001. A convenient, updated abridgment of the second edition of the *Oxford Companion to Canadian Literature* (1997). For topical overviews, the fuller version should be consulted.

Ware, Tracy, ed. *A Northern Romanticism: Poets of the Confederation—A Critical Edition*. Ottawa, Ont.: Tecumseh Press, 2000. Focuses on the poets who emerged in the last two decades of the nineteenth century to raise their art to new heights. Includes extensive selections from their poetry, biographical introductions to each poet, notes, bibliographies, and critical essays.

Rosemary M. Canfield Reisman

CARIBBEAN POETRY

From its earliest beginnings in the eighteenth century, Caribbean, or West Indian, poetry has been an elusive but dynamic art. Though sometimes static, it has always been an evolving art form. According to one scholar, Lloyd W. Brown, the first 180 years of West Indian poetry were uneven at best; however, Brown was appraising only the formal aspect of Caribbean poetry, a poetic tradition that was imposed on the peoples of the West Indies first by a slavocracy and later by an imperialist regime. There has always been an oral tradition in the Caribbean, and although this tradition has been suppressed, it could never be destroyed. It has existed in children's ring games, in calypso, and in the combined arts of carnival, Junkanoo, and other folk and religious celebrations. Then, too, the unwritten tradition of the Amerindians has enriched the art of Caribbean poetry. Ironically, after years of suppression, the folk and oral traditions, combined with other aspects of Afro-Caribbean cultural experiences, are theorized, by Edward Kamau Brathwaite, as the wellspring of "nation language."

EIGHTEENTH CENTURY

Slavery in the Caribbean was extremely harsh, and people of African descent had very little opportunity to develop the art of composing poetry. Therefore, the first poems to be published by an Afro-Caribbean came as a result of an experiment centered in the noble savage concept. Francis Williams of Jamaica, a free black, was the first to publish a poem. John, the second duke of Montagu (and at one time Jamaica's governor), believed that if blacks were given the same educational opportunities as Caucasians they would be able to compete successfully with Caucasians. Williams, under the patronage of the duke, was educated in England. On his return to Jamaica, the duke was unable to establish his protégé in Jamaican society, so Williams opened a school in Spanish Town.

In 1759, Williams wrote "An Ode to George Haldane, Governor of the Island of Jamaica" to celebrate the arrival of the governor at his new office. Written in Latin, the poem, the only extant work of Williams, attests to the poet's abilities, but it also suggests the subservient position in which Williams found himself:

> Established by a mighty hand (God the creator gave the same soul to all his creatures without exception), virtue itself, like wisdom, is devoid of color. There is no color in an honorable mind, nor in art.

Williams then bids his black muse not to hesitate but to "mount to the abode of [the new governor] the Caesar of the setting sun," and bid him welcome.

The other acknowledged poet of the eighteenth century is James Grainger, a Scottish physician who made his home in Jamaica. His extended poem *The Sugar-Cane* (1766) is often described as a pastoral epic that discusses the vicissitudes of life on the island. The poem is based on Western European forms that underscore European stereotypes, as in this description of the slaves:

> Adroit they [slaves] form; nor inexpert
> A thousand tuneful intricacies weave,
> Shaking their sable limbs; and oft a kiss
> steal from their partners; who, with neck reclin'd
> and semblant scorn resent the ravish'd bliss.

Grainger depicts a Romantic pastoral but also indicates that, should the slaves drink alcohol or hear the drum they will immediately revert to their savage ways, and "bacchanalian frenzy" will ensue. Despite the idealistic picture presented in *The Sugar-Cane*, the poem has come to typify the long-lived tradition of the Caribbean pastoral.

NINETEENTH CENTURY

Williams and Grainger represent the poetry of the eighteenth century; the poets who typify the tradition during the nineteenth century are the Hart sisters of Antigua and Egbert Martin of Guyana. Elizabeth Hart Thwaites and Anne Hart Gilbert were two women of African descent who have not received much exposure. Their parents, Anne Clerkley Hart and Barry Conyers Hart, were free African Caribbeans. The father, a plantation owner, was also a poet who published his poems in the local newspaper. Although slavery prevailed in Antigua, both sisters married white men and devoted their lives to educating other African Caribbeans. The sisters were known for writing religious poems and hymns. Anne Hart Gilbert affirms that, although race prejudice was pervasive, her light complexion exempted her and her family from racial prejudices. In "On the Death of the Rev. Mr. Cook," Elizabeth Hart Thwaites praises the missionary for his work among all races:

> With rapture [he] heard the diff'rent tribes converse,
> In Canaan's tongue redeeming love rehearse,
> And Afric's sable sons in stammering accents tell
> Of Jesu's love, immense, unspeakable.

Like the Hart sisters, Egbert Martin had his roots in the Caribbean Basin and was considered the most prominent poet of his day. The son of a Guyanese tailor, Martin wrote poetry that followed the traditional modes of European models. He did, at times, paint realistic word-pictures of Guyanese landscapes, and in some of his better poems he makes his readers aware of the poverty of his people. Perhaps he is not as patriotic as his "National Anthem" suggests, but in it, he calls for Britain to close its "Far-reaching wings" over all its "Colonial throng." Written for Queen Victoria's Jubilee in 1887, the poem won an award for his patriotic efforts.

TWENTIETH CENTURY

Caribbean poetry came into its own during the twentieth century. The nineteenth century poets were cautious. They protested against the oppressive rule of the colonials, but they saw themselves as British. The poets of the early part of the twentieth century were militant. They were nationalistic. The poets who best represent this period are Jamaica's Claude McKay, Jamaica's Louise Bennett, Guyana's Arthur J. Seymour, St. Lucia's Derek Walcott, and Barbados's Edward Kamau Brathwaite.

CLAUDE MCKAY

One of the strongest voices to come out of the Caribbean during the early twentieth century is that of Claude McKay, born in 1889 in Sunny Ville, Jamaica. Before leaving his home, he published two volumes of dialect poetry *Constab Ballads* (1912) and *Songs of Jamaica* (1912). Shortly after publishing these volumes, McKay migrated to the United States, where he became the voice of oppressed blacks not only in the Caribbean but also throughout the world. He insisted that he was "never going to carry the torch for British colonialism or American imperialism." Using the sonnet as his major mode of expression, McKay describes America as a vicious tiger that "sinks into my throat her tiger's tooth/ stealing my breath of life. . . ." The poet warns America that he "sees her might and granite wonders. . . . Like priceless treasures sinking in the sand." The poet insists that if America kills him, "she" will be killing herself because it is he who makes America strong. In "If We Must Die," McKay's persona encourages the oppressed not to die "like hogs/ Hunted and penned in an inglorious spot," but to die nobly facing the enemy: "Pressed to the wall, dying but fighting back!" Although McKay was probably not thinking of the British as oppressed (the British for Mckay were always the colonizers, the oppressors), during World War II, when the Germans were blitzing London, British prime minister Winston Churchill quoted McKay's poem in the House of Commons to rally the nation, and British soldiers carried copies of the poem in their pockets.

Although McKay never returned to Jamaica to live, he did write about the beauty of the island. In "Flame Heart," he admits that he has forgotten much about Jamaica, but what he has never forgotten is "the poinsettia's red, blood red in warm December." His romantic nostalgia is also evidenced in "The Tropics in New York": In passing a store that displayed tropical fruits in a window the persona admits: "And, hungry for the old, familiar ways,/ I turned aside and bowed my head and wept." McKay, then, represents the new thrust in Caribbean poetry that came to the fore in the early part of the twentieth century. He is sophisticated enough to use the traditional British literary tradition, but instead of writing romantic pastorals he instructs the oppressed to fight and he warns the oppressors of disastrous times should they continue their oppression.

LOUISE BENNETT

Jamaica-born Louise Bennett (1919-2006) is an important poet in the development of Caribbean poetry because she had the courage not to develop her talents in the accepted English literary tradition. Bennett admits that she was not taken seriously as a poet. She started out writing in the traditional Caribbean pastoral tradition, but she was not doing what she wanted to do, so she followed the folk/oral tradition. A nationalist and a womanist, Bennett makes her philosophical statements through humor. In "Colonization in Reverse," the poet informs Miss Mattie, a persona in much of her poetry, that England is in for a surprise because Jamaicans now have the whip hand. They "Jussa pack dem bag and baggage;/ An tun history upside dung." The Jamaicans are giving Britain a dose of its own medicine by moving to Britain. The poet insists that the British folk are known for being calm when faced with adversity, yet she muses: "But ah wonder how dem gwine stan/ Colonization in reverse." In "Jamaican Oman," Bennett explains that Island women have always been liberated and have always supported their men. Long before other women of the world sought to be liberated "Jamaican women wassa work/ Her liberation plan!" Bennett was not always held in high esteem as a poet, especially prior to the 1960's. However, with independence, poets became more concerned with finding their own voices rather than imitating British models. Bennett became the spirit of the age.

ARTHUR J. SEYMOUR

Arthur J. Seymour, from Guyana (1914-1989), was pivotal to the development of poetry in the Caribbean as both a writer and a publisher. As a poet, his longevity allows us to see the transition that was occurring in the Caribbean. His poetry of the 1930's has very little if any protest and is tempered by a "colonial quiescence." Later, however, Seymour combines his Guyanese nationalism with an embracing of the entire Caribbean. In "For Christopher Columbus," the reader, like Columbus, sees weaving palm trees in the tropical breezes "And watches the islands in a great bow swing/ From Florida down to the South American coast." While he seems to fall back on the earlier English model of the Caribbean pastoral, Seymour does not forget to remind his audience of the degradation of slavery and of the suffering that African Caribbeans have endured.

DEREK WALCOTT AND EDWARD KAMAU BRATHWAITE

Derek Walcott of St. Lucia and Edward Kamau Brathwaite of Barbados are the two writers who bridge the gap between poets of the colonial period and the New World poets. These artists have witnessed the harshness of colonialism. They have known what it means to be isolated as artists and as individuals, for they came into adulthood and began their writing when the Caribbean nations were still Crown colonies. As a poet and a dramatist, Walcott has used his talents to accentuate Caribbean speech patterns and cultural traditions in works such as *Omeros* (1990) and *The Odyssey: A Stage Version* (pr. 1992). He has used the Homeric legends and Homeric characters to crystallize the Caribbean experience. In 1992, he won the Nobel Prize in Literature, thereby bringing great visibility to Caribbean writers as a whole.

Brathwaite, also a poet of international fame, has brought notoriety to Caribbean poetry not only through his writing and his oral presentation but also through his scholarly endeavors in Caribbean language and culture. Both Walcott and Brathwaite have transcended their Caribbean ethos to become world-renowned po-

Derek Walcott (Getty Images)

ets, and both have brought Caribbean poetry from its colonial vision into the international arena and have turned Caribbean dialect into what Brathwaite calls "nation language" of the Caribbean.

POST-INDEPENDENCE PERIOD

The poetry of the post-independence period in the Caribbean is more exuberant than the poetry of the colonial era. Brathwaite affirms that Caribbean poets have found a new mode of expression that he calls "nation language." This New World language might sound like English, "but in its contours, its rhythm and timbre, its sound explosions, it is not English. . . ." Three poets who demonstrate this new language are Grace Nichols, Fred D'Aguiar, and Bongo Jerry.

GRACE NICHOLS

Grace Nichols (born in Guyana in 1950), whose roots are in Guyana, insists that her poetry comes out of "a heightened imagistic use of language that does things to the heart and head." She is at ease with both languages, standard English as well as creole or nation language, because for her, the two languages are "constantly intercepting." The blending of these languages is evident in the poem "I Is a Long-Memoried Woman." Here the persona states:

> From dih pout
> of mih mouth
> from dih
> treacherous
> calm of mih smile
> you can tell
> I is a long-memoried woman.

FRED D'AGUIAR

Fred D'Aguiar (born in 1960 in London and sent to Guyana as a child) fuses folk tradition with standard English and nation language. In "Mama Dot Learns to Fly," D'Aguiar explores the myth of the flying African. Mama Dot, looking at a film of inventors trying to fly, decides that she wants to see an ancestor, so with "Her equipment straightforward/ Thought-up to bring the lot/ To her: *come leh we gaff girl*." The idea here, as Toni Morrison suggests in *Song of Solomon* (1977), is that people of African descent do not need the invention of flying machines because they have the natural ability to fly. Much of the flying concept is suggested in the final line of the poem when Mama Dot says: "Come let us go off, girl."

BONGO JERRY

Unlike Nichols and D'Aguiar, who fuse standard English and nation language, Bongo Jerry, a Rastafarian poet, uses a language that Brathwaite calls "the roots and underground link of all the emerging forces" of the New World literature. Bongo sees the new language as a liberating tool for people of the Caribbean. In the poem "MABRAK" the poet proclaims:

> Save the YOUNG
> from the language that MAN teach,
> the doctrine Pope preach
> skin bleach
> HOW ELSE? . . . MAN must use MEN language to
>   carry this message.

The message is that the language that has been taught by the European, "BABEL TONGUES," must be silenced, and the poets of the Caribbean must "recall and recollect BLACK SPEECH."

Caribbean poetry has evolved from an imitation art into a dynamic expression of the cultural traditions of the people. In reclaiming their submerged language, a language of African origins, poets are affirming their heritage and their pride in their newfound freedom. This pride is also reflected in the determination of Caribbean women poets to attain the same status as their male counterparts without sacrificing their gender identity and their poetic voice. At the beginning of the twenty-first century, women scholars and poets were uniting in an effort to achieve the recognition that for so long had been denied to them.

In the past, Caribbean artists often left home to pursue success abroad. However, advances in communication technology have increased contact between the Caribbean and the rest of the world. Also, independence has resulted in an affirmation of cultural liberation, making migration less likely, and freedom has nurtured a spirit of creativity in Caribbean poets.

BIBLIOGRAPHY

Baugh, Edward. *Derek Walcott*. New York: Cambridge University Press, 2006. A definitive guide to

Walcott's works, demonstrating how his ideas and his techniques have changed over the course of his career. Bibliography and index.

Brathwaite, Edward Kamau. *A History of the Voice: The Development of National Language in Anglophone Caribbean Poetry*. London: New Beacon Press, 1984. The text explores Brathwaite's theory of the development of a Caribbean language that is centered in an African rather than a British tradition.

Brown, Stewart, and Mark McWatt, eds. *The Oxford Book of Caribbean Verse*. New York: Oxford University Press, 2005. Includes poems from Caribbean writers in English, French, and Spanish, with translations of the French and Spanish poems. A comprehensive guide.

Burnett, Paula, ed. *The Penguin Book of Caribbean Verse in English*. London: Penguin Global, 2006. Traces the development of both the oral and the literary traditions. Also has a good general introduction, glossary, biographical notes, and index of poets.

Dance, Daryl Cumber. *Fifty Caribbean Writers: A Bio-Bibliographical Critical Sourcebook*. New York: Greenwood Press, 1986. Contains biographical sketches, major works, themes, critical reception, and bibliographical information.

Ferguson, Moira, ed. *The Hart Sisters: Early African Caribbean Writers, Evangelicals, and Radicals*. Linds: University of Nebraska Press, 1993. Contains an extended critical introduction, the major works of the Hart sisters, and an appendix with information about people who were involved with the sisters.

Hamner, Robert D., ed. *Critical Perspectives on Derek Walcott*. Boulder, Colo.: Three Continents, 1997. This text has both criticisms by Walcott and criticism of his works by other scholars.

Jenkins, Lee M. *The Language of Caribbean Poetry: Boundaries of Expression*. Gainesville: University Press of Florida, 2004. An analysis of Caribbean poetics, pointing out the influence of the English, Scottish, and Irish literary traditions on Caribbean poets, as well as their response to modernism and postmodernism. Bibliography and index. A major study.

Markham, E. A., ed. *Hinterland: Afro-Caribbean and Black British Poetry*. Glasgow, Scotland: Bloodaxe Books, 1990. Contains several selections by each of the major poets included, as well as their essays about their works. Index.

Miller, Kei, ed. *New Caribbean Poetry: An Anthology*. Manchester, England: Carcanet, 2007. Selections from the works of eight contemporary poets demonstrate the continuing vigor, as well as the healthy diversity, of the Caribbean poetic tradition.

Narain, Denise DeCaires. *Contemporary Caribbean Women's Poetry: Making Style*. New York: Routledge, 2002. In the first detailed study of the subject, the author analyzes the reasons Caribbean female poets have been marginalized and traces the development of an authentic female voice in Caribbean poetry. Provides detailed readings of poems by relatively unknown women. Notes, extensive bibliography, and index.

Williams, Emily Allen. *Anglophone Caribbean Poetry, 1970-2001: An Annotated Bibliography*. Westport, Conn.: Greenwood Press, 2002. In addition to bibliographical references, includes time line and useful lists of conference proceedings, critical works, interviews, and recorded works.

Ralph Reckley, Sr.
Updated by Rosemary M. Canfield Reisman

CATALAN POETRY

Catalan, a romance language that serves as a bridge between the Ibero-Romanic and the Gallo-Romanic languages, is spoken today mainly in Spain, in the regions of Catalonia, Valencia, and the Balearic Islands. In addition, it is the official language of the tiny nation of Andorra, which lies in the Pyrenees Mountains on the border between Spain and France. Although clearly related to its sister Romance languages, it is not a dialect but a fully developed language with a venerable history and literature of its own. It flourished from the Middle Ages through to the twentieth century, but during Francisco Franco's totalitarian rule (1939-1975), it was banned from use in schools, government agencies, and the media. It did not die, however, but was reborn, along with a sometimes radical sense of nationalism, in the late 1970's after Franco's death. In 1979, both Spanish and Catalan were officially recognized in Catalonia, and in 1983, the Linguistic Normalization Act reinvigorated the language's use in official and commercial contexts. In 1997, the Catalan Language Act actually required broadcast media in Catalonia to offer programming in Catalan. Schools expose children to Catalan from a young age. This rebirth of the language has given rise to a revived interest in Catalan poetry both new and old.

MIDDLE AGES

Catalan first produced its own poetry in the thirteenth century. Before that time, and for the next two hundred years, many powerful poets whose vernacular was Catalan chose instead to write in Provençal. The Provençal poets, neighbors geographically, had provided the forms and the lexicon of courtly love and had developed the prestige of *amour courtois* in lyric poetry. Although some Catalan poets of this period did occasionally write in Catalan, their best-known works are in the more prestigious Provençal. The troubadour Catalan school began to flourish in the late twelfth century; among its members were Count Ramon Berenguer IV, Guillem de Cabestany, Guerau de Cabrera, Guillem de Bergadà, Cerverí de Girona, and Ramon Vidal de Besalú. The latter two were jongleurs or troubadours. Their sensitive love lyrics and highly sophisticated rhyme schemes were faithful to earlier Provençal models; among their themes were *amour courtois* of a political nature and satiric social verse.

Provençal, the language of art, was noticeably different from daily speech in Catalan. An important factor in maintaining the predominance of Provençal was the poetic Consistory of Toulouse, "de la Gaya Sciencia," at which Catalan poets writing in Provençal were winning contestants more often than not. This poetic contest, later named the Jocs Florals, has been revived in Toulouse and Barcelona since the nineteenth century, although Provençal is no longer the requisite language.

RAYMOND LULL

A chronological study of the masterpieces of Catalan poetry begins with the *Cancó de Santa Fe* (c. 1075), which represents an early, still formative Catalan that nevertheless resembles modern Catalan much more closely than the language of the *Chanson de Roland* (twelfth century; *The Song of Roland*, 1880) resembles modern French. Into the formless genre of Catalan poetry, there suddenly burst the most brilliant, fecund author and thinker of all Catalan literature, Raymond Lull (c. 1235-1316). His stature in Catalan letters is comparable to that of Dante, Giovanni Boccaccio, and Petrarch in Italian literature.

Although Lull's writings encompass a broad literary range, he is particularly appreciated for his poetry, including *Libre d'amic e amat* (c. 1285; *The Book of the Lover and Beloved*, 1923), *Lo desconhort* (c. 1295; lamentation), and *Cant de Ramon* (c. 1299; song of Raymond). Lull, a Franciscan, wrote almost innumerable philosophical and theological treatises in Latin, Arabic, and Catalan. His Catalan novel *Libre d'Evast e Blanquerna* (1283; English translation, 1925), composed in five parts that symbolize the five wounds of Christ, is considered his masterpiece; embedded in this novel is the highly poetic, internally rhyming prose poem *The Book of the Lover and Beloved*, which echoes the biblical Song of Songs and anticipates Saint John of the Cross in its celebration of the mystic ecstasy of lover and beloved.

Lull's encyclopedic *Libre de contemplació* (1273; *Book of Contemplation*, 1985) is a doctrinal work, while his *Libre de meravelles* (1288-1289; *Felix: Or, Book of Wonders*, 1985) is concerned with the revelation of God in nature, particularly in the section titled *Libre de les bèsties* (c. 1290; *The Book of the Beasts*, 1927), in which animals assume anthropomorphic roles. Among his other Catalan texts is the *Libre de l'orde de cavalleria* (1279; *The Book of the Order of Chivalry*, 1484), which became a manual for medieval knighthood and which was closely imitated by Don Juan Manuel in Castilian. Lull's *Opera latina* is principally theological and rigorously Scholastic in approach, while *Libre del gentil e dels tres savis* (1274-1276; *The Book of the Gentile and Three Wise Men*, 1985) is a balanced discussion of the respective religious positions of a Christian, a Jew, and a Muslim. Lull produced many other works in both Latin and Arabic.

A noble and amoral courtier as a young man, Lull underwent a dramatic conversion at the age of thirty. He left his wife, children, and rank to become a Franciscan, dedicating himself to study, teaching, writing, and converting Muslims and Jews. He traveled and taught widely, writing in different languages for widely divergent audiences. He made more than one trip to Tunis, perhaps dying while he was there or soon thereafter as a martyr, stoned by a mob. He is venerated not only as a great scholar, thinker, and poet but also as a religious figure, having attained the rank of Blessed.

Lull was the first great poet to write in Catalan. It is almost certain that, during his dissolute and courtly youth, he practiced versifying in Provençal, but after his conversion, he wrote in Catalan, using poetic forms borrowed from Provençal, except in *The Book of the Lover and Beloved*. In addition to being the first champion of Catalan poetry and prose, Lull was the first Catalan poet to delineate the Franciscan approach to God through nature, a tradition that has persisted in Catalan poetry to the present day. Lull's desire to demonstrate the rationality of the Christian faith and to recognize the universe as a manifestation of the Divine informed his philosophical and poetic quest.

Lo desconhort is one of Lull's best-known poems. Written in monorhymed Alexandrines, it is a highly personal analysis of his failures, imbued with pessimism and personal frustration. Readers today sense the poet's personality quite strongly, while recognizing the theme of unfulfilled personal aspirations as universal and timeless.

Lull employed poetic form not to exhibit his artistry but merely to provide a vehicle for his deeply felt religious expression. Concept and emotion take precedence over art, which had become hollow to him after his conversion. He was perceived during his own lifetime as a scholar, theologian, and prose writer, and a full appreciation of his poetry developed in the twentieth century. Lull was able to free himself from ritual Provençalisms and artistic rigidity precisely because of his overwhelming religious purpose.

After the uniquely personal poetry of Lull, the fourteenth century passed without the emergence of another significant Catalan poet. While the popular vernacular lyric did exist, the more erudite court poets continued the Provençal tradition, and the Catalan epics of the period were written exclusively in prose.

THE RENAISSANCE

The Catalan Renaissance began with the reign of Martí L'Humà in 1396, extending to 1516 and covering the reigns of Ferdinand Alfons IV of Catalonia, Alfons V of Aragon, Joan II, and Ferdinand II. Under Alfons, the center of the Catalan kingdom was Naples, which served as a meeting ground for Catalan and Italian poets and other intellectuals. Italian poets and writers, particularly Dante, Petrarch, and Boccaccio, were influential in the middle and late phases of the Catalan Renaissance in both poetry and prose. Provençal influences continued to be dominant in the early stage of the Renaissance, especially in the poems of Gilabert de Pròixita and Andreu Febrer, the latter also a translator of Dante's *La divina commedia* (c. 1320; *The Divine Comedy*, 1802) in terza rima.

JORDI DE SANT JORDI

Jordi de Sant Jordi (c. 1400-1424), poet, courtier, and soldier, was the outstanding poet of the young Catalan Renaissance. His love poetry appears in his collection *Estramps* (c. 1420; free verses). The flavor of his unrhymed, decasyllabic verse is Petrarchan, though still with a hint of Provençal. He was much appreciated for his adaptation of Italianate love themes, reminiscent of the *dolce stil nuovo*. The elegance of his Catalan was innovative and raised Catalan poetic diction and versification to new heights of expressiveness and sensitivity, achieved through sophisticated harmonizing of vocabulary and syntax.

AUSIÀS MARCH

The greatest poet of the Catalan Renaissance was Ausiàs March (1397-1459). His influence has been so far-reaching that he is still the most highly respected poet of classic Catalan literature. Catalan poets of the nineteenth and twentieth centuries continuously studied, imitated, and drew inspiration from March's controlled emotional torment. Among the Renaissance Castilian poets who admired and cited him were the Marqués de Santillana, Garcilaso de la Vega, Gutierre de Cetina, and Francisco de Herrera.

March, poet and soldier-statesman, came from a noble literary family. He sings of the paradox of carnal love and its purification, the path from *eros* to *caritas*. His verse is poetically intense, involved actively in the Renaissance, but retaining vestiges of the late Middle Ages. His profound suffering in the course of a carnal and impossible love, followed by the death of his youthful mistress, provided him with his single, obsessive subject. What remained to be done after his personal tragedy was to replace *eros* with *caritas* in the manner of Dante and Beatrice. The death of the beloved created the possibility of this replacement, but since March was sincere in his moral code, this death was not a sufficient expiation; it robbed him of the possibility of attaining a "perfect" love in the course of life in this world. His expiation then became a unique experience, interiorized and always present to conscience and consciousness.

In March's *Cants d'amor* (c. 1450; songs of love), love is carnal, forbidden, guilty. His preoccupation with sinful love marked a transition in Catalan poetry. In March's time, many Catalan poets were still writing in Provençal, following the traditional precepts of courtly love. In contrast, March was absolutely sincere in his recognition of the iniquity of carnal love, but hesitant to deny it totally in his desire for the unattainable Teresa Bou, who assumed for him a role very similar to that of Beatrice for Dante.

March renounced the cult of form to write a dense, cerebral poetry. His language, like his style, is sober, measured, and direct, nakedly expressing his tortured passion. His preferred form is the decasyllabic line, the same form later used by Maurice Scève in the sixteenth century. March's poems are a conversation, a dialogue and debate between the lover and his soul; their concerns are as vital in the twenty-first century as they were in the fifteenth.

JOAN ROIÇ DE CORELLA AND JAUME ROIG

After March, two other Valencian poets of note appeared in the Catalan Renaissance: Joan Roiç de Corella and Jaume Roig. Roiç de Corella wrote *Tragèdia de Caldesa* (fifteenth century), lyric love poetry devoted to his beloved, Caldesa; he also wrote religious poetry devoted to the Virgin.

Roig is remembered for the narrative poem *Spill o llibre de les dones* (c. 1460; *Mirror: Or, Book of Women*), the most violent misogynistic diatribe of the Hispanic peninsula and one of the most extreme antifeminist works written in any century. Composed in a brusque, five-syllable line, it is full of crude descriptions that contrast radically with the tradition of lyric poetry; indeed, its content is essentially novelistic, and the choice of form has made the work an oddity in Catalan letters.

THE DECADENCE

In the fifteenth century, Catalan literature and culture fell into a decline that continued into the nineteenth century. With the ascendancy of Castile, power shifted away from the Catalan-speaking lands. As a result, Catalan poetry suffered; typical was the case of Juan Boscán (c. 1490-1542), a Catalan who wrote only in Castilian. Only Pere Serafí (c. 1505-1567), Francesc Vicenç Garcia (1582-1623), and Francesc Fontanella (1622-1685?) attempted to keep formal Catalan poetry alive during the decadence. Poetry continued on the popular level, however, particularly in the sixteenth century. It has survived in the anonymous *Romancer/ Canconer* (poem collection), which contains many famous ballads, such as "Els estudiants de Tolosa" (the students of Tolosa), "El testament d'Amelià" (Amelia's will), "El Comte Arnau" (Count Arnau), and "La dama d'Aragó" (the lady of Aragon); many of these ballads are written in a fourteen-syllable line of rhyming couplets with a caesura at the hemistich.

THE RENAIXENÇA

The nineteenth century brought a renewed sense of patriotism to Catalonia, and this renewal had intellectual overtones. Poetry was to play a great part in the Catalan cultural resurgence; indeed, it can be said that the lifeblood of modern Catalan literature is its poetry, which has nourished the culture with regular infusions of contemporary masterpieces.

One must begin an appreciation of modern Catalan poetry with the remarkable poetic event that initiated the Renaixença (rebirth) of Catalan letters: the newspaper publication in 1833 of "La Pàtria," an ode by Bonaventura Carles Aribau (1798-1862). After a lapse of three centuries, Aribau had captured the spirit of Catalonia in a nostalgic, Romantic evocation of landscape. The Catalan population had continued speaking Catalan during the three centuries since Serafí, and scholarly interest in the language had increased in the eighteenth century. The nineteenth century brought a renewed interest in the Middle Ages and in past grandeur; in this climate, "La Pàtria" provided the necessary impulse for the Renaixença. Once under way, the Catalan cultural revival was eagerly supported by intellectuals, scholar-poets such as Milà i Fontanals, archivists, and the Catalan people in general.

One consequence of the Renaixença was the reestablishment of the Jocs Florals in 1859, with the stipulation that Catalan be used exclusively. One of the winners was the epic and lyric poet Jacint Verdaguer (1845-1902). Verdaguer, often called Mossén Cinto, is the best known and most highly esteemed poet of the Renaixença. His complete works were available during his lifetime, and he was a living inspiration to and symbol of the Catalan people during the nineteenth century. Catalan scholars now consider Verdaguer's works to represent the long first flowering of the Renaixença, with its Romantic, religious, patriotic, and epic tendencies. Verdaguer's Franciscan humanism, his enrichment of the Catalan language, and his evocation of Catalan history and landscape combine in a formula that has given him a unique place as the patriarch of modern Catalan literature.

THE MALLORCAN SCHOOL

While Verdaguer was writing near Barcelona, Maria Aguilo was laying the foundations for poetry and literature in Mallorca in the nineteenth century, influencing Valencian poetry as well. Teodor Llorenc and Vicent Querol were nineteenth century poets of the simple life. Josep Lluis Pons i Gallarça, another Mallorcan poet, led the way for Miquel Costa i Llobera (1854-1922), the most famous Mallorcan poet of the early twentieth century. Costa i Llobera, a priest and admirer of Horace, combined a sensitivity to the beauty and serenity of Mallorca with Christian fervor. His poetic intensity is refined, controlled, but deeply felt. Joan Alcover, Gabriel Alomar, Llorenç Riber, Miquel dels Sants Oliver, Maria Antònia Salvà, Bartomeu Rosselló-Pòrcel, and J. M. Llompart are other Mallorcan poets who followed the example of Costa i Llobera.

JUAN MARAGALL

Juan Maragall (1860-1911) was a contemporary of Verdaguer but differed from him as much as the Mallorcan school did in its own way. Maragall was concerned with aesthetics and the act of creating poetry, and his personal wealth, happy marriage, and social status allowed him the luxury of composing on his own terms. He relied on the moment of inspiration for his lyric poetry, not on forms, styles, or foreign influences. More of an intellectual than Verdaguer, his themes are love, death and resurrection, and Catalonia.

Maragall's admiration for German and Greek literature led him away from the Romantic tendencies of the Jocs Florals. His inner fire and his belief in his own inspiration helped him to create his own style, highly personal, negligent in form, and new in approach. His "Canto espiritual" has been compared by numerous scholars to works of March and Lull. Maragall remains a pivotal figure in Catalan letters, because he moved Catalan poetry forward aesthetically and stylistically.

MODERNISM

Maragall's influence brought about an explosion of Catalan poetry in the early and mid-twentieth century; Josep Carner, Jaume Bofill i Mates, and Josep Maria López-Picó were particularly indebted to Maragall. Joaquim Folguera (1894-1919), Joan Salvat-Papasseit

(1894-1924), and the Mallorcan Bartomeu Rosselló-Pòrcel (1913-1938) were unable to fulfill their great potential; all three died young. Salvat-Papasseit's soul-wrenching intensity gives his verse a peculiarly modern flavor and makes it among the most powerful in Catalan literature of any period. Other outstanding poets who were contemporaries of Salvat-Papasseit are Agustí Esclasans, Clementina Arderiu, J. V. Foix, Marià Manent, Josep Maria de Sagarra, Tomàs Garcés, Ventura Gassol, Carles Riba, and Josep Sebastià Pons of Roussillon, a Catalan in that now-French region. Several of these poets were associated with the movement known as *Noucentisme* ("1900-ism"), which rejected the late Romanticism of Verdaguer and the provincialism of nineteenth century Catalan culture.

Josep Carner (1884-1971) spent much of his life outside Catalonia, but his influence still places him at the apex of modern Catalan poets. Whereas Maragall sought the "living word" of inspiration, Carner, a lover of wordplay, was a master of form and controlled emotion. He was a "poet's poet" of great inner serenity. Riba (1893-1959) ranks with Carner in importance. Riba, a professor of Greek, was a highly intellectual poet, yet his work is informed by a deep sensitivity to human concerns.

Foix (1893-1987) was the outstanding figure of twentieth century Catalan literature. Many of his works defy categorization in traditional genres. His poetry is an extraordinary fusion of native Catalan elements with influences assimilated from the European avant-garde. He was particularly influenced by Surrealism and maintained a lifelong interest in the visual arts; his close association with Joan Miró and other painters in the post-World War I period had an important impact on his work.

Foix was a major force in introducing the European avant-garde to Barcelona and Catalonia through his extensive journalistic writing. Many of his poems have been immortalized in paintings of Salvador Dalí, Miró, Joan Ponç, and Antoni Tàpies, who recognized in him a kindred spirit. Foix regards the poet as an "investigator," a "researcher," whose medium is words. He is an anguished twentieth century poet who combines the syntax and emotion of March with the vision of Giorgio de Chirico, René Magritte, Dalí, and Miró.

SALVADOR ESPRIU

Salvador Espriu (1913-1985), author of *La pell de brau* (1960; *The Bull-Hide*, 1977) and *El llibre de Sinera* (1963; the book of Sinera), is perhaps the best-known modern Catalan poet—one of the few whose works are known outside Catalonia. Whereas Foix was a writer of "pure poetry," Espriu was concerned with political actualities. Foix's poems are sung in cathedrals by choirs, while Espriu's are sung by the modern "troubadours" of popular music. His eclectic use of literary and cultural influences and his satiric wit contribute to his unique appeal.

REVIVAL OF INTEREST

What is most significant about Catalan poetry is that it has been able to renew itself after a significant historical lacuna. In the 1980's, the Spanish government agreed to the demands of Catalan nationalists, supported by a majority of the Catalan-speaking populace, to make Catalan the official language of their region, and legislation since then, such as the Catalan Language Act of 1997, has furthered those goals. Even though Spanish remains dominant, Catalan poets have continued to appear on the scene: Maria Ángels Anglada (1930-1999), Miquel Martí i Pol (born 1929), Marta Pessarrodona (born 1941), and Francesc Parcerisas (born 1944) are only a few.

BIBLIOGRAPHY

Barkan, Stanley H., ed. *Four Postwar Catalan Poets*. Rev. ed. Translated by David H. Rosenthal. Merrick, N.Y.: Cross-Cultural Communications, 1994. Provides translations of and critical commentary on twentieth century Catalan poets.

Carner, Josep. *Nabi*. Translated by J. L. Gili, edited by Jaume Coll. London: Anvil Press Poetry, 2001. Offers a translated version of Carner's Christian-themed poetry and an introduction by Arthur Terry.

Crowe, Anna, ed. *Light off Water: Twenty-five Catalan Poems, 1978-2002*. Translated by Iolanda Pelegri. Manchester, England: Carcanet Press, 2007. Twenty-five poems, each by a different poet, demonstrate the revival of the Catalan poetic tradition after years of suppression.

Espriu, Salvador. *Selected Poems of Salvador Espriu*.

Translated by Magda Bogin. New York: W. W. Norton, 1991. A bilingual collection that includes selections from nine of Espriu's books of poetry. Also includes an introduction by the Catalan poet Francesc Vallverdu, which provides valuable insight into Espriu, the man and the artist.

Foix, J. V. *When I Sleep, Then I See Clearly: Selected Poems of J. V. Foix*. Translated by David Rosenthal. New York: Persea Books, 1988. The selection spans the entire career of Catalonia's major avant-garde poet, Foix, who won Spain's 1985 National Prize for Literature.

Gaunt, Simon. *The Troubadors: An Introduction*. New York: Cambridge University Press, 1999. Leading scholars in Britain, the United States, France, Italy, and Spain trace the development of the troubadour tradition (including music), engage with the main trends in troubadour scholarship, and examine the reception of troubadour poetry in manuscripts and in Northern French romance. A series of appendixes offer an invaluable guide to more than fifty troubadours, to technical vocabulary, to research tools, and to surviving manuscripts.

Lull, Ramon. *The Book of the Lover and the Beloved*. Translated by Mark D. Johnston. Warminster, England: Aris & Phillips, 1995. An English translation from original manuscripts of the work considered one of the greatest mystical texts of the Middle Ages. Foreword by Geoffrey Pridham. Bibliography.

McNerny, Kathleen, and Cristina Enriques de Salamanca, eds. *Double Minorities of Spain: A Biobibliographic Guide to Women Writers of the Catalan, Galician, and Basque Countries*. New York: Modern Language Association of America, 1994. Alphabetically arranged listings provide brief biographies of a heretofore neglected group of authors, with evaluative descriptions of their work. Following each entry is a listing of books and other publications in which their writing has appeared, works that have been translated into Castilian or English, and critical studies.

Rosenthal, David H. *Postwar Catalan Poetry*. Lewisburg, Pa.: Bucknell University Press, 1991. Critically examines the trends in twentieth century Catalan poetry. Includes a bibliography and an index.

Solà-Solé, Josep M., ed. *Modern Catalan Literature: Proceedings of the Fourth Catalan Symposium*. New York: Peter Lang, 1995. Presents the topics and discussions of the Fourth Catalan Symposium, held at the Catholic University of America in 1993. Topics range from general surveys of modern Catalan poetry to studies of specific poets, poems, novels, and modern folktales. Also discusses women writers and stylistic relationships between writers. Includes translations of two new collections by poets Olga Xirinacs and Miquel Martí i Pol.

Terry, Arthur. *A Companion to Catalan Literature*. Woodbridge, Suffolk, England: Tamesis, 2003. An updated and enlarged replacement for the author's *Catalan Literature* (1973). Traces the subject chronologically, emphasizing major figures and movements. Includes bibliography of critical works, list of English translations, and index.

Triadú, Joan. *Anthology of Catalan Lyric Poetry*. Berkeley: University of California Press, 1953. Critically examines and provides translations of the works of Catalan's lyric poets.

Walters, D. Gareth. *The Poetry of Salvador Espriu: To Save the Words*. Woodbridge, Suffolk, England: Tamesis, 2006. The first extensive study of Espriu in English. Considers such matters as the poet's development through time, his status as a symbol of resistance to oppression, and his reputation for obscurity. Bibliographical references and index.

Patricia J. Boehne

CHINESE POETRY

China has traditionally been a nation of poets. From ancient times through the first decade of the twentieth century, Chinese poetry held a position of importance unequaled by poetry in any other nation. By virtue of several important factors—linguistic, cultural, social, educational, and political—Chinese poetry, until the downfall of the monarchy in 1911, manifested certain unique characteristics.

ANCIENT CHINESE WRITING

The earliest known examples of Chinese script were inscribed on tortoise shells and animal bones around 1300 B.C.E., the time of the Shang Dynasty (c. 1600-1066 B.C.E.). These objects are referred to as "oracle bones" because they were employed by shamans, or priests, to predict future events. Later in the Shang, inscriptions were made on bronze vessels. When the Zhou (Chou) Dynasty (1066-221 B.C.E.) succeeded the Shang, its bronzes were also inscribed. A series of hunting songs carved on boulders, erroneously termed "stone drums," dates to around 400 B.C.E. In 219 B.C.E., by order of Shi Huangdi (Shih Huang Ti), the first emperor of the Qin (Ch'in) Dynasty (221-206 B.C.E.), the Chinese script underwent a standardization process. Two new types of script were devised: One, to be used for formal and official purposes, was called *xiao juan* (*hsiao chüan*); the other, intended for general use, was called *li shu* (clerk's style). Because it was found that the speediest and most efficient way of writing *li shu* was with brush and ink, such writing soon developed into an art in itself, the art of calligraphy. By the time of the Han Dynasty (206 B.C.E.-220 C.E.), calligraphy had achieved equality as an art with painting and poetry. Calligraphy and painting not only were seen as twin arts of the brush but also were intimately associated with poetry. This attitude is shown in the famous remark made by Su Dongpo (Su Tung-p'o) about the great Wang Wei, who was outstanding as a calligrapher, a painter, and a poet: "In his poetry there is painting, and in his painting, poetry."

The distinctive visual properties of Chinese script that made its writing an art transcend its pictographic origins. Although Chinese writing began with pictographic word-signs, these word-signs were soon conventionalized into almost complete abstractions. Single characters were then combined to form not only compound but also complex characters, many simply with determinants of the broadest meaning and others with signs to indicate sound. The Chinese written language thereby expanded from around twenty-five hundred characters in early times to between forty thousand and fifty thousand by the Qing (Ch'ing) Dynasty, which was founded in the seventeenth century.

Writing such characters demands skill in drawing, a sense of form and proportion, and a sensitivity to the qualities of line, dot, and hook. Although a number of single characters can be combined into one, the resulting character must occupy the same amount of space and have the same square appearance as that of any other character. Furthermore, calligraphers tended to view the strokes in their characters in terms of natural objects and forces. To them, a horizontal stroke was a mass of clouds; a hook, a bent bow; a dot, a falling rock; a turning stroke, a brass hook; a drawn-out line, an old dry vine; a free stroke, a runner on his mark; and so on. Painters considered calligraphy their training ground, and poets saw their art as a kind of word painting. The three arts of calligraphy, painting, and poetry can be seen woven together in that school of composite art known as *wenrenhua* (*wen-jen-hua*; literary "men's painting"). Here, the scholar-artist would display his calligraphy in the brushstrokes he used to fashion trees, rocks, or bamboo shoots. Then he would balance his picture with a poem inspired by his painting, written in his best calligraphy, as an integral part of his composition. Later, his friends or other connoisseurs might write additional poems or laudatory inscriptions on his painting that would add to its value.

Although the visual was preeminent in the development of Chinese poetry, it must not be thought that the musical quality of the words, even in silent reading, was ignored or considered unimportant. The sounds of spoken Chinese in its various dialects have their phonetic systems of vowels and consonants and also their distinctive tonal systems, which depend on the movement of or the holding of the pitch of the voice.

At the same time, however, classical Chinese written characters are independent of any particular pronunciation or dialect. The origins of this literary language can be traced to a period sometime after the establishment of the Zhou Dynasty, when a new class of men began to replace the Shang priesthood as magical religion gave way to a philosophy of history. This new class was the scholar class; only such men could memorize the large number of characters that their language then contained. These scholars, later called the literati, were responsible for the transmission of China's cultural heritage to future generations.

CLASSICAL CHINESE

By the fall of the Han Dynasty in 220 C.E., the literati had so monopolized the Chinese script that it had broken away from the vernacular language and gone its separate way. Soon, it was recognized that writing need not be restricted to utilitarian purposes—that it was capable of producing aesthetic pleasure. This view elevated the status of belles lettres to a high position for the first time in Chinese history. In this way, *wenli* (*wen-li*; classical Chinese), or *wenyan* (*wen-yan*; literary Chinese), became the only form of the written language used everywhere for all serious purposes, quite divorced from the spoken language. Such written Chinese has no pronunciation of its own but is pronounced in as many different ways as there are dialects. All Chinese poetry considered as literature has been written in *wenli*, or classical Chinese, from its formulation until the advent of the Chinese literary renaissance in 1917, when it was almost entirely replaced by bai hua (*pai hua*), or the living language of the people, used for literary as well as practical purposes.

Regardless of the independence of *wenli* with respect to the sounds that are attached to it, Chinese poetry has its own peculiar sound structure, which includes metrical forms as well as rhyme and other auditory effects. In short, there is a "music" of Chinese poetry that has its own rules of versification relative to genre and purpose. Indeed, this sound structure of Chinese poetry is so peculiar to itself that it is impossible to render in translation.

A fourteenth century wenrenhua, *or literati painting, featuring a poem inspired by the artwork.*

CHINESE VERSIFICATION

Chinese versification is based on two principal auditory qualities that may be attached to the Chinese word-signs. Every character is monosyllabic when sounded, and each monosyllable has a fixed pitch, called a "tone," which is semantic—that is, gives a clue to its meaning. Hence, generally speaking, the number of syllables in a poetic line is equivalent to the number of characters in that line. The number of characters and their monosyllables, however, is not invariably equal to the number of "words" in a given line, because there are some characters that never appear alone and make up "words" of two or more characters. The regularity or the variation of the number of characters (or syllables) and the regularity or the variation of their fixed tones are the basis of Chinese poetic meter and play the major role in Chinese versification, together with some incidence of rhyme.

During the Tang (T'ang) Dynasty (618-907), classical Chinese had eight tones, which could be reduced to four pairs. By the Yuan (Yüan) Dynasty (1279-1368), the eight tones had been reduced to four. These pitches were distinguished, ranging from one to four, as level (*ping*, or *p'ing*), rising (*shang*), falling (*qu*, or *ch'ü*), and entering (*ze*, or *tse*). These four tones, however, were arbitrarily reduced for poetic purposes to two, the first being regarded as level while all the rest were simply considered as deflected. For example, in the demanding form of the *lüshi* (*lü-shih*; regulated poem), the requirement was that a poem be made up of eight lines of equal length with each line comprising either five or seven characters. The poet had various tone patterns from which he or she could choose, depending on whether five or seven characters was selected for the line length. The first full line might call for the following tone pattern: deflected (but level permitted), deflected, level, level, deflected. Each of the rest of the lines would have its specific tone pattern. Such regulated verse also required a particular rhyme scheme. In addition to varieties of pitch, the poet could use contrasts in the length or quantity of syllables, because the tones differ in length and movement. All this sound variation gives the recitation of a Chinese poem a singsong quality.

MUSIC AND FOLKSONGS

From the beginning, Chinese poetry has been intimately connected with music. The folk poems collected in the earliest anthology, *Shijing* (traditionally fifth century B.C.E.; *The Book of Songs*, 1937), were originally songs meant to be chanted or sung. Some were popular songs, others courtly songs or sacrificial and temple songs. The popular songs were intended to be sung to the accompaniment of music with group dancing. Early commentators on the *The Book of Songs* were musicians as well as literary critics.

The history of Chinese poetry shows the marked influence of folk songs. *The Book of Songs* established a poetic tradition that was to be followed by serious poets until the twentieth century. Its typical four-line character poem became an esteemed and standard form. Its tone of refined emotional restraint, its sympathy with human nature, and its general lack of malice toward others became a poetic ideal followed by many later poets. A number of other standard Chinese poetic forms were derived from folk songs, such as the Han *yuefu* (*yüeh-fu*), the Tang *ci* (*tz'u*), and the Yuan *qu* (*ch'ü*). All these standard forms were derived from the songs of the people, but once they became the standard fare of the literati, the words and music were divorced from each other, and the poetry was written to be read rather than sung, with little or no regard for its musical potential. The history of Chinese poetry also shows that once a form became too refined and overly artificial—too far removed from normal reality—poets would return to folk traditions for new inspiration.

THE POLITICS OF POETRY

Certain cultural factors peculiar to China, quite apart from the nature of its language and the relation of that language to the other arts, have also shaped Chinese poetry. Although philosophy and religion have played important roles (particularly Confucianism, but also Daoism and Buddhism), perhaps the major role has been played by government. From the time of the early Zhou Dynasty, the Chinese state took a decided interest in poetry. The government realized that the popular songs of the people could serve as an index to the ways in which the people felt about the government and their lives under it. Rulers or their emissaries would travel over the feudal states collecting popular songs and their musical scores. A department of music called the Yuefu (Yüeh-fu; "music bureau") was established for this purpose. Although it languished for a time, it was revived by Wudi, the emperor, in 125 B.C.E. Thus, folk poems were written down and preserved, inspiring sophisticated poets to imitate them in their own work.

Because the difficulty of the Chinese written script had led to the formation of a scholar class from whose ranks the government was obliged to select its officials, teachers such as the great Confucius (551-479 B.C.E.) were engaged primarily in educating and training students as prospective government servants. Confucius believed that the study of poetry had an important role in the development of moral character, a prerequisite of just and efficient government. For this reason, he selected from the government collections of the feudal states the poems that make up *The Book of Songs*, which he edited and used as a textbook in his seminars. After his death and the official sanction of the Confucian doctrine during the Han Dynasty, *The Book of Songs* became one of the five official classics, which, together with the four books, made up the nine official classics considered indispensable to the education of the scholar-official.

During the Han Dynasty, the government decided that the best way to discover "men of talent" suitable for public service was on the basis of merit, and a merit system based on competitive examinations was established. The government began to employ the Confucian-trained graduates of the National University. This practice indissolubly linked an education in the Confucian classics with an official career, and by the time of the Tang Dynasty, a nationwide system of public competitive examinations to recruit officials on the basis of merit had been established. Theoretically, these competitive examinations were open to all Chinese citizens except those who followed certain occupations classified as base or common. The subsequent major Chinese dynasties relied on these public examinations to obtain the best possible government officials until as late as 1905, when the system was abandoned as obsolete. Thus, for many centuries, the civil-service examination system provided the ruling class with an influx of new talent that had undergone intensive intellectual and artistic training, including skill in the writing of poetry.

The system required a candidate to acquire three successive degrees—taken, respectively, at the county, province, and national capital levels—before being eligible for official appointment. The first degree, that of *shengyuan* (*sheng-yüan*; "government student"), and the second degree, that of *xiucai* (*hsiu-ts-ai*; "budding talent"), were simply preparatory for the third and highest, that of *jinshi* (*chin-shih*; "metropolitan graduate"), the acquisition of which entitled the graduate to be appointed to some official post in the government. The *jinshi* degree required a thorough knowledge of the Confucian classics, skill in calligraphy, and the ability to write poems as well as essays. The standards were high, and only a few of the many candidates were passed by the examiners.

The prevalence of this system of competitive examinations had a profound effect not only on Chinese society, education, and politics but also on literature. Apart from its role in perpetuating poetic conventions from generation to generation, the civil-service experience furnished themes that are common to Chinese poetry as a whole. Indeed the vast majority of Chinese poets were government officials.

GRAMMAR AND SYNTAX

The grammar and syntax of Chinese have also played their part in the shaping of China's poetry. Some writers have declared that the Chinese language has no grammar and that its words may serve as any part of speech. Neither of these allegations is correct. Although Chinese has no inflection of number, case, person, tense, or gender—and more words in Chinese than in English have multiple functions—Chinese verbs do have aspects, and some words are normally nouns, whereas others are normally verbs. Although the basic pattern of the Chinese sentence is subject followed by predicate, the Chinese "subject" is the topic of the sentence, not necessarily the agent that performs the action of the verb. In addition, the subject or the verb of the Chinese sentence is often omitted, and coordinate constructions frequently lack conjunctions.

The Chinese language is, therefore, more compact and concise than English. In economy of expression, it resembles a telegram in English, and *wenli*, or classical Chinese, is even more abbreviated than *bai hua*, or everyday speech. If Chinese is more sparing in its words than English, however, it is also less precise. If this feature is a disadvantage in prose concerned with the particular, it is a distinct advantage in Chinese poetry, which is concerned essentially with the universal. Chinese poetry can therefore exploit its compactness and economy of expression in conjunction with its grammatical and syntactic fluidity to enhance its power to mean far more than it says.

ZHOU DYNASTY (1066-221 B.C.E.)

The earliest great monument of Chinese poetry is *The Book of Songs*, an anthology of folk poems selected and edited by Confucius. The poems themselves come from the earlier period of the Zhou Dynasty, from between 1000 and 700 B.C.E. Their collection and preservation by Confucius, China's greatest teacher, shows the importance he attached to the study of poetry, which he believed was essential to the proper moral development of man, and since his time, *The Book of Songs* has been regarded as one of the great classics of Chinese literature.

The Book of Songs not only possesses great aesthetic value but also is an important historical document that strongly influenced all subsequent Chinese poetry. Revealing the minds and hearts of the Chinese people during the ancient Zhou times, it established a poetic tradition that was followed by later Chinese poets down to modern times. Throughout the history and development of Chinese poetry, *The Book of Songs* has served as a model of poetic eloquence, a storehouse of words, images, themes, and poetic forms (its typical four-character line became a standard form), and a continual source of inspiration to later poets.

By the beginning of the fifth century B.C.E., the power of the feudal state of Zhou had begun to wane, and new national states emerged whose rulers appropriated the title *wang* ("king"). Of these new states, two emerged as the most powerful—Chu in the south and Qin in the northwest. Chu had become a prosperous and beautiful state with a high degree of refined culture. The leisurely cultivation resulting from its economic prosperity eventually produced a series of popular religious songs that were collected under the title *Jiuge* (*Chiu Ko*; nine songs). These elegant songs dating from the fifth century B.C.E. became the model for an irregular and flexible type of elegy that was to inspire sophisticated poets to create a new poetic genre, the *Chu ci* (*Ch'u tz'u*; "Chu elegy").

By the next century, an identifiable person emerged from the anonymity of collective authorship to become China's first known poet. This was Qu Yuan (Ch'ü Yüan; 343?-290? B.C.E.), author of the distinctive masterpiece "Li sao" (*The Li Sao, an Elegy on Encountering Sorrows*, 1929). A son of the nobility, he had served

his king as second in rank to the prime minister. Having for some reason lost his political office, however, Qu Yuan was exiled to wander throughout the land. Deciding to devote his life to poetry, he eventually composed *The Li Sao*, a poem that significantly influenced the course of Chinese poetry. Qu Yuan's work conferred distinction on the new genre of the *Chu ci* and inspired a school of poetry responsible for the establishment of a Chinese elegiac tradition that continued to exist until modern times. This tradition eventually led directly to the creation of another new genre, the Han *fu*.

QIN AND HAN DYNASTIES (221 B.C.E.-220 C.E.)

A struggle for power went on among the feudal states during what is called the Warring States Period (475-221 B.C.E.). This struggle was concluded when the state of Qin succeeded in crushing all opponents to form the first unified empire in Chinese history. Prince Zheng of Qin, who ascended the throne in 221 B.C.E. as Shi Huangdi, was a man of authoritarian mold: During his reign, all literature of which he disapproved was burned, and the Chinese script was standardized.

The earliest examples of Qin poems appear in *The Book of Songs*, but they do not differ significantly from the rest of the poetry in the collection. Other specimens of Qin poetry appear in the hunting songs carved on the so-called stone drums. The most important Qin scholar and poet was Li Si (Li Ssu; 280-208 B.C.E.), who was the scholar the emperor assigned to standardize the Chinese script and who initated a new poetic genre— the *song ci* (*sung tz'u*), or panegyric. When the emperor toured the country, large stone tablets were erected on which were carved panegyrics to commemorate his visits to various places. These imperial panegyrics were composed and inscribed by Li Si.

The Qin Dynasty did not last long. When Shi Huangdi died in 210 B.C.E., rebellions broke out, resulting in internal warfare. This anarchy was resolved with the establishment of the Han Dynasty in 207 B.C.E. During the Han Dynasty, two new poetic genres made their appearance—the *fu* and the *yuefu*. Generally, the word *fu* means "to display," and specifically, it means "to chant or to narrate." As a poem, the *fu* originally was one to be chanted rather than sung—that is, performed without musical accompaniment. Under the Han, the *fu* became a poem of social criticism, but later this motive was replaced by the desire to treat its subject in an elegant or refined manner. This later motive eventually resulted in cutting the poem off from the real world, and even some of the best writers of such *fu* considered them frivolous exercises, worthless as literature. Nevertheless, the *fu* dominated the Han period.

At its best, the *fu* is characterized by flowing rhythm, pleasant rhyme, and splendid imagery. An offshoot of the *Chu ci*, the form came to prominence when Wudi (r. 140-87 B.C.E.) became fascinated by the work of the great Han *fu* writer, Sima Xiangru (Ssu-ma Hsiang-ju; c. 180-117 B.C.E.). Author of such *fu* as "Zi xu fu" ("Master Nil"), "Shang lin fu" ("Supreme Park"), "Meiren fu" ("The Beautiful Lady"), and "Chang men fu" ("Long Doors"), Sima Xiangru was rewarded for his skill by appointments to important government posts.

The Han *yuefu* emerged from the popular folk songs collected by the government's music bureau. This sophisticated type came to maturity about 200 C.E., by which time it had been discovered that the form was particularly suited to narration. Perhaps the most famous writer of the narrative type was a woman, Cai Yan (Ts'ai Yen, fl. 206 C.E.), who composed two "Songs of Distress," which became famous. Taken captive by the Huns and forced to become the consort of a Hun chieftain for twelve years before she was ransomed, she tells of her life during her captivity and reflects on her experiences. Another Han narrative *yuefu*, titled "Kong jue dongnan fei" (author unknown; "Southwest the Peacock Flies"), is generally considered a masterpiece and is the longest medieval poem of China at 353 lines. Later, poems of this type based on the folk style and rendered in five- or seven character lines became known as *gushi* ("ancient verse").

SIX DYNASTIES AND SUI DYNASTY (220-618 C.E.)

With the end of the Han Dynasty, China again lapsed into disunity. Three independent kingdoms struggled with one another for power. Wei had retained much of the power it had usurped from Han, but soon it was challenged by Shu and Wu. This period of political contention is known as the Three Kingdoms period (220-265). The powerful house of Jin then arose and

eliminated both Shu and Wu to found the Jin (Chin) Dynasty (265-419). By 420, China had divided itself into the South and North Dynasties; this division lasted until 589. Finally, the Sui Dynasty took over and ruled China until 618.

Despite the political confusion and social unrest resulting from the power struggles of the Six Dynasties period (220-588 C.E.), it was an age of rapid development in poetry, in both form and content. Beginning in the third century, a profound change took place in the intellectual climate of China, the positivism of Han Confucianism being replaced by mystical Confucianism supported by the *yin-yang* cosmology. With this change, a new attitude toward poetry as an art emerged. *The Book of Songs* was interpreted in terms of mystical philosophy, the *Lunyu* (*Lun yü*; later sixth-early fifth centuries B.C.E.; *The Analects*, 1861) of Confucius was interpreted on Daoist principles, and the *Yijing* (*I Ching*; eighth to third century B.C.E.; English translation, 1876; also known as *Book of Changes*, 1986), the classic of spiritual or psychological transformation, became the dominating Confucian text. In short, a fusion was effected between Confucianism and Daoism, and Indian Buddhism was integrated into Chinese intellectual life. Buddhists and Daoists came to the fore, and a number of poets were predominantly one or the other.

During the time of the last Han emperor, the five- or seven-character poetic line had replaced the old four-character pattern of *The Book of Songs*. Although the irregular verse form of the popular folk song had been rejected, the poets had not entirely lost contact with the spontaneity of these songs. A master of this new type, called *shi* (later *gushi*; *ku-shih*), was Cao Zhi (Ts'ao Chih; 192-232), perhaps the most important member of the group called the Seven Masters of Jian An (Chien An). Another significant group, the Seven Worthies of the Bamboo Grove, was composed of poets who had abandoned the city for the country to escape the political confusion of the time. Ruan Ji (Juan Chi; 210-263) was the most outstanding member of this group; his eighty-two *yonghuai shi* (*yung-huai shih*; "poems expressing feelings") express the new attitude that poetry should be an honest disclosure of the poet's feelings and emotions. Poets termed this attitude *tou*, and *tou qing qing* (*t'ou ch'ing ch'ing*) means "to call up and expose one's inmost feelings."

In accord with the mysticism of the time, this attitude was linked to *tong* (*t'ung*), the ability to see into the nature of things—literally, "to go through things." At the same time, a number of poets rejected the orthodox Confucian idea that the main purpose of poetry was didactic and moralistic, a view that emphasized content over form. The poet and critic Lu Chi (261-303), for example, in his *wen fu* (literary *fu*), adamantly declared that form is as important as content and insisted that poetry has an intrinsic aesthetic value.

In addition to the five- or seven-character *shi*, another genre was developed during the Six Dynasties period: a new kind of *fu*, a shorter version that omitted dialogue and tried to capture the lyric quality of the *Chu ci*. It also employed the rhetoric of *pian wen* (*p'ien wen*; "balanced prose"). Lu Chi as well as Zuo Si (Tso Ssu, fl. 265-305) were both great masters of this new kind of *fu*. Later came the literary giant Tao Qian (T'ao Ch'ien; 365-427), also known as Tao Yuanming (T'ao Yüanming), a many-sided man. The scion of a great official family, he joined the civil service, but loving his freedom and independence more than official rewards, he resigned at the age of thirty-three and never returned to public life. His poem on retirement, "Homeward Bound," has been much admired, but he is most famous for his *fu* "The Scholar of Five Willows" and "Peach Blossom Spring." He is the greatest of the recluse poets of the Six Dynasties period.

Although China was unified once again under the Sui Dynasty (581-618), little need be said about that dynasty's poetry. No significant developments took place, and no great poets emerged. The two best poets were Yang Guang (Yan Kuang, 580-618), who succeeded his father on the throne in 605, and the Lady Hou, one of Yang Guang's concubines.

TANG AND FIVE DYNASTIES (618-960)

The Tang Dynasty, founded by Li Yuan (Li Yüan) after he crushed the Sui regime, was the golden age of Chinese poetry. Li Yuan reigned as Gaozu (Kao Tsu), then voluntarily stepped down in 626 in favor of his second son, Li Shimin (Li Shih-min), who reigned as Taizong (T'ai Tsung) and was a great patron of litera-

ture. Under these rulers and their successors, a new system of land tenure was put into effect, and the competitive trade that developed on a wide scale produced a new social class, the urban bourgeoisie. Changes also took place in the realms of philosophy, religion, the arts, and literature. Orthodox Confucianism was modified by the inclusion of mystical elements, new religions such as Nestorian Christianity came on the scene, and two new forms of *shi* made their appearance and became very popular: *jueju* (*chüeh-chü*, literally "cut short") and *lushi* (*lü-shih*, literally "ruled verse"). Until the Rebellion of An Lushan in 755, during the reign of Xuanzong (Hsüan Tsung; reigned 712-756), the nation enjoyed unprecedented peace, prosperity, and cultural development. The Tang Dynasty produced China's two greatest poets, Li Bo (Li Po; 701-762) and Du Fu (Tu Fu; 712-770), as well as a host of other major poets: Wang Wei (701-761), Han Yu (Han Yü; 768-824), Bo Juyi (Po Chü-yi; 772-846), Yuan Zhen (Yüan Chen; 779-831), Du Mu (Tu Mu; 803-852), and Li Shangyin (Li Shang-yin; 813-858). Although poetry flourished at the court of the early Tang, it was mostly of the occasional type, inspired by festivals and sumptuous banquets. With the appearance of the *jueju* and the *lushi* forms, poetry was taken more seriously. The *jueju* was a poem of four lines of equal length, with either five or seven characters to the line, a set tone pattern, and a rhyme scheme. The *lushi* was a poem of eight lines of equal length, again with either five or seven characters to the line, contrasting intonations in each pair of lines, and a rhyme scheme. Parallel construction was required in the four middle lines of the eight-line poem, rhyme was required in the even-numbered lines, and a set tonal sequence was required in all eight lines. Two masters of court poetry, Shen Juanqi (Shen Chüan-ch'i; c. 650-713) and Song Zhiwen (Sung Chih-wen; c. 660-712), are credited with crystallizing the *lushi* form.

Xuanzong was a lover of beauty and the arts, and he succeeded in bringing the best poetic talent of China to his court. Two of the poets he employed turned out to be the two greatest poets China has produced: Li Bo and Du Fu.

LI BO

As a boy, Li Bo developed two consuming interests—poetry and swordsmanship. At the age of ten, he was writing poetry and studying fencing. He apparently never entertained any political ambitions and did not study the Confucian classics in preparation for taking the examinations. Rather, he was a dabbler in Daoism and alchemy. He left home at the age of nineteen to seek adventure and wandered from place to place. Occasionally he sought employment as a bodyguard, and it is said that he thrust his sword through a number of opponents; otherwise, he indulged his passion for writing poetry. He eventually arrived at Changan, where his poetic talent was brought to the attention of the emperor, who employed him as a court poet for a brief period (742-744).

Xuanzong found that Li Bo was as fond of drinking wine as he was of writing poetry, and the two activities frequently went hand in hand. Independent in spirit and incapable of sycophancy, Li Bo soon lost his position and resumed his wandering. According to legend, he drowned while boating on a lake; having grown intoxicated from drinking wine, he tumbled out of his boat into the water in an effort to embrace the moon's reflection. True or false, this legend accurately reflects the spirit of Li Bo, a lover of nature and beauty who continually sought to plunge into the unknown.

A poetic genius in the romantic mold, Li Bo was intent on being himself, yet he sought to transcend the self as well. A visionary poet, he never lost his humanity. If he ascended the mountain to touch the stars, he descended to enjoy a bowl of rice and the welcoming pillow of a farmer friend. He relished listening to a Buddhist monk playing his lute as much as he did fencing or drinking wine. Poetry was always foremost in his mind.

DU FU

China's other great poet, Du Fu, was a man and a poet of a character quite different from that of Li Bo. A native of Gongxian, in what is now Henan Province, he was descended from a family of scholars and writers. He studied the Confucian classics with the object of qualifying himself for an official career, and at the age of twenty-five, he journeyed from his home to the capital to take the *jinshi* examinations. Failing to receive his degree, however, he decided to take up the career of poet and journeyed about the country riding on a donkey. At the age of thirty-eight, he submitted three *fu*

compositions to Xuanzong. Impressed, the monarch rewarded him with an official appointment. Soon, however, the An Lushan Rebellion drove Xuanzong from power and Du Fu into exile. The shock of the rebellion had a pronounced effect on him and on his subsequent poetry.

Following the accession of Suzong (Su Tsung), Du Fu returned to the capital to accept the dangerous office of imperial censor. His critical memorials to the throne, however, displeased the emperor, who, in effect, banished him by appointing him governor of a small town. Consequently, Du Fu resigned and retired to the country. Called out of retirement to serve on the board of works, Du Fu resigned again after six years and retired to the country, this time permanently. Dedicating his life to poetry, he grew old before his time and died in poverty at the age of fifty-eight.

Li Bo was a romantic, "a heavenly immortal in temporary exile on earth." His poetry tends to move away from the real toward the unreal; he sought not to reform the society of his time but to escape from it. Du Fu was a classicist, an earth-rooted man, a mortal with a social consciousness, a serious man with a heart full of sorrow and passionate indignation. His poetry tends to concentrate on the real and to avoid the unreal. He faced up to the hard facts of life: the suffering of the masses, social injustice, corruption in government, the extravagances of the rich, the horrors of war, the ravages of time, and the desires and fears of living people in the everyday world. He was a critical realist with a tragic sense of life. However, despite the sorrow he carried in his heart, he had his light side and never lost his sense of humor.

Du Fu's poetry can be divided into an early, a middle, and a late period. His early period (c. 750-755), that prior to the An Lushan Rebellion, is characterized by such poems as "The Eight Immortals of the Wine Cup," a clever piece of lighthearted satire, and the glittering satirical ballads "The Ballad of the Beauties" and "The Ballad of the War Chariots." The middle period (755-765), that of the rebellion and its aftermath, is characterized by such poems as "Lament of the River Bank" and "Lamenting of the Imperial Heir," both of which feature nostalgia, sadness, and cynicism. The late period (766-770) is characterized by poems such as "My

Thatched Roof Whirled Away by an Autumn Gale," a vivid picture of the hardships of poverty and old age. Du Fu called Li Bo the "unrivaled poet," yet Du Fu surpasses his friend in intellectual power and emotional range. No Chinese poet has displayed more mastery of the regulated form.

OTHER TANG POETS

Of the other major Tang poets, Bo Juyi stands above the rest. A very successful government official, he rose to high rank under Xuanzong. He was a leader in the development of the long narrative poem called the *xin yuefu* (*hsin yüeh-fu*; "new lyric ballad"). Despite their length, his two poems "Song of Everlasting Sorrow" and "Song of the Lute" were in their day extremely popular with both commoner and aristocrat. Wang Wei, poet, painter, calligrapher, and musician, followed a political career. His devotion to the Chan (Japanese Zen) school of Buddhism is evident in both his painting and his poetry. He was noted for his mastery of the *jueju* form. Han Yu was a highly successful government official and a noted essayist and writer of short romances as well as a poet. He was the leader of a reform movement that sought to free literature from its artificialities. His poems "Mountain Stones" and "Poem on the Stone Drums" were particularly admired.

Yuan Zhen is as famous for his thirty-year friendship with Bo Juyi as for his own poetry. A government official, his career was not very successful, but he is known for the poems and letters that passed between him and Bo Juyi. Du Mu (Tu Mu) had a moderately successful official career. He is regarded as a transitional figure between the middle and late Tang periods and was a sharp critic of both Li Bo and Du Fu. He is noted for the descriptive talent displayed in his "Traveling in the Mountains."

Li Shangyin also pursued a moderately successful political career while achieving a considerable literary reputation. In his poetry, he makes much use of myth, symbolism, and classical allusions, and his work is regarded by some as obscure. He is noted especially for his love poems and funeral elegies.

After the Tang restoration, which followed the suppression of the An Lushan Rebellion in 757, the imperial administration experienced increasing difficulties in maintaining control over the empire. Finally, in 907, a local military commander murdered the Tang emperor and proclaimed himself the founder of a new dynasty, the Liang. This dynasty, however, was short-lived and was followed by four others before China was reunited with the establishment of the Song (Sung) Dynasty in 960. This period between 907 and 960, known as the Five Dynasties period, did not produce distinguished poetry.

SONG DYNASTY (960-1279)

Under Emperor Tai Zu (T'ai Tsu), China became an empire again, with its capital at Kaifeng (K'ai-feng, then called Pien-ching, or Bianjing), just south of the Yellow River in East Central China. In 1126, the Jin Empire invaded the North China Plain, captured Kaifeng, and held the emperor prisoner. The Chinese court fled southward to establish a new capital at Hang (present Hangchow) on the lower Yanzi Plain, not far from the East China Sea. Hence, the Song is divisible into the Northern Song (960-1127) and the Southern Song (1127-1279).

Although the Song was a period of turmoil, warfare, and chaos, in many ways it was also an age of great culture and refinement. The dynasty is noted for its landscape painters as well as for its writers. Indeed, in the arts and literature, the Song nearly equaled the accomplishments of the Tang. The chief poets of the Song Dynasty were Ouyang Xiu (Ou-yang Hsiu; 1007-1072), Wang Anshi (Wang An-shih; 1021-1086), Su Dongpo (Su Tung-p'o; pen name of Su Shi; 1036-1101), Li Qingzhao (Li Ch'ing-chao; 1084-c. 1151), and Lu You (Lu Yu; 1125-1210).

OUYANG XIU

Ouyang Xiu was both a major political figure—he was president of the board of war—and the acknowledged leader of the literary world of his time. A great prose master and a major poet, he was a reformer and innovator. His position of influence and his own exemplary prose style were largely responsible for the success of the *guwen* (*ku-wen*) prose movement, which had originated with Han Yu several hundred years earlier. As for *shi* (*shih*), or regulated poetry, he was a master of the *jueju*, or quatrain. This can be seen in his "The Pavilion of Abounding Joy" and "Returning Home in the Rain," which are direct, simple, and fluent. Although he closely followed tradition in these works, his individual voice is apparent. His *ci*, or poems based on musical scores, are short but produce a distinctive musical effect. His most outstanding *fu* is "Qiu shenfu" ("Sounds of Autumn"). Ouyang Xiu was a painstaking writer and a tireless reviser of his work.

WANG ANSHI

Wang Anshi was a powerful political figure and a controversial social reformer. As prime minister under Shenzong, who ascended the throne in 1068, Wang instituted a reform program that caused great controversy and resulted in his resignation. He became the governor of what is now Nanjing and received many subsequent honors, but he never regained his former political power. He was an outstanding prose writer as well as a superb poet and was particularly famous for his direct and clear-cut memorials to the throne and for his funeral inscriptions. He invented the "five-legged essay," the precursor of the famous "eight-legged essay" later required in the public examinations. In poetry, his *jueju* were much admired. Poems such as "Night Duty" and "Early Summer" present concrete images in swift sequence with vivid realism.

SU DONGPO

The most original poet of the Song was Su Dongpo, an important public official and an outstanding calligrapher and painter as well as a major poet. He opposed Wang Anshi's reforms and was therefore banished. Su Dongpo returned to the capital in 1085, after Wang's fall. From 1089 to 1091, Su Dongpo was the governor of Hang. He returned to the capital but was soon banished again, first to Huizhou in Guangdong Province and then to Hainan Island. As a poet, he was a keen student of such previous literary greats as Tao Qian, Du Fu, and Han Yu. He was also a great admirer of his contemporary, Ouyang Xiu. He deliberately strove to break out of the limitations of Tang poetry and succeeded more spectacularly than his contemporary Wang Anshi. With a view toward perpetuating his technique, he drew around him some of the outstanding poets of his time. His school succeeded in dominating *shi* poetry for the remainder of the Song period.

Su Dongpo liked to write regulated poetry of the kind that allowed him maximum freedom—long, free-wheeling *fu* or short, seven-character *jueju*. His twin *fu* on the "Red Cliff" are memorable descriptions and meditations on history. His quatrain "Mid-Autumn Moon" shows his disciplined economy of expression. He broke away entirely from the conventions of the *ci* and wrote a meditative kind of poetry without much regard for its musical possibilities. Whatever kind of poems he wrote, he was always original. His poetry is noted for its range of vision, its inclusion of vernacular language, and its organic form.

LI QINGZHAO

Li Qingzhao and Lu You are perhaps the two most interesting poets of this group because of their unusual personalities and the peculiar circumstances of their lives. Li Qingzhao has been called the greatest woman poet of China. She was a native of Shandong Province, and her father was the renowned scholar and writer Li Gefei (Li Kei-fei). Having married scholar and antiquarian Zhao Mingcheng (Chao Ming-ch'eng), Li Qingzhao apparently had found an ideal relationship. When the Jin invasion forced the Chinese court to flee southward, she and her husband did likewise, but her husband died on the way, and she was obliged to continue her flight alone. This tragic loss profoundly affected Li Qingzhao for the rest of her life. After a few years in Hang, she removed herself to Zhejiang, where she spent the rest of her days. Li Qingzhao wrote both prose and verse, but the vast majority of her writings have been lost. She enjoyed a high reputation in her time, particularly for her *ci*. Her poetry displays a sensibility that is distinctively feminine. Many of her *ci* express her feelings regarding her widowhood and increasing age. Her images are precisely selected and her poems show a capacity for deep feeling.

LU YOU

Lu You, a native of Zhejiang Province, has been regarded as the greatest poet of the Southern Song. At the age of twelve, he wrote prose and verse sufficiently distinguished to attract the attention of the highest officials in the government, including the emperor himself. Lu You began a career in public life, but he soon encountered difficulties. His independent spirit and pronounced talent excited the envy of many, who spread malicious gossip about him; furthermore, he found great difficulty in conforming to the expectations of others. An ardent patriot who felt deeply dishonored by China's loss of its former territory, he consequently took a strong interest in the military. He served on the staff of Fan Chenda when that renowned poet was the military commander of Sichuan Province. He wrote a large body of nature poetry, but despite its high quality, the keys to his work are his patriotism and his respect for the art of war. He saw a special dignity in the profession of soldier and held that warfare was indispensable to national defense. He yearned to be a man of action but never could find the proper context in which to act. The most prolific poet in the history of Chinese literature, Lu You lived to the advanced age of eighty-five.

Although the Song Dynasty is noted for the production of some great *shi* and *fu*, the dominant poetic genre of the period was the *ci*. The *ci* was the most popular form of the age, despite the fact that it was rated below the *shi* and *fu* in terms of literary merit.

YUAN DYNASTY (1279-1368)

The ruling class of the Southern Song had believed in negotiation, appeasement, and opportunistic alliances rather than an aggressive foreign policy and a strong national defense. Militarily weak, its treasury exhausted by the payment of exorbitant tribute, the government sought an alliance with the Mongols against their common enemy, the Jin Tartars. This policy backfired when Kublai Khan, the grandson of Genghis Khan, suddenly grown powerful, blatantly annexed China to the Mongol Empire. The Chinese people awakened from their long dream to find themselves under the heel of a foreign conqueror.

To the imperialistic Mongols, China was simply a colony for exploitation. Ignoring Chinese tradition and customs, they did whatever they thought necessary to maintain control over the country. In place of the traditional Chinese class hierarchy of scholars, farmers, merchants, and soldiers, the Mongols instituted a hierarchy based on race: Mongols, useful foreigners, Northern Chinese, and Southern Chinese. At first, the Chinese as a whole were excluded from participating in the government, but soon realizing the enormity of its mission, the Mongol regime decided that such a policy might have dire results. Accordingly, the regime began

depending heavily on the Chinese official class. Many Chinese scholars, however, refused to cooperate with the Mongols and retreated to the country to become recluses and wanderers.

Thus, energies that might have been exerted in governmental administration were channeled into the arts, particularly into painting and musical drama. The Yuan Dynasty was a great age of *wenrenhua*, the art that combined painting, calligraphy, and poetry into a single unit and produced the Four Great Masters of the Yuan Dynasty: Huang Gongwang (Huang Kung-wang), Ni Zan (Ni Tsan), Wang Men, and Wu Zhen (Wu Chen). It was also the golden age of the Chinese opera, the Mongols being particularly fond of this theatrical form, and it produced four great masters of the Northern school: Guan Hanqing (Kuan Han-ch'ing; c. 1220-1307), Wang Shifu (Wang Shih-fu; c. 1250-1337), Ji Junxiang (Chi Chün-hsiang; fl. 1260-1280), and Ma Zhiyuan (Ma Chih-yüan; c. 1265-1325). Although the Northern style of drama predominated during the Yuan period, a Southern style had developed under the leadership of Gao Ming (Kao Ming; fl. 1345-1375).

In the realm of nondramatic poetry, the most important Yuan form was a new kind of lyric that developed from the *qu* (*ch'ü*), or dramatic verse, and was known as the *sanqu* (*san-ch'ü*), or "unattached song." Poets who were not dramatists began to write these "unattached songs" based on the style of dramatic verse but not intended to be part of any play. This new type of lyric was looser in its requirements than *shi* with respect to rhythm, diction, and treatment of subject matter. The most prominent author of *sanqu* after the year 1300 was Zhang Kejiu (Chang K'o-chiu; fl. 1275-1325). A songwriter who occupied various civil-service posts under the Mongols, he wrote mainly about his disappointments in life and his efforts to console himself.

MING DYNASTY (1368-1644)

The last years of the Yuan Dynasty were plagued by rebellions, the work of military adventurers and quasi-religious leaders; behind the scenes were the wealthy gentry, ambitious for political power. A Buddhist monk named Zhu Yuanzhang (Chu Yüan-chang), crafty and ruthless, was able to best all opponents and oust the Mongols at the same time. He became the founder of the Ming Dynasty and reigned as Hongwu (Hung Wu) from 1368 to 1399. An absolute monarch, he tightened the hold of the government on the everyday life of the nation.

Free of Mongol domination, the Chinese people welcomed native rule and reacted strongly against foreign practices. The emperor himself led this pro-Chinese movement by reviving ancient Chinese customs and ceremonies and emphasizing agricultural pursuits. He revised the civil-service examinations and introduced the very rigid format of the eight-legged essay, which was required of all degree candidates. As a consequence, candidates were driven away from poetry, which previously had been their main preoccupation, to concentrate on this rigid essay format. Indeed, the spirit of originality and innovation was suppressed altogether in favor of maintaining tradition and observing established conventions.

Although for a time the Ming experienced considerable trouble in keeping the Mongols at bay, the third emperor of the Ming Dynasty, Yongluo (Yung Lo; r. 1402-1424), succeeded in frustrating all their efforts, reestablishing the empire in most of the northwest. With peace restored, interest in art and literature increased. The technique of block printing was perfected, publishing flourished, and scholars were put to work selecting the best literature of the past and present for preservation and circulation. Illustrated encyclopedias, dictionaries, collections of stories, plays, and poems; treatises and monographs on the arts and sciences; and critical studies of art and literature were prepared and printed. It was an age of *tongshu* (*t'ung-shu*), or "collectanea." There was great activity in the writing and production of drama and in the writing of vernacular fiction. Much nondramatic poetry was written in the *shi* and *ci* forms, but it was the Southern *sanqu* that became a universal fad. Although superb craftsmen, the nondramatic poets were generally imitative and bound by tradition and conventions.

QING (OR MANCHU) DYNASTY (1644-1911)

In 1644, China was invaded by the Manchus, a nomadic Mongolian people. Unlike the Mongols, the Manchus were interested in China for its own sake, not merely as a colony to be exploited. They admired Chinese culture and gradually became completely assimilated, losing their own cultural distinctiveness. The second Qing emperor, Kangxi (Ka'ang Hsi), was not only a strong military leader and an able administrator but also a scholar and a lover of the arts and literature. From an early age, he had loved the Chinese language, Chinese literature, and Confucian philosophy. He encouraged Chinese scholarship to such a degree that scholarship became the dominating force of his time. Because of him, a great dictionary of more than forty thousand Chinese characters was compiled.

Massive compendia such as the *Gujin tushu jicheng* (1726; collection of pictures and writing) and the *Siku quanshu* (1773-1782; *The Emperor's Four Treasures: Scholars and the State in the Late Ch'ien-lung Era*, 1987) came into being. The former classified all the significant writings of the empire; the latter reedited all the major writings of the empire for inclusion and was so voluminous that it was never printed, although seven copies were made by hand. Interest in classical literature flourished, and vigorous creative efforts were made in drama and fiction. In poetry, all previous literary types were revived: the Tang *shi*, the Song *ci*, the Yuan dramatic and lyric *Chu ci*, and the Han *fu*. A similar revival took place in classical prose, with interest directed at the *guwen* of the Tang and Song Dynasties. Vernacular prose produced perhaps the greatest Chinese novel, *Hongloumeng* (1792; *Dream of the Red Chamber*, 1958), by Cao Xueqin (Ts'ao Hsueh-ch'in).

Most of the Qing poets were fine technicians, but few were able to free themselves from the old masters such as Li Bo, Du Fu, Bo Juyi, and Su Dongpo. Nevertheless, there were some poets whose independence of spirit penetrated their imitations so that they spoke in their own voice. The most outstanding of them were Qian Qianyi (Ch'ien Ch'ien-yi; 1582-1664), Wu Weiye (Wu Wei-yeh; 1609-1671), Wang Shizhen (Wang Shih-chen; 1634-1711), and Yuan Mei (Yüan Mei; 1715-1797). Important but less-skilled poets were Chen Zulong (Ch'en Tsu-lung; 1608-1647), Chen Weisong (Ch'en Wei-sung; 1626-1682), and Nara Singde, a Manchu (1655-1685), all of whom were noted for their *ci* during the early Qing. Among the noteworthy writers of *ci* during the late Qing were playwright Jiang Shiquan (Chiang Shih-ch'üan; 1725-1785), Wang Pengyun (Wang P'eng-yün; 1848-1904), and Huang Xing (Huang Hsing; 1874-1916).

By the end of the nineteenth century, Western ideas and the aggressive dynamics of Western power and technology had brought fear, dismay, turmoil, violence, and shame to the people of China. Despite pleas from its wise men for reforms that would enable China to survive as a nation and a civilization, the Dragon Throne and the power around it blindly opposed all change as capitulation to Western ideas and methods. Such intransigence brought about the revolt of the people in 1911, when, led by the revolutionary firebrand Sun Yat-sen, they overthrew the old autocratic system and established the Chinese Republic the following year.

POST-QING PERIOD (1911-1949)

In 1905, the civil-service examination system was abolished, and modern education along Western lines was introduced into China. Large numbers of students went abroad to study—to Japan, to North America, and to Europe. Depending on where they studied, they absorbed the influences of various foreign authors. They returned to their homeland with all sorts of Western ideas. In 1917, Hu Shi (Hu Shih), a philosopher trained in the United States, and Chen Duxiu (Ch'en Tu-hsiu) launched a radical literary movement advocating that literature be written exclusively in *bai hua*, the vernacular, and no longer in *wenli*, or classical Chinese. Furthermore, old genres, diction, and themes were to be abandoned, and a new value was to be placed on those novels, plays, and folk poems of the past that had been written in the everyday language of the people.

With the acceptance of this doctrine and the historical circumstances surrounding Chinese poets from 1917 to 1927, Chinese literature fell into turmoil. In 1923, a group of young writers gathered around Xu Zhimo (Hsü Chih-mo; 1895-1931) to form the Crescent Society. The aesthetic theoretician of this group was Wen Yiduo (Wen I-to; 1899-1946), who, under the influence of the French writer Théophile Gautier, championed the use of measured prosodic units to achieve a musical effect in the vernacular similar to that of the best classical poetry. Wen Yiduo believed in art free of politics, an orientation for which he was attacked by some. His volume *Sishui* (the dead water), published in 1928, has been admired as one of the finest volumes of poetry produced anywhere in the 1920's. Wen Yiduo may be the greatest Chinese poet of the twentieth century.

Another group, interested in expressing the relationship of humans to the universe, is represented by such poets as Feng Zhi (Feng Chih; 1905-1993) and Bian Zhilin (Pien Chih-lin; 1910-2000) advocating the use of metaphor to express metaphysical ideas.

Under the influence of French Symbolists such as Paul Verlaine and Stéphane Mallarmé, a group led by Li Jinfa (1901-1976) and Dai Wangshu (Tai Wangshu, 1905-1950?) attempted to suggest through symbols that only humanity's impressions of the world have substantial reality. In this period of ferment and experimentation, the theme common to all was freedom from the old classical restraints.

From 1927 to 1932, revolutionary ideas were in the air, and social protest became the watchword behind the slogan "From literary revolution to revolutionary literature." Many radical writers were imprisoned and executed as a result of their overt protests. Around 1932, revolutionary writing began to be replaced by what was called the New Realism; the sufferings of the masses were realistically described without recommendations for revolutionary action. The poetry of Zang Kejia (Tsang K'o chia; 1905-2004), Ai Qing (Ai Ch'ing; pen name of Chiang Hai-ch'eng, or Jiang Haicheng; 1910-1996), and Ren Jun (Jen Chün; born 1909) is typical of this period.

From 1937 to 1947, China was at war. In 1942, the Communist leader and poet Mao Zedong (Mao Tse-tung, 1893-1976) issued his famous dictum from Yenan calling for "Social Realism" in literature. By 1947, most writers had purged themselves entirely of classical ornament as well as of the conventions of Western literature, and the new vernacular medium had assumed its own Chinese shape. With the establishment of the People's Republic of China in 1949, however, Chinese literature became shackled in another manner: by communist ideology. It assumed the stereotyped role of supporting the new communist society in ways approved by the party leaders.

THE MAOIST ERA (1949-1976)

Though his regime was harshly repressive of poetic creativity, Mao himself fancied his own poetic abilities and took a general interest in the state of Chinese poetry. The delicacy, precision, and suggestiveness of traditional Chinese poetry made an uneasy fit with the sloganeering and propaganda of the Maoist belief system, but Mao nonetheless produced many fervid poems that inevitably received much comment from Chinese literary organs. In Maoist ideology, the cultural sphere was an important vehicle for disseminating the ideology of the state. However, the modernist poets of the Guomindang era were not entirely silenced under Mao. Guo Moruo (1892-1978), who wrote in free verse, bridged several generations and was a living link between past and present. Although he served as a functionary in the communist government (he was head of the Chinese academy of science), Guo's poetic integrity was never compromised, he continued to range widely over aesthetic, historical, and philosophical concerns. Even the harsh repression of the Cultural Revolution of the 1960's failed to extinguish the spark of poetic imagination totally. The underground poetry of this era erupted, ironically, as an enthusiastic echo of government-sponsored frenzy; the initiative and spirit that was generated, however, was felt to be threatening by the leadership despite its apparent ideological conformity. Poets such as Huang Xiang and Quo Lusheng suffered terribly for their independence during this era. Though poetry did not entirely grind to a halt, creativity was trammeled.

THE POST-MAO ERA

The literary generation immediately following the Cultural Revolution produced what is known as scar literature (*shanghen wenxue*), whose main purpose was to provide a testimony to the ravages of the immediate past. Scar literature emerged particularly after the death of Mao in 1976 and after the April 5, 1976, protests occasioned by the death of Mao's colleague Zhou Enlai. Although, as far as politically possible, it excoriated the crimes of the government, scar literature was still overwhelmingly public in orientation, and it continued, if perhaps only in the mode of trauma, the idea that literature is a rendition of external reality.

Around 1978, several poets decided to go a step further than scar literature. *Meng long* ("misty" or "obscure") poetry that sprang up in this era went in tandem with the Democracy Wall movement of 1978-1979, yet paradoxically turned away from public expression into a more indirect and introspective mode, concentrating on the self in natural surroundings. Misty poetry in this way seemed to resemble traditional landscape poetry, but it often contained hidden symbols of ideological dissent from the communist government. Misty poetry produced the major names that dominated Chinese poetry into the twenty-first century: Bei Dao, Gu Cheng, Shu Ting, Yang Lian, and Mang Ke. Bei Dao (Zhao Zhenkai; born 1949) was the first of the misty poets to come to public light with his poem "The Answer" (1979); still the most famous living Chinese poet at the end of the century, Bei Dao and his work made new demands of the reader, not remaining within the customary conventions of Chinese lyric, although its influence by Western models did not at all equate to mere imitation. Gu Cheng (1856-1993) is contemporary Chinese poetry's *poète maudit*; his psychological turmoil eventually led him to kill both himself and his wife in exile in New Zealand in 1993. Simpler and more confrontational in his language than Bei Dao, Gu Cheng wrote poems whose final meaning is nonetheless elusive. Shu Ting (born 1952) was the only major woman poet in the misty group; her signature poem "To the Oak Tree" reveals more rhythmical and musical tendencies than do the poems of her contemporaries. The poetry of Yang Lian (born 1955) is often rhapsodic and dense with natural images, yet replete with an underlying cynicism; he has tended to write about Tibet and the western portions of China itself. In later years, he became more interested in the roots of Chinese identity. Mang Ke (born 1950), with Bei Dao, was coeditor of *Jintian* (today), the leading magazine of misty poetry. Mang was one of the first of his generation to publish serious poetry, and his images, most famously that of the sunflower, are vivid and bridge the gap between objectivity and subjectivity, nature and human desire.

The government began to react against misty poetry

in the "anti-spiritual pollution" campaign of 1983, and some of the poets went underground or into exile. The misty poets nevertheless were still the most prominent group at the beginning of the twenty-first century, drawing increasing international attention. Their stature sometimes led to resentment on the part of less-well-known poets, many of whom began to adopt a more discursive and colloquial approach, one focusing less on the individual ego than on the intermittently intolerable conditions of human existence itself. Others, though, went in the opposite direction and introduced spiritual, sometimes explicitly Christian themes into their verse.

Chinese poetry in the 1990's was affected by a specific event and a long-term process: the Tiananmen Square massacre of June, 1989, and the onslaught of globalization that led Shanghai to be changed virtually overnight into a gleaming postmodern megalopolis. Although the communists adamantly retained control, Chinese writers were much more in touch with their counterparts abroad, especially in the Chinese diaspora. The government allowed freedom of expression in strictly literary matters, no longer aspiring to intervene in the cultural sphere or codifying a prescribed aesthetic, as in the Mao era. At the start of the twenty-first century, the main tension in Chinese poetry was between "vulgar," or *minjian* poets, who used the banalities of everyday life to express a pulse of authenticity, and more intellectual poets who sought to plug into advanced Western philosophical debates. The underground journal *Shi Cankao*, edited by Zhong Dao, tended to promote the *minjian* poets, especially Yi Sha (born 1966), who in "My Ancestors" took a completely anti-idealistic and antinostalgic view of his own relation to tradition. The *minjian* poets espoused an aesthetic that would have been out of fashion in the West, had they been Western, and thus provided a counterpoise to the inevitable cross-fertilization between Chinese and Western aesthetics. This cross-fertilization was expedited by the number of Chinese writers who, whether for political or for economic reasons, emigrated to Western countries.

Ouyang Yu (born 1955), for example, not only moved to Australia but also (in volumes such as *Songs of the Last Chinese Poet*, 1997) saw himself as much as an Australian as a Chinese poet and founded a bilingual journal, *Yuanxiang* (otherland). The translator Mabel Lee, also based in Australia, translated both Chinese poetry and fiction into English, making it more visible internationally. Other overseas poets, such as Bei Ling (born 1959), continued to be active in calling attention to human rights concerns within China. Bei Ling, with fellow exile Meng Lang (born 1961), in 1993 founded the literary periodical *Qing Xiang* (tendency), the most spirited and imaginatively comprehensive Chinese literary journal of its era. Bei Ling, who first left China in the late 1980's, returned to China and was arrested there in the summer of 2000 for his literary activities and was liberated only after international pressure. Bei Ling's poetry, praised by Western luminaries such as Joseph Brodsky, Seamus Heaney, and Susan Sontag, is measured in its diction and stance, yet is written with considerable emotion—one example of the many available new syntheses in the age-old tradition of Chinese poetry.

BIBLIOGRAPHY

Barnstone, Tony, and Chou Ping, eds. *The Anchor Book of Chinese Poetry: From Ancient to Contemporary, The Full 3,000-Year Tradition*. New York: Anchor Books, 2004. This massive anthology is an excellent source for the study of Chinese poetry, collecting more than six hundred poems written over the past three thousand years.

Birrell, Anne, trans. *Chinese Love Poetry: New Songs from a Jade Terrace, a Medieval Anthology*. 2d ed. London: Penguin, 1995. Collects poems from the Chinese medieval period; Birrell adds an introduction, notes, and a map.

Cai, Zong-qi, ed. *How to Read Chinese Poetry: A Guided Anthology*. Bilingual ed. New York: Columbia University Press, 2007. A historical and literary guide through Chinese poetry, featuring more than 140 poems, some with close readings. The book is organized chronologically, with each chapter written by an expert in the area, but has an alternative thematic table of contents. Include helpful explanations of such matters as sound, rhythm, and syntax. Glossary-index.

Cao, Zuoya. *The Asian Thought and Culture: The In-*

ternal and the External, a Comparison of the Artistic Use of Natural Imagery in English Romantic and Chinese Classic Poetry*. New York: Peter Lang, 1998. An examination of the different ways that the English Romantic poets and the classic Chinese poets connected the inner and outer worlds, as well as their different poetics—correcting previous wrong notions about Chinese nature poetry. Close readings of more than thirty poems. Notes, bibliography.

Chang, Kang-i Sun, and Huan Saussy, eds. *Women Writers of Traditional China: An Anthology of Poetry and Criticism*. Stanford, Calif.: Stanford University Press, 1999. Women have long played a role in Chinese literature; this massive (nearly nine-hundred-page) work is important to literary, Chinese, and women's studies. Bibliography, index, maps.

Hamill, Sam, trans. *Crossing the Yellow River: Three Hundred Poems from the Chinese*. Rochester, N.Y.: BOA Editions, 2000. Hamill's introduction and a preface by poet W. S. Merwin make this a valuable compendium.

Hightower, James Robert, and Florence Chia-ying Yeh. *Studies in Chinese Poetry*. Cambridge, Mass.: Harvard University Press, 1998. This monograph of more than six hundred pages covers the history of Chinese poetry and poetics into the twentieth century. Bibliography, index.

Lin, Julia C., trans. and ed. *Twentieth-Century Chinese Women's Poetry: An Anthology*. Armonk, N.Y.: M. E. Sharpe, 2009. Contains 245 poems by women poets, both from the Chinese mainland and from Taiwan. Introduction traces the history of contemporary Chinese women's poetry. Biographical headnotes.

Lupke, Christopher, ed. *New Perspectives on Contemporary Chinese Poetry*. New York: Palgrave Macmillan, 2008. An impressive collection of scholarly articles, reflecting a variety of theoretical viewpoints. The arguments advanced are illustrated and supported by close readings. Bibliography and index.

Owen, Stephen. *The End of the Chinese "Middle Ages": Essays in Mid-Tang Literary Culture*. Stanford, Calif.: Stanford University Press, 1996. An examination of Chinese literary and intellectual life during the Tang Dynasty. Bibliographical references, index.

_____. *The Making of Early Chinese Classical Poetry*. Cambridge, Mass.: Harvard University Asia Center, 2006. A study of poems written between the end of the first century B.C.E. and the third century C.E., demonstrating that despite differences in author and genre, they were remarkably similar. The writer argues that later classical poetry evolved out of this tradition. Introductory overview, seven appendixes, bibliography, and index.

Seaton, Jerome P., ed. *The Shambhala Anthology of Chinese Poetry*. Boston: Shambhala, 2006. This book compiles 380 poems by China's great poets, representing three thousand years of Chinese literature. The poems Seaton chose for this volume are representative of the poets' works, and all were translated by Seaton himself. He makes the poems easily accessible by grouping them into historical periods and writing an informative introduction to each group, lending to their historical, cultural, and literary significance.

Sze, Arthur, trans. *The Silk Dragon: Translations from the Chinese*. Port Townsend, Wash.: Copper Canyon Press, 2001. Translations into English of Chinese poems from the fourth through the twentieth centuries.

Weinberger, Eliot, ed. *The New Directions Anthology of Classical Chinese Poetry*. New York: New Directions, 2003. Contains 250 poems, some of them in translations crafted by Ezra Pound, William Carlos Williams, Kenneth Rexroth, and Gary Snyder, and others by the esteemed poet, scholar, and translator David Hinton. Includes essays by the translators and comments by the Chinese poets themselves. In his introduction, Weinberg discusses how American poets have been influenced by their Chinese counterparts. Biographical notes.

Wu, Fusheng. *The Poetics of Decadence: Chinese Poetry of the Southern Dynasties and Late Tang Periods*. Albany: State University of New York Press, 1998. Includes examination of Li Shangyin and other poets of the fourth to tenth centuries. Bibliographical references, index.

Yeh, Michelle, and N. G. D. Malmqvist, eds. *Frontier Taiwan: An Anthology of Modern Chinese Poetry*. New York: Columbia University Press, 2001. A substantial (nearly five-hundred-page) anthology of Taiwanese poetry. Bibliography and a map.

Yip, Wai-lim, ed. and trans. *Chinese Poetry: An Anthology of Major Modes and Genres*. 2d ed. Durham, N.C.: Duke University Press, 1997. A classic anthology, containing 150 poems in every major genre. Poems are printed both in calligraphic form, with word-for-word annotations, and in English translation. In an introductory essay, the editor explains Chinese aesthetics, and each section of the volume is preceded by a short commentary and followed by a bibliography.

Richard P. Benton
Updated by Nicholas Birns

CROATIAN POETRY

The beginnings of Croatian poetry coincided with the introduction of Christianity to the Croats in the ninth century, when the disciples of the missionaries Cyril and Methodius came to the South Slavic lands, bringing with them writings in Old Church Slavonic concerning church rituals. Unfortunately, most Croatian literary works of that period have been lost. The earliest extant Croatian poetry is contained in *Misal Kneza Novaka* (1368; the missal of Prince Novak), written in *glagolitsa*, a special alphabet devised by the missionaries on the basis of the local tongue. Numerous church songs from the fourteenth and fifteenth centuries show a great variety of rhymed and unrhymed metrics—from seven to twelve syllables—but there are also songs in free verse. All of this poetic activity, limited though it was in subject matter and scope, constituted the necessary preparation for, and transition to, the blossoming of artistic literature in general, and poetry in particular, in cultural centers along the Adriatic coast from the second half of the fifteenth century to 1835.

The Croatian territories on the Adriatic coast escaped Turkish rule and, as a result, were able to develop in every respect. This was especially true of the Republic of Dubrovnik (Ragusa). Culturally, this area was under the direct influence of Italian Humanism and Petrarchan poetry. Many Croatian poets were educated in Italy and wrote for the most part, or exclusively, in Latin. More important, even though the general tenor and spirit of their poetry were unmistakably under the Italian influence, the Croatian poets of Dalmatia were able to give their poetry a native slant and color, not only in language and setting but also in their own understanding of the function and purpose of literature and poetry.

FOURTEENTH TO SIXTEENTH CENTURIES

The first writer of stature who excelled in both Latin and Croatian was Marko Marulić (1450-1524). His many writings on religious and moral issues were widely circulated throughout Europe in the first half of the sixteenth century. Marulić was at times suspicious of the secular spirit of the Renaissance; his poetry is steeped in piety and Christian morality, often touching on the social problems of his time, especially the immoral behavior of some members in the hierarchy of the Catholic Church. He also warned repeatedly about the danger of the advancing Turks, who had besieged his native Split. His most ambitious work, the epic *Judita* (1501; *Judith*, 1990), uses a biblical story to reflect on conditions in Dalmatia in his time, particularly the Turkish threat and the need to preserve freedom.

Šiško Menčetić (1457-1527) and Džore Držić (1461-1501) were two of the early Dubrovnik writers who laid the foundations of Croatian medieval poetry with their somewhat scant poetic contributions. Menčetić was a patrician and Držić a priest; they complemented each other in that the former was a more conventional and the latter a more spontaneous poet. Menčetić's lyric poetry follows closely the spirit of Petrarch, while that of Držić reflects the spontaneity and freshness of folk poetry.

The works of these two poets soon began to exert influence on the second generation of Dalmatian poets in the first half of the sixteenth century. Hanibal Lucić (1485-1553) and Petar Hektorović (1487-1572) wrote love poems in the Petrarchan tradition and incorporated that tradition even in their longer works, the play *Robinja* (1520; English translation, 1585), by Lucić, and the epic *Ribanje i ribarsko prigovaranje* (1568; *Fishing and Fishermen's Conversation*, 1959), by Hektorović. A strong influence of folk poetry is also evident in their works; like many writers of their generation, they had begun to assert themselves as Croatian writers even as they assimilated foreign influences. One of the most fascinating poets in this respect is Andrija Čubranović, of whose life very little is known but who, in his love poem "Jedjupka" (the Gypsy), embellished his Petrarchan model with the octosyllabic line, which had become synonymous with the young but rapidly growing Croatian tradition.

Other noteworthy poets of the sixteenth century expanded the scope of their poetry while branching out into other genres; in fact, some of them are better known for their work in other genres. Mavro Vetranović (1482-1576), after starting in the religious and moralistic vein of his predecessors, developed into a pure lyric poet who was not reluctant to dwell on his personal concerns in a highly reflective manner. Marin Držić (c. 1508-1567), the author of many pastoral plays and comedies, expresses in his love poems, as in his drama, the joy of life, indulging in an unabashed glorification of youth, pleasure, and beauty. Dinko Ranjina (1536-1607) and Dinko Zlatarić (1558-1609) also endeavored to break away from the traditions established by older poets; although they lacked the strength to complete such an important task, they pointed in the direction that Croatian literature would take in the next century.

RENAISSANCE

On the strength of the solid foundation laid by almost a century of unhindered growth, Croatian poetry of the Renaissance reached its pinnacle in the seventeenth century. The greatest Croatian poet of the century, and indeed of the entire era, was Ivan Gundulić (1589-1638). Continuing in the Christian tradition of his predecessors, Gundulić added a pronounced nationalism in order to present the life of Dubrovnik and of his people in general. In *Suze sina razmetnoga* (1622; the tears of the prodigal son), his deep religiosity is reflected in the realization of the transience of all things and of the need to seek God. It is the long, unfinished epic poem *Osman* (1651; English translation, 1991), however, that qualifies Gundulić as one of the greatest poets in all the South Slavic literatures. *Osman* reflects Gundulić's preoccupation with the freedom of his people in their struggle against the Turks. The defeat of the Turkish sultan Osman by Poland is used by the poet to instill hope in the Slavs. What makes the epic outstanding is an artistic quality not previously seen in Croatian poetry: a richness of poetic expression, a strong rhythm and deft rhyming, and a skillful mixture of lyric and realistic elements.

SEVENTEENTH CENTURY

After Gundulić, the literature of Dubrovnik began a slow decline. There were only two other poets of note: Ivan Bunić Vučić (1591-1658) wrote Anacreontic poems with an emphasis on love and other sensuous experiences, composed in flowing octosyllables and couched in picturesque images. Ignjat Djurdjević (1675-1737) wrote most of his poetry in the eighteenth century, but in spirit, he belonged to the preceding century and, as such, concluded the golden age of the literature of Dubrovnik. Like Vučić, Djurdjević wrote love lyrics stressing sensuality and the unhappy ending of the love experience.

While Dubrovnik relinquished its leading position in Croatian literature, other parts of Croatia began to assert themselves. In the seventeenth century, there were three noteworthy poets in Croatia proper: Petar Zrinski (1621-1671), Fran Krsto Frankopan (1643-1671), and Pavao Ritter Vitezović (1652-1712). The first two belonged to aristocratic families, which furnished the leaders of Croatian society at that time. They were involved in a conspiracy against Austrian rule and, because of this, lost their lives while still very young. They managed to write only a few poems each, drawing from their great knowledge of foreign literatures and concentrating on translation from these literatures. In their own poetry, they were influenced by folk traditions and by the fashionable poetry of their time, including that of Dubrovnik. Vitezović, the first professional writer in Croatia, distinguished himself by his work in cultural matters and by his efforts toward the unification of all the Southern Slavs.

EIGHTEENTH CENTURY

In the eighteenth century, the poets of Croatia proper failed to match the achievements of the Dubrovnik literature of the past, but they prepared the ground for greater achievements that would soon follow. Andrija Kačić Miošić (1704-1760), for example, imitated folk poetry in a versified historical chronicle, *Razgovor ugodni naroda slovinskoga* (1756; a pleasant account of the Slavs), thus foreshadowing the importance of folk poetry during the national revival of the Southern Slavs in the next century. Matija Antun Reljković (1732-1798), primarily a didactic poet, endeavored in his main work, *Satir* (1762; the satyr), to help his people free themselves from foreign rule as well as from ignorance. Tito Brezovački (1757-1805) also wrote primarily to educate his people and, in the process, used their own language.

FOLK TRADITIONS

During these centuries, there was another literature—folk literature—which existed like an underground river. The folk poetry of the Croats developed simultaneously with that of the Serbs; sometimes it is impossible to tell them apart unless they deal with clearly identifiable historical events and figures. Like their Serbian counterparts, Croatian folk poems concern themselves with the basic conflict of the medieval history of the Southern Slavs—the struggle of Christendom against Islam. Croatian lyric folk poems are almost identical with those of the Serbs in that they, too, depict the everyday concerns of the common people. They are also rich artistically. While the Serbian folk lyrics are mostly decasyllabic, Croatian folk lyrics employ a greater variety of meters, most of them in a twelve-syllable meter known as *bugarštica*.

ROMANTICISM

Folk poetry gave a strong impetus to the national revival in all the South Slavic lands at the beginning of the nineteenth century. The sense of oneness among the Serbs and Croats, as evidenced by folk poetry that could be read and appreciated in all parts of the Serbo-Croatian linguistic and ethnic domain, led to the reawakening of national identity and to the formation of the so-called Illyrian movement. This movement originated in Croatia, where it also had its strongest and most eloquent support. It consisted of people from all walks of life, although writers, especially poets, predominated. The movement was influenced, somewhat belatedly, by Western European Romanticism, notably that of German literature. Nationalistic aspirations to free the country from the suffocating domination of Austrian, Hungarian, German, Italian, and Turkish rulers also contributed considerably to the birth of this movement. Its main leader, Ljudevit Gaj (1809-1872), proposed that the *Štokavian* dialect, the language of the vast majority of Serbo-Croatian folk poems, should serve as the official language of all the Southern Slavs, and many writers began to use this dialect exclusively.

The Illyrian movement in Croatia produced three excellent poets: Ivan Mažuranić (1814-1890), Stanko Vraz (1810-1851), and Petar Preradović (1818-1872).

Mažuranić is best known for his epic poem *Smrt Smail-age Čengijića* (1846; the death of Smail-aga Chengich), which glorifies the struggle of the Montenegrins against the Turks while presenting a dark picture of the Turkish atrocities. The epic embodies many elements of Croatian culture, even though it depicts the plight of another South Slavic nation, thus underscoring one of the basic themes of the Illyrian movement. The influence of epic folk poetry is reflected in the simplicity and immediacy of Mažuranić's language, in the poem's dramatic action, and in its decasyllabic meter. Vraz, a Slovene by birth and upbringing, started to write in Slovenian but then accepted the call of the Illyrians for a common language. He wrote his best works in Croatian, chiefly love poems collected in *Djulabije* (1840; red apples). Like most Illyrians, he believed that a poet should create artistic literature based on folk poetry, but he also wrote sonnets, ghazels (a form of Middle Eastern love poem popular among the Romantics), romances, ballads, satiric poems, and epigrams, introducing a more cosmopolitan spirit to Croatian literature. Preradović, an officer in the Austrian army who had almost forgotten his native language and had begun to write poems in German, "awoke" in later years and in the process, became one of the best-loved Croatian poets. He wrote love poems and reflective verse, but he particularly excelled in patriotic poems, which expressed his faith that one day, all Slavs would unite to form a single nation. The message of his poetry is complemented by an artistic prowess of a kind never seen before in Croatian literature.

Croatian Romanticism was carried on by the generation of poets around the middle of the nineteenth century, although without the intensity and high accomplishments of the Illyrians. The unsuccessful Revolution of 1848, when hopes for independence and a better future were dashed, also had a dampening effect. Of several Romantics during this phase (Mirko Bogović, 1816-1893; Luka Botić, 1830-1863; Franjo Marković, 1845-1914; Josip Eugen Tomić, 1843-1906), the most powerful was August Šenoa (1838-1881). A prolific writer of fiction and prose in other genres, he wrote poetry with the same attitude as he did his prose, combining a realistic method with many Romantic elements, including a preoccupation with the past, the rediscovery of folk literature and folklore, the primacy of emotion, and nationalistic pride.

REALISM

During the period of realism (1881-1895), there were only two significant poets: August Harambašić (1861-1911) and Silvije Strahimir Kranjčević (1865-1905). While Harambašić wrote light, musical poems in which he extolled freedom and exhorted people to fight for it, Kranjčević developed into a poet of fiery spirit. His four books of poetry constitute one loud cry of protest against the injustice and senselessness of contemporary social conditions and of human existence in general. Nevertheless, he expressed the hope that somehow conditions would improve. The author of several outstanding poems, he enriched Croatian literature like no other poet in the nineteenth century, and with his spotlight on human relationships and on the inequities contained therein, he made a sharp turn toward modernity in Croatian poetry.

MODERNISM

The modern spirit came into full recognition and expression with the next generation of poets, grouped around the movement fittingly calling itself *Moderna*. *Moderna* was keenly attuned to contemporary problems and concerns; it also welcomed the influence of foreign authors to a degree unprecedented in Croatian letters. Poetry was its strongest voice, although other genres and arts were also involved. Long strides were made in matters of form and poetics. The movement did much to free Croatian poetry from its provincial confines and to make it a worthy though still neglected partner on the international scene.

There were several competent poets in the *Moderna* movement. One of the first to achieve recognition was Milan Begović (1876-1948). His love poetry, collected in *Knjiga boccadoro* (1900; the book of the golden word), is bold, innovative, rebellious, uninhibited; it shocked older readers but endeared itself to the younger generation. Begović later became more active in drama and fiction and abandoned poetry altogether. Dragutin Domjanić (1875-1933), who made a more important contribution to the poetry of *Moderna* than

did Begović, reached his zenith in *Pesme* (1907; poems). He led a secluded and self-effacing life, reflected in his rather private and pessimistic poetry. Vladimir Vidrić (1875-1909) was the exact opposite of Domjanić, in both his upbringing and his approach to poetry. He wrote only about forty poems, in which he roamed the world and its history, from classical antiquity and Slavic mythology to the present, giving full vent to his Dionysian joy of life. Sparse in quantity but refreshing in quality, Vidrić's poetry has steadily gained in esteem and popularity. Ante Tresić Pavičić (1867-1949), during his long life and career, belonged for a while to *Moderna*, and with his broad erudition, attempted to adopt classical meters to contemporary Croatian. His importance lies more in his influence on younger poets than in his own output. Perhaps the most significant representative of *Moderna* was Antun Gustav Matoš (1873-1914), although his contribution was more important in other genres than in poetry. He wrote poems relatively late in his life, paying strict attention to form and the high aesthetic criteria he advocated in all of his works. His influence on subsequent Croatian writers has been considerable; he was one of the most important Croatian men of letters in the first two decades of the twentieth century.

VLADIMIR NAZOR

Vladimir Nazor (1876-1949) also began to write during this period and espoused modernistic tendencies, but because he was able to outgrow many literary periods and movements, it is difficult to tie him down to a single one. He wrote in many genres, but he was at his best in poetry, publishing more than ten collections. Central to Nazor's poetic outlook is his pantheistic reverence and love for nature in all of its forms. His ebullient optimism and faith in humanity despite all the seamy aspects of life, of which he was not oblivious, made him a bard of faith and hope. He undoubtedly derived his sunny disposition from his place of birth, an island in the Adriatic where he had grown up and spent his youth, and from the fact that his long life passed without much trouble. With his somewhat idealized depiction of the Croatian people, Nazor won favor with the broad reading public, who readily overlooked his shortcomings and lack of depth.

THE WORLD WARS

The advent of World War I brought about a decisive change in Croatian poetry, just as it did in other South Slavic literatures. New faces and forces occupied the central stage during and after the war, elbowing out the older ones, even the writers of *Moderna*. Most of the new poets considered it their first duty to protest against the horrors and madness of war. The strongest new voice belonged to Miroslav Krleža (1893-1981), a writer of remarkable power and breadth who would dominate Croatian letters for seven decades. A politically engaged intellectual, an insistent advocate of social justice, a passionate polemicist, a writer of unusual prowess and broad erudition, Krleža expounded his views in a highly artistic manner in all of his works, of which poetry constituted only a small part. He led Croatian literature during the period of feverish activity and artistically satisfying creativity between the two world wars.

There were other poets worth mentioning (in addition to prewar poets such as Domjanić and Nazor): Tin Ujević (1891-1955), Antun Branko Šimić (1898-1925), Gustav Krklec (1899-1978), Dobriša Cesarić (1902-1980), and Dragutin Tadijanović (1905-2007), to name only some of the most accomplished. The first two should be singled out. Ujević was a bohemian by nature and a highly original poet of intense, mostly pessimistic experiences. In his eight books of poetry, he trod the tortuous path of an often misunderstood loner in his struggle for inner freedom and identity. Šimić's poems strike a similarly tragic chord, intensified by illness and premonitions of early death. Both of these poets have exerted a strong influence on their younger counterparts and on contemporary Croatian poetry.

During World War II, most poets were silent, but a few gave expression to the tragic experiences of their people. Nazor joined the partisans and wrote poems extolling their struggle in his usual positive fashion. Those were the last noteworthy poems he wrote; he died soon after the war. A young poet, Ivan Goran Kovačić (1913-1943), also joined the partisans and gained prominence with his long poem *Jama* (1944; the pit). It is written in a very strict form, full of magnificent imagery and powerful use of language, raising to a tragic level the theme of human suffering and the horrors of war. Kovačić himself was a victim of the war.

POSTWAR AND LATE TWENTIETH CENTURY

In the first postwar years, several older poets—Ujević, Nazor, Krklec, Cesarić, Tadijanović, and others—reappeared with new works, but in almost all cases, their earlier poetry is much better. In the first postwar generation, Vesna Parun (born 1922) and Jure Kaštelan (1919-1990) occupy prominent positions. In 1947, Parun published her first book, *Zore i vihori* (daybreaks and whirlwinds), a collection that was influential among young poets and was at the same time denounced by the Socialist Realist critics. Primarily a poet of love, she combines sensuousness and great compassion with the rich texture of her spiritual intuition. For her, love is a redeeming force that can rescue the world, but from the beginning, one also detects a dark streak in her poetry, for ultimately she is a realist. The ideal she reaches for remains unattainable, and her numerous collections attest this struggle. Kaštelan brought a new, specifically personal tone into Croatian poetry, especially in his elegiac war poems. On one hand, he laments the dead; on the other, he reflects on the fate of those who survived. In his later poems, Kaštelan sought to find a new voice, replacing the themes of war with the problems of modern humans as social beings.

SLAVKO MIHALIĆ

The next generation produced a crop of excellent poets. Slavko Mihalić (1928-2007) wrote in an idiom remarkable for its simplicity, precision, and lyric fluency. His poetry is that of a contemporary man with a rich personal experience who is at the same time well aware of the whole range of intellectual history. His spirit is critical and self-conscious. Mihalić the poet could forget neither that he was writing a poem nor that he lived in the twentieth century. His poems are meditations on the fate of the individual attempting to find a synthesis in a world which feels no pressing need for one. It is the seriousness of his commitment that made Mihalić one of the most impressive figures in contemporary Croatian literature.

MILIVOJ SLAVIČEK

Milivoj Slaviček (born 1929) reveals a certain intellectual kinship with Mihalić, although his emphasis on rationalism and nonconformism is much greater. The intentional prosiness and even awkwardness of his lines result in poetry that is not devoid of emotion and that has its own original intensity. Slaviček at his best has the ability to bring out the absurd details of everyday life and give them poetic luminosity. He seems to carry on a running dialogue with his fellow humans and himself about the basic problems of existence, expressed in colloquial language.

IVAN SLAMNIG

Ivan Slamnig (1930-2001) was probably the most tireless experimenter in contemporary Croatian literature. Each of his poems is a subtle reworking of some aspect of traditional style, form, and imagery. What guided him in these experiments was his impeccable ear as well as his sense of the absurd. The result is a blend of black humor and high seriousness. Essentially an intellectual, he created a kind of metaphysical vaudeville, at once terrifying and comical, cool yet not lacking in compassion.

ANTUN ŠOLJAN

Antun Šoljan (1932-1993), who has of late turned to fiction and drama, has probably the greatest imagistic talent in postwar Croatian literature. The clarity and the resonance of his images give his poems an anonymous, timeless quality. At best, they appear to be parables of an intense inner life. Both Šoljan and Slamnig have been influenced by, and have translated, English and American poetry.

ZVONIMIR GOLOB AND VLADO GOTOVAC

Zvonimir Golob (1927-1997) shared Šoljan's interest in the image, although he leaned toward Surrealism and those who influenced him were to be found among Spanish and South American poets. Parallel to this imagistic tendency, a profound wish to write a poetry of ideas exists in Croatian literature. The prime example of this tendency is the poetry of Vlado Gotovac (1930-2000). His poetry is terse, austere, reduced to an absolute economy of expression whereby each line is almost a separate unit, a kind of epigrammatic building block of the poem. Still, beyond the Hermeticism of these poems there is an authentic lyric voice, in tone not unlike that of the Serbian poet Borislav Radović.

Dubravko Horvatić (1939-2004), Danijel Dragojević (born 1934), and Dubravko Škurla (1933-1957) belong to the next generation of poets. Horvatić steadily evolved his own universe of symbols, exploring the situation and the fate of humanity. Dragojević was a poet of intellectual parables, and Škurla a lyricist of great directness and purity. Many younger poets are slowly acquiring their own poetic profile and carving their own niche in Croatian poetry. The completion of that process is still some time away. As in Serbian poetry, there is bustling activity in contemporary Croatian poetry that bodes well for its future.

BIBLIOGRAPHY

Barac, Antun. *A History of Yugoslav Literature*. Ann Arbor, Mich.: Joint Committee on Eastern Europe Publication Series, 1973. A standard history of all Yugoslav literatures and poetry, including Croatian, by a leading literary scholar. Although somewhat outdated, it still provides reliable information, especially on the older periods.

Debeljak, Aleš. "Visions of Despair and Hope Against Hope: Poetry in Yugoslavia in the Eighties." *World Literature Today* 68, no. 3 (1992): 191-194. Debeljak looks at Yugoslav poetry, including Croatian, on the eve of tumultuous events and changes in Yugoslavia in the 1990's. Poetry of the 1980's in some ways foreshadows those events, giving vent to despair and forlorn hope.

Eekman, Thomas. "Form and Formlessness in Contemporary Serbian and Croatian Poetry." *Southeastern Europe* 9, nos. 1/2 (1982): 84-94. An expert analysis of formalistic aspects of Croatian poetry, based on copious examples and citations.

Hawkesworth, Celia, ed. *A History of Central European Women's Writing*. New York: Palgrave, 2001. Contains four essays on Croatian women writers, along with a number of others on relevant topics. Map, bibliography, and index.

Kadić, Ante. "Postwar Croatian Lyric Poetry." *Slavic Review* 17 (1958): 509-529. Kadić examines the first post-World War II generation of poets and their output, emphasizing their efforts to preserve their artistic freedom under political pressure to conform to nonartistic dictates.

Miletich, John S. *Love Lyric and Other Poems of the Croatian Renaissance: A Bilingual Anthology*. Bloomington, Ind.: Slavica, 2009. A revised and expanded edition of *The Lute and the Lattice: Croatian Poetry of the Fifteenth and Sixteenth Centu-*

ries (1971). Intended for use as an introduction to Croatian literature and as an aid to anyone learning the language of the period, as well as for specialized research. Extensive notes and bibliography.

Torbarina, Josip. *Italian Influence on the Poets of the Ragusan Republic*. London: Williams & Norgate, 1931. Torbarina traces the Italian influence on the poets of this very important period, which led to the blossoming of the literature of Dubrovnik in the Middle Ages.

Žmegač, Viktor. "On the Poetics of the Expressionist Phase in Croatian Literature." In *Comparative Studies in Croatian Literature*. Zagreb, Croatia: Zavod za znanost i književnost Filozofskog fakulteta u Zagrebu, 1981. A skillful treatment of expressionism in Croatian poetry in the 1920's and 1930's, covering a very important period.

Vasa D. Mihailovich
Updated by Mihailovich

CZECH POETRY

The oldest Czech poetry dates to the fourteenth century, although the literary history of Bohemia extends further back by several centuries, to include the Old Church Slavonic and medieval Latin poetry written in Bohemia before the use of the vernacular in literature. Arne Novák, the doyen of Czech literary historiography, includes even works written in German in his survey of Czech literature. A less controversial course, however, is to discuss only poetry written in Czech, considering it as Czech even if written by a Slovak, as was the case with Ján Kollár (1793-1852).

An overview of Czech poetry encourages an imperfect division into roughly four periods: the golden age (to 1409), the age of struggle (1409-1774), the age of revival (1774-1918), and the modern age (1918 to the present). In a terminology that includes the entire Western European cultural context, the four periods parallel the gothic, the Baroque, the Romantic, and the modernist periods; clearly missing is the Renaissance, marginalized in the religious wars, in the Reformation and Counter-Reformation. (Paradoxically, it was only in the second half of the nineteenth century that a "Renaissance" poet, Jaroslav Vrchlický, 1853-1912, appeared in Czech poetry.) Nevertheless, such schematic divisions should not be rigidly respected; they merely provide convenient orientation markers.

THE FOURTEENTH CENTURY

The magnificence of fourteenth century Czech literature lies in the breadth and quality of poetry that appeared so suddenly, situating Bohemia firmly in the Western European literary context. Verse chronicles, epics, didactic literature and satire, courtly love poetry, sacred hymns, profane lyrics—such was the rich spectrum of Czech poetry in the fourteenth century, unequalled in any other Slavic literature at the time. For present-day readers, this rich poetic tradition serves as a reminder of the cultural unity of Bohemia with Western Europe; like other Central European cultures, Bohemia has always been oriented toward the West, something that the unfortunate political locution "Eastern Europe" managed to obfuscate.

The rich treasury of fourteenth century Czech poetry was the product of many well-educated and practiced poets working at the court in Prague, at the Caroline University, or in the monasteries. The oldest attested Czech hymn, from the fourteenth century, was based on a Greek refrain and bears some traces of Old Church Slavonic forms. This hymn, "Hospodine, pomiluj ny" ("Lord Have Mercy on Us"), was preserved as an integral part of the coronation ceremony of the Czech kings, which explains its antiquity. The typical fourteenth century hymn appears in rhymed octosyllabic quatrains, or even longer stanzas, as in "Kunhutina modlitba" ("The Prayer of Lady Kunhuta"). More interesting and indeed regarded as representative of the best poetry of the century is the sophisticated fourteenth century epic poem *Legenda o svaté Kateňě* (the legend of Saint Catherine). The poem combines religious, Scholastic, and secular themes, perhaps reflecting the new situation of Prague, where, in 1348, Charles IV had established the Caroline University (Saint Catherine was the patron saint of its faculty of arts) and his magnificent court. In *Legenda o svaté Kateňě*, the story of the martyrdom of Saint Catherine and her miracles is supplemented both by skillful rhetorical arguments and by elements reminiscent of the Provençal love song.

In its synthesis of sacred and secular elements, the poem marks the transition from versified lives of the saints to the courtly love poetry then sweeping Western Europe. The Provençal love song and the German *Minnesänger* were not perceived as exotic imports in Prague. Rather, because of the cosmopolitan atmosphere encouraged by Charles IV, courtly love poetry developed almost simultaneously in Western Europe and in Bohemia, having found in Prague a fertile soil. In the work of the homegrown Czech love poet Záviš, a master of the Caroline University, there is proof of such encouragement of genre, as well as an indication that at least some poets of the period were connected with the university.

Apart from religious and scholarly poetry, the golden age also produced satirical poems that castigate shoemakers, blacksmiths, butchers, bakers, and others. These "satiry o řemeslnících" ("satires about trades-men") are simple moralistic exempla; much more elaborate are other satirical poems from the same collection of fourteenth century manuscripts, including the twelve hundred lines of the satirical *Decalogue*, wherein adaptations from *Gesta Romanorum* abound.

The art of poetry was only one facet in the many-sided jewel of Czech Gothic culture: the cathedrals, the painting, the advances of learning that, collectively, form the golden age. They all flourished in the fourteenth century, and it is difficult to say which of them was preeminent.

FROM 1409 TO 1774

After the magnificence of the fourteenth century, the fifteenth century seems disappointing. Hymnal poetry was all that remained from the rich fourteenth century heritage, but in the religious strife brought about by Hussite Wars, the hymn was forced to assume a military function, and poetry suffered accordingly.

The period of religious strife was not, however, completely unsuited for literature of any kind: Pamphlets were produced in large numbers, as befitted an age of controversy. Particularly rich too is the satirical poetry of the period. Here, the medieval form of the satirical exemplum combines with a new content, the fruit of the fifteenth century religious pamphleteering of such Hussite thinkers as Petr Chelčický (1390-1460). The didacticism of this satire works against its metaphorical elements to the extent that the latter are suppressed; the allegory in such works seems heavy-handed, so subservient is it to the propagandistic function of the Hussite cause. The Catholic cause did not remain undefended, and the result was a battle of pamphlets, and even a battle of satirical poems, in which both causes were ridiculed.

After the Hussite Wars, Bohemia found itself in a paradoxical position. Nationally—that is, from the point of view of the advancement of the Czech cause, Czech control of the main cities, the use of the vernacular, and so on—there was a clear victory. At the same time, the Czechs isolated themselves from the European context as heretics. This cultural isolation was sadly accompanied by the decline of the Caroline University, by the inability of the main European cultural movements of the Renaissance to establish themselves in Bohemia, and by the destruction of much of the Gothic heritage, including artworks of all kinds, but particularly manuscripts.

Thus, the Czech literary tradition was interrupted, and it was only at the end of the fifteenth century that a cultural revival began, under the influence of Italian Humanism. At first, this influence appeared primarily in translations from classical literature, and only later in original work. At the turn of the fifteenth century, there was a small poetic movement of Czech noblemen, some of whose works are preserved in the *Neuberg Anthology* (c. 1500). There, along with Humanistic irony and Renaissance joie de vivre, the reader encounters compositions of a medieval character close in spirit to the courtly lyric. Further developments—after the Habsburg Dynasty assumed control over Bohemia—strengthened the Humanistic influence, but at the price of turning Bohemia, culturally, into a German province. Humanism inspired the writing of original Latin poetry, while infusions of Italians and Spaniards further discouraged the production of Czech literature.

Given this situation, it is difficult to overestimate the impact made on Czech literature by the Kralická Bible (1579-1593). This landmark Czech translation of the Bible was comparable in its influence to Martin Luther's German translation: It standardized the Czech language, providing a model of usage and style. Its concreteness of expression, its precision, and its lively use of colloquial language make the Kralická Bible the acme of the literary production of its time. It has been particularly influential—indeed incalculably so—on Czech poetry.

The defeat of the Protestant cause and with it the Czech nationalist cause at the Battle of White Mountain in 1620 ushered in a period of religious intolerance that forced many into exile. Jan Ámos Komenský (1592-1670), better known as Comenius, was representative of this Czech exile. A pioneer of modern educational methods and a lexicographer, he was also the author of many Protestant hymns and the last bishop of the Czech Brethren Church.

The greatest personality of the Catholic period was

the Jesuit Bohuslav Balbín (1621-1688), whose historical and linguistic works as well as his poetry were written in Latin. A small group of Catholic Baroque poets wrote in Czech: Adam Michna z Otradovic (1600-1670), Felix Kadlinský (1613-1675), and—the most talented of the group—Bedřich Bridel (1619-1680). Bridel illustrates the positive aspect of the cultural situation that developed after the defeat of the Protestant and nationalist causes. There was in this period a strong Spanish influence under the sign of the victorious Counter-Reformation. Bridel, like Balbín, was a Jesuit, and his work can serve as a good example of Baroque poetry. His transcendentalism and mysticism are evident in such works as "Verše o nebeském paláci" (1658; verses about the celestial palace). This was also the age of hymnbooks, and the same Jesuits were highly productive in offering the people rich collections of hymns, an enormously popular genre at the time.

Worth noting among the various types of literature of the time is Czech folk poetry, which was discovered by the literate Czech writers at the end of the seventeenth century and gradually became the object of a Romantic cult. Assiduously collected, published, propagated, and eventually imitated, the folktales and folk songs of the Czech people are among the most impressive cultural achievements of the Slavs and deserve to be studied in their own right. It is not an exaggeration to say that Czech Romanticism without Czech folk literature would be unthinkable, for the revivalists needed something to revive.

THE AGE OF REVIVAL (1774-1918)

Rather than a revolution from below, a fiat from above—in the form of an imperial edict on religious tolerance—stands at the beginning of the Czech national revival. The revival of Czech as a literary language was also given impetus by the pan-European fascination with folk culture that preceded the Romantic movement. In particular, Johann Gottfried Herder's collection of folk songs, *Volkslieder* (1778-1779), directly influenced, after a delay of several decades, such Czech folklorists as Václav Hanka and František Ladislav Čelakovský. Hanka could not withstand the temptation to provide Czechs with an ancient epic compara-

ble to Ossian and so produced two forgeries of ancient epics. This basically Romantic impulse was rewarded, surprisingly, by an impressive result that played a positive role in firing the imagination of other revivalists.

The literary revival of Czech language was given further impetus by the nationalist reaction against the Germanizing tendency at the end of the eighteenth century, but the movement directly responsible for bringing into play all the forces conducive to revival was the Enlightenment. The Enlightenment brought the Counter-Reformation to a decisive end, symbolized by the suppression of the Jesuit order. Those active in the Enlightenment were also active in the nationalist, revivalist movement following the 1774 clash over the compulsory use of German in Czech schools—an edict that provoked massive resistance and heightened national consciousness.

As an overview of the entire revivalist period, Arne Novák's periodization seems particularly helpful: Enlightenment (1774-1815), classicism (1815-1830), early Romanticism (1830-1848), and late Romanticism (1848-1859). (Novák omits the period from 1860 to World War I, for by 1860, the revival was an accomplished fact.) In the period of Enlightenment inaugurated by the reforms of Emperor Joseph II, the literary revival profited from historical and linguistic scholarship; notable is the work of the learned Jesuit Josef Dobrovský (1753-1829), whose *Geschichte der bömischen Sprache und Literatur* (1792; history of Czech language and literature) laid the foundation for such revivalists as Josef Jungmann and Pavol Jozef Šafárik.

The revival of Czech poetry began with the Puchmajer group of poets. Antonín Jaroslav Puchmajer (1769-1820), influenced by Dobrovský, published *Sebrání básní a zpěvů* (1795; collection of poems and songs), an anthology of poems by young Czech poets.

At a time when Romanticism had already conquered Western Europe, Czech poetry went through a brief phase of classicism, exemplified in poetry by Jungmann (1773-1847) and his poetic school. Jungmann translated widely from both classical and modern European literature; his translations from English, French, and German poetry had an enormous impact on young Czech poets, although this impact was largely limited to formal imitation of Jungmann's hexameters. Jungmann's school included scholars and poets such as the professional soldier Matěj Milota Zdirad Polák (1788-1856), the author of a rare and precious lyric poem in six cantos, *Vznešenost přírody* (1813; the nobility of nature). The greatest poet associated with Jungmann, eclipsing him as the personification of the age of revival, was Ján Kollár (1793-1852), a Slovak writing in Czech and thus claimed, not unreasonably, by both nations as their national poet. His magnum opus is *Slávy dcera* (1824, 1832; the daughter of Sláva), organized into five cantos that situate the poem geographically and mythologically at the foci of five rivers: Elbe, Rhine, Moldau, Lethe, and Acheron. Following the form of the Petrarchan sonnet with trochaic meter, Kollár manages to be most inspiring when mourning the fate of the Lusatian or Sorbian Slavs— those Western Slavs who, by Kollár's time, had been almost completely absorbed by Germany.

František Palacký (1798-1876) and—a Slovak— Pavol Jozef Šafárik (1795-1861) were two other outstanding figures in the national revival: Palacký mainly as a cultural and literary historian, Šafárik as a Slavist, the author of the first comparatist history of Slavic literatures, published in 1826.

Palacký, folklorist Čelakovský, and others were much impressed by Bernard Bolzano (1781-1848), a Prague thinker of Italian origin but a German patriot. Bolzano influenced Czech religious thought and poetry in the rationalist direction, and his influence explains in part the distinctive character of the late-blooming Czech Romantic movement.

Unlike Western European Romanticism, which began as a reaction against the rationalist sensibility of the Enlightenment, Czech Romanticism, hampered by the Hussite heritage as well as by the influence of Catholic thinkers like Bolzano, was of a decidedly rationalist orientation. Folklore, which played an important role in the Romantic movement throughout Europe, was particularly significant in Czech Romanticism. Many Czech Romantics began as collectors of folktales and folk songs, and their immersion in the folk tradition and the poetics of folk literature distinguishes them from the scholarly classicists, with their finely honed versifying and precision of poetic expression.

KAREL JAROMÍR ERBEN

Karel Jaromír Erben (1811-1870) is known as the greatest poet of the ballad, a folk genre he enriched through his wide ethnographic experience. He was also an author who, aware of many native and foreign influences, was able to elevate a humble folk genre into a sophisticated vehicle of poetic expression. Of particular importance is the first part of his *Kytice z pověstí národních* (1853; a bouquet of folktales), containing twelve ballads that were immediately recognized as treasures of Czech poetry.

KAREL HYNEK MÁCHA

A contemporary of Erben, Karel Hynek Mácha (1810-1836) elevated Czech Romanticism to new heights. Within the Romantic period, widely regarded as the richest in the history of Czech poetry, Mácha reigns as the undisputed leader, largely on the strength of his poem *Máj* (1836; *May*, 1973), influenced as much by the native ballad as by his wide readings in Romantic literature: Lord Byron, Victor Hugo, Friedrich Schiller, Adam Mickiewicz. The poem is a mixture of lyric and epic built around two balladic motifs: the fate of a jealous murderer and the tragedy of a parricide who avenged the seduction of his beloved. Among Mácha's innovations were his fresh diction and imagery, his discovery of the iambic potential of the Czech language, and his novel combination of the philosophical reflection (often with nihilistic undertones) with a sensational plot (imperfectly developed) derived from tragic ballads. Uniformly rejected on its publication by established critics, *May* was passionately accepted by the young generation, who turned it into a sort of manifesto and even founded a literary journal, *Máj*, named after it. Mácha's masterpiece is still considered to be the greatest single Czech poem. After Mácha's death, pilgrimages to his grave were organized, and an entire cult of Mácha developed. Few Czech poets of subsequent generations (a notable exception is Jan Neruda) escaped Mácha's influence.

KAREL HAVLÍČEK BOROVSKÝ

In the 1850's a transitional period, poets gave way to translators and popularizers, with a few notable exceptions: the belated publication of Erben's *Kytice z pověsti národních*, Božena Němcová's lyric novel *Babička* (1855; granny), and the satiric poetry of Karel

Havlíček Borovský (1821-1856). Havlíček's poetry was a harbinger of the new, rationalist, critical age to come, paralleled on the ideological level by the switch from individualism to the collectivizing faith of socialism. Still, other movements were also present on the scene; such was the Mladá Čechie (Young Bohemia) movement, vaguely fashioned after the Young Germany movement, and the tendency to take into account more fully the works of foreign literatures and thus move away from the narrow, Slav-centered direction of the older revivalists.

Havlíček represents another awakening as well: Starting from the premise, so dear to the older revivalists, of the liberating potential of Russia, he became disenchanted after visiting Russia and bitterly opposed Russophilism in Bohemia. His great satire of sacred and profane absolutism, though unfinished, sounded a new note in Czech satiric poetry, particularly in *Křest svatého Vladimíra* (1876; the baptism of Saint Vadimir). Feuerbachian materialism and virulence reminiscent of the satiric polemics of the Hussite age join in this low burlesque based on the grotesque treatment of the legendary beginnings of Russia. The poem is a literary equivalent of Gustav Doré's *Histoire pittoresque, dramatique, et caricaturale de la Sainte Russie* (1854; *The Rare and Extraordinary History of Holy Russia*, 1971), though arguably less comical than the latter. Havlíček also excelled in the genre of epigram and was a journalist of genius, all of which is clearly reflected in his poetry.

Havlíček's acidic satire marked the end of the Romantic and revivalist period proper—which came to a close in 1860 when an imperial edict proclaimed constitutional liberties guaranteeing the Czechs the national freedoms (without the full national independence that was to come in 1918) for which the earlier revivalists fought so long and hard. Thus, the foreign tendencies—not merely literary influences—that appeared in literary movements as a full-fledged cosmopolitan orientation began to compete seriously with the narrower nationalist pan-Slav orientation that had characterized the revivalists. This development coincided with the rise of realistic convention in European literature and with the availability in Bohemia of a rapidly growing and increasingly sophisticated readership.

The problem of "catching up with the rest of Europe" suddenly became more pressing than the problem of preserving and strengthening the national identity. Of the latter, there were fewer doubts after 1860, and Czech poets began to look around more inquisitively.

JAN NERUDA

The distinct national and cosmopolitan movements had their own literary journals: *Máj*, the tribune of the nationalistic and Romantic movements, and *Lumír*, the forum of the more cosmopolitan but also tendentiously realistic movement. *Máj*, however, was not neglectful of foreign literature, and if it idolized first of all Mácha, Erben, and Havlíček, one should note that these three writers exemplified three quite different literary tendencies: a diversity challenging such simplifications as the national-cosmopolitan division. Thus, a "cosmopolitan" author, Jan Neruda (1834-1891), published in *Máj*, though he was a *Lumír* author par excellence. His *Hřbitovní kvítí* (1857; graveyard flowers), distinguished by its social motifs, its critique of hypocrisy, and its irony and skepticism reminiscent of the late verse of Heinrich Heine; his ballads after Erben; and his *Písně kosmické* (1878; cosmic songs), full of positivist zeal, all led to his final collection, *Zpěvy pátecní* (1896; Friday hymns), an amalgam of messianic and religious-patriotic hymns celebrating the future national victory in a manner found in Polish messianic poetry. The tortuous development of Neruda's poetry gives an indication of the complexity of this literary period.

ADOLF HEYDUK

Neruda's complex development can be contrasted with the career of his friend, the lyric poet Adolf Heyduk (1835-1923), a member of the *Máj* circle. Heyduk produced poetry that is remarkably even, influenced by Erben and by Slovak culture, which Heyduk grew to love and promoted among fellow Czechs. His forte was the intimate lyric, exemplified in *Cigánské melodie* (1859; Gypsy melodies), though his Slovakophile *Cymbal a husle* (1876; cymbalo and violin) complements Kollár's *Slávy dcera*.

SVATOPLUK ČECH

The contrast of Neruda and Heyduk was repeated in the next period by the contrasting pair of Jaroslav Vrchlický (1853-1912) and Svatopluk Čech (1846-1908). The latter has been called the last revivalist poet, influenced by Mácha, Mickiewicz, Alexander Pushkin, and Lord Byron, as were many revivalist poets before him. Čech's tendentious, nationalistic work often suffers from an artificial, academic, heavily periphrastic style. Thus, his ideological importance in Czech poetry outweighs his artistic contribution. Indeed, this late revivalist was not a match for Vrchlický in any sense other than a narrowly partisan one: Vrchlický was a giant and Čech his contemporary.

JAROSLAV VRCHLICKÝ

In his enormous output and his erudition, awesome scope, and fundamental importance for subsequent Czech poetry, Vrchlický has no rivals. His output alone dwarfs that of an entire poetic generation, including some eighty-odd volumes of original poetry, drama, and prose and an incredibly rich treasure chest of translations that in turn dwarfs his original work. It would be easier to list the names of those world authors whom he failed to translate than to enumerate those whom he rendered into Czech. Above all, Vrchlický preferred Italian literature, from which he translated Dante, Petrarch, Torquato Tasso, Ludovico Ariosto, and many others. From French, he translated Victor Hugo, Charles Baudelaire, Pierre Corneille, Molière, and Edmond Rostand; from English, an anthology ranging from James Thomson (1834-1882) to Alfred, Lord Tennyson, as well as Percy Bysshe Shelley, Edgar Allan Poe, Walt Whitman, and William Shakespeare; from German, Johann Wolfgang von Goethe, Schiller, and so on. Then there are the odds and ends: Henrik Ibsen, Mickiewicz, János Arany, Sándor Petöfi, Hafiz, and the Chinese *Shijing* (traditionally fifth century B.C.E.; *The Book of Songs*, 1937). In addition, Vrchlický did a number of prose translations. Vrchlický was a cosmopolitan figure of world stature whose literary orientation was a matter of daily practice and a practical vocation: He was a professor of comparative literature in Prague. The range of Vrchlický's translations suggests what was and was not available to the Czech reader before his time and gives a clear indication of the increasing cosmopolitanism of Czech literature. Vrchlický's immersion in foreign literature as well as in foreign life (he lived in Italy for a year and traveled widely in Western and Northern Europe) made him a figure without precedent in Czech poetry.

JOSEF SVATOPLUK MACHAR

Vrchlický (like Mácha before him) inspired a poetic school and a new generation of translators whose appetites Vrchlický had whetted. At the same time, poets such as Josef Svatopluk Machar (1864-1952) went in another direction entirely, following the realistic orientation of Havlíček and Neruda. Machar, in his attempt to follow Neruda, pushed Czech poetic diction closer to prose by purposely making it dissonant and ugly. Machar's poetry of social protest was echoed by a regional poet Petr Bezrucč (1867-1958), the author of *Slezské písně* (1903; Silesian songs).

KATOLICKÁ MODERNA AND MODERNIST MOVEMENTS

In turn, a reaction against this poetry of social protest was initiated by a group of poets known as *Katolická Moderna* (modern Catholic movement), the most important of whom were Antonín Sova (1864-1928) and Otokar Březina, (1868-1929). This group eclipsed, by both their artistic strength and their numbers, the movement of social protest.

Sova was an anti-Parnassian and thus was at odds with the Vrchlický school as well as with the school of social protest. A strong individualist, he crafted intimate lyrics, rejecting social values. With Březina, Czech poetry gained a fresh and original voice worthy of the fine tradition of Czech Catholic verse. Religious poets in modern Bohemia still find Březina refreshing and profound, for he is a poet of mystery, a reflective poet whose verse reveals his study of ancient and modern philosophy. In some literary histories, both Sova and Březina are mentioned in connection with the Symbolist movement, an identification made tenuous by the fact that in Bohemia, Symbolism appeared simultaneously with realism, metaphysical Romanticism, and other movements.

By the end of the nineteenth century, the Czech literary situation was complicated by a proliferation of movements under the general heading of modernism. The age of manifestos began in 1895 with the proclamation of the *Manifest ceské moderny*. This was the era of the Decadents, such as Jiří Karásek ze Lvovic (1871-1951), Hlaváček, and later, Otakar Theer (1880-1917): a period characterized by the glorification of death and of free love; by Satanism, irony, and nihilism; by the so-called Illusionist Baroque of Hlaváček and the tragic metaphysical vision of Theer's sensuous lyrics. Here, at the beginning of the modern age, one can find the origin of a basic division that has continued to plague twentieth century poetry: modernism versus social protest.

THE MODERN PERIOD

The year 1918 saw revolutionary changes: The Czechoslovak Republic was established after generations of poets and patriots had spent centuries hoping, dreaming, and writing about the day of independence. When independence finally came, however, euphoria was mixed with deep shame and despair following the moral disaster of World War I, which ushered in modernity in a way that few had expected. If anything, the fact of independence intensified many social problems, for there was no more national oppression to be used as a scapegoat. These social problems paled, however, when compared to the huge human losses that came twenty years later, following the debacle of the Munich Treaty of 1938 and subsequent occupation of Bohemia and Moravia by the Nazis in 1939. Czechoslovakia was reestablished in 1945, but in 1948, the communists took over and ruled until the collapse of communism in Europe in 1989. The democracy was reestablished. By 1993, the Czech and Slovak Federation broke up in an amicable divorce brokered by the political elite motivated by economic (Czech) and nationalist (Slovak) reasons. Since January 1, 1993, there have been separate Czech and Slovak republics. At the beginning of the new millennium, the Czech Republic, having joined the North Atlantic Treaty Organizaion, was poised to join the European Community, of which it had been a firm member already during its golden age, some six hundred years before.

During the twentieth century, for some poets, a red star was beckoning from Moscow, offering promises that were never fulfilled. For others, indeed for most, a far more attractive symbol was the Eiffel Tower: Paris, its poets, and its avant-garde. Finally, the Catholic Church and the rich tradition of Czech religious verse nourished another line of poets. The various movements of modern Czech poetry can largely be located with reference to these three trends.

The movements themselves can be briefly enumerated: the Proletarian movement, Poetism, Surrealism, and Socialist Realism. The last was a caricature of the original Proletarian phase, consisting of already forgotten "courtly" poetry (in honor of Joseph Stalin) and poetry about socialist construction, in which tractors, foundries, and mines, together with collective farms, were amply featured. As for Poetism and Surrealism, both were avant-garde movements of French origin. Poetism attracted a wider group of Czech poets than did its more widely known counterpart. By 1934, when the Surrealist movement reached the Czechs, the situation in poetry was highly polarized, politically and ideologically, and only a few of the Poetists became Surrealists. With Socialist Realism, matters were simpler still: Whatever was published was, by definition, Socialist Realist poetry, because during this reign of Stalinist dogma, only such poetry was deemed acceptable. Thus, poets had to acquire the new way of writing or be imprisoned or worse, unless they chose to remain silent.

It is a different story when one considers individual poets. Here a neatly schematic approach is inadequate, for a single poet may be associated with diverse and even contradictory movements. Stanislav Kostka Neumann (1875-1947), for example, spanned the spectrum from the Satanism of his decadent youth to anarchism, to naturalism, and on to Marxism, ending his life as a model Socialist Realist.

A more talented poet, Jiří Wolker (1900-1924), began his career with *Host do domu* (1921; a guest in the house), wherein he reflected on the miracle of existence, on the harmony of life in which the numinous penetrates the objects of everyday reality. Soon, however, he joined the Proletarian poets grouped around the Communist literary journal *Devětsil*. His next collection, *Těžká hodína* (1922; difficult hour), became a classic of Proletarian poetry, although it eschews the superficial contempt for tradition that the Proletarians shared with the avant-garde, harking back as it does to the ballads of Erben. A more interesting, if not more talented, member of *Devětsil* was František Halas (1901-1949), whose pro-worker sympathy is belied by his meditative, complex poetry collected in *Tvář* (1931; face), *Dokořán* (1936; wide open), and *A co?* (1957; so what?).

Instead of social commitment and collective spirit, the Poetists offered unbridled individualism and irresponsibility. This disdain of convention was personified in Vítězslav Nezval (1900-1958), whose individuality was apparent in his first collection, *Most* (1922; bridge), and particularly in *Podivuhodný kouzelník* (1922; the amazing magician). By 1930, the macabre and the graveyard atmosphere—all the rage in Czech poetry at the time—claimed him in *Poems of the Night*, which anticipated the advent of Surrealism in Czechoslovakia. Between 1934 and 1938, when the Surrealist movement in Czechoslovakia was dissolved (though continuing in Slovakia during the war with much success), Nezval published *Žena v množném čísle* (1936; woman in the plural), *Praha s prsty deště* (1936; *Prague with Fingers of Rain*, 2009), and *Absolutní hrobař* (1937; a total gravedigger). After the war, and after some forgettable collections of Socialist Realist poetry, Nezval returned with a modest volume of patriotic poems in the old style, *Z domoviny* (1951; from my homeland), subdued, without a trace of his Surrealist sparkle.

JAROSLAV SEIFERT

When Wolker was idolized after his untimely death, Jaroslav Seifert (1901-1986) coined the slogan "Down with Wolker"; in his view, Wolker's ballads were radically unsuited to the demands of the new age. In Seifert's *Samá láska* (1923; *Only Love*, 1990; revised as *Svatební cesta*, 1938; translated as *Honeymoon Ride*, 1990), traditional art is dead (including the ballad), and love and revolution meet. Seifert's *Na vlnách TSF* (1925; *Over the Waves of TSF*, 1990) is completely Poetist, but by 1933, he had broken with Poetism and the morbid death poetry of the period with his *Jablko z klína* (1933; *An Apple from Your Lap*, 1998). Seifert rejected social commitment as well as the iconoclasm of Poetism, devoting himself to the ideal of good art in the traditional sense and avoiding avant-garde tricks, morbidity, and conflict. The strongest feature of Seifert's poetry becomes his very personal lyric voice, and nowhere in his numerous collections is it as poignant as in his *Morovýacute; sloup* (1977; *The Plague Column*, 1979; also known as *The Plague Monument*, 1980), great poetry based on mature reflection against the stark background of his country's tragic history. In

1984, Seifert was the first Czech author awarded the Nobel Prize in Literature.

VLADIMÍR HOLAN

Vladimír Holan (1905-1980) would have amply deserved that prize, but he was a unique and controversial figure, towering with his talent above the discordant fray of Czech poetry. Movements were not to his liking, and after 1945, he refused to have anything to do with his epoch, isolating himself as if in solidarity with those who, like the fine poet Jan Záhradníček (1905-1960), the author of the apocalyptic *La Saletta* (1947), were imprisoned by the authorities. Holan's great poetry is meditative, prosodically demanding, and complex; his mastery was evident as early as in *Triumf smrti* (1926; triumph of death), and he continued to work at a high level in *Vanutí* (1932; breezing) and *Oblouk* (1934; the arch). His *Panychida* (1946; vigil) treats in a prophetic manner the monsters of "Satanocracy" and "Titanomania," while his *Noc s Hamletem* (1964; *A Night with Hamlet*, 1980) is widely translated and increasingly seen as a masterpiece of European, if not world, literature.

THE NEXT GENERATION

The following generation produced a trio of significant poets: Jan Skácel (1922-1989), Miroslav Holub (1923-1998), and Karel Šiktanc (born 1928). Of interest are Skácel's collection *Hodina mezi psem a vlkem* (1962; the hour between the dog and the wolf), Holub's *Achilles a zelva* (1960; Achilles and the turtle), and Šiktanc's *Slepá láska* (1968; blind love). Catholic poets such as Zahradníček and the older Jakub Deml (1878-1961) reentered the Czech literary consciousness in the 1990's after a long period of neglect and suppression during communism. This holds true as well for Václav Renc (1911-1973), Zdenek Rotrekl (born 1920), and Josef Palivec (1886-1975).

Poetry by women, who became more visible in the 1980's, made a strong contribution. The work of Marcela Chmarová (born 1951), Marta Gärtnerová (born 1948), and Marta Chytilová (1907-1998) should be mentioned. Exile, not always a good experience for poets, nevertheless enabled publication of such poets as Jirí Gruša (born 1928) and Ivan Diviš (1924-1999). It also helped popularize authors of protest songs, forbidden at home during the communist rule, such as Karel Kryl (1944-1994), Jaroslav Hutka (born 1947), and Svatopluk Karásek (born 1942).

BIBLIOGRAPHY

Büchler, Alexandra, ed. *Six Czech Poets*. Translated by Alexandra Büchler, et al. Todmorden, Lancashire, England: Arc, 2007. A volume in the New Voices from Europe and Beyond series. Introduction by the editor is in English. Poems are presented in bilingual form, with Czech text along with English translation.

Cejka, Jaroslav, Michael Cernik, and Karel Sys. *The New Czech Poetry*. Chester Springs, Pa.: Dufour Editions, 1992. The works of these three poets from the generation after Holub, all born during the 1940's.

French, Alfred. *The Poets of Prague: Czech Poetry Between the Wars*. New York: Oxford University Press, 1969. Historical and critical overview. Illustrations, bibliography.

_____, ed. *Anthology of Czech Poetry*. Introduced by René Wellek. Ann Arbor, Mich.: Czechoslovak Society of Arts and Sciences in America, 1973. Translations into English with original Czech text. Illustrated.

_____. *The Czech Avantgardists*. Rockville, Md.: Kabel, 1995. English translations of late twentieth century avant-garde Czech poets. Includes illustrations.

Hawkesworth, Celia, ed. *A History of Central European Women's Writing*. New York: Palgrave, 2001. Contains three essays on Czech women writers, along with others dealing with topics such as women readers and the development of self-awareness. Map, bibliography, and index.

Holý, Jiří. *Writers Under Siege: Czech Literature Since 1945*. Portland, Oreg.: Sussex Academic Press, 2008. A decade-by-decade study, ending with postmodernism and the early twenty-first century. Includes profiles of major writers, a list of anthologies of postwar literature in English, bibliographical references, and an index.

Kovtun, George J. *Czech and Slovak Literature in English: A Bibliography*. 2d ed. Washington, D.C.: Library of Congress, 1988. A useful reference work.

Lodge, Kirsten, ed. and trans. *Solitude, Vanity, Night: An Anthology of Czech Decadent Poetry*. Prague: Charles University, 2007. Poems by three major Czech Decadents are dominated by pessimism and a preoccupation with both perversity and death. This anthology is especially important because at the end of the twentieth century the Decadent movement had a sizeable a following among Czechs.

Novák, Arne. *Czech Literature*. Translated by Peter Kussi. Ann Arbor: Michigan Slavic Publications, 1976. A rare English-language history. Includes a bibliography and an index.

Pynsent, Robert. *Czech Prose and Verse: A Selection with an Introductory Essay*. Atlantic Highlands, N.J.: Humanities Press, 1979. Czech text with an English introduction. Index.

Volkova, Bronislava, and Clarice Cloutier, eds. and trans. *Up the Devil's Back: A Bilingual Anthology of Twentieth-Century Czech Poetry*. Bloomington, Ind.: Slavica, 2008. A collection that begins with works of the Symbolists and the Decadents of the 1890's and ends with postmodernists. Includes poems by sixty-five writers, as well as their biographies.

Peter Petro

EAST GERMAN POETRY

Any study of the literature of the German Democratic Republic (GDR) must tackle the problem of definition. What, exactly, is East German poetry? The question may appear trivial and the answer self-evident: This term is intended to apply to the verse literature produced in the German Democratic Republic, the socialist state that came into being on October 7, 1949, and that ceased to exist on October 3, 1990, when its member states joined the Federal Republic of Germany (FRG). Such a facile definition, however, is inadequate. To begin with, it fails to comprehend the literature produced between 1945 and 1949 in what was then the Soviet Occupation Zone of Germany. Another problem relates to residency and publishing conditions. Does the definition include writers who were expelled from the country, such as Wolf Biermann; who voluntarily left it permanently, such as Peter Huchel, Reiner Kunze, and Sarah Kirsch; who were granted long-term visas enabling them to take up residency in the West, such as Günter Kunert; or who had written their works in East Germany but could get them into print only in the FRG, as was the case with Biermann?

For the purpose of this essay, then, East German poetry will be defined very broadly as the poetry written (although not necessarily published) from April, 1945, to September, 1990, in the territory that once constituted the German Democratic Republic. This definition excludes works by writers such as Bertolt Brecht and Johannes R. Becher, which were produced before the authors settled in East Germany and those written by poets such as Kunze and Thomas Brasch after their departure from the GDR.

Another important preliminary question to be addressed is whether the literatures of East and West Germany did indeed represent two separate and essentially dissimilar literatures or whether they formed one body of writing, exhibiting only superficial differences as the result of external conditions. No agreement exists on this matter. The official East German position, formulated in 1956 by Walter Ulbricht, then first secretary of the ruling Socialist Unity Party of Germany (Sozialistische Einheitspartei Deutschlands, SED), was that there are two German states with two different cultures. That had not always been the East German view. When the first all-German convention of writers gathered in Berlin in 1947, the lyric poet Johannes R. Becher, who was to serve as the country's minister of culture from 1954 to his death in 1958, condemned attempts to bring about confrontations between the East and the West and to play off the Germans in the different occupation zones against one another. Becher declared emphatically:

> Thus, there is no West German or East German literature in this sense, neither a South German nor a North German one, but only a single one, a German one which does not allow itself to be hemmed in by the boundaries of occupation zones.

From a different vantage point, the East German novelist and dramatist Rolf Schneider, who was granted a long-term visa in 1979 and thereafter resided in the West, gave a similar assessment, although he phrased it much more polemically: "There is only one German literature, that of West Germany. Some of its authors are living in the GDR."

On the other hand, Fritz J. Raddatz, who had also chosen to move to the Federal Republic, started his 1972 book on East German literature with the flat statement: "There are two German literatures." As he explained, the political division of the country had so strongly affected what used to be the common language of the two German states that it was no longer possible to consider the literatures based on those differing modes of communication as one and the same. This essay, while not completely agreeing with Raddatz's premise, is also based on the conviction that the literature of East Germany, largely as the result of political and social factors, constituted an entity that developed separately and was relatively independent of trends and developments in the nonsocialist world, including the FRG. Obviously, East German poetry did not evolve in a vacuum, yet on the whole, the differences between the literatures of the two Germanies appeared more pronounced than those between contemporary works written in West Germany and in Austria or Switzerland. It is interesting that the Soviet critic Lev Kopelev (who was stripped of his Soviet citizenship in 1981 and later resided in Western Germany) maintained in 1965 that there were three German literatures: one characteristic of the GDR, one typical of the FRG, and a third one that, by reason of generality of theme and interest (and of artistic quality), transcended any political division.

THE SOCIALIST STATE

The Marxist position that all literature ought to be viewed in its economic, social, and political context may be debatable, but it is impossible to assess the work of the poets of a socialist society such as the GDR without regard to the environment in which they live. The SED and its cultural policies had an immediate impact on all creative writing, and the East German poets' attitude toward their audience often differed from that of their Western counterparts. While German literature has always had a strong didactic bent, East German novelists and dramatists, and also lyrical poets, have followed Brecht's example in defining their function as that of educators of the nation to a much greater extent than have writers in the West.

East German poetry, then, should be seen in direct relation to the evolution of a socialist ideology in the GDR. Several successive phases of this evolution can be distinguished. The years from 1945 to 1949 represent the period of building, of laying the foundation for a "socialist national literature." It was important to understand what had happened during the period when Adolf Hitler was chancellor and what had paved the way for the National Socialist movement. A new ideology had to be firmly anchored in the minds of the people. Thus, "anti-Fascist and democratic renewal" was the political as well as the cultural goal. With the formal establishment of the GDR, this first—and largely preparatory—phase was completed.

From 1949 to the early 1960's, the concept of a "socialist national literature" within an autonomous socialist state crystallized. In part, literature served to rally the people behind the effort to build a strong economy, although poetry played a less important role in this effort than did the other genres. In the light of this

declared goal of literature, the 1959 writers' conference in the industrial town of Bitterfeld was an important attempt to forge a strong alliance between authors and workers. The Bitterfeld movement encouraged industrial and agricultural workers to become writers and urged writers to gain direct experience in factories and collective farms. Socialist Realism was seen as the most appropriate stylistic approach, and Soviet literature provided models.

Although the overall goals to be attained were fairly clear, this period was by no means one of consistent and planned cultural development. Like all the countries in the communist bloc, East Germany was affected by Joseph Stalin's death in 1953 and the subsequent official denunciation of the personality cult. In the summer of 1953, widespread expressions of dissatisfaction with economic and social conditions led to unrest, labeled an "attempted Fascist putsch" by the SED. The Twentieth Congress of the Soviet Communist Party of February, 1956, and the discussions at the Fourth Writers' Congress in Berlin a month earlier seemed to signal a more flexible cultural policy. This "thaw" came to an end, however, with the October, 1956, uprising in Hungary. The construction of the Berlin Wall on August 13, 1961 (which was not breached until November 9, 1990) marked the conclusion of the phase of developing and protecting the new socialist state.

"Literature within a developed socialist society" is the label frequently attached to the works of authors since the early 1960's. This period has been characterized by growing self-confidence on the part of the government and by decreasing popular interest in a reunification of Germany. By the end of 1962, the lyric poet Peter Huchel had been replaced as the editor of the highly respected and influential journal *Sinn und Form*. He and many intellectuals in both German states had considered it one of the last cultural bridges between East and West. Under Huchel's successors, the character of this publication changed drastically, and any potential West German influence was eliminated. The Second Bitterfeld Conference in April, 1964, was unable to repeat the impact of the Bitterfeld movement of five years earlier, although the phenomenon of the "writing worker" was still a factor in contemporary East German literature.

The Eighth Convention of the SED, in the summer of 1971, marked the beginning of a period of cultural liberalization. A few months later, Erich Honecker, first secretary of the party's Central Committee, made clear that the restrictions imposed by the doctrine of Socialist Realism had at least been eased: "As far as I am concerned, no taboos can exist in the realm of art and literature, provided that one proceeds from the firm postion of Socialism." He emphasized that he was referring both to the choice of topics and to artistic style. That "firm position of Socialism," however, was by no means clearly defined, and it was the party that determined the extent to which an author might have strayed from that basis. In November, 1976, Biermann, who had moved to East Germany from Hamburg in 1953, was considered to have gone too far in his satiric poems and songs. He was allowed to leave the country for a concert in West Germany but was then denied permission to return and stripped of his East German citizenship. This action provoked strong protests from many of his fellow writers, prompting, in turn, official reprisals.

In June, 1979, Honecker repeated his 1971 statement about taboos having no place in literature, but he added a warning:

> However, what matters most is to know where one stands in the political struggles of our times. . . . The position between the fronts of the warring classes has always been the losers' position, a position that is as hopeless as it is ignominious, opposing the interests of the people who are the true patrons of the arts.

In the 1980's, official repression coincided with the government's willingness to let oppositional poets emigrate to West Germany, often under cover of long-term visas to the West. Other poets managed to have their poems published in the West and smuggled back into East Germany. As popular unrest grew against the socialist government, many poets who had remained in the East took part in the mass demonstrations which finally persuaded the authorities to open East Germany's borders on November 9, 1989, and permit free elections which swept them from power and led to the demise of the GDR in October, 1990.

THE FIRST GENERATION

One problem with generalizations about trends in East German poetry—apart from the implied disregard for the writers' individuality—was the coexistence of several different generations of poets, with each age-group representing different experiences and conceptions.

When the Nazi regime collapsed at the end of World War II, a number of outstanding writers returned to Germany from their wartime exile in the United States, in Mexico, in the Soviet Union, and elsewhere. Many of them had been supporters of communist ideology before Hitler came to power, and they saw a chance to help create a new society that would reflect their political philosophy. The role of these writers in the development of a "socialist national literature" is important. In West Germany, the year 1945 was considered "point zero," a new beginning after the near-total destruction of the country and much of its culture. East German writers and ideological leaders, on the other hand, emphasized the importance of the inheritance of progressive trends in bourgeois literature since the turn of the century and, even more significant, of a socialist tradition in German culture. Wolfgang Joho stated that position most clearly when he titled his 1965 article in the journal *Neue Deutsche Literatur* (new German literature), "We Did Not Begin in the Year Zero."

Thus, Brecht, Anna Seghers, Arnold Zweig, and a number of other writers provided an important link between positive aspects of the past and the hoped-for better future. Best known among these poets of the "first generation" were Erich Weinert (1890-1953), Johannes R. Becher (1891-1958), Brecht (1898-1956), Huchel (1903-1981), Erich Arendt (1903-1984), René Schwachhofer (1904-1970), Georg Maurer (1907-1971), Louis Fürnberg (1909-1957), and Max Zimmering (1909-1973).

THE SECOND GENERATION

For most of the writers of the second generation, the Nazi period and World War II had been a traumatic experience. Some had left Germany at an early age, others had fought in the war, and several had spent time as prisoners of war in the Soviet Union, where they had been exposed to a new ideology. *Das Judenauto* (1962;

The Car with the Yellow Star: Fourteen Days out of Two Decades, 1968), and autobiographical novel by Franz Fühmann (1922-1984) is perhaps the best document of the inner changes that these authors experienced. Characteristic of this group is the attempt to look both to the past and into the future. In prose narratives and dramas, but also in poetry, they attempted to come to terms with what had happened in the period of the Third Reich. At the same time, those who had lived through such dark years believed that the future held great promise, and many of their poems reflect this faith. In addition to Fühmann, prominent among these writers were Kuba (Kurt Barthel, 1914-1967), who had gone into exile when he was nineteen; Stephan Hermlin (1915-1997), who had left Germany in 1936; Johannes Bobrowski (1917-1965); Hanns Cibulka (1920-2004); Paul Wiens (1922-1982), who had emigrated with his parents in 1933; Günther Deicke (1922-2006); Walter Werner (1922-1995); and Helmut Preissler (born 1925).

THE THIRD GENERATION

The third generation is made up of East German poets who were between ten and twenty years old when Hitler's Reich ended. These writers came to maturity in a socialist society, and the war, which played a large role in the thinking of those only a few years older, was not as much of a decisive experience for most of them. They were diligent students, though by no means mere imitators, of the poets who had already established a reputation. Their works frequently praised the society in which they lived, combining personal expression with an affirmation of the socialist system. A significant number of writers from this group eventually chose to live in the West.

Well-known representatives of this generation are Christa Reinig (1926-2008), Werner Lindemann (1926-1993), Uwe Berger (born 1928), Günter Kunert (born 1929), Eva Strittmatter (born 1930), Heinz Kahlau (born 1931), Kunze (born 1933), Uwe Gressmann (1933-1969), Wulf Kirsten (born 1934), Rainer Kirsch (born 1934), Sarah Kirsch (born 1935, for several years Rainer Kirsch's wife), Karl Mickel (1935-2000), Helga M. Novak (born 1935), and Heinz Czechowski (1935-2009). Reinig, Kunert, Kunze, Sarah Kirsch,

and Novak all eventually moved to the West before the end of the GDR. Adolf Endler (1930-2009) belongs to the same age-group, although his background is different; he moved from West Germany to the GDR in 1955.

THE FOURTH GENERATION

Often the authors of the fourth generation, those who were not yet ten years old at the end of the war or who were born after it, are not considered a separate group because much of their work is similar in character to that of the writers who are slightly older. However, these writers, unlike their near-contemporaries, never knew a society other than the socialist German state, and that fact alone sets them apart. Furthermore, many of them were instrumental in bringing about what critics like to call the "new wave of lyrical poetry" of the early 1960's, a period marked by experimentation and an increased emphasis on personal modes of expression. A landmark poetry reading in December, 1962, at the Academy of Arts, organized by Stephan Hermlin and featuring among other young poets Sarah Kirsch, Volker Braun, and Biermann, focused attention on these attempts. Some politicians strongly objected to the "fear of life, nihilism, and skepticism" of these poets and condemned the "excessive individualism, ambiguity, and symbolism" exhibited in their works as essentially non-Marxist. With the 1966 discussion on the meaning and purpose of poetry in the journal *Forum*, in which party leaders and established critics eventually specified these objections, the new wave had come to an end.

Well known or very important among this last generation of GDR poets—although certainly not in every case representative of the new wave—are Biermann (born 1936), Joochen Laabs (born 1937), Peter Gosse (born 1938), Kito Lorenc (born 1938), Braun (born 1939), Harald Gerlach (1940-2001), Andreas Reimann (born 1946), Kristian Pech (born 1946), and Gabriele Eckart (born 1954). Biermann, as mentioned above, lived in West Germany after 1976, although he continued to consider the GDR his real home. Eckart belongs to those poets who were allowed to leave for the West in the 1980's. Lorenc holds a unique position within this group; he writes poetry both in German and in Sorbian (or Wendish), the West Slavic language of a small ethnic minority in the GDR that received special attention and encouragement from the government after 1945.

THE POETIC UNDERGROUND

From the mid-1980's to the end of the socialist regime, a group of young, urban poets, many of whom lived in the hip, working-class district Prenzlauer Berg of East Berlin, established a poetic "underground." Using a loophole in state censorship, which required publication permits only if one hundred or more copies were printed, the poets published their verses in magazines and folders of just five to ninety-nine copies. These mini-collections, which were often widely shared among readers, quickly became known by their Soviet name, *samizdat* (meaning self-publication). Among these young, oppositional poets, Elke Erb (born 1938), an accomplished poet herself, guided the work of writers like Uwe Kolbe (born 1957), who left the GDR in 1987, shortly before its demise. Among the exiles was another underground poet, Sascha Anderson (born 1953), who later was revealed to have worked as an informer for the Stasi (East Germany's secret police). While the government barely tolerated and, as Anderson's case proves, tried to infiltrate the community of underground poets, their impact and influence grew as that of the regime faltered. When Andreas Hegewald wrote of "frozen mummies" in his poetry, his readers caught the reference to the GDR's superannuated leadership. Soon, the "mummies" were gone, and the *samizdat* magazines, which bore titles such as *Anschlag* (assault), *Ariadnefaden* (Ariadne's thread), or *Grenzfall* (border case), became prized collectors' items.

POLITICS AND PATRIOTISM

Any comparison between East German poetry and that produced by authors in the FRG tends to be an oversimplification. All works of literature are statements by individuals, reflecting their personal temperaments, insights, and experiences. However, all the writers under discussion lived and created poetry within a socialist society. Some broad generalizations may be warranted in view of that fact. Certain trends in East Germany did not appear to have parallels in the West.

Perhaps the most obvious difference between East German and West German poetry was the choice of explicitly political themes by some East German writers. Poems praising the party and glorifying great leaders of the socialist movement, both dead and living, have no equivalents in West German literature. It should be pointed out, however, that such paeans became rare after the 1950's and that they are not representative of more modern East German poetry, either in quality or—contrary to the impression created by certain one-sided anthologies—in quantity.

In line with the clearly perceived goals of creating a new political consciousness after the Third Reich had collapsed and of pointing to new role models that would symbolize the ideals of socialism, the authors of the first generation and those beginning to write in 1945 and shortly thereafter produced a large amount of poetry that can be classified only as political propaganda. (It may be worth noting here that the term "propaganda" had essentially positive connotations in the East German vocabulary.) Their poems related important events in the history of socialism or praised the accomplishments of workers devoted to the welfare of the masses. Brecht's long narrative poem of 1950, "Die Erziehung der Hirse" ("The Education of Millet"), could serve as an example. It describes the developments leading to Soviet grain production sufficient to feed the Red Army during its defense of the homeland. Zimmering's "Die grosse Kraft" (the great power) celebrated the ambitious Stalin Plan to irrigate large areas of Siberia and to generate electric power by controlling and rerouting Russian rivers. A revival of this type of literature occurred in connection with the successful launching of the first Soviet Earth satellite. Typical of the flood of Sputnik poetry is Becher's "Planetarisches Manifest" (planetary manifesto), which hails the technical achievement of the Sputnik—the first artificial satellite placed in orbit around Earth—as the culmination of the revolutionary development that had started in Russia in 1917.

Other works glorify the heroes of socialism. Brecht, Becher, and many others related in their poems the sufferings and the unbroken spirit of Resistance fighters against the Third Reich during World War II. Martyrs for the communist cause, such as Rosa Luxemburg and

Karl Liebknecht, who were murdered by right-wing army officers in 1919, or Ernst Thälmann, who died in a Nazi concentration camp in 1944, were the topics of poems by Brecht, Becher, Bobrowski, Weinert, and other writers. Some of the poetry in praise of great communist leaders consciously evoked religious associations. Becher lauded Vladimir Ilich Lenin as the man who "touched the sleep of the world/ With words that became bread," and Kuba's "Kantate auf Stalin" ("Stalin Cantata") said about the Soviet leader: "The book in his hands, his eyes fixed on it,/ he stood against a world full of evil./ Upright he ascended the via dolorosa/ filled with compassion, with wrath, and with love." Stalin's death signified the demise of this type of poetry, which then largely disappeared from later East German anthologies. It is difficult to read such poems today without a sense of embarrassment, and one has to agree with the insight of Hans Magnus Enzensberger's important essay on poetry and politics that "authority, stripped of its mythical cloak, can no longer be reconciled with poetry."

When workers rebelled against increased work quotas on June 17, 1953, and the ensuing uprising had to be quelled by Soviet tanks to rescue the East German government, Brecht wrote "Die Lösung" (1953; "The Solution"), one of his few critical poems challenging the socialist government that had welcomed him with wide open arms. Brecht's angry poem quotes the official statement of the Secretary of the Writers Union that the people have lost the confidence of their government and can win back this confidence only through twice the work effort. With an irony worthy of Jonathan Swift, the poem proposes the following solution:

> Would it not be
> easier if the government
> dissolved the people and
> elected a new one?

In a similar vein, the young worker-poet Braun wrote in 1956, "Oh Lord, create space in my congested chest!" a clear cry for more political freedoms. Since the mid-1960's, fewer and fewer poems of a blatantly propagandistic, political nature have been published in the GDR. This does not mean, however, that political philosophy no longer has a significant impact. Characteristically, Sarah Kirsch said in connection with her 1973 collection *Zaubersprüche* (translated in *Seven Skins: Seven Poems*, 1981), which contains mainly love poems, "If I had no political interests, I could not write any verse." To many authors, socialism was an established and accepted fact in their society and in their lives, and it was no longer necessary to sing its praise or to educate the public about it.

Political poetry that criticizes and accuses could be found, too, but it was understandably not very common in an open forum, unless such criticism was veiled, published privately, or clearly directed against conditions and phenomena in capitalist society. Biermann's 1963 "Ballade von dem Briefträger William L. Moore" ("Ballad of the Letter-Carrier William L. Moore"), about the murder of a civil rights demonstrator in the United States, was made available to a wide audience. His satiric poems about shortcomings in GDR society, about pettiness and doctrinaire rigidity among party functionaries, could be published only in the West. There, the poems were welcomed as ammunition in the propaganda war against the East, although the author had intended them as contributions toward the improvement of socialist society. The state he had chosen, however, saw his writings as attacks on the foundations of Marxism-Leninism and would not tolerate lines such as the following from his 1962 "Rücksichtslose Schimpferei" ("Reckless Abuse"):

> I am the individual
> the collective has
> isolated itself from me
> Don't stare at me with such understanding!
> Oh, I know
> You are waiting with serious assuredness
> for me to float
> into your net of self-criticism.

The partisan interpretation of Biermann's poetry in the FRG points to a serious problem in the Western response to GDR literature. Western observers tended to read a rejection of socialism into many poems that actually convey no such message. It may be legitimate to see the five-line poem by Kunert, "Unterschiede" ("Differences"), as an expression of the writer's concern about a position that depends on official praise and is threatened by government sanctions:

> Sadly I hear a name called out:
> not mine.
> With a sigh of relief
> I hear a name called out:
> not mine.

Much more questionable, however, is the attempt to use some of Bobrowski's late poems as evidence of the author's alienation from his society. Bobrowski, a convinced Christian and an active member of the East German Christian Democratic Party, repeatedly expressed his basic agreement with the goals and principles of the Marxist state in which he lived.

It was not until the mid-1980's that poems expressing political protest gained a large audience. In 1988, Braun, the regime's previously celebrated worker-poet, wrote in "Verheerende Folgen mangelnden Anscheins innerbetrieblicher Demokratie" (disastrous consequences of a lack of appearance of intra-factory democracy):

> It is too soon. It is too late
> Summer is waiting outside the door
> A lighter time. But frozen still
> everything flowers, all thought. With what little freedom
> do we go out, lingering instead
> in our homes.

When the poem was published, glasnost (openness) and perestroika (restructuring) were propagated in the Soviet Union, but the East German leadership tried to freeze its country in the pre-Gorbachev past.

PLACES, PEOPLE, AND NATURE

At first glance, much of the nonpolitical poetry by East German writers appears somewhat more provincial than the work of their Western counterparts. Many poems clearly reflect very specific and often narrowly defined geographical and cultural settings. Frequently an attempt is made, however, to relate the specific to the general. Georg Maurer, whom many younger poets consider their teacher, demonstrated this relationship when he referred to a definite area near Leipzig where he lived: "I am sitting in the universe/ on a bench in the Rosental."

There are many references to recent history and present social and economic conditions and, even with writers outside the Bitterfeld movement, frequent attempts to re-create the atmosphere of the industrial or agricultural workplace. Although the many mediocre poems in praise of the tractor and its role in the battle for food are rightfully forgotten today, more modern authors often—consciously or unconsciously—employed the vocabulary of an industrialized world. In the poem that introduced his first volume of poetry, *Provokation für mich* (1965; provocation for myself), Braun compared the poems of his generation with "high pressure valves in the pipeline network of our longings" and "telegraph wires that endlessly vibrate with electricity." It is doubtful that such metaphors would have occurred to his West German counterparts.

In such cases, it is often difficult or even pointless to distinguish between political and nonpolitical poetry. In general, history—especially twentieth century history—was a popular theme. Bobrowski, who grew up in the region of East Prussia, where Germans and Slavs had lived together and struggled with each other for centuries, again and again inserted into his poems references to German oppression of other cultures and to the heritage of guilt he shared. What for him was a general theme was treated by Fühmann as a personal experience in his long poem of 1953, "Die Fahrt nach Stalingrad" ("Journey to Stalingrad"), the lyric companion piece to his *The Car with the Yellow Star*.

Related to the focus on the immediate surroundings, there was a greater emphasis on nature poetry than in the West. Huchel and Bobrowski (who saw himself as Huchel's pupil) wrote some of the finest German nature poems of his day. Occasionally, the tendency to depict nature and landscapes has been interpreted by outside observers as an escape from a stifling society, yet it is remarkable that in Huchel as well as in Bobrowski, nature does not exist for its own sake but becomes meaningful only through humanity's relationship to it. Consequently, few of the landscapes they describe are without a reference to humanity. Maurer said about his *Dreistrophenkalender* (three-stanza calendar) of 1951: "When, through Marx, I understood something about the essence of humanity, I comprehended the essence of nature at the same time. In this way, I personified it and sealed the relationship between me and it."

Beginning in the 1960's, however, the cityscape replaced the landscape in much East German poetry, and Gressmann's "Moderne Landschaft" ("Modern Landscape") of 1966 evokes a characteristic image:

> Steel trees are growing on the sidewalks
> And wires branch
> From tree to tree.
> Below, the electric animals
> With people in their hearts
> Are roaring past.

The passerby finds the sight quite normal, "For the landscape of stone/ Is his mother as well." In the industrialized world of the GDR, an unabashed nature poet such as Strittmatter has become the exception rather than the rule.

FORMALIST POETRY

Much of East German poetry in the early years after World War II was marked by an attempt to adapt traditional forms to new ideological content. Classical patterns and the structures once developed as vehicles for religious expression served to give dignity to socialism and the new world it appeared to open up. Numerous cantatas, oratorios, and hymns were created by Becher, Fürnberg, Kuba, Hermlin, Zimmering, and others. Their texts are virtually interchangeable and lack any mark of artistic individuality. Some authors also attempted to create modern folk songs in order to popularize political ideas. While those works found their way into the songbooks of the youth organizations of the GDR, few have enriched the literature of the country. Brecht's simple language and direct approach were often used as models, but few imitators approached the quality of his verse.

Other traditional forms were still far more popular in East Germany than in the West. East German poets wrote sonnets and adapted the classical ode to the language of the twentieth century. Similarly, the ballad, a convenient tool for the effective presentation of scenes from history, retained a firm position in the country's poetry and became a vehicle of antigovernment protest by the late 1980's. Brecht, Hermlin, Biermann, and

many others wrote ballads to illustrate political and philosophical views. Even the metric form of the medieval epic was revived, as in Fühmann's reinterpretation of the Nibelungen myth.

As a rule, East German writers are less given to formal experimentation and thus tended to produce more immediately accessible and concrete statements than some of the more adventurous poets of West Germany. It may be worth mentioning in this context that the very term "concrete" with respect to poetry assumed two quite different meanings in the two German states. Although some East German poets, such as Kunert or Endler, showed an inclination toward the condensation of a poem's idea into a few brief lines, the reduction to isolated words or even letters so characteristic of Western concrete poetry can hardly be found in East Germany. A perusal of East German magazines and anthologies suggests that even the renunciation of uppercase letters was seen as a daring experiment.

It is evident that the formal conservatism of East German poetry sprang from two distinct although closely connected sources. One was the tradition established by the party and its cultural policies. When the State Commission for Artistic Concerns was established in 1951, it listed among its goals "overcoming formalism" and carrying on the "fight against decadence." Despite Hermlin's 1964 statement that it is a sad sight indeed if the representatives of the world's most modern social order recoil when they come across the word "modern," there was little official encouragement of formal experimentation. Alexander Abusch's denunciation of poetry, "which stammers linguistic fragments, assembles combinations of letters and juggles with them," thus creating poetic "ephemeral sensations, written for the snobbish amusement of a bourgeois 'elitist' audience," remained the official SED position to the end.

It would be wrong, however, to attribute the formal conservatism of East German literature solely to government pressure. Many authors themselves had little appreciation for the self-centered, Hermetic poetry of some "elitist" Western writers who show disdain for their audience and who have consciously robbed poetry of its communicative function. Indeed, quite a few East German writers agreed with the lines from Fürnberg's poem "Widmung" ("Dedication"): "Oh, those who call themselves pure poets—/ if they only knew how poor they are!"

POETRY AS COMMUNICATION

Whereas lyric poetry is generally a much more private vehicle of expression than the other literary genres and thus tends to be monologic, East German lyric poets showed a definite inclination toward dialogue. With remarkable frequency, their works aim for a partnership with the reader and attempt to engage him or her directly. This popular view of the poem as a means of two-way communication was emphasized through the many public readings and discussions of poetry held throughout the country. More important, however, is its impact on the literary works themselves in terms of their language and structure.

Lorenc started his poem "Versuch über uns" ("Attempt About Us") with the—not completely rhetorical—question, "Or in which Language should I speak from us to us?" His ethnic and linguistic background adds a special meaning to this question, but many East German writers pondered the same problem. The plural "us" is also quite appropriate: The poet is addressing the people, the collective, of which he, too, is a part. This is important, because the poet no longer saw himself as a teacher, above and apart from the people, as in the earlier years of the GDR. Strittmatter and Kunert stated explicitly that they did not have any didactic purposes in writing poetry, but Kunert added that he was not engaging in a monologue. Poets had the feeling that they were needed by their audience, that poet and readers are searching for the same thing—which, according to Kunert, could be defined by reference to the African American term "soul food." Braun similarly saw himself as a "good friend" of his reader, not as a "barker." He and his colleagues did believe, however, that the poet has to transcend the merely personal and private to say something of relevance to the audience. Thus, as Kahlau's love poems show, even the intimate emotional relationship between two human beings can become part of a dialogue with the reader.

No dialogue can occur if the ideas to be discussed are obscured by linguistic patterns out of the grasp of one of the partners. This realization made many writers strive for *Volkstümlichkeit* (folksiness, or popular comprehensibility of poetry). In some cases, this attempt has led to an impoverishment of language. Hermlin's early poems, for example, demonstrate his skill in translating the idioms of German expressionism and French Symbolism into an artistic vehicle for the communication of his philosophy. His language was widely criticized as esoteric and obscure, and perhaps partly in response to such attacks, but surely also out of a desire to reach a broader audience and not merely an "elite," he deliberately changed his style, much to the detriment of his art.

HISTORICAL PARALLELS

Most of the specific features of East German poetry discussed above were directly related to the role of the writer in a socialist society, yet many of these phenomena also have a long-standing tradition in German literature. Political poetry has been written in Germany since the Middle Ages. Many authors were opposing prevailing conditions, to be sure, but from Walther von der Vogelweide (c. 1170-c. 1230) through Johann Wolfgang von Goethe (1749-1832) and Heinrich von Kleist (1777-1811) to some of the minor bards of the Third Reich, poets have sung the praise of the mighty.

The poetry of the *Biedermeier* period as well as that of German Realism emphasized the writers' immediate environment, but even before the nineteenth century, the outstanding lyric poet Friedrich Hölderlin (1770-1843) was able to embrace the universe by focusing on his South German surroundings. Nature poetry has been popular with German writers and their audiences from Friedrich Gottlieb Klopstock (1724-1803), whom Bobrowski called his "taskmaster," and Goethe to the Romantics and the Realists, with the works of Annette von Droste-Hülshoff (1797-1848) constituting an artistic peak. Some parallels exist between the poetry of certain East German authors, particularly Huchel, and the nature poetry of the 1920's and 1930's.

One of the outstanding accomplishments of the great German writers of the eighteenth century—from Klopstock and Hölderlin to Gotthold Lessing (1729-1781), Friedrich Schiller (1759-1805), and Goethe—was their successful adaptation of traditional literary forms to their language and their times. Some of those classical forms were still popular among the poets of the GDR. The Romantic writers not only collected folk songs but also imitated their style in their own creative efforts. Fühmann's interesting experiment of retelling fairy tales in linguistically simple poems, while giving them a contemporary socialist interpretation, is also reminiscent of Romantic literature. Historical ballads, elevated to a high level of lyric expression by Goethe and Schiller, were among the most characteristic literary forms of the nineteenth century. The conservative trend in German poetry is by no means a new phenomenon, and writers as well as critics have again and again eschewed experimentation and rejected "empty" formalism. The denunciation by the old Goethe of what he considered "unhealthy" in Romantic writing can serve as an example. Finally, the didacticism of much of German literature, from medieval polemical pieces to the exhortations of the expressionists, has always implied the reader's role as a silent partner in a dialogue.

These historical parallels are hardly surprising. The GDR considered itself the true heir to the cultural values of the German classical tradition. It assumed the role of guardian of a heritage that, so it claimed, was neglected and destroyed in the FRG. This attitude helps to explain why much East German poetry, especially that of the late 1940's and of the 1950's, strikes outside observers as dated and old-fashioned.

FINAL PHASE

By the 1980's, many of the old masters—Brecht, Bobrowski, and Huchel the most important among them—were gone. Some poets, such as Hermlin and Fühmann, had turned to other forms of literature. In reaction to government repression and swelling popular unrest and dissatisfaction with the socialist government, an increasing number of poets was leaving the country right up to the fall of the Wall in Berlin. However, among the younger generation, talents emerged that were well worth watching. The number of books of verse that were published in the GDR would amaze most Western observers, and even more so the fact that this poetry found readers. Politics played a heavy role in the literary life of the country, and the massive political changes bringing an end to the GDR saw many po-

ets at the vanguard of popular opposition and protest. Before the 1980's, many poems never made it into print for reasons unrelated to their artistic quality.

The English-speaking reader is handicapped still by the relative scarcity of East German poetry in translation. Except for much of Brecht's work, some of Bobrowski's poetry, isolated poems by other East Germans, and a few good anthologies of Eastern and Western German poetry, there is still relatively little opportunity for those who cannot read the originals to acquaint themselves with a once thriving and interesting verse literature.

The English-speaking reader is often further handicapped by ideological preconceptions. If John Flores, in an important 1971 study, singles out two 1947 poems, "Die Zeit der Wunder" (the time of miracles) and "Ballade nach zwei vergeblichen Sommern" (ballad after two futile summers), as "perhaps the finest Hermlin has written" and then adds that they are "poems of disappointment and disillusion," one cannot escape the impression that there is a causal connection between those two statements. Unless the reader in the West is willing to accept East German poetry within its own context, the mere availability of translations will not matter much.

BIBLIOGRAPHY

Deicke, Günter, ed. *Time for Dreams: Poetry from the German Democratic Republic*. Translated by Jack Mitchell. Berlin: Seven Seas Press, 1976. A good collection of East German poetry up to the mid-1970's.

Flores, John. *Poetry in East Germany: Adjustments, Visions, and Provocations, 1945-1970*. New Haven, Conn.: Yale University Press, 1971. Older and staunchly anticommunist, still a valuable discussion of the role of poetry in East Germany during the height and the eventual waning of the Cold War. Shows how in the West, East German poetry was often considered either propaganda or secret opposition to the socialist regime.

Hamburger, Michael, ed. *East German Poetry: An Anthology*. Oxford, England: Carcanet, 1972. A bilingual anthology that provides a good selection of poetry.

Hartung, Harald. "Lyric Poetry in Berlin Since 1961." Translated by Lorna Sopcak and Gerhard Weiss. In *Berlin Culture and Metropolis*, edited by Charles W. Haxthausen and Heidrun Suhr. Minneapolis: University of Minnesota Press, 1990. A brief but very important article shedding light on, among other things, the flourishing of an alternative, underground East German poetic culture in East Berlin. Poets from East Berlin were in the vanguard of those intellectuals demanding change from the socialist regime, resulting in its ultimate peaceful overthrow.

Ives, Rich, ed. *Evidence of Fire: An Anthology of Twentieth Century German Poetry*. Seattle: Owl Creek Press, 1988. Contains some significant and important East German poems. Nicely places East German poetry in the overall context of modern German poetry. A useful complement to Charlotte Melin's anthology.

Leeder, Karen J. *Breaking Boundaries: A New Generation of Poets in the GDR, 1979-1989*. New York: Oxford University Press, 1996. A comprehensive analysis that focuses on both official and underground poetry of the last decade of the GDR. Well written and critically informed, this is a very important study for any student of the topic. Includes bibliographical references and index.

Martens, Lorna. *The Promised Land? Feminist Writing in the German Democratic Republic*. Albany: State University of New York Press, 2001. By studying the prose and the poetry of women writers living in the GDR, the author questions whether the state was in fact a utopia for women. Especially important in that Martens's book is the first to deal systematically with this issue.

Melin, Charlotte. *German Poetry in Transition, 1945-1990*. Hanover: University Press of New Hampshire, 1999. One of the best anthologies for readers wanting to acquaint themselves with East German poetry. Excellent, informative introduction, valuable author biographies, good bibliography, index.

Owen, Ruth J. *The Poet's Role: Lyric Responses to German Unification by Poets from the GDR*. Amsterdam: Rodopi, 2001. In addition to a chapter on "The Poet's Role in the GDR 1949-1989," the book contains analyses of specific works written both during the period and after unification.

Sax, Boria. *The Romantic Heritage of Marxism: A Study of East German Love Poetry*. New York: Peter Lang, 1987. A perceptive study of the topic. Marxist positions on the topic are clearly expressed, and discussion, criticism, and analysis of the poems are of remarkable clarity and distinction. Bibliography and index.

Dieter P. Lotze
Updated by R. C. Lutz

ENGLISH AND CONTINENTAL POETRY IN THE FOURTEENTH CENTURY

Whan that Aprill with his shoures soote
The droghte of March hath perced to the roote . . .
Thanne longen folk to goon on pilgrimages,
And palmeres for to seken straunge strondes,
To ferne halwes, kowthe in sondry londes;
And specially from every shires ende
Of Engelond to Caunterbury they wende,
The hooly blisful martir for to seke,
That hem hath holpen whan that they were seeke.

With these words Geoffrey Chaucer begins *The Canterbury Tales* (1387-1400), arguably the poetic masterpiece of fourteenth century England and certainly a stout cornerstone in the monumental edifice of the English literary tradition. Critics have long praised Chaucer's choice of the pilgrimage as the overarching frame for a highly varied collection of individual tales, and readers are often advised of its particular virtues of providing a theme of religious renewal and community enterprise against which are set, for example, the delightful boorishness of the Miller, the outrageous iconoclasm of the Wife of Bath, the earnest pondering of how man and woman are to live together in what G. L. Kittredge called the "Marriage Group," and the insouciant extortion of the wily Pardoner. However, perhaps readers are not often enough reminded of the milieu in which *The Canterbury Tales* was created, the context which it in part reflects. It is crucial to a faithful reading of any literary work that readers take a moment to review its cultural and historical background, and never is such a review more needed than for this tumultuous period that proved to be the poetic flowering of the late Middle Ages.

Geoffrey Chaucer, in an illustration from The Canterbury Tales *(1387-1400).*
(©Bettmann/CORBIS)

HISTORICAL CONTEXT

The fourteenth century was an era of great literary achievement in the face of governmental, economic, and religious near-apocalypse. No sooner had Boniface VIII declared his own gaudy papal jubilee in the year 1300 than his chief secular opponents, Philip IV of France and Edward I of England, began to contest his power. Working from the solid church and state amalgam that was the bequest of the thirteenth century, Boniface had aroused the kings' resistance in 1296 with the *Clericis laicos* papal bull, which asserted the Roman Catholic Church's right to levy taxes. Two years after the jubilee, he issued the more famous *Unam sanctam*, intended to establish the primacy of the Church in unambiguous terms by subordinating all human creation to the authority of the pope in Rome. This anachronistic attempt at absolutism, destined to fail in an era in which social and political evolution was ever accelerating, precipitated the withdrawal of the Papacy from Rome to Avignon, initiating in 1309 the Babylonian captivity of popes that was to last until 1376 and presaging the ultimate schism in the Church, which was healed only two decades into the fifteenth century at the Council of Constance. With the loss of a generally accepted central government for Christianity, as well as numerous other disasters, many of the philosophical and religious syntheses of the previous century also foundered.

As prominent as any dogma inherited from the thirteenth century was Saint Thomas Aquinas's apparent reconciliation of faith and reason in his *Summa theologiaea* (c. 1265-1273; *Summa Theologica*, 1911-1921). Blending the newly rediscovered Aristotelian logic and his own brand of Christian humanism, Thomas erected a cathedral-like intellectual monument to celebrate the fusion of human reason and divine grace. John Duns Scotus (c. 1265-1308), a Franciscan, had begun to pry faith and reason apart, however, and William of Ockham (c. 1280-1350) finished the dismantling through the application of his well-known "razor." Ockham insisted that human knowledge should be restricted to the immediately evident, thus making it necessary to discard the grand latticework of categories assembled by Aquinas and others. The Nominalist movement, so called because of its dismissal of the Thomistic *nominae* (or categories), also provided the impetus for a series of scientific developments at the universities of Oxford and Paris. To replace the Aristotelian notions of streams of air as the medium for physical motion, for example, Jean Buridan (c. 1295-1358) offered a theory of original forces that was to be transferred fruitfully to studies of heavenly bodies. Remarkably, Nicholas of Oresme (c. 1330-1382) described the universe as a mechanical clock, an idea all the more brilliant since such timepieces had been perfected only in his century. Along with these discoveries, and others such as the cannon, eyeglasses, and the mariner's compass, came the evolution of modern scientific method in the nominalist emphasis on observed phenomena.

To be sure, however, Ockham's was not the only heresy to come to prominence in the vacuum of formal religious authority created by the withdrawal of the Papacy. As rationalism lost its footing in the Christian worldview, mysticism increased markedly and became a pan-European movement, finding its focus in Germany, for example, with the writings of Meister Eckhart (c. 1260-1327). Interest in astrology and alchemy was likewise on the rise; and Chaucer especially revealed a fascination with the courses of the stars and planets and their supposed influence on the world of men. One of the more engaging and curiously modern heresies involved the professions of the Free Spirit reformers, who advocated unrestrained sexual freedom and other apparent vices in the pursuit of individually achieved deification. Nearly as influential as Ockham's nominalist beliefs were the attacks of John Wycliffe (c. 1320-1384) on the presumptions of the Avignon popes. Refusing to credit any clergy with the power they claimed unless they were in a state of divine grace, he championed the Englishmen who resisted the financial demands of the Papacy and later questioned the existence of Church government and even the Eucharist itself. In many ways Wycliffe, a strident religious dissenter and yet the originator of the first English Bible, well represents the maelstrom that was Christianity in the age of Chaucer and his contemporaries.

As religion passed through a series of challenges, reforms, and counterreforms, losing in the process the comparatively well-regulated syntheses of the preceding century, secular developments followed suit. England and France entered the fourteenth century with their governments reasonably intact, but in both cases a succession of less-than-qualified leaders and a sequence of catastrophic events brought the countries to their political knees and, not inconsequently, to the Hundred Years' War. On the French side, Philip the Fair (Philip IV), opponent of Boniface, had placed the monarchy in a position of strength at the cost of considerable financial strain on his constituency. When he died in 1314, his successor Louis X was quickly forced to agree to charters limiting his power and transferring a great deal of authority to a confused baronial system. After two more Capetian kings of unremarkable achievement, the rule passed to the inept Philip VI, who set about establishing an adversarial relationship with his English counterpart Edward III, an ongoing conflict that led eventually to open warfare. In mid-century, John the Good assumed the throne, only to be taken prisoner at the Battle of Poitiers. Even as these monarchs followed one another to death or infamy, Edward III was in the process of declaring himself king of France; the French, in a weakened condition, had to curb his presumptuousness in 1360 by consenting to the conditions of the Treaty of Brétigny, awarding Gascony, Calais, and Ponthieu to the English in return for Edward's renunciation of his claim to their monarchy. While John's son Charles V (reigned 1364-1380) was able to reorganize his country and help the English to exhaust themselves and relinquish newly won territories, the century ended with France in the hands of the incompetent Charles VI, and the advantage once more passed to its opponent.

England likewise started the fourteenth century struggling with Boniface. Edward I (reigned 1272-1307) fostered a typical thirteenth century cooperation between the monarchy and the legislative powers, reformed the judicial system, gave order to ecclesiastical activity, and controlled feudal tendencies. His son Edward II, however, was at best a shadow of his father. He suffered a humiliating defeat by the Scots at Bannockburn in 1314 and gave no evidence whatever that he was qualified for leadership. In 1327, he was forcibly deposed by the parliament, and his fourteen-year-old son, Edward III, was appointed the nominal regent. At first the young man was only a figurehead manipulated by his mother Queen Isabella and her lover Roger Mortimer, but three years after his accession he toppled them both, sentencing Mortimer to death and stripping the queen of all power and holdings. With the monarchy in hand, this English Orestes then set about providing a focus for growing English nationalism by erasing the Shameful Peace with Scotland from popular memory through a series of successful battles to the north. Thus, Edward III showed his ambitions and talents early in his fifty-year reign and also revealed, not incidentally, a penchant for nationalistic assertion that was to lead to severe, even crippling, problems for the nation he so stoutly defended.

The most serious and debilitating result of this martial activity was the Hundred Years' War with France, which opened in 1337 when Edward ordered the Gascon fleet to attack shipping in the ports of Normandy. As mentioned above, a context for these actions already existed in the quarrel over the French crown and the efforts of Flanders to gain its independence, and this single event was merely one of many subsequent skirmishes along the English Channel. Important events included the naval encounter of 1340, the Treaty of Brétigny in 1360, and the gradual reversal in favor of the French in the late fourteenth century. At the same time, the spirit of British nationalism that fueled Edward's war machine also manifested itself in other ways: The Statute of Praemuniere (1353) forbade Englishmen to bring their appeals to a foreign (that is, papal) court, and the first of the Navigation Acts (1382) stipulated that English goods must be carried by domestic ships only. When the official change from French to English as the language of the law courts (1361) is added to this list, it becomes apparent that the rising tide of nationalism was nearing its peak. Unfortunately, the advent of Richard II in 1377 created another incompetent monarch to rival Edward II. The century closed in an undistinguished manner, with Richard desperately resorting to execution of his enemies in 1397 and suffering his own death two years later.

In Germany, the political situation was even worse. The inheritor of an unwieldy coalition of states headed by scheming princes and under attack by the Papacy, Albert of Habsburg tried to bring order to the empire but was murdered in 1308 by his nephew. The puppet emperor Henry of Luxemburg (VII) made a foolish expedition to Rome in an attempt to bring Italy back into the fold but was poisoned in 1313. His successor, Charles of Bohemia, dismissed papal claims with his Golden Bull of 1356, but his concentration on Bohemia at the expense of the empire as a whole left his nation vulnerable to attack, and the French and Swiss made steady gains throughout the fourteenth century. Notwithstanding this unrest, the German cities made some strides forward in urban management in the form of administrative innovations, paved streets, fire protection, and public health. At about the same time, the Serbian people made their first heroic effort to throw off the Ottoman yoke at the celebrated Battle of Kosovo (1389), where the Serbs and their leader Knez Lazar went down to a defeat that was to serve as the seedbed of a fierce nationalism and an extensive cycle of heroic poems.

In Italy, the internal strife characteristic of the period stemmed primarily from the withdrawal of the popes to Avignon. With Philip IV and Edward I in open defiance of Boniface's edicts, and with the time of absolute clerical authority on the wane, there was little choice but to abandon the politics of Rome and to seek refuge under the French imperial banner. Meanwhile, the customary infighting in Italy grew worse, with the merest and most superficial unity existing between the southern Kingdom of Naples and the northern despots. A touch of neoclassicism emerged for a moment in the reforms of Cola di Rienzi, who rose to power in 1347, but the age made his visions of reinstating antiquity anachronistic, and he was driven into exile and murdered in 1354. The popes began to try to return to Rome and reinstall themselves in 1367; nine years later, when Urban VI resisted all attempts to depose him, and his "successor" Clement VII retreated to Avignon to establish a rival papacy, the Great Schism was begun. All in all, Italy was not a pleasant place to live in the fourteenth century, as the writings of Dante confirm.

Almost precisely in the middle of the century, the Black Death struck Europe, reducing the total population of most countries by half to two-thirds. As the frequency of themes of morbidity, pessimism, and death in all of the arts indicates, this pestilence had a profound effect on the medieval mind, in addition to its decimation of the populace. Traveling along trade routes from China through Italy, Spain, and southern France, by July, 1348, it had reached Normandy and the English coast. Medieval medicine was apparently powerless against the more virulent of the disease's two forms, and it passed unchecked into Ireland and Wales over the next two years, only to return periodically throughout the rest of the century. In addition, people had earlier had to contend with the disastrous crop failure and famine of 1315, caused by floods that were also to recur regularly for many years to come. For these and other reasons, economic disaster became the rule of the day, and overtaxed market systems, alternating surpluses and shortfalls of agricultural and manufactured goods, the backsliding of emancipated serfs into the feudal equivalent of slavery, and general social upheaval led to the Peasants' Revolt of 1381.

As the authority of the Church and of secular government languished, the Thomistic unity of faith and reason unraveled, the Black Death claimed half of Europe, antifeminist and anti-Semitic movements gained momentum, and the economic and social institutions of the thirteenth century trembled and then fell, people were forced to experiment and adapt in order to survive. Reform and renovation proceeded in all areas, with various degrees of success and almost no visible effect until the fifteenth century. However, in the middle of the worst confusion and turmoil the Middle Ages was to know, the arts underwent truly radical change and produced a remarkable number of discoveries and true masters.

ARTISTIC AND LITERARY CONTEXT

Emblematic of this transformation was the Italian painter Giotto (c. 1266-1337), a genius who cast aside his shepherd's crook to become the first great postclassical painter. What Giotto accomplished was phenomenal: He replaced the formal, stylized, two-dimensional Byzantine representations with a more realistic artistic idiom that imitated nature in all its beauty and with all its flaws. His *Madonna Enthroned* (c. 1310) and *Death of St. Francis* (c. 1318-1320), for example, illustrate his technique of creating depth, movement, and fidelity to nature. While the Italo-Byzantine style continued in a modest way on a separate line (an example is Simone Martini's *Annunciation* of 1333), Giotto's techniques spread north rather quickly, first in the form of manuscript illumination (as in the work of Jean Pucelle, beginning c. 1325) and later in architecture and portraiture. Giotto's painting played a large part in bringing Europe to the brink of the Renaissance.

As the conventional use of Latin declined and the vernaculars became more prominent all over Europe, great authors began to mold the new tongues for literary purposes. Like Giotto, the Italian poet Dante (1265-1321) reached beyond traditional models and the tenor of the times to create his masterpiece, *La divina commedia* (c. 1320; *The Divine Comedy*, 1802). Dante wrote his epic poem while he was a political exile wandering through northern Italian cities in search of a patron; however, even though topical allusions to the political and social problems of his beloved Florence abound, his work rises above contemporary strife to glimpse the path to God: in the hands of his guides,

Vergil, representing human reason, and then Beatrice, who as the symbol of divine love leads the pilgrim Dante to the heaven where reason cannot take him, he accomplishes the journey of Everyman and allegorically points the way to the Christian's true reward. Dante's countryman Petrarch (1304-1374), who, in addition to establishing so many of the Italian sonnet conventions, contributed to most of the literary and philosophical genres of his day, stressed the importance of human mortality in the face of theological dogma and displayed an atavistic tendency to return to the ancient philosophers in his search for truth.

Giovanni Boccaccio (1313-1375), author of *Decameron: O, Prencipe Galetto* (1349-1351; *The Decameron*, 1620), a collection of ten "days" of ten stories each, tried to develop a more worldly poetic language. His famous tales are told by seven young women and three young men who flee Florence to escape the ravages of the Black Death and for ten days amuse themselves with stories of cuckolding, murder, and other fantastic pursuits. Especially since it now appears that Chaucer had not read *The Decameron* and thus conceived the analogous structure of his *The Canterbury Tales* independently, the genre of tales unified by a framing story should be considered a typically fourteenth century form in its originality and response to the demands of individuality on traditional genres.

MEDIEVAL TEXTS

Some characteristics of medieval texts were particularly prominent in this age of experimentation and reaction to change. Authors in this period suffered very little from the more modern "anxiety of influence," and there were compelling reasons for their resistance to this literary disease. In the fourteenth century—and virtually throughout the Middle Ages—no special value was placed on originality: Stories, characters, events, and situations were almost always borrowed, either from another source or from the word hoard of convention, or simply translated from Latin or one of the vernacular tongues, in whole or selectively. Poets did not so much strive after fresh and mysteriously engaging material as they molded known material to their own designs; they were in the main retellers rather than creators, and this procedure characterized not only

their subject matter but also the ways in which they shaped it. As has been shown time and again, the rhetoric of medieval poetry was codified by such writers as Geoffrey of Vinsauf, Bernard Silvestris, and Alanus de Insulis. Fourteenth century poets had available to them handbooks concerning such topics as the proper method of picturing a woman's beauty—proceeding vertically through a catalog of her features from "tip to toe." These conventional methods of description were advocated by poets and expected by their audiences, as were what Ernst R. Curtius has called topoi, or narrative commonplaces, such as the ubiquitous garden of earthly delights, the *locus amoenus*. Form as well as content was traditional, and each aspect of the poetry was all the more expressive because of its typicality in other works and consequent connotative power. Twice-told tales and time-tested rhetoric were the order of the day, and so modern notions of aesthetics must be adjusted to take faithful account of these medieval values.

Such stories and established methods of telling them imply a particular kind of text no longer extant in a modern literary milieu consisting of finely crafted objects virtually complete in themselves. The Romantic legacy of originality marks the end of texts with an active history behind them, but the poem that reaches out into its traditional context to complete its form and content is, par excellence, a medieval phenomenon. The process had begun with earlier medieval oral traditions—Anglo-Saxon, Old French, and Hispanic; in the case of the oldest texts, such as *Beowulf* (c. 1000) and the *Chanson de Roland* (twelfth century; *The Song of Roland*, 1880), the tradition is paramount, and the poet is a member of a succession of bards who transmit more than they compose. With later medieval texts, the individual author is firmly the master of his or her own literary fate, and yet the debt to tradition is still great. The medieval text, in short, has diachrony: It reaches back to earlier narratives or lyric moments and it speaks through a grammar of commonplaces and rhetorical figures assembled and approved by tradition. The more innovative writers of the fourteenth century grasped tradition with consummate ease, reformulating its lexicon of tales and grammar of rhetoric, and passed beyond it to create formerly unheard harmonies on the basic melodies of the canon. These original melodies remain, however, and give the newer compositions a fundamental strength. Indeed, it is well to remember that even the great iconoclast and innovator, Chaucer, was the inheritor of a rich traditional legacy, which he invested brilliantly with his often startlingly fresh ideas for literary works, and that both the intensely dramatic and psychological *Troilus and Criseyde* (1382) and the great send-up of medieval romance, "Sir Thopas," bear testimony to his creative use of poetic tradition.

ARTHURIAN LEGEND

One of the strongest of medieval traditions, and one that was to reach forward to the Medieval Revival of the Victorian era, to the classic American tale-telling of Mark Twain, and beyond, into the modern era, was the cycle of legends surrounding King Arthur and his knights. This central character of countless tales was probably a sixth century historical figure celebrated in Britain for his heroic defense against Saxon invaders; like the Serbian Knez Lazar after his fall at Kosovo in the late fourteenth century, Arthur was especially revered after the Celts were defeated and subjugated by the Germanic attackers. Of his earliest history little is known—some Welsh sources from about 600 (such as the elegy *Gododdin*) refer to his martial accomplishments, and the priest Nennius chronicles the victories over the Saxons as well as local legends, but by 1100, in Wales, he had become a full-blown legendary hero of romantic adventure and the leader of a band of men who were themselves larger than life. From this Welsh origin, the legend of Arthur spread to the Cornish, who claimed him for their own, and then to the Bretons, who through their French-Celtic bilingualism were able to spread the insular tradition to the Continent: Largely by means of oral transmission, a medium that was to remain a channel for diffusion of romance materials throughout the Middle Ages, the tales soon passed from Wales to France, Provence, Italy, Sicily, Germany, and parts of Asia Minor. Even the great Arthurian masterworks of Chrétien de Troyes in France and Wolfram von Eschenbach and Gottfried von Strassburg in Germany trace their origins to this Breton connection.

Arthurian legend entered the learned tradition through Geoffrey of Monmouth's *Historia regum Britanniae* (c. 1136; *History of the Kings of Britain*, variant version before 1155; vulgate version 1718), a delightful, wholesale fabrication that passed as the standard historical account until the sixteenth century and was even adapted into French by the Anglo-Norman poet Wace around 1155 as *Le Roman de Brut*, in which form it also enjoyed wide currency as a source for English romances, directly and through Layamon's *Brut* (c. 1205). Meanwhile, the French romancers were developing the attached legends of Lancelot, Tristram, Gawain, and the Grail. In the twelfth century, Arthur's knights and court occupied the center of their attentions, while in the thirteenth, they combined individual tales, greatly expanded the contemporary cycles of tales, and further Christianized the originally animistic and magical Grail stories. It is from this French efflorescence that the English tales of Arthur begin to develop in the second half of the thirteenth century, the legends having come full circle back to their origins in Britain, albeit in much modified form.

Of the considerable number of fourteenth century poems concerning Arthur or his knights, a handful stand out as deserving of special attention. Perhaps foremost among them are *Sir Gawain and the Green Knight* (c. 1400), by the Pearl-Poet, and the two poetic tales of Arthur's death, the alliterative *Morte Arthure* (c. 1400) and the stanzaic *Morte Arthur* (c. 1360). The former, composed in alliterative long lines in the same Northwest Midlands dialect that characterizes *Sir Gawain and the Green Knight* and the stanzaic version, derives mainly from Wace's translation of Geoffrey and legends of Alexander, and it presents its portrait in both epic and tragic terms. Because of its relatively high density of conventional diction and typical scenes, it has been described as either a memorized or a traditionally composed poem; it is not far removed from the oral tradition that spawned its phraseology and narrative design. The alliterative poem represents what Larry Benson calls the "chronical tradition," an ostensibly historical account of battles and warriors rather than of romance and carefully drawn, individualized characters.

The stanzaic version, *Morte Arthur*, however, is a true romance composed in eight-line stanzas of four-stress lines and represents a deftly managed condensation of the French prose *La Mort Artu* (c. 1225-1230). It includes Lancelot's encounter with the maid Astolat, his defense of the queen, the usurpation of the kingdom by Mordred, and the events leading up to Arthur's death. Unlike the alliterative version, this poem depends more on a fast-paced, streamlined narrative with emphasis on action rather than on conventional romance tropes, an economical texture that no doubt played a part in attacting the close attention of Sir Thomas Malory as he composed his classic Arthurian works in the next century.

GAWAIN POEMS

While no fourteenth century poems specifically about the wizard Merlin survive, owing perhaps to the lesser influence of Geoffrey of Monmouth's *Vita Merlini* (c. 1150) as compared to his seminal *History of the Kings of England*, and while the only verse tale involving Lancelot in any significant role is the stanzaic *Le Morte d'Arthur* (1485), by Malory, a great many poems about Arthur's knight Gawain survive from the late medieval period. Primarily because Gawain was prominent in both Geoffrey and Wace, as well as in the French romances of Chrétien, the English romancers celebrated his chivalric prowess and, it may be safely said, by their literary attention assigned him the highest rank of all who honored Arthur at the famous Round Table. Apart from *Sir Gawain and the Green Knight*, the best known of these tales is *Ywain and Gawain* (c. 1300-1350), a translation and condensation of Chrétien's *Yvain: Ou, Le Chevalier au lion* (c. 1170; *Yvain: Or, the Knight with the Lion*, c. 1300) and the only extant Middle English version of any of the great French romancer's works. As is the general rule with Anglo-Norman or French originals and their English descendants, the continental poem bristles with sophisticated literary conventions that reflect its intended courtly audience, while the English adaptation often uses proverbial or colloquial expressions more in keeping with its popular constituency. *Syre Gawene and the Carle of Carelyle* (c. 1400) is also aimed at a popular audience and shares with its better-known counterpart the elements of temptation and beheading. In addition, the second episode of *The Awntyrs off Arthure at the Terne Wathelyne* (after 1375) consists of the common challenge to Gawain and incorportes the hunting scenes that are juxtaposed to scenes of courtly wooing in *Sir Gawain and the Green Knight*. Finally, the *Libeaus Desconus* (c. second quarter of the fourteenth century), not much read today but extremely popular in its time, included the story of Gawain's bastard son Guinglain, whose emergence from personal obscurity combines the biographies of his father and Perceval. Possibly the work of Thomas Chestre, the author of *Sir Launfal* (c. 1430), this romance is ordinary enough in its execution but boasts a fair number of analogues, among them the Middle High German *Wigalois* (c. 1209) by Wirnt Von Grafenberg and the Italian *Carduino* (c. 1375) in addition to the inevitable French parallel *Le Bel Inconnu* (c. 1190).

PERCEVAL, GRAIL, AND TRISTAN POEMS

The Perceval legend is rare in the medieval English poetic tradition, but alongside Malory's later prose is found the fourteenth century romance *Sir Perceval of Galles* (c. 1300-1340) and the more ambitious and justly famous German *Parzival* (c. 1200-1210; English translation, 1894) of Wolfram and *Perceval: Ou, Le Conte du Graal* (c. 1180; *Perceval: Or, The Story of the Grail*, 1844), the last romance composed by Chrétien.

The Grail poems, Christianized in twelfth century French versions by association of the magic platter, and later cup, with already existing legends surrounding the Eucharist, are likewise few in English during this period, the only avatar being the fragmentary *Joseph of Arimathie* (c. 1350).

Tales of Sir Tristram prove scarcer still, the sole examples being found in the thirteenth century *Sir Tristram*, in Malory's *Le Morte d'Arthur*, and in a phantom twelfth century text by one Thomas of Britain that provided the basis for Gottfried's monumental but incomplete *Tristan und Isolde* (c. 1210; *Tristan and Isolde*, 1899). If the relative paucity of Arthurian poems in certain areas is frustrating, caused in part by the eternal problem of damaged, destroyed, and lost manuscripts, it should be remembered how freely and widely these tales circulated, even without the aid of writing, throughout the Middle Ages, and therefore how rich the Arthurian tradition must have been.

ALLITERATIVE REVIVAL

The latter half of the fourteenth century saw the burgeoning of unrhymed alliterative verse commonly called the alliterative revival. Like many terms canonized by usage in literary histories, this rubric is in some ways a misnomer. In the absence of hard and unambiguous information, it is customarily assumed that the rejuvenation of the alliterative verse form reflects a kind of continuity not only with the thirteenth century *Brut* of Layamon but also with the poems in the Anglo-Saxon type of alliterative meter five centuries earlier. Although the former connection is generally acknowledged, the latter is much more tenuous and cannot at yet be demonstrated. It would be better to consider the revival essentially a Middle English phenomenon, a poetic renaissance that took place when the cultural, linguistic, and historical time was right.

To appreciate the explosion that took place about the year 1350, one should note Derek Pearsall's striking observation that, while only twenty-eight lines of unrhymed alliterative verse survive from the period of 1275 to 1350, the figure rises to more than forty thousand lines during the period from 1350 to 1425. Clearly something significant happened to precipitate this poetic deluge, and scholars have long been laboring to uncover and describe the forces that were or might have been at work. One suggestion is primarily historical, although with innumerable ramifications in other areas: It explains the rapid rise of English alliterative poetry as a response to the vacuum created by the demise of the Anglo-Norman tradition, a reflex of the progressive reaffirmation of things English, and especially English language and literature. Other critics locate the impetus of the revival in the activity of monastic orders, which in the later Middle Ages were much involved in the social and economic as well as religious spheres. Still others have attributed this resurgence to the patronage of the ruling classes of the west of England, and some have found the verse to be propagandistic of this or that group or opinion.

Whatever the complex of origins at the root of the movement, however, most critics agree that the revival was a phenomenon that began in the north and soon spread to the northwest and southwest Midlands areas, that it was a typically fourteenth century flowering of

literary excellence far outstripping anything immediately before or after it, that the movement was transitional between oral and written composition and transmission in its often consciously artistic permutations of traditional conventions and patterns, and that it represents the increasingly English character of literary tradition.

POETIC GENRES

Literary traditions seldom follow well-worn or predictable pathways; rather, they seem to meander this way and that, ever evolving and changing their own defining characteristics. As so many editors of anthologies and teachers of medieval survey courses have come to recognize, this truism is particularly apt for the fourteenth century. Although the period was never at a loss for models in the various European literatures, and although not a few contemporary writers were content to follow unquestioningly the rules of composition bequeathed to them implicitly in the assortment of genres at hand and explicitly in sources such as the handbooks mentioned above, many poets struck out bravely beyond the frontiers of generic and rhetorical propriety to discover new modes of artistic expression.

The result of this iconoclasm is at once a rich legacy of experimentation and a correspondingly heterogeneous mix of poetic types. In confronting this achievement, one must be careful not to diminish its richness and complexity by insisting on too rigid a taxonomy to contain it. Some of the commonly used labels, such as the venerable "romance," do have bona fide literary identities and deserve the title of genre on the basis of classical critical criteria. Others, such as "didactic poetry," are obviously the offspring of descriptive necessity and can lay no claim to constituting an integral group within the poetic tradition; clearly, it would be difficult to locate many medieval poems that are not in some manner didactic. With this caveat in mind, then, some general remarks about the maze of fourteenth century genres can be made.

THE ROMANCE

Although it may boast of being the most widespread and significant poetic form of the fourteenth century, the romance is not a genre that lends itself easily to brief definition. A general profile of the English romance can be assembled, however, and certain cycles or groups among its extant representatives can be distinguished. The English romance, a creature of the mid-thirteenth through the fifteenth century, was composed in a bewildering variety of verse forms as well as in prose, the major types of versification being the four-stress couplet, the tail-rhyme stanza (with a large number of different rhyme schemes), and the four-beat alliterative meter, sometimes in stanzaic format. The romancer followed the typical medieval method of borrowing par excellence, the source most often being a French original that was adapted into English, with original touches added by the poet, or simply translated in whole or in part. Stories concerned the adventures, both martial and amorous, of knights and their opponents and ladies, and were told with the greatest "willful suspension of disbelief" imaginable, a fantastic quality that fairly characterizes the genre as a whole. The narrative voice of most romances leads one to the conclusion that the primary aim of their composers was entertainment, and in fact there is evidence that many of the poems were meant to be read before audiences, both popular and courtly. This tendency did not, however, absolutely preclude a didactic intent; in some of the more finely crafted romances, such as *Sir Gawain and the Green Knight*, the chivalric and religious undercurrents are plain in the overall design of the work.

Hand in hand with the fantasy element in medieval romance goes idealization, readily transmuted to instructive purpose, and convention. Because the genre made use of oral traditional forms by cultivating stock characters, attitudes, and action patterns, it tended to present the immediate and particular against the larger canvas of the generic. Commonplaces, story patterns, verbal tags and formulas, and stock scenes were all among the elements at the romancer's disposal, and the fantastic, the ideal, and the typical merge in a text enlivened by its traditional context. The responses of heroes, the undertaking of quests, the wooing of ladies, and the games of courtly love are expected subjects; the audience read (or better, listened) to the story of Sir Launfal or Morgan Le Fay with a deep sense of its "reality" in the romance tradition and without nagging worry that its content was in modern terms quite unrealistic. To enter the world of medieval romance, to join the poet's quest, was willfully to renounce the corporeal and mundane in favor of the mysterious, the adventurous, and the magical.

More often than not the quest proved successful, the journey culminating in the medieval equivalent of a Hollywood ending. Innocence and even naïveté prevail, as the Perceval tradition well illustrates, and virtue is almost always rewarded. With little regard for historical accuracy, the romancer felt free to embroider a dull sequence of events either with his own personal literary design or, more frequently, with a pattern that was part of his poetic inheritance. He favored feasts and public ceremonies of all sorts for his courtly audience, more worldly embellishments for a popular group. In either case, however, his English poems were, as remarked above, generally less sophisticated than their French originals, in part because their intended audience was also less sophisticated.

As the useful taxonomy in *Manual of the Writings in Middle English* (1967) by John Wells and J. Burke Severs indicates, the great variety of English romances can profitably be viewed in ten groups: poems that derive from legends concerning early Britain; King Arthur; Charlemagne; Godfrey of Bouillon; Alexander the Great; Troy; Thebes; the long-suffering Eustace, Constance, Florence, or Griselda; the Breton lay; and a miscellaneous category that includes works of Eastern origin, historical poems, and didactic pieces. An alternate method for classifying and interrelating romances is the approach of Laura H. Loomis and Maldwyn Mills, a tripartite division of chivalric, heroic, and edifying. The first group contains those verse tales most like earlier French romances in their primary concern with love and chivalry, inorganic combination and recombination of stock elements, and typical location in a magical or exotic domain. The second type characteristically treats the hero as a member of a collective force and highlights societal expectation in addition to heroic achievement. In the third group, the most important values are suffering and endurance in the face of just or unjust punishment, with the possibility of eventual transcendence as the protagonist's reward.

The most famous entry in the first Wells/Severs category, that of native English romances, must certainly be *King Horn* (c. 1225), a tale told and retold in many forms throughout the medieval period. Within the fourteenth century are *The Tale of Gamelyn* (c. 1350-1370) and *Aethelston* (c. 1355-1380), two poems that are probably English in origin and for which, unlike most other works in this group, no surviving sources in French have been discovered. *The Tale of Gamelyn* presents a lively composite of a number of familiar folktale elements, most prominently the benevolent outlaw behavior associated in the popular imagination with Robin Hood, and contemporary social commentary, as imaged in the hero's overturning of a corrupt judge and court. Moreover, there are criticisms of monastic and mendicant orders of clergy, humor, psychological realism, and the cherished happy ending, the last perhaps as much the gift of folktale as the emblem of the romance genre as a whole. The quite Anglo-Saxon *Aethelston*, a patently unhistorical tale of the victorious leader at the Battle of Brunanburh, is even more qualified for inclusion in the Loomis-Mills group of "heroic" romances, for not only is it unrelieved by episodes of love and chivalry but it also figures forth community values and obligations at the expense of individuals. Aethelston stands falsely accused until a trial by fire proves his innocence; the same trial determines the treason of his blood brother Wymound, and matters are soon set right through execution. A third verse romance, *William of Palerne* (c. 1350-1361), amounts to a popularized translation of the French *Guillaume de Palerne* (1194-1197) and follows the return pattern so common in this and other categories.

THE LYRIC

The miscellany of surviving Middle English lyrics extends throughout the period 1200-1500 and resists the application of general ordering principles and specific dating. Many of these works, however, take on a variety of identifiable aspects, even though the poets are themselves generally anonymous, and with good reason since many of the poems and virtually all of the constituent motifs and phraseology were in the public domain. As Raymond Oliver puts it, the poems have three intentions: to celebrate, to persuade, and to define. In the first case, the setting is a ritual occasion, such as the spring season, a wedding, Easter, or, preem-

inently, Christmas; the large collection of traditional carols belongs to this category. Lyrics intended to persuade customarily adopt a stance on particular actions and explain them in a coherent fashion, the *contemptus mundi* theme being a common subject for treatment. The third case, definition, bears on a position or doctrine and is almost always religious in nature. Other characteristics of the lyrics include their impersonal, generalized attitude and lack of interest in personality and psychology, features reflecting the poems' presentation in oral performance.

Many of the topics and themes common to other fourteenth century literature can be found in much abbreviated form in the lyrics. An example is the courtly lover's plaint, such as the justly famous "Blow, Northern Wynd" (c. 1320), or, perhaps most classically, in "Now Springs the Spray" (c. 1300): "Nou sprinkes the sprai./ Al for love Icche am so seek/ That slepen I ne mai." The employing of a seasonal marker to impart an archetypal momentum to a brief narrative, another familiar medieval device, also typifies many of the lyrics, such as this one (c. 1320):

> Somer is i-comen in,
> Loude syng cuckow!
> Groweth seed and bloweth meed
> And spryngeth the wode now. . . .

This famous poem preserves, as do others of the period, an elaborate set of instructions for performing its music. More than other contemporary genres, however, these poems manifest the influence of French and Latin traditions in their multilingual phraseology: Where they are not straighforwardly macaronic, they are often brimful of borrowings. Their rhetoric is also very different from that of other forms; again in keeping with their customary composition for oral performance, the rhetorical figures ordering the poems lean toward the paratactic in structures such as anaphora, parallelism, and repetition of words and phrases. Larger patterns follow suit, with emphasis on stanzaic organization, narrative patterns based on ritual, liturgical, or seasonal events, and repetition of segments. Alliteration and assonance occur frequently, and the meter is accentual; as a rule, Rossell Hope Robbins's suggestion that the levels of prosody and versification are commensurate with the complexity of the subject well summarizes the matter and takes account of the whole spectrum of lyrics, from the plainest and most popular song to the most sophisticated tract on human mutability.

As Oliver notes, surviving Middle English lyrics differ considerably from contemporary continental traditions in their anonymity and lack of concern with individual psychology. German, Latin, and French lyrics of the period often treated ostensibly biographical or other personal issues, most notably the poems of François Villon (1431-1463?) written in the form of a last will and testament, but also the works of Walther von der Vogelweide (c. 1170-c. 1230), Hugh Primas of Orléans (wrote c. 1150), and the German Archpoet (died c. 1165). Comparisons with Old English material, particularly with elegiac lyrics and gnomic poetry, show a large number of alliterative and rhetorical features in common, and the further development of the Middle English lyric can be seen in the poetry of John Skelton and William Dunbar in the late fifteenth and early sixteenth centuries. Those lyrics that can be placed in the fourteenth century (at least on the evidence of surviving manuscripts) show a representative spread of topics and concerns, from the sometimes vulgar recountings of nature in all its earthiness, to Christmas carols that have managed to survive to this day, to celebrations of spring and religious renewal, to earnest contemplations of the transience of human life and meditations on liturgical moments and their meaning. The lyrics constitute a rich miscellany, a backdrop of tradition that helps to contextualize the entire medieval period.

DIDACTIC POETRY

Under this heading are grouped, for the sake of convenience, poems whose intent is chiefly religious and instructional and that do not easily stand alongside better-defined counterparts in other genres. Although it is quite true that much of fourteenth century verse could be called didactic, this category should include only works not generically appropriate for inclusion elsewhere. One such work is Robert Mannyng's *Handlyng Synne* (1303-c. 1317), a thorough recasting of the Anglo-Norman *Le Manuel des péchés* (thirteenth century), by William of Wadington. The subject of Mannyng's

poem is vast: A good deal of Christian church doctrine, including the Ten Commandments, the Seven Deadly Sins, the Sins of Sacrilege, the Seven Sacraments, the Twelve Points of Shrift, and the Eight Joys of Grace, comes under his scrutiny. He occasionally leavens his theological lessons, perhaps intended for a specific audience of novices of Sempringham, with realistic detail and reaction, and, like Chaucer after him, he knows the edifying potential of a good story:

> For lewde men Y undyrtoke
> On Engylssh tunge to make thys boke;
> For many ben of swyche manere
> That talys and rymys wyl blethly here.

Mannyng also composed *The Story of England* (c. 1338), a chronicle of historical events from the Biblical flood to the reign of Edward I, and he may be responsible for an adaptation of Saint Bonaventure's *Meditations on the Life of Christ* (mid-thirteenth century).

Another primarily didactic poem of this century is the anonymous *Parlement of the Three Ages* (c. 1350), which employs two of the most characteristic medieval narrative devices, the dream vision and the debate. An example from the alliterative revival described earlier, this tale concerns the Nine Worthies and thus connects itself with the Alexander legends and their form as romances, but the most fundamental structure of the poem is as a moral lesson on the transience and mutability of all things earthly. The poet reviews the Worthies, wise men, and lovers, all from the perspective of the "vanity of human wishes," combining tried and true stories, topoi, and narrative patterns with a vigorous alliterative language that recalls at points the hearty realism of Anglo-Saxon heroic poetry as well as the later *Sir Gawain and the Green Knight*.

Less realistic but perhaps more rewarding stylistically and aesthetically, the elegiac *Pearl* (c. 1400), attributed to the Pearl-Poet, concerns the author's infant daughter who dies in her second year and inspires in her father a debate over divine wisdom and mortal expectation. After ascending to heaven, she tells him of her spiritual happiness and explains temporal misconceptions in God's ordering of the universe. Just as he tries to cross over to her, the poet awakes from his dream vision with his head on her grave, forever reconciled to her loss. A highly allegorical work, *Pearl* recalls numerous biblical figurations from Revelations and elsewhere and presents its simple dream-vision narrative and complex allegorical latticework in a style both nominally typical of the alliterative revival and yet uniquely its own in the concomitant development of stanzaic patterns. Many critics have sought, and arguably found, numerological sequences that relate in some way to biblical and patristic sources, a not uncommon phenomenon in medieval texts. Other poets likewise turned to the dream and debate as methods for active mediation of the earthly and spiritual worlds, but few achieved the delicate interweaving of alliterative idiom and theological instruction that the Pearl-Poet displays.

The same author is also credited with two other poems in the *Gawain* manuscript, *Cleanness* (c. 1400) and *Patience* (c. 1400). The former presents the tales of the Biblical flood, a popular subject since Anglo-Saxon times and usually thought to prefigure the Apocalypse; the destruction of Sodom and Gomorrah; and the fall of the sacrilegious Belshazzar, concerning itself chiefly with the impurity of the situations that incurred God's punishment. The poet counterposes the sinful figures in these three biblical stories—and again the numerology seems more than accidental—to the three positive figures of Noah, Abraham, and Nebuchadnezzar, whose respect toward God is rewarded with mercy. Although not so intensely allegorical as *Pearl*, *Cleanness* still motivates the reader to compare the three main stories with other biblical sources and, perhaps most of all, to consider the tropological implications for his own life. Similarly, *Patience*, the fourth of the poems in the *Gawain* manuscript, retells the narrative of the Book of Jonah, although the general medieval fascination with steadfast faith throughout the worst imaginable adversity, as evidenced so widely in the edifying romances of Griselda and company, must also serve as a background for this alliterative expatiation. This shorter poem is also the most personal of the four, portraying each of its characters with considerable realism and finesse, and offering a glimpse into the psychology of Jonah, particularly his human frailty. As a whole, the works of the Pearl-Poet must be numbered among both the best and most memorable of the didactic poems

of the fourteenth century and the most complicated representatives of the alliterative revival.

POLITICAL AND HISTORICAL POETRY

During the fourteenth century there arose a fair number of poems that chronicled various historical epochs and events with a political purpose in mind. The earliest of these are eleven poems by Laurence Minot (1300?-1352?), written between 1333 and 1352, on the successful campaigns by Edward III against the Scots and the French. Responding to earlier English defeats, in particular the Shameful Peace with Scotland following Edward II's defeat at Bannockburn in 1314, Minot sought to eulogize the king's achievement and foster the cause of nationalism. The first and best known of his works, *Halidon Hill* (c. 1333), commemorates the young monarch's retributive victory that regained control of the northern border and soothed the political as well as territorial wounds inflicted on the English psyche but warns against thoughtless celebration lest the nation be deceived by Scottish "gile."

John Barbour's *The Bruce* (c. 1375) celebrates Scottish nationalism in an account of the heroic actions of King Robert the Bruce and his faithful comrade-in-arms Sir James Douglas that stretches to more than thirteen thousand lines. Beginning with historical facts and bringing to his work classical and medieval models as well as a lively sense of mythic narrative, Barbour recounts the heroic accomplishments of Robert, including the Battle of Bannockburn and Douglas's unsuccessful attempt to bear the fallen king's heart to the Holy Land. As Charles Dunn and Edward Byrnes observe in *Middle English Literature* (1973), the poem finds its thematic center in Robert as the quintessential defender of Scottish liberty and in Douglas as the equally paradigmatic loyal follower. In this and other ways, *The Bruce* eludes categorization, whether as chronicle, political poem, epic, or myth; in the final analysis it remains a work sui generis, one most typical of the mélange of later fourteenth century verse forms.

The anonymous author of *Thomas of Erceldoun* (c. 1388-1401) also combined a number of stock medieval generic characteristics to forge a unique kind of narrative. Although parts of the story share with *Halidon Hill* and *The Bruce* certain real battles as subjects, and although the hero of the work, one Thomas Rymor of Earlston, is historical, the poem also interweaves common folktale elements and other features typical of medieval romance. The main narrative frame concerns Thomas's love affair with an underworld queen and his consequent ability to foretell the future. As well as the queen's predictions about clashes between Scotland and England, the poet presents certain other auguries of indistinct relation to the first group. Dunn and Byrnes note that *Thomas of Erceldoun* typifies a pan-European medieval technique in its assignment of known historical facts to the visions of a seer or prophet and attachment of especially attractive prophecies not yet fulfilled to the historical record; once assembled, the entire package was apparently submitted as a political tour de force.

PRECURSORS TO CHAUCER

Apart from the many engaging and accomplished poems treated above under various generic categories stand some individual authors and works that, by virtue of both their own artistic excellence and their influence and modern appeal, deserve special attention. Among this latter group are William Langland's *The Vision of William, Concerning Piers the Plowman* (c. 1362, A Text; c. 1377, B Text; c. 1393, C Text; also known as *Piers Plowman*), the Pearl-Poet's *Sir Gawain and the Green Knight*, and John Gower's *Confessio Amantis* (1386-1390; the lover's confession). Each in its own way helps to set the standard of poetic achievement that is the legacy of the late fourteenth century or "Ricardian" period, as J. A. Burrow has named it, and together these three poems constitute a crucial context for the genius of Chaucer.

PIERS PLOWMAN

William Langland's *Piers Plowman* is extant in three recensions, labeled the A, B, and C texts. The three combined are divided into two parts, "The Vision of William, Concerning Piers the Plowman" and "The Life of Do-Well, Do-Better, and Do-Best," which articulate, respectively, general and individual problems of evil and corruption, both offering solutions for the good Christian during his stay on earth. The vision portrays the ruin of contemporary society in allegorical terms and, perhaps responding in part to the social up-

heaval that racked the everyday lives of fourteenth century humanity, suggests the humble and simple virtue and obedience of the plowman as an antidote to temporal discord. In the second section, the poet conducts an allegorical search for the ideal Christian existence, starting within himself and then undertaking a quest through various liturgical and philosophical domains under the guidance of a series of mentors. With his journey complete, the dreamer's vision turns from its focus on higher abstract truths to their practical implementation in contemporary society.

Langland's poem is, as much as any medieval work, uniquely his own, but one can trace a few analogues and parallels to fill out its literary context. Tracts such as Mannyng's *Handlyng Synne* are typical of many such instructional poems and prose works of the period; some of the most familiar include Dan Michel of Northgate's *Ayenbite of Inwyt* (1340, a translation of *La somme des vices et des vertues* by Laurentius Gallus) and Chaucer's "Parson's Tale." These poems and similar works were commonly consulted by writers for liturgical details and traditional literary accounts associated with church dogma. Also of influence was the well-developed sermon tradition of the later Middle Ages, which became a learned craft memorialized in handbooks (*Ars praedicandi*), much like the *Ars rhetoricae* or *Ars poeticae* employed by poets in search of commonplaces of description or narrative action. In fact, several whole works are at least formally similar to *Piers Plowman*, such as Guillaume de Deguileville's *The Pilgrimage of Human Life, of the Soul, and of Jesus Christ* (c. 1330-1358), as well as more general classical and other foreign models of allegorical quests and seeking after divine truth. Although superficially *Piers Plowman* and *Sir Gawain and the Green Knight* appear to be strange bedfellows, the fact remains that Langland's poem is also a manifestation, and a brilliantly executed one, of the alliterative revival. Even so, as with all of the best works of the late fourteenth century, *Piers Plowman* is best assessed on its own merits as an earnest and able contemplation of its time, in this instance against the backdrop of the Christian drama.

To appreciate the earnestness of this finely crafted allegorical latticework, it is necessary to view the poem in its literary historical milieu. Recalling the desperate state of affairs in late fourteenth century England—the Church in corrupt disarray since the preceding century, the Avignon Papacy just coming to an end, the Black Death having run rampant only twenty-five years before, the long-standing social discontent crystallizing in the Peasants' Rebellion of 1381, the condemnation of Wycliffe's teaching in 1382, and the blatantly incompetent rule of Richard II, one can well imagine how a poem such as *Piers Plowman* came to be composed and why, if the extremely large number of extant manuscripts is any testimony, it found a large and sympathetic audience long before being taken up by scholars and critics as one of the masterpieces of its time. In a century racked by uncertainty, the spiritual journey of Everyman in search of truth must have served a social as well as aesthetic purpose; given the prevailing problems, it may not be too daring to characterize one function of this "poem of apocalypse," as Morton Bloomfield calls it, as cathartic or therapeutic. In the medium of poetic art, Langland and, vicariously, his countrymen could respond to a sometimes corrupt and vacuous clergy with satire and wit; they could counter a monumentally intransigent and self-centered government with lessons on taming Lady Meed; and, most crucial, they could combat the socially exacerbated sickness of mortality by imagining, in great allegorical detail, a religious restorative. Langland proposed a journey not unlike that of Dante, a dream of transcendence of the earthly sphere, and a vision of God uncomplicated and unsullied by the catastrophic events of his time. Even if *Piers Plowman* ends with the Antichrist in power, the Church under attack, and the world as yet unredeemed, the dreamer has a new understanding of what lies beyond his immediate environment as a defense against apocalypse. The search will continue.

Sir Gawain and the Green Knight

Another of the jewels in the crown of the alliterative revival, the Pearl-Poet's *Sir Gawain and the Green Knight* represents a very different sort of literary masterpiece from *Piers Plowman*. Melding together games and story patterns from Celtic folklore, attitudes and values from a highly developed and thoughtful Christianity, and the ritualistic procedures of courtly love, it achieves a fusion of medieval ideas unique in the four-

teenth century. An Arthurian hero, Gawain, in place of his monarch, takes up the challenge to behead the Green Knight and, should the marvelous fellow survive, to allow him the same privilege a year hence. Gawain accepts what critics have viewed as both a Christmas prank and the initial act in a story of vegetative renewal and cleanly lops off the Green Knight's head; not the least discouraged, his adversary gathers up his lost part and, reminding Gawain of his pledge, rides off to unknown regions. Too soon the annual cycle is complete and the day arrives for the honorable knight's departure to fulfill the bargain; Gawain leaves Arthur's court and eventually finds himself at the castle of one Bercilak and his lady, an honored guest enjoying their hospitality. Here the plot begins to thicken ominously. While the lord and master is off on his daily hunting expedition, not incidentally for three successive days, his wife acts as courtly temptress of their guest. Gawain finds himself suspended between two medieval romantic codes: Either he must follow the precepts of chivalric behavior and, refusing the lady's advances, honor his host's hospitality as a true knight of the Round Table, or he must gallantly bow to the pressures of courtly love and, accepting the lady, fulfill another set of expectations. Of course he cannot do both, especially since he agreed with Bercilak to exchange any booty won on their respective hunts, and so he is caught in a logically insoluble quandary. After weakening the third day and accepting a kiss, Gawain leaves the castle and soon encounters the Green Knight, who turns out to be Bercilak in disguise. Submitting to the promised return blow, the hero flinches once, receives a second feint, and on the third swing of the ax is slightly injured, just enough to compensate for his minor indiscretion on the third day of the earlier test. The Green Knight then gives him the lady's "girdle" or sash, a symbol of femininity since classical times, to wear around his belt in remembrance of the whole affair, and Gawain heads back to Arthur's court with his life and his knighthood intact.

The sources behind this lively tale include a mixture of originally Celtic elements and common romance motifs, but whatever the actual source materials with which he worked, the artistic achievement of the Pearl-Poet remains uniquely his own. The archetypal frame provided by the self-renewing Green Knight promotes ideas of recurrence and inevitability and is made to surround a series of ironic and playful games engaged in by the much-tried hero, the lady temptress, and the lord Bercilak. There is clearly no escape for Gawain, nor is there meant to be: The fall of Gawain as Everyman is in fact remarkably innocuous given the pressing circumstances, as the Green Knight's mercy (but justice) with his sharp edge illustrates. Gawain loses a battle as, from one point of view, the entrapment made inevitable by his mortality eventually draws blood; the Green Knight must be repaid, just as surely as the next Christmas season will announce the rebirth of God. The hero's fallibility also becomes his religious and moral sinecure. Chastised by a natural, postlapsarian error, he shows himself—and in the process humanity—to be the better for the test. What he loses with a kiss and a flinch from the blade he repays, Christlike, with his wound, and ever afterward the girdle remains as a symbol of his transcendence of mere mortal frailty. Gawain, like Oedipus, solves a riddle and wins a contest; by surviving the complex contest of conventions and circumstances, he comes to epitomize the triumph not only presaged by Christ but also, optimally, mirrored in Everyman's experience of earthly life. For all this, the vehicle for this highly serious investigation of mysteries remains a virtual *cadeau*, a Christmas jest: When all is over, when the tale is done and the poet adds "Honi soyt qui mal pence" ("Evil be to him who thinks evil"), Chaucer's immoral morality and playful hermeneutics seem very near indeed.

Confessio Amantis

Gower's much praised *Confessio Amantis* forms one third of a trilogy of poems by Gower on the evils that assail the individual and state and on methods for overcoming them and achieving virtue. He first completed the Anglo-Norman *Mirour de l'Omme* (1376-1379), and then the Latin *Vox Clamantis* (1379-1382); *Confessio Amantis* is universally proclaimed his masterpiece. A straightforwardly and severely moral work, it functions chiefly through a barer and more economical allegory than does *Piers Plowman*, but one that is in its way equally powerful. Again, there is the familiar dream-vision structure in book 1, with the poet Gower imagining a meeting with the God of Love, the Queen

of Love, and the Queen's priest Genius. The priest then treats the dangers of earthly love and the Seven Deadly Sins, one after the other, for most of the remainder of the work, teaching the poet-lover in good medieval style through a series of illustrative stories. Finding himself absolved of his afflictions, the poet is able to bid Venus farewell, turn to reason for guidance, and pursue the lasting spiritual rewards of moral virtue.

Several features of the *Confessio Amantis* deserve special comment. First, in addition to the dream vision, allegorical commonplaces, and discussion of the Seven Deadly Sins, the poem is thoroughly medieval in its juxtaposition of human versus divine love, a topic as old as the Anglo-Saxon elegies *The Wife's Lament* or *The Seafarer* (both c. tenth century). Of course, no poem could well function more differently from *Sir Gawain and the Green Knight*, but the two works do share the story of medieval man learning his human shortcomings and profiting from the lesson. The *Confessio Amantis* delivers its instruction in a less immediate, more austere manner, agreeing in tone and structure with *Piers Plowman*, but it seems worthwhile to note that Gower's moral allegory and the Pearl-Poet's romance do affirm the same values and, once the particulars deriving from generic differences are deemphasized, can be seen to offer similar prescriptions for getting on in the world. At the same time, one should remember that the *Confessio Amantis* is not, like *Piers Plowman* and *Sir Gawain and the Green Knight*, a product of the alliterative revival, and that both its subject and the rhymed couplets of its verse hark back to foreign as well as native models, as indicated by the vision's considerable debt for its story line to *Le Roman de la rose* (thirteenth century; *The Romance of the Rose*; partial translation c. 1370, complete translation 1900). The first portion of this work was written in the first half of the thirteenth century by Guillaume de Lorris and the second portion between 1275 and 1280 by Jean de Meung. As an obviously well-educated and widely read man, Gower had no shortage of models for his poetry, and he turned his conception of proper human attainments into a clear and readable narrative intended both to instruct and to entertain. That such a work, rigorously formal in attitude and design yet a paragon of literary attractiveness, could exist beside *Sir*

Gawain and the Green Knight and even complement its purpose is a measure of the poetic cornucopia of the fourteenth century.

THE CANTERBURY TALES

Towering over all of fourteenth century poetry are the poems of Chaucer. In nearly every imaginable manner Chaucer epitomizes his age and its literature. In the midst of social anguish and turmoil, he focused his genius on matters of supreme and permanent importance. As a thoroughly medieval author, he borrowed freely and imaginatively from English, French, Italian, and Latin sources. Refusing even more than his contemporaries to be hide-bound by generic or rhetorical constraints, he frequently pushed the rules of genre and poetic composition to the breaking point, creating in the process some works that defy classification in their brilliant originality. Especially typical of late fourteenth century or Ricardian masters, he managed to achieve affecting and enduring aperçus into the pilgrimage of humanity and the ceaseless ritual games between men and women.

Chaucer's most ambitious work, *The Canterbury Tales*, is also the most typical literary document of its age. At a time when uncertainty and doubt threatened to send most social and political institutions careening into disaster or disrepute, when Langland was composing his monumental allegory of salvation as a bulwark against religious and cultural apocalypse, Chaucer managed to assemble a company of remarkably disparate individuals and to lead them on a pilgrimage of hope, a journey that would discover their common humanity in a startlingly novel fashion. If creative response to the breakdown of hard-won but outmoded syntheses was an important theme in this period, then *The Canterbury Tales* epitomizes that solution: In presenting his panorama, Chaucer uses most of the major contemporary genres but subordinates them to a new design; he introduces God's plenty of personalities but finds a way to integrate them into a believable community; he has his pilgrims discuss many of the burning social, religious, and philosophical issues of the day but never lets debate or pedantry obtrude on the collective function of the group; and he achieves a realism and naturalism of characterization far beyond that of any contemporary work without ever abandoning either his

finely crafted, brilliantly conceived narrative voice or the structure, large and small, of the stories themselves and the work as a whole. When one adds the tremendous range of his learning, so apparent in the variety of sources and the skill with which he re-creates them, and the outright appeal of the poem for generations of audiences, it becomes no exaggeration to call *The Canterbury Tales* both Chaucer's masterpiece and the masterwork of the entire fourteenth century.

As might be expected, such a poem seems to have been largely the product of the poet's later years, of his mature style. Still influenced by the French tradition of romances and *dits amoureux* that served so importantly as models in his earlier writings, and having digested the contributions of the Italian poets and transmuted this literary gold into an indigenous English coin, Chaucer struck out on the kind of creative, original venture that only a lifetime of exposure to experience with traditional materials could foster. Scholars customarily associate the year 1386 with his conception of the plan for *The Canterbury Tales*, but he may well have been working on the project beforehand. Perhaps the next year he composed the immortal "General Prologue," from a textual viewpoint the key to all that follows. Opinions on other aspects of chronology vary as well, but the tales themselves probably occupied Chaucer for most of the rest of his life. The unfinished state of the work and its tangle of manuscripts indicate that he probably composed significant parts of the poem up until his death, but one should also remember that *The Canterbury Tales* was, like most medieval poetry, intended for oral performance and not primarily as a written text.

One of the influences on Chaucer's poem was the Italian novelle tradition, a loose aggregation of tales brought together by an outwardly unifying fiction. Although Giovanni Sercambi did write such a collection in the general form of a pilgrimage about 1374, it is important to note that neither this nor any other group of *novelle* could have provided more than a suggestion for the complex and dynamic frame of *The Canterbury Tales*. Likewise, the richness of the "General Prologue" derives not from the considerable number of sketches written at the time, but most vitally from Chaucer's genius for weaving conventional topoi, rhetorical rules, character types, and at least some real personalities into a fabric distinctly his own. Of the sources and analogues for the tales themselves, it may be said that the mélange of genres and possible parallels is as diverse as the company of pilgrims, including, besides the *novelle*, the French fabliau tradition, the romance, the saint's life, the folktale, the medieval sermon, the miracle story, the epic, and the mock-heroic poem. No form passed through Chaucer's hands without considerable elaboration or some sort of modification; often his contribution consisted of turning the genre to his favorite purpose of social satire, and at times his reworking was so complete that, as in the case of the superbly farcical "Sir Thopas," he created a virtually new genre.

To surround his tales of life and love, Chaucer constructed what is frequently called a frame but which might better be labeled a purpose or context. Unlike the Italian analogues that postulate a nominal unifying fiction and leave the matter quite undeveloped, the pilgrimage is ever evolving, with the poet shifting the focus this way and that to sustain the fiction and to allow his characters their remarkable range of expression and interaction. Intimately allied to the pilgrimage conceit is the naïve, impressionable narrator who keeps it alive—the poet-pilgrim Chaucer who mourns his lack of literary aptitude ("My wit is short, ye may wel understonde"). Behind this wide-eyed, good-natured fellow, of course, stands the poet Chaucer, manipulating the unbounded enthusiasm of his narrator with consummate skill and a keen sense of irony, allowing his audience a double perspective on characters and events. Indeed, it is impossible to separate the pilgrimage context from its somewhat clumsy but ever-willing rhapsode. If Chaucer's characters come alive and interact in ways unique to *The Canterbury Tales*, a large part of the credit is due to a combination of his narrator's unfailing and irrepressible humanity with the poet's own perspectives on the fascinating heterogeneity of humankind.

From this union of authorial design and naturalistic narration springs the vivacity of the "General Prologue." After setting the scene and creating the rationalizing fiction, the narrator begins an exacting introduction of his society in microcosm, epitomizing each character type and endowing each pilgrim with a memorable individuality. His small community allegorizes fourteenth century society—and it does not: Taking advantage of traditional associations, Chaucer not infrequently adorns a character with the "tell-tale detail," such as the Prioress's brooch, the Miller's wart, the Wife's deafness or scarlet hose, or the Pardoner's waxy yellow hair. Details and the actions and habits that they either imply or actually represent come nimbly into play, as the narrator balances expectations based on character types against the exceptions to those *règles du jeu*. Such is Chaucer's mastery of the poetic medium, however, that he expresses even these singularities in the form of medieval rhetorical commonplaces. Drawing on conventional techniques of poetic description, and especially on the *notatio-efficito* method of portraying inner qualities or liabilities in a character's specific physical features, he encodes some of his most subtle and iconoclastic observations on a character in the metalanguage prescribed by poetic handbooks. Sometimes an overabundance of one of the four humors—blood, phlegm, yellow bile, and black bile, postulated since the Greek physician Galen and common in medieval medical lore—leads to a judgment on a person; in another case a term with lascivious associations, such as the Wife's quality of being "gap-toothed," mitigates or seconds other aspects of a description. Employing to the hilt the narrator's unremittingly naïve euphemisms (only he could call as notorious a swindler and reprobate as the Pardoner a "noble ecclesiaste"), Chaucer delicately balances traditional expectation and individual design, managing to make time for implicit commentry that ranges from ironic to bawdy to sincerely religious.

Chaucer's portraits are elaborately crafted, to be sure, and just as certainly very carefully hung. Critics have pointed out various possible schemes for the arrangement, many of them founded on the ideas of the various estates or social classes of medieval provenance. Donald Howard suggests that the order of presentation is a mnemonic structure or aide-mémoire analogous to medieval formulations reported by Frances Yates; that is, three groups of seven, each group headed by an ideal figure: the Knight, followed by the Squire, Yeoman, Prioress, Monk, Friar, and Merchant;

the Clerk, followed by the Man of Law, Franklin, Guildsman, Shipman, Physician, and Wife; and the Parson and Plowman (brothers), followed by the Miller, Manciple, Reeve, Summoner, Pardoner, and Host. Howard argues that these mnemonic constructs were so much a part of medieval literary consciousness that it would be only natural for Chaucer to employ them in his art. This scheme for the introduction of the characters seems credible enough. It does, however, leave out a character who is in many ways the most important of all: Chaucer the pilgrim. Throughout the "General Prologue," but particularly in the thirty-two lines that intervene between the introductions of the Pardoner and the Host, the narrator is introduced as another in the company, an appealing fellow who begs his readers not to hold him directly responsible for what he reports because he can only repeat what was said by others. It is very much in the innocent nature of Chaucer the pilgrim to issue such a disclaimer before he begins the recital of romance, *fabliau*, and the other genres that make up *The Canterbury Tales*, and the reader may also sense the guiding hand of the poet finishing off the characterization of yet another pilgrim, the narrative liaison between poet and poem and the lifeblood of the pilgrimage frame.

Harry Bailly, the Host, soon takes nominal charge of the enterprise, sets the rules for tale-telling (two while riding to Canterbury and two on the way back from each pilgrim), and has the participants draw lots to determine who will start. The cut falls to the Knight, and the tales begin as they should in the social sphere of fourteenth century England with the pilgrim of highest rank opening the proceedings. "The Knight's Tale" turns out to be a story and a type of poem appropriate both to its teller and to its position in the work as a whole. As an adventurer in the service of the Christian God, and as "a verray, parfit gentil knyght" quite the opposite of that over-courtly bon vivant his Squire, he lends dignity and a sense of purpose to the community by relating an intricate Boethian romance that reaffirms the social order that he leads. Drawn primarily from Boccaccio's *Teseida delle nozze d'Emilia* (1339-1341; *The Book of Theseus*, 1974), with a great deal of the favorite medieval device of compression, this chivalric tale was probably first composed as a separate piece un-

connected with *The Canterbury Tales* and only later fitted into its present place. Whatever the nature of the lost version mentioned in the prologue to *The Legend of Good Women* (1380-1386), the extant tale chronicles the tragic and eventually ennobling love of the young knights Palamon and Arcite for a lady Emelye. The misfortunes of earthly life are seen as "perturbations of the spheres" and the story moves like Chaucer's *Troilus and Criseyde* from mortal myopia to a larger perspective under the aegis of Theseus. The variety of contributions to follow are to an extent rationalized by this tale, which remains a philosophical anchor and moral standard for the entire work.

No sooner has the stately knight finished justifying the ways of God to his fellow pilgrims than the drunken Miller counters the propriety and high style of the initial tale with his coarse, irreverent fabliau of carpenter John's cuckolding. The Miller is so impatient and rude, in every way the antithesis of the first teller, that he interrupts the Host's request that the Monk be next and, ever so characteristically, barges straight ahead to "quite the Knyghtes Tale." His own words introduce an important structural principle, that of "quiting" or repaying, which will account for the presence of the tale to follow as well. This lowlife character offers the furthest remove imaginable from the philosophical complexity of "The Knight's Tale" by telling an uproarious story of how Nicholas the clerk planned and carried off the seduction of the carpenter's wife virtually before her husband's eyes. Not only is the Miller "quiting" the Knight, but also, the lower class is challenging the views and values of the upper. Animal instincts and scheming are being played off against higher passions and earnest moral deliberations, and perhaps most significantly, the dynamics of the community of pilgrims—both as individuals and as representatives of their vocations or types—is starting to take shape. "The Miller's Tale" deals not with Boethius but with bawdiness: the clever Nicholas, the doltish John, the unspeakably fey parish clerk Absolon, and the concupiscible young wife Alison engage in a fast-paced charade that rides roughshod over courtly love, religious duty, matrimonial fidelity, and all available aspects of contemporary morality. At the same time, the Miller stumbles through a real, if homely, alternative to the deep pondering and austerity of "The Knight's Tale" and helps to set the tone and outer limits of Chaucer's investigation of humanity.

The lonely Reeve, who brings up the rear of the assemblage, then reacts violently against what he judges to be the Miller's personal insult of a trade he has practiced and, "quiting" his foe, responds with a fabliau about the cuckolding of a dishonest miller. Some tales later Chaucer introduces a justly famous character, Dame Alys or the Wife of Bath, as vigorous, self-serving, and lecherous as the Reeve is biting, sarcastic, and "colerik." Her prologue consists of a boisterous, happy biography complete with accounts of her five husbands and how she achieved mastery over all of them. Often linked to the antifeminist sentiment of the period, ironically evident in her fifth husband's book of misogynist exempla, the Wife commands the stage of *The Canterbury Tales* by misquoting and misapplying biblical and patristic authorities, by celebrating the lustful nature that led her to ogle Jankyn (her fifth husband) during her fourth mate's funeral, by discoursing on male and female genitalia with a crudity that would do the blockhead Miller proud, and generally by providing the community of pilgrims with an inextinguishable source of gleeful iconoclasm, good will, and high spirits. Very rarely in any literary period is there so vivacious and singular a character as the Dame; like a medieval Falstaff, she stands astride the work of which she is a part, to be remembered and cherished as a patroness of its art.

As the Wife boasts of her conquests in the prologue, the reader begins to understand that she is offering one possible solution to the problem of the contest for mastery between men and women. "The Wife of Bath's Prologue and Tale" is one in a series of seven tales that Kittredge identified as the "Marriage Group," a sequence that, he argued, was intended to present various possibilities for the seat of authority in marriage. The four most important members of this group are the Wife, the Clerk, the Merchant, and the Franklin. The Clerk tells a story of male dominance over a painfully patient Griselda which "quites" the Wife, and the Merchant spins the ubiquitous medieval tale of the elderly January and his young wife May, warning of the consequences that such a doomed alliance must bring. For

her part, the Wife fashions a prologue that finds distant analogues in the very antifeminist writings that it parodies, but which remains after all a brilliant original; her tale, on the other hand, is the common story of the Loathly Lady and her miraculous transformation, analogues of which are found in Gower's *Confession Amantis* and numerous contemporary romances. With the Knight under the thumb of the hag, whom he has promised to marry after she saves his life, Dame Alys makes her exit, no doubt supremely confident of the influence of her words on the audience she has been both entertaining and instructing. Even so, the reader may ask how well she has succeeded in making the patently outrageous palatable.

If the Wife, Clerk, and Merchant offer what are finally unsatisfactory alternatives for the problem of sovereignty in marriage, the Franklin, "Epicurus owene sone" and knight of the shire, provides a final solution in a tale that Chaucer adapted from Boccaccio's *Il filostrato* (c. 1335; *The Filostrato*, 1873) with elements from Geoffrey of Monmouth, the Breton lay tradition, and the common folktale motif of the rash promise. As Paul Ruggiers puts it in *Art of The Canterbury Tales* (1965), "The view of marriage which has in a sense been dismembered is reconstituted in terms of a balance between service and dominance, between human weakness and strength of character, between respect for self and respect for others." Even the announced genre of the tale, a Breton lay, promotes the resolution by creating a fairy-tale world wherein forbidding complexities can be magically simplified and the nagging temporal concerns of an imperfect world dissolved in a romantic suspension of disbelief. Taking as his topic and argument the already demonstrated reality that "Love wold not been constreyned by maistrye," the Franklin tells the story of Arveragus and his faithful wife Dorigen, whom Aurelius, the courtly lover par excellence, is, characteristically enough, pursuing. In resisting his suit, a rare abstinence in the world of *The Canterbury Tales*, she sets him a seemingly impossible task, saying that she will accede only if he manages to remove each and every stone from the coast of Britain. By consulting a clerk versed in Chaucer's favorite science of astronomy, the resourceful Aurelius accomplishes the task and calls the lady's hand.

The dilemma that now presents itself to Arveragus and Dorigen is clear-cut but morally insoluble: If she refuses Aurelius's love, she violates her solemn promise; if she accepts him, he violates her contract of fidelity with her husband. As much as the outcome seems "agayns the proces of nature," the quandary is real, at least for people as honorable and devoted to each other as this couple. Arveragus selflessly counsels his wife to uphold her part of the bargain and she reluctantly agrees, but such is the self-correcting nature of the world of "The Franklin's Tale" that the once crafty and unabashed suitor takes pity on Dorigen's obvious suffering and releases her from the promise, even proclaiming her fidelity as a virtue implicitly superior to the code of courtly love. True to its genre, the poem then completes the resolution by releasing Aurelius from his financial obligations through the kindness and mercy of the clerk he had surreptitiously hired to perform the impossible feat. *Gentilesse*, the Chaucerian idiom for nobility and delicacy of character, replaces *governance* as the ruling principle of conjugal relations, and the Marriage Group finds the answer it has been seeking throughout the community of pilgrims. "The Franklin's Tale" thus represents a kind of testament to order in the human world as well as a coda to a set of literary preludes. In the midst of real and expectable social chaos, there is a bit of magic, a moment of harmony in a generally discordant world.

That discord is never more baldly evident than in the shameless words of the Pardoner, a marvelously vile and altogether reprehensible character who will offer, so he claims, a "moral tale." It is difficult to see how such a man could bring it off: A seller of bogus absolutions and false relics, he takes as his theme the oft-quoted aphorism "Radix malorum est Cupiditas" ("The root of all evils is Greed") and goes on to make a case for himself as the contemporary personification of Cupiditas. He straightforwardly and pridefully boasts of swindling well-meaning people searching for religious comfort in the form of supposedly genuine pardons, happy to deprive even the poorest widow of the money that would keep her children from starvation. Ironically true to his claim to be able to instruct although he is himself fast-fettered by sin, the Pardoner launches into a moral exemplum presented as a sermon.

His tale, designed to illustrate the eventual retribution to be visited on gluttons and revelers and, by extension, on all those guilty of the deadly sins, is crudely told and leads into hollow strophes against what are of course his own flaws, followed by his customary shameless plea for money. His direct address of the Host as the pilgrim most in need of his services inflames Bailly and evokes his memorable threat to denature the Pardoner, a sentiment that the audience—especially the contemporary audience, who had to deal more and more with false sellers of writs as the authority of the Church continued to decline—must have applauded. It remains for the Knight, the embodiment of honor and social protocol and a tale-teller whose words have already served as balm for the ephemeral wounds of Everyman, to brave the verbal fray between these two and restore order to the pilgrim's community.

As an entire work, *The Canterbury Tales* seems to stand incomplete. Only twenty-three of the thirty pilgrims mentioned actually tell a tale, even though the Host's original arrangement called for no fewer than four apiece. The framing device, however, is a fiction that provides unity to a heterogenous collection; it is not a legal document. Especially since *The Canterbury Tales* were composed primarily for reading aloud before an audience, individual stories or groups of stories may well have enjoyed an existence of their own apart from the text as a whole. Chaucer may never have intended to "complete" his most lasting poem at all; having invented the fiction that would cause any number of tales to cohere, he may simply have turned his hand to those characters, issues, genres, and narratives that most attracted him. It seems more than a little pedantic, then, to insist that *The Canterbury Tales* remains incomplete, in the sense of "partial," for Chaucer's vision reached far beyond anything created by even his most talented contemporaries, and the tales he did compose bear eloquent testimony to the fertility of his design.

At the close of "The Parson's Tale" there is one final twist of the narrative thread in *The Canterbury Tales*. Here Chaucer places his "retraction," ostensibly a profession of faith accompanied by a confession of self-proclaimed wrongdoings in some of his poetic works. Critics have pointed out how the retraction has numerous literary precedents and analogues, perhaps the most striking of which is Boccaccio's own rejection of his often bawdy tales in Italian in favor of learned Latin treatises. A reader may also take Chaucer's protestation as another in a series of clever manipulations of his audience, accepting his prayer at face value as both a pious expostulation and a traditional tour de force but recognizing the retraction itself as a form of disclaimer—only this time on the part of Chaucer the poet rather than Chaucer the pilgrim. As has been seen, the narrator is more than adequate to the task of presenting *The Canterbury Tales* in a naturalistic and blameless way, and now the poet further relativizes not only this work but also all others that treat in any way lecherous, scatological, or otherwise irreligious subjects. If Chaucer's retraction honestly professes faith in Christ and hope for eternal salvation, it also allows the poet and audience yet another perspective on the wonderful variety of pilgrims who have trod the stage of *The Canterbury Tales:* They are real, they are complete in themselves, and they collectively figure forth a uniquely engaging pastiche of characteristics, attitudes, values, and beliefs typical of the fourteenth century in particular and of humanity in general. Chaucer cannot retract that achievement.

BIBLIOGRAPHY

Anderson, J. J. *Language and Imagination in the Gawain-Poems*. Manchester, England; Manchester University Press, 2005. A new interpretation of *Pearl*, *Cleanness*, *Patience*, and *Sir Gawain and the Green Knight*, which the author sees as reflecting the conflict between religious and secular groups that was waged throughout the century. Bibliographical references and index.

Andrew, Malcolm, and Robert Waldron, eds. *Poems of the Pearl Manuscript*. Exeter, Devon, England: University of Exeter Press, 2008. When this standard text, first published in 1978, appeared in 2007 in a substantially revised fifth edition, the new English prose translations were made available only on a compact disc. The 2008 volume contains the first print edition of these translations, which were intended to resemble the originals as closely as possible.

Armstrong, Dorsey. *Gender and the Chivalric Community in Malory's "Morte d'Arthur."* Gainesville: University Press of Florida, 2003. Demonstrates how markedly Malory's emphasis on gender identity departs from the treatment of gender in earlier Arthurian works, arguing persuasively that it is this theme that unifies the narrative.

Boitani, Piero, and Jill Mann, eds. *The Cambridge Companion to Chaucer*. 2d ed. New York: Cambridge University Press, 2003. Essays by various writers cover scholarship in the field and the application of new literary theories to Chaucer's works. Bibliographic essay, chronology, and index.

Burrow, J. A. *The Gawain-Poet*. Tavistock, Devon, England: Northcote House, 2001. A highly respected scholar discusses each of the Pearl-Poet's works, placing them in the context of medieval theory and practice. Bibliography and index.

Burrow, J. A., and Hoyt N. Duggan, eds. *Medieval Alliterative Poetry: Essays in Honour of Thoriac Turville-Petre*. Dublin: Four Courts Press, 2009. Includes several studies of *Piers Plowman*, as well as essays on the use of the alliterative form elsewhere.

Chaucer, Geoffrey. *The Riverside Chaucer*. 3d ed. Edited by Larry D. Benson. Based on *The Works of Geoffrey Chaucer*, edited by F. N. Robinson. Boston: Houghton Mifflin, 1987. Replaces Robinson's standard text. Contains the complete works, along with informative introductory materials, new explanatory notes, glossary, index of proper names, and bibliography. Indispensable for students of Chaucer.

Hirsh, John C., ed. *Medieval Lyric: Middle English Lyrics, Ballads, and Carols*. Annotated edition. Malden, Mass.: Blackwell, 2005. An anthology of fifty poems, all written between the thirteenth and fifteenth centuries, except for five American versions included for the purpose of comparison. Introduction and helpful commentaries by the editor. Punctuation and capitalization of the Middle English poems have been modernized, and side glosses explain unfamiliar words. Three appendixes contain additional lyrics. Annotated bibliography.

Holton, Amanda. *The Sources of Chaucer's Poetics*. Farnham, Surrey, England: Ashgate, 2008. Defines

Chaucer's poetic techniques by comparing several of his works with their textual sources. Bibliography and index.

Mehl, Dieter. *English Literature in the Age of Chaucer*. Harlow, Essex, England: Longman, 2001. A comprehensive survey of the period. In addition to discussions of Chaucer and his major contemporaries, there are chapters on the Scottish poets and the Middle English lyric. Notes and bibliography.

Newman, Barbara. *God and the Goddesses: Vision, Poetry, and Belief in the Middle Ages*. Philadelphia: University of Pennsylvania Press, 2003. A brilliant analysis of female figures in medieval Christian literature, suggesting that in fact the Church did not hold to inflexible monotheism. Bibliographical references and index.

Pearl-Poet. *Sir Gawain and the Green Knight*. Translated by Keith Harrison. New York: Oxford University Press, 2008. Annotated edition. An impressive new translation by poet Harrison. In the introduction, editor Helen Cooper places the work within the Arthurian tradition and comments on its poetic form and its narrative structure.

_____. *"Sir Gawain and the Green Knight," "Pearl," and "Sir Orfeo."* Translated by J. R. R. Tolkien. Boston: Houghton Mifflin, 1975. Tolkien is known to modern readers mainly as the author of *The Lord of the Rings* (1955), but he was better known during his lifetime as a medievalist and professor of English literature at Oxford University. His translations of Anglo-Saxon works are considered classics. His son Christopher Tolkien, who edited the work, includes a glossary and an appendix on verse forms.

Saul, Nigel, ed. *The Oxford Illustrated History of Medieval England*. New York: Oxford University Press, 2001. Provides a wealth of information on the social, cultural, and religious life of the period, covering topics as varied as the nature of national identity, the character of urban life, the great works of art and architecture, the details of religious practice, and the development of a vernacular literature. Illustrated with more than one hundred pictures—including twenty-four pages of color plates.

Scanlon, Larry, ed. *The Cambridge Companion to Medieval Literature, 1100-1500*. New York: Cambridge University Press, 2009. Essays on the major authors and the dominant genres of the period. Chronology and bibliography.

John Miles Foley

ENGLISH POETRY IN THE FIFTEENTH CENTURY

Dwarfed by the mighty accomplishments of Geoffrey Chaucer at one end and the great Elizabethans at the other, fifteenth century poetry has often seemed to stretch like a lesser plain between mountain ranges. There is some truth to this view: By no standard was this a distinguished age in the history of English verse. The English Chaucerian tradition, running from John Lydgate and Thomas Hoccleve to Stephen Hawes, can boast no major poet and only a paucity of significant minor ones, and rarely did fifteenth century works in the well-established popular genres of metrical romance, saint's life, and lyric match the high achievements of the century before. Indeed, the best-known literary productions of the 1400's—the prose Arthurian romance of Sir Thomas Malory and the dramatic cycles of the Corpus Christi season—belong to genres other than poetry. Poetry in this period may have suffered a general undervaluation owing to comparisons that it cannot sustain.

If one approaches fifteenth century poetry with chastened expectations and sensitivities attuned to the artistic aims of this period as distinct from others, one can find work of real interest and value. For example, although the age found little original stimulus in matters of poetic form, the carol attained its fullest development during this time, and the ballad was beginning to take shape. Finally, at the turn of the century, three Scots "makars"—Robert Henryson, William Dunbar, and Gavin Douglas—produced verse of a sufficiently high order to warrant labeling the reign of James IV a brief "golden age" of literary Scotland.

HISTORICAL CONTEXT

Although it is always hazardous to speculate on the connections between history and artistic felicity, it remains true that the political and social climate in the fifteenth century did not favor literary achievement. The international stage was still dominated by the Hundred Years' War with France; Henry V's successful invasion, crowned by the victory of Agincourt in 1415, committed his successors to a costly, protracted, and ultimately futile defense of this new French territory against the onslaughts of Joan of Arc and the French king. Meanwhile, in England itself the weakness of Henry VI encouraged factionalism and intrigue, which finally erupted in the Wars of the Roses between the Lancastrians and the Yorkists. It was a nation tired of war and depopulated of much of its nobility that welcomed the restoration of civil order in 1485 with the crowning of Henry VII and the establishment of the Tudor dynasty.

This political turbulence severely disrupted the patronage system on which art throughout the Middle Ages and into the Renaissance had always relied. Early in the century, Henry V had encouraged literary production, as had his brother, Humphrey of Gloucester. However, the decimation and financial impoverishment that subsequently exhausted the aristocracy could hardly serve to foster an atmosphere of courtly refinement such as had supported Chaucer and John Gower. Indeed, it is notable that the fifteenth century witnessed a contraction in most aspects of intellectual and cultural life. Architecture, the visual arts, philosophy, and theology all declined; only in music did the English excel, principally through the harmonic innovations of John Dunstable (1370?-1453). At the same time, the role of the poet seems to have been evolving from that of an entertainer in the tradition of medieval minstrelsy to one of an adviser to princes. Thus the prestige of erudition rose while the indigenous oral traditions fell further into disrepute.

SOCIAL CONTEXT

The rise of the middle class was another factor in the determination of literary tastes. Though depressed economically by the disorders in the middle of the century, this constituency ultimately gained in power as the aristocracy depleted its own ranks and resources. Simultaneously, education and literacy were spreading down the social pyramid. The gradual infiltration of Humanism from the Continent, particularly during the 1480's and 1490's, had as yet made no impression on the literary sensibility: What this new, conservative readership demanded was the familiar and time-honored—such as the lives of saints, or works of the revered Chaucer. This appetite fueled extensive copying of manuscripts, an activity culminating, as chance would have it, in a technological revolution when William Caxton established England's first printing press in 1476. The advent of widespread printing, following Johann Gutenberg's invention of movable type for the printing press, radically and permanently altered the availability of literary works and finally established the written text as the principal medium of poetic exchange.

GENRES AND VERSIFICATION

In their cumulative effect, these factors produced a literary conservatism that persisted throughout the century. Poets of this era turned to their own native tradition, particularly to Chaucer and Gower, for their models and stimulus, a practice contrasting radically with that of Chaucer himself, who wove into his verse many continental influences. Thus Chaucer's meters, the iambic pentameter and tetrameter, and his rhyme patterns, notably the ballade (*ababbcbc*) and rhyme royal (*ababbcc*) stanzas and the couplet, were widely imitated, even by poets with a most imperfect grasp of what they were imitating. These same poets likewise admired the poetic diction and the rhetorical elevation that Chaucer and Gower had standardized. This influence produced the inflated sententiousness, the rhetorical pomp, and the "aureation" (use of polysyllabic Latinisms) that modern readers often deplore in the verse of Lydgate and his followers.

However, fifteenth century poets adopted larger poetic forms as well. The many allegories and dream visions of the period clearly model themselves on Chaucer's work and that of his contemporaries. Other genres, such as the romance and lyric, continued to draw upon the same reserve of verse forms, topoi, story patterns, and subjects. Nowhere is the conservative character of the period better revealed than in the inclination toward verse translation. Of course, this was nothing new: The Middle Ages always had great respect for authority, and most writers—even the best worked from sources. The sheer bulk of fifteenth century translation obtrudes nevertheless, particularly in the number of major works that fall into this class. Lydgate's 36,365-line *The Fall of Princes* 1430-1438,

printed 1494), for example, was his longest poetic effort. Further, with the exception of Gavin Douglas's version of Vergil's *Aeneid* (c. 29-19 B.C.E.; English translation, 1553), seldom do the translations, despite their frequent expansion and supplementation of the originals, stand as significant poetic works in their own right; John Walton's competent yet poetically uninspired rendering of Boethius's *De consolatione philosophiae* (523; *The Consolation of Philosophy*, late ninth century) represents the best that the age produced. However sympathetically perceived, this widespread tendency to rely on the matter and inspiration of the past must ultimately be admitted as a weakness in much fifteenth century poetry, translated or otherwise. Rarely do the versifiers exhibit the ability of great traditional poets to return to and re-create the myths embedded in the traditional material.

THE CHAUCERIAN TRADITION

In the late fourteenth century Chaucer, drawing on the French tradition of courtly love and allegory that he found in *Le Roman de la rose* (thirteenth century), translated part of it as *Romaunt of the Rose* (*The Romance of the Rose*, complete translation 1900), and brought courtly poetry in England to its fullest perfection. His precedent inspired many imitations; allegories, love-debates, and dream visions throughout the fifteenth century attempted to recapture the Chaucerian magic. Although several of these labors show talent, one finds in this tradition little innovation or development beyond the point that Chaucer had reached.

Chaucer's first and historically most significant heir was John Lydgate (1370?-1451?), the prolific monk of Bury St. Edmunds whose influence and prestige over the next two hundred years rivaled those of his master. Written in almost every form and mode available to him, Lydgate's poetic corpus is staggering in its volume and variety: Taken collectively, his many allegories, romances, histories, courtly love poems, fables, epics, lyrics, hymns, prayers, didactic and homiletic works, and occasional pieces total some 145,000 lines. Lydgate's debt to Chaucer and the courtly love tradition appears most plainly in his early work of the first decade of the 1400's. *Complaint of the Black Knight* (wr. c. 1400; pb. 1885) features lovers' complaints in a dream-vision garden setting; in the 1,403-line *The Temple of Glass* (wr. c. 1403; pb. 1477), the poet in a dream visits a temple, styled after Chaucer's *House of Fame* (1372-1380), in which Venus joins a love-distressed knight and a lady. To this early period also belong versions of seven of Aesop's fables, representative of several didactic works in this vein composed by Lydgate at various times. Tales of Mariolatry loosely strung amid much digressive material constitute the 5,932-line *The Life of Our Lady* (wr. c. 1409; pb. 1484), another early work, and the harbinger of many later efforts in the genre of the saint's legend.

Lydgate's major works were the prodigious translations completed in his later years. Undertaken at the behest of Henry V, the *The Hystorye, Sege, and Dystruccyon of Troye* (wr. c. 1420; pb. 1513; better known as *Troy Book*) rendered Guido delle Colonne's Latin prose history of Troy into 30,117 lines in decasyllabic couplets. The tale of Oedipus and the rivalry of his two sons furnished the matter of the 4,176-line *The Siege of Thebes* (wr. c. 1422; pb. 1496), a tale embedded in a narrative frame attaching it to Chaucer's *The Canterbury Tales* (1387-1400). Begun in France in 1426 and probably completed two years later, the 24,832-line *The Pilgrimage of the Life of Man* (wr. c. 1426; pb. 1899-1904) translates and slightly expands Guillaume de Deguileville's fourteenth century *Pèlerinage de la vie humaine* (c. 1340). The lengthy and popular *Fall of Princes* (pb. 1494), composed for Humphrey of Gloucester between 1431 and 1439, generously renders into English Laurent de Premierfait's version of Giovanni Boccaccio's *De casibus virorum illustrium* (1355-1374; *The Fall of Princes*, 1431-1438), a compendium of medieval "tragedies" of men of greatness whom fickle fortune humbled. In addition to these major works, one finds myriad shorter pieces of every description poured forth profusely throughout the poet's long career.

Time has not smiled on Lydgate's literary reputation over the last two hundred years. Chief among his alleged sins is his prolixity, but critics also remark a prosodic weakness (especially in the prevalence of "broken-backed" lines), a tendency toward syntactic incoherence, and an infatuation with rhetoric and aureation. Other readers, however, finding these condemnations unduly harsh, note a human empathy, passages of lyric smoothness, and occasionally felicitous imagery, and a few have competently defended the poet's often-slandered craftsmanship. Although it is probable that Lydgate's poetic star will never rise to its former ascendency, it is also likely that future generations will find in his work merits that its amplitude has sometimes tended to obscure.

THOMAS HOCCLEVE

Less important historically yet in some regards more interesting is Thomas Hoccleve (1368?-1430?), a clerk of the Privy Seal whose attempts to secure patronage and pecuniary recompense would seem to have been less successful than desired. His magnum opus, the *Regement of Princes* (1412), occupies 777 stanzas of rhyme royal after the three-stanza envoi dedicating the work to Henry, prince of Wales. The body of the *Regement of Princes*, conflating material from three Latin sources, urges the young prince by means of exemplary tales to aspire toward virtue and to eschew vice. However, the most characteristic portion is the 288-stanza prologue, which amounts to an elaborate begging plea with many melancholy digressions and allusions to contemporary conditions. This autobiographical strain, allied with the many topical references and the poet's endearing love for Chaucer, whom he seems to have known personally, endows Hoccleve's verse with a human and historical interest that constitutes his main claim on posterity. On the other hand, his work lacks serious artistic intention, a sense of structural design, and stylistic distinction. Along with several shorter pieces, his other main poems are *La Male Règle* (1406), the *Letter of Cupid* (1402), and an autobiographically linked series including the *Complaint* (1422), the *Dialogue with a Friend* (1422), the *Tale of Jereslaus' Wife* (1422), *Knowing How to Die*, and the *Tale of Jonathas*.

JAMES I

Three other early "Chaucerians" require mention. Foremost among them is James I of Scotland (1394-1437), who spent most of his childhood as a prisoner of the English. Composed during his captivity, *The Kingis Quair* (1423-1424; better known as *The King's Choir*) pays tribute in 197 stanzas of rhyme royal to Lady Joan Beaufort, whom James married the next year (1424). In the poem the young monarch, complaining about his bad fortune, sees a beautiful woman through his cell window and is smitten with love. That night in a dream he visits Venus, Minerva, and Fortune, the last of whom promises the betterment of his affairs; on this hopeful note he awakes. Betraying a clear debt to Boethius's *The Consolation of Philosophy*, Chaucer's "The Knight's Tale," and Lydgate's *The Temple of Glass*, *The King's Choir* was written in the Scots dialect with Midlands admixtures and so occupies an important role in the emerging Scottish tradition.

OTHER WRITERS AND WORKS

Another captive nobleman, Charles d'Orleans (1391-1465) sprang directly from the French courtly tradition, writing in its language and traditional idiom. The main English translation, which Charles may have authored, is a three-part sequence of ballads and rondels dealing conventionally with the progress of several love affairs.

One further work from this early period was Sir John Thomas Clanvowe's *The Boke of Cupide* (1391). This May-time dream vision is dominated by a debate between a cuckoo, who slanders lovers, and a nightingale, who lauds them; the nightingale prevails, and the dream concludes with an assembly of birds. Composed in an unusual five-line stanza (*aabba*), this poem recalls such earlier works in the bird-debate tradition as the thirteenth century *Owl and the Nightingale* (c. 1250) and Chaucer's *Parlement of Foules* (1380).

The allegorical tendency found in *The Temple of Glass* emerges again in a group of poems from the later fifteenth century, most of which were at one time or another apocryphally attributed to Chaucer. One of the finest of these, *The Flower and the Leaf*, depicts through the eyes of a female narrator an amusing incident involving the followers of the Leaf (the laurel) and the followers of the Flower (the daisy). Skillfully composed in 595 lines of rhyme royal, *The Flower and the Leaf* invests its lightly allegorized narrative with much charm of image and detail. Somewhat heavier in its allegorical machinery, the 756-line *Assembly of Ladies* features such characters as Perseverance, Diligence, Countenance, Largesse, Remembrance, and Loyalty. Less courtly and more didactic, the *Court of Sapience*, sometimes attributed to Stephen Hawes, confronts a traveler with a more scholastic variety of allegorical personifications—such as Peace, Mercy, Righteousness, Truth, and the seven arts. Hawes's *The Pastime of Pleasure*, composed shortly before its publication in 1509, recounts the allegorical adventures of Graunde Amour on his road toward knightly perfection and the love of La Belle Pucel. Another early sixteenth century work, *The Court of Love*, far more skillfully narrates Philogenet's visit with Alcestis and Admetus at the Court of Love and recounts his successful wooing of Rosiall; the action closes with a celebration and birdsongs of praise. Thoroughly Chaucerian in form and intention, these poems mark the end of the courtly tradition in medieval English literature.

THE LYRIC

The term "lyric" suggests to most modern readers a highly individualized expression of some personal feeling in concrete language treating a subject of the poet's choice, yet this notion proves misleading in the case of the medieval English lyric. Although this body of poems indeed concerns itself with feelings, the individuality of the poet has been largely effaced; thus most of the surviving pieces are anonymous, not merely because the names of the authors are unknown (with a few exceptions, such as John Audelay and James Ryman), but in the nature of the expression. Moreover, the subjects, the basis on which these poems are usually classified, belong to a common cultural word hoard that also provides much of the standard imagery and diction. The consequence is a poetic genre expressive of what might be called "public experience"—moods, thoughts, and emotions defined and recognized in the public mind.

The essential continuity of the English medieval lyric from its beginnings in the mid-thirteenth century to the closing of the Middle Ages reveals itself in the persistence of certain lyric types, such as the Passion poem (treating Christ's Passion), the hymn to Mary, and the praise and complaint of lovers. The fifteenth century brought its share of changes. One new development was a growing literary self-awareness with a corresponding loss of freshness and spontaneity, characteristics that had distinguished early English lyrics from their more artificial French counterparts. New motifs came into prominence, such as the Marian lament; other poems elaborated old themes to greater lengths with an increasingly aureate diction.

The fifteenth century's most distinctive contribution lay in the flowering of a relatively new lyric form, the carol. Medieval English lyrics in general, employing a variety of metrical and stanzaic patterns, share no defining formal characteristics. The carol differs in this regard: R. L. Greene, the editor of the standard anthology, defines this lyric type as "a song on any subject, composed of uniform stanzas and provided with a burden." Sung at the beginning and repeated after every stanza, the burden is a group of lines, most often a couplet, that usually signals a major theme or subject in the poem. Some claim that the carol originated as a dance song. In any event, it is clear that during the fifteenth century the carol was developing a connection with the Christmas season; many explicitly celebrated the Nativity in a manner familiar to modern readers from Christmas carols of the present era. The genre was not restricted to this subject, however; one of the most beautiful and haunting of all carols is a Passion elegy whose burden runs, "Lulley, lulley, lulley, lulley;/ The fawcon hath born my mak away."

Medieval lyrics are usually classified on the basis of subject into two groups, the religious and the secular, with the religious poems being far more numerous. The most popular subject was the Virgin, whose cult still flourished in the late Middle Ages. Some of these Marian poems, adopting the conventions of secular love verse, proclaimed her inexpressible beauty, or praised her bodily parts, or begged for her mercy, or presented her with a Valentine's Day offering. More often, however, these lyrics derived from the Latin liturgical tradition. Many such pieces celebrated various of the Virgin's five joys—the Annunciation, the Nativity, the Resurrection, the Ascension, and the Assumption; "The Maiden Makeles" is a particularly famous Nativity song. God and Christ were often the objects of address; "Close in my Breast thy Perfect Love" harks in its intimate tenderness back to the fourteenth century mystical tradition of Richard Rolle. Christ's Passion provided another major subject in poems that tended toward a more extended narrative treatment and greater

didacticism than in previous periods. In one common and distinctive type of Passion poem, Christ himself addresses humanity directly from the Cross. A new fifteenth century trend introduced the theme of Mary's compassion and her participation in Christ's suffering. Lyrics in the *planctus* mode give expression to her grief; other poems present this theme through dialogues between the Virgin and Son.

Turning to the secular lyrics, one finds in the fifteenth century, as in most ages, a preponderance of love songs. All the expected types appear: praise to a lady and enumeration of her beauties, complaints about her cruelty and fickleness, laments on a lover's absence, and epistles, such as the one that opens "Go, litull bill, and command me hertely/ Unto her. . . ." Some lyrics take the form of antifeminist diatribes; others are plainly pornographic. One interesting anonymous series, *The Lover's Mass*, tastefully mimics the liturgy in fine love poems bearing such titles as the *Introibo*, *Kyrie*, and *Gloria*. A dramatic framework informs the highly praised "Nut Brown Maid," a debate between a woman and an earl's son disguised as a knightly outlaw which culminates in a self-revelation and a marriage offer. Other types of secular lyrics include drinking songs, charms and gnomes, and poems on historical events. In the meditations on fortune and worldly happiness, one can once more discern a growing religious tone in the contemplation of human affairs, a tone that emerges explicitly in the songs on death, the penitential confessions, and the homilies on virtue and vice. Cutting across this entire dichotomy of the secular and the religious are lyric types distinguishable by their objects of address. Poems addressed to the reader tend toward didacticism; lyrics addressing a third party (such as the Virgin or a human beloved) define themselves between the polarities of celebration and of complaint or petition. An appreciation for both strains, the didactic and the celebratory, is an essential prerequisite to any competent reading of medieval lyrics.

ROMANCES

During the fifteenth century two forms of popular narrative overlapped as the metrical romance declined and the ballad rose to supplant it. Though the relationship between these genres remains unsettled, both were probably circulated orally, and the traveling minstrel performers may have provided a line of continuity between them. This context of oral performance helps to explain in both cases the frequent verbal and narrative formulas that overly sophisticated readers are likely to condemn as "trite" and "stereotyped." At the same time, differences in subject matter and narrative technique clearly distinguish the two forms.

The first English romances appeared in the middle of the thirteenth century, at the very time when this aristocratic form had begun its decline in France. Descended from the chanson de geste, the French romance was a tale of knightly adventure that celebrated the ideals of bravery in battle, chivalric honor, courtesy, and service to a lady. Showing little concern for verisimilitude or psychological realism, these stories pitted their shallowly portrayed heroes against frequently supernatural and fabulous adversaries in a string of encounters joined less by a sense of "organic unity" than by a technique of narrative interlace. The English romances were regularly "translations" of such French works and exhibit many of these same characteristics. They also borrow most of their stories from the French cycles, specifically the "matters" of Britain (including the Arthurian cycle and unrelated "English" tales such as *Haveloc* written in the early thirteenth century), France (the Charlemagne cycle), and antiquity (including the cycles of Alexander, Troy, and Thebes). Other tales deal with the Orient, and a few bear no relation to any major cycle.

Fifteenth century romances have been relatively neglected in favor of Sir Thomas Malory's *Le Morte d'Arthur* (c. 1469, printed 1485), the greatest of the many prose narratives published by Caxton, yet the metrical romance persisted as a popular form: According to the *Wells Manual*, some thirty can be dated roughly from the fifteenth century, with a growing number from Scotland in the later decades. Lengths ranged from 516 lines in the cases of *The Grene Knight*, an unhappy condensation of the Pearl-Poet's *Sir Gawain and the Green Knight* (c. 1400), to the 27,852 lines of Henry Lovelich's *Merlin*, a translation of the prose French Vulgate. The most common verse patterns were rhyming octosyllabic couplets and tail-

rhyme stanzas, although occasionally other forms, such as the rhyme royal or ballade stanza, made their appearance. Although the alliterative revival had passed its prime, alliterative tendencies still persisted in Northumbria and Scotland, yielding late in the century such Middle Scots works as *Golagrus and Gawain* (c. 1500) and *The Taill of Rauf Coilyear* (c. 1475).

In their choice of subjects, fifteenth century romancers followed the established channels described earlier. One of the best-known Arthurian romances is the stanzaic *Morte Arthur* (c. 1360), a 3,969-line account of Lancelot's role in Arthur's downfall. Most of the romances from the Arthurian cycle depict the deeds of Gawain, who in the English tradition (unlike the French) remained for the most part a model knight. Two of the best Gawain romances are *The Avowynge of King Arthur, Sir Gawan, Sir Kaye, and Sir Bawdewyn of Bretan* (c. 1425), which follows each knight's separate path of adventure, and *Golagrus and Gawain*, whose plot hinges on a noble act of self-effacement by Gawain. After the Arthurian cycle, the next most popular source of lore for romance was the life of Alexander. *The Alliterative Alexander Fragment C* (c. 1450) verges on the epic; far more leisurely and episodic in its narrative style, the 11,138-line *Scottish Alexander Buik* (1438) is surpassed in length by another bulky Middle Scots poem, Gilbert Hay's 20,000-line *Buik of Alexander*. In other areas, the wars of Troy and Thebes inspired a handful of romances, two by Lydgate; a small group, including only *The Taill of Rauf Coilyear* and a Middle English *Song of Roland* (c. 1100), belong to the Charlemane cycle; five or six others, such as *Eger and Grime* (c. 1450) and John Metham's *Amoryus and Cleopes* (c. 1448), treat miscellaneous subjects. By 1500, the 250-year-old English metrical romance tradition had, with a few minor exceptions, reached an end.

BALLADS

David Fowler has argued that in the late Middle Ages, as the medieval minstrels were increasingly denied access to the courts of the higher nobility, the romance converged with the folk song to produce a shorter, simplified, less episodic narrative form that is now called the ballad. While the origins of balladry remain a controversial subject, it is certainly the case that the ballad is one of the few medieval forms that did not perish with the Renaissance and its aftermath, and as such it has a special claim to modern interest. The most thoroughly oral of the genres so far considered, the ballad could be defined as a short narrative poem, usually composed in two- or four-line stanzas, and distinguished by its concentration on a single event or episode. Unlike romances, which characteristically "tell" their stories, ballads tend to "show" their action directly through dramatic dialogue stripped of descriptive scene setting. The ballad style is formulaic: Tags, phrases, motifs, and episodes are repeated throughout the ballad tradition, and the poems themselves have survived in multiple versions. The general impersonality of the formulaic style is reinforced by the absence of a distinctive narrative persona. Although current opinion favors individual and not group composition, in its cumulative effect, balladry strikes one as reflecting the outlook of a community and tradition, not that of some particular person.

Although most extant ballads survive in collections from the seventeenth century and later, many of these poems may have originated in the fifteenth century or even before, for oral traditions have a well-demonstrated ability to transmit story patterns over remarkably long periods of time. The reconstruction of a specific ballad's evolution remains a speculative and subjective process, however, and there are a mere handful of documentably fifteenth century ballads, most of which narrate the adventures of Robin Hood. The choice of this legendary outlaw as a hero presents a departure from the usual practice of romancers with their knightly, aristocratic adventurers; indeed, later ballads do tend to draw subjects from middle-class life more often than romances had done. This point, however, should not be overemphasized: Ballads and romances retain many similarities of motif, story pattern, and even metrical form; in several cases, such as *Hind Horn* and *King Horn* (c. 1250), a ballad and romance relate the same story. However, during the fifteenth century the ballad had begun a life of its own that would lead in its peregrinations down to the modern day to a point far from its medieval origins.

OTHER FIFTEENTH CENTURY POETRY

The prestige of the courtly tradition did not obscure the power that religious narrative continued to exercise over the popular imagination. Indeed, collections of saints' lives of the type represented in the *South English Legendary* (thirteenth to fourteenth century) and the *Golden Legend* (c. 1260) enjoyed immense popularity throughout the century, although original composition in this vein was on the decline. Between 1443 and 1447, one of the most prolific of the religious versifiers, Osbern Bokenham, composed a group of thirteen saints' lives under the title *The Lives of Saints: Or, Legends of Holy Women*. The versatile Lydgate several times turned his hand to this genre; even John Capgrave, a learned friar who customarily wrote in prose, composed lives of Saint Norbert and Saint Katharine in rhyme royal. One must further note the numerous translations and verse paraphrases of books of the Bible, both Old and New Testaments, even if their literary achievement is slight.

A number of shorter poems address themselves to the events or conditions of the day. Major military conflicts such as the Battle of Agincourt and the Wars of the Roses inspired commemorative ballads and lyrics. A spirited series in prose and crude poetry, *Jack Upland* (c. 1389-1396), *Friar Daw's Reply* (c. 1420), and *Jack Upland's Rejoinder* (c. 1420), exchange blows on the subjects of friars and Lollardy. *London Lickpenny* (1515) vividly depicts life in the late medieval metropolis. Other poems in this satirical vein lament the state of the clergy and the general evils of the age.

A considerable bulk of the surviving poetry seems to be little more than versified prose. *The Libel of English Policy* (c. 1436), for example, makes recommendations on foreign trade policy in couplets and rhymed royal stanzas totaling 1,141 lines. Similarly, pragmatic intentions appear in John Russell's *Boke of Nurture* (c. 1460), an instruction on points of etiquette. By far the longest of these poems is Peter Idley's 7,000-line *Instructions to His Son*, which gives advice on a variety of subjects.

THE SCOTTISH MAKARS

In the fifteenth century in Scotland, an era concluding in military cataclysm as England crushed James IV and his Scottish forces at the Battle of Flodden Field in 1513, one finds a burgeoning literature with several poets or "makars" of real greatness. John Barbour, in many respects the founder of the English-language poetic tradition in Scotland, had already sounded a patriotic note in *The Bruce* (c. 1375), an epic romance celebrating the deeds of Robert the Bruce, national liberator and victor at the Battle of Bannockburn (1314). In 1423-1424, James I introduced a courtlier, more Chaucerian strain in *The Kingis Quair* (1423-1424; better known as *The King's Choir*). Two other poems sometimes ascribed to James, *Christis Kirk on the Green* and *Peblis to the Play*, initiate a Scottish comic tradition that continues in such works as *Sym and His Brudir*, *The Wyf of Auchtiramuchty*, *Cockelbie's Sow*, and even the romance *The Taill of Rauf Coilyear* (c. 1475). Exhibiting the superb mastery of an intricate, interlocking stanzaic pattern, *Christis Kirk on the Green* and *Peblis to the Play* are both distinguished for their vividly sketched rustic settings and their rough-and-tumble humor.

Meanwhile, the nationalistic and historical tradition of Barbour was carried on by Andrew of Wyntoun (1350?-1424) in his *Orygynale Chronikil of Scotland*, a lifeless history of the nation from Creation to the time of writing. Composed in octosyllabic couplets, Wyntoun's chronicle is best known now as the source of the Macbeth story that William Shakespeare found in Raphael Holinshed's *Chronicles of England, Scotland, and Ireland* (1577). By far the most popular and influential Scottish poem of the century was *The Wallace*, ascribed to a certain Blind Harry and completed before 1488. A companion piece to *The Bruce*, Harry's eleven-book heroic romance is based on the life of William Wallace (1272-1305), an unsuccessful Scottish insurgent a generation before Robert the Bruce. The first sustained Scottish work in decasyllabic couplets, *The Wallace* often irks modern readers with its chauvinistic romanticization, its repetitiveness, and its lack of psychological depth. At the same time, the poem does not lack enthusiasm, and many passages show real poetic power.

ROBERT HENRYSON

The work of Robert Henryson (c. 1425-c. 1505) and Dunbar is unrivaled in fifteenth century poetry, Scot-

tish or English. The label "Scottish Chaucerians" attached to these and other Middle Scots poets should be rejected, for it clouds their essential originality. Nevertheless, the poem for which Henryson is best known, *The Testament of Cresseid* (1532), is a 615-line continuation of the fifth book of Chaucer's *Troilus and Criseyde* (1382) in rhyme royal stanzas. Cresseid, rejected by Diomede, blasphemes against the gods, who accordingly punish her with leprosy. Troilus rides past one day and, pitying the wretched woman, whom he fails to recognize, tosses her a purse; learning the name of her benefactor, Cresseid repents, sends him a ring token, and dies. A poetic tour de force, *The Testament of Cresseid* presents a stern and uncompromising moral vision in which Cresseid falls as the result of her own wrongdoing; nevertheless, she ultimately finds redemption. Another major effort, the 633-line *Tale of Orpheus* (1508) interprets the Orpheus myth in a standard allegorical fashion. Of Henryson's some dozen minor poems, perhaps the best is "Robene and Makyne," a debate of wooing and rebuttal with an amusing dramatic reversal.

Henryson's magnum opus was his 2,975-line collection, *The Morall Fabillis of Esope, the Phrygian*, (1570; also known as *Fables*; twelve shorter poems of uncertain attribution). The didactic character of these thirteen fables of Aesop is reflected in the twenty to seventy-line *moralitas* following each one; composed in rhyme royal, the fables show in their ordering an awareness of total design. Henryson's poetry in general lacks the dazzling stylistic virtuosity of Dunbar's, although his meticulous craftsmanship cannot be faulted. His greatness lies more in his moral profundity, his detached, ironic humor, and his ability to depict the small and commonplace. In the sources of his learning and the tendency to allegorize, Henryson looks more to the Middle Ages than to the Renaissance; despite the usual Chaucerian influence and a competence in handling aristocratic themes, he belongs more to the parish pulpit than to the court.

WILLIAM DUNBAR

Henryson's temperamental opposite, William Dunbar (c. 1460-c. 1525), flourished in the court of James IV during the first decade of the sixteenth century until the demise of his royal patron at Flodden Field. Although he never attempted a work of much more than five hundred lines, his range of form and manner was otherwise matched only by the apparent fluctuations of his mood. "The Thrissill and the Rois" (1503), a dream vision in the Chaucerian allegorical fashion, celebrates the marriage of Margaret Tudor (the "Rose") and James IV (the "Thistle"). Another allegory of love, "The Goldyn Targe" (c. 1508), launches its poet-narrator into another dream vision before the court of Venus, where he is wounded by the arrows of Dame Beauty. Similar in spirit is "The Merle and the Nightingale," in which the two birds debate on the subject of love. "The Tretis of the Tua Mariit Wemen and the Wedo" treats love more satirically, as these depraved discussants contemplate sex and their husbands. Satire turns to invective in "The Flyting of Dunbar and Kennedy," a distinctively Scottish form in which the poetic contestants hurl at one another volleys of extravagant verbal abuse.

Dunbar also had his darker moments, as in "The Dance of the Sevin Deidly Synnis" (c. 1503-1508), in which the dreaming poet watches Mohammed preside over the grotesque festivities of his fiendish crew (Christian versus Muslim "infidels" being a common theme during the Middle Ages). "Lament for the Makaris" (c. 1508), with its refrain "Timor Mortis conturbat me" ("the fear of death disturbs me"), evokes the elegiac strain and the theme of the world's ephemerality that recur again in "This World Unstabille" and "In Winter"; a sonorous musical power adds weight to poems on the Nativity and the Resurrection. Among Dunbar's numerous remaining shorter poems, many were addressed to the king and the royal family. Some readers find Dunbar deficient in human sympathy and in his vision, but none can deny his imaginative inventiveness, tonal and emotional range, satirical humor tending toward the grotesque, and prosodic and stylistic genius that finds few equals in any period.

GAVIN DOUGLAS

Although Gavin Douglas (c. 1474-1522) turned to the classical world for his greatest literary attempt, the generality of his work, like that of his immediate peers and predecessors, belongs more to the Middle Ages than to the humanistic movements then stirring on the Continent and in England. His debt to the Chaucerian tradition appears in his early poems, *The Palice of Honour* (1501) and *King Hart* (attribution uncertain), both love allegories in the tired French and Chaucerian manner. His rendering of Vergil's *Aeneid* (c. 29-19 B.C.E.; English translation, 1553), into heroic couplets, completed just before Flodden Field in 1513, was the first; it remains one of the finest of all verse translations of this Vergilian masterpiece. Matching poetic style to social degree, Douglas employed heavy alliteration in passages relating to rustic characters and reserved a "noble" style for aristocratic matters. He also contributed an original prologue to each book. The total result, less a translation than a re-creation of the Roman epic into the Middle Scots language and idiom, exerted a regrettably minor influence on later poetry because of Scotland's political collapse and the rapid linguistic changes that followed. Flodden Field sounded the death knell to a literary era, but even as it did, English-language poetry was about to experience fresh influences and the revitalization of the Renaissance.

BIBLIOGRAPHY

Boffey, Julia, comp. *Fifteenth-Century English Dream Visions: An Anthology*. Annotated edition. New York: Oxford University Press, 2003. New editions of five dream visions. Introductory essays help to put each selection in context, and glossaries and annotations make the Middle English texts more accessible.

Boklund-Lagopoulou, Karin. *"I Have a Yong Suster": Popular Song and the Middle English Lyric*. Dublin: Four Courts Press, 2002. Discusses how serious poets often drew inspiration from popular songs, such as comic ballads, folk songs, ballads about outlaws or historical figures, and ballads of the supernatural. Bibliographical references and index.

Cooney, Helen, ed. *Nation, Court, and Culture: New Essays on Fifteenth Century Poetry*. Dublin: Four Courts Press, 2001. Essays by various scholars focus on the importance of courts and courtiers in the literature of the period. Among the topics discussed are courtly poetry, dream visions, complaints, and lyrics and carols. Bibliography and indexes.

Denny-Brown, Andrea, and Lisa H. Cooper, eds. *Lydgate Matters: Poetry and Material Culture in the Fifteenth Century*. New York: Palgrave Macmillan, 2008. Introduction by the editors; afterword by D. Vance Smith. Eight substantial essays on the background of Lydgate's poetry, his aesthetics, and his place in literary history.

Hirsh, John C., ed. *Medieval Lyric: Middle English Lyrics, Ballads, and Carols*. Annotated edition. Malden, Mass.: Blackwell, 2005. Introduction and commentaries by the editor. This anthology of fifty poems, forty-five of them in Middle English, includes five American versions printed with the originals. Punctuation and capitalization have been modernized, and side glosses explain unfamiliar words. Three appendixes contain additional lyrics. Annotated bibliography.

Mapstone, Sally, ed. *Older Scots Literature*. Edinburgh: John Donald, 2005. The first section of this volume consists of fourteen essays on fifteenth century writers and their works. One of the essays deals with the development of a Scottish "poetical anthology," and several discuss the poet and fabulist Robert Henryson.

Marshall, Simone Celine. *The Female Voice in The Assembly of Ladies: Text and Context in Fifteenth-Century England*. Newcastle upon Tyne, England: Cambridge Scholars, 2008. A study of a secular love poem that continues to interest scholars because it was written from a woman's perspective. By contrasting it with other fifteenth century texts, Marshall demonstrates how gender conventions influence women writers and readers.

Martin, Joanna. *Kingship and Love in Scottish Poetry, 1424-1540*. Farnham, Surrey, England: Ashgate, 2008. A thoughtful examination of the relationship between the relative youth of Scotland's rulers and the amatory themes found in many of the poetic narratives produced during their reigns, including those by Robert Henryson, William Dunbar, Sir David Lyndsay, and the lesser-known writers John Bellenden and William Stewart. Bibliography and index.

Scanlon, Larry. *Narrative, Authority, and Power: The Medieval Exemplum and the Chaucerian Tradition*. New York: Cambridge University Press, 1994. Explores the political and ideological significance of the medieval exemplum, a brief narrative form used to illustrate a moral, by studying four major works in the Chaucerian tradition (*The Canterbury Tales*, John Gower's *Confessio Amantis*, Thomas Hoccleve's *Regement of Princes*, and Lydgate's *Fall of Princes*).

Ward Parks

ENGLISH POETRY IN THE SIXTEENTH CENTURY

The poetry of the sixteenth century defies facile generalizations. Although the same can obviously be said for the poetry of other periods as well, this elusiveness of categorization is particularly characteristic of the sixteenth century. It is difficult to pinpoint a century encompassing both the growling meter of John Skelton and the polished prosody of Sir Philip Sidney, and consequently, past efforts to provide overviews of the period have proven unhelpful. Most notably, C. S. Lewis in his *English Literature in the Sixteenth Century Excluding Drama* (1954) contrived an unfortunate division between what he called "drab" poetry and "Golden" poetry. What he means by this distinction is never entirely clear, and Lewis himself further confuses the dichotomy by occasionally suggesting that his own term "drab" need not have a pejorative connotation, although when he applies it to specific poets, it is clear that he intends it to be damaging. Furthermore, his distinction leads him into oversimplifications. As Lewis would have it, George Gascoigne is mostly drab (a condition that he sees as befitting a poet of the "drab" mid-century) though blessed with occasional "Golden" tendencies, while Robert Southwell, squarely placed in the "Golden" period, is really a mediocre throwback to earlier "drab" poetry. Such distinctions are hazy and not helpful to the reader, who suspects that Lewis defines "drab" and "Golden" simply as what he himself dislikes or prefers in poetry.

The muddle created by Lewis's terminology has led to inadequate treatments of the sixteenth century in the classroom. Perhaps reinforced by the simplicity of his dichotomy, teachers have traditionally depicted the fruits of the century as not blossoming until the 1580's, with the sonneteers finally possessing the talent and good sense to perfect the experiments with the Petrarchan sonnet form first begun by Sir Thomas Wyatt early in the century. Students have been inevitably taught that between Wyatt and Sidney stretched a wasteland of mediocre poetry, disappointing primarily because so many poets failed to apply their talents to continuing the Petrarchan experiments begun by Wyatt. Thus, indoctrinated in the axiom that, as concerns the sixteenth century, "good" poetry is Petrarchan and "bad" poetry is that which fails to work with Petrarchan conceits, teachers deal in the classroom mostly with the poets of the 1580's and later, ignoring the other poetic currents of the early and mid-century. It has been difficult indeed to overcome Lewis's dichotomy of "drab" and "Golden."

Fortunately, there have been studies of sixteenth century poetry that are sensitive to non-Petrarchan efforts, and these studies deserve recognition as providing a better perspective for viewing the sixteenth century. In 1939, Yvor Winters's essay "The Sixteenth Century Lyric in England: A Critical and Historical Reinterpretation" focused on some of the less notable poets of the period, such as Barnabe Googe, George Turberville, and Gascoigne, who, until Winters's essay, had been dismissed simply because they were not Petrarchan in sentiment, and the essay also helped to dispel the notion that the aphoristic, proverbial content of their poetry was symptomatic of their simple-mindedness and lack of talent. By pointing out how their sparse style contributes to, rather than detracts from, the moral content of their poetry, Winters's essay is instrumental in helping the reader develop a sense of appreciation for these often overlooked poets. In addition to Winters's essay, Douglas L. Peterson's book *The English Lyric from Wyatt to Donne: A History of the Plain and Eloquent Styles* (1967), taking up where Winters left off, identified two major poetic currents in the sixteenth century: the plain style and the eloquent style. Peterson provided a more realistic and less judgmental assessment of the non-Petrarchans as practitioners of the "plain" rhetorical style, a term that was a welcome relief from Lewis's "drab." Thus, Winters's and Peterson's efforts were helpful in destroying the damaging stereotypes about the "bad" poets of the mid-century.

POETRY AS CRAFT

Despite the difficulties inherent in summarizing a century as diverse as the sixteenth, it is possible to discern a unifying thread running through the poetry of the period. The unity stems from the fact that, perhaps more than any other time, the sixteenth century was consistently "poetic"; that is, the poets were constantly aware of themselves as poetic craftsmen. From Skelton to Edmund Spenser, poets were self-conscious of their pursuits, regardless of theme. This poetic self-consciousness was manifested primarily in the dazzling display of metrical, stanzaic, and prosodic experimentation that characterized the efforts of all the poets, from the most talented to the most mediocre. In particular, the century experienced the development of, or refinement upon, for example, the poulter's measure (alternate twelve-and fourteen-syllable lines), blank verse, heroic couplets, rime royal, ottava rima, terza rima, Spenserian stanza, douzains, fourteeners—all appearing in a variety of genres. Characteristic of the century was the poet watching himself be a poet, and every poet of the century would have found himself in agreement with Sidney's assessment of the poet in his *Defence of Poesie* (1595) as prophet or seer, whose craft is suffused with divine inspiration.

SOCIAL CONTEXT

This process of conscious invention and self-monitoring is one key to understanding the poetry of the sixteenth century. It is a curious fact that whereas in other periods, historical and social factors play a large role in shaping poetic themes, in the sixteenth century, such extraliterary influences did little to dictate the nature of the poetry. Surprisingly, even though Copernicus's theory of a heliocentric universe was known by mid-century, the poetry barely nodded to the New Science or to the new geographical discoveries. Certainly, the century experienced almost constant political and religious turbulence, providing abundant fare for topical themes; a less apolitical period one can hardly imagine. It was the prose, however, more than the poetry, that sought to record the buffetings created by the fact that the official religion in England changed four times between 1530 and 1560.

It seems that the instability created by this uneasiness had the effect of turning the poets inward, rather than outward to political, social, and religious commentary (with the exceptions of the broadside ballads, pseudojournalistic poems intended for the unculti-

vated, and the verse chronicle history so popular at the close of the century), bearing out the hypothesis that good satire can flourish only in periods of relative stability. For example, despite the number of obvious targets, the genre of political satire did not flourish in the sixteenth century, and its sporadic representatives, in particular anticlerical satire, a warhorse left over from the Middle Ages, are barely noteworthy. A major figure in Spenser's *The Faerie Queene* (1590, 1596) is Gloriana, a figure depicting Queen Elizabeth, but she is an idealized rendering, only one of many such celebrations in poetry of Queen Elizabeth, not intended to provide a realistic insight into her character.

RISE OF VERNACULAR LANGUAGES

Thus, to the poet of the sixteenth century, the primary consideration of the poetic pursuit was not who or what to write about, but rather how to write. The reason for this emphasis on style over content is simple enough to isolate. By the middle of the sixteenth century, the English language was experiencing severe growing pains. In fact, throughout Europe the vernacular was struggling to overthrow the tyranny of Latin and to discover its essential identity. Nationalism was a phenomenon taking root everywhere, and inevitably, the cultivation of native languages was seen as the logical instrument of expediting the development of national identity. Italy and France were undergoing revolts against Latin, and Joachim du Bellay's *La Défense et illustration de la langue française* (1549; *The Defence and Illustration of the French Language*, 1939) proclaimed explicitly that great works can be written in the vernacular. In England, the invention of new words was encouraged, and war was waged on "inkhornisms," terms of affectation usually held over from the old Latin or French, used liberally by Skelton. Thus, George Puttenham, an influential critical theorist of the period, discusses the question of whether a poet would be better advised to use "pierce" rather than "penetrate," and Richard Mulcaster, Spenser's old headmaster, was moved to announce, "I honor the Latin, but I worship English."

It was no easy task, however, to legislate prescribed changes in something as malleable as language, and the grandeur of the effort nevertheless often produced comic results. Sixteenth century English vernacular, trying to weed out both Latin and French influences, produced such inelegant and uneasy bastardizations as "mannerlier," "newelties," "hable" (a hangover from Latin *habilis*), and "semblably," leading William Webbe in his *Discourse of English Poetry* (1586) to rail in a sneering pun about "this brutish poetry," with "brutish" looming as a veiled reference to "British." Although the sixteenth century was constantly discovering that the subtleties of perfecting a new language could not be mastered overnight, the effort was nevertheless sustained and paved the way for a future confidence in what the vernacular could achieve. Words that often strike the modern reader as outdated, stodgy pedantry are, in fact, the uncertain by-products of innovative experimentation.

Thus, to understand sixteenth century poetry is to ignore the stability of language, which is taken for granted in later centuries, and to understand the challenge that the poets experienced in shaping the new language to fit their poetry. Working with new words meant changes in the old classical syntax, and, in turn, changes in the syntax meant changes in the old classical versifications. These changes often resulted in frustration for the poet (and for the reader), but, depending on the skills of the poet, the result of all this experimentation could mean new rhyme schemes, new meters, and new stanzaic structures. In the wake of all the excitement generated by this constant experimentation, the poets cannot be blamed for often judging innovations in content as secondary to the new prosody. The volatility and flux of the language siphoned all energies into perfecting new styles not into content.

TRANSLATIONS

The zeal for metrical experimentation that characterized the sixteenth century is manifested not only in the original poetry of the period but also in the numerous translations that were being turned out. The primary purpose of the translations was to record the works of the venerable authorities in the new vernacular, and it is significant that Webbe refers to these works not as being "translated" but as being "Englished." Vergil's *Aeneid* (c. 29-19 B.C.E.; English translation, 1553) was a favorite target for the transla-

tors, with Henry Howard, the earl of Surrey, publishing a translation in 1553, Thomas Phaer in 1558, and Richard Stanyhurst in 1582. Stanyhurst translated only the first four books, and he achieved a metrical monstrosity by attempting to translate Vergil in English hexameters, reflecting the tensions of cramming old subject matter into new forms. Ovid was another favorite of the translators. Arthur Golding translated the *Metamorphoses* (c. 8 C.E.; English translation, 1567) in 1567, and also in that year, Turberville translated the *Heroides* (before 8 C.E.; English translation, 1567), featuring elaborate experiments with the poulter's measure, fourteeners, and blank verse. Most of the translations of the period may be dismissed as the works of versifiers, not poets (with the exception of George Chapman's Homer, which has the power of an original poem), but they are valuable reflections of the constant metrical experimentations taking place and, subsequently, of the ongoing process of shaping the new vernacular.

LITERARY THEORY

An overview of the poetry of the 1500's would be incomplete without an introduction to the critical theory of the period and the ways in which it recorded the successes and failures of the new vernacular experimentations. Not surprisingly, critical theory of the age was abundant. An obvious representative is Sidney's *Defence of Poesie*. The elegance and polish of this argument for the superiority of poetry over any other aesthetic pursuit has made it the most outstanding example of Renaissance critical theory. The easy grace of the work, however, tends to obscure the fact that the new experiments in prosody had created a lively, often nasty debate in critical theory between the guardians of the old and the spokespersons for the new. There were many other works of critical theory closer than the *Defense of Poesie* to the pulse rate of the arguments.

The turbulent nature of the critical theory of the period (and, by implications, the turbulence of the poetry itself) is reflected by Gascoigne, who in his "Certayne Notes of Instruction Concerning the Making of Verse" (1575) serves as a hearty spokesperson for the new vernacular, advocating a more widespread use of monosyllables in poetry and a rejection of words derived from foreign vocabularies so that "the truer Englishman you shall seem and the less you shall smell of the inkhorn," and decrying poets who cling to the old Latin syntax by placing their adjectives after the noun. In his *Art of English Poesy* (1589), Puttenham scolds those poets who "wrench" their words to fit the rhyme, "for it is a sign that such a maker is not copious in his own language." Not every critic, however, was so enchanted with the new experimentation. In his *Art of Rhetorique* (1553), Thomas Wilson called for continued practice of the old classical forms, and he sought to remind poets that words of Latin and Greek derivation are useful in composition. Contempt for new techniques in versification pervades Roger Ascham's *The Schoolmaster* (1570). He condemns innovations in rhyming, which he dismisses as derived from the "Gothes and Hunnes," and calls for renewed imitation of classical forms. In his *Discourse of English Poetry* (1586), William Webbe is even less charitable. He scorns the new experiments in prosody as "this tinkerly verse," and he campaigns for keeping alive the old, classical quantitative verse, in which the meter is governed by the time required to pronounce a syllable, not by accentuation. Clearly the severity of the critical debate needs to be kept in the forefront as one begins consideration of the poetry of the period; to fail to do so is to overlook what the poets were trying to accomplish.

ALLEGORIES AND DREAM VISIONS

The opening of the sixteenth century, however, was anything but a harbinger of new developments to come. Like most centuries, the sixteenth began on a conservative, even reactionary note, looking backward to medieval literature, rather than forward to the new century. Allegories and dream visions written in seven-line stanzas, favorite vehicles of the medieval poets, dominated the opening years of the sixteenth century. Under Henry VII the best poets were Scottish—William Dunbar, Gavin Douglas, and Sir David Lyndsay—and they were devoted imitators of Geoffrey Chaucer. The first English poet to assert himself in the new century was Stephen Hawes, who published *The Pastime of Pleasure* in 1509 which represented uninspired medievalism at its worst. The work is constructed as a

dream-vision allegory. An almost direct imitation of John Lydgate's work, *The Pastime of Pleasure* narrates the hero Grand Amour's instruction in the Tower of Doctrine, employing a profusion of stock, allegorical characters reminiscent of the morality plays. The old medieval forms, especially those combining allegory and church satire, were hard to die. In 1536, Robert Shyngleton wrote *The Pilgrim's Tale*, a vulgar, anticlerical satire directly evocative of Chaucer, and as late as 1556, John Heywood wrote *The Spider and the Fly*, a lengthy allegory depicting the Roman Catholics as flies, the Protestants as spiders, and Queen Mary as wielding a cleanig broom.

JOHN SKELTON

Another heavy practitioner of the dream allegory was John Skelton (c. 1460-1529), one of the most puzzling figures of the century. Skelton has long been an object of negative fascination for literary historians—and with good reason. He deserves a close look, however, because, despite his reactionary themes, he was the first metrical experimenter of the century. His paradoxical undertaking of being both metrical innovator and medieval reactionary has produced some of the oddest, even comic, poetry in the English language. His infamous Skeltonic meter, a bewildering mixture of short, irregular lines and an array of varying rhyme schemes, relies on stress, alliteration, and rhyme, rather than on syllabic count, and as a result, the reader is left either outraged or amused. His subject matter was inevitably a throwback to earlier medieval themes. He wrote two dream-vision allegories, *The Bowge of Court* (1499), a court satire, and *The Garlande of Laurell* (1523). Skelton is still read today, however, because of his fractured meter. The theme of his *Collyn Clout* (1522), a savage satire on the corruption of the English clergy (whose title, incidentally, was the inspiration for Spenser's *Colin Clouts Come Home Againe*, 1591), is of interest to the modern reader not so much for its content as for its versification. In the work, Skelton describes his own rhyme as being "Tatterèd and jaggèd/ Rudely rain beaten/ Rusty and moth-eaten." Skelton's rhyme arrives fast and furious, and it is possible to conclude that he may have been the object of Puttenhm's attack on poets who "wrench" their words to fit the rhyme.

CONTINENTAL INFLUENCES

Despite his original metrical experimentation, Skelton was still entrenched in inkhornisms and looked backward for his themes. Paradoxically, as is often the case, it can be the poet with the least talent who nevertheless injects into his poetry vague hints of things to come. Alexander Barclay wrote no poetry of the slightest worth, but embedded in the mediocrity lay the beginnings of a new respect for the vernacular. To the literary historian, Barclay is of interest for two reasons. First, he was the sixteenth century's first borrower from the Continent. Specifically, in his *Certayn Egloges* (1570), he was the first to imitate the eclogues of Mantuan, which were first printed in 1498 and which revolutionized the genre of the pastoral eclogue by making it a vehicle for anticlerical satire, although such satire was of course nothing new in England at that time. Barclay's second importance, however (and perhaps the more significant), lies in the fact that he was the first to use the vernacular for the pastoral.

TOTTEL'S MISCELLANY

It was not until mid-century that English borrowings from the Continent were put on full display. In 1557, a collection of lyrics known as *Tottel's Miscellany* was published, and the importance of this work cannot be overemphasized. It was innovative not only in its function as a collection of poems by various authors, some of them anonymous, but also in the profusion of prosodic experimentation that it offered. *Tottel's Miscellany* represented nothing less than England's many-faceted response to the Continental Renaissance. In this collection, every conceivable metrical style (including some strange and not wholly successful experiments with structural alliteration) was attempted in an array of genres, including sonnets, epigrams, elegies, eulogies, and poems of praise and Christian consolation, often resulting in changes in the older Continental forms. Truly there is no better representation of poets self-consciously watching themselves be poets.

Nevertheless, unfair stereotypes about the collection abound. Perhaps because of Lewis's distinction between "drab" age and "Golden" age poetry, students are often taught that the sole merit of *Tottel's Miscellany* is its inclusion of the lyrics of Wyatt and Surrey (which had been composed years earlier)—in particular, their imitations of the amatory verse of Petrarch. The standard classroom presentation lauds Wyatt and Surrey for introducing Petrarch and his sonnet form into England. Students are further taught that the long-range effects of *Tottel's Miscellany* proved to be disappointing since no poet was motivated to continue Wyatt's and Surrey's experiments with Petrarch for decades thereafter. Thus, *Tottel's Miscellany* is blamed for being essentially a flash-in-the-pan work lacking in any significant, literary influence. Such disappointment is absurdly unjustified, however, in view of what the publisher Richard Tottel and Wyatt and Surrey were trying to accomplish. Tottel published his collection "to the honor of the English tong," and in that sense the work was a success, as the conscious goal of all its contributors was to improve the vernacular. Furthermore, its most talented contributors, Wyatt and Surrey, accomplished what they set out to do: to investigate fully the possibilities of the short lyric, something that had never before been attempted in England, and, in Surrey's case, to experiment further with blank verse and the poulter's measure.

By no stretch of the imagination did Wyatt view himself as the precursor of a Petrarchan movement in England, and he made no attempt to cultivate followers. In fact, despite the superficial similarity of subject matter, Wyatt's poetry has little in common with the Petrarchan sonneteers of the close of the century, and he most assuredly would have resented any implication that his poetry was merely an unpolished harbinger of grander efforts to come. As Douglas L. Peterson has pointed out, Wyatt used Petrarch to suit his own purposes, mainly to perfect his "plain" style; and Yvor Winters maintains that Wyatt is closer to Gascoigne than Sidney. Whereas the sonneteers of the close of the century composed decidedly in the "eloquent" style, Wyatt expressed contempt for trussed-up images and pursued the virtues of a simple, unadorned style.

PLAIN STYLE

Thus, far from attempting to initiate a new "movement" of Petrarchan eloquence, many of the poems in *Tottel's Miscellany* sought to refine the possibilities of the plain style. As Peterson defines it, the plain style is characterized by plain, proverbial, aphoristic sentiments. It is a style often unappreciated by modern readers because its obvious simplicity is often mistaken for simplemindedness. The practitioners of the plain style, however, were very skilled in tailoring their verse to fit the needs of the poem's message, the pursuit of simplicity becoming a challenge, not a symptom of flagging inspiration. Skelton unwittingly summarizes the philosophy of the plain style when, commenting on his rhyme in *Collyn Clout*, he instructs the reader: "If ye take well therewith/ It hath in it some pith."

Thus, a plain-style poet expressing disillusionment with the excesses of love or extolling the virtues of frugality, rather than adorning his poem with an abundance of extravagant images, he instead pared his sentiments down to the minimum, with the intense restraint itself illuminating the poet's true feelings about love or money. The desiderata of the plain style were tightness and disciplined restraint. In the hands of an untalented poet, such as Heywood, who wrote *A Dialogue of Proverbs* (1546, 1963), the aphoristic messages could easily become stultifying; but as practiced by a poet with the skill of Wyatt, the economy of rendering a truth simply could produce a pleasurable effect. Interestingly, near the close of the century, when the eloquent style was all the rage, Sir Walter Ralegh, Thomas Nashe, and Fulke Greville often employed the techniques of the plain style.

FURTHER ANTHOLOGIES

The three decades following the publication of *Tottel's Miscellany* have been stereotyped as a wasteland when poetry languished desultorily until the advent of the sonneteers in the 1580's. Nothing could be more unfair to the poetry of the period than to view it as struggling in an inspirational darkness. Amazingly, such a stereotype manages to overlook the profusion of poetry collections that *Tottel's Miscellany* spawned. Though admittedly the poetry of some of these collections is forgettable, nevertheless the continual appearance of these collections for the next fifty years is an impressive indication of the extent to which Tottel's philosophy of prosodic experimentation continued to exert an influence.

The first imitation of Tottel to be published was *The Paradise of Dainty Devices* (1576), the most popular of the imitations. As its title would indicate, a number of

amatory poems were included, but the predominant poems had didactic, often pious themes, which offered ample opportunity for further experimentation in the plain style. A number of reasonably accomplished poets contributed to the collection, including Sir Richard Grenville, Jaspar Heywood, Thomas Churchyard, and Barnabe Rich. Another successful collection was *Brittons Bowre of Delights* (1591), interesting for its wide range of metrical experimentation, especially involving poulter's measure and the six-line iambic pentameter stanza.

Imitations of Tottel's works did not always prove successful. In 1577, *A Gorgeous Gallery of Gallant Inventions* appeared, a monotonous collection of poems whose oppressive theme was the vanity of love and pleasure, and it was as plagued with affectations and jargon as *Brittons Bowre of Delights* was blessed with fresh experimentation. Not everyone was pleased, however, with the new direction the lyric was taking after Tottel. In 1565, John Hall published his *Court of Virtue*, an anti-Tottel endeavor designed to preach that literature must be moral. In his work the poet is instructed by Lady Arete to cease pandering to the vulgar tastes of the public and instead to write moral, instructive lyrics, an appeal which results in the poet's moralizing of Wyatt's lyrics.

The experimental spirit of Tottel carried over into the works of individual poets, as well. From such an unlikely source as Thomas Tusser's *A Hundreth Good Points of Husbandry* (1557), an unassuming almanac of farming tips, explodes a variety of metrical experimentation, including Skeltonics, acrostics, and other complicated stanzaic forms. Despite his willingness to experiment, however, Tusser was not an accomplished talent, and thus there are three poets, Googe, Turberville, and Gascoigne, to whom one must turn to refute the stereotype of the mid-century "wasteland." Too often viewed as bungling imitators of Tottel, these poets deserve a closer look as vital talents who were keeping poetry alive during the so-called wasteland years.

BARNABE GOOGE

In his *Eclogues, Epitaphs, and Sonnets* (1563), Barnabe Googe's explicit poetic mission was to imitate Tottel. Working mostly in the didactic tradition, he wrote some epitaphs and poems in praise of friends, but his eclogues are of primary interest to the literary historian. He revived the Mantuan eclogue, which had been lying dormant in England after Barclay, and his eclogues were good enough to offer anticipations of Spenser's *The Shepheardes Calender* (1579). Another noteworthy work is his *Cupido Conquered* (1563), a dream-vision allegory, which Lewis dismissed as "purely medieval." The dismissal is unfair, however, because, despite the throwback to medieval devices, the plot, in which the languishing, lovesick poet is chided by his muses for his shameful lack of productivity, reveals Googe's self-consciousness of himself as craftsman, a characteristic pose for a poet of the sixteenth century.

GEORGE TURBERVILLE

George Turberville's dexterity with metrics in his translation of Ovid has already been mentioned. Like Googe, Turberville, in his *Epitaphs, Epigrams, Songs, and Sonnets* (1567), carried on with Tottelian experimentation, primarily in didactic poems employing poulter's measure and fourteeners written in the plain style.

GEORGE GASCOIGNE

George Gascoigne has been late in receiving the attention that he deserves, his poetry serving as the most impressive evidence disproving the existence of a post-Tottel wasteland. Predictably, Lewis describes him as a precursor of golden age poetry, ignoring Gascoigne's contributions to the plain style. In his *A Hundreth Sundrie Flowres Bounde up in One Small Poesie* (1573, poetry and prose; revised as *The Posies of George Gascoigne Esquire*, 1575), Gascoigne was the first to experiment with Petrarch and the sonnet form since Wyatt and Surrey, but he was no slavish imitator. Gascoigne's poetry is often coarser and more lewd than that of Petrarch, but he never sacrifices a robust wit. In addition, he is an interesting figure for his variations in the sonnet form, featuring the octave-sestet division of the Petrarchan form, but in an English, or *abab* rhyme scheme. Puttenham refers to his "good meter" and "plentiful vein."

ELIZABETHAN POETRY

Thus, the poetry of the latter part of the century, the great age of the eloquent style, must not be viewed as a semimiraculous phoenix, rising from the ashes between Wyatt's experiments with Petrarch and the advent of Sidney. Nevertheless, it must be noted that the Elizabethan era ranks as one of the outstanding poetic periods of any century, its development of the eloquent style ranking as an outstanding achievement. A valuable representative of what the eloquent style was trying to accomplish is Sir John Davies' *Orchestra: Or, A Poeme of Dauncing* (1596, 1622). In his *Elizabethan World Picture* (1943), E. M. W. Tillyard analyzes the poem at length as a fitting symbol of the Elizabethans' obsession with cosmic order. Though accurate enough, Tillyard's discussion places too much emphasis on the poem's content and does not pay enough attention to the style in which the message is delivered. In the poem, the suitor Antinous launches an elaborate discourse designed to persuade Penelope, waiting for her Odysseus to return, to dance. Through Antinous's lengthy and involved encomium to cosmic order and rhythm, Davies was not attempting a literal plea to Penelope to get up and dance. Rather, he was using Antinous as a vehicle for an ingenious argument, ostentatious in its erudition and profusion of images; in effect, Antinous's argument is the repository of Davies' experiments in the eloquent style. It is the dazzling display of the process of argumentation itself, not the literal effort to persuade Penelope, that is the essence of the poem. The way in which the poem is written is more important than its content, and in that sense (but in that sense only) the goal of the eloquent style is no different from that of the plain style.

PETRARCHAN AND "ELOQUENT" STYLE

When one thinks of sixteenth century poetry and the eloquent style, however, one almost immediately thinks of the Petrarchan sonnet sequence, and one explanation for the almost fanatic renewal of interest in Petrarch was the inevitable shift of interests in poetic style. The plain style, so dominant for almost half a century, was beginning to play itself out, a primary indication being the decline in use of the epigram, whose pithy wit held little appeal for Elizabethan poets. The more skillful among them were anxious to perfect a new style, specifically the "eloquent" style, almost the total antithesis of the plain style. Not particularly concerned with expressing universal truths, the eloquent style, as practiced by Davies, sought embellishment, rather than pithy restraint, and a profusion of images, rather than minimal, tight expression. The eloquent style effected some interesting changes in the handling of the old Petrarchan themes, as well. It should be noted that in his experiments with Petrarch, Wyatt chafed at the indignities suffered by the courtly lover. By contrast, the sonneteers emphasized with relish the travails of the lover, who almost luxuriates in his state of rejection. In fact, there is no small trace of fin de siècle decadence in the cult of the spurned lover that characterized so many of the sonnets of the period, most notably Sidney's *Astrophel and Stella* (1591), and it decidedly signaled the end of the plain style.

SONNETS AND SONNET SEQUENCES

The sonnet sequence, a collection of sonnets recording the lover's successes and failures in courting his frequently unsympathetic mistress, was practiced by the brilliant and mediocre alike. Of course, the two most outstanding poets of the century pioneered the form—Sidney in his *Astrophel and Stella*, who in the true spirit of the poetic self-consciousness of the century wrote sonnets about the writing of sonnets and wrote some sonnets entirely in Alexandrines, and Spenser in his *Amoretti* (1595), who, in addition to introducing refinements in the sonnet structure, also intellectualized the cult of the rejected lover by analyzing the causes of rejection.

In the next twenty years the contributions to the genre were dizzying: Greville's *Caelica* (wr. 1577, pb. 1633); Thomas Watson's *Passionate Century of Love* (1582); Samuel Daniel's *Delia* (1592); Henry Constable's *Diana* (1592); Thomas Lodge's *Phillis* (1593); Giles Fletcher's *Licia* (1593); Barnabe Barnes's *Parthenophil and Parthenophe* (1593); Bartholomew Griffin's *Fidessa* (1593); Michael Drayton's *Ideas Mirrour* (1594), noteworthy for its experiments with rhyme; *The Phoenix Nest* (1593), a collection of Petrarchan sonnets in a wide variety of meters by George Peele, Nicholas Breton, Thomas Lodge, and others—the list of accomplished poets and tinkering poetasters was almost endless.

By the close of the century, so many mediocre poets

had turned out sonnet sequences, and the plight of the rejected lover had reached such lugubrious proportions that the form inevitably decayed. The cult of the masochistic lover was becoming tediously commonplace, and one of the major triumphs of the eloquent style, the Petrarchan paradox (for example, Wyatt's "I burn, and freeze like ice") lost its appeal of surprise and tension as it became overworked, predictable, and trite. The genre had lost all traces of originality, and it is interesting to consider the fact that the modern definition of a sonneteer is an inferior poet. As early as 1577, Greville in his *Caelica* had perceived how easily in the sonnet sequence numbing repetition could replace fresh invention, and to maintain some vitality in his sequence his subject matter evolves from the complaints of the rejected lover to a renunciation of worldly vanity and expressions of disappointment in the disparity between "ideal" love and the imperfect love that exists in reality. (For this reason, of all the sonneteers Greville is the only precursor of the themes so prevalent in seventeenth century devotional poetry.)

The success and subsequent decline of the sonnet sequence left it wide open to parody. Many of the sonnets of William Shakespeare, who himself revolutionized the sonnet structure in England, are veiled satiric statements on the trite excesses of Petrarchan images ("My mistress's eyes are nothing like the sun"), indicating his impatience with the old, worn-out sentiments. Davies' collection of *Gulling Sonnets* (c. 1594) was an explicit parody of Petrarchan absurdities and weary lack of invention, and, following their publication, the genre spun into an irreversible decline.

MYTHOLOGICAL-EROTIC NARRATIVE

As the sonnet declined, however, another form of amatory verse was being developed: the mythological-erotic narrative. This form chose erotic themes from mythology, embellishing the narrative with sensuous conceits and quasipornographic descriptions. It was a difficult form to master because it required titillation without descending into vulgarity and light touches of sophisticated humor without descending into burlesque. Successful examples of the mythological-erotic narrative are Christopher Marlowe's *Hero and Leander* (1598; completed by Chapman), Shakespeare's

William Shakespeare performing before Queen Elizabeth and her court. (Library of Congress)

Venus and Adonis (1593), Chapman's *Ovid's Banquet of Sense* (1595), Drayton's *Endimion and Phoebe* (1595), and Lodge's *Scillaes Metamorphosis* (1589). Like the sonnet, the mythological narrative fell into decline, as evidenced by John Marston's *The Metamorphosis of Pygmalion's Image and Certain Satires* (1598), in which the decadence of the sculptor drooling lustfully over his statue was too absurdly indelicate for the fragile limits of the genre.

SATIRIC AND RELIGIOUS VERSE

As the mythological narrative and the sonnet declined, both social satire and religious verse experienced a corresponding upswing. The steady growth of a middle-class reading audience precipitated an increased interest in satire, a genre which had not been represented with any distinction since Gascoigne's *The Steele Glas, a Satyre* (1576). Understandably, though inaccurately, Joseph Hall labeled himself the first En-

glish satirist. Juvenalian satire flourished in his *Virgidemiarum* (1597), similar to Davies' *Gulling Sonnets*, followed by Everard Guilpin's *Skialetheia: Or, Shadow of Truth in Certain Epigrams and Satyres* (1598), which attacks the "wimpring sonnets" and "puling Elegies" of the love poets, and Marston's *The Scourge of Villainy* (1598).

Perhaps feeling reinforced by the indignation of the satirists, religious verse proliferated at the end of the century. Bedazzled by the great age of the sonnet, the modern reader tends to generalize that the latter decades of the century were a purely secular period for poetry. Such a view, however, overlooks the staggering amount of religious verse that was being turned out, and it should be remembered by the modern reader that to the reader of the sixteenth century, verse was typified not by a Sidney sonnet, but by a versified psalm. Throughout the century, experiments with Petrarch ebbed and flowed, but the reading public was never without religious writings, including enormous numbers of sermons, devotional manuals, collections of prayers and meditations, verse saints' lives, devotional verse, and, of course, an overflow of rhyming psalters. Versifying the psalter had begun as early as the fourteenth century, but its popularity and practice went unsurpassed in the sixteenth. Although many excellent poets tried their hand at the Psalms, including Wyatt, Spenser, and Sidney, who saw them as legitimate sources of poetry, these versifications were led by the Thomas Sternhold and John Hopkins edition of 1549, and it represents a mediocre collection of verse. Nevertheless, the uncultivated reading public hailed it as an inspired work, and people who refused to read any poetry at all devoured the Sternhold and Hopkins edition. Popular collections among the Elizabethans were William Hunnis's *Seven Sobs of a Sorrowfull Soule for Sinne* (1583) and William Byrd's *Psalmes, Sonnets, and Songs of Sadnes and Pietie* (1588).

By the close of the century, attempts at religious verse by more accomplished poets were surpassing the efforts of hack versifiers. While the satirists were ridiculing the atrophied sonnet sequence on aesthetic grounds, other writers were attacking it on moral grounds, and perceptions of what poetry should be and do were shifting as the sonnet lost its influence. Having put a distance of four years between his *Astrophel and Stella* and the publication of his *Defence of Poesie*, Sidney authoritatively proclaimed in the latter work that poetry should celebrate God and Divine Love. Nashe attacks verse in which "lust is the tractate of so many leaves." Physical love was no longer au courant. In his "A Coronet for his Mistress Philosophy," Chapman reflects the new vogue of Neoplatonism by carefully identifying the differences between divine and physical love, also investigated meticulously by Spenser in his *Fowre Hymnes* (1596). Joshua Sylvester's translations between 1590 and 1605 of the works of the French Huguenot poet Guillaume du Bartas helped to reinforce Protestant piety and further counteracted the Petrarchans. The most saintly poet of the period was Southwell, a Jesuit. In his preface to his *Saint Peter's Complaint, with Other Poems*

(1595), Southwell laments that the teachings of Christ go unheeded as poets would rather celebrate the glories of Venus. In *Saint Peter's Complaint*, Peter excoriates himself for his denial of Christ, and the fact that the work is oddly adorned with sensuous conceits is an interesting indication that Petrarchan images managed to survive stubbornly, even in works inimical to their spirit. Finally, in 1599, Davies published his *Nosce Teipsum: This Oracle Expounded in Two Elegies*, whose theme was self-knowledge, rather than carnal knowledge of one's mistress, as well as the proper relationship between the soul and the body.

EDMUND SPENSER

The tug of war between the sonneteers and the religious poets was only one of several noteworthy poetic developments near the close of the century. Edmund Spenser, the most talented poet of the century, contributed to both sides of the battle (the *Amoretti* and *Fowre Hymnes*), but his versatility as a poet enabled him to transcend any one category. Spenser's early poetic career is not without its mysteries. No literary historian

Edmund Spenser (Library of Congress)

would have predicted that at a time when a new poetry was being refined by means of the sonnet form, someone would choose to revive the old medieval forms, but that is what Spenser did. *The Shepheardes Calender* is a throwback to the Mantuan eclogues, at this point almost a century old, and *Colin Clouts Come Home Againe* is reminiscent of Skelton's anticlerical satires. His "Prosopopoia: Or, Mother Hubberd's Tale" is an imitation of a medieval beast fable, and even *The Faerie Queene*, his most famous work, is essentially a compendium of medieval allegory and Italian epic forms derived from Ludovico Ariosto and Torquato Tasso. Furthermore, many of Spenser's works were written in a deliberately archaic style.

Thus a major contribution to Spenser's fame is not the originality of his themes but the range of his metrical and stanzaic experimentations. In a century characterized by poets self-consciously aware of themselves exercising their craft, Spenser was the apotheosis of the poetic craftsman. Though his archaic diction violated the tenets of many critics who believed that the vernacular must grow, Spenser's experiments in versification furthered the cause of making English more vital. Despite its reactionary themes, *The Shepheardes Calender* explodes with experimentation in poetic forms. The "January" eclogue is written in the six-line ballad or "Venus and Adonis" stanza, "February" is written in Anglo-Saxon accentual verse, "March" is written in the romance stanza of Chaucer's "Sir Topaz," "July" is written in a rough, vulgar ballad meter, and "August" is a contrast of undisciplined folk rhythms and elegant sestinas. Though not Spenser's most famous work, *The Shepheardes Calender* is nevertheless a remarkable symbol and culmination of the poetic self-consciousness of the sixteenth century and a fusion of the experiments in poetic versification that had helped to shape English as a suitable vehicle for poetry.

VERSE CHRONICLES

As the century was drawing to a close, a popular genre flourishing outside the continuing battle between amatory and religious verse was the verse chronicle history. Of all the genres popular in the sixteenth century, the verse chronicle history is probably the most difficult for the modern reader to appreciate, probably because of its excruciating length; but more than any other genre, it serves as a repository for Elizabethan intellectual, historical, and social thought, especially as it reflects the Elizabethan desire for political order, so amply documented by Tillyard in his *Elizabethan World Picture*.

The first treatment of English history in poetry was the landmark publication of *A Mirror for Magistrates* (1555, 1559, 1563). It was a collection of tragedies of famous leaders in the medieval tradition of people brought low by the turning wheel of Fortune and was written in rime royal, the favorite stanzaic vehicle of medieval narrative. The structure of its tragedies was imitated from John Lydgate's *Fall of Princes* (1494), and the constant themes of the tragedies were both the subject's responsibility to his king and the king's responsibility to God; if either the ruler or the subject should fail in his proper allegiance, disorder and tragedy would inevitably ensue. *A Mirror for Magistrates* was extraordinarily popular with a reading public desiring both entertainment and instruction. It went through eight editions in thirty years, with Thomas Sackville's "Induction" being considered at the time the best poem between Chaucer and Spenser.

The major importance of *A Mirror for Magistrates* is the fact that it fulfilled Sidney's mandate in his *Defence of Poesie* that the poet take over the task of the historian, and *A Mirror for Magistrates* exerted a powerful influence on the late Elizabethan poets. Pride in the royal Tudor lineage led not only the prose chroniclers but also the poets of the Elizabethan period to develop a strong sense of Britain's history. Shakespeare's history plays are widely recognized as reflections of England's growing nationalistic fervor, and because of the magnitude of the plays, it is easy to overlook the contributions of the poets to English history, or, perhaps more accurately, pseudohistory. The troublesome murkiness of Britain's origins were efficiently, if somewhat questionably, cleared up by exhaustive embellishments of the legends of Brut and King Arthur, legends that spurred England on to a sharpened sense of patriotism and nationalism. An obvious example is Spenser's chronicle of early British history at the end of book 2 of *The Faerie Queene*. In 1586, William Warner published his *Albion's England*, a long work ambitiously taking as its province all of historical time from Noah's Flood down to the execution of Mary, Queen of Scots.

The following years saw the publication of Daniel's *The First Fowre Bookes of the Civile Warres* (1595, 1599, 1601), whose books represented the apotheosis of all attempts at versified history. Like Shakespeare in his history plays, Daniel focused on a theme common in Elizabethan political theory, the evil that inevitably results from civil and moral disorder—specifically, the overthrow of Richard II. The modern reader has a natural antipathy toward the Elizabethan verse chronicles because of their length and because of the chroniclers' penchant for moral allegorizing, for their tedious accounts of past civil disorder as illustrative of present moral chaos, and for their far-reaching, interweaving parallels among mythological, biblical, and British history (for example, the Titans' defeat of Saturn being contrasted with the victory of Henry V at Agincourt in Heywood's "Troia Britannica," 1609). Nevertheless, these versified histories and their championing of moral order and nationalism constituted much of the most popular poetry of the Elizabethan period, and their impact cannot be overemphasized.

GROWTH AND TRANSITION

In retrospect, it is indeed astonishing to consider precisely how much the poetry of the sixteenth century grew after Hawes's allegories first limped onto the scene in 1509. The pressing need for most poets at the beginning of the century was to imitate medieval forms as faithfully as possible. There was no question as to the superiority of the classical authorities, and there was no "English" poetry as such. In 1531, Sir Thomas Elyot mentions Ovid and Martial but not English poets, and, as late as 1553, Wilson was defending the rhetoric of the authorities Cicero and Quintilian. Gradually, however, by struggling with the new language and continuing to experiment with verse forms both new and original, poets were starting to shape a new English poetry and were achieving recognition as craftsmen in their own right. By 1586, Webbe respectfully addressed the preface to his *Discourse of English Poetry* to "the Noble Poets of England" and made mention of Skelton, Gascoigne, and Googe, finally recognizing Spenser as

"the rightest English poet that ever I read." Thus, by the end of the century the question of whether there could be an English poesy had been replaced by the question of what were the limits of the great English poets.

Because of the struggle to shape the new vernacular, the sixteenth century differs from other centuries in that many innovations were coming from the pens of not particularly gifted poets. Thus, working in a period of volatility and flux in the language, such men as Barclay and Skelton could exert an impact on the shaping of the poetry and earn their place in literary history. The first half of the sixteenth century did not witness the formation of new genres. The old reliables, dream-vision allegories, anticlerical satires, pastorals, ballads, versified psalms, and neomedieval tragedies, were the favorite vehicles of most poets. The extraordinary development of this period was the metrical experimentation, which never stopped, no matter how limited the poet. Perhaps more than any other period, therefore, the first half of the sixteenth century reveals as many noteworthy developments in its bad poets as in its talented ones.

After the publication of *Tottel's Miscellany*, poetry began to settle down somewhat from its pattern of groping experimentation as it gained confidence and stability working with the vernacular. Perhaps the surest indication that poetry had hit its stride in England was the parody of the Petrarchan sonnet. The parody of the first truly great lyric form in England was a significant landmark because only widely popular forms tend to serve as targets for parody. A further indication of the vitality of the poetry was the fact that its poets survived the parody and went on to create new forms. Furthermore, poetic tastes were flexible enough to produce a Spenser who, while forging ahead with prosodic experimentation, looked backward to the archaisms that English poetry had originally used.

As the sixteenth century waned and old genres, such as the sonnet, the pastoral, and the verse chronicle, faded, there were numerous hints of what the poets of the new century would be attempting. In particular, there were several suggestions of the Metaphysicals. The decline in popularity of the Petrarchan sonnet and its subsequent ridicule paved the way for John Donne's satires of the form in many of his secular lyrics. As was seen earlier, Greville's religious themes in his *Caelica* were a precursor of devotional poetry. The sensuous conceits of Southwell heralded the Baroque extravagances of Richard Crashaw. The pastoral, a favorite Elizabethan genre, was fast fading, as indicated by Ralegh's cynical response to Marlowe's "The Passionate Shepherd to His Love," a plea for living a romantic life in pastoral bliss. In his "Nymph's Reply to the Shepherd," Ralegh makes it clear that such idyllic bliss does not exist. The pastoral was being replaced, however, by a less idealized, more rational mode, the theme of self-contained, rural retirement, as embodied at the close of the century in Sir Edward Dyer's "My Mind to Me a Kingdom Is," a theme that became increasingly popular in the new century. Finally, the proliferation of songs and airs, found in such collections as Nicholas Yonge's *Musica Transalpina* (1588), John Dowland's *The First Book of Songs or Airs* (1597), and Thomas Campion's *A Booke of Ayres* (1601), created a vogue that influenced the lyrics of Ben Jonson and his followers.

The true worth of the poetry of the sixteenth century, however, lies not in the legacies that were inherited from it by the next century but rather in the sheer exuberance for the poetic undertaking that characterized the century from beginning to end. Because of the continuing process of shaping the new vernacular, the tools of the poetic craft are evident in every work, and in no other century did the poets better embody the original etymology of the word "poet," which comes from the Greek word for "maker." To use Webbe's term, they "Englished" the old poetry and proved to be untiring "makers" of a new.

BIBLIOGRAPHY

Bell, Ilona. *Elizabethan Women and the Poetry of Courtship.* Illustrated edition. New York: Cambridge University Press, 1999. Argues that women's voices can be heard not only in poems by women writers but also in the implied responses by women to poetry addressed to them. The book bears evidence of extensive research, combined with judicious analysis of the poems mentioned.

Blevins, Jacob. *Catullan Consciousness and the Early Modern Lyric in England: From Wyatt to Donne.* Farnham, Surrey, England: Ashgate, 2004. The purpose of this study is to demonstrate that like Catullus, some English poets departed from convention and used the lyric both to praise and to reject accepted cultural ideals, thus establishing a personal identity. The author is convinced that this process is essential to the creation of good lyric poetry. Bibliography and index.

Braden, Gordon. *Sixteenth-Century Poetry: An Annotated Anthology.* Hoboken, N.J.: Wiley-Blackwell, 2005. Selections from a wide range of poets and from the major genres, including both sacred and political poetry. Fully annotated. Contains both a conventional table of contents and an alternate, thematic listing, as well as a chronology, an index of titles and first lines, a bibliography, and a topical index.

Cheney, Patrick, Andrew Hadfield, and Garrett A. Sullivan, Jr., eds. *Early Modern English Poetry: A Critical Companion.* New York: Oxford University Press, 2006. A collection of twenty-eight essays, three of them dealing with cultural changes and poetic theories, the rest suggesting new approaches to major poems. Contains a list of suggested readings at the end of each chapter and a chronology of Renaissance poetry.

Huntington, John. *Ambition, Rank, and Poetry in 1590's England.* Urbana: University of Illinois Press, 2001. Points out evidence of social protest in the works of writers of relatively humble origins, such as George Chapman, Christopher Marlowe, Ben Jonson, Edmund Spenser, Matthew Roydon, and Aemilia Lanyer. Huntington's close readings indicate that there is a need for reinterpretations of the poetry written during the period.

Kinney, Arthur F., ed. *The Cambridge Companion to English Literature, 1500-1600.* New York: Cambridge University Press, 2000. Essays about such subjects as Tudor aesthetics, poetry and patronage, lyric forms, romance, the epic, and patriotic works. Bibliographical references and index.

Lewis, C. S. *Poetry and Prose in the Sixteenth Century.* Oxford, England: Clarendon Press, 1990. Originally published as *English Literature in the Sixteenth Century Excluding Drama*, Vol. 3 in *The*

Oxford History of English Literature, in 1954. A new version of Lewis's controversial work. Bibliography and index.

Mapstone, Sally, ed. *Older Scots Literature*. Edinburgh: John Donald, 2005. The second section of this volume consists of thirteen essays on sixteenth century writers and their works. One of the essays deals with the "female voice" in the poetry of the period, while others discuss ballads, comic verse, and the elegiac tradition. Writers who flourished both in the late sixteenth century and in the early seventeenth century are discussed in the third part of the volume. Bibliographical references and index.

Morotti, Arthur F. *Manuscript, Print, and the English Renaissance Lyric*. Ithaca, N.Y.: Cornell University Press, 1995. The author of this important study examines the tradition of manuscript transmission of poetic works and explains how the change to print publication was effected. He also notes the ways in which the new process altered not only the creative process but also the cultural milieu. Bibliography and index.

Rivers, Isabel. *Classical and Christian Ideas in English Renaissance Poetry: A Student's Guide*. 2d ed. New York: Routledge, 1994. Contains a number of chapters on classical philosophies and Christian doctrines, as well as one chapter on theories of poetry. Lists of authors, an author index, and a bibliographical appendix.

Vickers, Brian, ed. *English Renaissance Literary Criticism*. 1999. Reprint. Oxford, England: Clarendon Press, 2003. This invaluable work presents thirty-six texts, each preceded by a biographical and textual headnote. Annotations with every selection. Includes suggestions for further reading, a glossary, an index of names, and an index of topics.

Whitney, Isabelle, Mary Sidney, and Amelia Lanyer. *Renaissance Women Poets*. New York: Viking, 2001. Considers the lives and works of three English women poets who wrote during the Renaissance. Though their social and cultural backgrounds were very different, all of them used their poetry to voice their convictions and to establish their identities as women and as talented, intelligent human beings.

Elizabeth J. Bellamy

ENGLISH POETRY IN THE SEVENTEENTH CENTURY

A question that can be asked of any century's poetry is whether it owes its character to "forces"—nonliterary developments to which the poets respond more or less sensitively—or whether, on the other hand, the practice of innovative and influential poets mainly determines the poetry of the period. Clearly, great poets do not always shape the literature of their century, as the cases of the twin giants of seventeenth century England, William Shakespeare and John Milton, indicate. What Ben Jonson wrote of Shakespeare is true of both: They are "not of an age, but for all time!" John Donne and John Dryden, however, are poets who seem to have stamped their personalities on much of the poetry of their own and succeeding generations.

JOHN DONNE AND JOHN DRYDEN

John Donne (1572-1631) turned twenty-nine in the year 1601. John Dryden (1631-1700), busy to the last, died at the end of the century. Thus a century brimming with good poetry may be said to begin with Donne and

John Donne (Library of Congress)

end with Dryden. On most library shelves, Donne and Dryden are both literally and figuratively neighbors. If not the shaper of poetry in the first half of the century, Donne stands at least as its representative poet, while Dryden, born only a few months after Donne died in 1631, probably has an even more secure claim to the same position in the final decades of the century. They may indeed have determined the poetic climate; certainly they serve as barometers on which modern readers can see that climate registered. The distinctive differences between the writings of the two men testify to the diversity of seventeenth century poetry and to the likelihood that powerful forces for change were at work in the interim.

The differences are apparent even when—perhaps particularly when—roughly similar types of poems (and parallels between the two are inevitably rough) are chosen. Donne wrote two sequences of religious sonnets. One begins:

> Thou hast made me, and shall thy work decay?
> Repair me now, for now mine end doth haste,
> I run to death, and death meets me as fast,
> And all my pleasures are like yesterday.

Dryden is known for two longer religious poems, one of which, *Religio Laici* (1682), begins: "Dim as the borrowed beams of moons and stars/ To lonely, weary, wand'ring travelers,/ Is Reason to the soul. . . ." A long list of contrasts might be drawn up, most of which would hold true of entire poems and, for that matter, of the works of the two poets generally.

Donne addresses God directly, for example, and even ventures to command him, while neither in his opening nor anywhere else in 456 lines does Dryden apostrophize his maker, although several times he refers circumspectly to "God," "Godhead," or "Omnipotence." Donne not only personifies but also personalizes the abstraction *death*, which "runs fast" and "meets" the speaker. Dryden's chief abstraction, *Reason*, is grand but "dim," and another that he introduces soon thereafter, *Religion*, though described as "bright," remains inanimate. Donne's sonnet has an immediate, even urgent, quality; Dryden sets out in a more deliberate and measured way, as if any necessary relationships will be established in due time. Donne achieves that immediacy through a plain, simple vocabulary, thirty-one of his first thirty-five words having only one syllable. Although there are no striking irregularities after the first line, rhetorical stresses govern the rhythm. Dryden's diction is also simple, but there are more polysyllables, and their arrangement, as in "lonely, weary, wand'ring travelers," creates a smoother, more regular cadence.

In other ways, the poems elicit different responses. Donne is paradoxical. The reader senses in his third line that rigorous demands are being made on him. What does "I run to death" mean exactly? How can that be? Why is death said to do the same? Such questions have answers, no doubt, but the reader anticipates that he will have to work for them, that he must stay alert and get involved. Dryden, on the other hand, begins by making a statement that can be accepted without any particular mental activity (which is not necessarily to say that it should be, or is intended to be, so accepted). Whereas the person setting out to read Donne suspects that obscurities may lie ahead, the beginner at Dryden finds nothing to raise such expectations. (The reader will hardly be surprised to find Dryden saying, near the end of the poem: "Thus have I made my own opinions clear.")

Samplers of other poems by the two poets reveal similar contrasts right from the beginning. Frequently, in Donne's poems, a speaker is addressing someone or something—God, a woman, a friend, a rival, the sun—in a tone that is often abrupt, questioning, or imperious. The poems are often dramatic in the sense of implying a situation and a relationship. They make demands, both on the addressee and the reader, who is present in somewhat the same way as an audience in a theater. Dryden was a dramatist, and a highly successful one, but he seems to have reserved drama for his plays. In his poems, he is inclined to begin, as in *Religio Laici*, with statements, often in the form of generalizations: "All human things are subject to decay." "From harmony, from heavenly harmony,/ This universal frame began." "How blest is he who leads a country life." While not condescending to his readers, Dryden is much more

John Dryden (Library of Congress)

likely to go on to tell them something—something clear, measured, plausible.

THE ELIZABETHAN HERITAGE

The Renaissance came to England late. Sixteenth century Italian poetry is dotted with famous names—Ludovico Ariosto, Pietro Bembo, Michelangelo Buonarroti, Torquato Tasso—and French poets distinguished themselves throughout the century, Pierre de Ronsard and the Pléiade group overshadowing others of whom today's readers would hear much more but for that brilliant constellation of poets. The Elizabethan poets' debt to these older literatures, particularly to that created by their French elders and contemporaries, has been well documented.

After the appearance of *The Shepheardes Calender* (1579) by Edmund Spenser (c. 1552-1599), English poetry came on with a rush, while the post-Renaissance Baroque movement was already rising on the European continent. By 1600, both Spenser and Sir Philip Sidney (1554-1586) were dead, but many of their contemporaries from the 1550's and 1560's worked on, with many of their brightest achievements still ahead. As relief from the earlier but continuing Elizabethan tradition of ponderous, prosaic moralizing exemplified by the incessantly reprinted and expanded *A Mirror for Magistrates* (1555, 1559, 1563), the poets of later Elizabethan decades favored pastorals, love sonnets, mythological narratives, and of course songs and the verse drama.

As part of the last wave of poets to come of age under Elizabeth, Donne and Jonson might have been expected to rebel against their elders. Fifteen years or so of hobnobbing with Hobbinol (poet Gabriel Harvey, c. 1545-1630) and other literary shepherds and of agonizing with woebegone Petrarchan lovers over their unattainable or recalcitrant golden ladies goaded the new generation into staking out new territory. The sweetness and naïveté of much Elizabethan verse cloyed their literary taste buds. The serious side of Elizabethan endeavor ran wearyingly to themes of transience and mutability. There was room for more realism and sophistication, and new forms and conventions.

Donne responded by parodying the ideal Petrarchan mistress in his paean to indiscriminate love, "I can love both fair and brown," meanwhile reserving that standard vehicle for love laments, the sonnet, for religious purposes. Jonson refused to write sonnets at all, coolly praised a goddess named Celia, and claimed, with some exaggeration, that he did not write of love. As mythologizers, Elizabethans were accustomed to plunder from Ovid and the Ovidians, but Donne did not conduct his raids on the *Metamorphoses* (c. 8 C.E.; English translation, 1567), with its wistful accounts of lovers vanished into foliage and feathers; instead, he concentrated on Ovid's saucy prescriptions for both lovemaking and love-breaking in the *Amores* (c. 20 B.C.E.; English translation, c. 1597), *Ars amatoria* (c. 2 B.C.E.; *Art of Love*, 1612), and *Remedia amoris* (before 8 C.E.; *Cure for Love*, 1600). Later (or perhaps just alternatively) he drew on the pre-Petrarchan traditions, including Platonism and Scholasticism, to write of love as a refining and exalting experience. As for Jonson, where the Elizabethans were amply decorous, he tended to be blunt

and epigrammatic. More rigorously than Donne, he rejected the medieval trappings that clung to Elizabethan poetry.

Neither man, however, made anything like a clean break with Elizabethan values. In satirizing Petrarchan conventions, Donne was only continuing a tendency implicit in the Petrarchan mode almost from its beginning, Shakespeare already preceding him in English poetry in his sonnet "My mistress's eyes are nothing like the sun." The man most responsible for the English sonnet-writing mania, Sidney, had, in his *Astrophel and Stella* (1591) suggested all sorts of latent possibilities for the deployment of wit that the Elizabethans had barely begun to exploit. Elizabethan moral earnestness awaited poets who could bring fresh resources to its expression. The student of the drama can hardly escape the conclusion that Donne owed something of his penchant for dramatizing love and religious conflict to the fact that he grew up in London at a time of flourishing theatrical activity, when even writers deficient in dramatic talent strove to turn out plays. Jonson must have learned much about friendship from Sidney's *Arcadia* (1590, 1593, 1598), the fourth book of Spenser's *The Faerie Queene* (1590, 1596), and other romances of the sort before turning this subject to account in poetic forms more congenial to him. Again, Jonson's distinctive contribution to songwriting depended on his good fortune in maturing at a time when music was everywhere in the air, as Willa McClung Evans showed in *Ben Jonson and Elizabethan Music* (1929). In short, Elizabethan influences on these Jacobean poets were very far from exclusively negative ones.

EDMUND SPENSER

Seventeenth century developments originating with Donne and Jonson have absorbed much of the attention of literary students, but the Spenserian tradition must not be underrated. As its master, Edmund Spenser, was a many-faceted poet, the tradition is a rich and diverse one. Michael Drayton carried his adaptations of Spenserian pastoral to the verge of the new century's fourth decade. The greatest English poet after Shakespeare found in *The Faerie Queene* the best model for his own epic. Some poets imitated Spenser's idealism, some his sensuous and even sensual music, some his achievement in romantic narrative, and some his demanding stanza. No one like Spenser wrote in the seventeenth century, but the rays of his genius shone over the century and long afterward. The twentieth century emphasis on Donne and the Metaphysical poets has had the unfortunate effect of obscuring the illumination that Spenser furnished generations of respectful and admiring followers.

LONDON BROTHERHOOD

In few European countries was there such a concentration of talent and creative energy as in Renaissance London. England had no city to rival it in size or cultural pretensions, and to the city or to the court came all aspiring writers and all ambitious men. Literary associations blossomed easily in its square mile, as did rivalries and jealousies. Although London did not boast a university, many of its creative men came to know one another in school. Beginning in the last quarter of the sixteenth century, for example, and extending over the next seventy years, the roster of poets who attended just one school, Westminster, includes Jonson, Richard Corbett, Giles Fletcher, Henry King, George Herbert, William Strode, Thomas Randolph, William Cartwright, Abraham Cowley, and Dryden. Half of these men later gravitated to one Cambridge college, Trinity. A similar list of poets who claimed residence at London's Inns of Court might be made. It is likely that the richness of late Elizabethan and seventeenth century English poetry owes much to the cross-fertilization that is almost inevitable when virtually all of the poets of any given time know one another more or less intimately. Although poets have always come together for mutual support and stimulation, in the seventeenth century, the poets who did so were not beleaguered minorities without status in the intellectual world or insulated coteries intent on defending the purity of their theory and practice against one another. Poets constituted something of a brotherhood—although brothers are known to fight—and not a school or club where narrowness can prevail along with good manners.

Realizing the essentially close relationships among poets whose work scholars tend to classify and mark off from one another, modern commentators on seventeenth century poetry have emphasized the common heritage and shared concerns of writers once assumed to be disparate and even antagonistic. It is well to recall this shared heritage and common cause when distinguishing—as criticism must distinguish—among individual achievements and ascertainable poetic movements.

THE METAPHYSICAL SCHOOL

After Sir Herbert Grierson's edition of Donne's poems in 1912, critics spent some decades attempting to define and delineate "Metaphysical poetry." T. S. Eliot, in a 1921 essay, lent his prestige to the endeavor, and such studies as George Williamson's *The Donne Tradition* (1930), Joan Bennett's *Four Metaphysical Poets* (1934), J. B. Leishman's *Metaphysical Poets* (1934), Helen C. White's *The Metaphysical Poets* (1936), and Rosemond Tuve's *Elizabethan and Metaphysical Imagery* (1947) refined readers' understanding of the movement but created such a vogue that the term "metaphysical" came to acquire a bewildering variety of applications and connotations, with the understandable result that some critics, including Leishman, came to view it with suspicion. Nevertheless, it remains useful for the purpose of designating the kind of poetry written by Donne, Herbert, Richard Crashaw, Henry Vaughan, Thomas Traherne, Andrew Marvell (at least some of the time), and a considerable number of other seventeenth century poets, including the American, Edward Taylor. The earlier tendency to call these poets a "school" has also fallen into disrepute because the term suggests a much more formal and schematic set of relationships than existed among these poets. Douglas Bush, in his valuable contribution to the Oxford History of English Literature series, *English Literature in the Earlier Seventeenth Century, 1600-1660* (1962), refers to the Metaphysicals after Donne as his "successors," while Joseph H. Summers prefers another designation, as the title of his 1970 study, *The Heirs of Donne and Jonson*, indicates.

Because the bulk of English Metaphysical poetry after Donne tends to be religious, it has been studied profitably under extraliterary rubrics, especially by Louis L. Martz as *The Poetry of Meditation* (1954), in which the author demonstrates how many distinctive features of such poetry derive from the Christian art of meditation, especially from such manuals of Catholic devotion as Saint Ignatius of Loyola's *Ejercicios espirituales* (1548; *The Spiritual Exercises*, 1736) and Saint Francis de Sales's *An Introduction to the Devout Life* (c. 1608). More recently, Barbara Kiefer Lewalski has argued for the importance of Protestant devotional literature in her *Protestant Poetics and the Seventeenth Century Religious Lyric* (1979). Donne and some of his followers have been profitably studied as poets of wit, a classification that connects them with Jonson and the Jonsonians, in later books by Leishman (*The Monarch of Wit*, 1951) and Williamson (*The Proper Wit of Poetry*, 1961), as well as in the aforementioned book by Summers.

Students of literature continue to be intrigued by the word "metaphysical," however, and by the challenge of pinpointing its essential denotation. One of the most distinctive traits of this poetry is the Metaphysical conceit, an image that, as its name suggests, is intended to convey an idea rather than a sensory quality. The conceit, as exemplified by Donne's comparison of the quality of two lovers' devotion to the draftsman's compass in "A Valediction: Forbidding Mourning," or the pulley image in Herbert's poem of that title used to express the speaker's sense of the relationship between God and humans, is likely to be ingenious, unexpected, and apparently unpromising; the poet is inclined to develop it at considerable length (Donne uses three stanzas for his compass conceit, while Herbert builds his whole poem on the pulley image) and in a number of particulars; and the result, often arrived at through argumentation, justifies the seeming incongruity of the image. An interesting comparison between Donne's imagery and that of Shakespeare has been made by Cleanth Brooks (in *The Well Wrought Urn*, 1947) with the view of demonstrating the use of similar conceits by Shakespeare, who is never thought of as a Metaphysical.

Describers of Metaphysical poetry have most often cited a cluster of traits, no one of which differentiates this mode from others. Metaphysical poems are often dramatic, colloquial in diction and rhythm, and set forth in intricate and varied forms with respect to line lengths, rhyme schemes, and stanzaic configurations. Whether dealing with sexual or religious love, Metaphysical love poems develop the psychological aspects

of loving that are always implicit, sometimes explicit in the Petrarchan tradition. Sexual, Platonic, and religious love are frequently explored in terms seemingly more appropriate to one of the other types. Thus Donne assures God that he will never be "chaste, except you ravish me," and a lady that "all shall approve/ Us canonized for love." Crashaw can refer to a mistress as a "divine idea" in a "shrine of crystal flesh," and, in another poem, to God as a rival lover of Saint Teresa.

The chief trait of Metaphysical poetry in the eyes of Earl Miner (*The Metaphysical Mode from Donne to Cowley*, 1969) is its "private mode." He considers the most distinctive aspect of the love or religious experience in this poetry to be its individual and private character. Either because the poet senses a breakdown of social bonds or because these bonds threaten the integrity of private experience, the Metaphysical poet is in self-conscious retreat from the social realm. Thus Donne's love poems often evoke third parties only to banish them as early as the first line: "For God's sake, hold your tongue, and let me love." The earlier Metaphysicals, however, are familiar with the world that they reject, and its immanence contributes to the dramatic quality in their poetry. In later poets such as Vaughan and Traherne, the interfering world has receded; as a result the dramatic tension largely disappears.

Metaphysical poetry's reputed taste for the obscure and the "far-fetched" has been overemphasized by critics from Dryden to the twentieth century. That it is intellectual and that its allusions are likely to necessitate numerous glosses for modern readers there can be little doubt. The ideal audience for Metaphysical poetry was small and select. To pre-Restoration readers, however, the poems probably did not seem especially difficult. It is simply that Renaissance learning was replaced by a different learning. As the century waned, a gap widened between the old and new learning; as a result Dryden had more difficulty reading Donne than do modern readers, who enjoy the benefit of modern scholars' recovery of much of that older learning. The continuing popularity of Metaphysical poetry demonstrates readers' continuing willingness to absorb glosses without which the richness of the poetry is lost.

European Metaphysical Poetry (1961), an anthology by Frank J. Warnke with a long critical introduction, presents French, German, Spanish, Dutch, and Italian texts of selected poems with facing verse translations. The volume includes a number of poems analogous to the works of Donne and his followers and distinguishes between the Metaphysical and Baroque traditions, although clearly they overlap.

METAPHYSICAL POETS IN THE NEW WORLD

A Mexican nun, Sor Juana Inés de la Cruz (1648-1695), rivals Taylor (c. 1645-1729), who came to America in 1668, as the first Metaphysical poet of the New World. Like Crashaw, Sor Juana writes emotional, sexually charged religious verse, but also like him, she was a keen student of theology and something of an intellectual. In Taylor, the Metaphysical manner and a Puritan religious outlook produced a body of poetry unique in the American colonies or elsewhere. The influence of Richard Baxter's famous book *The Saints' Everlasting Rest* (1692) is heavier on Taylor than on any other Metaphysical poet, and many of his poems are cast as meditations. The language is that of a man who lived and worked on the late seventeenth century American frontier, cut off from the society of the learned and the artistic. Even his conceits, such as the one on which he bases "Huswifery"—"Make me, O Lord, thy spinning wheel complete"—have a homely, rough-hewn air.

RELIGIOUS POETRY AND OTHER TRENDS

Finally, the seventeenth century produced a body of poetry not usually classified as Metaphysical but having some affinities with that tradition. Much of it is religious. Emblem poetry, best exemplified by Francis Quarles (1592-1644), was a mixed-media art including a print that depicted a scene of religious or moral significance, a biblical quotation, a related poem, another quotation, and, in most cases, a concluding epigram. The engravings in emblem books are frequently more interesting than the poems, but the form seems to have made its mark on Spenser, Shakespeare, and several of the Metaphysical poets, notably Herbert and Crashaw. Herbert's great book *The Temple* (1633) contains several poems that, arranged to form figures, become in effect emblems of their subject matter. Another poet,

Henry More, in his fondness for allegory and the Spenserian stanza points to one large influence, but often reminds the reader of the Metaphysicals in his choice and handling of imagery, even though his work is more justly charged with obscurity than theirs. At the same time, More is one of the few seventeenth century poets who is known to have studied René Descartes and to have been directly influenced by the Cartesian dualism of mind and matter. If, as Basil Willey has argued in *The Seventeenth Century Background* (1934), Cartesian thought undermined confidence in the "truth" of poetry, it is in More that one should be able to read the signs of the decline, but More seems as sure of the truth of his poetical utterances as of his *Divine Dialogues* (1668) in prose. Other Metaphysically tinged poetry will be considered part of the mid-century transition below.

BEN JONSON

From a twentieth century perspective Ben Jonson (1573-1637) was overshadowed by Shakespeare as a playwright and by Donne as a lyric and reflective poet, but his importance in his time is difficult to overestimate. Before his time, England had produced classical scholars who edited texts, produced grammars and other educational tools, and wrote significant prose. Not until Jonson, however, did an Englishman combine classical learning with great poetic ability. Jonson's interpretation of the classical heritage, which involved (besides the drama) imitations of such distinctly classical forms as the epigram, ode, and verse epistle; the translation into verse of Horace's *Ars poetica* (c. 17 B.C.E.; *The Art of Poetry*) and the employment of poetry as an ethical, civilizing influence not only enriched poetry but also defined classicism itself for generations of Englishmen. Even present-day classicists are likely to conceive of its essential spirit as comprising such virtues as simplicity, clarity, symmetry, detachment, and restraint, although such qualities are hardly the hallmarks of Euripides, Pindar, Ovid, and any number of other Greek and Roman poets. Jonsonian classicism proved to be a timely antidote to Elizabethan verbosity and extravagance, however, and generated some of the best poetry of the seventeenth century.

All Jonson's favorite classical forms had been practiced in the sixteenth century, though often in an eclectic and self-indulgent way. Jonson showed that the discipline of strict classicism could be liberating. Bush has pointed out that his imitations of Martial not only capture the temper of the greatest Roman epigrammatist better than did any of his predecessors, but also display more originality than earlier poems in this genre. Although not a great love poet, Jonson wrote a series of song lyrics that are models of their type, one of them, "Drink to me only with thine eyes" being familiar to millions of people who know nothing of classicism or of Jonson himself. His verse letter "To Penshurst," though initially unexciting to a reader accustomed to Donne's pyrotechnics, achieves an unobtrusive but unforgettable effect. When, at the end, he contrasts the Sidney family mansion with other houses—"their lords have built, but thy lord dwell"—he has accomplished a tribute worth all the fulsome compliments that Elizabethans heaped on their benefactors. It was through his study of Horace, a quiet bastion of civility in the noisy Roman Empire, that Jonson was able to produce such an effect.

Like Donne, Jonson not only wrote fine poems but inspired others of a high order as well. Robert Herrick (1591-1674), to whom Jonson was "Saint Ben," sometimes approached his master in the art of epigram and sometimes exceeded him in the writing of cool, elegant lyrics. Poets such as Edmund Waller (1606-1687) who reached the heights only infrequently probably could not have done so at all without Jonson's example (and occasionally Donne's also). The delicacy of Waller's "Go, lovely rose" is an inheritance of the Tribe of Ben. If the same poet's Penshurst poems fall short of Jonson's, Marvell's "Upon Appleton House" is both marvelously original and indebted to Jonson. William Alexander McClung, in *The Country House in English Renaissance Poetry* (1977), has shown how the poets after Jonson were able to set forth both an ideal of environment and an ideal of virtue through their reflection in a house.

Neither Jonson nor his followers necessarily came by their Horatian restraint and moderation naturally. As a young man, Jonson flashed the same hot temper that many another Elizabethans did not bother to control. In 1598, he plunged a rapier six inches into the side of a fellow actor named Gabriel Spencer, killing him

instantly. He escaped with a branding on the thumb by pleading benefit of clergy—a dubious privilege possible for an educated man in or out of holy orders. Pen in hand, however, he modeled his work on that of Horace, who counseled, and perhaps practiced, moderation as a "golden mean." Horace did not prevent Jonson from lashing out verbally at his critics from time to time, but the Roman poet probably saved the impetuous Jonson from many a poetical gaucherie.

Many of Jonson's followers were political conservatives, advocates of royal supremacy and others who had most to fear from the intransigent Puritans, whose power grew steadily throughout the first half of the century until they forced Charles I from his throne and, in 1649, beheaded him for treason. Thus Jonsonian classicists overlapped, but did not subsume, the Cavalier lyric poets, who celebrated the not particularly Horatian virtues of war, chivalry, and loyalty to the monarchy. Just as paradoxically, the great classicist of the generation after Jonson turned out to be Latin secretary of Oliver Cromwell's Commonwealth, the militant Puritan Milton.

At their best, the Jonsonians wrote graceful and civilized lyrics reflecting a philosophy that was, in the best sense of the term, Epicurean. Like the Elizabethans, they were attracted to the theme of human mortality, but whereas the earlier poets had responded to the inevitability of decline and death with lugubrious melancholy, the Tribe of Ben had imbibed Horace's advice: carpe diem, or "seize the day." They wrote the most beautiful lyrics on this theme ever written in English: Herrick's "To Daffodils," "To the Virgins, to Make Much of Time," and "Corinna's going A-Maying," Waller's "Go, lovely rose," and Marvell's "To His Coy Mistress."

Another subject dear to the heart of Jonsonians was one relatively rare in previous (and many later) eras: children. Jonson wrote, with deep feeling yet immense restraint, of the deaths of two children. "On My First Daughter" does not repeat the personal pronoun of the title, although the reader learns that her name was Mary. The parents, however, are referred to in the third person, only the final phrase, "cover lightly, gentle earth!" betraying the speaker's involvement in the child's demise. An even finer poem, "On My First

Son," has only six couplets and yet achieves enormous poignancy through the most economical means. Jonson could have expressed his love no more forcefully than by saying: "Here doth lie/ Ben Jonson his best piece of poetry." The lesson he draws is more Horatian than Christian: "For whose sake, henceforth, all his vows be such/ As what he loves may never like too much." Although Jonson wrote a few religious lyrics, it seems to be the classical legacy that he cherished most deeply.

Among those who gathered with Jonson at the Mermaid Tavern, Corbett also wrote of family members, including one poem "To His Son, Vincent" in which he characteristically sets forth moderate wishes for his offspring, "not too much wealth, nor wit," and on the positive side, the graces of his mother, friends, peace, and innocence at the last. Among the poets who wrote poems about other people's children was William Cartwright, who expressed wishes for a friend's newborn son, and Herrick, who penned two short epitaphs and two graces for children to recite at meals. Obviously the range of childhood poems in the seventeenth century is very narrow, even if Traherne's mystical poems "Shadows in the Water," "Innocence," and others are included. Even so, that children figure in poetry at all is an indication that Jonson's disciples do not consider commonplace subjects beneath their notice.

As might be expected of admirers of Horace and Martial, Jonsonians favored short lines and short stanzas, though without the intricacy and irregularity often seen in Metaphysical lyrics. They often wrote in couplets, though the form known as the heroic couplet does not appear much before mid-century and does not become important until the age of Dryden. The couplets mirror the unassuming quality of so much early English classicism but commonly betray careful craftsmanship. The diction is rather plain, the metaphors few, and not often unusual. The words and images are carefully chosen, however, with an eye to precision and euphony. The tone is tender and affectionate toward friends and loved ones, sarcastic toward those who, like fools, deserve it. There are few high flights, but neither are Jonsonian lapses likely to be very gross. Speech, Jonson wrote, in *Timber: Or, Discoveries Made upon Men and Matter* (1641) is "the instrument of society." Furthermore, "words are the people's." The poet is

someone who uses the people's resources for the people's good.

BAROQUE POETRY

Probably because it arose as a reaction against a Renaissance classicism that had no parallel in England before Jonson, the Baroque movement, beginning around 1580 and continuing for the better part of a century, had few manifestations in English poetry. First applied to architecture and later to sculpture and painting, the term described in particular the style of certain sixteenth century Venetian painters, particularly Jacopo Robusti Tintoretto, and of those, such as El Greco, who were influenced by the Venetians. The Baroque disdained formal beauty and placidity in favor of asymmetrical composition, rich color, energy, and even contortion.

Applied to prose style, "baroque" signifies the revolt against full and rounded Ciceronian elegance, a tendency to place the main sentence element first, the avoidance of symmetry by varying the form and length of constructions, and a greater autonomy for subordinate constructions, which tend to follow the main sentence element. English had developed a Ciceronian prose style, but a recognizably anti-Ciceronian prose arose in the seventeenth century, notably in such works as Robert Burton's *The Anatomy of Melancholy* (1621) and Sir Thomas Browne's *Religio Medici* (1642).

In poetry, the Baroque has some affinities with the Metaphysical, but the differences are suggested by the adjectives used to describe the Baroque: "ornate," "sensuous," "pictorial," and "emotional." The Baroque is more likely to reject logic and reason, which are useful to Metaphysical poets of an argumentative bent. In his *European Metaphysical Poetry*, Frank J. Warnke distinguishes between a Baroque inclination to use contrast and antithesis for the purpose of separating opposites and a Metaphysical preference for paradox and synthesis to produce a fusion of opposites. The Baroque was cultivated chiefly—not exclusively—by Roman Catholics as an expression of the Counter-Reformation spirit; it stands in contrast to the austerity of much northern European Protestant art.

The only English poets commonly associated with the Baroque are Fletcher and Crashaw (c. 1612-1649).

Although Crashaw left more than four hundred poems, he is best known for his Saint Teresa poems, especially his florid "Upon the book and picture of the seraphical Saint Teresa" called "The Flaming Heart." The poem blazes to a finish in a series of oaths that illustrate the Baroque manner:

> By thy large draughts of intellectual day,
> And by thy thirsts of love more large than they;
> By all thy brim-filled bowls of fierce desire
> By thy last morning's draught of liquid fire. . . .

By these and other oaths he asked to be emptied of self and enabled to imitate her example. It is no surprise to learn that Crashaw lived for some years on the Continent, that he renounced his Anglican priesthood to become a Roman Catholic, and that he died in Italy.

Fletcher (c. 1585-1623), on the other hand, stands as a caution against too facile generalizations. He is best known for his devotional poem, *Christ Victorie, and Triumph in Heaven, and Earth, Over, and After Death* (1610). He remained English and Anglican, and although his poetry reminds some readers of the baroque pioneer Guillaume du Bartas, he usually causes readers of Spenser to think of *The Faerie Queene*. The case of Fletcher underlines the fact that English writers of the earlier seventeenth century felt no compulsion to wage war with the Renaissance, since its greatest non-dramatic poet, far from being a doctrinaire classicist, synthesized elements classical, medieval, and Renaissance.

The Baroque style in poetry, as in the visual arts, contained more than the usual number of the seeds of decadence. Baroque poets were liable to grotesqueness, obscurity, melodrama, and triviality. Its excesses no doubt helped pave the way for the later neoclassical resurgence. Again by analogy with architecture, some literary historians have seen the Baroque also leading to the rococo, understood as a fussy, overdecorative, playful style that nevertheless might serve a serious purpose for a neoclassicist engaged in playful satire. The most obvious example in English literature, Alexander Pope's *The Rape of the Lock* (1712), comes early in the eighteenth century.

MID-CENTURY TRANSITION

To argue for too neat a mid-century transition between the earlier classical, Metaphysical, and Baroque styles, on the one hand, and the neoclassical age on the other, is perhaps to betray an obsession with the neoclassical virtue of symmetry, but in a number of ways the mid-century marks a turning point. England's only interregnum straddles the century's midpoint, while on the Continent the Thirty Years' War came to an end with the treaties of the Peace of Westphalia in 1648. Both of these political events involved poetry and poets, the English Civil War more strikingly. The continental wars, insofar as they involved Protestant-Catholic clashes, represented nothing new, but they exhibited several modern features. Because they involved most European states in one way or another and required a general congress of nations to achieve even temporary peace, these conflicts augured the modern situation, in which local conflicts can trigger unforeseen large-scale involvement. Armorers preparing soldiers for battle had to devise protection against traditional weapons such as the sword and also new ones such as the pistol; the latter were often used as a kind of last resort, as clubs, or thrown at enemies more often than they were fired. All over Europe men were getting a preview of the mass destruction they could expect in future wars. The necessity of compromise and toleration—never before recognized as virtues—was beginning to dawn. More and more it seemed essential that reason and judgment, not passion and force, reign.

England had embarked on its internal war in 1642. The Puritans, who had already succeeded in closing London's theaters, alarmed conservative Englishmen by closing down the monarchy itself. The execution of Charles I and the proclamation of the Commonwealth in 1649 culminated nearly a decade of violence that had driven Sir John Denham, Sir William Davenant, and Thomas Hobbes, among others, into exile, and the Cavalier poet Richard Lovelace into prison, where he penned several immortal poems. The political transition ended in 1660. Young Dryden wrote *Astraea Redux* (1660), an elaborate poetic tribute to a great event: the return of Charles II, son of the executed king, in glory. The adjustments made by all the former belligerents signal a new era. The next revolution, in

1688, despite ingredients seemingly as volatile as those which had precipitated the mid-century war, was not bloody.

Miner (*The Metaphysical Mode from Donne to Cowley*) has referred to the decade between 1645 and 1655 as a "microcosm" of the century as a whole. Certainly it was a productive time for poets. In only the first half of that decade appeared Waller's *Poems* (1645), Sir John Suckling's *Fragmenta Aurea* (1646), Crashaw's *Steps to the Temple* (1646, 1648), Herrick's *Hesperides: Or, The Works Both Humane and Divine of Robert Herrick, Esq.* (1648), Lovelace's *Lucasta: Epodes, Odes, Sonnets, Songs, &c. to Which Is Added Aramantha, a Pastorall* (1649), and Vaughan's *Silex Scintillans* (parts 1 and 2, 1650, 1655), all studded with still familiar anthology favorites. Although Marvell's posthumous poems are difficult to date, at least some of his best are presumed to have been written in the early 1650's, as were a number of the finest of Milton's sonnets, while *Paradise Lost* (1667, 1674) was evolving in Milton's imagination. Miner's point, however, is that the poets at work at this time are difficult to classify as Cavalier, Puritan, Metaphysical, or neoclassical. The distinctive earlier voices—those of Donne and Jonson and Herbert—had been stilled, and the most distinctive later one had not yet developed. The teenage Dryden's notorious foray into Metaphysical imagery in his 1649 poem "Upon the Death of the Lord Hastings," where Hastings's smallpox blisters are compared to "rosebuds stuck in the lily-skin about," and where "Each little pimple had a tear in it/ To wail the fault its rising did commit," presages the great neoclassicist only in its use of rhymed pentameter couplets—and those are not yet particularly "heroic."

That particular form, the end-stopped couplet with its potential for balance, antithesis, and memorable precision, was being hammered out in the 1640's by such poets as Waller, Denham, and John Cleveland (otherwise remembered chiefly as a decadent Metaphysical) in a series of spirited anti-Puritan satires. The latter's 1642 poem, "Cooper's Hill," now faded, looks forward to the Augustan Age with its blend of Horatian and Vergilian sentiments, its lofty abstractions, and its skillful handling of rhythm. The pentameter couplet was as old as Geoffrey Chaucer, but as a distinct unit,

sometimes virtually a stanza in itself, it was capable of generating quite different effects. Detachable, quotable, suited for uttering the common wisdom, the great truths apparent to all, it embodied the neoclassical concept of wit, which was variously defined from this period on, but most memorably (because so well-expressed in a couplet, of course) by Pope in 1711: "True wit is nature to advantage dressed,/ What oft was thought, but ne'er so well expressed."

At the very middle of the century appeared a work by a man whose profession was neither poet nor critic but whose terse genealogy of a poem marks off the distance between the ages of Donne and Dryden. Hobbes was responding to remarks on epic made by Davenant in the preface to his fragmentary heroic poem *Gondibert* (1651) when he wrote:

> Time and education beget experience; experience begets memory; memory begets judgment and fancy; judgment begets the strength and structure, and fancy begets the ornaments of a poem.

It is impossible to imagine Donne countenancing the splitting asunder of "structure" and "ornaments," or for that matter acknowledging "ornaments" at all—for where were they in his poetry?

The following year, 1651, saw the publication of Hobbes's magnum opus, the *Leviathan*. There he made explicit what his answer to Davenant had implied: "In a good poem . . . both judgment and fancy are required: but the fancy must be more eminent." In other words, "ornament" is more important than "structure." To be sure, Hobbes was only stating succinctly a view that had already surfaced in Francis Bacon's philosophy: Poetry is make-believe ("feigned history," as Bacon put it in *The Advancement of Learning* back in 1605) and has nothing to do with truth. This reproach becomes more damning when seen in the context of the linguistic theories set forth elsewhere by Hobbes and by the Royal Society of London in the following decade.

Another work of the mid-century marks a beginning rather than a transition. In 1650, *The Tenth Muse Lately Sprung Up in America* was published in London. Supposedly the manuscript had been spirited across the Atlantic without its author's consent. It was the first book of poems by an American woman, Anne Bradstreet. Discounting the doggerel of such works of piety as *The Bay Psalm Book* (1640), it was in fact the first book of poems by any American. More than two hundred years would pass before another woman poet would do as well as Bradstreet, who, twenty years earlier, as a teenage bride, had emigrated to Massachusetts.

POETRY AND THE SCIENTIFIC REVOLUTION

Of the nonliterary forces on seventeenth century poets, the New Science may well have been the most uniformly pervasive throughout the Western world. Whereas social, political, and even religious developments varied considerably in nature and scope, the scientists were busy discovering laws that applied everywhere and affected the prevailing worldview impartially. Some artists and thinkers discovered the New Science and pondered its implications before others, but no poet could fall very many decades behind the vanguard and continue to be taken seriously. The modern reader of, say, C. S. Lewis's *The Discarded Image* (1964) and E. M. W. Tillyard's *The Elizabethan World Picture* (1943) observes that the Elizabethan "picture" had not changed substantially from the medieval "image" described by Lewis. Between 1600 and 1700, however, the worldview of educated people changed more dramatically than in any previous century. Early in the century Donne signaled his awareness of science's challenge to the old certitudes about the world. By Dryden's maturity, the new learning had rendered the Elizabethan brand of erudition disreputable and its literary imagination largely incomprehensible.

In *The Breaking of the Circle* (1960), Marjorie Hope Nicolson uses a popular medieval symbol, the circle of perfection, to demonstrate the effect of the New Science on the poets' perception of their world. The universe was a circle; so was Earth and the human head. The circle was God's perfect form, unending like himself, and all its manifestations shared in the perfection. It was easy—one might almost say "natural"—for Donne to begin one of his sonnets: "I am a little world made cunningly." Significantly, Donne did not say that he was *like* a little world. Not only did he use a metaphor instead of a simile, but also he used the metaphor confident that he was expressing a truth. In another son-

net, Shakespeare refers to his soul as "the center of my sinful earth." Two thousand years earlier, Aristotle had said that "to make metaphors well is to perceive likeness," and this judgment still stood firm. Already, however, a succession of thinkers from Nicolaus Copernicus in 1543 to Sir Isaac Newton in 1687 were at work breaking up the circle of perfection.

A special irony attaches to the contribution of Copernicus, a pious Roman Catholic who took the concept of the circle of perfection for granted when he set forth his heliocentric theory of the solar system. His insight was to see the Sun, not Earth, as the center of God's operations in the visible world. To him, it was perfectly obvious that God would impart perfect circular motion to the planets. Unfortunately his new model provided even less accurate predictability of planetary motions than the old geocentric theory that it was intended to replace. Thus he had to invent an ingenious system of subordinate circles—"eccentrics" and "epicycles"—to account for the discrepancies between the simple version of his model and his observations of what actually went on in the heavens. Thus, although his heliocentric theory incurred condemnation by Protestant and Catholic alike, his cumbersome model did not attract many adherents, and for decades intelligent people remained ignorant of his theory and its implications.

Two contemporaries of Donne changed all that. In 1609, Galileo built a telescope; by the next year, he was systematically examining not just the solar system but other suns beyond it. Johann Kepler discovered, virtually at the same time, the elliptical orbit of Mars. He did this by breaking the old habit—his own as well as humankind's—of regarding physical events as symbols of divine mysteries, and thereby swept Copernicus's eccentrics and epicycles into a rubbish heap. When Donne wrote *An Anatomy of the World: The First Anniversary*, in 1611, he showed his familiarity with the new astronomy:

> And new philosophy calls all in doubt,
> The element of fire is quite put out;
> The sun is lost, and the earth, and no man's wit
> Can well direct him where to look for it.

Even before the confirmation of Copernicus's theory, the greatest literary geniuses of his century raised versions of the great question provoked by the new science. Michel Eyquem de Montaigne put it most simply in his *Essais* (books 1-2 1580; rev. 1582; books 1-3, 1588; rev. 1595; *The Essays*, 1603): "What do I know?" The word "essays" signifies "attempts," and the work can be described as a series of attempts to answer his question. Miguel de Cervantes, setting out with the rather routine literary motive of satirizing a particularly silly type of chivalric romance, stumbled on his theme: the difficulty of distinguishing appearance from reality—even for those who, unlike Don Quixote, are not mad. The second part of Cervantes's novel, *El ingenioso hidalgo don Quixote de la Mancha* (1605, 1615; *The History of the Valorous and Wittie Knight-Errant, Don Quixote of the Mancha*, 1612-1620; better known as *Don Quixote de la Mancha*), written like the first out of an understandable but pedestrian literary ambition (to reclaim his hero from the clutches of a plagiarist), raises the disturbing possibility that the madman interprets at least some aspects of reality more sensibly than the "sane" people among whom the idealistic Don Quixote was floundering. Shakespeare, having already endorsed the ancient concept of the poet as a divinely inspired madman in *A Midsummer Night's Dream* (pr. c. 1595-1596), created, at the very beginning of the new century, a "mad" hero who raises an even more profound question: Can knowledge of the truth, even if attainable (and Hamlet gains the knowledge of the truth that concerns him most—the circumstances of his father's death—through ghostly intervention), lead to madness and paralysis of the will?

Unlike Eliot's twentieth century figure of J. Alfred Prufrock, who asks, "Do I dare disturb the universe?," medieval man did not disturb, and was not disturbed by, the universe. Even the presumed decay of the world from its original golden age did not alarm him, for it was all part of the plan of a wise and loving Creator. In *An Anatomy of the World*, the decay of the world has become profoundly disturbing, for the very cosmic order itself seems to be coming apart: "'Tis all in pieces, all coherence gone." Shortly before writing this poem—and perhaps afterward—Donne was able to write poetry of the sort quoted earlier, in which he moves easily from macrocosm to microcosm; but he

also recognized that the "new philosophy calls all in doubt."

Astronomical discoveries were not the only form of knowledge. In 1600, William Gilbert wrote a book on magnetism. He was, like Copernicus, a good sixteenth century man and could talk about lodestones as possessing souls; his important discovery, however, was that the earth is a lodestone. In 1628, when William Harvey published his findings on the circulation of the blood, he referred to the heart as the body's "sovereign" and "inmost home," but in the process, he taught the world to regard it as a mechanism—a pump. The old worldview was being destroyed quite unintentionally by men whose traditional assumptions often hampered their progress, but whose achievement made it impossible for their own grandchildren to make the same assumptions or to take the old learning seriously. As a result of Robert Boyle's work, chemistry was banishing alchemy, a subject taken seriously not only by poets but also by the scientists of an earlier day. At century's end, to talk of a person as a "little world" was mere quaintness, for Harvey had taught everyone to regard the body as one sort of mechanism, while the astronomers insisted that the solar system was another. It was merely idle to make connections between them.

As the scientists focused more clearly on their subjects, the poets' vision became more blurred. Astronomy is only one such subject area, but it is a particularly useful one for the purpose of demonstrating the change. Around 1582 Sidney's Astrophel could exclaim: "With how sad steps, O moon, thou climb'st the skies,/ How silently, and with how wan a face." Astrophel is a disappointed lover, of course, and need not be taken too seriously. What strikes the reader is the ease with which his creator sees parallels between the moon and the earthbound lover. In a more serious context, Herbert addresses a star: "Bright spark, shot from a brighter place/ Where beams surround my Savior's face." Herbert almost surely knew what Galileo had been doing, but his "brighter place" still lay, as it were, beyond the reach of the telescope. In 1650, Vaughan could begin a poem: "I saw Eternity the other night/ Like a great Ring of pure and endless light,/ All calm, as it was bright." The reader's first inclination is perhaps to marvel at the facility of the utterance, but is the tone as matter-of-fact as it seems? Might not Donne and Herbert have seen eternity every night? On second thought one wonders whether the moments of insight are getting rarer. Five years later, Vaughan published "They are all gone into the world of light," a poem reflecting an awareness of the transience of the heavenly vision:

> And yet, as Angels in some brighter dreams
> Call the soul, when man doth sleep:
> So some strange thoughts transcend our wonted themes,
> And into glory peep.

At the end of the poem the speaker begs God to "disperse these mists." Any reader can verify that in later Metaphysical poetry the view of heaven gets cloudier. Traherne, almost surely writing in the Restoration, sees heaven not through the earthly eye but mystically with a sight often blurred by dream, shadows, and mists. In "My Spirit," for example, his soul "saw infinity/ 'Twas not a sphere, but 'twas a power/ Invisible." In *Religio Laici*, Dryden can see none of this and counsels submission to the Church. By 1733, Pope has banished all thought of reading heavenly meanings in the heavens: "The proper study of Mankind is Man"—unless, of course, one happens to be an astronomer.

NEOCLASSICISM FROM 1660 TO 1700

By the Restoration, the poets had turned their attention primarily to public and social themes. The comedy of this period has given readers the impression of a licentious age determined to bury the memory of Puritanistic domination and live as fast and loose an existence as possible. Such behavior could not have characterized more than a tiny percentage of the people of later Stuart England. It was an age struggling for order through compromise. Wit might entertain, but life required sober judgment.

The classical tradition survived the New Science better than did the Metaphysical. It did not aspire to compete with science in the realm beyond everyday human and social experience. The Jonsonian tradition of short lyric and reflective poems no longer flourished, but the neoclassicists of the Restoration rediscovered satire and the heroic poem—the latter primarily in the remarkable triad of Miltonic poems published between 1667 and 1671: *Paradise Lost* (1667, 1674), *Paradise*

Regained (1671), and *Samson Agonistes* (1671). Horace was not neglected, but the study and translation of the Homeric and Vergilian epics gained in popularity. The time might have been ripe for a great patriotic epic (Milton considered a true Arthurian epic that would rectify the deficiencies of Spenser's episodic one before he finally settled on the yet nobler idea of justifying God's way to humans), but whether because Milton's accomplishment had preempted the field or because history as Restoration poets knew it could not be hammered into the Vergilian mold, it was not written.

Instead, Dryden produced something new: a political satire in a heroic style based on a contemporary controversy over the attempt to exclude Charles II's Roman Catholic brother James from the royal succession. It was a serious matter, laden with danger for the principal in the struggle, for Dryden, and for the nation. He did not use blank verse, as Shakespeare and Milton had in their greatest works, but the heroic couplet, a form that Dryden had been honing for twenty years. The result is a poem of peculiar urgency, yet by virtue of Dryden's skillful representation of Charles II as the biblical King David and of the earl of Shaftesbury as "false Achitophel," who attempts to turn Absalom (Charles's illegitimate son, the duke of Monmouth) against his father, the poem takes on universality. It is by far the most impressive poem of the period: *Absalom and Achitophel* (1681, 1682).

The drama aside, satire is the greatest literary achievement of the Restoration, and it is also the most diverse. From Samuel Butler's low burlesque of the Puritans in *Hudibras* (1663, 1664, 1678, parts 1-3) to Dryden's sustained high style in *Absalom and Achitophel*, from a butt as small as one undistinguished playwright (Thomas Shadwell in Dryden's 1682 mock-epic *Mac Flecknoe: Or, A Satyre upon the True-Blew-Protestant Poet, T. S.*) to one as large as humankind, vain aspirer to the status of rational being (the earl of Rochester's "A Satire Against Mankind," printed in 1675), verse satire flourished, providing models for even greater achievements in the first part of the following century. The Renaissance notion of decorum as the delicate adjustment of literary means to ends, of the suitability of the parts to the whole, governed these diverse attempts at diminishing the wickedness and folly that Restoration poets considered it their duty to expose and correct. Even *Hudibras*, with its slam-bang tetrameter couplets and quirky rhymes, seems the perfect vehicle for flaying the routed Puritans, and its levels of irony are far more complex than superficial readers suspect. When satire began to invade prose, as it increasingly did in the eighteenth century, its narrative possibilities increased, but it lost subtle effects of rhythm, timing, and rhyme.

Compared with the first sixty years of the century, the Restoration seems a prosaic age. A considerable number of its most accomplished writers—John Bunyan, the diarists Samuel Pepys and John Evelyn, Sir William Temple, John Locke—wrote no poetry worth preserving, and Dryden himself wrote a large proportion of prose. Does the preponderance of prose and satire confirm Eliot's early charge that a "dissociation of sensibility" had set in by the time of the Restoration? Is it true that writers no longer could fuse thought and feeling, with the consequence that prose was used for conveying truth and poetry for the setting forth of delightful lies?

Hobbes, who had little use for poetry in general, praised the epic as conducive to moral truth, and he admitted that satire can be defended on moral grounds also. The Restoration poets in England were the successors of a classical tradition that emphasized the ethical value of poetry, so they might as plausibly be considered carrying out, on a somewhat larger scale, the dictates of Jonson as those of Hobbes. The Royal Society of London, of which Dryden was a member, was founded in 1662 for "the improving of natural knowledge," and among its ambitions it numbered the improving of the language by waging war against "tropes" and "figures" and "metaphors." One cannot imagine Donne having anything to do with such an organization, all the more because the Society on principle did not discuss "such subjects as God and the soul." It is difficult to see how Dryden's association with it substantiates the charge of dissociated sensibility, however, for there is certainly both thought and feeling together in *Absalom and Achitophel*, even if it is, like the Royal Society itself, earthbound and relatively unmetaphorical, and, while it is no doubt instructive, gen-

erations of readers have taken delight in it also.

One is tempted to offer a different explanation for Restoration writers' greater attachment to prose and to satire. The reading audience expanded greatly in the seventeenth century, and increasingly it became the business of the writer to satisfy its interests, which for a variety of reasons were political and social. The early Metaphysical writers possessed a very small audience (one another and a few more who shared the same interests); very much the same situation obtained for Jonson and his followers. When the readership increased, poets modified their work accordingly. When Dryden did write of religion, he wrote of it as he and his contemporaries understood it. That Dryden took little delight in Donne's poetry is clear from his remarks in "A Discourse Concerning the Original and Progress of Satire" (1693):

> Donne affects the metaphysics, not only in his amorous verses, where nature only should reign; and perplexes the minds of the fair sex with nice speculations of philosophy, when he should engage their hearts and entertain them with the softnesses of love.

Dryden did not understand Donne's intentions very well, but he understood his own political intentions very well indeed.

In his own and the century's final years, Dryden worked primarily at translation, promising in his "Preface to *Fables Ancient and Modern*" (1700), "if it should please God to give me longer life and moderate health." He added another provision: "that I meet with those encouragements from the public, which may enable me to proceed in my undertaking with some cheerfulness." This is the remark of a public figure—a former poet laureate, author of a stream of plays and published books since the 1600's, a veteran attraction at Will's Coffee House in London.

Poets had not always expected such encouragements. When Donne died in 1631, only four of his poems had been published. Herbert, Marvell, and Traherne saw few or none of their poems in print. Jonson, on the other hand, had offered his work to the public, even inviting ridicule in 1616 by boldly calling his volume *Works*. Like Dryden after him, he had developed a healthy sense of audience in his career as a playwright. He had even more reason to fear an unhappy audience than Dryden, for along with John Marston and George Chapman, he had been imprisoned and very nearly mutilated by a gang of Scots retainers of James I whom the trio had outraged by some of their jests in their play *Eastward Ho!* (pr., pb. 1605). Nevertheless, Jonson promised a translation of Horace's *Ars poetica* (c. 17 B.C.E.; *The Art of Poetry*), with no provisions whatsoever, that same year. The fact that he did not deliver the translation until long afterward does not seem to have had anything to do with readers' wishes. Jonson usually conveyed the impression that whatever he had to say amounted to nothing less than a golden opportunity for any sensible reader or listener.

Even if one assumes that Dryden's hope for encouragement may have been only an expression of politeness, that politeness itself signifies a change of relationship with the "public." Most of the poetry written in the time of Donne and Jonson has the quality of being overheard. It is as if the poet is praying, making love, or rebuking a fool, and the reader has just happened to pass by. If the poem is a verse epistle, the reader experiences the uncomfortable feeling that he is reading someone else's mail—and quite often that is so. By 1700, the poet seems conscious of producing a document for public inspection and proceeds accordingly, with all the implications—fortunate and unfortunate—of such a procedure. He will not tax the public with too many difficulties, for some of them—too many, perhaps—will not understand. He had better polish his work, and he had better not be dull. He might produce one of those "overheard" lyrics once in a while, but the chances are that they will yield few excellences not imitative of earlier poets whose circumstances favored that type of poem.

The neoclassical sense of audience would continue, as the neoclassical period would continue, for nearly another century—at least in those poets with access to a public. The poet's public stance would give rise to more fine satire and reflective poems of great majesty and sustained moral power. The knack of lyric would be largely lost, and, when recovered, the lyrics would be romantic. No one would ever write poems like "A Valediction: Forbidding Mourning" or "To His Coy Mistress" again.

BIBLIOGRAPHY

Baker, David J. *Between Nations: Shakespeare, Spenser, Marvell, and the Question of Britain*. Stanford, Calif.: Stanford University Press, 1997. Fusing historiography and literary criticism, this book places Renaissance England and its literature at a meeting of English, Irish, Scottish, and Welsh histories.

Barbour, Reid. *English Epicures and Stoics: Ancient Legacies in Early Stuart Culture*. Amherst: University of Massachusetts Press, 1998. Part of the Massachusetts Studies in Early Modern Culture series. Portrays the intricate dialectical influence of the ancient Greek philosophies of Epicureanism and Stoicism on seventeenth century England and analyzes how these disparate legacies served as touchstones for discourse in the theater, poetry, and political, religious, and scientific literature of the period.

Campbell, Gordon, and Thomas N. Corns. *John Milton: Life, Work, and Thought*. New York: Oxford University Press, 2008. A biography by two eminent Milton scholars, emphasizing the relationship between Milton's imaginative works and the rapidly changing times in which he lived. Includes illustrations and maps. Extensive notes and bibliography. Index.

Cummings, Robert, ed. *Seventeenth-Century Poetry: An Annotated Anthology*. Malden, Mass.: Wiley-Blackwell, 2000. A selection from the works of more than fifty poets, including all the major figures of the period, as well as a number of writers recently added to the literary canon, many of them women. Modernized spelling and in-depth annotations. Index of authors, index of titles and first lines, and bibliography.

Cunnar, Eugene R., and Jeffrey Johnson. *Discovering and (Re)Covering the Seventeenth Century Religion Lyric*. Pittsburgh, Pa.: Duquesne University Press, 2001. A collection of fifteen essays whose primary purpose is to consider devotional lyricists of the seventeenth century who have previously been neglected. Among those discussed are Robert Southwell, Aemilia Lanyer, William Alabaster, William Austin, and Mary Carey. Bibliography and index.

Fowler, Alistair, ed. *The New Oxford Book of Seventeenth Century Verse*. 1992. Reprint. New York: Oxford University Press, 2008. This indispensable anthology contains 861 selections from works of major and minor poets and from a wide range of genres, including popular verse. Notes, index of first lines, and index of authors.

Lewis, Jayne, and Maximillian E. Novak, eds. *Enchanted Ground: Reimagining John Dryden*. Toronto: University of Toronto Press, 2004. A volume in the University of California, Los Angeles, Clark Memorial Library series. Subjects of these essays by various scholars include Dryden's political poetry, religious beliefs, connections to the literary heritage, plays, and songs. An audio compact disc of Dryden's songs is included with the book. Illustrated. Bibliographical references and index.

Mapstone, Sally, ed. *Older Scots Literature*. Edinburgh: John Donald, 2005. The third part of this volume contains essays on seventeenth century Scottish poets, including those associated with Scotland's James VI after he ascended the English throne. Bibliographical references and index.

Morotti, Arthur F. *Manuscript, Print, and the English Renaissance Lyric*. Ithaca, N.Y.: Cornell University Press, 1995. Examines the tradition of manuscript transmission of poetic works and explains how the change to print publication was effected. Morotti notes the ways in which the new process altered not only the creative process but also the cultural milieu. Bibliography and index.

Post, Jonathan F. S., ed. *Green Thoughts, Green Shades: Essays by Contemporary Poets on the Early Modern Lyric*. Berkeley: University of California Press, 2002. Twelve noted contemporary poets contemplate the poetry of their sixteenth and seventeenth century predecessors in the first publication of its kind. The keen insights and the lively style of these essays has elicited enthusiastic comments from scholars and critics. Highly recommended. Index.

Rawson, Claude, and Aaron Santesso, eds. *John Dryden (1631-1700): His Politics, His Plays, and His Poets*. Newark: University of Delaware Press, 2004. Essays produced for Yale University's celebration of the tercentenary of Dryden's death. Part 1 of the volume focuses on Dryden's plays, part 2, on connections between Dryden and other poets. Bibliography and index.

Reid, David Stuart. *The Metaphysical Poets*. Harlow, England: Longman, 2000. The author devotes a chapter to each of the six major Metaphysical poets, emphasizing their unique qualities as well as their similarities. The theme of diversity is then carried into a concluding chapter, which deals with other types of "seventeenth century wit" and with the differences between Metaphysical poets and the Augustans. A brief biography precedes each of the six main chapters. Illustrations, bibliographical references, and index.

Young, R. V. *Doctrine and Devotion in Seventeenth-Century Poetry: Studies on Donne, Herbert, Crashaw, and Vaughan*. Studies in Renaissance Literature 2. Rochester, N.Y.: D. S. Brewer, 2000. Argues that the devotional poetry of John Donne, George Herbert, Henry Vaughan, and Richard Crashaw owed more to the tradition of continental Catholicism than to Protestantism. The author also challenges postmodern interpretations by pointing out that such matters as subjective identity have long been basic to Christian thought. A landmark scholarly study. Bibliography and index.

Zwicker, Steven N., ed. *The Cambridge Companion to John Dryden*. New York: Cambridge University Press, 2004. Among the topics of the essays in this diverse collection are Dryden's plays, his satire, his politics, and his poetics. Chronology, bibliography, and index.

Robert P. Ellis

ENGLISH POETRY IN THE EIGHTEENTH CENTURY

The eighteenth century in Britain saw the blossoming of seventeenth century poetic modes and the sprouting of modes that would blossom into Romanticism. It was an age of reason and sentiment, of political turbulence, of growing colonialism and wealth, of beautiful landscapes and parks, of gin addiction and Evangelicalism, of a burgeoning middle class and growing respect for middle-class values, of increasing literacy and decreasing dependence on patronage, and of cantankerous Tories and complacent Whigs. As England became the center of world commerce and power, so, too, it became the center of literary achievement.

John Dryden died in 1700, but his death signaled no dramatic change in poetic style. Poets walked in his footsteps, moving away from Metaphysical conceits—from the style of those poets who glittered "Like twinkling Stars the Miscellanies o'er"—to search for smoothness and a new style of thinking. Symptomatic of the eighteenth century's passion for order and regularization was the tinkering by Alexander Pope (1688-1744) with the poetry of John Donne: He made Donne's numbers flow melodiously and corrected his versification. Heroic couplets and lampoons and political satires such as Dryden's were written throughout the century. Common Restoration subjects such as the imperious mistress and the cacophony of critics continued to be used.

Dryden named William Congreve (1670-1729) his poetical successor, but Pope was his true heir. From the appearance of his *Pastorals* in 1709 until William Wordsworth's *Lyrical Ballads* in 1798, Pope dominated poetry. His influence, for example, pervades Robert Dodsley's *Collection of Poems, by Several Hands* (1748), and it is evident in William Mason's *Museaus* (1747), in the half dozen other poems concerned chiefly with Pope, and in the many others that refer respectfully to him. If the poets of the latter part of the century did not imitate him, they at least grudgingly admired him while reacting against him.

The "ancients"—Homer and Vergil in particular, but Horace, Pindar, Juvenal, Martial, and Anacreon,

too—were devoutly followed. As school boys, the poets did countless exercises translating Latin and Greek verse, and, like John Milton before them, poets such as Joseph Addison (1672-1719) and Samuel Johnson (1709-1784) began by writing Latin verse. In the middle of his career, Pope translated the *Iliad* in 1715-1720 and the *Odyssey* in 1725-1726; he spent his later career writing imitations of Horace. Johnson chose to write imitations of the other great Roman satirist, Juvenal. These imitations were not strict translations; rather, they picked up hints from the classics and made the subject relevant to contemporary life. Even at the end of the century, William Cowper (1731-1800) translated Homer, though his style was too heavily Miltonic.

William Shakespeare and other Elizabethans provided a third important example for eighteenth century poets. Both Pope and Johnson edited Shakespeare: Pope's edition was valuable chiefly for restoring "prose" passages to the original blank verse, Johnson's for his criticism founded on common sense. Joseph Warton (1722-1800) and Thomas Warton (1728-1790) and other mid-century poets appealed to the example of Shakespeare to free themselves from the classical doctrine of the superiority of judgment and taste to the imagination. Shakespeare helped inspire *An Ode on the Popular Superstitions of the Highlands of Scotland, Considered as the Subject of Poetry* (1788), by William Collins (1721-1759), and even William Blake (1757-1827) was drawn to Elizabethan poetry. For the eighteenth century, Shakespeare represented unlearned genius, and his quality of irregularity, of "great beauties and blemishes" was highly praised.

Although less influential than Shakespeare, Edmund Spenser had his followers. *The Castle of Indolence* (1748), by James Thomson (1700-1748), imitated Spenserian melody and descriptive techniques, and William Shenstone (1714-1763) parodied Spenser in *The Schoolmistress* (1742). *The Minstrel* (1771-1774), by James Beattie (1735-1803), was one of the longest and best poems of the century written in Spenserian stanza. Another poet who owed much to Spenser was the tragic Thomas Chatterton (1752-1770. Like

Spenser, Chatterton wrote vigorous lyrics and showed much metrical originality.

When eighteenth century poets sat down to write a poem, they did not pour forth images of their souls; they attempted certain genres and looked to the ancients for inspiration and example. Their voices and emotions were public rather than private, and they wrote about the present rather than about their own pasts. The poet was the spokesperson for his age and his subject was humans as social creatures. The personal did, however, creep into eighteenth century verse: The best work of Matthew Prior (1664-1721) best work was personal, if not autobiographical, and Pope used the epistle form to speak personally.

Eighteenth century poets valued elegant ease and noble urbanity. "Decorum" was a key word: The eighteenth century classicists sought to control the abundant energy that characterized earlier English classicists. Augustan poets tried to achieve the effect of apparent casualness of structure with definite coherence under the surface. Their use of noble Roman tone and classical patterns familiar throughout Europe gave them a Continental audience, something the Elizabethans never had.

EPICS AND MOCK-EPICS

The most popular genres were epic, ode, satire, elegy, epistle, and song. To show their fealty to Homer and Vergil, nearly every eighteenth century poet at least thought of writing an epic. Pope, for one, was planning an epic on Brutus when he died. None of the plans for writing epics or the epics that were written brought forth anything but sour fruit (Aaron Hill's biblical epic *Gideon*, 1749, is a prime example); however, the mock-epic form in this possibly nonheroic age brought forth delicious fruit, including Pope's *The Rape of the Lock* (1712, 1714) and *The Dunciad* (1728-1743).

ODES

Eighteenth century poets had more success writing odes than they did writing epics. In the early years of the century, poets looked to Pindar or to Horace as models for writing odes. They used Pindaric odes for exalted subjects and Horatian odes for various urbane,

personal, and meditative themes. In the seventeenth century, Abraham Cowley had popularized irregularities in the Pindaric odes; after Congreve denounced them in his *A Pindarique Ode on the Victorious Progress of Her Majesties Arms* (1706), most poets knew the duty of Pindaric regularity but still preferred the laxness of Cowley's form. Thomas Gray (1716-1771) was an important exception: He wrote two Pindaric odes—"The Bard" and "The Progress of Poesy"—in rigidly correct form.

In the second quarter of the century, a new type of ode appeared, inspired by Milton's "L'Allegro" and "Il Penseroso." The "descriptive and allegorical ode" centered around a personified abstraction, such as pity or simplicity, and treated it in a descriptive or pictorial way. Collins and the Warton brothers did much to popularize this mode in the 1740's.

SATIRE

The eighteenth century was, of course, the golden age of satire. Satirists such as Jonathan Swift and Pope attacked the frivolity of polite society, the corruption of politics, and false values in all the arts. The aim of satire, as Pope explained it, was not wanton destruction: Satire "heals with Morals what it hurts with Wit." Satirists, he claimed, nourished the state, promoting its virtue and providing it everlasting fame.

Eighteenth century poetry has been accused of monotony and weak feeling. The zeal of the satirists for truth and virtue, however, blazes through many lines, and the warmth of their compassion for the poor, the sick, the mistreated, and the aged glows through many others. Pope, in the *Moral Essays* (1731-1735), for example, pities the ancient belles of court: "See how the World its Veterans rewards!/ A Youth of Frolicks, an old Age of Cards." The age, particularly the state under the administration of Sir Robert Walpole, may not have been as black as the satirists painted it—it was an age of increasing wealth and progress—but the satirists were obsessed by the precariousness of intellect and of civilization, by the threat of fools and bores and pedants, by the fear of universal darkness burying all. In a world where human intellect alone keeps society from the disintegration caused by unthinking enthusiasts and passionate pig heads, dullness is morally objectionable—

an aspect of vice. Satirists thus became moral crusaders for truth, virtue, and intelligence. They believed in an ancient state of purity which humans could not re-create; humans could, however, "relume the ancient light" (in Pope's words) for the future.

ELEGIES

Elegies in Latin and Greek were composed in ele-giac couplets rather than the hexameter lines of the epic and the pastoral. Donne wrote amatory elegies in the seventeenth century, but by the eighteenth century, ele-gies were meditative pieces, often about death. Gray's "Elegy Written in a Country Churchyard" (1751), said by some to be the best poem of the eighteenth century, is an elegy for all "average" and obscure men. It achieves the ideals of its day in its attempt to work in universal terms and in its purity and harmony of dic-tion; it approaches Romanticism in its placid melan-choly and rustic setting. In "Elegy to the Memory of an Unfortunate Lady" (1717), the other important elegy of the eighteenth century and one of the only works of Pope that the Romantics could tolerate, Pope laments the mortality of a young suicide victim and his own mortality, stressing the threats to human feeling and the glory of its intensity.

EPISTLES

The epistle, or verse letter, an important form in the seventeenth century, reached its height in the epistles of Pope in the 1740's, and continued to be popular until the end of the nineteenth century. Horace provided the classical model for the verse epistle. The familiar form of the epistle allowed poets to seem to speak sincerely and intimately to a close friend while addressing the public about general issues. Almost all epistles were written in heroic couplets, began in a rather rambling way, and finally came to a point about halfway through the poem. Charles Churchill's *Epistle to William Hogarth* (1763), for example, begins with a miscella-neous discussion of satire. The effect of this structure is comic and optimistic: Order is brought out of disorder.

LYRIC POETRY

Lyric poets used the song to achieve brevity and, at times, elegance. Songs were collected and written throughout the period, but the greatest of the song-writers—Robert Burns (1759-1796)—came at the end. He not only composed his own songs but also reconsti-tuted and invigorated old Scottish songs, turning a drinking song into "Auld Lang Syne" and a disreputa-ble ballad into "John Anderson My Jo."

EPIGRAMS

Other popular genres included the epigram, the fa-ble, and verse criticism. The tradition of the epigram, modeled on Martial and on Horace, began in the Re-naissance and appealed to the eighteenth century be-cause of its conciseness and the opportunity it provided to display wit. The average epigram was at most six lines long, beginning with something to arouse curios-ity or anticipation and closing with humor or surprise. Common topics included love and the characters of people, though some epigrams were obscene. A spe-cialized form of the epigram was the epitaph, which several poets composed for themselves. John Gay's ep-itaph reads: "Life is a jest, and all things show it/ I thought so once; but now I know it," and Swift's Latin epitaph, roughly translated, says that he is now gone where bitter indignation no longer lacerates his heart.

FABLES

The fables of the eighteenth century demonstrate the ability of Augustan writers to enrich and vary a genre. The favorite form for the fables was the iambic tetrameter couplet. Gay wrote the best English fables (1727-1738), though Swift, Bernard Mandeville, Prior, Christopher Smart, Cowper, Beattie, and Johnson also wrote them. Far from being childlike, Gay's *Fables* (1727, 1738) expressed a disillusioned cynicism to-ward humankind, particularly emphasizing foolish hu-man pride. No English fable, however, could measure up to those written in France by Jean de La Fontaine in the seventeenth century.

CRITICAL POETRY AND *AN ESSAY ON CRITICISM*

The critical poem was popular in the Restoration and came into full bloom in the eighteenth century. Fol-lowing the pattern set by Horace in his *Ars Poetica* (c. 17 B.C.E.; *The Art of Poetry*), the Italian poet Marco Girolamo Vida wrote *De arte poetica* (1527; *Vida's Art of Poetry*, 1725) and the French poet Nicolas Boileau-Despréaux wrote *L'Art poétique* (1674; *The Art of Poetry*, 1683). In England, John Sheffield's *Essay on Poetry* (1682), Wentworth Dillon, earl of Roscommon's *Essay on Translated Verse* (1684), and Lord Lansdowne's *Essay upon Unnatural Flights in Poetry* (1701) bore testimony to the increased interest in literary criticism and theory.

Pope's *An Essay on Criticism* (1711), the zenith of this genre, condensed eighteenth century poetic standards. *An Essay on Criticism* is actually a poem on how to judge a poem and on what morals are requisite for a critic. The first requirement is to follow nature, then to follow the ancients who "discov'red" and "Methodiz'd" the rules of nature. The "laws of Nature" to the Augustans meant, roughly, the right principles that every person of common sense and goodwill would follow in thought and conduct. The French called nature *la belle nature*, and Pope maintained that it is "the source, and end, and test of Art." The faith that humans have in a world of universal human values underlies the concept of nature.

From *An Essay on Criticism* comes such neoclassic advice as: "The Sound must seem an Eccho to the Sense," "Avoid Extreams" (the Augustan ideal of the golden mean), "In all you speak, let Truth and Candor shine," and "Men must be taught as if you taught them not." The poem's merit lies in its compressed phrasing of current standards, not in any originality of thought. Early eighteenth century poets or their audiences were not as much impressed by originality as by memorable expression: Pope said that true wit is "What oft was *Thought*, but ne'er so well *Exprest*," and Addison in *The Spectator* 253 wrote that "wit and fine writing doth not consist so much in advancing things that are new, as in giving things that are known agreeable turn."

POETRY, PATRONAGE, AND POLITICS

Eighteenth century poets generally came from good families in much reduced circumstances. Prior, Swift, and Johnson fit this generalization, though Pope was the son of a wealthy linen draper. Poets still sought patrons, praising their parks and estates, but more and more their writings at least partially supported them. Prior, for example, apparently netted four thousand guineas from his *Poems on Several Occasions* (1707, 1709). The audience for literature was growing, thanks in large measure to the graduates of charity schools and the newly founded grammar schools. Political preferment also proved lucrative for poets. Addison served as undersecretary of state and later secretary to the lord-lieutenant of Ireland, and Burns collected excise taxes. Johnson's letter to Lord Chesterfield on his tardy recognition of the *Dictionary of the English Language* (1755) is said to have given the final blow to patronage, though the letter was not printed until near the end of the century.

In the first half of the century, poets aligned themselves according to politics. Addison and Whigs such as Ambrose Philips reigned at Button's coffeehouse. The Tories—Swift, Gay, Thomas Parnell, Pope, and John Arbuthnot—formed the Scriblerus Club and met at Arbuthnot's apartments in St. James's Palace. Parnell and Gay both worked closely with Pope and yet remained independent: Parnell published his Miltonic poems chiefly in miscellanies, and Gay became the king of burlesque. Barbs flew back and forth between the Whig and Tory parties, the deadliest of which was Pope's portrait of Addison in *Epistle to Dr. Arbuthnot* (1735).

HUMOR AND SATIRE

Though there undoubtedly was venom in these attacks, there was also a good measure of humor written in the early decades of the century. Gay was a chief contributor with *Wine* (1708), a burlesque of Milton and John Philips's *Cyder* (1708) and *Trivia: Or, The Art of Walking the Streets of London* (1716). Swift, Lady Mary Wortley-Montagu, and others helped to popularize "town eclogues." The most delightfully imaginative and amusing of the exposés of society was Pope's mock-heroic *The Rape of the Lock*, with its sylphs and gnomes and diminution of Homeric epic. *The Rape of the Lock* is much more complicated than Dryden's *Mac Flecknoe: Or, A Satyre upon the True-Blew-Protestant Poet, T. S.* (1682): Pope reveals the confusion of moral values in society in such catalogs as "Puffs, Powder, Patches, Bibles, Billet-doux." Pope simultaneously laughs at the foibles of society and warns of the fragility of beauty.

Most poets wrote in heroic couplets, a pair of rhyming pentameter lines. In Shakespeare's time, couplets closed sonnets or scenes in blank verse dramas; in the later seventeenth century, couplets were adapted to correspond to the elegiac couplet of classical verse and to the heroic, unrhymed Greek and Latin hexameter. Pope was the master of the heroic couplet; he knew how to build two or three couplets, each technically closed, into a unified, easy period. Throughout the century, poets in England and America tried to equal his artistry. By the end of the century, poets such as Cowper still attempted heroic couplets, but with little success. Cowper could achieve the Horatian simplicity admired in the eighteenth century, but his verses lacked Horatian polish and piquancy.

Even in the early part of the century, however, poets such as Swift and Prior ignored heroic couplets in favor of tetrameter couplets. Prior criticized the heroic couplet, complaining that it

> cuts off the Sense at the end of every first Line, which must always rhime to the next following, and consequently produces too frequent an Identity in the Sound, and brings every Couplet to the Point of an Epigram.

Short poems and irregular meters, on the whole, were not highly regarded.

THE NATURE OF HUMANKIND

After the 1640's, England's civil war left deep scars that lasted well into the eighteenth century. Religious and political factions still strained the country, and the atmosphere was at once one of compromise and tolerance and one of skepticism. It was a time when writers questioned and strove to understand the nature of humanity, human limitations, and the limitations that must be set on human passions. Answers to these questions differed significantly: Some optimistic moralists believed in the essential goodness of humankind, some satirists and cynics bemoaned humanity's incorrigible pride, which would forever keep people from the truth, and some realists insisted that humanity and the world must be accepted as they are, in all their ugliness.

In *Characteristics of Men, Manners, Opinions, Times* (1711), the Anthony Ashley-Cooper, third earl of Shaftesbury, promulgated a belief in the perfection of the universe and the naturalness of virtue in humans.

Opposing Hobbes's belief in the natural selfishness of humans, Shaftesbury wrote that it is

> impossible to conceive that a rational creature coming first to be tried by rational objects, and receiving into his mind the images or representations of justice, generosity, gratitude, or other virtue, should have no liking of these or dislike of their contraries. . . .

He asserted that unselfishness is as natural to humans as selfishness and that humans have "social instincts" and "social passions" as well as egotism. Although Shaftesbury had many detractors, including Bernard de Mandeville in his *Fable of the Bees* (1714), his beliefs gained wide acceptance in England, France, and Germany.

Pope's *An Essay on Man* (1733-1734), another influential document on these ethical questions, reflects Pope's own attempts to balance optimism and a sense of fact. He describes the "great chain of being" and the place of humanity in this "isthmus of a middle state" as "A Being darkly wise, and rudely great." He tried to build his rational system of ethics without denying religion but by being independent of it. Thomson, who was influenced by Shaftesbury, anticipated Pope in declaring in *The Seasons* (1730, 1744, 1746) that what seems evil is seen only in part, because the whole is good, that order may be threatened yet will survive in a larger sense. He did not, however, attack the problems of evil and humanity's moral responsibility directly.

A corollary to the question about human nature was the problem of happiness. As the wealth of the citizenry increased, leisure time, sports, recreation, and the search for happiness became important. "Happiness" replaced "property" as one of the inalienable rights of human beings. In searching for happiness, people become disillusioned, and many a writer from Prior through Johnson to Oliver Goldsmith expressed the pessimism that neither knowledge, riches, pleasure, nor power can avail against the assault of time and human weakness. John Dyer voiced the feeling well in these lines from *Grongar Hill* (1726):

> A little Rule, a little Sway,
> A Sunbeam in a Winter's Day
> Is all the Proud and Mighty have,
> Between the Cradle and the Grave.

This pessimism led Prior to urge people to cherish fleeting joys as the only respite in the human world of suffering and led Edward Young in *The Complaint: Or, Night-Thoughts on Life, Death, and Immortality* (1742-1744; commonly known as *Night-Thoughts*) to insist on the latent divinity of humans and their power to fly above worldly claims to the blessed realms of infinity. Gray, in his "Hymn to Adversity" (1742), which Johnson termed both "poetical and rational," cautioned against expecting more of life than life can give. Chastising men for chasing "treacherous phantoms" and deluding themselves with visions of "airy good," Johnson in *The Vanity of Human Wishes* (1749) urged people to study, exertion, and prayer. All these poets evince the increasing concern and compassion of the century with the lot of humanity.

LANDSCAPE AND PHILOSOPHICAL DISCOURSE

While Pope inherited satire and heroic couplets from Dryden, there was another poetic movement in the eighteenth century whose ancestors were Milton, reflective poetry, and blank verse. Poets increasingly used landscape as material for their poetry and wedded it to philosophical discourse. Thomson's *The Seasons* was both the crowning effort of this movement and a stimulus to its further development. Thomson patterned *Autumn* (1730) and *Winter* (1726) on the chronological progress of the season and *Summer* (1727) on the events of a typical day. The passages alternate between description and meditation, with description being the most innovative. Thomson excelled in the presentation of exuberant motion and tightly packed detail. Pope and Philips had written lovely pastorals earlier in the century, and Gay incorporated much folklore and the sights and sounds of the country in his *Rural Sports* (1713) and *The Shepherd's Week* (1714); but Thomson's work differed sharply from the pastoral in its description of nature for its own sake, with human incidents as background rather than nature as background for human drama. *The Seasons* started a tradition of descriptive poetry, which at its extreme became a love of what Shenstone called "odd picturesque description." The descriptive poem usurped the place of the epic as the most honored poetic form, and Thomson was invested as the preeminent

English poet of nature until Wordsworth succeeded him.

Thomson has been accused of having an overly latinate style with false ornamentation. His strength lies in his minute observation of nature, in his almost scientific curiosity. A professed deist, Thomson saw in nature a revelation of the attributes of God; other deists, and even the more orthodox, upheld him in this belief. The scientist in Thomson admired the orderliness of the mathematical universe. Like Pope, Thomson insisted on intelligence and reason; he believed that a study of nature frees people from superstition and ignorance. He, too, reflected on the wants and miseries of human life.

DIDACTIC POETRY

Encouraged by *The Seasons* and *An Essay on Man*, many poets began to write in a moralizing, didactic manner, including William Somerville (*The Chace*, 1735), Henry Brooke (*Universal Beauty*, 1735), Mark Akenside (*The Pleasures of the Imagination*, 1744), and Young (*Night-Thoughts*). Akenside's *The Pleasures of the Imagination*, based on Addison's discussion of the same subject in *The Spectator*, insists on the interconnection of truth, goodness, and beauty. Akenside's training in religion, philosophy, science, and art is evident throughout the poem, which is more a document for a historian of ideas than for an appreciator of poetic beauty.

Night-Thoughts is essentially a Christian book of piety, but its appeal lay in its concentration on death and its autobiographical elements. Its main theme is that death's inevitability should sober both the reckless libertine and the complacent deist. Its moral reflections are addressed to a "silken son of pleasure" named Lorenzo, whose "fond heart dances while the siren sings." The pious gloom of *Night-Thoughts*, which was mistranslated and misinterpreted, caused a sensation on the Continent and was gradually incorporated into the European tradition of romantic *Weltschmerz*.

SENSIBILITY AND MELANCHOLY

Another important movement in the literature of England and the Continent in the first half of the eighteenth century has been named "sensibility." By this is meant an exquisite sensitiveness to the beautiful and the good, a sensitiveness that induces melancholy or sorrow. All that is noble and generous in human conduct was thought to have its source in this exquisite sensitivity, and nature assisted as a moral tonic to the human heart. The pensive mood, even though it induced melancholy, also induced pleasure because it freed the emotions and the imagination from the conventions of civilization and from the vanity and corruption of humankind. Milton's "Il Penseroso" partly influenced this new mode, and Richard Steele promoted melancholy in *Tatler* 89: "That calm and elegant satisfaction which the vulgar call Melancholy, is the true and proper Delight of Men of Knowledge and Virtue." In *Grongar Hill*, Dyer employed picturesque ruins and other devices to summon a mood of gentle melancholy, and Shenstone asserted his independence from the satirists and wits, writing that the eighteenth century had "discovered sweets in melancholy which we could not find in mirth." Thomas Warton's celebratory "The Pleasures of Melancholy" (1747) avoided the didacticism of some of Milton's followers and cultivated relaxed and idyllic moods instead. In some ways, sensibility was a natural reaction to the Restoration, to its moral cynicism and its exclusive culture. Sensibility was a movement toward moral feeling and conduct, toward middle-class values, and, politically, toward the Whigs.

FROM SOCIETY TO THE INDIVIDUAL

The latter half of the century produced no English poet equal to Pope, but it did produce a large number of important writers and did serve as a transition period from concentration on society as the preserver of the best in humanity to concentration on the nobility and potential of the individual. The beautiful city of Bath was built in the classical style, and the Adam brothers designed and built new streets and squares in Edinburgh. Advances were made in the art of writing history because men had come to believe with Pope that the "proper study of mankind is man." Shaftesbury's doctrine of humanity's natural goodness coupled with materialistic rationalism had led to optimistic political programs based on the perfectibility of humanity.

Writers did not rebel overtly against the classical tradition but increasingly began to write about realistic matters of everyday life. Gray's "Elegy Written in a Country Churchyard" is one of the best examples of this new poetic material. Humble life is treated humorously as well as realistically and much less idyllically. Writers began to claim that absolute standards are impossible and to believe in progress and novelty. With increasing doubts about Pope's assertion that truth is "one clear, unchanged, and universal light," the pendulum swung from fear of individualism and enthusiasm (which had led to civil war) to love of diversity (which, in turn, led to revolutions).

Poets became expressers of mood rather than eloquent preachers of general truths. The poet was exalted as a mysterious and sacred natural force that mere intelligence could not comprehend and training could not bestow. "Genius" supplanted wit as the creative force in the poet's mind. Abbe Yart in his sketch of Pope distinguished between the two: "Wit consists in adorning well-known thoughts, but genius is creative." William Duff in his *Essay on Original Genius* (1767) wrote that genius combines a "plastic and comprehensive imagination" with "an acute intellect, and an exquisite sensibility and refinement of taste." Imagination, the key ingredient in genius, was for Johnson a lively, delightful faculty that objectifies truth, recombines experience, and produces novelty by its varied combinations. For Blake, the imagination was the highest power in humans, the organ of morality, art, and spiritual illumination. It had a demonic power and, indeed, was said to be the voice of nature itself speaking through the poet's soul. Genius, which was subject only to its own laws, produced "natural" literature of wild irregularity or homely simplicity. Giving a suprarational source to poetic genius eventually created problems, particularly in Blake's works. It served to weaken the poet's powers of self-criticism and control.

Moving away from the Renaissance and neoclassic idea that poetic genius should be learned, mid-eighteenth century audiences believed in "natural" or unlearned genius. Johnson, however, while affirming that "no man ever became great by imitation," insisted that genius must be trained by study. Belief in "natural" genius went hand in hand with a return to folk and national literature. In Germany, Johann Gottfried Herder developed his famous distinction between *Volkspoesie*, poetry that springs spontaneously from the people, and *Kunstpoesie*, poetry that the educated produce within the traditional culture. In England, Collins's *Ode on the Popular Superstitions of the Highlands of Scotland, Considered as the Subject of Poetry* used folklore to inspire the poetic imagination and voiced the view that literature should have its source in the indigenous folk culture rather than in Greco-Roman literary tradition.

The better poets imitated Horatian and French models inexactly. Even the conservative Goldsmith could write *The Deserted Village* (1770) without setting out to write an elegy or a pastoral. In Pope's time, imitation was supposed to be creative rather than servile, but by mid-century, critics such as Young were writing that it is the poet's duty and highest possible achievement to be "original." Originality, not to be confused with novelty, meant going back to the originals of things, not going to the "copies" of others. As one newspaper critic wrote, "striking out new Paths" rather than "treading very circumspectly in old ones" is of primary importance (*Daily Gazetteer*, 1741). The classical soil had been tilled out.

GOTHICISM

In addition to the fertile soil found in humble, everyday life, poets found new material in the Middle Ages, in castles and ruins and anything "Gothic." The Frenchman Paul Henri Mallet and his work *Northern Antiquities* (1770) did more than any other individual to set Europe ablaze with enthusiasm for ancient Germanic mythology and the medieval manners and customs of the North. In England, Horace Walpole built his monument to Gothicism, Strawberry Hill. Thomas Warton, the elder, wrote "A Runic Ode," and Thomas Warton, the younger, wrote three volumes on the history of English poetry from the twelfth to the close of the sixteenth century (1774-1781). Pope earlier in the century had chronicled love pangs in an *Epistle from Eloisa to Abelard* (1717), though this also had its source in Ovidian elegy, Dyer described Welsh ruins in *Grongar Hill*, Thomas Warton set his "The Pleasures of Melancholy" in the yard of a partially ruined Gothic church, and Gray published two odes "from the Norse tongue"— "The Fatal Sister" and "The Descent of Odin"—and

some translations of Welsh stories. The poetry of Gray, in fact, provides a useful example of the turn from Greco-Roman traditions to Northern antiquities: He began his career writing classically correct elegies and odes and finished his career imitating the primitive minstrelsy of the North.

Even though James Macpherson's Ossian tales were not authentic, they were extraordinarily successful, praised by Gray because they were "full of nature and noble wild imagination." The tales of Ossian reveal what eighteenth century audiences thought they saw in medieval writings: primitivism and sentimentalism. The idea of a Centic bard such as Ossian who could rival Homer thrilled Macpherson's contemporaries. They also enjoyed the sententious melancholy they could feel in such tales as that of the warrior Carthon whose father Clessámmoor unknowingly kills him. The sentimentality and melancholy of the tales is increased by double distancing: The tales themselves are supposedly old and the poet Ossian is writing longingly of a time past. Macpherson owed more to the Bible, Homer, Milton, and more recent authors, however, than he did to an oral tradition.

BALLADS

Concurrent with the interest in medievalism came the reawakening interest in the ballad. Popular ballads in the first half of the century include Henry Carey's *Sally in Our Alley*, Gay's *'Twas When the Seas Were Roaring* (1715) and the ballads in his *The Beggar's Opera* (1728), and Henry Fielding's *Roast Beef of Old England* (1731). Even Swift's two saints found broadside ballads plastered on the walls of the cottage of Baucis and Philemon. Many of the ballad songs are narratives. Allan Ramsay, an important publisher of ancient Scottish ballads, modernized and "improved" the texts. In America, many complaints against the British took the form of ballads.

Considered a rather rude and plebeian amusement, the ballad gained respectability with the publication of Thomas Percy's collection, *Reliques of Ancient Poetry*, in 1765. The ballad's simple style profoundly affected the changing tastes of the writers and public of the eighteenth century. In the latter part of the century, Cowper's "The Diverting History of John Gilpin" had tremendous success; Cowper adapted it from the true story of a wild horseback ride taken by John Beyer, a Cheapside linen draper. Cowper credited the popularity of the ballad to its nationalism (he believed the ballad form was peculiar to England), its flexibility in being used for both humorous and tragic subjects, and its simplicity and ease.

Percy's *Reliques of Ancient Poetry* caught the imagination of its German readers. Addison, Swift, and Pope had had followers in Germany, and, then, Thomson, Milton, and Young. Sentimental verse won approval in the writings of F. G. Klopstock and Ewald Christian von Kleist. H. W. von Gurstenberg, F. F. Kretschmann, and Michael Denis (the translator of Ossian) led the "bardic" movement. It was Percy's collection, however, that directly influenced the poets who in 1772 founded Gottinger Hain, or the Brotherhood of the Grove, and who belonged mainly to the peasant or bourgeois classes.

PRIMITIVISM

The same yearnings that the eighteenth century felt for native poetry and nature stimulated the glorification of the "noble savage." Particularly in the latter half of the century, writers expressed longing for a "return to Nature" and brought primitivism into vogue. They contrasted the innocent child of the wilderness with the selfish adult of artificial civilization. Urban life and civilization departed from the "natural." Jean-Jacques Rousseau, the greatest European supporter of the "Return to Nature," believed that nature had originally made people good and happy but that civilization had made them criminal and miserable. Poets such as Cowper escaped to the countryside for tranquillity, and in those times nature was easily found: One could walk into the country even from central London, the largest of the few large towns in England. Cowper expressed the sentiments of many when he wrote, "God made the country, but man made the town."

CHILDREN'S POETRY

The spread of education and the longing for innocence produced another new literary form, literature for children. Before the eighteenth century, poets wrote about children, particularly about their deaths, in hopes

of parental patronage, but few poems were written for children. At the beginning of the century, Isaac Watts wrote *Divine and Moral Songs for Children* (1715) and at the end of the century Blake wrote *Songs of Innocence and of Experience* (1794) specifically for children. Blake did not condescend to children or indulge in humorous play to amuse the adults who read to children. His verses are childlike but never childish. Other writers for children include Philips and Prior. Philips, a writer of pastorals, earned the nickname "Namby Pamby" for his syrupy children's verses. Much better were Prior's mock-serious verses like the one in which Kitty begged Mama for the chariot and "set the world on fire."

HYMNS

Another new flowering in the eighteenth century was hymn writing. As more and more sects formed in opposition to established churches, new music for worship had to be created. In the first part of the century, Watts was one of the best and most scholarly of the Dissenting writers. His hymns, including "God our help in ages past," expressed the popular view that the universe displays the Almighty's hand. With fresh and independent critical ideas, Watts believed that the cultivation of faith can elevate poetry. Watts's hymns and others in the early part of the century tended to be "congregational" in point of view.

In Germany, pietism revived and left its traces in the sphere of religious poetry. The main emphasis lay in the individual's spiritual experience, not in conformity. A comparable revival in England was Evangelicalism. Just as literature had reacted to excessive cynicism and rationalism by growing in emotional intensity, so religion, both within and without the Anglican Church, reacted to skepticism and deism by emphasizing the passions and conversion of the individual soul. John Wesley and Charles Wesley, ordained Anglican ministers, felt forced by the hostile Established Church to break off and form an independent sect of Methodism. Methodism rapidly gained converts, especially among the humble and less educated. It brought them solace for their sorrows, gave them a moral force and feeling of personal importance, and added to the stirrings of democracy within society. The Wesleys themselves wrote hymns, mostly personal in nature. Charles Wesley's most famous hymn is "Jesus, Lover of My Soul." Another famous hymn written at this time is "Rock of Ages, Cleft for Me" by the now unknown writer, Augustus Toplady. Many hymn writers, unfortunately, committed the error of mixing secular metaphor and symbolism, with ludicrous and unsavory results.

Cowper, the poet of the Evangelical revival though still an Anglican, wrote sixty-five *Olney Hymns* (1779) in conjunction with Reverend John Newton, the most famous of which is "Light Shining Out of Darkness" ("God moves in a mysterious way"). For the most part, his hymns express the beauty and serenity of the religious experience, although self-doubts darken "Light Shining Out of Darkness." Cowper was obsessed by the idea that God's grace had been withheld from him and that his eternal damnation had already been decided. His poetry expressed despair and hope and made firm doctrinal assertions which were typical of his day.

PROGRESS POEMS

The two best poets of the new belief in secular progress were Collins and Gray. Both accomplished scholars, they expressed their poetic ideals of liberty and simplicity in historical surveys or "progress poems." Collins excelled in writing odes: His "Ode to Evening" is particularly beautiful in its delicate "dying fall" of cadence. His "Ode Written in the Beginning of the Year 1746" has a delicate and pensive melody. Emotional apostrophes fill Collins's work, making it more exclamatory than reflective and making it less warm and personal. He chiefly appeals with his curious, ornate fantasies and his creation of dim and dreamlike effects.

Even though Gray and Collins resembled each other in temperament and literary principles, Gray was the better and more popular writer. Among the most learned of English poets, Gray read widely in Latin and Greek, in his English predecessors, and in Old Norse and Welsh. His range in various meters was unmatched in his century: He could write ceremonious heroic quatrains in "Elegy Written in a Country Churchyard," energetic effluences in his Pindaric odes, and primitive chants in his later period. His poetry dealt with emotions more directly than that of Collins. "The Bard" and "The Progress of Poesy," which combine tight organi-

zation with wild imaginative flights, approach the sublime as few other attempts at this time did. Gray's fastidiousness and habit of endless revision limited the number of poems he published.

SAMUEL JOHNSON

Although the spring and summer of neoclassicism had passed, there still remained the colorful autumn in the writings of Samuel Johnson and his friends, writings that insisted on presenting life realistically. The impressive figure of Johnson dominates the later half of the eighteenth century. The last major Augustan figure, he excelled in writing poetry, essays, and criticism, and in compiling the great *A Dictionary of the English Language*. His first major poem, *London* (1738), satirized the city's corruption in imitation of Juvenal's denunciation of Rome. It came out on the same day as Pope's *Epilogue to the Satires* and was thought to compare favorably with it. In 1747, Johnson composed a prologue for the opening of the season at Drury Lane, a poem remarkable for its compressed and intelligent dramatic criticism. His greatest poem, *The Vanity of Human Wishes*, expressed Christian pessimism about humanity's earthly lot. Johnson opposed the currents of his age in criticizing Milton, the pastoral tradition, and blank verse, and in condemning the elevation of instincts and emotions over reason.

OLIVER GOLDSMITH

Johnson's friend Oliver Goldsmith displayed a similar range of talent in writing poetry, a novel, essays, and plays. In *The Traveller* (1764), representative of the "survey" convention of eighteenth century verse, he scrutinizes and judges the national temperaments and political constitutions of several European nations. He explains the doctrine of the principle of compensation, yet another eighteenth century exegesis on the idea of happiness: Every state has its own particular principle of happiness, which in each may be carried to "mischievous excess." In *The Deserted Village*, he chastizes large estate owners for razing country villages and scattering the villagers to increase their holdings. He describes the economic plight of the villagers and warns of the dangers of luxury and "trade's unfeeling train." Both poems, written in heroic couplets, display the gentle humor and kindness of their author.

GEORGE CRABBE

Another poet who insisted on portraying life realistically was George Crabbe. Crabbe despised the weak idealism of the pastoral and poured his energy into describing the sordid and humble life of the Suffolk villagers of his youth. Crabbe was no devotee of Shaftesbury: He had no sentimental confidence in the goodness of human nature. Unlike earlier classicists, he emphasized individual responsibility rather than societal responsibility for crime and distress.

CHARLES CHURCHILL

Charles Churchill, a dissipated clergyman who turned poet in his later years, continued the classical tradition of satire with all the faults of Pope and fewer merits. In his first important poem, *The Rosciad* (1761), he vigorously attacked theatrical personalities (some critics have named this poem the best satire between Pope's *The Dunciad* and Lord Byron's *English Bards and Scotch Reviewers*, 1809). Churchill's satires have the energy and venom of Pope's satires, but they lack deftness and elegance. Churchill wrote many of his satires in support of his friend John Wilkes. Wilkes had condemned the Scottish people in *The North Briton*, a weekly political periodical; Churchill continued the outcry in *The Prophecy of Famine* (1763). William Hogarth had drawn a caricature of Wilkes in the courtroom; Churchill took revenge on him in *Epistle to William Hogarth*. Wilkes dueled with Samuel Martin; Churchill defended him in *The Duellist* (1763). The fourth earl of Sandwich was Wilkes's enemy; Churchill attacked his hypocrisy in *The Candidate* (1764). Contemporaries of Pope and Churchill could relish the frequent personal allusions, but to succeeding generations, they have meant little.

WILLIAM COWPER AND ROBERT BURNS

William Cowper tried to add to the satirical tradition, but he was too gentle and gracious a man to be a great satirist. In "Table Talk," he commented on the poetry of the century; in "Retirement" and "The Progress of Error," he attacked the follies of high life; and in "Expostulation," he condemned patriotic poems, including the lyric "On the Loss of the Royal George."

Cowper could write moving realistic poetry. In *The Task* (1785), he accurately and delightfully sketched country life, recording the sights and sounds and shrewdly portraying human character. *The Task* satisfied the hunger of the eighteenth century for long poems (a hunger that soon began to be satiated), for rambling structure, and for reflective description. "Domestic happiness" and gardening, he rejoiced, give "blest seclusion from a jarring world." Humor at this time was becoming rare and precious in poetry. Cowper wrote *The Task* on the urging of his friend Lady Austen, who wanted him to try blank verse and who told him, when he complained of not having a subject, "Oh, you can never be in want of a subject; you can write upon any—write upon that sofa!"

Cowper's poetry blended and harmonized the new and sometimes disquieting elements of his era: evangelical religion, sensibility, and democratic rumblings. Unlike his predecessors, Cowper seldom philosophized about the abstraction "Nature" when he described and reflected about the landscape. Unlike his contemporaries, he did not follow the rationalist tradition of placing the "Book of Nature" beside the Bible, although he did believe in creation as "an effect whose cause is God." Unlike the Romantics, he found no strangeness in beauty and felt no intense passion for nature; he was simply and genuinely attached to it.

Unlike Thomson and Young, the other two great descriptive poets of the century, Cowper had a natural fluency and could choose his polysyllables well. He avoided the stereotypical "poetic diction" used for objective detail and wrote easy, graceful blank verse. Although his verse lacks the concentration and intensity of the greatest poetry, it nevertheless remains faithful to reality and does so in natural, nearly conversational diction.

Cowper and Burns were among the late bloomers of the cult of simplicity, writing of rural domesticity and using subjective, autobiographical material. More intimate and emotional than their predecessors, they saw their roles as poets more as individuals speaking to themselves or to small audiences about their own experience than as the loud voice of the public. As such, they were transitional poets. Although less intellectual than Dryden or Pope, Cowper wrote intelligently about prison reform, slavery, and the French Revolution, and Burns wrote cogently about the oppressive Church of Scotland. Unlike Dryden, Swift, or Pope, Cowper never zealously burned for causes, but he did defend George Whitfield, an eminent Methodist who had been slandered.

Like Cowper, Burns wrote satire and realistic verse in natural and spontaneous style. He too was a poet of domestic emotion, but he described his environment not for itself but for the human relationships implied in it. Although he lived among and wrote of the common people of the Scottish lowlands, he was a highly educated man and a worthy inheritor of the ancient tradition of vernacular song and poetry. He wrote about Scottish life and manners in Scottish dialect and used his local Ayrshire neighborhood for inspiration. His manner, though not original, struck his non-Scottish audience as fresh and unusual.

Earlier Scottish poets had been ignored in London. In the cases of Allan Ramsay and Robert Fergusson, this was perhaps understandable; they wrote unpretentiously about their native land. Ramsay's work resembled that of Gay in many ways: He displayed hearty humor and shrewd observation for vivid rustic detail. Like Gay, he used the pastoral form for realistic ends and attempted a ballad opera, *The Gentle Shepherd* (1728). John Home, the author of *Douglas* (1756), who was known as the "Scottish Shakespeare," and William Wilkie, the author of *The Epigoniad* (1757), who was known as the "Scottish Homer," had also been slighted.

Working with stanzaic types popular with Scottish poets since the Middle Ages, Burns added vigor and musicality to his inheritance. (The stanza of "The Holy Fair," for example, is adapted from the old "Christis Kirk on the Green" stanza.) In his most effective satires—"Holy Willie's Prayer," "The Holy Fair," and "Address to the Unco Guild"—Burns savagely exposed religious hypocrisy. He wrote at the height of the liberal-minded rebellion against the doctrine of election and the impossibly strict rules of conduct enforced by the orthodox Presbyterian Church and its courts.

Like Cowper, Burns sympathized with the growing democratic tendencies: He believed in the essential worth of a person, whether rich or poor. His mind was free and modern, and his powers of observation accurate and penetrating. His nature poetry was the plain, simple observation of a Scottish farmer, not the reflective scientific musing of a devotee of Thomson. Above all, he was an extraordinarily gifted lyricist. He became the voice and symbol of his people, pleasing non-Scots with his "primitive" and "native" verse and focusing the national feelings of his own people.

TOWARD ROMANTICISM

The most significant event of the end of the eighteenth century was, of course, the French Revolution. In German literature, it was regarded as a warning about the problem of liberty. In English literature, it kindled enthusiasm in poets, but their celebratory poetry did not sparkle. Cowper and Burns saw in the revolution a declaration of the worth of all people, a manifesto of the political rights of the people. Beyond this, the revolution generated a millennial movement in English thought and life. Blake was the greatest of the millennial prophets, imagining a day when a new Jerusalem would arise in England after the reconciliation of Urizen (reason) with Los (imagination) and Luvah (passion).

The classical myths were dead, but the millennial era provided a seedbed for new myths. In *The Book of Thel* (1789), Blake introduced his own myths to symbolize philosophical ideas, which he later expanded in his "Prophetic Books." Against the character Urizen, the spirit of reason, custom, and institutions, Blake could vent all his revolutionary ire.

It is easy to write generalizations about the poetry of a particular period; it is less easy to make the poetry fit the generalizations. One can say, though, that the eighteenth century is a garden of exotic and diverse blooms. (Any century that included Blake, Gray, and Pope would have to be.) With some reservations, one can generalize that the century began with the glories of satire, the desire for improvements in society, and ended with the uncertainties of a new individualism and emerging social order. In between grew the love of description, reflection, and moralizing; an appreciation for everyday life and the common person; a yearning to know humanity, its native land, its history, and its place in the universe; a burning for feeling as well as reason; and a search for truth and beauty. The garden was ready to blossom into the fresh colors of Romanticism.

BIBLIOGRAPHY

Brunström, Conrad. *William Cowper: Religion, Satire, Society*. Lewisburg, Pa.: Bucknell University Press, 2004. A re-assessment of Cowper, emphasizing his attempt to reconcile the idea of retirement into rural life with his own version of social responsibility. Torn between these extremes, Cowper symbolizes a conflict that was not uncommon among eighteenth century intellectuals. Bibliographical references and index.

Fairer, David. *English Poetry of the Eighteenth Century, 1700-1789*. Annotated edition. Harlow, Essex, England: Longman, 2003. Discusses a variety of topics, ranging from ways of feeling, such as the search for sublimity, to types of writing, such as the mock-heroic mode and the verse letter. An excellent introduction to the subject. Bibliography and index.

Fairer, David, and Christine Gerrard, eds. *Eighteenth Century Poetry: An Annotated Anthology*. Malden, Mass.: Blackwell, 1999. Provides the widest possible range of texts and places work of the traditionally prominent figures (such as Alexander Pope, Jonathan Swift, Anne Finch, Christopher Smart, Robert Burns, and William Cowper) alongside work by other writers, particularly women with strong and distinctive voices (Sarah Egerton, Mary Jones, Mary Collier, Mary Leapor, Ann Yearsley, and Anna Laetitia Barbauld). All the poems have full annotations and generous head notes.

Ferguson, Moira. *Eighteenth Century Women Poets: Nation, Class, and Gender*. Albany: State University of New York Press, 1995. Examines the poetry of Anne Yearsley, Janet Little, Mary Scott, and Mary Collier through various lenses, including women's labor, patriotism and resistance, and class identity.

Frushell, Richard C. *Edmund Spenser in the Early Eighteenth Century: Education, Imitation, and the Making of a Literary Model*. Pittsburgh, Pa.: Duquesne University Press, 1999. A study of eighteenth century imitations and adaptations of the works of Spenser.

Gerrard, Christine, ed. *A Companion to Eighteenth-Century Poetry*. Malden, Mass.: Blackwell, 2006. Contains essays on contexts, genres, and critical issues, as well as close readings of individual poems. The recent expansion of the literary canon is evident in the inclusion of works by a considerable number of women poets. Bibliographical references and index.

Goodridge, John. *Rural Life in Eighteenth Century English Poetry*. New York: Cambridge University Press, 1996. Compares poetic accounts of rural labor by James Thomson, Stephen Duck, and Mary Collier, and explores the purpose of rural poetry, revealing an illuminating link between rural poetry and agricultural and folkloric developments of the time.

Irlam, Shaun. *Elations: The Poetics of Enthusiasm in Eighteenth Century Britain*. Stanford, Calif.: Stanford University Press, 1999. Examines the aesthetic theory of the period and reassesses the poetry of James Thomson and Edward Young, two poets seldom read today but very popular in their time. The book also explores the genesis and construction of moral authority through a variety of competing discourses appropriated by poetry.

Kaur, Savil. *Poems of Nations, Anthems of Empire: English Verse in the Long Eighteenth Century*. Charlottesville: University Press of Virginia, 2000. Describes the formal features and thematic concerns of the long poems written in the Restoration period of the mid-eighteenth century and how they tie in with England's, and Britain's, empire of the sea.

McIlvanney, Liam. *Burns the Radical: Politics and Poetry in Late Eighteenth-Century Scotland*. East Linton, Scotland: Tuckwell, 2000. A thoroughly researched study of the poet as the product of Scottish Presbyterianism, the Whig tradition, and the Scottish Enlightenment, leading to new conclusions about his political ideas and new interpretations of his major works.

Sitter, John, ed. *The Cambridge Companion to Eighteenth-Century Poetry*. New York: Cambridge University Press, 2007. The editor's excellent introduction on the "future" of eighteenth century poetry is the first of thirteen essays by various writers, ranging from such topics as nature poetry and the poetry of sensibility to more general subjects, including the possibility of a "national" poetry and the worth of poetry in general. Illustrated. Chronology, bibliography, and index.

Starr, G. Gabrielle. *Lyric Generations: Poetry and the Novel in the Long Eighteenth Century.* Baltimore: Johns Hopkins University Press, 2004. While it has been generally accepted that in the eighteenth century, lyric poetry and the novel had nothing in common, the author of this highly original study argues convincingly that as the novel developed, it had a profound influence on lyric poetry, and that the lyric, in turn, inspired novelists. Bibliographical references and index.

Ann Willardson Engar

English and American Poetry in the Nineteenth Century

The literary nineteenth century is commonly divided into periods or phases, more or less arbitrarily. There was clearly a Romantic period in England from about 1786 to 1832, followed by a more sedate Victorian reaction that itself began to disintegrate after 1860. American literature remained minor and derivative until about 1820, when William Cullen Bryant emerged. While the 1830's were comparable on both sides of the Atlantic, with significant interaction, Romanticism lasted longer in America—to which it was more applicable. The traumatic American Civil War of 1861 to 1865, however, soon drew American letters toward the increasing pessimism already common in England. During the last third of the nineteenth century, British and American literature were widely separate, and the uniqueness of American writers was generally acknowledged. Nevertheless, the two literatures were deeply interdependent at the beginning of the century, with Britain's dominating, as the young United States of America were less united than a collection of states with strong ties to Britain and the Continent.

Despite its geographical separation from England, the East Coast of what is now the United States was very strongly British during the eighteenth century, not only politically but also culturally. The American Revolution (1776-1783), which justified itself on grounds derived primarily from British thought, changed nothing in that respect, for though American writers such as John Trumbull, Timothy Dwight, and Philip Freneau soon turned toward American subjects, they continued to see them through British eyes and to imitate British literary models, which were still of the neoclassical type. Neoclassicism was appropriate to a society in which religious and social values were well assured and stability was more evident than change. However, this stability was vanishing rapidly throughout the latter eighteenth century, in both England and America.

Political, economic, and social revolutions

It was an era of revolutions, through which much that has since characterized the West came into being. Not all of these revolutions were sudden or dramatic, but their cumulative force was irresistible. For example, population increased enormously throughout the latter eighteenth century in England and the United States as better sanitation, nutrition, and medicine increased longevity and reduced infant mortality. This larger and healthier population strained available resources, pressured an outmoded economic system, and gave both countries unusually large numbers of the young, who used the increasing availability of books to effect political, agricultural, technological, scientific, and social revolutions on behalf of the abundance and freedom with which their own interests were identified.

Two of the most obvious revolutions were political, as the United States broke away from England in 1776 and France attempted to discard its outmoded monarchy and religious establishment in 1789. Less precipitously, agriculture was revolutionized by the development of improved plows, crop rotation schemes, selective breeding, and (in England) an improved network of canals and turnpikes that allowed farmers to market specialty crops over greater distances. The superior transportation of the latter eighteenth century was also broadly effective in extending the boundaries of urban culture beyond London to provincial and even rural centers, so that authorship (for example) was more widespread. As mail service improved, men of letters everywhere corresponded more meaningfully, and even American colonials such as Benjamin Franklin were effective participants in the European ferment. Other aspects of technological change were also rapid, as both England and the United States responded ever more fully to the development of mechanical power. The steam engine, developed by James Watt, inaugurated the first phase of the Industrial Revolution, which would then transform the two countries for a second time during the nineteenth century with the advent of railroads and steamships; these latter inventions made the territorial ambitions of Britain and the United States—Britain's, beyond its shores, and America's, toward the west—feasible. The factory system, with its emphasis on regulated labor and standardized parts, was not only of economic and social importance—it strongly influenced nineteenth century literature and thought as well. Prior to the American Revolution, however, because British law prevented the full development of American manufacture (finished goods had to be imported from England), much colonial ingenuity was devoted instead to improved nautical technology—at which New England quickly became outstanding—and eventually to exploring the resources of the constantly retreating western frontier.

The sea, the frontier, and foreign countries attracted young adventurers who would otherwise have been victimized by the economic inequities of hereditary wealth. Thus, in the nineteenth century, the Industrial Revolution fostered a new entrepreneurial class that gained both economic and social prominence. These aggressive and often uncouth opportunists challenged the increasingly moribund landed aristocracies of England and the United States, wresting a larger share of political power and social respectability for themselves. If the eighteenth century was, at its beginning, dominated by hereditary nobility, its internal conflicts gave rise to a nineteenth century in which an aristocracy of talent was more important.

The internal conflicts of the eighteenth century derived in large part from a crosscurrent of ideas known as the Enlightenment, which originated in seventeenth century England with Francis Bacon, John Locke, and Sir Isaac Newton, then spread during the next hundred years to France, where ideals of cosmopolitan urbanity, rational humanism, and religious toleration (if not outright disbelief) were popularized by Voltaire, Denis Diderot, and Jean-Jacques Rousseau, all of whom advocated freedom and change. A second eighteenth century center of Enlightenment initiative was Scotland (then experiencing a nationalistic revival), which contributed the skepticism of David Hume, the economic theories of Adam Smith, and an impressive series of historiographic, scientific, technological, and literary achievements. The American phase of the Enlightenment, including Benjamin Franklin, Thomas Jefferson, and James Madison, guided restless colonials toward independence, economic self-sufficiency, and a radically new theory of government. However, both the Declaration of Independence and the Constitution of the United States were based on Enlightenment ideals

that derived in large part from those of Republican Rome.

INFLUENCE OF THE PAST

Nineteenth century minds never forgot their indebtedness to the past, and one of the most reliable characteristics of nineteenth century literature is its historicism. The science of archaeology, for example, arose during the 1740's with systematic digging at Pompeii and Herculaneum, leading to a revival of visual classicism in architecture, sculpture, and painting. Then the nineteenth century began with French archaeological discoveries in Egypt, including the Rosetta stone. As a result, pyramids recur throughout nineteenth century arts as symbols of death, the sphinx and hieroglyphics appear as mysterious embodiments of knowledge denied to humanity, and Egypt itself becomes the new symbol (replacing Rome) of antiquarian grandeur. Incremental archaeological enthusiasm soon overwhelmed Europe and its more creative minds with statuary from the Parthenon, winged lions from Assyria, relics from Troy, many now-familiar classical masterpieces, and vast new sites, art forms, and religions from the Americas, Asia, and Africa. During the nineteenth century also, the concept of geological time was established, with all its vast duration and wondrous legacy of vanished giants. Thus, the nineteenth century past no longer began with Adam, but instead an immensely complex progression through incalculable time from uncertain beginnings to the illustrious present. No other century in the history of the West experienced such a readjustment of its time sense as did the nineteenth.

Although overwhelmingly Protestant, nineteenth century writers in England and the United States were often attracted to the Catholic Middle Ages. Gothic architecture was popularly revived in Britain, and there was a resurgence of medieval craftsmanship in the Pre-Raphaelite movement of Dante Gabriel Rossetti and William Morris, which (together with the aesthetic and social criticism of John Ruskin) did much to reduce the ugliness of overindustrialized Victorian minor arts. Poets likewise returned to the Middle Ages for inspiration, though seldom realistically. For Sir Walter Scott, John Keats, Alfred, Lord Tennyson, James Russell

Lowell, Morris, and other writers, medievalism was a utopian alternative to the deficiencies of the present, but one that the cold scrutiny of history could not fully corroborate.

To some extent, the same disparity characterizes the nineteenth century's image of classical Greece, which overshadowed Rome in cultural prestige and was accepted as a symbol of liberty, whether political, intellectual, or behavioral. For the many Hellenists of the nineteenth century, Greek mythology was a major inspiration. Among the most popular myths was that of Prometheus, which attracted William Blake, Thomas Campbell, Lord Byron, Elizabeth Barrett Browning, Robert Bridges, and especially Percy Bysshe Shelley, for whom Prometheus was the mythological embodiment of enlightened, technological man. In related contexts, Byron died on behalf of Greek independence, and Keats revered its artistic legacy. Mid-Victorian writers, such as Tennyson, valued Greece primarily for its writers, particularly Homer, while later ones such as Matthew Arnold and Thomas Hardy admired the realism of Greek tragedy. Greek lyric poetry found readers throughout the century and influenced A. E. Housman, especially. Combining the lyric and dramatic traditions of classical Greece, Shelley attempted two lyric dramas on Greek subjects, *Prometheus Unbound: A Lyrical Drama in Four Acts* (pb. 1820) and *Hellas: A Lyrical Drama* (pb. 1822), which would be imitated later by Arnold ("Empedocles on Etna," 1852), Algernon Charles Swinburne (*Atalanta in Calydon*, pb. 1865), and Hardy (*The Dynasts: A Drama of the Napoleonic Wars*, pb. 1903, 1906, 1908, 1910). The pagan, libertarian, and sometimes erotic influence of Greece was taken very seriously.

Nineteenth century writers admired individuality and boldness. They found the heroic age of exploration particularly congenial, as poems about Christopher Columbus (for example) were written by Joel Barlow, Samuel Rogers, William Lisle Bowles, Tennyson, Walt Whitman, Joaquin Miller, and Lowell. Samuel Taylor Coleridge's *The Rime of the Ancient Mariner* (1798) was based on exploration literature and the voyage of Magellan; Keats mistook Cortez for Balboa; while Bowles and Whitman celebrated Vasco da Gama and the spirit of discovery in general. Other heroes of the century included George Washington, Napoleon Bonaparte, the duke of Wellington, and Abraham Lincoln. There were also many poems and essays about writers, including Homer, Vergil, Dante, William Shakespeare, Torquato Tasso, John Milton, Johann Wolfgang von Goethe, the British Romantic poets, Ralph Waldo Emerson, and Whitman. Artists of the Italian Renaissance were often extolled for their individuality—the Renaissance as a whole was popular—and various Enlightenment figures (Bacon, Newton, Voltaire, and Rousseau primarily) were either praised or damned, according to the religious preferences of the writer. Surprisingly little was written, however, in praise of religious heroes as such.

RELIGIOUS DOUBT

Traditional religion was sorely pressed throughout the nineteenth century (its latter half particularly) to retain credibility in the face of pervasive doubts which arose on all sides—from biblical criticism, undermining the literal word; from Enlightenment objections to religious authority and intolerance; from the diversity of religious observance and the insipidity of orthodox spirituality; and from the currently popular philosophies of materialism and utilitarianism, neither of which found much use for the inanities of a debased theological tradition that, during the eighteenth century, had clearly become part of an oppressive church-and-state establishment. One of the most pervasive features of nineteenth century literature, therefore, is religious doubt, which frequently resolved itself in any of several ways: by regarding history as a manifestation of God, turning from God to humans, abandoning religion in favor of art, or returning to orthodox belief. Though there were also a number of alternative faiths, including spiritualism, the guiding light of the century was science.

BRITISH ROMANTICISM

The century began with the English Romantics, who were influential in both England and America. Neoclassical literature, which dominated the first half of the eighteenth century in England, emphasized practical reason, social conformity, emotional restraint, and submission to the authority of classical literary techniques. It was generally allied to political and religious conservatism as well. As life in eighteenth century England was transformed by political, economic, social, and technological innovations, however, the old manner of literary expression seemed increasingly obsolete to younger and more audacious writers who had absorbed the Enlightenment philosophy of humanism and freedom.

ROBERT BURNS

Among the first of these new men in literature was Robert Burns (1759-1796). Though he did not live quite long enough to experience the nineteenth century at first hand, Burns strikingly exemplified a number of its tendencies. Far from apologizing for either his Scottish burr or his rural origins, at a time when both were disparaged in polite society, he appealed to the 1780's as a supposedly untutored genius, a natural poet whose verses arose not from the inkwell but from theheart. Beneath his colorful regionalism and earthy rural sensuality there remained a stubborn dignity, an antiaristocratic humanity, and a concentration upon his own emotions that favored meditative and lyric poetry. Burns's carefree morality and religious satire signaled the approaching end of religious orthodoxy in British poetry (it would last longer in the United States) and effectively countered the turgid morbidity into which so many midcentury versifiers had fallen. In his egalitarian social attitudes ("A man's a man for a' that"), Burns portended the imminent French Revolution of 1789. His literary influence throughout the next century extended to Scott, Tennyson, John Greenleaf Whittier, Lowell, Hardy, and Rudyard Kipling, all of whom profited from Burns's use of dialect in serious literature and from his revolutionary insistence that the right of an individual to worth and dignity is not dependent on the urbanity of his speech.

WILLIAM BLAKE

If William Blake (1757-1827), of Burns's generation, was not so obviously an outsider as the Scottish poet, he soon became one through the seeming incomprehensibility of his highly individualistic poetry and art. A firm supporter of the American and French Revolutions, Blake was also the first important author to sense the underlying dynamism of his times. No other poet, for example, perceived the historical importance of either the Industrial Revolution or the political upheaval in the United States so clearly. Similarly, no other poet has influenced twentieth century theories of literature so much. However, Blake was dismissed as a madman in his own times, and his influence on nineteenth century literature became important only toward the end, with Swinburne, Rossetti, James Thomson, and William Butler Yeats. It is now clear, however, that Blake's concerns with innovation, energy, myth, lyric, and sexuality were extremely prescient.

WILLIAM WORDSWORTH

Though William Wordsworth (1770-1850) was more in accord with late eighteenth century restraint than Blake, he effected the most significant theoretical

William Wordsworth's cottage in England. (Time & Life Pictures/Getty Images)

change ever seen in English literature and did more than any other individual to give nineteenth century literature its distinctive character. With its explicit rejection of neoclassicism and the aristocratic tradition in literature, Wordsworth's *Lyrical Ballads* of 1798 (first American edition, 1800), written with Coleridge, is often considered the official beginning of the literary nineteenth century. Its famous preface, added to the English edition of 1800, outlined Wordsworth's new criteria for literature, to which virtually all the significant poets of his century would subscribe. His influence is evident in Coleridge, Byron, Shelley, Keats, Tennyson, Arnold, and Hardy, among major British poets, and in Bryant, Emerson, Henry David Thoreau, Whitman, Henry Wadsworth Longfellow, and Whittier, among American ones. He was the most written-about poet of the century. Wordsworth also had a significant impact upon non-poets such as John Stuart Mill; even Charles Darwin read him. Nineteenth century literature in all its forms is immensely indebted to Wordsworth's preoccupations with rural life, childhood, mental and emotional development, language, history, and nature.

SAMUEL TAYLOR COLERIDGE

Although Wordsworth's collaborator, Samuel Taylor Coleridge (1772-1834), was also an accomplished poet, his substantial influence on later writers (Emerson in particular) came primarily through his prose. As a poet, however, he influenced Wordsworth, Scott, Shelley, Keats, and Edgar Allan Poe, preceding the latter as a symbolist of sometimes uncanny power. Coleridge was also a foremost theorist and critic of English Romanticism, as well as an effective transmitter of German Romantic thought to both England and America.

SIR WALTER SCOTT

Wordsworth and Coleridge now seem far greater poets, but Sir Walter Scott (1771-1832) and Lord Byron were more immediately popular, not only in Britain and the United States but also throughout Europe. In his narrative poems and many novels (all too hastily written), Scott further popularized regionalism, historicism, and folk traditions. His novels influenced Washington Irving and James Fenimore Cooper, thus virtually beginning nineteenth century literature in

America, and created an immense vogue for historical literature of all kinds; his poetic insistence on a nationalistic Scottish muse helped to inspire the Irish harp of Thomas Moore, the Indian one of Bankim Chatterjee, and the "barbaric yawp" of Whitman. Longfellow was also indebted to Scott's influence for his well-known longer poems on American themes, but went beyond Scott in the amazing cosmopolitanism of his literary sources. In his pseudomedieval manor house at Abbotsford—much copied by his fellow artisans—Scott played the gracious host to innumerable literary visitors, several of them American. Throughout his lifetime, he was the kindest and most accessible major literary figure in Europe. During the first decade of the nineteenth century, when Britain was preoccupied with its resistance to Napoleon and travel on the Continent was scarcely possible, Scott was also his country's most popular poet.

LORD BYRON, PERCY BYSSHE SHELLEY, AND JOHN KEATS

Lord Byron (1788-1824) dominated the Regency, when from 1811 to 1820 England was governed by their heir apparent (later George IV), George III having been declared hopelessly insane. Byron's contradictory but forceful verses, cynical and witty as they were, appealed to a disillusioned younger generation who had seen its hopes for political reform quashed by the failure of the French Revolution and its taste for heroics eradicated by the unnecessary holocaust of the Napoleonic wars. After 1816, however, as England reverted to peacetime reconstruction, Byron's immorality and religious heterodoxy became too much. He was forced into exile on the Continent that year, soon to be followed by Percy Bysshe Shelley (1792-1822), against whom the same charges were leveled, and (primarily for reasons of health) by John Keats (1795-1821), who appeared to some imperceptive critics as nothing more than a sensuously explicit Cockney. These judgments, of course, did not prevail as Byron's influence extended to John Clare, Tennyson, Arthur Hugh Clough, Elizabeth Barrett Browning, Emily Brontë, Poe, Whitman, and Miller; Shelley's to Arthur Henry Hallam, Thomas Lovell Beddoes, Tennyson, Browning, Swinburne, Thomson, Hardy, and Yeats; and Keats's to Tennyson, Thomas Hood, Rossetti, Morris, Emily Dickinson, Lowell,

Swinburne, and innumerable minor poets. The Byronic hero also became a familiar type in Victorian fiction, Shelley had a major impact upon freethinkers and labor leaders, and Keats became almost a model for both writers and artists during the latter half of the century. Thus, the major English Romantic poets as a group were highly influential in and beyond literature throughout the nineteenth century.

AMERICAN TRANSCENDENTALISTS

The Transcendentalist movement in the United States during the 1830's and 1840's, centering on Emerson (1803-1882)—who disassociated himself from the term—was an awakening of new literary possibilities comparable to, and in part derived from, the literary revolution initiated by Wordsworth and Coleridge. Whereas British Romanticism was often a rebellion against social oppression within the country itself, however, much of its American equivalent was pitted against the tyranny of British literary predominance and European snobbishness generally. William Ellery Channing concluded in 1830 ("Remarks on National Literature") that a truly American literature did not yet exist, and there were many subsequent laments regarding the Yankee failure to achieve cultural independence. "We have listened too long to the courtly muses of Europe," proclaimed Emerson in his famous oration on "The American Scholar" in 1837. Nathaniel Parker Willis, a minor poet from New York, was even more emphatic two years later. "*In literature,*" he claimed,

> *we are no longer a nation.* The triumph of Atlantic steam navigation has driven the smaller drop into the larger, and London has become the center. Farewell nationality! The English language now marks the limits of a new literary empire, and America is a suburb.

Like many desperate pronouncements, this one soon proved wrong, but it was by no means clear in 1839 that those then living would witness the remarkable effulgence of American letters that was to come.

The significant American poets whose emergence showed Willis to be a false prophet included Emerson,

Emily Dickinson

Thoreau, Jones Very, Poe, Whitman, Dickinson, Longfellow, Whittier, Oliver Wendell Holmes, and Lowell. Emerson himself was a major influence on contemporary and later American poets, including Thoreau, Very, Whitman, and Dickinson. His essays influenced such remarkable British thinkers as Thomas Carlyle, Arnold, Clough, John Sterling, James Anthony Froude, Herbert Spencer, and John Tyndall. Poe, eventually a force in France, was significant in England only for Swinburne, Rossetti, and Thomson. Whitman appealed to a number of late Victorians, influencing Tennyson (in "Vastness"), Swinburne, William Michael Rossetti, John Addington Symonds, Lionel Johnson, Edward Dowden, and even Robert Louis Stevenson. Those who appreciated his accomplishments were generally also fond of Blake and Shelley. Longfellow became the most popular poet in the English-speaking world around the mid-century, so beloved in Britain and elsewhere that hundreds of his editions appeared, including one of *The Song of Hiawatha* (1855) illustrated by Frederick Remington. Although Longfellow has come to be considered only a genial minor figure in world literature, he alone among American poets was accorded by his British admirers a memorial in the Poets' Corner, Westminster Abbey. As for the others, Whittier, Holmes, and Lowell had only moderate international appeal, while Thoreau, Very, Dickinson, and Herman Melville were virtually unknown. Even so, it could no longer be said that literary influences between England and America ran only in one direction.

From certain Germanic sources, often transmitted through the philosophical prose of Coleridge and Carlyle, Emerson and his associates derived a fundamental conviction that all material facts are emblematic of spiritual truths, which led them to believe that religious revelation was continuous. This openness to factual and spiritual enlightenment prompted American writers to read widely, often in untraditional sources. Thus, classical works of Asian religion, the *Bhagavadgītā* (c. 200 B.C.E.-200 C.E.; *The Bhagavad Gita*, 1785) and others, were of interest. The Orientalism of Emerson, Thoreau, and Whitman, more serious and better informed than that to be found in the work of earlier English poets such as Moore (*Lalla Rookh*, 1817), helped them to accept the benevolent impermanence of nature.

Because of their belief in progressive revelation, American Transcendentalists were also more able than their British literary counterparts to accept the current findings of natural science—astronomy, geology, and biology—by which many nineteenth century writers were influenced. Though these three sciences were together discrediting the Creation narrative in Genesis (a task virtually completed by 1840), and suggesting the relative insignificance of humans in a mechanistic world of vast time and space, the American Transcendentalists remained almost sanguine in denying the unique status of any one religious tradition, for they regarded the world of nature (whose cruelty they overlooked) as God's most reliable revelation of himself and as a corrective to the mythological understanding of all earlier peoples.

Attitudes toward nature

Attitudes toward nature remained benign in America well after they had become suspect in Britain, where a skeptical tradition among the unorthodox had

been articulated by Shelley and soon reasserted itself through Tennyson (1809-1892), who was the official and most influential poet of Victorian England. However, just after Emerson had published his idealistic, Wordsworthian essay *Nature* (1836), he and Tennyson both read Charles Lyell's *Principles of Geology* (1830-1833), which emphasized the immensity of geological time and raised fundamental questions about the history of life. The book exhilarated Emerson, who regarded it as a demonstration of the pervasiveness of natural law, and hence of morality. Tennyson, however, had still not reconciled himself to the premature death of his friend Hallam at the age of twenty-two and was led by Lyell into agonizing despair over a seemingly amoral world in which whole species perished routinely.

Tennyson's doubts were eventually assuaged by his reading of Goethe, his friendship with Carlyle, and a conviction (reinforced by several naturalists) that life's record in the rocks was purposeful and upward. However, his literary resolution of the dilemma in *In Memoriam* (1850), the greatest long poem of its time, only temporarily delayed the specter of amoral, indifferent nature that would come to haunt the remaining half of the nineteenth century. In the United States, on the contrary, the prevailing attitude toward nature long remained that of Thoreau's *Walden* (1854) or even became symbolic of national greatness, as western exploration revealed mountains, rivers, and other scenic wonders unequaled in England; surely they were emblematic of the country and its future. The future that most concerned Americans at mid-century belonged to this life rather than the next, for their nation had been imperiled by issues of slavery and states' rights, despite the glitter of California gold.

Victorian reforms and doubts

In general, the first third of the literary nineteenth century in England was preoccupied with political questions, as public concern responded in turn to the French Revolution and its failure; to the subsequent rise, threats, and necessary defeat of Napoleon; to the internal dislocations of the Regency; to the complicated international situation after Waterloo; and especially to needed reforms at home—for inequities between social classes were rife, and England seemed to be on the brink of insurrection. After 1832, however, when the first Reform Bill (enfranchising the middle class) was enacted, it became clear that social betterment would be achieved through legislation and education rather than revolution. Poets such as Ebenezer Elliott, Hood, Elizabeth Barrett Browning, and (in America) Lydia Huntley Sigourney joined Carlyle, Charles Dickens, and other writers of prose in depicting the hard lot of the underprivileged, particularly children and the working poor. Black slavery was no longer at issue in Britain because the slave trade had been abolished in 1807 and slavery itself (common only in the West Indies) in 1832. It would last until 1865 in America. There was also feminist agitation, but this was a social revolution for which the Victorian world was not yet prepared; Victoria herself (crowned in 1837) opposed it.

Even so, a remarkable transformation took place within mid-century England as enlightened advocates uncovered inequities old and new. Among the revolutionary bills passed by reforming parliaments were the Factory Act of 1833, regulating child labor; the Poor Law Amendment Act of 1834, regulating workhouses; the Municipal Reform Act of 1835, unifying town governments; an act of 1842 prohibiting the employment of women and children in mines; another in 1843 prohibiting imprisonment for debt; the first public health act in 1848; another factory act, shortening hours and days, in 1850; a second major political reform in 1868; and, finally, the great public schools act of 1870. If there were fewer reforming acts in less-developed America, it was in part because fewer were needed. Whatever the indigenous shortcomings of British industrialism, its problems were taken seriously by both workingmen and writers. One of the few European states to avoid armed revolution during the nineteenth century, Britain was perhaps the most socially advanced nation in the world, as well as the most industrialized, for humanitarianism and progress had become its prevailing creeds.

This humanitarianism increasingly superseded orthodox religion, which had begun to experience severe problems of credibility. The Oxford movement toward a more historical Christianity, less dependent on the precise text of the Bible, had begun under John Keble in

1833, but this promising doctrinal initiative on the part of the Anglican Church (official in England) lost effectiveness when John Henry Newman, its most persuasive advocate, announced his conversion to Roman Catholicism in 1845. The high road to orthodoxy having proved disastrous, Anglican theology was afterward dominated by the Broad Church movement (to which the poets Coleridge and Clough were important), which scarcely emphasized doctrinal conformity at all. Except for Newman, Christina Rossetti, and Gerard Manley Hopkins, few English poets after 1850 were orthodoxly religious.

Tennyson's *In Memoriam* managed a dubious immortality for the young skeptic that it commemorated, but other poets of the time were less sure, as Clough and Arnold remained agnostics at best. In *Christmas Eve and Easter Day* (1850), Robert Browning rejected both doctrinal and evangelical Christianity in favor of a theistic religion of love, and Arnold implied much the same in "Dover Beach" (1851). While meeting the equivalent American spiritual crisis with more gusto, Whitman observed in *Leaves of Grass* (1855) that "Creeds and schools" were "in abeyance." His own faith derived from all religions and did not include curiosity about God. In a poem of 1871 addressed to Whitman, however, Swinburne admitted that "God is buried and dead to us." Among American poets, Melville and Dickinson became religious seekers; Emerson, Whittier, and Longfellow, among others, remained relatively confident of supernatural goodness throughout the 1850's and 1860's, but their optimism (shared by Tennyson and Browning to some extent) seemed increasingly tenuous to younger readers.

One by one, traditional verities disappeared from English and American literature, and more rapidly in Britain. God was doubtful, nature cruel, history vindictive, love impossible, and humans animalistic and corrupt. The poet who articulated the new disillusionment most forcefully, Arnold (1822-1888), saw himself as an isolated wanderer through a post-Christian, postrationalistic wilderness of historical and personal estrangement. Like Shelley's poet in *Alastor* (1816), Arnold sought for love and could not find it; of all men he wrote, "Thou hast been, shalt be, art, alone." Several later Victorian poets, including Robert Browning (*Men*

A drawing by artist Florence Harrison illustrates Christina Rossetti's poem "The Lowest Room." (Hulton Archive/Getty Images)

and Women, 1855), Dante Gabriel Rossetti, George Meredith, and Coventry Patmore, wrote extensively of their relationships with women, and of the failure of love; others turned from normal eroticism altogether. Compare these works with other long poems of the times which concentrate on women, including Tennyson, *The Princess* (1847), and "Guinevere," taken from *Idylls of the King* (1859-1885); Clough, *The Bothie of Tober-na-Vuolich* (1848); Elizabeth Barrett Browning, *Aurora Leigh* (1856); Longfellow, *The Courtship of Miles Standish* (1858); and Morris, *The Defence of Guenevere* (1858).

INFLUENCE OF NATURAL SELECTION

As for nature, history, and humanity, all three had become suspect by mid-century and all three coalesced in the theory of natural selection publicized by Darwin's *On the Origin of Species by Means of Natural Selection* (1859), which transformed nineteenth century skepticism into disillusioned pessimism and savage exploitation. Darwin's work inspired a major literary movement called naturalism and certainly ennobled the tragic sense of such powerful, effective poets as Hardy (1840-1928) and Stephen Crane (1871-1900). In both England and America, Darwin's harsh view of nature was coupled with the reality of war (India, 1857; Charleston, 1861; Havana, 1898). Perhaps even more disillusioning, however, was the incremental recognition in both countries that the optimism of previous decades regarding human nature was implausible. Throughout the last quarter of the nineteenth century authors repeatedly proclaimed, though usually in prose, that human beings are defiled on the surface and ugly to the core. Though the century could bear its religious losses with stoic fortitude, it could not maintain an essentially optimistic outlook against the pervasive antihumanism of its final years.

ALLIED WITH ART

Throughout the nineteenth century, literature had been closely allied with art. Much of its descriptive poetry, for example, was based on painted forebears or similar contemporary work; thus, Wordsworth is often compared with John Constable, Shelley with J. M. W. Turner, Coleridge with German Romantic art, Byron with Eugène Delacroix, and Browning with the Impressionists. Several important writers, including Blake, Ruskin, Morris, and Dante Gabriel Rossetti, were authentic artists in their own right; others combined their verbal work with others' art to collaborate on illustrated editions. That poets were makers of pictures, as the Roman poet Horace had declared, was assumed throughout the century. They became interpreters of pictures also, as can be seen in Bowles, Wordsworth, and especially Browning. For many later nineteenth century poets, however, the writer was no longer a prophet but a critic, concerned less with cosmic purpose than with humanity's revelation of itself through art.

TRANSITION TO A MINOR ART

It is symptomatic of the times that poetry became more personal, less prestigious, and even private (Dickinson, Hardy, Hopkins) as public utterances turned instead to evaluation of the literary past. Thus, Arnold virtually abandoned poetry for criticism of various kinds, while Dante Gabriel Rossetti, Lowell, Swinburne, and William Watson all reveal critical aspirations overtopping creative ones. Major anthologies of the time, edited by Edmund Clarence Stedman and Francis Palgrave, show that poetry appealed to the later nineteenth century more as conventional verbal prettiness than as original thought; a great deal of it was essentially decoration. Fanciful, but not imaginative (in the searching, Romantic sense), late Victorian poetry soon became, with only a few exceptions, a minor art, as statements of intellectual importance tended increasingly to be made in prose.

The Pre-Raphaelite Brotherhood of Dante Gabriel Rossetti (1828-1882) and his circle, which fostered both poetry and art, was a major attempt to defend creative imagination against the economic, social, and intellectual forces that were depressing it, which is to say, against the impersonality of manufacture, the bad taste of the rising middle class, and the unidimensional reality of empirical science. William Michael Rossetti (1829-1919) was, with his brother, largely responsible for bringing Whitman, Miller, and Edward FitzGerald's the *Rubáiyát of Omar Khayyám* (1859) to critical attention, while reviving interest in the work of Blake and Shelley. Only a small coterie in London, however, fully appreciated how desperate the artistic situation had become. From them emerged Yeats (1865-1939), an Irish cultural nationalist influenced by Moore and Scott, who based his major poems (mostly twentieth century) on the bold visions of Blake and Shelley, while rejecting Tennysonian doubt and the depressing outlook of scientific materialism. Tennyson, Robert Browning, Whitman, Arnold, Hardy, and Yeats have come to be regarded as the most significant British poets of the latter part of the nineteenth century, and all have had their impact on subsequent writers.

BIBLIOGRAPHY

Armstrong, Isobel, Cath Sharrock, and Joseph Brigtow, eds. *Nineteenth Century Women Poets: An Anthology*. Reprint. New York: Oxford University Press, 1998. Presents the work of more than one hundred women writers and achieves range and depth by reprinting poems by working-class, colonial, and political poets, in addition to very substantial selections from the work of major figures.

Axelrod, Steven Gould, Camille Roman, and Thomas Travisano, eds. *Traditions and Revolutions, Beginnings to 1990*. Vol. 1 in *The New Anthology of American Poetry*. New Brunswick, N.J.: Rutgers University Press, 2003. The first volume of an ambitious three-volume work in progress. Part 2 of this book covers the period from the beginning of the nineteenth century through the Civil War; part 3, from the Civil War to 1900.

Beach, Christopher. *Politics of Distinction: Whitman and the Discourses of Nineteenth Century America*. Athens: University of Georgia Press, 1996. Demonstrates how Walt Whitman differentiated his work from previous literary models, while he sought to portray daily life and the concerns of the common people in an idiomatic, rather than a high-minded literary manner.

Blyth, Caroline, ed. *Decadent Verse: An Anthology of Late-Victorian Poetry, 1872-1900*. London: Anthem Press, 2009. Expands the traditional definition of decadence so as to apply it to writers such as Alfred, Lord Tennyson, Elizabeth Barrett Browning, and Thomas Hardy, as well as to the Pre-Raphaelites and to many lesser-known poets. Fifty women writers are included in this extensive collection. Critical commentaries put the works into a historical context, and chronologies list developments in prose and in the visual arts.

Chapman, Alison, ed. *Victorian Women Poets*. Cambridge, England: D. S. Brewer, 2003. A collection of essays commissioned by the English Association. Many suggest new interpretations of the canonical poets, while others focus on recently discovered writers. Recurring themes in the essays include poetics, politics, publishing, the expansion of the British Empire, and the passion for social justice.

Gray, F. Elizabeth. *Christian and Lyric Tradition in Victorian Women's Poetry*. New York: Routledge, 2009. Investigates how Victorian women used

Christian texts in their poetry, reinterpreting passages to support their own experiences and to challenge gender repression. An illuminating study.

Gray, Janet, ed. *She Wields a Pen: American Women Poets of the Nineteenth Century*. Iowa City: University of Iowa Press, 1997. Includes sixty-eight American women writers and their works, which appeared in print in the context of social purposes—the abolitionist movement, the temperance movement, the Hawaiian nationalist movement, the Sunday School movement, the Zionist movement, and the woman suffrage movement.

Helsinger, Elizabeth K. *Poetry and the Pre-Raphaelite Arts: Dante Gabriel Rossetti and William Morris*. New Haven, Conn.: Yale University Press, 2008. Explores the relationship between the visual and the verbal achievements of the two poet-artists and explains how their example influenced later poets and poetics. Plates and illustrations. Bibliography and index.

Jackson-Houlston, C. M. *Ballads, Songs, and Snatches: The Appropriation of Folk Song and Popular Culture in British Nineteenth Century Realist Prose*. Brookfield, Vt.: Ashgate, 1999. Focuses on nineteenth century British literary allusions to folk songs and popular culture. Examines the work and attitudes of authors of the period who attempted to mediate the culture of the working classes for the enjoyment of middle-class audiences.

Lambdin, Laura Cooner, and Robert T. Lambdin. *Camelot in the Nineteenth Century: Arthurian Characters in the Poems of Tennyson, Arnold, Morris, and Swinburne*. Westport, Conn.: Greenwood Press, 1999. Examines how four poets used figures, events, and ideas from the Arthurian legends in their work and for their own ends. The authors conclude that the poets sought not to reflect historical reality but to produce religious, aesthetic, and political systems of representation.

O'Gorman, Francis, ed. *Victorian Poetry: An Annotated Anthology*. Malden, Mass.: Wiley-Blackwell, 2004. Illustrated. Includes all the major poets and some lesser-known writers. All the poetic genres of the Victorian era are represented. Biographical headnotes for each poet, and every poem is prefaced by a useful introduction and is fully annotated. Chronology.

Olson, Steven. *The Prairie in Nineteenth Century American Poetry*. Norman: University of Oklahoma Press, 1995. Examines the poetry of Herman Melville, Emily Dickinson, Walt Whitman, Oliver Wendell Holmes, James Russell Lowell, and Henry Wadsworth Longfellow. Explores the idea of the prairie as the principal metaphor for embodying the issues present in the political, social, and cultural life of nineteenth century America.

O'Neill, Michael, and Charles Mahoney, eds. *Romantic Poetry: An Annotated Anthology*. Malden, Mass.: Wiley-Blackwell, 2008. Illustrated. Contains selected works of ten Romantic poets and a variety of poetic forms. Excellent introduction, chronology, headnotes, and annotations.

Storey, Mark. *The Problem of Poetry in the Romantic Period*. New York: St. Martin's Press, 2000. Examines the relationship between the various Romantic manifestos and the major poetry of the time, finding that despite the apparent confidence of many writers, there was an underlying unease about the validity of poetry.

Wagner, Jennifer Ann. *A Moment's Monument: Revisionary Poetics and the Nineteenth Century English Sonnet*. Madison, Wis.: Fairleigh Dickinson University Press, 1996. Argues that the history of the sonnet in the nineteenth century is more than a decorative strand in its literary fabric. This book is mainly about William Wordsworth, who discovers, through Milton, that at the heart of the sonnet's power as a form is the trope of synecdoche, which he connects up with the very moment and act of representation—thereby "inventing" the visionary Romantic sonnet.

Dennis R. Dean

ENGLISH AND AMERICAN POETRY IN THE TWENTIETH CENTURY

Twentieth century poetry has been variously characterized as romantic, antiromantic, impersonal, highly personal, chaotic, orderly, classical, symbolist, wholly untraditional, reasoned and measured, or incomprehensible—depending on the critic whom one reads. This radical diversity suggests a fundamental problem with poetry in the twentieth century: It has no clear path to follow. Finding previous poetry inadequate to deal with the situation in which they find themselves, modern poets must create anew, must, in Wallace Stevens's phrase, "find out what will suffice." The modern poem is an act of exploration. In the absence of givens, it must carve out its own niche, make its own raison d'être.

Not surprisingly, then, twentieth century poetry is marked by astonishing variety. What logic could successfully yoke together Robert Frost and Allen Ginsberg, Philip Larkin and William Carlos Williams, Sylvia Plath and Ezra Pound? None, so long as the category of modern poetry is understood to be a fixed entity; such definitions always aim at closure and exclusion. Nevertheless, it is possible to see all of modern poetry as a piece, and that possibility is what this essay hopes to explore.

THE RISE OF MODERNISM

Modern poetry began with a sense of discontinuity, a sense that the world of the twentieth century was not merely different as one century always is from another but decisively different, qualitatively different from all the centuries past. This sense of discontinuity was shared by the other arts; it was "on or about December 1910," Virginia Woolf wrote, that "human character changed." This shared conviction of radical change gave rise to the far-flung, loosely defined movement in the arts known as modernism, characterized in poetry by the fragmented, elliptical, allusive styles of Pound and T. S. Eliot.

To believe that the poetry of the Pound-Eliot school constitutes the whole of important modern poetry, however, or that modernism was a cohesive, unified movement, is to ignore many of its characteristic elements. As early as the first meetings of the Imagist group, gathered around Pound in England in 1912, the diversity of talent, ideas, and aesthetics among modernist poets was already clear. Modernism was not a unified movement even in its early stages. Moreover, there were significant poets who did not buy into modernism at all. Against Pound's famous injunction to "compose in the manner of the musical phrase, not the metronome," there is Frost's equally well-known statement that writing free verse is like "playing tennis without a net." Against the heavily idea-laden poetry of Eliot and the New Critic/Fugitive poets—John Crowe Ransom and Allen Tate, in particular—stand Williams's "no ideas but in things" and Archibald MacLeish's "a poem should not mean but be." The pillars of what is commonly regarded as modernism, then, found themselves flanked right and left by dissenters, as well as faced by independent thinkers within their camp. Mod-

William Carlos Williams

ernist poetry, as commonly construed, represents a fairly limited if important range of the whole of modern poetry. If discussion of that entire range (and the diversity of British and American poetry is staggering) is to go forward, "modern" must be reclaimed from "modernist." As distinguished from the self-consciously modernist, "modern poetry" can be understood to be roughly synonymous with twentieth century poetry, excepting the occasional reactionary or nostalgic poet and a few carryovers from Victorianism.

THE END OF VICTORIANISM

Modern literature is less united in what it stands for than in what it opposes. In a sense, almost all writing in the twentieth century attempts to throw over the nineteenth century, particularly those aspects of it generally classified as Victorian. Both the sociopolitical and the literary elements of Victorianism come under fire from the modern artist, and the combination of targets should not be surprising, since politics and economics combine with literature in the nineteenth century to form what appears to modern eyes to be a uniform culture. While this uniformity may be largely mythical, it nevertheless has become one of the givens in discussions of Victorianism.

Behind most of the philosophical, social, and political inquiries of the nineteenth century, not merely in England and America but throughout the Western world, lies the idea of progress, of a goal toward which society is moving perceptibly. One of the clearest manifestations of this idea is Karl Marx's *telos*, the goal or endpoint of civilization's quest for utopia. Marxism depends on this idea as on no other; the supposition that one can chart the course of societies with certainty that each will follow the same line of development rests on the unstated assumption that all societies are moving in the same direction, and that therefore there must be some goal toward which all, willingly or not, tend. Marx is not alone, of course, in so thinking. The utilitarianism of Jeremy Bentham and John Stuart Mill, with its emphasis on "the greatest good for the greatest number," builds on similar foundations: That act is best that, since it offers maximum benefits to the most members of society, promotes the greatest social progress. Other progress-centered developments in thought range from

American manifest destiny (and other nations' quest for empire, as well) to Mary Baker Eddy's "Every day in every way things get better and better."

Nor is this phenomenon limited to social thought; the single greatest scientific contribution of the century bears the mark of its time. Charles Darwin's evolutionary theory is every bit as dependent on the notion of *telos* as is Marx's: The result of the fittest members of the species surviving to mate with one another is that newer and fitter forms of life constantly come into being. The newest and fittest form, naturally, is the human being. That Darwinian thought is a logical extension of nineteenth century notions of progress is borne out by the readiness with which evolution was accepted not by biologists, but by social thinkers. Social Darwinism combines evolutionary thought with the already accepted mode of utilitarianism.

CULTURAL BREAKDOWN

Against this concept of progress lies its opposite, and what may even be seen as its necessary, complement. A society that is constantly progressing is undergoing constant change, which in turn means that traditional institutions and ways of life must break down. In *The Education of Henry Adams* (1907), Henry Adams expresses this idea in terms of the twin images of virgin and dynamo. The virgin, representative of traditional culture, symbolizes stability and order, a manageable, if static, society. The dynamo, the modern society, spins constantly faster, changing incessantly, leaving its members with a sense of chaos and confusion. While modern society shows progress, it also falls into relativism, since the traditional institutions on which absolutes are based are breaking down. Whereas the idea of progress was a product of mid-nineteenth century thinkers, the time of the Great Exhibition in London, the notion of cultural breakdown achieved its widest circulation late in the nineteenth century and into the twentieth, receiving its fullest development, perhaps, in the work of Eliot.

Nineteenth century literature, particularly in England, mirrored the development of thought in the period. It should not be surprising, therefore, that the chief poet of High Victorianism, Alfred, Lord Tennyson, was tremendously popular as well as critically acclaimed, and that the same should be true for the novelist Charles Dickens. The artists of mid-century specialized in giving the people what they wanted. Walt Whitman, the nineteenth century poet to whom American moderns so often look, would seem to be an exception. One must remember, of course, that Whitman's work was largely ignored during his lifetime, that he was not a popular poet by any means when his work first appeared, and that the recognized poets of the era, such as John Greenleaf Whittier and Henry Wadsworth Longfellow, worked with the public's desires more firmly in mind. Then, too, even Whitman wrote directly to his audience much more than the typical modern poet (if there be such a thing) does, and his great poem, *Leaves of Grass* (1855), is a public celebration of the people.

DECADENCE

The late nineteenth century produced the expected countermovement, in which the characteristic poem is much darker, more decadent, and suspicious of the openness and health of the High Victorians. Under the influence of the darker Romantics and the French Symbolists (who got their own dose of dark Romanticism from Edgar Allan Poe), the late Victorians from the Pre-Raphaelites on demonstrate a tendency toward the sinister and the unhealthy, toward madness and dissipation. Prostitutes, drug addicts, criminals—all those, in short, from the underside of society, from the social strata largely ignored by Tennyson—figure heavily in the work of Dante Gabriel Rossetti and Algernon Charles Swinburne, Ernest Dowson, Lionel Johnson, the early William Butler Yeats, and, of course, Oscar Wilde. Their fascination with dark subjects and dark treatments shows a suspicion of the methods and beliefs of the earlier Victorians analogous to Adams's suspicion of progress. Their work collectively embodies the fin de siècle sense of impending change, the exhaustion of old modes, the existential ennui of a society in decline. The late Victorian poets were not a new beginning but a clear end, a cry for the new, while in the United States the cry was silence, the absence of any major poetic talents. On both sides of the Atlantic, poetry in English was a gap waiting to be filled, and awaiting of something as yet unknown.

EARLY MODERN MOVEMENTS

The early years of the twentieth century produced three separate groups of poetic innovators: the Georgian poets, the Sitwell group, and the Imagists. Although all three failed to sustain movements, each contributed elements to the large field of modern poetry.

The first two groups were decidedly minor, producing little work that has continued to be held in high esteem by the critical or poetic communities. The Georgians are often dismissed as the old guard that the true modernists struggled to overthrow; yet such an easy dismissal overlooks the radical nature of the movement. As Geoffrey Bullough pointed out in *The Trend of Modern Poetry* (1934), Georgian poetry, while a throwback to Romanticism, represents a break with the Imperial poetry of the same period, and the established poets of the day looked on it with some horror. Moreover, while the movement itself died down, some of its work in loosening the reins on traditional verse forms has survived, as one can see in the repeated comparisons of Larkin's work with the Georgian poetry of Edward Thomas. The conversational diction and simplicity of their poetry, as Bullough further notes, has become something of a standard feature in certain strains of modern poetry. Similarly, the work of the group gathered around the Sitwells ultimately came to little, yet there is much in that poetry that foreshadows developments in other, more important poets. The spiritual despair, the often forced gaiety, the combination of wit and bleakness of Sitwellian poetry shows up in many other writers' work in the century. Ultimately, their work is for the most part ignored or forgotten because they had very little to say; their poetry had much surface but lacked substance.

IMAGISM

Of the three, Imagism is by far the most important school for modern verse at large. The goal of the movement, as the name implies, was to bring to poetry a new emphasis on the image as a structural, rather than an ornamental, element. Growing out of French Symbolism and taking techniques, styles, and forms from Japanese haiku, *tanka*, and *hokku*, from Chinese ideograms, and from classical Greek and Provençal troubador lyrics,

Imagism reflects the diverse interests of its founders and their rather dilettantish nature.

While there were a number of very fine practitioners, among them F. S. Flint, D. H. Lawrence, T. E. Hulme, H. D. (Hilda Doolittle), Richard Aldington, Williams, Carl Sandburg, and Amy Lowell, it is Pound who stands as the major spokesperson and publicist for the group. Pound, along with Aldington and H. D., formulated the three cardinal rules of the movement in "A Retrospect": direct treatment of the thing discussed; absolute economy of diction; and composition "in the sequence of the musical phrase, not in the sequence of the metronome." At various times, others from the group expanded on or modified those three initial rules, yet they stand as the basis for Imagist technique. In fact, they are descriptive of the movement rather than prescriptive; the Imagist group had been meeting in one form or another for several years when Pound formulated these precepts. Much of the philosophical basis for the school comes from Hulme's study of Henri Bergson's thought. Under Hulme's influence, the varied interests of the members jelled into a more or less cohesive body of theory, at least for a short time.

The poetry produced by the group, although by no means uniform, shared certain characteristics. First of all, it was an attempt to put the creation of images at the center of the poetic act. The image is a sudden moment of truth, or, as Pound describes it, "an intellectual and emotional complex in an instant of time." It shares a good deal with other modern moments of revelation, from Gerard Manley Hopkins's "inscape" to James Joyce's "epiphany." The brevity of the Imagist poem, another defining characteristic particularly of those produced early in the group's history, is a logical extension of the emphasis on the image. As an attempt to eschew rhetorical and narrative forms and to replace them with the "pure" poetic moment, the Imagist poem, existing almost solely for the creation of the image, completes its mission with the completion of that image. A long poem of the type would simply be a series of discrete images whose relation to one another could only be inferred, since explicative transitions would be a violation of precept. The longer poems produced under the leadership of Lowell evidence a loosening of form and a laxity of craftsmanship. The late Imagist poems are not so much transitional, pointing toward some new development, as they are decadent, indicative of the movement's demise.

That Imagism would be short-lived was almost inevitable. The goals and techniques of the movement were antithetical to sustaining even a poem of any considerable duration, let alone a school. The tiny Imagist poem is much too limiting to allow its creator much variety from one poem to the next. The chance to explore themes, ideas, and beliefs simply does not exist, since that sort of argument-oriented poetry is what Imagism sought to replace. Even the proponents of Imagism had larger plans than their espoused methods would allow. Pound, for example, even while he was most closely associated with the group, was working on his plan for the *Cantos* (1925-1972). Nevertheless, even if Imagism lacked the qualities to make it a sustained movement, its methods have been adopted in the great majority of poems written in the twentieth century. Imagist techniques appear in Williams's *Paterson* (1946-1958) and in the *Cantos*, but they also appear in the work of such non-Imagists as Tate, Eliot, Plath, and Dylan Thomas, and make possible such later developments as Surrealism and the Deep Image poetry of James Wright and Robert Bly.

Symbolism

Imagism, itself a product of diverse influences, is only one of a great many influences on modern poetry. Perhaps the single most important influence has been nineteenth century French Symbolism. Ironically, the source of much Symbolist theory was Poe, whose work was largely ignored by Anglo-American critics. The French, however, saw in his darkly Romantic speculations, in the bleakness and horror of his work, even in his impulse toward dissipation, the vehicle appropriate to poetry on the modern predicament. In his own country, he may have been a Gothic oddity; in France, he was a prophet. The work produced by his French followers—Jules Laforgue, Tristan Corbière, Charles Baudelairc, Stéphane Mallarmé, Arthur Rimbaud, and Paul Verlaine—incorporated much from Poe: the darkness, the exploration of life's underside, the penchant for urban landscapes, and, most important, the centrality of the symbol.

Certainly symbols have always been used in poetry, and little that the Symbolists accomplished with symbols was entirely new. What was fresh and unique, however, was their insistence on the symbol as the structural raison d'être of the poem. No longer relegated to the status of ornament or occasional item, the symbol became for these poets the goal one actively sought to achieve in the poem. Like so many of their modern followers, they were reacting against the Scylla and Charybdis of loose, discursive verse on one hand, and didactic, allegorical verse on the other. Also like their followers, they mistrusted language, having seen too much bad poetry turned out by following conventional use of "poetic" language. They therefore felt that the achievement of poetry must lie elsewhere than in the play of words. Their solution was to place heavy emphasis on the poetic moment, the symbol. They attempted to separate radically the symbolic from the allegorical use of imagery, and there is about much Symbolist poetry a vagueness that refuses to let the symbol be quite pinned down. In some of the followers of Symbolism, particularly in the work of the English poets of the 1890's, that vagueness drifts off into airy realms too thin for habitation.

Symbolism found its way into Anglo-American modern poetry by so many routes that it is nearly impossible to chronicle them all. Nevertheless, a few of the points of entry require mention. The earliest important mention of Symbolism is in Arthur Symons's famous book of 1899, *The Symbolist Movement in Literature*. Symons, along with Yeats and other poets of the Rhymers' Club, introduced the work of these Frenchmen to English audiences not only through essays and defenses but also through original English poetry on Symbolist models. Giving as much attention to prose writers as to poets, Symons hailed the new literary wind blowing from Paris as one that did not shrink from neurosis, nightmare, and decadence. Of Mallarmé, he says, "All his life he has been haunted by the desire to create, not so much something new in literature, as a literature which should be itself a new art." This sense of newness, of shocking, appalling novelty, was immediately grasped by defenders and vilifiers alike, and Symbolism itself became a symbol. Wilde could not have set the character of Dorian Gray so well in ten pages of de-

scription, at least for his immediate audience, as he did by having Dorian reading, at several key points, Joris-Karl Huysmans's *Á rebours* (1884; *Against the Grain*, 1922). This first wave of enthusiasm, however, was mainly a matter of imitation, and if it largely died out before producing any major works of interest, it was because the writers who experimented in the mode were playing with an exotic toy, not working with an instrument fitted to their own machinery.

The second major attempt at importation, this one aiming for domestication, grew eventually into Imagism. If the work of Symons and Yeats was important because it showed that such a thing as symbolism existed, Imagism's importance lay in the translation of a movement from one century and one place into another movement in another century and another place. Imagism sought to refine the terms of the symbol; Pound, writing of the aims of Imagism, said that symbolic function was one of the possible uses of the image, but that it should never be so important that the poem is lost on a person for whom "a hawk is simply a hawk."

The third major importer of Symbolism into English was Eliot. He wrote extensively about the Symbolists; he copied their style, even to the point of writing in French in some early poems; he openly acknowledged his debt in direct borrowings from their work; and, most important, he produced the most complete example of a Symbolist poem in English, *The Waste Land* (1922). In the use of urban landscape, the feverish, nightmarish quality of the imagery, the darkness of the vision, the layering of symbols and images within symbols and images, *The Waste Land* demonstrates its creator's overwhelming debt to the Symbolists. The poem's centrality in the modern canon lends weight to the significance of Symbolism for modern Anglo-American poetry. Knowingly or not, all poets who have found themselves affected by Eliot's great work have also been affected by Laforgue and Baudelaire.

THE METAPHYSICAL INFLUENCE

Symbolism was not, however, the only major influence on modern poetry. Another example of Eliot's importance as an arbiter of poetic taste and style is the resurrection of the English Metaphysical poets as models for modern verse. Long ignored by English critics, the Metaphysicals—John Donne, in particular—offer the modern poet another use of a controlling metaphor. If the Symbolists reintroduced the poet to the symbol, Donne and his contemporaries—Andrew Marvell, George Herbert, Henry Vaughan, Richard Crashaw—showed him how to use it in extended forms. The conceit of the Metaphysical poem, like the symbol of the Symbolist poem, is an example of figurative language used not as ornament, but as structural principle. Since the conceit of a Donne poem is used as a way of integrating metaphor with argument, the model served to overcome the limiting element of Imagism and, to a lesser extent, of Symbolism itself. Both the latter movements, since they eschewed argument as a poetic method, shut themselves off from the possibility of sustained use. The Metaphysical conceit (and what is the image of the wasteland if not a conceit, a unifying metaphor?) allows Eliot to adapt Imagist and symbolist techniques to a long, elaborately structured poem.

WALT WHITMAN AND THOMAS HARDY

Another, very different model for long poems was found in Walt Whitman's *Leaves of Grass*. Whitman's great contribution is in the area of open form. The sometimes chatty, sometimes oratorial, usually free-wheeling style of his poetry has done more than anything else to show the path away from iambic verse. His influence is clear on such poets as Williams, Lawrence, Ginsberg and his fellow Beat poets, and Charles Olson and the Black Mountain poets, yet he also often moves through less obvious channels, and virtually any poet who has experimented with open forms owes him a debt. Even a poet as strongly opposed in principle to the looseness of his verse as Pound accorded Whitman grudging respect.

Against this characteristically American model stands the typically British example of Thomas Hardy. Where Whitman's poetic is antitraditional and iconoclastic, open and rhythmic and boisterous, Hardy's is tight-lipped, satisfied to work within established forms, dour and bleak. Hardy's work was not merely traditional; while he worked within standard forms, he often pushed their limits outward, expressing the modern dissatisfaction with form not by rejecting it but by bending it to suit his needs. Very much Victorian, he

still anticipates the modern, standing as a threshold figure for such followers as W. H. Auden, Larkin, Roy Fuller, and perhaps the entirety of the British Movement poets of the 1950's.

Both Whitman and Hardy offer alternatives to the mainstream of modernist poetry as embodied by Pound and Eliot, the Fugitive poets, William Empson, and such later poets as Geoffrey Hill. Modern Whitman-esque poetry—such as Olson's *The Maximus Poems* (1953-1983), which also are strongly indebted to the *Cantos*, and Ginsberg's "Howl"—is commonly regarded as avant-garde, that in the Hardy line as reactionary or antimodern. To accept such labels is to misunderstand the nature of modern poetry. These three camps represent not so much three separate attitudes toward art or aesthetics as three attempts at dealing with the world poetically, those attempts being based on regionalism as much as anything else. The poetics of the Eliot-Pound camp are essentially cosmopolitan, the result of ransacking international literary history from the classics and Chinese lyrics to the Provençal poets to the Symbolists. The other two schools are much more closely related to place, to national identity. Auden is not less modern than Williams; he is more British. Moreover, to insist on too clear a dividing line among the camps is to falsify the situation. While the influence of one figure or school of poetry may be more pronounced on some groups or individuals, there is also a general influence on the whole of modern poetry, so that the struggle of a poet such as Larkin to loosen forms may be the result of the undetected (and probably undetectable) influence of Whitman, who has caused a general trend toward openness. On the other hand, if there is a rancor in Ginsberg that is not present in Whitman, it is perhaps that the later poet has picked up the typically modern ambivalence that is present in Hardy. In short, one should not be too hasty in excluding any potential influence, nor in assessing a poet's "modernity."

AFTER WORLD WAR II

The foregoing discussion, while it has applicability to the entire century, fails to address some of the significant developments since World War II. Poetry after that war underwent a mid-century crisis, during which time it made a number of motions that appeared to indicate rejection of the poetry that had immediately preceded it. The Movement in England, the Beats and Black Mountain poets in the United States, confessional poetry, and Surrealist poetry were all symptomatic of change, and the critical tendency has been to read that change as sweeping, as a revolution. There is, however, much evidence to suggest just the contrary—that what took place after 1945 was not revolutionary but domestic: a periodic housecleaning occasioned by changes in fashion and perhaps also by changes in the world around the poet.

It is not entirely unfair to say that modern poetry came into being when the dilettantism of Georgian and Sitwellian and Imagist poetry ran into World War I. The utter inability of those movements to deal effectively with a world in which such a cataclysm possibly forced poets to abandon certain precepts that had failed them. It is no mere coincidence, for example, that Imagism flourished in the years immediately preceding the war when, as Paul Fussell notes in his study *The Great War and Modern Memory* (1975), England was blithely, even determinedly ignorant of impending events, or that it faltered and died during the war years. The Imagist poem did not offer sufficient scope for the creation of a work of "a certain magnitude." Eliot's great contribution, as mentioned earlier, lay in grafting Imagist (and symbolist) technique onto forms that allowed greater expansiveness.

Similarly, the tremendous destruction brought about in World War II caused a shift in attitudes and, by extension, in poetic practices. In World War I, the destruction was limited largely to combatants; battle was a distant thing. By the end of World War II, the bombing of population centers, the unveiling of atomic weaponry, and the revelation of genocide had made warfare both more personal and more terrible. The poetics of impersonality and detachment as sponsored by Eliot suddenly seemed outmoded, and the movement in much of modern poetry since that time has been toward a renewed involvement with the self. Eliot's self is an extension of culture; a member of church, state, and critical school; a representative of agencies and institutions. His concern with the self, from "The Love Song of J. Alfred Prufrock" to *Four Quartets*

(1943), is a curiously impersonal involvement. After the war, however, many poets turned their verse inward, examining the self with all its flaws, hungers, and hidden violence.

SURREALISM

Another branch of postwar American and English poetry has been heavily influenced by Surrealism. Whereas the early modernists went directly to the Symbolists, these postwar poets first encountered Symbolism through its later development, Surrealism. The French Surrealism of André Breton had comparatively little impact in England, where only a handful of writers—notably David Gascoyne and Thomas—employed its techniques with any regularity. It had even less impact in the United States. Spanish Surrealism, on the other hand, was imported into American poetry through the work of Bly, Wright, and W. S. Merwin, all prolific translators, and into English poetry in small bits through Charles Tomlinson's association with Octavio Paz. The Deep Image poetry of Bly and Wright, owing much to Federico García Lorca, César Vallejo, and Pablo Neruda, often reads like a Symbolist rendering of deep consciousness. The New York School of Kenneth Koch, Frank O'Hara, and John Ashbery also demonstrates its indebtedness to earlier, continental Surrealists.

RENEWED ROMANTICISM

Earlier native poets have been reevaluated in the postwar period as well. Hardy has become even more important to certain strains of British poetry than he was before the war, while the reappraisal of Whitman and the discovery of Dickinson as a poetic resource has led American poets to a new sense of tradition. If Beat poetry would be impossible without Whitman, then confessional poetry would also be impossible, or at least radically different, without Dickinson. Her intense concern with self and soul, her death obsession, her striking use of associative imagery, her use of very simple poetic forms for very complex ideas, all show up in the work of Robert Lowell, Plath, Sexton, and John Berryman.

As the interest in Dickinson suggests, the renewed emphasis on the self in postwar poetry leads to a new involvement with Romanticism. Often, though, it is with the darker side of Romanticism that poets interact—with Symbolism, with Lawrence and Dickinson—with those elements, in short, that show the self on the edge of disaster or oblivion. There is, of course, the buoyant optimism of Whitman to counteract this trend, yet even his influence often appears darker than the original. The return to favor of Romanticism might be the sole real break with earlier moderns, with modernism, with Eliot's classicism.

Even here, however, such a generalization is dangerous. One must remember that Lawrence, Williams, Stevens, Thomas, Robert Graves, and even elements in Eliot's work belie the anti-Romantic stance usually accepted as a basis for modernism. Similarly, the more positive attitude toward the Romantics is by no means universal. The Movement poets, for example, adopted a vigorous anti-Romantic position in their dryly ironic verse, while there is much in Romanticism that even those poets who seem closest to it find unappealing. The modern Romantics, like the modern classicists, select only those elements that fit the modern platform they happen to be building.

EASTERN, MYTHIC, AND ARCHETYPAL INFLUENCES

Not all influences on twentieth century poetry were domestic. Like the earlier moderns, the postwar poets made forays into exotic poetics. Indeed, the postwar period might be called the Age of Translation, in which English-language poetry became open to the riches of world poetry as never before. Both Japanese and Chinese poetry were particularly influential in the postwar years, notably in the work of Kenneth Rexroth and Gary Snyder. In this period, there was a marked trend toward going below the surface of Asian culture to the deep structure of its modes of thought. Snyder, for example, spent several years in a Zen monastery in Kyoto, and while the experience did not turn him away from Western society entirely, it caused him to reexamine more familiar cultural forms in the light of another perspective.

Another distinctive characteristic of modern poetry is its preoccupation with myth and archetype. To be sure, much of the poetry in the Western tradition, from Homer and Ovid to Percy Bysshe Shelley, from Dante

to Tennyson, is explicitly concerned with myth, yet the modern sense of the mythic differs from anything that went before. In modern poetry, everyday life is frequently seen as a series of rituals, often acted out unawares, by which humankind expresses its relation to the universal.

In part, this distinctively modern awareness of myth and archetype can be attributed to the influence of the new science of anthropology as exemplified in Sir James Frazer's pioneering work *The Golden Bough* (1890-1915). The work of Sigmund Freud and Carl Jung early in the twentieth century added to the modern writer's interest in myth. Where Frazer examined mythic patterns as cultural phenomena, Freud and Jung demonstrated the ways in which individuals internalize such patterns. Myth and archetype derive their power, then, from their timeless hold on the individual consciousness.

The result of this thinking was a tremendous explosion of genuinely new literature, of poetry and fiction in which the quotidian acts of ordinary individuals take on meaning beyond their understanding. Among the fruits of this new flowering were the two most important works produced in English in the twentieth century, both too significant for subsequent writers to ignore and too awesome to copy. One was the story of a single day in Dublin in 1904, during which the ramblings of an Irish Jew parallel the wanderings chronicled in Homer's *Odyssey* (c. 725 B.C.E.; English translation, 1614): Joyce's *Ulysses* (1922). The other, of course, was Eliot's *The Waste Land*. In his essay "*Ulysses*, Order, and Myth," Eliot announced that in place of the traditional narrative method, the modern artist could henceforth use the mythic method, that fiction and poetry would gain power not from their isolated stories, but through the connection of the stories to a universal pattern.

Yeats, of course, had been working in the field of myth in poetry for a long time and had been actively creating his own mythology, through the work surrounding *A Vision* (1925), for several years. Lawrence, too, was a mythmaker, both in his poetry and in his fiction. However, both of these writers' uses of myth constitute dead ends of sorts, for their mythologies are largely private, unusable by others. The mainstream of poetic use of myth in the twentieth century runs, not through the mythmakers, but through myth-followers. From Eliot and Pound to Plath and Seamus Heaney, modern poetry has produced a great deal of work that follows mythic patterns.

MORAL AMBIVALENCE

A final defining characteristic of modern poetry is its ambivalence. The modern poet seems, on the whole, constitutionally incapable of wholeheartedly loving or hating the world in which he or she lives. The foremost example of ambivalence is the work of Yeats, in which he simultaneously strives for release from the world and regret at the possibility of release. Indeed, Yeats carries this double attitude further than anyone else, turning it into an elaborate system. Yeats provides an elaborate image of that ambivalence with his "whirling gyres": The interlocking gyres stand for ideas, beliefs, and qualities that, while completely opposed to one another, nevertheless require each other for completion. In Yeats, one idea is never whole; it must have its opposite idea, for only the interlocking pair are completed, as the tower is incomplete without the winding stair (to use his own symbols).

As a result, Yeats is virtually incapable of rendering a wholehearted judgment in his poetry. He sees both good and bad, the positive and the negative, in all things. In his poems about the Irish Civil War, for example, although he supports Irish independence, he can see the destruction brought about by members of the IRA as well as by the British Royal Irish Constabulary. In "Easter 1916," he celebrates the courage of the insurrectionists, yet at the same time questions their wisdom. Even that questioning is edgy, incomplete; he says that perhaps it was unwise, that perhaps it will set back the cause of Ireland; he refuses either to denounce the uprising or to praise it unreservedly. The most famous example of Yeatsian ambivalence, mirroring the pair of gyres, is a pair of interlocking poems about Byzantium. In "Sailing to Byzantium," the speaker is old and world-weary. He seeks the quietude, the tranquillity of the artificial world represented by Byzantium; he speaks longingly of the work of the city's artisans, of escaping out of the world of flesh into the world of pure beauty. In "Byzantium," he finds himself looking back

across the ocean, again longingly, at the world of flesh and mire. Here he is weary of the world of timeless beauty, and the imagery of the poem's desires is of living creatures, particularly of the dolphin that could carry him back to the living world.

The Byzantium poems embody a fundamental feature of modern poetry: The chaos and contingency of the modern world lead the poet to distaste, to a desire for escape, to a retreat into the sheltered world of aesthetics that Edmund Wilson referred to in *Axel's Castle: A Study in the Imaginative Literature of 1870-1930* (1931). However, contrary to Wilson's contentions, that move is very much an act of engaging the world, every bit as much as Rimbaud's rejection of poetry (the example that Wilson cites as the alternative) for the life of a gunrunner. The characteristic attitude is not rejection but ambivalence; the poet, while wishing to withdraw from the world, is nevertheless caught in it, is a part of it, and can never escape from it. Poetry, therefore, although an attempt to hold the world at arm's length, still remains in contact with it and is constantly a response to, not an escape from, life.

Yeats and Hardy are models for this attitudinal complex, along with the late Victorians—such as Swinburne, Dowson, and Dante Gabriel Rossetti—and the French Symbolists. British poetry tends to be dominated by ambivalence more than its American counterpart does; the Beats, for example, seem less ambivalent than the British Movement poets. In general, however, modern poetry may be characterized fairly as the poetry of ambivalence.

NEW CRITICISM

In turn, much of the attitudinal bias of the New Criticism—the influential critical movement spawned by modernism—can be explained on the basis of ambivalence: the emphasis on irony, tension, ambiguity, as keys to poetry; the elevation of the Metaphysical poets and the concomitant devaluation of Romantic and Victorian verse; the blindness to poetry that is open or singleminded. Despite its shortcomings, the New Criticism's great contribution was that it taught readers (and still teaches them) how to read modern poetry. That most of the illustrious practitioners of the New Criticism—Tate, Robert Penn Warren, Ransom, Empson—

were also poets of considerable accomplishment should come as no surprise. The New Critics, despite the claims of Cleanth Brooks and others, did not read all kinds of poetry equally well, yet their sensitivity to modern poetry remains unequaled, because they were so attuned to the various forms that ambivalence can take in a poem.

Disjuncture and discontinuity

Modern poetry—particularly after *The Waste Land*—is characterized by deliberated discontinuities. Several impulses came together more or less at once to create the disjointed poetics of modern verse. One, of course, was the inheritance of Imagism, the concentration on the intensely poetic moment almost to the exclusion of everything else. More fundamental was the sense of fragmentation in society and in consciousness that many modern writers express, a sense of radical discontinuity with the past. One consequence of this sense of fragmentation was a distrust of language. The ambivalence of modern writers toward the world lead them to suspect received forms, particularly those forms that suggest continuity and wholeness. Such completeness contradicts a writer's experience of the world, in which things are fragmented, discontinuous, chaotic, intractable. To blithely write long, flowing poems in the manner of Tennyson would be to violate one's own experience of the world and one's own consciousness. Other literary forms come under suspicion as well, but the modern poet is particularly wary of sustained, regular forms. Even such artists as Larkin or Yeats, who work in received forms, often take great pains to change them, to make them less regular. The corollary—a suspicion traceable to the Symbolists—is that language itself is unreliable, a debased medium encrusted with connotations from previous usage.

These several forces came together to move the modern poem toward disjuncture and discontinuity. Again, in this respect as in so much else, *The Waste Land* was seminal work. The poem leaps from image to image, throwing unconnected and even antithetical elements violently together to produce a work that, although it draws heavily on earlier literature, is like nothing that had gone before. The links between the five main sections of the poem have particularly troubled readers, since they are not related in any immediately identifiable manner. Still, they do cohere, they do move toward some final point as a group that none of them achieves individually. Their cohesiveness is a function of each section's relation to the whole, rather than, as one might expect, the relations between pairs of successive sections.

The poem sequence

When the disjunctive poetics of modern verse are practiced in works of large scale, as in *The Waste Land*, traditional forms must necessarily be scrapped. In very short lyrics, of course, there is no problem with the connection between sections, but in longer works the sections must stand together in some logical fashion or risk the outrage heaped on Eliot's work when it first appeared. Even so, a poem can go on piling image upon image without respite for just so long before it breaks down, before the reader becomes hopelessly lost in the morass. To circumvent the problems raised by continuity in a disjunctive poetry, the modern writer has turned to the poem sequence. The sequence has been variously defined, but perhaps it is most satisfactory to think of it as a series of poems that are capable of standing alone but that take on greater significance through their mutual interaction.

Thus, a sequence is a long poem made of shorter poems; the modern poem sequence has its opposite number in what Joanne V. Creighton, in her study *Faulkner's Craft of Revision* (1977), calls the "short-story composite." The composite is a book composed of chapters that are themselves stories; the stories can be read separately, as in an ordinary collection, but they also form a unified whole when read together. She cites Ernest Hemingway's *In Our Time* (1924) and William Faulkner's *Go Down, Moses* (1942) as such works, in which the writer has given as much planning and work to the book's larger structure (as in a novel) as he has to the individual parts (as in a normal short-story collection).

The poem sequence is not the exclusive property of the twentieth century, of course. Many earlier examples can be cited, depending on how one judges such matters: Rimbaud's *Une Saison en Enfer* (1873; *A Season in Hell*, 1932), Whitman's *Leaves of Grass*, Dante

Gabriel Rossetti's sonnet sequence *The House of Life* (1869), William Morris's *The Earthly Paradise* (1868-1870), perhaps even Dante's *La divina commedia* (c. 1320; *The Divine Comedy*, 1802). However, in almost every case, the premodern sequence attempts to justify its disunity by displaying the unity among its sections, by talking its way through or over the gaps. By contrast, the modern sequence often works through silence, by exploiting the interstices, allowing ambiguity or multiple meanings to slip in through the cracks. The unexplained juxtaposition of elements adds to the possible meanings of the work; the reader must participate in the construction of the sequence.

In the loosest possible sense, any book of poems is a sequence; so, in the twentieth century, sequences come in all denominations. Both Lawrence and Yeats experimented with sequencing fairly informally in their work. Lawrence often collected his poems in a book around a theme or a method of creation, and strung poems together by resonant phrasings, as in the group of poems whose central piece is "The Ship of Death." Yeats also carefully arranged the poems in his books, and in his revisions, he not only changed poems but the order as well. At the other end of the scale stands *The Waste Land*, which is not, strictly speaking, a sequence at all, yet which shares some characteristics of the sequence: fragmentation, separate titles for its sections, length, and scope. Still, it fails to meet one of the criteria: Its separate sections cannot stand alone as poems. One cannot dissect the poem without making hash of it. It looks like a sequence, and indeed it is often listed as one, but it is not. It is a long, fragmentary, truly modern poem. To find a real poem sequence in Eliot, one must look to the end, to *Four Quartets*.

The Waste Land owed its striking discontinuity in large measure to the blue pencil of Pound. Pound's editorial assistance, as in the case of Hemingway's *In Our Time*, nearly always took the form of radical deletion, and in this poem, he cut much transitional and explanatory material, resulting in a formal jumpiness that reinforces the cultural and personal neurasthenia. It is to Pound's own work, though, that one must look to find an early example of a poem sequence.

Both *Homage to Sextus Propertius* (1934) and *Hugh Selwyn Mauberley* (1920) are early sequences by Pound,

and, while not mere exercises, are trial pieces for his major life sequence, the *Cantos*, which he had already begun. Both are attempts at sustained works made up of smaller units. *Homage to Sextus Propertius* is a single poem made up of twelve loose translations or renderings of poems by Sextus Propertius, each of which had stood alone in the original. The effect, in Pound, is of a series of more or less autonomous pieces that have an affinity for one another, a common language or flavor, a function in part of the latinate diction employed by the poet. His *Hugh Selwyn Mauberley* is a more recognizable sequence, unified by the persona of Mauberley. When read as a whole, the poems take on much greater meaning through their collective resonance. The renderings of Propertius's work are loosely affiliated, are similar to one another; the poems in *Hugh Selwyn Mauberley* are parts of a whole.

It is in the *Cantos* that Pound works most concertedly in the poem sequence. Taking Dante's *The Divine Comedy* as its extremely loose model (Pound once said he was writing a *commedia agnostica*), the poem works its way through ancient and modern history, Eastern and Western thought and art, economics, literature, politics, music, architecture, and personal experience. The *Cantos* is a record of a modern poet's experience, an epic-scale work of the person of sensibility in the world.

The unity of the sequence is established through purely internal means: echoes, repetitions, thematic and ideological ties. The apparent obscurity of a given canto is a function of the unity of the poet's mind: The obscure utterance will likely be expanded, explained, revised, rearticulated at some later point in the proceedings. Thus the *Cantos* have a Hermetic quality that can make reading a single canto difficult, while rewarding a comprehensive reading of the whole. The publication history suggests that the parts of the *Cantos* can be read singly or in groups, coming out as they did by fits and starts over fifty years, but they prove most rewarding when taken as a total work, when read as the epic they were intended to be. They are the Ur-sequence of modern poetry. Tate said of them that they beg for a ceaseless study at the rate of one a year in depth, the whole to be read through every few weeks to maintain perspective. His comments are suggestive of the demands that twentieth century literature makes on its readers; works such as *Ulysses* and the *Cantos* are pitched away from the popular audience and toward the professional reader who can give them the kind of constant and loving attention they demand.

THE BRIDGE

At about the same time that the first thirty cantos were appearing, Hart Crane was writing another sequence that would become a refutation of the wanderlust and classicism of Pound's work and of the wasteland-mentality of Eliot's. *The Bridge* (1930) is a sequence much closer to Whitman's than to Pound's, celebrating America and the American people, very much a home-grown thing. Where Pound is something of a literary Ulysses, traveling the known world for his materials, Crane relies primarily on native sources, native images, native speech, native treatments. Like most poets of his time, he had wrestled with the influence of Eliot and the Symbolists, learning much from them but unwilling to remain in that camp. He found his liberation through Whitman, whose buoyant optimism

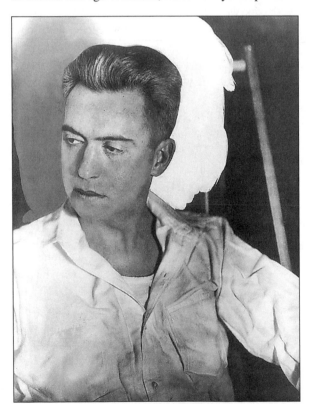

Hart Crane (Library of Congress)

and sense of universal connectedness countered Eliot's pessimism and exhaustion.

The result of that influence is impressive: If Eliot can connect nothing with nothing, then *The Bridge*, with its emphasis on connections, is the antithesis of Eliotic aesthetics. Crane finds connections everywhere, and the poem's two major symbols, the bridge and the river, are both connectors, uniting distant or separate elements of the country. They are a brilliant pair of symbols, necessary complements. While the river connects one end of the country with another, it also divides it and requires a counter-symbol; the bridge, ridiculous without a river underneath, provides the literally overarching symbol of unification. The poem also strives to unify its disparate elements in ways that neither Eliot's nor Pound's work needs to do. The individual poems in *The Bridge* are much more genuinely separate than the individual cantos, certainly than the sections of *The Waste Land*. They are, for the most part, fully capable of standing alone, poems of unquestionable autonomy. What they lack, when separated from the whole, is the thematic power of Crane's emphasis on unity and wholeness. It is the constant harping on the theme that drives it home for the reader, the continual transformations of the quotidian into the symbolic, the universal. A bridge in New York becomes the symbol of America; a river becomes the Mississippi, which becomes another symbol of the enormous variety and range of experience in the country; a woman becomes Pocahontas, whose presence in the poem leads toward an exploration of American history. Crane shared with his contemporaries Sandburg and John Dos Passos a desire to write works that encompassed the whole of the national experience, which remained open to the promise of America. Dos Passos's novel trilogy, *USA* (1937), has many affinities with *The Bridge* and with Williams's *Paterson*.

PATERSON

Two other significant modern poets have sought to capture America in poem sequences, but they have differed from Crane's method in their insistence on the local as the key to the universal. Both Williams's *Paterson* and Olson's *The Maximus Poems* (both of which appeared over a number of years) portray American life by concentrating on individual cities. Neither work shows the kind of boundless enthusiasm and optimism that Crane displays, probably because their very close relationships with the microcosms of Paterson, New Jersey, and Gloucester, Massachusetts, force them to see society with all its warts. Crane's general view, like Whitman's before him, allows him the luxury of not seeing the country close up, of blithely ignoring what does not suit him. Williams, on the other hand, can see all the squalor and pollution of the Passaic River and show them to the reader, but he can also see the falls. His optimism is a greater achievement than Crane's because it is harder won. So too with Olson, who, even while railing against the economic exploitation of nature and what he calls the "perjoracracy" of American society, can still see its possibilities.

While the two works share many similarities, they are also different in many ways. *Paterson* reflects Williams's scientific interest in minutiae, his Imagist background, his passionate attachment to place. The poem focuses almost entirely on the city of Paterson and environs, scarcely bothering to suggest the ways in which it is representative of the larger society. That connection Williams leaves to the reader to make. He says repeatedly in the poem, "No ideas but in things," and he holds fast to this precept. He makes a collage of newspaper accounts, essays, personal recollection, and direct observation. One of the poem's great innovations, in fact, is Williams's use of unreworked materials, such as newspaper reports, personal letters, and historical accounts. *Paterson* proceeds not by wrenching its materials into poetic form, but by building the poetry around the materials that are evidence of life; it is a genuinely organic work in the most exact sense of its growing out of, and thereby taking its form from, the materials it employs. Williams criticized Eliot for the elitism of his poetry and his criticism; in *Paterson* he demonstrated his commitment to an egalitarian poetry. Unlike Eliot, he does not shy away from the contingency and chaos of life, does not feel obliged to superimpose an artificial order, but instead is content to live with what order he can discover in the world around him. He is closer to Crane and Whitman than to the method of the *Cantos*.

THE MAXIMUS POEMS

It is Olson who employs Pound's poetics toward a Whitmanian vision of America. Like *Paterson*, The

Maximus Poems are grounded in a specific place, but they employ the sweeping style, the cross-cultural borrowing, the often declamatory tone of the *Cantos*. Tate says of Pound's work that despite all the allusions, quotations, and foreign sources, the structure and method of the *Cantos* is simply conversational, the talk of literate men over a wide range of subjects. *The Maximus Poems* are also heavily conversational, relying on a listener for all the speaker's pronouncements. They embody a curious paradox: Despite their ostensible epistolary structure (Olson calls the separate poems letters, and even addresses them to various individuals), their principal unit of structure is speech-related.

These poems are the major work exemplifying Olson's theory of projective verse. In an attempt to break the tyranny of the traditional poetic line and the iambic foot, Olson proposes a system of "composition by field," of thinking in terms larger than the line, of composing by means of, not a formal unit, but a logical one. The line of poetry should reflect the thought it contains and be limited by the breath of the speaker. A line, therefore, is roughly equivalent to an utterance, and should be controlled by it, rather than forcing the thought to conform to the limitations of the line, as in traditional verse. Although few of the other practitioners of projective verse—Robert Duncan, Robert Creeley, Denise Levertov, Edward Dorn—have insisted on a "breath unit" as an essential part of the definition of what they do, Olson does insist on it as the standard for the poetic line, and the result in *The Maximus Poems* is that the letters have a strikingly oral quality. Each poet, Olson believed, must strike his own rhythm in poetry as personal as a signature.

PERSONAL SEQUENCES

Of course, not all sequences have dealt with issues of such enormous scope. When poetry took a confessional turn in the 1950's, so did the poem sequence. Two of the most notable examples of the genre are Robert Lowell's *Life Studies* (1959) and Berryman's *The Dream Songs* (1969), both of which employ the techniques of sequencing toward highly personal ends. Lowell's career moved from the highly formal poetry he learned under the influence of Ransom at Kenyon College to a looser style. By the time of *Life Studies*, he was able to include a long prose section, "91 Revere Street," something that would have been unthinkable even a few years before. Since each poem deals with a discrete event or mental state or person from a poet's past, little is lost when individual poems are read out of sequence.

By contrast, Berryman's *The Dream Songs* gain greatly by their association with one another. Forming as they do a more or less unified narrative of the life of their protagonist, Henry, the poems develop as they go along, and to excerpt one or a few is to lose much of the flavor of the whole. Alternately riotous and melancholy, boastful and mournful, the songs careen through moods and events at a furious pace. Even the voices are unstable. Henry uses a variety of ways of talking about himself, sometimes "I," sometimes "Henry," sometimes even "you," and there is even a voice of a heckler, which may or may not be a separate person, who addresses him as Mr. Bones and who speaks in the parlance of nineteenth century minstrel shows. The poems gain a formal tension in the play between the looseness of the story and the rigid structure; while a given song may use multiple voices, employ jumps in logic or time frame, or tinker with silences and double entendre, it will always contain eighteen lines in three six-line stanzas, a form that the poet says he learned from Yeats. The poems, like Lowell's, chronicle the weaknesses, failures, successes, and torments of their creator, although Berryman's are always masked by the story line.

ENGLISH AND IRISH POEM SEQUENCES

While much of the most interesting work in sequences has been done by American poets, some very fine sequences have come out of England and Ireland, including the work of some recent poets, among them Hill, Ted Hughes, Heaney, and Tomlinson.

CROW

Hughes worked with sequences on several occasions, and the most notable product of those experiments was his *Crow* (1970). The book was his first effort at creating a mythology, at overthrowing the tired mythology of Christianity. Where Christ is human, loving, gentle, compassionate, soothing, and bloodless, representing the human desire for order and tranquil-

lity, Crow is lusty, violent, animal, raucous, deceitful, cruel, unsympathetic, and, perhaps worst of all, cacophonous. He represents those qualities of disorder and chaos that humankind tries to control with such myths as Christianity, the side that will not be controlled or denied. However, Crow is not human; he tries at one point to be, but fails, and the closest he comes is in acquiring language. As an effort at wholesale myth-making, *Crow* is best read as a complete sequence, since the function of Crow himself is often not fully explained by a single poem.

Hughes furthers the project of sequence making to greater or lesser extents in other work, including *Gaudette* (1970), *Moon-Whales, and Other Moon Poems* (1976), and the very late *Birthday Letters* (1998). This last is a series of poems written over a period of a quarter century and beginning just a few years after the death of Hughes's wife, poet Plath. Hughes's investigation of her genius and pain is raw, honest, careful, and sensitive, opening with his first sighting of her in a photo of newly arrived Fulbright scholars. In "Freedom of Speech," he considers her sixtieth birthday party, if it had happened, and finds everyone concerned—her parents living and dead, her children, even her horse Ariel—smiling and in a sense satisfied, all except Hughes and Plath themselves. In the last poem, "Red," he notes that while red was her chosen color, blue was her color of life; the adoption of red, while leading her into some of her greatest poetry, also leads her away from life and sanity and toward the death that came, over the years, to seem so inevitable.

MERCIAN HYMNS

Hill, the maker of several sequences, including "Funeral Music," "The Songbook of Sebastian Arrurruz," "Lachrimae," and "An Apology for the Revival of Christian Architecture in England," created a figure similar to Crow in his domination of the poetic landscape in King Offa of the *Mercian Hymns* (1971). Offa is the presiding spirit of the West Midlands, the setting of the work, a figure out of medieval history whose presence explains and unifies the poem as Williams's Paterson and Joyce's Finn do in *Paterson* and *Finnegans Wake* (1939), respectively. Whereas *Crow* takes on the whole of Western experience and culture, Hill satisfies himself with the problems of the England he knows. He is deeply rooted in place, in the sense of history and geography of his England, and the mythology he creates is local, as opposed to the universality of the Crow myth.

In *Mercian Hymns*, a series of thirty prose poems (although Hill objected to the phrase, he offered nothing in its place) present scenes from past and present English life—especially that of the West Midland region—so juxtaposed that Hill and his grandmother and Offa all appear as figures in the work. Hill drew from literature, history, philosophy, architecture, and anthropology for his materials, weaving them into a tapestry of place.

THE TRIUMPH OF LOVE

Like Hughes, Hill has continued his work in sequences, most notably in "An Apology for Christian Architecture in England" from *Tenebrae* (1978) and the book-length *The Triumph of Love* (1998). In these works, so different from each other in numerous ways, Hill investigates the intersection of history, morality, religion, and literature from a perspective of personal outrage. In the 150 small sections of *The Triumph of Love*, he looks back at the barbarity and horrors of the century just ending, considering the role of language, poetry (Donne and Herbert and Dryden and Milton as well as more recent practitioners), the uses of religion, genuine faith, and personal culpability. If in the end he indicts humanity, himself included, for its shortcomings, he does so because he believes, he knows, that we can be better than we are. Redemption, although not likely based on past evidence, is not beyond humanity's reach. He has been compared to Eliot in his concern for the relation of the modern world to traditional society, the function of belief in personal life, the impulse to withdraw from the world; yet he is unlike Eliot in his insistence on locale, as well as in his distrust of his impulse to reform the world. Hill's verse has a built-in heckler, a questioner of motives and achievements. If he owes much to Eliot (and of that there can be no doubt), he also shares many qualities with Hughes, including the recognition of man's animal side and the ferocity of some of his poetry.

NORTH

Heaney also sets his poem sequences in a specific place. Throughout his work, Heaney, an Ulster Catholic, is concerned with the relation of his language and the literary forms in which he works to the history of his people and their current troubles. That concern culminates in *North* (1975), in which he explores the history of Irish oppression through poetic excavation. Probing back into literary history, he settles on a modification of Old English poetics, with its heavy alliteration, its pounding rhythms, and its cacophonous vocabulary, as a means of transporting himself out of contemporary Ireland and back to the beginning of the conquests of the Celts by Germanic, Roman, and English armies. He finds an analogous archaeological situation in the excavation of the bog people in Jutland.

The book is made up of two very loosely structured sequences, within which are smaller and more tightly controlled sequences. The first section of the book is the historical exploration and an attempt to turn the intractable forces of history and politics into a workable personal mythology. The section is framed with poems dealing with Antaeus, the earthbound giant of Greek mythology, and indeed all the poems gather their power as well as much of their material from the land. The poems about the bog people and Heaney's reaction to them lie at the very heart of the section, forming a smaller sequence of their own. The poet is also concerned in this first section, through his interest in the bog people, with the Viking occupation of Ireland, and out of that interest grows a small sequence, "Viking Dublin: Trial Pieces." The poem's six sections carry the poet, by means of an ancient whalebone carved as a child's toy, into the Ireland of the Vikings and into those aspects of culture, the poet's culture, that are remnants of that time.

Having made his peace with the past, Heaney turns in part 2 to present social and political conditions. Like the first, this section is a loose thematic sequence, all of the poems building around the same set of subjects: violence, oppression, and suspicion in occupied Ulster. Within the section is the powerful sequence "Singing School." The poem takes its title from Yeats's "Sailing to Byzantium," which hints at his ambivalence toward the conditions in his homeland. Like Yeats, he finds himself torn between the desire to escape the mayhem and violence surrounding him and his need to remain attached to the land. The sequence is composed of six poems recounting Heaney's personal encounters with the forces of oppression, with the highly charged emphasis on personal dialect and language, with the frustration that leads to violence and the fear that violence spawns. "Singing School" is one of the few modern poems to rival Yeats in the authentic presentation of emotional and intellectual responses to social turbulence and personal danger.

Renga

One of the most interesting efforts at writing a poem sequence in the mid-century period is the collective poem *Renga* (1971), written by Tomlinson, with Paz, Jacques Roubaud, and Edoardo Sanguinetti. The *renga* is a traditional Japanese form, a chain poem written collectively, an effort to overcome the ego by blending one's poetry with that of others, sometimes many others. The emphasis is on continuity rather than individual brilliance, and as such is another form of that strain of Eastern thought whose goal is self-effacement. These four Western poets broke with tradition in establishing as the basis of their *renga* a Western form, the sonnet. Each one began a section which was to run for seven sonnets, and each contributed part, a quatrain, a tercet, or a couplet, to each of the first six. The seventh was then to be written by the poet who had begun the series. Sanguinetti declined to write a sonnet at the end of his cycle, declaring that it was complete, so the sonnets total twenty-seven instead of the expected twenty-eight. The multilingual poems, translated into English by Tomlinson, have as their goal the laying aside of ego and personal style for the greater goal of the poem's unity.

Confessional poetry

One of the important divergences from the modernist program in the wake of World War II was the turn toward a more personal poetry, even a painfully personal, confessional poetry. No doubt the shift was motivated in part by politics; a number of those writers who had espoused the impersonal theory of art had also veered dangerously close to totalitarian political thought. Eliot had openly proclaimed himself a reactionary in politics and religion, while Pound, institutionalized at Saint Elizabeths Hospital, provided an irrefutable link between modernism and fascism. Moreover, the turn toward personal poetry was part of a larger move away from the academic, often obscure verse of Eliot and Pound and toward a more open, more accessible poetry. Among the models for such a move were Whitman and Dickinson, although Whitman's contribution to the proletarianization of poetry was not in confessional but in Beat poetry.

The confessional school was, in its beginnings, a specifically regional movement; indeed, it had deep historical roots in Puritan New England. Puritan literature characteristically revealed the struggle of the soul with belief and with evil; in a world where the devil was so ominously and constantly present, the soul could never be at rest, and the writings of Edward Taylor and Jonathan Edwards, along with a host of lesser preachers, show the vigilance that the believer must maintain in his war with the powers of darkness. Those highly personal revelations are often public in nature; that is, the purpose for telling of the pits and snares into which one has fallen and out of which one has endeavored to climb is to better equip one's neighbors or one's congregation to fight off the blandishments of the forces of Hell. However, this is not the only function of such revelations.

In the poetry of Anne Bradstreet, the purpose of such personal revelations is much more private, cathartic; she seems to need release from the pressures and torments of her life, and in writing about them, she externalizes them. In the frequency with which her poems deal not with salvation and temptation, but fear of death, anxiety for children's well-being, hope, aspirations for the future, and love for her husband, she displays the privacy of her revelations. These are not pulpit-poems, as so many of Taylor's are, not poems of a person who is first of all a citizen of God's City on the Hill, but rather of a woman, mother, and wife.

Another major model for confessionalism was Dickinson. Her poetry, in its patterns of thought, its death-obsession, its simultaneously domestic and violent imagery, its self-absorption, and its veerings toward the insane and the clairvoyant, exemplifies many of the themes and treatments that show up in confessional poetry. Dickinson's fiercely personal verse concerns itself not with the workings of self-in-society, but with the self-in-its-own-society. In poem 465, "I heard a Fly buzz—when I died," for example, she writes not of death as a universal experience nor of the communal effects of death, but of the personal experience of dying. The poem gains its power from the tension between the commonplace of a buzzing fly and the extraordinary circumstance of a dying person's taking notice of it. Certainly death itself is a commonplace, but Dickinson's attempt to portray the workings of the mind of a dying person, or one who is already dead, makes the reader's experience of that death extraordinary. In other poems, she makes equally astonishing leaps into madness, despair, delight, grief, solitude, even into closed coffins, and in each of those poems, the most remarkable feature is the stark, unmediated sense of reality that she conveys. The states of being in her poems are almost never filtered through the grid of literature; rather, they come directly from her experience, either real or imagined. Like Whitman, she insists on the genuineness of experience and shuns conventions and received forms or modes of expression. Often their very genuineness makes the poems grate on the reader; their cumulative effect can be very nerve-jangling, owing in large measure to her intense rendering of emotion.

It is possible to see the beginnings of contemporary confessional poetry in Pound's *The Pisan Cantos* (1948), which demonstrate a radical departure from the poet's earlier work, focusing much more heavily on personal experience in the nightmare world of his Italian captivity. However, Pound was never properly speaking a "confessional poet," and perhaps no such thing existed until 1959, when W. D. Snodgrass's *Heart's Needle* and Lowell's *Life Studies* appeared. Lowell has claimed that teaching Snodgrass at the University of Iowa was the greatest single factor in the conversion of his poetry from the intricately formal style of *The Mills of the Kavanaughs* (1951) to the immediacy of *Life Studies*. Certainly it was more than coincidence that the two works appeared in the same year and displayed such similarity in their use of personal material.

However, there are important differences, as well. Snodgrass, even while looking squarely at the events of his life, incorporating them unglossed into his poetry, maintains a cool irony. *Heart's Needle*, for example, deals directly with his relationship with his daughter

in the wake of his divorce. The sequence is filled with moments of melancholy and pathos, rue and self-recrimination. All the while, though, the poet keeps a certain distance from the Snodgrass who is his subject, or attempts to, for the detachment is in constant danger of breaking down. His concentration on the versification, on the syllabics in which he writes, on ironic self-deprecation, on himself as spectator of a scene in which he is also the principal actor, all wrestle with the impulse to bare his feelings. That impulse is most victorious on the edges of poetry: the ends of verses and the ends of sections, at those interstices where the momentum of the conscious poetic necessarily falters. The effect on the reader is a periodic jarring, as the rhythm of the waltz around Snodgrass's true feelings is tripped up by their sudden appearance, by the protruding foot of honest emotion that refuses to be denied. This struggle between alternating sides of the poet's self is paradigmatic of the inner war that manifests itself in all of the chief confessional poets. In Snodgrass, however, it is more gentle, more intellectualized, perhaps, than in any of the others. One rarely has the sense in reading his work that his struggle is of a self-destructive, violent nature, as it is with the others.

The poems of Lowell's confessional mode, similarly, while they may display a greater urgency of self-revelation, are often gentler in tone than those of Plath, Sexton, or Berryman. Still, it is important to remember that not all of Lowell's work is confessional, not even at the time when he was most closely identified with the movement. Two of the sections of *Life Studies* deal with material that cannot be called confessional, and part 1 cannot even be termed personal. Nevertheless, both of those sections show affinities with the work in part 4, "Life Studies," for which the book is most commonly remembered. In the poem about Ford Madox Ford, for example, the laughing, trivializing reminiscence suddenly gives way in the last sentence to "Ford,/ you were a kind man and you died in want." Like Snodgrass's poems, Lowell's often turn on final switchbacks, reclaiming the poet's memory from the trivial, the quotidian, the petty details of scenes and relatives. Those final moments can be quiet, as in the recollection of his father's last words in "Terminal Days at Beverly Farms." However, those quiet endings thinly veneer a dangerous, even violent reality trying to break through, as the poet, holding a locked razor in "Waking in the Blue," cannot be trusted any more than the wife in "To Speak of Woe That Is in Marriage" trusts her drunken husband. The madness and violence of Lowell's poetry contends with the understatement and irony he learned from the Fugitives Tate and Ransom. The controlled diction of his verse gives a greater cutting edge, in its implicit denial, to the wild swings of his mental and emotional life.

Not all of the confessional poets attempted to control those swings as did Lowell and Snodgrass. Berryman, for one, actively exploited the extremes of his emotional states for comic and grotesque effects in *The Dream Songs*, and even invented separate voices to accommodate separate levels of consciousness. Henry speaks of himself in both the third and the first person and goes through periods of wild elation and equally wild despair, through paranoia and delusions of grandeur, and through it all there is the voice of the heckler, the voice of Mr. Bones that undercuts and mocks all other voices. The result is a multilayered narrative in which the various states exist not quite simultaneously but nearly so, on different levels, reflecting the layering of an embattled consciousness. Numerous writers, among them Berryman's first wife, Eileen Simpson, in her book *Poets in Their Youth* (1982), have commented on the wild swings of mood to which Berryman was subject, the turbulence of his personal life, including his alcoholism, his difficulty with his mother, and his extreme, myopic intensity when he was writing. Those various strains find their mythologized way into *The Dream Songs*, and their much more direct way into *Delusions, Etc. of John Berryman*, published shortly before his death in 1972.

Plath and Sexton, too, fought their wars much more openly than Lowell, their one-time teacher. Plath in particular dissected her life with a ferocity that, while it is certainly descended from Dickinson's work, is not comparable with any other poet's self-revelation. One of the most disturbing features of the public reception of the work of Berryman, Plath, and Sexton is the morbid fascination with the personal details that their poems reveal. Clearly, Plath fuels such interest; she spares the reader nothing, or virtually nothing, of the pain and despair of her life, yet her poetry is far from the mere raving of a madwoman. She controls, directs, and mythologizes her material rather than remaining its victim. In "Lady Lazarus," from the posthumous *Ariel* (1965), she becomes not simply a woman with suicidal tendencies, but a mythological goddess who dies periodically to rise revivified from the ashes, phoenixlike, to "eat men like air."

In "Daddy," she uses the same material, the pattern of repeated suicide attempts, in the opposite direction. No longer a power-goddess but the victim of abandonment by her father (who died when she was eight), she assumes the role of archetypal victim, a Jew of the Holocaust, casting her father, whom she comes to associate with all Germans, as her Nazi oppressor. Her great ability to find in the world around her the correlatives of her personal suffering, or perhaps her ability to bring the events and cultural institutions around her into focus through the vehicle of her personal disorder, turns her poetry into a striking, if at times repellent, force. One almost certainly will not feel at ease reading her work; one will almost as certainly be impressed with its power, with the force of her imaginative wrestling with her demons. Such poetic revelation of spiritual turbulence is rarely seen in English literature; perhaps not since Hopkins has a poet bared psychic anguish so totally.

Each of the celebrated confessional poets has produced very impressive work, although not all of it is of a kind, yet the slackness and self-parodic nature of some of Sexton's and Berryman's later work point to a weakness of the genre: The self can be bared only so often, it seems, before the reader has seen quite enough. The profusion of terrible poetry by followers of these writers has suggested its limitations as well as its attractions. It is very easy to write wretched confessional poetry, since the subject matter is always at hand. It is much more difficult to turn that subject matter into art.

This is reactionary poetry, and like most things reactionary it remains on the fringe; it is extremist. There has been a marked movement in poetry after World War II toward personal, autobiographical poetry (sometimes termed postconfessional poetry). Writers as different as Duncan, Ginsberg, Creeley, Stevie Smith (who, although British, most resembles Dickinson), Thom Gunn, and Jon Silkin all make use of material from their own lives. Very few writers now shy away from autobiographical material as Eliot would have them do and as writers of the first half of the century often did. Confessional poetry, then, although not of the mainstream itself, however much its apologists, such as M. L. Rosenthal in *The New Poets* (1967), may argue for its centrality, has turned the course of poetry toward the personal.

The work of its main practitioners will probably survive despite, not because of, the confessional nature of the poetry. The ironic self-observation of Snodgrass, the wistful, mournful verse of Lowell, with its tension between the trivial and the painful, the hilarious mythologizing of Berryman's *The Dream Songs*, the power and ferocity of Plath's imagery and phrasing will stand with the work of any group of poets of any age. It is well to remember that much poetry remains important despite some major component, be it subject matter, thematic treatment, or political orientation. There is much that modern readers find disagreeable, after all, in Geoffrey Chaucer, John Milton, and William Shakespeare.

BEAT AND MOVEMENT POETRY

Confessional poetry provided, if not the answer for modern poetry after World War II, at least an articulation of the problem. During the 1950's two other literary groups sprang up, one in America and one in Britain, both of which were also concerned with the plight of the individual in an intractable world. Beat and Movement poetries are violently dissimilar expressions of similar revulsions to the same world situation. Both react against the formalist art of the modernists, against uptight, bourgeois, philistine society, against the repressive political and cultural institutions of the period. The differences between the two lie more in national attitudes and predispositions than in first principles. Moreover, both show affinities with existentialism.

The self underwent a series of shocks beginning with World War II, with its death camps, its blitzkriegs, its atomic bombs. The twentieth century was distinguished by a new scale of violence and terror—the virtual destruction or totalitarian suffocation of vast areas,

of whole nations or peoples. In the face of that leveling destruction, the individual was quite lost. Furthermore, the prevailing ideologies of the century did not given the individual much room to maneuver. Both communism and fascism, of course, are anti-individual in their very orientation and quite willing to sacrifice the autonomy of the self for the good of the state. However, free-enterprise capitalist democracy also partook of its dollop of statism in the modern world, the most outstanding example of which was the McCarthy-era witch-hunts, those exercises designed not so much to ferret out saboteurs and seditionists as to enforce conformity and steamroll deviation from the average. As already mentioned, the impersonal theory of poetry put forth by Eliot and his circle coincided historically as well as theoretically with the rise of totalitarian politics, and it was that entire complex that writers of the 1950's sought to overthrow. To see the argument in purely literary terms is to miss a great deal of the significance of the action.

Both the Beats and the Movement poets, then, wrestled with the problem posed by existentialism: namely, how does the individual maintain his or her autonomy in the face of an overwhelming, repressive society? Their answers, while divergent, displayed certain similarities that can perhaps be understood in terms of various strains of existentialism. The Movement writers leaned more toward despair and quiet rebellion from within the ranks, while the Beats were open insurrectionists, confronting a hostile world with wild romanticism.

Larkin has written of life at Oxford during the war, showing how, at the very moment when students normally developed their grandest ideas of themselves, the privation, uncertainty, and anxiety of wartime undercut their natural tendencies. He suggested that his own self-effacing poetry and that of his contemporaries were in large measure a by-product of Nazi aerial technology, that the Blitz and the V-2 rockets reduced the range of options available to the undergraduates, and that he never broke out of that range. One has the sense in Larkin's work that he is trapped, that society closes in around the individual before he has a chance to stake out his own territory. That sense is shared in the work of many of his contemporaries, although it takes many different forms.

The generation preceding the Movement, including the Auden circle, was at times highly political. Many writers became involved in the urgent issues of the day; many actively sought roles in the Spanish Civil War. Empson accompanied Mao Zedong on the Long March. Most, although by no means all, of the writers of the 1930's embraced leftist politics to some degree, and a great many of them, like Auden himself, later either repudiated or quietly slipped away from their earlier beliefs. The Movement writers, even while sometimes claiming kinship with the writers of the 1930's, particularly Empson, shied away from the grand political gesture, as indeed they seemed to suspect all large gestures.

The Movement poets were in some respects a strikingly homogenous group—much more so than the Beats. All of the principals attended one of the two major English universities: Larkin, Kingsley Amis, Robert Conquest, John Wain, Elizabeth Jennings, and John Holloway went to Oxford, while Donald Davie, D. J. Enright, and Gunn were at Cambridge. They were from, or at least they celebrated in their writings, middle-class or working-class backgrounds. For many, education was interrupted by war, and as a result they seemed, in Hughes's analysis, to "have had enough."

The Oxford group, for the most part, emerged from the penumbra of neo-Romanticism. Larkin, for example, recorded his struggle to free himself from the influence of Yeats, and, through Vernon Watkins, of Dylan Thomas. His early poetry is largely a rehash of Yeats's style and imagery, neither of which sounds at all natural coming from Larkin. Not until the privately printed *XX Poems* of 1951 did his true voice begin to assert itself. Similarly, much of Jennings's early work fairly drips with syrup, wending its way through enchanted woods on the trail of unicorns. Like Larkin, and, for that matter like most of the Oxford writers, she began to find herself only around 1950, although glimmers of her distinctive style had begun to show themselves earlier.

The Cambridge three took a more direct route, one that led straight through their studies under F. R. Leavis. As Blake Morrison points out in *The Movement: English Poetry and Fiction of the 1950's* (1980), all three credit Leavis with shaping their thought and, to a

great extent, their poetry. His skeptical rationalism served as a natural springboard to the highly rational, un- or even antimetaphorical poetry of the Movement.

The Movement, then, was a cultural and social phenomenon as well as a literary clique. A great many British writers from about the same time, some of whom turned out to be highly averse to the Movement views, have at one time or another been seen as belonging in some sense or other. The Movement was a reactionary school, looking back to Edward Thomas and the Georgians as well as to the writers of the 1930's for its models, looking away from both the modernism of Eliot and Pound and the Romanticism of such 1940's poets as Dylan Thomas, David Gascoyne, and Edith Sitwell. It was anti-Romantic, antimetaphorical, highly rationalistic, and formally very traditional. It stressed colloquial diction and concreteness against both highly wrought "poetic" diction and the airy abstraction of neo-Romanticism and English Surrealism. The tone is often flat, neutral, especially in Larkin, and a chief mode, as one might suspect, is irony. The irony, like the formal precision, is a stay against the isolation and the alienation that lies behind much of this writing.

Nearly everything about the Movement writers points to their alienation as an almost necessary state of young, thinking people of that time. They stood outside the institutions, either looking in the windows or ridiculing those inside, but in either case they were outsiders. Amis's Jim Dixon in *Lucky Jim* (1954) is a textbook case of a Movement hero, an outsider who suddenly finds himself on the inside, who is suddenly confronted with the smallness and tackiness and pomposity and arrogance of the powerful and well-heeled. Typically, he causes disaster wherever he goes.

Larkin lived perhaps closer to the Movement program than any of the others, always isolated, always provincial, always alienated, reeking of spiritual exhaustion and cultural bankruptcy to the point that he could barely bring himself to write at all. (By his own count, he averaged three to five short poems per year.) His poetry has also remained closest to the original line; much of his late work is very similar in spirit and tone, and even technique, to that written in the early 1950's. Its poetic qualities lie in its tight control and its compression rather than in any overtly poetic devices. It crawls rather than leaps, uses reason and intellection rather than surges of spirit. His is a highly Apollonian poetry.

To find the Dionysian poetry of the 1950's, one must leap an ocean and a continent, to San Francisco. If one were to take as a starting point the same basic rejection of values and suspicion of social and cultural institutions that prompted the Movement, and add to it the rejection of values and styles adopted as a makeshift solution by the Movement (and perhaps also of the personal, Freudian anguish of the confessional poets), one would be left with approximately the Beat mentality. While the Beats rejected the cozy middle-class complacency of the 1950's, they did so with characteristically American flamboyance, as opposed to the typically British reserve, tightness, and control. The Movement fought by withdrawing; the Beats fought by setting the enemy on his ear.

At its broadest, the Beat generation can be considered to include not only those San Francisco writers (and occasional drop-ins from the East Coast) normally associated with it—Lawrence Ferlinghetti, Snyder, William Everson, Ginsberg, Jack Kerouac, Philip Whalen, Michael McClure, Gregory Corso—but also, as John Clellan Holmes suggests in an essay in Lee Bartlett's *The Beats: Essays in Criticism* (1981), the Black Mountain group of Olson, Duncan, Creeley, Dorn, and Levertov, and perhaps even the New York circle centered on Ashbery, Koch, and O'Hara. Most of these writers share certain attitudes toward literature and toward their audience.

One of the first calls-to-arms was sounded in Olson's 1950 essay "Projective Verse," in which, among other things, he calls for an end to the pedestrian verse line. Olson felt that the tyranny of the accentual-syllabic line, which had ruled since the Renaissance in English prosody, was strangling creativity. He therefore made his plea for an open-form poetic line, a variable line based on the requirements of phrasing and the poet's own natural voice—and on the devices peculiar to the typewritten poem. What Olson really argues for is the primacy of the poet in the poetry. No longer, he says, should the poet wrench verse around to meet the standards of an exhausted poetics. Rather than emerging from the head only (and this is perhaps the importance of the breath-unit), the poem must emerge from the effort of the whole person. Olson even gives form to his idea in the essay itself. This is no textbook example of essay writing; its form is a large part of its function. The reader knows simply by reading it whether he is one of the chosen, for it is designed to call to the loyal and heap confusion on the enemy; it is intended to perplex the sturdy specimens of traditionalism simply by its language. This exclusionary technique became a hallmark of the entire Beat experience.

Certainly the Beat lifestyle was designed to be offputting to nonhipsters, with its slang, sexual and drug experimentation, and rootlessness. The poetry itself also challenged its audience, with its free-flowing forms, often incantatory rhythms, wild flights of imagination, and sometimes coarse language. These qualities established themselves very early, so that when Robert Lowell, then a rising young poet with a formidable reputation, went to San Francisco to give readings in 1956, he found the audiences bored with his work because they had already become accustomed to hearing verse best typified by the then still unpublished "Howl" of Ginsberg.

If confessionalism looked to New England for its source, then the Beats looked to Camden, New Jersey. There could have been no Beat poetry without Whitman. The movement followed him not only in the openness of its form and in its attitudes but also in its declamatory poetic voice. Ginsberg was particularly indebted to Whitman in the matter of a public poetic voice. Whitman was not the only source, of course, although he was the most important one. Others would include Blake (whose voice, says Ginsberg, came to him in 1948, reciting poems), Lawrence, Henry Miller, Williams, and Rexroth. These last three were early champions of the fledgling movement as well as models, and Rexroth especially offered intense verbal support. Williams had said that Eliot set back American poetry twenty years or more, that his highly academic, closed poetry flew in the face of the proletarian, egalitarian verse toward which Whitman pointed. When the twenty years (more or less) were up, the new proletarian uprising made itself felt.

In a movement that is overtly social as well as literary, there are always social as well as literary sources.

Black culture, especially jazz; Mexican peasant culture for dress; and even behavioral models, Zen Buddhism, Hinduism, and Asian culture in general, were among the origins of the exoticism of Beat life. However, much of what the Beats adopted they turned upside down. There was a demonic quality about their movement, an urge toward self-immolation and willful dissipation and disintegration, that was lacking in the originals. While it could be argued that the fiery urge toward dissolution was a by-product of the jazz influence, that the Beats learned self-destruction from Charlie Parker and Billie Holiday, it seems more likely that such an impulse was a fairly natural outgrowth of the rejection of safe, "straight" values. The movement was angelic as well as demonic; "Beat," as Everson reminds the reader, means "Beatific." While Everson may stand closer than any of his compatriots to a traditional Christian mysticism, an ultimate goal of the Beats was a kind of godliness. If they employed the tigers of wrath rather than the horses of instruction, it was nevertheless to arrive at wisdom. It is easy for an outsider to mistake the methods of the Beats for their ends. Certainly there have been many figures both famous and obscure who have used the movement's ideals as a shield for intellectual or moral slovenliness, but just as surely it is a mistake to fail to discern the difference between the pilgrimage and the destination.

Generalizations are dangerous, particularly when dealing with a group of writers so obviously devoted to individualism in life and art, yet there were features common to the generality of Beat poetry. There was a formal openness. The projective verse of Olson and Creeley becomes a wholly subjective form, a totally personal and even unconscious matter in much of Beat writing. Kerouac, who can be considered the discoverer of the movement, since it was he who named it, hated revision, and his version of revision was to remove and expand sections until they became new works. In many of his novels, he wrote in a state of semicontrol, surrealistically allowing his material to take over. In like manner, the poetics of "Howl," for example, work very close to the unconscious. Its rhythmic, pulsating regularities, its incantatory insistence, its word and phrase repetitions insinuate themselves into the reader's (or the auditor's) consciousness, al-

most without requiring intellectual understanding. It is a poem to be felt as much as to be comprehended. In Snyder's work, crumbled and reassembled syntax creates the effect of compression of thoughts and ideas, of puzzles and conundra stumbled onto in the act of creation. While his poems are considerably more ordered than the prose of William Burroughs's cut-up method, they seem to be springing naturally from the psyche, newly freed from the constraints of rationality.

The formal openness of Beat writing, in fact, is a function of its emphasis on the unconscious, on some aspect of humanity divorced from intellection. The Dionysian impulse is always away from reason, from order, from control, and toward those elements that modern society would have humankind erase or submerge under the great weight of orthodoxy. The use of drugs, of primitive cultures, of Christian mysticism, Asian meditation, and Hasidic prophecy are all aimed at freeing the kernel of preconscious truth from the centuries-old and miles-deep husk of social conformity and "rational" behavior.

Most of the Beats believed, with Snyder, that if the inner being could be liberated and made to speak for itself, society could be changed. In his essay "Buddha and the Coming Revolution," Snyder quotes the World War I slogan "Forming the new society in the shell of the old," and that slogan can stand as well for the society of one, the primary object of reform for the Beats. Once the individual has learned how to live, the new society can be developed. Only in a society in which people have given up their individuality, where they have willingly immersed their differences in the stagnant waters of conformity, can such a thing as McCarthyism occur. Inevitably, then, the Beats went to the greatest lengths imaginable to assert their individuality. One cannot, after all, write in one's native rhythms unless one knows one's own mind and spirit. The act of writing, then, like living itself, is a political act, and the Beats were as politically visible as any literary group of the twentieth century.

Their work was both important in its own right and tremendously influential. While Ginsberg's *Howl, and Other Poems* (1956) and *Kaddish, and Other Poems* (1961) and Snyder's *Riprap* (1959), *Myths and Texts* (1960), and *Six Sections from Mountains and Rivers*

Without End (1965) are probably the best-known works, there are a host of others. Corso's *The Mutation of the Spirit* (1964) is clearly a major work, a wrestling with important issues, as is much of Everson's work, including the pre-Beat *The Residual Years* (1968). The sheer mass of good poetry by Everson ensured his continued importance in the movement, although none of it found the audience that Snyder's or Ginsberg's did. McClure, particularly in his drug poems, became a valuable recorder of a phase of experience vital to the movement. It was Ferlinghetti, however, who chronicled the Beat experience and attitude most carefully, and who consciously played the role of Beat poet— sometimes to the point of seemingly losing himself in it. In such books as *A Coney Island of the Mind* (1958) and *The Secret Meaning of Things* (1969), and particularly in such poems as "Autobiography," he captured the essence of Beat life. Perhaps more important, he gave life to the movement through publishing its poets and by overseeing the physical center of the movement in San Francisco's City Lights Bookstore.

WHITHER?

Literature is always an act of becoming, a dialectical process between the mind of a writer and the literary and social-historical forces around him or her. However, literature at the end of the twentieth century—and to the present—is perhaps uniquely in a state of flux. Its rejection of the past has been so vehement, its condition of upheaval so prolonged, its experimentation so striking that writers and critics alike have come to look on it as an arrival, as what literature has become. That constant upheaval within modern poetry, however, suggests that such is not the case. Rather, the overthrows and insurrections point to the extremely transitory nature of the modern experiments. In a body of poetry in which versification changed relatively little from Shakespeare to Dante Gabriel Rossetti, but in which no school of poetics has held sway for much more than a decade since then, the impermanence of modern poetry can hardly be avoided. It may well be that it has arrived at a state of perpetual dislocation, but that is hardly the same as consensus.

The problem lies as much in the modern world as with the writers themselves. When Stevens says that the modern poem must "find out what will suffice," he implies that the traditional givens of poetry will not suffice because the world has changed. After the myth-analysts and the psychoanalysts of the last one hundred years, after the awful destructions of two world wars, after the rise of modern multinational corporate entities, after the end of traditional society, in the face of post-Cold War terrorists and daily uncertainty, how can poetry be expected to remain where it was? All is certainly less than right with the world. So the writing of modern poetry constitutes an incessant quest for form, a struggle to find a form that works in the modern context, that will suffice. The range of attempts can seem utterly baffling, yet it is possible to break them down into several loose categories.

The antimodernist poet recoils from the world, refusing also its chaotic poetics, which he or she often sees as symptomatic. Instead, antimodernists retreat into traditional forms, writing in regular meters and rhyme schemes, in recognizable stanzaic patterns. Included among the ranks of antimodern poets would be Frost, Housman, Edwin Arlington Robinson, the Georgian poets, the Movement poets, and some of the poetry of the Fugitives, particularly some of the work of Ransom and Donald Davidson. Their tradition is primarily English, looking back through Hardy and the Victorians.

By contrast, the modernist poet is, simultaneously, constantly reminded of the literary past and struggling to use it to create a new work of art, to "make it new." This artist's method is probably best described in Eliot's essay "Tradition and the Individual Talent," in which he says that a new work of art is not merely added to the collection of existing monuments, that a new work both alters and is informed by those already in existence. Eliot is the preeminent modernist poet. Others would include Pound, Stevens, Robert Lowell, Hill, Heaney, Tate, Warren, Auden and his circle, Plath, Berryman, and Merwin. The modernist literary inheritance is much more eclectic, and much more continental, than that of the antimodernists, and looks to France, to the Symbolists, for much of its immediate impetus.

Postmodernist poets openly reject the forms and styles of literary tradition in an attempt to create a radically new poetry to engage the world they find. Post-modernists generally choose open forms, employ loose structures, and write out of their own experience. They are much more personal poets than Eliot's modernists, feeling the world move through them, sensing that the necessary forms can be had through self-knowledge rather than through a study of tradition. On the Continent, postmodernists have appeared as Dadaists or Surrealists, and nearly everywhere they are experimentalists. Early types would include Sitwell (sometimes), Lawrence, Williams, Rexroth, Louis Zukofsky, Gascoyne (also sometimes), and Sandburg, while later manifestations can be found in the Beat poets, Olson's Black Mountain group, Hughes, the Liverpool group, and Bly, James Wright, Ashbery, and their fellow Surrealists.

There is, finally a fourth category, not so much a group as an assortment of leftovers, poets whose work is so individual, whose vision is so much their own, that they defy taxonomic classification. Yeats is such a poet, certainly, and so too are Crane, Thomas, Galway Kinnell, and perhaps others already located in one group or another, such as Lawrence, Hill, or Merwin. There are those writers who find themselves confronted with a specific social or political situation that forces their poetry in a direction that it might not otherwise have taken. Such is very likely the case with the Irish poets from Yeats and Louis MacNeice to Heaney, John Montague, Thomas Kinsella, and Tom Paulin. It may also be that their situation is paradigmatic of modern poetry generally: It is not merely that literature is changing but rather that the context of literature is changing so drastically and so rapidly that writers find themselves in a mad scramble to keep up.

Language poets

Both sides of the Atlantic have experienced developments in this last, largely unclassifiable realm in the postmodernist era. Beginning in the late 1970's, the United States in particular began to see an extreme twist on the postmodernist program in the form of the Language poets. The movement grew out of a number of radical poetry journals, most notably $L=A=N=G=U=A=G=E$, from which it takes its name, and rejects the author-dominated model of traditional poetry, choosing instead indeterminate forms and incomplete meanings that require the reader to take an active role in creating meaning. The poets and apologists base their approach on a pantheon of radical literary and political thought: deconstruction as practiced especially by Jacques Derrida, the Marxism of the Frankfurt school, the language theories of Jacques Lacan, the experimentalism of Gertrude Stein, the Dadaists, and the poetic practices of such writers as Creeley, Zukofsky, the Objectivists, Ashbery, and the Russian Futurist Velimir Khlebnikov.

The Language poets use these influences to do battle with what they see as the tyranny of the single-image "voice poem," the poem of individual experience culminating in a dominant image that seeks to explain and justify the poem's existence and control the reader's response. This model of the interaction between active, controlling writer and passive, controlled reader is the point of attack for the Language poets in their prose statements and in their work: Bruce Andrews's *Wobbling* (1981) and *Love Songs* (1982); Charles Bernstein's *Controlling Interests* (1980) and *Islets/Irritations* (1983); Lyn Hejinian's *Writing Is an Aid to Memory* (1978); Ron Silliman's *Tjanting* (1981) and *The Age of Huts* (1986). Their work is often striking in its strangeness, sometimes recalling in its apparent randomness the work of Dada poet Tristan Tzara or various forms of conceptual art. Whether the movement will last or, like Tzara and Dadaism, become a curious byway, an interesting footnote to poetic history, may not be determined for many years.

Martian poets

Pound's dictum to "make it new" has found new and curious adherents in Britain and Ireland since the late 1970's, through a movement and individuals who have sought to bring whimsical observation and satiric scrutiny to the poetic tradition. Craig Raine provided the name of the movement known as the Martian school with the title poem of his collection *A Martian Sends a Postcard Home* (1979). In that poem, the eponymous spaceman observes many of the mundane elements of Earth life and makes them alien to the Earthling-reader: A car, for instance, becomes a motion picture with the screen in back so that riders can see what they have passed, a telephone is an infant picked up when it cries yet sometimes deliberately awakened by tickling (in dialing a number). This practice of radical re-vision of the world is taken up not only by Raine but also by Christopher Reid and James Fenton, among others. While the Martian poets show a great deal of formal and stylistic variety from one to another, what they share is an emphasis on wit and invention in the treatment of their subjects.

WIT AND HUMOR

Other writers not specifically in the Martian group who nevertheless rely on wit and humor would include the Ulster poet Paul Muldoon and Wendy Cope. Muldoon's verse is consistently wry and arch; his response to a split national identity (is he British or Irish?), to a history of internecine conflict, is not anger or tragedy but irony. Like Raine, he tests the possibilities of perception and language in *Mules* (1977), *Quoof* (1983), and *Meeting the British* (1987).

Cope investigates the tradition by undermining it. Working in the realm of satire and parody in *Making Cocoa for Kingsley Amis* (1986), she deflates the grandeur of *The Waste Land*, for example, with a series of limericks. Her poems stand as feminist commentaries on a male-dominated tradition of "significance." The nature of her wit is cutting and subversive, and the results are often delightful.

VOICES OF DIVERSITY

One of the major developments in late-century poetry was the development of the voice of the outsider. American minority writers have become increasingly strong. Certainly there have been waves of African American poetry throughout the century, from the Harlem Renaissance between the wars through the Black Arts movement of the 1960's and beyond, from such poets as Langston Hughes, Gwendolyn Brooks and Robert Hayden to Amiri Baraka, Lucille Clifton, Etheridge Knight, Sonia Sanchez, and Audre Lorde. African American poets throughout the century have given voice to people too often silenced by the mainstream culture, while bringing new and dynamic rhythms and forms to American poetry.

Hughes's use of jazz and blues in his work, for instance, together with the marvelous voices of the disenfranchised in poems such as "Madam and the Rentman," "Theme for English B," or "Mother to Son" point the direction for the black poets who follow. While there is a remarkable diversity in the sort of poetry written by those who come later in the century, many subsequent poets—from his near-contemporary Brooks, who died in 2000, to Thylias Moss, whose career began in the last two decades of the century—share with him a great facility with the dramatic monologue, and many of the best remembered African American poems of the century will prove to be those voiced not for the poet, but for characters drawn from the community.

Native American poetry is a somewhat more recent phenomenon on the national scene. Many of the important Native American novelists since 1960 have also written poetry: N. Scott Momaday, Leslie Marmon Silko, James Welch, Louise Erdrich, and Sherman Alexie. Often, their work mixes intimate knowledge of tribal life with strong academic influences. Momaday, for instance, draws on his Kiowa ancestry and his experience as a teacher on various reservations in a poetics informed by his graduate studies at Stanford University, where he studied under the formidable Yvor Winters.

Other American Indian poets, such as Simon Ortiz and Joy Harjo, are primarily poets. Ortiz is much more heavily grounded than Momaday in his home community, the Acoma Acumeh Pueblo of New Mexico. His concerns with Native American identity, with resistance to assimilation, and with the role of language and poetry in that resistance run through his books, including *Going for the Rain* (1976), *From Sand Creek: Rising in This Heart Which Is Our America* (1981), *Woven Stone* (1992), and *After and Before the Lightning* (1994), which records his stay on South Dakota's Rosebud reservation.

The waning century also saw increases in Latino (Alurista, Bernice Zamora, Gloria Anzaldúa) and Asian American (Lawson Fusao Inada, Janice Mirikitani) voices. Despite the many differences among these writers, they share a concern with both the place of their ethnic group in the larger culture and the dynamics within the group. While Zamora and Anzaldúa, for example, concern themselves with Mexican American struggles in Euro-America, they also critique the macho, sexist culture of the La Raza movement, as represented by Alurista.

The United Kingdom has also seen this increased diversity. A great deal of "British" or "English" poetry—like its fiction—in recent times has come from beyond the customary centers of privilege and power. Gone are the days when poetry was dominated by London, Oxford, and Cambridge, the era of Auden, MacNeice, Spender, and C. Day Lewis. As the century came to a close, the poetry scene was increasingly reflecting the provincial, the postcolonial, the racially and sexually diverse nature of contemporary British life.

IRISH POETRY

The final four decades of the twentieth century saw a tremendous flowering of Irish poetry, particularly of poetry from the North. Of that group Heaney is clearly the most prominent feature, although he is joined by Tom Paulin, Muldoon, Derek Mahon, Ciaran Carson, Michael Longley, and Medbh McGuckian as major figures from all points of the political and religious compass. Their work is informed by their experience of the Troubles that began in 1969 and continued throughout the remaining years of the century, although not all of them address the political situation as directly as Heaney. Muldoon's obliqueness often hides his social awareness inside fantastic structures, as in *Madoc: A Mystery* (1990), his epic poem of colonization and cultural domination focusing not on Northern Ireland but on North America. Muldoon asks what might have happened had Southey and Coleridge followed through on their project to found a utopian settlement in the United States. The poem follows wild leaps of time, place, person, and philosophical school to conclude that, ultimately, British efforts at colonization do not generally end well.

McGuckian brings a woman's sensibility to the experience in Ulster; she is also one of the few poets to have remained in her native province throughout the Troubles. In such collections as *The Flower Master* (1982), *Marconi's Cottage* (1992), and *Captain Lavender* (1995), she marries the intensely personal with the

political in a verse characterized by sudden juxtapositions and surreal imagery to create a poetry that is intense, fascinating, sometimes forbidding, and always intriguing.

The Republic of Ireland also has produced many impressive poets during the same period: Kinsella, Paul Durcan, Montague, Paula Meehan, Matthew Sweeney, and Eavan Boland. Boland provides an interesting case in her treatment of her status as woman and poet as a postcolonial condition. Her work, particularly in *Outside History: Selected Poems, 1980-1990* (1990) and *In a Time of Violence* (1994), addresses the customary treatment of women in male Irish poetry and seeks to reclaim the female experience from the mythologizing impulses of that male tradition. That her work has found a very large and enthusiastic audience in America among readers not usually concerned with Irish issues testifies to the timeliness and aptness of her poetry. Her work investigates not merely the power arrangements between genders but also the ways in which language and literary practice have served to reify those arrangements. Beyond that diagnosis, however, the great power of Boland's poetry lies in her ability to offer alternatives, to reenvision the dominant myths of the female and invest them with new vigor.

WOMEN'S POETRY

Poetry by women, indeed literature by women, that reexamines male-female relations has been quite prominent in the final decades of the century. The late Angela Carter, for instance, reworked fairy tales and Shakespearean plots to subvert the masculine assumptions of the originals in her fiction. Carol Ann Duffy works similarly in her poetry, which is dominated by the dramatic monologue. If her preferred form is that of Robert Browning, author of "My Last Duchess," the voice she chooses is that of the duchess herself. The title poem of her first volume, *Standing Female Nude* (1985), is a monologue by the model of a Degas-like painter of the female form who takes her existence for granted. Boland also has poems about artists' females—Edgar Degas's washerwomen and Pierre-Auguste Renoir's grape pickers—and arrives at much the same conclusion, although without giving those women voices. Duffy's nude model is stiff from posing, angry, but spunky and insightful and altogether engaging. Her book *The World's Wife* (1999) is filled with monologues by the wives of famous men in history, myth, and literature: Aesop, Freud, Pilate, Darwin, Faust. These compelling and often hilarious soliloquies remind readers of the extent to which traditional culture has shut out the voice of the woman and either ignored or minimized the contributions of women in the lives of "great men." Because, for so much of the century, British poetry was a men's club, the contributions of writers like Duffy in causing readers to revise their understanding of human nature are immense indeed.

POSTCOLONIAL POETS

It is worth noting that the last two Nobel Prizes in Literature won by English-language poets in the twentieth century went to outlanders: Northern Ireland's Heaney and St. Lucia's Derek Walcott. Walcott is only one representative of a movement in contemporary poetry: the increasing presence of poets who were either born in or descended from residents of former European colonies in Africa, Asia, and the Caribbean. E. A. Markham, Louise Bennett, James Berry, A. L. Hendricks, Linton Kwesi Johnson, and Edward Kamau Brathwaite from the Caribbean; Fred D'Aguiar, Grace Nichols, Martin Carter, and Jan Carew from Guyana; and Mahmoud Jamal and H. O. Nazareth from India testify to the dynamic poetry scene in the minority communities of England and in the former colonies. Those voices often sound odd to British poetic traditionalists, in the same way that, in the United States, the poetry of Langston Hughes or Baraka or Brooks may have initially seemed outside the mainstream even in a country where the example of Whitman has always provided a greater openness.

Walcott is clearly the towering figure among the Caribbean writers—winner not only of the Nobel Prize in 1992 but also of numerous other literary prizes, holder of endowed chairs at American universities, and commander of prime book-review space when a new collection appears. While he has been publishing work since the late 1940's, his reputation, if it needed such help, was firmly cemented with the publication of *The Arkansas Testament* (1987) and *Omeros* (1990). The latter is an epic poem about Caribbean fishermen and

their world seen through the filter of Homer's *Iliad* (c. 750 B.C.E.; English translation, 1611) and *Odyssey* (c. 725 B.C.E.; English translation, 1614)—"Omeros" is a local corruption or variant of "Homer." In tracing out the passions, rivalries, conquests, and calamities of his characters, Walcott reminds readers that Homer's epics were themselves the tales of fishermen and farmers forced out of their own normal orbits by circumstances larger than themselves, and in so doing, he invests his tale, and his people, with a nobility and a grandeur as old as myth.

Poetry has not found itself in such turmoil since Western society careened its way out of the Middle Ages and into the Renaissance. Perhaps when and if society once again settles onto some stable course (and modern weapons technology and multinational economics make that seem unlikely enough), then the course of poetry may also become more uniform. As things stand, though, both society and poetry appear to be headed for a very protracted period of transition. If that is so, then readers of verse will continue to be blessed, or cursed, with the astonishing variety that has characterized modern poetry.

BIBLIOGRAPHY

Acheson, James, and Romana Huk, eds. *Contemporary British Poetry: Essays in Theory and Criticism.* Albany: State University of New York Press, 1996. Offers a wide-ranging look at the work of feminists and "post feminist" poets, working-class poets, and poets of diverse cultural backgrounds, as well as provocative re-readings of such well-established and influential figures as Donald Davie, Ted Hughes, Geoffrey Hill, and Craig Raine.

Axelrod, Steven Gould, and Camille Roman, eds. *Modernisms, 1900-1950.* Vol. 2 in *The New Anthology of American Poetry.* New Brunswick, N.J.: Rutgers University Press, 2005. A collection of more than six hundred poems by sixty-five poets, representing a wide variety of movements and schools. Songs and poems from popular culture are included. There are also critical essays by some of the poets. Good introductions, notes, and bibliographies.

Altieri, Charles. *The Art of Twentieth-Century Ameri-*

can Poetry: Modernism and After*. Malden, Mass.: Blackwell, 2006. Traces history of modernism, from Ezra Pound and William Carlos Williams to Wallace Stevens and W. H. Auden, concluding with postmodernist trends. Includes new readings of works by major poets. Bibliographical references and index.

Beach, Christopher. *The Cambridge Introduction to Twentieth-Century American Poetry*. New York: Cambridge University Press, 2003. A concise, chronological study of the major twentieth century movements, concluding with contemplative lyricism and the avant-garde. Glossary, notes, bibliography, and index.

Broom, Sarah. *Contemporary British and Irish Poetry: An Introduction*. Illustrated edition. New York: Palgrave Macmillan, 2006. Comments on both well-known and newer, experimental poets, pointing out how their works are influenced by economic and political issues, as well as by conflicts based on race, class, and gender. Extensive bibliographical references and index.

Corcoran, Neil, ed. *The Cambridge Companion to Twentieth-Century English Poetry*. New York: Cambridge University Press, 2007. Essays by prominent scholars, some dealing with general topics, others with movements or groups, still others on the works of a single poet, such as D. H. Lawrence or Philip Larkin. Bibliography and index. An invaluable resource.

Dowson, Jane, and Alice Entwistle. *A History of Twentieth-Century British Women's Poetry*. New York: Cambridge University Press, 2005. Explores the subject by means of thoughtful, imaginative essays, grouped into three chronological sections, each of which is preceded by an excellent overview. Extensive bibliographical references and annotations.

Gioia, Dana, David Mason, and Meg Schoerke, eds. *Twentieth-Century American Poetry*. Boston: McGraw-Hill, 2003. This remarkable volume, compiled by three poet-scholars, offers students a comprehensive view of the entire century. Extensive selections from the works of the poets included are arranged chronologically and grouped by school or movement, beginning with realism and naturalism,

moving through the Harlem Renaissance and open-form poetry, and concluding with internationalism. A historical and critical overview precedes each section.

_____. *Twentieth-Century American Poetics: Poets on the Art of Poetry*. Boston: McGraw-Hill, 2004. Published as a companion to the volume above, this book consists of fifty-eight essays by fifty-three poets. Index of authors and titles and bibliography.

Grennan, Eamon. *Facing the Music: Irish Poetry in the Twentieth Century*. Omaha, Neb.: Creighton University Press, 1999. Sympathetic readings give the reader a powerful sense of how Irish poetry in the twentieth century kept pace with the often intractable public and private life of the Irish island, both north and south.

Hamilton, Ian, ed. *The Oxford Companion to Twentieth-Century Poetry in English*. New York: Oxford University Press, 1996. Comprehensive guide to modern English-language poetry. The works of fifteen hundred poets from New Zealand to Zimbabwe are discussed in the context of the literary and cultural movements that spawned them.

Pratt, William C., ed. *The Fugitive Poets: Modern Southern Poetry in Perspective*. Rev. ed. Nashville, Tenn.: J. S. Sanders, 1991. Chronicles the impact of literary modernism on Southern poets such as Robert Penn Warren, John Crowe Ransom, Donald Davidson, and Allen Tate as their region was taking its "backward glance" before stepping into the modern world.

Roberts, Neil, ed. *A Companion to Twentieth-Century Poetry*. Malden, Mass.: Blackwell, 2001. Forty-eight essays, covering a wide range of topics, such as the relationship between poetry and science or poetry and politics. Several essays focus on post-colonial poetry in English; a number of others offer new interpretations of specific poems. One of the most comprehensive volumes of its kind.

Silkin, Jon. *The Life of Metrical and Free Verse in Twentieth-Century Poetry*. New York: St. Martin's Press, 1997. Presents a premise that two modes of verse, free and metrical, engage the creative energies of current poetry. The poetic work of Walt Whitman, Gerard Manley Hopkins, T. S. Eliot,

Ezra Pound, D. H. Lawrence, Dylan Thomas, Basil Bunting, and ten British poets from the post-World War II era illustrate how free and metrical verse create—separately or together—a poetic harmony.

Tate, Allen. *Four Decades of Essays*. 1968. Rev. ed. Wilmington, Del.: ISI Books, 1999. A classic collection of nearly fifty essays by one of the twentieth century's most acclaimed poets and literary critics. Speaks poignantly to the concerns of students, teachers, and general literature readers alike and covers the broad sweep of Tate's critical concerns: poetry, poets, fiction, the imagination, language, literature, and culture.

Tuma, Keith, ed. *Anthology of Twentieth-Century British and Irish Poetry*. Annotated edition. New York: Oxford University Press, 2001. Contains 450 poems by 126 poets. A biographical and critical introduction is provided for each poet. Notes, bibliography, and index.

Wilson, Edmund. *Axel's Castle: A Study in the Imaginative Literature of 1870-1930*. 1931. Reprint. New York: Random House, 1996. A landmark work, this book established Wilson's reputation as one of the twentieth century's foremost literary critics. Traces the development of the French Symbolist movement and its influence on six modern writers: William Butler Yeats, Paul Valery, T. S. Eliot, Marcel Proust, James Joyce, and Gertrude Stein.

Thomas C. Foster

European Oral and Epic Traditions

"Literature," as the word is most often used, means written works: poetry, fiction, prose. The term itself, derived from the Latin word for "letter of the alphabet," enshrines a particular notion of what literature involves—namely texts. The concept of a nonwritten, oral "literature," therefore, might seem a contradiction in terms. Nevertheless, before modern literate culture valued one form of language (written) above the other, before there was even any one word such as "literature" to cover the disparate forms of verbal art often tied to social functions, there existed poems, songs, dramas, and narratives. In contemporary nonliterate societies, there are many examples of flourishing "literary" forms, while even in modern Western society, the most popular verbal artistic modes are "oral" in that they are transmitted without the use of writing. How many people, for example, read the text of a popular hit song, a Broadway play, or a television show?

The fundamental orality of all literature, then, can be seen to reassert itself, even in the most literate of all cultures. Indeed, the audiovisual revolution has helped broaden the notion of literature; no longer does one limit it to that which can be printed and cataloged in libraries. Consequently, it has become possible to conceive of a traditional oral literature that lies at the roots of modern written Western literature. This overview surveys monumental works of that tradition in the light of research on all kinds of oral literature, explains how and why these works might be called "oral," and draws out the implications of their "oral" character. Finally, some aspects of the influence of oral tradition on later written work will be examined.

Definitions

Oral literature comprises a vast range of verbal products, including modern blues lyrics, African drum songs, ancient Greek epic poetry, urban legends, the latest jokes or limericks, ballads, folk songs, folktales, children's rhymes, and streetcorner games such as the "dozens" (a series of rhyming insult verses that can be extended to any length by improvisation). On one hand, it is quite useful for an investigator to know about all of these genres of oral literature, to take the term at its most inclusive, so that one can learn by comparison exactly what makes each given composition "oral" and therefore different from its written counterpart. On the other hand, some restriction of the term is needed to examine in any detail the workings of such literature. This essay, then, focuses on one narrow area of oral literature that has exerted influence of a disproportionate magnitude. While at times referring to African and Asian literature, most of the essay discusses Western literature. Unfortunately, this means excluding such great compositions as the Babylonian *Gilgamesh* (c. 2000 B.C.E.) story, the Iranian *Shāhnāma* (1010 C.E.), and the Sanskrit *Rāmāyaṇa* (c. 500 B.C.E.; *The Ramayana*, 1870-1874) and *Mahābhārata* (c. 400 B.C.E.-200 C.E.; *The Mahabharata*, 1834), as well as the hymns of the *Rig Veda* (c. 2500 B.C.E.), all of which have importance for the student of epic poetry in the Western tradition.

This survey will be further limited to poetry thought to be composed, and not merely transmitted, without the aid of writing. This restriction necessarily raises some questions: What of ballads or songs which change as they are transmitted? Is not this a form of composition without writing, even if the original composition were "written"? Such questions might be answered when discussion turns to longer compositions, such as narrative songs, which at times seem to exhibit the same behavior. It will be seen that the interplay of "oral" and "written" makes up a separate problem within the field of oral poetics, and ballad study requires critical notions different from those applied to other oral genres.

Finally, this article makes a further distinction between freely improvised poetry existing within a literate culture alongside written work—for example, the work songs and insult-contest verses that can be heard today—and preliterate compositions, which necessarily transmit large amounts of traditional language, motifs, and themes, and so cannot be called improvised in the same way. These poems, usually lengthy and narrative in nature, demand trained composers using generations-old techniques; at every turn of the poem, one comes across fusions of the individual's creative improvisation with traditional material.

The traditional poems to be discussed are the Greek *Iliad* (c. 750 B.C.E.; English translation, 1611) and *Odyssey* (c. 725 B.C.E.; English translation, 1614); the Old English *Beowulf* (c. 1000); the Icelandic *Poetic Edda* (ninth to twelfth centuries; English translations 1923, 1928, 1962, 1997); the *Nibelungenlied* (c. 1200; English translation, 1848), in Middle High German; and the Old French *Chanson de Roland* (twelfth century; *The Song of Roland*, 1880).

GREECE

Modern Western culture, for which "illiterate" is a pejorative word, takes writing for granted as something both necessary for civilization and good in itself. However, those who set out to read ancient Greek literature must divest themselves of this, among many other modern attitudes, and think themselves back into a culture which, while it valued speech above most things, did not have at all the same regard for the written word. Ancient Greece was an oral culture, and its early literature is oral literature; it is only when one understands the exigencies of oral composition and the expectations of an audience attuned to the oral art that Greek epic and lyric poetry—even history, oratory, and drama—become fully intelligible.

In Plato's dialogue *Phaedros* (c. fourth century B.C.E.; *Phaedrus*, 1804), Socrates relates the story of the invention of writing; his account provides a good starting point from which to examine Greek attitudes to written art. As Socrates tells it, in the Egyptian region of Naucratis lived the god Thoth, inventor of numbers, geometry, astronomy, and writing. Thoth once asked Thamus, king of the land, to pass on these arts to the citizens, for the good of all. "My discovery will enable the Egyptians to become wiser and better at remembering," said Thoth, when talk came to the new craft of writing. Thamus refused, however, saying, "This will make men forget, seeing that they will neglect memory and remember things not from within themselves but by faith in the exterior signs." Writing, concluded the king, would give Thoth's pupils only the appearance of wisdom; they would lack true teaching (the sort Socrates practiced by dialogue).

Plato's myth of Thoth focuses attention on three important aspects of oral culture: the role of the performer, that of the audience, and the inevitable effects on both brought about by the technological innovation of writing. Even if widespread literacy is not assumed, writing has a powerful impact. In Plato's time, the art probably belonged strictly to an educated elite. In the period surveyed in this essay, the Archaic Age (750-490 B.C.E.), even fewer Greeks are likely to have known how to use writing in daily life; writing was, after all, a recent invention, having been introduced by Phoenicians in the eighth century B.C.E. The attitude expressed by the Egyptian Thoth is consistent with early Greek notions about the role of writing as an aid rather than an end in itself, and even then, as an aid appropriate only for certain activities. It was certainly useful for inscriptions, to mark tombs or objects to be dedicated at temples, or to record laws—these are, in fact, the first recorded uses of the art of writing in Greece. The two oldest inscriptions, from the eighth century B.C.E., comprise some verses scratched on ceramic ware: "Whoever of all the dancers now sports the most, gets this," says a line on a jug found at Dipylon. A drinking vessel says, "Nestor's cup is good to drink from," then adduces, by means of a favorable contrast, its own capacity for giving wine. Whereas the first mention of a book comes in the late fifth century B.C.E. and the oldest actual surviving manuscript dates to a century later, writing intended to show possession or to memorialize had long been in use. Entertainment and instruction were the province of oral performers, not of written texts.

Thus, *Phaedrus* reflects the status of writing and oral performance in early Greek society. Thoth's conception of writing resembles that of Archaic Age Greeks, who thought in terms of one-way communication directed toward an unspecified audience, including future generations. For example, the Dipylon vase could be passed on, like some modern athletic trophies, annually, without change, its general statement always appropriate to the occasion of a dance contest. The attitude of Thamus, on the other hand, would match archaic modes of thinking about poetry as entertainment: It is an oral performer's attitude.

It is known from twentieth century fieldwork that

oral poetry always involves interaction between performer and audience. Even if the audience does not interrupt to make specific requests or suggestions about the poet's tale, the poem is shaped by the context of the performance: the time available, the occasion (whether ritual or secular), and, especially, the poet's perception of what the audience wishes to hear. They may want the "good old stories" or, as Telemachus says in the *Odyssey*, they may desire "the latest song." "Old" and "new" are relative terms; the poet's method of composing remains the same. He relies on his store of memorized traditional material, including both verbatim phrases and large plot structures, to create "new" compositions for each new audience. Every poem is both old—in the sense that each poet's repertoire comes to include only audience-tested material—and new, since the oral poet always competes with others in the craft and with himself as well, attempting to hone and polish his own compositions.

All of these observations are based on scholarship concerning composition techniques of oral poetry as it exists in many parts of the world today (principally Africa, the Balkans, and Asia), but Archaic Greek poetry makes explicit reference to the same techniques. A principal example is the poet's reliance on memory. Archaic Greek poetry consistently invokes the Muses, mythological daughters of Mnēmosunē (memory, or reminding). In Homer, as well as in lyric poetry, the Muses are viewed as the repository of all traditions, precisely because they are immortal goddesses and therefore were eyewitnesses to past events (as Homer says in calling on them to remind him of the catalog of ships in the *Iliad*, book 2). From the Greek standpoint, all poetry is therefore impossible without divine aid in the form of a divinized memory; the poet is automatically a religious figure and his art an act of faith, although the Greeks never make this formulation explicit.

What does the Greek poet remember? The simplest answer is "tradition," taking that word to mean traditional lore about heroes, ancestors, gods, and events, and also traditional expressions—unusual old words and noncurrent word endings (compare the *-th* third-person singular verb ending of English "poetic" language), as well as the traditional adjectives attached to

certain nouns. These latter adjective-noun combinations preserve a traditional way of looking at reality, and many are extremely old; for example, Homer often describes "fame" (*kleos*) as "unwithering" (*aphthiton*). Since the same adjective is frequently used of natural phenomena, a Greek audience would be attuned to think of "fame" as somehow growing like a plant. This perception is not the poet's invention, but rather an inherited piece of tradition. Sanskrit, a language related to Greek, preserves in its old poetry the exact equivalent of this phrase, in cognate words (*śravas ákṣitam*). Because Sanskrit and Greek speakers had split from a unified group and taken up residence in their respective lands by 2000 B.C.E. at the latest, this agreement in poetic language must go back to the time when both languages had a common dialect and common art; this is an Indo-European poetic tradition, as modern scholars believe. The idea of "undying fame"—what Achilles in the *Iliad* seeks and wins—is preserved because this phrase reflects the very ideology of the poetry itself: Personal heroic reputations are undying because they are recalled and renewed through generations of poets and audiences.

To put this in other terms and to return to the example of Plato's Thoth, one might say that for an oral poet to reject or pit himself against his tradition would be a contradiction in terms. The poet lives by tradition, as it lives through him. The powerful invention of writing, however, begins to erode tradition, offering a competing means of ordering reality, one which purports to be more authoritative. As the work of Albert Lord and others has shown, oral poetic technique begins to die out when a region's poets begin to accept the idea of writing and of "songbooks." Plato's Thamus, then, is absolutely correct in reprimanding the inventor of writing. The unease produced by the introduction of writing into ancient Greece appears in subtle hints near the end of the Archaic Age, when poets such as Xenophanes begin to criticize traditional concepts of the gods and the idea begins to take hold that myth is something subversive, false, or marginal. In contrast, for Homer, at the beginning of the Archaic Age, the word *muthos* is simply an authoritative speech act: a word, tale, or command.

A word should be added about the oral audience.

Far from being primitive consumers of art who merely wished to hear the names of famous ancestors, they were doubtless so familiar with oral art in everyday life that a high standard of criticism could evolve among them. The author of the *Hymn to Apollo* (third century B.C.E.), one of the so-called Homeric hymns, commends his poem to the audience in the personal note intruded at the end of the composition and bids the audience to compare his work with that of others which they hear, to spread his fame. A group of listeners valued for the potential favor they might do a poet, preserving his reputation, would always be treated to the height of a performer's art. Such interaction between artist and audience nourished the high art of Homer.

ILIAD AND ODYSSEY

Any discussion of traditional Western poetry should begin with Homer, because the study of the monumental poems attributed to him has continued throughout the Western literary tradition and first sparked the rediscovery of oral literature's distinctive techniques. From antiquity, there have been questions about the date, composition, and authorship of the two epics. In essence, the Homeric Question (as this collection of uncertainties has come to be called) grows from a lack of knowledge concerning a certain period in Greek history, the Dark Age, which extended from the fall of Mycenaean civilization (c. 1600-1100 B.C.E.) to the eighth century B.C.E., when writing in alphabetic form came to Greece from the Phoenicians and when Greek social institutions assumed their classical shapes.

The Homeric poems can be dated to the eighth century B.C.E. through certain indications of language and content (for example, mention of an oracle at Delphi, of iron, of seated statues). Why not assume, then, that a gifted literate poet of the eighth century, perhaps living in a Greek colony of Asia Minor (as tradition maintained), realized the usefulness of the newly imported alphabet for recording poetry and set himself to write one or two lengthy heroic poems about nearly mythical events of four hundred years before, the siege and fall of Troy? More is currently known, however, about the Mycenaean Age than about the Dark Age. The remains of a great city close to the traditional site of Troy were found at the end of the nineteenth century by Heinrich

Schliemann. In 1952, Michael Ventris, a British linguist, finally deciphered the language of the clay tablets found at Mycenaean Age sites on Crete and mainland Greece and discovered that it was an early form of Greek, used to record details of palace administration. These discoveries indicated that Homer's poems contain exact reminiscences of the heroic age they celebrate: a boar's tooth helmet in the *Iliad*, book 10, a body shield in the *Iliad*, book 6, and many other objects that are known to have gone out of use by 1000 B.C.E. are matched by real objects actually dug from Greek earth. Even the long catalog of ships in the *Iliad*, book 2, has been found to contain traces of very old authentic information. Words found elsewhere only in the newly deciphered Linear B Greek tablets appear in Homer's poetry.

Without a written tradition, one might ask how the memory of such words and objects could be preserved in the four-hundred-year gap between the war at Troy and Homer's own time, if not orally? Linear B writing certainly died out with the downfall of Mycenaean sites around 1100 B.C.E., and, at any rate, it seems never to have been used for literary purposes. On the other hand, if one attempts to explain the *Iliad* and the *Odyssey* as memorized poems, recited verbatim for centuries, there remains the obvious objection that the poems do not present a consistently archaic, Mycenaean picture, but rather a cultural mélange. Even the argument that an eighth century B.C.E. poet could have had access to nonpoetic, oral recollections of distant objects and customs, which he then incorporated into a chronologically haphazard poem, fails to explain the uniqueness of Homeric poetry, for such an argument leaves aside the most important obstacle, the peculiarly mixed Homeric dialect, which linguists affirm could never have been the speech of one poet, time, or place. In other words, the very diction, as well as the content, of the *Iliad* and the *Odyssey* is the product of a long evolution. What does this make of Homer? A series of poets? An editor?

One tradition of Homeric scholarship maintained that the poems were not both the work of one poet, the shadowy Homer, but showed differences of approach and style, leading critics to postulate several authors. With renewed vigor, the scientific nineteenth century

German tradition of scholarship, equipped with more exact observations about inconsistencies of plot and language between and within the poems, began to "analyze" the *Iliad* and the *Odyssey* into constituent smaller parts—"lays" or "songs" about separate themes, such as the wrath of Achilles or the return of Odysseus, which had been stitched together to form larger compositions. F. A. Wolf's *Prolegomena ad Homerum* (1795), which proposed a sixth century B.C.E. editing of the shorter lays into longer poems, can be seen as the first of such "analyst" attempts at explaining Homer's legacy. When, however, by the end of the nineteenth century, these critics had still failed to agree on the scheme of subdivision for the poems, the field was left open for fresh interpretations.

In 1928, a young American scholar, Milman Parry, convinced of the essential unity of Homer's poems, demonstrated in detail how it was possible that Homeric poetry could be traditional—the product of evolution—yet the work of one man. Parry investigated the occurrence of "formulas" in the poems, the recurring groups of words "used under the same metrical conditions to express an essential idea," as he defined the term. He pointed out that the use of certain adjectives or "epithets" to modify proper names, such as "much-enduring Odysseus" or "swift-footed Achilles," followed a system that was metrically controlled. Thus, noted Parry, Odysseus would be called "much-enduring, shining Odysseus" (*polutlas dios Odusseus*) when the hexameter line that the poet was composing required an ending of a certain metrical shape; when the poet needed an adjective to modify the name Odysseus in a line one syllable longer at its break, or caesura, he would invariably use "wily" (*polumetis Odusseus*).

Two principles governed the system. First, for each commonly used proper name there was, with fractional exception, one and only one epithet to fit each possible metrical position; this tendency Parry referred to as the "thrift" of the system. Second, the system was extensive, applying to some fifty or more figures in the poems and accounting for the epithets used in a variety of metrical conditions. The important conclusion that Parry drew from the existence of such a thorough system was this: No literate, writing poet could or would have wished to develop it. It could have evolved only

through some generations of poets who needed a system to enable rapid composition, in which an epithet would be ready at hand whenever they had to mention a proper name. Parry's investigation of the diction of Vergil and Apollonius Rhodius supported his conclusion. The writing poets used multiple epithets for one and the same metrical position and for proper-name combinations.

In his 1928 work on the traditional epithet, Parry hinted at his next ground-breaking hypothesis but did not make it explicit. Only after an initial trip in 1933 to Yugoslavia, where he studied the singing of contemporary nonliterate epic poets, did Parry suggest that Homer resembled modern "singers of tales," the Yugoslavian *guslars*. Homer was an oral poet, and the formulaic nature of his language confirmed this, for the Serbo-Croatian songs that Parry collected between 1933 and 1935, with the help of his student and co-worker Albert B. Lord, were highly formulaic in precisely the same ways. After Parry's accidental death in 1935, Lord continued his teacher's brilliant work, extending his investigations into such matters as traditional motifs and themes in the epic poetry of Greece, Yugoslavia, and medieval England, France, and Germany.

Lord's book *The Singer of Tales* (1960) contains valuable observations from his field experience that can be applied to all oral traditional poems. First, Lord pointed out that the performance of poems using the traditional style of formulaic composition differed from singer to singer, from region to region, and even from performance to performance of the same poem by the same singer. It is consequently not possible to speak of any fixed text for any given song in the tradition; put another way, the *Iliad* or the *Odyssey* that is available to the modern reader is only one performance of a long line of poems on the same subject. This fluidity of tradition explains why inconsistencies of plot may occur: not because a poet cannot keep details straight, but because there are "formulaic" themes and motifs, offering at each turn various possibilities for elaboration or condensation of traditional material.

A modern oral poet, such as Lord studied, might sing a version of a Serbo-Croatian epic at a coffeehouse during the Muslim Ramadan festival; when asked to sing for a collector of poems, the same poet could expand his version, add other plot details, yet still claim to be telling the same story. Lord found that for these singers and thus, by extension, for other oral poets, "the same poem" usually meant the same basic theme, not word-for-word correspondence. From their boyhood apprenticeships, the *guslars* had soaked up thematic variations, which they developed in a style of semi-improvisation, always with a view toward their audience and its knowledge of hundreds of other performances. One master singer, Avdo Medjedović (whose poems are in the Parry collection), knew fifty-eight epics in 1935. Medjedović dictated to Lord at least two poems that were more than twelve thousand lines in length, thus providing evidence that the *Iliad* and the *Odyssey*—sixteen thousand and twelve thousand lines, respectively—could have been the result of actual performances. In addition, Lord's observation that the songs that Medjedović sang were "finer," in the singer's opinion, when sung to the attentive individual audience that had requested the performance led him to postulate that the same dictation situation was the origin of the Homeric poems.

Lord's hypothesis would account for the perplexing question of the manner in which oral compositions, such as the *Iliad* and the *Odyssey*, finally were handed down as texts. Such a scenario also avoids the pitfalls of postulating an oral poet who becomes a literate poet. As Lord found, such poets gradually lost their ability, and within a generation or two of the introduction of songbooks, the oral art of the singers tended to die out. A true oral poet would, in fact, have no desire to use writing—certainly not as an aid to memory, for which he already possessed an economical nonliterate system; and, in the traditional mode of performance before an audience, there would be no reason to switch modes, to write for an unseen audience. There remains the possibility that Homer, coming at the end of an oral tradition already threatened by literacy in nonpoetic spheres, foresaw the usefulness of the new medium and found a scribe to record his masterpieces. In this way, the poems would be at once "oral" and "written." Lord later noted that, for a literate person living in an area where oral poetry is performed, the traditional oral style is easy to imitate, and thus, there can be "transi-

tional" poetry of a mixed character. Lord was willing to view much of Old English religious poetry, which appears to be formulaic to a degree, as transitional.

The Parry-Lord theory, as it is called, is not the only way to examine oral literature, but it is the most useful for traditional narrative poetry. Lyric, ballads, praise poems, and other genres may require different methodology, as Ruth Finnegan pointed out in *Oral Poetry* (1977). Aside from this, there have been misunderstandings and overextensions of the Parry-Lord type of analysis. The classicist H. T. Wade-Gery said in *The Poet of the Iliad* (1952) of the opposition to the theory of Parry and Lord, "As Darwin seemed to many to have removed the finger of God from the creation of the world and of man, so Milman Parry has seemed to some to have removed the creative poet from the *Iliad* and the *Odyssey*." Lord was the first to admit that his studies of Serbo-Croatian poems were valid only as outlines of broad principles, not as normative models for oral poetry, but sometimes his strictures went unheeded. Perhaps the most concerted reaction to the theory came immediately after the widespread dissemination of its principles in the 1960's, following the publication of *The Singer of Tales*.

Later, however, such concern with "creativity" was seen for what it is: a remnant of the Romantic conception of the poet. Neither Homer nor the *Beowulf* poet nor the countless anonymous singers of oral poems were concerned with being "creative" in the modern sense; instead, the oral poet sought fresh variation within a traditional structure of themes and diction. To use the Greek poet Pindar's metaphor (a very old one), "there are many roads of song."

The seminal work of Parry and Lord, then, taught literary critics to view poetry from traditional oral cultures in a new way. Rather than misapplying standards based on written texts to the repetitive elements of oral poetry—whether of word, phrase, scene, or theme—one must focus on just such formulaic elements to see how the individual singer has modified and rearranged the tradition in order to make meaning.

The *Iliad* and the *Odyssey* provide countless examples of such repetition. One does not have to insist on the noun-epithet as the basis of the formulaic analysis of these poems. In fact, the term "formula" and its definition are in dispute, especially in Homeric studies. There is much to be learned from the poet's manipulation of higher-level formulaic elements of a poem: the motif and the theme. The motif, or type-scene, is the recurring use of many of the same details—but not necessarily in the same words—to tell about arming for battle, sending off messengers or a ship, feasting, getting up, going to bed, dueling, and a number of other actions that give weight and texture to long poems.

One such type-scene depicting the sacrifice and consumption of cattle, builds in the *Odyssey* to a central theme. The suitors' continual sacrifice of Odysseus's cattle is both the generating circumstance for Telemachus's decision to rescue his father's house and the reason Odysseus, on returning to the island of Ithaca, must slaughter the suitors. The seemingly inconsequential sacrifice scenes at other points in the poem gain resonance from the centrality of these first and final cattle-kills.

As an example, when Telemachus arrives at Nestor's city of Pylos in book 3, he encounters the old Trojan War veteran performing a huge sacrifice of cattle on the shore; there follows the most detailed use of the type-scene, describing in each particular the gilding of the beasts' horns, the ritual cutting, the cooking, and the feast. Homer expands here on the capsule motif of sacrifice, it seems, precisely because Pylos is meant to form a contrast to the situation on Telemachus's Ithaca, where (with fatal consequences) sacrifice and feasting are conducted in an incorrect manner. Again, sacrifice becomes all-important during the wanderings of Odysseus. The episode of the Cyclop's cave in book 9 presents another "improper" sacrifice which, by repetition of certain key phrases, hauntingly recalls the real purpose of sacrifice—nourishment of men and honor of gods—but refers to the eating of men, raw, by the monster. Finally, the same double allegiance, of reference and resonance, gives added meaning to the sacrifice of the Sun's cattle by Odysseus's disobedient crew, described in book 12: Here, the type-scene of sacrifice once more applies to a wrong sacrifice but foreshadows the "right" (in Greek terms) killing of the suitors, who, like Odysseus's crew, ate what was not theirs.

The type-scene is similar to a musical refrain, except that it never has to be repeated exactly to be effective. The theme, on the other hand, is more like the key signature of a musical piece: It establishes the limits within which the piece is to be "played" against the possible range of all themes. The theme is not bound to any one situation in the plot but, rather, underlies many plot events and can surface in the form of imagery or action or speech. The *Iliad* and the *Odyssey* illustrate the tendency of themes to combine, contract, or expand in narration. In this way, long narratives approach both myth and ritual (sharing common narrative progressions, such as the "return from the dead" theme) as well as the folktale. The latter can be analyzed in terms of "multiforms"—that is, variant tellings of the same essential action, with changes of detail in each version. The theme, too, is multiform—the return of Odysseus from Troy is simply another form of the theme (also narrated in the *Odyssey*, in book 11) of the return from Hades. In the *Odyssey*, this theme is combined with two others, also familiar from folktales: the initiation of a youth and the waiting of a wife (in this case, further combined with a wooing theme, which is found by itself in other Greek poems, such as the "Suitors of Helen" attributed to Hesiod).

The *Iliad* offers an even clearer example of the combination and reduplication of traditional themes. The main plot is centered on the narrative theme of the "withdrawal in anger" of the hero Achilles from battle. Introduced in the first book of the poem, the theme does not find its conclusion until the return of Achilles and the death of Hector. Along the way, it engenders another traditional theme, the "death of a substitute"—clearly a ritual theme as well—in this case, the death of Patroclus, Achilles' alter ego. Important as it is in connection with Achilles, the theme is not confined to him within the poem. Instead, like the type-scene, it is employed to counterpoint Achilles and other characters in the epic.

The theme of withdrawal exists as a narrative possibility whenever a hero retires from the fighting. A striking example occurs when Hector, returning during a lull in the fighting to his home in Troy, encounters Paris, who has been dallying with his abducted bride, the Greek Helen. "It is not good to put anger in your spirit like this," Hector tells Paris on their meeting, as he berates him for leaving the fight. In reality, anger has nothing to do with the withdrawal of Paris; he had been snatched magically back to Troy by Aphrodite when he was about to lose a duel with Menelaus on the plain. Why does Hector mention anger? An earlier generation of critics maintained that Homer here bungled his plot. Now, however, one can explain such words on Hector's part as the working of thematic intrusion: Withdrawal in the tradition, as a theme, usually implies the anger of the hero. Here, the lesser figure Paris only becomes more distinct from the heroic Achilles by the poet's mention of this theme, tied as it is in the main narrative to the anger of Achilles. It is an artful use of traditional material.

Similarly, Homer uses the withdrawal theme to structure another tale-within-a-tale, the story of Meleager, told by Phoenix in book 9 to induce Achilles, his ward, to go back to the fight. The Meleager story mirrors Achilles' own situation: He has retired in anger from a war and cannot be made to return until it is too late. Again, the smaller narrative (like the type-scene of sacrifice in the *Odyssey*) is used to foretell part of the larger story; indeed, Achilles will return to battle too late to save his dearest companion, Patroclus. In this example, one sees the essence not only of narrative themes but also of the importance in an oral culture of the narrative itself: Oral culture needs oral poetry to enforce its morality. The story becomes an exemplum, indicating the best heroic behavior for the young Achilles by reminding him of past heroic deeds and their consequences. Action as well as story is governed by tradition.

Homeric poetry is worth dwelling on because it is preeminently aware of its heritage as oral poetry. In invoking the Muse, the source of all traditional lore concerning the past, the poet acknowledges that what he hears from the goddess is more important than anything he himself might invent. In celebrating Achilles and Odysseus, the *Iliad* and the *Odyssey* make the same acknowledgment: Both heroes are also poets, Achilles singing the deeds of the ancestors as he sits in his hut, Odysseus telling his own adventures to the Phaeacian court.

NON-HOMERIC ORAL POETRY

Although the earliest extant Greek lyric poetry postdates Homer, one cannot assume that epic poetry was "invented" before lyric; indeed, it is clear from the *Iliad* and the *Odyssey* that Homer knew other genres of poetry. He pictures the social use of genres which were to become familiar from later poets. Wedding songs can be paralleled in the work of Sappho in the late seventh and early sixth century B.C.E.; laments are the first songs in a long oral tradition that is alive today in rural Greece; choral maiden songs were composed later by Alcman and Pindar; and hymns to the gods were later elaborated as long narrative poems such as the Homeric hymns. It must be assumed that these later poems simply continued a tradition of oral poetry as old, if not older, than that of Homeric epic. It may even be that epic verse developed from the simpler meters of lyric poetry, as some scholars suggest (see G. Nagy, *Comparative Studies in Greek and Indic Meter*, 1974). This would explain some of the richness of Homer's poems: They incorporate the varied themes and emotions of the range of concurrent lyric poetry known to the poet Homer, that poetry that closely preserves the folk traditions of the Greek people.

Early Greek lyric poetry shows its oral heritage in several important ways: first, by its directness of style, simple syntax, and use of concrete, often stunning, images (qualities much admired by Ezra Pound and the Imagists in the early twentieth century); second, by its use of formulaic expressions, many of which are also found in Homer ("golden Aphrodite"; "shining children"; "blazing fire"). These devices were meant to be appreciated by an audience of listeners rather than by page-turning readers; therefore, clarity and immediate effect were crucial for the oral composer. Another consequence of this poetry's constant attention to the presence of an audience is its "social" quality. There is no such thing as "confessional" poetry in early Greece. Instead, there are a number of personas, or masks, for the poetic performer, which can also be found to be traditional. A good example occurs in the work of the Boeotian composer, Hesiod.

HESIOD

Hesiodic poetry seems to be contemporary with Homeric epic, with which it shares dactylic hexameter meter and traditional formulaic style, but the two major works attributed to Hesiod are markedly unlike the *Iliad* and the *Odyssey*, particularly in that Hesiod's poetry refers to its own maker. In the opening section of *Theogonia* (c. 700 B.C.E.; *Theogony*, 1728), Hesiod describes his encounter on Mount Helicon with the Muses, while he was pasturing sheep, and he tells of how he received a scepter, a symbol of power, along with the gift of singing about the origins of the gods. This "song" which the Muses taught him (note the oral figure) is then resung by the poet as the substance of the remaining *Theogony*. The origin of all from Chaos and Night, the overthrow of Uranus by Cronus and of Cronus by Zeus, who then orders the cosmos—all of these remind one of portions in the *Iliad* in which a wisdom figure (Nestor, for example, or Phoenix) refers to semidivinized abstract notions in order to explain the workings of the world. Clearly, the *Theogony* is in an old genre; similar explanatory cosmologies are known to have been recited at kingship rituals in the ancient Near East, whence some of Hesiod's own tales also seem to have originated. The innovation in Hesiod's own treatment appears to be his singing of the song in the role of a shepherd (a motif remarkably similar to that in the story of Caedmon, the Old English poet). That this shepherd is a persona, and not necessarily the "real" poet, becomes clear from Hesiod's *Erga kai Emerai* (c. 700 B.C.E.; *Works and Days*, 1618), in which the poet is at one time a farmer and is also a cunning "adviser" to his brother Perses, as well as to local princes. The brother, says Hesiod, wronged him over a dispute about their patrimony. Zeus is also counseled, along with the princes (his earthly representatives), as Hesiod employs the traditional and widespread "Instruction of Princes" genre. An intriguing poem, the *Works and Days* uses the myth of the Five Ages of Man, as well as the stories of Prometheus's invention of fire and of Pandora's box, to point its instruction. Ethics for Hesiod includes "works" as well as a kind of faith, so that the detailed agricultural and ritual admonishments that conclude the poem are organically related to the myth section. Furthermore, it is the persona of the farmer/adviser that unites the two seemingly disparate parts.

Like that of Hesiod, all Greek poetry in the early period instructs and addresses its audience, at times explicitly, at other times by implication, through the exteriorizing of inner emotions. The startling variety of me-

ters and dialects in which Greek lyric is composed cannot conceal the basic similarity in function: The poetry is targeted for limited, local, chosen groups but uses a common Greek store of images and formulas to underline its poetic messages. Inevitably, the poet is viewed as a craftsperson—for example, as a maker (*poiētēs* in Greek) of words; his craft is a social institution. The following survey of lyric poetry centers on the ways in which the poets' view of their craft, as reflected in their verses, and their acknowledgment of an audience, point to the oral origins of such poetry.

ARCHILOCHUS

For the soldier-poet Archilochus of Paros (c. 680-c. 640 B.C.E.), poetry is clearly delineated as a craft, one on a level with his other trade: "The servant of Ares I am, and I understand the Muses' lovely gift as well," he writes in one elegiac couplet. Some of Archilochus's poems are set immediately before or after battles—the poet warns about the tactics of an enemy or talks of his bread "won by the spear and eaten while I lean on the spear"—but Archilochus was most noteworthy in the eyes of later antiquity for the attitude he takes toward military life. His persona is that of the dissident warrior; perhaps the audience was meant to think of Achilles. In one poem, Archilochus bids farewell to the shield that he has thrown away in flight from battle; in other verses, he encourages a watch party to get drunk and pours scorn on a dandified general. Allegiance to the Muse overrules that to the god of war. Archilochus's own martial career as an early colonizer of the northern Aegean island Thasos may have inspired the poems; more likely, this "warrior" is another persona. The poet has a second mask, like Hesiod: He is a dangerous satirist, a practitioner of the art known as *iambus* (from which the term "iambic" derives, although the word originally designated a genre). *Iambus* is the art of blame-poetry, venomous attacks of which are said to have led Archilochus's victims to suicide. Scholars know from other oral cultures that such beliefs in the power of destroying reputation are taken seriously and have real effect. Archilochus practices his invective artfully, attacking in the voice of another, for example, a woman who spurned him, when he makes a character in a dialogue poem say "her bloom has withered" and insinuates that she is less than chaste.

Archilochus's poetry often resembles a conversation that the audience is invited to overhear. Perhaps the best example is his address to his own soul: "Spirit, boiling with incurable woes, get up. Defend yourself, hurl your chest against the foes." It is preeminently Archilochean in combining war images (soul as fighter) with advice ("Do not boast when you win or weep in your house when you lose") and ending with a pragmatic command ("Know what sort of rhythm moves men"). All of his verse convinces and holds an audience through such devices, but rather than being deceived into identifying Archilochus as the first genuinely individual voice in the European lyric tradition (a claim that is often made), one should recognize that his art was the product of a long oral tradition of personal poetry, as conventional as epic poetry in its use of framing techniques, imagery, and personas.

Archilochus, both personal and public composer, warrior as well as poet of the drinking party, provides a good starting point from which to approach two poles of the later Greek tradition, which may be termed the "personal"—represented by Alcaeus and Sappho—and the "social"—as seen here in the Athenian lawgiver Solon's poems and those of the sixth century Theognis of Megara.

ALCAEUS AND SAPPHO

Alcaeus and Sappho both lived on the island of Lesbos in the late seventh and early sixth century. They enormously influenced later European poetry, but because later poets, in their imitations, popularized the images of a jovial, bibulous party poet (Alcaeus) and an intensely personal bluestocking poetess (Sappho), modern critics find it difficult to hear the authentic voices of these consummate lyricists. This is particularly true because later written poetry, as often happens, also adapted Sappho's and Alcaeus's oral-oriented devices and settings, the immediate addresses and allusions to ongoing festivities or rituals among a small circle of friends. Consequently, one comes to their poetry with a false sense of familiarity. What is conventional in the written poems of Horace, for example, should very often be treated as actual utterance in poems by Sappho and Alcaeus: Horace, in Rome of the first century B.C.E., could not have known firsthand the sort of social occasions about which he writes, whereas

Sappho and Alcaeus could not have avoided participating in such local institutions as the *kōmos* (festival with procession), the wedding feast, maidens' festivals, or the symposium (men's drinking party). In an oral culture, it makes no sense to compose poems "as if" one were attending such occasions, because the actual occasions demanded poetic accompaniment to be performed on the spot.

Alcaeus explicitly acknowledges an audience at such occasions, while Sappho hints at one, keeping in the foreground her own persona. Still, the assumption that both poets are composing for a present audience must guide interpretation. For Alcaeus and Sappho, the audience can include ancestors; as in Homer, the notion of fame through poetry alone is the overriding incitement to correct behavior. Thus, Alcaeus, in one of his many poems dealing with the local politics of Lesbos, uses an enduring image as he calls on his companions to "bail out" the ship of state, lest it sink, and tells them to "run to harbor" lest they "shame by cowardice the good forebears beneath the ground." Sappho similarly speaks of memory in an address to an unnamed woman, implying that only poetry can give true immortality—a persistent theme of Archaic poems, one easily understood in a culture where even the word for fame (*kleos*) means, literally, "that which is heard": "Dead, you will lie, neither memory nor desire of you will there be," says Sappho, "for you do not have any of the roses of Pieria [the home of the Muses]." To exercise memory, in composing poetry, is to ensure that one is remembered.

In their use of the hymn genre, Alcaeus and Sappho illustrate the ways in which traditional public poetic forms can have personal reference. Alcaeus, who wrote hymns to Apollo, Dionysos, and the Dioscuri, among other deities, calls on the gods to aid in defeating his enemies in the city-state and to bring him back from exile. He combines hymns with symposium poems—the sort of verses designed to muster his group of friends by self-reference, similar to his "ship of state" poems. Sappho, on the other hand, uses the hymn form several times in calling for rescue from love affairs. Her most famous and only completely intact poem beseeches Aphrodite to withdraw her forces; Sappho fills the hymnic framework of the poem with an exquisite flash-back description of Aphrodite's previous aid—how she came in a sparrow-drawn chariot and promised to make Sappho's lover reciprocate. Aphrodite is doubly praised in the poem, which attests that her promise was so great in the past as to involve the poet in new love difficulties, prompting the new cry for help.

Aside from their use of traditional, socially fixed oral forms, and their nod to the role of memory in poetry, Sappho and Alcaeus alike compose poetry to consolidate their audiences—that is, their "friend groups" (the *philoi*, or "beloved," a concept strange to English). In this, they show the tight bond that oral poetry enforces between performer and audience: Sappho's laments for young women who are growing up, moving away, or marrying can be understood as addressed to the remaining group of girls (in a culture where gender segregation was the norm). This applies even to her famous ode that seems to detail with clinical precision the physical effects of jealousy that Sappho feels on seeing a girl she knows next to a man. In reality, this was probably an elaborate praise poem for the *girl*, using traditional metaphors and the device of a "foil," or fictitious rival figure. Alcaeus's most apparently "personal" poems—for example, his exhortations to come drink with him—are also public in that the drinking is understood to take place at a symposium, where serious political talk mixes with philosophical meditation and relaxation.

SOLON

In an oral culture such as that of Archaic Greece, the role of poetry in politics cannot be underestimated; even in the "enlightened" fifth century, rhetoric and poetry swayed Athens to a disproportionate and dangerous degree. Solon (639-559 B.C.E.), the Athenian lawgiver, exemplifies the alloy of poetic and political craft. In one poem, he admits to using the "arrangement of words" (*kosmos*), rather than political speeches, to persuade Athens. This is a sort of sympathetic verbal magic: ordering words begets order in the state. In other poems, he urged the Athenians to remember his reforms. As does Hesiod, Solon frames his poetry as "instruction" to the audience—in this case, the entire city. The instructions often take the mythic form of Hesiodic discourses on abstract concepts which are half divine, such as Justice (*Dikē*). Solon's long poem addressed to

the Muses, daughters of memory, for example, describes in parts the way in which Zeus pursues wrongdoers through their descendants: Like the poet, dependent on memory, Zeus, too, "does not forget," and it is essential that the audience, also, remember this. Memory, therefore, works on three levels, making this poem a paradigm for the role of poetry in oral society.

THEOGNIS

How do audiences remember? In an oral culture, they must be constantly reminded, and this is where oral art comes to the fore. With the increasing use of writing, such functional poetry as Solon's, meant for performance, was soon being memorialized for future generations. A valuable hint of the procedure survives in the traditional lore about another "political" poet, Theognis of Megara (sixth century B.C.E.), a city near Athens. His poetry, in elegiac couplets, about fourteen hundred lines of which survive, may have been put on deposit in a local temple. An allusion to a "seal" on the poems preventing theft may mean that Theognis actually sealed the verses up with wax on the papyrus roll; it has been suggested that the "seal" may also have a metaphorical significance, indicating that the specific performer-audience relationship which this instructional poetry illustrates between an adviser (Theognis) and his young friend (Kyrnos) will never be duplicated. Because the poet has given Kyrnos immortality ("I have given you wings with which to fly over the sea," as the poet says), the bond will never slip. As it appears, Theognis uses Kyrnos as a foil in order to counsel his city, Megara, and the poetry, like Solon's, thus embodies the reciprocal relationship characteristic of oral culture: Performers need audiences; Greece remembered Theognis.

CHORAL POETRY

A discussion of the unique combination of public and personal which defines early Greek poetry would not be complete without mention of choral poetry, that elaborate art form that used words, music, and dance to celebrate important community rites. The earliest representative of the form, Alcman, active in Sparta in the seventh century B.C.E., displays the characteristics marking this increasingly important poetry. In his *parthenion* (maiden song), for example, the local mythology of Sparta combines with gnomic utterances ("Do not try to fly to heaven; no one should try to wed Aphrodite") and details of the immediate occasion, such as the praise of the local maidens through extensive comparisons to traditional beauties: stars, sun, moon, horses, and goddesses. Only the introduction of strophic structure (the format in which two identical verse units are capped by a third, differing in meter), which might have occurred in the sixth century B.C.E., differentiates Alcman's choral song from those composed in the fifth century flowering of the genre, both in the choruses of Athenian tragedy and in the works of Bacchylides and Pindar.

BEOWULF

"One might say that each song in oral tradition has its original within it and even reflects the origin of the very genre to which it belongs." This observation by Albert Lord, though meant to be general, might apply specifically to *Beowulf* (c. 1000), the earliest full-length Germanic language epic that has survived. Although this poem was probably composed in the eighth century, its historical context is that of the early sixth century on the Continent and in Scandinavia; the story was likely brought to England by the migrating Angles and Saxons. This is prima facie evidence for the conservative nature of the poem, a trait often noticed in other oral compositions: The Serbo-Croatian songs that Lord and Parry found were often about battles fought five hundred years previously, such as that at Kosovo Polje in the fourteenth century. The *Nibelungenlied* (c. 1200; English translation, 1848), *Cantar de mío Cid* (early thirteenth century; *Chronicle of the Cid*, 1846; better known as *Poem of the Cid*), and *The Song of Roland* all share this characteristic.

In the case of *Beowulf*, as clearly as in the Greek epics, the oral origin of the poem is made explicit by the poet's own references to oral poems in the narrative, so that *Beowulf* is conservative in its view of poetry as well as in its historical outlook. As in the *Iliad* and the *Odyssey*, when bards are presented composing poetry, one should not expect exact depiction of the process by which the narrative itself was composed: There is always the possibility that the poet is archaizing, recalling the more glorious poetic as well as heroic past, when oral composers held a higher place in society.

The very existence of this "backward look" is important; it is the seal of a poem's traditional content.

The origin of a poem such as *Beowulf* can be viewed within the Old English epic in the important scene starting at line 867. As the Danes return on horseback from the site of Grendel's plunge, a retainer of their king recites the exploit,

> A man proved of old, evoker of stories,
> Who held in his memory multitude on multitude
> Of the sagas of the dead, found now a new song
> In words well-linked: the man began again
> To weave in his subtlety the exploit of Beowulf.

This sort of instant praise poetry is not, however, simply a direct restatement of the hero's deed. The "evoker of stories" instead praises Beowulf by beginning with the story of Sigemund, who had a similar exploit (killing a dragon), and he ends with a mention of the blameworthy Heremod, an early Danish king, the complete opposite of Beowulf. There is no mention of the way in which he actually praised the maiming of Grendel by the contemporary hero; it could well be that what the old retainer composed in fact made little or no reference to Beowulf. Surprising as this might seem, it would fit with what can be seen in the *Iliad*, in the episode just mentioned above: The present is continually set into its past heroic context in this oral traditional material.

That something like the horseback poem of the retainer could have occurred in early times is suggested by the Roman historian Tacitus's account of Germanic tribesmen, who, he reported, sang the histories of their ancestors before battles and at night in their camps. This urge to turn the past into incentive for the present lies at the root of heroic poetry as well as praise poetry, the kernel form of the epic. In the song of the retainer, which resembles Greek praise poetry in its use of a "negative foil" figure (the blamed character), one can see the kernel blossoming into a full-fledged narrative.

As in the analysis of the Greek epics, the notion of type-scene and theme proves useful in establishing connections between *Beowulf* and oral composition. The analysis of the low-level formula—the repeated phrase or word—is less conclusive; *Beowulf* appears to be oral because it appears to have a high percentage of formulas or formula-types (repeated syntactical groupings such as epithet and noun), but the statistical method should not be relied on completely. It has recently been shown that poems known to have been written and signed by Cynewulf, probably in the ninth century, would have to be classified as "oral" if the same counting methods were applied. It could be that both Cynewulf's poems and the epic *Beowulf* are transitional products of the meeting of an oral tradition with a learned, Christianized, literate society. This would explain the seemingly incongruous elements of Christian faith in the heroic poem. Whatever the results of the diction-oriented analysis, the occurrence of traditional type-scenes and themes in *Beowulf* is important in itself and may be taken to show the poem's oral heritage.

Beowulf has its start in an arrangement of type-scenes remarkably like that of the *Odyssey:* A hero sets out by boat, is met on landing, is greeted and entertained, finds important information, and acts on it to the advancement of his own heroic career. In the *Odyssey*, the sequence is repeated, once for Telemachus (like *Beowulf*, a young hero accompanied by a small group) and once for Odysseus (books 5 through 13). Beowulf, however, acts immediately; the poem is consequently much shorter. Odysseus and Telemachus, on the other hand, act only on return to Ithaca, where their reunion and slaying of the suitors forms the grand finale. In this development, conditions of performance must dictate which themes will be doubled and which contracted, how many type-scenes will be inserted, and how large they will be allowed to grow.

The *Beowulf*-poet handles themes with as much dexterity as Homer, although his stock of type-scenes seems smaller. An example is the "taunt of Unferth" scene. The taunt is itself a genre in oral society, as the Homeric epics and modern African examples make clear. Here, the taunt is expanded to contain a thematic narrative remarkably like the theme of the surrounding poem: the underwater exploits of Beowulf. Unferth, a retainer of the Danish king Hrothgar, asks Beowulf on arrival whether he is the man who lost a swimming-match against Breca. Beowulf's reply is an elaborate, suspenseful narrative of a fight with sea-demons—the "correct" version of the story, unlike Unferth's, and a foreshadowing of his defeat of Grendel's mother be-

neath the lake. Beowulf (like Odysseus) acts the part of the oral poet. Is it not significant, then, that he wins over the final monster, not with Unferth's donated sword Hrunting, but with the "blade of old-time" found in the den of Grendel, which only Beowulf among heroes can lift? His personal weapon, like his personal story, is the one to surpass the competing stories of heroic action; fame, in an oral culture, tunes out the noise of rumor.

As well as containing hints of its own origin, *Beowulf* has one scene that might point to the kind of poetry that ultimately replaced it. The introduction of Grendel into the narrative describes his approach to the hall of the Danes where he had daily heard singing—and the song consists of nothing less than the creation of the world by God. As such, this singing strongly resembles the compositions attributed to Caedmon in a well-known section of Bede's history of the English Church. Caedmon was in the habit of leaving the nightly entertainments at Whitby Abbey because he had never learned songs, Bede reports. One night, guarding the stables, Caedmon dreamed that he was asked to sing the creation of the world; he did so, and the next morning recited the poem to his superiors, who from that time on used him to put stories from religious works into verse. Caedmon clearly was an oral composer; from Bede's viewpoint, his gift was "divine," since he knew no literature. However, it was through such recruits to Christian tradition that the oral art of the older native singers eventually was lost—the beginning of the end can be seen in the *Beowulf*-poet's knowledge of this theological genre.

POETIC EDDA

The Icelandic compositions known as the *Poetic Edda* or the *Edda* (ninth to twelfth centuries; English translations 1923, 1928, 1962, 1997) provide more valuable evidence for a quite ancient traditional diction and meter in Germanic poetry. Phrases composed of the same words (with slight sound changes) can be found in the *Poetic Edda* and in Old High German and Old English poetry, and must therefore be considered common Germanic. This means that the art of composing such poetry came about before the Germanic dialects had split into separate languages. Furthermore, the preservation in both Old English and Icelandic verse of the same four-stress, alliterative metrical line, composed of two clearly distinguished half lines, argues for a common metrical heritage—this would explain, in part, why similar phrases are preserved in different languages.

What are the implications of these discoveries for the criticism of the poetry? Given that the form of Eddic and other Germanic verse is very old, one is encouraged to look for signs of antiquity both in content and in structural elements—the type-scenes and themes.

The most obvious common inheritances on these higher levels are those of subject matter. Both Eddic poems and the *Nibelungenlied*, for example, focus on historical events of the fifth and sixth centuries C.E.: the deaths of Gunther and Hagen, and the revenge on Attila the Hun. Other Eddic poems (no one composition consists of more than one hundred or so lines) treat episodic, mythological incidents—encounters between Odin or Thor and giants or dwarfs, for example. Here, too, one can see resemblances to other Germanic poems: *Beowulf* is just such an encounter theme, extended to epic proportions in 3,182 lines. It has even been proposed that later, epic-length poems such as the *Nibelungenlied* are no more than collections of short plays that would resemble Eddic poems. The theory, attributed to Karl Lachmann, a nineteenth century German scholar, runs up against the same problems that plague the analysts' division of Homer into separate songs: Where does one make the divisions? Of more importance is the Eddic poems' distinctive viewpoint. Rather than simply narrating an incident from myth or history, the *fornskáld* (Eddic poet) most often used dialogue and allusive speeches in rhetorical settings: arguments, riddle contests, or *flyting* (mutual abuse matches). From such poetry, then, one gets a picture of actual heroic age genres of discourse in a preliterate society. The genre of *flyting*, in fact, helps one to understand the occurrence of episodes, such as Unferth's abuse of Beowulf, in longer compositions. A few examples in this vein will illustrate the ways in which Eddic poetry is conscious of its own role as the repository of the collective memory of the Icelandic people.

First, it is clear from a poem such as "The Words of the All-Wise" that knowledge, in such a preliterate culture, is knowledge of tradition, especially of the traditional formulas—legal, religious, or poetic. The

same message is transmitted (subliminally, perhaps) by Homer, who makes his heroes into traditional singers. In the Eddic poem, Alvis ("all-wise"), a dwarf, is questioned by Thor about the names of various things—clouds, sea, wind, and so on. Alvis must answer with the learned lore of poetry; for example, the heavens are called "*Heaven* by men, *The Arch* by gods,/ *Windweaver* by vanes,/ by giants *High-earth*, by elves *Fairroof*,/ By dwarves *The Dripping-Hall*." Thor eventually wins this contest, not by any deficiency in Alvis's answers, but because dawn arrives and Alvis turns to stone. That Alvis's feat was expected of every learned poet in the tradition is evidenced by the so-called *Prose Edda* (c. 1220), a later work by the thirteenth century Icelandic scholar Snorri Sturluson, who wrote the *Skáldskaparmál* or "Poetic Diction" portion specifically for the instruction of a generation of poets whose grasp of the traditional lore was slipping.

The Eddic poems, preserving large amounts of traditional material, including mythological as well as practical advice in the form of gnomic utterances, might be compared with the work of Hesiod. As Hesiod in the *Works and Days* offers gnomic advice for every phase of social life, so the *Hávamál* (ninth and tenth century; *The Sayings of the High One*, 1923) provides guidelines for behavior, stressing (as does Hesiod) reciprocity in friendships, moderation in eating and drinking, and distrust of women. As Hesiod's *Theogony* traces the genesis of gods and men, so the *Words of Vafthrudnir* (ninth and tenth century), another Eddic poem, recounts the origin of the world, of seasons and giants, and even the fate of the gods. This apocalyptic strain in Icelandic poetry takes over completely the *Völuspá* (c. 1000; *Völuspá: The Song of Sibyl*, 1968), serving as a reminder to comparatists that poetry and seer craft in traditional preliterate societies are closely related activities: Knowing past lore is the key to the future.

Where words themselves are so important, their bestowal or refusal is crucial if one's heroic deeds are to be considered heroic; the *Poetic Edda* is conscious of this fact, as the *Hávamál* proclaims: "Cattle die, kindred die/ Every man is mortal;/ But I know one thing that never dies:/ The glory of the great dead." Not only is word-craft the mark of the wise and the guarantee of heroism, but it also brings about social integration, being the means by which an audience is united in pleasure and therefore bonded together in understanding. Again, the *Hávamál* realizes this, in concluding with an audience statement in the form of a wish: "Joy to him who has understood,/ Delight to him who has listened."

NIBELUNGENLIED

It is a long distance, chronologically and generically, from the archaic lore of the *Edda* to the courtly life depicted in the *Nibelungenlied*, or "song of the Nibelungs," a nine-thousand-line composition dating from around 1200. While the Eddic poems exhibit concise diction (sometimes obscure) and dramatic organization, the *Nibelungenlied* has often been criticized for being threadbare, disorganized, and padded in its verse. This may be the effect, partly, of adapting older material to a more modern meter (a longer, three-stress-per-half-line, rhymed verse) and changed social situation, which demanded longer and more "courtly" poetry. Whatever the cause, these surface differences should not stand in the way of an appreciation of the similarities between the Icelandic, Old English, and Middle High German poems. All are rooted primarily in the past.

The *Nibelungenlied* announces itself as an "old story" of heroic action, feasts, and laments; from the first, one perceives its relationship, thematically, to the "wail after wassail" outlook of *Beowulf*, the *Seafarer* (one of a collection of poems found in the *Exeter Book*, copied about 975 C.E.), and other Old English poems. At least figuratively, the poem characterizes itself as oral by promising that all who wish can hear the story of Kriemhild, Gunther, Siegfried, and Etzel. Other marks of its actual oral heritage are visible in the presence of formulaic language (speech introductions, epithets, and repeated lines) and the picture of a society it presents—one in which traveling entertainers can be given gold for singing praise.

Although often compared to the *Iliad* as a story of heroes resigned to destruction, the *Nibelungenlied* might better be thought of as the thematic equivalent of the *Odyssey*: Both are revenge poems. In this case, it is the revenge of the woman Kriemhild for the murder of her husband Siegfried by Hagen, a vassal of Gunther, Kriemhild's brother. Siegfried's alleged insult to Brun-

hild, Gunther's wife, brings about a quarrel between sisters-in-law, and Hagen takes it on himself to save the honor of his mistress. Hagen pays for the murder of Siegfried when Kriemhild, later married to a Hun and living far away, invites her relatives to visit her, where she then has them killed by loyal troops of her husband, Etzel: The woman-in-waiting theme of the *Odyssey* is melded with the revenge-of-the-returning-hero theme.

On the level of type-scene, as well, the *Nibelungenlied* resembles the *Odyssey*. Here, oral theory might answer the objections of critics who find the continual references to clothes—the wearing and giving of them—to be a flaw in the poem. First, consideration of the heroic status symbolism involved in clothing would lessen such criticism: The *Odyssey* offers the examples of clothes as proper gifts and concerns of heroes. The bestowing of expensive woven goods is a mark of hospitality in epic; in the Greek as well as in the German poem, it marks high points in the action—the solution of conflict, the happy return or arrival of heroes. Thus, this particular custom behind the type-scene has roots in heroic society.

It has been shown above that the sacrifice type-scene became important for Homer's *Odyssey*. In the same way, the refrainlike recurrence of the clothing scenes in the *Nibelungenlied* prepares the way for a reversal of rhythms. The rules of hospitality, always adhered to in the first half of the poem (and marked by the clothing type-scenes), are subverted after the marriage of Kriemhild to the Hun, Etzel. It is not surprising that the poet made use of this repeating device to mark a change in mood; the audience would have been alert to any variations in such traditional scenes. The change is most marked when Hagen crosses the Danube with Gunther and the rest. The crossing itself, which makes clear Hagen's tragic recognition of certain death when he shatters his boat to prevent return, is curiously signaled beforehand by some water sprites whom Hagen encounters. He steals the sprites' clothing: the exact opposite of type-scene behavior up to this point. By so doing, Hagen learns his future—as in the *Odyssey*, the abnormal occurrence of the type-scene involves foreshadowing of plot events.

At the Huns' city, the growing gulf between traditional significations of clothing and the new, more menacing meanings is underscored by Hagen again. Seeing his companions dressed in their new clothes (the normal type-scene before a courtly event), Hagen reprimands them: "You want breast-plates, not silken shirts." In the remainder of the poem, the type-scenes of hospitality (of which the clothes scenes are most important) are used with ironic bitterness as negative metaphors for the entire action. "This hospitality to the guests leaves much to be desired," says Hagen as he surveys the slaughter wreaked by his hosts. Even the fiddler, the stock accompanist of hospitable entertainments, is presented here in a negative way: Volker, Hagen's companion, is both musician and warrior, and, in a horrific metaphor, he is said to have "red rosin on his bow." Once again, the metaphors find their fullest resonance precisely because the normal repetitive devices of an oral poem—here, the type-scene—have been subverted in an artful and meaningful manner.

THE SONG OF ROLAND

Nearly one hundred French *chansons de geste* (songs of heroic action) survive; the earliest among them, the twelfth century *The Song of Roland*, is also that with the most-sung theme: the defeat, through treachery, of Count Roland, nephew of Charlemagne, at Roncesvalles in the Pyrenees on August 15, 778, by a Saracen army. The poem is in four thousand ten-syllable lines, arranged in assonating groups of varying length, called *laisses*. Metrically, it is distinct, as are the other chansons, from the romance form that was composed contemporaneously. In content and viewpoint, the chanson is also distinct: While the romance tries to analyze emotions and offers fictional episodes, the chanson commemorates historical actions, from a neutral (or, at least, a third-person omniscient) point of view. As Joseph Duggan has shown, the degree of formulism in the language of *The Song of Roland* marks it as orally composed. The poem perhaps signals the end of a tradition, which must have been flourishing three hundred years before, when the events described by the poem occurred. The new type of poetry— romance—was a literary, written phenomenon, soon to become widespread, and evolving in several centuries into the modern novel. Meanwhile, the older, oral tradition must have been equally widespread in its day.

There is evidence of a Spanish equivalent to *The Song of Roland*, the thirteenth century *Cantar de Roncesvalles*. *Cantar de mío Cid* (early thirteenth century; *Chronicle of the Cid*, 1846; better known as *Poem of the Cid*), the great Castilian epic, must have grown out of a deep tradition like that behind the French poem. The transmission from performance by a *jongleur* to written text is still problematic, as is the case with other compositions of the oral style, but once again, the recognition that these poems arise from an oral heritage tends to focus attention away from criticism of the poems as allegory or psychological studies and toward the proper study of oral technique: diction, type-scene, theme, and repetition in all its forms.

The structure of *The Song of Roland* recalls once more the revenge poems. Here the revenge is dual: Charlemagne's punishment of the Saracens who have attacked the rear guard of his army on its return to France, and the later revenge of Ganelon, a Frankish peer who conspired with the Saracens to prompt the attack, in which his enemy Roland was killed. Within the framework of revenge is the description of the battle itself. In turn, this rhythmic unit is structured by smaller units—not the type-scene, but repeated triplets sharing similar diction. As in the *Odyssey* and the *Nibelungenlied*, the repeated units gain resonance as the poem progresses. Thus, in *The Song of Roland*, the use of triplets is common early in the poem for emphasis on any scenes that the poet considers to have important impact, or to be emotionally dense. The agreement between Ganelon and the Saracens, for example, is marked by a triple presentation of gifts to the Frank by the pagans' peers.

The poet can expand the use of triplets to cover wider areas in the poem; one such expansion verbally frames the kernel scene of the composition—that is, the sounding of Roland's ivory horn to summon help from the distant Charlemagne. Three times Oliver asks Roland to sound the horn, and each time Roland, in a slightly varied form, replies that the act would shame him. The hero of an oral poem, it should be noted, is more often than not bound by the very tradition that immortalizes him. Roland cites "what people will say" if he sounds the horn because of the Saracens—like Achilles or Beowulf, he must think of the fame or blame accorded him by later tradition. When the Franks fare badly in the battle, and Roland decides to sound the horn after all, the poet marks the event with a reversal of the triplet structure. This time, Roland speaks first of his resolve, then Oliver answers. Ideological positions are also reversed: Now it is Oliver who cites shame as reason for silence, Roland who seeks help. The device of repetition increases the drama of this tragic reversal; it is clear that Roland's rash arrogance has caused the defeat. When Roland finally sounds the horn, a final triplet echoes the call, describing the repeated, agonized attempt to make the sound, on Roland's part, and the repeated, disbelieving hearing on Charlemagne's. It is a stroke of poetic genius to duplicate the aural image of Roland's despair—the horn call—in an aural device, repetition; this is oral poetry using its traditional techniques to full advantage.

OTHER ISSUES

Although not discussed here, other oral traditions are rich, if not as thoroughly documented in Western literature. A fuller account of the sources and methods of oral traditional narrative poetry is needed. Even if it were to be restricted to Europe, such an account would have to examine Russian poems such as *Slovo o polku Igoreve* (c. 1187; *The Tale of the Armament of Igor*, 1915), the large field of Romance poetry other than *The Song of Roland* and the *Poem of the Cid*; and nonepic genres such as Greek and Irish praise poetry (Pindar and Bacchylides, bardic verse) and Icelandic skaldic compositions.

Of interest too is the relation between written and oral forms: It is clear that the two modes interact; it is equally certain that there is no one sure marker of oral or written style, since copying goes on from one sort to the other. However, while there has been much work done to "prove" that certain works have roots in oral traditionals, the student of modern literature would benefit most from the study of the figure of "speech" in known written literature. Repetition of words, motifs, themes—all of these in written works, such as the novel, are in fact the heritage of a "literature" that was not written but spoken to an audience that responded to such symmetries. What is the true written work—the epistolary novel? How deeply is the idea of speech and

hearing ingrained in all literature? These are questions that an interplay of oralist and modern critical methods might have a better chance to solve.

BIBLIOGRAPHY

Acker, Paul. *Revising Oral Theory: Formulaic Composition in Old English and Old Icelandic Verse*. New York: Garland, 1998. Places oral-formulaic analysis within the larger context of folklore and mythology theory, concentrating on Eddic poetry, *Beowulf*, and Old Norse rune poetry.

DuBois, Thomas A. *Lyric, Meaning, and Audience in the Oral Tradition of Northern Europe*. Notre Dame, Ind.: University of Notre Dame Press, 2006. By looking at the ways lyric songs are interpreted by various Northern European cultures, the author points out significant differences between audiences and notes the characteristics they have in common. Includes comments on lyrics within epics, religious lyrics, and the songs of Shakespeare. A unique and valuable work.

Foley, John Miles. *Homer's Traditional Art*. Philadelphia: University of Pennsylvania Press, 1999. Addresses the question of how an understanding of oral tradition can illuminate the understanding of the *Iliad* and the *Odyssey* and other ancient poetry.

_____. *The Singer of Tales in Performance*. Bloomington: Indiana University Press, 1995. Covers the theory of oral-formulaic composition and offers specific analyses of Serbian charms, Homeric hymns, and Old English poetry using the theory.

_____. *Traditional Oral Epic: The "Odyssey," "Beowulf," and the Serbo-Croatian Return Song*. Berkeley: University of California Press, 1990. A comparative study of oral techniques in Greek, Anglo-Saxon, and Yugoslavian epics.

Haymes, Edward R., and Susann T. Samples. *Heroic Legends of the North: An Introduction to the Nibelung and Dietrich Cycles*. New York: Garland, 1996. Covers the two major cycles of medieval Germanic epic poetry, with special attention to theories of oral composition.

Lönnrot, Elias. *The Kalevala: An Epic Poem After Oral Tradition by Elias Lonnrot*. Translated by Keith Bosley. New York: Oxford University Press, 2009.

A new translation of the great Finnish epic. The translator, an English poet as well as a prize-winning translator, has provided a lengthy and informative introduction.

Lord, Albert B. *The Singer of Tales*. 2d ed. Cambridge, Mass.: Harvard University Press, 2000. The classic work on Serbo-Croatian *guslars*, first published in 1960 and based on fieldwork carried out by Lord and Milman Parry, showing what illumination their techniques of oral composition can throw on the composition of the *Iliad* and the *Odyssey*.

_____. *The Singer Resumes the Tale*. Edited by Mary Louise Lord. Ithaca, N.Y.: Cornell University Press, 1995. A collection of Lord's essays, published after his death.

Palmer, R. Barton, ed. and trans. *Medieval Epic and Romance: An Anthology of English and French Narrative*. Glen Allen, Va.: College Publishing, 2007. Included in this collection are Modern English versions of the epics *Beowulf* and *The Song of Roland*, as well as a selection from Guillaume de Machaut's epic *The Taking of Alexandria*. The romances in the anthology are Chrétien de Troyes's *Yvain: Ou, Le Chevalier au lion* (c. 1170; *Yvain: Or, the Knight with the Lion*, c. 1300), translated by William W. Kibler; *Havelok*; *The Chatelaine of Ve*; and the complete *Lais* (c. 1167; *Lays of Marie de France*, 1911; better known as *The Lais of Marie de France*, 1978). Historical introduction by the author, as well as introductions to each genre. Chronology.

Parry, Adam, ed. *The Making of Homeric Verse: The Collected Papers of Milman Parry*. Reprint. New York: Oxford University Press, 1993. All of Milman Parry's important works, collected, edited, and in some cases translated by his son.

Reichl, Karl, ed. *The Oral Epic: Performance and Music*. Berlin: Verlag für Wissenschaft und Bildung, 2000. Papers presented at an international colloquium at the University of Bonn, dealing with such subjects as the words and music of Balkan and old French epics, south Slavic epics, and old Norse Eddic poetry. Bibliographical references.

Zatti, Sergio. *The Quest for Epic: From Ariosto to Tasso*. Translated by Sally Hill with Dennis Looney. Edited by Looney. Toronto: University of Toronto Press, 2006. Essays by a major Italian critic, translated for the first time into English, dealing with the development of narrative from the chivalric romance to the epic. An introduction by Albert Russell Ascoli highlights Zappi's contributions to literary criticism.

Zumthor, Paul. *Oral Poetry: An Introduction*. Translated by Kathy Murphy-Judy. Minneapolis: University of Minnesota Press, 1990. A comprehensive introduction to oral poetry, its performance contexts, composition, and evolution.

Richard Peter Martin

FRENCH POETRY TO 1700

The history of French poetry in the early centuries is in fact the history of French literature as a whole. Prose was not cultivated as a literary medium until the thirteenth century, and for centuries after that the poetic genres continued to predominate. It thus seems appropriate to begin this essay with a brief survey of the history of the French language and of the forces involved in the creation of the nation-state of France.

Before France, there was Gaul. The French language developed out of the popular form of Latin spoken in Gaul under the Roman administration, which went back to Caesar's conquest of the region in the first century B.C.E. and endured until the fifth century C.E. By the time the Western Roman Empire had succumbed to waves of barbarian immigration, this language had already developed a character of its own and could be distinguished from the "purer" Latin of the cleric, scholar, and diplomat (which was to remain the language of learning and international intercourse for many centuries—although it, too, continued to evolve). The barbarian group that assumed political leadership of Gaul in the sixth century was the Franks, and while they gave their name to the territory and the language, they introduced few changes in the latter, which they learned from the Gallo-Roman population. "French" continued to evolve quite rapidly and was the first of the Romance languages to be recorded in writing.

The oldest document in the French language, preserved in a tenth century manuscript, goes back to C.E. 842 and consists of the oaths sworn in ratification of a treaty by Charles the Bald and Louis the German, two grandsons of Charlemagne. From the late ninth or early tenth century there survives a sequence, or liturgical poem, on the martyrdom of Saint Eulalia. It is important to realize that at that time, and for many centuries thereafter, French was not a single language but a group of related dialects, divided along regional lines. By the eleventh century, these dialects could be said to fall into two broad groups, called *langue d'oc* (language of *oc*) and *langue d'oïl*, after the word for "yes" in each. The *langue d'oc*, or Occitan, as it is known to modern linguists, was spoken in the south of France and included

Provençal, the dialect of the troubadours. The *langue d'oïl* was a group of northern dialects, used by the authors of the chansons de geste. The Parisian dialect, which eventually came to dominate the others, grew in importance from the late twelfth century to the fifteenth, when it became the literary language of the country as a whole.

The first French literature of real importance appeared in the eleventh century. By that time, several institutions that were to play major roles in the development of France—and of French literature—had been established. The most important of these institutions, whose power was enhanced by their alliance, were the Roman Catholic Church and the monarchy. A brief survey of their early history seems in order here.

The Church had the deeper roots and was the stronger of the two for many centuries. The Christianization of Roman Gaul had begun as early as the first century C.E., although the new faith encountered persecution there as it did in Rome. (Saint Denis, who gave his name to the basilica where French kings were buried for twelve centuries, was an early martyr, about C.E. 250.) By about the year 400, Christianity was well established, and it was adopted, along with the vernacular, by the Germanic immigrant-invaders of the fifth century. Church organization, modeled on the Roman imperial administration, survived this turbulent period intact and remained a source of stability throughout the Dark Ages that followed.

The baptism of the Frankish chieftain Clovis in 496 created the first link between the Church and what was to become the French monarchy, for Clovis was the founder of the Merovingian Dynasty, which continued to rule the Franks until the mid-eighth century, adding Burgundy and Provence to their realm. The Carolingian Dynasty, which followed, likewise obtained the sanction and support of the Church: Pepin I, its first representative to reign, was anointed at Saint-Denis by the Pope himself, and Charlemagne, Pepin's son, was crowned Holy Roman Emperor in Rome in the year 800. Charlemagne's empire, though short-lived (it fell apart almost immediately after his death), was responsible for a brief revival of classical learning. Indeed, the renewed interest in the classical form of the Latin language at this time helped to preserve Latin as the instrument of scholarship and diplomacy for the rest of the medieval period. Another enduring legacy of the Carolingian Empire was created by the sense of heroic possibility and divine sanction, which was embodied in the figure of Charlemagne himself, who quickly assumed legendary proportions.

The ninth century saw the division of the kingdoms that were to evolve into the states of France and Germany; it also saw violent inroads by the Vikings, Muslims, and Magyars (ancestors of the Hungarians) into Western Europe. During this period of unrest, political control was often reduced to its lowest terms, which meant smaller units of organization based on land tenure and on the capacity for self-defense. When Hugh Capet, founder of the Capetian Dynasty, was anointed by the Archbishop of Reims and succeeded the last Carolingian in 987, the territory under his control amounted to roughly one-fiftieth that of modern France. The centuries to come would see a continuing struggle between kings and nobles as the former sought to increase their lands and influence at the expense of the latter. The alliance between Church and monarchy, already a firmly established historical precedent, would prove a powerful fulcrum in this struggle. The monarchy would triumph, however, only with the help of a "third estate" still to emerge: the bourgeoisie.

THE ELEVENTH CENTURY

French literature, like the literature of ancient Greece, may seem to have sprung up full-blown, for the earliest surviving works—the eleventh century chansons de geste—are epics of great power and considerable sophistication. Like the Greek epics, however, they reflect both a period of poetic development (to which they owe their form) and a sense of history—specifically, the sense of looking back to a heroic past. The poetic development is very difficult to trace because of the dearth of evidence; it seems to owe much to the Latin verse forms used in the liturgy of the Church, and it may also reflect the memories of classical (especially Vergilian) epic preserved by the more educated of the clergy, who continued to produce Latin narrative verse through-

out the medieval period. The impetus behind the flowering of the chanson de geste seems, however, to have been largely historical and to some extent religious: Its appearance coincides with the beginning of the Crusades and with the consolidation of the feudal system, both eleventh century developments. Heroic songs celebrating the exploits of Charlemagne and his vassals may well have existed in Carolingian times and in the intervening centuries, yet it was in the eleventh century that these songs came into their own, and the glimpses they give of social and political organization correspond to the conditions prevailing during that period.

The heroic songs do not have anything to say (except incidentally) about the life of the peasant class, nor indeed much about the life of women of the noble class. They reflect the point of view and interests of the feudal lords for whose entertainment and edification they were composed. They also reflect to some extent the interests and teachings of the Church, for some were written by clerics, or at least by men of some education—and at this period all education was under the aegis of the Church. As Sidney Painter has demonstrated in his 1940 book, *French Chivalry*, there were conflicts throughout the Middle Ages between the views of the clergy and those of the secular nobility concerning the duties and virtues of a "true knight." However, within certain bounds, clerical writers on chivalric conduct tended to accommodate Church teachings to the realities of feudal existence, which of necessity were dominated by the interests of the knightly class.

FEUDAL SOCIETY

The feudal system was neither created nor destroyed at a single blow; it evolved out of the confusion of the ninth and tenth centuries, reached its high-water mark in the eleventh, and declined gradually in the face of royal and bourgeois inroads over the course of the next four centuries. Because of its intimate connection with the chanson de geste and with the slightly later developments of romance and troubadour poetry, it deserves detailed consideration here.

The feudal social and political structure was based on land tenure and military might. These two factors were interdependent because of the technology of warfare: The knight needed both means and leisure to equip and train himself for combat on horseback in heavy armor. Because the economy was almost exclusively agricultural (until the twelfth century saw the revival of town life), knights depended for their income on the surplus produced by the peasants, serf or free, who tilled their lands. These lands were held as fiefs granted by the king or by one of the greater nobles in return for the knight's service in battle. Many fiefs were also held by the Church, and in early days bishops and powerful prelates were often themselves knights; a prominent literary example is Archbishop Turpin, one of the heroes of the *Chanson de Roland* (twelfth century; *The Song of Roland*, 1880). The system proved well adapted to an age in which the absence of any strong central authority left the field open for brigandage and made communication and travel difficult. Under these conditions, such control as could be exercised was usually local and based on force or the threat of force. The knight was not seen as a parasite but as a professional soldier who performed the vital service of protecting those who lived on his lands—that is, those who fed and clothed him. The lack of central authority also made him a virtual sovereign, responsible for keeping the peace, enforcing the law, and judging those who broke it within his domain.

From the perspective of the chansons de geste, the most important aspect of the feudal system is the network of relationships it fostered among the knights themselves or between the knights and their overlords. The relationship of vassalage, whereby a man vowed his allegiance and loyal service to a more powerful lord in return for a fief, had both Roman and Germanic antecedents. On the fringes of the empire, men were often given land in return for (ongoing) service in the Roman army, and the German chieftains gathered about them groups of loyal retainers, each of whom could in turn call on the freemen under his authority for help at need. Under the decentralized conditions prevailing after the breakup of Charlemagne's empire, local ties grew stronger, while allegiance to a far-off king grew tenuous. The effective control of much of France reverted to those barons, or lesser nobles, who were themselves the best fighters and could command the most loyal troops.

It is easy to see how important the friendships and

rivalries between individuals might become in such a situation. Like Homer's warriors, the knightly heroes of the chansons de geste are bound by ties of strong affection and divided by fierce hatreds; each insists on his own prerogatives and is mortally offended by slights to his honor. It is probably no coincidence that Homer's age was also one of decentralized power and of recovery following the collapse of a palace-centered economy. In medieval France as in prehistoric Greece, these conditions gave an unusually wide scope to the ambitions of individual nobles. At the same time, the awareness in each case that a previous age (the Mycenaean for Homer, the Carolingian for the eleventh century poet) had seen achievements on a grander scale focused interest on heroic stories of the past. The historic accuracy of these stories is often questionable and sometimes nonexistent; the historic interest they convey is genuine and significant.

THE SONG OF ROLAND

One of the three major cycles, or series of related chansons, deals with the court of Charlemagne and in particular with the prowess of his nephew Roland; the best known, and indeed the earliest, is the *Chanson de Roland* (twelfth century; *The Song of Roland*, 1880), which describes his last battle. As in the *Iliad* (c. 750 B.C.E.; English translation, 1611), the hero of the poem is not the commander in chief but one of his younger retainers, whose strength and daring make him more valuable in battle than men with more lands or larger contingents. The tragic plot of the poem is set in motion by the resentment and hatred of Roland's stepfather, Ganelon, whom Roland nominates for a dangerous embassy. (Roland has himself volunteered for the embassy, but Charlemagne has refused on the grounds that he is too valuable to risk.) Ganelon betrays Roland by urging the Saracens to ambush him in the Pyrenees as he commands the rear guard, covering Charlemagne's retreat from Spain. Overly confident of his own strength, Roland refuses to sound his horn (to summon help) until it is too late; at last, surrounded by dead and dying comrades, he sounds the horn, so that their deaths may be avenged, and dies extending his glove to God in an ultimate act of homage.

In a book-length study, *The Chanson de Roland* (1969), Pierre Le Gentil has shown how complex are the motives of both heroes and villains in the poem, and how subtle are the poet's means of characterization. Because of the directness of the narrative and the relative simplicity of the language, the modern reader may be tempted to dismiss it as "primitive"—from a twenty-first century perspective, the absolute antagonism of Christian and "infidel" and the notion of "holy war" do seem both primitive and alien. To appreciate the poem's complexity and coherence, one must try to approach it on its own terms, within its eleventh century feudal context.

An important element of this context which remains to be discussed is the relationship between Christianity and the code of knightly conduct. The Church consistently tried to curb the excesses to which knights were prone, condemning tournaments and private war between Christians as vainglorious and homicidal. However, war for profit (through plunder and ransom) remained a common occupation of the barons as long as the power of the king and his chief vassals was weak, while tournaments grew in popularity as the possibility of waging local wars waned. The Church did succeed in promulgating two more limited curbs on private warfare: The *Pax Dei*, or "peace of God" (late tenth century), laid a curse on those who plundered churches or the poor or harmed women or clergy, and the *Truga Dei*, or "truce of God" (eleventh century), forbade private war from Wednesday night to Monday morning and during the seasons of Christmas and Easter. Beginning in the twelfth century, ecclesiastical writers also urged the inclusion of a religious ceremony in the dubbing of new knights, to make them aware of belonging to a special "order" bound to uphold the faith (and, of course, the Church) as well as the behests of their secular lords.

The Church's greatest success, however, was in galvanizing the nobility of France for two great series of Crusades—in Spain and in Palestine—against the Islamic world. Although it is clear that the hope of profit was as important a motive in these wars as in local campaigns among rival barons, it would be as wrong to discount the religious motive as to give it sole consider-

An eighteenth century illustration from the twelfth century epic poem Chanson de Roland. *(Hulton Archive/Getty Images)*

ation. Nor should the hope of secular glory—which plays such an important part in the chansons de geste—be ignored. The truth is that in this case, religious duty and individual ambition or hopes of profit could be made to coincide. Thus, Roland's love of battle and craving for glory are justifiable when used in the service of God, and spoils taken from Saracens are not considered ill-gotten gains but rewards for upholding a sacred cause. Painter quotes an especially apt passage from the troubadour Aimeric de Pégulhan: "Without renouncing our rich garments, or station in life, courtesy, and all that pleases and charms, we can obtain honor down here and joy in Paradise." Although considerable opportunism was involved, there is no reason to read such a passage as merely cynical. The chansons de geste, no less than the Crusades, undoubtedly reflect, among other motives, a genuinely religious impulse. Like their pagan ancestors, these knights had no trouble reconciling piety and prosperity—or, as in the case of Roland, piety and glory.

EVOLUTION OF THE FEUDAL REGIME

The Crusades were only one factor, although an important one, in the prospects of the feudal class as they evolved over the course of the following centuries. In addition to carving out a Latin Kingdom of Jerusalem (whose first king, or "advocate," Godfrey of Bouillon, became the hero of several late chansons de geste), French knights led or took part in a number of foreign campaigns in the second half of the eleventh century which resulted in the creation of new fiefs and kingdoms: William of Normandy's invasion of England in 1066, Norman conquests in Sicily and southern Italy, Burgundian and Champenois inroads in Spain and Portugal. The younger sons of nobles, who had the least to gain by remaining at home, were drawn to these adventures in especially large numbers, and some slackening of feudal warfare at home ensued. During the same period, improvements in agricultural technique and equipment permitted the cultivation and resettlement of great areas within France that had lain fallow since the ninth century. This simultaneous external and internal expansion greatly increased the prosperity of France as a whole, and at first the knightly class was in a position to profit most by it. Alfred de Jeanroy, in *La Poésie lyrique des troubadours* (1934), has suggested that the resulting wealth and leisure were largely responsible for the rapid development of poetry in this period.

A further development of the age, however—the growth of a money economy—was to prove a transitory blessing to the lesser nobility, for it led, in the course of the following centuries, to a centralization of power in the hands of the king and his chief vassals, such as the dukes of Normandy and Burgundy and the counts of Flanders and Champagne. The growth of towns and the proliferation of trade fairs at first provided nobles with sources of cash in the form of rents and market tolls, but their increasing dependence on such sources of income was eventually to make them vulnerable to royal devaluations of currency (in the fourteenth and fifteenth centuries) and inflation (in the sixteenth century). Meanwhile, the greatest gains were being made by the lords whose dependencies included the largest towns, and within the towns a class was rising that would seriously undermine the financial and even the political position of the nobility. Already by the end of the twelfth century, the king and dukes of France were using armies composed largely of poorer knights, who fought not in return for land tenure but for cash. At the same time, the great lords employed townsmen—bourgeois—as overseers of their estates, while the king, mistrustful of noble ambitions, began to rely increasingly on bourgeois civil servants. The lesser nobility had had a taste of prosperity, and some were not ready to relinquish it, even if it meant abandoning their status as seigneurs and attaching themselves to the army or court of a richer lord. Thus, as Painter puts it, "the nobles of France entered on their metamorphosis into courtiers."

Prevented from waging private war, they increasingly engaged in tournaments for glory and profit, while those who had the leisure and the inclination cultivated the arts of poetry, music, and dance. The chanson de geste was not yet past its prime, but it began to face competition. At the richer courts, noble women took a more prominent social role and began to exert a distinct influence on ideals of chivalric conduct. The more powerful of these women, including Eleanor of Aquitaine and her daughter, Countess Marie of Champagne, became patrons of poets working in new lyric and narrative genres that gave a more prominent place to profane love. Originating in the south of France with the troubadours, the new theme soon spread to their northern counterparts, the trouvères; meanwhile, the "matter of France" (the Carolingian cycle) was gradually supplanted by the "matter of Britain" (tales of Arthur and his knights) and the "matter of Rome" (tales from classical mythology) as sources of plots for narrative verse. Thus, the chanson de geste was finally eclipsed by the roman (romance).

THE ROLE OF THE CHURCH

The twelfth and thirteenth centuries saw the highwater mark of the Church's independence and secular power, as well as of its hold on the intellectual life of France. Its independence was the result of a papal effort, begun in the eleventh century, to wrest control of clerical appointments from the nobility and kings of Europe, who had come to consider bishoprics and monastic offices as political plums—a means of rewarding and enriching their favorites. Using the powerful threat of excommunication, popes and their legates had insisted on the right of monks to elect their abbots and of canons (clergy attached to a cathedral) to elect their bishops. Most Church property was also freed from feudal dues and appropriation. The new abbots and bishops were often men of integrity and considerable learning. In the eleventh and early twelfth centuries, the monastic orders of Cluny and Cîteaux took a leading role in the reform, and their efforts were largely responsible for the surge of church building known today as Romanesque.

During the course of the twelfth century, as towns grew in size and importance, leadership passed to the canons and bishops, and the Gothic phase of church building was focused on the cathedral. Episcopal schools also eclipsed the monasteries as centers of learning and became the seedbeds of what has been called the "twelfth century renaissance." In Chartres and Paris especially, there was a revival of classical learning and a spurt of literary activity in Latin, which remained the language of the schools (as the name of Paris's Latin Quarter recalls). An especially important development was the renewed interest in logic and dialectic as keys to learning. Thanks to contacts with Byzantium and with the Arabs, ancient texts that had been lost to the West were rediscovered, and an interest in Aristotle, the great logician, was stimulated by the commentaries of Islamic scholars. Logic was applied even to the "mistress of the sciences," theology, by Pierre Abélard and his students. Despite the fierce reaction this generated (under the leadership of the stern but charismatic Bernard of Clairvaux), the new schools continued to grow and to attract students from all over Europe; by the thirteenth century, Paris had become the intellectual capital of the West. (The Sorbonne, the first college of the University of Paris to be endowed, was founded in 1257.)

The thirteenth century was also the century of Saint Thomas Aquinas, and it saw the triumph of Scholasticism, a system of philosophy and theology that forged a synthesis of ancient (Aristotelian) and Christian learning. It was chiefly through the cathedral schools and universities that the vernacular literature of France was enriched by contact with the classical legacy of dramatic, lyric, and epic poetry. The tradition of Latin didactic verse, which had been maintained throughout the Middle Ages by such clerics as had any learning, also flowed into the vernacular mainstream at this time, inspiring historical chronicles and other didactic works, at first in verse and then in prose.

LYRIC POETRY

The first real flowering of lyric—as opposed to narrative or liturgical—poetry in France took place early in the twelfth century, in the southern regions of Aquitaine and Provence. This poetry was written not in the *langue d'oïl*—the language of the chanson de geste and the parent stock of modern French—but in the *langue d'oc*, often referred to as Provençal (something of a misnomer, since Provençal was only one of four dialects involved). It deserves more than a passing mention in the history of French poetry, and indeed in that of European poetry as a whole, for its influence on later poets was profound. This is especially true of its major theme—courtly love—but the complexity of its form was also admired and emulated for centuries, especially in France.

The south was at this period the most cosmopolitan region of France, thanks to its coastal towns, which carried on a growing trade with Italy, Spain, and the Middle East. The debt of troubadour poetry to Arabic forms of lyric is still a matter of some debate. It seems clear that there was at least some influence, traceable to contacts between the Occitan (southern French) and Islamic cultures in the course of the Spanish Crusades. In particular, the form known as the *zadjal* may have suggested the intricacy of verse forms and the theme of refined love characteristic of the troubadour lyrics. The influence of contemporary Latin verse, especially hymns, has also been demonstrated. Whatever its sources, this sudden flowering owed much to the newfound wealth and leisure of the nobles of Aquitaine and Provence in the early twelfth century; the first known troubadour was in fact the powerful duke of Aquitaine, Guillaume IX (grandfather of Eleanor), and nearly all troubadours were of the noble class. Indeed, the decline of troubadour poetry—and of the *langue d'oc* as a literary language—may well be linked to the so-called Albigensian Crusade of the early thirteenth century, which in suppressing the Catharist or Albigensian heresy destroyed many of the noble families of southern France.

Troubadour poetry—all of which was written to be sung, either by the *trobador* (poet) himself or by a *jonglar* (French *jongleur*, professional singer)—comprises a number of distinct genres, each with its characteristic form, vocabulary, and themes. Thus, for example, the *planh* laments the death of a noble knight (usually the poet's lord); the *sirventes* explores a political or moral issue (such as prospects for war or peace, or the virtues and vices of different groups—young and old, Italian and German); the *tenson* takes the form of a debate in which opposing views are presented in alternating stanzas. By far the most popular forms, however, were those devoted to the theme of love, such as the *alba* (the lovers' parting at dawn) and the *canso d'amor* (love song). Indeed, even the *tenson* was often devoted to the fine points of courtship. Within an amazingly short time, a highly elaborate system of conventions evolved, and the elaboration was deliberate and self-conscious. It suited both the courtly milieu in which the troubadours moved and their necessarily indirect praise of a passion that was often adulterous.

A key metaphor in this system of conventions was feudal: The knight vowed homage and service to the lady of his heart, as to his liege lord, and (at least in the earlier poems) he often had some hope of recompense—if not in the form of sexual favors, then at least in the form of smiles, looks, kind words, or other "platonic" tokens of affection. A common complaint is that the lady is cruel or haughty and will not respond, although the lover's happiness—indeed, his very existence—depends on her. Sometimes it emerges that she is not unmoved but must feign indifference to protect her reputation or deflect her husband's jealousy, for the nature of this courtly or refined love (*fin' amor*) is such that it is rarely compatible with marriage—an institution more often used to further economic or political

ends than to gratify the desires of individual men and women.

Women in particular were rarely consulted about their destined marriage partners, and it is easy to understand their craving, as increased prosperity gave them leisure to imagine such things, for the attentions of men who were attracted not to their houses and lands but to their persons and sensibilities. Although by far the greater number of troubadours were men (there were a few women), noble women seem to have played a considerable part in elaborating the ethic of courtly love; at the very least, they must have come to see themselves as worthy of gentle treatment and long courtship, withholding their favors from men who did not approach them with the proper deference.

As Frederick Goldin has indicated in his anthology *Lyrics of the Troubadours and Trouvères* (1973), adherence to the new ethic very soon became a condition of acceptance into the exclusive circles where it prevailed. The result was a new definition of the man of worth. In addition to noble birth and prowess in battle, he was to demonstrate the courtly qualities of fair speech, good manners, and a certain delicacy of feeling; above all, he was to find in love the source and focus of the knightly virtues. One of the fullest expositions of this new code is the *De amore* of André le Chapelain. A Latin prose treatise of the twelfth century, the *De amore* was translated into French in the thirteenth century and later into Italian and German; its author, a northerner (probably a protégé of Marie of Champagne), was one of the men responsible for the diffusion of courtly ideals among writers in the *langue d'oïl*. Needless to say, there were many discrepancies between the ideal and the reality, but the troubadours themselves were the first to acknowledge that, adopting an array of poetic voices—from the resigned "platonic" lover to the coarse womanizer—and playing them off against one another, sometimes within a single poem.

Efforts have sporadically been made to associate the troubadour ethic with the so-called Catharist heresy, the violent suppression of which in 1209 decimated the southern nobility and broke up the courts that had bred and sustained the troubadours. Among the attributes of the poetry that suggest such a connection are its hermetic style (*trobar clus*), which permitted the expression, in a kind of literary code, of ideas and feelings the "vulgar" were not to share, and the quasi-mystical attitude taken by some troubadours toward their ladies. (Women could attain to the highest positions within the Catharist sect and could be counted among "the Perfect," who were considered living saints.) It is difficult, however, to reconcile the often frankly erotic content of troubadour verse with the ascetic practices of the Cathars ("the pure").

The heresy was able to gain ground because, despite the twelfth century reforms, the Church was still a secular power, with all the abuses of its own doctrines that fact entailed. The Cathars, by contrast, preached a return to the austerity, simplicity, and charismatic fervor of early Christianity. The sect earned the respect of the peasants, but most of its adherents were of the noble and bourgeois classes. The Church could not ignore such a powerful challenge to its authority, and when attempts at conversion failed, Pope Innocent III ordered the Cistercians to preach a crusade against the sect. Most of the nobles of northern France took part, spurred by regional antagonisms and hopes of gain as well as by religious promptings. (Many southern nobles were in fact dispossessed of their lands.) The bloodshed was fearful, and the victims included many women and children. In addition, libraries were destroyed, a fact that may account for the dearth of surviving chansons de geste in the Occitan dialects.

The troubadour poems survived because they were esteemed and emulated (and thus recopied) in Italy and in the north of France. In this way, they became the antecedents of the *stil nuovo* or "new style" of Dante and his contemporaries, as well as of the lyrics of the French trouvères and the German *Minnesänger*. The trouvères in particular took over much of the original system of "courtly" images, themes, and forms, although they were less given to the Hermetic style. As Frederick Goldin has shown, they also abandoned the troubadour's lively attention to his courtly audience, concentrating instead on the inner experience of the lover and "the possibilities of figurative language"—extended metaphor and simile. Finally, they enriched the repertoire of lyric forms by borrowing from folk song such genres as the *chanson de toile* (sewing song) and by re-

viving the classical taste for bucolic poetry (thus, the genre called the *pastourelle* portrayed knights wooing shepherdesses).

THE ROMANCE

In the mid-twelfth century, a new genre of narrative verse appeared which absorbed the courtly love ethic and fused it with plot material unknown in the chanson de geste. This was the romance. The chansons de geste did not disappear but were forced instead to yield first place in popularity to the new genre, which seems to have been inspired by the rediscovery of Roman epic (Vergil, Statius) and Greek romance (in Latin retellings). Another prominent influence was that of Ovid, whose interest in love and in the psychological states of his characters struck a chord in the courtly circles where romance took root. As in the chansons de geste, historical accuracy is not a matter of much concern; thus, one of the most famous romances, the twelfth century *Roman d'Alixandre* (from which the twelve-syllable line, or Alexandrine, may take its name) portrays Alexander the Great as a typical twelfth century knight, who holds tournaments and adheres to the chivalric code. Despite such contemporary elements, the world of the romances is largely a never-never land, a fabulous past in which magical powers operate and the courtly ideal is incarnated in "perfect knights." This is true not only of the classically inspired romances but also of the Arthurian group, the plots of which, borrowed from Celtic legend, probably entered French literature by way of the Anglo-Norman court of the Plantagenets (where, it should not be forgotten, Eleanor of Aquitaine reigned as queen during the second half of the twelfth century).

In the greatest romances, the flight from reality characteristic of the genre is mitigated by an interest in psychology—especially that of love—and by an exploration of real contradictions within the chivalric ethic. The work of Chrétien de Troyes (1150-1190) is outstanding in these respects. His romance *Érec et Énide* (c. 1164; *Eric and Enid*, 1913) probes the conflict between the demands of prowess and courtly love: Erec is distracted from knightly pursuits by his love for his young wife, and he tries to right the balance by forcing her to follow him—without speaking—as he goes in search of adventure. *Cligès: Ou, La Fausse Morte* (c. 1164; *Cligès: A Romance*, 1912) examines the quandary of a woman who is betrothed to a man she does not love and who has vowed fidelity to another. (Although a magic potion helps her keep her vow and evade her husband, her dilemma—and her husband's fierce jealousy—are unmistakably real.) *Lancelot: Ou, Le Chevalierà la charrette* (c. 1168; *Lancelot: Or, The Knight of the Cart*, 1990), Chrétien's treatment of the Lancelot story, offers the most extreme version of the knight's "love service" to his lady and the frankest endorsement of adultery. It is interesting that Chrétien takes pains in his prologue to explain that his patroness, Marie de Champagne, suggested the story and the theme: It was at her command he says, that he undertook the work.

Finally, Chrétien's last (and unfinished) romance, *Perceval: Ou, Le Conte du Graal* (c. 1180; *Perceval: Or, The Story of the Grail*, 1983), undertaken for a later patron, Philip of Flanders, describes the process by which an untutored boy becomes one of Arthur's greatest knights. Despite its fairy-tale quality, the story deals realistically with the pains and pleasures of growing up, as Perceval struggles to assimilate the courtly ethic and reconcile it with his duties as a Christian. (The legend of the Grail quest, which appears in *Perceval* and other early French romances, was reworked by Wolfram von Eschenbach, the German *Minnesänger*—who in turn inspired Richard Wagner's *Parsifal*, 1882—and by English writers in verse and prose, of whom the last and best known was Sir Thomas Malory.)

THE ROMANCE OF THE ROSE

The romance continued to enjoy unabated popularity for centuries, but as early as the thirteenth century it began to be recast in prose, which would thenceforth eclipse verse as a medium for narrative. One of the last great verse romances, *Le Roman de la rose* (*The Romance of the Rose*, partial translation c. 1370, complete translation 1900), was composed in two sections from 1230 to 1240 (by Guillaume de Lorris) and from 1275 to 1280 (by Jean de Meung). It has been called "the most popular single work of the thirteenth century and perhaps of the whole medieval period" by Geoffrey Brereton in *A Short History of French Literature* (1954). It was also destined to enjoy great influence

with the French poets of the sixteenth century. Its popularity seems to have resulted from the success with which it combined the dominant themes and interests of its age: the courtly, the didactic, and the satiric. The first of its two authors was of noble birth, the second bourgeois, and their attitudes toward their subject—the allegorical struggle of a lover to obtain the Rose of his desire—are antipathetic in several ways, yet complementary. Guillaume de Lorris, the greater poet of the two, is a faithful spokesperson for the courtly tradition, which he sums up with exquisite grace and psychological subtlety. Jean de Meung, a product of the University of Paris and its Scholastic learning, is a rationalist who looks on love somewhat cynically and indeed seeks to undermine, through satire, the courtly conventions and the supremacy of the class that produced them.

COMIC AND SATIRIC POETRY

Virtually all the works discussed thus far, with the exception of the second part of *The Romance of the Rose*, were written by and for the members of the noble class; similarly, nearly all the characters portrayed in them are noble. The fabliaux, short narrative poems written in the meter proper to romance (octosyllabic rhyming couplets), offer a different view of thirteenth century society, one that includes bourgeoisie, peasants, and the lower clergy as well as knights and ladies. Some of the fabliaux are known to have been the work of nobles and wellborn clerics, and the genre undoubtedly had a place in courtly circles as a kind of comic foil to romance. However, it was also used by the *jongleurs* and by the *goliards* (poor students, usually clerics), who tended to live from hand to mouth and were seldom of noble birth.

As the bourgeois class grew and prospered, it, too, sought the entertainment these itinerant singers had to offer, and found it in the down-to-earth fabliaux. Although the genre encompasses a wide variety of subjects, fabliaux may be distinguished from other short narrative genres, such as the courtly *lai*, pious *miracle*, and polemical *dit*, by their comic tone and ordinary, everyday setting. Although a good number end with a moral, the real focus of interest is usually the tale itself. Sometimes the moral is frankly ironic. In *De Brunain et de Blérain* (thirteenth century), a peasant and his wife give their cow to the local priest, who has assured them that God returns twofold what is offered him; when the cow breaks free and returns home leading the priest's cow, with which it has been tethered, the peasant is overjoyed and believes God has kept his promise. The poet closes with the moral the priest had preached—"He is rich who gives to God, not he who hides and buries [his goods]"—but its religious meaning, discounted by the story, is replaced by a worldly one: Nothing ventured, nothing gained. Although a satiric vein is often visible in the fabliaux, as a group they neither spare nor single out any one class. Covetous priests, arrogant nobles, credulous peasants, and grasping bourgeoisie are all portrayed; the joke may be on any or all of them, depending, presumably, on the sympathies of the poet and of his audience.

ROMAN DE RENART

The thirteenth century likewise saw the creation of longer and more directly satiric poems inspired by the various serious genres and by indignation at specific social abuses. Thus, the *Bible Guyot* (1205-1218), written by a monk, details the abuses of the clergy, while the mock-epic *Audigier*, in rebuttal of the romances and *chansons de geste*, portrays the nobility as cowardly and coarse. The most successful of all of these attempts, however, was the *Roman de Renart* (c. 1175-1205; *The Most Delightful History of Reynard the Fox*, 1681; most commonly known as *Roman de Renart*), which grew from an initial long poem into a vast cycle—indeed, into a veritable genre. Its oldest "branches," as they are called, were probably inspired by medieval Latin versions of the beast fable, a genre ultimately traceable to Aesop's fables (sixth century B.C.E.) but, as the shadowy figure of Aesop himself should indicate, owing much to folktale and thus susceptible to additions and reshapings from popular as well as literary sources.

The various poems of the cycle have in common a wily and unscrupulous hero, Renart the fox—usually known as Reynard in English—whose ability to outwit his "betters" (including not only Ysengrim the wolf and Brun the bear but also King Noble the lion) suggested very early, if not from the beginning, a social satire in which the lower orders manage to get the better of their oppressors among the nobility and clergy. It is worth noting that the genre enjoyed its greatest popularity in the northeastern regions of Picardy and Flanders, where the bourgeois class was particularly strong and conscious of its rising economic power. However, Renart is not a comfortable hero, and in one poem, *Le Couronnement Renart* (coronation of Renart), written about 1250, he actually obtains the crown—only to favor the rich while continuing to oppress the poor. In later branches, as in *The Romance of the Rose*, the stories are increasingly allegorical and didactic, becoming almost encyclopedic in scope; at the same time, political and social criticism is less veiled, and *Renart le Contrefait* (fourteenth century; the title suggests both "Renart the Misshapen" and "Renart the Dissembler") has been seen as a foreshadowing of the Jacquerie, a fourteenth century peasant uprising.

THE FOURTEENTH AND FIFTEENTH CENTURIES

By the early fourteenth century, a series of strong Capetian monarchs had succeeded in extending the royal domain—the portion of French territory not held as fiefs but administered directly by the king—until it included almost three-fourths of the entire realm. With the help of the Church, which upheld the monarchy's "divine right" to rule, of the legal profession, which consolidated their power on the basis of Roman legal precedent, and of the bourgeoisie, who manned their civil service and whose growing wealth filled their coffers with tax revenues, the Capetians made themselves the most powerful monarchs of Europe. The apex of their fortunes was reached under Philippe le Bel (Philip the Fair, thanks to his good looks), who dared to defy the Pope—and carried the day.

The struggle began in 1296, when Boniface VIII declared that Philip had no right to tax the clergy without papal consent, and ended in 1303, when the aging Pope died, reputedly of shock, after being held under arrest by Philip's agents on charges that included heresy. The king's diplomatic maneuvers next secured the appointment of a French pope, Clement V, who actually transferred the papal court to Avignon in Provence, from which his French successors continued to reign until 1377. A number of important institutions of government were also established or strengthened during this period. Philip was the first French king to convene a meeting of the Estates General, made up of representatives of the country's three "estates," or classes: clergy, nobility, and bourgeoisie (referred to as the "third estate"). The first meeting, in 1302, was designed to align the nation solidly behind Philip in his struggle with the pope. Later meetings were usually convened to raise general taxes, for which the king had to obtain the consent of feudal lords and independent towns; through its control of taxation, the Estates General wielded considerable power in the fourteenth century and during the Hundred Years' War. Although it lost this power to the monarchy in the late fifteenth century, the precedent had been set for a governing body that was to include representatives of the nation as a whole. Finally, Philip IV enhanced the authority of the Parlement of Paris (a court of justice, not a parliament in the British sense), to the detriment of the nobility, who lost many of their judicial rights; by the fifteenth century, it had become independent even of the king, over whose legislation it held de facto power of judicial review.

At the accession in 1328 of Philip VI, the first king of the Valois line, the monarchy seemed stable and powerful; the kingdom was prosperous, and even the peasantry seem to have been feeling the good effects of two centuries of economic growth. In the course of the next two centuries, however, France was to be ravaged by the long, cruel conflict known as the Hundred Years' War. The steady concentration of power in the hands of the monarchy would be interrupted, to the temporary advantage of the feudal class. At the same time, the self-esteem of the French as a people would be shaken, a deep hatred of the English would be sown among them, and the costs of war, in lives and in resources, would prove staggering.

None of this was apparent until the war was well under way. The source of conflict was the issue of the French royal succession after the Capetian line ran out. After initially acknowledging Philip of Valois (a first cousin of the last Capetian king, Charles IV), Edward III of England decided to press his claim (through his mother, Isabel, Charles IV's sister) to the throne of France. As duke of Aquitaine and Guyenne—which Eleanor had brought as a dowry to Henry II—Edward Plantagenet was a vassal of the French crown; the encroachments of the French monarchy on feudal privi-

leges made some sort of confrontation between the two kings inevitable. At this date, Anglo-Norman, a dialect of the *langue d'oïl*, was still spoken by the ruling class of England, who shared a common culture with the nobility of France. Edward thus had no trouble picturing himself as king of France; he had everything to gain and relatively little to lose by the attempt. In the event, his success surprised even him. Although France was the richer kingdom, its army—composed of heavily armored knights—proved inferior to the English, whose longbows were able to pierce armor while permitting greater mobility. The battles of Crécy and Poitiers, in 1346 and 1356 respectively, were not only military victories for the English but also severe blows to the prestige and chivalric ideology of the French nobility.

A more serious blow to the French cause was the capture of Philip IV's successor, King John, who had to be ransomed at incredible cost. A striking proof that the chivalric code still had substance at this period is the fact that when one of John's sons, who had been sent to England as hostage pending full payment of his father's ransom, broke his word and escaped, John himself returned voluntarily to London. The Treaty of Calais (1360) gave the French a breathing space, and John's canny successor, Charles V, who renewed the conflict, might have driven the English from France had he lived; he died however, at the age of forty-three, leaving a twelve-year-old son, Charles VI, who went mad in his early twenties and became a puppet of his unscrupulous and ambitious uncles. The latter took advantage of the king's weakness to extend their own power, and a feudal order reemerged in which chronic struggles among the French lords themselves further bled the country.

The vigorous Henry V of England, capitalizing on this state of affairs, allied himself with the dukes of Burgundy and made deep inroads into France between 1415 (the date of the Battle of Agincourt) and 1429, when the tide was finally turned by Joan of Arc, who believed she had been called by God to cast the English out of France. Although she was captured by the Burgundians in 1430 and burned by the English as a witch in 1431, her military victories, and chiefly the coronation of Charles VII, which she brought about, restored French morale. By 1436, Charles was able to reenter

Paris, which the English and Burgundians had occupied since 1418. The country was so exhausted by the long struggle that it took until 1450 to expel the English from Normandy and until 1453 to take Guyenne, their last stronghold. (Only Calais, on the Channel opposite Dover, remained in English hands.)

Despite their ultimate victory, the French suffered far more in the war than did their enemies, many of whom were enriched by the spoils they took and whose prestige as a nation waxed as that of France waned. The war was fought almost exclusively on French soil, and the civilian population was subjected to plundering by French as well as English soldiers. The war likewise interfered with the cultivation of crops and the distribution of food, so that famine was widespread. Still more victims were claimed by the Black Death, or bubonic plague, which reached France in 1348 and 1349, recurring, less severely, in 1361. The disease is believed to have killed about a third of the population of Europe, including half the inhabitants of Paris (fifty thousand people) and thousands more throughout France. The death toll was undoubtedly increased by ignorance of the process of contagion; the same ignorance, in the face of such devastation, fostered the conviction that God had chosen this means to punish his people for their sins. Many believed the end of the world was near. That the plague was no respecter of persons and did not respond to collective acts of penitence struck terror in the believers; the varied responses included fanatical outbreaks of anti-Semitism, attempts to legislate morality, and discontent with the clergy, some of whom avoided ministering to the dying for fear of catching the disease. Although there were upsurges of piety, so that the Church was enriched by bequests, it was seen as having failed to mitigate or even to explain the suffering.

For other reasons as well, the moral authority of the Church declined steadily in the course of the fourteenth century. Corruption was perhaps the greatest single factor: The hierarchy resorted increasingly to simony (the sale of Church pardons, appointments, and dispensations) to satisfy its taste for luxury. At the papal court in Avignon—which Petrarch, writing in the 1340's, called "the Babylon of the West"—cardinals and prelates vied with one another in extravagance of dress;

many had private palaces and mistresses. The Avignon "captivity" of the Papacy, which lasted until 1377, was immediately followed by the Great Schism (1378-1417), during which two and even three rival popes simultaneously laid claim to the office. Still, the hold of Catholicism was not easily shaken. It continued to provide the terms in which most men understood their existence and the rituals with which they faced life's crucial moments. Like the idea of chivalry and the prestige of the knightly class, the moral ascendancy of the Church and the prestige of the clergy were undermined by events of the fourteenth and fifteenth centuries, but they did not collapse. Indeed, as Johan Huizinga argued in his important book *The Waning of the Middle Ages* (1924), the pomp of Church and court and the elaborate distinctions of rank observed by both may well have been alternatives to, or forms of compensation for, the widespread pessimism of the age. It was not an age of reform, and in that respect it was, as Huizinga saw, a prolongation of the Middle Ages.

EVOLUTION OF LITERARY FORMS

The art and poetry of the fourteenth and fifteenth centuries reflect a similar tendency to elaborate old forms and themes rather than to seek new ones. In architecture and sculpture, the "flamboyant" style (so named for the flame-like motif it favored) was an outgrowth of the Gothic. In literature, the romance and even the chanson de geste were still in vogue, while the heirs of the trouvères continued to celebrate courtly love in intricate lyric measures. However, new trends were visible as well. Poetry no longer held a monopoly of the literary genres; narratives, including romances and historical chronicles, began increasingly to be written in prose. At the same time, while many poets still wrote works intended to be sung, lyric poetry began to disengage itself from song, as narrative poetry had done at the appearance of the romance. Finally, lyric poetry made room for a certain realism, inspired by the harsh conditions of the age. The supreme poetic achievement of the age is that of François Villon, who combined his contemporaries' attention to form with his own uniquely realistic perspective on the ills—and the sins—of his generation.

In the fourteenth century, the repertoire of lyric

forms inherited from the trouvères was enriched by the ballade (not to be confused with the English ballad), the rondeau, and other fixed forms that were to predominate for several centuries. In contrast to the sonnet, a highly versatile form developed in Italy at this period (but which would not enter French literature until the sixteenth century), these forms were both complex and rigid. To borrow a comparison from Geoffrey Brereton,

> the composer of the shortest *ballade* has to find fourteen similar rhymes of one sort, six of another, and five of another—besides working in an identical line four times. The sonneteer needs a maximum of only four rhymes of the same sort and he does not have to repeat any of his lines.

It was inevitable that such forms should suggest a certain artificiality, especially in the hands of their less skillful practitioners. However, some skill in poetry was evidently expected of the average "gentleman," as in Elizabethan England, and a collection of one hundred ballades by various hands (none of them professional) attests a fairly high standard of competence.

There were also more or less professional poets attached to the courts of princes; thus, Guillaume de Machault (c. 1300-1377) was chaplain, secretary, and court poet to John, king of Bohemia, while Eustache Deschamps (c. 1346-1406) served at the courts of Charles V and of his son Louis, duke of Orléans. Jean Froissart was a protégé of Philippa of Hainault, the queen of Edward III of England; he is best known for his prose *Chroniques* (late 1300's; *Chronicles*, 1523-1525) of contemporary history, but he wrote lyric poetry as well. One of the most popular poems of the age, *La Belle Dame sans merci* (1424), was the work of Alain Chartier, secretary to Charles VI and historiographer of Charles VII. Although none of these men was of noble birth, they fully espoused and promoted the chivalric ideology still prevailing in the noble circles in which they moved. The same is true of Christine de Pizan, one of the first professional women of letters, who sought the patronage of various nobles in order to support her three children (she was widowed as a young woman). It is interesting that while these writers made autobiographical allusions in their prose works, most of them clung to conventional courtly themes—the lovers' debate, the allegorical journey—and put relatively little of their personal experience into their poetry.

CHARLES D'ORLÉANS

The same may be said of the most talented of them, who happened also to be the highest-born: Charles d'Orléans (1391-1465), a nephew of Charles VI and father of Louis XII. Taken prisoner at the Battle of Agincourt, he spent twenty-five years in England because his family could not afford the ransom demanded. Thanks to his rank, he was not harshly treated, and he took advantage of his enforced leisure to cultivate his talents as a poet. Although he used the same rigid forms as his contemporaries, his verse is distinguished by an impression of spontaneity—which is the result, however, of a thorough mastery of his medium. With Charles d'Orléans, the medieval taste for allegory finds a culminating expression (his earliest poem is a kind of *The Romance of the Rose* in miniature) and at the same time begins to shift toward true metaphor. It seems fitting that the last great representative of the courtly tradition should have been—like the first, Guillaume IX, the troubadour—a *grand seigneur*, a high-ranking member of the class that tradition had celebrated.

FRANÇOIS VILLON

François Villon (1431-1463?), the other great poet of the fifteenth century and one of the greatest of all time, offers a striking contrast in every respect to his noble contemporary, whose court at Blois he seems to have visited. A poor boy, son of an illiterate mother (for whom he wrote a moving prayer to the Virgin), Villon was educated at the University of Paris, thanks to a priest who became his benefactor. He might have made a career in the Church but instead was drawn to the headier, if more dangerous, life of the tavern and the street. He was tried for various crimes, ranging from murder to church robbery, and was certainly guilty of some of them. Banished from Paris in 1458, he wandered about the country and may have belonged—as did two of his friends—to a gang of thieves. Certainly, he saw the miseries of the age at first hand, and he describes them in vivid detail, from the point of view of the poorest classes. Although he used the poetic forms current in his day and made no technical innovations, his subject matter and tone are strikingly new. There were precedents for confessional poetry in the thirteenth century works of Ruteboeuf (a poor student and defrocked cleric), Jean Bodel, and Adam de la Halle; the latter two wrote *congés* (leave-takings) that seem to look ahead to Villon's *Le Grand Testament* (wr. 1461, pb. 1489; *The Great Testament*, 1878). Villon's entire oeuvre, however, is infused with the confessional impulse.

It is especially revealing to compare Villon's entry in a poetic contest sponsored by Charles d'Orléans with Charles's own entry. The theme assigned to all, "I die of thirst beside the fountain," suggested to Charles the unreliability of Fortune, who leads him in good times and in bad, yet the terms of his complaint are general and his tone even, although melancholy. The one specific reference, to "the fire of lovers," even makes it possible to read the poem as a conventional lover's complaint, although this theme is not developed and a broader interpretation seems preferable. To Villon, however, the paradox of want in the midst of plenty immediately suggests his own precarious existence; as his refrain stresses, he is "bien recuilly, debouté de chascun" ("welcomed and rebuffed by everyone"). It has been suggested that the envoi, or closing stanza, addressed by convention to an unspecified "prince," is in fact an oblique appeal to Charles for support. In any case, the urgency of Villon's tone is unmistakable; he brings a new subject matter to the courtly form, to powerful effect. Of all the poets considered thus far, Villon offers the most immediate and compelling look at his own world. His poems capture the brutality and pessimism of the age that produced the *danse macabre* (a common motif in the visual arts—a procession containing people of all classes, being led away by Death, a grinning skeleton). However, Villon also sees, and makes his readers see, the humor and the faith that made it possible to survive in that world.

THE SIXTEENTH CENTURY

The sixteenth century in France was dominated by two related movements best known to twentieth century readers as the Renaissance and the Reformation. Both were made up of smaller and disparate movements, yet while it is important to acknowledge the diversity this implies, the labels have stuck because they point to consistent trends amid the diversity. The century was characterized by a revival of interest in forms of art and learning stemming from classical models, and it saw the appearance of "reformed" Christian churches whose definitive rejection of Roman Catholicism led to long and bloody struggles. Both movements affected the whole of Europe, and neither began in France. It makes sense to speak of a French form of each, however—particularly since the sixteenth century saw the first appearance of strong national feeling among the French. Although this feeling would be seriously threatened by the religious wars of the second half of the century, it would reemerge upon the accession of Henry IV, the first of the line of Bourbon kings.

The Renaissance or "rebirth" of arts and letters had economic underpinnings: It was made possible by a gradual recovery (after the Hundred Years' War), followed by a boom in trade that favored French merchants and artisans because they were in a position to provide the finished goods Europe was seeking. Spain had silver and gold from her New World colonies but wanted cloth, leather, tools, and even food (Spanish agriculture as well lagged behind that of the French). All of these commodities the French had for sale. This was the era in which the modern form of capitalism can be said to have made its appearance, as the merchant class assumed the upper hand in the disposition of the country's wealth: The nobles spent money lavishly, but the bourgeoisie loaned and invested—and earned. Since the reign of Louis XI (1461-1483), who had picked up (or stolen or bought back) the pieces of his realm after the Hundred Years' War, the bourgeoisie had also provided the backbone of the royal administration. The noble class might live extravagantly—indeed, were expected to do so—and win glory in foreign campaigns, but they were chronically in debt and thus dependent on both the bourgeoisie (the moneylenders) and the king (the dispenser of offices and pensions). Meanwhile, a new order of nobility—the *noblesse de robe*, so called because they held judgeships—was being culled from the ranks of the bourgeoisie by kings anxious to reward their faithful officers and to win allies among this newly powerful class. Although social distinctions were carefully maintained between the *noblesse de robe* and *noblesse de sang* (the hereditary nobility), the former imitated the latter as much as they could, and often lived more sumptuously, as did many of the *grands bourgeois*.

Despite these far-reaching changes in economic and social organization, French kings continued to rule by "divine right" and to have the final word in most policy decisions, especially those regarding foreign policy. Indeed, thanks to increased control over the debt-ridden nobility and the rising bourgeoisie, the power of the monarchy was more far-reaching than ever before, to the point that the term "absolute" is often applied to the monarchy of this and the following two centuries. The concordat, or agreement with the pope, of 1516 increased royal power and finances further by making the king the de facto head of the Church in France, with authority to name successors to all major ecclesiastical posts. Because of the concordat, French kings were not tempted to use the stirrings of religious reform as an excuse to break with Rome, as did Henry VIII of England. The early years of the century were thus years of relative tolerance, in which religious questioning was but one symptom of the new approach to intellectual inquiry.

A combination of surplus wealth, absolute control of foreign policy, and old chivalric ideas permitted three French kings in succession to invade Italy in the late fifteenth and early sixteenth centuries. Although their territorial gains were short-lived and costly, they brought back with them to France a passion for the way of life they had tasted in Italy and a determination to transplant it to their native soil. They and their officers patronized artists such as Raphael, Michelangelo, and Leonardo da Vinci (the latter died at Francis I's château of Amboise); they built new, airy palaces and decorated them in a style inspired by that of Renaissance Italy, then in its culminating phase. Above all, they collected books and manuscripts and patronized scholars who had rediscovered the learning of the ancient world. Nor was it a simple matter of recovering lost texts and cultivating skills that had waned (such as the knowledge of classical Greek); the old texts were read in a new spirit.

In the first place, an avid intellectual curiosity was fed by new admiration for the powers of the human mind. The work of establishing accurate texts and translations called for critical acumen and self-confidence; instead of resorting to unquestioned authorities, scholars such as Guillaume Budé and Lefèvre d'Étaples produced their own commentaries. They also tended to focus their studies on humanity rather than on God—but this does not mean that they were irreligious. Although most of them criticized the temporal abuses of the Church, only a few took the further step of rejecting its authority in spiritual matters. While marveling at the purely human virtues they saw in the old pagan authors, they also re-edited the Bible and translated it into French; the study of Hebrew was revived along with that of Greek. Moreover, when the first printing presses appeared in France in the late fifteenth century, the majority of works published were not the classics but missals and other devotional books.

As Lucien Fèbvre emphasized in his influential essays on Renaissance France, printing was from the first a business, requiring considerable capital and hinging on possibilities of profit. The classics were printed later, and in smaller quantities, because they appealed to a smaller public, clustered in a few centers of learning: Paris, the Loire Valley (where the new royal châteaus were rising), Lyons (the great trading center of the age). It is important to realize, however, that the new learning was not confined to the upper classes; in fact, the chivalric ideal, which maintained its hold despite—and perhaps in compensation for—the dwindling power of the nobility, valued social graces and feats of arms above learning, and proportionally fewer nobles than one might expect became scholars.

The Reformation owed as much to the revival of classical learning as it did to the rise of the bourgeoisie. To approach sacred texts in a critical spirit is ultimately to assert the autonomy of the scholar, and of his conscience. John (Jean) Calvin, who became the leader of the reform movement in France, was a student of the Humanist scholar Guillaume Budé; at the Académie, Calvin's seminary in Geneva (established in 1559), his preachers received a thorough training in the classics as well as in theology. The same was true, however, of the preachers recruited by Saint Ignatius and his Society of Jesus, founded in 1534 to stem the tide of the Reformation; reformers and counterreformers alike turned to the classics as models of clear exposition and—perhaps most important—of effective argument. The struggle between them was a fierce one, and it was not confined to the lecture hall and the pulpit; as nobles, *grands bourgeois*, and even cities took sides, it immediately became a political issue, with bloody consequences.

During the first third of the century, as the ideas of Martin Luther began to circulate in France, Francis I took a tolerant attitude while remaining orthodox himself. (His sister, Marguerite of Angoulême, was still more receptive to the new doctrines, and not only patronized but also protected many of the Huguenot—French Protestant—writers, including the poet Clément Marot.) Francis did not adopt a policy of repression until 1534, when the so-called "affair of the placards" made him fear for his own power. His son, Henry II, pursued this policy in a more fanatic spirit, and great numbers of Protestants were executed as heretics—although martyrdom had the effect of reinforcing Protestant convictions.

The event that led to civil war, however, was the death of Henry II in 1559. His three sons, who succeeded him one after the other, proved unable to control the state, and feudal ambitions, newly fused with religious animosities, erupted in a series of eight wars between 1562 and 1598. Both sides were guilty of fanaticism and atrocities; the most appalling single incident was the massacre of Protestants that began on the feast of Saint Bartholomew in 1572. The struggle was further complicated and intensified by the participation of foreign troops (Spanish and Italian Catholics, English and German Protestants), whose ostensible motive was to aid their coreligionists but who were often used to further the ambitions of foreign monarchs.

With the death of Henry III in 1589, the dynasty of the Valois came to an end and was succeeded by that of the Bourbons, whose first representative, Henry IV, had to renounce his Protestant faith to secure the allegiance of Paris. The bourgeois Parlement, as well as the Estates General (convened in 1592), clearly expressed public resentment of foreign intruders and weariness of religious strife. The Edict of Nantes, which Henry promulgated in 1598, granted freedom of worship to Protestants and Catholics alike, while a treaty with Spain in the same year marked the end of foreign intervention. Henry was not slow to gather the reins of absolute power into his hands, thereby setting the stage for the glories and abuses of the century of Louis XIV.

A CENTURY OF POETS

The sixteenth century saw a great efflorescence in French poetry. Although none of the individual poets had quite the stature of Villon, there were so many of them, and of such high quality, that the term "Renaissance" may be applied without hesitation. It is doubly appropriate because the new poetry was both a reflection of Italian influence at the height of that country's Renaissance and a genuinely French development, infused with confidence in the literary potential of the French language.

The century began with a school of poets known to critics as the Rhétoriqueurs because of their fondness for elaborate rhetorical figures. They represent both the end of a phase of development—the obsession with form that had marked the lyric poetry of the fourteenth and fifteenth centuries—and the beginning of the new Renaissance phase. Thus, despite their fondness for old forms, whose complexity they increased wherever possible, and for old themes (allegorical treatments of courtly love), they also took pride in their native language. One of the most talented of them, Jean Lemaire de Belges, even composed a treatise interspersed with poems, whose object was to demonstrate the equality of literary merit between French and Italian. Finally, two of the Rhétoriqueurs, Jean Marot and Octovien de Saint-Gelais, had sons who became better poets than their fathers—but who owed to those fathers their early formation as poets.

French Renaissance poetry, like that of the Rhétoriqueurs, was superior to all court poetry. Most of its practitioners were not themselves nobles but courtiers, attached to noble patrons who appreciated the arts. The most coveted places were at the royal court, where some of the century's best poets, including Clément Marot and Pierre de Ronsard, served in various capacities. (Poetic excellence was not sufficient, however, to ensure permanent favor: Marot fell from grace because of his Huguenot sympathies, and Ronsard because of the death of his royal patron, Charles IX.) However, there were other milieus in which poetry could flourish. The new passion for learning gave rise to circles or salons among the bourgeoisie, of which the most famous was that of Louise Labé, called "la Belle Cordiére" because both her father and her husband were prosperous ropemakers. She was herself a poet of considerable merit, and her circle, in Lyons, attracted other poets of both genders who drew inspiration from the style of Marot and the Italian Petrarch. The circle of seven poets known as the Pléiade (after the constellation of the Pleiades) took shape at a school in Paris and was made up of students of the Humanist scholar Jean Dorat. Earlier in the century, before the Catholic repression set in, there had been circles united by an interest in religious reform as well as in Humanist learning; the most brilliant of these was the court of Marguerite d'Angoulême, sister of Francis I.

The two most striking characteristics of the new poetry fostered by these circles were its adaptation of Italian and classical forms and its steadily increasing sophistication of style and tone. From Petrarch, the fourteenth century Italian poet, it borrowed the sonnet sequence, and as Petrarch had celebrated the stages of his idealized love for "Laura," so Maurice Scève explored his for "Délie" (1544) and Joachim du Bellay his for "Olive" (1549). Ancient forms of lyric verse were borrowed—the ode, the epistle, the elegy—and attempts were even made to revive the epic in its classical, Vergilian form. (Classical tragedy was also revived at this period, with considerable success.) A school of so-called neo-Latin verse flourished in Humanist circles, and many of the poets best known for their French verse also composed in Latin.

There was an ongoing debate concerning the relative merits of Latin and French, which prompted the members of the Pléiade to issue a kind of manifesto (composed by du Bellay) called *La Défense et illustration de la langue française* (1549; *The Defence and Illustration of the French Language*, 1939). In addition to defending the merits of French as a medium for great poetry, du Bellay recommended that it be further "ennobled" or "elevated" through emulation of the classical genres and by borrowings from Latin vocabulary and syntax. Because of differences in the structures of French and Latin, and notably because Latin (like

Greek) is an inflected language, some of these borrowings proved too artificial and were not naturalized into the poetic repertoire of French. In general, however, the emulation of ancient models brought a new sophistication to French lyric, which is perhaps best appreciated by comparing the poetry of the earlier generations of Renaissance poets with that of the Pléiade. This is scarcely to denigrate Marot and his contemporaries, whose style some will prefer because it is less polished or more "Gallic" (Marot was, after all, the contemporary of François Rabelais). It is merely to acknowledge a prominent trend, which produced some outstanding results and set the tone for half a century of French verse.

It remains to acknowledge the striking range of theme and mood visible in French Renaissance poetry—a range corresponding to the variety of genres it rediscovered and adapted, but corresponding as well to the range of emotions generated by the events of the century. Thus, side by side with the graceful and often passionate love poetry inspired by Petrarch, one finds the melancholy but stately sonnets of du Bellay's *Les Regrets* (1558; *The Regrets*, 1984), inspired by classical elegy, and the unfinished epics attempted by Ronsard and Guillaume du Bartas; one also finds Ronsard's eloquent defense of his Catholicism in the *Discours des misères de ce temps*, 1562; discourse on the miseries of these times) and Agrippa d'Aubigné's fierce blend of satire and indignation (in the Protestant cause this time) in his *Les Tragiques* (1616). Not infrequently, a considerable range is to be found in the work of a single poet. Marot, for example, though best known for his badinage (or light, playful wit), was equally capable of fervent lyricism (as in his translation of the biblical Psalms) and of vehement satire in the vein of d'Aubigné ("L'Enfer," or "Inferno," was inspired by his imprisonment for his Protestant beliefs). For sheer versatility, Ronsard was unequaled; he tried his hand at dozens of genres, and even his failures—such as an attempt to emulate the Pindaric odes—are the result of lapses of taste rather than any lack of poetic vigor. The rediscovery of Greece and Rome had enriched the repertoire of poetic forms and themes, but the passion conveyed was the poets' own—the faith and the anguish, the loves and the ambitions of a turbulent century.

THE SEVENTEENTH CENTURY

In the seventeenth century, the French monarchy, the ancien régime, reached its apogee and began its decline. In an important sense, Louis XIV can be held responsible for both of these developments, although it is arguable that he did more to hasten the decline than to gain the summit, which had been the long-sought objective of Cardinal Richelieu and Cardinal Mazarin before him (not to mention Henry IV and Francis I). It was Louis XIV, the Sun King, who sought to formalize and demonstrate his power in the visible symbol of Versailles—a court whose every grace and virtue (and extravagance and whim) was ultimately an expression of his own will. Clearly, this was in many ways a fiction, and a pernicious one insofar as it blinded Louis himself to important social and economic developments in his realm. It was, however, a fiction of great power, which many seventeenth and eighteenth century rulers tried to emulate and which left its mark on French culture well beyond the Revolution.

Like their predecessors since Philip IV, both Louis XIII and Louis XIV—whose reigns together spanned nearly the entire century—based their power on the employment of bourgeois ministers while reducing the nobility to the status of dependents of the crown. Because both acceded to the throne in childhood, two of their ministers, the cardinals Richelieu and Mazarin, were virtual rulers of France for long periods. Richelieu was responsible for rebuilding the French military, crushing noble intrigues against Louis XIII, and humbling the Habsburg dynasty in the Thirty Years' War, thereby securing the borders of France. Mazarin pursued Richelieu's policies after the latter's death, and, despite the four-year setback of the Fronde (1648-1652), managed to complete the submission of the nobility and the containment of Habsburg Spain.

The Fronde was in fact the last real attempt of the French nobility to recoup the power they had been steadily losing to the monarchy since the thirteenth century. By allying themselves with the bourgeois Parlement and the Parisian masses, incensed by Mazarin's attempts to tax them, a coalition of princes managed for a time to expel "the Italian," whose foreign birth inspired suspicion and hatred. A quarrel between the rebellious factions, however, which coincided with

Louis XIV's coming of age, spelled the end of the uprising. Moreover, the fear and humiliation which the young Louis experienced during the Fronde made him determined never to share his power with the nobility—nor, indeed, with the higher clergy. After Mazarin's death, he served as his own first minister and chose his other ministers from among the lower classes. He refused to convene the Estates General, suppressed what political initiative the Parlement had acquired, and brought even provincial administration under his direct control by the use of agents known as *intendants*.

Considering himself the spiritual as well as the temporal head of the French Church, he took the disastrous step of revoking the Edict of Nantes. This had the practical effect of driving numbers of Huguenots into exile, to the great detriment of French industry. The worst abuse of Louis's reign, however, was his utter disregard of fiscal realities. In planning Versailles and in waging continual war for what he considered the greater glory of France, he stubbornly refused to count costs. When combined with a bureaucratic control of industry and a cruelly unfair system of taxation (which exempted the rich while crushing the peasantry), Louis's prodigality paved the way that was to lead, in another century, to revolution. (A number of tax revolts among the peasants marked the decade of the 1670's.)

Despite its claims to absolutism, the monarchy was not the only institution in seventeenth century France, nor did Louis have a monopoly on the ideas of the age. It was an age in which religion still held great power, not only over the minds of individuals but also over institutions (such as the Sorbonne) and intellectual life—though its premium on philosophical truth would be challenged in the course of the century. If the French Church was largely subordinate to the king in temporal matters, it retained much authority in spiritual matters and could use this authority to political as well as spiritual effect. Thus, the international order of the Jesuits played a role in both the Thirty Years' War and the revocation of the Edict of Nantes.

Louis XIV's confessor was a Jesuit, and the king seems to have been following his advice in suppressing the ideas of Cornelius Jensenius and his French followers. The Jansenists, though Catholics, had ideas on predestination that resembled those of John Calvin. Their adherents included brilliant men of letters such as Jean Racine and Blaise Pascal, whose *Lettres provinciales* (1656-1657; *The Provincial Letters*, 1657) were at once a defense of Jansenist teachings and an attack on the moral "casuistry" of the Jesuits. The Jesuits, and the pope, focused their attacks on the Jansenists' notion of grace, but there can be little doubt that the moral austerity and integrity of the latter also made them a source of embarrassment to a corrupt Church and a corrupt court. Among the orthodox, too, there were initiatives toward reform, such as the creation of new religious orders and of a secret society, the Compagnie du Saint-Sacrement, whose efforts ranged from charitable works to persecution of Protestants, Jansenists, and freethinkers—Jean-Baptiste Molière criticized its excesses in his verse play *Tartuffe: Ou, L'Imposteur* (pr. 1664; *Tartuffe*, 1732).

Religious questions were rendered still more pressing by the growth of skepticism or "libertinism." Pascal's *Pensées* (1670; *Monsieur Pascal's Thoughts, Meditations, and Prayers*, 1688; best known as *Pensées*) consists of notes for an ambitious project he never completed: a "Defense of the Christian Religion," addressed to the *mondain*, or "man of the world," who in Pascal's day would have been increasingly likely to doubt or neglect religious teachings. Both the hypocrisy of the clergy and the luxurious life of the court were factors in this skepticism, but a new factor was philosophical doubt, sown by the growing split between religious and scientific truth. The Copernican theory of the solar system, developed in the sixteenth century, had been reaffirmed by Galileo in 1632. Although the Inquisition forced Galileo to recant, this proved to be a rearguard action, and by 1687, Sir Isaac Newton had laid the foundations for a wholly new science of physics. Pascal himself was a great mathematician as well as religious thinker, contributing to the creation of calculus and probability theory. Pascal's own faith, and the sense of mission that drove him to undertake a defense of Christianity, took on urgency precisely because he glimpsed the vast, indifferent universe science was to reveal and could no longer accept the rationalistic proofs of God's existence offered by the Scholastics. The most influential thinker of the age in France was René Descartes, who was not a solitary genius but the most successful of his contemporaries in formulating the new philosophical problems. His work proved seminal because it provided not a system but a method of research, inspired by mathematics and rejecting the testimony of tradition—including religious tradition. Although Descartes himself was a religious man and made room in his theories for a Creator, others went further and denied the existence of God. Those who rejected tradition as the basis of their beliefs were commonly referred to as *libertins* (an epithet that originally meant simply "freethinkers"). An important group of *libertins* gathered about the philosopher Pierre Gassendi, who also espoused the Copernican theory but borrowed his ideas on physics from the ancient "atomists," Democritus and Epicurus. In addition to elaborating new theories, many of these seventeenth century scientists also conducted experiments and shared their results with one another through the creation of *académies*, or scientific societies. *Académies* flourished in Dijon, Rouen, and other provincial cities, as well as in the capital.

Thus, behind the facade of Louis XIV's absolutism, a variety of social, spiritual, and intellectual movements were struggling to define and maintain themselves. In this respect, the history of the eighteenth century was essentially a working out of trends already perceptible in the seventeenth.

AN ECLIPSE OF LYRIC POETRY

Great French poetry was written in the seventeenth century, but almost all of it was dramatic poetry—the tragedies of Jean Racine and of Pierre Corneille, the comedies of Molière. Even the fables of Jean de La Fontaine are narrative and satiric, rather than lyric, poetry. Granted that great lyric genius is rare and owes much to inborn gifts, there is still call to ask why this century should have failed to foster such talents as there were. (The sixteenth and nineteenth centuries offer especially striking contrasts in this regard.) At least a part of the answer lies in the milieus where poetry was produced.

From the beginning, French lyric poetry had flourished chiefly in aristocratic circles, whether the poets were themselves noble or not. This did not change in the seventeenth century; the new element was the over-

whelming force of centralization drawing all such circles into the orbit of the king. Hippolyte Taine argued
in his history of the ancien régime that the creation of a
single court as the source of all royal patronage (and the
simultaneous reduction of all aristocrats to dependency
on the king) had a great effect on both language and
thought, which extended throughout the eighteenth as
well as the seventeenth century. Because the court was
"worldly" but not learned, the more erudite Renaissance borrowings from the ancient world were rejected
as pedantic or eccentric; the sophistication that continued to be sought was of a social and not an intellectual
order. The exploration of individual emotion, an essential element in most lyricism, was likewise discouraged, as art became preeminently public. Thus, while a
certain elaboration of form and refinement of expression might be approved as proper to the exclusivity of
court circles, ideas, themes, and syntax were to be clear,
logical, and accessible.

This ideal of clarity was expressed both at the beginning and near the end of the century by two influential critics, François Malherbe and Nicolas Boileau-
Despréaux. Both were poets, but they are best known as
the theoreticians of French "classicism," which they
did not invent but did much to propagate. Malherbe laid
down a set of rules for the composition of verse that forbade hiatus (the juxtaposition of two vowels) and
enjambment, while prescribing that rhymes and metrical breaks (caesuras and line ends) should coincide
with syntactic breaks. Boileau wrote a treatise on the art
of poetry that owed much to Aristotle and Horace, the
ancient theoreticians of style, but his work is clearly a
product of its own time in its emphasis on reason,
which it exalts above the other faculties involved in the
creation of poetry.

Although Boileau also upheld the ideal of sublimity
and looked to the ancients, as well as to the Bible, for
models, his emphasis on logic and his tendency to
equate reason with common sense actually had a leveling effect. In Taine's assessment, Boileau and his contemporaries could insist on the transparency of "truth"
and "nature" because they shared a language and a
perspective shaped by the court, where intense social
pressure eliminated both individual and regional ("provincial") idiosyncrasies. It is worth noting that the sev-

enteenth century also saw the creation (by Cardinal
Richelieu) of the French Academy, an officially sanctioned group of writers charged with maintaining the
"purity" of the French language.

This is not to say that a dull uniformity of style prevailed in seventeenth century poetry. There were in fact
a variety of different trends, yet each reflected to some
degree the effects of court pressure. The trend sometimes identified as Baroque because of its affinity with
that style in the plastic arts is chiefly concerned with appearances and their instability. Jean Rousset's *Anthologie
de la poésie baroque française* (1968; anthology of
French Baroque poetry), which offers a selection of
this poetry, arranged by theme, includes sections on
metamorphosis, disguise, bubbles, clouds, and water,
both as a reflecting or shimmering surface and as a
flowing—hence inconstant—element. The influence
of Italian poetry, and in particular of Giambattista Marino (who lived in Paris from 1615 to 1622), is visible in
these works, but the attention to surfaces is also a characteristic of court life. A curious feature of seventeenth
century religious art, which Rousset associates with the
Baroque tendency, is a fascination with death and physical decay. This feature is obviously related to the spiritual struggles of the age, but it, too, reveals an obsession with appearances, for the living—including the
beautiful and the powerful—may be transformed at any
time into corpses. Thus, the spiritual anguish of the age
was perhaps increased by the contrast, inherent in court
life, between apparent beauty, favor, or power, and its
instability.

Some critics, however, deny the existence of a true
Baroque style in France and speak instead of *préciosité*
and burlesque. These related trends share an exaggerated concern for form, but whereas *préciosité* takes
form seriously and makes its observance almost a point
of honor, burlesque reveals its ridiculous side. The
précieux poets flourished in the salons, which emerged
as miniature courts in the orbit of the royal court. The
most famous and influential of these was that of the
marquise de Rambouillet, whose poor health often prevented her from going out and who, in compensation,
assembled about her a circle of literary and social luminaries. During the years of its existence (1620-1665),
her salon welcomed Richelieu, Malherbe, Marino,

Corneille, and Madame de Sévigné, among others, as well as many of the higher aristocracy.

Though serious works were read and discussed, the salon was primarily a social gathering, where time might be spent in parlor games and above all in polite conversation. Other salons were formed in emulation of the Hôtel de Rambouillet; the most prominent was the bourgeois salon of Madeleine de Scudéry, author of multivolume novels in true précieux style. Though chosen for its original meaning, "of great price or value," the term précieux came to mean a style of writing or behavior that sought consciously to elevate its practitioners. Exotic or abstract words might be substituted for ordinary ones; farfetched or hyperbolic comparisons were sought; medieval poetic forms such as the ballade and rondeau were revived for the sake of their complexity. Insofar as most salons were organized by women and devoted considerable attention to the refined expression of love, they bear comparison with the courts where troubadour lyrics evolved. However, the fact that many courtly themes had become clichés forced poets to seek ever more exaggerated treatments of them, while the dependent, courtier status of the people involved offered an implicit contrast to the virtues convention ascribed to them.

The situation invited parody, and indeed some précieux poetry verges on self-parody. Writers in the burlesque vein took advantage of this situation, pushing précieux tendencies to ridiculous extremes or deflating them with doses of realism. It is interesting to note that the burlesque poets—Paul Scarron, Saint-Amant, Cyrano de Bergerac—tended to occupy more ambiguous or marginal positions in society, while virtually all were *libertins*. Although some of these men frequented the salons, they also gathered in the cabarets and cafés of Paris, where there were no refined standards of etiquette to repress their flights of satiric and obscene humor.

JEAN DE LA FONTAINE

Granted that the centralized court life of the age did not foster lyric poetry, it nevertheless had a positive effect on some other forms of literature, for it encouraged the close study of human character under what might almost be called laboratory conditions. Thus, the genius of La Fontaine, the greatest nondramatic poet of the age, found ample matter in the observation of his fellow courtiers. Like Villon, La Fontaine is remarkable for the range of tone he achieved in a poetic idiom that imposed great formal restrictions. In contrast to Villon, however, La Fontaine is himself absent from his poetry, except as a sharp and sometimes pitiless observer of human foibles. His *Contes et nouvelles en vers* (1665; *Tales and Short Stories in Verse*, 1735) and *Fables choises, mises en vers* (1668-1694; *Fables Written in Verse*, 1735) have been compared to the great dramatic poetry of his age, which sought to portray universals of human behavior yet in so doing inevitably revealed much about its own time and place.

Thus, La Fontaine's fables manage to give vivid glimpses of contemporary life in the guise of the beast fable. La Fontaine has even been accused (by Jean-Jacques Rousseau, among others) of teaching his readers how to rise in the world by dissembling and well-placed flattery, yet it can more plausibly be argued that his fables unmask the baser motives of courtiers, by attributing these motives to animals and by identifying them in plain words. In fact, the most striking feature of the fables, given La Fontaine's proximity to the court of Louis XIV, is their directness; nor does it come as a surprise to learn that the king was cool toward the poet. It should be noted as well that La Fontaine—who was himself a bourgeois from the provinces—did not limit his purview to the court but peopled his menagerie from all the ranks of seventeenth century society. Although his models were classical, he thus rejoined the French medieval tradition of the fabliaux and the *Roman de Renart*, offering a pungent antidote to the artificiality of much court poetry.

BIBLIOGRAPHY

Banks, Kathryn. *Cosmos and Image in the Renaissance: French Love Lyric and Natural-Philosophical Poetry*. London: Legenda, 2008. Explores the relationship between Renaissance imagery and poetic language and the ways that poetic language, in turn, influenced Renaissance thought. Bibliography and index. Bilingual edition.

Gaunt, Simon, and Sarah Kay, eds. *The Cambridge Companion to Medieval French Literature*. New York: Cambridge University Press, 2008. A guide to French literature from the ninth century to the Renaissance. Detailed analyses of major poetic works, from lyrics to romances. Chronology and suggestions for further reading.

Hollier, Denis, with R. Howard Bloch et al. *A New History of French Literature*. Cambridge, Mass.: Harvard University Press, 1994. A translation of *De la literature française*. A unique work, consisting of 164 succinct essays on a wide range of subjects, all written by scholars who are known for their extensive knowledge in a particular area. Bibliographical references and index.

Kay, Sarah, Terence Cave, and Malcolm Bowie. *A Short History of French Literature*. New York: Oxford University Press, 2003. A reliable but accessible overview of French literature, told as a series of stories that describe major writers and place them within the context of their times. Ideal for general readers as well as for more advanced students of French.

Kelly, Douglas. *The Art of Medieval French Romance*. Madison: University of Wisconsin Press, 1992. Uses statements made by the authors of medieval romances to answer questions about the genre that are raised by modern readers.

Kenny, Neil. *An Introduction to Sixteenth-Century French Literature and Thought: Other Times, Other Places*. London: Duckworth, 2008. This thoughtful study attempts to account for the fact that in the French Renaissance the writers whose primary concern was the improvement of their society so often wrote about other times and distant places. Illustrated. Bibliographical references and index.

Moss, Ann. *Poetry and Fable: Studies in Mythological Narrative in Sixteenth-Century France*. New York: Cambridge University Press, 2009. Through studying changes in the treatment of mythological subjects, the writer shows how both aesthetic theories and the attitudes of readers were changing during the period.

Shapiro, Norman R., ed. and trans. *French Women Poets of Nine Centuries: The Distaff and the Pen*. Baltimore: Johns Hopkins University Press, 2008. Introductions by Roberta L. Krueger, Catherine Lafarge, and Catherine Perry; foreword by Rosanne Warren. Contains more than six hundred poems by fifty-six different writers, with originals and translations on facing pages. A monumental volume.

Shaw, Mary Lewis. *The Cambridge Introduction to French Poetry*. New York: Cambridge University Press, 2003. An exhaustive survey of French poetry, with topics ranging from verse forms and genres to the relationship between poetry and politics. Glossary of poetic terms, bibliography, and indexes.

Stephens, Sonya, ed. *A History of Women's Writing in France*. New York: Cambridge University Press, 2000. A collection of essays, each focusing on a different period. Includes bibliography and a guide to more than 150 writers and their works.

Willett, Laura, trans. *Poetry and Language in Sixteenth-Century France: Du Bellay, Ronsard, Sébillet*. Toronto: Centre for Reformation and Renaissance Studies, Victoria University, 2004. Contains key texts in development of poetic theory. Introduction and notes by Willett. Bibliography.

Lillian Doherty

FRENCH POETRY SINCE 1700

It has often been said that the most poetic works of eighteenth century France were written in prose—works such as François de Salignac de la Mothe-Fénelon's *Télémaque* (1699; *The Adventures of Telemachus*, 1720), Jean-Jacques Rousseau's *La Nouvelle Héloïse* (1761; *Eloisa: Or, A Series of Original Letters*, 1761) and especially *Les Rêveries d'un promeneur solitaire* (1782; *The Reveries of a Solitary Walker*, 1783), Bernardin de Saint-Pierre's *Paul et Virginie* (1787; *Paul and Mary*, 1789), and Constanin Volney's *Les Ruines* (1791; the ruins). Here, true poetic feeling and sentiment, as those terms were defined by the Romantics, are indisputably present. However, the eighteenth century, turned toward reason and progress, was not without poetry of a different sort, and critics who view the period as a mere lacuna in poetry between classicism and Romanticism have not studied the major authors or their influence on the following centuries. There was indeed a great output of poetry, although in many cases quantity substituted for quality.

The eighteenth century was one of the most vibrant periods of French history, yet it has two faces: the face of the salon, the court, the ball, and the masque, preserving the past, and the forward-looking face of the philosophes. In the eighteenth century, France was the idol of culture; European monarchs spoke French and built imitations of Versailles. At the court of Louis XV, although luxury and frivolity flourished, so did such cultural accomplishments as the architecture of Jacques Gabriel, the paintings of François Boucher, Jean-Honoré Fragonard, and Antoine Watteau, and the exquisite cabinets and commodes of Georges Jacob and Jean-Henri Riesener. In Paris, men and women of society gathered in the salons of the Duchesse de Maine, the Marquise de Lambert, Madame de Tencin, and Madame de Geoffrin. It was here that much poetry of the period gained its inspiration; it was inferior to the great seventeenth century masterpieces and somehow displayed in its shallow forms the end of an era.

The more vibrant aspect of the *siècle des lumières*, the Age of Enlightenment, was the activity of the philosophes, the great thinkers and writers who ultimately affected the destiny of France and the modern world with their emphasis on reason and their belief in human progress. At first relatively restrained and committed to popularizing scientific discoveries, as in the works of Pierre Bayle (1647-1706) and Bernard le Bovier de Fontenelle (1657-1757), they began to address more delicate issues. Charles-Louis de Secondat, known by his title of Montesquieu (1689-1755), wrote an anonymous satire of religious and political institutions in his *Les Lettres persanes* (1721; *Persian Letters*, 1722) and produced a scholarly study on law in *De l'esprit des lois* (1748; *The Spirit of Laws*, 1750). The great Voltaire, who so dominated every aspect of the eighteenth century that it is known as the Age of Voltaire, used his clever and ironic pen to satirize virtually everything and everyone, particularly religious intolerance and superstition. Denis Diderot (1713-1784), known especially as the editor of the great résumé of eighteenth century knowledge, *L'Encyclopédie* (1751-1780), was himself a writer of sensibility, already foreshadowing Romanticism, and a man of cold reason bordering on atheism. Finally, Rousseau (1712-1778) argued for a return to the simple life, to a new morality and religion based on the heart, and a new type of government under which equality would reign.

Although the philosophes used prose as their principal means of expression, they all began a literary apprenticeship with poetry, and Voltaire expressed many of his important ideas, and all of his tragedies, in verse. Poets touched philosophical ideas, often tangentially, especially in science, nature, and morals, and Voltaire judged each of them by their conformity to his ideas. Poetry, on the whole, kept to classical models, faithful to the precepts of Nicolas Boileau-Despréaux (1636-1711). The great genres—ode, elegy, eclogue, and satire—were the most practiced. Rhythm and rhyme were decorously employed, and allusions to antiquity proliferated. At the beginning of the century, subjects were rarely personal, but after 1750, sentiment and nature themes began to appear. Poems of circumstance were frivolous, sensual, and pagan in inspiration, illustrating the degradation of morals, yet there was a surprising quantity of religious poetry in this age of anticlericalism, Deism, and even outspoken atheism. The century ended with a more lyric poet, André-Marie Chénier, a victim of the very revolution that he had supported in verse and in action.

GUILLAUME AMFRYE, ABBÉ DE CHAULIEU

Poetry in the eighteenth century, as in the seventeenth, originated in the salons. The elegant Society of the Temple was the meeting place for libertines of the time, and at the turn of the century, a period of literary aridity, Guillaume Amfrye, Abbé de Chaulieu (1639-1720), could be found among the poets of the salons. His works were not published until 1724, but he composed many madrigals and poems of circumstance inspired by the music of Jean-Baptiste Lully. Well versed in the classics, he employed classical allusions and classical verse forms with accuracy, though without poetic feeling. His "Apologie de l'inconstance" (1700; apology for inconstancy) links two centuries and foreshadows future currents. More oriented to the theater, where he enjoyed a moderate success, Antoine Houdar de la Motte (1672-1731) shows greater simplicity and freshness in his style. Though occasionally original, his verse is not brilliant.

JEAN-BAPTISTE ROUSSEAU

The greatest poet of the early eighteenth century is generally acknowledged to be Jean-Baptiste Rousseau (1670-1741), also a member of the libertine Temple group. Jealous of his reputation, he spent the last thirty years of his life in exile after being convicted of calumny. His poetry, much appreciated in his own day though now forgotten, reveals a sensitivity to language and rhythm that anticipates Paul Valéry's preoccupation with language: Rousseau in his *Art poétique* insists on patience, work, and inspiration, much as Valéry was later to do. Rousseau's main sources of inspiration were antiquity and the Bible. Although many poems are imitations of Pindar, Rousseau has original compositions in his *cantates* (love allegories), of which the best is his "Cantate à Circé." His *Odes sacrées* (sacred odes) on biblical themes are his best, but "Ode à la Fortune," "Ode à Adonis," and "Ode à Bacchus"

are also excellent, as is his "Paraphrase du Cantique d'Ézéchias," written for a convalescing person, in which the sick man recalls his brush with death in realistic terms.

VOLTAIRE

François-Marie Arouet, known to his contemporaries and to posterity as Voltaire (1694-1778), dominates the history of eighteenth century poetry as he does the entire *siècle des lumières*. His earliest poem, "Sur la religion naturelle" (on natural religion), was written in 1722; shortly before his death he was still composing epistles (*Épîtres*) to friends and enemies, living and dead, with the same acerbic pen. Voltaire dreamed of creating a great French epic, and early in his career composed *La Ligue* (1723, revised as *La Henriade*, 1728; *Henriade*, 1732). Lacking imaginative life, the poem fails utterly to comprehend the meaning of its subject, the religious wars of the sixteenth century. Voltaire immediately turned to another source of epic

Jean-Baptiste Rousseau (Time & Life Pictures/Getty Images)

inspiration, Jeanne d'Arc, in *La Pucelle d'Orléans* (1755, 1762; *The Maid of Orleans*, 1758; also as *La Pucelle: Or, The Maid of Orleans*, 1785-1786), which he began in 1730 and concluded in 1762 with twenty-one cantos. Although Jeanne, the beloved French heroine for all ages, is presented with sharp sarcasm and irony, the work sold some 300,000 copies and was parodied and burlesqued many times.

Although all of Voltaire's work is satiric, he wrote many poems that are satires proper. *Le Temple du goût* (1733; *The Temple of Taste*, 1734), in prose and verse, is surprisingly conservative in matters of taste and quite perceptive when discussing architecture. Voltaire also assigns a number of writers from the seventeenth and eighteenth centuries to a room in his temple, and he is particularly offensive toward his enemies, dead or alive. The same vein reappears in *Le Pauvre Diable* (1758; the poor Devil), published under the name of the then recently deceased Jean-Joseph Vadé, and likewise a harsh invective against contemporary writers. Voltaire excelled in all the small genres; in fact, it was for them that he was most appreciated by his contemporaries.

Voltaire could also be serious, even reflective. The great Lisbon earthquake in 1755 had shaken his faith in progress and had caused him to reflect more deeply on the role of Providence in human life. Voltaire, though anticlerical, was never atheistic, professing a rather moderate Deism. His "Poème sur le désastre de Lisbonne" (poem on the disaster of Lisbon) is a serious meditation on life and death. "Poème sur la loi naturelle" (poem on the natural law), written in the same year, 1756, stresses the importance of reason in directing humans to God, without the need of formal religion.

Although Voltaire believed that his tragedies, all written in Alexandrines, and his epics would assure his future fame, it is rather for his *contes philosophiques* that he is remembered. As a poet, he is the greatest of the eighteenth century after Chénier, which is not to make him great, since Chénier is perhaps the only true poet of that century. Voltaire was an adequate poet, however, and his philosophical works in verse are still read today, though most of his other poetry is forgotten.

DIDACTIC AND RELIGIOUS POETRY

In the camp opposed to Voltaire and the philosophes were several didactic and religious poets. Among the best of the religious authors were Jean-Jacques Lefranc, marquis de Pompignan (1709-1784), and Louis Racine (1692-1763), son of the great Jean Racine, author of seventeenth century classical tragedies. Pompignan is known for his "Ode sur la mort de Jean-Baptiste Rousseau" (ode on the death of Jean-Baptiste Rousseau), but his best works are his *Poésies sacrées* (1734, 1751, 1763; sacred poems), paraphrases of biblical texts, many of which have real literary value. Their lyric accents and ease of versification anticipate the achievements of Alphonse de Lamartine.

LOUIS RACINE

Louis Racine, like his father, reveals the influence of Jansenism, though without his father's passion and depth. "La Grâce" (written 1720), a poem in honor of the Holy Spirit, is overtly Jansenist, yet some of its passages anticipate the tone of Lamartine's *Harmonies poétiques et religieuses* (1830). "La Religion," also written in 1720 and widely read at the time, is Racine's most important work. It celebrates God the Father, with many literary exaggerations, such as Christ walking on the waters surrounded by nymphs, receiving the homage of Neptune. Racine's *Odes saintes* (1730-1743; holy odes), the most famous of his twenty-two odes, honor God the Son. Racine's most original ideas are expressed in "Réflexion sur la poésie," his *art poétique*, which insists on the necessity of enthusiasm, harmony, and passion. Unfortunately, he did not incorporate these principles into his work, although his was an erudite mind, formed by the classics and the great Christian thinkers, such as Saint Thomas Aquinas, Saint Augustine, Jacques-Bénigne Bossuet, and Pascal.

JEAN-FRANÇOIS, MARQUIS DE SAINT-LAMBERT

Eighteenth century didactic poetry was not always religious, as in Pompignan and Racine. A great deal of it was directed to nature and science, such as *Les Saisons* (1769; the seasons), by Jean-François, marquis de Saint-Lambert (1716-1803). Better known for his articles in *L'Encyclopédie* and his amorous adventures with Madame Du Châtelet and with Madame d'Houdetot, Saint-Lambert wrote this lengthy poem in four cantos in imitation of Hesiod, with observations on the natural phenomena that accompany the changes in the seasons. It was greatly praised by Voltaire because of its philosophical implications. Other contemporaries, such as Diderot and Baron Melchior von Grimm, recognized the exhaustion of this genre, which was to attract inferior poets until the end of the century.

JACQUES DELILLE

More original in his descriptive poetry was Jacques Delille (1738-1813), a professor of Latin and translator of Vergil's *Georgics* (37-30 B.C.E.) in 1770. Delille's best-known work is *Les Jardins* (1782; *The Gardens*, 1798), a long poem in eight cantos that speaks of the art of gardening and the embellishment of the countryside. Though often monotonous, it does have poetically sensitive passages, especially in its appreciation of autumn, later echoed by Lamartine. Delille's "Les Trois Règnes de la nature" (the three kingdoms of nature), although written in 1809, is entirely in the spirit of the eighteenth century; the work possesses historical value for the richness of its vocabulary, including a number of neologisms.

JEAN-ANTOINE ROUCHER

Jean-Antoine Roucher (1745-1794) also represents the rustic tradition with his *Les Mois* (1779; the months), a poem in the tradition of Saint-Lambert's *Les Saisons*. Although Roucher's verse has a certain charm and delicacy, his sensitivity is obscured by an excess of rhetoric. He was guillotined the same day as Chénier and had not lived long enough to develop his poetic talent.

PONCE-DENIS ÉCOUCHARD LEBRUN

Hoping to unite Lucretius and Sir Isaac Newton in his poetry, Ponce-Denis Écouchard Lebrun (1729-1807), known in his time as Pindare-Lebrun, aimed to replace the mannerism of his age with classical simplicity. Less faithful to his allegiances, he composed poetry in honor of Robespierre during the Revolution and for the glory of Napoleon under the empire. Lebrun projected a great poetic masterpiece, "La Nature: Ou, Le Bonheur philosophique et champêtre" (nature, or philosophic and rustic happiness), but only the section called *Le Génie* (1760; the genius) was completed. In this work, Lebrun anticipates the Romantic conception of genius, but the poem is overburdened with erudite references. Like Voltaire, Lebrun was inspired by the

earthquake of Lisbon, and in 1755, he composed two pseudoscientific odes on that disaster. His "Ode sur le vaisseau *Le Vengeur*" (1794; ode on the ship, *Le Vengeur*) is a poem in honor of revolutionary patriotism. Hailed by Diderot as the ideal poet-philosopher, Lebrun occasionally wrote some excellent passages. Inspired by Louis Racine, Lebrun was to become the master of Chénier.

ANTOINE-LÉONARD THOMAS

Toward the middle of the eighteenth century, a pre-Romantic spirit, very evident in the prose of Diderot and Rousseau, also appeared in poetry, though it did not fully triumph until Lamartine's *Méditations poétiques* (*Poetical Meditations*, 1839) in 1820. Antoine-Léonard Thomas (1732-1785), author of numerous epistles and odes, none of which has durable value, does, however, show a pre-Lamartinian spirit in his "Ode sur le temps" (ode on time). Certain phrases definitely foreshadow Lamartine's "Le Lac" ("The Lake"), such as "l'océan des âges" and "en vain contre le temps je cherche une barrière." Lamartine evidently knew and admired the poem, which lacks the love element of "The Lake." Thomas evokes the flight of time, the ephemeral life of humans on earth, and the hope of eternity—themes that were to become very popular in the nineteenth century.

NICOLAS-JOSEPH-LAURENT GILBERT

Even more Romantic and fiercely independent was Nicolas-Joseph-Laurent Gilbert (1751-1780), who attacked the philosophes in satirical works and showed real poetic promise before his untimely death. Although his fate was associated with that of Thomas Chatterton by Alfred de Vigny, Gilbert's death was in fact the result of an accident, and his harsh invectives against his society, such as in *Le Dix-huitième Siècle* (1775; the eighteenth century), were well understood by his contemporaries. In this poem, he condemned the philosophes, inveighing against atheism and immorality accompanied by lack of real art. His "Ode sur le jugement dernier" (1773; ode on the Last Judgment) is pre-Romantic in tone. His most touching work, with a distinctly Romantic feeling for death, "Ode imitée à plusieurs psaumes" ("Ode—Imitated from the Psalms") or "Adieux à la vie" (farewell to life), was written in 1780, shortly before his own death.

ISLAND-BORN FRENCH POETS

Romantic exoticism characterized the works of three poets born in French semitropical islands: Nicolas-Germain Léonard (1744-1793), born in Guadeloupe, and Antoine Bertin (1752-1790) and Évariste-Désiré de Forges de Parny (1753-1814), both born on the Île Bourbon, now the Île de la Réunion. The *Idylles* (1766) of Léonard are dreamy and delicate, recalling James Thomson (1700-1748) and Oliver Goldsmith in inspiration, though not without a classical influence. Léonard's more descriptive passages anticipate Alfred de Musset and especially Lamartine, who knew and read his works. Bertin, a friend of Parny, is best known for his *Les Amours* (1780), written in the manner of the sixteenth century poet Pierre de Ronsard. They are erotic, lighthearted, and sensual, with overtones of melancholy such as one finds in Watteau's painting *Fêtes galantes*.

The best poet of the three was Parny. He was much appreciated by Voltaire, who—alluding to the Roman elegist Tibullus—called him "mon cher Tibulle"; to posterity, Parny was known by the less flattering diminutive Tibullinus. A poet of love and sensuality, Parny took as his Elvire a woman named Eléonore, whom he was not permitted to marry. His best love poetry is found in *Poésies érotiques* (1778; erotic poems). He addressed patriotic themes in his "Épître aux insurgents de Boston" (1777). His most original works, however, are his *Chansons madécasses traduites en françois* (1787), which are really poems in prose, although the distinction of inventing the genre usually goes to Aloysius Bertrand. Sensual and even licentious in the manner of the eighteenth century, Parny's poetry is not without the melancholy that was to inspire nineteenth century Romantics.

PRE-ROMANTICISM

As the nineteenth century dawned, minor poets already were writing in Romantic accents, yet Romantic poetry did not come into prominence until 1820. A transitional writer, Charles-Hubert Millevoye (1782-1816), began with classical epistles, translations of Vergil, and biblical and historical poems. Millevoye's "Chute des feuilles" (falling leaves), "La Demeure abandonnée" (the abandoned dwelling), "Le Poète mourant" (the dying poet), and "Priez pour moi" (pray

for me) are true Romantic poems, distinguished by their melancholy, appreciation of nature, and meditations on death and by their early expression of the cult of the individual.

ANDRÉ-MARIE CHÉNIER

The eighteenth century, so little known for true poetic inspiration, ended with the voice of a real poet, André-Marie Chénier (1762-1794), whose brother Marie-Joseph Chénier (1764-1811) at first eclipsed him in fame. Born in Constantinople of a mother who falsely claimed Greek ancestry, Chénier was to be haunted throughout his life by the Greek concept of beauty. His early poetry, mostly elegiac, was written in the style of the eighteenth century, yet he gradually attained a masterful simplicity, especially in *Les Bucoliques* (wr. 1785-1787, pb. 1819). Aiming, like Voltaire, to write an epic, he began two, *Hermès* and *L'Amérique*, neither of which was ever completed, although *L'Amérique* shows his gift for cosmic vision. In 1794, Chénier wrote *Iambes*, attacking the Jacobine tyranny that would send him to the guillotine the same year.

Chénier was not a Romantic: There is in his verse no cult of the individual, no restless melancholy or evocation of nature and death. If anything, he was a classical poet: His own line, "Sur les pensers nouveaux, faisons des vers antiques" ("On new thoughts, let us make ancient verses"), sums up his aesthetic. Some of his finest poems, such as "L'Aveugle" (the blind man), the story of a meeting of three shepherds with Homer, anticipate the work of Victor Hugo. "La Jeune Tatentine" (the young Tatentine), a classical story of a young woman drowned at sea, is told in sober and clear lines. "La Jeune Captive" (the young captive), inspired by Chénier's meeting with the young Aimée de Coigny in prison, expresses their desire to cling to the young and vibrant life that the revolution was about to snatch from them. Chénier was at least able to attain immortality through his work, for although Romantic poetry was not to follow his style, it did continue his genuine lyrical inspiration. More directly, the Parnassians emulated his sculptural beauty and his love of ancient Greece.

ROMANTICISM

The nineteenth century in France, as in England, Germany, Poland, and Russia, opened under the sign of

Romanticism. While this was the Romantic period par excellence, Romantic themes in literature and ideas ebb and flow in alternation with the serenity of classicism. It is the opposition of a Greek temple to a Gothic cathedral, one representing a single, perfect idea repeated endlessly; the other, freedom in original creativity. Authors such as Madame de Staël have romanticized Romanticism, seeing in it the Christian expression of melancholy, the incompleteness of existence, and the somber gray of foggy northern climates. Finally, Romanticism expresses the turbulence of the human spirit as it strives for independence and emancipation from the rules and restraints of classical order and reason.

In France, the Romantic period spanned a century, from the late eighteenth century to the late nineteenth, achieving its fullest expression during the first third of the nineteenth century. Romanticism first appeared in France during the years between 1760 and 1775, largely in prose rather than poetry. It was from England and Germany, however, rather than from Rousseau and Diderot, that the French Romantic movement, especially in poetry, was to take its primary inspiration.

Madame de Staël's *De l'Allemagne* (1810; *Germany*, 1813) places the roots of Romanticism in Germany, and in the years that followed, French Romantics such as Victor Cousin, Jules Michelet, Charles-Augustin Sainte-Beuve, Hugo, Lamartine, Musset, and others would visit Germany as a hallowed shrine. In France, the most influential German Romantics were Johann Wolfgang von Goethe (1749-1832), whose Werther was the ancestor of René and Adolphe; Friedrich Schiller (1759-1805); and especially the teller of fantastic tales, E. T. A. Hoffmann (1776-1822), whose influence is directly evident in the works of Charles Nodier, Gérard de Nerval, and Théophile Gautier.

For the French Romantics, English inspiration meant William Shakespeare, whom many authors, such as Stendhal in *Racine et Shakspeare* (1823, 1825; *Racine and Shakespeare*, 1962), were to exalt in place of the French classicists. Voltaire, in the eighteenth century, had already proclaimed Shakespeare's superiority; both poets and dramatists were to discover him in the nineteenth. The sentimental novelists of eighteenth century England, such as Samuel Richardson (1689-1761),

not only influenced French Romanticism, but inspired changes in the literature of far-off Russia as well. The two greatest contemporary influences from England were Sir Walter Scott (1771-1832), whose novels of medieval chivalry inspired Vigny, Alexandre Dumas, père, Honoré de Balzac, Hugo, Prosper Mérimée, and Gautier as well as writers in Italy, Germany, and Russia, and Lord Byron (1788-1824). The Byronic hero became the model for Romantics throughout Europe.

Although literary historians usually date the flowering of French Romanticism from François-René de Chateaubriand's novels *Atala* (1801; English translation, 1802) and *René* (1802; English translation, 1813) and his treatise *Le Génie du christianisme* (1802; *The Genius of Christianity*, 1802), there was actually a prolonged silence in literary production from the beginning of the French Revolution in 1789 to the exile of Napoleon Bonaparte in 1815. With the exception of Chénier, there was practically nothing of great value in poetry during this period—in fact, not until Lamartine's *Poetical Meditations* in 1820. The intensity of the Revolution was no doubt responsible for the early years of this lacuna, although poetry did not have a remarkable history in the eighteenth century. The role of Napoleon (1769-1821) in the history of Romanticism is more problematic. A classicist in taste and philosophy, he launched the most severe and correct of all styles, the Empire style, and he took the ancient Roman Empire as the model of his conquests. No one, however, understood better than he the message of the Revolution: liberty, equality, fraternity, the need for newness, mobility of class structure, patriotism. Although he dreamed of French supremacy in Europe, his "liberation" of Germany and Italy taught the inhabitants of these countries to seek their own roots, and thus he sowed the seeds of nationalism throughout Europe.

French Romanticism, not unlike the Romantic movements in England, Germany, Poland, and Russia, stressed freedom from classical restraints. Since the classical tradition was strongest in France, where the distinction between comedy and tragedy was adhered to with Aristotelian exactness, the call to freedom did not immediately abolish classical forms. Lamartine still wrote in Alexandrines and evoked pagan deities and classical heroes. It was through the emancipation of the theater that poetry was to find new forms of expression, although Hugo's early verse is marked by formal experimentation. Where classicism insists on universal themes, Romanticism stresses the individual: Racine's *Phèdre* (1677; *Phedra*, 1776) dramatizes every woman's jealousy; "The Lake" is Lamartine's personal lament at the loss of love. Classicism made reason the primary law—in the words of Boileau, "aimez donc la raison." Romanticism, echoing Pascal's "raisons du coeur," the reasons of the heart, insisted that emotion had a more powerful role to play.

French Romantic poetry also exalted nature. As Rousseau discovered the mountains of Switzerland, so Lamartine heard the echoes of the Lac du Bourget in the surrounding hills of Burgundy, and Vigny evoked the purple and gold of Mount Nebo in exotic grandeur. However, for the Romantics, nature is more than a setting or, as in the eighteenth century, an object of study. Rather, it reflects the moods of the poet: Chateaubriand's melancholy, for example, becomes the autumn leaves that he hopes will carry him off to the land of happiness and oblivion. Death, too, is a Romantic theme, perhaps best illustrated by Chateaubriand's cult of the tomb. The Romantics, for the most part, share a spiritual orientation, though most of them reject traditional religious forms. Like Rousseau's Savoyard vicar, they call on the God of the heart, whom they find in nature as well. Hence, they believe in immortality and resurrection, with the possible exception of the stoic Vigny, who stresses the silence of God in response to man's sufferings.

The revolt against classicism further implied a rejection of antiquity and a preference for the Middle Ages. As writers examined their individual memories in meditative introspection, so nations sought their origins in what, until then, had been despised medieval institutions and buildings. Gothic architecture was again respected. Eugène-Emmanuel Viollet-le-Duc (1814-1879) restored cathedrals and chateaus; medieval manuscripts were collected and studied. Folktales about Renard and *chansons de geste* about Roland were evoked more than Ulysses and Aeneas. Along with medieval themes, exoticism was cultivated. Chateaubriand idealized the New World, the domain of the noble savage; Lamartine and Vigny were inspired by the Holy Land; Eugène Delacroix's somber paintings took on the sunny skies of Algeria after his visit there.

Romanticism, as Madame de Staël observed, is profoundly bathed in melancholy. The French spoke of a pervasive mal du siècle, suggesting a mood of restlessness and ennui, a distaste for one's society, a superabundance of life. This state of mind anticipates the dilemma of modern humanity, overwhelmed by too many options and rejecting traditional and stable values: Romantic melancholy deepens and sours under Charles Baudelaire, and eventually becomes the Absurd of Albert Camus.

Although Chateaubriand was the most profoundly Romantic of all French writers, his works are in prose, albeit with a poetic rhythm and orientation. The great French Romantic poets are Lamartine (1790-1869), Vigny (1797-1863), Musset (1810-1857), and Hugo (1802-1885). Since Romanticism implies freedom, each one was very different, yet they, like all French writers, gravitated to a salon—in the early 1820's, to Charles Nodier's salon at the Arsenal, and after 1827, to Hugo's Cénacle, rue Notre-Dame-des-Champs. Their greatest period of literary productivity was between 1820 and 1850, although Hugo's major poetic works, *Les Châtiments* (1853) and *Les Contemplations* (1856), appeared later. This was a period of relative conservatism in France: The restoration of the Bourbons had already taken place in 1815. The revolution of 1830, however, which brought Louis-Philippe to power, inspired a wave of lyric poetry.

ALPHONSE DE LAMARTINE

The publication of Alphonse de Lamartine's *Poetical Meditations* in 1820 revolutionized French poetry as William Wordsworth and Samuel Taylor Coleridge's *Lyrical Ballads* had revolutionized English poetry in 1798. Immediately, Lamartine became famous, and though he later wrote more profound and scholarly works, it is for his first brief collection that he is remembered in French literature. In it, he immortalizes Elvire, an idealization of Madame Julie Charles, whom he had met at the Lac du Bourget in 1816 and who died shortly afterward. His best-known poem, and one of the most beloved in all of French literature, is "The Lake," in which he evokes the passage of time and the role of memory in keeping alive past happiness. Other poems in the volume treat such Romantic themes as nostalgia for one's childhood and the beauty of the Burgundian countryside. Lamartine continued in the Romantic vein in *Nouvelles méditations poétiques* (1823, new poetic meditations), *La Mort de Socrate* (1823; *The Death of Socrates*, 1829), and *Le Dernier Chant du pèleringe d'Harold* (1825; *The Last Canto of Childe Harold's Pilgrimage*, 1827), inspired by Lord Byron's *Childe Harold's Pilgrimage* (1812-1818, 1819).

Harmonies poétiques et religieuses (1830; poetic and religious harmonies) was inspired by a desire to write modern psalms and reveals a deeply religious orientation in the tradition of eighteenth century poets such as Louis Racine and Thomas. Lamartine had spent the years from 1826 to 1828 in Italy with the French embassy in Florence, and an Italian strain is evident in these volumes. Lamartine writes often of death and immortality, paraphrasing Pascal's comparison of the grandeur of God and the finiteness of humans, similar to the disparity between the immensity of nature and the insignificance of humanity. After 1830, Lamartine became more deeply involved in French politics, and by 1848, he was part of the provisional government in the Second Republic. Hence, his late works are more often explicitly political. Lamartine also dreamed of a vast epic poem that was to be his "Légende des siècles." He realized it in part in two enormous works: *Jocelyn* (1836; English translation, 1837) and *La Chute d'un ange* (1838; the fall of an angel). Both are for the most part forgotten today, although *Jocelyn* was immensely successful when it was published. It tells the story of a seminarian, put to flight by the Revolution, who falls in love with another fugitive. Their love cannot be consummated because of his subsequent ordination, yet when she dies, he lovingly buries her, in a scene recalling Chateaubriand's *Atala*.

Lamartine's is lyric poetry in the original sense of the word: poetry that sings. Simple diction, melodic alliteration, repetition, and a gift for memorable formulations make his verse easy to recite and learn by heart. Lamartine's ideas are clear; although he uses symbols and images, they are easily intelligible and they touch the ordinary reader. Lamartine is also noted for his sincerity, both in his personal poetry and in his political verse. M. F. Guyard, however, editor of Lamartine's poems in the Pléiade edition, finds him not exacting enough, too uneven in style, mistaking quantity for quality. Nevertheless, Lamartine introduced into French literature the Romantic and lyrical style, which, after undergoing diverse mutations, profoundly influenced the development of modern literature, not merely in France but virtually worldwide.

ALFRED DE VIGNY

Very different from Lamartine's gentle lyricism is the stoicism and revolt of Alfred de Vigny. Conscious of his ancient family nobility and hostile to the revolution and all that it symbolized, Vigny supported the conservative government of the Restoration and that of Napoleon III. At the same time, his work foreshadows the modern concept of the Absurd, which Albert Camus was to popularize in the mid-twentieth century. A solitary like the existentialists, who see humans as thrown into a hostile universe without recourse to divinity or human fellowship, Vigny projected himself in the title figure of his play *Chatterton* (pr., pb. 1835): the poet misunderstood by society. In contrast to Lamartine, whose voluminous work touched on many topics, Vigny wrote little and well. He is known especially for *Poèmes antiques et modernes* (1826, 1829, 1837; ancient and modern poems) and *Les Destinées* (destinies), published posthumously, in 1864.

Although much of Vigny's poetry is declamatory and shows the influence of Chénier, Byron, and Chateaubriand, one of his best works, "Moïse" (1822; Moses), is faithful to its biblical inspiration in its spirit of uncompromising moral solitude. The greatest of the Old Testament prophets, a figure for the poet, is symbolically called by God to the top of the mountain, yet when he complains of his solitude, he receives nothing but silence. In symbolic language, he recalls his mission with pride and distress and seeks only to sleep the sleep of the earth. Later, Vigny was to exalt the fierce and stoic pride of refusal to submit to one's fate in "La Mort du loup" (1838; the death of the wolf), while in "Le Mont des oliviers" (1844; the Mount of Olives), Christ, like Moses, faces a silent and impassive God. Like the Symbolists who followed him, Vigny gradually came to a religion of art.

Essentially a philosophical poet, Vigny builds his poems on a structure of symbols, often weaving a stanza around a single image. In contrast to Lamartine, Vigny's stance is aloof; detached from his creation, the poet expresses his intimate thoughts under the guise of the symbol. Vigny the dramatist is also present in his poetry, where dialogue and gesture reveal the idea to be expressed, as in his account of the wounded she-wolf who does not deign to address her mate's killers, or the dialogue of Christ with his Father. Vigny used the Alexandrine consistently: *Les Destinées* includes eleven poems totaling about two thousand lines, with regular classical rhyme. Vigny has often been accused of living in an ivory tower, but he sought to flee the vulgar crowd in order to bring humanity to a higher level, and he expressed through his own paradoxical nature the eternal conflict of hope and despair.

ALFRED DE MUSSET

Known as the "enfant gâté," the spoiled child of Romanticism, Alfred de Musset exemplifies the suffering Romantic youth full of passion and desire. The volume of his poetry is not great, yet he wrote some of the finest plays of the period, notably *Lorenzaccio* (pb. 1834; English translation, 1905). He wrote his best works between the ages of twenty and thirty and spent the final years of his short life in frivolity, forgotten by those who had praised him so highly for his first volume, *Contes d'Espagne et d'Italie* (1829; *Tales of Spain and Italy*, 1905), a collection of charming, lighthearted poems about countries Musset had never visited. Musset, the quintessential Romantic, mocked Romanticism in his witty "Ballade à la lune" ("Ballad to the Moon"), as he mocked contemporary drama in such works as "Une Soirée perdue" ("A Lost Evening").

After Musset's liaison with George Sand—an affair that ended in betrayal and suffering—his poetry took on a new tone; the period after his rupture with Sand (1835-1840) was also his most productive. He is best known for the cycle of poems titled *Les Nuits* (nights), written between 1835 and 1837. Apart from "La Nuit de décembre," in which the poet meets his double at critical moments of his life, the poems of the cycle constitute a dialogue between the poet and his Muse, who calls him forth to poetic creativity. The month determines the image: May, springtime, brings an invitation to love and breathes the perfume of flowers and voluptuousness. August is a more triumphant evocation of

the poet's victory over his suffering, though without any definitive result. In "La Nuit d'octobre," the last of the series, the Muse takes on a maternal stance and attempts to cure the poet of his sickness by counseling him to gather the flowers of today's garden, forgetting the past.

Much criticized by contemporaries and later nineteenth century critics for his frivolity and lack of depth, Musset appeals to many twentieth century readers, particularly in his emphasis on the double: The poet engages in dialogue with himself and analyzes his dreams in a strikingly modern manner. Musset's poetry is musical, brilliant, and varied; he employs the Alexandrine and the newer experimental forms with equal facility. Many of his lyrics belong to the genre of the popular song, very much appreciated in the nineteenth century. His subtle wit places him in the French comic tradition, though not in the overt "esprit gaulois" of François Rabelais and Voltaire. Perhaps Musset's greatest contribution to French Romanticism is a spirit of youth and verve, sensitivity and passion, and a desire to enjoy life and profit from the sufferings it imposes.

VICTOR HUGO

The one figure who unites all French Romantics and towers over them in gigantic proportions is Victor Hugo. Born in the year made famous by Chateaubriand's *René* and *The Genius of Christianity*, Hugo declared, early in life, that he wished to be "Chateaubriand or nothing." Indeed, there is a great similarity between the two: an Olympic vision; a fascination with the *gouffre*, or the abysmal whirlpool, and with the tomb; a sense of the rhythm of words and a facility in manipulating them. Known universally as a thoroughgoing Romantic, Hugo was still publishing lengthy collections in the 1870's and the 1880's, long after Baudelaire had redirected poetry into the path of Symbolism and in the very years in which Stéphane Mallarmé was cloaking it with Hermetic obscurity. A prolific novelist and playwright as well as a poet, Hugo proclaimed the Romantic revolution in the theater and opened the path for experimentation in poetry, allowing *rejets* and enjambments, verses of all meters and lengths, and new types of rhyme.

Hugo began to publish poetry in 1822, about the same time as Lamartine and Vigny, and with them, he formed a poetic triumvirate recognized by their contemporaries. Hugo at first seemed the most conservative, yet in 1826, with *Odes et ballades*, and in 1829, with *Les Orientales* (1829; *Les Orientales: Or, Eastern Lyrics*, 1879), he launched a wave of medievalism and orientalism that was to dominate early French Romanticism. The second period of Hugo's poetic career, before his exile in 1851, was marked by personal suffering and political involvement. His most important volumes of poetry from this period are *Les Feuilles d'automne* (1831; the leaves of autumn), *Les Chants du crépuscule* (1835; *Songs of Twilight*, 1836), *Les Voix intérieures* (1837; interior voices), and *Les Rayons et les ombres* (1840; the rays and the shadows). The manner of the poems is varied, as is Hugo's wont; there are poems about his love for Juliette Drouet and about his family, as well as French history and the revolution of 1830. He defines the role of poet as seer and manifests an awareness of the vast panorama of human history.

In 1851, Napoleon III carried out a coup d'état and shifted to a conservative rightist position, openly allying himself with the Church and the nobility. Hugo was disillusioned with the leader whom he had previously supported and denounced him with such vehemence that Hugo was obliged to leave France, at first traveling to Belgium and then to the English islands of Jersey and Guernsey. The fruit of his political invective is a volume of poetry titled *Les Châtiments* (the chastisements), in which he compares Napoleon I to Napoleon III or Napoleon le Petit. Some of the poems are mere political insults; others are exalted verse, especially the lengthy *Expiation*. While in exile, however, Hugo's wrath cooled, and he began to reflect on more universal topics. His poetic masterpiece, *Les Contemplations* (1856), deals with intimate themes, such as the death of his daughter Léopoldine, the role of the poet, the problem of suffering humanity, and the exaltation of the simple and the poor. The volume expresses Hugo's personal vision of the world and its destiny, mingling Christianity, Illuminism, and eclectic mystical doctrines. It is in this collection of poems that Hugo the visionary emerges: The beggar's cloak becomes a constellation, the sower of plants in the sky, and the harvester's sickle is reflected in the crescent moon as the union of Boaz and Ruth prefigures the birth of Christ.

Victor Hugo (Hulton Archive/Getty Images)

Hugo continued to work on his vast epic after his return to France in 1870, dreaming of a historical masterpiece that would embrace all time in *La Légende des siècles* (1859-1883; *The Legend of Centuries*, 1894). He also planned for it to include *Dieu* (1891; God) and *La Fin de Satan* (1886; the devil). At the same time, in *L'Année terrible* (1872; the terrible year), he recounted the ravages of war and revolution—the bloody birth of the Third Republic in 1870. The heyday of Romanticism was by then long past, yet Hugo remained a living legend. Political deputy and member of the Opposition, spokesperson for the Romantic theater, Hugo led as well as wrote. In his vast collection of works, he left models for all meters and all topics. Although often trite, he is seldom without wit or sentiment. At times painfully long-winded, he can also compress deep emotion into a few lines, as in a poem about his pilgrimage to his daughter's grave, "Demain, dès l'aube. . . ."

Visionary and Olympian, rivaling God in his pride and consumed by sensuality, Hugo was also a poet of delicacy and humility; he has left an indelible mark on French literature.

PARNASSIAN POETS

Romanticism was perhaps the last great literary movement. Others, such as Symbolism and Surrealism, have since appeared, but they have lacked the unity of doctrine and the sweeping appeal of Romanticism. Nevertheless, they have left a profound mark on modern society, itself fragmented and confused.

By 1850, Romantic themes had begun to lose favor. In the novel, realism had already made its appearance: Balzac, in his *La Comédie humaine* (1842-1848; *The Human Comedy*, 1896), showed men as pawns of social forces and victims of their own monomaniacal passions. Romantic emotion was still present, yet it was not the introspective *mal du siècle* of Chateaubriand's *René*. The cult of the individual broadened to a concern for society, particularly in Hugo's poems and novels, where the downtrodden and the unfortunate became heroes rather than the noble savage or the disillusioned noble. In *Le Rouge et le noir* (1830; *The Red and the Black*, 1898), Stendhal, too, had chosen for his protagonist a provincial young man who is a far cry from the Byronic heroes of Romantic fiction.

Although the novel was to turn to the middle class for its inspiration, a number of poets turned away from the changing society of the mid-nineteenth century to take refuge in a detached ethereal atmosphere. These Parnassian poets, as they were known, who never constituted a full-fledged literary school with a unified doctrine, edited a journal called *Le Parnasse contemporain* (contemporary Parnassus), named for the home of the Muses. Its first issue, in 1866, contained poems by Gautier, Théodore de Banville, Charles-Marie Leconte de Lisle, Baudelaire, José-Maria de Heredia, François-Édouard Coppée, Sully Prudhomme, Verlaine, and Mallarmé, several of whom were to gain fame as Symbolists or as talented independent writers. The Parnassians' second volume appeared in 1871; the third volume, issued in 1876, is little more than an anthology, with no unifying theme.

The single doctrine that loosely linked the Parnassian poets was their commitment to art for art's sake. Reacting against Hugo's metrical freedoms and Romantic introspection, the Parnassians proclaimed the necessity of perfection in form. They wished to remain objective, not revealing their personal emotions or opinions. They sought serenity, equilibrium, and purity in their work, striving for sculptural perfection and a close affiliation with the plastic arts in general. Often finding inspiration in classical sources, they did not abandon the Romantic cult of the Middle Ages or love of the exotic. Although the main representatives of Parnasse are Leconte de Lisle (1818-1894), Banville (1823-1891), Heredia (1842-1905), and Prudhomme (1839-1907), these poets acknowledged the inspiration of Gautier (1811-1872) and Nerval (1808-1855), whose individualistic voice was claimed by many poetic schools, ranging from the Symbolists to the Surrealists. The Parnassians also greatly admired André Chénier.

THÉOPHILE GAUTIER

Equally Romantic and Parnassian, Gautier was both a poet and a painter in verse. It was the latter quality in particular that attracted the Parnassians, who sought affinities with the plastic arts. Gautier's first volume, *Poésies* (1830; English translation, 1973), set a new tone in such poems as the calm "Paysage" (countryside). *La Comédie de la mort* (1838; *The Drama of Death*, 1909) is Romantic in its cult of death, yet it lacks the fantastic element so characteristic of Romantic verse on this theme. It was with *Émaux et camées* (1852, enlarged 1872; *Enamels and Cameos*, 1900) that Gautier found his own style. In this enormously influential work, Gautier states his intention to treat a limited number of subjects in a restrained form. He seeks durability rather than movement, noting that he prefers "the statue to the woman." Indifferent to social problems and human suffering, he seeks "plastic poetry." All passes, he writes in his *Art poétique* (1857). Only art will endure: The bust survives the city.

In his "Symphonie en blanc majeur" ("Symphony in White Major"), Gautier seeks to evoke in poetry a fusion of music with the visual arts. He speaks of the swan-maidens (the Valkyries) as impassive statues in icy white, and likens them to a woman whose beauty is self-contained. He carves a poetic statue in solid marble, articulating each part of the body in tones of white, and uses the harmonies of the sounds to create a musical atmosphere. Gautier's combination of Romantic and often ethereal subject matter with poetic forms aspiring to the qualities of sculpture opened new directions in French poetry and, later, through Ezra Pound's Imagism, influenced a generation of poets who did not know the French Symbolists at first hand.

GÉRARD DE NERVAL

Gérard Labrunie, known as Gérard de Nerval, lacked Gautier's sense of aesthetic distance. For Nerval, poetry was exorcism, an attempt to clarify his clouded emotional and mental state. A feminine figure, based on the actress Jenny Colon, with whom he fell in love in 1836, dominates his work. She is named Aurélia or Sylvie and appears in his tales as well as in his poetry. Nerval's eclectic religion of art borrows elements from traditional Christianity as well as from alchemy, the Kabbalah, and other occult systems; he also places much hope in dreams. For him, "le rêve est une autre vie" (dreams are another life), and the Surrealists were to hail him as their predecessor. Nerval's symbols possess an absolute reality for him. He becomes the Prince of Aquitaine evoked in "El Desdichado."

Nerval's principal collection of poems is the sequence of sonnets titled *Les Chimères* (English translation, 1965; also known as *Chimeras*, 1966; best known as *The Chimeras*, 1982), published in 1854 with his tales *Les Filles du feu* (*Daughters of Fire*, 1922). The poems are full of paradox and mystery, like the legendary Chimera; Nerval himself said of them that they "lose their charm if they are explained." Rich in classical allusions loosely woven together, they evoke the unlikely juxtapositions of a dream. The sonnets have the clear, sculptured quality of Gautier's verse mingled with uninhibited fantasy. Nerval's is a private mythology, in which plants and animals have a secret meaning. Translator of Goethe's *Faust: Eine Tragödie* (pb. 1808, 1833; *The Tragedy of Faust*, 1823, 1838) and Hoffmann's tales, Nerval was enamored of German poetry and remained throughout his life under the spell of the Faustian quest for privileged knowledge. Long considered a poet of the second rank—although his admirers included Gautier, Baudelaire, and Marcel Proust—Nerval has been reevaluated by modern crit-

ics, who see in him and his "supernaturalism" an important step in the exploration of the subconscious.

CHARLES-MARIE LECONTE DE LISLE

If both Gautier and Nerval inspired the Parnassians, Charles-Marie Leconte de Lisle was their uncontested master. After an apprenticeship in political verse, which revealed his attraction to the ideas of Félicité-Robert de Lamennais and Charles Fourier, Leconte de Lisle found his own style in *Poèmes antiques* (1852; ancient poems), *Poèmes barbares* (1862; barbarian poems), *Les Érinnyes* (1873, the Erinyes), *Poèmes tragiques* (1884; tragic poems), and *Derniers poèmes* (1895; last poems). Intransigent in his aestheticism, he made art his religion, not unlike Mallarmé, Valéry, and Proust. Leconte de Lisle's salon became the meeting place of the young poets of his generation, who came to accept his definition of art as the cult of beauty. In his conception, art is reserved for an elite, independent of truth, morality, and utility.

Leconte de Lisle translated the Greek classics to earn his livelihood, and his works are permeated by classical figures. In his poems, he often reworks classical myths to convey his message. Like Gautier, Leconte de Lisle resembles a painter or a sculptor, and in classical fashion, exhibits serenity and perfect control of his material. He also draws on Asian myths and Hindu philosophy, the source of his concept of the *néant divin* (divine nothingness). Leconte de Lisle's nature poems are beautiful for their clear and precise evocations. In contrast to Chateaubriand's identification with autumn leaves and misty shores, Leconte de Lisle invites the reader to enter through nature into the *néant divin*, since nothing is real and all is the dream of a dream.

BANVILLE, HEREDIA, AND PRUDHOMME

Among the Parnassians who frequented Leconte de Lisle's salon, the three most important are Théodore de Banville, José-Maria de Heredia, and Sully Prudhomme. Banville shows more concern for form than for content, and his early publications, *Les Cariatides* (1842) and *Les Stalactites* (1846), reveal his admiration for Greek art and for a sculptured effect in verse. Inspired by such diverse themes as acrobatic exercises (*Odes funambulesques*, 1857) and the Middle Ages (*Trente-six Ballades joyeuses à la manière de François*

Villon, 1873; joyous ballads in the manner of François Villon), Banville worked especially to achieve "rich rhymes."

Heredia, of Cuban origin, is known for his mastery of the sonnet; his most important collection, *Les Trophées* (1893; *Sonnets from the Trophies*, 1898), contains 118 sonnets evoking past grandeur and exotic countries. Erudite and exact, his gallery of sonnets presents a series of perfect miniatures. Prudhomme, the poet of the "Vase brisé," the broken vase like a broken heart, differs from the other Parnassians in his sensibility, evident in his earlier work, *Stances et poèmes* (1865), *Les Épreuves* (1866; trials), *Les Solitudes* (1869), and *Les Vaines Tendresses* (1875; vain tenderness). His later works, *La Justice* (1878) and *Le Bonheur* (1888; happiness), are oriented toward didactic and philosophical themes.

PROSE POEMS

Romanticism, with its call for new forms and experimentation, coupled with Parnassian emphasis on style, provoked a new type of poetry in the mid-nineteenth century. Generally called the *poème en prose*, or prose poem, its origination is credited to Aloysius Bertrand (1807-1841), although Parny, in his *Chansons madécasses traduites en françois* in 1787, had anticipated it by almost a century. Bertrand's *Gaspard de la nuit* was published in 1842, a year after his death. Delicate and exact like a sculpture or a miniature, his work inspired a flurry of interest in the prose poem. Two prose poems, *La Bacchante* and *Le Centaure*, by Maurice de Guérin (1810-1839), were published posthumously in 1840, and many critics regard Lamennais's *Paroles d'un croyant* (1834; words of a believer) as a prose poem. This work of mystical socialism expresses religious and political beliefs in vibrant and inspiring terms. It was, however, with Baudelaire, Lautréamont, and Arthur Rimbaud that the prose poem was to become an important literary form. Lautréamont (1846-1870), whose real name was Isidore-Lucien Ducasse, anticipated the Surrealist revolution in his *Chants de Maldoror*, a prose poem published in 1869.

CHARLES BAUDELAIRE

With Charles Baudelaire (1821-1867), a new generation of poets—and, in fact, modern poetry—was born. At first grouped by literary historians with the Romantics and the Parnassians, Baudelaire was soon linked with the Symbolists, whose work he inspired. His famous poem "Correspondances," included in *Les Fleurs du mal* (1857, 1861, 1868; *Flowers of Evil*, 1909), expresses in its first stanza the ethos of the entire Symbolist movement:

> Nature is a temple, in which living pillars
> Sometimes utter a babel of words;
> Man traverses it through forests of symbols,
> That watch him with knowing eyes.

Flowers of Evil, Baudelaire's great volume of poems, admits good and evil; moral, immoral, and amoral; beautiful and ugly, as fit matter for poetry. The greatest modern vice, Baudelaire proclaims, is ennui,

Charles Baudelaire (The Granger Collection, New York)

and he pictures Satan Trismégiste smoking his pipe as he prepares to swallow the world in one gaping yawn. Baudelaire's ennui is far removed from the romantic *mal du siècle*; it is connected with bourgeois conformity and mediocrity, an absence of true feeling and individual values. It is the same ennui that devours the parish of Georges Bernanos's country priest, and not unlike that which is subjected to a *reductio ad absurdum* in Eugène Ionesco's portraits of society. Modern society gravitates toward the city, and Baudelaire was one of the first poets of the city in all of its faceless anonymity. He sees the dark and seamy side of Paris—the nightlife, the underworld, the beggars, and the prostitutes—and with true compassion, pities their helplessness.

Baudelaire was constantly torn between two extremes, the desire for spirituality and the pull toward sensuality, and his poetry reveals the torment of guilt and despair. Woman becomes the symbol of this "double postulation": Idealized women, chaste and semi-divine, are opposed to the figure of Baudelaire's mulatto mistress, Jeanne Duval, a sensuous Eve whose flowing hair, like the waves of the sea, leads him off into exotic climates and voluptuous paradises, yet whose very sensuality inspires his contempt. The epitome of modern humanity, Baudelaire seeks the "artificial paradises" of drugs and alcohol, hoping to overcome ennui and disgust and intensify his perceptions.

A brilliant art critic as well as a poet, Baudelaire discovered the talent of Delacroix; as a literary critic, he was perhaps the first to grasp the depth of Edgar Allan Poe indeed, Baudelaire introduced a veritable Poe cult in France, and his translations of Poe greatly influenced Mallarmé. In his slim volume *Petits Poèmes en prose* (1869; also known as *Le Spleen de Paris*; *Poems in Prose*, 1905, also known as *Paris Spleen, 1869*, 1947), Baudelaire perfected the new form of the prose poem.

In his prose poems, Baudelaire expresses his hatred of bourgeois conformism and his faith in art as the path to salvation. Somewhat akin to the Parnassian cult of beauty, this idea was to become the credo of Mallarmé and Verlaine, and it launched a new phase of poetry, not only in France but abroad as well. If Hugo is the greatest Romantic poet, then Baudelaire is the most original and the most modern of the nineteenth century.

SYMBOLISM

Symbolism is more difficult to define than Romanticism or Parnassianism, although it shares elements with both. From the Romantics, the Symbolists inherited an emphasis on subjectivity and the image of the poet as seer, an isolated figure rejected by society. From the Parnassians, the Symbolists took the notions of perfection in art and the importance of language for its own sake. Symbolism is oriented toward the ideal, the vague, the world of dreams and unreality. Closely associated with Impressionism, Symbolism reflects the impression of a moment that changes; it poses the question of the relation of the individual to time. Subtlety, fluidity, harmony—all are Symbolist virtues. To name an object, says Mallarmé, is to deprive it of much of its interest. Opposed to the world of materialism and bourgeois society, the Symbolists sought the Platonic and Hegelian universe of the ideal. Mystical without religious aspirations, the Symbolists nevertheless recognized a world of the spirit. They were also closely allied with music: Verlaine proclaimed, "De la musique avant toute chose" (music before everything else), and his works inspired many composers. Mallarmé's *L'Après-midi d'un faune* (1876; *Afternoon of a Faun*, 1956) is perhaps better known to foreign readers through Claude Debussy's tone poem of the same name.

Unlike Romanticism, which came to France primarily by way of England and Germany, Symbolism was born on French soil. The critic Robert Sabatier (*La Poésie du XIXeme siècle*, 2 volumes, 1977) calls the Symbolist movement a "calm revolution." It accompanied the more violent battles of the Franco-Prussian War of 1870, followed by the bloody Commune of 1871. This struggle, shorter but more intense than the revolution of 1789, eventually subsided into the tumultuous Third Republic. Social agitation was great; workers demanded their rights, protesting against low wages, child labor, and other evils. At first, it seems a contradiction to place Verlaine's "pure poetry" in *Romances sans paroles* (1874; *Romances Without Words*, 1921) into such an atmosphere; Symbolism, however, was predicated on a rejection of reality and a quest for perfection.

PAUL VERLAINE

Paul Verlaine (1844-1896), whose verse had appeared in *Le Parnasse contemporain* of 1866, nevertheless epitomizes the quest for suggestion, pure poetry, the vague, and the imprecise. His poetry is pure music, as he himself affirms, written in a minor mode, with an exquisite delicacy markedly opposed to his violent and impulsive character. Friend of the Parnassians, encouraged by Mallarmé and inspired by Rimbaud, Verlaine was well known and appreciated in literary circles. His first work, *Poèmes saturniens* (1866), was an accomplished performance for a young man of twenty-two, its dreamlike verse always verging on melancholy and grim fantasy. *Fêtes galantes* (1869; *Gallant Parties*, 1912), in the manner of Watteau, recalls Pierrot, Columbine, Harlequin, and the *commedia del l'arte*, though once again with a mood of impending disaster. *La Bonne Chanson* (1870) was written for Verlaine's fiancé, Mathilde Mauthé; the marriage, however, was destined not to survive, just as the dancing figures in *Gallant Parties* disappear with the dawn.

Romances Without Words, the most Verlainean of all Verlaine's works, is a volume in which the symbol alone has reality and all else disappears like the "interminable ennui" of the snow-covered plain. The poet is perfectly identified with the simple aspects of nature, such as rain, snow, or the shadow of the trees, hauntingly evocative in the French musical vowels "l'ombre des arbres." Only the music remains, even the verb disappears, as aptly analyzed by Jacques Borel. Verlaine's later work, including *Sagesse* (1880; wisdom), written after his conversion in prison, and *Jadis et naguère* (1884; formerly and long ago), is good but pales in comparison to his few but exquisite works composed during his sojourn with Rimbaud, who brought him both ecstasy and suffering.

ARTHUR RIMBAUD

If Verlaine represents the mystery and subtlety of poetry etched in tones of gray, Arthur Rimbaud (1854-1891) is Prometheus, the rebel, the rival of the gods and the thief of their fire. Rimbaud's credo was to become a seer, a *voyant*, by unleashing all of his senses. In 1871, he foreshadowed his spiritual autobiography in "Le Bateau ivre" ("The Drunken Boat"), where he saw himself drunk with adventure and soon bored with life. In the same year, he attempted a Baudelairean *correspondance* with "Voyelles" ("Vowels"), seeing himself as the inventor of the colors of letters. Like

Nerval's, Rimbaud's work is enigmatic, full of private symbols.

Rimbaud also produced one of the most important volumes of prose poems ever written. *Les Illuminations* (1886; *Illuminations*, 1932)—the title meaning, according to Paul Verlaine, "colored plates"—was written in 1872, in a burst of poetic inspiration. In this exercise in pure Symbolism, Rimbaud, like the Surrealists, tries to wipe away the former world with another deluge and to create a new world with the innocence of childhood and the pure brightness of the sun. He embraces the dawn like a child caressing a beautiful woman, yet, at the same time, he satirizes contemporary society and its bourgeois mediocrity in the style of Baudelaire. There is a mystical quality also in such prose poems as "Conte" ("A Tale"), "Génie" ("Genie"), and "À une raison" ("To a Reason"), which influenced Paul Claudel.

Rimbaud's rupture with Verlaine provoked *Une Saison en enfer* (1873; *A Season in Hell*, 1932), his farewell to poetry. Here, he mixes traditional verse with the prose poem. More coherent in plan and structure than *Illuminations*, it is a kind of spiritual autobiography in which Rimbaud confesses his sadism, cruelty, and inconsistency, especially in his relationship with Verlaine. The critic Enid Starkie (*Arthur Rimbaud*, 1961) sees three principal motifs in the work: sin, God, and life. After believing that he has attained Heaven, Rimbaud discovers that it was really Hell. He had hoped to escape his heritage, but the Christian sense of sin is too strong, and he finds himself "the slave of his baptism." He confesses his Promethean desires, his rivalry with God, and admits that his desire to create the word has ultimately reduced him to silence. Thus, at the age of nineteen, Rimbaud abandoned poetry.

STÉPHANE MALLARMÉ

Stéphane Mallarmé (1842-1898), like Baudelaire and Verlaine, began his career by publishing ten poems in *Le Parnasse contemporain* in 1866. Among them, "Les Fenêtres" ("The Windows") and "Brise marine" ("Sea Breeze") are echoes of Baudelaire's "Les Phares" ("The Beacons"), "Le Voyage" ("The Voyage"), and "Parfum exotique" ("Exotic Perfume") and the prose poem "Anywhere Out of the World" (original title in

English). In fact, the early Mallarmé is hardly distinguishable from Baudelaire, with images of escape, the haunting sound of the sea, and the sick man who always desires another life. It was with *Hérodiade* (1945, 1959; *Herodias*, 1940) and *Afternoon of a Faun* that Mallarmé found his own style. Fame and recognition gradually followed, and he became the center of a salon that included such writers as Jules Laforgue, Henri de Régnier, Maurice Barrès, Claudel, André Gide, and Valéry.

Mallarmé's style is Hermetic, mysterious; in his conception, poetry is addressed to an elite and should speak only in halftones, never revealing the complete message, for to name an object is to rob it of its suggestive magic. Mallarmé's is the poetry of absence, of the inability to realize one's poetic vocation. The azure sky is inaccessible, and the swan is forever imprisoned in the icy lake, haunted by flights that might have been. The faun is perhaps the best image of Mallarmé's poetry; playing sensual music on his flute, the faun evokes the two nymphs that he may or may not have seen, may perhaps have dreamed: "Aimai-je un rêve?" (Did I love a dream?).

Deliberately discouraging the casual reader of his verse, Mallarmé sought to eliminate the beginning and the end of the "plots" of his poems; in his later work, he also introduced dislocations of syntax, so that the words themselves became puzzles to be solved. Images of tombs, of mirrors, of lakes and eyes, sensuous images of women's hair and seductive nymphs grace his poetry. Most of them convey many levels of symbolism, from self-knowledge to artistic creation. The tension between dream and reality, life and death, absence and presence, is at the heart of Mallarmé's work—which, despite its enigmatic quality, has influenced an entire generation of writers, among them Valéry and Marcel Proust, and has provoked numerous exegeses.

DECADENT POETS

Ironically, Baudelaire, Rimbaud, Verlaine, and Mallarmé, who represent the best of Symbolism, did not refer to themselves as Symbolists; the term was applied to them retrospectively. Around 1885, a group of less-skilled poets influenced by these masters grouped together to form what they called the Symbolist school.

Today, they are known to the world of letters by such various names as Decadents and vers-librists. They wrote in ephemeral journals such as *L'Hydropathe*, *Tout-Paris*, *La Nouvelle Rive Gauche*, and *Lutèce*. They wrote manifestos, such as Jean Moréas's *Manifeste du symbolisme*, published in *Le Figaro* in 1886, and René Ghil's *Traité du verbe*. They produced poems of mixed quality but always inferior to the works of the great masters who preceded them.

Among those who were labeled Decadents, the most noteworthy are Charles Cros (1842-1888), a scientist, inventor, and poet, and Corbière (1845-1875), whose *Les Amours jaunes* (yellow loves) was published in 1873. Laforgue (1860-1887), despite the brevity of his life, was perhaps the best known of the group. His principal collections, *Les Complaintes* (1885; complaints) and *L'Imitation de Notre-Dame la lune* (1886; imitation of Our Lady of the Moon), are marked by poetic fantasy and deep sincerity. His later poems are written in free verse, with trivial familiarity, revealing at the same time a preoccupation with death and with the problem of evil. Tormented by the image of Hamlet, Laforgue sought unity through the double. Like Baudelaire, Laforgue observed the monotonous and sad existence of the city; T. S. Eliot acknowledged a considerable debt to Laforgue.

ÉMILE VERHAEREN

The Symbolist tradition continued into the twentieth century. The Flemish-born Émile Verhaeren (1855-1916) was a poet of the modern city. His *Les Campagnes hallucinées* (1893; hallucinatory countrysides) and *Les Villes tentaculaires* (1895; tentacled cities) evoke the city of the future, the labor of workers, and faith in humanity. In style and inspiration, Verhaeren resembles Walt Whitman. In the five volumes of *Toute la Flandre* (1904-1911; includes *Les Tendresses premières*, 1904; *La Guirlande des dunes*, 1907; *Les Héros*, 1908; *Les Villes à Pignons*, 1909; and *Les Plaines*, 1911; all of Flanders), he praised modern progress in his native country.

HENRI DE RÉGNIER

Quite the opposite is Henri de Régnier (1864-1936), who, after an apprenticeship with Parnasse from which he retained the cult of art and beauty, and a number of Symbolist poems, returned to classicism and the inspiration of the seventeenth and eighteenth centuries. *Les Médailles d'argile* (1900; medals of clay) was written in memory of André Chénier. *La Cité des eaux* (1902; the city of waters), inspired by Michelet, evokes Versailles, which Régnier describes in sculptured motifs. One can find in his work echoes of Ronsard, Racine, Chénier, and Mallarmé. Even in the 1920's, Régnier continued to write in the same style, and newer modes eclipsed his fame, though his work is excellent in composition and inspiration.

FRANCIS JAMMES AND PAUL FORT

A return to a simple and natural style marks the works of Francis Jammes (1868-1938) and Paul Fort (1872-1960). Discovered by Mallarmé, Gide, and Régnier when he was thirty years old, Jammes charmed audiences by the simplicity and sincerity of his work. Profoundly Catholic in his orientation, beginning with *Clairières dans le ciel, 1902-1906* (1906; clearings in the sky), he pleased Claudel. Jammes's religious convictions are especially evident in *Géorgiques chrétiennes* (1911-1912; Christian georgics), in which he extols the family and praises God.

Fort's ballads, which at first glance appear to be in prose, feature rhyme, assonance, and other poetic devices. His work is voluminous, and includes plays as well as poetry; in 1890, he created a *Théâtre d'Art* to represent Maurice Maeterlinck's work and Poe's raven. Although Fort's poetry is international, it is also very French; his diction alternates between a simple vocabulary not unlike Francis Jammes's and archaic expressions from the past.

SAINT-POL-ROUX AND BLAISE CENDRARS

Paul-Pierre Roux, known as Saint-Pol-Roux (1861-1940), has the distinction of being claimed by Catholics and Surrealists alike. He lived in seclusion for almost forty years, and his work is a strange mixture of mysticism and what he calls poetic *surcréation*. His *Les Reposoirs de la procession* (1893-1907; repositories of the procession) illustrates his use of free verse, hallucinatory juxtapositions, and mystical language. Also anticipating Surrealism was Blaise Cendrars (1887-1961), whose travels, ranging from New York to Manchuria, in the years before World War I inspired *Pâques à New York* (1912; Easter in New York) and *La Prose du Transsibérien et de la petite Jehanne de France*

(1913; English translation, 1931). The latter includes a dialogue between the author and the legendary Petite Jehanne de France, in which the railroad, in cinematographic fashion, becomes the focus of various images; Cendrars referred to this technique as *simultanéisme*. The original edition was illustrated by Sonia Delaunay and suggests the music of Arthur Honegger's *Pacific 231*. The Swiss-born Cendrars (whose real name was Frédéric Sauser) was also a gifted novelist.

EARLY TWENTIETH CENTURY POETS

The period between 1905 and 1914 was a brilliant one for Paris. The city became, as in the seventeenth and eighteenth centuries, the center of European culture. Impressionists such as Claude Monet and Pierre-Auguste Renoir continued to paint; Paul Cézanne and Henri Matisse had already launched new artistic forms; Pablo Picasso had come to Paris from Spain. Maurice Ravel and Debussy wrote their music for orchestra and ballet; the dance was revolutionized by the appearance of the director Sergey Diaghilev and the Ballets Russes in 1909, with the impetuous and genial dancer Vaslav Nijinsky, and the collaboration of the great Russian composer Igor Stravinsky in *The Fire-Bird* (1910), *Petrouchka* (1911), and *The Rite of Spring* (1913). The theater resumed life again in André-Léonard Antoine's *Théâtre Libre* and Jacques Copeau's *Vieux Colombier* in 1913.

However, this high degree of culture, calling forth poets and artists from Europe and America, had its dark side. The year 1905 was a year of wars and strikes throughout Europe, especially in Russia, where the shadow of the Revolution was already threatening. European alliances were fragile, and Germany, a victor over France in 1870, was once again a menace. In 1914, World War I broke out. For France, it was a moment of patriotism. The war, however, was long and difficult; soldiers spent months and years in the trenches, and the final victory was marred by great losses, both human and financial. The years immediately following, the 1920's, were years of exuberance and exaltation, of joie de vivre and new beginnings. The 1930's, in contrast, were dismal, with the Depression, unemployment, and yet another threat of German rearmament.

It was only natural that poetry should respond in

various ways to such circumstances. The great cultural renaissance of the prewar years kept alive the Symbolist quest for beauty in Valéry, Claudel, and Gide, and Proust's autobiographical novel in poetic prose, *À la recherche du temps perdu* (1913-1927; *Remembrance of Things Past*, 1922-1931, 1981). The *renouveau catholique* (Catholic renewal), which had already attracted Jammes, Ernest Psichari, Jacques Maritain, and others, drew Claudel and Charles-Pierre Péguy, for it promised stable values in a changing world. At the same time, the unprecedented carnage of the war led to a cult of destruction of all traditional values. Freudian discoveries provoked exploration of dreams, and here the Surrealists found inspiration for their poetry, following the leadership of Guillaume Apollinaire and his nineteenth century predecessors, Lautréamont and Rimbaud. Surrealism touched almost every major French poet during and after the 1920's, and it exercised a considerable international influence as well; no other school of comparable influence is identifiable in twentieth century French poetry.

CHARLES-PIERRE PÉGUY

Part of the *renouveau catholique* at the turn of the twentieth century, though never officially returning to the Church, Charles-Pierre Péguy (1873-1914) turned to poetry for inspiration toward the end of his life. A militant Socialist in his *Cahiers de la quinzaine* (1900-1914; notebooks of the fortnight), Péguy expressed his religious beliefs in the idiosyncratic free verse of *Mystères: Le Mystère de la charité de Jeanne d'Arc* (1910; *The Mystery of the Charity of Joan of Arc*, 1950), *Le Porche du mystère de la deuxième vertu* (1911; *The Portico of the Mystery of the Second Virtue*, 1970), and *Le Mystère des saints innocents* (1912; *The Mystery of the Holy Innocents*, 1956). The *Tapisseries* (tapestries), comprising *La Tapisserie de Sainte Geneviève et Jeanne d'Arc* (1912), *La Tapisserie de Notre-Dame* (1913), and the unfinished *Ève* (1913), were written in more traditional meters, as were the interminable and incomplete *Quatrains* (1939). In his verse, Péguy evokes the Middle Ages and the heroism of old France.

Péguy's verse line is often prosaic; a single "line" may take up an entire page or more. He also employs extensive digressions and thematic repetitions. As a result,

the texture of his poetry is often forbidding, and he has been most widely read in brief selections that fail to convey the overarching structure of his work. Péguy was to gain fame for his patriotism. Chauvinistic in his conception of France as specially favored by God, Péguy wrote of the glory of dying for one's country in a just war. He joined the army at the outbreak of World War I when he was past forty and was immediately killed in the First Battle of the Marne. Immortalized as a hero, Péguy was revered even during World War II, when his mix of religion and nationalism was less in vogue. He is still respected today, although in many ways, he stands apart from the mainstream of twentieth century poetry.

PAUL CLAUDEL

An ardent convert to Catholicism and a champion of the Church, Paul Claudel (1868-1955) was a career diplomat as well as a poet. His work took him all over the world, from Asia to the United States and South America, and his poetry reflects this wide experience in its cosmic vision. Claudel himself traced his roots to Rimbaud, in whom he found a liberation of language and of the spirit. Claudel was a playwright as well as poet, and most of his dramatic works are written in symbolic poetry and in his own peculiar rhythmic style. His principal nondramatic poetic works are *Cinq Grandes Odes* (1910; *Five Great Odes*, 1967) and *Corona Benignitatis Anni Dei* (1915; *Coronal*, 1943). Toward the end of his life, he again returned to poetry in "Paul Claudel interroge . . ," (1948-1955; Paul Claudel questions . . .), a series of invocations of various saints.

Claudel regarded poetry both as a means of *connaissance* and as a means of *co-naissance*, knowledge and birth. His verse is characterized by the primitive structure of dialogue and monologue. To express his sense of time as rhythmic rather than merely sequential, he invented a type of line known as the *verset claudélien*. Recalling the biblical Psalms in both form and inspiration, Claudel's line resembles human breathing or the ebb and flow of the sea, "la dilatation de la houle." Since language for Claudel is essentially oral communication, the poet is the person who names an object or an idea; as in Symbolist theory, he becomes a seer and a prophet. In his "Magnificat," one of the *Five Great Odes*, he compares his life-generating paternity in the physical sense to poetic creativity, both of which reflect God's creation of humans in his image.

In *Five Great Odes*, Claudel uses his principal images of the Muses, water, and grace to symbolize his poetic creation. Jubilant and triumphant, his work is a vast symphony to the arts and to the divine presence in the world. The fourth ode, "La Muse qui est la grâce" ("The Muse Who Is Grace"), is an *ars poetica* as well as a profession of faith. More accessible than the others, the third ode, "Magnificat," celebrates the birth of Claudel's daughter Marie and articulates his own spiritual autobiography. Claudel is also much appreciated for his simple works in traditional verse, such as "La Vierge à midi" (the Virgin at noon), deeply religious and more human than the cosmic explosion of his more elaborate creations. It is precisely this cosmic dimension, however, along with his verbal experimentation, that places Claudel in the mainstream of twentieth century poetry, and his original use of images and symbols constitutes a worthy succession to Baudelaire, Rimbaud, and Mallarmé.

PAUL VALÉRY

Paul Valéry (1871-1945) also was indebted to the Symbolists. Influenced by J. K. Huysmans's *Á rebours* (1884; *Against the Grain*, 1922) and by Verlaine and Mallarmé, he began to write poetry in 1889, making the acquaintance of such poets and artists as Mallarmé, Pierre Louÿs, Gide, and Debussy, and later Renoir and Edgar Degas. As Mallarmé's earlier works are close in style to Baudelaire's, so Valéry's first poems, later collected in *Album de vers anciens* (1920; *Album of Early Verse*, 1971), resemble Mallarmé's. "La Fileuse" ("The Spinner") evokes Mallarmé's "Sainte" and breathes the Symbolist tradition. In 1892, after a spiritual crisis during which Valéry reflected on the dangers of art and sentiment, he abandoned poetry for twenty years. During this time, he worked, married, and exercised his mind through the study of mathematics, without, however, abandoning his literary and artistic friends.

In 1917, Valéry returned to poetry with *La Jeune Parque* (*The Youngest of the Fates*, 1947; also known as *The Young Fate*), soon to be followed by *Charmes: Ou, poèmes*, (1922; *Charms*, 1971). The style of these works is noticeably different from that of the earlier ones. Serene and controlled, they nevertheless show the influence of Symbolism and the subtleties of Mallarmé. Valéry is a poet who searches for purity of language and action in the here and now. He sees poetry as a sublime vocation, necessitating time and patience, a theme beautifully expressed in the simple "Les Pas" ("Footsteps"), where the poet awaits the Muse as the lover awaits his beloved: The essence of inspiration is the waiting. Valéry's conception of art is perhaps best exemplified in his masterpiece, "Le Cimetière marin" ("The Graveyard by the Sea"). Here, classical serenity blends with realism and idealism to express man's failure to attain absolute perfection and his need to attempt to live.

Not strictly a philosopher, Valéry was, in the fullest sense of the word, a thinker, and poetry was only one of the forms that his thinking took. His essays and his voluminous notebooks, a lifelong project, have significantly influenced modern French poetry, particularly in arguing the primacy of language—language, that is, regarded not as a means of communication but as a field in which the poet can pursue his autonomous art.

GUILLAUME APOLLINAIRE

Guillaume Apollinaire (1880-1918) is a poet of the twentieth century in a way that Valéry is not. While Valéry was a product of the fin de siècle Symbolist milieu, Apollinaire was energized by the artistic renaissance centered in pre-World War I Paris—the Paris of Picasso. Apollinaire, without a father and without a country, assumed an international and paternal role in the development of a new style of poetry. He saw temporal and spatial relations as essentially different from what they had been in the past. In his verse, he articulates the profound discontinuity and disorientation of modern society, without, however, falling into Baudelairean spleen or the Romantic *mal du siècle*.

Apollinaire introduced striking innovations in form: the removal of all punctuation, the use of free verse with irregular rhyme and rhythm, and the *calligramme*, or picture-poem. His poetry was influenced by his collaboration with the revolutionary painters of his time: Marie Laurencin, Henri Rousseau, Raoul Dufy, Robert Delaunay, and especially Pablo Picasso. Writers who were to be associated with Surrealism, including Philippe Soupault, André Breton, and Tristan Tzara, acknowledged him as their precursor, and Pierre

Reverdy and Francis Picabia printed his works in their avant-garde journals.

After 1912, Apollinaire definitely espoused modern art, and the publication of *Alcools: Poèmes, 1898-1913* (*Alcools: Poems, 1898-1913*, 1964) in 1913 was its first poetic manifestation, although *Le Bestiaire* (*Bestiary*, 1978) in 1911 already foreshadows this orientation, with woodcuts by Raoul Dufy. In *Alcools*, the first and last poems, "Zone" and "Vendémiaire," are the most revolutionary in their dislocation of space and time and use of startling images. Many poems in the volume are relatively traditional, including the much appreciated and nostalgic "Le Pont Mirabeau" ("Mirabeau Bridge"). In *Calligrammes* (1918; English translation, 1980), Apollinaire's picture-poems immediately catch the reader's eye, but the most genuinely innovative poems in the volume are to be found in the first section, "Ondes" ("Waves"), rich with disconcerting juxtapositions and unusual images. In the final poem in *Calligrammes*, "La Jolie Rousse" ("The Pretty Redhead"), Apollinaire bequeaths "vast and strange domains" to anyone willing to take them.

SURREALISM

Only a few years before poets and antipoets came to explore these kingdoms, Apollinaire had subtitled his play *Les Mamelles de Tirésias* (pr. 1917; *The Breasts of Tiresias*, 1961) a *drame surréaliste*. The Surrealist movement, touching art, poetry, and music, traced its roots to Apollinaire, and even further back to Lautréamont and his *Chants de Maldoror*. Like Romanticism, Surrealism was an international movement, exerting a powerful influence on the development of modern poetry in Greece, Latin America, and other nations and regions with widely diverse poetic traditions.

In part, Surrealism was a reaction to World War I, reflecting a loss of faith in traditional values. At the same time, there was also a feeling of euphoria at the end of the war, a sense of limitless possibilities. There were discoveries to be made in other worlds, especially the world of dreams, opened by the work of Sigmund Freud.

Early Surrealism found a kindred spirit in the Romanian Tzara (Sami Roesenstock; 1896-1963), who, in 1916, in Zurich, launched a movement called Dada,

which was aimed against all logic, reason, and social organization. In 1918, the Dadaists published a manifesto that expressed their gospel of destruction and celebrated the "fertile wheel of a universal circus in the real powers and fantasy of each individual."

The founding Surrealist group included Soupault (1897-1990), René Crevel (1900-1935), Robert Desnos (1900-1945), Paul Éluard (1895-1952), Louis Aragon (1897-1982), Benjamin Péret (1899-1959), and Francis Picabia (1879-1953), all of whom acknowledged Breton (1896-1966) as their master. In their manifesto of 1924, they defined Surrealism as "psychic automation . . . in the absence of any control exercised by reason, and outside of any aesthetic or moral preoccupation." Thus, one of their most important techniques was "automatic writing," in which one wrote whatever occurred to him, without any reflection or concern for sense, grammar, or punctuation. They also practiced a faithful transcription of dreams, the "other life" so exalted by Nerval.

Many artists became members or associates of the Surrealist group, including the Spaniard Salvador Dalí (1904-1989), who was also a poet and an essayist, and who baptized his method "paranoic-critic"; Marcel Duchamp (1887-1968), who brought Surrealist art to the United States; the German Max Ernst (1891-1976), who used collages, among other media of expression, and was interested in depth psychology; and the Belgian René Magritte (1898-1967), whose works evince a metaphysical and disconcerting character. The cinema was also an important vehicle of expression for Surrealism, especially the films of the Spanish director Luis Buñuel, such as *Le Chien andalou* (1928) and *L'Age d'Or* (1930). The Surrealists also produced periodicals, such as *La Révolution surréaliste*. In 1930, the name of this journal was changed to *Le Surréalisme au service de la Révolution*, marking an internal rupture in the Surrealist movement between those who wished to maintain an apolitical stance and those who had embraced communism.

The most faithful Surrealists were Breton, Péret, Soupault, and, erratically, Desnos. With the exception of Breton, the poets who remained within the Surrealist camp achieved only limited success. It is rather those who received their first inspiration and liberation through Surrealism, and who then followed their own creative instincts, who are among the most representative of modern poetry. Indeed, as noted above, there is hardly a modern French poet who was not touched in some way by Surrealism.

ANDRÉ BRETON

André Breton was both the chief theoretician of the movement and its supreme practitioner. His work is difficult to classify by genre, since the Surrealist philosophy is predicated on the breaking down of such categories. *Nadja* (1928; English translation, 1960) is a sort of poetic novel, emphasizing the role of chance. *Les Vases communicants* (1932; *Communicating Vessels*, 1990) and *L'Amour fou* (1937; *Mad Love*, 1987) resemble Baudelairean poems in prose, with poetic evocations of the city. *Arcane 17* (1944; *Arcanum*, 1994), written in the United States during Breton's lengthy sojourn there during World War II, is a beautiful appreciation of nature and an idealization of woman. The collection is composed of vignettes loosely connected to one another as travel impressions; the work is a lengthy meditation on Nerval's "ma seule étoile est morte" (my only star is dead), into which are woven observations on contemporary life and society.

ROBERT DESNOS

Robert Desnos was a specialist in the language of dreams. He was a faithful adherent to the Surrealist gospel until 1936, when he proclaimed his own originality. This independence naturally led to a rupture with Breton, but it enriched Desnos, whose poetry showed genuine talent. During his early involvement with Surrealism, he used many *jeux de mots*, as in his and Duchamp's *Rrose Sélavy* (1922). Desnos's most important collections are *Je me vois* (1926; I see myself), *La Liberté ou l'amour* (1927; liberty or love), and *État de veille* (1943; state of waking). During World War II, like Aragon and Éluard, he composed patriotic verse in simple and accessible meters. His other works often take the form of prose poems and of a new type that he invented for the radio, called *poème radiophonique*. A man of varied interests, he was the friend of artists and writers, especially Picasso and Ernest Hemingway. Poetry for Desnos was essentially the meeting of the unusual and the spontaneous, the natural and the surreal, often mingled with wit and humor. His

best love lyric, "Poème à la mystérieuse" ("Poem to the Mysterious Woman"), was written as he lay dying in a concentration camp.

PAUL ÉLUARD

Paul Éluard, born Eugène Grindel, published several early collections under the sign of Surrealism, including *Les Nécessités de la vie et les conséquences des rêves* (1921; the necessities of life and the consequences of dreams) and *Capitale de la douleur* (1926; *Capital of Pain*, 1973); the latter volume also introduces the orientation toward beauty in expression and the faith in the omnipotence of love that mark Éluard's mature work. In the 1930's, Éluard evolved toward humanitarian idealism, expressed in *La Vie immédiate* (1932; the immediacy of life) and *Les Yeux fertiles* (1936; fertile eyes). Very active in the Resistance, he wrote simple lyric poetry in *Poésie et vérité* (1942; *Poetry and Truth, 1942*, 1949). His *Poésie ininterrompue* (1946; uninterrupted poetry) expressed his quest for a human community in the face of human solitude. Almost medieval in his idealization of woman in the courtly tradition, Éluard wrote some of the finest love poetry of the twentieth century. He seeks fraternity and solidarity, along with love, to break through human loneliness. Fundamentally positive and optimistic, Éluard assumes a constructive attitude toward life, especially through poetry.

LOUIS ARAGON

Louis Aragon evolved in much the same way as Éluard and addressed similar themes, such as love and war, although in a different style. A prolific writer, he was a novelist, a critic, and a journalist as well as a poet. Aragon's style is deceptively casual; his verse has affinities with popular music and medieval ballads, mixed with a certain intellectual cruelty and satire. His most popular poetry was associated with the Resistance; in it, he compares France with his wife, Elsa, the ideal woman of his poetry, whom he celebrates in *Le Crève-coeur* (1941; the heartbreak) and *Les Yeux d'Elsa* (1942; Elsa's eyes). *La Diane française* (1944) reflects his humanitarian and patriotic response to the suffering created by the war. Committed to communism, he touches on political themes in *Les Beaux Quartiers* (1936; *Residential Quarter*, 1938) and *La Semaine sainte* (1958; *Holy Week*, 1961).

JACQUES PRÉVERT

A popular poet, like Aragon, yet with a style unique among modern artists, Jacques Prévert (1900-1977) was a poet, screenwriter, and composer of popular songs. His collaborator, the film director Marcel Carné, described him as the one and only poet of the French cinema. Joseph Kosma set many of his poems to music, including the well-known "Les Feuilles d'automne" ("Autumn Leaves") and "Barbara." Prévert's poetry began to appear after World War II, and his first volume, *Paroles* (1945; words), became a best seller, unusual for poetry in France. Other popular collections include *Histoires* (1948; stories), *Spectacle* (1941, 1951), and *La Pluie et le beau temps* (1955; rain and good weather). Witty and satiric, varied in theme, full of wordplay and understatement, and including traditional verse and prose poems, Prévert's poetry has its roots in the oral tradition. Prévert can be both tender and mocking; he charms the reader with his facile verve and down-to-earth subjects. He is critical of all institutions, and he speaks of nature, birds, and animals with delicate intimacy. Prévert is regarded as the most genuinely popular poet of modern France and the only songwriter who is at the same time a true poet.

JEAN COCTEAU

Also involved with theater and cinema was Jean Cocteau (1889-1963), whose work has a fantastic quality best expressed by the figure of Orpheus, Cocteau's favorite image. Poet, painter, screenwriter, and novelist, Cocteau himself classified all of his works as poetry. He regarded his films as "poems in action"; the theme of metamorphosis recurs throughout his oeuvre. Among his works more strictly poetic in the traditional sense are *Poésies, 1917-1920* (1920), *Vocabulaire* (1922), *Plain-Chant* (1923), *Allégories* (1941), and *Le Chiffre sept* (1952; the number seven). Mystery, communication with death, *préciosité*, and a certain obscurity characterize all of his work.

MAX JACOB

Himself a legend and an influence on Cocteau, Max Jacob (1876-1944) belonged to Apollinaire's circle on rue Ravignan in the period before World War I. Jewish in origin, he became a Catholic in 1915, and his poetry shows a mixture of mysticism and humor. Although Jacob was less talented than Apollinaire, his poetry has remained durable: It is a mixture of satire, sarcasm, popular lyricism, and parody, free of all literary affectation. Like so many of his contemporaries, Jacob was also an essayist, novelist, and moralist. Among his best collections are *Le Cornet à dés* (1917; partially translated in *The Dice Cup*, 2000), *Le Laboratoire central* (1921), *Ballades* (1938), and *Derniers poèmes en vers et en prose* (1945). Like Reverdy, Jacob spent much of his life in the shadow of a monastery, Saint-Benoît-sur-Loire, until his capture and execution by the Germans in 1944. He is especially noted for his mastery of the prose poem and for the narrative, rather than the rhythmic, quality of his poetry.

JULES SUPERVIELLE

More influenced by Symbolism (primarily through Jules Laforgue) than by Surrealism, the Uruguayan-born Jules Supervielle (1884-1960) became a link between modern French verse and poetry in Latin America. Popular in style, like the poetry of Prévert and Aragon, his work has strong lyric quality. Supervielle believed in everything and therefore had a strong orientation toward hope, in the manner of Hugo and Péguy. Simplicity, together with a sense of mystery, characterizes his verse: Supervielle is the poet of children and animals. At the same time, he often speaks of death, though without a trace of morbidity. Although he began to write at a very young age, his first success was *Gravitations* (1925). Other important collections include *Le Forçat innocent* (1930; the innocent criminal), *La Fable du monde* (1938; the fable of the world), *Poèmes de la France malheureuse* (1941; poems of unhappy France), and *Oublieuse mémoire* (1949; forgetful memory). He also wrote tales, novels, and plays in a charming poetic style.

PIERRE REVERDY

In 1928, Breton hailed Pierre Reverdy (1899-1960) as the greatest poet living at that time. Incapable of sustaining his bonds with the Surrealists, whom he had supported in his journal *Nord-Sud*, or with anyone for that matter, Reverdy spent much of his life in the shadow of the great abbey of Solesmes. He is the most secret and most solitary of the Surrealists, and his poetry reveals the same quality, thus expressing better than his contemporaries the great void that exists in modern society. While most of the Surrealist generation responded to World War II with a burst of patriotic fervor, Reverdy never mentions the war; *Plupart du temps* (1945; most of the time) speaks of lack of comprehension, clouds and shadows, winter, an expected arrival that never occurs, the world in pieces, and similar themes. The critic J-P. Richard, writing on Reverdy, says that a poem for him is a path that goes nowhere yet one that orients the reader to the innermost part of his being. Such is the wartime message of Reverdy.

Reverdy's other principal collections, *Poèmes en prose* (1915; *Prose Poems*, 2007), *La Lucarne ovale* (1916), *Sources du vent* (1929; sources of the wind), *Étoiles peintes* (1921; painted stars), and *Main d'œuvre: Poèmes, 1913-1949* (1949), are all secret and mysterious, situated in a fragmented universe in which walls recede and corridors wind into a labyrinthine abyss. Friend of the cubists, Reverdy gives his poetry a geometric quality, with ovals, circles, and other forms. Bodily shapes are curved, like Mallarmé's swan, in an eternal question mark. Like Verlaine's, Reverdy's poetry has a resonance all its own, with cavernous and metallic sounds and steps that disappear into the distance. Reverdy writes more by negation than by affirmation; as Claudel observed, to give a name (*nom*) is to say no (*non*). Again like Verlaine, Reverdy writes a poetry of absence, yet he somehow seeks for a desired presence. The critic Robert Greene allies Reverdy with the existentialist philosophy of Camus and Jean-Paul Sartre, expressing fundamental human solitude. One senses a mystical quality in Reverdy's work that addresses the dark night of the soul more than the union with the beloved. Although critics may be tempted to "decode" his work, Reverdy, like Rimbaud, who alone possessed the key to his visions, left only "pure poetry" which is itself the message.

MODERN POETRY

All modern poetry goes back to Baudelaire, Mallarmé, and Rimbaud. Symbolists, Surrealists, and religious writers alike took their inspiration from a vague doctrine that none of these poets explicitly enunciated. The critic Wallace Fowlie, writing in the 1950's, defined the legacy of Symbolism as a quest for "purity" in poetic expression; in his view, the progressive "spiritualization" of modern art in all of its forms is the principal characteristic of modern-day poetry. Here, "spiritualization" is not meant in a religious sense; rather, it suggests the emancipation of poetry from a mission, from the necessity to signify, to point to a meaning, to deal with personal or social issues. Thus, the modern poet becomes not a prophet—the role played by Hugo and his contemporaries—but rather a magician or a visionary, in the tradition of Rimbaud, an explorer of hidden realms and of the interior kingdom of the subconscious. The modern poet is also in search of the lost paradise of childhood, in the tradition of Baudelaire.

The Surrealists, under the sign of Melusine, defined the poetic vocation as that of the seer and the magician. Poets are not to change society; they are, rather, to illuminate it, to show it visions of another life. The Surrealists insisted on the primacy of language, its independence and its importance in its own right—hence the *jeux de mots*, the startling juxtapositions, the fragmentation of sentences, the popularity of the prose poem, and the abolition of genre distinctions in the practice of what is called simply *écriture*, writing.

Robert Greene, writing at the end of the 1970's, saw a further distinction in contemporary French poetry. He divided contemporary poets into two groups, one associated with the journal *Tel Quel* (the title of which comes from Valéry's essays), increasingly Marxist in its orientation, and the journal *L'Éphémère* (1967-1972), with its successor *L'Argile*, founded in 1973. The *telquelistes* are Hermetic writers with links to the analytical and neoclassical tradition of Valéry; they regard the poem as a reflection on itself, with no structure or meaning other than that given it by the reader. Writers who share this orientation also consider themselves as successors to Lautréamont. They ignore all genre distinctions and view all types of writing simply as *écriture*. To this group, Greene assigns Francis Ponge and Marcelin Pleynet, both of whom are regular contributors to *Tel Quel*.

The second group in Greene's schema trace their descent from Rimbaud and Apollinaire. They are orphic poets who seek adventure: For them, poetry exists to take humanity beyond the everyday to a realm of deeper knowledge. These poets continue the quest of the Surrealists for a reality beyond reality. Like Apollinaire and the Surrealists, they maintain close ties with the world of the plastic arts (Greene feels that the cover of *L'Éphémère*, with an emaciated nude by Alberto Giacometti, is especially significant). Greene sees Reverdy as a predecessor of this second group, which includes Yves Bonnefoy, René Char, Jacques Dupin, and André du Bouchet.

All modern French writers, whose principal works appeared after 1940 and Germany's occupation of France, are marked by the existentialism articulated by Camus and Sartre. Victims of a senseless war, profoundly humiliated by the Occupation, and psychologically and spiritually shaken by the apparent loss of values, they look for meaning in the fundamental solitude of existence. The fragmentation of society is visible in their fragmented lives; the poetry of such authors as Henri Michaux verges on the absurd, and the linguistic experimentation of Raymond Queneau (1903-1976), whose work knows no genre, expresses a revolution in language and has had a strong influence on modern writing. Other writers, such as Pierre-Jean Jouve (1887-1976), who really belongs to the preceding generation, Patrice de la Tour du Pin (1911-1975), and Pierre Emmanuel (1916-1984), are among the most important representatives of poetry with a religious orientation.

SAINT-JOHN PERSE

A giant among modern poets, recipient of the Nobel Prize in Literature in 1960, is Alexis Saint-Léger Léger, known as Saint-John Perse (1887-1975). Like Claudel, who became his friend and encouraged his early attempts at poetry, he traveled widely, and his poetry is informed by a cosmic vision. He is a poet of disciplined but luxuriant sensuality, a great visionary who identifies flesh with spirit in a burst of life, although without the religious dimension that characterizes Claudel. Images of the sea are frequent in Perse's work, as are images of wind, rain, and sky, archetypal images symbolizing the primitive forces of fertility, passion, and vitality. His epic of the earth and the cosmos is situated in a vast space that has its own time and rhythm.

Perse's first collection, *Éloges* (English translation, 1944), appeared in 1911. In 1924, he published *Anabase* (*Anabasis*, 1930), regarded by many critics as his mas-

terpiece. Among the important volumes that followed are *Exil* (1942; *Exile*, 1949), *Vents* (1946; *Winds*, 1953), *Amers* (1957; *Seamarks*, 1958), and *Chronique* (1960; English translation, 1961). Although all these works are written in a kind of free verse or are in fact prose poems, Perse is a classical poet in both form and inspiration, for like Valéry, Perse subordinates his sensuous images to a strict and serene discipline. Many of his titles and images are taken from classical Greek culture: *Anabasis* takes its title from the march of Xenephone, while *Seamarks* evokes the setting of an ancient Greek theater. The altar is the sea, and the fragments of humanity around its edges play out in dialogue the conflict between the human and the divine. The sea is also the main actor in *Exile*, written in New Jersey when the poet was in exile from Vichy France; the Atlantic Ocean, which separates him from his homeland, symbolizes the march of a cosmic army. Richard sees in Perse's work a reflection of the decomposition of Occidental civilization, with an invocation to the primitive forces of life, especially water, to cleanse and reinvigorate the world.

HENRI MICHAUX

Where Perse's rolling lines present a cosmic flow of images, the works of Henri Michaux (1899-1984) are disconcerting and abrupt in style and content. Some critics regard him as one of the most important and original of modern French poets, yet he is largely undiscovered. Like many of his contemporaries, Michaux abolished the distinction between poetry and prose; his essays, travelogues, and personal journals are all distinctly "poetic." Michaux excels in the small incident rather than in sustained poems, and he shifts grammar as he shifts ideas, for his vision is destructive of syntax. Michaux has described his many experiments with hallucinogens in brilliant poetic prose; he is a poet of magic and ritual, and many of his works are incantations and exorcisms, asserting above all the power of self. Michaux is an artist as well as a poet, and his drawings, equally mysterious and enigmatic, often accompany his poetry. Although it is difficult to distinguish genres in Michaux, *Un Barbare en Asie* (1933; *A Barbarian in Asia*, 1949), *Plume: Précédé de lointain intérieur* (1938), *Ailleurs* (1948; elsewhere), and three long poems in verse, *Paix dans les brisements* (1959;

peace in the breakings), "Iniji," and *Vers la complétude* (1967; toward completeness), are among his principal poetic works. These three long poems relate his experiences with drugs; he seeks to represent rather than to explain his hallucinatory visions. Later volumes included *Émergences-Résurgences* (1972; *Emergences-Resurgences*, 2000) and *Chemins cherchés, chemins perdue, transgressions* (1982).

FRANCIS PONGE

The grammatical and linguistic dislocation found in Michaux is even more evident in Francis Ponge (1899-1988). To read him, observes Greene, one must change one's idea of what poetry is, for Ponge's work is totally removed from the traditional concept of poetry. Ponge does not attempt to explain, for he believes that the reader holds the key to a poem. Not unlike Samuel Beckett's prose, Ponge's work exemplifies the total loss of self as the center of self-consciousness. He invents words, variously christening his new genre *objeu*, *objet*, and *jeu de mots*, or "metapoem." He reveals an obsessive concern for words, which—frequently in defiance of their etymology—he treats as onomatopoeic or iconic. He employs puns, false starts, repetitions, reversals, and other such means to express the senselessness of the world and his inability to express it. In his view, the contemporary writer is reduced to describing the world by means of a *littérature littérante*.

Francis Ponge (AFP/Getty Images)

Ponge has been "discovered" three times: in the 1920's, by the *Nouvelle Revue française*; in 1944, by Sartre; and in the 1960's, by *Tel Quel*. In his work from *Proêmes* (1948) to *Nouveau Recueil* (1967), which includes such significant works as "Le Pré," Ponge assumes the stance of a post-existentialist poet, one who, like Descartes, sees nature as a clock but goes on to conclude that the wheels of the machinery mean nothing beyond their spinning.

MARCELIN PLEYNET

Much younger than Ponge, Marcelin Pleynet (born 1933) expresses his rapidly accelerating disengagement from contemporary culture, which he finds politically repressive and spiritually bankrupt. He began writing during the Algerian War (1954-1962) in a style reminiscent of such disparate writers as Perse, Char, Éluard, and Reverdy. Pleynet's early collections were *Provisoires amants des Nègres, 1957-1959* (1962; provisory lovers of Negroes) and *Paysages en deux* (1963). With *Comme* (1965) and *Stanze* (1973), he achieved an individual style not unlike the metapoetic mode invented by Ponge. In *Comme*, metaphor is not the matter of poetry; it is its sole subject, and form mimes meaning. This change in Pleynet can be attributed in part to the events of May, 1968, when all French institutions came under examination; his stylistic development has also been influenced by a growing admiration for China. Pleynet engages in creative disordering of words to reveal the deep structure of language and mind. His critical works reveal an admiration for Matisse and James Joyce, and he seeks to follow Joyce's example in developing a new *littérature d'engagement*, in which language will play the major role. *Stanze* reveals the diverse influences of Ezra Pound, Lautréamont, Sigmund Freud, Karl Marx, and Mao Zedong in its willful transgression of sexual, political, and syntactic taboos. Although Pleynet's work points to a radically new style of poetry, it is also a work still in the process of evolving and therefore difficult to evaluate with any certainty.

RENÉ CHAR

Among the poets designated by Greene as orphic or meaning-oriented, the greatest is René Char (1907-1988). A convinced Surrealist from 1929 to 1934, he wrote *Artine* in 1930, considered the most classically Surrealist work. Breaking from Surrealism because he did not wish to accept the Surrealists' narrow definition of dreams, he nevertheless links Surrealism with present-day writing in the journals *L'Éphémère* and *L'Argile*. His masters include Heraclitus and Georges de La Tour, who embody for him the Greek concept of *energeia*; more immediately, he shares affinities with Martin Heidegger and especially with Camus, who greatly valued his work. He thus manifests a philosophical orientation and, like Camus, an authentic search for human dignity.

Influenced by his Surrealist heritage, Char employs the technique of contradiction—the juxtaposition of semantically incompatible worlds in place of traditional images. This procedure corresponds to his philosophy of poetry as a means whereby the individual self is lost in order to accede to the impersonal fullness of being. It is also an expression of Char's quest for perfection of expression. Char's prose poems are superior to his more traditional verse, where his rhythm is flowing, breathless, and intense. Among his collections are *Commune présence* (1964; common presence), *Le Poème pulvérisé* (1947; the pulverized poem), *Les Matinaux* (1950; *The Dawn Breakers*, 1992), and *Dans la pluie giboyeuse* (1968; in the game-stocked rain). A later collection, *Aromates chasseurs* (1976; aromatic hunters) uses Orion and the archipelago as a cluster of contradictions and an evocation of the cosmos and outer space. Char maintains throughout his work, much like Nerval, that true life is inaccessible (*ailleurs*) but that one must clutch the bits and pieces within one's grasp and live them authentically.

ANDRÉ DU BOUCHET

Two contemporary poets who have worked together on *L'Éphémère* and *L'Argile*, André du Bouchet (1924-2001) and Jacques Dupin (born 1927), are united in their approach to art through the study of Giacometti, yet each uses his own individual manner to resolve the

problem of art and consciousness. Du Bouchet studied in the United States and reveals not only American but also English and German influence, especially that of Shakespeare, Joyce, Friedrich Hölderlin, and Celan. Although du Bouchet experiments with language, he declares expressly that language is not the primary object of his work. Richard, noting in du Bouchet's work a resemblance to Reverdy, adduces the presence of obstacles, nudity of vocabulary, and monochromatic tones typical of du Bouchet's verse. In *Dans la chaleur vacante* (1961; in the vacant heat) and *Où le soleil* (1968; where the sun), du Bouchet shows a Mallarméan preoccupation with consciousness as well as an artistic awareness of the problem of space. It is in the arrangement of his lines, recalling both Mallarmé and Péguy, that this awareness is most evident, for du Bouchet fractures his sentences and leaves blocks of interlinear white, which he considered integral to his poetic expression. Later works, such as *Qui n'est pas tourné vers nous* (1972; who is not turned toward us), are what he called *poésies critiques*, critical essays of a sort, but the distinction between poetry and criticism is rather tenuous in this highly experimental writer, who maintained that what interested him above all is the human condition. With *L'Incohérence* (1979; incoherence), *Désaccordée comme par de la neige* (1989; made discordant as if by snow), *Pourquoi si calmes* (1996; why so calm), and *Carnet 2* (1999; notebook 2), du Bouchet continued his varied productivity and concern with the aesthetics of language. The influence of Mallarmé persists all the way to *Carnet 2*, with the use of the single, extended poetic sentence. His is the tendency of modern poetry that attempts to define poetry itself.

JACQUES DUPIN

Du Bouchet's associate, Jacques Dupin, is also situated in the line of Reverdy and Rimbaud, seeing life and poetry alike as a process of continual creation and destruction. A disciple and protégé of Char, Dupin, in his first volume, *Gravir* (1963; to climb), shows the influence of his mentor, both in his lyrical and lucid passages and in his sibylline utterances. *L'Embrasure* (1969) is more original and questions the very role of language. Finally, *Dehors* (1975; outside) sees *écriture*, the modern appellation for both poetry and prose, as a vehicle for transcendence. Greene sees in Dupin a poet who unites the two principal trends of modern French poetry, suggesting a common ground between the poets preoccupied with language for its own sake and those concerned with meaning, and perhaps indicating the direction that poetry will take in the future. In *Matière du souffle* (1994; stuff of breath), Dupin still attempts to define the poem and the act of poetic creation, essentially making a poem of his own poetic process. Unfortunately, such self-preoccupation has brought poets since Mallarmé to a sense of emptiness that is again reflected in Dupin's *Le Grésil* (1996; sleet).

PHILIPPE JACCOTTET

The need to clarify the enigmas of the world recurs in the poetry of Philippe Jaccottet (born 1925) whose *Cahier de verdure* (1990; green notebook) expresses cautious optimism amid the doubt of earlier poetry. With *Cristal et fumée* (1993; crystal and smoke), the experience of eternity poses questions which lead to a contemplative serenity in *Après beaucoup d'années* (1994; after many years). Expressions in both prose and poetry encourage faith in the transcendent, but doubts return in *La Seconde Semaison* (1996; the second sowing).

YVES BONNEFOY

The influence of Mallarmé persists with Yves Bonnefoy (born 1923), who has given considerable attention to it in the extensive critical work which supplements his poetry. His poetic productivity, including volumes such as *Ce qui fut sans lumière* (1987; *In the Shadow's Light*, 1991) and *Début et fin de la neige* (1991; beginning and end of the snow), returns to themes of poetic continuity and of mortality. Poetic beauty has aspects that are both permanent and ephemeral. Different aspects of transcendence appear, from the recognition of divine elements in nature to the valorization of dream experiences. However, problems persist with the inadequacy of language to translate these ideas.

MICHEL DEGUY

Like many of his contemporaries, Michel Deguy (born 1930) offers pieces in both poetry and prose. His *Aux heures d'affluence* (1993; rush hour) takes a combative, philosophical tone analyzing various problems of the modern world while continuing to deal with fundamental poetic problems of the inadequacy of language and the inevitability of death. *A ce qui n'en finit pas* (1995; to what does not finish) seeks to reconcile oppositions that threaten to fragment life. Amid menaces of disintegration, love may become a unifying force, and along with personal reconciliations may come both poetic unity and solidarity in the world outside it. *L'Énergie du désespoir* (1998; the energy of despair) returns to the poem as both varied expression and unifying utterance of all and nothing.

BERNARD NOËL

Bernard Noël (born 1930) returns to the theme of death in both its harsh and elegiac aspects. *La Peau et les mots* (1972; skin and words), *Bruits et langues* (1980; sounds and tongues), *La Chute des temps* (1983; *Time-Fall*, 2006), *L'Ombre du double* (1994; shadow of the double), and *Les États du corps* (1999; states of the body) sometimes approach a form of freedom or catharsis amid more negative concerns of a material culture that inform also Noël's writings in art criticism and philosophy.

JUDE STÉFAN

The hope and despair inspired by modern life reappear in the work of Jude Stéfan (born 1930). *À la vieille Parque* (1989; to the old muse), *Elégiades* (1993; elegies), *Povrésies: Ou, 65 poèmes autant d'années* (1997; poor poetry), and *Epodes: Ou, Poèmes de la désuétude* (1999) employ tones of satire or of bittersweet irony in the face of threats but still posit ideals of both sensual and poetic beauty. Stéfan returns to the poetry of antiquity, of the Renaissance, and of the close of the nineteenth century to recall the concept of poetry as music.

ANDRÉE CHEDID

The end of the twentieth century, as women were entering in great numbers into other fields of activity, saw a notable increase of female authors. Andrée Chedid (born 1920) poses central poetic questions with *Textes pour un poème, 1949-1970* (1987; texts for a poem), *Poèmes pour un texte* (1991; poems for a text), and *Par-delà les mots* (1995; beyond words), and with *Territoires du souffle* (1999; realm of breath), moves to an optimism in poetic expression.

BEYOND FRANCE

Female voices also emerged in Canadian literature in French, where Anne Hébert (1916-2000), after having summed up her work with *Œuvre poétique, 1950-1990* (1992; poetic work, 1950-1990) continued with *Poèmes pour la main gauche* (1997; poems for the left hand). Nicole Brossard (born 1943) published *Vertige de l'avant-scène* (1997; dizziness from center stage). These represent only a sample of the poetry being written by women in Canada.

Meanwhile, the canon of French literature, so long focused on the writers of the mother country, has expanded to include works from a variety of former colonies. Following the immense attention to the poetry of Léopold Senghor (1906-2001), who, as president of Senegal, enjoyed a unique ability to be heard on the international level, Aimé Césaire of Martinique (1913-2008) found a wide audience for a poetic work ranging from his early *Les Armes miraculeuses* (1946; *Miraculous Weapons*, 1983) to *La poésie* (1994).

In some ways the twentieth century resembled the eighteenth in that other literary forms threatened to upstage poetry. The modern novel, with its many forms ranging from popular romance and adventure to more serious intellectual and psychological works, has proliferated. At the same time, new technology has brought films and other electronic forms of publication to be considered on a par with literature. Amid this diversity of forms, however, poetry continues both to be widely written and to cultivate new voices. For the first time since the Renaissance, a significant number of these voices are female. Global communication has brought poets from Canada, Africa, and the Caribbean into the cultural sphere of France. As these many voices are raised, readers are able to choose from a rich variety of texts in the twenty-first century.

BIBLIOGRAPHY

Blackmore, A. M., and E. H. Blackmore, eds. *Six French Poets of the Nineteenth Century: Lamartine, Hugo, Baudelaire, Verlaine, Rimbaud, Mallarmé*. New York: Oxford University Press, 2000. Includes generous selections from the six nineteenth century French poets most often read in the English-speaking world today. Modern translations are printed opposite the original French verse, and the edition contains more than a thousand lines of poetry never previously translated into English.

Breunig, L. C., ed. *The Cubist Poets in Paris: An Anthology*. Lincoln: University of Nebraska Press, 1995. This compilation, a synthesis of the collaboration between cubist art and literature, draws mainly on the works of fifteen Parisian cubist poets of the first two decades of the twentieth century, including Guillaume Apollinaire, Max Jacob, and André Salmon, who, with Pablo Picasso, formed the nucleus of the French cubist movement.

Caws, Mary Ann, ed. *Surrealist Painters and Poets: An Anthology*. Cambridge, Mass.: MIT Press, 2001. Contains materials produced by self-defined Surrealists, including memoirs, dreams, journal entries, poetry, and art. Lavishly illustrated. Bibliographical materials and index.

_____. *The Yale Anthology of Twentieth-Century French Poetry*. New Haven, Conn.: Yale University Press, 2004. This excellent collection includes poets representing Symbolism, post-symbolism, cubism, simultanism, Dada, and *L'Éphémère*, and ends with the new generations writing from 1967 to 2002. Bilingual. Bibliography and indices.

Flores, Angel, ed. *The Anchor Anthology of French Poetry: From Nerval to Valéry in English Translation*. Rev. ed. New York: Doubleday, 2000. First published in 1958, this collection introduced an indispensable corpus of Western poetry to countless Americans. The poetic and cultural tradition forged by the Symbolist poets—Baudelaire, Rimbaud, Verlaine, Apollinaire, and others—reverberated throughout the avant-garde and countercultures of the twentieth century, including modernism, Surrealism, abstract impressionism, and the Beat movement, an influence examined in a new introduction by poet-singer Patti Smith.

Kay, Sarah, Terence Cave, and Malcolm Bowie. *A Short History of French Literature*. New York: Oxford University Press, 2003. A highly readable volume, presenting an overview of French literature in narrative form. Describes major writers, pointing out their relationship to the times in which they lived. An ideal starting point for students of the subject or for general readers.

Kelly, Michael G. *Strands of Utopia: Spaces of Poetic Work in Twentieth-Century France*. London: Legenda, 2008. An unusual study, drawing attention to the links between utopian themes and poetic practice, especially as seen in the works of Victor Segalen, René Daumal, and Yves Bonnefoy.

Metzidakis, Stamos, ed. *Understanding French Poetry: Essays for a New Millennium.* New York: Garland, 1994. Focusing on the ebbing influence of poetry, this volume provides the theoretical grounding for understanding how and why French verse has become overshadowed by critical and artistic prose. The essays included are mostly original contributions by some of the foremost scholars of French poetry currently writing in the English-speaking world.

Prendergrast, Christopher. *Nineteenth Century French Poetry: Introductions to Close Readings.* New York: Cambridge University Press, 1990. Essays on eleven different poets from Lamartine to Mallarmé and Laforgue, by eminent scholars representing a wide range of critical and theoretical viewpoints. Each of these essays focuses on the detailed organization of a single poem and opens pathways for further study and discussion.

Shapiro, Norman R., ed. and trans. *French Women Poets of Nine Centuries: The Distaff and the Pen.* Baltimore: Johns Hopkins University Press, 2008. Introductions by Roberta L. Krueger, Catherine Lafarge, and Catherine Perry; foreword by Rosanne Warren. Contains more than six hundred poems by fifty-six different writers, with originals and translations on facing pages. A monumental volume.

Shaw, Mary Lewis. *The Cambridge Introduction to French Poetry.* New York: Cambridge University Press, 2003. An exhaustive survey of French poetry, with topics ranging from verse forms and genres to the relationship between poetry and politics. Glossary of poetic terms, bibliography, and indexes.

Sorrell, Martin, ed. and trans. *Elles: A Bilingual Anthology of Modern French Poetry by Women.* Afterword by Jaqueline Chénieux-Gendron. Exeter, Devonshire, England: University of Exeter Press, 1995. Introduces English-speaking readers to some of the best French poetry published by women during the last three decades of the twentieth century. Each poet introduces herself with an essay on her conception of poetry and her own position as writer.

Stephens, Sonya, ed. *A History of Women's Writing in France.* New York: Cambridge University Press, 2000. A collection of essays, including general essays on women writers of various periods and one specifically on twentieth century women poets. Includes bibliography and a guide to more than 150 writers and their works.

Thomas, Jean-Jacques, and Steven Winspur. *Poeticized Language: The Foundations of Contemporary French Poetry.* University Park: Pennsylvania State University Press, 1999. Explores the way in which contemporary French poetry places great emphasis on language itself and analyzes the innovations crafted by more than fifty writers. With its eleven chapters and extensive bibliography, this is one of the most comprehensive English-language introductions to French poetry.

Irma M. Kashuba
Updated by Dorothy M. Betz

German Poetry to 1800

Poetry as a pleasant distraction from life, as a conventional ornament for social occasions, as linguistic play or experiment, even as the sincere expression of heartfelt emotions, belongs to comparatively recent times. In its beginnings, humankind used the magical power of patterned, rhythmic speech to impose meaning and order on the world. Through poetry, humankind hoped to gain mastery of both the natural and the social environment. Certainly this was true of the Germanic tribes: The first writer to mention Germanic poetry, the Roman historian Tacitus (c. 55-120 C.E.), expressly refers to the Germanic custom of celebrating gods and heroes in song. Religion (humanity's relation to God) and history (humanity's relation to the community in time) were to remain poetry's central domain for centuries to come. Thus, the historical and cultural context can never become a matter of indifference to those who care for poetry. What might appear to later generations as mere background was related strictly to the purpose and theme of poetry in its own day. In ancient times, few deeds were unaccompanied by the poetic word, and fewer still would be remembered were it not for poetry.

Germanic tribes lived on the shores of the North and Baltic seas as early as 2000 B.C.E. Some time after 500 B.C.E., when climatic changes forced most of them to migrate south, they divided into three distinct groups. The North Germanic tribes (Normans, Danes, Jutes) were those that stayed behind; the East Germanic tribes (Goths, Vandals, Burgundians) slowly drifted southward into present-day Hungary, Romania, and Bulgaria; and the West Germanic tribes (Saxons, Franks, Angles, Swabians, Alemanni) moved into the middle of Europe, present-day Germany, northern France, Belgium, and the Netherlands.

The Germanic tribes had barely settled in their new environment when the Huns, a fierce Mongolian people, swept into Europe around 400 C.E. The impact of the Hunnish invasion was most directly felt by the East Germanic tribes. Pushed forward by the relentlessly advancing Huns, the Germanic tribes fell on an already tottering Roman civilization, gaining and losing power over the nations in their path with spectacular speed. The Vandals established kingdoms in Italy, Spain, and North Africa; the Goths, in Italy and Spain; the Burgundians, on the Rhine.

Origins to Eleventh Century

Two hundred years later, these tribes had all but disappeared, exhausted and decimated by their heroic exploits, absorbed by the cultures and people they had overrun, yet they disappeared only after leaving behind a lasting record of their remarkable feats. If history demands patterned, poetic order, it certainly demanded it here, in the face of the splendid achievements and the tragic end of the East Germanic tribes. Soon, the scop, the warrior-poet, sang in the lord's hall of heroic courage and loyalty, of betrayal and revenge, of inscrutable fate and man's fortitude when confronted with its cruel decrees. For centuries, this oral poetry informed and stimulated the imagination of the Germanic tribes until, several hundred years later, some accounts were finally given literary form.

Though naturally influenced by the tumultuous events around them, the West Germanic tribes underwent a gradual development. The most notable migratory action was that of the Angles and some of the Saxons, who, after the Roman forces had pulled out of Britain, began to settle there in the fifth and sixth centuries. On the Continent, historical progress took place under the steady ascendancy of the Franks. Clovis I (481-511) united all major West Germanic tribes, with the exception of the Continental Saxons, under Frankish leadership. When Clovis converted to Roman Catholicism, Latin culture quickly accompanied Christianity on its missionary journeys. The ensuing political and cultural unification was underscored by a growing linguistic unity among the tribes. Starting among the Alemanni of Germany's southern highlands, a consonant shift spread through the West Germanic tribes, differentiating their language from that of their North Germanic neighbors as well as that of the Angles and Saxons. This language, Old High German, is considered the first distinct forerunner of modern German.

The unity of the West Germanic tribes reached its culmination under the rule of Charlemagne (768-814). Charlemagne was not only a brilliant political leader but also a farsighted patron of the arts; the earliest extant literary fragments in the vernacular date from his reign. Baptismal vows, creeds, and prayers give evidence of the importance that church and state placed on the vernacular in their concerted effort to convert the Germanic peoples to Christianity. Nevertheless, cultural life under Charlemagne and his Carolingian successors proceeded mostly in Latin. Of lyric poetry in Old High German, only two fragments of poems have survived. Both are religious in nature, though secular poetry did exist, as is indicated by an ecclesiastical injunction against the writing or sending of *Winileodos* (songs of friendship). The "Wessobrunner Gebet" (c. 780; "Wessobrunn Prayer") contains in twenty-eight lines a fragmentary account of creation, while the "Muspilli" (c. 830), almost four times as long, describes the Day of Judgment.

The most important poetic work of the ninth century, however, is an epic, the religious epic *Der Heliand* (c. 840; *The Heliand*, 1966). In its six thousand lines of dramatic alliterative verse, Christ has been transformed into a magnanimous Germanic lord and his apostles into retainers who, moving with him from castle to castle, believe in his mission with unflinching loyalty. Unfortunately, the epic did not have its deserved impact on German literature, because it was not written in Old High German, but in Old Low German (Old Saxon), a Germanic dialect as yet unassimilated by the developing German language. Thus, it was quickly forgotten and not rediscovered until, in the sixteenth century, the Protestant Reformation searched high and low for a historical tradition.

Charlemagne's liberal cultural policies also encouraged a collection of heroic songs reaching back into the pre-Christian days of the Great Migrations. This collection is said to have been burned by Charlemagne's son, the weak and bigoted Louis the Pious. A glimpse of what such a collection might have contained is provided by a brief fragment, the sixty-eight lines of the *Hildebrandslied* (c. 800; *The Song of Hildebrand*, 1957). It commemorates in a terse and somber style the tragic conflict which pits Hildebrand's loyalty to his liege against his affection for his son, who, with an equally fervent loyalty, has embraced the cause of Hildebrand's sworn enemies. Though the poem breaks off before the issue is decided, it is clear that Hildebrand's ideals of heroic conduct will force him to kill his son rather than forsake his lord in battle.

The future of German poetry did not lie with *The Heliand* or with *The Song of Hildebrand*, but with Otfrid von Weissenburg's *Krist* (c. 865; Christ). An Alsatian monk, the first German poet whose name is known, Otfrid incorporated a most promising metrical innovation into his otherwise lackluster disquisitions into the life of Christ. Influenced by the style of Latin church hymns, Otfrid decided to rhyme his poetry. With his work, rhyme—until the ninth century essentially foreign to the alliterative verse of the Germanic tribes—was to establish a hold over German poetry that would not be relinquished until the twentieth century.

Whatever promise Old High German poetry might have held, historical changes brought it to a most ignoble end. Charlemagne's vision of a politically, culturally, and linguistically unified Europe disintegrated in the dynastic feuds of his grandsons. Scarcely thirty years after his death, his empire divided along lines that foreshadowed the borders between the future states of Germany and France. The political split was ratified by a linguistic one: The oaths confirming the Frankish division were no longer sworn in one Frankish language, but in two: Old High German and Romance, the ancestor of modern French.

During the declining years of the Carolingian Empire, the religious unity of Western Europe provided the only force against the centrifugal tendencies of the Germanic tribes. With the growing influence of the Church, Latin inhibited the development of German poetry. This situation became even more serious following the accession of the dukes of Saxony to the throne of what by then had become Germany. With forceful single-mindedness, the Saxon emperors achieved a degree of political and administrative unity that allowed Germany to dominate European politics for more than two centuries. On the other hand, these emperors had neither the time nor the inclination for poetry. Moreover, Saxon—as has been mentioned before—was the only major West Germanic dialect on the Continent that had not yet adopted the consonant shift of Old High German. It was only to be expected that a house of Saxons would have no particular interest or stake in the advance of an Old High German language or literature. The results are certainly striking: Not a single poem in German is extant from a period of some one hundred and fifty years. During these dark ages of neglect, Old High German starved to death. It was only after further linguistic changes, which led to the new language patterns of Middle High German, that German poetry received a second chance.

ELEVENTH TO FOURTEENTH CENTURY

In an effort to weaken tribal independence in their realm, the Saxon emperors had relied increasingly on the prelates of the Church for the administration of the country. Unmarried, the higher clergy would obviously be less likely to form dynastic interests of their own and would be more inclined to give their unreserved loyalty to the man who had invested them with their office. In the course of a century, the Church in Germany had thus been transformed into an effective branch of imperial government. Under the Frankish line of the Salians, which followed that of the Saxons, this practice had finally overtaken Rome itself. Henry III (1039-1056) considered it simply one of his personal responsibilities to install and depose popes as he saw fit. Against this glaring political abuse of the Church, the Burgundian monastery of Cluny started a campaign that struck at the heart of the German Empire. The battle cry of Cluny was that all further lay interference in appointments to high ecclesiastical office should cease. Henry IV (1056-1106), politically dependent on a Church hierarchy willing to do his bidding, had no choice but to defy this religious reform. The confrontation lasted for about fifty years and ended in a devastating defeat of the imperial cause, resulting in a dramatic loss of German power without and German unity within.

The effect of the rigorously ascetic revival on poetry proved, at least immediately, no less intimidating. Heavily dogmatic and didactic poetry dominated the second half of the eleventh century. However, it was the very same religious enthusiasm of Cluny that made another spiritual call possible, a spiritual call that was soon to overwhelm Cluny's monastic objectives with

a renewed worldliness. Unforeseen adventures arose from the fervent appeal to free the Holy Land from the Saracens, to organize a Crusade. For almost two centuries—the First Crusade began in 1096, the last ended in 1270—the European imagination was captivated by the ideal and the reality of the Crusades as nothing had captivated it since the Great Migrations half a millennium before. The joys of the world quickly crept back into poetry. Narrative poems were told for the sheer fun of telling tall tales of exotic lands. What these poems still lacked, however, was some organizing principle that would lift their episodic style to the level of a unified theme and ethos. This vacuum was soon to be filled by the new, ideal man of the Crusades, the Christian knight.

Knighthood, or chivalry, could trace its origins most directly to the political and economic conditions during and after the Great Germanic Migrations. At a time of rapid tribal expansion and in the absence of the necessary logistical means for the operation of large-scale armies, the tribal lord stood in need of a highly mobile and well-equipped fighting elite. To maintain this force and to gain its unswerving loyalty, the lord rewarded its members by granting them land, the surplus of which would support them and their military craft befittingly. When not called up to serve his lord, the vassal administered his land. He would also be free to grant land to some of his retainers on similar conditions. In this way, there arose over the centuries a whole pyramid of intricate dependencies—the system of feudalism.

Feudalism, however, had slowly begun to deteriorate. The property which the lord had lent to those who had served him faithfully tended to become hereditary. As tribal expansion within the limits of Western Europe could not go on forever, the lords found themselves increasingly hard put to reward those they needed for the exercise of their power, while at the same time and for the same reason, many young noblemen saw themselves excluded from the lifestyle of their fathers.

In this deepening crisis, the Crusades provided European society with a momentary easing of its social and economic dilemmas. Through the Crusades, the inevitable decline of the feudal system was delayed.

Knighthood received a reprieve during which it rose to heights of artistic splendor and ethical idealism that were to dazzle the people of Europe long after knighthood itself had lost its historical relevance.

What was new about the ideal of the Christian knight was that, for the first time, Germanic political and social realities were sanctioned by Christian idealism. The perfect knight was to strike a balance between the primarily Germanic virtues of courage, loyalty, and honor and a more tempered set of Christian values such as moderation, chastity, generosity, and mercy. Self-interest, class-interest, and Christian idealism joined forces, allowing the knight to prove himself, through endless adventures, worthy before God and the world.

France was the first nation in which the ideals of chivalry gained a firm hold on literature and life. In Germany, it was only during the rule of Frederick I (1152-1190) of the Swabian house of the Hohenstaufen that chivalry was accepted as an indigenous element of Germanic culture. An extraordinarily brilliant period of German poetry was soon to follow. In the short span of merely two decades (1190 to 1210), several poetic masterpieces were produced which not even the great works of German Romanticism can be said to have surpassed.

NIBELUNGENLIED

The *Nibelungenlied* (c. 1200; English translation, 1848), an epic composed by an unknown Austrian monk, is built on specifically Germanic conceptions in its effort to explore the true values of knighthood. At least two Germanic oral traditions—the Frankish legend of Siegfried and the narrative of the downfall of the Burgundians (or Nibelungs) under the onslaught of the Huns in 437 C.E.—are here combined to create the German national epic. It tells the story of Siegfried, the perfect knight, at the court of the Burgundians and of Kriemhild, his wife, a Burgundian princess, who swears revenge on her kinsmen when she learns that they killed Siegfried—jealous of his unequaled prowess. For thirteen years, she has brooded on the wrong done to her, when Attila offers her his hand in marriage. She accepts and another thirteen years later lures the nobles of her homeland to the court of Attila, where they are slaughtered in a bloodbath which finally engulfs even the vengeful queen. Behind a veneer of

courtly decorum and Christian morality, there arises before the listener the most profound image of the heroic age in the German language. A world holds sway in which the joys and sorrows of life are experienced with stark intensity, in which the virtues and vices of men are as bold as the actions they engender, but also a world in which fate, not the deeds of heroes, ultimately determines the course of all events.

ROMANCE

More directly indebted to French influence and the newly established ideals of chivalry are the court epics of Hartmann von Aue (c. 1160-1165 to c. 1210-1220), Wolfram von Eschenbach (c. 1170-c. 1217), and Gottfried von Strassburg (fl. c. 1210). In contrast to the heroic epic, the court epic, or romance (so called because of its origins in the Romance languages), does not restrict itself to the praise of national heroes. Even great men of classical antiquity such as Aeneas and Alexander become heroes of courtly epics. Neither are the fates of nations the concern of romances. Instead, the romance is focused on an individual knight whose valor is tested against the temptations and afflictions of the world. To make these tests as representative as possible, a romance will prefer ideal knights in ideal settings to anything that might smack of mere reality.

The most famous and most popular locale of the German romance is the legendary court of King Arthur and his Knights of the Round Table. Hartmann von Aue introduced the Arthurian theme into the German language. His two Arthurian romances, *Erek* (c. 1190; *Erec*, 1982) and *Iwein* (c. 1190-1205; *Iwein: The Knight with the Lion*, 1979), closely follow court epics of the French poet Chrétien de Troyes in their devotion to the typical preoccupation of the French romance: the discussion and exemplification of ethical conflicts arising within the knightly code of values. Erec neglects his duties as a knight for love of his wife; Iwein neglects his wife for love of knightly adventures. In both cases, harmony is reestablished as soon as the knights have learned the lesson of the golden mean.

The discussion of these neatly, dialectically arranged conflicts proved to be more French than German. The two greatest masters of the German court epic moved away from such delicate planning to pursue the very limits of all courtly conventions. Wolfram, much less learned than Hartmann, proceeded in his *Parzival* (c. 1200-1210; English translation, 1894) with a decidedly unconventional style and theme. Highly individualistic, often obscure in his use of metaphors, he created a world of daring and immoderate yearnings. The story is that of Parzival's vicissitudes on the way to an understanding of life, suffering, and death. During this journey, King Arthur's Round Table is recognized as little more than a stage on the long and narrow path to perfection. Only by abandoning the security of all previous values—not merely by balancing them in an aesthetically pleasing order—only by a complete change of heart does Parzival finally discover the source of all inner peace in the total submission to the will of God. For Wolfram, perfect knighthood is nothing less than sainthood.

It is hard to believe that two works of such contrasting styles and themes as Wolfram's *Parzival* and Gottfried's *Tristan und Isolde* (c. 1210; *Tristan and Isolde*, 1899) were written in the span of less than a decade. What they obviously have in common is their determination to follow courtly ideals beyond all courtly conventions. However, where Wolfram was consciously obscure and other-worldly, Gottfried wanted to be consciously lucid and human. *Tristan and Isolde* is also an epic of immoderation: It speaks of the earthly, sensual passion that Tristan and Isolde feel for each other. Tristan is a vassal of King Mark of Cornwall and Isolde is Mark's young wife, yet Tristan and Isolde persist in their love and build an illicit relationship through long adventures of deceit and subterfuge. The willful, often mocking breach of the knightly ideal of chastity was in itself nothing new for courtly poetry. What was new was the total seriousness, the total lack of frivolity with which Gottfried treated this adulterous union as a troubling human predicament.

LYRIC POETRY

Lyric poetry, too, experienced an amazing surge of creativity under the auspices of the chivalric ethos. It was poetry devoted primarily to an extremely stylized, extremely idealized form of loving adoration of the "fair sex," a love which in German was to be known as *Minne*, the practitioners of which would become known as *Minnesänger*. This lyric poetry reached its most elaborate form in the song of the troubadour, the *canso d'amor* (love song) of southern France. With ever new variations, the poet describes in his song the typical stages through which he courts a lady who is almost always of a higher station than himself and married to another man. Arduous periods of wooing and pleading are often rewarded by shows of the lady's favor. These shows of favor—smiles, acknowledgments, the wearing of the knight's colors (sexual favors are granted only rarely)—are, nevertheless, constantly jeopardized by malevolent friends and cold conventions, frequently by the fickle or obdurate heart of the lady herself. Thus, brief moments of bliss are usually followed by long spells of mournful longing and dejection. Though a poet's love did at times stray from the elevated plane of these platonic feelings, *Minne* was not incompatible with marriage and should not be misunderstood as an actual challenge to the harsh and dreary marriage conventions of the day. More often than not, *Minnelieder* (songs of *Minne*) were barely more than a fashionable parlor game. In spite of the assumed intimacy of the confessional style, little of what is expressed in them should be taken for more than the polite gallantry of a professional singer in his attempt to gain the protection of a powerful lady at court.

WALTHER VON DER VOGELWEIDE

Walther von der Vogelweide (c. 1170-c. 1230) gave the conventions of the troubadours their most creative adaptation in the German language. His strong and unabashed zest for life filled his *Minnelieder* with a surprising vitality. It was this zest for life which convinced Walther that *Minne* cannot be bound to social station, that it can be felt toward any woman, and that true nobility of heart is found more often outside rather than inside the nobility of rank. There, too, love seems so much freer to give itself to the beloved. Walther refused to consider a *Minne* that is predicated on the notion of its remaining unfulfilled anything but a false and inhuman emotion.

In a similar vein, Walther's spontaneous appreciation of nature enlivened the many threadbare metaphors inherited from the troubadours. Even the tradition of the troubadour's *sirventes* (poems exploring political and moral questions) assumed in Walther's hands an unusual urgency. Fights between emperor and pope had erupted again; civil war had returned to Germany; and the lyricist of fervent love threw himself into the partisan struggle with political verse of equal ardor. Walther was undoubtedly not only the greatest but also the most versatile poet of the Middle Ages. Love, nature, politics, and religion were themes for his inspiration, creating an unmatched lyric summa of medieval culture on the eve of that culture's collapse.

FOURTEENTH TO SIXTEENTH CENTURY

With the execution of the last of the Hohenstaufens at the hands of his enemies in Italy (1268), the fabric of medieval politics in Germany unraveled rapidly. The election of Rudolph of Habsburg (1273) ushered in an era in which imperial power forsook its claim to European leadership and restricted itself to the politics of dynastic self-aggrandizement. Of even greater importance for the future of medieval culture was the glaring failure of the Crusades in 1270. European nobility in all of its heroic posturing saw itself confronted initially with a serious loss of face and ultimately with an even more serious loss of legitimacy.

While knighthood had weakened itself in seven Crusades, its adventures in the East had helped another class to gather unforeseen strength. As it turned out, the Crusades had opened wider horizons not only for the idealistic imagination of chivalry but also for the decidedly materialistic imagination of the middle class. Trade was flourishing, and so were the cities of Germany. A money economy, originating in Italy, replaced the complex relations of loyalty with the simple cash nexus. Armies of loyal knights gave way to armies of mercenaries; light infantry and gunpowder relegated the heavily armored knight to eventual obsolescence. Even where the knights did manage to redirect their crusading spirit—as did the Knights of the Teutonic Order when they declared the conversion and colonization of Prussia to be a new goal—their efforts could no longer be sustained without the ever more obtrusive money of the burghers. The Middle Ages had entered a period of complex yet obvious transition. The effects of this transition on poetry were equally complex but not nearly as obvious.

The demands of the changing times were felt in the nobility itself. In search of novel themes and renewed vitality, *Minnelieder* strove to combine, rather incongruously, the overwrought ideals of *Minne* with intentionally crude peasant settings. Much of this lyric poetry reads like a deliberate satire of itself. Didactic poems, on the other hand, tried desperately to explain chivalric ideals to a less and less receptive audience. Furthermore, the court epic, sensing the need for a closer grasp of reality, admitted historical events and characters into the never-never land of romance. Soon, the peasant epic evolved to debunk the whole conceited glitter of courtly perfection. *Meier Helmbrecht* (c. 1250; peasant Helmbrecht), the most famous peasant epic in the German language, tells the story of a young man who, seduced by social ambition and the airs of chivalry, joins a band of robber barons. At the end of a short life of tragic illusions and suffering, he is turned away by his own father and finally hanged by the people of his own village.

Social and economic power shifted from the knightly courts to the towns and their burghers. The rising middle class, however, was slow to realize a class consciousness of its own. The cultural vacuum that arose as a result of this hesitation was not easily filled. Instead of creating values appropriate to its interests and aspirations, the middle class felt that its socioeconomic power entitled it at long last to the values of its erstwhile betters. The resulting disparity between the anachronistic idealism of what was believed and the materialism of what was practiced led to a whole culture of satire, a culture castigating itself for its lack of authenticity.

The pretensions of the court epic were lampooned in the mock epic, while the excitement of knightly adventures gave way to stories about the pranks with which clever rogues exploited the vanity of others. The animal fable, derived from Greek and Oriental sources, finally broadened the social critique to include all classes of society. *Reynke de Vos* (1498; Reynard the fox) no longer poked fun at the nobility, but at all the social climbers who, like their archetype, the cunning and unprincipled fox, spare no effort on their way into the antechambers of the king. The international best seller of late medieval satire was Sebastian Brant's *Das Narrenschiff* (1494; *The Ship of Fools*, 1509), a poem whose author viewed his own times with an utterly jaundiced eye. Brant, who is considered one of Germany's earliest Humanists, was in fact no reformer. He favored no trend or class and offered no prospect of any solution. More than one hundred follies and vices are paraded around and soundly thrashed by an impartially venomous tongue, leaving a vivid picture of the cultural uncertainty that gripped the waning Middle Ages.

The curious inability of the middle class to move beyond the cultural values of a society whose economic and social restrictions it had long left behind is evidenced in the appropriation by sturdy and conscientious burghers of the courtly *Minnelieder*. From a wide variety of *Minnelieder*, which they carefully collected and studied, artisans in the towns culled a system of twelve rigid patterns. These they proceeded to employ, with slavish adherence, for their own songs on moral and didactic themes. *Minnesänger* had turned into *Meistersänger* (master singers), well-intentioned craftspeople who made up for their lack of imagination by a display of pedantic learning and a bizarre ingenuity in the arrangement of their metrical schemes. Inventiveness reached fantastical heights when it was felt that only those singers could be declared *Meistersänger* who had added at least one original "tone" (verse arrangement) to their guild's stock in trade. In his middle-class smugness and with his matter-of-fact imagination, the cobbler Hans Sachs (1494-1576)—one of the last and certainly the most accomplished of the *Meistersänger*—assumed an almost patriarchal stature in German literature. Nine years before his death, he proudly counted among his numerous literary works no fewer than 4,275 *Meistersänge* (master songs) in 275 strophic forms, 13 of which he had invented himself.

The *Volkslied* (folk song)—to the modern sensibility, the most appealing poetic achievement of the fourteenth and fifteenth centuries—occupied a very marginal place in the literary world of its day. It, too, had its origins in the *Minnelied*, but, in contrast to the *Meistersäng*, the *Volkslied* refused to live up to the formality of its courtly predecessor and instead infused the conventional themes of love and longing with the simplicity of experience. In simple rhymes, repetitive im-

ages, and catchy refrains, the *Volkslied* deals with typical situations of easily identifiable classes of people: hunters, millers, students, soldiers, and so on. Over the centuries, many of the *Volkslieder* were overlaid with the patina of a garbled text, a naïve nonsense which, if anything, seems to have added to their perennial charm.

In spite of its popularity, the *Volkslied* did not possess the formative power to fill the cultural void that the receding chivalric society had left behind. Other forces had to originate to fashion a new image of world, humans, and society. When these forces arrived on the scene, they were not particularly related to poetry, nor were they particularly productive of it. The origins of modern humans were accompanied by a tremendous loss of the power of poetry. The culture of knighthood had been an unmistakably poetic one; prose virtually did not exist as a literary form. The new society arose almost in the absence of poetic formulation and evolved a decidedly prosaic culture.

Like the eleventh century, the fourteenth century was marked by a wave of religious fervor. In contrast to the earlier revival, however, this religious enthusiasm championed no ecclesiastical cause. The secular power of the Church had reached its high point at the end of the thirteenth century when, with almost no transition, it found itself embroiled in every imaginable ecclesiastical and political trouble. The Babylonian Captivity of the Papacy in southern France (1309-1377) and the following forty years of schism—in which two, then three popes stood against one another—had driven the religious aspirations of the people upon themselves and into the arms of mysticism. Mysticism, a form of religious individualism which strives for a direct union with God through contemplation, found its most creative expression in the philosophical sermons of Meister Eckhart (died 1327). The imaginative prose style used to explain his difficult and often highly paradoxical thoughts greatly extended the scope of the German language.

At a time when northern Europe developed in mysticism a religious version of individualistic self-reliance, the Italian city-states—for once uninhibited by the presence of either pope or emperor—advanced a strictly secular counterpart. Believing themselves the rightful heirs of classical Rome, the Italians accepted it as their duty to resurrect the classical ideal of a human perfection to be achieved without interference of church or state. Faith in a rebirth (renaissance) of classical antiquity soon spread to other parts of Europe. What the Humanists of the German Renaissance lacked in natural links to the classical spirit, they eagerly compensated for by a meticulous adherence to its letter. Preoccupied with the editing and translating of classical texts, German Humanism quickly degenerated from a rebirth of humanity to a mere rebirth of philology. It is true that with the image of the *poeta doctus* (poet-scholar), Humanism gave the poet a fresh and lofty mission. As a learned educator, he was no longer to be subservient to anything outside the demands of his chosen profession. At the same time, however, Humanism clipped the wings of German poets by insisting that Humanist poetry could only succeed in the clarity of Latin, not in the murky barbarisms of the German language. The rich harvest of Latin poetry produced by German poets during the Renaissance yielded some impressive fruit. Nevertheless, it has remained a harvest unclaimed, a literature relegated to the limbo of unread and forgotten books.

As admirable as the goals and values of the German Humanists in all of their balanced sanity might have been, no cultural reform is likely to succeed that sets itself up in opposition to the imaginative propensities of the people it wants to educate. Humanism was destined to remain the ideal of a small elite of literati. It was quickly swept away by a reform that did speak to the imagination of the people, Martin Luther's Protestant Reformation.

SIXTEENTH TO EIGHTEENTH CENTURY

When Martin Luther (1483-1546) posted his ninety-five theses against indulgences on a church door in Wittenberg, nobody, least of all Luther, could have predicted the repercussions this act would have for him and his country. Despair about the prevailing corruption of the Church was general, and there was nothing in Luther's theses that had not been said before. Still, the object of his attack was chosen with the instinct of a true rebel.

In the granting of indulgences, the Church had given itself the power to remit some of the punishment a sinner had to expect after death even for those sins that had been forgiven in the sacrament of penance. This remittance of future punishment for past sins was usually tied to some spiritual or material sacrifice on the part of the sinner: fasting, praying, almsgiving, pilgrimages, and so on. In the fifteenth century, a financially strapped Papacy had made monetary "sacrifices" by the sinner—to be paid into the Papacy's always empty coffers—the center of its dealings with indulgences and a regular item in its fiscal planning. Soon, unscrupulous monks roamed the countryside, promising nothing short of salvation to those willing and able to pay for it. The poor, who of all classes were most dependent on the hereafter for any hope of a happier life, felt excluded from the spiritual benefits of these transactions. The selling of indulgences represented simply too much of what people in Germany had hated for so long: the Church's heavy-handed interference in people's most personal affairs, its greedy exploitation of foreign countries, and its un-Christian preference for the rich. Thus, a devotional practice which had existed in the Church for a long time galvanized the discontented masses of Germany almost overnight.

The initial strength of a movement is rarely a reliable indication of its staying power. What made Luther's reforms survive was that Luther himself, appalled by the widespread anarchy he had caused, directed his reform into the rigid channels of a new ecclesiastical organization. Excommunicated by the pope and under imperial ban, he turned for support to the only authority that could still profit from his cause: the power of Germany's territorial princes. Lured by the promise of the confiscation of Church property, they were only too willing to become Luther's *Notbischöfe* (emergency bishops). When the emperor finally found the time and means to intervene, he saw himself confronted by a well-entrenched state church. Reluctantly, he accepted its existence in the Peace of Augsburg (1555).

It remains astounding that the sixteenth century, which stirred so many political, social, and religious emotions, produced almost no poetry. It is less surprising that the important contributions that were made came during the first two decades of the Reformation and were the work of Luther himself.

Luther's greatest literary achievement was his extraordinarily successful translation of the Bible. It is hard to think of any book in the German language that has influenced German literature more than has the *Lutherbibel* (1522, 1534). For more than a century, Middle High German had been in transition. The imperial chancery had long attempted to arrive at a uniform German language for its own legal and diplomatic affairs. Whatever effort may have gone before, Modern High German came alive only when Luther, through his ingenious use of dialect and idiom, transformed the German of the chanceries into a language that could serve all people for all purposes. Luther's language spread even faster than his Reformation. By the end of his life, more than 100,000 copies of the *Lutherbibel*—an amazing number for those days—were in circulation. For the first time in its history, Germany had a standard written language.

Luther contributed most directly to poetry through his composition of thirty-six hymns, the only lasting poetic creations of the whole of the sixteenth century in Germany. Spiritual songs had certainly existed before, often as converted versions of popular secular songs. What distinguishes Luther's hymns—one has only to think of the rousing "Ein feste Burg ist unser Gott" ("A Mighty Fortress Is Our God")—is that they express not only the communing of an individual with his God but also the common faith of the whole congregation. Luther's *Geistliche Lieder* (1524; *Spiritual Songs*, 1853) started a tradition of hymnal poetry in Germany which was to remain creative well into the nineteenth century.

It must have seemed clear from the beginning that the Peace of Augsburg had been arranged as little more than a truce between the warring parties. By the early seventeenth century, Catholic and Protestant princes began to arm and organize their hatred in opposing leagues. The bloody Thirty Years' War (1618-1648) started in Prague when the Protestant nobility of Bohemia refused to acknowledge the accession of the Catholic emperor, Ferdinand II, to the throne of Bohemia. With the help of the Catholic League, Ferdinand proved victorious in 1620, and the war appeared to have come to a quick end. Too much, though, rode on the Protestant cause. Alarmed by the Catholics' easy victory

and their brutal reprisals, the Protestant princes, under the leadership of Danish King Christian, resolved to try for another outcome. Once again, Ferdinand prevailed in 1626, this time with the help of his celebrated general Albrecht von Wallenstein. The next Protestant willing to try improving Protestant fortunes was Swedish King Gustavus, and under him—not without the financial support of Catholic France—the Protestant cause finally triumphed, though Gustavus himself was killed in the decisive battle in 1632. With the death of Gustavus and the murder of Wallenstein in 1634, it looked as if the war had spent itself, yet as no one seemed satisfied with the resulting stalemate, hostilities were resumed on an even larger scale. France entered the war on the side of the Protestants, while Spain fought for the imperial and Catholic party. In 1635, chastened by seventeen years of grueling war and appalled by its widening dimensions, the Protestant princes arranged a peace with Ferdinand. The task of ridding themselves of their former allies, however, proved to be a lengthy and frustrating affair. None of these friends wanted to leave Germany without having something to show for his pains. War and negotiations dragged on for another thirteen years, until the Peace of Westphalia, in 1648, ratified the total exhaustion and despoiling of Germany.

About half of the German population died as a result of the Thirty Years' War. Agriculture almost ground to a halt as hundreds of villages simply ceased to exist. Trade had been interrupted for too long to be resumed without great delay; neither was there any capital to restart even the most essential industries. The country had been bled white. Only political systems, the most parasitic of all human organizations, increased and multiplied with prodigious fertility. By 1648, Germany had disintegrated into eighteen hundred independent territories, fifteen hundred of them averaging a population of about three hundred people. Even among the remaining territories, barely a handful could be classified as states. The nobility survived the war nearly intact, and the reconstruction of Germany proceeded under its leadership and on its terms, delaying the assertion of a middle-class consciousness for more than a century.

In the context of this momentous national decline,

German literature tried belatedly to absorb the Humanism of the Italian Renaissance into the vernacular. For guidance and inspiration, poets and critics turned to France, the country in which such an assimilation of the Italian Renaissance had been accomplished most successfully. What the French poet and aesthetician Joachim du Bellay had done for France with his *La Défense et illustration de la langue française* (1549; *The Defence and Illustration of the French Language*, 1939), Martin Opitz wanted to do for his compatriots seventy-five years later.

MARTIN OPITZ

Das Buch von der deutschen Poeterey (1624; book on German poetry), by Martin Opitz (1597-1639), although a very slim volume by the standards of German scholarship, became the most influential treatise on German poetry for more than a century. Its program was as simple as it was practical. For the Renaissance, poetry was a branch of rhetoric, a rhymed form of oratory whose ultimate aim lay not within itself, but in the pleasing instruction and persuasion of its reader. Since Aristotle's treatment of the subject, rhetoric had always been thought to follow objective, teachable rules. All that needed to be stated more explicitly was simply how German poets could profit from these rules in their efforts to construct more persuasive poems. First, Opitz suggested, rhetorical poetry, like any other argument, needs to be organized rationally, avoiding everything that might startle or confuse. Second, rhetorical poetry ought to be elegant, employing the fitting word while never offending with even the semblance of crudity. Finally, rhetorical poetry must be dignified, a goal to be achieved by borrowing as many lofty metaphors from the ancients as can reasonably be accommodated by the text.

In his poetry—very mediocre stuff—Opitz conformed to the letter of his own law. It is poetry in which virtuosity of form and coldness of feeling stand in direct proportion to each other. As with the classical Sophists, who prided themselves on the fact that they could argue with equal conviction on both sides of any issue, Opitz's poetic persuasiveness comes across as strangely opportunistic, even indifferent to the ostensible purpose for all of his rhetorical posturing: the themes of his poetry. The vanity of all earthly things, the praise of love, the inconstancies of fortune, the sorrows of war, and the longing for peace are all treated with an equally detached expediency.

BAROQUE POETRY

Soon, however, the frightening insecurities of life, made so obvious by the horrors of the Thirty Years' War, asked more from poetry than Opitz's rationalistic disdain and stoic equanimity. Life could no longer be treated as a mere occasion for the making of good poetry. The resulting seriousness about subject matter also placed greater demands on the rhetorical form, straining it to the breaking point in the service of a poem's passionate pleading. The period characterized by this new strain, this contorted urgency, is called the Baroque (a word of Portuguese origin describing the contorted shape of irregular pearls).

ANDREAS GRYPHIUS

The poet most often identified with German Baroque poetry is Andreas Gryphius (1616-1664). Having experienced the brutalities of war in a traumatic childhood that left him an orphan at an early age, Gryphius became obsessed with the Christian message of humanity's utterly fallen state. In contrast to Opitz, Gryphius was a man of unshakable conviction, and it was the strength of this conviction which made his rhetoric so Baroque, so forced in its effort to persuade at all costs. At no point did it occur to Gryphius that the direct expression of his personal experiences might be the most appropriate theme for his poetry. The rhetoric of the Renaissance valued the persuasiveness of the representative, not the individualistic or existential. Gryphius, therefore, clothed his fears and pains in the verbal pomp of grandiose metaphors, expanding, recapitulating, polishing his unvarying message in an endless drive for more perfect rhetorical strategies.

If in Gryphius's poetry representative rhetoric and existential message still fused in a creative though distorted vision, by the end of the seventeenth century, the power of rhetoric overwhelmed even the most serious subjects and finally disentangled itself from all of them. Opitz had not been very particular about his themes, but at least the comparative simplicity of his rhetoric had allowed no jarring disparity between elaborate form and superficial content. By the end of the seventeenth century, however, rhetoric resolved to disguise the absence of original themes by a most ornate extravagance in its treatment of traditional ones. This trend toward rhetorical affectation was by no means peculiar to German poetry; Italian and Spanish poets had set the example of virtuosity for its own sake.

CHRISTIAN HOFMANN VON HOFMANNSWALDAU

In Germany, the leading exponent of ultimate refinement and the mastery of all technical skills was Christian Hofmann von Hofmannswaldau (1617-1679). Hofmannswaldau's cherished subject was the vanity of all earthly joys, particularly the futility of erotic pleasure, yet his painstaking search for the most exquisite epithet, the most luxuriously sensuous metaphor, the most sensational analogy seemed to circumvent rather than to promote his somber faith. The feverish obsession with which Hofmannswaldau dwelled on the erotic pleasures he condemned betrayed him for what he really was: an eroticist with a bad conscience. In this respect, Hofmannswaldau was quite typical of Baroque culture at the end of the seventeenth century. Those espousing this culture no longer were convinced of what it said yet lived under the compulsion to say it ever more vehemently, as if repeating its faltering beliefs might rouse them to their former vigor. Instead, a less troubled generation started to react to the whole phantasmagoric display of the Baroque with swift retribution. At the turn of the eighteenth century, middle-class rationality still prided itself on its own good conscience and felt absolutely no qualms about dismissing the bad conscience that had preceded it.

EIGHTEENTH CENTURY

The politics of continental Europe in the eighteenth century—until the French Revolution of 1789—were taken up with a series of dynastic struggles that led to several international wars: the War of the Spanish Succession (1701-1714), the War of the Polish Succession (1733-1735), the War of the Austrian Succession (1740-1748), and the War of the Bavarian Succession (1778-1779). The absolute control which royal and princely families exercised over their states transformed any dynastic haggling among the intricately related ruling houses of Europe into an immediate and serious international power struggle. If these prolonged

family feuds had a common concern, it was their desire to let no upstart join their illustrious ranks and thus destroy whatever balance of power they had orchestrated. However, it was the rapid rise of just such an upstart house and nation that provided Germany with its most important political development of the century. Prussia under the rule of the Hohenzollerns was the last state in Europe to emerge as one of its leading powers. Not even a kingdom before 1701, Prussia had become, under the hands of frugal and disciplined rulers, a power that half a century later was able to hold its own against the combined forces of Austria, France, and Russia.

Oddly enough, these dramatic political events did not influence German culture significantly. While the nobility had reserved for itself the theater of international politics, it had, at the same time and by an unspoken agreement, granted the middle class a considerable degree of private security and peace. After the hardships of the Thirty Years' War, the middle class was eager to accept such a bargain, at least until it would be able to rebuild its economic stamina. Thus, the eighteenth century presents the picture of a Germany in which the nobility was responsible for matters of politics and the middle class was responsible for everything else.

In the running of its affairs, the middle class was greatly helped by the spirit of rationalism and empiricism. Rationalism had become the philosophy of the bourgeoisie in France since René Descartes had declared reason, rather than tradition or precedent, as the sole authority in the management of human conduct. Empiricism, an elaboration of rationalism developed in England by John Locke (1632-1704), specified that reason needs to be based on experience and that no rational judgment ought to be made without prolonged observation of the facts. French rationalism and English empiricism combined to inspire the Age of Enlightenment. The middle class, which had nothing to lose by the abolition of a tradition that kept it out of power and had everything to gain from the rational observation of political, social, and economic facts, embraced the Enlightenment as its most sacred mission.

To the poets of the Enlightenment, the contorted rhetoric of the Baroque appeared neither rational nor based on facts. A first reaction against Baroque poetry had occurred in France, where Nicolas Boileau-Despréaux, in his *L'Art poétique* (1674; *The Art of Poetry*, 1683), had insisted on the sober standards of truthfulness, naturalness, and reasonableness in the writing of poetry. In 1730, Johann Christoph Gottsched (1700-1766) presented his countrymen with a German version of Boileau's creed in his *Versuch einer critischen Dichtkunst vor die Deutschen* (1730; attempt at a critical art of poetry for Germans). How quickly, though, attitudes were beginning to change in Germany is evident from the fact that Gottsched and his theories of rational poetry turned into the laughingstock of German poets in less than twenty years.

The reaction against Gottsched was led by two Swiss professors, Johann Jakob Bodmer (1698-1783) and Johann Jakob Breitinger (1701-1776). Both men were admirers of the English scene and favored its literature over that of the French. In typically empiricist fashion, they suggested that it might prove more profitable to deduce a good poetic theory from the study of good poetry, rather than to hope for good poetry to be written in accordance with some preconceived poetic theory. In short, the theory of poetry must follow, not precede, the practice of poetry. Looking at poems without prejudicial expectations, Bodmer and Breitinger discovered that a good poem is, above all, imaginative and that reason played a very secondary role in its creation. The ensuing fight between the two camps ended with the total defeat of Gottsched and of the French influence over German poetry. In the end, what turned the tide in the acrimonious squabbles was the fact that Bodmer and Breitinger could point to a young poet who substantiated and justified all of their claims, while Gottsched, as hard as he tried, could not.

FRIEDRICH GOTTLIEB KLOPSTOCK

This young, amazingly original poet was Friedrich Gottlieb Klopstock (1724-1803). Klopstock's poetry, with its outbursts of feeling and its flights of the imagination, caught the reading public totally by surprise. Klopstock made it his personal responsibility to restore to poetry the honorable function which it once had exercised within the Germanic tribes: to guide and express humanity's relation to God, nature, and society. As the prophet of an all-powerful poetry, he naturally felt no inhibition to dismiss what small-minded academicians had laid down as poetic law. Language, Klopstock believed, belongs to poets, and only they can determine its possibilities. In incomplete sentences, in irregular syntax, often in free rhythms, Klopstock stammered in awe before the grandeur of his themes (God, nature, love, patriotism) as much as before the sublime emotions these themes evoked in him.

It was Klopstock's faith in the power of poetry that impelled him to write in the genre in which poetry had exercised its power over society most forcefully: He set out to write an epic. Klopstock's genius, unfortunately, was lyric rather than epic, and his *Der Messias* (1748-1773), which swelled to twenty thousand lines, has remained one of the most monotonous and unreadable epics of all time. The passion which gave Klopstock's shorter poems their distinction could not be sustained over the course of twenty-five years; his emotions turned flat and belabored, exhausting and finally grating on the sensibilities of the reader.

Not even Klopstock's lyric poems withstood the test of time as well as one might have expected. In spite of his emotionalism, Klopstock abided by the basic principles of rhetorical poetry: His feelings did not spontaneously transform themselves into words. To create a poetic effect, it was not enough for Klopstock to relate his experience poetically. That experience, however personal, needed to be made representative of all experiences under similar conditions. To arrive at this representative quality, the poet had to generalize the intimacy of what he felt until the feeling became comprehensible, not to say reasonable, to the reader. Klopstock, who was a very emotional poet, almost never lets the reader share in the immediacy of his emotions. Even when Klopstock seems to have been sincerely overwhelmed, one almost always senses the rational scaffolding that supports the poetic expression of his ecstasies.

In the second half of the eighteenth century, faith in human experience as representative and rational received a mighty jolt when it became clear that experiences are neither shared nor accessible to reason. On the contrary, each person's experiences create a unique world—a strictly individualistic world and therefore (as one needs a point of reference outside oneself for rationality) beyond the power of reason.

JOHANN GOTTFRIED HERDER

From these disturbing insights, the philosopher and critic Johann Gottfried Herder (1744-1803) drew some surprisingly fruitful conclusions for poetry. As language originally was meant to express the emotional responses to experiences, and as these emotional responses are as individualistic and irrational as the experiences which caused them, the most primordial form of language could not have been rational prose but must have been irrational poetry. Poetry is the mother tongue of the human race, because it is in poetry that humanity's first and only appropriate interpretations of the world occurred.

Most existing poetry, sadly enough for Herder, served as pleasing ornament or rhetorical confirmation of an already charted human environment. This trend needed to be reversed; poetry needed to reassume its primary function. Above all, it had to regain access to basic human experiences within the tradition to which it wanted to speak. Attempts to rejuvenate German poetry in accordance with the standards of Greece, Rome, or France were doomed to fail. Instead, a conscious effort was necessary to enable German poetry to reestablish its ties to the life of the German people. To this end, the poetic language would have to cleanse itself of all artificiality and return to the simplicity and spontaneity exemplified in the creations of folk poetry.

JOHANN WOLFGANG VON GOETHE

The success of Herder's ideas was not, as has often been claimed, immediate or sweeping. Of the young poets of the time, only one showed himself deeply affected, yet one poet was all Herder needed for his theory to triumph, for this young man was Johann Wolfgang von Goethe (1749-1832).

Goethe met Herder in 1770, and one year later Goethe's poems usually designated as *Sesenheimer Liederbuch* (1775-1789, 1854; *Sesenheim Songs*, 1853) made Herder's program come true. The twenty-two-year-old poet speaks of his love for the pastor's daughter at Sesenheim in tones of boundless joy, as if such love had never existed before and would never exist again. With a relaxed innocence, he trusts the poetic quality of all that is natural and recovers for the language of poetry, without the slightest tinge of embarrassment, love and heart, flowers and kisses, the sun, the moon, the air, and the clouds.

Still, for Herder, the poet was not merely an innocent participant in the world's harmony. As a creator, the poet also carried grave responsibilities for the state of human affairs. In a series of forceful odes, Goethe explored the challenges of any creative response to earthly existence. Through a study of great prototypes (Prometheus, Mohammed, Ganymede) and their rhythms of life, Goethe felt confirmed in his belief that equal creativity is required for rebellion against and submission to the flow of things in this world. A poet can prefer one of these attitudes to the other only at the expense of constraining his or her most vital gifts, an infinite capacity for experience.

Goethe's career as an administrator at the court of Weimar (1775-1786) demanded a firmer, more realistic response from the poet. In view of humanity's innumerable limitations, moderation had the last word. Emotional introspection was replaced by objective overview,

The year 1999 marked the 250th birthday of Johann Wolfgang von Goethe. Hundreds of lamp busts, in Goethe's likeness, were displayed as part of a celebration in Weimar, Germany. (AP/Wide World Photos)

as the typical rather than the extraordinary in life received Goethe's attention. Only in an occasional lyric sigh for release—as in Germany's most famous poem, the weightless, dreamlike "Über allen Gipfeln ist Ruh" ("Over All the Hilltops It Is Still")—could Goethe admit to himself the strain which his search for order and objectivity had placed on him.

Emotional release in the midst of order and objectivity became Goethe's great discovery on his journey through Italy (1786-1788). Goethe lived and celebrated this release upon his return to Weimar in his cycle of *Römische Elegien* (1793; *Roman Elegies*, 1876). The unashamed eroticism of the classical age is praised here in the strict order of classical meters. Emphasizing the sensual, often outright licentious foundations of antiquity's formal achievements, Goethe freely mocked his compatriots' prudishly ideal conception of classical perfection. Almost a quarter of a century later, Goethe would reaffirm his faith in sensuality as a precondition of great art—this time encouraged by his discovery of Persian poetry—in a similar cycle of poems, his *Westöstlicher Divan* (1819; *West-Eastern Divan*, 1877).

Goethe's lyric poetry reached its last peak in the eighteenth century between 1797 and 1798 when, in friendly competition with Friedrich Schiller, Goethe wrote several of his finest ballads.

FRIEDRICH SCHILLER

Friedrich Schiller (1759-1805), the greatest dramatist of the eighteenth century, was a primarily speculative mind, and his poetry rarely achieves the confessional intimacy which so often makes Goethe's poems read like fragments of an autobiography. Schiller philosophized in his poems on the painful antagonism between what is and what ought to be, between the innate freedom of humans and the acquired constraints of a person's conventional mind and heart.

These differences of poetic perspective also distinguish Goethe's and Schiller's ballads. The ballads of Goethe remain close to their popular roots; they focus on the inexplicable omnipresence of demonic powers, as in the well-known "Der Zauberlehrling" ("The Sorcerer's Apprentice"). Schiller's ballads, by contrast, dramatize ethical or philosophical conflicts: The downfall of pride is the theme of "Der Taucher" ("The Diver"); the jealousy of the gods, that of "Der Ring des Polykrates" ("The Ring of Polycrates"); and "Die Bürgschaft" ("The Pledge") proclaims the invincible power of friendship. With their easy combination of dramatic narrative and didactic intent, Schiller's ballads enjoyed an unparalleled popularity throughout the nineteenth century; in modern times, they are often unjustly dismissed.

FRIEDRICH HÖLDERLIN

Schiller's poetry of ideas and Goethe's poetry of experience were fused at the beginning of the nineteenth century by Friedrich Hölderlin (1770-1843). Hölderlin wrestled for a few intense years with such apparent abstractions as freedom, love, fatherland, divinity, and fate in intensely existential, at times opaque poems until the onset of a severe mental illness at the age of thirty-three broke up his creative struggle.

Classical Greece was Hölderlin's model of a harmonious society, and the French Revolution raised his hopes for a reconstitution of such a society even in his own country. Hölderlin wanted to be the prophet of this great advent. To be a worthy prophet, he was ready to bridge the gulf between future and present, ideal and reality, knowing full well that this would mean to be exiled from both, to exist as a lonely wanderer in time, a victim of his own promises. His having been exiled by God and humanity—expressed in poems such as "Die Heimat" ("Homeland") and "Abendphantasie" ("Evening Fantasy")—Hölderlin considered a great suffering and a great distinction, the suffering and distinction of a heroic fate. Hölderlin's only fear was that he might not be equal to the demands of this calling. His unquestioning faith in the power of poetry he shared with the Romantics of his era, while the humility with which he lived his vocation foreshadowed a much more modern sensibility.

BIBLIOGRAPHY

Becker-Cantarino, Barbara, ed. *German Literature of the Eighteenth Century: The Enlightenment and Sensibility.* Rochester, N.Y.: Camden House, 2005. Essays ranging from historical contexts to dominant ideas in the works of major writers. Bibliography and index.

Beiser, Frederick C. *The Romantic Imperative: The*

Concept of Early German Romanticism. Cambridge, Mass.: Harvard University Press, 2003. Explains how early German romanticism differed from later romanticism. One chapter defines "Romantic Poetry," which the writer insists dominates and defines the Romantic movement. An important reinterpretation.

Classen, Albrecht, ed. and trans. *Late-Medieval German Women's Poetry: Secular and Religious Songs*. Rochester, N.Y.: D. S. Brewer, 2004. Through intensive research, the writer has discovered and identified a number of German women who wrote lyric poetry in the fifteenth and sixteenth century and undoubtedly will be added to the literary canon. An important contribution to medieval studies. Introduction, notes, and interpretive essay by the editor.

Cocalis, Susan L., ed. *German Feminist Poems from the Middle Ages to the Present: A Bilingual Anthology*. New York: Feminist Press, City University of New York, 1986. Introduces and rediscovers German women poets dating back to the thirteenth century.

Dobozy, Maria. *Re-membering the Present: the Medieval German Poet-Minstrel in Cultural Context*. Turnhout, Belgium: Brepois, 2005. Examines performance art from 1170 to 1400, pointing out both how the fact of performance influenced the poet's techniques and how the poet-performer used his art to mold his society. Bibliography and index.

Gentry, Francis G., et al., eds. *German Epic Poetry*. New York: Continuum, 1995. Heroic poetry from the great epics of German literature, including *Jungere Hildebrandslied*, *The Battle of Ravenna*, *Bitterolf and Dietlieb*, and *The Rose Garden*.

Haymes, Edward R., and Susann T. Samples. *Heroic Legends of the North: An Introduction to the Nibelung and Dietrich Cycles*. New York: Garland, 1996. Traces the origins of epic tales in the Dark Ages and follows their spread throughout medieval literature. Surveys the medieval literary versions: the hero, heroic poetry, and the Heroic Age.

Hutchinson, Peter, ed. *Landmarks in German Poetry*. New York: Peter Lang, 2000. Examines the scope of German poetry, providing critical essays and history.

Newman, Jane O. *Pastoral Conventions: Poetry, Language, and Thought in Seventeenth Century Nuremberg*. Baltimore: Johns Hopkins University Press, 1990. Traces the development of the seventeenth century Nuremberg pastoral poetry society Pegnesischer Blumenorden as a historical, interpretive community of theorists and poets, and offers a detailed analysis of their writings, through which are explored issues at the center of scholarly debate about the Renaissance and early modern period.

Resler, Michael, ed. and trans. *German Romance I*. Rochester, N.Y.: D. S. Brewer, 2003. In this first volume of a series, Middle High German versions of Arthurian romances and translations into English are presented on facing pages. Extensive notes, bibliography, and index.

Walsøe-Engel, Ingrid, ed. *German Poetry from the Beginnings to 1750*. Foreword by George C. Schoolfield. New York: Continuum, 1992. These translations into English are an excellent starting place for the study of early German poetry. Bibliography and index.

Joachim Scholz

German Poetry: 1800 to Reunification

The French critic Hippolyte Taine (1828-1893) once wrote that between 1780 and 1830, Germany brought forth all the ideas of his age. Although somewhat hyperbolic, Taine's pronouncement should not be taken lightly. These fifty years span the period of Romanticism in German literature, art, and philosophy, and its many innovations in poetry left their mark in a pervasive, if occasionally discontinuous, tradition.

ROMANTICISM

German Romanticism can be said to have an early and a late phase. The early period is identified chiefly with August Wilhelm von Schlegel (1767-1845), his brother Friedrich (1772-1829), Ludwig Tieck (1773-1853), Novalis (Friedrich von Hardenberg, 1772-1801), Friedrich Schiller (1759-1805), and Friedrich Schleiermacher (1768-1834). The early phase was more critical and theoretical than late Romanticism, which counted more poets among its adherents, including Achim von Arnim (1781-1831), Clemens Brentano (1778-1842), and Joseph von Eichendorff (1788-1857).

Walter Benjamin has maintained that the German Romantics confronted their times not primarily on epistemological terms, even though these were in fact significant (for example, the philosophy of Johann Gottlieb Fichte, 1762-1814), but instead primarily through the medium of art. Friedrich von Schlegel saw the potential of the new age in the spirit of poetry. His essay "Progressive Universalpoesie" ("Progressive Universal Poetry") addresses a fundamental design of early Romanticism: the universal poeticization of life. Conceptually, Romantic poetry (in the broad sense) embraces all traditional genres of literary and philosophic discourse within its totalizing system. This view radically reformulated the mimetic possibilities of nature and privileged poetic perspective in new, epoch-making ways.

Novalis once wrote:

> Romanticism is nothing other than a qualitative sublimation. . . . By giving the commonplace exceptional signifi-

cance, the habitual an air of mystery, the familiar the dignity of the unfamiliar, the finite an infinite meaning—in so doing I romanticize.

Viewed against its cultural and sociohistorical context, a basic feature of early Romanticism is its systematic desystematization of what were perceived by the Romantics to be restrictive and rigid norms. Abhorring the profane and mourning the loss of life's poetic qualities, the Romantics were among the first to recognize and react against the modern forces of social and economic alienation. They blamed the rationalization and instrumentalization of Enlightenment ideology for having emptied life of its poetry and in contrast projected the Middle Ages as the last great harmonious historical age.

The revolutionary ideas advanced in philosophy and aesthetics have their parallel in Novalis's collection of poems *Hymnen an die Nacht* (1800; *Hymns to the Night*, 1897, 1948). Novalis suffered greatly at the deaths of his brother and his fiancé in 1797, and in 1799, he composed these six hymns, the poetic manifestation of his encounter with death (a central experience of German Romanticism). *Hymns to the Night*, a combination of ecstatic prose and strophic hymns, asserts that true perception of the world comes only after having acquired complete knowledge of the self. This view, related to Fichte's philosophy, is pivotal, for it locates the human being at the center of comprehending the universe.

Novalis's collection recounts both personal and individual experience and, through a quasi-mystical vision, projects the situation onto the dimensions of the historical-eschatological course of humankind. The objectification of Novalis's vision reveals the central transformation of the metaphoric function of light and dark, day and night, whereby night becomes the primal force of the universe. This transvaluation of their respective ranges of meaning takes place through a foregrounding of paradox and oxymora. Evolving ultimately into myth, Novalis's *Hymns to the Night* is a classic example of Romanticism, especially along those lines where its symbolism intersects with that of Christianity.

While Novalis's work is indisputably central to any discussion of early German Romantic poetry, the fact that critics are able today to speak of a "Romantic poetry" is largely a result of other factors. One of them was the publication, in 1805, of *Des Knaben Wunderhorn* (the boy's magic horn), a collection of German folk songs compiled by Achim von Arnim and Clemens Brentano. Interest in folk literature had been generated earlier by the young Johann Wolfgang von Goethe (1749-1832) and Johann Gottfried Herder (1744-1803), who in fact coined the German word *Volkslied* (folk song) in 1775. The work of Arnim and Brentano revived this interest, a task made easier by the current of nationalism running through Germany at the time.

Nearly all writers associated with German Romanticism wrote poetry, but, in the spirit of Schlegel's "Progressive Universal Poetry," these poems generally formed part of a larger text, most often a novel (the privileged genre within Romantic aesthetics). Typically, the heroes of Romantic novels are poets, or at least lead "poetic lives," and they are prone to express their emotional states—whether joy or sorrow, exhilaration or despair—in the relatively spontaneous form of the lyric poem. These factors, then, also help define the contours of Romantic poetry.

CLEMENS BRENTANO

Clemens Brentano had a great affinity for the folk song and used its features in his own verse. (The folk-song strophe, common to much nineteenth century German verse, is easily recognized by its alternating *abab* masculine/feminine rhyme scheme.) Brentano was a diverse and creative writer with an exceptionally active imagination. Although his poems are sometimes formally inconsistent, the tenor of his work is constant: musical, synesthetic, crafted, rich in texture. "Auf dem Rhein" ("Upon the Rhine") reveals a characteristic fascination for the macabre, manifested (from the Romantic perspective) in the eerie dimensions of the twilight. Appearance and reality become indistinguishable and effect a strikingly modern sense of disorientation. "Sprich aus der Ferne" ("Speak from Afar") uses the refrain as magic incantation. A desire to see all things as related informs this poem's lyric voice: the individual

and the universe, the near and the far. The structured dimensions of casual (and causal) reality give way and flow together, presented through synesthesia and oxymora. The poem's closing rhetorical gesture reflects the universalizing tendency of Romanticism.

JOSEPH VON EICHENDORFF

Joseph von Eichendorff's poetry displays a longing for unity and simplicity. He uses nature as a medium for understanding human existence and not merely as an object of imitation. Nature becomes a grand hieroglyph, and the poet's task is to render the most approximate translation. A fundamental Romantic dualism—nature as both demonic and divine—informs his work. The mood evoked by Eichendorff's landscapes often suggests impending danger, perhaps the risk of losing one's way in the dark. One critic has said of Eichendorff—who, unlike his contemporary Brentano, a late convert to Catholicism, was a devout Catholic throughout his life—that he "is not so much the poet of romantic longing as the poet of the *dangers* of romantic longing."

PATRIOTIC ROMANTICS

The poetry of Ernst Moritz Arndt (1769-1860), Max von Schenckendorff (1783-1817), and Karl Theodor Körner (1791-1813) represents another dimension of German Romanticism. According to E. L. Stahl,

The patriotic verse of these soldier-poets expresses the satisfaction of an urge to share in communal life. In the same way conversion to Catholicism fulfils religious Romantic longings, Patriotic activity and traditional religiosity cause the primary Romantic impulse to abate and new attitudes to prevail. The wanderer returns home and settles down to perform his acknowledged civic and domestic tasks. The age of "bürgerlicher Realismus" [Bourgeois Realism] begins with this change in outlook which was imposed on German writers by the social developments and the political events of the post-Napoleonic era.

BIEDERMEIER AND VORMÄRZ

Between 1830 and 1849, two distinct trends appeared within German poetry. The first, known as *Biedermeier*, was an introspective turn in response to the severe social and political repression exercised by Prince

Metternich (1773-1859). The second, referred to as *Vormärz*, was an effort to politicize literature in the hope of effecting social and political reform. The public at large still preferred poetry to the popular novel, and in its various forms (verse epic, cycles, and ballads) its purpose was mainly to entertain and (from an ideological point of view) "distract." Tomes of poetry, mostly traditional and derivative, depicted a charming poetic world of tranquil harmony. Against this numerically significant backdrop, the Young Germans, idealists and political activists, advanced their theory of prose. Between 1830 and 1848, social tensions grew and the political spirit turned more radical.

Heinrich Heine (1797-1856) recognized that even the conservative patriotic verse of the Romantic poets could play into the interests of social and political liberals, since as an ideological instrument, poetry was capable of stirring great enthusiasm among the people. Interest in the "political poem" accrued because—viewed pragmatically—it was the most appropriate literary form for subversive agitation and propaganda. Heine derided the hackneyed declarations of freedom and the ponderously didactic reflections often found in the more cumbersome representatives of ostensibly political verse. Concerned with matters of immediate social and political relevance, this poetry was often subjected to the mechanisms of censorship in Metternich's control. (The reports of his spies frequently referred to the danger posed by these political "folk poems," an indication that the liberals had succeeded in part in redefining the readership of poetry as well as the genre's objectives.)

Not all poets wrote within this mainstream of events. Two of note who remained relatively aloof from political affairs are Annette von Droste-Hülshoff (1779-1848) and Eduard Mörike (1804-1875). Although they did not enjoy the recognition they deserved during their lifetimes, their poetry has come to be highly valued for its complexity and its moral intensity.

ANNETTE VON DROSTE-HÜLSHOFF

Annette von Droste-Hülshoff, perceptive and intelligent, recognized the changed social conditions of her times, but family ties and the traditions of conservatism and Catholicism, coupled with a deep attachment to the countryside of her home region, Westphalia, exercised

a strong authority in her poetry. Westphalia becomes the locus of her search for harmony and order between the individual and nature. In contrast to the Romantic nature imagery of forests and streams, one finds in Droste-Hülshoff for the first time in German literature the poetic treatment of the moors and heaths of her own Westphalia. The realism of her verse lies in its attention to minute detail both in nature and in human nature. The senses of sight and sound play important roles throughout her work. She felt the presence of a demoniac undercurrent in all of existence, and thus her poems are often ballads or at least balladesque. The Catholic Church provided a sanctuary for Droste-Hülshoff. She understood her role as author to be a "power by the grace of God." Her confessional poems, such as "Geistliches Jahr" ("Spiritual Year"), show her coping with the dilemma of sin and the fall from grace.

EDUARD MÖRIKE

Eduard Mörike is often called the greatest German lyric poet of the nineteenth century. His poetry shares features with that of late Romanticism, and his use of classical forms and themes shows his affinity with classicism. Some consider his work *Biedermeier* because of its introspective and unpretentious nature; still others refer to the "impressionism" of his poetry. All in all, these varying assessments give testimony to the artistic complexity of his work. His poetic technique is marked by a sensitivity for chiaroscuro and for the minutely observed symbolism of the divine within nature.

Mörike sought to reconcile the ideal with the real; his poems are accompanied by a sense of despair, helplessness, and resignation. The landscape of the country idyll provides order and security. Isolated and alienated, Mörike views love and nature in his poems with melancholy. Still, his deep Christian faith seems to have counteracted his melancholy. He always returned to the central problem of death; he preferred a life of the soul, but he failed to find the ultimate harmony he desired. Unlike his contemporary Nikolaus Lenau (1802-1850), Mörike managed to contain his despair at least enough to resist nihilism. Showing the tensions between what Sigmund Freud later described as the pleasure principle and the reality principle, Mörike's poems register important sociohistorical antagonisms of nineteenth century Germany.

NIKOLAUS LENAU

Nikolaus Lenau is a figure of several contradictions. At once a great Austrian revolutionary poet and a late Romantic poet of *Weltschmerz*, Lenau suffered the isolation characteristic of the bourgeois intellectual, and his works turn around a central moment of melancholy. His poetry documents both the individual's revolt against the instrumentalization of human beings and the rejection of bourgeois complacency. His early poem "Einsamkeit" ("Loneliness") best illustrates his *Weltschmerz*, bordering on existential dread. In his verse epic *Die Albigenser* (1837; the Albigensia), on the other hand, Lenau acknowledges Georg Wilhelm Friedrich Hegel's *Weltgeist*. Lenau's reworking of historical material (the fate of the Cathars, against whom Pope Innocent III waged war from 1209 to 1229) reveals his interest in the struggle for economic and political power, an interest not merely antiquarian. The poem begins: "Nicht meint das Lied auf Tote abzulenken" ("Not of the dead shall the song give pause to think").

HEINRICH HEINE

Probably the most fascinating and enigmatic poet of the nineteenth century, Heinrich Heine is most often identified with his first volume of poetry, *Buch der Lieder* (1827; *Book of Songs*, 1856). With these poems, it became clear that Heine was both the heir and the bane of German Romantic poetry. In the vein of Romantic poets, he could create moods and turn nature into a mirror for subjective feelings, but he no longer shared their belief in the mysterious whole. For Heine, the integrity of the whole is an illusion (even though one that is longed for), and in its place there appears a sense of disintegration, nature as a collage of signs and indicators of his own subjectivity. His Byronic irony draws on both sentiment and sharp criticism. His right hand creates a sentimental mood or atmosphere which his left hand all the while is busy undermining through critical observation, exposing its illusory dimensions, rejecting them as unrealistic. The result of this double labor is the special tension characteristic of Heine's work, the central poignancy behind his poetic voice.

Heine's attraction and aversion to German Romanticism resulted from the fact that by 1830, Romanticism was a greatly inflated commodity. Backward-looking and conservative, it no longer offered appropriate solutions for dealing with the changed conditions. Heine thus distanced himself from its ideological subtext, while on the surface employing to his own advantage its artistic conventions. Thus, the special shape of Heine's wit, a kind of "double take," is evidenced in the poem "Ein Jüngling liebt ein Mädchen" ("A Young Boy Loves a Young Girl"). Here, the final lines reaffirm the validity of feeling after exposing it to mockery. In another poem, "Ich wandle unter Blumen" ("I Amble Among Flowers"), Heine, as the critic Robert M. Browning has observed, "does not so much ridicule feeling, the 'romantic' attitude, as reveal its inappropriateness as a mode of social behavior. Such is the world and we have to accept it." In "Mein Herz, mein Herz ist traurig" ("My Heart, My Heart Does Sorrow"), the antithesis of the pleasant surroundings and the sorrowful observer/narrator suggests at first that the cause for his mood is misfortune in love (although this is not stated explicitly). Instead, the poem is a remarkable example of the more general historical conditions of despair. When contrasted with the expressed death wish of the observer in the final line, the peaceful, serene summer landscape appears as reified and proplike, testifying to Heine's alienation both as lover and vis-à-vis nature. Heine's works thus contain the central ambivalences of his time.

In "My Heart, My Heart Does Sorrow," for example, the ambivalence of the summer idyll is juxtaposed to the ambivalence of the nostalgia expressed for an unattainable restored world. On one hand, Heine indulges his *Weltschmerz*, while, on the other, he exposes it as a pose, as illusionary game playing. The characteristic result is the combination of haunting appeal to sincere emotional states and their frequent reversal through pungent intellectual stimulation. The different tone of Heine's later poetry results from its more explicit politicization. Rejecting aesthetic banality as well as profane content, such as could be found in much of the tendentious poetry of the *Vormärz*, Heine's own political poetry offers successful counterexamples, as in "Die schlesischen Weber" ("The Silesian Weavers").

A CHANGE IN STYLES

The political poetry typical of the *Vormärz* virtually disappeared with the failed revolution of 1848. Complacency, disillusionment, and a conservative patriotism prevailed. Derivative didactic poetry predominated, represented by the work of the Munich Circle of poets, the most popular of whom was Emanuel Geibel (1815-1884). The more significant writers and poets of the genre known as Bourgeois Realism relied on the tradition of the *Erlebnislyrik*, or poetry of personal experience, such as that initiated by Goethe and practiced widely by the Romantics. This tradition, as well as that of the *Stimmungsgedicht*, or mood poem, ran its course in the period from 1850 to 1880.

REALISM

It is not customary to speak of lyric poetry in terms of realism, although one can consider it from this point of view, keeping in mind that the term "realism" has a range of meanings. Gottfried Keller's (1819-1890) realism is to be found in the unpretentious experience of his *Erlebnislyrik* and in the restraint of emotion. Friedrich Hebbel (1813-1863) and Conrad Ferdinand Meyer (1825-1898) showed an exacting attention to poetic form and rejected the highly rhetorical declamatory mode of earlier lyric diction. The realism of Theodor Storm (1817-1888) resides in his affinity for the folk song and in the acoustic sensitivity of his poems. Theodor Fontane (1819-1898) used everyday speech and eschewed the predominant bombastic style of the ballad of his day. The realists sought poetic experience in a balance or harmony among the divergent forces acting upon the self and the world around them, forces of alienation and isolation. On the whole, their poems display a preference for simple motifs and rhythms, uncomplicated strophes and lines of verse. Brevity and modesty proved more conducive to a sincere personal tone. Antiquated forms, viewed as rhetorically empty, fell into disrepute. Themes of love and nature, joy and sorrow, longing and remembrance prevailed, with an underlying tone of resignation evident. With some poets, especially Storm and Meyer, one senses an aura of *Spätzeitlichkeit*, the feeling of having been born too late, a condition suggested by the increasing artistic stylization of their poetry. Meyer's symbolic imagery finally broke with the conventions of the *Erlebnisgedicht* (poem of personal experience) more completely than any of his predecessors, and he stands at the threshold of what we commonly acknowledge to be modern poetry.

FRIEDRICH HEBBEL

Friedrich Hebbel's poetry is pensive and intellectual. He rejected the tendentious poetry of his day, but his own verse sometimes suffers because of its highly intellectualized reflection, especially evident in his later sonnets and epigrams. As a postclassicist, Hebbel was drawn between the reflection and speculation characteristic of Schiller's work and the emotion and immediacy essential to Goethe's. Hebbel's imagery tends to be static, with the intellectual tension and the unnatural syntax of his poems countering the illusion of immediacy. He treats the themes of dream and night, pain and death, in a dialectic fashion. The antithesis of the individual and the universe provides a central tension at the core of his lyric ego. The poetic symbol overcomes the fundamental opposition of self and universe.

THEODOR STORM

With Theodor Storm, the poetic symbol loses its comprehensive meaning and evolves into something more psychological and impressionistic, an attribute of a given mood, disposition, or atmosphere. Storm always proceeds from a single experience and then, through precise observations—particularly acoustic ones—achieves the artistic translation of this moment into compelling figurative language. Aware of the interdependency of form and content, Storm considered the brevity of the lyric poem structurally appropriate to the intense communication of states or moods. After 1848, his often sentimental lyric subjectivity gave way to a preoccupation with external reality in distinct, descriptive language. His nature poems, like those of Droste-Hülshoff, reveal close ties with his own home region, Schleswig-Holstein. Storm's later poems became more acerbic and, as with Meyer, the strong presence of death and isolation within Storm's lyric voice suggests a sense of *Spätzeitlichkeit*.

CONRAD FERDINAND MEYER

Conrad Ferdinand Meyer's poetry marks a significant historical moment between the realists' reformulation of the *Erlebnisgedicht* and the Symbolism of Rainer Maria Rilke (1875-1926). Some scholars therefore speak of Meyer's poetry as "anachronistic," while others stress those features of his work which point toward the future and the predominant course of modern poetry into the twentieth century. Meyer dealt continuously and in various ways with the problem of existence. Caught in the historical currents of pessimism and the accompanying sense of the loss of values which afflicted the late nineteenth century, Meyer preached the instructive and redemptive power of poetry. His own poetry evolves toward the poetic figuration of a subjective moment. His collection of poems from 1882 evidences a new kind of language, one intent on uncovering the essence of things through objectification. Even the most personal experience undergoes a transformation that objectifies it as a symbol or an allegorical image. In contrast to the more conventional mode of the *Erlebnisgedicht*, direct speech in Meyer's poetry is rare and generally recedes entirely behind the distance of intellectuality. The formal perfection of his poems is one means of coping with suffering and death, as in, for example, "Eingelegte Ruder" (inlaid rudder) or "Im Spätboot" (in the late boat). In "Zwei Segel" (two sails), the fundamental experience of human love is transformed and objectified in a symbolically rich texture of images.

NATURALISM

The publication of *Moderne Dichtercharaktere* (characters of modern poets) in 1885, an anthology showcasing the revolutionary bravado of the younger generation and its new aesthetic program, introduced naturalist poetry. Few of the original contributors, however, became significant poets, perhaps because the aesthetics of naturalism were not compatible with the conventions of lyric poetry.

ARNO HOLZ

Arno Holz (1863-1929), an avid experimentalist, was the most accomplished poet among the German naturalist writers. His *Buch der Zeit* (1885; book of this time), a pithy, coarse, and "thoroughly modern" collection of poems, rejected the artifice and pretense of conventional poetic diction. *Phantasus* (1898, enlarged 1916, 1925, 1929, 1961) shows his indebtedness to Walt Whitman's rhythms, his pathos, and his nontraditional use of form.

DETLEV VON LILIENCRON

Although unaffiliated with any literary movement, Detlev von Liliencron (1844-1909) realized in his verse many of the objectives of naturalist aesthetics. He achieved a naturalist effect in his combination of simple and precise perceptions, a technique which could just as well be called impressionistic in several instances. (Some critics have remarked that Liliencron's poems are "impressionistic" insofar as they are snapshots of reality as viewed from the surface, evocative glimpses of life, strung together according to the principle of juxtaposition and showing disdain for conventional rules of grammar and syntax.) His poems display spontaneity, rich imagery, and sensitivity to rhythm. The evocative atmosphere of his poems creates a depth which haunts the imagination. *Adjutanternritte* (1883; rides of an adjutant), his first book of poems, proved to be his most lasting; the quality of his later work generally did not live up to its promise.

TURN OF THE TWENTIETH CENTURY

While the naturalist poem per se remained more a concept than a reality, the abundance of poetry written around the turn of the twentieth century displayed a variety of forms, styles, and graces. There was the neo-Romantic balladry of Agnes Miegel (1879-1964), Börries Freiherr von Münchhausen (1874-1945), and Lulu von Strauss und Torney (1873-1956), generally traditional in form and content and conservative in ideology. There was also a revival of nature poetry in the vein of *Heimatkunst* (provincial art). At the same time, the style known as *Jugendstil*, or Art Nouveau, emerged. With its penchant for the charming and the ornate, *Jugendstil* was naturally drawn toward poetry. Some of Stefan Zweig's (1881-1942) poems can be considered representative of this style: They deal frequently with death, particularly its paradoxical relation to the centrifugal forces of life. *Jugendstil* experiences nature as a palliative for moroseness, pain, and suffering.

Around the same time, Frank Wedekind (1864-1918) and others were writing much satirical poetry, often with a political thrust, popular above all in the cabarets of large cities such as Berlin and Munich. The work of Christian Morgenstern (1871-1914) was singular in the tenor of his keen, penetrating questions of reality. Then as now, his poems have proved to be enormously popular. The work of Richard Dehmel (1863-1920) met with great success during his own lifetime, but today Dehmel's passionate vitalism is chiefly of historical interest. Erotic and sexual overtones dominate his later poems, and his equation of "poetic power" with "divine power," influenced by Friedrich Nietzsche, reveals a fundamental ideological interest of the time.

SYMBOLISM

Of more lasting significance for modern poetry was Symbolism, which includes the works of Stefan George (1868-1933), Rilke, and Hugo von Hofmannsthal (1874-1929).

STEFAN GEORGE

As Robert M. Browning has said, "modern poetry in the eminent sense begins in Germany" with Stefan George. George sought to retrieve the forces of creativity that the forces of materialism had either inhibited or destroyed. Through beauty, he sought to restore magic and majesty to art. Incorporating the tradition of Symbolism from the French poets Charles Baudelaire, Stéphane Mallarmé, and Arthur Rimbaud, George was a language purist, striving for precision and perfection in his highly sculptured works. His aesthetics of art for art's sake evolved to accommodate a view of the poet as seer and teacher. George identified himself with Dante and with Hölderlin and advocated a kind of pagan beauty and aristocratic conservatism, behind which resided an ideology of hero-worship. The manner in which George flaunted his "eccentricity"—from his homosexual Maximin cult and his antiphilistine typographical innovations to the liturgical earnestness with which he read his own verse—repelled and impressed his contemporaries, frequently both. His highly aristocratic view of poetry and his technique of pictorial stylization, whereby the meaning of life can be grasped only as an aesthetic phenomenon, reveal a debt to Nietzsche.

HUGO VON HOFMANNSTHAL

Nearly all of Hugo von Hofmannsthal's poetry was written between 1890 and 1900, between the ages of sixteen and twenty-six. His *Ein Brief* (1901; *Letter to Lord Chandos*, 1952) is a central document for understanding much of the poetry that preceded it. Here, Hofmannsthal confronts the language crisis which plagued him at the time (for a period immediately be-

fore and after the fictitious letter, he produced almost nothing). The letter envisions a way out of the dilemma—by seeking a new language, one of ciphers and symbols which allow objects to speak directly. This path was, however, to be Rilke's, not Hofmannsthal's; the latter rejected this kind of aestheticism. One of Hofmannsthal's best-known poems is the "Ballade des äusseren Lebens" (ballad of external life). While the title addresses the external life, it implies an internal—and qualitatively superior—plane of existence, which the poem reveals through an aesthetics of the moment that rescues objects and life from transitoriness and gives meaning to an otherwise meaningless existence. As such, it anticipates the magic exorcism of language as described in the Chandos letter.

RAINER MARIA RILKE

The poetry of Rainer Maria Rilke is unrivaled in its aesthetic richness and its capacity to induce new modes of vision. After reading Rilke's poetry, one simply sees the world differently from before. The best example of this transforming power can be found in "Archaischer Torso Apollos," with its thematization of art's redemptive value, as expressed in the final line: "Du musst Dein Leben ändern" ("You must change your life"). This notion of "art's redemptive value" was not new with Rilke, but it is articulated with particular force in his works. It is a notion basic to what one might term the "ideology of art" as it first developed with Romanticism: namely, that art can claim a specific visionary power not common to other forms of human activity and production. Coupled with this fundamental tenet is the assumption that art is not divorced from life, that it has real, affective functions—which is why the lyric voice in Rilke's poem on Apollo, itself a work of art, is compelled to acknowledge its "redemptive effect." Rilke's first volume, *Leben und Lieder* (1894; life and songs), was followed by five more before 1900. Much of the early work reveals that Rilke was still struggling for a distinctive poetic voice. This he found by the turn of the twentieth century, beginning with *Die frühen Gedichte* (1909; early poems), *Das Buch der Bilder* (1902, 1906; *The Book of Images*, 1994), *Das Stundenbuch* (1905; *Poems from the Book of Hours*, 1941), and culminating in his *Neue Gedichte* (1907, 1908; *New Poems*, 1964). In *The Book of Images*, he moved tentatively toward a more objective poetry. From Auguste Rodin, Rilke had learned a new definition of artistic creativity, emphasizing craftsmanship rather than inspiration. In these poems, and later ones, he sought to be as plastic as possible. *Poems from the Book of Hours* depicts a Russian monk seeking God and the essence of all things through confession and prayer. Ultimately, this search proves futile, but the prayers are from the very start imbued with an underlying sense of doubt; all of Rilke's overtly religious poetry is informed by a modern skepticism. Rilke then abandoned his search for God and concentrated on creating a type of poem known as the *Dinggedicht*, or "object poem." Instead of a conventional portrayal of the symbolic confluence of the individual and nature, Rilke sought an "objective art." "Der Panther" ("The Panther"), from *New Poems*, was the first text in which Rilke realized this technique to an absolute degree. The poem articulates no sentimentality or "human" sympathy; instead, the affective possibilities of the poem are left entirely to the dimensions of the object itself, the panther.

Rainer Maria Rilke (Hulton Archive/Getty Images)

Rilke's later volumes of poetry, *Duineser Elegien* (1923; *Duinese Elegies*, 1931; better known as *Duino Elegies*) and *Die Sonette an Orpheus* (1923; *Sonnets to Orpheus*, 1936), written after a decade of silence, celebrate the transmutative power of feeling, a power capable of transforming the material world into spirit. By rendering the physical world "invisible," Rilke hoped to rescue it from the forces of transitoriness, to secure it forever within a dimension beyond space and time. As Browning has commented:

> The world is here to be felt and we are in the world to feel it. We *can* feel it because of our awareness of transiency, i.e., because we know death. Death is therefore Rilke's theme of themes. But for the poet feeling is not enough; the poet must also say. In saying, the rest of humanity is given to understand what is to be felt. In this way, the poet's work extends our consciousness.

EXPRESSIONISM

Rilke's work spans the period of German expressionism, although he should not be identified with it. The strident bravado of the new poetry of expressionism was chiefly concerned with shocking the complacent bourgeoisie. Moralistic pathos and visionary élan exploded the baser constraints on form and material, and the boldness of imagery challenged established perspectives and advocated novel and free modes of perception. Kurt Pinthus (1886-1975), editor of the influential anthology *Menschheitsdämmerung* (1920; twilight of humanity), wrote in 1915 that the new poetry surged forth "out of torment and scream, out of admiration and disdain, analysis and honor . . . toward the essential, toward the essence not only of appearance, but of Being." Expressionist poetry countered the forces which rendered language automatic and void of meaning by introducing innovative syntax and imagery, thus creating novel dimensions within the newly discovered relations of space and time and making manifest a new hermetic reality. Reality was transformed into word and sign, transfigured as cipher. Alienating meter and rhyme effected a grotesque refraction of reality, also an essential feature of expressionist poetry.

The first phase of German expressionism in particular (roughly from 1911 to 1914) discarded the "sensibility wasting in reflection" of much nineteenth century poetry and urged a sensibility animated and absorbed in construction, in presenting simultaneously the "what" and the "how" of perception. Expressionist poetry experimented with the possibilities of metaphor, substituting a fusion of image and idea for the older parallelism of image and idea. Reality and referentiality were thus made problematic. Foreign influence was also a factor. George's translation in 1901 of Baudelaire's *Les Fleurs du mal* (1857, 1861, 1868; *Flowers of Evil*, 1909) was an important contribution to the German literary scene. Whitman was introduced to the German public in 1868, but the popular edition of his poems appeared only in 1901, translated by Johannes Schlaf (1862-1941). Translations of François Villon and Rimbaud also appeared. Rimbaud's influence was chiefly in the realm of imagery, and his idea that "the Poet becomes a seer through an extended, immense and consistent disordering of all the senses" compelled Georg Trakl (1887-1914) and others to break with the concept of purely rational continuity. Filippo Tommaso Marinetti and Italian Futurism also encouraged German poets to experiment with linguistic innovations.

"Weltende" ("End of the World"), by Jakob von Hoddis (1887-1942), is typical of the apocalyptic visions manifest in early expressionist poetry; its discontinuities were intended to reflect the dissolution of civilization. After undergoing psychiatric treatment in 1915, von Hoddis was finally committed to a mental institution in the 1920's. Still, his work struck a central nerve of the time. Writing initially in the fashion of Symbolism, von Hoddis found a distinctive character in his apocalyptic projections. His compression of contemporary thought and emotion into signs and iconic formulas typified the grotesque and cynical expressions of the crisis-consciousness of these years. Similarly, "Der Gott der Stadt" ("The God of the City"), by George Heym (1887-1912), locates the source of eschatological anxiety in the modern metropolis, where Baal rules as the god of material pleasure. The poem "Morgen" ("Morning"), by Alfred Lichtenstein (1889-1914), is yet another example of the expressionist vision of the world on the brink of destruction, where failure to communicate forebodes the ultimate demise of society.

This basically imagist poetry, which privileged visionary experience over visual experience (*ex*pressionism versus *im*pressionism), resulted in a diversity of individual poetic dictions. The contours of the early years of German expressionism are marked by a sharp disdain for the bourgeois conventions of poetry and by experimentation with new techniques of montage and imagery. After 1914, as the critic and translator Michael Hamburger has written, "its craft of imagery was vulgarized and, at the same time, its mental climate became predominantly political." Behind the outrage and the utterances—sometimes cynical, sometimes grotesque—one senses the urgent longing for the "New Man."

GEORG HEYM

Despair, fear, and the presentiment of catastrophe are the constant themes of Georg Heym's poetry. Heym experienced life as a prison-house and suffered existential ennui, from which even death promised no escape. Melancholy pervades his eschatological visions; elements of Christian belief are transformed, as with Trakl's poetry, into apocalyptic images. His verse is largely paratactic, and this simple poetic syntax is supported by a predominance of iambic pentameters or rhymed tetrameters. As the poems develop, however, along simple syntactic lines, images are superimposed, one over the other, creating a density and tension that belie the surface simplicity of the discourse.

ELSE LASKER-SCHÜLER

The poetry of Else Lasker-Schüler (1876-1945) is charged with anxiety, *Weltschmerz*, and ennui. Her poems exhibit a longing for a return to the beliefs of the "fathers" and celebrate mythical origins in transparent and yet enigmatic language. Expressionism with Lasker-Schüler becomes a liberation of the imagination. Her poems exude the sense of security peculiar to dreams.

GEORG TRAKL

Georg Trakl viewed in his poems an "all too faithful reproduction of a godless, cursed century." Hyperaccentuated guilt and the experience of horror and degeneration inform his poems. Trakl claimed that his work was an "incomplete attempt" to expiate "guilt," both of the individual and of humankind. Nature objectifies his own inner strife and reveals the lack of harmony within Trakl's poetic world. The recurrence of a few central images in his poems has led one critic to speak of Trakl's oeuvre as "one poem." Trakl's experimentation with drugs heightened his apocalyptic visions. Remembrance, dream, and drug-induced intoxication, along with lines from Maurice Maeterlinck and Rimbaud, produce an evocative poetry, a singular accomplishment of German expressionist writing.

Hamburger maintains that Trakl best understood the nature of the crises that he and his generation faced, exploring how it is that modern men and women relate to death and to evil, whereas Heym (to cite a counter-example) avoided analysis of the crisis by projecting onto the landscapes of his text images of death and evil and suggesting their omnipresence and inexorability. Hamburger also notes that a distinction can be made between Heym's consistently dark view of nature and Trakl's more variable imagery. The effect of the latter's, even if only vague and highly mediated, is to uncover the traces of a paradise that is perhaps not forever lost.

A NEW FREEDOM

Expressionism was the first literary movement in Germany that made the anticlassicist tendency a mass phenomenon, but the disruption of old realities and old poetic conventions created at the same time a new freedom, or at least the perception that freedom (and novelty) were real possibilities. From then on, every poet had to decide what to do with this potential freedom. Since the time of expressionism, there has been no authoritative norm governing the production and reception of poetry which one could manipulate in order to shock and to draw attention to the work of art ("épater les bourgeois") and to the possibility of new experiences. Expressionism broke with all norms and thereby created an utterly new situation (which, significantly, itself soon became an established and "authoritative" convention).

ERNST STADLER

Ernst Stadler (1883-1914), thoroughly versed in the European literary tradition, experienced the early years of the twentieth century less as an end than as a beginning, seeing in them not the disintegration of modern society but the promise of its transformation. Initially, he had difficulty achieving an individual tone and style. Ultimately, after experimenting with Symbolism, he adopted a dithyrambic voice of political activism—what he called a "new joyous, all-embracing world feeling." His verse espouses an ecstatic devotion to fellow human beings, a longing for freedom, and an acceptance of life's abundance. Rather than viewing the city as the locale of degenerate corruption and destruction, Stadler saw it as a cause for celebration, as the facilitator of ecstatic union.

JOHANNES R. BECHER

The early radical poems of Johannes R. Becher (1891-1958) struck out at the bourgeois world in which he grew up. Immoderate and shrill, their forceful imagery "spits in the face" of his immediate milieu and social mores; rhetorical exposition disrupts the traditional form of these poems. With the advent of war, he sent out an urgent appeal for a "new syntax," a "catastrophic syntax" that would raze conventions: Word and deed were coterminous for Becher the political activist. Much later, his voice lost resonance; his visions largely unfulfilled, Becher wrote that "The poem cannot survive without truth."

FRANZ WERFEL

The dithyrambic prophecies of human redemption and reconciliation found in the work of Franz Werfel (1890-1945) struck a resonant chord among his generation. As the conscience of his time, Werfel, whose poetry sought to transform feelings into music, represents a significant dimension of expressionism. Werfel celebrates the redemptive value of the poetic word and projects an optimism utterly open to the world, while at the same time humbly acknowledging the presence of God. Art and theology thus blend; political activism yields to a "Christian mission" sustained by verbal dynamism and full-toned musicality. Werfel experienced his poems acoustically and was more concerned with emotive charge than with formal consistency.

GOTTFRIED BENN

Gottfried Benn (1886-1956) drew upon Nietzsche's philosophy of art to form his concept of artistry and perspectivism, whereby form becomes the "primary instance," taking precedence over all contextual considerations. Benn's first volume of poetry, *Morgue, und andere Gedichte* (1912; morgue, and other poems), used montage and calculated scientific jargon mixed with profane colloquialisms to achieve a shocking alienation. Benn confronted the empty prophecies and shabby progress of his time with the final reality of death. Disease, decay, and death are his themes in the early poems; humans are portrayed as helpless creatures—miserable, pitiful, despicable. The volume *Söhne* (1913; sons), the central theme of which is the characteristically expressionistic father-son conflict, reveals a futuristic aspect (again typical of expressionism) with its projection of a "New Man," an artist who will overcome death in ecstatic vision.

ALFRED LICHTENSTEIN

Alfred Lichtenstein (1887-1914) applies the grotesque to expose reality as absurd—a juxtaposition of the ridiculously banal and the sublimely tragic. His lyric voice, marked by alienation and the dislocation of images and motifs, is often compared with that of Jakob von Hoddis. Objects in Lichtenstein's poems are always distorted and displaced, always perceived from bizarre, radical, and unsettling perspectives.

AUGUST STRAMM

The poetry of August Stramm (1874-1915), characterized by a constructivist style, is not easily accessible. A tremendous diversity is evident within his modest oeuvre, and estimations of his work range from "thoroughly expressionistic" to "pretense and sham." Striving to reunite meaning and sound, Stramm dispenses with tradition in order to allow the individual word to appear in untrammeled isolation. Such deformation effects an unusual concentration of expression. In allowing the word to exercise its own effect, his poems turn programmatically from empirical reality. The resulting abstraction is charged with the currents of eros and chaos.

THE 1920'S THROUGH 1940'S

Following the strong element of subjectivity evident in the poetry of expressionism, the 1920's ushered in a new responsiveness to the factual and the objective. The human being was of such central interest to the poetry of German expressionism that nature as such found little room there. By the mid-1920's, however, nature

was once again a central theme of poetry, often perceived as the only medium through which objectivity and precision of detail could be achieved. As Alfred Döblin proclaimed in 1925: "Art is boring, we want facts, facts." In part, this trend encouraged a revival of nature poetry, in German referred to as *naturmagisch*, focusing on the objective details of nature and celebrating their cosmic relevance. The particular dimensions of this cosmic order vary among poets. For Elisabeth Langgässer (1899-1950), for example, the order is largely determined by Christian ideas, while Günther Eich (1907-1972) concentrates on the parameters of language per se.

NATURE POETS

Both Langgässer and Eich worked in a circle of poets connected with a poetry journal called *Kolonne* (column), whose contributors included Peter Huchel (1903-1981), Hermann Kasack (1896-1966), and Georg von der Vring (1889-1968). In the works of these *naturmagische* poets, visible nature is considered "wondrous"; their realism is thus "magical" to the extent that their poetic diction is a kind of invocation. Lyric expression is thus an act of revelation as well as of interpretation.

PETER HUCHEL

Peter Huchel wrote nature poetry typical of the *Kolonne* group. Nature here appears not as a romantic object of poetic longing, for an elegiac tone is mixed with contemporary metaphors of struggle and warfare. Natural processes are depicted in crystalline, precise language that often reveals their underlying violence. Huchel's nature poetry never simply flees into boundless and timeless space; the poet delivers testimony as an eyewitness.

GÜNTHER EICH

Günther Eich first began writing poetry in the company of the *Kolonne* group. His early nature poems are both subjective and reflective; one can see in them the first steps toward the dispassionate stance and the extreme brevity which characterize his poems after 1945. Contemplating specific, concrete objects, such as the blue feather in "Die Häherfeder" ("Jay Feather"), Eich searches for the deeper reality behind "signs" and "omens." Still, language—at least the cognitive, rational faculties of the mind—proves unyielding, for the "sly answer" lies somewhere just beyond the dimensions of habituated thought and perception. The sudden surprise initiated by the sign is thus a central moment for Eich's work.

WILHELM LEHMANN

Wilhelm Lehmann's (1882-1968) poetry deals with nature and myth, the dual constituents of meaning and order in his universe. The individual, subjective ego of the poet recedes behind the objectivity of language, which, through precise concentration on objects, attempts to open vistas to that level of order which transcends the individual. The unreal and the dreamlike are also part of Lehmann's poetic world. There is a certain consistency within or behind Lehmann's poetic landscape, but the imagery is not static; instead, it moves as part of a larger cosmic cycle, as the passing of seasons relates to mythical signs.

ELISABETH LANGGÄSSER

Depictions of nature and the presence of myths also determine the imagination of Elisabeth Langgässer, but are used as portals through which to recognize the underlying order of Christianity. This sense of order is not always achieved in her poetry, but where it is absent one at least senses that a struggle has taken place to realize it. During the war, Langgässer held on to the "magical" qualities of reality as a vehicle for hope and for redemption in the Christian sense.

OSKAR LOERKE AND GEORG BRITTING

The poetry of Oskar Loerke (1884-1941) gives expression to the complete poetic universe. Balancing intellect and emotion, the static and the fluid, Loerke achieves a consistency and sense of order that extends beyond his own subjectivity. Loerke's concise observations result in a spiritualization of nature.

Georg Britting (1891-1964) was the poet of the Bavarian landscape. He stressed the idyllic and the bucolic but experienced nature as magical, disclosing it as a sign of a larger cosmic order. This combination of the sensuous and the intellectual makes Britting's poetry representative of the so-called Magical Realism.

TOPICAL POETRY

The objectivity of another group of poets, including Kurt Tucholsky (1890-1935) and Erich Kästner (1899-

1974), was directed toward social conditions. Their poems read like warnings of imminent catastrophe; their efforts to awaken the public rested on a faith in the social efficacy of the poetic word. In the 1920's, this objective poetry was best represented by the song, the broadsheet, and the ballad. The work of Tucholsky falls into this category, as does that of Kästner and Bertolt Brecht (1898-1956).

The epic quality of Brecht's anti-Aristotelian theater figures in his poetry as well: It is distancing, descriptive, and critical rather than sentimental and empathetic. His poems break with the bourgeois tradition of aestheticism, nature, and confessional poetry. His description of these years as a "bad time for poetry" did not imply a rejection of poetry altogether, but rather only a rejection of the conventional forms and traditional subject matter of poetry, which were no longer adequate to the changed historical circumstances. Brecht thus tried to rejuvenate art, but not (like Rilke) exclusively through formal and aesthetic means, although he was sensitive to the historical necessity of formal experimentation. In his verse, Brecht admits to a longing for the conventional elements of lyric poetry, but since "a talk about trees is almost a crime/ because it implies silence about so many horrors," he does not indulge this desire. His vocabulary and poetic diction are strict and sober, marked by clear and unsentimental precision.

Countermovements against the new objective tone are visible in the poetry of Rudolf Alexander Schröder (1878-1962) and Hans Carossa (1878-1956), whose conservative political and aesthetic orientation drew them toward the classical heritage in both form and content. They were more interested in the timeless aspects of poetic diction than in the merely topical. With the advent of National Socialism, their posture became a kind of inner emigration, problematic because, if from the point of view of the individual, political abstinence was a kind of mute contradiction to the Hitler regime, as a whole the totalitarian system was able to disenfranchise their voices, if not actually coopt them altogether. Schröder's work represents a consistent effort to preserve the Western cultural heritage. He had a keenly developed sense for form, which he applied to his humanistic religious poetry. Carossa strived in his verse for harmony and moderation; his artistic perspective was that of a pious humanist, his models Goethe and Stifter. Carossa's conservatism and classicism were manipulated to the advantage of Nazi ideology.

THE NAZI REGIME

Poetry written in accordance with the ideology of National Socialism largely eschewed the principles of precise objectivity. Characterized by the frequent use of archaic words and phrases, it shied away from formal innovation. Josef Weinheber (1892-1945) studied the example of the classics and was concerned primarily with questions of form and aesthetics. He became well known with the volume *Adel und Untergang* (1932, 1934; nobility and decline) and was supported at the time of its publication by the Nazis. Some of his later writings reciprocated this support, and toward the end of the war, suffering from severe depression after having acknowledged his misguided affiliation with National Socialism, he took his own life.

The most significant party-line poet was Erwin Guido Kolbenheyer (1878-1962). The stylistic diversity of his work reveals its fundamental confusion. He greeted the rise of National Socialism as a historical necessity, explaining its emergence through digressions on philosophy, politics, history, economics, biology, religion, and culture. The appeal of his work is utterly totalitarian. Party slogans and verse become indistinguishable in his monumental panegyric to the supremacy of the German spirit in all of its manifestations. As a member of the Prussian Academy of Poets and as the recipient of several distinctions, Kolbenheyer was one of the most forceful poetic voices on the literary scene of the Third Reich. Other party-line poets included Hanns Johst (1890-1978) and Gerhard Schumann (1911-1995).

POSTWAR POETRY AND MODERNISM

The situation for poetry after 1945 was at first ambivalent. On one hand, historical conditions presented German writers with an enormous challenge. On the other hand, the devastation, frustration, and overwhelming loss of orientation made a direct confrontation with the immediate past something to be avoided. Poets inherited a language corrupted in the Nazi era,

and they recognized the need to replace it with a new idiom.

Under these circumstances, it is not hard to understand that, initially at least, issues of content mattered more than issues of form. The immediate task of assessing the relation of the present to the past rendered aesthetic considerations secondary. Historically, this phase was probably necessary, because postwar German poetry could become credible once again only after having expunged its affiliation with National Socialism. Gradually, however, aesthetic considerations emerged from the background. A critical factor in this development was the influence of foreign literatures, in particular the force of modernism.

One could therefore consider postwar German poetry along two lines: the political-social, and the linguistic-formal. Progressive experimentation in poetry was impeded by the presence of hackneyed lyric phrases and the failure to confront sociopolitical reality. Formal traditionalism and a social isolation resulting in escapism and indifference toward politics coexisted. It is significant that the most important mode of expression for the immediate postwar years was not poetry but narrative prose, above all the short story. Here, authors pursued the necessary confrontation with contemporary sociopolitical issues, while poetry continued its preoccupation with the vestiges of Surrealism, on the one hand, and the tradition of nature poetry, on the other. These coexisting trends can be visualized as four principal constellations dominating the postwar poetry scene. One of these was a political conscience combined with formal traditionalism. A second resided as well within traditional poetic forms but shied away from political commentary. The other two possibilities were a combination of formal modernism with either a political or an apolitical attitude. While such a scheme is helpful, it should be noted that a distinction between "political poetry" and "poetic escapism" can be misleading. One need only read the works of Hans Magnus Enzensberger (born 1929) to realize that these two descriptions are not mutually exclusive.

Poem after poem of the postwar years revealed that poetry in the service of spiritual and ethical rejuvenation could afford little room for new aesthetic solutions. In this regard, the poetics of Benn—namely, the rejection of everything contextual in the attempt to approximate the "absolute poem"—appears as a historically necessary step in the development of postwar German poetry. Theodor Adorno (1903-1969) pronounced that, after Auschwitz, it was no longer possible to write a poem, necessitating a reconsideration of the content, the form, and the function of poetry.

Postwar poetry can be said to have begun not in 1945 but in 1948, for it was in the latter year that the first postwar poems of Benn, Eich, Huchel, and Karl Krolow (1915-1999) appeared, not to mention the first volume by Celan (1920-1970). These poets are all identified with the tradition of Hermetic poetry, and they represent the primary avenues through which postwar German poetry drew upon the traditions of modernism. In a sense, then, German postwar modernist poetry represents no really new beginning, but instead the realization, continuation, and extension of established modernist movements. The resonance with which modernism appeared on the postwar German literary scene suggested something radically new; the war obscured lines of development reaching back into the 1930's and earlier.

The overwhelming presence of this obscured tradition was best articulated not by a poet but by a scholar. In 1956, Hugo Friedrich published *The Structure of Modern Poetry*, an attempt to reveal the unity of European-American poetry since the mid-nineteenth century through a study of its genesis and its various typologies. His work dominated scholarly discussions of poetry in Germany for some time. Tracking the development of modern poetry from its origins in Mallarmé, Friedrich isolated its more significant features, such as the rejection of old taboos, a preoccupation with darkness, an overwhelming sense of isolation and anxiety, and an insistence on the logic of discontinuity. Friedrich's book has much in common with the spirit of postwar German poetry, for he neglects the sociohistorical constituents of modern poetry and highlights instead its phenomenological-existential dimensions. Benn epitomizes this orientation among poets.

KARL KROLOW

Karl Krolow once wrote that metaphor determines "the economy of the single poem." Krolow's imagery reveals the development of his poetry as a whole, as well as the shift in poetics which marked the postwar years. Krolow's first metaphors belong to the category of "traditional nature." Later, he moved to more aggressive, expressionistic, and even surrealistic metaphors. Then, he focused on decidedly intellectual images, gradually relying less and less on rhyme or regular strophes while developing a laconic style.

INGEBORG BACHMANN

Ingeborg Bachmann (1926-1973) published her first volume of poems, *Die gestundete Zeit* (borrowed time), in 1953 and immediately established her reputation as a poet with a keen ability to articulate her doubts about the meaning of history and her anticipation of catastrophe, an anxiety shared by many Western European intellectuals during the Cold War. The specific accomplishment of this volume lies in its suggestive interrelation of societal perplexity and individual despair. Several of her poems combine poetic diction and utopian thought, while others suggest their ultimate irreconcilability. In the tension between "superfluous objects" and words "for the lowest classes," Bachmann exposes as illegitimate the traditional mode of poetic speech and in its place suggests the possibility of a documentary, didactic literature.

PAUL CELAN

The difficulty in understanding the poetry of Paul Celan results less from the allusions embedded in his texts than from his concentration on the expressive possibilities and limits of language. This problem is often the central preoccupation of his poems. The "incontrovertible testimony" of the poet can be achieved only after the utmost exertion, where language is pressed to its limits. Celan's poems are always "under way," in search of a partner in conversation.

HANS MAGNUS ENZENSBERGER

By the late 1950's, the tradition of nature poetry had run its course. Already during the mid-1950's, West German poetry was becoming more explicitly political. A fundamental problem thus emerged: that of achieving the aesthetic political poem, of articulating both literary and political progressiveness. The new politicized poetry displayed a certain disenchantment with the state of things, preferred sobriety to ceremony, and, in a sense—because of its basic distrust of any "magical powers" residing in the poetic word—depoeticized poetic diction and renounced the traditional notion of "lyrical" by presenting primarily a cerebral appeal.

The successful articulation of both aesthetic and political progressiveness is perhaps best illustrated in the work of Hans Magnus Enzensberger. Initially, Enzensberger relied on Edgar Allan Poe's "Philosophy of Composition" for the theoretical basis of his work but soon incorporated the philosophy of Adorno. In the 1950's, Enzensberger conceived experimental poetry and social criticism as mutually dependent. The background of his early poetry is the Cold War, the atomic threat, the rearmament of West Germany, and in particular, the economic recovery of the Konrad Adenauer era, a process which Enzensberger viewed as threatening to the integrity of the individual. In the 1960's, Enzensberger turned increasingly toward political writings. He remains impatient with the cheap (commodified) utopias of would-be reformists. A socialist by choice, a skeptic by nature, and a realist through practice of acute observation, Enzensberger always imbued his poetry with his unmistakable mark. The work of Erich Fried (1921-1988) is likewise politically keen. Fried's poetry achieved recognition in the turbulent decade of the 1960's and is noted for its laconic style, coupled with Brechtian techniques of paradox, antithesis, and dialectic reversal.

MID- TO LATE TWENTIETH CENTURY

A significant experimental phase of West German poetry, one which shared a skepticism of traditional metaphoric expression and poetic diction, was concrete poetry, best represented by Eugen Gomringer (born 1925), Franz Mon (born 1926), and Ernst Jandl (1925-2000). The term was introduced by Gomringer in analogy to concrete art, and by it he meant to distinguish a linguistically experimental literature which reflected and thematized its own raw material—that is, language. Applying the principles of functionality, clarity, simplicity, communicability, objectivity, and play, concrete poetry sought to reintegrate literature into social life. Using techniques of reduction and permutation, concrete poetry focused on the presentation of language and linguistic elements and not on the representation of reality beyond language. Ultimately, however, the experimentalism of concrete poetry soon rigidified into rather predictable patterns. Challenging (and entertaining) material was written by Jandl, whose keen wit and linguistic sensitivity inform the foreground of his work. While focusing on the acoustic and optical valences of language, Jandl at the same time recognized the social implications of his work, for language as the material of his art was also the material of his thought and speech and, as such, material shared by a significant portion of Western society.

In 1965, Walter Höllerer (1922-2003) presented a call for the "long poem," understood as an alternative to the then predominant Hermetic poem. This reformulation of poetic diction was carried out by Günter Herburger (born 1932), Rolf Dieter Brinkmann (1940-1975), and Nicolas Born (1937-1979), among others, who advocated a new subjective realism in the 1970's. For Jürgen Theobaldy (born 1944), a significant representative of the youngest poets, the long poem of the late 1960's gave way to the "new poem" of the 1970's, when several younger poets tried to relocate the self, rearticulating the individual as socially and politically relevant. This renewed emphasis on the self becomes most comprehensible when viewed as a reaction to the agitprop poetry of the late 1960's and the disillusionment of the intellectual Left in the early 1970's.

Poets of this New Subjectivity movement flourished throughout the 1970's, and their concern with personal experience and the intricacies of daily life struck a chord with the public. Theobaldy's "Schnee im Büro" (snow at the office) details the daydreams of an office worker for whom the evenings and vacations with his lover barely compensate for his mundane eight-hour workday, during which he feels "imprisoned" and a mere "number."

More women poets saw publication of their works, and gained prominence and attention to their poetry, which often defied categorization and invigorated the poetic scene. Elisabeth Borchers (born 1926) displays an acute awareness for the nuances of language, and the poems of her *Gedichte* (1976; poems) use startlingly ironic imagery such as "solid" ruins, and are infused with her personal experience, as in "Das Begräbnis in Bollschweil" (the funeral in Bollschweil). Here, memory fails the poet to compose a proper eulogy, and the death of a close one leaves behind nothing but "small, slow ghosts" scurrying between the mourners.

Hilde Domin (1909-2006) similarly includes allusions to her personal life in her poetry, which is also concerned with the play of language, and occasionally conjures up Surrealist images and associations. In "Mauern Sortieren" (sorting walls), in her *Gesammelte Gedichte* (1987; collected poems), a look at "textile patterns" in a mail-order catalog reminds the persona of "patterns of walls," which later form the alliterative "Mauern aus Menschenfleisch" (walls of human flesh) to crescendo in the paradoxical coupling of "Mutter/ Mauer" (mother/wall) which lies "zwischen Geschwistern/ jeder auf seiner Seite/ Berlin" (between siblings/ each on his own side/ Berlin), bringing the poem to a personal conclusion.

The 1980's saw a surprising return to formal poetry, with rhymes and meters replacing the ubiquitous free verse of the preceding two decades. Poets such as Krolow returned to rhymed lines, and Ulla Hahn (born 1946) abandoned her earlier, political poetry in exchange for poems following traditional forms, and quite surprised her readers. Enzensberger and Jandl returned to traditional reflections on the meaning of being, and even love poetry was read by a serious audience again.

On the other hand, the political issues of the decade, most noticeably environmentalism and the squatter movement in some of the larger cities like Hamburg and Berlin, spawned a flurry of poetic activities, often arising out of the alternative scene. Concerns over America's stationing of short-range nuclear missiles in Germany briefly brought back political passions in poetry. In 1989, the momentous changes in the Soviet Union and in Eastern Europe caught quite a few German poets in the West by surprise. By October 3, 1990, before one year had passed after East Germany allowed the breaching of the Berlin Wall in November, 1989, Germany became reunified. German poets in the West and the East now had to grapple with the challenges brought forth by the reintegration of two quite different societies.

BIBLIOGRAPHY

Appleby, Carol. *German Romantic Poetry: Goethe, Novalis, Heine, Hölderlin*. Maidstone, Kent, England: Crescent Moon, 2008. Contains a discussion of the themes that were basic to the literature of Romanticism, along with critical studies of the major poets and philosophers of the period.

Baird, Jay W. *Hitler's War Poets: Literature and Politics in the Third Reich*. New York: Cambridge University Press, 2008. An analysis of the ideas that motivated Germany's Nazi poets, including their interpretation of history and their hopes for the future. Also includes their life stories and assesses the influence of what are now recognized as inferior works. Bibliographical references and index.

Bohm, Arnd. *Goethe's Faust and European Epic: Forgetting the Future*. Rochester, N.Y.: Camden House, 2007. By placing *Faust: Eine Tragödie* (pb. 1808, 1833; *The Tragedy of Faust*, 1823, 1838) within the context of earlier works in the genre, the author supports his belief that the work should be viewed as a Christian epic. An important new study by a highly respected scholar. Bibliography and index.

Boland, Eavan, ed. and trans. *After Every War: Twentieth-Century Women Poets*. Princeton, N.J.: Princeton University Press, 2004. One of Ireland's major woman poets has collected poems by German women who survived the war, some of them well known for their literary works, others obscure. The German and English versions of the poems are on facing pages. Illustrated. Bibliography and index.

Donahue, Neil H., ed. *A Companion to the Literature of German Expressionism*. Rochester, N.Y.: Camden House, 2005. Essays on the philosophical background of expressionism, as well as on specific writers, including all the major poets involved in the movement. Also contains critical overviews and textual analyses.

Fachinger, Petra. *Rewriting Germany from the Margins: "Other" German Literature of the 1980's and 1990's*. Montreal: McGill-Queen's University Press, 2001. Looks at the views expressed in the writings of German minorities, including immigrants from other countries, German Jews, and Germans who grew up in the German Democratic Republic. A much-needed study. Bibliography and index.

Harper, Anthony, and Margaret C. Ives. *Sappho in the Shadows: Essays on the Work of German Women Poets of the Age of Goethe, 1749-1832*. New York: Peter Lang, 2000. Includes translations of the poems into English and further bibliographical references. Highlights a freshly emerging aspect of German Romanticism from a mostly feminist perspective.

Hofmann, Michael, ed. *Twentieth-Century German Poetry: An Anthology*. New York: Farrar, Straus and Giroux, 2008. A collection of superb translations of the works of major German poets, assembled by a noted poet and translator. Bilingual format.

Koelb, Clayton, and Eric Downing, eds. *German Literature of the Nineteenth Century, 1832-1899*. Rochester, N.Y.: Camden House, 2005. Volume 9 in the Camden House History of German Literature series. Sums up the political, cultural, and literary movements of the period and discusses important writers in detail. Includes list of primary and secondary sources.

Nader, Andrés José, ed. *Traumatic Verses: On Poetry in German from the Concentration Camps, 1933-1945*. Rochester, N.Y.: Camden House, 2007. Combines a study of the motivations that impelled inmates of the camps to write poetry with the poems that survived, presented both in the original and in translation. A valuable contribution to Holocaust studies and to the history of German poetry.

Vanchena, Lorie A. *Political Poetry in Periodicals and the Shaping of German National Consciousness in the Nineteenth Century*. New York: Peter Lang, 2000. An innovative approach to the subject, with detailed bibliographical references and index. Shows how some poets were quite ardent German Nationalists, and illustrates how popular periodicals helped disseminate nationalistic ideas among educated citizens.

Richard Spuler
Updated by R. C. Lutz

GERMAN POETRY SINCE REUNIFICATION

The dramatic events leading to the sudden collapse of the socialist regime of East Germany in 1989 came almost as a complete surprise to many German poets in West Germany. By the late 1980's, most poets in the West had come to accept the separation of Germany into two separate states. In spite of an increasing stream of East German poets who were either forced, like Wolf Biermann (born 1936) in 1976, or allowed, like Uwe Kolbe (born 1957) in 1987, to leave East Germany, the socialist regime of the German Democratic Republic (GDR) in the East was considered durable. Western poets were locked in their own debate about the sudden rise of traditional form in poetry and took scant notice of the massive changes in the East.

A year after the reunification of Germany in 1990, the West's Hans Magnus Enzensberger (born 1929) revisited the effects of this surprise in his collection *Zukunftsmusik* (1991; future music) when he wrote:

> Future Music
>
> That what we can't anticipate
> Will teach itself.
>
> It shines, is uncertain, distant.

Here, the poem acknowledges that great changes may actually catch the human poet unawares. Similarly, the negative ending of the poem that the music of the future "isn't there for us,/ never was there,/ is never there,/ is never," articulates the mood of the post-reunification hangover, with rising Western resentment at the cost of the bailout of the East, and Eastern nostalgia for a time when the state guaranteed employment for all, for example. Enzensberger's conclusion that in spite of all the changes, the future is not "for us," the common people, and echoes popular misgivings surfacing in Germany in the early 1990's.

In the years before reunification, many Western poets looked at their East German counterparts who had stayed in the GDR with a mixture of disdain and indifference, often regarding East German poetry as backward in form and provincial in theme. However, relatively unbeknownst to the West, East German poets often found themselves at the vanguard of rising popular unrest. After reunification, the "underground" poets of the big cities like East Berlin, Leipzig, and Dresden found themselves in a certain vacuum.

Elke Erb (born 1938) had been an influential, nurturing presence for the initially only loosely associated group of young poets residing in the hip Prenzlauer Berg district of East Berlin. In 1991, she published her collection *Winkelzüge: Oder, Nicht vermutete, aufschlussreiche Verhältnisse* (shady tricks). These poems, which were actually written just before the fall of the Berlin wall, already foreshadow the poet's uncertainty about the future. "The heroine, led by her history . . . so uncertainly/ that she can identify herself neither in the present/ nor the future" stands at a new path. The old (socialist) directives have vanished, "swallowed up by the Earth," and she has to carve her own way without any external spiritual guidance. Erb's *Poet's Corner 3* (1991) hammers home this point of disillusion with the past coupled with apprehension for the future. Here, her poem "Thema verfehlt" (off the topic) calls upon the ghosts of past communist leaders, who appear "like someone without a home/ someone who holds a sail, not his own,/ into the wind, which is not his own." There is a gathering of restless spirits, whose borrowed ideals have failed them in a world not of their own making, and yet the direction for the future is indeterminable.

For the poets of the East, reunification thus brought a moment of pause after the heady days which had seen the toppling of the repressive regime. Erb's friend and protégé Kolbe expressed a common nostalgia for the days of struggle and togetherness in his volume *Vineta* (1998). The title poem "Vineta" alludes to a mythical Nordic Atlantis, whose greedy inhabitants caused it to sink forever to the bottom of the Baltic Sea. Ironically, Vineta Street is also the terminus of the subway line running through Prenzlauer Berg, where Kolbe lived and worked before leaving for West Germany in 1987. In his poem, Kolbe reflects:

> Do you still remember, back then, when we knew the
>   name, when we
> knew every name, when the chestnuts were talking to
>   us, burst open
> with their horny shoots

The poet laments the passing of the vitality of the poets' gatherings in the backyards of residential apartment buildings graced by old chestnut trees. In reunified Berlin, modernization increasingly gets rid of these old trees, just as the subversive political journals of the East (*samizdat* literature) died out for lack of state oppression, which had forced them to be self-published in editions of less than one hundred copies. Some of the famous literary journals to which Kolbe and his associates had contributed poetry survived past 1993, but their character had become more mainstream since the flair of the forbidden had vanished with the advent of freedom of speech after reunification.

Ironically, the opening of the archives of the Stasi, East Germany's secret police, revealed that one of the Prenzlauer Berg poets, Sascha Anderson (born 1953), who later emigrated to West Germany, was one of the Stasi spies himself. Thus, the socialist regime had tried to subvert the opposition, but it had collapsed in spite of these secret machinations.

In the West, poets found themselves less forced to embark on a quest to redefine their position in regard to their art and their audience. There, the continuous strong output by women poets like Elisabeth Borchers (born 1926), Karin Kiwus (born 1942), Ulla Hahn (born 1946), and Ursula Krechel (born 1947) has substantially defined much of German postreunification poetry.

KARIN KIWUS

Karin Kiwus's *Das chinesische Examen* (1992; the Chinese Examination) focuses on the power of personal memories and the various attitudes toward change. Drawing from the author's cultural exchange with East Asia, Kiwus informs the reader that for a certain kind of Chinese examination, the student has to remember and write down everything he or she is thinking about while sitting in a barren room for a set amount of time. Reminiscent of modernism's fascination with the so-called stream-of-consciousness approach to writ-

ing, Kiwus's painter-protagonist Soutine, in "Bonjour Monsieur Soutine," remembers a grisly scene in his studio:

> And the flayed ox in my studio
> Don't you know that I must rescue
> Its flesh from decay, pouring buckets of
> Blood over it

While flesh and the organic is in danger of decay, statues contain at least the promise of timelessness. However, timelessness invites stasis, and the world changes around its leftover monuments. "Dieser eine Russe" (this one Russian) is a statue commemorating the Soviet Union's victory over Nazi Germany, such as can be found in the Treptow Park Soviet War Memorial in (East) Berlin. While his expression, literally cast in stone, never changes, history has moved on and has obliterated not only the vanquished Nazis but the victorious Soviets as well. What meaning, the poem inquires, can still be attached to these statues?

ULLA HAHN

Symptomatic of the unexpected lasting power of the traditionalist revival in German poetry since the 1980's, Ulla Hahn, who had begun her career as a radical left-wing poet, continued to surprise her audience with a return to more traditional, formal poetry. In 1993, she published *Liebesgedichte* (love poems), but she reminded her readers that her poems were not the lyric equivalent of easy listening when she wrote that "The poem my lady is not eau de cologne . . . no deodorant for the sweaty smell of fear." Invigorating love poetry with a strong feminist bent, Hahn has developed a devoted readership who welcomed *Epikurs Garden* (1995; the garden of Epicurus).

URSULA KRECHEL

Feminist rebellion is alive and well in Ursula Krechel's collection *Technik des Erwachens* (1992; techniques of awakening). The poet expresses disgust with societal strictures designed to keep women complacent in traditional roles. "Weisheit" (wisdom) exhorts the reader that "in the margin the woman does not become womaner," ironically using the grammatically incorrect comparison "womaner" to bring home her point of the impossibility of being "more of a woman" if content with a marginal role. Similarly, teachers in the employment of the government, with its conservative rules and regulations, are to be mistrusted regardless of their gender, as "Nachlass" (last will) admonishes:

> I do not believe in the entrails of women teachers
> Girded with principles and ordinances

In Krechel's *Verbeugungen vor der Luft* (1999; obeisances to the air), she combines the political with a more formalist interest in the intricacies of language and sound, almost returning to some of the preoccupations of Germany's concrete poetry of the 1970's. She insists that her poems are mere "projections," plays on words, yet also attacks conservatism with cynicism and occasional obscenity. Krechel's poem "Goya, späte Jahre" (Goya, later years) plays fast and lose with history and insists that artistic work has to go on in spite of political pressures. Her nineteenth century Spaniard Goya shouts, "world, stay outside, I'm painting."

ELISABETH BORCHERS

Elisabeth Borchers's *Was ist die Antwort?* (1998; what is the answer?) brought a return of a well-regarded poet who had been silent for a while. Most of her poems are very short, but contain strong moral messages, as in her "Wohnungen" (residences): "Everything returns/ And has reached its end."

There is no escape from history, a point especially relevant as Germany still has to live with its Nazi past. If many of Borchers's poems remain somewhat impersonal and distant, the reader is confronted with an author who generally rejects the autobiographical style in search of a larger truth.

HELGA M. NOVAK

In a career which began in the East and by force moved to the West, Helga M. Novak (born 1935), who was stripped of her East German citizenship in 1966, saw a steady revival of her poetry in the 1990's. Her collection *Silvatica* (1997), was praised for its use of the metaphor of the hunt to comment on womanhood. Here, Novak returns to the Greek myth of the hunter-goddess Artemis, reviving an interest in classical allusions. Her massive collection of a life's worth of poetry, *Solange noch Liebesbriefe eintreffen* (1999; as long as love letters still come in) met with mixed criticism. Her political poems were criticized for a lack of

aesthetic achievement, and her moral focus on the underdog was found lacking in sophistication. However, her power to evoke emotions with her socially engaged poetry was welcomed by many.

HEINZ CZECHOWSKI

Heinz Czechowski (1935-2009) straddled the East and the West. In *Nachtspur* (1993; night track), he gives voice to his despair of having lost his bearings and calling in life, when he writes in "Damals zuletzt" (back then, for the last time):

> Thus I give up
> To search for my lost identity
> It is sufficient to be here
> And to know that one is still here. . . .

Five years later, in *Mein westfälischer Frieden* (1998; my peace of Westphalia), Czechowski alludes to the peace treaty of Westphalia, which ended the devastating Thirty Years' War in 1648, as an allusion to the peace he has made in his life with his move, in 1995, from his native Dresden in the East to Western Germany. While his voice is still full of sorrow, there is a sense that the poet has forgiven history for having disappointed him. It is a time to make peace and enjoy the beauties of the day.

JOACHIM SARTORIUS

Reunified Germany's renewed weight in international affairs was echoed by the internationalist poems of Joachim Sartorius (born 1946). A prolific collaborator with international visual artists, Sartorius's poetry celebrates a masculine sensuality that unifies the global sphere. In *Der Tisch wird kalt* (1992; the table turns cold), Sartorius imagines world peace to feel like the first breath after ejaculation: "A final joyous breathing . . . so clear a breath as if it journeyed/ around the whole of the world." In *Vakat* (1993; vacant), Sartorius provides poems to Nan Goldin's pictures of deserted brothel and hotel rooms around the world, reveling in a sex worker's joy that "The evening is young/ Money from beauty/ Jingles in the pockets."

GERHARD FALKNER

Internationalism takes a different turn in the poetry of Gerhard Falkner (born 1951), who continues to remind Germany that, for example, in spite of winning the soccer world championship in 1990, "there are shadows/ abrupt poems" which function "like supreme tribunals" to remind the reader of the powers of words like "Auschwitz" and the evils of the past that continue to cast a shadow on the joyous present.

THOMAS KLING

Instruments of information technology populate the work of Thomas Kling (1957-2005), who dedicated himself to incorporating the language of the new technology and issued collections like *nacht.sicht.gerät* (1993; night.vision.apparatus), *morsch* (1996; rotten), and *Fernhandel* (1999; long distant trade). Embracing a technocratic, computerized world, he offers love poems that express age-old sentiments in the language of Silicon Valley.

DURS GRÜNBEIN

Refocusing on the human body, yet maintaining an almost clinical distance, has become the trademark stance of celebrated poet Durs Grünbein (born 1962). Growing up in East Germany's Dresden, Grünbein developed his craft by pointing out the absurdities of socialist society. After reunification, he continued to dissect the fabric of comfortable lies attempting to hold together postmodern society. His caustic vision of the loneliness of the Internet age strikes a chord with his urban readership. "Apart from the screen, as you can see/ the image of the screen is a nothing" is his verdict on the empty, self-referential nature of cyberspace, in his poem "Ultra Null" (ultra zero) in *Schädelbasislektion* (1991; skull crash course). His *Nach den Satiren* (1999; after the satires) carries his theme of an impending bio-apocalypse further. His witty satires on the new Berlin, which evokes in the brain "something which cries for destruction," and his somewhat stereotypical denunciation of California's body culture have made Grünbein one of Germany's most widely read contemporary poets.

REVITALIZATION

In the decades after the fall of the Berlin Wall, Germany's poets have embraced a broad variety of styles, themes, and forms in their literary attempt to work through the political, social, and intellectual ramifications of reunification. Their vibrant poetry ranges from a vigorous revitalization of old traditions to a keen awareness of the new self in a newly reconfigured coun-

try. The urge to express the impact of the Internet society, to envision integration of East and West, and to give a voice to the female perspective has inspired vivid poetry that continues to connect to an interested, wide-ranging audience.

BIBLIOGRAPHY

Berman, Russell. *Cultural Studies and Modern Germany: History, Representation, Nationhood.* Madison: University of Wisconsin Press, 1993. Poetry is discussed in the light of a general interest in cultural studies, encompassing art and popular culture. Spotlights topical intellectual concerns in the reunified Germany. Bibliography and index.

Brockmann, Stephen. *Literature and German Reunification.* New York: Cambridge University Press, 1999. An excellent study of the interplay of literature and culture. Ample room is given to discussing poetry and poets' roles in the reunified Germany. One of the best books on the subject in English. Bibliography and index.

Donahue, Neil. *Voice and Void: The Poetry of Gerhard Falkner.* Heidelberg, Germany: Winter Press, 1998. Donahue, Falkner's translator into English, places the poet's work in the context of modernist and postmodernist thought and debate in Germany. The final two chapters link Falkner's work to contemporary German poetry in general, with an interesting comparison to Durs Grünbein.

Durrani, Osman, Colin Good, and Kevin Hilliard, eds. *The New Germany: Literature and Society After Unification.* Sheffield, England: Sheffield Academic Press, 1995. Among the many essays in this collection are two that deal with poetry, both in English. Bibliography and index.

Eigler, Friederike, and Peter Pfeiffer, eds. *Cultural Transformations in the New Germany: American and German Perspectives.* Columbia, S.C.: Camden House, 1993. Contains an interesting essay by Peter Geist on German poetry immediately after reunification. Other essays focus on the Prenzlauer Berg poets of Berlin. Each essay has its own bibliography. Informative in-depth essays.

Fachinger, Petra. *Rewriting Germany from the Margins: "Other" German Literature of the 1980's and*

1990's. Montreal: McGill-Queen's University Press, 2001. Looks at the views expressed in the writings of German minorities, including immigrants from other countries, German Jews, and Germans who grew up in the German Democratic Republic. A much-needed study as Germany deals with a new, multicultural society. Bibliography and index.

Grimm, Reinhold, and Irmgard Hunt, eds. *German Twentieth Century Poetry*. New York: Continuum, 2001. A useful anthology providing well-translated texts. Concise introduction. Includes bibliographical references and indexes.

Hofmann, Michael, ed. *Twentieth-Century German Poetry: An Anthology*. New York: Farrar, Straus and Giroux, 2008. A new collection of the works of major poets, presented in bilingual form. Includes writers of the 1990's.

Owen, Ruth J. *The Poet's Role: Lyric Responses to German Unification by Poets from the G.D.R*. Amsterdam: Rodopi, 2001. Examines the changes in poets' feelings about their roles in society after the reunification of Germany. Extensive bibliographical references and indexes.

Rolleston, James, ed. *Contemporary German Poetry*. Special issue of *Studies in Twentieth Century Literature* 21, no. 1 (Winter, 1997). An outstanding choice of essays and newly translated poetry. The best English text on many of Germany's contemporary authors. Each essay comes with notes and bibliographies, even though most secondary material quoted is written in German. An comprehensive overview of the subject that combines detailed analysis with broader studies.

R. C. Lutz

GREEK POETRY IN ANTIQUITY

The earliest Greek poetry was unlettered, oral, and traditional. For centuries before the appearance of the alphabet in the eighth century B.C.E., Greek poets were creating songs, probably in dactylic hexameter, for entertainment, ritual, and religious purposes. Some of these poems were probably short lyrics and others were longer tales about their heroes and gods. Most, if not all, were probably intended for public performance by individuals or by choruses. Especially in longer, narrative poetry, fixed phrases such as epithets and formulas were used as mnemonic devices and compositional tools to tell and retell tales through generations.

HOMER

While the texts of the earliest surviving Greek poetry, the Homeric epics *Iliad* (c. 750 B.C.E.; English translation, 1611) and *Odyssey* (c. 725 B.C.E.; English translation, 1614), were probably not written down in definitive form until the eighth century B.C.E., the tales on which they are based may have existed in oral form at least by the late second millennium B.C.E. Although the very existence of their author is clouded in controversy, few challenge their author's debt to a long chain of earlier poets who helped establish tales about a ten-year-long war between the Greeks and the Trojans and the troublesome homecomings of the Greeks after their victory. Homer's *Iliad* deals only with the tenth year of the war and the consequences of the quarrel between the Greek leader Agamemnon and his chief warrior Achilles. The *Odyssey* focuses on the ten-year wanderings of the Greek warrior Odysseus following the war and the troubles he faced when he finally arrived home in Ithaca. Many other tales surrounding these events were part of a tradition called Trojan cycle. Some were concerned with the events leading up to the war or with the nine years of conflict prior to the *Iliad*, others with events following the *Iliad* and with the end of the war. There were also other homecoming tales besides that of Odysseus, and even stories about other wars, such as that known as the Seven Against Thebes, but none of these survives except in fragments.

Also surviving under Homer's name, but probably written by a number of anonymous authors, are the Homeric hymns, a collection of thirty-three songs to individual Greek deities. Thought to have been sung as preludes or introductions, especially for performances of Greek epics, these hymns use the dactylic hexameter and vocabulary of Homer and usually include the traditional parts of a prayer, with an invocation, sanction, and entreaty to the god. A few of these hymns, specifically those to Demeter (2), Apollo (3), Hermes (4), Aphrodite (6), and Dionysus (7), incorporate significant narrative sections telling stories about these deities.

HESIOD

In his two surviving poems *Theogonia* (c. 700 B.C.E.; *Theogony*, 1728) and *Erga kai Emerai* (c. 700 B.C.E.; *Works and Days*, 1618), the poet Hesiod (fl. c. 700 B.C.E.) also uses the hexameter and language of Homer but in an often personal, didactic tone. In *Theogony*, Hesiod focuses on the birth of the gods and the violent succession of divine rulers from Uranus to Cronus to Zeus. *Works and Days*, usually described as a farming manual, is rather a statement of Hesiod's own philosophy and worldview. In his personal poetic voice, he celebrates the justice of Zeus, describes the evils of women, and reflects on his own divine calling to be a poet. Other well-known myths told by Hesiod in these poems include the stories of the Titan Prometheus and of the first woman, Pandora.

FIRST-PERSON POETRY

Hesiod's poetry marks a transition in the seventh century B.C.E. from the traditional, oral poetry represented by the surviving Homeric epics to shorter, more individualized verse that often uses this traditional language in novel ways. In most cases, this poetry, like the Homeric epics, continues to be composed for performance rather than for publication. Most of this poetry survives only in short fragments culled from references in later works or found on scraps of Egyptian papyri. These poems are written in a variety of meters, styles, and dialects. Some, like elegy, use the traditional dactylic hexameter, but accompanied by a second line, in dactylic pentameter, to form an elegiac couplet. It is possible that the origin of the word "elegy" is derived from a non-Greek word for flute. This poetry was, in fact, often sung to the accompaniment of such musical instruments. Occasionally the Greeks themselves mistakenly assumed that the word meant "lament," but such poetry is especially associated with commemoration of the dead only in the Greek tombstone inscription tradition. Ancient Greek poems written in a variety of other meters are usually called "lyric," after a stringed-instrument the Greeks called the lyre. A third important type of personal verse used an iambic meter especially for invective or poetry of personal attack. While metrical form and theme are closely associated in Greek poetry, such metrical features are rarely discernible in English translation. All of these varied verse forms, however, share an emphasis on personal self-expression, reflection, and, especially, the use of the first person.

ARCHILOCHUS

One of the earliest surviving poets of elegiac and iambic was Archilochus (c. 680-c. 640 B.C.E.). In a famous fragment about losing his shield in battle, Archilochus used Homeric vocabulary to question traditional Greek military values and priorities, which demanded that a warrior return either with his shield or on it. Archilochus argued that saving his life and being able to fight again for his country were more important than the shield, which he lost. Much of Archilochus's poetry seems to have centered on his relationship with a woman named Neobule. When her father Lycambes suddenly broke off Archilochus's engagement to his daughter, the poet turned to violent, abusive invective against both father and daughter, who are said to have committed suicide as a result of Archilochus's attacks. An alternative interpretation of this invective poetry, usually written in a metric form called iambic, is that such poetry is actually ritualistic rather than personal and autobiographical. The relationship between the name Lycambes and iambic argues strongly in favor of such a ritualistic context for Archilochus's poetry.

SEMONIDES

Greatly influenced by Archilochus's invective iambic poetry was Semonides of Amorgos (fl. late seventh century B.C.E.). His most significant surviving fragment is a strongly misogynistic iambic poem in which various animals are compared to different types of women. Only the industrious woman, compared to a bee, earns the poet's approval.

SAPPHO AND ALCAEUS

Sappho and Alcaeus, both of Lesbos, wrote their lyric poetry in the early sixth century B.C.E. Both experimented with metric forms and created meters named after them. Both suffered exile from their homeland due to political upheavals on the island during the reigns of the tyrants Myrsilus and Pittacus. Alcaeus replied to Archilochus by losing his shield in one of his poems. In addition to contemporary politics, the poet wrote drinking songs, love songs, and hymns. He is best known as the possible inventor of the "ship of state" metaphor. Sappho is one of the few female voices in ancient Greece. Her poetry deals occasionally with politics and myth, but especially focuses on apparently autobiographical themes, especially her love for other women. Her only complete poem is probably her

Calliope, the Greek muse of epic poetry. (AP/Wide World Photos)

"Prayer to Aphrodite," which transforms the public prayer poem into a description of a personal relationship with the goddess.

ALCMAN

The lyric poet Alcman worked in Sparta in the late seventh century B.C.E. and wrote hymns to the gods, love poems, and especially songs for choruses of young women. These choral songs, probably sung at festivals and perhaps in competition, may have used a central mythic narrative to make a moral point.

ANACREON

Anacreon of Teos (c. 571-c. 490 B.C.E.) is especially associated with the courts of the tyrants Polycrates of Samos and Hipparchus of Athens, for whom he wrote joyful and reflective lyrics about love, drinking songs, and occasional elegiacs. While his surviving fragments occasionally refer to the political turmoil of his day, Anacreon's poems seem to seek escape from such concerns in the sophisticated pleasures of the aristocratic symposium or drinking party.

THEOGNIS

One of the few Archaic elegists whose work survives substantially in manuscript is Theognis (c. seventh century-c. sixth century B.C.E.). Theognis's poetry is addressed to a friend named Cyrnus and includes drinking and love songs. Theognis's emphatic aristocratic bias is revealed in his strong feelings about politics and morality.

OTHER EARLY POETS

The poetry of other early elegists reflects the frequent warfare of the period as Ionian Greeks struggled to resist the great empires of the East and generations of Spartans fought on the Greek mainland against their neighbors the Messinians. Poets like Tyrtaeus of Sparta (fl. seventh century B.C.E.), Callinus of Ephesus (fl. early seventh century B.C.E.) and Mimnermus of Colophon (fl. 632-29 B.C.E.) wrote about war and exhorted their contemporaries to fight on behalf of their cities. Occasionally Mimnermus turned to more personal themes, such as the difficulties of old age.

Archaic Greek poetry was also used for philosophic and political purposes. The pre-Socratic philosopher Xenophanes of Colophon (fl. late sixth century B.C.E.) wrote in a variety of poetic forms, including epic, el-

egy, and satirical iambics and hexameters. His surviving fragments challenged many of the assumptions and norms of Greek society, including the anthropomorphism of the Greek gods and the honors awarded to Greek athletes. The Athenian statesman Solon (fl. early sixth century) used poetry to justify the political and economic reforms he instituted as archon in 594-593 B.C.E.

THE CLASSICAL PERIOD

The fifth century B.C.E. saw the finest flowering of poetry in Greece. The tragedies of Aeschylus, Sophocles, and Euripides and the comedies of Aristophanes are the best-known and most influential products of this period, associated with the civic life of Athens, which grew to be the center of Greek culture of the time. Practitioners from many places in the Greek-speaking world, however, helped to raise poetry to a high state in the century that saw the defeat of Persia and the downfall of democratic Athens. Pindar's brilliant choral odes celebrating victors in the national games, important philosophical verse, elaborate dithyrambic poetry—all had their roots and flourished outside Athens. Although the achievement of Athenian dramatists came to overshadow the other poetry of the period, a true appreciation of their highly synthetic art form requires a sense of the fifth century poetic "climate"; only then can what is innovative and fresh in the drama of the period be contrasted with that which continues Archaic trends.

POPULAR POETRY AND SKOLIA

The parties, or symposia, at which Greek men gathered regularly to discuss the latest politics, to drink, and to talk on all topics, from the trivial to the philosophical, often featured informal songs as well. Plato's dialogue *Symposion* (fourth century B.C.E.; *Symposium*, 1701) offers a look at the procedures on such occasions: Each member of the party must contribute a performance, poetic or rhetorical. An antiquarian writer of the second century C.E., Athenaeus, preserved about twenty-five examples of various types of songs that might be sung on such occasions. The topics that most occupied the minds of the Athenian leisure class are in kernel form here. It should be remembered that this class gave Athens its preeminent writers and that, in general, Greek literature was the creation of an elite. The audience for the public poetry of the drama, however, was mixed in a democratic fashion because admission was provided by the city-state; on other occasions, the poetry was performed at free festivals.

What might a fifth century Greek have sung, then, at an evening's entertainment? He might well have chosen a poem by a sixth century lyric poet such as Anacreon or Alcaeus, a poem celebrating the joys of drinking and sporting among friends. For variety, the participants in a symposium, especially those with good voices, might have invented new words for a traditional tune, or they might have had verse-capping contests (like those of Japanese party poetry, *renga*) in which the song would zigzag among the guests. Both of these latter sorts of entertainment seem to have fallen under the heading of *skolia* (crooked songs).

Politics, love, social life, and light philosophy were the most popular subjects of *skolia*. In these occasional poems, several points of interest appear. First, the political allusions, although they may refer to figures of a century earlier, concern the present day. The continuing call for *isonomia* (equal portioning) was a democratic slogan in Athens, so that this *skolion* was no doubt sung among members of the political clubs opposed to aristocrats. Again, the songs reveal glimpses of alternative myths (also a powerful political weapon in Greek culture): Nowhere in the tragedy of the *Iliad*, for example, is it hinted that Achilles will survive death at the hands of the Trojans, but a *skolion* on this theme has a different version. One is reminded that popular Greek culture knew hundreds of myths and bits of lore, many more than have survived, all of which provided an essential background to an understanding by Athenians of Greek tragedy, where some dramatists used alternative versions for the sake of making dramatic points. Thus, the *skolia* serve as reminders of the bulk of fifth century Greek poetry, which has been lost to later generations.

Tragedy also deals with the ethical values of the group, as represented by the *polis* (city-state), and here also, popular poetry can offer insights, providing evidence for a view of life that might have been held by many Athenians in the audience of a dramatic perfor-

mance. What is a crisis, in ancient Greek terms? Does it resemble anything so terrible as the fates of tragic heroes? One might revise the answer to these questions on reading in a *skolion* that "for a mortal, health is the first best thing; second, fine looks; third, honest wealth; and fourth—to be among friends and be young." These are far from the heroic virtues that many critics take tragedy as teaching.

The friends (*philoi*) mentioned above indicate that in the fifth century, the ethics of an earlier age had not died out. The bulk of extant verse from the Archaic period was meant for performance before friends and directed toward the consolidation of the group which constituted the audience. Such friend groups still determined the course of politics and social life in Greece at a later stage. The fifth century songs continue this emphasis on knowing who one's friends are (although they fail to mention the usual Archaic converse of the statement that one should hate one's enemies). One poem expresses the wish to open up and look inside the heart of a man in order "to consider, by his guileless mind, whether a man is dear [*philos*]"; other verses call on companions to "drink with me, be young with me, with me love and wear festive crowns; go mad when I'm out of my mind, and be sober when I am."

Finally, a short poem warns, in the manner of earlier didactic poetry: "Friend, a scorpion's under every rock; make sure that he doesn't strike you. All treachery goes with what is hidden." This constant urge to bring out into the light the hidden spaces of the heart—among friends at least—is at the root of Athenian drama, it might be said; tragedy, the highest art form of Greece, is the bringing forth in public (where the friends are those of the city/audience) what is hidden in the souls of enigmatic heroes such as Ajax and Oedipus, so that the public can learn. Although the genres differ widely in scale and occasion, they share a common ideology and a goal of group consolidation.

ELEGAIC POETRY

The historic events of the fifth century B.C.E. brought new demands for such social cohesion as poetry could offer. In the early part of the century, the Greek city-states banded together under the lead of Sparta and Athens to defeat the might of the Persians, first in 490 B.C.E., then in a more protracted struggle ending in 480 or 479 B.C.E. with Greek victories at Salamis and Plataea. This surprising outcome ushered in an era of self-confidence and inspired serious high art that attempted to understand the world system anew: What kind of virtue did Greece have that it could win against such odds? The drama of Aeschylus (525-456 B.C.E.), which attempted to reconcile cosmic problems by pointing to the example of Athens's institutions, is but one indication of this trend. Aeschylus also wrote the only surviving Greek tragedy that deals with a historical rather than a mythic event: His *Persai* (*The Persians*, 1777), produced in 472 B.C.E., only eight years after the Athenian victory at Salamis, pictures that battle as the inevitable result of the clash between Athenian piety and godless Persian arrogance.

As always in Greece, poetry and politics mixed. Many battles of the Persian War were commemorated shortly after they occurred, as cities paid poets to honor those who had fallen. For this purpose, the type of verse used was an old form called elegiac, dating at least to the seventh century B.C.E. and consisting of couplets in the form of a dactylic hexameter followed by a dactylic pentameter. Elegy had long been used for consolatory or lament poems, but it was also a vehicle for light verse, as examples by Archilochus show, and for instructional poetry, as in the work of Theognis, in the sixth century B.C.E. The examples of the genre in the fifth century B.C.E. are mainly serious in tone, with a laconic expressiveness that arises from the contrast between the longer first line and the pungent, short second line of the couplet.

Simonides of Ceos (556-468 B.C.E.) is credited with the best epitaphs written for Persian War heroes. A poet with a wide reputation in his time for both choral and elegiac verse, his is the famous inscription for three hundred Spartan dead at Thermopylae: "Friend, to the Spartans report that here, obedient to their words, we repose." Poignant brevity and meaningful understatement are the mark of Simonides' craft; to the memory of the entire Greek force buried at Thermopylae were inscribed his words: "Here, once, fought against three hundred thousand, four thousand from the Peloponnese." For a contingent of sailors who died in the last naval battle of the war, he wrote: "Friend, once we lived

in the town that had good harbors—Corinth; now the island of Ajax holds us—Salamis."

When read in bulk, this sort of elegiac verse, most often the work of anonymous poets, offers glimpses of Greek feeling on the heroic, on death, and on the afterlife, in an unvarnished manner. Those who died in battle were often given the status of "hero"—a word usually indicating a revered warrior of the distant past. Tragedy looks back to the Trojan War era for its heroes and makes them contemporary with the Athenian fifth century; just so, elegiac verse enshrines contemporary heroes in the tradition of the past, so that there is recompense for their having died—the granting of fame through poetry.

Paradoxically, the complex art form of tragedy is most successful when it attains the elegant simplicity of sentiment and expression characteristic of such epitaphs. Aeschylus and Sophocles are known to have written some elegiac verse, and it perhaps benefited their art. At any rate, this is another instance of the influence of the "poetic climate": A Greek audience, imbued with the spirit of inscriptional verse encountered daily, would be properly primed to appreciate the clarity and seriousness of tragic drama, the convention that left the worst out of view (murder, for example, which was never displayed on stage). Sepulchral verse hardly mentions the fact of dying but renders its significance. Finally, the premise of the epitaphs—that the dead live or are speaking to passersby—illuminates central assumptions that underlie tragedy: One must reenact the hero's sufferings onstage because heroes still "live," at least in annual cult observances. Indeed, so many Greek tragedies actually deal with the death or burial of the hero and so much detail is accorded to the burial site in the plays—as in Aeschylus's *Choēphoroi* (458 B.C.E.; *Libation Bearers*, 1777), for example—that it has been suggested that tragedy grew out of the religious act of hero worship, a ritual process which took place at tombs throughout Greece. Thus, the connections between epitaph and tragedy may go deeper than an affinity of tone.

PHILOSOPHICAL POETRY

Greek tragedy is philosophical poetry; both in the choruses and in the speeches of actors, humanity's fate, a person's relation to the gods and to other people in the *polis*, continually occupies the minds of the tragedians.

How does one reconcile God and humans? What takes precedence, the family or the city? These and other questions force Greek tragedy to become thoughtful, wide-spirited, and therefore universal.

Philosophy in poetic form, however, was by no means confined to tragedy. Both the popular poetry of the symposium and the laconic art of tombstone verse reveal a particular Greek fascination with the large questions of life. Choral poetry (to be discussed below) also traditionally is interwoven with philosophical statements in the form of "gnomes"—pithy moral statements such as that by Alcman: "From the gods comes retribution."

SIMONIDES

Simonides, who also wrote elegiac poetry, was much admired in the fifth century for verse that attempted to deal with ethical questions. His poetry, which explores and expands on common gnomic statements, might well be labeled philosophical. His poem in praise of the Thessalian aristocrat Scopas seems to have been particularly well known, so much so that Plato, in his philosophical dialogue *Prōtagoras* (fourth century B.C.E., *Protagoras*, 1804), could represent his master Socrates and other intellectuals as alluding to Simonides' poem as though each knew the verses by heart. "For a man to become truly good, shaped four-square and blameless in foot, hand and mind, is hard," wrote the poet. Like a philosopher, he proceeds to take issue with earlier formulations: He voices disagreement with the saying of the wise man Pittacus, that "It is difficult for a man to be good." It is noteworthy that the professional philosopher Protagoras, in Plato's dialogue, treats Simonides as an equal and begins to argue that the poet was inconsistent in preferring his own statement to that of Pittacus. The correct explanation must be that Simonides intentionally contrasted his verb use (to *become* good) with his predecessor's (to *be* good), for, as the poet goes on to say, "it is hard for one to avoid being *bad* if unfightable chance overcomes him." Only a god can choose to *be* good, while man must evolve from a given lot determined by the divine: He can *become* good, not *be* good. Simonides concludes that the most one can hope for is not to do shameful things willingly—"even the gods do not contest coercion."

The poem is cast in an Archaic fashion, with the poet arguing that one side is to be praised, another blamed, as Archilochus and Alcman did two centuries earlier when the existence of an oral culture made the meting out of proper reputation the primary task of the poet. Simonides, therefore, finds fault with Pittacus; he praises those who act ethically. Moreover, the entire composition is framed as a praise poem to Simonides' patron, in a centuries-old genre. Finally, the poem treats themes with a long history in Greek lyric and epic: The idea of being good in diverse activities is found in the *Iliad*, and the notion that fate and the gods are "unfightable" (*amēkhanos*) is a key theme from the seventh century on. What, then, is new about Simonides' poem?

Surely to devote an entire poem to gnomic morality, rather than using these statements as asides, is innovative, but also fresh is the fashion in which Simonides attempts to make precise linguistic revisions in the statements of his predecessors. The art of "correct speaking" was actually a discipline practiced by the word-conscious members of the Sophistic movement, the most important intellectual movement in fifth century Greece. The Sophists (some of whom figure in the dialogue of Plato discussing this poem) claimed to be able to teach anything, for a fee, including how to become virtuous. Tragedy, politics, history, and rhetoric were to feel the effects of the Sophists' teachings, but it was primarily poetry which became the battleground of old and new in Greek culture, for, even into the early fifth century, poets laid claim to practice the highest form of wisdom (*sophia*) and to be called wise. With the coming of Sophistic philosophy, poets faced a challenge for the title. Simonides, accepted as *sophos* (wise) by both poets and philosophers, represents the coming trend of intellectualizing poetry; although he clung to established poetic forms, he extended the limits of poetry in attempting to make it do the work of analytical thought.

PARMENIDES

The fusion of traditional forms with startlingly new content also characterized the work of two fifth century pre-Socratic poets, Parmenides of Elea (writing about 490 B.C.E.) and Empedocles of Acragas (active in mid-century). Both were from the colonies of Magna

Graecia (southern Italy and Sicily), and both sought, in different ways, to solve the problem that preoccupied Simonides in the poem on virtue: the conflict between being and becoming. Some critics might object to a consideration of their writings as poetry, because it is clear that the pre-Socratic poets were interested mainly in argument rather than poetic form. However, they had good precedents if they had wanted to write prose philosophy; that they chose verse is important to understanding fifth century poetry as a whole. It is another indication of the seriousness attached to poetic craft and marks the difference in social structure that in ancient Greece allowed poets to be regarded as serious thinkers. There are further implications in their choice of verse rather than prose. Using epic meter, the two philosophers immediately signaled their connection with the oldest Greek literary tradition (and it must be remembered that Homer, too, was often treated as a philosopher).

Parmenides, in fact, often recalls by his diction several passages in the *Odyssey* as he describes his own journey toward enlightenment in his preface to the poem "The Way of Truth." Like Odysseus, he poses as the "knowing man" who is carried through many towns by the influence of a goddess (unnamed here; compare Athena in the *Odyssey*) until he reaches the gates of Night and Day. There the goddess promises that he will learn "the unshaken heart of rounded truth" as well as the untrustworthy opinions of humans. For Parmenides, then, the *Odyssey* is a model of plot (featuring, as it does, a return to the land of light and the living) as well as of diction, but the truth, as Parmenides has it, is the opposite of Homer's notion and is, in fact, an enemy of poetry, it seems. Homer takes the world as it appears, describing it in shining epithets; Parmenides considers sense impressions to be inherently false. Working from a premise that "not-being" is unthinkable, the philosopher denies the void, the existence of divisions in nature, and such phenomena as opposites, which imply change (for example, night and day). The possibility which Simonides holds out to humans, that of "becoming," is in Parmenides merely another misperception of helpless humans, based on illusion. Here, then, is a final reason for Parmenides' use of poetry as vehicle: Seeing so clearly, he is on the side of the gods; although

his thought seems to undercut the possibility of poetry to express truth, his instinct is to use the voice of authority and tradition. After all, the divine oracles of Delphi were always composed in dactylic hexameter.

EMPEDOCLES

Empedocles' two poems of several thousand lines each, *Peri physeōs* (fifth century B.C.E., *On Nature*, 1908) and *Katharmoi* (fifth century B.C.E., *Purifications*, 1908), remind one at every turn of Homeric epic, but once again the insistent logical argumentation bears the mark of the fifth century intellect. One example from the more completely preserved nature poem will suffice to point out the gulf between the philosopher and the epic poet. In explaining how he believes respiration works, Empedocles introduces a simile much in Homer's lengthy manner. The blood and air regularly interchange through the pores, pushing one another, he explains,

> just as when a girl plays with a *klepsydria* [water clock] of gleaming brass. When she puts the mouth of the pipe against her shapely hand . . . no liquid enters the vessel, but the bulk of air within holds it back until she uncovers the dense stream.

The close observation of everyday scenes is a virtue of Homeric poetry, one which may have helped later Greek poetry by developing a language for seeing things, but never does Homer go this far or use description thus for its own "scientific" ends.

Empedocles, however, rightly uses poetry for his vehicle of expression. His system, a refinement of that of Parmenides, explains change and motion within Being as caused by the constant rearrangement of four eternal elements; this, in turn, is effected by the actions of Strife and Love. By employing the key words of the *Iliad* (which is about strife between a soldier and his chief, resolved through the love of the soldier's companion), Empedocles defines the phenomenal world as a grand Homeric struggle.

DITHYRAMBIC POETRY

Parmenides and Empedocles represent one extreme in fifth century poetry—its highly intellectual strain. A Greek audience, for whom the Delphic maxim "nothing in excess" was usually an unattained ideal, could find a counterbalance in another extreme form of poetry—dithyramb. This highly emotive art form, thought to have begun with worship of the revel god Dionysus (patron of poets), remains important for students of Greek literature because, according to Aristotle, the genre gave birth to tragedy. In fact, at the annual Dionysian festivals of Athens, at which tragedy and comedy were performed in the fifth century, dithyrambic competitions still had a place of honor, and huge choirs strove to win singing prizes. During the course of the century, dithyramb declined as a serious form as its offspring tragedy reached its zenith, so that, near the end of the century, the comic poet Aristophanes could poke fun at the dithyrambists as either effeminate or crazy. He parodied their art in songs such as this one from *Ornithes* (414 B.C.E.; *The Birds*, 1824): "Thou author of Aitna, Father/ At whose dire doom do foregather/ All the high hierarchs—Och! wad, thy nod, some giftie/ gi'e me: I don't care what, just a token of your regard." Seeking to compete with the tragedians, the dithyrambists merely produced a stiff and highly mannered art.

Earlier fifth century dithyramb, however, must have retained some of the vigor that had led, in distant times, to the creation of tragic poetry. It had dialogue, used episodes from myth, and most important, often divided portions between a chorus and a chorus leader. This led to the existence of similar features in tragedy, which was still performed for the Dionysian religious rites in the fifth century. Some idea of the state of dithyrambic art at mid-century can be gained from the poems of Bacchylides, the nephew of Simonides, who excelled in the genre. A poem of his on the Athenian hero Theseus's encounter with Minos of Crete employs an unusual meter, with many short syllables in succession, to create an atmosphere of excitement. One episode in the mythical visit is focused on Minos's challenge to Theseus to prove that he is the son of Poseidon, god of the sea, by diving to recover a sunken ring. Direct speech enlivens the narrative, giving it an epic tone, while newly coined compound adjectives distance the poem from Homeric epic. Perhaps the most original feature of the work is Bacchylides' incorporation of a dramatic audience within the poem in the form of the group of fourteen youths whom Theseus is bringing as

a tribute to Minos. They tremble in fear at their leader's dive and shout in joy as he returns from undersea. It is not difficult to see how dithyrambic art that had attained this stage earlier—using a chorus to sing about a chorus in myth—could have led to the beginnings of drama. Bacchylides himself, in fact, wrote other dithyrambs entirely in dialogue form, which could easily be acted. The main nontragic element in the poems is not in their outward form but in the particular selection of mythic moment. Rather than centering his compositions on the life-or-death crises of the hero, enlarging the drama by speeches in the mouths of main actors, Bacchylides picks small details in heroic life stories to dramatize. It is miniature art, in contrast to the large-scale Athenian drama, anticipating the Alexandrian Greek art of the *epyllion* (little epic) of the third century B.C.E.

VICTORY ODES

Bacchylides had a nearly contemporary rival, the Boeotian poet Pindar (c. 518-c. 438 B.C.E.), who competed for patronage from great aristocratic families all over Greece by writing dithyrambs, maiden songs, praise poems, and, most important, odes to commemorate the victories of youths at the four national games. Competitions were held in events ranging from boxing to flute playing, and victors, although rewarded only with crowns of leaves, gained instant reputations all over the Greek world. Like much Greek poetry, victory odes were performed at religious occasions, since the games were sacrosanct (even warring states suspended hostilities to attend) and were thought to have been instituted by heroes at sites sacred to particular gods. In Pindar's words, the ode itself was "repayment" for the agony of the athlete in winning. That agony (from the Greek *agon*, meaning "contest") was in Greek terms itself a repayment for the similar trials of the distant hero: Because heroes suffered, carrying out martial or civilizing acts, the athlete, representing the community, did likewise in memory of his predecessors. This complex set of ideas underlies tragedy also, because there are indications that in some city states, dramas were staged to reenact the sufferings of a god or hero. Like the dithyramb, odes coexisted with tragedy and served a functional purpose on the local level. An athlete could be accompanied home from the games by a poet paid to sing his praises, or spontaneous odes might be performed on the site of the victory itself, at the crowning ceremonies in Olympia, for example. Here again, it is important to note the way in which Greek poetry associates the contemporary in all its homely detail with the heroic past.

A good example is provided by one of the surviving forty-five odes, written for a victor from Pindar's favorite city-state, Aegina. Phylakidas had won the *pancratium* event at the Isthmian games in Corinth around 480 B.C.E. In his ode, Pindar combines the three main elements of choral poetry: mention of the specifics of the occasion, myth, and transitional gnomic statements, relating victory to myth. After beginning with an invocation to Theia, divine light, mother of the sun, Pindar immediately shifts his focus to the victor: "In the struggle of the games he has won the glory of his desire." In a fashion characteristic of choral poetry and especially of his own, Pindar then abruptly shifts his attention again, to the lesson which the victor's example illustrates: "Men's valor is judged by their fates, but two things alone look after the sweetest grace of life—if a man fares well and hears his good name spoken. Seek not to become Zeus." The sudden shift to the warning is understandable in the context of the occasion, because success, according to Greek views, tempted the anger and jealousy of the gods. Tragedy continually reinforces the same message by showing the fates of those heroes who sought to become godlike.

After enumerating Phylakidas's past and present victories, the poet proceeds to the victor's homeland, Aegina, and its accomplishments. He praises its wealth of heroes, including the forebears of Achilles. He concludes with a reference to the recent Battle of Salamis, where sailors from Aegina had played a large part in gaining the victory. Because Aegina had such heroes in the past, it still produces hero-sailors and hero-athletes, Pindar implies. For the poet, as for Greek poetry in general, the past is continuous with the present and explains it.

HELLENISTIC POETRY

After the Peloponnesian War and Athens' surrender to Sparta in 404 B.C.E., Greek poetry gradually becomes less public and performative and more scholarly

and literary. One exception is comedy, which continued to thrive, especially in Athens, for much of the fourth century and into the third century B.C.E. The only surviving comic writer is the Athenian Menander (c. 342-c. 291 B.C.E.), some of whose work was rediscovered on papyri in modern times. Together with a number of scenes from other plays, his complete *Dyskolos* (317 B.C.E.; *The Bad-Tempered Man*, 1921; also known as *The Grouch*) reveals an emphasis on contemporary, everyday concerns. Unlike the often biting political satire of Aristophanes' Old Comedy, Menander's New Comedy deals with problems with children, spouses, money, and slaves. Like the earlier dramatic tradition, New Comedy is written in a variety of metrical forms, often with musical accompaniment.

The period following the reign of Alexander the Great (336-323 B.C.E.) is marked by a revolution in Greek poetry, which becomes more cosmopolitan, more sophisticated, and more learned as the Greek world expands to include the eastern half of the Mediterranean. The center of this new Hellenistic poetry was the Ptolemaic city of Alexandria in Egypt. To this city and its famous library flocked poets from all over the Greek world. Two poets, in particular, define the poetic milieu. Callimachus (c. 305-c. 240 B.C.E.) emphasized short, learned poetry like the aetiological legends he collected in an elegiac poem called *Aitiōn* (n.d.; *Aetia*, 1958), while his student and rival Apollonius Rhodius (between 295 and 260-late third century B.C.E.) used the more traditional epic form in his *Argonautica* (third century B.C.E.; English translation, 1780) about the legendary quest of the Argonauts for the Golden Fleece and the story of the Greek hero Jason and his relationship with the Colchian witch Medea.

Related to the shorter, highly polished poetry of Callimachus are the bucolic or pastoral poems produced by Theocritus of Syracuse (c. 308-c. 260 B.C.E.), Bion of Phlossa (fl. c. 100 B.C.E.), and Moschus of Syracuse (fl. 150 B.C.E.). Probably based on traditional songs sung by shepherds, usually with flute accompaniment, these more sophisticated Hellenistic poems incorporate singing contests between shepherds, laments, refrains, and stanzaic structures into highly refined, dramatic, and descriptive verse. Occasionally the rural setting is replaced by more urban themes. The iambic mimes of Herodas (fl. third century B.C.E.) share with pastoral poetry an emphasis on the dramatic and the descriptive. Little is known about the author or the context of his work, which may have even been intended for performance, but the surviving seven poems create vivid pictures of various character types, including a bawd, a pimp, a schoolmaster, and a shoemaker.

Another significant use of poetry in the Hellenistic period is for learned, didactic treatises. Aratus of Soli (c. 315-240/239 B.C.E.) produced the *Phaenomena*, a poem about astronomy which was widely read and imitated for centuries. Nicander of Colophon (fl. second century B.C.E.) used epic hexameters in a variety of poems, including the surviving *Theriaca* (about poisonous snakes and their antidotes) and *Alexipharmaca* (about other poisonous substances and their antidotes).

The Greek lyric tradition, especially the epigram, continued in the Hellenistic period. Some important representatives of the genre in this period are Asclepiades of Samos (fl. 290 B.C.E.), who introduced the theme of love to the epigram and may have been the first to give Eros (Cupid) wings; Anyte of Tegea (fl. early third century B.C.E.), best known for her tombstone epigrams; Corinna of Tanagra (of uncertain date), whose choral lyrics with a narrative element were probably written for women; Philodemus of Gadara (c. 110-c. 40/35 B.C.E.), an Epicurean philosopher whose highly polished but racy love poems may have influenced the Roman poets Horace and Ovid; and Meleager (c. 140-c. 70 B.C.E.), a Cynic philosopher noted not only for his lost Menippean satires, in which he mixed prose and poetry, but also for his love epigrams.

The survival of many lyric poems from the Hellenistic period as well as Archaic and Classical periods, is due to Meleager's publication of the first poetic anthology, *Stephanos* (c. 90-80 B.C.E.; *Fifty Poems*, 1890; best known as *Garland*) in which he included outstanding examples from approximately fifty earlier poets, including Archilochus and Anacreon, as well as his own work. Unfortunately, Meleager's *Garland* survives only within anthologies of later date.

THE ROMAN PERIOD AND LATE ANTIQUITY

The Hellenistic Age is usually said to end with the defeat of Anthony and Cleopatra at the Battle of Actium by the Roman Octavian (later, Augustus) in 31 B.C.E. Rome's annexation of Egypt following the death of Cleopatra marked the final stage in the Roman conquest of the eastern Mediterranean in the second and first centuries B.C.E. During the subsequent Roman period, Greek literature in general, and poetry in particular, went into decline.

Several anthologies of Greek lyric and epigram in the tradition of Meleager's *Garland* were made during this period. The most comprehensive of these was probably done by Constantinus Cephalas, a Byzantine official in Constantinople in 917 C.E. Like Meleager's earlier *Garland*, however, Cephalas's anthology survives only in the *Greek Anthology*, the work of an unknown scholar (or scholars) in the late tenth century C.E. This anthology of approximately thirty-seven hundred epigrams, arranged thematically in fifteen books, includes works from all periods, from the Archaic through the Byzantine. Some of the thematic groupings include *ekphrasis*, or descriptive poems, love poems, dedicatory poems, homosexual love poems, and poems of Christian devotion.

One of the few major pieces of Greek poetry in the Roman period is the *Dionysiaca* of Nonnus of Panopolis in Egypt (fl. fifth century C.E.), an epic in forty-eight books about the god Dionysus, and, especially, his conquest of India.

In 529 C.E., the emperor Justinian ordered the closing of the Academy in Athens. This event effectively marks the end of the ancient Greek world and the beginning of Byzantine history.

BIBLIOGRAPHY

Budelmann, Felix, ed. *The Cambridge Companion to Greek Lyric*. New York: Cambridge University Press, 2009. A collection of twenty essays, grouped by subject matter. Includes maps and illustrations, chronology, glossary, and index, as well as lists of editions, commentaries, translations, lexicons, and bibliographies. Extensive bibliographical references and excellent index.

Constantine, Peter, et al., eds. *The Greek Poets: Homer to the Present*. New York: W. W. Norton, 2009. Introduction by Robert Hass. A landmark publication, containing more than one thousand poems by two hundred poets. Essential for any student of Greek poetry. Map.

David, A. P. *The Dance of the Muses: Choral Theory and Ancient Greek Poetics*. New York: Oxford University Press, 2006. A new theory of ancient Greek poetry, which is based on harmony rather than metrics and emphasizes the importance of dance in performance. Well reasoned. Bibliography, general index, and index locorum.

Ford, Andrew. *Homer: The Poetry of the Past*. Ithaca, N.Y.: Cornell University Press, 1992. The Homeric poems are used to define the nature of traditional Greek poetry, especially the Homeric epics, and the role of the oral poet in society. In five chapters, Ford deals, in succession, with the function of traditional poetry as a means to transmit the past, epic poetry as a record of the past known only in full by the Muse, the poet as performer, the relationship between oral song and written text, and a view of ancient poetry as a form of "divine singing." Indexes.

Green, Ellen, ed. *Women Poets in Ancient Greece and Rome*. Norman: University of Oklahoma Press, 2005. The first collection of essays to examine the poetry written by Greek and Roman women, based mostly on surviving fragments, and accounts of their creative lives, as reported by their male contemporaries. Bibliography and index.

Green, Peter. *Alexander to Actium: The Historical Evolution of the Hellenistic Age*. Berkeley: University of California Press, 1990. Several chapters in this sweeping history of the Greek world—from the death of Alexander the Great in 323 B.C.E. to the victory of Augustus over Anthony and Cleopatra at the Battle of Actium in 31 B.C.E.—deal with Greek poetry. Of particular interest are chapter 11, "The Poet as Critic,", on Callimachus, Aratus, and Lycophron; chapter 13, "Armchair Epic,"; on Apollonius of Rhodes' and chapter 15, "Urbanized Pastoralism," on Theocritus and Herodas. Thirty maps, chronology, four genealogical tables, 217 figures, notes, bibliography, and index.

King, Katherine Callen. *Ancient Epic*. Malden, Mass.: John Wiley, 2009. An introduction to six epics, including Homer's *Iliad* and *Odyssey*. Includes chronologies, map, chart of Olympian gods, glossary, and index. A source that is both reliable and accessible.

Nagy, Gregory. *Poetry as Performance: Homer and Beyond*. New York: Cambridge University Press, 1996. A prominent scholar of Greek and Homeric poetry traces the development of the Homeric poems from oral performances in the mid-second millennium B.C.E. to the composition of written texts of the *Iliad* and the *Odyssey*. Nagy describes a process that assumes not a single, original text, but rather a "multitext" or series of coexisting oral variants. Includes significant observations on the composition of lyric poetry such as that of Sappho. Preface, bibliography, and index.

Raffel, Burton, trans. *Pure Pagan: Seven Centuries of Greek Poems and Fragments*. New York: Random House, 2004. Introduction by Guy Davenport. Part of the Modern Library Classic series. Works by poets highly regarded in their historical period but now almost forgotten have been re-created by an award-winner translator, making them available to English-speaking readers for the first time. Biographical sketches and a "Finding List."

Taplin, Oliver, ed. *Literature in the Greek and Roman Worlds: A New Perspective*. New York: Oxford University Press, 2000. This collection of seventeen essays by twelve classical scholars is arranged chronologically, beginning with Homer and ending with the culture wars of the second century C.E. and beyond. The authors offer a special focus on audiences and the way that this literature was received by its readers and spectators. Special attention is given to Greek poetry in the essays on Homer, Archaic Greek poetry, Greek literature after the classical period, and Greek literature in the Roman period. Includes eleven maps, forty illustrations, a time line of chapters, a detailed chronology, a bibliography, and an index.

West, M. L., trans. *Greek Lyric Poetry*. 1993. Reprint. New York: Oxford University Press, 2008. Contains a large collection of poems written between 650 and 450 B.C.E., many of them never before translated. Generously annotated. Bibliography and index.

Richard Peter Martin and Thomas J. Sienkewicz

GREEK POETRY SINCE 1820

EDITORS' NOTE: This essay uses the system of transliteration recommended by the Modern Greek Studies Association, in which stress marks are eliminated. Essays in the *Critical Survey of Poetry: European Poets* on individual modern Greek poets use a system of transliteration that comports with the most often cataloged forms of titles and names seen in the Library of Congress. The index for *Topical Essays* uses the latter form to conform to all other indexes in *Critical Survey of Poetry*.

In an essay written around 1950, the poet George Seferis defined one of the major obstacles to a contemporary understanding of modern Greek poetry:

> The rarest thing in the world is a foreign author . . . who knows Greek. Even now, according to the general perception of foreigners, and perhaps of our own people, classical Greece, Byzantine Greece, and modern Greece are countries which are unrelated and independent. Thus, everyone is limited in his own area of specialization.

As Seferis argued, in order to appreciate the full scope of modern Greek poetry one must see it as "a living art which belongs to a living tradition"—a tradition that extends from ancient Greece through the centuries of the Byzantine Empire to the renaissance of Greek poetry in the twentieth century.

HISTORICAL OVERVIEW AND THE LANGUAGE PROBLEM

Modern Greek poetry has its roots in a vernacular tradition that is unique among European literatures. Throughout its long history, the Byzantine Empire (300-1453) strongly discouraged the development of a written vernacular. Instead, the fledgling nineteenth century nation-state despots imposed the difficult and exclusive language of purist Greek (*katharevousa*, an artificial derivative of the classical Attic dialect of 500 B.C.E.). The language of the common person, demotic Greek, was officially nonexistent.

With the fall of Constantinople in 1453, Byzantine domination gave way to Turkish rule. In addition, the Turks conquered all Greek territories formerly occu-

pied by the Venetian Empire: Rhodes (1522), Crete (1669), and Corfu (1716). From 1453 to 1821, Greeks lived under the Ottomans. During these centuries of oppression, the demotic poetry of the Greek folk song expressed the yearnings, joys, and laments of a people who had once defined the principles of Western democracy and freedom.

Throughout the early years of the Greek state—and, with few exceptions, for most of the twentieth century—the purist tongue has been the official language of the nation, the language taught in schools and used for all official communications. Finding little of lasting value in this oligarchical tradition, Greek poets for the most part wrote in demotic, laying the foundation for a regeneration in the poetry of their new republic, which manifested itself in the twentieth century, when Greece earned two Nobel Prizes and became a leader in the art of the "poetic word."

FOUNDATIONS OF DEMOTICISM

The first Greek to grapple with the split identity of the Greek language strictly in terms of poetry was Dionysios Solomos, recognized today as the founder of modern Greek poetry. The story of his achievements begins in 1822, when Spyridon Trikoupis, a well-known Greek diplomat, historian, and libertarian, paid the young aristocrat a visit at Solomos's birthplace on Zakynthos, one of the Ionian Islands. Trikoupis's self-assigned mission was to find and promote a Greek poet who would speak out for a liberated Greece in the Greek vernacular. The Greek War of Independence from the Ottoman Empire had begun in 1821. Solomos had recently published a slender volume of poetry in Italian (*Rime improvvisate*, 1822), and Trikoupis knew him to be a man with revolutionary sympathies.

During one of their first meetings, Solomos (who demanded that they speak only of poetry) recited his most recent Italian composition. After an uncomfortable silence, the young poet demanded a response. Trikoupis answered by assuring Solomos that he would certainly secure an undisputed position among the great Italian poets. The diplomat added, however, that "the Greek Parnassus has not yet found its Dante." Dante had released Italian literature from the strictures of Latin and had solidified the written foundations of his native Tuscan (the *lingua vulgaris* which eventually became modern Italian) through his bold and expert style. Five centuries later, Solomos struggled against the use of *katharevousa* to rescue the Greek vernacular from possible extinction as a written form of expression. For centuries, Italy and Greece had dragged along the linguistic chains of their ancestry: the one in classical and church Latin, the other in an imitation of the formal (unspoken) dialect of Plato and Demosthenes. Solomos's early exposure to Dante's victory over Latin proved decisive for the future development of a poetic idiom which, for the first time, reached out to the vast majority of Greeks, who neither understood nor had any hope of understanding *katharevousa*, the language of the few.

At the time of Trikoupis's first visit, there was still a significant language barrier for the young poet; although he spoke Greek, his formal education had taken place in Venice (from 1808 to 1818), where he was trained exclusively in Latin and Italian. Solomos's lessons in the Greek vernacular began immediately following his first interview with Trikoupis. His new tutor taught Solomos the rudiments of his native tongue. Trikoupis must have known that this isolated struggle for written expression in a language that all Greeks might understand would meet with formidable opposition. Most of Solomos's contemporaries, in politics as well as literature, scorned demotic speech with its vulgarities and grammatical irregularities. In his only surviving prose work, *Dialogos* (1824), Solomos stated the problem in Greece with simplicity and exasperation: "Our own learned men want us to write a language that is neither spoken now, nor has ever been spoken in any other period, nor shall ever be spoken in the future."

The most important features of demotic Greek for the evolution of a written poetic idiom were its simplicity and widespread usage among Greek-speaking people, in both Greece and the countries of the Hellenic diaspora. Their long oral tradition provided a wellspring of folk songs and ballads, narrative poems, and early mystical church literature.

In the absence of a poetic mentor in his own time, Solomos turned to whatever he could salvage from the demotic past. For his textbooks in Greek prosody, he studied the two narrative masterpieces of the Cretan Renaissance (1600-1669): *Erofili* (c. 1585), by George Chortatsis, and, in particular, *Erotokritos* (1713; *The Erotocritos*, 1929), by Vitzenzos Kornaros, an epic romance of 10,052 lines. These works, in addition to an immense body of demotic folk songs, provided the linguistic guidelines for Solomos's instinctive sense of metrical balance and line structure. Through his poetic genius, the standard fifteen-syllable line of the demotic folk song gained deeper tones and new dimensions of meaning.

Written in 1823, shortly after his first lessons with Trikoupis, *Imnos is tin Eleftherian* (1823; *The Hymn to Liberty*, 1825), a poem of 158 quatrains and Solomos's first work in modern Greek, received immediate international recognition. Among its early admirers were Victor Hugo, Alphonse de Lamartine, and François-René de Chateaubriand, while Johann Wolfgang von Goethe hailed the young Greek as "the Byron of the East." The first few quatrains of *The Hymn to Liberty* were soon put to music and, after Solomos's death in 1857, were established as the national anthem of the new republic.

Solomos's major accomplishments, however, began to take shape only after 1824. During these years, many of them spent in Corfu, he completed his most sustained and influential poems: "Sack of Psara," "The Dream," *Lambros* (1834, 1859), "The Poisoned Girl," "The Nun," *To Kritikos* (1859; the Cretan), and *Porphyras* (1859). He completed the third sketch of *Eleftheri poliorkimeni* (1859; the free besieged) in 1848. This poem preoccupied him for nearly twenty years and is considered his finest and most mature work. In the last version of *Eleftheri poliorkimeni* one can detect the outline of Solomos's entire poetic development, from the early patriotic eulogies to the adoration of nature that characterized his middle period to the intense mysticism that infused his later works.

It is characteristic if unfortunate that most of the aforementioned poems are, to greater or lesser degrees, fragmentary or incomplete. Nevertheless, poetically as well as linguistically, Solomos achieved his goals, giving the vernacular of his people a firm base of inspiration and poetic invention for generations to follow.

AN ISOLATED STRUGGLE FOR EXPRESSION

In 1824, one year after the appearance of Solomos's *The Hymn to Liberty*, Andreas Kalvos (1792-1869) published ten poems in a volume titled *I Lira* (lyre) and in 1826 another collection of ten poems under the title *Lirika* (lyrics). These two thin books represent his only contribution to Greek poetry, but of their generation, these twenty poems had an impact on twentieth century Greek poetry second only to that of Solomos. Kalvos, also from Zakynthos, was born six years before Solomos, in 1792. Kalvos's mother was an aristocrat of the Zantiot landed gentry, while his father was a villager who could not adjust to the aristocratic way of life. When Kalvos was only ten years old, his father took him and his younger brother away from their birthplace and their mother to live in Livorno, Italy. Kalvos never saw his mother again. After his father's death in 1812, Kalvos settled for a short time in Florence, where he worked as a private tutor. There, he met Ugo Foscolo, the eminent Italian-Greek poet and libertarian, who hired Kalvos as his personal secretary.

In 1816, Kalvos dedicated his first poem to Napoleon Bonaparte. What is significant about his first composition is not the dedication or the subject matter, but the poet's decision to write in Greek. Kalvos had no formal knowledge of written or spoken Greek; his everyday means of communication was Italian. As a result, the diction of the poem is strained and uneven, mixing elements of demotic, classical, and purist Greek. Still, the poem embodies a potency of expression that foreshadows Kalvos's later achievements.

By 1820, Kalvos had lived in Zakynthos, Italy, Switzerland, and England, where he parted company with Foscolo. Kalvos then returned to Florence to become a member of the Carbonari, the most radical and progressive political force in Italy at the time. He was so active that the Italian government banished him from the country in the year of his return. Having gone back to Geneva, Switzerland, in 1821, Kalvos immediately involved himself with the movement for Greek independence. There, among the Philhellenes, he attempted to coordinate a revival of classical Greek culture with the movement for Greek independence.

By then twenty-nine years old, Kalvos had spent his most impressionable years among devoted if not fanatic European intellectuals. For these French and English Philhellenes, the independence of Greece symbolized a return to the ancient glory that had spawned Western civilization. While in Europe, Kalvos shared this political fervor. In his poetry, however, Greece was to be transformed into a spiritual landscape of magical and mythical elements.

In 1824, while still residing in Geneva, Kalvos issued *I Lira*. It is noteworthy that these ten poems were accompanied by detailed commentary, footnotes, and a lexicon, all in French. It was important to Kalvos that his audience be international and that his poems communicate universal messages, even though they expressed patriotic sentiments in support of the Greek revolution. His second collection, *Lirika*, was published in 1826 in Paris, where he lived for one year before his first return to Greece after twenty-four years of an active but difficult absence. Kalvos went directly to Nafplion, the first capital of the new state and a hotbed of political activity. He was, however, quickly disillusioned and left after a few days. His abrupt departure from Nafplion marked the end of his involvement with the movement for Greek independence. Embittered by the political infighting that he encountered in Nafplion, he also stopped writing poetry.

For the next twenty-six years, Kalvos lived in Corfu (not far from Solomos), where he taught, wrote philosophical articles, and eventually became a professor at the Ionian Academy. Little else of his life there is known except that his temperament was irascible, and his poetic silence was absolute. In 1852, after having been expelled from the Ionian Academy, Kalvos departed once again, this time for Great Britain, where he spent the last years of his life. In this self-imposed exile, he married an Englishwoman, helped her run a girl's school, and translated religious texts into English for the Anglican Church. Kalvos died in 1869 and was buried in Louth, England.

In his poetry, Kalvos attempted to release his exile's longing for a free fatherland. His idealistic vision of Greece was rooted in the austere mythological world of Pindar. Often Kalvos mentions the Olympian gods—not for ornament but to indicate the living presence of a timeless mythic reality. His twenty odes extol the struggle for liberty, the virtue of a heroic death, and similarly exalted themes characteristic of the Romantic poetry that was flooding Europe throughout the early nineteenth century. Kalvos's distinctive genius emerged not from his subject matter but from his unique mode of expression. He confronted the same problem that challenged Solomos—isolation from the mother tongue—but Kalvos's solution was drastically different.

Whereas other poets of this period tried to unite form and romantic emotion in harmony, Kalvos accentuated their opposition. In contrast to the harmonic, lilting flow of Solomos's poems, Kalvos's odes were classically concise and rigid. He utilized a strict verse form (unrhymed stanzas of four seven-syllable lines and a last line of five syllables) modeled after the Pindaric odes. With severe formal simplicity, Kalvos expressed his intense longing for an end to his own exile.

Although Kalvos had a thorough knowledge of classical Greek, the vernacular was a foreign language to him. His twenty poems are studded with words and phrases borrowed from classical lexicons and old texts. Though the syntax is basically demotic, his inclusion of archaisms and grammatical elements of classical Greek reveal his need to create his own rules out of a language that had many conflicting personalities: classical, Byzantine, purist, demotic. The undercurrent of Kalvos's lyrical genius infuses this awkward, artificial language with poetic substance and vitality.

Though Kalvos was far from prolific, and his devotion to the art of poetry short-lived, his work served as a stepping-stone for many Greek poets of the twentieth century. Odysseus Elytis was one of the first modern Greek poets to discuss the contemporaneity of Kalvos's unusual technique, while George Seferis speculated as to what new peaks of poetic expression Kalvos would have reached if he had continued to write for the duration of his life. Kalvos finally received recognition as a major national poet when his burial place was moved from Great Britain to Zakynthos in 1960, a year that was officially declared as the Year of Kalvos.

KOSTIS PALAMAS

Kostis Palamas (1859-1943), a native of the Greek mainland (Missolonghi), is one of the greatest poets in the history of modern Greek literature. With his first publication of poems in 1886, he quickly surpassed his contemporaries and established himself as a central figure in Greek letters. In the poetry he wrote between 1880 and 1920, Palamas embodied the living heritage of Solomos and consolidated what his Ionian predecessor had left unfinished.

Throughout these years, Greek literary life broadened its perspectives beyond the limits of the Romantic school and the aging followers of Solomos. As founder of the New School of Athens, Palamas pioneered new directions in the development of a contemporary demotic poetry. Recognizing humanity's spiritual and social fragmentation in his own time, Palamas attempted to reconcile the divisive forces of twentieth century history through his poetry and critical studies in Greek and world literature.

While other poets at the turn of the century were able to adopt surface elements of the works of Solomos or the European Romantics, Palamas aspired to integrate the essence of these influences into the main body of his work. One of his greatest desires was to bring the demotic tradition into the mainstream of European art and literature. Palamas achieved his goal by looking in two complementary directions. For linguistic continuity, he turned to Solomos and the evolution of the demotic tradition, which, for Palamas, could be traced back from Solomos through *The Epic of Digenis Akritas* (1100-1150) to the epic narratives of Homer. Palamas's philosophical perspective, which is consistent throughout his work, emerged from a lifelong adoration of Goethe, who stirred Palamas to poetic inspiration and discipline much as Dante had awakened Solomos to his final purpose.

Although Romantics such as Lord Byron and Victor Hugo continued to influence Greek literature toward the end of the nineteenth century, of greater immediacy and impact for Palamas were the French movements, Parnassianism and Symbolism, while in his later years Palamas turned to the lyric mysticism of Rainer Maria Rilke. One could go on for pages listing the poets and thinkers whose works Palamas knew better and more intimately than any of his contemporaries in Greece. This vast accumulation of knowledge is unified by his ability to synthesize and subordinate these influences to the demands of his deep visionary voice.

After having published his first book of poems *Tragoudia tis patridos mou* (songs of my homeland), in

1886, Palamas titled his next volumes *O imnos tis Athinas* (1888; hymn to Athena) and *Ta matia tis psychis mou* (1892; the eyes of my soul), the latter a phrase borrowed from Solomos. This last choice of title indicates how strongly Palamas felt about establishing a bond of continuity between his own efforts and those of his Ionian predecessor. Unlike the epigones of Solomos, Palamas's works were not mere imitations of the father of Greek poetry; instead, Palamas used Solomos's works as stepping-stones to radical innovations in the poetry of his own time.

With *Iamvi ke anapesti* (iambs and anapests) in 1897, Palamas broke from the traditional demotic form of the fifteen-syllable line and, for the first time, introduced Symbolism into Greek poetry. In addition, the stanzaic structure of these poems (three quatrains each, composed of four interchanging anapestic and iambic lines) reveals the unmistakable mark of Kalvos. Indeed, Palamas was the first poet-critic not only to recognize Kalvos publicly as a major Greek poet, but also to acknowledge his poems as a determining influence on his own work.

In 1904, Palamas published *I asalefti zoi* (*Life Immovable*, 1919, 1921), a large collection of poems that included many written a decade earlier. At a critical stage in the evolution of a Greek poetic idiom, these new poems confirmed a world of poetic truth in a lyrical realization of the Greek poet's personal and historical endurance. The volume constituted Palamas's first mature attempt to create a unified metaphysical domain. In reference to these poems, the foremost scholar of Palamas, Thanasis Maskaleris, has maintained that "the whole collection is a song of all life elevated to the harmony and immutability of poetic sublimation."

Finally, it was in his long visionary poem, *O dodekalogos tou giftou* (1907; *The Twelve Words of the Gypsy*, 1964), that Palamas made his most sustained contribution to modern Greek poetry. Published in 1907, thirty-six years before his death in 1943, these twelve cantos of brilliant metrical diversity bring together the wisdom, lyricism, and visionary acuity that Palamas had been striving for in his constant struggle for self-expression and universal transference. The Gypsy-Musician, the protagonist of the poem, records his metamorphosis as a symbol for freedom and art,

against the historical background of Byzantine Greece prior to the conquest of Constantinople in 1453. First, through an agonizing process of renunciation, he becomes a Greek patriot who finally embraces a mystical vision that allows him to become a true Hellene—a citizen and teacher, not of one nation, but of all the world. Palamas's preoccupation with the universal emerges with great intensity throughout the poem. Once again, it is the poet's lyric genius that provides this poem with its greatest source of energy and impact. Permeating the poem is a dreamlike flow of time that foreshadows much of modern poetry's conscious disorder and disregard for the classical concept of chronological narrative. *The Twelve Words of the Gypsy* is an epico-lyrical dream narrative, certainly the first of its kind and quality in modern Greek literature.

By the time he died in 1943, Palamas had published eighteen volumes of poetry and nearly 2,500 essays and articles concerning Greek and world literature. Some critics have suggested that Palamas should be remembered primarily for his contribution as an incisive, knowledgeable critic, and not so much for his poetry. Today, however, there is little question among Greek poets and scholars of contemporary literature that his influence as a poet has been paramount. As Seferis was to observe not long after the death of Palamas: ". . . the work of Palamas is the landscape in which the total realization and resurrection of the Greek poetic idiom take place in life itself."

CONSTANTINE P. CAVAFY

By the turn of the century, Athens had evolved into the center of political, cultural, and intellectual life for the Greek people. The climate was often frenetic, sometimes violent. In 1901, the New Testament was published for the first time in demotic. Rioting was the initial response at the University of Athens. Such a translation was considered a sacrilege by the conservative establishment; students' lives were sacrificed, and many were seriously wounded. At this time, demoticism began to stand for much more than simply a radical change in the language; it suggested social and political alternatives as well. Until recently, demotic was the official language of the Greek Communist and Socialist parties, while *katharevousa* was employed by Greek royalists and other right-wing parties.

Another orientation, unassociated with the demotic-purist controversy, was needed in order to awaken Greek poetry to the universal crisis of meaning and art that was preoccupying the masters of twentieth century world poetry. While the demoticists were still singing the praises of the Greek landscape and Greek history in terms of borrowed European models, their contemporaries abroad were weighing the existence and validity of the poetic word itself. The demotic tradition—alone or in combination with European models of Romanticism, Parnassianism, or Symbolism—no longer sufficed as a "center" for Greek poetry. It took a Greek poet who spent practically his entire life outside Greece, in Alexandria, Egypt, to perceive this problem and propel Greek poetry into the mainstream of twentieth century poetry: Constantine P. Cavafy (1863-1933). Untouched by the constant turmoil and linguistic confusion in mainland Greece, Cavafy created a mythic world that enabled him to see beyond the temporal issues into the heart of the universal. From his vast readings in Hellenic and Alexandrian history, Cavafy pieced together a poetry not of glory or heroic conquests, but of defeats, human frailties, decadence, and the often ironic tragedies behind every conquest and success. As the poet and critic Howard Moss has observed, Cavafy's slim oeuvre embodied "the commonplace life of the streets and the splendor of ancient tales and legends, in which the ordinary man of the first could become the unwitting hero of the second" (*Whatever Is Moving*, 1981).

Cavafy was born in Alexandria in 1863; his family was of a long line of wealthy Alexandrian aristocrats. When the father died in 1869, the Cavafy family inherited the dignity of their lineage but not its fortune. Three years later, at the age of nine, Cavafy began his most extended stay outside Alexandria. Hoping to find better opportunities for her older sons, the mother took Constantine and his brothers to Great Britain. After seven years there, the Cavafy family returned to its beloved city. At the age of sixteen, Cavafy was fluent in English and French and precociously familiar with European history and culture. With the exception of two years of forced exile in Constantinople and four short trips to Europe and Greece, Cavafy spent the remainder of his uneventful life as a civil servant in Alexandria.

Later in his life, Cavafy referred to the poems he wrote before 1900 as "trash." Most of this verse was clearly a result of both his early exposure to French and English Romanticism and his initial use of *katharevousa*. In contradiction to his blunt rejection of his early work, however, several poems written between 1896 and 1900 indicate another direction in his poetics that eventually led to masterpieces such as "The God Abandons Anthony" and "Alexandrian Kings." During these years, Cavafy wrote five poems that characterized the fruits of this metamorphosis: "Walls," "Candles," "The First Step," "The Horses of Achilles," and "The Funeral of Sarpedon." His early romantic tendencies vanished, to be replaced by a unique, historical sensibility that preferred the stark truths of man's ironic failures and tragic dignity. Between 1900 and 1904, his art came into full flower, with poems such as "Thermopylae," "The City," and, in 1904, "Waiting for the Barbarians," the poem that would place him beside T. S. Eliot, William Butler Yeats, and Ezra Pound. In this same year, he printed a pamphlet of fourteen poems, including the aforementioned, for private distribution to friends and loyal readers. During this period, Cavafy was also writing more lyrical and erotic poems such as "Voices," "Desires," "He Swears," and "One Night."

In his maturity, Cavafy delineated three categories to which all of his completed poems could be individually referred: historical, erotic, and philosophical. Although these boundaries may apply to the form and manifest content of his poems, beneath the surface there is a constant overlap and interaction among these three categories.

What Cavafy called his historical poems had the greatest impact. They all emerge from an ancient city which, in the poet's mind, is of mythic though always human proportions. They are gestures of history that reveal the repetitive conditions of human existence and the humble dignity required to "bid her farewell, the Alexandria that is leaving." In 1911-1912, Cavafy printed three poems that established him as Greece's first poet with a thoroughly modern sensibility: "The God Abandons Anthony," "Philhellene," and "Alexandrian Kings." In this last poem, Cavafy's ironic bite could not be more incisive or less understated. Of the Alexandrians praising Caesarion, Cavafy observes:

Him they hailed oftener than his younger brothers,
him they hailed King of Kings.

The Alexandrians understood of course that
these were only theatrics and mere words.

In the service of his irony, Cavafy developed a new poetic idiom that cultivated, for the first time in modern Greek poetry, some of the qualities of prose. The musical cadences of the demotic tradition are absent in these antimelodic poems. Their characteristic rhythm is that of a man speaking in a matter-of-fact voice, objectively recording the tragic and necessary ironies of the human condition.

Although his mode of expression is fundamentally demotic, Cavafy often adds a touch of realism by including colloquial phrases of *katharevousa* that had become just as much a part of everyday speech as demotic. In keeping with his devotion to "Mythic Alexandria," he also gave linguistic authenticity to his narrative poems with his discreet use of the Alexandrian idiom and spelling.

Cavafy's frank, erotic poems express irrepressible memories of sensual longings that excite the senses but torture the mind. Although many of these poems reflect his much-discussed homosexuality, Cavafy's eroticism has a universal relevance. Often, his seemingly distant but detailed recollections of fleeting erotic encounters provide the only redeeming element in the otherwise monotonous flow of time and destiny.

Cavafy's philosophical poems, such as "Thermopylae," are often historical as well: Here, the categories break down. As a whole, this group reflects Cavafy's belief in the ineluctability of fate and in the dignity to be won when humans encounter and accept the dramas of their tragic nature.

The first publicly available edition of Cavafy's collected poems did not appear until 1935, the same year that Seferis issued his third collection of poems, *Mythistorema* (English translation, 1967). Seferis was thirty-five years old at the time; Cavafy had died two years before, at the age of seventy. Seferis was perhaps the first poet of his generation to recognize and understand Cavafy's essential breakthrough into modern poetry. In the following decades, Cavafy's Alexandrian voice became increasingly influential; today, widely translated, he is recognized as one of the major poets of the twentieth century. Ahead of his time, in almost magical isolation, Cavafy paved the way for a new generation of poets who would make Greek poetry one of the richest literatures in modern Europe.

ANGELOS SIKELIANOS

In the early years of the twentieth century, most young Greek poets of the mainland were overwhelmed by a Baudelairean obsession with ennui and self-annihilation. Born on the Ionian island of Leucas, Angelos Sikelianos (1884-1951) was an important exception. Disregarding the melancholy of his contemporaries, Sikelianos celebrated life and death through intensely lyrical realizations of ancient oracular mythology and folk religion. Rooted in the pre-Socratic metaphysics of Ancient Greece, his best poems unveil the confluence of the natural and the supernatural. Sikelianos believed the poet must assume the role of prophet, oracle, and teacher; so strong was this belief that he actively promoted the reestablishment of Delphi as a contemporary center for mystagogues of all persuasions. Here, Sikelianos envisioned the emergence of "the universal soul of the world." Although this vision was never fully realized, it provided him with the spiritual fortitude and poetic resources to create an affirmative alternative to the Greek version of Baudelaire's "generation of the damned."

The pre-Socratic tradition remained archetypal for Sikelianos throughout his life. The teachings of Pythagoras, the Mysteries of Eleusis, Orphism and the cult of Dionysus, and the mantic center at Delphi represented the four main bodies of mystic wisdom that Sikelianos sought to enshrine in his poetry. He perceived this wisdom as the primal undercurrent of the Greek Christian ethos; consequently, Sikelianos had no qualms about including "my Christ, and my Dionysus" in one breath. Similarly, in "The Village Wedding," the poet invokes both the Christian "Word of God" and "Leto giving birth to Apollo. . . ." In the folk rituals of Greek Orthodoxy, Sikelianos discovered the subconscious continuation of the religious principles he derived from the pre-Socratic world of ancient Greece.

From the rich language of his demotic heritage,

Sikelianos assembled his poetic visions. His vocabulary is rooted in the vernacular, particularly in the dialectal variations of his birthplace in the Ionian Islands. In early poems such as "Return" and "The Horses of Achilles," Sikelianos experimented with free-verse alterations of the normal pattern of modern Greek metrics (the fifteen-syllable line). The new rhythms he created served to stress his central motifs of iconoclastic and pantheistic concerns. It is unfortunate that translations cannot capture the forceful and intensely lyrical cadences that flow, unimpeded, through the original Greek of these poems, for it was in his rhapsodies of religious feeling that Sikelianos established himself as a virtuoso of modern Greek poetry.

For the most part, Sikelianos was a traditional poet. By 1920, he had rejected free verse, focusing his attention instead on formal structures of poetic composition: sonnets, fifteen-syllable couplets, and other strict forms of his own devising. Of his short poems, "Songs of Victory I" (a series inspired by the Balkan Wars), "Pan," "Thalero," and "The Mother of Dante" are among his best. By 1917, with the completion of "Mother of God," Sikelianos also had mastered the long poem. "Mother of God" has been praised as the most musical poem written in Greek since the death of Solomos.

Three years before the composition of "Mother of God," Sikelianos's beloved sister, Penelope, died. In the poem, Sikelianos gathers symbols of Christianity, matriarchal goddesses, divinities of the natural world, and the spirit of his dead sister to provide a new consciousness of death that might release humans from their futile efforts to comprehend death in their own limited terms. The poet's reconciliation with death is a central concern in his poems written between 1927 and 1942.

Sikelianos's output during these years was sporadic, for he began to devote his energies to establishing a Delphic university and Delphic festivals that would feature performances of classical Greek tragedies, exhibitions of folk art, Byzantine music and dancing, even naked athletic contests in the original stadium of ancient Delphi. Though the combined efforts of Sikelianos and his wealthy American wife, Eva Palmer, were originally rewarded with success, the venture was doomed to failure by eventual lack of support

and the German occupation of Greece from 1940 to 1945.

From 1935 to 1942, however, Sikelianos made great strides in his poetry. The symbolic texture is tighter and the language more deeply reflective in poems such as "The Sacred Way," "Attic," "Apology of Solon," and "Agraphon." In the last ten years of his life, Sikelianos turned to the composition of lengthy tragedies that were unwieldy and difficult to stage. His zenith as a mystical poet with a tragic vision had already been reached in "Mother of God" and in the shorter poems written during the 1930's and early 1940's.

By the time of his death in 1951, Sikelianos had established an international reputation. In 1946, he had been nominated by the Society of Greek Writers for the Nobel Prize, and a year later he was elected president of this same society. Many of his finest poems had already been translated into Italian, French, and English. In its lyrical spontaneity and its religious identification with nature, his work has been instructive and influential for many Greek poets of subsequent decades.

KOSTAS VARNALIS

Another poet whose work remained unscathed by the engulfing despair that characterized Greek poetry in the 1920's was Kostas Varnalis, born in Pirgos, Bulgaria, in 1884. As a student in Bulgaria, Varnalis nurtured an idealized vision of Greece, sustained by his early and intensive studies in the classics. His first poetic compositions were in *katharevousa*, with traditional form, meter, and rhyme. When he arrived in Greece for university studies at the age of nineteen, his romantic conception of Greece soon gave way to a bitter and ironic realism.

From 1913 on, Varnalis chose to write only in demotic, completely rejecting his early purist orientation. Moreover, like Palamas and Sikelianos, he began to accept the influences of the Parnassians and the Symbolists. Adhering to the strict forms of the sonnet and the quatrain, Varnalis reconstructed his dreams of classical glory. Images of ancient Greece abound in poems such as "Alcibiades," "Orestes," and "Aphrodite." In this last poem, however, the satiric mood of his later and more significant work begins to surface. Sarcasm, parody, and invective satire eventually became the vehicles for Varnalis to express his growing disenchantment with modern Greece and the futility of his earlier nostalgic hopes.

By 1920, after a year of studies in the postwar atmosphere of Paris, Varnalis came to embrace dialectical materialism and the Marxist ideology of historical and social change. The tragic outcome of the Balkan Wars and the Asia Minor Catastrophe in 1922 solidified his new political radicalism. Nevertheless, his finest poems lacked the bombast and rhetoric that characterized the emerging wave of leftist writings in the early twentieth century.

While still in Paris, Varnalis had written "The Burning Light," a poem in three parts which combined his early lyricism with poignant satire. Prometheus, Christ, and a contemporary leader of the proletariat are depicted as carriers of the burning light through ages of darkness and repression. Introducing himself, the leader shouts: "for I am the child of Necessity and the mature offspring of Wrath." "The Burning Light," published in 1922, was the first important left-wing poem to be written in Greece.

Varnalis's next major project was "The Enslaved Besieged," an obvious parody of Solomos's major poem, *Eleftheri poliorkimeni* (the free besieged). Divided into four sections, the poem is long and epic in scope. The poet lashes out against an ideology that promoted the mass acceptance of enslavement and fascism. Varnalis described the essence of the poem as "antiwar and anti-idealistic."

Apart from his original poetry, Varnalis is also widely known in Greece for his brilliant and witty translations of Aristophanes. In addition, Varnalis wrote a great deal of literary criticism informed by his Marxist beliefs. He died in 1969 during the dictatorship of the Colonels (1967-1974).

KOSTAS KARYOTAKIS

The life and death of Kostas Karyotakis (1896-1928) had two strikingly different consequences for the development of twentieth century Greek poetry. His reputation as a melancholy and dispirited poet along with his dramatic suicide in 1928 inspired a large following of poets who, unlike Sikelianos or Varnalis, remained outside the mainstream of modern Greek poetry. Karyotakis's poetry itself, however, became a strong undercurrent in this mainstream, from which

emerged the voices of Seferis (1900-1971), Elytis (1911-1996), Yannis Ritsos (1909-1990), and Andreas Embirikos (1901-1974). In contrast to these strongly individual poets, the epigones of Karyotakis were content to repeat clichés of romantic and confessional despair. Indeed, in recent years the term *karyotakismos*, or Karyotakism, has denoted the Greek offspring of Baudelaire's "generation of the damned." Whereas their last echoes were heard in about 1940, the poems of Karyotakis continue to influence even the current generation of leading Greek poets, such as Lefteris Poulios, Yannis Kondos, Vasilis Steriades, and Jenny Mastoraki. It is therefore essential that Karyotakism be clearly distinguished from Karyotakis's poetry which has established itself as a haunting presence on the contemporary scene.

Karyotakis wrote and published three books of poems in his lifetime. The first, *O ponos tou anthropou ke ton pragmaton* (1919; the pain of men and things), maps out the domain of his concerns; at every destination there is fear and oblivion. In his second book, *Nipenthe* (1921), Karyotakis continued his stark explorations of hopeless and self-deceiving lives. Published in 1927, one year before his death, his last book, *Elegia ke satires* (elegies and satires), was both his finest and most unsettling. In its pages were grim and mournful expressions of a voice that found no solace in demotic or classical literature. Arthur Rimbaud, Charles Baudelaire, and Jules Laforgue influenced Karyotakis more than his Hellenic heritage. For Karyotakis, human existence was a limitless void. Beauty existed, but only as a mocking reminder of "the tears, the sweat, and the vast sky's nostalgia, all the bleak wastelands."

In the structured verse of rhymed stanzas, he recreated the emotional abyss that eventually overpowered him. However, in this formal style that exemplified the end of French Romanticism in Greek poetry, Karyotakis experimented, taking unusual liberties with diction, imagery, and rhythms, for only by pushing to its limits this already exhausted poetics could he make room for the utter desolation he so effectively expressed.

In place of the self-pity that abounded in the works of his contemporaries, Karyotakis adopted a satirical self-abnegation that would not allow for sentimental flirtations with romantic despair. His unique brand of satire is humiliating and tragic. Most of his images are derived from Greek life in the provinces (which he regarded as a kind of Hell). In this landscape, Karyotakis found his characters, bringing to the surface the painstaking routine of their empty lives.

The actual story of this poet's death hauntingly reflects the burden of having been the most profound Greek spokesperson of the "generation of the damned." On the night of July 21, 1928, the poet attempted, for several hours, to drown himself in the sea. The next day, having purchased a pistol, he sat in a seaside tavern, the Heavenly Garden, wrote a suicide note, and then, in the shade of a nearby eucalyptus tree, shot himself. Like his poems, the details of his death are satiric and uncomfortably self-conscious. He concluded his suicide note with the following postscript: "I advise all those who swim well not to try death by drowning. . . . At the first opportunity I shall write of my impressions as a drowned man." Although many younger poets were drawn to his work by the dramatic nature of his death, others were deeply disturbed by the poetic impasse that his poems exemplified.

GENERATION OF 1930

In 1931, at the age of thirty-one, Seferis published a small book of poems titled *Strofi* (*Turning Point*, 1967). In its subject matter and tone, *Turning Point* signaled the first significant turn away from the unrelenting, romantic despair of the previous generation; in spirit and sensibility, these poems were much closer to the tragic dignity of Cavafy. In fact, throughout his life, Seferis considered Cavafy to be his truest and, sometimes, most overwhelming forerunner. Seferis became the primary force in the modernization of Greek poetry for the next twenty-five years.

GEORGE SEFERIS

George Seferis (the pen name of Giorgos Stylianon Seferiades) was born in 1900, in Smyrna, a city of Asia Minor widely known as an intellectual center for Greeks of the Hellenic diaspora. In 1914, the Seferiades family moved to Athens, where the poet completed his secondary education, and from 1918 to 1924, he studied law in Paris. Encouraged by his father, a professor of law, to familiarize himself with all facets of

European customs and thought, Seferis spent an additional year (1924-1925) in London, where he first became acquainted with the works of Eliot. During these formative years abroad, Seferis became increasingly aware of the intellectual and poetical forces that changed the accepted forms of literature soon after World War I. As a young student in Paris, he learned of the Asia Minor Catastrophe and the violent destruction of his beloved birthplace, Smyrna. In his later poetry, this experience helped define one of his central motifs: the constant urge to return to a home that exists only in terms of a frayed and bitter memory.

Seferis returned to Athens in 1926 and immediately entered the diplomatic service, in which he made a lifelong career. From 1936 to 1962, his work took him to Albania, Egypt, South Africa, Italy, Turkey, Lebanon, Syria, Jordan, and Iraq. His last post was as ambassador to Great Britain from 1957 to 1962.

In 1946, Seferis was awarded the coveted Palamas Prize. In 1960, he received an honorary doctorate from Cambridge University, and in 1963, he won the Nobel Prize in Literature. Honorary doctorates soon followed from Oxford, Thessaloníki, and Princeton universities. Finally, an honorary fellowship from the American Academy of Arts and Sciences gave him the opportunity to study, lecture, and write for six months as a poet in residence at Princeton University (1966). From this time onward, he lived in retirement in Athens until his death on September 20, 1971.

Although unique in their content and austere tone, the poems of *Turning Point* and those of Seferis's subsequent collection *I sterna* (1932; *The Cistern*, 1967) were thoroughly traditional in form. In particular, Seferis proved himself a contemporary master of the fifteen-syllable line in the longest and most lyrical poem of *Turning Point*, "Erotikos Logos." The influence of both *The Erotocritos* and Solomos is evident in Seferis's melodic and sensitive use of the demotic language. Unlike the narcissistic ego that is heard in the poetry of Karyotakis, Seferis's voice is collective, expressing a personal drama that is elevated to the general character of universal tragedy.

It was not until 1935, however, with the publication of *Mythistorema* (English translation, 1960), that Seferis was able to inject the poetry of his time with elements that would alter decisively the course of modern Greek poetry. Perhaps the most significant element that Seferis introduced in the poems of this collection was a free-verse form perfectly suited to a simple but intensely lyrical demotic idiom and spelling. Sikelianos had experimented with free verse but only for a short period. Varnalis also had abandoned free verse early in his career, while Karyotakis took few chances in the framework of his European influences. In contrast, from 1935 to the end of his career, Seferis used free verse almost exclusively.

Mythistorema, which can mean either "novel" or "myth" of history, consists of twenty-four parts. The physical and spiritual landscape of this poem is rooted in Greek mythology. In the persona of the poet himself, the characters who travel endlessly in the dry world of *Mythistorema* have been lost in other times as well: the Argonauts, Odysseus, Elpenor, Orestes, Agamemnon, Astyanax. As they search for signs of life and light, their dreamlike anxieties reflect the real anxieties of contemporary man:

> I woke up with this marble head in my hands;
> it exhausts my elbows and I don't know where
> to put it down.

In Seferis's next collection of poems, *Imerologio katastromatos I* (1940, *Logbook I*, 1967), the apprehension of war is accompanied by a sure and tragic awareness of whom its victims will be. There is an atmosphere of anxiety and decay, but also of historical resolve and the courage to endure, a persistent characteristic of Cavafy's finest poems as well. In the last poem of this volume, "The King of Asine," Seferis presents the image of an ancient mask behind which is the void and "the poet a void." Unlike the rootless desperation of Karyotakis, however, the despairing feelings in this poem are mythic in context and therefore more historically enduring and tragic. This mythic aspect persists in all of Seferis's poetry.

Imerologio katastromatos II (*Logbook II*, 1967), completed in 1944, is a poetic summation of Seferis's bitter war experiences. Written in the places of his diplomatic exile during the war, many of these poems are dated with the names of the foreign cities that provided his exiled government with political asylum while the

Germans occupied Greece: Transvaal, October, 1941; Pretoria, 1942; Cairo, August, 1943. The speaker of these poems, who speaks for many, expresses the fragmented identity of the wandering exile. *Logbook I* and *Logbook II* record Seferis's journey through the spiritual netherworld of World War II Europe.

In 1946, Seferis completed a major poem that had been incubating for years. He titled it "Thrush," after the name of a ship sunk by the Germans in the harbor of Poros, the island where Seferis actually wrote the poem. The ship is a symbolic vehicle for the continuation of a voyage that Seferis had begun to chart in *Logbook I*. The tapestry of images and symbols in this poem reflects the influence of Eliot and especially of Cavafy, with "beds . . . that can haunt you" and "images in the mirror, bodies once alive, their sensuality."

The publication of this four-part work (Seferis's longest poem) in 1946 was followed by a poetic silence that lasted for ten years. A decade later, in 1955, *Emerologio katastromatos III* (*Logbook III*, 1967) appeared—another mythic journey of wandering spirits, inspired by Seferis's close ties to the island of Cyprus. In the best-known poem of this collection, "Helen," myth surfaces as actuality; Seferis addresses Teucer (brother of Ajax in the *Iliad*) as his own brother, and finally asks him: "What is god? What is not? And what is there between them?"

Although several collections of Seferis's poems were issued between 1940 and 1961, after *Logbook III*, no new poems appeared until 1966, with the publication of *Tria krifa piimata* (*Three Secret Poems*, 1969). These relatively short poems are regarded by many critics as Seferis's most esoteric. His central motifs of light and dark, which are heard with a disturbing clarity in "Thrush," are emphasized again in the staccato verse of Seferis's last major composition.

Throughout his life, Seferis also contributed enormously to the growth of modern Greek poetry with his critical writings. *Dokimes* (1962; the collected essays of George Seferis) includes penetrating and contemporary appraisals of *The Erotocritos*, Cavafy, Kalvos, Solomos, the sixteenth century painter El Greco, the Homeric hymns, and an important record of Seferis's discussions with Eliot. Seferis's principal prose works are *Treis meres sta monasteria tes Kappadokias* (1953;

three days in the monasteries of Cappadocia), *Delphi* (1962; English translation, 1963), *Discours de Stockholm* (1964), and *'E glossa stèn poiésé mas* (1965) and volumes of personal diaries which reveal the painstaking groundwork that preceded each of his published poems. Also significant were his translations into Greek of Rimbaud, Paul Valéry, Paul Éluard, Yeats, Pound, Archibald MacLeish, and, in particular, *The Waste Land* (1922) of Eliot. In one of his essays, Seferis pointed to the three peaks of modern Greek poetry: Solomos, Kalvos, and Cavafy. By consensus, his own name must be added to this list.

ANDREAS EMBIRIKOS

While Seferis linked modern Greek poetry with its rich native heritage, another strong current in modern Greek verse was defined by its radical break with indigenous traditions. Surrealism made its first appearance in Greece in 1935 with the publication of a series of prose poems titled *Ipsikaminos* (blast furnace), by Andreas Embirikos (1901-1975). From 1925 to 1931, Embirikos lived in Paris, closely allying himself with André Breton and his school of Surrealist painters and poets. During these crucial years in the European capital of artistic and literary activity, Embirikos also devoted himself to the study of psychoanalysis.

Born on September 2, 1901, in Braila, Romania, Embirikos was brought to Athens in his infancy. There, he completed his primary and secondary education, going on to study philosophy at the University of Athens. In 1922, he moved to London, where he worked three years for a steamship company owned by his family of international shipbuilders and shipowners. After these years in London, he joined his father in France until 1932, when he returned to Greece. In 1934, Embirikos resigned from the family business and established himself as Greece's first practicing psychoanalyst. He retired in 1951, devoting the rest of his life to writing and photography.

The poems of *Ipsikaminos* were received in Athens with ridicule and critical antagonism. Few were able to understand the often startling but productive method of "automatic writing." In the poem "Light on a Whale," Embirikos begins: "The original form of woman was the braiding of two dinosaurnecks." By juxtaposing images that seemed to bear little or no relationship to

each other, the poet was not simply trying to surprise or shock the reader. Rather, his intent was to provide a flow of subliminal motifs drawn from the creative and unifying wellspring of the subconscious.

Embirikos's preoccupation with female sensuality and its mythic origins provided a focal point for his later growth as a poet who could no longer make use of the formless nature of pure Surrealism. In his second collection of poems, *Endohora* (1945; the hinterland), symbols of the Freudian libido appear frequently and with great urgency: "erupting shock of a huge volcano," "the canals' lips," "a very small daughter . . . fondling the day's nipples," "the breasts of youth," "petals of pleasure." These sexual images come to life in mystical exaltations of eroticism that bind humanity to nature in joyful and immortal embraces. A master of both demotic and purist, Embirikos often used puns and other forms of wordplay to bolster the latent meanings of his consistently Freudian interpretation of humans and nature in the modern world. *Endohora* consists primarily of poems written in highly structured but idiosyncratic verse forms. This emerging need for form indicated his growing distance from pure Surrealism. Nevertheless, Embirikos always perceived himself as a child of Surrealism.

From the beginning of his lifelong involvement with poetry, Embirikos repudiated the self-annihilating pessimism of Karyotakis. For Embirikos, life always triumphs in love—the spiritual apprehension of the universally erotic. As a result, his poetry also rejected the tragic necessity of guilt voiced by Cavafy and Seferis.

Embirikos was not alone in his discovery of Surrealism. There were other important Greek poets who also used the principles of Surrealism to create poems of intense vision and lyric power. Among the most outstanding of his contemporaries were Nikos Engonopoulos (1910-1985) and Nikos Gatsos (1911-1992), whose only book, *Amorgos* (1943), has been translated four times into English.

ODYSSEUS ELYTIS

In 1935, a new literary periodical titled *Nea grammata*, published under the direction of Andreas Karandonis and George Katsimbalis, began to promote the forthcoming masters of twentieth century Greek poetry. Finding an audience responsive to their work, Cavafy, Sikelianos, Seferis, Gatsos, and Embirikos appeared frequently in its pages. Toward the end of 1935, *Nea grammata* also published the first poems of Odysseus Elytis, who until his death in 1996 reached new heights of poetic expression with each passing decade.

Born on November 2, 1911, in Iraklion, Crete, Elytis (the pen name of Odysseus Alepoudhelis) was truly a child of the Aegean Islands. Even though his family moved to Athens in 1914, Elytis spent his summers on the Aegean Islands between Crete and Lesbos, where his family had originated. It is the natural and historical elements of this brilliant, ancient landscape that later provided the foreground for his most important achievements in poetry. After completing his secondary education in 1928, Elytis decided to study law at the University of Athens in 1930. At about the same time, he began reading the poems of the French Surrealist Éluard, who opened a whole new vista of poetic experience and feeling for the young, impressionable Elytis. In 1935, while still a student at law school, he heard Embirikos's first lecture on Surrealism and its potential significance for modern Greek poetry. During this year, which also saw the first important publication of his poems, Elytis withdrew from law school, having chosen to devote the rest of his life to poetry and art.

Even the advent of World War II could not deter Elytis from pursuing his dream. In 1940, he served as a second lieutenant on the Albanian frontier to help organize Greek resistance against Benito Mussolini's impending invasion of Greek territory. Elytis's experience at the front became the subject of a long elegiac poem, *Azma iroiko ke penthimo yia ton hameno anthipolohago tis Alvanias* (*Heroic and Elegiac Song for the Lost Second Lieutenant of the Albanian Campaign*, 1965), which was first published in 1945. Later, discouraged by the violent repercussions of the war in his own country (the Greek Civil War, 1946-1949), he went to live in Paris (1948-1952). There, he spent much of his time among poets and painters such as Breton, Éluard, Tristan Tzara, René Char, Giuseppe Ungaretti, Henri Matisse, Pablo Picasso, Alberto Giacometti, and Giorgio de

Odysseus Elytis (AP/Wide World Photos)

Chirico. Many of these artists had also befriended Embirikos, who was to be Elytis's first Greek mentor and a lifelong friend. Since 1952, Elytis has lived primarily in Greece, traveling once to the United States in 1961 and shortly afterward to the Soviet Union. During this period, he has played a leading role in Greek literary and artistic life as president of the Greek Ballet (1956-1958) and as a governing member of Karolos Koun Art Theater (1955-1956). In addition to writing art criticism, he has also translated the works of Éluard, Pierre-Jean Jouve, Federico García Lorca, Rimbaud, Vladimir Mayakovsky, and others. Elytis's contribution to modern poetry, increasingly recognized abroad as well as in his native land, was decisively acknowledged with the Nobel Prize in Literature in 1979.

With the publication of his first two books, *Prosanatolizmi* (orientations) in 1939 and *Ilios o protos, mazi me tis parallayies pano se mian ahtidha* (sun the first) in 1943, Elytis unveiled a poetry of Surrealistic inspiration brimming with images from his mystical experiences of the Aegean Islands. His early relationship with

Surrealism served as a catalyst, allowing him to express the inherently lyric spirit not only of his youth but also of Greece itself. The tone of these poems is highly personal, full of celebration, movement, and metamorphosis. In his poem, "Windows Toward the Fifth Season," for example, Elytis exemplifies his belief in the sensuality of poetic thought: "How beautiful she is! She has taken on the form of that thought/ which feels her when she feels it devoted to her. . . ."

Elytis's major poem, *Heroic and Elegiac Song for the Lost Second Lieutenant of the Albanian Campaign*, depicts in patriotic and lyrical language the Greek defense against Mussolini's invasion of Greece in October of 1940. The Italian invasion is remembered in Greece for its unifying effect on the Greek people. Against seemingly insurmountable odds, the Greeks managed to defeat the Italians quickly, pushing them back into Albania. In the midst of the oppressive years that followed, Elytis felt the need to account for and praise this sudden burst of mass heroism. Divided into twelve cantos, this poem, fertile with images of a living landscape and its magical properties, takes the reader through a verbal metamorphosis from dead body to the living and immortal spirit. By the end of the poem, the lost soldier has been resurrected and deified as "He ascends alone and blazing with light." These twelve songs mark the poet's first important encounter with the tragic elements that distiguish the poems of his maturity.

Though first published in 1960, the poems of *Exi ke mia tipsis yia ton ourano* (*Six and One Remorses for the Sky*, 1974) were written between 1953 and 1958. The dominant voice is somber, finely attuned to the desolating aftermath of both World War II and the Greek Civil War that immediately ensued. The joyful, unhampered spirit of Elytis's early poems is here tempered by a greater consciousness of "dark forces" and their human price.

Following the composition of this collection, Elytis completed *To axion esti* (1959; *The Axion Esti*, 1974), a work much longer and more intricate than anything he had written before. The title phrase, meaning "worthy it is," is a Greek Orthodox ecclesiastical expression dating back to the early years of the Byzantine Empire. More specifically, the phrase was used for both the title

of a Byzantine hymn glorifying the Virgin Mary and the name of a holy icon depicting her. The religious connotations of this expression along with its suggestions of song and image suggest the complex intention of the poem: a spiritual quest of music and imagery leading to a victorious emergence from the "Vast Dark Places." Even the formal structure of the poem is tightly modeled after the structures of Byzantine liturgy and hymnology. In all of its features, this poem illustrates the poet's growing faith in the absolute purity of poetry and its sanctified nature as a means of expression and communication.

The Axion Esti is divided into three sections. In the first, called "Genesis," the persona is born, and grows toward awareness and acceptance of mythic identity. The second section, titled "The Passion," charts the development of a now less innocent but unified consciousness through the experiences of World War II and its tragic aftermath. The last part, "The Gloria," is a long group of hymns that praise and celebrate everything from "the light and man's first prayer carved out of rock" to "a woolen sweater left to the frost."

This ambitious composition is also rich in allusions to Elytis's predecessors in the Hellenic tradition. In the struggles and praises of *The Axion Esti*, there are echoes of Homer, Heraclitus, Byzantine hymnographers, Saint John, Solomos, Kalvos, and the heroes of the Greek War for Independence, whom the poet sanctifies as saints. Because of its musical construction and contemporary breadth of vision, *The Axion Esti* was soon set to music by Mikis Theodorakis, who, in 1964, orchestrated and conducted the piece with a full choir and orchestra. Since then, the poem has received international recognition.

At about the same time that Elytis finished *The Axion Esti*, he began preparing yet another long poem, *Maria Nefeli* (*Maria Nephele*, 1981), which did not appear in its entirety until 1978. It consists of two parallel monologues spoken respectively by Maria, a symbol for the younger generation, and the Antiphonist, a more ancient, atavistic persona. These voices represent two divergent personalities that nevertheless belong to the poet himself. Though they search along different paths, their goal is the same: "to be slowly united with the grandeur of sunrise and sunset."

The most distinctive characteristic of Elytis's productive commitment to poetry has been his belief that devotion to art, in its purest form, might counterbalance the forces of horror and evil in the modern world. His efforts have often been incorrectly labeled as naïve; even a cursory inspection of a work such as *The Axion Esti* reveals that Elytis is no more a naïve optimist than was Eliot in his *Four Quartets* (1943): Both works seek metaphysical salvation through a poetic realization of tragedy. To achieve this end, Elytis has created a poetry grounded in a synthesis of complementary realities: contemporary, ancient, mythic, surreal, religious. The concatenation of these realities in his poems is always informed by his unique sensibility.

YANNIS RITSOS

Although Yannis Ritsos belongs to the Generation of 1930, he did not participate in the intellectual exchange and ferment that characterized the early years of *Nea grammata*, around which poets such as Seferis, Elytis, Embirikos, Nikos Gatsos, and George Sarantaris had enthusiastically clustered. Nevertheless, by the 1950's it was clear, especially in Europe, that Ritsos had added an important dimension to the poetry of his times. Born on May 14, 1909, his life story is one of family tragedy, sickness, and political persecution. His constant exposure to the presence of death and suffering forced him to confront the essential problems of human existence. Poetry for Ritsos did not serve as a kind of introspective consolation but as sustenance essential to the life of his body and spirit. In his work, especially in his later poems, personal experience is transformed into metaphor. His growth as a poet was characterized by his efforts to learn and create from the wounds of his experience.

Even Ritsos's childhood was scarred by misfortune and loss. His father was a chronic gambler who squandered the family fortune and later suffered a breakdown so severe that he was committed to an asylum in the late 1920's. When Ritsos was twelve years old, his mother and eldest brother died of tuberculosis, the same disease that has tormented the poet himself throughout his life. Afflicted for the first time in 1926, he spent most of the next five years confined to various sanatoriums and clinics. In 1931, Ritsos moved to Athens, where he became involved with Marxist groups. His commitment

to Marxism emerged from the overcrowded conditions and mass suffering he witnessed and shared during his years of confinement.

Ritsos's first book of poems, *Trakter* (tractor), appeared in 1934. Traditional in form and belligerent in tone, these early poems reflected his conversion to Marxism. The titles alone provide obvious clues: "To Marx," "To the Soviet Union," "To Christ," "The Intellectual," "The Undecided." Evident throughout is the desperation of Karyotakis and the politically satirical bite of Varnalis, who was Ritsos's first teacher and a lifelong friend. In their poetry, Ritsos and Varnalis had much in common at first. Later, however, Ritsos developed a style indicative of a more profound and introspective orientation.

Ritsos's first major poem, *Epitaphios* (1936), divided into twenty songs written in the rhymed couplets of the traditional Greek folk lament, is the dirge of a mother whose son has been killed in a street riot during the calculated and murderous breaking of a strike by government forces in 1936. Issued the same year, the poem elicited such an immediate and empathetic response from the Greek people that the presiding dictator, General Joannes Metaxas, banned the book and ordered that it be burned before the Temple of Zeus in Athens. The title of the poem is taken from the Greek Orthodox liturgy, from the lament of the Virgin Mother kneeling before the dead Christ. Though political on one level, the poem is fundamentally religious, echoing the mourning of a collective psyche.

The years between 1936 and the advent of World War II marked Ritsos's final break from the confinements of traditional form. The four books that were issued during this period all had controlling musical themes: *To tragoudi tis adelfis mou* (1937; the song of my sister), *Earini symphonia* (1938; spring symphony), *To emvatirio tou okeanou* (1940; the march of the ocean), and *Palia mazurka se rythmo vrohis* (1943; old mazurka to the rhythm of rain). In many of these poems, such as "Rhapsody of Naked Night" and "A Glowworm Illuminates the Night," the poet's synthesis of Surrealism, Impressionism, and Imagistic continuity overshadows the early political rhetoric and pessimism of *Trakter*.

During the Nazi occupation of Greece in World

War II, Ritsos played an active role as cultural liaison for the resistance organization EAM-ELAS, whose purpose was to undermine the Nazi regime and reinstate democracy in Greece. Written between 1945 and 1947, *Romiosyne* (1954; *Romiossini: The Story of the Greeks*, 1969), his last long poem of a revolutionary spirit, captured the pain, the longing, and spiritual sacrifice of the war years. Published a number of years later and set to music by Theodorakis in 1958, this poem served as a symbolic reference point for the members and sympathizers of the Greek resistance. With praise and exaltation, Ritsos links the courage and heroism of these rebel forces with the enduring nature of their ancestors, such as Odysseus and the Byzantine folk hero Digenis Akritas.

Because of his active membership in EAM-ELAS, Ritsos was exiled to government detention camps between 1948 and 1953. It was during this bleak period of his life that he turned away from the doctrinaire and theoretical concerns that characterized much of his earlier work. Under the oppressive circumstances of prison life, Ritsos began to write with more urgency than before, often jotting his poems on scraps of paper which he would stuff into bottles or tin cans to be retrieved at a later date. These were primarily short pieces that record his existential struggle for sanity and resolve in the face of constant physical and psychological deprivation. At times cryptic, these poems are consistently subtle and poignant, indicative of the poet's expanded consciousness of human suffering and solitude.

In the next fifteen years following his liberation in 1952, Ritsos wrote prolifically, gaining international acclaim from writers such as Jean-Paul Sartre, Pablo Neruda, Ilya Ehrenburg, and Louis Aragon, who insisted that Ritsos was "the greatest living poet." One of his finest poems of this period is the dramatic monologue *I sonata tou selinofotos* (1956; *The Moonlight Sonata*, 1979). The speaker is a woman dressed in black who yearns to leave her home, which she describes as stifling and decadent—a house that "persists in living with its dead." However, by the end of the poem, she has chosen to remain. No longer capable of change, this person is trapped by her own fears and memories of a past which is embedded in the house it-self. This haunting poem depicts solitude that engenders slow internal decay, leading finally to complete impotence.

Throughout the 1960's, Ritsos concentrated on expanding the poetic dimensions of the dramatic monologue. His efforts were productive, resulting in four consecutive masterpieces of the genre: *Philoktetes* (1965; English translation, 1975), *Orestis* (1966), *Ismene* (1972; English translation, 1977), and "The Return of Iphigenia." In each poem, a character taken from the ancient tragedies of Aeschylus and Euripides is transformed into a lonely spokesperson for contemporary reality. Through the dramatic realization of each character's true identity in metaphorical terms, Ritsos reveals the tragic uncertainties of human existence.

In 1967, when the junta of the Colonels seized power, Ritsos was quickly arrested. In exile on the barren landscape of Yiaros and Leros, the poet reached further into himself, distilling short poems in a language that is extremely compressed. Their tone is often reminiscent of Cavafy, who inspired Ritsos to write *Twelve Poems for Cavafy*, published in 1974. These poems, like those from *O tihos mesa ston kathrefti* (the wall in the mirror), also written in 1974, confirmed Ritsos as a master of irony, metaphor, and understatement—all the qualities he admired in Cavafy.

During the military dictatorship from 1967 to 1974, the government banned Ritsos's books, but before and after that period, he received a number of honors: the Grand International Prize for Poetry of the Biennale of Knokkele-Zoute, Belgium, 1972; the Alfred de Vigny Poetry Prize, Paris, 1975; the Etna-Taormina International Poetry Prize, Italy, 1976. The most meaningful honor of all for the poet came, finally, from Greece itself in 1976 when Ritsos was awarded an honorary doctorate from the University of Salonika. In addition, he was frequently been mentioned as a candidate for the Nobel Prize. In keeping with the high and difficult standards of his generation, Ritsos produced a body of work that is destined to influence contemporary poetry on an international scale. He died in 1990.

NIKOS KAZANTZAKIS

Another important poet of the prewar generation was Nikos Kazantzakis (1883-1957), internationally celebrated for novels such as *Vios kai politeia tou Alexe*

Zormpa (1946; *Zorba the Greek*, 1952) and *O Cristos xanastaronete* (1954; *The Greek Passion*, 1953; also known as *Christ Recrucified*), who initially made a name for himself in Greece for his poetry and drama. In 1938, he published a modern sequel to Homer's *Odyssey* in the form of a remarkable epic of 33,333 seventeen-syllable iambic verses, *Odysseia*, which took him fifteen years to complete. The nihilistic Odyssean hero encounters in his travels various modes of thought that he explores, but that end in nihilism. Kimon Friar spent many years translating this epic, published in English to much acclaim in 1958 as *The Odyssey: A Modern Sequel.*

TAKIS SINOPOULOS

In the minds of most critics familiar with modern Greek poetry, Takis Sinopoulos (1917-1981) stands firmly beside the more widely known poets such as Cavafy, Seferis, Elytis, and Ritsos. Of these four poets, Sinopoulos often contrasted his work to the poetry of Elytis. For both, the sun is a recurrent image that plays a central and unifying role in their poetry. For Elytis, the sun illuminates reality with its purity, grandeur, and beneficence. The sun of Sinopoulos, on the other hand, is invested with a demoniac power that burns, maims, and transforms the surrealistically bucolic landscapes of Elytis into a ravaged geography of the dead that will not permit the poet to forget.

The devastating qualities of this light, which is Sinopoulos's most prominent leitmotif, are derived in part from his intense involvement as a medical officer serving the government forces during the Greek Civil War of 1944 to 1949. Throughout these years of fratricidal horror, Sinopoulos, who had graduated from medical school in 1944, was confronted by death in a ruthless way. His poems are populated with the dead and their living gestures.

Sinopoulos's first book of poems, *Metehmio I* (midpoint I), appeared in 1951. At this time, he had just begun to set up his practice as a physician in the Athens area, attempting to start a new life after his horrifying experiences on the front. The wounds were still fresh, as evidenced in this first book of poems, which begins: "Landscape of death. Sea turned to stone, black cypress trees/ low sea-shore ravaged by salt and light" ("Elpenor"). So pressing was the physician's need to

express his rage and his tragic impressions of the war years that he published five more books of poems within the decade: *Asmata I-XI* (1953; cantos I-XI); *I gnorimia me ton Max* (1956; acquaintance with Max); *Metaichmio II* (midpoint II) and *Eleni* (1957); and *I nihta kei antistihi* (1959; night and counterpoint). Many of these poems draw on ancient Greek literature and mythology; as in the works of Seferis and Ritsos, ancient characters emerge frequently, always to express loss and tragic realization.

Another important feature of Sinopoulos's verse is his highly personal and imagistic awareness of his roots in the landscape of his birthplace, Pirgos, in Ilias. The specific nature of this landscape is not so much symbolic as it is a common reference point for the unity and continuity of his most important motifs: time, memory, and human frailty. In "Origin," published in 1962, Sinopoulos concludes: "This is where I was born. This is where I grew up./ So these are what I need for my rage and my pride/ in order to hold and be held./ I have no gods. No fear."

The publication of "Deathfeast" in 1972 solidified Sinopoulos's permanent place beside his already famous contemporaries. This poem—the title piece of a collection—is Sinopoulos's most moving tribute to the comrades and loved ones whom he lost during the war. Scarred, dismembered, and disoriented, these ghosts of his tormented memory approach him. Their names appear as in a Homeric catalog of the dead. In the introduction to his translation of Sinopoulos, *Landscape of Death* (1979), Kimon Friar observes:

> The guests who have come unbidden to this deathfeast are not those so grandiloquently summoned by Ángelos Sikelianos in his "Greek Supper for the Dead," to a table spread with silver candelabra, scarlet roses, and crystal cups, but are like those who herd around a fire or a pit of blood and beg for resurrection in the poet's memory.

"Deathfeast" echoes not only Sinopoulos's sense of fragmentation and guilt but that of an entire generation still hounded by its memories of war and devastation.

During the last years of his life, Sinopoulos became one of the first Greek poets to exploit fully a subtle combination of prose and poetry. He had used this technique in *I piisi tis piisis* (1964; the poetry of poetry), a collection of aphorisms that expose the awesome but sustaining nature of his art. More so than in his later works, this small book reveals another, less desperate side of the poet's characteristically dark preoccupations. Like Cavafy, it is only in the strange domain of poetry that Sinopoulos finds his "myth of reality, where things rejoice in the absurd aspect of their existence."

This introduction of prose elements into poetry characterizes much of the work that Sinopoulos completed in the late 1970's, including *To hroniko* (1975; the chronicle), *O hartis* (1977; the chart), and *Nihtologio* (1978; the nightlogue). The consciousness that emerges in these works is dreamlike and, as the poet himself often indicated, cinematic. Although they are written in diary form as recollections of his past, they do not follow chronological sequence. Dream, memory, thought, and feeling mingle freely in these "notes toward a poem" as they do for the poet in reality. In structure and content, *Nihtologio* and *O hartis* reveal the influence of the French poets Char and Maurice Blanchot. Like Sinopoulos, they too were men with war-torn memories who constantly sought the most effective means to express the necessity of poetry in times of destruction and human waste.

Considered by many critics to be Sinopoulos's most mysterious and obscure poem, "The Grey Light" (1980) was also the last work he completed before his death in 1981. Divided into eight short sections, it is an intricately organized web of personal experiences, places, and objects which are linked together to provide a kind of mystical order for the fragmented but meditative reality in which Sinopoulos lived and created. "The Grey Light" is also a final homecoming; it takes Sinopoulos back to "the sky of Pirgos" beneath which "the river sleeps by your side."

The poets who represent the next generation of modern Greek poetry came to regard Sinopoulos as the father of the postwar period. This is confirmed not only by his poetry but also by his personal involvement as a mentor and guide for many of the younger poets. During the oppressive years of the Colonels' regime, the doors of his home in suburban Athens were always open to writers and poets who were in need of guidance and support. Aside from his taxing profession as a physician and the constant demands of his poetry, Sino-

poulos also found time to write criticism, edit literary publications, translate, and paint. What is most striking about his contribution as a poet is the high degree of excellence that he was able to maintain throughout his work, from his first publication in 1951 to his last, just prior to his death in 1981.

POSTWAR YEARS

The horror of World War II and the civil war that followed was also visible in the work of Sinopoulos's contemporaries—Manolis Anagnostakis (1925-2005), Miltos Sahtouris (1919-2005), Eleni Vakalo (1921-2001), Nikos Karouzos (1924-1990), Aris Alexandrou (1922-1978), and Ektor Kaknavatos (born 1920). Along with Sinopoulos, these were foremost among the poets known as the First Postwar Generation. Like Sinopoulos, they were affected by the Symbolist trends of the previous generation, although they wrote largely in free verse and were interested in more experimental forms and diction.

MANOLIS ANAGNOSTAKIS

Manolis Anagnostakis was a schoolboy during the war years, and came of age toward the end of the German occupation of Greece. He belonged to a leftist group of students in Thessaloníki who established the literary magazine *Ksekinima* (beginning) in 1944 and took part in the leftist resistance. During the Greek Civil War, he, along with numerous other freedom fighters, was arrested by the right-wing government and was sentenced to death. Though he was later released, many of his fellow students and comrades in arms were executed. As the Greek critic Dimitrios Tsakonas put it, Anagnostakis was "a dead man who survived the firing squad, or rather a man with multiple rifle wounds made by the bullets that killed others." If Sinopoulos's poetry is the reaction of a young man facing horror and carnage at the front, Anagnostakis's poetry is the more desperate reaction of the adolescent facing horror and carnage at home. His first book of poetry, *Epohes* (the times) was published at the end of World War II in 1945. In it there is no sign of joy at Greece's newfound freedom from the Germans. Instead, his poetry expresses a helplessness and feeling of defeat, the individual falling victim both to the injustice of the powers that be and the evil within himself. In his poem "Epilogue" (translated by Connolly), Anagnostakis writes:

> These verses may well be the last
> The last of the last that will be written
> For the future poets are no longer living
> Those who would have spoken all died young. . . .

Anagnostakis expressed the despair of his generation, which fought for freedom in the resistance only to face persecution after the war. Among the poets of the First Postwar Generation, Anagnostakis painted the most vivid picture of the fatal split within Greek society after World War II. Greek critics have described his poetry as a personal version of wilder and more desperate postwar Karyotakism.

MILTOS SAHTOURIS

Miltos Sahtouris is considered, along with Sinopoulos and Anagnostakis, to be one of the more important poets of the First Postwar Generation. In his first three books of poetry, *I Lismomenin* (1945; the forgotten woman), *Paraloges* (1948; ballads), and *Me to prosopo ston tiho* (1952; with the face against the wall), one can see panic stemming from the chaos of a confused and shattered world. The stylistic trademark that sets Sahtouris apart is his distilled and succinct verse. He continued prewar Surrealism, but in a new direction: The transformation of humanity, combined with a personal dimension that has strong undertones of sexuality—the private, sensitive person within a murderous society. In the poem "Desolate" (again in a translation by Connolly), he writes:

> . . . crows have dressed in red
> like whores
>
> the church cracked
> under the heavy rain
> saints were to be found
> running in the streets.

ELENI VAKALO

Eleni Vakalo, the foremost woman poet of the First Postwar Generation, dealt with the terrors of war by turning her back on civilization and focusing on nature, but in stark language that rejects lyricism. European civilization had brought war and destruction. The human

beings she evokes are people in their pristine form, stripped of their Europeanness. Vakalo was particularly interested in visual arts and was considered a major art critic, the effects of which can be seen in her poetry. Her attention to the poetics of postmodernism left a mark on the poetry of the next generation of poets, particularly the women poets of the generation of the 1970's.

NIKOS KAROUZOS

Nikos Karouzos distanced himself from the Surrealist, Symbolist, and political poetry of his generation. His poetry is wild and passionate, containing an uneasy and very original mixture of religious and sexual themes. One of Karouzos's interesting characteristics is the use of elements of purist Greek (*katharevousa*), which gives his poetry a controlled and cerebral dimension even at its most passionate.

SECOND POSTWAR GENERATION

The Second Postwar Generation spent their childhood in war and civil war, but came of age in the mid to late 1950's. Some of the notable poets of this generation are Kiki Dimoula (born 1931), Niltos Fokas (born 1927), Vyron Leondaris (born 1932), and Titos Patrikios (born 1928). These poets were interested in keeping and developing the Greek tradition, but after the disruptive years of war were also interested in allying themselves with international poetry movements.

THE 1960's AND 1970's

In the late 1960's, politics once more played a crucial role in the development of Greek poetry. The 1950's and early 1960's had been a period of relative calm, as Greece set about rebuilding the infrastructure shattered by World War II and the civil war. On April 21, 1967, a right-wing military junta seized power in a coup d'état. One of the new government's first actions was the enforcement of strict censorship. Some major poets, such as Karouzos, continued publishing, as did Elytis, who avoided the censor by publishing abroad, but the majority of Greek poets, following the example of Seferis and Ritsos, countered the new strictures by refusing to publish their work.

In November, 1969, the Junta government abolished official censorship, replacing it with an equally stringent Press Law, which stipulated that a headline or the title of a book had to correspond exactly to the content. The first book of poetry representing the generation of the 1970's was consequently titled *Eksi piites* (six poets). The poets were Lefteris Poulios (born 1944), Vasilis Steriades (born 1947), Katerina Anghelaki-Rooke (born 1939), Nana Isaïa (born 1934), Tasos Denegris (born 1934), and Nasos Vayenas (born 1945). Other important anthologies followed: *Katathesi '73* (deposition '73) and *Katathesi '74* (deposition '74).

The new generation of poets was the first to attempt a full demystification of ancient Greek myth, recasting it within the parameters of modern reality. The poets were influenced by Western European and American trends, particularly American Beat poets such as Allen Ginsberg and Lawrence Ferlinghetti. While earlier generations of Greek poets had striven to retrieve and re-create the traditions of the Greek past, the new generation juxtaposed these traditions with the increasingly ubiquitous popular culture, weaving classical motifs into modern reality. One of the poems that best demonstrates the clash of old and new (translated here by Karen Van Dyck) is from Jenny Mastoraki's first poetry collection, *Diodia* (tolls):

> Then the Trojan horse said
> no, I refuse to see the Press
> and they said why, and he said
> he knew nothing about the massacre
> after all,
> he always ate lightly in the evening
> and in his younger days
> he had worked a stint
> as a wooden pony on
> a merry-go-round.

Of the generation of the 1970's, Yannis Kondos (born 1943) proved himself master of the short epigram as well as of satire and wry humor, while Poulios reflected the alienation and rhetoric of the American Beat generation. Poulios was most closely associated with the Beat movement, although while the American "beatniks" were reacting against the strictures of daily life in American society, Poulios was reacting to the strictures of an increasingly dominant alien culture—American and Western European—which was making ever deeper inroads into modern Greek culture.

While the generation of the 1970's was primarily centered on society and the city, Anghelaki-Rooke stood out as a nature poet grounded in the physicality of the female body. In the early 1970's, she was perceived as the Greek poet with the closest affinity to the contemporary nature poets of northern Europe and the United States. The poetry of Mihalis Ganas (born 1944), on the other hand, focused on themes that centered on the life of provincial Greece, particularly Ioannina, relying on provincial idiom and images.

The Junta fell in 1974, after which freedom of expression was restored. Interestingly, it was the women poets—Vakalo, Dimoula, Anghelaki-Rooke, Rea Galanaki, Maria Laina, and Mastoraki—who continued experimenting with the elliptical language that had been a product of the censorship period, creating compelling and innovative work.

THE 1980'S ONWARD

The generation of the 1980's saw a greater diversity of poetic themes and forms than ever before. Among its foremost poets were Nikos Davettas (born 1960), Thanassis Hatzopoulos (born 1961), Yorgos Houliaras (born 1951), Dyonisos Kapsalis (born 1952), Ilias Lagios (born 1958), Stratis Paskalis (born 1958), Haris Vlavianos (born 1957), and Spiros Vrettos (born 1960).

In the 1990's, Dimoula's work gained attention for its linguistic playfulness and specifically Greek themes—particular appealing for readers who are wary of the threat of Greece's losing its cultural and linguistic integrity with the increasing homogenization of Europe. In an era when the Greek language is seen as vulnerable to the onslaught of English—as evidenced by the deep opposition to the proposal in 2001 that English be the second official language in Greece—Dimoula chooses topics viewed by many as privately Greek and untranslatable, in the sense that the poems have a topical meaning for the Greek reader. "Single-Room Symptom" (translated by Connolly) offers an example:

> No different in Pylos either
> the same disorderly retreat from Syros the year before
> twice as bad in Kalamata last year
> the train was full and the weeping demanded
> we go back to Athens on foot.

An interesting phenomenon has been the increase in the number of Greek poets living and writing outside Greece, often referred to as the poets of the Greek diaspora. Notable among these are the Australian poet Dimitris Tsaloumas (born 1921) and the American poets Olga Broumas (born 1949) and Eleni Sikelianos (born 1965), the latter the great-granddaughter of Angelos Sikelianos.

BIBLIOGRAPHY

Beaton, Roderick. *Introduction to Modern Greek Literature*. Rev. ed. Oxford, England: Clarendon Press, 2004. The second revision of the volume published in 1994, which had the distinction of being the first book-length study of modern Greek literary works—those published since 1821. Greek quotations are translated into English. Maps.

Bien, Peter, et al., eds. *A Century of Greek Poetry, 1900-2000*. Bilingual edition. Westwood, N.J.: Cosmos, 2004. Includes 456 poems by 109 poets, including Greece's two winners of the Nobel Prize. This collection is especially significant because many of the poets are relatively unknown outside Greece, and many of the poems have not previously been translated.

Constantine, Peter, et al., eds. *The Greek Poets: Homer to the Present*. New York: W. W. Norton, 2009. Introduction by Robert Hass. Covers three millennia of Greek poetry and includes more than one thousand poems, many in new translations. Essential. Map.

Hadas, Rachel. *Merrill, Cavafy, Poems, and Dreams*. Ann Arbor: University of Michigan Press, 2000. A wide-ranging collection of essays by a noted poet, translator, and scholar, many of them pointing out how Greek myths and themes have influenced other writers, such as the American poet James Merrill. Includes essays on Constantine P. Cavafy, George Seferis, and Kostas Karyotakis.

Keeley, Edmund. *Inventing Paradise: The Greek Journey, 1937-1947*. Evanston, Ill.: Northwestern University Press, 2002. A noted scholar and translator recalls a time before the war when he was a member of a literary group that included George Katsimbalis and George Seferis. Though it is rich in biographical details and scenic descriptions, along with a good deal of literary criticism, the primary purpose of the volume is to suggest how literature helped the Greek spirit to survive the Nazi occupation intact.

Nagy, Gregory, and Anna Stavrakopoulou, eds. *Modern Greek Literature: Critical Essays*. New York: Routledge, 2003. Essays on various subjects, including the poetry of Constantine P. Cavafy and bilingual elements in the works of Theodor Kallifatides. Bibliographical references and index.

Ricks, David, ed. *Modern Greek Writing: An Anthology in English Translation*. London: Peter Owen, 2003. A selection of Greek prose and verse written since 1821. Introductory notes on each writer.

Valaoritis, Nanos, and Thanasis Maskaleris, eds. *An Anthology of Modern Greek Poetry*. Jersey City, N.J.: Talisman House, 2003. The editors of this outstanding collection, who are both noted poets and critics, translated most of the works included. Almost a hundred poets are represented, some of them established, others relatively new.

Van Dyck, Karen. *Kassandra and the Censors: Greek Poetry Since 1967*. Ithaca, N.Y.: Cornell University Press, 1998. Focusing on poetry produced since 1967, the author shows how the tactics women poets used to deal with censorship were also helpful as they sought to change traditional assumptions about gender and replace them with feminist ideas and ideals. Indexes.

_____, trans. *The Rehearsal of Misunderstanding: Three Collections by Contemporary Greek Women Poets*. Lebanon, N.H.: University Press of New England, 1998. Includes Greek and English versions of *Keik (The Cake)*, by Rea Galanakē; *Histories gia ta vathia (Tales of the Deep)*, by Tzenē Mastorakē, and *Diko tēs (Hers)*, by Maria Laina. Bibliographical references.

James Stone; Peter Constantine
Updated by Karen Van Dyck

HUNGARIAN POETRY

Along the well-worn path the Hungarians (Magyars) took westward during the centuries preceding their entry into the Carpathian Basin in 896 C.E., they shaped a peculiar folk culture and folk poetry. Ethnographers, linguists, and researchers of comparative literature have arrived at this conclusion, even though no written trace of ancient Hungarian literature has survived. The runic alphabet of the seminomadic Hungarians was not used for recording literary texts, but the wealth of ancient poetry is attested by later allusions, although after Christianization in about 1000, both the state and the Church made every effort to eradicate even the memory of the pagan period. The chant of the shaman, an improvised incantation for the purposes of sorcery, prophecy, necromancy, or healing, often combined with music, dance, and a primitive form of drama, thus survived primarily in children's rhymes and other simple ritualistic expressions. The secular counterparts of the shamans, the minstrels (*regősök*), provided the first examples of epic poetry, recounting the origin of the Hungarians. Two of these epics are known (in their later reconstructed forms) as the *Legend of the Miraculous Stag* and the *Lay of the White Steed*. The versification is believed to have been similar to that of other ancient European poetry; it is thought, for example, that the Hungarian minstrels did not use rhyme, relying instead on alliteration.

The culture of medieval Hungary was influenced by both Roman and Byzantine Christianity, but it was most effectively shaped by the various monastic orders (Benedictines, Cistercians, Dominicans, and Franciscans, among others) who settled in the land from the tenth to the thirteenth centuries. Learning remained almost entirely theological until the middle of the fourteenth century, and writing continued even longer in Latin, the language of the Church.

The Latin hymns and laments of Hungarian monk-writers were mostly dedicated to the praise of Hungarian saints, and their subject matter generally derived from the legends associated with these saints. Because only later copies of these creations survived, little is known of their origins or of their authors.

The earliest known poetic text in Hungarian originates from about 1300: The "Ómagyar Mária-siralom" ("Ancient Hungarian Lament of Mary") is an adaptation from the "Planctus Sanctae Mariae" of Geoffroi de Breteuil (died 1196). The original liturgical hymn was transformed into a pious lay song with strong mystical undercurrents. Written in the ancient Hungarian line, consisting of eight syllables, with stress on the first and the fifth, the poetic technique of the "Ancient Hungarian Lament of Mary" is so accomplished that centuries of literary practice must be assumed to have preceded it.

While epic romances and troubadour songs began to flourish in the fourteenth century, the poetry of chivalry left relatively scarce evidence of its existence in Hungary. Its best-known example is the *chanson de geste* woven around the figure of Miklós Toldi, a popular strongman-soldier. Elements of this epic passed into folklore and formed the basis of works several centuries later, including a masterful epic trilogy by János Arany.

By the fifteenth century, secular poetry in the vernacular had made its presence strongly felt in Hungary. The untutored minstrels and rhymesters were joined by clerks and scribes (the *deák*), who supplemented the works of the bards with their own compositions, including "historical" songs as well as love poems and satirical lays. One good example of their work is the narrative song titled *Szabács viadala* (1476; the siege of the Szabács), which recounts an episode of warfare against the invading Ottoman army. Its contradictions continue to intrigue scholars; while its language is bleak and it reads like a school exercise, it exhibits a strikingly modern vocabulary and flawless technique in its use of decasyllabic rhymed couplets.

THE RENAISSANCE AND THE REFORMATION

While indifference toward literacy and the written word continued to be the rule of the period, there arose in Hungary important centers of Renaissance culture during the reign of the Anjou kings (1308-1382) and especially during that of Mátyás (1458-1490). His efforts to establish a strong central authority were well served by the professional men in his employ, recruited from a variety of countries. Besides these learned foreigners, a new crop of Hungarian intellectuals appeared as a result of schooling in the universities of Western Europe.

Outstanding among these was Janus Pannonius (1434-1472), a Ferrara-educated bishop of Pécs, the creator of finely chiseled epigrams, elegies, and panegyrics and the first Hungarian man of letters whose fame transcended the borders of his homeland. His topics included affairs of state, the growing Ottoman peril, the love he felt for his homeland (while missing the culture of Italy), and his disenchantment with the policies of his sovereign. Renaissance luxury and the contemplative atmosphere of court literature were shattered during the stormy period following Mátyás's death, but the tradition of Humanist poetry domesticated by Pannonius and his circle of followers has remained alive in Hungarian literature to this day. The large number of Hungarian poems surviving from the sixteenth century indicates that a considerable body of verse already existed in the Middle Ages, even if most of it is unknown today.

The major impulse for this cultural growth was the Protestant Reformation. The literature of Hungary became a battleground for the various new tenets. Hymns, didactic verses, and rhymed paraphrases of biblical episodes, written in Hungarian, became weapons that assured the rapid acceptance of Protestantism among the people. Of the secular minstrels of the century, the best known and most prolific was Sebestyén Tinódi (died 1556), who was more a storyteller than a poet. His accounts of battles and sieges were accurate, but his verse was monotonous and repetitive, made enjoyable only by musical accompaniment. Free adaptations of Western European poetry abounded during the century, the principal genre being the *széphistória* (named after the Italian *bella istoria*) interwoven with elements of Hungarian folklore, thus reflecting a strong native character.

BÁLINT BALASSI

Representing the finest achievements of Hungarian Renaissance is the poetry of Bálint Balassi (1554-1594), a nobleman whose turbulent life was spent in constant pursuit of love, wealth, and adventure, often under the shadow of political suspicion. His works have something of the flavor of the English Cavalier poets, something of François Villon, with the additional feature of an intimate knowledge of nature. Proficient in eight languages and familiar with the works of the great Humanists, Balassi wrote poetry with great dexterity. His cycles of love poems remained unsurpassed for centuries, and the intensity of his Christian verse, in which he disputed with God while seeking solace in him, foreshadowed the thoroughly personal religious works of later Hungarian poets. The intensity of a soldier's life made itself felt through the discipline of his lines. His most perfectly composed and most frequently quoted poem is a *cantio militaris*, "A végek dicsérete" (1589; "In Praise of the Marches"), an eloquent hymn to life on the marches and to the beauty of nature, ending with a moving grace and farewell. Balassi developed a verse form for himself, a nine-line stanza consisting of six-, six-, and seven-syllable cycles, with an *aab-ccb-ddb* rhyme scheme; named after him, this pattern became a favorite of Hungarian poets.

THE COUNTER-REFORMATION AND BAROQUE

Much of the seventeenth century was characterized by the militant spirit of the Counter-Reformation, resulting in an enormous output of religious poetry, mostly by Roman Catholic writers. The outstanding Hungarian poet of the century, Miklós Zrínyi (1620-1664), a thoroughly Baroque man of letters, bore one significant resemblance to Balassi: He also had a firsthand knowledge of combat, and his descriptions of battle scenes, especially in his epic carrying the Latin title *Obsidio Szigetiana* (wr. 1645-1646; *The Peril of Sziget*, 1955), are particularly graphic and authentic. In his narrative, as well as in his prose writings, Zrínyi displayed the explicit and fervent political commitment which was to become an integral part of much Hungarian poetry. Although the influence of Vergil, Ludovico Ariosto, and Torquato Tasso is discernible in *The Peril of Sziget*, the presentation of details and the use of atmosphere make it a profoundly original Hungarian creation.

The cultivation of sentimental rococo poetry became a fashionable pastime during the seventeenth century. Even highborn ladies tried their skill at it, most of them producing religious or domestic verse. The epic tradition of Zrínyi was carried forward by an inventive, widely read courtier who stayed away from actual battles. The heroes of István Gyöngyösi (1629-1704) were genuine nobles and ladies; in his numerous epithalamia he revealed their love secrets to his\ readers in great detail and with obvious relish. He was the typical poet-follower of lords, adjusting his politics and principles to those of the "great family" he served. His works are nothing more than family or society stories, but their accomplishment is undeniable. Gyöngyösi's honest craftsmanship, especially in his descriptions of the countryside, presages the works of the great Romantic and realist poets of the nineteenth century.

With the growth of readership, an eager public appeared for secular as well as religious poetry. For some time, these writings circulated in handwritten copies, but by the 1680's a number of printed songbooks were in popular demand. The vulgarized versions of Renaissance poems in the form of verse-chronicles constituted the bulk of the poetry of the age, with a number of rhymed greetings, soldiers' songs, laments, and dirges also in evidence. The proliferation of love poetry was striking; entire songbooks appeared filled with these often ribald verses, attempting to follow the high standards set by Balassi and Gyöngyösi. Among students, the traditions of goliardic poetry were revived, with sharp expressions of social discontent.

Political and religious intolerance resulted in the outbreak of the *kuruc* wars during the late seventeenth and early eighteenth centuries. Reflecting the makeup of the rebelling armies, many popular songs of this period voiced the complaints of fugitives, outlaws, and impoverished, vagrant students. A large body of (mostly anonymous) poetry was produced during the successive rebellions and campaigns. Written in the simplest folk idiom, suitable for musical adaptation, such songs and laments provide gripping descriptions of the miseries and joys of *kuruc* life. The most famous among them (such as "The Rákóczi Song") later inspired Franz Liszt and Hector Berlioz to compose stirring Romantic music.

EIGHTEENTH CENTURY

From 1711, when the *kuruc* armies of Prince Ferenc Rákóczi II were defeated, to the 1770's, Hungarian literature experienced a period of relative decline. Only the continuing flood of imitative, mannerist rococo verse indicated the survival of poetry. The poets of this period showed a remarkable command of form and diction, and some of them were important in the development of modern poetic techniques. Baron László Amade (1704-1764), a sophisticated cultivator of *poésie galante*, produced poems worthy of mention. Ferenc Faludi (1704-1779), a Jesuit abbot, also became interested in secular poetry. In spite of its rococo affectations and style, his verse was firmly grounded in reality and took much from Hungarian folk literature. With his earthy realism and his prosodic experimentation, Faludi became one of the early exponents of truly modern poetry.

The Enlightenment reached Eastern Europe by the 1770's and—even though the absolutist Habsburg authorities thwarted any political organization—its effect on the cultural life of Hungary was profound. Intellectual renewal was rapid and irresistible. One of its centers was Vienna, where Hungarian noblemen were educating their sons. French, German, and English-language treatises and literature filtered into Hungary, resulting in the founding of great private collections of books and art, the formation of literary societies, and the publication of periodicals. French (later German) Neoclassicism became the dominant trend in poetry. The earliest prominent figure of Hungarian Enlightenment, György Bessenyei (1747-1811), while known mostly for his essays and his plays, also wrote a number of philosophical poems. Had they appeared in print during his lifetime, they would have been pioneering works.

FERENC KAZINCZY

Much more influential was Ferenc Kazinczy (1759-1831). Although writing relatively few poems, of modest merit, he was for nearly forty years the central figure of Hungarian literary life; he organized, criticized, encouraged, and educated the writers and poets scattered throughout Hungary by maintaining an extensive correspondence from his rural manor. All the good, and many of the bad, poets of the period were indebted to him. While they considered style, presentation, and construction to be of supreme value, attaching secondary importance to the thoughts conveyed, Kazinczy and his circle soon came to the conclusion that, in its uncultivated state, the Hungarian language was inadequate to communicate the timely ideas of literature and the arts. They made reform, refinement, and development of the language a question of primary importance. Proclaiming these aims in their sharply worded epigrams, epistles, and critical essays, they initiated the struggle between "neologists" and "orthologists" which persisted through much of the nineteenth century.

MIHÁLY CSOKONAI VITÉZ

While the early reform generation produced few outstanding poets, one of their contemporaries, Mihály Csokonai Vitéz (1773-1805), exhibited the fruits of his search for new forms of expression. He made use of everything he learned from European literature, transmitting it into his own sphere of experience and producing from the synthesis something original and integrally his own. He was the first Hungarian who attempted (unsuccessfully) to make a living from his literary efforts. Despite the fact that he lived in a state of squalor and acutely felt rejection, many of his poems are marked by a subtle grace and cheerfulness. They range from Rousseauesque philosophical ponderings to drinking songs and village genre pieces. His love cycles written during his many periods of courtship happily blend light passages of rococo fancy with more sober thoughts. Csokonai Vitéz could be compared to the Scottish poet Robert Burns (1759-1796), except that this would overemphasize the populist element of his poetry.

ROMANTICISM

While the Enlightenment gave rise to philosophical and didactic verse, disposed to abstraction and aridity, lyric poetry found another impetus. The reformers and experimenters encouraged originality and aesthetic individuality, in sharp contrast to both neoclassicism and the earlier Baroque orientation. The campaign for national independence revealed a set of common feelings shared by all Hungarians and resulted in anxious efforts to preserve the native tongue and indigenous customs. The intensive exploration of traditional literature, the

growing awareness of literary history, and the Romantic influence of Ossianic poetry combined to open the way for unrestrained experimentation. In the area of versification, for example, Western European patterns were adopted by Hungarian poets as if based on stress alone. Consequently, the French Alexandrine was assimilated as a twelve-syllable accented line of two beats, each having six syllables. Four of these lines were arranged into a stanza, at first all lines rhyming, later following the Western example of rhyming couplets. Even more significant was the introduction of a metrical principle that could be based on the length of syllables. Since the Hungarian language makes a clear distinction between long and short syllables, this practice is perfectly suited to it. Some of the poets introduced the purely metrical, nonrhyming forms of Greek and Roman poetry, while others adapted rhyming verse forms from the West. The flexibility and smoothness resulting from these experiments was unprecedented in Hungarian poetry.

The typical attitudes of Romantic literature—the glorification of history, the preference for a noble and often affected "sublimity," which went hand in hand with a healthy respect for reason—were made more complex in Hungary by an exaggerated emphasis on folk poetry and a contradictory predilection for new techniques of versification. The resulting torrent of poetry during the early decades of the nineteenth century presented a sharp contrast to that of the previous epoch. Lyric ballads, elegies, and epic romances prevailed, in accordance with the requisite extremes of desolation and melancholy on one hand and exhortation and pride on the other. As elsewhere in Eastern Europe, Romantic literature in Hungary contributed to the birth or revival of national consciousness and to the forging of a national identity. With its maturation and with the strengthening of political processes, this literature assisted in democratizing the atmosphere for a national culture. The patriarchal-feudal mode gave way to a semibourgeois one: Writers and poets were able to earn a living from their writings, making noble patronage unnecessary. Publishing became a profitable business; men of letters combined their work with editing and journalism, and they began to be recognized and respected on their own.

One of the architects of the transition to Romanticism was Sándor Kisfaludy (1772-1844), a scion of wealthy landholders, whose two-hundred-verse cycle *A kesergő szerelem* (1801; sorrowful love) combined strong traditional elements with Renaissance, Baroque, and rococo influences. The form he created to harmonize with his message, the "Himfy-stanza," composed of eight- and seven-syllable accented lines, came to be one of the favorites of Hungarian poets. Dániel Berzsenyi (1776-1836) did not bring innovations in style or in form, but the emotional intensity with which he proclaimed enduring virtues—moral integrity, courage, love of freedom and justice—accounted for his great popularity during the reform period, when politics and ethics were considered intertwined. His terse and vigorous images and phrases are charged with classical allusions, but his elevated style and antique pose conceal the wounded soul of a modern person. His disillusionment with his morally deficient contemporaries was great; while his intensely disciplined art continued to reflect a remarkable self-control, behind the wisdom of antiquity lay the resignation of a Christian longing for contentment. Although Berzsenyi was disappointed because Hungarian poetry did not develop along his guidelines, his influence on future poets was strong and lasting.

FERENC KÖLCSEY

Ferenc Kölcsey (1790-1838) was the most profound thinker among the Hungarian Romantics. A saintly man of uncompromising standards, he embodied the national aspirations of the age. The earlier examples of his relatively small poetic output were clearly influenced by the notion of a *Weltliteratur*, but later he showed a predilection toward a vigorous, striking, though often grave and pessimistic, nationalistic poetry. His best-known poem is "Himnusz" (1823; "Hymn"), a somber invocation to God on behalf of the Hungarian nation, which was put to music and is now the national anthem of Hungary.

MIHÁLY VÖRÖSMARTY

Mihály Vörösmarty (1800-1855), the greatest Romantic poet of Hungary, introduced a new element into the literary life of the nation. His works were much more than reflections on the events around him; they expressed well-considered and inspired judgments on the vital questions of the age as dictated by the poet's genius. In "Szózat" (1836; "The Summons"), he addressed the world on behalf of his nation: "The sufferings of a thousand years call for life or death." This appeal remains unmatched in its confidence and its effect on the reader's conscience. Familiar with the inherent contradictions in the societies and cultures of his age, Vörösmarty also inquired whether humankind "ever advanced through the medium of books" in his "Gondolatok a könyvtárban" ("Thoughts in the Library"). The ensuing images suggest a pessimistic answer, but the poet appears unable to accept such a dark conclusion: "A new spirit finds its way ahead," he insists in this and in other poems, which shows him to be a true poet of humankind. There is a nagging doubt and a touch of despair in his mature poems, and the defeat of the nationalist revolt by combined Russian-Austrian forces in the Hungarian War of Independence (1848-1849) released the floodgates of his bitter, almost demoniac imagery.

POPULISM

In Hungarian literary history, the decade preceding the 1848 Revolution is referred to as the "era of the people and of the nation." Romanticism was very much alive, but by this time some of the best poets found even Romanticism too narrow and infused it with plebeian-democratic ideals expressed in an increasingly realistic manner. The stylistic trend best suited for the purposes of this period was the populist (*népies*) approach. It fused Romantic and realistic elements, steadily (although cautiously) increasing stress on the latter. During the 1840's, a courageous, involved commitment to critical realism became dominant, especially among members of the younger generation. The immediate aims of literature were to rediscover folk poetry, to depict the life of the common people, and to give voice to their aspirations. In a domestication of the universal Romantic philosophy, the concept of the "true man" was adapted to that of the "true Hungarian." The indirect aim of the young writers and poets was the modern expression and interpretation of national character. What they could not foresee was that this national character was to undergo radical transformation during the second half of the nineteenth century.

SÁNDOR PETŐFI

In the person of Sándor Petőfi (1823-1849), many of these ideals found their consummation. Petőfi was endowed with everything a national poet must have: innate talent, a fiery commitment, the right historical situation, and a sense of manifest destiny. After a brief life (he died in his mid-twenties), he left behind a body of works that, both in quality and in volume, cannot be ignored in any assessment of world literature. (He also shared Lord Byron's fate in that he died a tragic death which made him both a symbol and a myth.) After imitating the folk style so successfully that many of his verses are popularly known as folk songs, he signaled his break with the strict Romantic approach in a spirited parody of the heroic epic, *A helység-kalapácsa* (1844; *The Hammer of the Village*, 1873). His most popular epic, *János Vitéz* (1845; *Janos the Hero*, 1920; revised as *John the Hero*, 2004), also indicated this transition. The tale and its trappings are stock Romanticism, while the treatment and the picture projected are closer to realism.

Political themes became increasingly interwoven with his poetry during the 1840's. Even in his genre-pieces, the setting sun was compared to a bloody ruler, and the clink of wineglasses to the clanging of chains enslaving men. In a letter, he proclaimed his guiding principle: "When the people rule in poetry, they will be close to ruling in politics as well, and this is the task of our century." Not surprisingly, this kind of thinking led him away from a Romantic admiration for the past. Petőfi produced some of the most powerful love poetry of the century, and his descriptive poems (mostly about the plains region between the Danube and Tisza rivers) are imbued with folksy, evocative humor, particularly when presenting the life-style of the Hungarian nobility. He developed a style and a language quite clearly his own, which grew to accommodate the whole spectrum of Hungarian life. As a result of his "democratic style," his readers understood him immediately. While moving away from strict Romanticism, Petőfi found the direct and natural approach his predecessors sought. He moved effortlessly from one type of poetry to another, adopting new techniques at will and solving the most difficult problems of versification with ease and grace.

JÁNOS ARANY

János Arany (1817-1882) was a friend of Petőfi. They agreed on a number of issues and were both committed to making the life of the people the central theme of literature. While Petőfi was a fiery radical, quite conscious of his genius, Arany was an exemplary office-worker who wanted to be "just like everyone else." He first attracted attention by writing the epic poem *Toldi* (1847; English translation, 1914), a thoroughly Romantic historical story with a hero of folk imagination who avenges the outraged feelings of the common people—a natural, simple, untainted soul, unselfish but self-respecting and conscious of his own worth. In Arany's epic, the Hungarian nation is presented as it once was (according to the Romantics): a family community, governed by the rules of justice and nature. The defeat of the Hungarian Revolution and the death of his friend Petőfi injured Arany deeply. In poems that were highly subjective, empirically analytical, and soberly reflective, he tried to bridge the conflict between his ideals and the realities of life in subjugated Hungary. The language of his poetry was something he deliberately created. It was not the straightforward, unambiguous voice of folk poetry, but rather a precise literary speech of carefully chosen words and expressions, bearing the widest variety of meanings and associations. Arany's poems may be immediately comprehensible to the reader, but they are, at the same time, among the most difficult in Hungarian literature to render in a foreign language.

In spite of his considerable lyric output, in which a wide variety of subjective topics were treated, Arany saw himself primarily as an epic poet, and as such, he considered it his task to revive in a contemporary context the common and single-minded national consciousness. This vision explains his predilection to treat a variety of historical subjects in his epics. He avoided the pseudohistorical idealization of the peasant by incorporating into his writings a distinctly un-Romantic view, according to which, even though national character is best preserved by the common people, it may also become primitive because of its isolation, and it should be enriched with values originating in other cultures. Apart from *Toldi*, Arany is best remembered for his ballads, the themes of which were taken from the sad and trying periods of Hungarian history. This outmoded genre, extant only in the villages and marketplaces, was salvaged through Arany's masterful handling of the Hungarian sentence and especially through his use of numerous psychological associations.

Legacy and change

The success of Petőfi and Arany resulted in a veritable cult of populist poetry. Petőfi's numerous imitators, not all of them without talent, copied his style and themes with genuine fervor but seldom achieved his level of consistency and brilliance. Thus, the Petőfi cult soon degenerated into absurd virtuosity and buffoonery. Arany's followers were somewhat more successful. Their writings are characterized by literary skill, an effective use of common speech, and a scrupulous concern for details of versification. These poets led long and blameless lives and filled many of the leading positions in the nation's cultural affairs during the late nineteenth century. It was largely as a result of their efforts that the poetic guidelines of Petőfi and Arany, imbued with excessive nationalistic and isolationist tendencies and referred to as populist-nationalism, became the official dogma of Hungarian cultural life. Lyric poetry, its position already weakened by the appearance of new, more subjective prose genres, became even more monotonous and irrelevant to the growing urban and semiurban readership.

The 1880's brought about a flurry of revival in Hungarian poetry, when a few solitary writers, almost completely ignored by the academic establishment, attempted to infuse new vigor into the literary life of Hungary. The name of János Vajda (1827-1897) became synonymous with opposition and stubborn refusal to conform to artificial standards. Largely because of his aggressiveness and lack of objectivity, his antitraditional, pantheistic, and symbol-studded poetry was never even acknowledged, let alone respected by the critics. Seeking visions of glory and greatness in an age when such were outmoded, he spent his declining years in angry meditation, writing more good lines than good poems. Among the younger outcasts, Gyula Reviczky (1855-1889) merits mention for his melancholy, reflective poetry, in which impressionistic and

Symbolist elements were first expressed in Hungary. József Kiss (1843-1921) was not an outcast; indeed, for a time he was among the most popular poets of Hungary. As the successful editor of the country's first bourgeois literary weekly, *A hét*, he strongly influenced contemporary taste, and his lyric poems and ballads introduced the life of Hungary's Jews into the mainstream of Hungarian literature.

Modern poetry

The turn of the century witnessed the rise of a wealthy liberal middle class in the cities of Hungary. Their desire to gain recognition for their tastes and values alongside traditional Christian-national ones contributed to a spirit of literary secession. Passive and late-blooming as this "secession" was, it achieved a grudging acceptance of relative (as opposed to absolute) values, and by introducing free association into the practice of poetry, it loosened the structure of Hungarian verse. At the same time, a "great generation" of writers and poets appeared on the scene. Their artistic power was too elemental and their appeal too overwhelming to be stopped. Not all of them wanted to change Hungarian society, but most of them agreed in wanting to open all avenues for describing the realities of Hungary as "a country of contradictions."

Endre Ady

Among those contributing to the periodical *Nyugat*, one may find some of the brightest names in twentieth century Hungarian poetry. In influence, quality, and complexity, none of them approached Endre Ady (1877-1919). When he published his first important volume, *Új versek* (1906; *New Verses*, 1969), he embodied the shocking newness of modern European literature, and critics promptly declared him incomprehensible, immoral, unpatriotic, and pathological. Unrelenting, Ady poured forth (besides his numerous newspaper articles) a series of poetry volumes, the titles of which reflect the break he made with traditional poetry: *Vér és arany* (1908; *Blood and Gold*, 1969), *Az Illés szekerén* (1909; *On Elijah's Chariot*, 1969), *Szeretném, ha szeretnének* (1910; *Longing for Love*, 1969), *A minden titkok verseiből* (1910; *Of All Mysteries*, 1969), *Ki látott engem?* (1914; *Who Sees Me?*, 1969), and *A halottak élén* (1918; *Leading the Dead*, 1969). Everything about which he wrote was universal yet at the same time very Hungarian: his enthusiasm to struggle against existing wrongs, his desire for an explainable, "whole" world, his ambivalent attitude toward revolutionary change, and his view of the modern man-woman relationship as a ruthless struggle. He was deeply concerned about the loneliness of his nation in the dangerous modern world and the tragedy this position portends. He was never able to break the bonds of Calvinist determinism, but in his religious poems he presented the most tormented disputes with God and the most complete submission to his will ever witnessed in Hungarian poetry. His technique for creating a strange and mysterious world using the simplest language was supreme. Fusing iambic meter with the stressed rhythm of Hungarian poetry, his uncomplicated sentences evoke a variety of colors and shifting hues.

MIHÁLY BABITS

The most intellectual poet of the first *Nyugat* generation was Mihály Babits (1883-1941), who was willing to experiment with every form, style, and technique. Disdaining the emotional, enthusiastic approach to literature, he emphasized craftsmanship. In the face of significant social issues, however, he revealed that behind the mask of the aesthete, there was a noble, caring soul, devoted to human dignity.

DEZSŐ KOSZTOLÁNYI

Like Babits, Dezső Kosztolányi (1885-1936) is most often referred to as a "bourgeois humanist." Overcoming the strong Decadent influence of his youth, he continued to display occasional moments of theatricality. The child who lived in him juggled rhyme and rhythm with great dexterity, sometimes in sheer delight, sometimes ironically. The wonder of all things, the desire to discover every secret, compelled him to blend Impressionism and Symbolism almost spontaneously, in a variety of poetic forms. Later, no longer limited to recording the events of everyday life, he wrote poems concerning the eternal image of human action. His titles became unadorned, his structure well ordered, the stanzas often ending with vigorous Sapphic lines. Thus, he moved away from the bourgeois decadence of the fin de siècle and fused the modern immediacy of his poems with traditionally conceived forms.

OTHER NYUGAT POETS

If Ady represents an energetic and open commitment to social action and Babits represents a bourgeois humanism, passive until forced by desperation into action, then the other *Nyugat* poets may be described as taking positions between these two extremes. Early twentieth century Hungarian poetry was divided between an emphasis on self-expression and a subservience to the eternal demands of art, between the desire to change and the recognition of supreme permanence. The ambience of *Nyugat*, however, was such that the writers of its circle never became sharply polarized.

Gyula Juhász (1883-1937), probably the most "autobiographical" Hungarian poet of the twentieth century, voiced powerfully the distress of the solitary and oppressed individual. His poems, whether evoking images of the physical world or depicting the misery of the peasants, blend the delicate colors of Impressionism, the lethargy of fin de siècle, and the most realistic, even radical, tendencies with ease. Frequently recalling the past (especially in his love poems), he used a rich variety of adjectives, thus inducing a mood of melodious sweetness.

The poetry of Árpád Tóth (1886-1928) was tired, fragmented, melancholy, expressing a vague desire to break out of the drabness of his world. In a number of other ways, too, he showed an affinity with poets of the West such as Paul Verlaine and Oscar Wilde. Rarely using any Symbolist devices, Tóth's poems were exceptionally rich in word pictures, similies, and metaphors. Lacking in his verse was any sympathy for the masses, as he believed it was in vain to hope to reach other souls in one's isolation.

Milán Füst (1888-1967) used the brightest of colors in his relatively few poems, which evoked figures and images from the past. This was no mere return to Romanticism: Füst spent months polishing a single poem, merging the restlessness of Art Nouveau with classical monumentalism and a desire to achieve tranquillity. Füst's poems reveal a shrewdly designed private world in which the struggles with everyday problems of life and artistic destiny can be resolved.

During the politically and materially ruinous period between the two world wars, Hungary experienced a flowering of literary life. *Nyugat* continued to be the most resilient and effective forum for the modern poets of Hungary, in spite of repeated attacks from the Right and the Left alike. The growth of authoritarian nationalism evoked a corresponding wave of humanist opposition, although the latter was often tinged with a sense of hopelessness. The interwar poets broke with the idyllic worldview of the prewar decades, and many of them began seriously to doubt the viability of an "inner man." In order to escape the mannerism of the fin de siècle, they reached back to older forms, trying thereby to create order out of chaos. Few poets adhered to avant-garde principles, but their influence was significant.

Lajos Kassák (1887-1967) was the first genuine worker who achieved a name for himself in Hungarian literature, largely through his poems exhibiting a bewildering array of expressionist, Futurist, and Decadent influences. His extravagant hopes for humankind were balanced by the firm structure of his verse, which was achieved without relying on rhyme, stress, or regular rhythm. In spite of the personal voice he employed, he did not speak for himself, instead expressing humankind's vehement response to the phenomena of modern technology.

If Ady's task was to initiate a literary revolution, that of Attila József (1905-1937) was to carry on and fulfill its promises. During his tragically short life, marred by poverty and neurosis, this gifted poet absorbed a great variety of influences. From Kosztolányi, he learned to respond to the immediacy of the moment; from Juhász, he gained an intimacy with his country and his fellow men; from Babits, the pursuit of classical values. József's daring use of and dexterity with construction reveal the influence of Kassák, while his interest in the simple forms and rhythm of Hungarian folk songs shows that he was not immune to the sway of modern populism. His poetry, nevertheless, shows a striking originality and uniqueness. True to his time and its influences, József intermingled material phenomena with the subjective stream of his moods, thus presenting an artistic experience which varied and dissolved according to the state of his mind. He demonstrated great facility in his use of traditional forms, achieving particularly striking effects with the sonnet. He may have solved the paramount artistic dilemma of

his time, fully experiencing and giving poetic expression to the shattered and shattering twentieth century. He paid a price, however, for this achievement: "My heart is perched on nothing's branch," he wrote during the last year of his life, before he killed himself.

One of József's most original contemporaries was Lőrinc Szabó (1900-1957), who, exhibiting many traits of the bourgeois avant-garde, cannot be placed in any single category. He forged his individualistic style from a blend of strident expressionism and the influence of the Neue Sachlichkeit (New Objectivity), tolerating no affectation. Szabó's poems always have a direct message without recourse to suggestion, invocation, or magic. An early theme of his poetry is the loss of illusions, which he later combined with the ruthlessness of nature and the futility of human struggle. It was only a short step from this to a solipsistic position and a fascination with Eastern philosophy, which may have served the poet well during the years of silence enforced upon him by the cultural policy of post-World War II Hungary.

While the claim is frequently made that the "official" literature of interwar Hungary was conservative and nationalistic, the artists of dissenting views, including those of the noncommunist Left, had considerable access to literary forums such as the periodicals or newspapers. Many of the middle-class poets, from socialist idealists to adherents of Catholicism, were characterized by an intellectual hunger, strong humanist convictions, and an "urbanist" attitude, the latter becoming the collective name under which they were known. Their best-known representatives were Zoltán Jékely (1913-1982), a poet of wry, melancholy erudition, and György Rónay (1913-1978), whose modern verse was based on Christian humanism and rational sobriety.

The poetry of Miklós Radnóti (1909-1944) was characterized by the affirmation of order and harmony, respect for reason, and a strong interest in the classics. His early attraction to pastoral themes, emphasizing the joys of life and containing a wholesome eroticism, soon gave way to the realization that fateful social forces were at work in his Hungary. Aware of the terrible inhumanity looming over the horizon, he broke the superficial calm with powerful volumes, such as *Járkálj csak, halálraítélt!* (1936; *Walk On, Condemned!*, 1980). His poetry blossomed on the verge of his violent death, when, as a prisoner of the Nazis, he penned some of his best lines during his final days.

Sándor Weörcs (1913-1989) turned away from the objective reality of his surroundings and used his instinctive skill to produce an unbelievably varied poetic output, which emphasized his interest in the sound of words and in the myths and rites of the eternal human condition.

NEW POPULISTS

Quite distinct from this group, a large heterogeneous body of writers and poets began to appear during the 1930's, whose special emphasis on rural themes marked them as the new populists. They believed that it was the peasantry who, after a meaningful land reform, would provide the ideology and the energy for a national revival, and that they would also produce a new, dedicated intellectual leadership. They visualized Hungary as forming a bridge between East and West, although most of them had no sympathy for the Soviet system. The rift developing between the new populists and the urbanists proved to be one of the great misfortunes of modern Hungary. Neither group was able to prepare the nation for the changes that were obviously coming after the end of World War II, and neither group was powerful enough to bring about a thorough "moral revolution" which would implement much-needed social reforms.

The outstanding figure of the populists, Gyula Illyés (1902-1983) is generally regarded as one of the foremost Hungarian poets of the twentieth century, as well as a versatile prose writer and playwright. Early in his career, he was strong enough to ignore traditional rules and seemed to delight in a stylized, disciplined "primitiveness." Persuasiveness and originality characterize his best poems, which are heroic in mood and subject, with a touch of melancholy discernible throughout. During the late 1930's, he was the spokesperson of the populists, and his radical leftist past made him acceptable to every political group after the end of World War II. His enthusiasm for Soviet-imposed change soon cooled, and in 1956, he wrote *Egy mondat a zsarnokságról* (1956; *One Sentence on Tyranny*, 1957),

which may be called the Hungarian poem of the twentieth century. He wrote some of his finest poems in his old age, in verse characterized by musicality, gentle resignation, and introspection.

The end of World War II hardly signifies a milestone in the history of Hungarian literature, although thorough changes were implemented in the makeup of the country's intelligentsia. Hundreds of promising talents were destroyed by the war and its sordid aftermath, and as many or more were silenced later under various pretexts. After a few years of tenuous coalition, which offered genuine opportunities for free cultural development, the message was brought home that in the same manner that "there is no separate solution to Hungary's political problems," there would be no independent Hungarian cultural life, either. The pseudoprinciples of Socialist Realism were enforced in Hungary for only a few years, but their effects proved to be long lasting. Literature was placed completely in the service of daily politics, with bewildering and (in retrospect) amusing results.

Few dramatic changes resulted from the aftermath of the 1956 Revolution. After a handful of writers and poets were imprisoned, and a much greater number thoroughly intimidated, the "new" government declared that it was permissible for an artist to ignore politics. The Writers' Association was disbanded in order to create a "sounder" atmosphere, and the nation's best writers and poets quietly ceased publishing their creations. An eager coterie of political adherents tried to fill the gap, and authorities permitted many blameless and harmless apolitical poets to have their works printed, after years of muzzling them. The 1960's brought amnesties, the renewal of cautious debates, and the admission that there may be more than one kind of Socialist Realism. During the 1970's, with most of the real dissidents safely dead or out of the way, the authorities saw fit to open many avenues for literary experimentation and aesthetic debate, and exceptions to the Marxist hold on the country could be seen to demonstrate the resilience of the people's creative spirit.

POST-COLD WAR POETRY

In post-Cold War Hungary, in which literature and poetry of the prior several decades had functioned as a moral opposition to the Communist government, there was great expectation of a flowering of literature once the political obstacles were removed and the writer finally could freely explore his or her imagination. However, critics have found this has not happened, for several reasons. After the fall of the previous system, the dissident writer lost the poetic mission, a point of reference. Many writers also became politicians and had no time to write. Economics played a large role as well, with the cessation of government subsidies, the disintegration of state book-distributing giants, and steep increases in prices of new books. Living under high inflation and suffering from rising unemployment, the public was unable to afford as many books as it once purchased. Also, writers complained that, in the new commercial markets, unless a book promised profit, it would not be published regardless of its merit. The publishers that managed to stay in business tended to be those that published lurid potboilers, criminal and adventure stories, and soft-core pornography. As a reaction to the prohibition of erotic images and thrillers during the Communist rule, the Hungarian public often favored such publications over more serious literature.

The literary landscape of the "new" Hungary also found increasing tension between traditional nationalist and religious ideas and those of the modern era. The populists—those who claimed themselves as the cultural arms bearers of nationalism—started an offensive against cosmopolitan writers, known collectively as "urbanites," for the control of ideology and cultural lifestyle in Hungary. While the roots of this conflict stemmed from a decades-old rivalry between the city and the countryside, the more recent rise of multiparty politics has encouraged rivalry and resentment to increase. Populist authors regard the urbanites as arrogant because of their advantages in education, travel, and knowledge of languages—a gap that will take a generation or more to close. Urban liberals assume that the rural group is burdened by ideology. A glimpse into the populist mentality can be found in contemporary Hungarian poet Ferenc Juhasz's long poem "A szarvassá változott fiú kiáltozása a titkok kapujából" ("The Boy Changed to a Stag Cries Out at the Gate of Secrets"), based on a Transylvanian folktale. The theme "you can't go home again" is evident here, in that the provincial cannot return to the old way of life but also does not fit in with the liberal intellectual world of Budapest.

Despite the factionalism and political and cultural hurdles facing modern Hungary, it remains a country with an active literary culture. Fortunately, in the 1990's and at the beginning of the twenty-first century, the works of several major contemporary Hungarian poets—Csoori, Illyés, Ágnes Nemes Nagy, Radnóti, Gyozo Ferencz, György Petri—have become readily available in translation, widening the narrow conduit between Hungarian and world literatures.

SANDOR CSOORI

Sandor Csoori (born 1930), a leading contemporary Hungarian poet, essayist, and scriptwriter, has been called "the genius of discontent" and is considered to be one of the most prominent artistic spokespersons for the Hungarian people in the last decades of the twentieth century. A recipient of the Attila József Prize in Poetry, he also won the prestigious Kossuth Award, Hungary's greatest honor for achievement in artistic and scientific work. He serves as a modern voice for the populist movement, albeit a moderate one, and his poems and other literary works exhibit a never-ending concern over a threatened culture and national identity. For Csoori, the village represents a simpler society, the rudiments of a human community, a rough-hewn harmony beyond the experience of a more complex city. His cynicism is evident in "My Mother, a Black Rose," a tender and sensitive evocation of his mother's daily struggle for existence. Although not well, she still milks the cow, sweeps, and launders. "Unwelcome strangers," a code name for communist functionaries, talk to her "rudely" and, fearful, she tightens "her black shawl as if it were her loneliness." There are "wonderful new machines" around but no one comes to help her. "One night she falls to the ground/ Small, broken, shattered/ A bird will come/ And carry her away in his beak."

GYÖRGY PETRI

One particular poet who received both critical and public acclaim was György Petri, who died of cancer at the age of fifty-six in 2000. Readers appreciated Petri's combination of ideas and the language used to express these ideas. When it was still dangerous, he berated the "socialist regime" and kept the torch of the 1956 revolution burning. With the fall of communism in 1989, he then turned on himself, opposing the fragments of a society that seemed indestructible in its evilness, and he revoked memories, half heroic, half satiric, and issued statements on death. His poetic stance was rejection; he used the most ingenious devices to free himself of bile, but it seemed the more he got rid of, the more there was. His poem "Electra" displays his bitterness and is powerful not only because it serves as a powerful allegory of vengefulness in the wake of the abusive communist regime but also because it in part turns the myth around, to highlight universal guilt:

> Take my little sister, cute sensitive Chrysothemis
> to me the poor thing attributes a surfeit of moral passion,
> believing I'm unable to get over
> the issue of our father's twisted death.
> What do I care for that gross geyser of spunk
> who murdered his own daughter!

Reality as equated with sorrowful-history-turning-into detestable-sociology is not a matter to laugh about or something to play with. However, the poet would have liked to have played, if only his fearful honesty and his temperament had let him. Although well known as a love poet, Petri sullied what might be tender verses with obscenity and fierce irony to reflect how living under Hungary's dishonest, brutal communist regime cheapened even the finest feelings. He did not see an easy way to assuage the psychological damage inflicted by the Communists, even in the wake of communism's fall in 1989: "The epoch expired like a monstrous predator./ My favorite toy's been snatched."

BIBLIOGRAPHY

Gömöri, George. *A History of Hungarian Poetry, 1945 to 1956*. Oxford, England: Clarendon Press, 1966. Provides a thorough history. Bibliographical footnotes.

Gömöri, George, and George Szirtes, eds. *The Colonnade of Teeth: Modern Hungarian Poetry*. Chester Springs, Pa.: Dufour Editions, 1996. A collection of the works of thirty-five major Hungarian poets, all born between 1900 and 1954. Members of Hungar-

ian minorities living in other countries are included. Useful notes on the poems and biographical notes.

Hawkesworth, Celia, ed. *A History of Central European Women's Writing*. New York: Palgrave, 2001. Contains four essays on Hungarian women writers, along with others dealing with topics such as women's self-adjustment and feminist self-awareness. Map, bibliography, and index.

Kolumban, Nicholas, ed. and trans. *Turmoil in Hungary: An Anthology of Twentieth Century Hungarian Poetry*. St. Paul, Minn.: New Rivers Press, 1996. Generous selections from the works of nineteen poets. Illustrated.

Makkai, Adam, ed. *In Quest of the "Miracle Stag": The Poetry of Hungary, an Anthology of Hungarian Poetry in English Translation from the Thirteenth Century to the Present*. Foreword by Árpád Göncz. Urbana: University of Illinois Press, 1996. Provides a wide selection of Hungarian poetry. Includes biographies.

Pilinszky, János. *Metropolitan Icons: Selected Poems of János Pilinszky in Hungarian and English*. Studies in Slavic Language and Literature 8. Edited and translated by Emery Edward George. Lewiston, N.Y.: E. Mellen Press, 1995. Contains about a third of the poet's verse, including selections from all of his major collections. Introduction, notes on the poems, and bibliography.

Schwartz, Agatha. *Shifting Voices: Feminist Thought and Women's Writing in Fin-de-Siècle Austria and Hungary*. Montreal: McGill-Queen's University Press, 2008. Subjects include the fight for suffrage and independence, the dangers of a return to tradition, and the effects of urbanization. One appendix contains authors' biographies; the other is a bibliography of Hungarian women writers of the period.

Suleiman, Susan Rubin, and Éva Forgács, eds. *Contemporary Jewish Writing in Hungary: An Anthology*. Lincoln: University of Nebraska Press, 2003. A volume in the Jewish Writing in the Contemporary World Series. Introduction by the editors. Features a broad selection of writings by Jewish authors in Hungary. Bibliographical references.

Szirtes, George, ed. *Leopard V: An Island of Sound: Hungarian Poetry and Fiction Before and Beyond the Iron Curtain*. New York: Random House, 2004. The editor of this important anthology, himself an award-winning poet, has arranged literary works so as to trace the history of change in Hungary from wartime into the Stalinist period and eventually to postmodernism and to anxiety or despair. Published to coincide with the Hungarian Year of Culture (2003-2004).

Tezla, Albert, ed. *Ocean at the Window: Hungarian Prose and Poetry Since 1945*. Minneapolis: University of Minnesota Press, 1980. Contains a substantial introduction by the editor, followed by selections from the works of twenty-four writers and biographical-critical essays. Also has a guide to Hungarian pronunciation and a bibliography of literature in translation.

András Boros-Kazai
Updated by Sarah Hilbert

INDIAN ENGLISH POETRY

Before Asian Indians could write poetry in English, two related conditions were necessary. First, the English language had to be sufficiently Indianized to be able to express the reality of the Indian situation; second, Indians had to be sufficiently Anglicized to use the English language to express themselves. The first of these two conditions, the Indianization of the English language, began much before the second, the Anglicization of Indians. Hence, though the first Indian poet to write in English was Henry Derozio, in the early nineteenth century, the Indianization of English had begun about three centuries earlier, in 1498, when Vasco da Gama, sailing from Lisbon, landed in Kerala. It was almost another century before the first Englishman came to India, but by the time Father Thomas Stephens arrived in Goa in 1579, a considerable body of Indo-Portuguese words were already being assimilated into English. Such lexical borrowing accelerated with the increasing British presence in India after 1599, when the East India Company was launched. For nearly 150 years after the charter of the East India Company, Englishmen in India wrote only travel books for the public and journals and letters in private. Nevertheless, by the end of the seventeenth century, a number of Indian words had been naturalized into English. The following is a selection from G. Subba Rao's catalog in his book *Indian Words in English* (1969):

Amuck, Arrack, Bazaar, Bandicoot, Brahmin, Bungalow, Calico, Cash, Cheroot, Chintz, Chit, Compound, Cooly, Dhobi, Divan, Dungaree, Fakir, Ghee, Guru, Gunny, Hakim, Hookah, Imam, Jaggery, Juggernaut, Maharaja, Mongoose, Nabob, Pariah, Pucka, Punch, Pundit, Shampoo, Shawl, Tank, Toddy, Yogi, Zamindar.

Because the functional and pragmatic context of the language changed in India, English began to adapt itself to its new environment. This nativization process continued as the use of English increased, as schools were established to teach it, and as the number of Indians using it increased.

More important than this large-scale lexical borrowing was the fact that, by the end of the eighteenth century, Englishmen in India had started to write poetry on local Indian subjects, whereas earlier, they had written only travelogues, journals, and letters. Of these Englishmen in India, the most important was Sir William Jones (1746-1794), one of the first British Indian (or Anglo-Indian) poets. An accomplished linguist and translator, his familiarity with Indian traditions is reflected in his eight hymns to the various Indian deities. These poems are strictly Indian in both style and theme; in writing them, Jones demonstrated for future Indian poets that the English language could be a fit vehicle for Indian subject matter. Hence, by the beginning of the nineteenth century, the prospective Indian English poet inherited not only an English whose expressive range had been enlarged by a substantial lexical borrowing of Indian words, but also an English which, as British Indian poets such as Jones had shown, was richly amenable to Indian subject matter.

The second precondition, the Anglicization of Indians, began when the British became a powerful colonial power in India. This happened more than 150 years after the East India Company was chartered. In 1757, the British won the historic Battle of Plassey, which gave them control of Bengal. In 1772, they assumed the *Diwani*, or revenue administration, of Bengal, and in 1790, they took over the administration of criminal justice. Not until the British had changed from traders to administrators did the large-scale Anglicization of India begin. This Anglicization around the turn of the eighteenth century was marked by several crucial events. First, in 1780, India's first newspaper, *Hickly's Bengal Gazette*, was published in English. Second, in 1817, Raja Rammohan Roy, a prominent social reformer, helped found the Hindu College of Calcutta, which later, as Presidency College, became the premier educational institution of Bengal. Third, and most important, by 1835, the British government had laid the foundations of the modern Indian educational system, with its decision to promote European science and literatures among Indians through the medium of the English language. The result was that English became in India, as in other British colonies, a passport to privilege and prestige.

A study of the social and cultural contexts of Indian English poetry reveals several important insights into its origin. First, Indian English poetry began in Bengal, the province in which the British first gained a foothold. In addition, Indian English poetry was an urban phenomenon centered in Calcutta. In fact, for the first fifty years, Indian English poetry was confined entirely to Bengalis who were residents of Calcutta. Then, gradually, it moved to other urban centers, such as Madras and Bombay; even today, Indian English poetry is largely urban. Finally, because English was an elite language in India, Indian English poets belonged to the upper class. Thus, in its early years, most of the practitioners of Indian English poetry came from a handful of prominent Calcutta families.

CRITICAL APPROACHES

There are basically three ways of approaching Indian English poetry: as an extension of English poetry, as a part of Commonwealth poetry, or as a part of Indian poetry. The first approach is largely outdated today, while the second, though still current, has gradually yielded to the third.

When Indians first began to write poetry in English, they were outnumbered by Eurasians and Englishmen who also wrote poetry on Indian subjects. Hence, poetry by Indians was not distinguished from poetry by non-Indians. Indeed, both types were published by the same publishers, the Indian subsidiaries of British publishers such as Longman or Heinemann, or by the English newspapers and magazines of India, which were usually owned and edited by Eurasians or Englishmen. Most Indian English poets were educated by Englishmen in Anglophone schools; like other English poets, they studied English literature. Because India was a part of the British Empire, Indian English poets did not have a strong national identity, and their early efforts were considered to be a tributary of the mainstream of English literature. Anglo-Indian literature was the term used to denote their poetry, the implication being that this was English literature with Indian themes. The term referred primarily to the literature produced by Englishmen and Eurasians in India, though it also included work by "native" Indians. The first scholarly work on Anglo-Indian literature was Edward Farley

Oaten's *A Sketch of Anglo-Indian Literature* (1908), a condensed version of which was included in the *Cambridge History of English Literature* (1907-1914), edited by A. C. Ward. Oaten's primary concern was with English writers such as Jones, Sir Edwin Arnold, and Rudyard Kipling, and Oaten made only passing reference to Indian writers in English. With India's independence from Britain and the withdrawal of the British from India, Anglo-Indian literature, defined as literature written by Englishmen in India, more or less came to an end. On the other hand, literature by Indians in English increased, gradually evolving an indigenous tradition for itself. Consequently, Oaten's approach became untenable in dealing satisfactorily with Indian English literature. Nevertheless, it continues to have a few adherents—among them George Sampson, who, in *The Concise Cambridge History of English Literature* (1970), contends that Indian English literature is a tributary of mainstream English literature.

Another approach, initiated by scholars in England in the early 1960's, is to consider Indian English literature as a part of Commonwealth literature or the literature of former British colonies and dominions such as Canada, Australia, the West Indies, and countries in Africa, South Asia, and Southeast Asia. The *Journal of Commonwealth Literature*, based at the University of Leeds, has done much to foster such an approach. Later, academics in the United States attempted to see Indian English poetry as a part of a global literature in English. The journal *WLWE: World Literatures Written in English* represents this approach. These approaches are fairly useful when the focus is large and the scholar is located in the United States or the United Kingdom, but they share the problem that the literatures of the various nationalities have little in common and often belong to different traditions: for example, Nigerian English literature and Australian literature. Nor does such an approach serve very well when one literature, such as Indian English poetry, is studied in depth. It then becomes clear that labels such as "Commonwealth literature" or "world literature in English" simply help to provide a forum for these litcratures in Western academia and that detailed study is still pursued by nationality.

The most widely accepted approach to Indian English poetry is to regard it as a part of Indian literature. This approach might seem the obvious one, but it took nearly a century to gain wide acceptance and is not without its problems. In the first place, there is no such thing as Indian literature per se: Indian literature is constituted of literatures in the several Indian languages, including Hindi, Tamil, Bengali, and Manathi. Most of these literatures, however, have their roots in the Sanskrit tradition of Indian literature which flourished from roughly 1500 B.C.E. to 1500 C.E. After the latter date, the regional literatures in the various Indian languages emerged. Hence, it is possible to argue that a unified tradition in Indian literatures does exist. Once that is granted, the task of the critic is to place Indian English literature into such a framework. Considering that English is not traditionally an Indian language, that is not easy, although at the time that Indian English literature began to emerge, there was a renewed efflorescence in the other regional languages of India as well. Moreover, the "renaissance" of regional literatures occurred under a stimulus similar to the one that caused the emergence of Indian English literature—namely, the impact on India of British rule, Western knowledge, and the English language. It is reasonable, then, to regard Indian English poetry as a limb of the larger body of Indian poetry, a creation of the same sensibility that has produced other regional-language poetry in India since the nineteenth century.

This approach was first propounded by Indian critics during the 1930's and 1940's, the most influential among them being K. R. Srinivasa Iyengar, whose *Indo-Anglian Literature* (1943) was the first book-length discussion of Indian English literature. Iyengar used the term "Indo-Anglian" to distinguish this literature from Anglo-Indian literature and to suggest that it was a part of Indian literature. In his introduction to *Indian Writing in English* (1982), Iyengar mentions that the phrase "Indo-Anglian" was used "as early as 1883 to describe a volume printed in Calcutta containing 'Specimen Compositions from Native Students.'" Probably, "Indo-Anglian" was merely an inversion of "Anglo-Indian," used to distinguish the poetry written by Indians from that of the Englishman. Alongside the term "Indo-Anglian," "Indo-English" was also used by critics who did not like the former. Both terms were used

until the early 1970's, after which Indo-English gradually acquired greater acceptance. The term "Indian English" was used from the 1960's as synonymous with "Indo-English." It is being used increasingly in preference to other terms.

HENRY DEROZIO

Henry Derozio (1807-1831) is generally credited with being the first Indian English poet. His father was of Portuguese descent and his mother an Anglo-Indian. Derozio was Indian not only by birth but also by self-definition. This was especially remarkable because Derozio, a Christian, was reared among Eurasians and Englishmen, and many of his Hindu Bengali contemporaries strove hard to identify themselves with the British. Derozio's love for India is revealed in several of his poems. In his short life of twenty-three years, Derozio had a remarkable career as a journalist, a teacher at Hindu College, a leading intellectual of his day, and a poet. He has often been compared to John Keats.

Derozio wrote short poems for several magazines and newspapers of his day, but only one volume of his poems, *The Fakeer of Jungheera* (1828), appeared during his lifetime. A selection of his poems, published in 1923 by Oxford University Press, has subsequently been reprinted. As a poet, Derozio showed great promise, though he did not live to fulfill it. His poems reveal the great influence of the English Romantic poets, particularly Lord Byron and Sir Walter Scott. Derozio's sonnets and short poems, such as "To India My Native Land" and "The Harp of India," are his most accomplished works. His ambitious long poem *The Fakeer of Jungheera* is an interesting attempt to fuse the Byronic romance with the realities of the Indian situation. Despite the fact that Derozio's output was uneven and meager, he is counted as one of the major Indian English poets for both historical and artistic reasons.

KASIPRASAD GHOSE

A contemporary of Derozio, the Indian English poet Kasiprasad Ghose (1809-1873), published *The Shair and Other Poems* in 1830. Ghose has the distinction of being the first Hindu Bengali Indian to write English verse. He continued Derozio's efforts to deal with Indian subjects in his poems. An interesting example is his semicomic poem "To a Dead Crow," in which

Ghose uses the unglamorous, common Indian crow as a subject. The persona Ghose created for himself was that of the *Shair*, or the poet in the Indian Persian tradition, indicating that although he wrote in English, his stance was that of an Indian poet.

MICHAEL MADHUSUDAN DUTT

Michael Madhusudan Dutt (1824-1873), whose long narrative poem *The Captive Ladie* (1849) was published about twenty years after Ghose's book, is an interesting figure in Indian English poetry. Dutt is remembered today not as an English poet but as the first and one of the greatest modern Bengali poets. After his failure at English verse, he turned to Bengali, his mother tongue. Dutt's case is frequently cited by those critics who believe that Indians cannot write good English poetry and should write only in their mother tongue. Since Dutt, there have been several other poets who began to write in English but turned to their native languages after being dissatisfied with their efforts in English. Dutt is also interesting because, though he acquired fame as a Bengali poet, he was extremely Anglicized. He not only converted to Christianity but also married an Englishwoman and qualified for the bar in England.

OTHER EARLY POETS

Another family of the Dutt name brought out *The Dutt Family Album* in 1870, featuring about two hundred pieces by Govin Chunder Dutt (1828-1884), his two brothers, and a nephew. Earlier, the whole family had converted to Christianity and, in 1869, had left India to live in England and other parts of Europe. The volume sheds light on the literary atmosphere prevailing in the aristocratic Dutt family, which was to produce another generation of poets in Govin's daughters Aru and Toru Dutt. Another notable poet of this time was Ram Sharma, born Nobo Kissen Ghose (1837-1918), who published three volumes of verse between 1873 and 1903. Sharma, who practiced yoga for several years, tried to bring an Indian religious dimension to Indian English poetry.

In this period, Indian English poetry moved out of Bengal for the first time with the publication of the Bombay poet B. M. Malabari's *Indian Muse in English Garb* (1876). Soon Cowasji Nowrosi Versuvala's *Count-*ing the Muse* (1879) and A. M. Kunte's *The Risi* (1879) were published in Bombay and Poona, respectively. Though still an upper-class hobby, Indian English poetry was slowly spreading to metropolitan centers outside Bengal.

The poetry of the first fifty years of Indian English poetry (1825-1875) is generally considered imitative and derivative by critics. Certainly, the poems from this period which are usually anthologized do not show signs of very great talent. A judgment on the quality of these poets, however, must not be passed hastily, because most of their books are out of print and hence not easily available for critical scrutiny.

TORU DUTT

There is almost complete critical consensus that the talent of Toru Dutt (1856-1877) was an original one among Indian English poets. Like Derozio, she died young, and like Emily Brontë, her life has been the object of as much interest as her poetry. Toru Dutt left for Europe with her family when she was thirteen and attended a French school in Nice with her elder sister, Aru. The Dutts then moved to Cambridge, England, where Toru participated in the intellectual life of the university. Though converted to Christianity and very Anglicized, the Dutts felt alienated in England, and they returned to Calcutta four years after they had left, when Toru was seventeen. In 1874, soon after their return, Aru died. Earlier, when Toru was nine, her elder brother Abju had died. One year after her sister's death, Toru published *A Sheaf Gleaned in French Fields* (1875), which also featured eight pieces by Aru. These poems, "renderings" from the French, were enthusiastically received in India and England and soon went into three editions, the third published by Kegan Paul, London, with a foreword by Arthur Symons. In that same year, 1875, Toru took up the study of Sanskrit, and ten months later she was proficient enough in it to think of producing "A Sheaf" gleaned from Sanskrit fields. This volume was published in 1882, after her death, as *Ancient Ballads and Legends of Hindustan*, with a foreword by Edmund Gosse. Meanwhile, she had written one French novel and left incomplete an English novel, both of which were published after her death. Weakened by tuberculosis, she died in 1877 at the age of twenty-one.

The most significant aspect of Dutt's literary career was her return to her Indian heritage after her sojourn in the West. In *Ancient Ballads and Legends of Hindustan*, she converted popular myths from the *Rāmāyaṇa* (c. 500 B.C.E.; *The Ramayana*, 1870-1874), the *Mahābhārata* (c. 400 B.C.E.-200 C.E.; *The Mahabharata*, 1834), and the *Purāṇas* into English verse. In this, she pioneered a way for several later Indian English writers who had similar problems regarding their literary identity. Dutt's English versions, except in a few instances, are without condescension to the original and without authorial intrusions. In addition to longer "ballads" and "legends" from Sanskrit mythology, Dutt wrote short lyrics, odes, and sonnets. The best of these, probably her best single poem, is "Our Casuarina Tree." This poem, reminiscent in both form and content of Keats's odes, is about the beautiful Casuarina tree in the poet's garden at Baugmaree. The tree, by the end of the poem, becomes a symbol not only of the poet's joyous childhood but also, through an extension in time and space, of the poet's longing for permanence and eternity. The poem is a masterpiece of craftsmanship, a fine blending of thought, emotion, and form. Though her output as a poet was not particularly prolific, *A Sheaf Gleaned in French Fields* and *Ancient Ballads and Legends of Hindustan* show sufficient accomplishment to entitle Dutt to her place in the pantheon of Indian English poets.

SRI AUROBINDO GHOSE

Sri Aurobindo Ghose (1872-1950) probably has the best claim to be regarded as the greatest Indian English poet. In a poetic career of more than fifty-five years, his output and range were truly staggering. Sri Aurobindo wrote lyrics, sonnets, long narrative poems, poetic drama, and epics. He was fluent in a variety of conventional meters, such as iambic pentameter and hexameter, and he also experimented with quantitative meter and mantric poetry.

His reputation rests most securely on the posthumously published *Savitri* (1954), an epic of some twenty-four thousand lines. In *Savitri*, Sri Aurobindo used the story of Savitri's conquest of death in *The Mahabharata*—a story that has influenced Indians for centuries as an exposition of perfect womanhood—and expanded it to create his epic. In this epic, Savitri real-

izes her divine potential as a human being and, like Christ, defeats death; after her conquest of death, she returns to earth as a symbol of what humanity can achieve. A mystic and a seer, Sri Aurobindo claimed merely to have described his own, palpable experience in writing the poem. In his "Letters on *Savitri*," which are attached to the authoritative edition of the poem, Sri Aurobindo says that the work was written under the highest possible poetic inspiration, which he called "over-mind poetry," a state in which there was no effort on his part and in which he was merely the scribe of a "vision" which descended, perfect and complete, upon him. *Savitri*, one of the longest poems in the English language (it is roughly twice the length of John Milton's *Paradise Lost*, 1667, 1674), is the most discussed poem in Indian English literature. It took about fifty years to finish—from the germ of the idea to the final written product—and a complete reading demands a long time; nevertheless, year after year it continues to attract and challenge critics, students, and readers.

As *Savitri* is the most discussed Indian English poetic work, Sri Aurobindo is the most discussed of the Indian English poets. His was a multifaceted personality—he was a seer, mystic, Vedantist, poet, philosopher, revolutionary political activist, literary critic, and thinker. Like many other major Indian English poets, he was born into an upper-class Anglicized family and was educated in England. Finding himself completely Westernized, he strove to find his roots, to realize himself, after returning to India. Remarkably successful in this, he is considered one of the greatest thinkers of modern India. As a poet, he was extremely well-versed in the European tradition of literature as well as the Indian tradition. Sri Aurobindo was fully conscious of what he was doing as a poet; he had a comprehensible theory of poetry and a clear view of what he sought to accomplish, both formally and thematically. His appraisal of the nature of poetry is clearly formulated in *The Future Poetry* (1953), and it is with this knowledge that his later, more difficult poetry is to be approached. Sri Aurobindo's poetry is easily available in the centenary edition of his *Complete Works* (1972).

SAROJINI NAIDU

If Sri Aurobindo is the greatest Indian English poet, Sarojini Naidu (1879-1949) is certainly the most popular, accessible, and moving—in a sense, the best Indian English poet. Naidu's poems are all songs, meant more to be heard than read. She is a lyric poet whose work shows a mastery of rhyme and meter. Her typical poem is short, usually consisting of fewer than twenty lines, although she did write some long sequences of short poems. The chief quality of her poetry is melody—the sound and sense combine to produce emotion, as in music. Within this musical, lyric paradigm, Naidu is extremely versatile. Like Rabindranath Tagore, she was a truly all-Indian poet, drawing upon the poetic traditions of several Indian languages and inspired by different regions of India and by different religious traditions.

The most remarkable feature of Naidu's poetry is its complete authenticity as Indian poetry. She achieves an Indian quality of both form and content without the slightest self-consciousness. She uses both the rhythms and the conventions of Indian folk songs as inspiration for much of her poetry. The range includes songs of professions ("Palinquin Bearers," "Wandering Singers," "Indian Weavers"), love songs ("Indian Love-Song," "Love-Song from the North," "A Rajput Love-Song"), lullabies ("Cradle-Song," "Slumber-Song for Sunalini"), seasonal songs ("The Call of Spring," "Harvest-Song," "The Coming of Spring"), and devo-tional songs ("Lakshmi, the Lotus-Born," "Hymn to Indra, Lord of Rain," "Songs of Kanhaya"). Naidu's imagery, too, is strikingly Indian, transferred into English from conventions in Indian poetry. In "A Rajput Love-Song," for example, she says, "O Love! were you the *keora*'s soul that haunts my silken raiment?" and "O Love! were you the scented fan that lies upon my pillow?" Both of these images are stylized and sophisticated, not naïve or simplistic. Naidu also uses discourse-types from Indian folk songs: Some of her songs are monologues, others duets, and still others are communal songs in several separate voices and in chorus. Naidu uses several Indian words as well as quotations from Indian languages to enhance the Indian flavor of her poems. These words and quotations, however, are harmonized completely in the poem and not used indiscriminately. All in all, Naidu's attempts to locate herself in an Indian tradition of poetry were highly successful.

During Naidu's lifetime, four volumes of her poems were published: *The Golden Threshold* (1905), *The Bird of Time* (1912), *The Broken Wing* (1917), and *The Sceptered Flute* (1943), a collection of the first three books. *The Feather of the Dawn* (1961) was published by her daughter after Naidu's death. Naidu's poetry shows no major change or development from her first to her last book; although the tone becomes more somber, the metric felicity is the same. Naidu was chiefly a love poet, and her poetry explores the many facets of love as outlined in the Sanskrit tradition of love poetry: love in union, love in longing, love in separation; the pain of love, the joy of love, the sin of love, the desire of love; earthly love, divine love. Toward the end of her career, she became increasingly a *bhakti*, or devotional, poet, expressing in poem sequences her transcendent love for the Almighty. Although her work is unpopular with a number of recent Indian English poets, Naidu remains the most critically acclaimed Indian English poet after Sri Aurobindo.

Indian English poet Sarojini Naidu, left, with Indian leader Mahatma Gandhi. (Hulton Archive/Getty Images)

RABINDRANATH TAGORE

Aside from Sri Aurobindo and Naidu, the period from the 1880's to the 1920's produced two other major poets. Chief among these is Rabindranath Tagore (1861-1941). Strictly speaking, Tagore is not considered an Indian English poet. He wrote only one long poem, *The Child* (1931), directly in English, writing all of his other works in Bengali, translating some later into English. Nevertheless, it was Tagore's 1912 English rendering of his famous Bengali poem *Gitanjali* (1910) that won for him the Nobel Prize in 1913. After that, Tagore "translated" several of his works into English, deviating considerably from the originals in the process. These renderings into English pose a unique, theoretical problem for the student of Indian English poetry: Should these works be regarded as originals or as translations? This problem has not been solved satisfactorily, but the consensus is that they are translations. Tagore, as the greatest Bengali writer, obviously belongs rightfully to Bengali; his influence on Indian English poets, however, is so great that he cannot simply be ignored in that area of study. The least that can be said is that Tagore is another example of a bilingual poet, a phenomenon not at all uncommon in the traditionally multilingual society of India.

MANMOHAN GHOSE

Another important poet of this period is Sri Aurobindo's elder brother, Manmohan Ghose (1869-1924). Some of Ghose's early poems appeared in *Primavera* (1890) while he was still in England. During his lifetime, only one volume of his verse, *Love Songs and Elegies* (1898), appeared, but when he died, he left in manuscript several volumes of poetry—short poems; two incomplete epics, *Perseus, the Conqueror* and *Adam Unparadised*; and one long, incomplete poetic drama, *Nollo and Damayanti*. After his death, his longtime English friend Laurence Binyon published some of these lyrics as *Songs of Life and Death* (1926), prefaced by a memoir of Ghose. Recently, Calcutta University published Ghose's complete poems in five volumes, under the supervision of his daughters. Ghose's life was tragic. Returning to India after a completely English upbringing, he found himself out of place—in his own words, "de-nationalized." His wife's health had deteriorated, and she died after being paralyzed for years. Finally, the poet himself went blind. The most common criticism of his poetry is that it is totally un-Indian in form and content. This is largely true, though he did try to write his long poetic drama, *Nollo and Damayanti*, on an Indian theme. Ghose came close to being an English poet despite being Indian, but at that, too, he was doomed to fail. Today, despite his metric virtuosity, neither do his poems appeal to Indian readers nor has he found a place in the canon of English poetry. Ghose, at best, is uneasily an Indian English poet. His example, unfortunately, has not deterred other Indians from completely Westernizing themselves.

TWENTIETH CENTURY: 1920'S-1950'S

The period from the 1920's to the 1950's was marked by a great efflorescence of Indian English poetry. It produced literally scores of poets, each with several volumes of verse to his or her credit. For the first time, a large mass of Indian English poetry was created, no longer confined to the upper class. Unfortunately, though this period produced a large quantity of poetry, it has been neglected by critics, primarily because the modernist poets of the 1950's were so united in their aversion to their predecessors.

Though this period produced a large quantity of poetry, it is the most neglected and underrated period in Indian English poetry. The chief reason for this is the severe reaction against this poetry by the post-1950's poets. Indeed, contemporary Indian English poets have been so united in this aversion that most recent anthologies totally omit the poets who came to maturity in the preceding generation. Although it is common in literature for the present generation to react against the previous generation, this reaction has reached allergic proportions in contemporary Indian English poetry. Much of the poetry of the period from the 1920's to the 1950's is becoming scarce—many of the publishers of that era are now defunct, and no serious attempt has been made to preserve these texts. Few libraries outside India possess texts from this period, and even in India, they are scattered in different places. Consequently, the poets of this period have received very little critical attention.

The best-known poet of this period is Harindranath Chattopadhyaya (1898-1990). Starting with his *Feast of Youth* (1918), he regularly published volumes of verse and poetic drama into the 1960's. He was easily one of the most prolific poets in Indian English poetry. The range of his content was very diverse, covering a whole spectrum of ideologies from extreme Aurobindonian idealism to revolutionary Marxist materialism. His formal range, however, was limited; he usually wrote rhymed, metric verse which, though competent, is sometimes predictable and cloying.

Most of the other poets of this period can be divided into three groups: the Aurobindonian and religious poets, the lyric and Romantic poets in the tradition of Naidu and Tagore, and the poets whose work reflects a transition from this Romanticism to the modernity of the post-1950's poets.

This period produced several poets who were inspired by Sri Aurobindo; they are sometimes called the Pondicherry school, because they lived in the Aurobindo ashram in Pondicherry and were disciples of Sri Aurobindo. The most famous of them are K. D. Sethna (born 1904) and Dilip Kumar Roy (1897-1980). Others, also inspired by Sri Aurobindo, are Nirodbaran (1903-2006), Nolini Kanta Gupta (1889-1983), Prithwi Singh Nahar (1898-1976), Anil Baran Roy (1901-1952), Punjalal (1901-?), and Romen Palit (born 1920). Some of their poetry has seemed obscure to readers because of its mysticism. Other religious and devotional poets are Ananda Acharya (1881-1945), T. L. Vaswani (1879-1966), and Jiddu Krishnamurti (1895-1986).

The largest number of poets in this period practiced the lyric, Romantic mode of Naidu and Tagore. It is perhaps because of these two poets that the impact of European modernism on Indian English literature was considerably delayed. Many of these neo-Romantics were professors of English in India; examples are P. Seshadri (1887-1942), N. V. Thadani, Shyam Sunder Lal Chordia, Govinda Krishna Chettur (1898-1936), Armando Menezes (1902-1983), Hymayun Kabir, V. N. Bhushan (1909-1951), and P. R. Kaikini. There are many more, and their total output is massive. Their poetry has long been out of fashion, seeming effusive and quaint, but certainly not all of it can be dismissed outright, as has often been the case.

Several poets of this period effected the transition from Romanticism to the modernism of the post-

1950's poets. These transitional poets introduced concrete, commonplace imagery, irony, the language of common speech, and a personal, psychological dimension to Indian English poetry. Probably the earliest "new" poet of Indian English was Shahid Suhrawardy (1890-1965), whose *Essays in Verse* (1937) was avowedly influenced by T. S. Eliot and other modernists. Though some of his poetry seems to be merely self-conscious muttering and vague, allusive cerebration, Suhrawardy certainly brought a new tone to Indian English poetry. His work, however, was lost to most Indians after he migrated to Pakistan after the partition of India in 1947. Another poet who struck a new, realistic note was Manjeri Iswaran (1910-1968). Bharati Sarabhai created a sensation in English literary circles with her poetic drama *The Well of the People* (1943), in which she used several of Eliot's techniques.

Joseph Furtado (1872-1947) was another talented poet of this period who experimented considerably with language. Though he was predominantly a lyric poet, he brought an element of realism and rustic humor to Indian English poetry. His chief contribution was his use of Indian English pidgin and code-mixed varieties in poems such as "Lakshmi" and "The Old Irani." In these poems, Furtado not only anticipated contemporary poets such as Nissim Ezekiel, who exploit pidgin in their poetry, but also helped to bring the language of Indian English poetry closer to the language of the bilingual speech community in which English is actually used in India. What is interesting is that Furtado's use of pidgin, unlike Ezekiel's, is not parodic or condescending; whereas for Ezekiel, the joke is at the expense of an Indian variety of English, for Furtado, the comedy derives from authentic characterization.

A REVOLUTION IN TASTE

During the 1950's, the dominant tone in Indian English poetry shifted from Romanticism to irony. The revolution in taste did not occur overnight, but once established, its impact was swift and sweeping. What had been minority voices suddenly became the majority: A whole generation rejected its immediate past. This rejection is nicely voiced in Nissim Ezekiel's first book, *A Time to Change, and Other Poems* (1951).

The new poets were a vocal group and did not hesitate to denigrate openly their predecessors. P. Lal, for example, attacked Sri Aurobindo at length, though Lal retracted his strictures a few years later; dividing readers into those who could appreciate Sri Aurobindo and those who could not, Lal firmly placed himself and the poets of his generation in the latter category. This debunking of poetic ancestors continued. In the influential article "The New Poetry," published in *The Journal of Commonwealth Literature* (July, 1968), the poet Adil Jussawala required fewer than three pages to dismiss Indian English poets from Derozio to Naidu, claiming that the best Indian English poetry was being written by poets of his generation. Eight years later, R. Parthasarathy, another contemporary poet, introducing his now widely used anthology *Ten Twentieth Century Indian Poets* (1976), reiterated Jussawala's claims. Many other poets of this generation echoed the notion that theirs was the only Indian English poetry worthy of the name. However, these "new" poets soon divided into two main factions, those who practiced the dominant ironic mode and those who preferred a more traditional lyricism and Romanticism.

Besides Ezekiel, some of the poets who practice the ironic, clipped mode are Parthasarathy, A. K. Ramanujan, Gieve Patel, Shiv K. Kumar, Arun Kolatkar, and Jayanta Mahapatra. A typical poem in this mode involves an alienated speaker observing a typically Indian situation with detachment. Examples are numerous: In Keki Daruwala's "Routine," a police officer cynically regards yet another violent mob that he has to disperse. In Ezekiel's "Background, Casually," the poet assesses ironically his own lack of identity. In Kolatkar's *Jejuri* (1974, 1976), a place of pilgrimage is seen through the eyes of a detached and nonconformist visitor. Mahapatra's "The Whorehouse in Calcutta Street" shows a detached, self-critical observer recording his impressions of a brothel. In "Homecoming," Parthasarathy records his homecoming experience with self-critical irony. In "Naryal Purnima," Patel sits apart, commenting on a religious tradition from which he is alienated. In "Obituary," Ramanujan views the death of his father with ironic detachment. The same paradigm repeats itself. The situation is Indian; the observer is a self-critical, detached outsider. The poets use this mode to write both about themselves and, as in

Mahapatra and Daruwala, about the external world. Often, as in Kamala Das, the early poems of A. K. Mehrotra, or in Pritish Nandy, the irony turns to anger. Most of these poets write free verse in a language that is as precise and close to "standard" English as possible. Exceptions, such as Ezekiel's poems in Indian English, are usually parodies.

There were, however, some poets who chose to write in the lyric and Romantic strain. The chief practitioners of this mode include V. K. Gokak, Keshav Malik, Karan Singh, Shankar Mokashi-Penekar, and, in their later works, Lal and Nandy.

INDIAN WOMEN POETS

In the final years of colonial rule and even in the first decade after Independence, there were far fewer women poets in India than men. In the 1960's, Kamala Das (1934-2009) established her reputation by writing striking, confessional poems exploring female sexuality and arguing for women's sexual rights. However, it was not until the middle 1970's that works by women poets began appearing in significant numbers. *The Bird's Bright Ring: A Long Poem*, by Meena Alexander (born 1951), was published in 1976, and her collection *Without Place*, in 1978. In 1979, the Goan Eunice de Souza (born 1940) published her first volume, *Fix*. The telling portraits of de Souza's fellow Catholics made this book not only the writer's most controversial but also probably the most distinctive of her many fine works. *Fix* is also important in that it was published by Newground, a cooperative started by three poets, including Melanie Silgardo (born 1956), another of the many outstanding women writers who came to the attention of readers late in the 1970's.

It should be noted that controversial ideas and radical views were also expressed by women writing in the regional languages, such as the Bengali poet and social worker Maitreyi Devi (1914-1990), who voiced her concern for peasants and for tribal people, and Amrita Pritam (1919-2005), whose poems in Punjabi focus on the mistreatment of women after her native area of India became part of Pakistan. Pritam herself settled in India, and her experiences help to explain why there are so many more women writers in India than in Muslim Pakistan. However, in *We Sinful Women: Contemporary*

Urdu Feminist Poetry (1991), seven Urdu women poets protest the ongoing repression of their gender by the religious and civil authorities of Pakistan. This collection was recognized throughout the world as an important expression of feminist feeling within the Muslim world. Wisely, the editor of this collection, Rukhsana Ahmad, had made wide circulation of the volume possible by translating all of the poems into English and printing her versions beside the Urdu originals.

Although not all of the women writers who have emerged since the 1960's are preoccupied with sexuality, feminism, or social justice, they are far more concerned with such issues than with that of language, which loomed so large in the minds of the first postcolonial generation of writers. It now seems to be generally accepted that English is no longer to be regarded as the language of an oppressor, but instead is seen as a convenience, as a common means of expression, which can be adapted to reflect everyday life on the Indian subcontinent and which will probably ensure a much wider distribution of one's work than publication in a regional language. On the other hand, those who choose to write in one or another of the regional languages are no longer faced with almost insurmountable difficulties in finding a translator. As Vinay Dharwadker comments in his preface to *The Oxford Anthology of Modern Indian Poetry* (1994), there are now a great many excellent translators actively seeking new materials for new audiences throughout the world. Whether they write in regional languages or in English, Indian poets of both genders can now aspire to international distribution.

WRITERS AND THE WIDER WORLD

If Partition displaced some writers, many more left their native areas as international travel became less costly and as opportunities for them to study and to teach abroad multiplied. Since the new multiculturalism among Western readers was creating a rapidly expanding market for works by Indian writers, whether written in English or translated into English, it was only natural that those writers would go west to meet this new and highly appreciative public, some of them to visit or to stay for a time, some of them to remain permanently.

AGHA SHAHID ALI

These new developments made the old nationalistic objections to writing in English seem irrelevant; now the question was whether or not the writers of the diaspora should even be classified as Indian writers. The English-language Muslim poet Agha Shahid Ali (1949-2001), for example, was born in Delhi, grew up in Kashmir, and returned to Delhi for his education before moving permanently to the United States in 1976. One might expect exile to be the theme of Ali's poems. However, he drew upon his own experiences primarily as a basis for his definition of the human condition. Wherever people live, Ali suggested, they are subject to change, and as a result they will suffer from a sense of loss and of longing for what is past.

DOM MORAES

Displacement and loss are also major themes in the poetry of Dom Moraes (Dominic Frank Moraes, 1938-2004). Born in Bombay, educated there and at Jesus College, Oxford, Moraes was a great success in England, both personally and professionally, from the time his first book of poems, *A Beginning* (1957), written when he was only nineteen, won the 1958 Hawthornden Prize. However, he did not feel at home there or in his native Bombay, where he finally settled after a journalistic career that took him all over the world. Like Ali, Moraes believed that one always feels like an exile, even if technically one is "at home."

KEKI N. DARUWALLA

Keki N. Daruwalla (born 1937) would agree. Although he was born and educated in India and made his home in New Delhi, Daruwalla does not feel any sense of stability. Again and again he points out in his poetry that no place on earth is exempt from change. What bothers him about history, which Daruwalla defines as no more than a record of changes, is that it records public events rather than private tragedies. In "Hawk" and "A City Falls," Daruwalla stresses his conviction that what transpires in the life of an individual, caught in cataclysmic change, is more significant than what happens to a city or even to a society.

VIKRAM SETH

In his revised edition of *Modern Indian Poetry in English* (1987), Bruce King credits Vikram Seth (born 1952) with altering the Western world's attitude toward Indian poetry in English, which up to that point had been classified more as a hobby for a few readers than as part of mainstream English literature. Seth's volume *The Humble Administrator's Garden* (1985) so delighted the London reading public, King explains, that critics began talking about including the title poem in future anthologies of English poetry. Their approval was due as much to Seth's evident rejection of the excesses of modernism in favor of a more polished style as to his captivating wit. Seth was soon just as popular in New York as he had become in London, and with the publication of his novel in rhymed verse titled *The Golden Gate: A Novel in Verse* (1986), he gained an international reputation.

Seth is a typical representative of the new cosmopolitanism among Indian writers. He was born in Calcutta and eventually made his home in New Delhi. However, Seth was educated at Oxford, at Nanjing University in China, and at Stanford University in California, where for several years he also was an editor for the Stanford University Press. Tibet was the setting of Seth's award-winning travel book, *From Heaven Lake: Travels Through Sinkiang and Tibet* (1983). Perhaps it was not surprising that his verse novel, which is set in San Francisco, drew criticism in India for not being "Indian" enough. These critics were happier with Seth's story of an Indian family, the best-selling novel *A Suitable Boy* (1993).

SUJATA BHATT

Wherever they live and whatever their subject matter, however, it is evident that Indian poets remain conscious of their roots. For example, Sujata Bhatt (born 1956), who was born in Ahmedabad of a family originally from Gujarat, was educated in the United States and eventually made her home in Germany. However, not only does she translate Gujarati poetry into English, but she also uses Gujarati words and even whole lines of Gujarati in her own poems. It has been pointed out that good intentions do not necessarily make for good poetry. Often Bhatt's bilingual experiments do not work. Nevertheless, her attempts to express the multicultural experience must be noted, and some of her poems, especially those in *Brunizem* (1988) are very good indeed.

At the beginning of the twenty-first century, Indian poetry written in English, as well as regional poetry translated into English, was at last attaining the recognition it deserved. Critics were enthusiastic about the new generation of Indian writers; publishers in Great Britain and in the United States were anxious to bring out their works; and readers throughout the world were becoming familiar with poets hitherto unknown to them. In this case, at least, change was all for the better.

BIBLIOGRAPHY

Agrawal, K. A. *Toru Dutt: The Pioneer Spirit of Indian English Poetry—A Critical Study*. New Delhi: Atlantic, 2009. Analyzes the works of the Bengali woman who is often called the first Indian writer to produce English poetry of high quality. The writer concludes that Dutt not only is important historically, but also remains one of the finest Indo-Anglian poets.

De Souza, Eunice. *Talking Poems: Conversations with Poets*. New Delhi: Oxford University Press, 1999. Interviews with ten important Indian poets, conducted by a writer and editor who is herself a major poet.

_____, ed. *Early Indian Poetry in English: An Anthology, 1829-1947*. New Delhi: Oxford University Press, 2005. Includes the works of twenty poets, ranging from epics, ballads, narratives, and romantic verse to devotional poetry. Notes on each poet and an informative introduction by the editor.

_____. *Nine Indian Women Poets: An Anthology*. New Delhi: Oxford University Press, 1997. Two generations of post-Independence Indian writers, selected because their poetry is of consistently high quality, are represented in this volume. Contains biographical notes, critical commentaries, and an index of first lines.

King, Bruce. *Modern Indian Poetry in English*. Rev. ed. New Delhi: Oxford University Press, 2006. An important critical work, which first appeared in 1987. Chronology, useful appendexes, and index.

_____. *Three Indian Poets: Ezekiel, Moraes, and Ramanujan*. 2d ed. New York: Oxford University Press, 2005. Since the publication in 1991 of the first edition of this book, all three of these important modern poets have passed away. In this revised volume, the author reconsiders the total output of three distinguished but very different writers. Excellent introduction.

Naik, M. K., and Shyamala A. Narayan. *Indian English Literature, 1980-2000*. Delhi: Pencraft International, 2004. A critical survey of the fiction, poetry, drama, and nonfictional prose produced during an exceptionally active literary period. Includes a comprehensive bibliography of secondary sources.

Prasad, G. J. V. *Continuities in Indian English Poetry: Nation, Language, Form*. Delhi: Pencraft International, 1999. A new and original study of the history of Indian English poetry, discussing all the major writers and presenting new readings of many of their poems. The author considers such matters as the poets' attempts to place themselves within the context of their native country despite the fact that they are writing in a nonnative language.

Singh, Kanwar Dinesh. *Contemporary Indian English Poetry: Comparing Male and Female Voices*. New Delhi: Atlantic, 2008. Various critical approaches are used to determine the influence of gender and sexuality on the themes of poets and on their poetic practice. The works of twelve important Indian poets, five men and seven women, are discussed at length.

Thayil, Jeet, ed. *The Bloodaxe Book of Contemporary Indian Poets*. Cambridge, Mass.: Bloodaxe, 2008. An anthology covering fifty-five years of Indian poetry in English. Contains poems by seventy Indian poets, living all over the world, who nevertheless write out of shared traditions and express themselves in a common language.

Verma, K. D. *The Indian Imagination: Critical Essays on Indian Writing in English*. New York: St. Martin's Press, 2000. In addition to an introductory discussion of "Structure of Consciousness, Literary History and Critical Theory," contains chapters on Sri Aurobindo and Nissim Ezekiel. Notes and an index.

Makarand Paranjape
Updated by Rosemary M. Canfield Reisman

Italian Poetry to 1800

Poetry and literature in the Italian vernacular, the common language that sprang from the ashes of Latin, arose in Italy around the beginning of the thirteenth century and soon displayed itself in literary works of major importance. This linguistic success is so extraordinary that one wonders how it was possible that such a literary phenomenon could take place in a language whose written tradition is so recent. The spoken language, however, had a long history, which is represented by the development of Latin into several vernaculars. The heritage and cultured structures of Italian have roots that are deep and extensive, developing from the culture and literature of the medieval period, the time from the fall of the Western Roman Empire to the beginning of the thirteenth century.

From Latin to Italian

During that long period of time, Italy developed a literature that, on one hand, was no longer in Latin but, on the other, was not yet in Italian. This language maintained the appearance of Latin but was quite different from classic Latin; it was the Latin used by the Roman Catholic Church and by educated people, a language that, after the fall of the Roman Empire, spread throughout Europe as the cultured language and remained as the official language of science until the modern age. Medieval literature, however, was not developed extensively, and its quality, from an artistic point of view, was rather limited.

During the Middle Ages, the Church had become the major source of knowledge and culture, and it had inherited from Rome its characteristic of universality. The major documents of medieval Christian thought profoundly shaped the values of the new vernacular literature; particularly influential were the works of the Scholastic philosophers, among whom towers Saint Thomas Aquinas and in which one can find the vital roots of Dante's writings.

Italian vernacular poetry began in the thirteenth century with the simultaneous flowering of written literature in several of Italy's competing dialects. In the twelfth century, it had appeared that the Sicilian dialect was going to acquire the status of a national language; Sicily, at the time of Emperor Frederick II (1194-1250), had become an important center of cultural life and art. This Sicilian superiority was ephemeral, however, vanishing after the death of the emperor. It was instead the Florentine tongue that, for several reasons, became the national language. The Florentine dialect prevailed primarily because, during the period of assertion of the vernacular, some of the greatest masterpieces of Italian literature were written in that dialect.

Early vernacular works

The earliest extant poetic compositions in the vernacular are religious works intended for doctrinal instruction; typical examples of this genre are Bonavesin della Riva's *Libro delle tre scritture* (c. 1300; book of the three scriptures) and Fra Giacomino da Verona's *De Jerusalem celesti* (c. 1230) and *De Babilonia civitate infernali* (c. 1230). In the field of specifically religious poetry, which contains a clear and pure effusion of spiritual feelings, there is the *Laudes creaturarum* (c. 1225), by Saint Francis of Assisi, and the oeuvre of Jacopone da Todi, which includes 102 laudes. Though the majority of these religious poems narrate the deep mystical experience of the author, there are also several that are of a moral and satiric nature.

Of greater importance from an artistic and cultural point of view is the development in Italy of a lyric poetry of Provençal origin, which reflected a courtly concept of love that was conceived as an homage to "the lady" according to the principles dictated by the codes and rules of feudal society. The courtly content of this poetry and the very elaborate style rarely offered the possibility of expressing truly sincere and deep feelings. The poetry created by this style gave more importance to the artifice of the form than to the originality of the inspiration and was therefore characterized by a certain coldness.

The poetic genre had some success in northern Italy as a result of the troubadours, who traveled from court to court from Provence into northern Italy. The most consistent achievement of this lyric style, however, took place in Sicily at the court of Frederick II, where it assumed the status of a school. Among its most celebrated poets were Frederick himself and his sons, Enzo and Manfredi. In addition, there were resident courtiers such as Jacopo da Lentini and Giacomino Pugliese. The aesthetic value of the poetry of the Sicilian school is minimal; there, the worst traits of Provençal poetry were accentuated. Nevertheless, the historical significance of the Sicilian school is great: It constituted the first attempt to use the vernacular with a clear artistic intention. At this historical moment, as earlier mentioned, Sicilian could have become the national language. Historical events, however, prevented that. Frederick II died in 1250, and with his demise the power of his court soon disappeared and the cultural and literary effort which he so strongly supported collapsed.

DOLCE STIL NUOVO

The poetry of the Sicilian school had, nevertheless, already found a fruitful development in Tuscany, where its poetic themes were enriched with political and religious elements—particularly in the works of Guittone d'Arezzo and in the amorous poetry of Chiaro Davanzati. Furthermore, the Sicilian experience was instrumental in suggesting a new development, a new conception of love poetry that was proposed by the advocates of the *dolce stil nuovo* ("sweet new style"). In this new style, feelings are based on a bourgeois experience—the culture of the communes—not on a feudal one as was the case with Provençal poetry. Supported by a mystical consciousness, the new poetry exemplified a greater sincerity of expression and was supported by deeper sensitivity and more ardent feelings. Guido Guinizzelli's lyric poem "A cor gentile ripara sempre amore" ("Love Seeks Its Dwelling Always in a Gentle Heart") established what could be considered the schematic structure of the new school. Originating in Bologna, this innovative way of creating verses reached Florence, where Guido Cavalcanti further developed it in his poem "Donna mi prega" ("A Lady Asks Me"). Cino da Pistoia brought to the *dolce stil nuovo* a new psychological concept of love, substantively humane, with a potential that Dante was to explore in *La vita*

nuova (c. 1292; *Vita Nuova*, 1861; better known as *The New Life*), written shortly after 1292. *The New Life* narrates the spiritual unfolding of his pure love for Beatrice, a girl whom he met early in his life and who died young in 1290, leaving the poet grief-stricken. Under the influence of the *stilnovisti*, Dante cultivated his love for Beatrice as a pure—almost religious—feeling through which he might be led to spiritual perfection. This concept would be developed extensively in his masterpiece.

DANTE

Dante (1265-1321) was born in Florence into a Guelph family that claimed ancient noble origins. He received his early education from the Franciscan friars of Santa Croce Church in his native town and, from the poetry of the Sicilian school that had spread into central Italy, he learned to write verses in the vernacular. Like many other citizens of Florence in his social condition, Dante participated in the tumultuous political life of the commune. As a consequence of these activities, he was exiled when the Black faction of the Guelph party, which was supported by Pope Boniface VIII, won political dominance over the White faction, to which Dante belonged. The Blacks banished the leaders of the Whites from Florence and its territory. Military attempts to regain power organized by the White faction failed. Dante resigned himself to the life of an exile and stayed at several courts in northern Italy, finally settling down in Ravenna at the court of Guido da Polenta. In Ravenna, he devoted his attention to completing his sacred epic, *La divina commedia* (c. 1320; *The Divine Comedy*, 1802). He died in Ravenna in 1321.

It is significant that Dante composed his masterpiece in exile. After a long period of tumultuous events, the moment for deliberation had come. On the one hand, the recent past appeared to him as a forest of mistakes; on the other hand, he could visualize the possibility of a transcending order, embracing Heaven and Earth. Dante believed that the misled and corrupt humanity of his time could organize itself into a new order which could reach the goal of temporal and eternal happiness. This empire would be universal and divinely ordained, and the emperor would be independent in his temporal power, his authority granted directly to him by God and not by the pope. Other motives that certainly influenced the composition of the poem were Dante's love for Beatrice and the desire to glorify her, his desire for justice, and his need to express his aesthetic insight and creative imagination.

In *The Divine Comedy*, Dante describes being lost in "una foresta oscura," a dark forest which represents the confusion of life. As a result of his experience, he acquires a consciousness of the sad condition of his spirit. He wants to free himself from this anguished state, but with human resources alone the soul cannot save itself. If a man with a soul in distress shows good intentions, however, he deserves the help of God; the Holy Virgin, representing "Divine Mercy," comes to his aid. She calls on Lucia (Saint Lucy), the "Enlightened Grace," who, in turn, goes to Beatrice, the symbol of knowledge in divine matters. Beatrice—who is also the human woman loved by Dante—descends into Limbo and begs Vergil, who represents "right reason," to bring help to Dante. Reason tells Dante that he cannot go suddenly from a sinful life to one of perfection; he must first face the dreadful consequence of sin by visiting Hell. He must then continue to Purgatory to make amends for his sins. Only then, after having reached the condition of natural perfection (the Terrestrial Paradise), will Dante be able to go to the Celestial Paradise and therefore reach the supreme reward, undergoing the beatific Vision of God. In this last part of Dante's mythical voyage, Vergil, "right reason," will not be a sufficient guide, and Dante will visit Paradise with the help of Beatrice.

The Divine Comedy is an epic poem of one hundred cantos. These cantos are collected into three parts, each of which is dedicated to one of the kingdoms of the life beyond: *Inferno, Purgatorio* (*Purgatory*), and *Paradiso* (*Paradise*). The *Inferno* is described in strong and vivid terms: the terrible heat and fires of the underworld, the agonies of the suffering, the terrors of the devils. In *Purgatory*, where the passions are appeased, there predominates a condition of melancholy generated by the recollection of the flawed past life and the interminable waiting for the state of eternal beatitude. In *Paradise*, Dante acknowledges the impossibility of conveying absolute happiness and holiness in earthly terms.

Although *The Divine Comedy* is Dante's master-piece, he left other notable works as well. In addition to the poems that are included in *The New Life*, pervaded by mystical love, he composed a collection of *canzoniere* (lyric poetry) that documents the further artistic development that the poet had to undergo in order to reach the richness of motive that characterizes *The Divine Comedy*.

Dante's achievements mark a moment of great cultural change in the history of Italy. On the one hand, he summarizes the thought, life, and aspirations of the Middle Ages; on the other hand, he opens the door to a modern conception of life and culture. If Dante's gaze is fixed toward Heaven, he is not blind to temporal happenings, and he observes the Earth in all of its aspects and details. He does not ignore the mystery of the human soul. Rather, as exemplified in one of the cantos of *The Divine Comedy*, he embraces the courage of Ulysses, who ventured to discover new worlds. Thus, Dante anticipates the questing spirit of the Renaissance.

PETRARCH

The political ideas of Petrarch (1304-1374), the other major poet of the thirteenth century and one of the major figures of Italian literature, present a historical ambience quite different from that of Dante. Politically, Petrarch is far removed from the conception of a universal empire. His interest is clearly concentrated on Italy seen as a country geographically and ethnically different from any other country beyond the mountain chain of the Alps. Culturally, Petrarch departs from the medieval worldview; for him, the classical world acquires a new interest. Thus, Petrarch could be considered a precursor of Humanism.

From a psychological point of view, Petrarch does not possess the self-assurance that is typical of Dante. He appears to be more introspective, with a tendency toward self-analysis, which may have accounted for his uncertainty and unhappiness—elements that constitute the essence of his poetry. The conflict between his religious desires and his worldly attitudes is never fully resolved. There is no serenity or dramatic resolution for him, only the constant melancholy that is characteristic of the modern spirit.

Petrarch was born Francesco Petrarca in Arezzo, the son of Pietro di Parenzo (commonly known as Ser Petracco), a Florentine notary who belonged to the

White political faction and was exiled in 1302, the same year in which Dante was exiled. In 1312, the family moved to near Avignon, in France, where Petrarch's father had found employment with the papal court. Petrarch studied law at the universities of Montpellier and Bologna, but his interest was oriented more toward literature than law. In 1327, in the Church of Santa Chiara in Avignon, he first saw Laura, the woman who was the major source of inspiration for his poetry. Petrarch served several lords in Italy, especially those of Colonna, a powerful Roman family that contributed several popes to the Church. Petrarch traveled through the many regions of Italy as well as in France, Flanders, and Germany. Later, he returned to Provence and retired to Vaucluse, a small town not far from Avignon. He spent his time writing a long epic poem in Latin, *Africa* (1396; English translation, 1977), his most extended work in that language. The poem was inspired by Vergil's *Aeneid* (c. 29-19 B.C.E.; English translation, 1553) and was written in hexameter and subdivided into nine cantos. Petrarch felt this epic to be his major contribution to the literature of his time. It was successful during his lifetime, and in 1340, Petrarch was rewarded with the title of poet laureate by the Senate in Rome. During this period, he continued his activities as a diplomat at the service of various courts in Italy. He also continued with his literary endeavors, which included collecting ancient texts by Latin authors. Later, he went to live in the territories of the Republic of Venice and died in 1374 in Arquà, a small town near Padua, where he had gone into seclusion.

The true poetic glory of Petrarch, however, derives almost exclusively from the lyrics he wrote in the vulgar tongue, *Rerum vulgarium fragmenta* (1470, also known as *Canzoniere*; *Rhymes*, 1976). Though he dismissed these lyrics as *nugellae* ("little things"), he refined and edited them throughout most of his life. *Rhymes* consists of 366 poems, most of them sonnets recounting the melancholy story of his love for Laura, a love that did not cease even with Laura's death, which occurred in 1340 during the plague. Well acquainted with the love poetry of the Provençal troubadours, the Sicilian school, and the *stilnovisti*, Petrarch derived from these traditions elements that became vital and inseparable parts of his own poetic world. Nevertheless,

the imprint, the essence of *Rhymes*, stems from his passion for Laura, the focus of an intense conflict between the seductions of the world and the enduring values of spiritual love.

The work is divided into two parts, usually designated "In vita di madonna Laura" (in the lifetime of Laura) and "In morte di madonna Laura" (after the death of Laura). In the first part, Petrarch's love has great impulses, prostrations, enthusiasms, and a gloomy bitterness. The poet blesses the moment of his falling in love and swears eternal fidelity to his feelings for Laura. Only rarely does sensuality appear in his verses, but at the same time the poet does not attempt to transform his feelings into a mystical thought that will raise him—through his love of the woman—to love of God. In the second part, those poems written after Laura's death, there is at first an expression of grief, the torture of separation, the tormenting thought that Laura's beautiful face, the "dolce sguardo," the endearing glance, are gone forever. Then, the image of Laura begins to live a new life in the soul of the faithful lover; she is no longer a temptress. Instead, Laura becomes a maternal figure and the consoler of Petrarch's sufferings. Also, with this new vision, Petrarch believes that his love, even if spiritualized, is still love for a human creature and therefore a distraction from the love for the Creator. Petrarch's *Rhymes* has been among the most influential poetic works not only of Italian literature but also of world literature. With a psychological acuity that anticipates the modern discovery of the self, Petrarch describes refined and sophisticated feelings, spellbinding in their perplexity but at the same time never completely detached from a lived human experience.

GIOVANNI BOCCACCIO

The third of the great Italian writers of this period is Giovanni Boccaccio (1313-1375), whose fame is founded on *Decameron: O, Prencipe Galetto* (1349-1351; *The Decameron*, 1620). A literary work in prose, it is a collection of one hundred short stories related to one another by a frame story.

Of limited artistic value, Boccaccio's poetry is nevertheless of historical interest. For the most part, it is allegorical, reflecting Dante's model and the general pattern of the medieval literary tradition. His most significant early works include *Il filostrato* (c. 1335; *The Filostrato*, 1873), a lyric composition somewhat biographical in style, which was followed by *Teseida delle nozze d'Emilia* (1339-1341; *The Book of Theseus*, 1974), an epic poem imitating the style of Vergil's *Aeneid* and Statius's *Thebais* (c. 92 C.E.; English translation, 1766). There is also *La caccia di Diana* (c. 1334; Diana's hunt), a mythological poem describing the life at the court of Naples where Boccaccio spent some time during his youth. Other works written before the *Decameron* are *Il ninfale d'Ameto* (1341-1342; also known as *Commedia delle ninfe*), an idyllic poem of popular love, and *L'amorosa visione* (1342-1343; English translation, 1986), an allegorical poem inspired by Dante's *The Divine Comedy*.

ITALIAN RENAISSANCE

Between the end of the fourteenth century and the beginning of the fifteenth century, there appeared in Italy the first signs of a profound change in Western culture. The typical representative of this period, which would be later called the Renaissance, sought above all the full and balanced development and enjoyment of his human potential. Transcendence was not explicitly denied but was simply neglected. The Renaissance person did not feel the need of divine grace to achieve these goals, and the ideal of the ascetic, who runs away from the world so that the spirit will thrive, was completely foreign—indeed, almost incomprehensible.

At the beginning of this period, there was a great interest in the studies of classical languages and literature. This interest in classical culture and the new critical sense with which these cultures were analyzed bred a large cultural movement called Humanism. In the infancy of the new movement, in the first part of the fourteenth century, there was little interest in the vernacular, since the aspirations of learned individuals were oriented toward classical languages. Among the Humanists who distinguished themselves as poets in this first part of the century, Giovanni Pontano entrusted all of his creative literary efforts to the Latin language; his works include an astrological poem, *Urania* (1505); an epic poem, *Lepidina* (1505); and three books of elegies, *De amore coniugalis* (1480-1484; conjugal love), which are dedicated to his wife.

LORENZO DE' MEDICI

At this historical moment, Tuscany no longer held predominance in the national literature but nevertheless was, along with Florence, a very active cultural center because of the patronage of Cosimo de' Medici and of his grandson Lorenzo the Magnificent (1449-1492). Lorenzo has a place in the history of Florence and Italy because of his great abilities as a politician and administrator and his munificent and intelligent patronage of the arts; in addition, he distinguished himself as a man of letters.

In Lorenzo's oeuvre one finds the influence of the most contrasting poetic currents of his time. His *L'altercazione* (after 1473) reveals the influence of the Platonist Center founded in Florence by the renowned Humanist Marsilio Ficino. In *Selve* (1515), Lorenzo narrates an allegorical love story which, as in Petrarch's *Trionfi* (1470; *Tryumphs*, 1565; also known as *Triumphs*, 1962), goes through several stages—jealousy, hope, despair—to conclude finally in the contemplation of the eternal beauty, God. In his *Rime* (1680), dedicated to Lucrezia Donati, he was inspired by the *stilnovisti*, whose philosophical ideas were close to Platonism. Also deserving of special consideration are *Nencia da Barberino* (c. 1474), a short lyric poem in which the peasant Vallera gives vent to his passionate love for the beautiful shepherdess Nencia, and *Canto trionfale di Bacco e Arianna* (c. 1490), a work in which Lorenzo becomes the interpreter of the soul and spirit of the Renaissance with the accomplished skill of a highly developed artist.

POLIZIANO

The most eminent poet of his century, Poliziano (1454-1494), was born in the Tuscan town of Montepulciano. Although born into a family of humble condition, Poliziano was able to educate himself at the school of noted Humanists in Florence. He also attracted the attention of Lorenzo the Magnificent, who took him into his house as the tutor of his children.

Poliziano was a brilliant Humanist and wrote verses both in Latin and in Greek. Some of his poems in classical languages have remarkable taste and artistic value, but his reputation as a poet is based on his vernacular poetry, especially on *Stanze cominciate per la giostra del magnifico Giuliano de' Medici* (1518; *The Stanze of*

Angelo Poliziano, 1979; commonly known as *Stanze*), *Orfeo* (pr. 1480; English translation, 1879; also known as *Orpheus*), and *Rime* (wr. 1498, pb. 1814).

Stanze is an incomplete lyric poem, of which Poliziano wrote only the first book and part of the second. This work was supposed to celebrate the joust won in Florence in 1475 by Lorenzo's brother Giuliano, who was later killed during Pazzi's conspiracy in 1478. The poem describes how Giuliano, a handsome and vigorous young man, is living an intense and happy life in close contact with nature, spending most of his time riding and hunting and giving little attention to love and sentiment. Cupid is offended by this young man's attitude and plans to take revenge by making Giuliano fall in love with a beautiful nymph, Simonetta. In the second book of the poem, Venus and Cupid send Giuliano a dream that instills in him the desire for warlike glory, which is necessary in order that he be deserving of Simonetta's love. He prepares to organize a joust, and it is at this point that the poem is interrupted. The poem interprets with admirable grace that moment in which the sentimentally immature young man, who is completely involved with the exterior world, withdraws into himself and achieves for the first time a new awareness, noticing the rise of unsuspected love feelings.

Poliziano wrote *Orfeo*, his second major literary work, during his stay at the Gonzagas' court in Mantua. The tone of this composition is dramatic, but it lacks a true conflict of passions. The poem places instead a greater importance on the lyric and elegiac motives, but they seldom reach the expressive intensity of *Stanze*. Of more significant artistic value, from the lyric point of view, is *Rime*, a collection of love poems that also includes the famous "I' mi trovai fanciulle un bel mattino" ("I Went A-Roaming, Maidens, One Bright Day"). This poem ends with an invitation to capture the fleeting moment and to "gather ye therefore roses . . . ere their perfume pass away"—a topos which was to become one of the most pervasive in Renaissance poetry throughout Europe.

JACOPO SANNAZZARO

The same accents are found in the poetry of the Neapolitan author Jacopo Sannazzaro (1458-1530), who, lacking the depth of inspiration, the vitality, and the human understanding of Poliziano, succeeds neverthe-

less in reaching a respectable artistic sophistication. Sannazzaro's reputation rests on *Arcadia* (*Arcadia and Piscutorial Eclogues*, 1966), a pastoral poem published in 1504. To his contemporaries, *Arcadia* appeared to be a unique combination of all the various motives of pastoral poetry, deriving its inspiration from classical poets such as Vergil, Ovid, and Theocritus.

LUIGI PULCI

Another author of the fifteenth century, Luigi Pulci (1432-1484), profited from the enlightened patronage of Lorenzo the Magnificent. Pulci tried several forms of traditional poetry without great success, achieving fame only when he turned to an epic poem, *Morgante*, which he started almost as a joke. Instead, it introduced a genre that acquired a large popularity in Italy. The poem took up the subject matter of the *Chanson de Roland* (twelfth century; *The Song of Roland*, 1880) and the legend of Charlemagne—a theme that had found an unusual popularity among the simple people in Italy and had created a rich florescence of epic poems, none of which had arrived at any reputable artistic level. These epic poems had gradually taken a very definite structure, a structure that was monotonously repeated. The plot usually revealed the treacheries and evil deeds of the members of the House of Maganza, which had expelled from France the members of the House of Chiaromonte and called the Saracens to fight against Charlemagne, the leader of the Chiaromonte. These same adventures, usually narrated by storytellers in the streets, reappear in Pulci's *Morgante*. Pulci, however, succeeds in bringing the story to a level that is artistically moving and epic in scope.

Pulci ended his poem at the twenty-third canto, and his work was published as it was, incomplete, as *Morgante* (1481). Later, urged by a friend to complete it, the poet added another five cantos that tell of the defeat at Roncesvalles, where the rear guard of Charlemagne's army, returning from Spain and being led by the Paladin Roland, is destroyed by the Saracens. Thus completed, the epic poem was titled the *Morgante maggiore* (1483).

MATTEO MARIA BOIARDO

This new literary genre was continued by Matteo Maria Boiardo (1440 or 1441-1494), who freed it from the popular tradition that still existed in Pulci's work and initiated with refined artistic awareness the poetic theme of the old chivalry, or Romantic epic. His major work, the *Orlando innamorato* (1483-1495; English translation, 1823), a grandiose enterprise originally planned to include 120 cantos divided into four parts (though interrupted after the second part), merges the two major themes of chivalric poetry: the events narrating the story of Charlemagne, from which Boiardo obtained his major characters and the plot of the Christian world fighting the Saracens, and the Arthurian legend, from which he deducted the individualistic spirit of love and adventure as well as the fair land aspect.

Love and adventure are evident in the *Morgante maggiore*, but both seem somewhat incidental to the story, lacking the well-organized and well-planned structure found in this new poem. In the *Orlando Innamorato*, love and adventure are closely connected, and it is indeed love that drives the restless knights to undertake the most unusual and risky endeavors. Boiardo is also credited with having created numerous characters with well-defined personalities; in turn, these characters were taken up by Ludovico Ariosto.

Several parts of Boiardo's *Orlando Innamorato* have a high poetic value, but the poem is not considered a true masterpiece: It lacks a unifying spirit that would give life to all parts of the story. There is, however, in Boiardo's poem an interesting taste for the primitive, from which stems a grandiosity that is not handicapped by exceptional or complicated psychological depth. One also perceives in his stories a fascinating and uncontrolled indulgence in the simple and powerful passions of love, vengeance, and a desire to conquer that is clearly an asset to his work and poetic conception. This raw energy, however, cannot be sustained throughout the poem. Little by little, the rich vein of inspiration exhausts itself, and the episodes of the story monotonously repeat themselves until the reader's interest in the adventure weakens and disappears. The spirit of the Renaissance, so deeply different from the one of the Middle Ages, demanded an entirely new vision of the world of the chanson de geste, and it was Ariosto who met this demand.

LUDOVICO ARIOSTO

Ludovico Ariosto (1474-1533) was born in Reggio Emilia. His father was in the service of the lords of that region, the Este family, and Ludovico inherited the position when his father died. He worked at first for the Cardinal Ippolito d'Este and then for the Cardinal's brother, the duke Alfonso d'Este, who had his court in the city of Ferrara. Often, however, the poet had to leave his favored city, sent by his patrons on missions to various parts of the duchy and Italy. Later in life, he was able to live in a house that he bought on the outskirts of Ferrara, where he could dedicate himself completely to writing, the greatest passion in his life.

In his youth, under the Humanistic influence, Ariosto wrote only in Latin, imitating Catullus and Tibullus. Ariosto first published a Latin ode, "Ad Philiroen" ("To Philiroe"), in 1494. After 1503, however, the poet rarely wrote in Latin; his lyric poetry was composed primarily in the vulgar tongue.

Ariosto began writing his masterpiece *Orlando furioso* (1516, 1521, 1532; English translation, 1591) around 1503 and published a first edition of sixteen cantos in 1516. After extensive revision, he published a second edition in 1521. Finally, yet another version, with several cantos added, was published in 1532. This careful revision produced a poem that for its excellent style could be compared to Petrarch's *Rhymes*. Moreover, the form in which the poem is written, the ottava rima, gave such musicality to Ariosto's verses that it was called the "golden octave."

Orlando Furioso is a continuation of the *Orlando Innamorato*; Ariosto's poem more or less begins where Boiardo concluded his story. Although the *Orlando Furioso* has an extraordinary number of episodes, its plot is based solidly and clearly on a few fundamental events. The multiplicity of the facts narrated does not create confusion or boredom but unfold in harmonious and orderly ways. All the characters, who may at times appear scattered, are intermittently collected at a specific point, be it the palace of the sorcerer Atlante or under the walls of Paris, walls from which they subsequently depart in search of new, wonderful adventures.

The spirit of the poem should be sought in the vision of life as a changing scene, a continuously changing spectacle, a vision that Ariosto had obtained from the Renaissance conception at its highest and most balanced stage of development. According to this conception, life should be observed with a certain detachment, without bitterness and without moralizing.

LATE SIXTEENTH CENTURY

In the second part of the sixteenth century, the great magnificence of the Renaissance faded, perhaps because of the natural exhaustion of the intense fervor of life, both elegant and merry, that had charmed the Italian courts. Politically, the change was particularly severe. The Spanish domination of Italy drastically changed life in the courts of several states. From a literary point of view, artistic production was tightly controlled and dominated by the rules and suggestions of several learned societies, especially the Accademia della Crusca ("academy of the chaff"), founded in 1583 with the intention of purifying the literary language.

There was, however, in the late sixteenth century an interesting ferment of new ideas. The theoretical elements implicit in the Renaissance conception of life became explicit only during this period. They were expressed in organized philosophical thought by thinkers such as Giordano Bruno (1548-1600), Bernardino Telesio (1509-1588), and Tommaso Campanella (1568-1639), a prolific author whose masterpiece is *La città del sole* (1623; *City of the Sun*, 1880). Inspired by Plato's philosophy, Campanella describes a utopian, egalitarian society ruled by a priest-philosopher in *City of the Sun*.

An important influence on Italian literary development after the Renaissance was exercised by the sweeping religious movement known as the Counter-Reformation. This Catholic movement tried to contain the spread of the Protestant revolution while renewing the life of the Catholic Church. In this period, literature followed the natural consequence of the exhaustion of the Renaissance, and the Counter-Reformation ideals succeeded from time to time in animating literary production with renewed religious spirit. Included among these works is the oeuvre of Torquato Tasso, who closed the Renaissance that Petrarch had opened.

TORQUATO TASSO

Torquato Tasso (1544-1595) was born in Sorrento, near Naples. His father, Bernardo, was an accomplished man of letters and had written a lyric poem, the *Amadigi* (1560), which had been somewhat successful. Bernardo Tasso was the secretary to the prince of Salerno, Ferrante di San Severino, and when the prince was forced to leave his state and go into exile for politi-

cal reasons, Bernardo, accompanied by his son, followed his patron. This exile brought the Tassos to the courts of several Italian princes, and young Torquato pursued his studies in different universities, finally graduating from the University of Padua with a degree in literature. He was soon admitted to the retinue of Cardinal Luigi d'Este, to whom he had dedicated his pastoral drama *Aminta* (pr. 1573; English translation, 1591), a work that showed artistic maturity and that expressed in lovely forms the serenity of Tasso's spirit at that time in his life. Distinguished by this serenity and by its lighthearted sensuality, *Aminta* is the culmination of the Renaissance pastoral tradition.

Aminta was followed by *Gerusalemme liberata* (1581; *Jerusalem Delivered*, 1600), Tasso's major work. This period was not only the most prolific for the poet but also the happiest in his life. After 1575, the year in which *Jerusalem Delivered* was read publicly to the duke of Ferrara and his court, Tasso's mental health began to deteriorate. His sensitive mind was racked by doubts about the critical and religious soundness of his poem. He also became very suspicious of his friends and benefactors, and after some irrational episodes, the duke of Ferrara was compelled to confine Tasso to an asylum, where he remained for seven years. When he was released in 1586, the poet went to live at the court of the Gonzagas in Mantua, but only for a short time. He soon returned to his wanderings: Naples, Florence, back to Mantua, and Rome, where Pope Clement VIII planned to crown him with laurel. Tasso, however, could not manage to extend his life to the day of the coronation. Exhausted, he found shelter in the convent of Sant' Onofrio of the Giannicolo and there he died, on April 25, 1595.

Tasso had begun to work on his masterpiece, *Jerusalem Delivered*, with a greater concern than had characterized his earlier works. At the end of the sixteenth century, it was not conceivable that a poet would be starting to work on what was considered the most noble of the literary genre, the *poema epico* (the romantic poem), so much discussed by the supercilious academicians, yet without an adequate critical preparation. Tasso, therefore, expressed his ideas about the romantic poem in a short treatise, *Discorsi dell'arte poetica* (1587; discourses on the poetic art). The poet believed that the purpose of literature was more to entertain than to instruct and that in the romantic poem one should strive for credibility. For this reason, the poet should turn to history; tales of marvels and miracles should be religious in inspiration, it being undesirable for Christian people to believe in the prodigies of pagan divinities. Finally, Tasso asserted that the poet should seek greatness and nobility in the characters and the events, excluding ridiculous, comical, and vulgar facts and creatures.

During his youth, Tasso had conceived a romantic poem on the Crusades and had written the first book of a work titled "Il Goffredo." Later he undertook the project again and, working intensively, completed it in twenty cantos of ottava rima in 1575, publishing it in the final form in 1581 as *Jerusalem Delivered*. In this literary composition, the poetic world of Tasso manifests itself in all of its richness and depth. At first it appears that, from an artistic point of view, one is confronted again by the world of the Renaissance with major elements including glory, expectation, anticipation, anxiety, heroic efforts, idyllic visions, pleasure, power, and melancholy. Moralistic and religious elements are present only in rhetorical and artificial forms, and there are only a few passages of sincerely felt spirituality and mysticism. If one observes the essence and the structure of the poem with greater care, however, one realizes that in those Renaissance motives there is hidden a new spirit, a new feeling that, without dissolving them, without transforming anything, gives to these realities a new expression, a new and deeper significance. Desire, expectation, enthusiasm, and heroic efforts are no longer an end in themselves, a pure expression of exuberant energies; they need now an ideal that will support and fulfill them. Force, power, has lost its barbaric beauty and opens itself to human feelings. Melancholy is not regret for the fleeting, transitory aspect of happiness, but rather an anxious desire for a more spiritual happiness and fulfillment, a fulfillment that Tasso's religiosity circumscribes. In this correct merging and balancing of the two opposing and contrasting forces—the love for the world and the attraction toward spirituality—Tasso supersedes his mentor, Petrarch.

After Tasso completed *Jerusalem Delivered*, his in-

stability worsened. He began a new version of his epic, titled *Gerusalemme Conquistata* (1593; *Jerusalem Conquered*, 1907), an artistic failure on which he expended enormous labors. He also wrote a tragedy, *Il re Torrismondo* (pb. 1587; the King Torrismondo), inspired by Sophocles' *Oidipous Tyrannos* (c. 429 B.C.E.; *Oedipus Tyrannus*, 1715), as well as a poem of religious inspiration, *Le sette giornate del mondo creato*, published posthumously in 1607. None of these works could duplicate the intensity and the artistic fervor of his masterpiece.

BATTISTA GUARINI

Another work deserving of recognition and written in the same period is the pastoral tragicomedy *Il pastor fido* (pb. 1590; *The Faithful Shepherd*, 1602; translation by John Fletcher), by Battista Guarini (1538-1612), a poet from Ferrara who was for several years at the court in his own town and then in Florence and Urbino. More than for its dramatic qualities or artistic prominence of the protagonist, *The Faithful Shepherd* is famous for its musicality of expression, which brings Guarini's characters closer to those of the melodrama, a genre that had tremendous success in the seventeenth and eighteenth centuries.

The melodrama, as an artistic form, was created at the end of the sixteenth century by the Camerata dei Bardi, a group of literati and musicians who gathered at the Bardi's palace in Florence. Their intention was to effect a closer relationship between music and poetry, following the example of classical Greek authors. The first melodrama (or *favola per musica*) produced was *Dafne* (1600), written by Ottavio Rinuccini (1562-1621) with music by Jacopo Corsi and Jacopo Peri. In 1600, Rinuccini wrote *Euridice*, also with music by Peri, for the marriage of the king of France, Henry IV, and Marie de Médicis. A few years later, in 1608, he wrote the libretto for the opera *Arianna* (1608), by Monteverdi, which was performed at the court of the duke of Mantua.

Considerable success was enjoyed in the sixteenth century by lyric poetry that imitated Petrarch (*petrarchismo*), and among the numerous poets who wrote verses in this style, several are notable: Luigi Tansillo (1510-1568), Annibal Caro (1507-1566), Giovanni Della Casa (1503-1555), and Galeazzo di Tarsia (1520-

1553), who is perhaps the best in this group. In addition, two women poets achieved artistic renown in this period: Vittoria Colonna (1492-1547), a member of the Roman aristocracy and a good friend of Michelangelo (1475-1564), the great sculptor and painter (who also wrote noteworthy poetry), and Gaspara Stampa (1523-1554), from Padua, whose powerful and passionate verses are regarded by many modern readers as among the finest in European literature of her time.

SEVENTEENTH CENTURY MANNERISM

Poetry in seventeenth century Italy was characterized by a phenomenon that is usually identified as *secentismo* or *Marinismo*, from the name of the poet Giambattista Marino (1569-1625), who, more than anyone, was responsible for the vogue of this new poetic style throughout Europe. This new poetry gave an extraordinary importance to form, partly in consequence of slavish imitation of classical authors, a practice that gradually gave the impression that form was something detached from content. Artists used style as a means of attracting the attention of the reader. To generate a sense of wonder and amazement, poets tended to emphasize oddity, a characteristic that typified the literary production of the seventeenth century.

The most daring and applauded representative of this style was Marino himself, who was born in Naples. After a restless and adventurous youth, Marino, who had distinguished himself as a gifted and brilliant writer of verses, spent some time at the pontifical court in Rome and then was a guest in Turin at the court of Duke Carlo Emanuele I of Savoy, where he found glory and honor. Soon, however, he fell out of favor and was imprisoned. As soon as Marino was free, he left Italy for France, where he resided for many years in Paris, honored and admired at the court of Marie de Médicis. His reputation, especially after the publication of his major work the *L'Adone* (1623), was immense. When Marino returned to Italy, he was received with great celebration in Rome and Naples. He died in Naples shortly after his return in 1625.

Marino's lyric poems, which present various subjects, are collected in a book titled *La lira* (1615). Other compositions are *La galeria* (1619), a group of icono-

graphic poems; *La sampogna* (1620), a pastoral idyll; and the sacred epic *La strage degli innocenti* (1632; *The Slaughter of the Innocents*, 1675), which enjoyed widespread and popular success.

L'Adone is by far Marino's most important work. It embodies both the strengths and the shortcomings of his art, and it stands as the most representative expression of the spirit of its epoch. *L'Adone* is a mythological poem, conceived at first as a short idyllic poem and then enlarged, with extraordinary richness of digressions and episodes, to reach the impressive size of five thousand verses. These five thousand verses were then subdivided into twenty long cantos which center on the love of Venus and Adonis.

OTHER POETS

Although *secentismo* was predominant in this period, a number of other poets wrote according to the principles of more orthodox forms, those classical writers who opposed the group represented by Marino and his followers. They cannot, however, be separated from the previous group, because they, too, followed the same abstract conception that form and style are completely separate from content.

Among these poets, the best known is Gabriello Chiabrera (1552-1638), who lived at the courts of the Medici in Florence, the Gonzagas in Mantua, and the Savoias in Turin, and who was rewarded for his services and his art with honors and generous stipends. Chiabrera acquired his reputation through his *canzonette*, the pastoral poem "Alcippo," and his several odes imitating Horace, Anacreon, and particularly Pindar. His fame did not reach the heights of Marino's, but it was more constant, even if his artistic achievement was by far inferior.

Another poet who was also inspired by the classic tradition was Fulvio Testi (1593-1646), a courtier of the Estes in Ferrara. His artistic model was the lyric poetry of Horace, from which he drew erotic inspiration and moralistic reflections. Testi's poems have survived not because of their artistic achievement, but rather for their political significance: denouncing the political dominance of Spain over Italy during that historical period.

Among the minor poets of this century one could

mention Francesco Redi (1626-1698), a poet who gained some reputation for a dithyrambic poem, *Bacco in Toscana* (1685; *Bacchus in Tuscany: A Dithyrambic Poem*, 1825), written in praise of the wines of his region.

To the creation of a new literary genre—the mock heroic or heroicomic—the poet Alessandro Tassoni (1565-1635) contributed *La secchia rapita* (1622, 1630; *The Rape of the Bucket*, 1825). A poem written in ottava rima, subdivided into twelve cantos, it narrates in epic style the struggle between the towns of Modena and Bologna over the possession of a bucket, which is a caricature of some of the trivial aspects of the life of his times. The poem is fragmentary and, with the exception of some shorter parts, is of rather limited importance.

Among the writers of dramatic poetry in this century was Federico Della Valle (1565-1628), author of several tragedies of substantial value. The *Reina di Scotia* (wr. 1590-1600, pb. 1628) projects the powerful figure of Mary Stuart, human in her grief and elevated in her dignity as queen. A second tragedy that had a good success is *Judit* (wr. 1590-1600, pb. 1627), in which the Jewish heroine hides in her heart the austere and dreadful duty that she must carry out against the savage figure of Holofernes, a primitive man dominated by his instincts. The pair tower over a background of Oriental splendor. Both of these works are of remarkable artistic quality; they are superb as dramatic works and could be considered comparable to some of the best tragedies of Vittorio Alfieri, who is, perhaps, the most outstanding Italian tragedian.

EIGHTEENTH CENTURY NEOCLASSICISM

Toward the end of the seventeenth century, fourteen scholars and men of letters in the circle of Christina, queen of Sweden—who, after her abdication and conversion to Catholicism, resided in Rome—founded a literary academy, the Accademia dell'Arcadia, whose purpose was to exterminate the bad taste of *secentismo* and to return to Italian poetry the qualities of natural candor, simplicity, and classical purity. The members of the Accademia dell'Arcadia took names that were supposed to be of pastoral inspiration, and branches of the academy were soon established in every major Italian town.

The simplicity which the Accademia dell'Arcadia was planning to set against the despised mannerisms of *secentismo* was itself, however, a purely literary convention, and new affectations substituted for the old: Poetry remained imprisoned by the entanglements of rhetoric. Nevertheless, there were some positive aspects to this new literary movement. The Accademia dell'Arcadia represented a return to the pure classicism of the sixteenth century, and classical poets, both Greek and Latin, were once again the object of the attention that had been usurped by the dazzling Mannerist poets of the seventeenth century. Style and structure meant the reassumption of a composed and dignified form in poetry. The ideal of beauty was no longer confined to the expression of the unusual or the surprising, and poets were once again under the influence of the logic that had already guided men of letters during the sixteenth century, a logic that elaborated on the concepts of Aristotle's *De poetica* (334-323 B.C.E.; *Poetics*, 1705).

The only true poet produced by the Accademia dell'Arcadia was Pietro Metastasio, whose works constitute the fullest poetic expression of the Italian society of his time. Metastasio was born Pietro Trapassi in Rome in 1698. At a very young age, he showed an exceptional ability in improvising verses. This dexterity attracted the attention of G. V. Gravina, who was one of the founders of the Accademia dell'Arcadia. Gravina was convinced that the renovation of poetry had to take place through the restoration of the concept of classical art. He thought that the young Trapassi, properly educated, could achieve what he, Gravina—who was a theoretician, not a poet—would never be able to do. Gravina then took the young poet to live with him, changed his last name to the Greek-sounding Metastasio, and saw that he was instructed in the philosophy of René Descartes and in Latin and Greek literature and language. Gravina never imagined that with that kind of education his pupil could have brought to the maximum height a dramatic genre that any true follower of Aristotle's poetic theories should have considered at least spurious.

At the death of his mentor, Metastasio almost abandoned his art, but a dramatic sketch, *Gli orti esperidi*, which he had written in 1721 for a festivity at the court of Naples, opened the gates to his fortune as a dramatist and a poet. Diva "La Romanina" (Marianna Bulgarelli) took a liking to the young Metastasio; she saw that he was educated in the art of music and introduced him to the melodramatic genre. In 1724, Metastasio completed his first melodrama, the *Didone abbandonata* (*Dido Forsaken*, 1952), which was received with great favor and was followed by *Catone in Utica* (pr. 1727-1728; *Cato in Utica*, 1767) and *Semiramide* (pr. 1729; *Semiramis Recognized*, 1767), all of them works of unusual mastery.

During the second part of the seventeenth century, the poetic aspect of the melodrama had been completely overwhelmed by musical and choreographic dramas. Early in the 1700's, Apostolo Zeno, a learned Venetian who was the official poet at the court of Vienna, attempted a reform of the melodrama and tried to make the plots less absurd in order to bring them closer to historical truth. Zeno was not a gifted poet, and he believed that what he himself had not been able to accomplish could be done by Metastasio, who was an extremely talented writer of verse. Zeno, therefore, recommended Metastasio as his successor at the Viennese court, where, free from financial concerns, the latter would be able to continue his artistic pursuits. After some hesitation, Metastasio went to Vienna in 1730. The decade that followed was the most prolific in the career of the poet. Besides *oratori* and other short dramatic compositions, Metastasio wrote eleven melodramas, among them some of his best: the *Olimpiade* (pr. 1733; *The Olympiad*, 1767), *Demofoonte* (pr. 1733; *Demofoone*, 1767), *La clemenza di Tito* (pr. 1734; *The Mercy of Titus*, 1767), *Temistocle* (pr. 1736; *Themostocles*, 1767), and *Attilio regolo* (pr. 1750; *Atilius Regulus*, 1767). Though his poetic inspiration weakened, his reputation remained unchanged for the rest of his life, and when he died in 1782, he was honored and remembered as the Italian Sophocles.

In spite of the dramatic and serious subjects with which Metastasio's melodramas dealt, it could be said that in reality they are lacking in the heroic and dramatic spirit that they presuppose; the protagonist on whom the action is centered never acquires the warm personality of a real character, because Metastasio has for these heroes an admiration that he has learned through books rather than an attraction that grows from an innermost conviction of feeling. The elegiac elements of his plays have instead a singular poetic consistency and find their most complete realization in the *ariette* (usually two stanzas that are supposed to be sung). In these brief compositions of crystalline clarity, the poet is free from any obstacle of heroic travesty, and he finds the way to convey the best expression of the Arcadian spirit.

THE ENLIGHTENMENT

In the second part of the eighteenth century, a crisis began in Europe that would eventually find its resolution in the French Revolution. In only a few years, this revolution would cause a deep transformation in people's ways of thinking, of living, and of expressing themselves, through the demolition of all the surviving forms of the Renaissance and of the period that followed. A new philosophy developed that had its precedents in the works of the Frenchman René Descartes, the German Gottfried Wilhelm Leibniz, and the Englishman John Locke—a philosophy that placed humans at the center of the universe. Humans were regarded as the supreme judge of reality, capable of subjecting any question to strictly rational analysis.

This movement was known as the Enlightenment; its spirit was epitomized by the Frenchman who created *L'Encyclopédie* (1751-1780), a rational and scientific dictionary of all the sciences and arts. This encyclopedia was published in France under the direction of Denis Diderot (1713-1784) and Jean le Rond d'Alembert (1717-1783), with the precise design of divulging new ideas and illustrating through the light of reason all the theoretical, moral, artistic, economic, and practical problems with which humans could be confronted. The representative members of this movement, even if they moved intellectually in different directions and carried different points of view, were other intellectuals and artists such as Charles de Montesquieu (1689-1755), Voltaire (1694-1778), and Jean-Jacques Rousseau (1712-1778). This movement, which affected all the ways of life and thought of European society, had a significant effect on literature as well.

GIUSEPPE PARINI

In Italy, the highest poetic expression of the moral and spiritual renewal proposed by the Enlightenment was the work of Giuseppe Parini (1729-1799). Parini was born into a humble family in Bosisio, a small rural town near Milan. He appeared to be a very intelligent boy and was brought to Milan to study. In Parini's time, for a bright but poor youngster who wanted to acquire an education, the best course was to undertake a religious career. Parini entered a seminary and became a priest. He was very interested in literature and published, when still very young, a collection of poems. As was then fashionable for a poet, he became a member of the Accademia dell'Arcadia. From 1754 to 1762, he was a tutor in the house of Duke Serbelloni. He left his job and was for several months in severe financial difficulties. The publication of the first part of what is considered his major work, *Il giorno* (1763-1801; *The Day: Morning, Midday, Evening, Night*, 1927), a satiric poem in which he criticizes the sterile life of the aristocracy, brought him to the attention of the public and also of Count Firmian, who was the minister of Maria Theresa in Milan. Firmian was glad that Parini, with his writings, was calling on the aristocracy to assume more responsibility in their position in society. Firmian made Parini director of the *Gazzetta di Milano* for a year, and in 1769, Firmian appointed Parini as professor of literature at the Scuole Palatine.

When Napoleonic troops occupied Milan in 1796, Parini was called to be part of the new government; mistrusting any demagogic excess, he refused the offer and retired to private life. When the Austrians returned to Milan in 1799, he greeted them with joy. He died, on August 15, 1799.

Parini wrote several odes that reflect the credo of the Enlightenment and are of didactic and moralistic inspiration. Some of his poems expressing deep moral emotions include *La caduta* (1766), *A Silvia* (1795), and *Alla Musa* (1795). Others such as *Il pericolo* (1787), *Il dono* (1790), and *Il messaggio* (1793), are written in flattery of women; they are sparkling in their courtly, gallant fashion and full of aesthetic admiration for feminine beauty.

Parini's moral spirit and his conception of poetry are more fully expressed in *The Day*, the satiric and didactic poem in which he describes the futile day of a young lord of the Milanese aristocracy. The same Arcadian touches that are present in the *odi* are also part of the structure of *The Day*. A masterpiece that foretells the French Revolution, it nevertheless reflects Parini's excessive dependence on the conventions of his time. Proceeding with a slow documentary style, it is encumbered with too many details, and it has not aged well.

VITTORIO ALFIERI

The renewal of Italian moral consciousness in the eighteenth century had its first suggestive poetic expression in the works of Parini, but it was the work of Vittori Alfieri (1749-1803) that unambiguously announced the political renewal of the country. Vittorio Alfieri was born in Asti, into a family of the Piedmontese aristocracy. His father died when he was only a year old, and his mother soon remarried. As a child, Alfieri was withdrawn, dominated by a melancholy unusual in one so young. In 1758, he entered the Royal Military Academy of Turin, from which he was graduated after eight years of *ineducazione* (ineducation) with the rank of *portainsegna* (lieutenant) in the regiment of his own town. Military life did not attract him, since he was intolerant of any discipline. He was very fond of traveling, and between 1766 and 1772, he made three trips, the first within Italy, the other two through Europe, visiting all the major countries from Spain to Russia. When he returned to Turin, he allowed himself to luxuriate in a life of idleness and passion for horses. Even this rootless life, however, left him restless and dissatisfied, as reflected in the pages of his diary. Actually, his continuous discontent, his furious search without any apparent goal or purpose, was in reality caused by the clash of spiritual energies as he looked for a way of expressing his talents.

This expression he finally found in 1744 while assisting a sick friend. Alfieri scribbled down the sketch of a tragedy, *Antonio e Cleopatra* (pr. 1775; *Anthony and Cleopatra*, 1876), which after going through a process of painstaking revision, was staged with success at the Carignano Theater in Turin. This success did not make Alfieri vainly proud, but it made him conscious of his literary and moral mission and of the tremendous effort that he had to make in order to become worthy of his success. Until that moment, his education had been rather modest and fragmented, and he decided therefore to put aside horses, friends, and other pleasures and immerse himself in the study of letters. To improve his knowledge of the literary language, he went to live in Tuscany, and, to be more free in his pursuit, he renounced his aristocratic rights in favor of his sister and kept for himself a life annuity that would allow him to live comfortably. His tragedies were written one after the other, interspersed with other literary works, and all of them were pervaded by the burning ideal of freedom.

Alfieri was supported in his effort, which he thought was an artistic as well as a political mission, by a great love: his love for the countess Maria Luisa Stolberg of Albany, whom he met in Florence. In 1785, Alfieri went to live in France with Stolberg, whose husband, Charles Eduard Stuart, had died. There he had the opportunity to witness the outbreak of the French Revolution, which he greeted with a panegyric poem, *Parigi sbastigliata* (1789). He also had welcomed the American Revolution with a collection of five poems, *L'America libera* (1784; *Alfieri's Ode to America's Independence*, 1976). When the French Revolution degenerated into anarchy and terror, Alfieri left Paris and returned to Florence with Stolberg, living a quiet life while concentrating on his studies, until his death in 1803.

During the last years of his life, Alfieri wrote an autobiography in which he presented an interesting artistic version of his life and of the evolution of his personality. The same autobiographical spirit is present in his *Rime* (1789, 1804), which often is an analysis of his feelings and of his moods.

Alfieri's vocation as a tragedian was dictated by his desire to contribute to the Italian culture in a literary field that was not developed as it had been in France and other countries. The poet, in planning the structure of his tragedies, considered both the classical tragedy and the French tragedy as it had been developed by Corneille and Racine. He maintained in his work the three dramatic unities of time, place, and action, which had been imposed by the Renaissance interpreters of Aristotle's *Poetics*, as well as the division of each play into five acts. He did not continue the tradition of chorus and messengers, and he excluded the confidants that, in the French tragedy, through complicated introductory scenes, informed the public about the preceding action. Alfieri also minimized the love scenes and limited the number of characters so that he could con-

centrate the action on one or, at most, two of them. In Alfieri's tragedies, there is no description of the development of passion and spiritual tension. When the scene opens, these emotions have already reached the limits of human tolerance, and the tragic consequence cannot be avoided.

Because of these structures, the tragedies of Alfieri appear to be very close to the classical example and definitely classical in the precise clarity of his psychological implications as well as the precise separation between good and evil and the monolithic representation of the protagonist in his moral and spiritual composition. It is apparent, however, that all of these characters of unusual and solitary stature do not belong to the measured correctness of the neoclassical art at the end of the eighteenth century. Instead they predict the burgeoning Romantic movement, which established a drastically changed and renewed physiognomy of European art. This unusual aspect of Alfieri's tragedies is even more evident in those plays in which the protagonists have complex personalities full of contradictions and whose actions are projected on an anxious background which is threatened by obscure forces. Most representative of these dark plays are *Oreste* (pr. 1781; *Orestes*, 1815), *Rosmunda* (pr. 1784; English translation, 1815), *Agamennone* (pb. 1784; *Agamemnon*, 1815), *Saul* (pb. 1788; English translation, 1815), and *Mirra* (pr. 1789; *Myrrha*, 1815), which also represent some of his best works.

VINCENZO MONTI

Both Romantic and neoclassical elements are present in the poetry of Vincenzo Monti (1754-1828), a poet who in many respects concludes the literary activities of the eighteenth century and opens those of the nineteenth century and Romanticism. Monti was born in Fusignano, near Ferrara. As a young man, he received an education strongly based on classical culture, and since he had the unusual ability to write poetry, he captured the attention of Cardinal Scipione Borghese, who brought him to Rome to the papal court in 1778. There, Monti was soon involved with the dramatic political events of his times. At first he condemned the horrors and the excesses of the French Revolution in his poetic work *In morte di Ugo Bassville* (1793; *The Penance of Hugo: A Vision on the French Revolution*,

1805), commonly known as *Basvilliana*; subsequently, as a result of Napoleon's successful military campaign in Italy, he became a supporter of the new hero and wrote several panegyric poems in his honor. With the end of the Napoleonic Empire and the return of Austrian influence in Italy, Monti returned his support to the old master with new poems and other writings.

Among Monti's best-known work of his Roman period is "Presopopea di Pericle," which celebrates the finding of an ancient bust of the famous Athenian statesman. In *Al Signor di Montgolfier* (1784), he honors, according to the fashion of the Enlightenment, the greatness of the human mind. *The Penance of Hugo* is his best-known political work, and during the Napoleonic period, Monti's most noted works were *Il prometeo, Il bardo della Selva Nera* (1806), and *La spada di Federico II* (1806). This latter poem celebrates the victory of Napoleon over Prussia and has strong Romantic characteristics. After the fall of Napoleon, Monti celebrated the Austrian return with *Il ritorno di Astrea* (1816).

Unusually powerful and emotionally direct is his canzone "Per il giorno onomastico della sua donna" (for his lady's name day). Later in life, Monti resumed work on an earlier poem, "Feroniade," which was left unfinished; in it, he narrates the activities surrounding the draining and reclamation of the Pontine Marshes. This theme was dear to the hearts of the followers of the Enlightenment. Monti was not quite capable of creating the vital and complex structure of an extended or more engaging poem, although he had exceptional technical abilities in the composition of verses and therefore was greatly successful in his translations. Particularly masterful were his translations from classical languages, of which his translation of Homer's the *Iliad* (c. 750 B.C.E.; English translation, 1611) is considered his masterpiece.

NEOCLASSICISM

Monti's oeuvre is characteristic of the period during which the ground was being prepared for Romanticism. At this time, art, literature, and public life in Italy were inspired by classical culture to a degree unprecedented even in the Renaissance. For the most part, this was a rather superficial and gaudy phenomenon fos-

tered by the caesarism of the Napoleonic age and, perhaps, by an instinctive reaction of the Latin world against the surging German Romanticism. Thus, Italian neoclassicism, as this movement was called, bore the seeds of a Romantic sensibility. There was in Romanticism a torment and restlessness, an unsatisfied aspiration toward a perfected beauty—an unreachable region symbolized for the Romantics by classical Greece. This myth of Greece, present in all the best-known national literary compositions of the early nineteenth century, was the Romantic aspect of neoclassicism.

Monti is the most representative poet of this period, for his poetry is by nature oriented toward external forms. The new Romantic sensibility, preoccupied with the content of artistic reality, is not well assimilated in his art. This assimilation was to be the task of the poets who followed him, from Ugo Foscolo to Giacomo Leopardi, from Giosuè Carducci to Gabriele D'Annunzio. In D'Annunzio's poetry, the myth of the ancient world is no longer a serene and somehow superficial vision, but rather an island dreamed of and lost, a land of perfect beauty sought without hope.

BIBLIOGRAPHY

Barnes, John C., and Jennifer Petrie, eds. *Dante and His Literary Precursors: Twelve Essays*. Dublin: Four Courts Press, 2007. A publication of the Foundation for Italian Studies, University College, Dublin. Scholarly essays on Dante's political and intellectual environment and on new ways of reading his works. Bibliography and indices.

Brand, Peter, and Lino Pertile, eds. *The Cambridge History of Italian Literature*. 2d ed. New York: Cambridge University Press, 1999. In this new, definitive volume, the first of its kind in four decades, leading scholars provide information about a wide range of writers, their works, and their significance. Translations are included. Maps, chronological charts, and bibliographical references.

Cavallo, Jo Ann. *The Romance Epics of Boiardo, Ariosto, and Tasso: From Public Duty to Private Pleasure*. Toronto: University of Toronto Press, 2004. The author combines analyses of the three poets, discussion of the literary tradition, comments on their social and intellectual environments, and summaries of previous criticism in order to provide the basis for a persuasive new theory about the relationship between them. An impressive achievement. Bibliography and index.

Everson, Jane E. *The Italian Romance Epic in the Age of Humanism: The Matter of Italy and the World of Rome*. New York: Oxford University Press, 2001. Demonstrates how the romance, or chivalric epic, owed its appeal to a successful fusion of traditional, medieval tales of Charlemagne and Arthur with the newer cultural themes developed by the revival in classical antiquity that constitutes the key to Renaissance culture.

Holmes, Olivia. *Assembling the Lyric Self: Authorship from Troubador Song to Italian Poetry Book*. Minneapolis: University of Minnesota Press, 2000. Examines the change in the concept of authorship that occurred in the thirteenth century when, because of the increase in literacy, poetic expression changed from oral to written form. Notes, bibliography, and index.

Jacoff, Rachel, ed. *The Cambridge Companion to Dante*. 2d ed. New York: Cambridge University Press, 2007. An updated edition of the standard introduction to Dante. Contains three new essays on *The Divine Comedy*, a current bibliography, and references to online resources.

Mallette, Karla. *The Kingdom of Sicily, 1100-1250: A Literary History*. Philadelphia: University of Pennsylvania Press, 2005. Applies postcolonial theory to the period when Sicily was a multilingual, multicultural country, producing literature in Arabic, Latin, Greek, and Romance dialects. Contains an extensive selection of poems in translation. Bibliography and index.

Stortoni, Laura A., and Mary P. Lillie, eds. *Women Poets of the Italian Renaissance: Courtly Ladies and Courtesans*. New York: Italica, 1997. This bilingual anthology contains eighty poems by nineteen poets, ranging from love lyrics to spiritual meditations. Includes introductory essay, biographies, first-line index, notes, and bibliographies.

Zatti, Sergio. *The Quest for Epic: From Ariosto to Tasso*. Translated by Sally Hill with Dennis Looney. Edited by Looney. Toronto: University of Toronto Press, 2006. Introduction by Albert Russell Ascoli. In this work, translated into English for the first time, one of Italy's most important critics traces the development of the narrative genre from chivalric romance to the epic and points out how that form, in turn, predates the modern novel. Notes, bibliography, and index.

Patrizio Rossi

ITALIAN POETRY SINCE 1800

At the time of Italy's unification in 1861, Alessandro Manzoni was the only living member of the great triad of early nineteenth century writers (composed of Manzoni, Ugo Foscolo, and Giacomo Leopardi), and he had written little poetry after the completion of his masterpiece, the novel *I promessi sposi* (1827, 1840-1842; *The Betrothed*, 1828, 1951). Also surviving were a trio of late Romantic poets, Aleardo Aleardi (1812-1878), Giovanni Prati (1814-1884), and Giacomo Zanella (1820-1888). The first was a patriotic poet; the second, although he was famous for his long Byronic poem of contemporary Venetian life, *Edmenegarda* (1841), had abandoned Romanticism and turned classicist; and Zanella, who has withstood the test of time somewhat better than the other two, was a priest interested in reconciling science and religion. His masterpiece, "Sopra una conchiglia fossile nel mio studio" ("On a Fossil Shell in My Study"), often compared to Henry Wadsworth Longfellow's "The Chambered Nautilus," is an imaginative history of Earth and a reflection on the higher destiny that awaits humanity.

The unification of Italy robbed its writers of one of their main inspirations; without a direct political mission, Italian literature lost some momentum during the last third of the century, fragmenting into various movements. Some writers wished to cling to a dying Romanticism, some returned to the classical past, and some looked ahead to realism. Those who championed realism, called *Verismo* in Italy, were chiefly novelists and dramatists.

The Scapigliatura movement

In the 1860's, there flourished a movement in Milan called the *scapigliatura*, from the disheveled or Bohemian appearance of its members, who reacted against the traditional forms of late Romanticism in their desire to achieve a spontaneous artistic expression. They looked toward such non-Italian poets as Gérard de Nerval, Charles Baudelaire, Henri Murger, Paul Verlaine, Arthur Rimbaud, and Heinrich Heine, and their work exhibited overtones of Decadence (art for art's sake), realism, and Satanism. At their worst, they substituted allegory and symbol for genuine thought and feeling.

Emilio Praga (1839-1875), a painter as well as a poet, wrote in the style of Baudelaire and died of alcoholism. The nostalgic motifs of his poetry are couched in pessimism and sensuality and can hardly be classified as examples of realistic writing. Arrigo Boito (1842-1918), offspring of an Italian father and a Polish mother, who ranks second after Giuseppe Verdi among Italian composers of the late nineteenth century, wrote poetry that sadly and sternly evokes the past, but his best lyric work, such as the legend of *Re orso* (king bear), has today been forgotten. Giovanni Camerana (1845-1905), also a painter, who committed suicide at the age of sixty, wrote landscape poetry with a painter's eye for color and form.

Peripheral to the *scapigliati* were Vittorio Betteloni (1840-1910), who was drawn to realism—a translator of Lord Byron and Johann Wolfgang von Goethe and a forerunner of the crepuscular movement—and his friend Olindo Guerrini (pseudonym of Lorenzo Stecchetti; 1845-1916), known for his peculiar brand of realism that approached pornography and for his satirical view of politicians.

While the *scapigliatura* movement failed to produce any great work of poetry, it created a commotion of new ideas from which other rebellious movements arose. Indeed, it could be argued that the decadent aspect of the poetry of Giovanni Pascoli and Gabriele D'Annunzio represents a continuation of the precepts of the *scapigliati*.

Giosuè Carducci

At that time, there arose a giant of a poet who would command and receive such respect from the Italian people as is rare in modern times, and who would receive the first Nobel Prize awarded to an Italian (1906). The Tuscan Giosuè Carducci (1835-1907)—rebellious, republican, and anticlerical—presented a drastic contrast to Abbe Zanella, who had fought for the Catholic ideal of a confederated Italy under the authority of a liberal pope. Carducci instead wrote "Inno a Satana" ("Hymn to Satan"); although Carducci's Satan is a pro-

Giosuè Carducci (Library of Congress)

gressive "avenging force of Reason" rather than a prince of darkness, Carducci continued for many years to harbor a grudge in response to what he deemed Pope Pius IX's betrayal of Italy in the secular interests of the Vatican.

Carducci was hostile toward Romanticism for its emotionalism and its deficiencies in formal expression. He equated Romanticism with the Middle Ages. Classicism for him was the glistening and gladdening Sun, while Romanticism was the infecund ghost of the moon (whose "stupid round face" Carducci said he hated), the haunter of ruins and cemeteries. Although his father admired Manzoni and had encouraged the young Carducci to read him, the poet was instead attracted to Homer and Vergil and the pre-Manzonian and pre-Romantic classicists (as well as these aspects in the poetry of Foscolo).

Carducci tried to subdue Romantic impulses by successfully adapting Greek and Latin quantitative meter to Italian verse, an achievement that his Italian predecessors (including Gabriello Chiabrera, 1552-1638; Leon Battista Alberti, 1404-1472; and Tommaso Campanella, 1568-1639) had attempted but had not at-

tained. To the critics, his use of unrhymed Alcaics, Sapphics, hexameters, and Asclepiads seemed like nothing less than an insult to the Italian language. Carducci had foreseen this reaction and ironically called his three-volume collection *Odi barbare* (1877, 1882, 1889; *The Barbarian Odes of Giosuè Carducci*, 1939), not because the odes offended Italian readers but because Horace and Vergil would have been offended to hear their language corrupted in Italian. In his unbounded admiration for the sculptural lines of ancient Latin poetry, Carducci sometimes indulged a fascination with mere sound. His poetry is not often tender, but it is always cast in a mold of majestic form.

It is precisely Carducci's more tender poems, however, with their highly controlled emotionality, that are most alive for modern readers. His "Alla stazione in una mattinata d'autunno" ("To the Station on an Autumn Morning") is an impressive love poem reflecting the mood of his passion for Carolina Piva ("Lidia"); in the poem "Pianto antico" ("Ancient Lament"), while observing the greenness of a flowering pomegranate tree, he is reminded that his infant son, who once stretched out "his little hand" toward that very tree, is now dead.

Significantly, the poets whom Carducci chose to translate into Italian were Hellenistic Germans of the earlier part of the century, Friedrich Gottlieb Klopstock, August Platen, and Heine. Also revealing of his tastes are his eulogies for figures such as Giuseppe Garibaldi, the redeemer of Italy; Queen Margherita, the accomplished consort of King Umberto I; Homer; Vergil; Dante, whom he could appreciate but not love; Victor Hugo, to whom he writes: "Sing to the new progeny, O divine old man,/ time-honored song of the Latin people;/ sing to the expectant world: Justice and Liberty"; and even Jaufre Rudel and Martin Luther. A great orator, Carducci was often asked to make public addresses on literary figures of the past; at Pietole, he spoke on Vergil, at Arqua on Petrarch, at Certaldo on Giovanni Boccaccio, at Recanati on Leopardi. In Bologna on June 4, 1882, two days after the death of Garibaldi, Carducci delivered an extemporaneous tribute that has hardly been surpassed in any time or place. Carducci's heavy glorification of the past ("I stand on the mount of centuries"), however, became a suffocating burden from which his successors felt the need to free themselves.

As dogmatic as he was, Carducci was capable of changing his opinions and evolving with the times. The poet who wrote of ancient Rome, "No more she triumphs since a Galilean/ with russet hair, the Capitol ascending,/ thrust on her back a cross," gradually accepted a vigorous and loving morality touched with the divine, and even came to appreciate the historic mission of the Church. Indeed, the author of a savage poetic invective against Pope Pius IX mellowed to such an extent that he poetically invited "Citizen Mastai" (Count Giovanni Maria Mastai-Feretti, later Pope Pius IX) to drink a toast to liberty.

Though foremost a classicist, Carducci came to appreciate modern literature, both foreign and Italian. His "Colloqui con gli alberti" (conversations with the trees) even recalls one of Zanella's poems that Carducci admired, "Egoismo e carita" (selfishness and charity). In pre-Risorgimento days, Carducci was a staunch republican, but he slowly came to agree with Camillo Bensodi Cavour that Italy was not ready for democratic government, and he endorsed a kingdom under the House of Savoy. This decision led to a deep friendship with Queen Margherita, who in fact purchased his personal library a few years before his death to prevent it from being scattered.

OTHER NEOCLASSICISTS

There were other Italian neoclassicists at that time, many of whom were devoted followers of Carducci and many, like Carducci himself, who were professors in the new lay university system. This group gave rise to the term "professorial poetry," characterized by its solemn tone and pedagogical intent. Carducci's lifelong friend Giuseppe Chiarini (1833-1908), with whom he had founded the literary society of the Amici Pedanti in 1856, is known for his *Lacrymae* (1879; tears), a collection of simple verses on the premature death of his son, Dante. Other *carducciani*, such as Enrico Panzacchi (1840-1904), Giovanni Marradi (pseudonym of G. Labronio, 1852-1922), Severino Ferrari (1856-1905), and Guido Mazzoni (1859-1943), were evokers of historical landscapes or poets of personal fantasies uninterested in realism. Another poet of rebellious

spirit, but one antagonistic to Carducci, was the Sicilian Mario Rapisardi (1844-1912), professor and translator of Lucretius and Catallus and singer of the fatal unhappiness of humans and of the assault of science on long-accepted dogma. The same concern for the problem of human destiny is found in the poetry of Arturo Graf (1848-1913), the son of a Bavarian father and an Italian mother and, like Rapisardi, a professor.

GIOVANNI PASCOLI

Toward the end of the century, Carducci's position as unofficial poet laureate was assumed by his former student Giovanni Pascoli (1855-1912), who, like Carducci, was a professor and was interested only in the genre of poetry. As a humanist, he even surpassed Carducci, writing the finest Latin poetry since the age of Poliziano (1454-1494). By his emphasis on everday objects and activities, he shifted the focus of Italian poetry from the bourgeois to the petite bourgeoisie. As an outgrowth of his appreciation for the language of the common people, he incorporated many common and dialectal words into his Italian, and his example led to a more hospitable atmosphere for the ultimate acceptance of dialectal words into the standard language. His use and sometimes abuse of the onomatopoeic resources of language (for example, the *tellterell-tellteretelltell* of sparrows, the *siccecce siccecce* of stonechats) was widely imitated. Because of his great love for little things, his poetry has been loosely termed "religious," yet, in his conception, religion was hardly more than a cause around which people could rally in order to become closer to one another.

In his youth, Pascoli was for a brief time partial to socialism, and in his maturity he lived always without material pretensions. However, the long years of prosperous peace that followed the unification of Italy were materialistic years during which social and religious concerns played a minor role, and Pascoli's message of simplicity and appreciation for small things had to be tempered somewhat. It was to Italy's classical past and to its more recent patriotic and historical themes that he turned in his last years. His treatment of the classical world, however, was peculiarly his own; his classical heroes are not remote ideals but rather real people with the problems of all people. Thus, Alexander the Great is portrayed not as a conqueror but as a man who laments that there are no more worlds to conquer. Pascoli also acted as spokesperson for the hopes and dreams of the Italian people for an empire in Africa. When the Italians were repulsed by the Ethiopians at Adua in 1896, Pascoli mourned the defeat in a poem, and when Italians wished to annex Libya in 1912, he wrote a treatise in agreement with their imperialistic ideals.

Pascoli presented his ideas about poetry in an essay called "Il fanciullino" (1897; the little boy), where he argues that the true poet sees things as a child sees them, spontaneously finding the analogies necessary to express his wonder. Pascoli, himself a child at heart, found fault with literary Italian, cramped by classical tradition and a limited poetic vocabulary, and he led a campaign for a "svecchiamento del lessico" ("updating of the poetic lexicon").

About the same time, Edmondo De Amicis (1846-1908), who also esteemed the childlike sense of wonder that is so often stifled in adulthood, was finding similar fault with literary Italian. In *L'idioma gentile* (1905; the noble language), he recommended that aspiring poets study the specialized vocabularies of the peasant trades; the aesthetician Benedetto Croce (1866-1952), who valued ideas above the words that dress them, asked in rebuttal if young Italians should become cooks in order to become poets. Croce, like other critics then as well as now, attacked Pascoli for his informality, sentimentality, and emotionalism, and was especially offended when Pascoli allowed his mother to address him in "La voce" ("The Voice") by his childhood (and dialectal) nickname, Zvanì. However uncontestable these charges seem, Italian (rather than British or American) critics today generally view Pascoli as the primary forerunner of most twentieth century Italian poetry.

GABRIELE D'ANNUNZIO

Pascoli's younger friend and admirer, Gabriele D'Annunzio (1863-1938), the third and last surviving member of the triad, was born "of pure Sabelian race" at Pescara, halfway down the Adriatic coast of Italy. A figure of European stature who occupies a significant place in the political and social, as well as literary, history of Italy, D'Annunzio was the most versatile of the triad, for when he realized that poetry no longer counted as the highest art, he applied himself to the

novel and to drama. The crass sensuality of his novels and the exaggerated rhetoric of his plays, however, caused them to be forgotten in due time, while his poetry has proved to be of more lasting value. Because he attempted such a phenomenally wide range of stylistic and metrical possibilities in his poetry, D'Annunzio's legacy to subsequent generations has been great. To separate the enduring from the ephemeral in his vast output (a complete edition of his works, published by Mondadori from 1927 to 1936, makes up forty-nine volumes) has been an ongoing challenge to critics.

At the age of sixteen, D'Annunzio published an ode on the birthday of King Umberto I, written in the sapphic meter of Carducci. His first book of poems, *Primo vere* (1879, 1880; early spring), written while he was still at school, and his second, *Canto novo* (1882, 1896; new song), are imitative of Carducci and Olindo Guerrini and exhibit most of the characteristics for which he would become known—classical allusions *ad nauseam*, graphic description, linguistic and metrical dexterity, and an overwhelming joie de vivre. Another trait that became associated with him is his excessive use of the imperative mood, expressive of his sense of superiority and suggesting a master-novice relationship with his readers. The poems *Elegie romane* (1892) and *Poema paradisiaco—Odi navali* (1893) mark his attempt to free himself from the compulsion of the senses by means of human pity and sympathy—an attempt inspired by Leo Tolstoy and Fyodor Dostoevski.

D'Annunzio was also inspired by his mistress, Eleonora Duse; during the years of their affair (1894-1903), he produced his best works. His most ambitious undertaking bore the impressive title, *Laudi del cielo del mare della terra e degli eroi* (1899); he intended to expand this work into a series of seven books—each named for one of the seven Pleiades—but he never completed the project. The first book, *Maia* (1903), subtitled "Laus vitae" (praise of life), contrasts the myths of Hellas with the dogmas of Christianity in an ideal journey undertaken by the poet through Greece, celebrating joy in the perception of the natural beauty inherent in art, poetry, and legend. *Maia* takes up the theme of Carducci's *Barbarian Odes* and ends, in fact, with a tribute to Carducci. *Elettra* (1904), the second book of the proposed seven, offers an epic glorification of Garibaldi's efforts to liberate and unite Italy and sings the praises of other national heroes, of Hugo, and of Friedrich Nietzsche. *Alcyone* (1904; English translation, 1977), the third book, renews the Mediterranean tradition of the pastoral genre with its consummate simplicity and contains many of D'Annunzio's best-known poems; this volume is generally considered to represent the height of his poetic achievement.

Influenced by the French Parnassians and Symbolists, the English Pre-Raphaelites, and the German rhetoric of Richard Wagner and Nietzsche, D'Annunzio evolved a cult of Decadence centered on the relationship between beauty and decay. Not at all Christian, although always respectful to the clergy, D'Annunzio cultivated a fascination for Saint Francis of Assisi and went about his retreat, Il Vittoriale, in a dressing gown reminiscent of the Franciscan habit. The title of his poetic masterpiece, *Le laudi* (1949; expanded version of 1899 title, also includes *Maia*, *Elettra*, *Alcyone*, *Merope*, and *Asterope*), is from the *laudes* of the saint, and *Alcyone* includes pantheistic addresses that are paraphrased from the refrain of the "cantico delle creature." *Elettra* includes the poem "Assisi," in which D'Annunzio evokes Saint Francis from the very landscape, observing the "tortuous windings of desire" first in the "fresh breath of the evening prayer" and then in the "flesh of Francis/ inflamed by the demon of the flesh,/ bleeding on the roses' thorns." Daring to add outrageous detail to Christian myth, his boundless ego empowers him to transfer the turmoil of his own erotic fury to the landscape of Assisi and even to the saintly Francis himself, transforming his fantasy to the likes of a fertility rite. The same morbid mixture of carnality with Catholic myth and ritual is evident in D'Annunzio's mystery play, written in French, *Le Martyre de Saint Sébastien* (pr., pb. 1911), which was condemned as blasphemous by the bishop of Paris.

As a result of his fascist connections and his sympathy for Benito Mussolini (which, however, has been exaggerated by his detractors), D'Annunzio's fame faded rapidly after World War II. In the 1960's, glimmerings of a D'Annunzio revival began to appear: Some of his plays reopened; in 1976, Luchino Visconti made a film from the poet's novel *L'innocente* (1892; *The Intruder*,

1898); critics began to write about him again, and today tourists flock to his last home, Il Vittoriale, on Lago di Garda, to savor its historical implications. Two of D'Annunzio's more successful followers were women, Sibilla Aleramo (1876-1960) and Vittoria Aganoor Pompili (1857-1910). The suffocating influence of D'Annunzio's rhetoric, though less pervasive than Carducci's, did much to suppress genuine poetry and to push it to the sidelines of Italian literature, whence it had slowly to begin its way to recovery.

SIBILLA ALERAMO

The gifted and alluring Sibilla Aleramo (pseudonym of Rina Faccio) grew up in the Marches, where her Northern Italian father had been forced to take a position and where she made a bad marriage. Her free verse, often egocentric and cloyingly sensual, reaches lofty heights only when she describes the vanity of temporary carnal gratification. Her claim as Italy's foremost woman writer in the first century of the country's existence rests on the success of her novel, *Una donna* (1906; *A Woman at Bay*, 1908), in defense of women's rights. Among her lovers were the poets Vincenzo Cardarelli (1887-1959), Dino Campana (1885-1932), Clemente Rèbora (1885-1957), Giovanni Papini (1881-1956), and Giovanni Cena (1870-1917); she is sometimes compared to George Sand, whose correspondence with Alfred de Musset she translated into Italian. Although at earlier and later stages of her life she embraced socialism, in her poverty, she was obliged to use her literary talents on behalf of Mussolini. With hindsight, she expressed her envy of D'Annunzio, who died before the fascist debacle.

REGIONAL AND DIALECTIC POETRY

Traditional Italian poetry before the unification of Italy, as Ruth Phelps has noted, often lacks the "feeling of place" so evident in English poetry. Pascoli was the first of many modern Italian poets to convey this "English" love for a particular corner of the world. Salvatore Quasimodo (1901-1968), in *Il falso e vero verde* (1954), notes that Italian poets who are engaged most intensely by a world gathered up in a narrow landscape are often from the South, the tragic and much maligned South that has inspired even Northern poets to reflect on its destiny. Quasimodo himself wrote a

"Lamento per il sud" ("Lament for the South") in which he noted that "the South is tired of hauling the dead/ on the banks of malarial marshes,/ is tired of solitudes, of chains,/ is tired of the curses/ in its mouth," and elsewhere in his poems he frequently alludes to his childhood in Sicily. The heat of the Sicilian midday sun is a major force in the amatory poetry of Giuseppe Villaroel (1889-1965), and Lucio Piccolo (1903-1969) sought to preserve the Baroque Sicily of agave plants, sirocco nights, and colored wagons in his poetry. The savage terrain of isolated Basilicata has inspired such native poets as Rocco Scotellaro (1923-1953), who wrote of "Backbones of mountains/ touched by the light winter sun," and Leonardo Sinisgalli (1908-1981), who celebrated this "Land of huge mamas, of fathers dark/ and radiant as skeletons, overrun by roosters/ and dogs."

Libero de Libero (1906-1981) conveys his deep attachment to the land of his native Ciociaria (between Rome and Naples) in his allusive and elliptical poetry written in the Hermetic tradition. Ada Negri (1870-1945), in *Canti dell'isola* (1924; songs of the island), paints the transcending beauty of the dream island of Capri. Diego Valeri (1887-1976) celebrated Venice, his city of adoption, in both poetry and prose. Umberto Saba loved Trieste and mentions his native city, "beautiful between the rocky mountains and the luminous sea," as one of the personal treasures denied him by the "vile Fascist and greedy German." Andrea Zanzotto (born 1921) writes of his bucolic Pieve de Soligo among the foothills of the Dolomites (especially in *Dietro il paesaggio*, 1951; beside the landscape) and assails real-estate developers poised for ecological rape. Pier Paolo Pasolini (1922-1975) tenderly sprinkles Friulian place-names throughout his poetry.

Eugenio Montale (1896-1981), who spent most of the first thirty years of his life in Genoa, painted the Ligurian landscape in terms of *petrosita*, *scabrezza*, and *aridita* (stoniness, roughness, aridity), and Camillo Sbarbaro (1888-1967), who also wrote lovingly of Liguria, is in fact mentioned in Montale's "Caffè a Rapallo" ("Cafe at Rapallo") as part of the beachside landscape. Other poets who used Ligurian themes in their poetry or drew upon the Ligurian Riviera for local color and veristic imagery include Ceccardo Roccata-

gliata Ceccardi (1872-1919), Mario Novaro (1868-1944), and Giovanni Boine (1887-1917), who turned his eyes yearningly back to his native town on the Ligurian coast from a sanatorium in the Swiss Alps.

Closely linked to poetry celebrating a particular region is that which employs a dialect in the face of pressure to employ the standard language. When Italy became a united nation in 1861, only slightly more than 2.5 percent of the population could speak Italian in addition to their native dialect. Although the Italian dialects all share the same Latin origin as the national language, and in fact share a vast quantity of lexical and grammatical features, there are also bewildering dissimiliarities that can make mastery of standard Italian a difficult task. As a result of the prescriptivist stance of linguistic arbiters since the time of Pietro Bembo (1470-1547), who argued for the purity of the Tuscan variety of Italian to the exclusion of borrowings from other dialects, the Italian language that the nation inherited in 1861 was a rigid medium of expression whose parameters would not be broadened until Pascoli undertook the task—a half century before television and radio would do the job more efficiently.

Coinciding with the rise of *Verismo* during the second half of the nineteenth century, an impressive number of talented poets chose to write occasionally or exclusively in their native dialects, and they have given to Italian literature a curious offshoot that is neglected in many surveys of Italian poetry. Although poets have been writing in their local dialects since the literary emergence of those dialects in medieval Italy, and although such preunification poets as the Sicilian Giovanni Meli (1740-1815), the Milanese Carlo Porta (1775-1821), and the Roman Giuseppe Gioachino Belli (1791-1863) enjoyed local followings, it was not until there was a united Italy that dialectal literature won a wider audience, and it was not until the emergence of Salvatore Di Giacomo (1860-1934) that Italian critics began to take dialectal literature seriously.

SALVATORE DI GIACOMO

The Neapolitan Salvatore Di Giacomo, who ranks as one of Italy's greatest lyric poets, employed a dialect that is musical, refined, and polished, not at all like street talk, though he frequently depicts street scenes in his poetry. Since Di Giacomo believed that his fame would rest on his scholarly studies (thirty-four volumes) treating the history and sociology of Naples, he wrote those works and some of his novelle in Italian, reserving his use of dialect for his poetry. He began writing during the vogue of *Verismo* and folklore studies, but his treatment of subject matter is sentimentalized and subjectivized to such an extent that the effect it achieves is quite different from that of *Verismo*. His poetry is dreamy and melancholy, sentimental but not mawkish, as in the sonnets of *O munasterio* (1887; the monastery), about a jilted sailor who becomes a monk and still longs for the freedom of the outside world, for green things growing, and for the water of the bay in the moonlight. Simple and innocent, Di Giacomo displays a childlike enchantment with the stars and moon. At times, too, he is fascinated by macabre elements. In his ghastly dream of a winter night, "Suonno 'e na notte 'e vierno," he sees before him all the women he has loved; when he fails to recognize one of them, who is veiled, she invites him to embrace her, and he realizes that she is Death.

CESARE PASCARELLA

Two poets of the same period, both writing in the dialect of modern Rome (*romanesco*), were also widely read and appreciated: Cesare Pascarella (1858-1940) and Carlo Alberto Salustri (1871-1950), called Trilussa. Pascarella wrote his *Sonetti* (1900; sonnets) in a medium close enough to standard Italian as to be understood easily (the glossary that accompanies the collection contains a mere forty words). The twenty-five sonnets of his *Villa Gloria* (1886) recount the ill-fated attempt by a group of patriots to wrest Rome from the Papacy (1867), and *Scoperta dell' America* (1894; the discovery of America), consisting of fifty sonnets, portrays Columbus, Ferdinand and Isabella, the Spanish sailors, and the American Indians all speaking the Roman dialect with humorous effects as they reenact the drama of discovering America.

CARLO ALBERTO SALUSTRI

Carlo Alberto Salustri, or Trilussa, employed the *romanesco* dialect in its aspects of low-life (*gergo furfantino*) to construct fables in a variety of metrical forms. His art is witty, cynical, melancholy, epigrammatic, and not without a religious vein (as in "Sermone

1914," an antiwar poem). His cynicism is sometimes excessive, as in "L'omo inutile" (the superfluous man), about a six-month-old fetus under alcohol in a vat in a museum who claims that he is happier watching the people in the museum than dying as an adult in somebody's war; more often, his fables are simply delightful, as in "La carita" (charity), in which the president of an association for mistreated animals refuses to spare a dime to a beggar, claiming that only animals qualify for his sympathy, whereupon the beggar renews his appeal by displaying a headful of lice. Trilussa is probably best known for his political fables, which concern the freedom lost as a result of the fascist *ventennio*.

OTHER REGIONAL POETS

Having produced Di Giacomo and a host of other poets during its centuries as the largest city in Italy (a distinction it retained for several decades even after the Risorgimento), Naples has been the most prolific source of dialectal literature. Next to Di Giacomo is his contemporary and competitor for recognition, the *verista* Ferdinando Russo (1866-1927), whose poetry portraying Neapolitan life is more dramatic and less tragic than that of Di Giacomo. His poems, like those of Di Giacomo, often deal with unrequited or impossible love. Other Neapolitan poets, less accomplished than Di Giacomo or Russo, clung to the melic tradition and contributed to the repertory of Neapolitan *canzonette*.

After Naples, the area around Venice has produced the richest vein of dialectal poetry. The Venetian Giacomo Noventa (1898-1960), who, with Alberto Carocci and Franco Fortini, in 1936 founded the Florentine review *Riforma letteraria* (which was closed down by the fascists three years later), was an aristocratic popular poet who embraced liberal, socialist, and Catholic views. The Veronese poet Berto Barbarani (1872-1945) wrote of the humble people and of his own loves and sorrows, depicting children with the warmth and sympathy of someone who has not had any of his own. Writing in the dialect of Trieste, Virgilio Giotti (1885-1957), abjuring historical and folkloric themes, elaborated a crepuscular inwardness, while Biagio Marin (1891-1985) is essentially a religious poet. In Friulian, Pietro Zorutti (1792-1867), author of humorous and sometimes sentimental sonnets and impressive epigrams, wrote his *Strolic furlan* (1847; Friulian almanac), a title echoed in the name of a poetry magazine, *Stroligut di cà da l'aga* (little almanac from this side of the water), published by a modern Friulian, Pasolini. Pasolini founded the Academiuta di Lenga Furlana at Casarsa, an institution that was active from 1946 to 1950, and compiled, in collaboration with the *romanesco* poet Mario Dell'Arco, an anthology of contemporary dialectal poetry from the entire Italian peninsula, *Poesia dialettale del Novecento* (1952; dialect poetry of the twentieth century). To the socialistic Pasolini, the dialect of his mother's native Friuli represented a sacred language spoken by the blessed poor, and he began his career as a poet describing the Alpine enclave, which for him represented an idyll of sexual (in his case, homosexual) freedoms opposed to the sexual corruption offered by the cities. Ironically, however, it was in Friuli that Pasolini's sexual activities with local male youths first led to blackmail and to lawsuits.

The Milanese dialect was represented by Delio Tessa (1886-1939), whose work embodies an invigorated crepuscularism, and the Ligurian dialect by Edoardo Firpo (1889-1957), whose poetry evokes the harsh Ligurian earth and the rigorous lives of those close to it. Nearer to the historical seat of the national language in Tuscany is the Pisan dialect, used by Renato Fucini (1843-1921) in his sonnets, which present vignettes of everyday life.

Writing in the harsh and little-known dialect of Basilicata is Albino Pierro (1916-1995), whose printed poems are characteristically accompanied by translations in Italian, as in *Nd'u piccicarelle di Tursi/Nel precipizio di Tursi* (1967; on the cliff of Tursi). Coming to poetry not from literary study but from inner need, he writes of the mystery of life and death, of the ancient landscape of the Italian South. From neighboring Calabria came the philosophizing poet Vincenzo Padula (1819-1893), who occasionally wrote in his Calabrian dialect.

Sebastiano Satta (1867-1914) is regarded as the national bard of Sardinia, even if his best poetry was written in Italian. His work is often shallow and his diction stilted, but at moments in *Canti barbaricini* (1910), he evokes a primitive epic grandeur.

CREPUSCOLARI, FUTURISTI, AND VOCIANI

In the twentieth century, Italian poetry escaped the provincialism that had dominated it for some time. Even the great figures Carducci and D'Annunzio came to represent a limiting classicism and an overblown rhetorical nationalism. To be sure, such figures exercised an influence on poets following them, but on the whole, the turn of the century saw a reaction against them. Of the triad, only Pascoli can be said to have anticipated contemporary poetry. The reaction took three forms: the style of the *crepuscolari* (crepuscular poets), that of the *futuristi* (Futurists), and the poetics of the writers associated with the magazine *La voce*, the *vociani*.

The crepuscular poets never constituted a school as such. Their name, which means "twilight," was derived from an article by Giuseppe Antonio Borgese (1881-1952) assessing the poetry of the turn of the century. In Borgese's view, the triad's achievements were so great that the younger generation of poets, men such as Sergio Corazzini (1886-1907), Guido Gozzano (1883-1916), Corrado Govoni (1884-1965), and Aldo Palazzeschi (pseudonym of Aldo Giurlani; 1885-1974), could hardly hope to express themselves in new ways; theirs could be only a waning poetry. Borgese found these poets to be filled with world-weariness and an unnaturally early awareness of death; the language of their works he thought Pascolian in its simplicity, its emulation of ordinary linguistic rhythms, and its concern for "small things." Though none of these poets was to become great, they established the Pascolian vocabulary and concern for ordinary cadences later employed by the great Italian modernists.

The poets identified by Borgese as *crepuscolari* wrote for only a short time. Either they died young, as did Corazzini, or they turned to other literary forms, as did Palazzeschi. Nevertheless, some of these writers should be given serious attention. In the poetry of Gozzano, for example, the danger of the crepuscular style, a self-indulgent melancholy, is balanced by a mordant irony, an irony especially incisive when directed against the foibles of the poet-self. In his fine poem "Totò Merumeni," Gozzano elaborates on a Prufrockian caricature. Totò, a fallen aristocratic type with "culture up to his ears," struggles, but without too much anguish, to comprehend his circumstances. He is a man with sensibilities but without will: "He's the *good man*, that fool of/ Nietzsche's. . . ." Totò incarnates an overripe culture and the malaise of a spirit without direction because its greatness is past. A chilly objectivity prevents any sentimentality. One line that could otherwise have been excessive states the theme of the poem: "One by one Life took all of its promises back."

The weakness of the crepuscular style, and the reason for its short vogue, is evident in Govoni's "La trombettina" ("The Little Trumpet"). This poem opens clearly and interestingly with a direct statement that all the magic that is left from a fair is in a trumpet carried across a field by a girl. The poet goes on to add: "But within its forced note/ are all the clowns, white ones and red ones,/ the band . . ." and so on. These added lines are not necessary and reduce the powerfully imagistic opening to pretty description that sinks to easy nostalgia. Even though the poet provides a surprising reversal of tone as an ending—finding "the wondrousness of spring" in the "flicker of a firefly"— he does not balance the sentimentality of the larger part of the poem. In fact, the ending substitutes another kind of sentimentality.

It was not the crepuscular poets who succeeded in reentering the European world. In 1909, publishing in the Parisian newspaper *Le Figaro*, Filippo Tommaso Marinetti (1876-1944) issued the *Manifeste du futurisme*. The Futurist movement, which embraced sculpture and painting as well as poetry, took one side of the Nietzschean philosophy of will and elevated it to a religion. Marinetti praised courage and boldness, unabashed egotism, and the purifying air of war. The machine age transcended all previous ages: Noise, speed, and mastery were its central values. Men such as Marinetti, Ardengo Soffici (1879-1964), Govoni, Papini, Palazzeschi, and even Giuseppe Ungaretti wrote under the Futurist banner.

Marinetti's call for the destruction of culture, though absurd in one way, was, in another way, prophetic, for World War I, which many of the Futurists foresaw and welcomed, threw European culture into a whirlwind of self-questioning. By the end of the war, it appeared as if Carducci had been forgotten. Ironically, the Futur-

ist advocacy of war and its identification with fascism assured its fate: The reaction against the war meant that most writers turned their backs on Futurism as well.

Marinetti's "words in freedom," a poetic style in which syntax is interrupted or destroyed in order to achieve unusual juxtapositions of words, and in which words are stretched and given new, or absurd, meanings, became an element in a new poetic style emerging in Italy in the 1920's and focusing on the magazine *La voce*. Arturo Onofri (1885-1928) and Ungaretti were the major exponents of this style.

La voce saw its first number in December of 1908 under the editorship of Giuseppe Prezzolini (1882-1982). A center of social, political, and literary debate for eight years, the magazine became progressively more literary until, in December of 1914, under the editorship of Giuseppe De Robertis (1888-1963), it became completely literary. The writers published in *La voce* came from every side of the political spectrum. Even Mussolini and the dialectal poet Di Giacomo published in the magazine, but the writers who came to be known as *vociani* were men such as Sbarbaro, Papini (who had collaborated with Prezzolini on the magazine *Leonardo*), Rèbora, Piero Jahier (1884-1966), Palazzeschi, Cardarelli, Saba, and Campana.

Like Soffici, Palazzeschi, and Papini, Jahier had been a Futurist. For him, social issues were crucial in poetry, and in this belief he was typical of the *vociani*. His social concerns might have been colored, however, by his strict Protestant upbringing. Jahier's poetry was an antecedent of Ungaretti's, for it was fragmented, analogical, and aimed at an almost mystical apprehension of reality beyond any rational order.

Onofri had seen a crepuscular and Futurist phase, but his mature voice is identified with his *La voce* years. Following the French Symbolists, he insisted that the poem was a reality unto itself that had to be taken on its own terms. As Onofri's poetry developed, it became progressively more mystical, and his aesthetics reflected the influence of German Idealism, for he sought a union of the creative ego with the cosmos.

De Robertis, the editor of *La voce* from December, 1914 to December, 1915, saw the magazine through its most significant phase. With Ungaretti, De Robertis played an important part in the revaluation of Giacomo Leopardi, establishing the nineteenth century poet as perhaps the dominant native influence on Italian poetry in the first half of the twentieth century. The critic Silvio Ramat further asserts that this period in the history of *La voce* represented the beginnings of the Hermetic school, the most important movement in twentieth century Italian poetry.

DINO CAMPANA

Dino Campana, often called one of the *vociani*, must be treated separately, for he defies categorization. His association with the magazine was by default, for Soffici, to whom Campana had entrusted the manuscript of *Canti orfici* (1914; *Orphic Songs*, 1968), lost it; Campana thus had to publish his work himself. When Soffici read it, he praised it highly and was instrumental in arranging for a second edition.

Campana was influenced by the American poet Walt Whitman. A restless traveler, pathologically lonely and eventually mad, Campana wrote impassioned poetry. Imitating Whitman, he wrote in free verse, with erratic syntax and disquieting imagery. His sole work, *Orphic Songs*, lyrically depicts travels, women, loneliness. His writing is reminiscent of Vincent van Gogh's expressive power—as, for example, when he describes Genoa, making it any modern city: "And The City is aware/ And lights up/ And the flame titillates and swallows up/ The magnificent residues of the sun. . . ."

Campana's poetry is spontaneous, filled with brilliant insight, but sometimes without sustaining integument. True to their name, these poems seem, at their best, inspired in a demoniac fashion, and it is that quality that keeps them safe from pathos. Ironically, it might have been Campana's madness that preserved his work from melancholy. His life, however, was not thus preserved, for soon after the publication of his poems he was committed to a mental hospital at Castel Pulci near Florence, where he remained until his death in 1932.

GIUSEPPE UNGARETTI

Giuseppe Ungaretti (1888-1970) is the central figure of twentieth century Italian poetry. Next to him are Montale and Saba, and in the succeeding generation, Quasimodo. Only Ungaretti, Montale has said, could benefit from the air of freedom around the time of World War I. Though Saba was writing at that time also, his poetry remained derivative of Pascoli until he encountered Ungaretti.

Ungaretti was born in Alexandria, Egypt. His education was French, which probably accounts for the decidedly Symbolist influence on his poetry. His style brings together Symbolist, Futurist, and Leopardian techniques. The use of fragmented lines, analogy, nonmetrical but rhythmic cadences, and mysterium characterizes his early writing, the works of World War I: *Il porto sepolto* (1916; the buried port) and *Allegria di naufragi* (1919; the joy of shipwrecks).

In describing his verse, Ungaretti spoke of a poetics of the word, suggesting that words have a plethora of significations which it is the task of poetry to unearth. Ungaretti's spare style was a consequence of this belief. "I flood myself with light/ of the immense." So goes the poem "Mattina" ("Morning"); such a poem is evocative, incantatory. Even in those poems based on a narrative, Ungaretti removed all spare words—anything that served a merely decorative or metrical function—in order to get at the significant elements only. Such a narrative poem is "In memoria" ("In Memoriam"), about the suicide of his friend Mohammed Sheab. On its surface, the poem appears to be simply a whittled-down account of a tragic event, but when the reader takes into account the role of the poetic speaker, his condition as a soldier at the Italian front during World War I, and the fact that the poem stands as a successful song, such lines as "And he could not/ set free/ the song/ of his abandon" or "And only I perhaps/ still know/ he lived," it becomes clear that the apparent simplicity and directness of the poem conceal depths of meaning. This poem is not, in any simple sense, an effort to memorialize its subject through art; indeed, the poem suggests that the precariousness of things and of people is the very precondition of song.

After his first collections, Ungaretti turned to an intensive study of traditional Italian lyrics: Petrarch, Tasso, Leopardi. From the highly condensed line and music of his first works, he turned to traditional metrics as an inspiration, seeking, he said, "true Italian song." Without abandoning the lean quality of his early verse, Ungaretti managed in volumes such as *Sentimento del tempo* (1933; the feeling of time) and *La terra promessa* (1950; the promised land) to infuse his work with the music of the hendecasyllabic line. At the same time, his syntax became more complex, and he introduced subtle allusions to the classics. These features of his poems provoked resistance among some critics and inspired the label Hermetic—that is, requiring secret knowledge.

For Ungaretti, poetry and experience are in dialogue with each other (he called poetry "seemly biography"), so that a more complex poetry reflects a deepening experience. In fact, poetry is the vehicle by which experience is deepened, or, to put it in a more Ungarettian fashion, restored to its purity. Such an understanding of the role of poetry reveals how central language is to Ungaretti's worldview. For most human beings, caught up in a fragmented or clichéd language, experience is alienated from them at the very moment of its occurrence; though the poet might not come closer to the moment of experience, in recollection through poetry, he can uncover the truth of experience. Others, like Ungaretti, move from atheism to faith, suffer the loss of an only son, and confront old age, but they cannot capture the truth of these experiences as Ungaretti was able to do in his poetry.

Ungaretti's dialogue with tradition is an extension of his dialogue with experience. The essentials of experience do not change—love, death, memory—and the truth of these is held in the collective memory of tradition. The poet cannot work alone, but must return to the past creatively as a source. In one of his last poems, "Per sempre" ("For Ever") and written, perhaps, in memory of his wife, Ungaretti captured something of the sense of this twofold dialogue: "With no impatience I shall dream,/ Bend to the work/ That has no end. . . ."

Ungaretti gained an international reputation, lectured widely, and influenced almost every major modern poetic movement in Italy. He, along with Montale, Quasimodo, and others, was also active as a translator, helping to lead Italy out of cultural provincialism.

EUGENIO MONTALE

While contemporary Italian poetry begins with Ungaretti, its greatest figure may be Eugenio Montale, though the bulk of Montale's work makes up only four modest collections: *Ossi di seppia* (1925; partial translation, *The Bones of the Cuttlefish*, 1983; full transla-

tion, *Cuttlefish Bones*, 1992), *Le occasioni* (1939; *The Occasions*, 1987), *La bufera, e altro* (1956; *The Storm, and Other Poems*, 1978), and *Satura, 1962-1970* (1971; English translation, 1998).

Montale's earliest poems are in the crepuscular mood, showing especially the influence of Gozzano as well as of Pascoli, but D'Annunzio is also present. Though Montale is not really a regional poet, his reflection of Sbarbaro, a fellow Ligurian, gives his poetry a regional feel. Unlike Sbarbaro's landscapes, however, Montale's settings verge on metaphysical realities, providing images emblematic of the human condition.

Not completely a pessimist, Montale nevertheless wraps whatever sense of extraordinary reality is attained in his poems in a language of desolation and spiritual fragmentation. In the poem "I limoni" ("The Lemon Trees"), for example—which many critics treat as thematically central to Montale's first collection, *Cuttlefish Bones*—there are several suggestions of a breakthrough into a heightened reality: "Here by a miracle is hushed/ the war of diverted passions,/ here even to us poor falls our share of riches,/ and it is the scent of the lemon trees. . . ." These openings, however, are quickly obscured: "But the illusion wanes and time returns us/ to our clamorous cities. . . ." In Ungaretti, the desolate landscape of modern existence is likewise seen as resulting from the reality of time, but for him there is also a way beyond depersonalized time; in Montale, the landscape is bleaker, the music more muted.

Montale's greatness lies in his ability to evoke cosmic order in the midst of ordinary things and events. A thunderstorm holds back ultimate reality, for example, in "Arsenio," a poem many critics take to be a self-portrait. Montale commented that at the time of the writing of this poem, he was under the influence of Henri Bergson, the French philosopher: "Miracle was as evident for me as necessity." For Montale, however, there was never a complete breakthrough to extraordinary reality; thus, Arsenio, after contemplating the possibility that the sound of castanets holds the key to a heightened reality, is suddenly swept along in a thunderstorm: "Everything about you is washing with overflow, the loose awnings/ flap in the wind, and immense rustling skirts/ along the earth, and down collapse with strident sounds/ the paper lanterns. . . ."

Montale's later poetry, beginning with *The Occasions*, became more difficult, more Hermetic: "I wanted a fruit that could contain its motives without revealing them, or better, without flaunting them." He was after an extreme concentration of meaning, an obscurity he considered good. The title of *The Occasions* suggests the difficulty of these poems; in them, one is immersed in occasions without introduction and must make one's way in the midst of objects suggestively arranged, but without any obvious relationships among them. Montale's is often a poetry of things imbued with meanings and memories.

For Montale, the central drama of existence is a striving for harmony with the self and the cosmos. Neither of these is finally achieved in life, but the poems themselves stand as a testament that Montale will not sink into cynicism or complete pessimism; although the poems do not offer ultimate consolation, they do limn a heightened experience. Thus, there is a kind of faith in beauty underlying these works, not aestheticism but an aesthetic stoicism: "The life that seemed/ so vast is briefer than your handkerchief."

UMBERTO SABA

Umberto Saba (1883-1957) lived and wrote during a period of tremendous poetic innovation in Italy, yet his own work remained close to the lyric tradition of Petrarch and Leopardi. To be sure, his poetry reveals the influence of his contemporaries (he himself acknowledges the influence of Ungaretti on his style), but the great body of his work cannot be categorized as belonging to any of the schools of twentieth century Italian poetry. Even though he is said to be a major force in the development of neorealism after World War II, he never shared any of the political themes of this school. Saba's poetry is fundamentally autobiographical. His recurring subjects are ordinary things, animals, and the people close to him—his mother, his father, and, above all, his wife.

Saba was born in Trieste, a city to which he remained passionately attached throughout his life. His mother was Jewish, and it was her religious identity that the poet chose for himself. His father deserted the family when Saba was a young boy. When he met his father years later, at the age of twenty, Saba says it was then that he discovered the origin of his poetic spirit.

The images of Trieste found in his poetry were connected in his imagination with his wet nurse, a woman Saba loved; his emotional allegiance to her caused his mother some jealousy and pain. Saba suffered often during his adult life thinking of the pain he had given his mother, and it was probably only with his marriage that he found some sense of peace with himself.

Saba's major opus, *Il canzoniere* (1921, 1945, 1948, 1961, 1965), bears the title of Petrarch's great work—no doubt in homage to it. Written between 1900 and 1954, these poems are addressed to Saba's daughter Linuccia in an ironically offhand, self-deprecating way. The book is an autobiography in verse, and critics have often commented that the poet becomes self-indulent and technically lax in some of the poems, but, taken as a whole, the work has a greatness that is undeniable. Indeed, Saba's *Il canzoniere* is one of those rare masterpieces that combine unswerving artistic vision with great popular appeal.

A Pascolian, Saba balances potentially sentimental themes, such as the love he has for his wife, with a muted and ironic language. In "A mia moglie" ("To My Wife"), he develops a series of similes between his wife and barnyard animals. These images never become cute, and by the end of the poem, they ring with surprisingly passionate power: ". . . as in all the females/ of the peaceful animals,/ close to God;/ and in no other woman." Saba was a master of classical meters and forms. His career as a poet was traditional in the sense that he apprenticed himself to his craft, learning more and more difficult forms. This painstaking craftsmanship in the service of emotional authenticity made for great poetry. Though he valued simplicity, Saba was in no way simple.

SALVATORE QUASIMODO

Salvatore Quasimodo, born in Modica, Sicily, stands with Ungaretti, Montale, and Saba as one of the great poets of modern Italy. His winning of the Nobel Prize in Literature in 1959 aroused a great deal of critical debate, for many had expected the older Ungaretti or Montale to win. Quasimodo, furthermore, won the Nobel Prize based on his later work, such as *Giorno dopo giorno* (1947; day after day), which he wrote after his turn away from Hermeticism to a more socially and politically engaged poetry. For those critics who considered his early work superior, the Nobel Prize seemed a mistake. There is no doubt today, however, that Quasimodo is held in the highest critical esteem.

Educated as an engineer, though he discovered his love of poetry early in life, it was not until his late twenties that Quasimodo sought publication. His first poems were published in *Solaria*, a magazine whose internationalism, intellectualism, and political nonalignment were considered antifascist. In 1930, his collection *Acque e terre* (waters and lands) appeared, immediately establishing Quasimodo as a major new voice. These first poems were obscure, subdued, mysterious—Hermetic in the manner of Montale and Ungaretti. Though his early work revealed a strong sense of landscape, Quasimodo's main concerns—like Montale's—were spiritual. His was a voice of human loneliness and anguish. In "Ed è subito sera" ("And It Is Suddenly Evening"), this mood is beautifully, if epigrammatically, conveyed: "Each alone on the heart of the earth,/ impaled upon a ray of sun:/ and suddenly it's evening."

Quasimodo often evokes classical music, as in "Vento a Tindari" ("Wind at Tindari"); "Tindari, I know you mild/ among broad hills, above the waters/ of the god's soft islands. . . ." In the Italian, the cadences of classical Greek structure the line and add to the evocative power of the landscape. Like Ungaretti, Quasimodo sought a promised land which poetry somehow prefigured. In this case, it is Sicily sung in such a way that it becomes a mysticized realm. Just as Quasimodo practiced what Ungaretti called the "excavation of the word," so, too, he uncovered classical resonances in the scenes of his native island.

Quasimodo, along with many other Southern writers, lived in the North because of the deplorable condition into which the South had sunk, but in his writing, he remained a southerner, even ascribing to men of the South a capacity for creative invention because of their destitution. It was during his first stay in the North that Quasimodo encountered an important influence, Monsignor Rampolla del Tindaro, who encouraged him to study the classics. After teaching himself Greek and Latin, Quasimodo went on to the study of poetry and philosophy in the classical languages. In 1940, he published a powerful, controversial volume of translations,

Lirici greci (1940; Greek lyrics), establishing himself as a major translator of the classics.

During World War II, Quasimodo went through a critical change. The involuted, obscure poetry of the 1930's came to seem to him a manifestation of self-indulgence, and he turned to a more socially engaged poetry. In this new poetry, he sought to communicate with a wider audience and to bear witness to the absurdity of the contemporary situation. In poems such as "Auschwitz," he called for a rejection of inhumanities: "Upon the plains, where love and lamentation/ rotted . . . , a no/ to death. . . ." His project, which he shared with many other artists of this century, was the remaking of humanity. The cry that closes "Uomo del mio tempo" ("Man of My Time") is as old as Greek tragedy, expressing, perhaps, humanity's only real hope: "Forget, O sons, the clouds of blood/ risen from the earth, forget the fathers:/ their tombs sink down in ashes,/ black birds, the wind, cover their heart."

HERMETICISM

There are many ways of understanding the phenomenon called *Ermetismo*, or Hermeticism. Essentially an extension of Symbolism into Italy, the movement nevertheless developed distinctively Italian features. The term "hermetic" was first used in a 1936 article by the Crocean critic Francesco Flora (1891-1962), who deplored the lack of clarity in the poetry of Ungaretti and his fellow spirits. Flora criticized Ungaretti in particular for practicing an art that was French, an "analogical art"; like the French Symbolists, Ungaretti employed metaphor and ellipsis to bring out an inherent richness in words that went beyond any logical order. Flora's analysis, however, failed to acknowledge the native Italian influences that also shaped Ungaretti's art, particularly the "poetics of memory" elaborated in Leopardi's *Zibaldone* (1898-1900; notebook of thoughts).

Ungaretti, Montale, and later Quasimodo were the most important poets associated with Hermeticism; other poets identified with this school were Mario Luzi (1914-2005), Vittorio Sereni (1913-1983), Alfonso Gatto (1909-1976), and Sinisgalli. Sandro Penna (1906-1977) is also counted in this group, but the character of his poetry—like that of Saba's, to which it is sometimes compared—defies categorization.

Sinisgalli, a Lucanian poet, wrote of his region but also of urban life; his poetry is characterized by a remarkable precision that reflects his study of mathematics. As a poet, Sinisgalli moved from revelation to revelation. In his later poetry, leaving behind the mannerisms of Hermeticism, he became more epigrammatic, simpler and more direct. As he says of the poet in "Alla figura del poeta": "Like a rabbit in a hutch, every morning he finds—under his paws, before his eyes, near his nose—his portion of syllables and signs."

Of the other Hermetic poets, Luzi is perhaps the most significant, for he emerged, after the war, as a major spokesperson in defense of Hermetic poetry, which was coming under attack at that time by the emerging neorealists. The war had an effect on Luzi himself, however, and by the 1950's, his style had broadened considerably from that of his earlier poetry. Luzi's work is allusive, refined, and complex. He said of poetry: "The great adventure of modern poetry consists . . . in its attempt to reconstruct through language that unity lost by the ideal, practical, expressive world."

Gatto and Sereni both began in the analogical style of Hermeticism, and both changed direction as a result of the war. Gatto's earlier poetry—impressionistic, filled with landscapes—was highly melodic, perhaps reflecting his Neapolitan heritage (Gatto was born in Salerno). Sereni explored the historical and ideological questions raised by the war.

RELIGIOUS POETRY

The patriotism that produced the Risorgimento and the prosperity that followed it were not conducive to the writing of lofty religious poetry. An exception is the poetry of the Calabrian Antonino Anile (1869-1943), a neoclassicist and follower of Carducci as well as a university professor of anatomy who saw no irreconcilable conflict between science and faith. Always deeply religious, his poems portray the beauty of nature as a manifestation of God.

Many of the *vociani* wrote what might be called religious poetry. Papini converted to Catholicism after the trauma of World War I and wrote his famous *La storia di Cristo* (1921; *The Life of Christ*, 1923), a work neither theological nor scientific but charged with love and hope. From 1921 until his death, he was constantly concerned with deepening his faith, as in "Domande al Signore" ("Requests of the Lord"), where he asks for simplicity, humility, a serene smile, the cleansing of his "turbid soul that reeks of the sewer," and the burning of his heart "so that, in pursuing pain, it would find/ Your irrefutable will."

The Milanese Rèbora, another of the *vociani*, started to write poetry as an atheist. The victim of shell shock in World War I, he was discharged in 1915, and the experience forced him to do more than ask the usual existential questions about war. In 1929, he retired to a monastery, was ordained a priest in 1936, and abjured the writing of poetry until 1955, when he wrote "Curriculum vitae," an autobiographical meditation on his spiritual pilgrimage.

The response of *vociani* such as Rèbora, Onofri, and Jahier to the rhetoric of the nineteenth century was a moral indignation. Rèbora became traditionally religious, Onofri became a mystic, and Jahier expressed himself in philosophical terms. Jahier, unlike Rèbora, saw war as the symptom of a corrupt capitalistic society and as such saw it as God's way of destroying that corruption. Onofri, on the other hand, embarked upon a mystical quest that produced poems less successful than his earlier attempts.

The spiritual crisis that Ungaretti underwent after 1928 led to his return to Catholicism and ultimately is reflected in the most important part of his collection *Sentimento del tempo*. In the central poem of the section, titled "La pietà" ("Pity"), the poet expresses serious doubts about the power of his poetry and seems to waver between two poles: the solipsism of a poetry pursued in a world without God, and the certitude of a renewal of faith. Though Ungaretti expresses a tone of greater harmony in his later works, the struggle persists. Ungaretti remained the paradoxical agnostic believer; every introduction of a Christian value or image in his verse is balanced by a pagan or a humanistic counterweight.

Always insistent that he belonged to no school, Carlo Betocchi (1899-1986) cultivated his own style and his own sympathetic outlook toward objects of ordinary life. Although his post-World War II poetry is more somber, all experiences are interpreted as proof of his love for God and humanity. A land surveyor and construction engineer, Betocchi was instrumental in the organization of *Il frontespizio*, a Florentine review for Catholic poets (1929), of which he and Papini were coeditors.

Quasimodo was probably the most conventionally religious of the first-rank poets of this era. His work translating the New Testament and his knowledge of the Old Testament are echoed allusively in all of his poetry, and religious references are not always treated Hermetically. His poem "Man of My Time" takes on the directness of a sermon: Man, with his "exact science bent on extermination," is "without love, without Christ," and the poet then includes a scriptural quotation: "The blood smells as on the day/ when one brother said to the other brother: 'Let us go out to the fields.'" His great antiwar poem "Alle fronde dei salici" ("On the Branches of the Willows"), in which the poet asks, "And how could we have sung/ with the alien foot upon our heart?" and in which lyres hung on willow branches swaying in the sad wind form a counterpart to the "black howl" of a mother who meets her son crucified on a telegraph pole, was inspired by the Psalm 137, in which the children of Israel, who have hung their harps "upon the willows in the midst thereof," ask "How shall we sing the Lord's song in a strange land?" The most important lesson that Quasimodo learned from his faith was the acceptance of suffering, an acceptance that gives his mature poetry great moral authority.

The poet-priest David Maria Turoldo (1916-1992), of Friulian origin, published his first book of poetry, *Io non ho mani* (1948; I have no hands), in the painful years after World War II, establishing himself as a lover of all living things, even of the earth itself. His imagery is sensuous and uninhibited ("And while the kisses of others/ stopped at the mouth,/ I ate You at every dawn"). Although he inveighs against the destructiveness of the Western world, he can praise even the cities and the machines of the world, for they are human handiwork and are not in themselves profane.

LA RONDA AND THE RONDISTI

The review *La ronda*, founded by Cardarelli and published in Rome between 1919 and 1923, represented an attempt to encourage a renewal of Italian letters after World War I. The *rondisti* wished to restore good writing in poetry and prose by a return to classical tradition, well-constructed syntax, clear style, and a literary vocabulary. The creation of literature was once again to be viewed as a craft with as few infractions of the rules as possible. In their task of reeducating Italians in the art of writing, they chose as their model Leopardi, ultimately emphasizing his prose over his poetry. They failed for the most part to achieve these goals, for the world was changing, and although they rejected fascism, the academicism that gradually developed from their aims came dangerously close to suiting the needs of fascism.

Only in the work of Cardarelli did the *rondisti* produce a significant contribution to poetry. Cardarelli, whose critical work revealed a particular distaste for Pascoli and a virtually idolatrous regard for sixteenth century literature, wrote of the seasons as emblems for the cycle of human life, of landscapes in the harsh light of a sun that often obliterates hopes and dreams. Some of the other writers associated with *La ronda*, such as Emilio Cecchi (1884-1966) and Riccardo Bacchelli (1891-1985), were influential in propounding the vision of art as an autonomous sphere, a notion that became an important aspect of Hermeticism. Initially Ungaretti, from 1919 to 1920, was involved with the *rondisti*, but he split with them because he felt they wanted prose poems instead of creations approaching song.

Like the *rondisti*, Ada Negri (1870-1945), who was the first woman member of the Italian Academy, held traditional views about poetry. In her poems, she exalts the virtue of the working classes and, in those written after her marriage to a wealthy Piedmontese industrialist, the joys of motherhood. After a period of disillusionment, she wrote *Il libro di Mara* (1919), a powerful love poem that has been likened to the lyrics of Sappho and the Song of Solomon.

POETRY OF THE RESISTANCE

It is an understatement to say that for the Italian people, the experience of World War II was traumatic and that they emerged from it with changed values. The fact that virtually all postwar literary movements are introduced with the prefix "neo-" (for example, neorealism, neoexperimentalism) is but a single example of the rupture caused by the war. A great polemic arose after the war over charges that Italian poets had done little or nothing to stop the rise of Fascism. One result of the charges was that previously Hermetic poets such as Quasimodo, Sereni, and Luzi underwent profound changes of attitude; another was that poetry reflecting on the mission of the Resistance movement came to be highly esteemed. In an attempt to unify poets, some critics have amplified the meaning of "Resistance" poetry to include any antiwar poetry of the period. Thus, the very fine *Antologia poetica della resistenza italiana*, edited by Elio Accrocca and Valerio Volponi and published in 1955, includes poets such as Ungaretti, who initially admired Mussolini and only later became disillusioned, and Sereni, who was imprisoned by the Americans in North Africa.

Italian poets sympathetic to the Resistance poured forth torrents of verse to commemorate the heroism of the fallen, and torrents of deeply felt invective, such as Saba's refrain, "All this the vile Fascist/ and the greedy German took from me," or Palazzeschi's cry, "Death to the Germans." Italians of Jewish descent were especially vocal: Saba, Natalia Ginzburg, and Franco Fortini, who wrote, speaking of Italy, "Now it is not enough just to die/ for that empty ancient name." The death of Corrado Govoni's son at the Fosse Adreatine (the massacre in Rome by the Germans of 335 partisans on March 24, 1944, about which De Libero also wrote movingly) inspired an elegy, *Aladino: Lamento su mio figlio morto* (1946; Aladino: lament for my dead son), reminiscent in breadth and length of Alfred, Lord Tennyson's *In Memoriam* (1850).

Especially significant among the Resistance poets are Cesare Pavese (1908-1950), Pasolini, and Gatto. Pavese, one of those who attacked the Hermeticists for their failure to speak out against Fascism, was arrested for antifascist activities in 1935 and then imprisoned. He was profoundly affected by the deaths of his friends Giaime Pintor and Leone Ginzburg, killed in their partisan undertakings, but his feelings about the period were given fuller development in his novels than in his poetry.

Pasolini was just as deeply affected by the death of his younger brother Guido at the beginning of 1945, and it is Guido's tale that Pasolini tells in "Il testamento Coran" (the Qurʾān testament), later incorporated into *La meglio gioventì* (1954; the finest youth). For Pasolini, who was drafted into the Italian army in September, 1943, but who deserted after a mere week, the Resistance was "a style all light, memorable/ awareness of sun."

Like Pavese and Pasolini, Gatto was a Communist. Seeds of his moral dilemma were evident in his *Amore della vita* (1944), and in 1944 and 1945, his verses circulated secretly; in 1949, they were assembled in *Il Capo sulla neve* (the head on the snow).

Because he failed to join the Fascist Party, Montale was investigated by the Questura of Florence in 1937 and in the following year was discharged from his employment at the Gabinetto Vieusseux, at that time the largest lending library in Europe. Adolf Hitler's visit to Florence in the spring of 1938 is recalled in Montale's "Primavera hitleriana" ("Hitlerian Spring"), in which the poet observes the cries of "alala" and the swastikas (the Italian term for which means "hooked crosses") with consternation and irony. Some readers, however, felt that in his later poetry, Montale did not make that consternation explicit enough.

Quasimodo, who was active in the Resistance and was imprisoned by Mussolini for a time at Bergamo, felt impelled after the war to reconsider his role as a poet. His conversation was no longer with a vague and generalized humanity but with humans specifically. He emerged from his poetic seclusion and became committed to helping humans remake themselves. His Resistance poems are contained in *Giorno dopo giorno*, in which there abound references to this change in self-perception, to the difference between his previous and his present poetic mission ("I can no more return to my elysium"), and denunciations in savage terms of human inhumanity toward other people ("You are still the one with the stone and the sling,/ man of my time"). In "Auschwitz," he tells the soldier that he will find the smoke-immolated victims within him, but adds as an afterthought, "or are you, too, but ash/ of Auschwitz, medal of silence?"

HERMETICS VERSUS NEOREALISM

The passions released by the ordeal of World War II and the bitter civil strife of the Resistance could not help but spill over into literary debate, and this was especially the case in Italy, where poetry aligned itself with schools in which political ideology was explicitly or implicitly supported. Because of their passive resistance, the Hermetic poets came under attack from the Left; the attack was initiated in an article published in *La rinascita* in 1944 and went on for several years, finally wasting itself in mere verbal exercise. In the meantime, the political realities of Italy had changed considerably, for the Italians, along with other Europeans, entered a period of economic well-being.

Several of Italy's most significant writers participated in the debate. More significant, however, these were the years in which neorealism emerged as the most vital form of Italian artistic expression, and though neorealism is associated to a large extent with the novel and the cinema, this movement also had its poetic exponents.

Pavese anticipated the neorealist art of the postwar period in *Lavorare stanca* (1936; *Hard Labor*, 1976). These poems are generally expressions of unromanticized landscapes filled with people from daily life. Though they have lyrical moments, they are informed by a pervasive bitterness. In "Instinct," Pavese speaks of dogs copulating and then refracts the attitudes of various emblematic persons through this act in such a way as to humble human pretenses: "Anything can happen out in the/ open. Even a woman, shy when face to face with a man,/ stands there. . . ."

Of all the exponents of neorealism, it is Pasolini who stands out as the central figure. Born in Bologna but at heart a Friulian, Pasolini was the quintessential *homme engagé*. A filmmaker, novelist, and political essayist as well as a poet, he showed not only a love for the great classics and for the Hermetic style of Ungaretti, but also a devotion to leftist apologetics and Roman Catholicism. Pasolini was lionized and rejected by almost every group with which he came in contact. His poetry cannot be said to follow any specific style, but it is clear that his interests are in an art of social relevance. His volume *Le ceneri de Gramsci* (1957; *The Ashes of Gramsci*, 1982) was in part an act of homage to Antonio Gramsci, the head of the Italian Communist Party who was imprisoned under Mussolini but who managed to send out letters and journal entries expressing his vision of society and art.

In the title poem, "The Ashes of Gramsci," Pasolini combines historical reflections on the years before World War II with personal confession: "I live in the non-will/ of the dead postwar years: loving/ the world I hate. . . ." It may be that there is no resolution for the conflict between the artist's absorption in art and the artist's moral duty to communicate with his fellow humans; in Pasolini, one finds a man living this contradiction.

A simpler case of neorealism is evident in Scotellaro, whose poetry is of a regional character. Scotellaro was born in Basilicata in 1923; a Socialist, he became mayor of his town but died at an early age in 1953. His poetry expresses his understanding of the peasantry, from which he himself came; his lyrics depict the life of his region and its ancient, even atavistic, character.

Fortini (pseudonym of Franco Lattes; 1917-1994) began as a Hermetic poet but turned to a poetry of social engagement. A prominent Marxist critic, Fortini, a Jew, went through a period of disillusionment during the war. Despite his Marxist orientation, his poetry maintains classical references and style; he writes, as Ramat puts it, in the Petrarchan-Leopardian tradition.

Although neorealism was dominant in the years after World War II, several prewar poets, among them Luzi and Sereni, continued in the postwar era to write in the Hermetic style. In the 1950's, a number of younger poets associated with Luzi came to be regarded as neo-Hermetic; two principal figures of this group are Zanzotto and Luciano Erba (born 1922). What distinguished them from the Hermetics of the 1930's was a greater concern for language per se—an attempt to regain a poetically significant language in a world in which language itself has been technologized.

Zanzotto's poetry, beginning with *Dietro il paesaggio*, poems written between 1940 and 1948, shares with Hermeticism a surface difficulty, a highly condensed but personal symbolism suggesting the need to penetrate appearances in order to apprehend the real. In his later poetry, access to the real is permitted only by linguistic experimentation, for the language of everyday usage has been enslaved for superficial, purely utilitarian ends. Shattering syntax, struggling to unearth what he calls a "nether language," Zanzotto has much in common with that of the avant-garde experimentalists.

At its most radical, Zanzotto's poetry virtually eschews content, suggesting the fragmentation, asymmetry, and nonnaturalism of much modern music.

Erba's development was the reverse of that of many later poets, for he began as a socially committed poet and then moved to neo-Hermeticism, one of a group of Lombard poets who sought to move beyond the heroics of neorealism to the expression of disillusionment. In many ways, there is a Pascolian streak in the poetry of Erba, for he develops a poetry of "small things" in order to focus on the insignificant lives of modern humanity. Erba's poetry has a clarity of line that gives the people portrayed in his work a vividness belying their ordinariness. This quality is exemplified in "Tabula rasa?": "Do you see me going along as usual/ in the districts without memory?/ I have a cream tie, an old burden/ of desires. . . ."

Another important postwar poet is the Sicilian Bartolo Cattafi (1922-1979). A recurring motif in Cattafi's poetry is the figure of a traveler or nomad set in a precisely and vividly described landscape. Cattafi strives to build blocks of words, to create poems that are thinglike assemblages of images: "Ex nihilo God/ from tatters scraps/ carrion trash me."

AVANT-GARDE AND LATER POETS

Other changes in poetry in the 1950's all centered on the role of language. The avant-garde focused on the absurdity of any rational philosophy—even worldviews as diverse as those of Croce and Gramsci—in the modern world. The poets of this avant-garde, such as Antonio Porta (1935-1989), Alfredo Giuliani (1924-2007), Nanni Balestrini (born 1935), Edoardo Sanguineti (1930-2010), and Elio Pagliarani (born 1927), are reminiscent of Surrealism in their insistence that art must reflect the schizophrenia of modern society. They also employ the open form of American poets such as Charles Olson and William Carlos Williams. Influenced by literary theory, often to a crippling degree, the avant-garde poets reflect the ideas of the New Novel in France (in their insistence on an art of things) and of semiotics (in fact, Umberto Eco, a noted semiotician, is usually considered a poet of this group).

As the twenty-first century began, Italian poetry was characterized by a bewildering diversity, in marked contrast to the time-honored Italian tendency to form schools. In part, this fragmentation seemed to be the result of the failure of the protests that swept Europe in 1968 to effect genuine social change. Italian poetry after the Cold War embraces computer poets and experimentalists who tear language apart and attempt to rebuild it in new forms, but also more traditional poets who continue to ply their trade.

BIBLIOGRAPHY

Blum, Cinzia Sartini, and Lara Trubowitz, eds. and trans. *Contemporary Italian Women Poets: A Bilingual Anthology*. New York: Italica Press, 2001. Selections from the works of twenty-five women poets published in the last half of the twentieth century. Though they represent various literary traditions and different regions of Italy, they are alike in having produced memorable poetry. Introduction, notes, and bibliography.

Bohn, Willard, ed. and trans. *Italian Futurist Poetry*. Toronto: University of Toronto Press, 2005. A bilingual collection of more than one hundred poems, arranged in chronological order, reflecting the diversity and the very real creativity of a movement that the editor believes has previously been mislabeled. Bibliographical references and index.

Brand, Peter, and Lino Pertile, eds. *The Cambridge History of Italian Literature*. 2d ed. New York: Cambridge University Press, 1999. In this definitive volume, the first of its kind in four decades, leading scholars provide information about a wide range of writers, their works, and their significance. Translations are included. Maps, chronological charts, and bibliographical references.

Cary, Joseph. *Three Modern Italian Poets: Saba, Ungaretti, Mondale*. 2d ed. Chicago: University of Chicago Press, 1993. Focuses on the work of Umberto Saba, Giuseppe Ungaretti, and Eugenio Montale. Biographical and critical studies of three poets who flourished in the first half of the twentieth century, along with a thoughtful discussion of the historical period in which they lived. Bibliography and index.

Condini, Ned, ed. and trans. *An Anthology of Modern*

Italian Poetry in English Translation, with Italian Text. New York: Modern Language Association of America, 2009. The thirty-eight poets in this collection represent all the dominant poetic genres and movements of post-Unification Italy, from symbolism and feminism to neo-avant-gardists and neorealists. Excellent introduction by Dana Renga, who also provided notes. Bibliographical references.

Frabotta, Biancamaria, ed. *Italian Women Poets*. Translated by Corrado Federici. Toronto: Guernica Editions, 2002. A volume whose purpose is to address the issue of gender differences among poets. Included are poems by twentieth century Italian women poets and interviews in which specific poems are discussed, as well as such topics as a definition of poetry.

Payne, Roberta L., ed. *Selection of Modern Italian Poetry in Translation*. Montreal: McGill-Queen's University Press, 2004. A bilingual collection that surveys Italian poetry between the 1860's and the 1960's, with special attention to groups that the editor feels have been neglected by critics, such as the Futurists and women poets. Includes ninety-two poems by thirty-five poets. An excellent introduction to modern Italian poetry.

Picchione, John. *The New Avant-garde in Italy: Theoretical Debate and Poetic Practices*. Toronto: University of Toronto Press, 2004. Describes the theoretical tenets of the experimental movement that flourished between the late 1950's and the late 1960's and explains how those ideas were applied in the creation of poetry. Of particular interest is the author's account of the growing friction between members of the movement and the split that eventually occurred. Bibliographical references and index.

Ridinger, Gayle, and Gian Paolo Renello, eds. *Italian Poetry, 1955-1990*. Boston: Dante University of America Press, 1996. This anthology of the work of three generations of Italian poets presents the poems in Italian followed by their English translations. Provides examples of recent experimental works, such as prose poetry. Biocritical essay and list of publications for each poet are included.

Jack Shreve and Robert Colucci

JAPANESE POETRY TO 1800

The history of Japanese poetry begins indisputably with the eighth century anthology *Manyōshū* (mid-eighth century; *The Collections of Ten Thousand Leaves*; also as *The Ten Thousand Leaves*, pb. 1981, and as *The Manyoshu*, 1940) although the earlier historical chronicles *Kojiki* (c. 712 C.E.; *Records of Ancient Matters*, 1883) and *Nihon shoki* (c. 720; *Nihongi: Chronicles of Japan from the Earliest Times to A.D. 697*, 1896), as well as a few stone inscriptions, also preserve scattered early poems and sacred songs. The significance of *The Manyoshu* is manifold. As the most literal translation of its title, "collection of myriad leaves," suggests, it is a work of imposing bulk; containing more than 4,500 poems, it is by virtue of its age and size simply not to be ignored. Another interpretation of its title, "collection of (or for) myriad generations," hints at the importance accorded poetry in eighth century Japan.

THE MANYOSHU

The Manyoshu was assembled at a stage of Japanese cultural development roughly comparable to that of northern and western Europe at the close of the Dark Ages. In both cases, literacy was confined to very small groups, elite islands of advanced culture in a sea of what was by comparison barbarism. In the European case, literacy was a legacy of the Roman conquests, held in trust by the Roman Catholic Church until an ebbing in the tide of barbarian invasion allowed it to infiltrate secular courts. Literacy was in a sense indigenous, a skill that, from the viewpoint of the early Middle Ages, had been known (although not widely practiced) from time immemorial. The written word came to Japan, however, as the central monument of a flourishing, contemporary foreign civilization, embodied in the energetic culture of the Sui (581-618) and Tang (618-907) Dynasties. Chinese culture and the idea of literacy did not come with a conquering army but rather, it appears, by choice. The future imperial court, having consolidated its sway over competing tribal or regional groups, began in perhaps the fifth century to maintain what seems to have been fairly regular intercourse with China by way of the land route up the Korean peninsula. It was at this time, most agree, that written records began to be kept in Japan, but they were in Chinese, the work of Chinese and Korean scribes imported by the court.

The rich sophistication of Chinese culture in comparison with that of Japan, Korea, and Vietnam must have been almost absurdly evident to the first generations of Japanese who set themselves the task of learning Chinese and its complex writing system, through which medium the entirety of more than a thousand years of literary culture was suddenly visible in an undigested mass. In addition to the native Chinese classics, there was a huge body of Buddhist texts in Chinese to contemplate. By the end of the seventh century, however, the emerging Japanese state, headed by an aristocratic court, had accomplished much by way of assimilating the new culture. Governmental forms and court rites were modeled on Tang examples, and alongside the native animist religion, Shintō, Chinese Buddhism was officially established and encouraged, for the power of Tang in China—where Buddhism was enjoying a short-lived ascendancy—was thought to rest in part on the magical efficacy of Buddhist ritual. Under such circumstances, where political power was legitimized by Chinese precedent and the spiritual realm was increasingly dominated by a complex Indian faith that the Japanese could approach only in Chinese, the dominance of Chinese in the field of letters is no surprise. The true cause for wonder is that *The Manyoshu* testifies to a vigorous parallel tradition of sophisticated literary activity in Japanese—a tradition that was a century and more old by the time the collection was compiled.

The poetry of *The Manyoshu* dates largely from the first half of the eighth century, but a significant portion of it was composed in the preceding century, and a small number of verses seem to be authentic survivals, if perhaps retouched by later hands, from even earlier. The poetry of *The Manyoshu* and the history of the *Records of Ancient Matters* are written with Chinese characters, but because the Chinese ideographs are used for their phonetic values, these texts may be read as pure Japanese. However absorbed they may have been, therefore, in making Chinese culture their own, the Japanese were occupied as well with the difficult task of adapting the new tool of writing to record in their own language what they most valued in the native tradition, at a very early time in comparison with other East Asian societies.

The Manyoshu and the *Records of Ancient Matters* thus may be viewed as evidence of a persistent Japanese determination to maintain a significant degree of independence from foreign cultural influence, but their existence also ironically underlines the power of Chinese example, for poetry and historiography occupied the vital center of the Chinese literary canon as it reached the Japanese. These works can thus also be thought of as part of a broader enterprise on the part of the Japanese aristocracy to equip itself with all the trappings of a modern Asian state in the age of the Tang. That *The Manyoshu* exists at all is symbolic of the ambitions of the imperial court, an assertion of cultural equality with China, the emulation of which was not simply a matter of fashion but a conscious policy designed to enhance the power and dignity of the state.

It would be a mistake, however, to dismiss *The Manyoshu* as nothing more than an exercise in imitation, for it contains some of the most technically sophisticated, imaginative, and emotionally satisfying poetry in the entire Japanese canon. It does show a great deal of Chinese influence, as in its "songs of the East" and "songs of the border guards," the inclusion of which may echo one of the supposed functions of the *Shijing* (traditionally fifth century B.C.E.; *The Book of Songs*, 1937), the oldest Chinese anthology of verse—namely, the gathering of intelligence about the temper of the people of the realm. More broadly, the poetry in *The Manyoshu* in general is strongly colored by Chinese poetic practice, and some individual verses can be shown to have been based on specific Chinese sources. Nevertheless, this is genuinely Japanese poetry in its language and special emphases. *The Manyoshu* is also an anthology that can give considerable pleasure to modern readers, for its poets possess, to a surprising degree, individuality of voice.

KAKINOMOTO HITOMARO

Manyoshu poet Kakinomoto Hitomaro (fl. 680-700) is usually accorded primacy of place as the earliest master of poetry in Japanese. He wrote in both of the dominant verse forms of the period, the *tanka*, or short poem, and *chōka*, or long poem. The *tanka* was short indeed, fixed at a length of thirty-one syllables which were distributed in five lines or, more properly, in units of five, seven, five, seven, and seven syllables. This would become the standard form of Japanese poetry in succeeding centuries—so dominant, in fact, that another name for it would be *waka*, simply "Japanese verse," as opposed to *kanshi*, Japanese poetry written in the Chinese language. The *chōka*, despite its name, was long only in comparison with the *tanka*; the longest example in *The Manyoshu* occupies only four pages in an English translation with generous margins, hardly an extended composition by the standards of other literary cultures. The *chōka* was of indeterminate length, a formally simple sequence of alternating five- and seven-syllable phrases ending in a couplet of seven-syllable lines. The *chōka* was usually followed by one or more verses in standard *tanka* form that were called *hanka* (envois or responses). Hitomaro originated neither of these forms, but his consummate mastery of both helped to establish them at the core of the Japanese poetic tradition.

Rhyme schemes and metrical feet play no part in the formal apparatus of Hitomaro's poetry, for they are simply meaningless in Japanese. Rhyme is more or less trivial, because every syllable in Japanese ends in a vowel or *n*, and there are only five vowels in the language, meaning that rhyme occurs randomly and frequently without poetic intercession. All syllables in Japanese are stressed so nearly equally that metric patterns based on alternation of stress are impossible. Nor does assonance or alliteration play any role in the formal rules of composition, again because of the simplicity of the sound system. Thus the prominence of syllable count in Japanese poetic structure: It is virtually all that is left by way of effects based on sound alone. Why units of five and seven syllables have proved so congenial to Japanese poets is unknown, but Hitomaro's importance lies in part in his success in demonstrating the ample sufficiency of this simple scheme, which has prevailed until the present alongside blank-verse forms introduced in the nineteenth century. In Hitomaro's verse, these small building blocks are built into phrases and sentences of great length and complexity; some entire *chōka* can be construed as consisting grammatically of single extended sentences with a complicated structure of parallel independent and dependent clauses rolling forward in rhythmic cadence to a final predication in the concluding couplet. Hitomaro showed the way for later poets, developing in both the expansive *chōka* and the terse *tanka* an armory of techniques to bridge the natural pauses at the end of metric units with the momentum of syntax or imagistic association.

Little is known of Hitomaro's life, but it appears that he may have functioned at least quasi-officially as a poet laureate, for many of his poems were occasioned by events important in the life of the court or nation—elegies on the death or interment of royal personages, for example, and celebrations of more auspicious events. These public poems are suffused with a sense of the awesome, even divine dignity of the sovereign and his or her (women could still occupy the throne in Hitomaro's day) immediate family. This sense of immanent divinity extended to the land itself. Place-names, for example, figure prominently in Hitomaro's poetry, recalling other *Manyoshu* poems that are actually attributed to emperors themselves, rulers of generations even earlier than that of Hitomaro, whose compositions seem sometimes to be little more than ritual incantations of the names of the mountains and plains of Yamato, the region south of modern Kyoto from which the imperial clan ruled early Japan. Hitomaro reinforced this invocation of place-names, originally no doubt a way of claiming hegemony by "naming" the bounds and features of the realm, through the use of *makurakotoba* (pillow words), which were either epithets traditionally coupled with certain place-names (or other parts of speech) or similar attributive phrases coined by Hitomaro himself on traditional models. Thus, epithets such as "Izumo of the eight-fold clouds," "Yamato which fills the skies," and "Sanuki of gemlike seagrass" make the earthly landscape glow with hints of the heavenly connections of high places and the mysteries of the depths. Such poems have as their purpose the exaltation of imperial rule, but they succeed as art because of Hitomaro's mastery of language and a particular gift for personalizing verse on even the most

public occasions by relating them to the individualizd human emotions they evoke in their participants.

The elegance and grandeur of Hitomaro's public commemorations are complemented in a body of highly personal verse of great emotional power, the most impressive of which is a sequence of *chōka* laments honoring his love for his wife (or wives—his biography is unclear) at partings in this life and at the final, awful parting of death. These poems share with his public verse a nice manipulation of *makurakotoba* epithets (such as "seagrass-lithe and bending girl"), which serve here not to add mythic significance to the landscape, but rather to relate the emotional substance of the poem to the phenomena of the natural world, a technique that gives this poetry a universality that transcends its intimate particularity.

The balance of majesty and individuality in Hitomaro's poetry moves both his public and nominally private verse toward a tonal middle ground precisely suited to poems composed for public recitation—which, authorities agree, was probably their original mode of presentation. Hitomaro was not, however, the last bard of a preliterate tradition, despite his use of the *makurakotoba* technique, which is obviously related to similar phenomena in indisputably oral traditions. The public recitation of poetry would continue to be a formal part of court life for centuries, making that aspect of his practice doubtful proof that Hitomaro was a late survivor of a diminished breed of oral poets. There is, moreover, substantial evidence of Chinese influence in Hitomaro's choice of imagery and subject matter and in the strong parallelism that structures his longer pieces. Finally, there is in his verse an idealization of a simpler past close to nature that can best be called pastoralism, clearly the product of a poet who still had access to the oral past but could speak in a complex and sophisticated voice trained in the methods and attitudes of a foreign, written literature.

OTHER EARLY POETS

Poets of the generation immediately following Hitomaro's wrote in an idiom even more clearly shaped by contact with Chinese poetry. Yamanoe Okura (c. 660-733), for example, is represented in *The Manyoshu* by a group of *chōka* on such subjects as poverty, destitution, and old age that can be read almost as a translated pastiche of Chinese poetic statements on the same themes, although his masterly use of Japanese has made them an admired (if rarely emulated) part of the native canon. Ōtomo Tabito (665-731), a close associate of Okura, left a series of *tanka* on the virtues of rice wine in which his adopted persona, that of the talented literary bureaucrat languishing in an enforced retirement, is as Chinese as anything by Okura, though Tabito's poetry is in a Japanese quite free of Chinese linguistic influence and in a form quintessentially Japanese. Both men were members of what was probably one of the earliest generations thoroughly at home in the world of Chinese letters, and their poetry may be read both as an homage to Chinese verse and as an intelligent experiment with expanding the range of Japanese poetic expression. They represent an extreme, however, for few later poets went as far as they did toward a Sinification of Japanese poetry, perhaps because the pessimism and intellectuality of their verse was believed to be simply too Chinese, too much a violation of the sunnier precedents of Japanese poetry.

Tabito's son, Ōtomo Yakamochi (718-785), may safely be called the most important and influential of the final generation of *Manyoshu* poets, both because of the quality of his verse and because he appears to have taken the leading role in the compilation of the anthology itself. Yakamochi's poetry marks him genuinely as a transitional figure. He is among the last masters of the *chōka*, which seems to have fallen from fashion rather soon after *The Manyoshu* was put together; at the same time, his work foreshadows what would become the dominant traditions of Japanese poetry for centuries to come.

There is a strong element of nostalgia in Yakamochi's poetry, most especially a longing for a glorious martial past, because the Ōtomo were a warrior clan. Later poets would not focus on this particular past—too redolent of violence for courtly tastes—preferring a more generalized evocation of antique timelessness; still, the stance toward the present, which is somehow drab, pedestrian, and ephemeral, is much the same as Yakamochi's, and quite different from Hitomaro's pastoralism. In Yakamochi's time, too, poetry moves indoors, or at least into the urban noble-

man's garden; gone are the grand vistas of mountain and plain, replaced by the singularities of garden plantings viewed close up over a balcony rail. Here Yakamochi was following one strand of Chinese verse, but he was also writing poetry germane to his time and place, since his was the first poetic generation to know the distinctive qualities of settled urban life; until 710, when a permanent capital city modeled on the Chinese metropolis was laid out on the site of modern Nara, the capital of Japan was wherever the emperor's court happened to be, and the court was mobile, for in accordance with Shintō belief, death rendered the sovereign's palace irremediably unclean, unfit for the sacral duties of the throne.

KOKINSHŪ

The next great landmark in Japanese poetry after *The Manyoshu* is another anthology, the *Kokinshū* (905; *Kokinshu: A Collection of Poems Ancient and Modern*, 1984), which is dated to 905 by its introduction. The *Kokinshu* marks the maturation of a tradition that has become known in English as court poetry. It is significant that it is once again an anthology that Japanese literary historiography singles out as important rather than, say, the achievements of a single poet or innovative poetic school, and doubly significant that this collection should bear the title it does—together these facts attest a conception of poetry as a collective cultural endeavor to which tradition and precedent are as important as innovation. Important also is the fact that the *Kokinshu* was an imperially commissioned collection, the first in a series of twenty-one that would appear at irregular intervals until 1433, and thus an early symbolic declaration of how important a part of court life poetry was and would be thereafter.

The scope and variety of the poetry of the *Kokinshu* are much constricted in comparison with *The Manyoshu*. The collection is smaller—it contains only some eleven hundred poems—and the overwhelming majority of the verses in it are *tanka*. There is little doubt, moreover, that this was a highly selective anthology. The *Kokinshu* was not meant as a representative sampler of the best of Japanese poetry, but rather, it appears, as a normative guide to what its compilers thought poetry should be. Principal among the compilers was Ki no Tsurayuki (884-946), whose introduction to the collection, the earliest extant piece of literary criticism in Japanese, would stand for centuries as the definitive statement of the proper concerns of the poet. Tsurayuki's most famous dictum is his metaphoric definition of Japanese poetry, which "takes as its seed the heart of man, and flourishes in the countless leaves of words." Emotion and its direct expression, he is saying, are what poetry is all about; in short, lyricism is at the core of Japanese poetry, and from Tsurayuki forward it would not be displaced. The classical Japanese canon would simply never admit the more expansive and multidimensional allegories, ballads, epics, and poetical discourses on religion, philosophy, and even politics that constitute so much of the high classical tradition of Western verse.

The *Kokinshu* is for the most part arranged topically, grouping together in the first books of the collection, for example, poems with seasonal subjects, season by season. Within each of these books, the poems are arranged roughly according to the order in which their dominant natural images occur as the seasons progress, so that in the first spring book, the flowering plum precedes the cherry. Love poems are arranged in like manner, to echo in the aggregate the pattern of a love affair, from initial infatuation through tentative courtship and passion to the inevitable abandonment. Not all topics allow this kind of mimetic organization—the books of celebratory poems, poems on parting, and poems based on wordplay are instances—but nowhere do Tsurayuki and his colleagues seem to have in mind the usual literary-historical objectives of Western anthologizers, grouping poems by author or in some way chronologically, to show stylistic changes over time.

The *Kokinshu*, it appears, was assembled not as a work of scholarship or preservation, but rather for the use of practicing poets, to whose needs its finely tuned topical organization was ideally suited. Despite Tsurayuki's insistence that poetry be an expression in "the leaves of words" of the movements of the heart, all the evidence—fiction, diaries, annotations to private and official anthologies—argues that poets in the age of the *Kokinshu* composed for specific occasions, not when seized by a lyric impulse. In this context, the *Kokinshu* and subsequent anthologies look very much like handbooks that were assembled as authoritative guides to the sort of poetry sanctioned by tradition and contemporary taste as appropriate to any number of clearly defined circumstances. As works such as the eleventh century novel *Genji monogatari* (c. 1004; *The Tale of Genji*, 1925-1933) illustrate so well, court poetry was a social art practiced either in full public view—at poetry contests, on flower-viewing expeditions, at banquets—or, if in private, as a form of communication between friends or lovers; any courtier or lady of the court with pretensions to social grace had to be ready to produce passable verse whenever called upon. The *Kokinshu* and other anthologies were organized to allow quick consultation for an appropriate model or for a poem that could be alluded to in one's own composition.

Within the narrowed confines of the poetry of the *Kokinshu*, there is still much to be admired, for its special province, the human heart, is after all not an easily exhausted subject. Poetry of love and courtship is not surprisingly one of the long suits of the collection. Particularly engaging is the work of such ninth century poets as Ariwara no Narihira (825-880), a courtier who quickly became a model of the ideal courtly lover, and the court lady Ono no Komachi (834-880), whose passionate verse threatened to escape the bounds of seemly reserve that most other poets were at pains to observe. Narihira's is a poetry of great wit and elegance, but it is colored also by a much-admired Buddhist awareness of the inconstancy of the temporal world and the deceptiveness of the emotions. Komachi, on the other hand, is a very subjective poet whose immersion in her own sometimes violent emotional states cost her admirers in a world that valued the pose, at least, of detachment more than direct cries from the heart. She and Narihira stand at the head of a long line of poets, male and female, whose *Kokinshu* verses established love poetry as one of the honored genres of court poetry.

By the time the *Kokinshu* was compiled, Buddhism had become a powerful force in shaping the Japanese poetic sensibility, which it entered indirectly through the influence of Chinese verse and directly as it became more and more a part of Japanese life. It did not, however, result in the development of an explicitly religious or devotional poetry. Rather, it provided a fundamental point of view for the poet in its insistence on a radical conception of phenomenal reality as a slippery, ever-changing flux given an illusory substance and stability by fallible human perception and rationalization. Impermanence and the unreliability of subjective observation are seldom spoken of explicitly in *Kokinshu* verse, which like all premodern Japanese poetry shies away from abstract nouns and overt philosophizing, but an acceptance of them as fundamental truths underlies much of the literature of the time.

There is a dark quality of resignation in the Buddhist conception of human experience that seems to be at odds with the more life-affirming, unreflective vision of humans and their world that characterizes Shintō animism, but in fact court poetry frequently manages a resolution of the conflict by finding a paradoxical comfort in the wholly reliable way the natural world eternally reaffirms the truth of universal flux; nature continues to be invested with meaning, but the meaning changes. Viewed in this way, nature is a rich repository of metaphor directly relevant to the human condition, which is why natural imagery comes to play such a large role in the lyric poetry of the Japanese court, particularly imagery that underlines change as a constant in nature and in human affairs. The beauty of spring blossoms is less interesting to the poet than the fact that they will fall or that fallible human eyes mistake them for a late spring snow.

Several techniques peculiar to Japanese poetry were exploited to their fullest for the first time by *Kokinshu* poets. The first is the *kakekotoba*, or pivot word, which takes advantage of both the special features of Japanese syntax and the existence in the language of a large number of homophones in what amounts to a highly refined form of wordplay. In the phrase *ko no me no haru ni*, for example, the word *haru* carries two distinct meanings. As a verb, it means "to swell," and with *ko no me*, "tree buds," and the subject-marking particle *no*, it produces the phrase, "tree buds swell." As a noun, however, *haru* means "spring," the season, and with the locative *ni* it makes an adverb of time, "in spring." Here, *haru* is therefore a *kakekotoba*, a word that "pivots" between two overlapping phrases that together mean something like, "in spring, when tree buds swell." The effect in Japanese is far less contrived than it would be in English, as in a phrase such as "in the grass spring blossoms forth," where "spring" and "blossoms" could be called pivot words of an awkward sort. In the Japanese example, as in the English, the *kakekotoba* consists of two superimposed homophones of different meaning and grammatical function. In other cases, the meaning of the pivot word is unchanged, but its syntactic function is different in the two phrases it links. In practiced hands, the *kakekotoba* technique—whose compact "punch" can almost never be translated adequately—is an effective method not only of adding a few precious syllables of meaning to the *tanka*, but also of greatly enriching the texture of a poem by involving the reader (or listener) in unraveling its overlapping meanings and functions.

A second device frequently exploited by *Kokinshu* poets is the *jokotoba* or *joshi*, a "preface" of one or more lines that forms part of the poem proper but is not directly related to its primary statement, to which it is most often linked by a pivot word. The *jokotoba* preface is similar to the *makurakotoba* epithet, but it is more complex, usually longer, rarely conventional, and more likely to be used consciously by the poet to establish a metaphoric relationship between two otherwise unrelated images. The *jokotoba* virtually disappears in translation, where it becomes simply a simile or metaphor, but it is a distinctive feature of classical *tanka* in Japanese.

A third technique polished in the *Kokinshu* and often used in conjunction with both *jokotoba* and *kakekotoba* to enrich the *tanka* is *engo* (related words). The *engo* technique is a refinement of diction in which the poet chooses his or her words in such a way that they both carry the intended meaning of the poem and at the same time relate to one other semantically or by sound alone in ways quite unrelated to the primary content of the poem. "Giving her a frosty glance, he leaves; from crimsoned lips fall raging storms of words" will have to serve as an English illustration of the principle of *engo*. The Japanese classical poet would recognize two parallel statements here—a surface description of an angry lovers' parting and an embedded evocation of late autumn in the sequence of related words: frosty-leaves-crimsoned-fall-raging-storms. Once again, the English example is labored because the technique is alien, but the conception is not inappropriate, since autumn in Japanese poetry is the season to reflect on the transience of life and love. In its native environment, when the *engo* technique is used in conjunction with other devices, the result is poetry of great complexity that can carry two or more serious messages simultaneously—no small feat in the compass of thirty-one syllables.

These techniques clearly functioned to allow far more to be said in the scant confines of a *tanka* than would otherwise have been the case, and it is probably no accident that they came into use at a time when the conventions of the form were becoming ever more clearly defined and restrictive. As previously noted, certain sorts of discourse and subject matter were felt to be more properly the province of Chinese poetry than Japanese, but diction itself was regulated as well. Loan words from Chinese, for example, were out of bounds to the *tanka* poet, even though by the time of the *Kokinshu* they had begun to enter everyday language in considerable numbers; no doubt they were prohibited in part because of their phonetic inelegance, but there may well have been an element of linguistic chauvinism at work as well. In any case, from the *Kokinshu* forward, poetic language would necessarily move further and further from the spoken language, which continued quite naturally to assimilate a great deal of Chinese vocabulary.

Perhaps even more important, the poetic consensus seems to have been that entire categories of imagery and native Japanese vocabulary were simply unpoetical. Bodily functions, for example, are almost entirely absent from classical Japanese poetry, even as metaphor—no poet would seriously "drink in" the beauty of a landscape or even "breathe" the fragrance of a blossom, much less "hunger" for a lover's "touch." Given the strong Buddhist influence in poetry of the classical period, it is perhaps a little surprising that even birth and death and any words clearly associated with them have no place, except by the most oblique sort of reference. This particular taboo probably had something to do with the preoccupation of Shintō ritual with cleanliness and purification, but more generally, it appears that there was an unspoken agreement among poets that poetic language simply did not admit of reference to the grosser stuff of human existence, not out

of prudery but rather in the spirit of what is best called courtliness, a set of attitudes that valued above all else stylization, refinement, restraint, cultivation, and a disdain for the pedestrian and coarse in all aspects of behavior.

SHINKOKINSHŪ

The courtly pose could and did sometimes result in a facile and shallow poetry in a world where versification was widely practiced as a social art, but it is a tribute to the high seriousness of purpose of the court poets that it did not produce, on the whole, a mannered and precious body of poetry. In the centuries following the appearance of the *Kokinshu*, the ever-growing canon of court verse took on the status almost of secular scripture, a collaborative text to be elaborated by each succeeding generation of poets. The culmination of this process is aptly symbolized in another great anthology, the *Shinkokinshū* (new *Kokinshu*), which appeared as the eighth in the series of imperial collections about 1206. The title was more than a token homage to the *Kokinshu*: It was a declaration affirming the primacy of tradition in the world of court poetry. The intervening anthologies had all, in a general way, taken the *Kokinshu* as their model of organization, but the *Shinkokinshū* makes constant reference to the earlier collection in ways alternately explicit and extremely subtle.

To explain the complex relationship between the "new *Kokinshu*" and its antecedent requires an acquaintance with the poetic technique known as *honkadori*—literally, "taking from a source verse," or incorporating into a new verse recognizable elements of an older poem in the canon. *Honkadori* is nothing more than a specialized variety of allusion requiring a clear quotation from an earlier poem, but that does not begin to explain its significance, for in many ways it is a key to understanding how poetry developed after the *Kokinshu*.

First, *honkadori* gave the poet another escape route from the confines of the classical *tanka*. The canon of "quotable" poetry was relatively manageable, being limited to the imperial anthologies and a small number of widely circulated private collections and prose works, such as *The Tale of Genji*, that contained poetry; this meant that in the elite subculture of the court, a poet could be confident of having an audience that would recognize his allusions. A poem using a *honkadori* allusion, therefore, expanded in the minds of its readers or listeners to include the entirety of the excerpted source poem. Thus, for example, a *Shinkokinshū* verse describing the desolation of a deserted village in autumn gains significant depth because the village, identified by name, is described with words borrowed from a pair of *Kokinshu* love poems, set in the same place, which dwelt on the sorrows of parting.

Beyond their effects within individual poems, *honkadori* allusions had a second important role to play in court poetry—namely, their function in tying new poems into an expanding canon that was not merely an accumulation of successively newer strata of poetry, but a complex fabric of allusion, cross-reference, and echo that worked continuously to revivify old poems while at the same time adding depth and the authority of tradition to new ones. The process was supported by the remarkable conservatism of poetic language, which came to be defined as the language of the *Kokinshu*. Because the language of the new poems was essentially of the same age as that of the source poems, it was possible to weave words and phrases from poems centuries old into original compositions with virtually no seams showing. The difficulty of composing poetry in antique language was mitigated for the poets of the *Shinkokinshū* and later periods by their intense absorption in the poetic canon, whose language became a natural mode of expression, neither dead nor artificial.

The loyalty of the compilers of the *Shinkokinshū* to the idea of precedent in poetry is most strikingly revealed at a number of places in the collection where entire sequences of poems, a dozen or more at a time, are selected and arranged so that they allude individually and collectively to precisely parallel sequences in the *Kokinshu*. Such feats of creative editorship required not only erudition and artistic sensitivity but also painstaking care on the part of the poets who assembled the anthology, a group led by Fujiwara Teika (1162-1241) under the active, involved sponsorship of the retired poet-emperor Gotoba (1180-1239). At a distance of eight centuries, it is possible only to speculate about what motivated such labors. One cause may have been simply the sheer intellectual and aesthetic pleasure of this complex interplay of old and new, a pleasure de-

nied the modern reader but no doubt quite unaffected among poets to whom the *Kokinshu* was an old friend and who were thoroughly accustomed to the effects of *honkadori*. Their purpose may have been also in part didactic, insofar as the elaborate juxtaposition of modern poems to their *Kokinshu* analogues illustrated what was meant by the contemporary injunction to "old words, new heart" in the writing of poetry—that is, to compositions that obeyed the iron rules of diction but were informed by contemporary sensibilities that saved them from a sterile antiquarianism.

The "new heart" of *Shinkokinshū* poetry is often defined with reference to an elusive aesthetic concept known as *yūgen*, whose definitions include allusiveness, evocativeness, "dark mystery," "mysterious vagueness," "mysterious depth," and even, simply, "elegance." A poem embodying *yūgen* points to a world beyond words whose outlines a true artist can evoke in the inner eye of his or her audience. *Yūgen* is in a way a specialized instance of the more general Buddhist philosophical preoccupation with the problematic relationship between perception and reality. The primary concern of the poet remained the authentic expression of emotion, but the true poet was moved by what a refined sensibility could see behind superficial reality—not by beauty, but by its transience, not by love, but by the inevitability of its loss. The characteristic mood of the *Shinkokinshū* is therefore emphatically not a sunny one but rather thoughtful and somber. That it is so clearly defined is remarkable, for this is a poetry that leaves much unspoken, the truths with which it concerns itself being of a sort that cannot be explained directly in the limited vocabulary of the court poet, from which all of the immense Chinese philosophical lexicon was banned. *Shinkokinshū* poets relied instead on highly concrete language and objective description devised to evoke in the reader, without intermediation, the same subtle vision that inspired the poetic act in the first place.

The tendency of *Shinkokinshū* poetry to reveal its "heart," its real meaning, not in its words but rather in the spaces between them, as it were, or in the history behind them, bespeaks a highly sophisticated understanding that "poetry" is not merely words on a page but the result of a very complex interactive process involving poet, ideas, words, and the reader. That this understanding was not subliminal but fully conscious is borne out by the evidence of modern Japanese scholarship.

As noted above, the *Shinkokinshū* closely follows the lead of the *Kokinshu* in its organization. Like the *Kokinshu*, the *Shinkokinshū* arranges poems so that they mimic natural progressions in the real world, be they those of the seasons or that of a love affair. Konishi Jin'ichi and other scholars have discovered that such sequences in the later collection were also ordered, however, in accordance with certain rules quite independent of the natural progressions they follow. Specifically, each poem in a sequence seems to have been chosen not only to forward the movement in question but also with a clear awareness of how it "fit" with the poems before and after it. Each successive, overlapping pair of verses must therefore be in harmony, sharing a common or closely similar tone, image, or point of view. A sequence of early-spring poems might thus begin with a verse containing the image of scattered patches of snow in a garden where flowering plums have begun to bloom; the next verse might then mention water trickling out from under melting snow, to be followed in its turn by one describing a swollen hillside freshet; the scene might then shift to a mountain village still snowbound but wreathed in wisps of springlike haze.

The reader supplies continuity to such a series by sensing, perhaps not always even consciously, that there is a logic operating in multiple dimensions here which makes for a natural movement from poem to poem. The location, for example, gradually shifts upward in space from garden to hillside (linked by the common image or implied image of melting snow) to mountain village, while at the same time the successive scenes are rendered from an increasingly distant point of view. The mood changes from the domesticity of a garden to the daunting isolation of the mountains, but the changes come slowly and naturally, thanks to the intervening verses. The sequence in effect reverses the natural progress of spring by beginning with blossoms and ending with a snowbound village, but the geographical shift up into the mountains explains the retrogression, which itself has the secondary effect of reaf-

firming the larger framework of early spring, always a time of false starts and late snows.

How aware any given reader might have been of this complex manipulation of images and associations is problematic, but it seems quite undeniable that the compilers themselves were fully conscious of the effects they created. Nothing else can really account for what is otherwise a puzzling randomness in the order of the verses when they are considered from the point of view of age or authorship, or for the inclusion of a surprising number of verses that by any standard are not the best the age produced, but that turn out to be precisely what is needed to effect transitions between pairs of clearly superior poems which carry associations that would otherwise clash or at least not dovetail neatly.

HAIKU AND RENGA

While the *Shinkokinshū* marks a high point in the classical poetic tradition, it by no means marks its end, which in a sense has come only in the past century with the decay of the custom of rote memorization of the poetic canon (or at least large parts of it)—a custom that was integral both to the appreciation and to the practice of court poetry. Indeed, until the first decades of the twentieth century, *tanka* in the court style, still subject to the ancient rules of diction and style, were a natural part of the repertoire of the literary-minded elite, and they are still far more a part of the popular conception of what poetry is than any specific poetic form of comparable age in the West.

This survival is all the more remarkable in view of the fact that the classical tradition itself engendered an entirely new world of poetic practice as early as the fifteenth century, culminating in the haiku, the only form of Japanese poetry generally known in the West and the only serious challenge in Japanese literary history to the preeminence of *tanka*. The seventeen-syllable haiku is a direct descendant of a form of poetry known as *renga* (linked verse), which in its origins was both an elaboration of and a challenge to the attitudes that shaped the poetry of the *Shinkokinshū* and the late classical age.

Renga developed originally as a pastime among court poets, a formalization of poetic games that included "verse-capping," in which contestants had to supply the second half—the seven/seven-syllable "lower verse"—of either a well-known *tanka* or an opponent's original composition, and *utaawase* poetry competitions, in which teams of poets publicly composed poems on a series of set themes. The term *renga* refers specifically to a sequence of alternating five/seven/five- and seven/seven-syllable units, each verse except the first being written in response to the verse preceding it. Each pair of verses, written by two different poets, was expected to be able to stand alone as a coherent *tanka*, even though every second pair necessarily inverted the upper and lower verses of the standard *tanka* form. The resulting chain, usually of thirty-six or one hundred links, was in effect a single poetic composition by multiple authors (most commonly three) who took turns supplying each successive verse. There was, however, no requirement that the *renga* sequence be restricted to a single theme. In fact, as it developed, one of the requirements of *renga* was that the subject matter of the verses in a sequence be varied to include as many of the traditional topics—seasons, love, grievance, and so on—as possible. There was therefore no overall unity to a *renga* chain, only the serial unity within each overlapping pair of verses. That late-classical poetics favored concrete imagery and objectivity aided the *renga* poet, because verses with those qualities were subject to multiple interpretations. A verse centering on the image "dew at daybreak," for example, could function nicely as a companion to a spring poem before it, and equally well as a lead-in to a verse describing a lover stealing away after a nighttime tryst.

Renga began as a light entertainment but soon began to be taken seriously as a poetic form of great potential. By the fifteenth century, two varieties of *renga* were being practiced, a light or comic form labeled *mushin* (frivolous, or lacking heart) and a serious form called *ushin*. In the hands of its most accomplished practitioners, such as the poet-priest Sōgi (1421-1502), serious *ushin renga* became what some regard as the supreme achievement of Japanese classical poetry. *Renga* was not, however, a form of poetry whose practice or appreciation could ever be widespread, since it required skills and erudition not to be found outside a small population of dedicated practitioners. As an outgrowth of classical *tanka*, serious *renga* conformed to all the rules of the court tradition within its constituent verses; in addition, it developed a detailed, elaborate set of conventions governing the poetics of the sequence as a whole.

A typical *renga* chain shares a number of characteristics with the carefully constructed *Shinkokinshū* sequences described above, but there are also major differences. In both cases, adjacent verses are linked on any of several levels—imagery, subject, point of view, and so on; *renga* sequences also often contain very complex links formed on the basis of *honkadori* in which a source poem called to mind by an allusion in one verse supplies materials that inspire the next. Both kinds of sequence depend for their coherence on manipulation not only of poetic materials but also of the actual experience of reading or hearing each verse as it is added to the chain, for it is the totality of all the associations a verse evokes in the mind's eye with which the compiler or poet works in building links from verse to verse.

The *renga* chain differs fundamentally from *Shinkokinshū* precedents, however, in two vital ways. First, it is an original composition, not compiled from existing materials; second, there is no external framework corresponding to the progression of a season or a love affair as is seen in the *Shinkokinshū*. The formal rules of *renga* composition no doubt developed as a strategy for averting the shapelessness that these characteristics made likely. The rules sometimes seem to have been needlessly minute and almost arbitrary in their specifications—as of exactly which verses in a sequence could and must contain the word "moon"—but their effect was to establish a tension between imagination and tight control that in the best surviving sequences results in a very pleasing rhythm of excitement and relaxation as the poets deal, verse by verse, with the difficulty of submitting inspiration and free association to discipline.

The sheer difficulty of serious *renga* made it the province of a small elite of professional poets, often Buddhist priests or laymen who adopted a priestly lifestyle to free themselves of ordinary social concerns. *Renga* poets were no longer courtiers for whom poetry was a polite art, but full-time artists who subsisted either on inherited means or the largesse of patrons. The imperial court itself, for so long the locus of poetic activity, had ceased to be an institution of any but symbolic political significance by the time *renga* became an important poetic mode. Patronage had therefore passed into the hands of a new class, the military leaders who gradually assumed control of the country as power slipped away from the court, beginning as early as the twelfth century. The old court culture enjoyed a brief resuscitation under the hereditary military dictators or shoguns of the Ashikaga clan, whose power base was the old imperial capital of Kyoto, but by the first decades of the fifteenth century, real power began to pass into the hands of local magnates known as *daimyō* or "great names," petty warlords who maintained their own courts and, as their means permitted and their tastes inclined them, extended patronage to poets and other artists. The stable, refined world that had nurtured the genteel ideal of the courtly poet, however, was gone forever. It is little wonder that the *renga* poets, men of immense learning and sensitivity surrounded by people who in an earlier age would have been thought unimaginably coarse, produced a poetry whose predominant moods were melancholy and nostalgia.

SIXTEENTH AND SEVENTEENTH CENTURIES

The sixteenth century brought change and upheaval on a scale that had not been seen since the earliest years of imperial expansion and the importation of Chinese culture nearly a thousand years before. Civil war touched all corners of the country, its destructiveness magnified by the use of firearms, which were introduced by Portuguese traders when they reached Japan in the middle of the century. Except in this one respect, the West would not have a profound effect upon Japan for another three centuries, but until Japan was officially cut off almost completely from foreign contacts in the seventeenth century, a small but steady stream of Portuguese, Spanish, Dutch, and English missionaries and traders destroyed forever the complacent Japanese view of civilization as something coterminous with the self-contained Chinese cultural sphere. The nearly total collapse of the old order—one famous story has a sixteenth century emperor peddling samples of his calligraphy to make ends meet—raised men to power who

had only the most tenuous of connections with the courtly values of the past, and it was inevitable that when peace finally came again at the end of the century, the art of poetry would emerge no less profoundly changed than any other sphere of Japanese life.

The year 1600 (or, by some reckonings, 1603) marks the beginning of a dynamic new era known to Japanese historians either as the Tokugawa period, after the dynasty of shoguns founded by Tokugawa Ieyasu, or the Edo period, after the city that was the seat of Tokugawa rule, modern Tokyo. Through a combination of political negotiation and brute force, Ieyasu brought the civil wars to an end after more than a century, and peace was soon followed by unprecedented prosperity. The democratization of formerly elite kinds of artistic endeavor that this new prosperity fostered would prove to be the most dramatic cultural development of the new era.

The activities of Matsunaga Teitoku (1571-1653) illustrate how profoundly poetry in particular was affected by these changes in the larger cultural environment. Teitoku was trained in the ancient traditions of classical *tanka*, which by his day were treated as a hermetic body of secret lore by the remaining court poets in Kyoto. He shared with his teachers the Confucian attitude that the practice of literature was an essential element in the cultivation of moral rectitude, but he saw that literature could never be accessible to the greater mass of the population, among whom literacy was spreading rapidly, if it continued to be treated as the private property of a hereditary poetic priesthood. He therefore undertook a career as a popularizer, giving public lectures on the classics in direct defiance of his mentors and—most important for the development of Japanese poetry—promoting a new style of linked verse that met what he believed were the needs of the time for a form of literature that could be practiced by the educated common man but that at the same time was not vulgar. Teitoku's chosen vehicle of literary instruction was *haikai*, more formally *haikai no renga*, or "comic *renga*," a descendant of the *mushin* mode in linked verse.

Before Teitoku, *haikai* was most decidedly a comic poetry of dubious morals. Its humor came in part from wordplay, parody, scatology, and other obvious comic effects, but also in considerable measure from the deliberate violation of the rules of serious *renga*, particularly those regarding diction—there was humor, for example, in the mere presence of as innocent a word as "nose" in a verse that otherwise followed thousand-year-old conventions of decorum. Teitoku lamented the unabashed vulgarity of *haikai* but recognized certain virtues in it. The proficient *haikai* poet still honored, if in a backhanded way, the principle that poetry was a matter of precedent and convention, without which much of the humor of *haikai* was meaningless, and *haikai* also admitted the use of colloquial language, which meant that it could become a poetry accessible to people who lacked a thoroughgoing education in the classical idiom.

Teitoku did not single-handedly make *haikai* the characteristic verse form of the Edo period, but his tireless promotion of it, aided by the beginnings of a printing industry, was certainly important in its spread. His attitude was condescending and didactic, but he attracted a great number of literary disciples from classes previously uninvolved in literary activity, particularly the middle and lower ranks of the samurai military caste and newly wealthy urban merchants. There quickly arose, however, a reaction against the uneasy compromise between vulgarity and traditional belletrism that characterized *haikai* of Teitoku's school. It is significant that the reaction came not, as might be supposed, from poets who protested against Teitoku's vulgarization of the high classical tradition, but rather from those who believed he was destroying the straightforward, comic irreverence of *haikai* by trying to turn it into an ersatz "serious" poetry for the masses.

The fight against what they considered to be the pretentious stuffiness of the Teitoku school was led by a group known as the Danrin school of *haikai*, disciples of Nishiyama Sōin (1605-1682), a traditional *renga* poet turned *haikai* partisan. Danrin *haikai* was a short-lived phenomenon, defeated by its excesses in combat with the Teitoku school in the first public literary feud Japan had seen. The Danrin poets steadfastly refused to credit the Teitoku school's insistence that *haikai*, if only it would accept the discipline of serious *renga* while changing with the times to allow everyday language and subject matter, could become a form of poetry with real depth and dignity.

There is an element suggestive of Dadaism in Danrin-school reactions against the Teitoku-school attitude toward *haikai*, best illustrated, perhaps, by the brief poetic career of Ihara Saikaku (1642-1693), better known as a fiction writer who was the first to chronicle the new, vigorous life of the urban middle classes. Saikaku's claim to fame as a poet comes from his practice of the extemporaneous solo composition of *haikai* sequences in public. His first great success came in 1675, when he produced a thousand verses at a single sitting. He finally retired from competition—actually, there was no competition—in 1684, after composing a record 23,500 linked verses in the space of a day and night, a tour de force that earned for him the sobriquet Niman'ō, "Old Man Twenty Thousand." (No record of the poems survives, since Saikaku produced them orally faster than a scribe could follow.)

MATSUO BASHŌ

Haikai survived and flourished, despite the guerrilla tactics of Sōin's Danrin-school followers and the excesses of Teitoku didacticism, thanks largely to the artistry of Matsuo Bashō (1644-1694), who is probably the only poet of the premodern period whose name is known to practically every Japanese person and whose poetry, rightly or wrongly, has come in the minds of Western readers to represent Japanese poetry in general. Bashō's early training in *haikai* was in the Teitoku school, favored in the conservative rural samurai milieu of his youth. After moving to Edo to pursue a career as a poet and teacher in 1672, however, he came under the influence of the Danrin poets, who found the openness of the shogun capital, still something of a boomtown, more congenial than the tradition-bound atmosphere of Kyoto.

Bashō did not join in the Teitoku-Danrin conflict; instead, he borrowed elements of both styles to produce his own, distinctive poetry in what came to be known as *shōfū*, the Bashō manner. In Teitoku *haikai*, Bashō found a commitment to discipline, polish, and technical skill essential to any real poetry. From the Danrin school, Bashō learned the importance of direct observation and objective description of the world of the senses, unmediated by artificial ideas of what was and was not "poetic." To this synthesis, he added a certain philosophical depth derived from his study of Chinese poetry and Zen Buddhism. His poetry, quickly disseminated in printed form, struck such a responsive chord that even by the time of his death, Bashō had become a national institution; some two thousand poets all over Japan claimed personal discipleship.

Interestingly, the immense popularity of Bashō's poetry played no small part in the demise of the *haikai* form, for the haunting beauty and technical sparkle of his individual verses overshadowed their role in linked-verse sequences. Bashō himself almost always composed in a group linked-verse setting, and much of his critical writing concerns itself with the paramount importance of keeping the linking process foremost in mind when writing *haikai*. Poetic practice and the

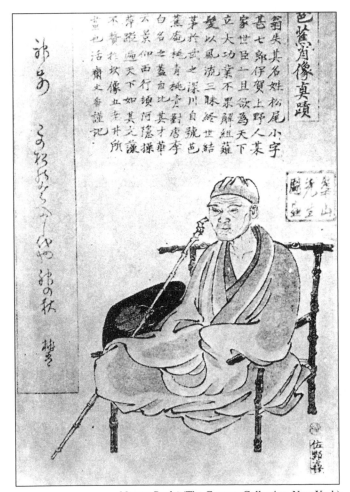

Matsuo Bashō (The Granger Collection, New York)

spread of publishing, however, were at work even in his day to put greater emphasis on the individual units of the *haikai* chain, particularly the *hokku*, the first verse in a sequence. The *hokku* was of great importance in *haikai*, as it had always been in *renga*. First, it was the only verse in a sequence that was specifically required to have reference to anything outside the other poems in the chain—the rules dictated that it specify as clearly as possible the setting, circumstances, and season in which the poets were gathered. Further, the *hokku* was by tradition the responsibility of the most accomplished poet present, who was by convention, if not in actuality, treated as an honored guest. The *hokku*, therefore, could be and often was composed beforehand; its distinctive status encouraged its author to take special pains.

The great majority of the verses by which Bashō's poetry came to be known in Japan were originally composed as *hokku*, whose distinctive qualities and special status made them attractive candidates for inclusion in published handbooks of *haikai* practice. Furthermore, one important means by which Bashō's work was disseminated was his published travel diaries, which recorded a number of poetic pilgrimages he took late in life, visiting sites important in the classical tradition. Bashō was by that time a literary celebrity, and so at nearly every stop on these journeys he was put up by local poets, in return for whose hospitality he participated in *haikai* sessions. As a guest, he invariably had responsibility for the *hokku*, and naturally enough it was his *hokku* that he chose to preserve in his diaries, for they alone were uniquely tied to the places he visited.

These circumstances conspired to help make the seventeen-syllable *hokku* an independent verse form, called haiku, which is nothing more than a *hokku* composed with no thought of its being part of a *haikai* sequence. Linked verse in the modern *haikai* style continued to be practiced, but poets after Bashō tended increasingly to concentrate on single haiku, which proved to be highly satisfying vehicles for poetic expression, insofar as they partook of the special qualities of the *hokku*—the polish that was possible in a verse that need not be an impromptu public performance, for example, and the way in which it took much of its inspiration from the immediate surroundings of the poet.

EIGHTEENTH CENTURY

Bashō was followed by a legion of notable *haikai* (or haiku—the terms were for some time interchangeable) poets, among whom might be singled out Takarai (or Enomoto) Kikaku (1661-1707), who added the kaleidoscope of city life to the poet's palette, restoring something of the earthiness that Bashō's otherworldliness had temporarily banished from *haikai*; Kikaku's poetry was not, however, any less touched with meaning than that of Bashō. Another poet deserving special note is Yosa Buson (1716-1783), whose verse is very elegant and at the same time sentimental. It is difficult to generalize about haiku. One of its chief virtues, fostered by Bashō's insistence on combining craftsmanship with authenticity of observation and emotional content, is that it allowed the expression of greater individuality than any poetic form that had preceded it, save perhaps the *chōka* a thousand years earlier.

The revolution that the haiku brought to Japanese poetry by disencumbering it of the most stifling aspects of classicism is characteristic of the diverse, iconoclastic creativity of Edo-period culture—a culture that flourished in spite of its near-total isolation from the currents of social and economic change that were reshaping other traditional cultures elsewhere in the world. Some of the important innovations of Edo literary culture lie beyond the scope of this essay, but the eighteenth century was not lacking in significant developments. Even the *tanka*, so long the embodiment of traditionalism, began to change as haiku poets redefined the purposes of poetry; *tanka* admitted colloquial language and prosaic subject matter and generated its own lively comic derivative, the *kyōka* ("mad verse"), which was wildly popular in the 1780's among a slightly jaded coterie of avant-garde intellectuals in Edo. Nativist scholars such as Kamo Mabuchi (1697-1769) and Motoori Norinaga (1730-1801) experimented with revivals of *chōka* and *tanka* in the style of *The Manyoshu* with a decidedly chauvinistic, anti-

Chinese coloration. At the same time, however, the intense involvement of many eighteenth century intellectuals in the study of Chinese literature also produced much verse written in Chinese, some of it of remarkable quality. Together, these trends foreshadowed the explosion of creativity in all fields of literature that would occur when Japan once more opened its doors to outside influence in the nineteenth century.

BIBLIOGRAPHY

Bownas, Geoffrey, and Anthony Thwaite, eds. and trans. *The Penguin Book of Japanese Verse*. Rev. ed. London: Penguin Books, 2009. A volume in the UNESCO Collection of Representative Works, Japanese series. A collection of Japanese verse from its beginnings through the Edo period. Introductions by the editor-translators, both of them distinguished scholars, noted for their expertise in Japanese culture.

Brower, Robert, and Earl Miner. *Japanese Court Poetry*. 1961. Reprint. Stanford, Calif.: Stanford University Press, 1988. Still the standard history of the development of the standard thirty-one-syllable *waka*, from its beginnings through the medieval period.

Carter, Steven D. *Waiting for the Wind: Thirty-six Poets of Japan's Late Medieval Age*. Reprint. New York: Columbia University Press, 1994. Part of the Asian Classics series. Presents more than four hundred poems by a range of poets from Japan's late medieval age (1250-1500), along with biographical sketches and critical evaluations of each.

_____, comp. and trans. *Traditional Japanese Poetry: An Anthology*. Stanford, Calif.: Stanford University Press, 1991. A collection of more than eleven hundred poems dating from the earliest times to the twentieth century. Though emphasis is placed on poets of literary or historical importance, there are also examples of such genres as poetic diaries, linked verse, and comic verse. Illustrations and maps. Bibliographical references and indexes.

Keene, Donald. *Seeds of the Heart*. 1993. Reprint. New York: Columbia University Press, 1999. The definitive account of the development of Japanese literature from the beginnings through the late sixteenth century. A good deal of space is dedicated to the development of Japanese poetry in all forms.

_____. *World Within Walls*. 1976. Reprint. New York: Columbia University Press, 1999. A continuation of Keene's history of Japanese literature until 1867. Provides useful analyses of poets and poetry in all styles.

Miner, Earl. *Japanese Linked Poetry*. Princeton, N.J.: Princeton University Press, 1979. A detailed history of medieval linked verse, or *renga*, with copious translations.

Ooka, Makoto. *The Poetry and Poetics of Ancient Japan*. Translated by Thomas Fitzsimmons. Santa Fe, N.Mex.: Katydid Books, 1997. Explores the great library of poetry anthologies compiled by the Imperial order. Re-creates in detail the social, political, and cultural realities surrounding the development of Japanese poetry from ancient until modern times.

Sato, Hiroaki. *One Hundred Frogs: From Renga, to Haiku, to English*. 1983. Reprint. New York: Weatherhill, 1995. Provides definitions, history, the forms, and the rules of these poems, with many useful insights into the techniques of translating Japanese poems, and adds many examples of poems and translations.

Shirane, Haruo. *Traces of Dreams*. Stanford, Calif.: Stanford University Press, 1998. A history of the development of haiku, concentrating on the career and accomplishments of Matsuo Bashō.

_____. *Traditional Japanese Literature: An Anthology, Beginnings to 1600*. Rev. ed. Translated by Sonja Arntzen et al. New York: Columbia University Press, 2007. A comprehensive anthology, containing a wide variety of texts, representing both elite and popular cultures. Introductions to the works provide information on historical and cultural contexts. Illustrations and maps. Extensive bibliographies. Index.

_____, ed. *Early Modern Japanese Literature: An Anthology, 1600-1900*. Translated by James Brandon et al. New York: Columbia University Press, 2002. Of special interest to students of Japanese poetry is the section in this massive book devoted to the prose and poetry of Matsuo Bashō. Another section deals with comic and satiric poetry. Introductions and commentary by Shirane. Illustrations and maps. English-language bibliography. Index.

Robert W. Leutner
Updated by J. Thomas Rimer

JAPANESE POETRY SINCE 1800

At the beginning of the nineteenth century, the long and powerful tradition of Japanese poetry continued to make possible the production of accomplished and moving poems in the great forms that had developed during various periods in the past: the thirty-one-syllable *waka* (also known as *tanka*, the name by which the form is familiar to many Western readers), the seventeen-syllable haiku, and the more philosophical medium of *kanshi*, or poetry in Chinese, which permitted both greater length and the kind of philosophical abstraction that had long been deemed unsuitable for the shorter forms of classical Japanese verse. These traditions might well have ossified but for the spread of literacy and learning and the inspiration of Chinese poetry available from the continent, which made it possible to achieve new variations within old forms. For example, Kobayashi Yatarō, known as Issa (1763-1827), a farmer from the mountainous countryside, had been able to create a style of haiku that could capture both the joys and the anguish of the plebeian world in which he lived, while Ōkuma Kotomichi (1798-1868) extended the boundaries of *waka* to include an interest in human personality and psychology that gave his poems a strikingly modern flavor. Rai Sanyō (1780-1832), writing in Chinese, dealt with extremely diverse subject matter—including the presence of the Dutch in Nagasaki—in his lengthy and sometimes polemical poetry. The traditions of Japanese poetry, then, were by no means moribund.

On the other hand, Japan's self-imposed seclusion from other nations, dating from the early 1600's, had denied its poets the opportunity to gain any real perspective on their own traditions, as they had always done before, through an exposure to literary traditions from other cultures. Thus, in the closing decades of the nineteenth century, when young Japanese finally were permitted to go abroad, an awakening interest among them in European literature brought about a profound change in the development of the Japanese poetic sensibility. Native traditions were continued, although much expanded in range of subject matter and vocabulary permitted, but a whole new form of poetry, based

on Western models and usually referred to as *shintaishi* ("new style verse" or "free-style verse"), developed into the standard vehicle for modern Japanese poetry. Both the traditional forms and the new forms grew and developed in response to the profound interest taken by Japanese poets in Western verse, which led to their attempts to understand, translate, and make use of those forms themselves.

FIRST EXPERIMENTS

Before it became possible to write effective poetry in the new forms, a period of experimentation was required. These experiments were undertaken by a variety of gifted poets and usually involved their attempts to translate Western poems into Japanese (a language itself moving quickly, under the influence of Western example, toward a closer alignment between the written and spoken forms than had ever before seemed possible). Their various enthusiasms assured that, by the first decade of the twentieth century, there would be examples in good modern Japanese of some of the finest examples of European and American poetry from all periods. These translated poems, in turn, inspired an efflorescence of high poetic accomplishment in the Japanese language that continues unabated today.

The first significant contribution to the acculturation of Japanese poetry appeared in 1882, when three Tokyo University professors, two of whom had studied in the United States, produced a series of fourteen translations and five poems of their own based on Western models. This small collection, the *Shintaishisho* (selection of new style verse), included a number of poems quite popular with nineteenth century English and American readers, including Alfred, Lord Tennyson's "The Charge of the Light Brigade" and "The Captain," Thomas Gray's "Elegy Written in a Country Churchyard," and Henry Wadsworth Longfellow's "A Psalm of Life," as well as a few bits and pieces of William Shakespeare, including Hamlet's famous soliloquy, "To be or not to be." In presenting these works in translation, the authors stressed their conviction that such poems could well serve as models for the future, since both *waka* and haiku were too short to express any sustained mood or argument and too bound by traditional vocabulary and subject matter. This small collection remained very influential with young writers, and the interest it generated was reinforced by the publication, in 1889, of *Omokage* (vestiges). This collection of translations included selections from the German Romantic poets, Johann Wolfgang von Goethe, Heinrich Heine, Nikolaus Lenau, and E. T. A. Hoffmann; the volume also included selections from Shakespeare by way of the German translation of Friedrich von Schlegel and from Lord Byron by way of Heine's German version. The translations were prepared by Mori Ōgai (1862-1922), one of the foremost novelists of early modern Japan, who had lived in Germany from 1884 to 1888 and had learned to appreciate the great German poets in the original. He prepared his translations with a group of colleagues, sometimes attempting a literal rendering, sometimes developing forms that captured the content but strove to achieve a more natural expression in Japanese.

These widely read translations brought Japan closer to a truly modern poetry, but the most influential models were those provided by Ueda Bin (1874-1916) in his 1905 collection *Kaichōon* (the sound of the tide), which brought the first adequate versions of Symbolist poetry to Japan. Through these elegant and still widely appreciated translations, Japanese readers were first able to read important poems by Charles Baudelaire, Paul Verlaine, Stéphane Mallarmé, Gabriele D'Annunzio, Christina Rossetti, Dante Gabriel Rossetti, and Émile Verhaeren. Response to these poems suggested a certain congruence between European Symbolist values, with their suggestion of an unspoken and mysterious beauty, and the traditional values of Japanese poetry, with its emphasis on such qualities as the hidden depths of beauty captured in the courtly ideal of *yūgen*. Indeed, for several decades, the influence of French poetry was to remain paramount in Japan, and it was very much under the French influence that the first great collection of modern Japanese poetry, Hagiwara Sakutarō's *Tsuki ni hoeru* (*Howling at the Moon*, 1969), appeared in 1917.

CHANGES IN TRADITIONAL FORMS

The same influences that were to create the new forms in Japanese poetry also helped bring about enormous changes in the traditional forms. In fact, four of the most important poets of the modern period continued to write in the traditional modes, using the possibilities of personal involvement and fresh vocabulary that had opened up to them by the turn of the century. The first of these was the poet Masaoka Shiki (1867-1902), who wrote both haiku and *waka* and did much to introduce the element of real and observed life into these forms. For Masaoka, the composition of poetry involved going out into nature to record what the poet himself could observe, and his principle of *shasei*, or "sketching from life," brought new vigor and reality to traditional forms that had tended to be restricted to a fixed vocabulary and a narrow range of emotional attitudes. Yosano Akiko (1878-1942), a poet whose vibrancy recalls the women writers of the early classical period such as the *waka* poet Ono no Komachi (834-880), instead plumbed the depths of her own emotional responses to life in order to produce *waka* full of emotional force and sensual consciousness. In a somewhat similar vein, Ishikawa Takuboku (1886-1912) wrote *waka* that told unsparingly of himself, his moods, and his defeats. Toward the end of his short career, Takuboku also began to introduce an element of political consciousness into his poetry that gave him another important role in the development of the modern poetic consciousness.

Saitō Mokichi (1882-1953) began his career as a doctor and studied neuropsychiatry in Vienna, yet he continued to make use of the *waka* form to record his intimate feelings and responses to the emotional complexities of his experiences. In the work of all of these writers, poetry became in a highly significant way an extension of their own personalities, permitting new possibilities for the *waka* and haiku forms. Thus, the democratization of poetry that began with Matsuo Bashō (1644-1694) and the Tokugawa (1579-1632) haiku has continued into the contemporary scene, where collections by dozens of poets provide for the continuity of a now comfortable tradition, which, while no longer at the cutting edge of modern poetry, still serves an honorable purpose in Japanese letters.

Other poets experimented with the older forms to make them as spare and flexible as possible. Several of the finest haiku poets of the period withdrew from conventional society and dedicated themselves to the service of Buddhism and the pilgrimage ideal. Their poetry thus shows powerful ties with the past wedded to complex contemporary sensibility. Ozaki Hōsai (1885-1926) was an insurance executive who after a period of instability abandoned his employment to serve as a Buddhist sexton in a small temple, where he wrote most of his remarkable free-style haiku. Taneda Santōka (1882-1940) led a dissolute life until becoming a mendicant monk; in the style of his great predecessor, Ryōkan (1758-1831), Taneda walked through the countryside, seeking salvation and writing down his trenchant and striking responses to the lonely life that he led. Ogiwara Seisensui (1884-1976) also did much to develop the style of free-form haiku and so make the tradition more available to modern writers and readers as a mechanism for expressing genuine contemporary concerns. Indeed, the work of these three men revealed the enormous range of which the venerable seventeen syllable form was capable.

Kanshi also remained a possibility for those Japanese writers in the late nineteenth and early twentieth centuries who had been educated in classical Chinese, although, by the turn of the century, German, English, and French had replaced Chinese as the most important foreign languages to be studied in Japan, and as a result interest and skill in composing traditional Chinese verse waned. Perhaps the finest *kanshi* poet in the early years of the twentieth century, and indeed perhaps the greatest in the history of Chinese poetry written in Japan, was the novelist Natsume Sōseki (1867-1916), one of the pivotal figures in modern Japanese culture. Educated in English literature and the author of the most sophisticated psychological novels of his time, Sōseki nevertheless summoned up his classical training to write down his private thoughts in a series of Chinese poems that tell more about his aspirations, disappointments, and spiritual life than most of his other, more accessible works. By Sōseki's time, very few Japanese were capable of reading, let alone appreciating, such poetry; perhaps it was precisely Sōseki's realization that he was writing in what was destined even in his

time to become a kind of private code that made it possible for him to be so open about himself in this most ancient form.

JAPAN AND THE EUROPEAN AVANT-GARDE

Japanese free-style verse came of age with the publication of Hagiwara's *Howling at the Moon*, a short book of poems, which, despite its debts to European Symbolism, revealed a mastery of colloquial language in the service of an authentic rendering of Hagiwara's inner world—troubled, ironic, and highly colored. Hagiwara himself had never been abroad ("I thought I'd like to go to France," he wrote in one of his poems; "France is too far away"). *Howling at the Moon* and the collections that followed contained poems filled with images that served as objective correlatives to elements in Hagiwara's own neurotic sensibility. Some of these are drawn from nature ("blurred bamboo roots spreading"), some from his own imagination. The most famous poem in *Howling at the Moon* begins: "At the bottom of the ground a face emerging,/ a lonely invalid's face emerging."

Reading Hagiwara's poetry while living in Europe, Nishiwaki Junsaburō (1894-1982) realized that it might be possible after all to write poetry in Japanese rather than in English or French. Nishiwaki, who once described himself as a "beggar for Europe," had decided that to participate in the creation of modern poetry, he would have to leave his homeland in order to shake off the weight of old traditions. Nishiwaki met Ezra Pound and T. S. Eliot (he was later to become the definitive translator of Eliot's works into Japanese) and began to publish in little magazines in London, but his encounter with Hagiwara's revolutionary volume of poems brought him back to Japan and the beginnings of a genuine avant-garde movement there. Nishiwaki had become interested in Surrealism while in Europe and found a means to adapt for his own work that method of piercing through everyday reality ("like looking at a hole in a hedge into eternity," he wrote). Nishiwaki's difficult verse, filled with references to Blaise Pascal, Rainer Maria Rilke, Pablo Picasso, and other figures of European culture, represents the high tide of Japanese poetry in the international style. Nishiwaki's high accomplishments seem to owe relatively little to the Japanese tradition and set him apart from his more conservative contemporaries in somewhat the same way that Pound's work constituted a break with the conservative traditions of English poetry. Both are eclectic, highly committed, and utterly individual, and both, in a special way, represent the literary ideals of the period in which they lived. Translations of a wide variety of Nishiwaki's best work can be found in Hosea Hirata's *The Poetry and Poetics of Nishiwaki Junzaburō: Modernism in Translation* (1993).

Other poets traveled to Europe but remained more within the developing traditions of modern Japanese poetry. Takamura Kōtarō (1883-1956) went to France, where he studied sculpture with Auguste Rodin, and returned to become one of the major lyric voices of his day. His poems were modern in style and spirit, but not aggressively so, and his best-known poems deal with the growing madness and death of his wife, Chieko, who haunts the pages of these remarkable lyrics like the ghost in a traditional Nō play. Extensive translations can be found in Hiroaki Sato's *A Brief History of Imbecility: Poetry and Prose of Takamura Kōtarō* (1992). Others, such as Kitahara Hakushū (1885-1942), Kaneko Mitsuharu (1895-1975), and Miyoshi Tatsuji (1900-1964), added other elements from European and American poetry to the expanding vocabulary of techniques available to modern Japanese poets and left behind important collections that are still widely appreciated.

While it may be correct to say that European models suggested possibilities for modern Japanese poetry, it would be wrong indeed to hold that the poetry produced was merely derivative. The work of Nishiwaki and the others described above is, as is clear even when read in translation, distinctly individual. In terms of authenticity of voice, no modern Japanese poet is more appreciated than Miyazawa Kenji, or Kenji Miyazawa (1896-1933), as he is known in the West. Miyazawa was a devout Buddhist. After training at an agricultural college, he taught poor farmers in Iwate Prefecture, far to the north of Tokyo, how to better their lives. Miyazawa was little read during his lifetime, but later he became a powerful presence in modern Japanese poetry, even a cult figure. His remarkable verse, which owes more to Buddhist sutras than it does to European

models, develops its metaphysical stance with an almost hallucinatory force. Miyazawa's work first became known to English-speaking readers through a series of translations by the American poet Gary Snyder, included in his collection *The Back Country* (1968); Sato produced a much more extensive collection of translations in *Miyazawa Kenji: Selections* (2007). In addition, Miyazawa's *Haru to shura* (1924) appeared in translation as *Spring and Asura* in 1973. As a result, Miyazawa's utterly individual voice is widely appreciated in translation. The best of his work is a rich and dazzling mixture of language and imagery that stretches modern Japanese to its limits and reveals possibilities of the congruence of sound and meaning unexplored in Japanese poetry before or since.

WAR AND POSTWAR YEARS

The rich and sophisticated mix of poetry produced in the 1920's and early 1930's came to an end with the dark days leading up to World War II. Some poets, such as Hagiwara, retreated to the use of traditional forms; some, such as Takamura, wrote patriotic poetry. Cut off from European developments and beleaguered at home by a repressive government and the difficulties of everyday living, Japanese poets seemed to turn inward. It was not until the end of the war that new trends could develop. When they did, it was perhaps not surprising that, in the wake of the war and the destruction that it had caused, younger poets came to distrust their own cultural past, which in their view had permitted a complicity with Japanese war aims. For them, the Japanese past seemed tainted, and beginning in the 1950's, poets looked again to Europe for their inspiration. In a sense, then, the war could be looked upon as an interruption in the internationalization of Japanese literature that had begun by the 1920's. In the postwar period, however, the break with the past became more definite and often assumed political significance.

Two trends in particular characterized the immediate postwar years. Following the example of Nishiwaki, who remained an immensely powerful figure in literary circles, a number of younger poets drew on European poetry in their effort to create a new tradition for themselves out of the ruins of the past. Considering that time of despair, it is perhaps not so surprising that in 1947, Ayukawa Nobuo (1920-1986) and his colleagues formed a group they called Arechi (the wasteland), suggesting both the impact of Eliot and their own sense of destruction and hopelessness. Others, such as Yoshioka Minoru (born 1919), continued to develop highly idiosyncratic symbolism and poetic forms that call to mind the commitment to the expanding mechanisms of language first undertaken by Nishiwaki. In the work of writers such as these, the legacy of European experimentation was still predominant.

A second trend placed a number of poets in the role of social critics who used the insights of the lyric mode to deepen and intensify their critique of postwar society. In this position, they had a powerful predecessor in the figure of Takuboku, who toward the end of his life had become increasingly wary of what he took to be reactionary trends in the development of the Japanese government and had begun to write poems that expressed his interest in socialism, even anarchism. Among the postwar poets who wanted to put society and its concerns back into the scope of their poetic vision, some were humanists horrified by the war, by the way in which human character had been degraded by destruction on the battlefield, and by the destruction caused by the atomic bomb. A few were Marxists. Little of this poetry has been studied or translated by Western scholars, but the work of early figures such as Oguma Hideo (1901-1940) certainly deserves proper study. Poets such as Ando Tsuguo (born 1919), most of whose work has been written in the postwar period, perhaps capture best this need of a generation to look back in an attempt to understand—emotionally, intellectually, and politically—what has happened to them. A reader who encounters their work in English may find it difficult to appreciate. A wider understanding of, say, Bertolt Brecht's poetry in England and the United States has now made it possible to write ironically in English on political issues, but the lyric thrust of the Japanese tradition applied to the war brings an overloading of images that may remain difficult for a reader from the Western tradition to encompass. Still, a search for authenticity in the early postwar period doubtless required this kind of linguistic travail, and the best of the works produced have a somber power that cannot be denied.

As the United States became involved in the Cold War and the Korean War as well, Japanese intellectuals began to react to what seemed to them a usurpation of their own sovereignty by the collusion of the Japanese and American authorities. Thus, there was a strain of contemporary Japanese poetry that, paralleling political movements, was largely reactive, particularly against the American involvement in Vietnam. Some of this political poetry had a satiric bite that was undeniably as effective as it was bitter.

A still later generation of poets, those who now have pride of place in Japanese literary circles, were born too late to have any direct experience of the war. These writers reached their maturity at a time when powerful changes had been wrought upon the fabric of Japanese society, where the processes of democratization and equalization of social class begun by the American occupation after World War II had altered the language as well as the society. Accordingly, Japanese poetry has tended to become increasingly colloquial, emphasizing the interior life of the poet, oppressed by the flatness, emptiness, and arbitrariness of modern life. As in English and American poetry, the grand gesture has been reduced to the ironic shrug, the powerful spiritual insight transformed into a wry and temporary awakening of sensibility. With the commercialization of communication, poets have found themselves more popular, and more vulnerable, than ever before. The work of Tamura Ryūichi (1923-1998), who owes something of his development to the Arechi school, has moments of a certain somber grandeur, but Tanikawa Shuntarō (born 1931) writes of the small disappointments and pleasures of his private world in a fashion that recalls the horizons, if not the style, of John Updike. His poetry is extremely popular in Japan and widely translated; the authenticity of his stance, which accurately reflects the spiritual condition of men and women in so many countries of the world, seems unquestioned.

Other writers among the postwar poets have attempted to strike out against this lassitude—some highly sophisticated, such as Anzai Hitoshi (1919-1994), whose work is characterized by brilliant language and a suggestive and ironic treatment of the Japanese past, and others, aggressively plainspoken, such as Ishigaki Rin (1920-2004), who used her experience as a working woman as the basis for moving and often wryly humorous verses.

LATE TWENTIETH CENTURY ONWARD

In more recent decades, it has become more difficult to make any definitive generalizations about poetic practice, as the quantity and diversity of poetry published, both in traditional and contemporary forms, remain enormous. It is perhaps too early for the reputations of younger writers to be settled in the minds of the multitude of readers attracted to poetry. In the midst of such continuing vitality, the increasing prominence of women poets, among them Tada Chimako (1930-2003), Shinkawa Kazue (born 1929), and Yoshihara Sachiko (born 1932) is an important and welcome development. A range of new themes have also become possible, as the high reputation of Takahashi Mutsuo (born 1937), a poet dealing extensively with homosexuality, makes evident.

Tanka (*waka*), the thirty-one-syllable form that goes back more than one thousand years, are still being composed. Certain poets have declared themselves as avant-garde poets in the genre and are anxious to set aside much of the traditional vocabulary in order to work towards what they consider a more unsentimental style. In any case, the form can still remain widely attractive. Indeed Tawara Machi (born 1962) achieved an international best seller in her fresh and often piquant collection of *tanka* titled *Salada kinenbi* (1987; *Salad Anniversary*, 1989).

Haiku, the seventeen-syllable form, also continues to attract a wide variety of poets, both professional and amateur. The kinds of expanded subject matter and fresh uses of the form which helped set the trends for more recent generations can be found in the seminal work of Saitō Sanki (1900-1962), with some of his best translated in *The Kobe Hotel* (1993).

Modern forms of verse, not surprisingly, retain pride of place as a privileged means of poetic expression. At least three larger trends might be noted here. The first involves the continued influence of French poetry and poetics in Japan. In those terms, such French poets as Baudelaire, Arthur Rimbaud, Paul Éluard, Mallarmé, André Breton, and Paul Valéry remain important; indeed, many contemporary Japanese poets who work and teach in university circles have done academic research on the French school and incorporate many of those principles into their own poetics. The resulting poetry is the most international in style of that composed in Japan at the end of the twentieth and beginning of the twenty-first centuries. More often than not, poems are produced that are about words or the nature of language itself. Such work is particularly difficult to translate, since the subject matter itself involves the nature of the Japanese language. Some poets, such as the popular and highly respected Ōoka Makoto, (born 1931) can sometimes link their work to the classical language of the traditional *tanka*, while the use of patterns and sounds is important in the work of such prominent "intellectual" poets as Hiraide Takashi (born 1950) and Asabuki Ryōji (born 1952).

In contradistinction to these kinds of verse, which overtly aim at the status of high art, a more popular kind of verse has also emerged, also often international in atmosphere, but one which makes use of elements in popular culture, such as the rhythms of jazz, and seeks to move poetry closer to a living oral culture. These poets in particular have revived the custom of poetry readings, long a feature in classical times, and come closer to expressing in their work an overt expression of political and social concerns. The best-known poet working in this vein, and arguably the best-known Japanese poet outside the country is Shiraishi Kazuko (born 1931), whose wit, feminist point of view, and antiestablishment stance have won her many friends and admirers around the world.

A third trend is the emergence of important longer poems and poetry sequences. Such efforts go back to the prewar generation of Nishiwaki, but more and more of these extended efforts have captured and sustained public interest. Here, three widely appreciated poets might be noted. Gōzō Yoshimasu (born 1939), who at one point studied in the United States, has expressed his admiration for Rimbaud. For many of his readers, he seems uniquely successful in capturing a certain sense of the emptiness and vacuum he finds in contemporary Japanese life. His poetry has sometimes been characterized as a series of voyages away from that felt sense of futility. Soh Sakon (born 1919) belongs to an earlier generation but began writing poetry after World

War II, inspired by his reading of Rimbaud and Valéry. His book-length poem *Moeru haha* (mother burning), published in 1967, now a classic of modern Japanese poetry, deals with the death of his mother in a 1942 fire bombing. Hara Shirō (born 1924), like other contemporary Japanese poets, is widely traveled and has been especially attracted to France. His highly regarded 1985 book-length poem *Ishi no fu* (*Ode to Stone*, 1990), uses as its links a series of stones, which serve as narrators from a variety of cultures and historical periods. These sections are interspersed with a continuing focus on a famous stone bridge in the southern city of Nagasaki, the town where Hara was raised.

Whatever the experimental nature of the language employed by all these poets, the very length of their work puts a necessary emphasis on larger themes, rather than merely a focus on the words themselves. This scale of verbal architecture creates a larger and more unified scale impossible to achieve in the shorter forms of poetry written in the Japanese classical and modern traditions.

Poetry has always been a highly respected form of artistic practice in Japan, and that pattern persists today. Most Japanese with a high school diploma can make an educated stab at writing haiku, perhaps even *waka*, and the relative evenness of vowel and consonant patterns in the Japanese language makes the composition of free verse relatively easy in a technical sense. Poetry magazines abound, and many accomplished writers compose for a circle of friends rather than for a national audience; indeed, some critics would maintain that this personal interchange between poets and their friends, so much a part of the Japanese poetic tradition since its beginnings in the *Manyoshuōshū* (mid-eighth century; *The Collections of Ten Thousand Leaves*; also as *The Ten Thousand Leaves*, pb. 1981, and as *The Manyoshu*, 1940) and the *Kokinshū* (905; *Kokinshu: A Collection of Poems Ancient and Modern*, 1984), helps explain why so many achieve some real sense of craft and why the best of the poets have become supreme manipulators of the language. The popularity and acceptance of poetry in Japanese life may debase it on the lower end of the scale, where businessmen without sensibility scribble down haiku, the imagery of which is worn clear of genuine meaning. However, on the other end of

that scale, those who write and rewrite for their poetic colleagues have achieved a level of accomplishment that is remarkably high.

Translation of any language is slippery enough, and good translations of poetry are particularly difficult to achieve; certainly, the barrier of the difficult Japanese language prevents most Western readers from discovering one of the most active poetic traditions in the world today. It may well be, however, that in the generations to come, the increasing number of good translations of contemporary Japanese poetry will create and sustain the same kind of excitement among readers and writers of poetry in English that European artists felt one hundred years ago when they first saw woodblock prints imported from Japan.

BIBLIOGRAPHY

Beichman, Janine. *Embracing the Firebird: Yosano Akiko and the Birth of the Female Voice in Modern Japanese Poetry*. Illustrated edition. Honolulu: University of Hawaii Press, 2002. A study of the early life and work of Yosano Akiko, whose first book, *Midaregami* (1901; *Tangled Hair*, 1935, 1971), radically changed *tanka* poetry and became a modern classic. The author has included her own masterful translations of poems by Yosano and her contemporaries. Bibliographical references and index.

Bownas, Geoffrey, and Anthony Thwaite, eds. and trans. *The Penguin Book of Japanese Verse*. Rev. ed. London: Penguin Books, 2009. A volume in the UNESCO Collection of Representative Works, Japanese series. Poetry of the Edo period is included in this anthology, followed by selections from the works of modern poets such as Tamura Ryūichi and Tanikawa Shuntarō. Bibliographical references and index.

Carter, Steven D., comp. and trans. *Traditional Japanese Poetry: An Anthology*. Stanford, Calif.: Stanford University Press, 1991. A collection of more than eleven hundred poems in traditional genres by poets selected for their merit or their historical significance. Illustrations and maps. Bibliographical references and indexes.

Heinrich, Amy. *Fragments of Rainbows: The Life and*

Poetry of Saitō Mokichi, 1882-1953. New York: Columbia University Press, 1983. A useful account of developments in the use of classical forms in the modern period, centering on the work of Saitō Mokichi.

Keene, Donald, ed. *Modern Japanese Literature: From 1868 to the Present Day*. 1956. Reprint. New York: Grove Press, 1994. Contains historical introduction by the editor, as well as brief introductions to the writers. Selected bibliographical references. A landmark work.

Koriyama, Naoshi, and Edward Lueders, eds. and trans. *Like Underground Water: Poetry of Mid-Twentieth Century Japan*. 1995. Reprint. Port Townsend, Wash.: Copper Canyon Press, 2000. Presents 240 poems by eighty poets, each of whom is introduced in a brief biographical headnote. Poetic styles range from conventional lyricism to surrealism, symbolism, anarchism, and nihilism. Excellent introduction.

Morton, Leith. *Modernism in Practice: An Introduction to Postwar Japanese Poetry*. Honolulu: University of Hawaii Press, 2004. This long-overdue study traces the modernist movement in Japan from its prewar origins to its emergence in the works of seven outstanding poets, presented in flawless translations and analyzed in detail. Other topics discussed at length are poetry by women and poetry from Okinawa.

Rimer, J. Thomas, and Van C. Gessel, eds. *The Columbia Anthology of Modern Japanese Literature*. 2 vols. New York: Columbia University Press, 2005-2007. The first volume of what has been called a "monumental" collection covers the years 1868-1945, the second, from 1945 to the present. Part of the Modern Asian Literature series. Includes fiction, poems, plays, and essays, organized both chronologically and by genre.

Sato, Hiroaki, ed. and trans. *Japanese Women Poets: An Anthology*. Armonk, N.Y.: M. E. Sharpe, 2007. Selections from the works of more than one hundred Japanese women poets in a broad range of genres, from ancient folk songs to court poetry, from *chōka* to free verse. Explanatory headnotes precede each section. Glossary, chronology, and bibliography.

Shirane, Haruo, ed. *Early Modern Japanese Literature: An Anthology, 1600-1900*. Translated by James Brandon et al. New York: Columbia University Press, 2002. One section of this book focuses specifically on haiku of the early nineteenth century. Introductions and commentary by Shirane. Illustrations and maps. English-language bibliography. Index.

Solt, John. *Shredding the Tapestry of Meaning*. Cambridge, Mass.: Harvard University Press, 1999. An account of the rise of avant-garde poetry in Japan, centering on the career and work of Kitasono Katsue.

Ueda, Makoto. *Modern Japanese Tanka: An Anthology*. New York: Columbia University Press, 1996. The poems of twenty writers appear in this collection. Each writer's work is preceded by a biographical and critical introduction. Selected bibliography.

J. Thomas Rimer
Updated by Rimer

LATIN AMERICAN POETRY

The panorama of Latin American poetry spans five hundred years, from the sixteenth to the twenty-first centuries. The first "Renaissance" in the New World (1492-1556) was the era of discovery, exploration, conquest, and colonization under the reign of the Spanish monarchs Ferdinand and Isabela and later Carlos V. The origins of Latin American literature are found in the chronicles of these events, narrated by Spanish soldiers or missionaries. The era of colonization during the reign of Philip II (1556-1598) was a second Renaissance and the period of the Counter-Reformation. During this time, Alonso de Ercilla y Zúñiga (1533-1594) wrote the first epic poem, *La Araucana* (1569-1589). The native saga narrated the wars between the Spanish conquistadors and the Araucano Indians of Chile. This is the first truly poetic literary work with an American theme.

SOR JUANA INÉS DE LA CRUZ

During the period of the Austrian Habsburg kings (1598-1701), this Renaissance was gradually replaced by the Baroque era. While the Golden Age of Spanish letters was declining in the Old World, Sor Juana Inés de la Cruz (1648-1695) reigned supreme as the queen of colonial letters. She was the major poet during the colonial era. The autodidactic nun, who wrote plays and prose as well as poetry, was known as the tenth muse, *la décima musa*. Her poetic masterpiece, the autobiographical "Primero sueño," combines Baroque elements with a mastery of Spanish and classical languages and her unique style. Her shorter poems, with their lyrical verse phrasing and native themes, capture popular Mexican culture. Some of her most famous sonnets are "Este que ves, engaño colorido" (what you see [is] dark deception), "¿En perseguirme, mundo, qué interesas?" (in pursuing me, world, what interests you?), "Détente, sombra de mi bien esquivo" (stop, shadow of my elusive love), and "Esta tarde, mi bien, cuando te hablaba" (this afternoon, love, when I spoke to you). Her most recognized *redondillas* (or "roundelays," stanzas of four octosyllabic lines rhyming *abba*) are "Este amoroso tormento" (this tormented love) and "Hombres necios" ("Foolish Men"). Her charm and brilliance won her many wealthy and royal patrons. While she initially accepted their admiration, she died a recluse after rejecting her literary career and denouncing her precocious fame and vain pursuits.

NEOCLASSICISM

During the Wars of Independence (1808-1826), Neoclassicism and other French influences dominated literary production. Andrés Bello (1781-1865) is better known for his prose, but he was also a prolific verse writer who followed the European neoclassical movement. He wrote the poems "Alocución a la poesía" and "La agricultura en la zona tórida" with American themes and European style. José Maria Heredia (1803-1839) was a Cuban exiled in Mexico and the United States who wrote about the beauty of the countries that adopted him. Romanticism characterized his poems about Niagara Falls, "Niágara," Aztec ruins, "En el Teocalli de Cholula," and other wonders such as a storm in "En una tempestad." His ode "Himno a un desterrado" relates his experience as an exile in adopted nations.

Gertrudis Gómez de Avellaneda (1814-1873) left Cuba to write in Spain because of the greater freedom she could enjoy there as a female poet. Romanticism influenced her poems about love, God, and her homeland, such as "Noche de insomnio y el alba" (night of insomnia and dawn), "Al partir" (upon leaving), and "Amor y orgullo" (love and pride).

José Hernández (1834-1886) wrote about the Argentinean gauchos in *El Gaucho Martín Fierro* (1872; *The Gaucho Martin Fierro*, 1935) and *La vuelta de Martín Fierro* (1879; *The Return of Martin Fierro*, 1935; included in *The Gaucho Martin Fierro*, 1935). His Romantic verses followed the structures and lyrical rhythms of popular songs that romanticized the gauchos as a dying breed in the wake of industrialization.

MODERNISMO

By 1875, the roots of a poetic movement had grown into a new poetic era. The Latin American *Modernistas* were innovators and critics of the conservative thematic and stylistic structures that persisted from the colonial period. In Latin American society, global industrialization, capitalism, North American cultural and economic imperialism, and Spain's loss of all its colonies had a significant impact on artistic development.

A definitive moment in the progress of the movement resulted from José Martí's publication of *Ismaelillo* in 1882. The poet and hero, who died fighting for Cuban independence (1853-1895), published *Versos libres* that same year, a collection that followed *Versos sencillos*, published in 1881. All three collections characterized the existential angst of the era as they experimented with new lyrical forms and themes. Martí approached language as a sculptor approaches clay and molded words into new forms. His innovations have allowed him to be considered the first great visionary Latin American poet as he sought to define *Nuestra América*, a Latin American identity struggling for artistic as well as political and economic independence. Throughout the movement, the anguish, emptiness, and uncertainty of modernity provided a unifying thread for poets seeking innovation.

The Mexican modernist Manuel Gutierrez Nájera (1859-1895) was a journalist renowned for his prose writings in his own time. He founded *La Revista Azul*, a literary review that promoted *Modernismo* throughout Latin America. His contemporary Rubén Darío (1867-1916), however, defined the *Modernista* poetic. Darío's poetry was a reaction to the decadence of Romanticism in which he sought a unique voice while reinvigorating the Spanish language. He led a movement that borrowed themes popularized by the European Romantics and stylistic models of the French Parnassian movement. Darío not only was an instigator and initiator of the vindication of his language, but also served as a bridge to the second stage of *Modernismo*. His *Azul* (1888; blue) and *Cantos de vida y esperanza, Los cisnes, y otros poemas* (1905; songs of life and hope, the swans, and other poems) represent Darío's dynamic style, respect for beauty, search for harmonious words, and celebration of pleasure. Despite the Decadence of his later poetry collections, Darío maintained confidence in the saving power of art and its use to protest against social and historical injustices and resolve existential enigmas. The *Modernistas* de-

fended humanism in the face of economic progress and international imperialism, which devaluated art. They elevated art as an end in itself.

Leopoldo Lugones (1874-1938) was the major Argentinean *Modernista* poet. His poems "Delectación morosa," "Emoción aldeana," and "Divagación lunar" lament ephemeral beauty captured and immortalized by perfectly placed words. Alfonsina Storni (1892-1938) was influenced by postmodernist tendencies. Her intense verse experimented with Symbolism and other twentieth century innovations. Her vivid sensual poems include "Tú me quieres blanca," "Epitafio para mi tumba," "Voy a dormir," "Hombre pequeñito," and "Fiera de amor." The Uruguayan Delmira Agustini (1886-1914) wrote intensely emotional and erotic poems that highlighted the dualities of human nature. Pleasure and pain, good and evil, love and death create and maintain verbal tension. These opposites struggle for dominance in poems such as "La musa," "Explosión," and "El vampiro."

All of these individual elements come together in these poets' faith in the artistic power of the word. This autonomous aesthetic power opposed the *fin de siglo* (turn of the century) angst resulting from industrialism, positivism, and competing ideologies. While reflecting on their predecessors, the *Modernistas* created original verse with unique usage of sometimes archaic or exotic words. The language was sometimes luxurious and sensual, adapting classical and Baroque usage, from elements of the Parnassians to those of the Pre-Raphaelites to the Art Nouveau and European Symbolist movements and tendencies of decadent Romanticism. The symbolic impact of words characterized the movement as a whole. This all-encompassing factor defines the movement and its existential nature. This poetry is the living expression of an era of spiritual crises, personal and societal anguish, and uncertainty about the future of art as well as humanity's direction as it embarked upon the twentieth century.

POSTMODERNISM AND THE VANGUARD

No exact date marks the transition from Latin American modernism to postmodernism or to a vanguard movement. A combination of historical and societal factors influenced the artistic development of individual Latin American countries. In the first two decades of the twentieth century, World War I and the Mexican Revolution interrupted artistic and literary exchange between the Old World models and the New World innovators. The urban bourgeoisie, who were patrons of the arts, were displaced. The United States had gradually replaced the European masters in science and industry as well as politics, and its dominance permeated all levels of Latin American society.

Altazor (wr. 1919, pb. 1931), by Chilean Vicente Huidobro (1893-1948), marks a break with the past. Huidobro originated stylistic practices never seen before in Latin American poetry. In *creacionismo*, his personal version of creationism, he sought to create a poem the way nature made a tree. His words, invested with autonomous linguistic and symbolic significance, reinvent themselves by creating a world apart from other words. They are antilyrical, intellectual, and disconnected from emotional and spiritual experience. Nevertheless, Huidobro's world, created by his unique use of words, was a human creation because in it the poet experiences alienation and existential angst. Huidobro's poems "Arte poética," "Depart," and "Marino" voice his despair in isolation.

Huidobro had a significant influence on younger poets, particularly in his development of a school of thought that centered on the theory of *Ultraísmo*, which attempted to construct alternative linguistic choices to those offered by the external world. *Ultraísmo* synthesized Latin American with Spanish and European tendencies.

Among those influenced by *Ultraísmo* were Jorge Luis Borges (1899-1986), and in fact, Borges became its main proponent. While his short stories have repeatedly caused him to be nominated for the Nobel Prize in Literature, his poetry reveals a linguistic expertise and lyrical genius unparalleled by his contemporaries. He believed that lyricism and metaphysics united to justify the means of the poetic process. This fusion provides the genesis of his most representative poems, "Everything and Nothing," "Everness," "Laberinto," "Dreamtigers," and "Borges y yo."

The Peruvian César Vallejo (1892-1938) developed a unique and distinctive poetic voice. His *Los heraldos negros* (1918; *The Black Heralds*, 1990), *Trilce* (1922;

English translation, 1973), and *Poemas humanos* (1939; *Human Poems*, 1968) demonstrate the impossibility of mutual communication and comprehension, the absurdity of the human condition, and the inevitability of death.

In 1945, Gabriela Mistral (1889-1957) was the first Latin American writer to receive the Nobel Prize in Literature. Her verses echo the folksongs and traditional ballads of her native Chile, the Caribbean, and Mexico. They naturally blend native dialects with Castilian in a lyrical fusion. Some of her best poems include "Sonetos a la muerte," "Todos íbamos a ser reinas," "Pan," and "Cosas."

Mistral's countryman Pablo Neruda (1904-1973) also won the Nobel Prize in Literature, in 1971. During his formative years he was influenced by *Modernismo*, experimenting with various styles while serving as an

Gabriela Mistral (AFP/Getty Images)

international diplomat. The last stage of his poetry was marked by didacticism and political themes, and he was exiled for his activity in the Communist Party. Neruda sought to create a forum for "impure" poetry that encompassed all experience. His *Canto general* (1950; partial translation in *Let the Rail Splitter Awake, and Other Poems*, 1951; full translation as *Canto General*, 1991) voiced his solidarity with humanity in his political and poetic conversion. *Odas elementales* (1954; *The Elemental Odes*, 1961) continued his mission of solidarity with the humblest members of creation. Other landmark collections include *Los versos del capitán* (1952; *The Captain's Verses*, 1972) and *Cien sonetos de amor* (1959; *One Hundred Love Sonnets*, 1986). Neruda believed that America and clarity should be one and the same.

The Mexican literary generation known as the *Taller* was led by Octavio Paz (1914-1998). He was awarded the Nobel Prize in Literature in 1990 for his brilliant prose and poetry that defined the Mexican culture and connected its isolation and universality to other cultures. His landmark analysis of poetic theory is proposed in *El arco y la lira* (1956; *The Bow and the Lyre*, 1973). The poetic evolution of linguistic progression considered "signs in rotation" culminated in *Piedra de sol* (1957; *Sun Stone*, 1963) and synthesized all twentieth century poetic theories into a highly original yet distinctly Mexican work. Representative poems include "Himno entre ruinas," "Viento entero," and "La poesía."

The Chilean poet Nicanor Parra (born 1914) developed a unique yet popular style. He called his poems *antipoemas* for their super-realism, sarcasm, self-criticism, and humor. Parra's poetry speaks to the masses and rejects pretension, as the poet revitalizes language and innovates with words in action. His masterwork, *Poemas y antipoemas* (1954; *Poems and Antipoems*, 1967), epitomizes antirhetorical and antimetaphorical free verse. "Soliloquio del individuo" and "Recuerdos de juventud" are representative.

The work of Sara de Ibañez (1910-1981) represents the antithesis of fellow Uruguayan Agustini. Her intellectual and metaphysical themes and neoclassical style allude to the poetry of Sor Juana and Golden Age masters such as Spain's Luis de Góngora y Argote. Love

and death are analyzed in "Isla en la tierra," "Isla en la luz," "Liras," and "Soliloquios del Soldado."

The "impure" poetry of Ernesto Cardenal (born 1925) unites political ugliness and the beauty of the imagination. It is characterized by *exteriorismo*, a technique that incorporates propaganda, sound bites, advertisements, and fragments of popular culture into poetry that seeks to convert and enlighten. The aesthetic value of these poems is not overshadowed by their political and spiritual message. Representative collections include *La hora O* (1960), *Salmos* (1967; *The Psalms of Struggle and Liberation*, 1971), *Oración por Marilyn Monroe, y otros poemas* (1965; *Marilyn Monroe, and Other Poems*, 1975), and *Cántico cósmico* (1989; *The Music of the Spheres*, 1990; also known as *Cosmic Canticle*).

Rosario Castellanos (1925-1974) is best known for her novels and essays about social injustice in her native Chiapas. Because she focused on the status of women within the Mayan culture and within Mexican society as a whole, she was considered a feminist. Her poetry and prose are concerned with the human condition, not only with the plight of women. Her most representative poems are "Autorretrato," "Entrevista de Prensa," and "Se habla de Gabriel."

Thematically and stylistically more militant and radical, Rosario Ferré (born 1938) writes overtly feminist poetry using elements of symbolism and irony. Her poems include "Pretalamio," "Negativo," "La prisionera," and "Epitalamio." As editor of a literary journal, Ferré introduced feminist criticism to Latin American literature.

Movements on a smaller national scale characterize present-day poetry. They are characterized by experimental and politically and socially conscious efforts. The twenty-first century heralds the work of *los nuevos*, the new poets whose work is linked to national as well as international issues.

Individual postvanguard poets do not identify with particular ideologies. The poetry of Argentineans Mario Benedetti (1920-2009) and Juan Gelman (born 1930) deals with personal exile as well as the universal experience of exile. Since the 1980's, women have emerged with empowered poetry that serves as liberation from oppression. Poets including Alejandra Pizarnik (1936-

1972), Rosario Murillo (born 1951), Giaconda Belli (born 1948), Claribel Alegría (born 1924), Juana de Ibarbourou (1895-1979), and Ana Istarú (born 1960) have given voice to the silent struggles of women striving to realize their potential in a male-dominated society.

Poetry written since the 1980's has focused on oppression and exile. The focus on the withdrawal from history as a condition for the poetry of Paz has shifted to the poet belonging in the historical moment so that poetry has a public place and common concern. Contemporary Latin American poetry has become the process of naming the word and rewriting history in a lived world. The making of that world is the creative act that celebrates the word.

BIBLIOGRAPHY

Agosín, Marjorie, ed. and trans. *These Are Not Sweet Girls: Latin American Women Poets*. Fredonia, N.Y.: White Pine Press, 1994. Bilingual edition. Agosín is a prolific and influential poet as well as a distinguished professor and literary critic. This volume from the Secret Weavers series focuses on the poetic production of Hispanic women since the advent of feminism as expressed through their work, written predominantly during the last thirty years of the twentieth century.

Agosín, Marjorie, and Roberta Gordenstein, eds. *Miriam's Daughters: Jewish Latin American Women Poets*. Foreword by Agosín. Santa Fe, N.Mex.: Sherman Asher, 2001. Twenty-eight poets are represented in this anthology, which includes the Spanish or Portuguese texts, along with English translations. Author biographies.

Gonzalez, Mike, and David Treece. *The Gathering of Voices: The Twentieth Century Poetry of Latin America*. New York: Verso, 1992. This study addresses a wide range of topics. The contradictions of Latin American *Modernismo* are explored, including its elements of shock and despair that distinguished it from its predecessors. The roots of the vanguard movement are examined, and the enduring poetry of Neruda is discussed in detail. Special topics are discussed, such as Brazilian *Modernismo* and the Guerrilla Poets of Cuba. The work concludes with studies of Postmodernism in Brazil and Spanish-language poets in exile.

Green, Roland Arthur. *Unrequited Conquests: Love and Empire in the Colonial Americas*. Chicago: University of Chicago Press, 1999. This volume offers insight into Spanish colonialism, European imperialism, and their influences upon literature. Colonial love poetry is analyzed within its socio-political and historical contexts. Chapters are devoted to Sor Juana's fascinating life and works. Illustrated. Bibliography.

Rowe, William. *Poets of Contemporary Latin America: History and Inner Life*. New York: Oxford University Press, 2000. This study discusses contemporary Latin American poets who bridge the centuries, including Nicanor Parra, Carmen Ollé, and Ernesto Cardenal. Williams explores two major influences on late twentieth century and early twenty-first century poetry: the avant-garde movement and politically motivated poetic writing. He examines these roots from contextual and historical perspectives.

Smith, Verity. *Encyclopedia of Latin American Literature*. Chicago: Fitzroy Dearborn, 1996. This reference of nearly one thousand pages contains essays of at least fifteen hundred words on major poets, novelists, dramatists, other writers, movements, concepts, and other topics relating to South American, Central American, and Caribbean (including Spanish, French, and English) literatures. Overview essays cover literatures of individual countries, eras, and themes (such as science fiction, children's literature, and indigenous literatures), as well as the literatures of the major U.S. Latino communities: Cuban, Mexican, and Puerto Rican.

Sonntag Blay, Iliana L. *Twentieth-Century Poetry from Spanish America: An Index to Spanish Language Poetry and Bilingual Anthologies*. Lanham, Md.: Scarecrow Press, 1998. Three indexes provide access to more than twelve thousand Latin American poems from seventy-two anthologies: an author index, a title index, and an index of first lines. An important reference for serious scholars.

Tapscott, Stephen, ed. *Twentieth-Century Latin American Poetry: A Bilingual Anthology*. Austin: University of Texas Press, 1996. This is the first bilingual collection of the most important Latin American poets. Portuguese as well as Spanish poems are translated, and the selections cover the full range of the century, from the *Modernistas* to the postmoderns, the vanguardists, and contemporary political and experimental poetry. Tapscott provides background material and introductions to eighty-five poets in a well-organized volume with excellent translations.

Vicuña, Cecilia, and Ernesto Livon-Grosman, eds. *The Oxford Book of Latin American Poetry: A Bilingual Anthology*. New York: Oxford University Press, 2009. This impressive anthology contains poems by more than 120 poets. Includes such often over-looked traditions as native chants, mestizo poetry, and invented languages. Excellent introduction by the editors. Biographical notes and bibliography.

Washburne, Kelly, ed. *An Anthology of Spanish American Modernismo: In English Translation, with Spanish Text*. Translated by Washbourne with Sergio Waisman. New York: Modern Language Association of America, 2007. Superb translations of poems by eighteen *Modernista* poets from Argentina, Bolivia, Colombia, Cuba, Mexico, Nicaragua, Peru, and Uruguay. Introduction, suggestions for further reading, and bibliography.

Carole A. Champagne

LATIN POETRY

Extant Latin poetry dates from 240 B.C.E., when the Greek Livius Andronicus made his first Latin translations of Greek dramas, but there is ample evidence of a poetic tradition in Rome prior to this date. Most literary histories of Rome terminate their surveys with the close of the second century C.E., yet a strong Latin poetic tradition continued in Europe well into the seventeenth century. Further, even if one were to limit the chronological range of Latin poetry to the period between 240 B.C.E. and 1700 C.E., or, yet more narrowly, between 240 B.C.E. and 200 C.E., the diversity of style and language within the field is striking. The term "Latin" implies a common language, yet Latin itself changed greatly over its active literary life. Just as the English language evolved between the time of Geoffrey Chaucer and William Shakespeare and, again, between that of Shakespeare and William Butler Yeats, so does the Latin of the earliest poets differ markedly from that of the great first century B.C.E. poet, Vergil, and Vergil's Latin from Latin poetry of the Renaissance.

Latin poetry is at times termed "Roman." The word "Roman" links the poetry with the city that controlled the Mediterranean world between the second century B.C.E. and the fourth century C.E., yet remarkably few Latin poets were native Romans. Many were from other areas of Italy—areas that did not receive full-citizen status until the first century B.C.E.; others came from scattered parts of the Roman Empire, including Spain and North Africa. Like the empire in which it evolved, then, Latin poetry was diverse and cosmopolitan, and its development cannot be separated from the political and social history of Rome and its empire.

To allow discussion of such a complex poetic tradition in a manageable way, the history of Latin poetry is here divided into seven chronological periods: its origins to 264 B.C.E.; early Republican poetry, from 264 to 100 B.C.E.; late Republican poetry, from 100 to 27 B.C.E.; Augustan Age poetry, from 27 B.C.E. to 14 C.E.; Silver Age poetry, from 14 to 138 C.E.; Latin poetry in late antiquity, from 138 to 476 C.E.; and medieval and neo-Latin poetry, from 476 to 1700 C.E. Discussion of each period includes a historical overview that focuses on events of major significance in the evolution of Latin poetry, an outline of contemporary literary trends, and a survey of several important poets of the period in the context of these historical and literary perspectives.

ORIGINS TO 264 B.C.E.

Compared to societies in the eastern Mediterranean, Rome was a late bloomer. At the peak of Egyptian civilization, the ancestors of the Romans apparently had not yet inhabited central Italy. In the seventh century B.C.E., by which time Greece had already produced Homer, Hesiod, and Sappho, the inhabitants of Latium were still primitive herdsmen and farmers. The social organization was patriarchal. The basic unit was the *familia*, which included not only the immediate but also the extended family, as well as slaves and other members of the household, over which the *paterfamilias*—that is, the oldest living male—held absolute authority.

Roman society's agricultural and familial orientation was reflected in its religious life, which revolved around a host of divinities: Jupiter and Mars, who controlled fertility; the Lares and Penates, who were the personal gods of each household; Vesta, who was the goddess of the hearth; and a host of others. Civic worship paralleled private cults, and the city of Rome had its own Lares and Penates as well as virgin priestesses of Vesta who oversaw the state hearth. To a great extent, the traditional relationship of a Roman to his state was considered to parallel that of a member of the *familia* to his *paterfamilias*, and a Roman was expected to exhibit the same *pietas*, or sense of piety and respect, toward the state that he demonstrated toward his own father. In addition to *pietas*, other traditional Roman virtues were distinctly agricultural in character and included industry, obedience, and seriousness. All of these qualities played an important thematic role in Roman literature from its inception.

Beyond the *familia*, the basic social units were the *pagi*, villages or cantons, which were only loosely united into several population groups (Latins, Sabines, Umbrians, and Lucanians, among others) partially based upon dialects such as Latin, Oscan, or Umbrian.

There was little unity among these groups and frequent warfare.

A significant change occurred in central Italy around 650 B.C.E., when Latium was invaded by the Etruscans, a mysterious people who had inhabited Tuscany in north-central Italy for at least several centuries. The provenance of the Etruscans lies outside the scope of this essay, but their influence upon the Latins politically, socially, and culturally cannot be underestimated. It was the urban-oriented and highly civilized Etruscans, many scholars believe, who caused the tribal Italians to settle in cities, and through whom the Italians were first exposed to Greek civilization.

In matters of religion, the Etruscans brought the Latins a more formal set of rituals, especially pertaining to augury. Under Etruscan influence, the taking of auspices by special priests called *augures* became customary prior to many public and private acts. Further, Roman temples and cult statues came to be based on Etruscan models. Such features of Roman religion became important themes in Latin literature, which, throughout its development, was continuously affected by changes in Roman religious beliefs and practices.

The founding of the city of Rome, traditionally dated to 735 B.C.E., is shrouded by diverse myths and legends, but archaeological evidence suggests that the site was inhabited early in the first millennium B.C.E., principally by Latin tribes, although there is a possibility that the city was founded under Etruscan influence.

Etruscan rule for at least part of Rome's early history is well supported by ancient evidence. Of the seven legendary kings of Rome, two, Tarquinius Priscus (commonly known as Tarquin the First) and Tarquinius Superbus (commonly known as Tarquin the Proud), were Etruscan in origin. Traditionally, the expulsion of the latter from Rome in 510 B.C.E. marked the end of Etruscan rule of the city and the founding of the Roman Republic.

Very early in their urban history, the Romans developed a two-tiered social structure. The small, privileged class of patricians were large landowners who controlled and protected numerous tenants and laborers under a patron-client relationship. In the early Republic, only members of patrician families could hold important political offices, such as the consulship, or become members of the Roman Senate. The mass of people were called the *plebs* or plebeians, and much of the history of the early Roman Republic is marked by the struggle of the plebeian class to wrest itself from the political and economic stranglehold of the patricians. Despite periodic compromises, this class conflict was never resolved during the lifetime of the Roman Republic. To a large extent, literature, as it developed especially in the Republican period, was composed by and for the patrician class. Plebeians usually achieved only limited literacy in this period and generally lacked the leisure time to read and to create literary texts.

In addition to class conflict, the early years of the Republic are marked by a series of wars between Rome and her neighbors and by the gradual absorption of the Italian Peninsula into the Roman sphere of influence. The Latin peoples were brought into a voluntary military federation called the Latin League, which gradually evolved into a Roman dependency: Keeping the name *socii* (allies), the Latins retained their local self-government and local citizenship but were forced to yield all foreign policy decisions to Rome. The invasion of north Italy by a Celtic tribe of Gauls and their brief capture of Rome in 390 B.C.E. were traumatic events which left a permanent mark on the Roman psyche. Threat of foreign seizure thenceforth became a frequent political rallying point for the Roman people. The fourth century B.C.E. was also marked by the gradual conquest of Etruscan cities by Rome, beginning with the Roman capture of Veii in 396 B.C.E. The same century witnessed a series of conflicts called the Samnite Wars, fought against Italian tribes in the southern peninsula, which led ultimately to Roman control of all Italy south of the Po Valley. This territorial expansion by Rome during the fourth century B.C.E. was the beginning of a remarkable military growth leading to Roman rule of the entire Mediterranean basin by the end of the millennium.

Such rapid expansion was not without its ramifications on Rome itself. The city may have absorbed Italy politically, but at least two centuries passed before her allies became completely Romanized; the intervening period was marked by revolts by various *socii*. Further, Rome's growth brought her suddenly into contact with two more advanced civilizations, the Etruscans in the north and the Greeks in the south. Such contacts transformed Roman society profoundly, not the least in the area of poetic expression.

Writing appears to have been introduced to Latium by the Etruscans, since it was the Etruscan alphabet rather than its Greek parent which was adapted to the Latin language. The earliest surviving inscriptions can be dated to about 500 B.C.E., and there are no extant literary pieces prior to about 240 B.C.E. The written Latin of the period from 500 to 240 B.C.E. is primarily legal and religious in character. Extant examples of primitive Latin include such legal documents as the *Leges regiae* (*The Laws of the Kings*) and the famous Twelve Tables, both of which survive in late prose adaptations but which were probably originally composed in verse. A priestly literature developed around formalized Roman ritual, and fragments of texts listing the order of ceremonies and lists of feasts (*fasti*) survive. Other extant documents include epitaphs (such as the famous inscriptions on the Scipios) and a few fragments from political and dedicatory monuments.

The Romans themselves maintained a tradition of oral literature but unfortunately lacked a Latin Homer or Hesiod to transform their oral compositions into written texts. Because none of this oral Latin poetry survives, many modern scholars deny the existence of any Latin poetry prior to 240 B.C.E. Such a view is extreme. Like other primitive cultures, the early Latins probably possessed some native forms of oral poetic expression. While these oral forms did not survive Rome's transformation from an oral to a literate culture and the exposure of Rome to Etruscan and Greek literary traditions, these native Latin forms were nevertheless remembered by later Romans and left their mark on written Latin literature.

The earliest Latin verse was composed in a metrical system that was probably accentual, like native English verse, rather than quantitative, like the system that later Latin poets adapted from Greek models. These later poets named the native form *versus saturnius* (Saturnian verse), referring to the mythical golden age of the god Saturn. A few examples of this verse survive, but the texts are so corrupt that it is impossible to reconstruct the actual metrical system with certainty. The ancient evidence suggests that Saturnian verse was used for a variety of literary purposes: religious verses, such as the extant *Carmen Arvale* (*Song of the Arval Brothers*, a hymn to Mars); popular forms, such as lullabies and aphorisms; *carmina triumphalia*, greetings to triumphant generals; epitaphs; dirges; and perhaps even epic songs about heroes of the past.

Two native literary forms warrant special mention because of their influence on later Latin poetic genres: *versus fescennini* (Fescennine verses) and *satura*. The Fescennine verses were probably connected originally with agricultural festivals but came to be used also at such celebrations as weddings and military triumphs. Significant features of this form include banter or repartee, which is often cited as a primitive stage in native Italian drama, and ribaldry or invective, thought to have been originally apotropaic in character and to have been influential in the development of later forms of Latin ribaldry, such as the harsh invectives of Catullus and Martial and the biting satires of Juvenal.

Another native genre was the *satura*, although there is a possibility that the form was actually imported from the Etruscans. The name *satura* may have derived from a Latin word referring to a dish with a variety of foods; ancient references suggest that the *satura* was essentially a medley, a performance in various forms, materials, and moods, including a mixture of singing, dancing, music, and spoken parts. Like the Fescennine verses, the *satura* may have been an early form of Roman drama and was certainly an important stage in the development of Latin satire.

Thus, prior to the Greek-influenced tradition of Latin literature beginning in 240 B.C.E., there was a poetic tradition in Latin that was ancient, indigenous, and oral. Though little survives of this literature, it is clear that it exhibited native Roman characteristics which affected later Latin poetry. Roman *gravitas* was offset by a basic respect for verse and an instinctive awareness of the role of poetry in the sacred and festive occasions of public life. Later Latin literature could not have developed if the Roman character were completely unfamiliar with and unresponsive to such forms of literary expression.

EARLY REPUBLICAN POETRY (264-100 B.C.E.)

This period marks not only the first Roman expansion outside Italy and the beginnings of the Roman Empire, but also the first extant Latin literature. Politically, the period was dominated by Rome's struggle with the city of Carthage, a Punic city on the coast of present-day Tunisia, in a series of three wars usually called the Punic Wars. This conflict, which saw military encounters in Italy, Africa, Spain, and the eastern Mediterranean, led ultimately to the destruction of Carthage in 146 B.C.E. and the recognition of Rome as the political and military power in the Mediterranean. During this period, too, Rome acquired its first provinces—in Sicily, Cisalpine Gaul, Spain, Narbonese Gaul (modern Marseilles), Africa, Greece, and Asia Minor—and first encountered the complex difficulties of foreign occupation and provincial administration. By the end of the second century B.C.E., the demands of the empire had made Rome critically dependent on its far-flung armies and politically ambitious generals.

During this period, Rome's political situation continued to be affected by problems of class conflict and social change. In the fifth and fourth centuries B.C.E., the plebeians had wrested several political concessions from the patrician class, including recognition of the legislative rights of the *concilium plebis* (the plebeian assembly) and the veto of the *tribuni plebis* (tribunes of the plebeians). The same period also witnessed the granting, to a few wealthy plebeian families, of political privileges once exclusively patrician, such as admission to the Senate and election to the consulship. The latter changes resulted not so much in increased power for the plebeian class as in a new alliance of wealthy plebeians with patricians, who together came to be called *nobiles* (nobles). During the third and second centuries B.C.E., it was this political group, as members of the Senate, which controlled the city and its growing empire. At the same time, the majority of plebeians, in effect, lost political ground; as the citizen population of Rome was dispersed with the expansion of the franchise, fewer and fewer plebeian citizens could make the long journey to Rome to cast their votes, and the plebeian assemblies were increasingly composed, not of small independent farmers as formerly, but of poor urban masses, including dispossessed peasants and freedmen. Systematic bribery of the urban plebeian population, via such methods as free food distribution and public entertainment, was already

common in the second century B.C.E. and demonstrated the widening social and political gap between nobles and plebeians, between Roman citizens and the disenfranchised Italian and provincial populations.

Futile attempts to remedy some of the worst social inequalities were made by the Gracchi brothers, Tiberius and Gaius, toward the end of the second century B.C.E., but the Gracchis' plans for land reform and political enfranchisement of the Italians met with effective opposition by the nobility.

To a large degree, Roman society was unprepared for the dramatic changes brought by the growth of her empire. The necessity for standing armies created both political problems and social difficulties. The need for farmland for retiring veterans, especially in the first century B.C.E., led to widespread land confiscations. No longer were Italian farms worked on a small scale by a single family. The tendency was toward *latifundia*, large estates owned by wealthy absentee landholders and worked by slave labor. The growth of the slave population in Italy was in direct proportion to the growth of the empire, since war captives were the primary source of slaves. A slave-based economy gave Roman nobility more leisure to pursue other interests, such as literature, but it also led to another social problem, slave revolts, which increased in the first century B.C.E.

Empire also brought great wealth into the city, by way of military plunder, taxation, and economic opportunities in the provinces. Many a Roman governor made a quick fortune in the year he spent in his province. The largest fortunes, however, were made not by the nobility, who traditionally despised commerce, but by a growing merchant class, called *equites* (knights), who were not part of the governing nobility. Traditional Roman virtues (such as industry and frugality) were put to a severe test by the city's new wealth, as is evidenced by the need for sumptuary laws in the city as early as the late third century B.C.E.

In addition to wealth, the empire affected Roman society in another basic way by exposing it to foreign and, often, more sophisticated cultures. Although the introduction of exotic religious cults was strictly regulated and officially discouraged, the popularity of rituals such as that of the Eastern goddess Cybele demonstrates the futility of this regulation. The transformation of Roman society from its rustic Latin origins into an urban cosmopolitan center was inevitable.

More than any other conquered people, it was the Greeks who profoundly changed the traditional Roman way of life. Actually, Rome had long been exposed to Greek civilization, especially through commercial contact with the Greek cities of southern Italy and Sicily, called collectively Magna Graecia, but Roman society remained generally unaffected by these early Greek contacts. Roman subjection of the Greek cities on Italian soil, such as Tarentum and Rhegium in the early third century B.C.E., and the founding of Roman provinces in Sicily in 227 B.C.E. and in Greece itself in 197 B.C.E. made inevitable the Hellenization of Roman society. Greek works of art and Greek literary texts began flowing into the capital. Especially in the third century B.C.E., Greek war captives began to educate their masters in Greek ways and customs, and many Romans started to adopt Greek ways. Bilingualism in Greek and Latin became a political and cultural necessity. A famous statement by the Roman poet Horace in his *Epistles* (c. 20-15 B.C.E.; English translation, 1567; includes *Ars poetica*, c. 17 B.C.E.; *The Art of Poetry*) summarizes well the relationship of Greece to Rome: "Captive Greece took its rough victor captive and brought the arts to rustic Latium." In reality, the initial Roman reaction to Hellenism was a combination of admiration and distrust, best demonstrated by the attitudes of two second century B.C.E. statesmen, Cato the Censor (234-149 B.C.E.) and Scipio Aemilianus (185 or 184-129 B.C.E.). Cato the Censor spent most of his career advocating traditional Roman values and education and condemning Greek voluptuousness and duplicity. By contrast, Scipio Aemilianus—the conqueror of Carthage and adopted son of Scipio Africanus, the defeater of Hannibal—was a staunch Hellenophile and the leader of an intellectual group that included some of the outstanding Greeks and Romans of his day. Members of this "Scipionic circle" included the Greek historian Polybius, the Stoic Greek philosopher Panaetius of Rhodes, the Latin dramatist Terence, and the Latin satirist Gaius Lucilius. Later enthusiastic Hellenists included the Gracchi brothers. The resolution of this conflict was presaged by Cato the Censor himself, who

toward the end of his life took up the study of Greek.

The third and second centuries B.C.E. were also marked by dissemination of Greek philosophical ideas in Rome. The three popular Hellenistic schools—the Platonists, the Epicureans, and the Stoics—all sent representatives to Rome and all had their Roman advocates, but of the three, Stoicism, with its emphasis on virtue and endurance, proved to be most appealing to the Roman character. Except for a few attempts at philosophic poetry, the period was largely given to the assimilation of Greek philosophy; there were no noteworthy Roman attempts at philosophy, in either prose or poetry, until the first century B.C.E. By the time of Augustus, Greek philosophy had become completely assimilated, and it is nearly impossible to read a passage in Latin literature that does not reveal the influence of Greek philosophy in some form.

The earliest extant Latin literature is datable to the period just after the First Punic War, and it is perhaps not coincidental that the first known Latin author, Lucius Livius Andronicus, was a war captive from the Greek city of Tarentum in southern Italy. Indeed, all the Latin poets of the period came from conquered territory, and it is only in prose that a few native Roman authors are known. This early period of Latin literature was marked by the assimilation of Greek literary themes and genres into the Latin language and by the blending of these Greek types with the native Roman literary temperament and forms of expression. Indeed, while these earliest poetic attempts were mostly Latin translations or adaptations of Greek works, within one generation after Livius, Latin authors were putting a distinctively Roman imprint on the foreign literary forms which they had assimilated and Latin literature was launched on a life of its own. It is unfortunate that this early Latin literature, with a few exceptions, survives only in fragments; it was apparently read and admired by Romans for many generations, but its influence on later authors is difficult to gauge from its fragmentary state.

The earliest Roman prose appears at the time of the Punic Wars, and Greek influence is demonstrated by the fact that the first Romans to write history, Quintus Fabius Pictor and Lucius Cincius Alimentus, wrote in Greek. The first Roman to write history in Latin was

Cato the Censor, whose seven books of *Origines* (lost work, 168-149 B.C.E.) covered the history of Rome to 149 B.C.E. and were a landmark in Latin prose. Cato the Censor also demonstrated his skill in prose composition in several didactic works, including the extant *De agricultura* (c. 160 B.C.E.; *On Agriculture*, 1913), and in his speeches, some of which he published. Roman oratory, a native field of expression, was encouraged by Rome's political system and eventually fused with the Greek rhetorical tradition. The periodic prose of Cicero in the first century B.C.E. was the result.

The history of Latin poetry begins with a Latin translation of Homer's *Odyssey* (c. 725 B.C.E.; English translation, 1614) by the Tarentine Greek, Lucius Livius Andronicus (c. 284-c. 204 B.C.E.). Livius's *Odyssey*, in Saturnian verse, apparently originated as a school text and was quickly followed by adaptations of Greek comedies and tragedies which were actually produced in Rome and in which Livius introduced Greek meters into Latin. Greek quantitative meters were quite different from the apparently accentual, native Saturnine verse, and many Latin words would not fit the Greek quantitative patterns. However, within a generation, Greek meters had replaced the Saturnian as the normal poetic medium in Latin. Livius, who is often justly called the "founder of Latin literature," also composed some lyrics, about which little is now known.

Gnaeus Naevius (c. 270-c. 201 B.C.E.), an Italian from Campania, continued Livius's adaptations of Greek literature into Latin, but with a bit more originality in that he sometimes replaced Greek stories with Roman ones. This is true in drama, where he not only adapted Greek comedies to Latin but also composed *fabulae praetextae*, plays on historical Latin themes. It is also true in epic, where he produced the first original epic in Saturnian verse, *Bellum Punicum* (*The Punic War*). Thus began the nationalistic vein which became a near constant in later Latin literature. Naevius's career also shows another, more unfortunate link between poetry and politics in Rome: the personal risks with which the Latin political poet often was confronted. Naevius, who died in exile for offending in verse the powerful Metelli family, was but the first of many Latin poets to suffer political oppression.

While the history of Roman drama generally lies outside the scope of this essay, it should be mentioned that the trends begun by Livius and Naevius were continued by several generations of playwrights, including the extant comic authors Plautus (c. 254-184 B.C.E.) and Terence (c. 190-159 B.C.E.), as well as the tragedians Marcus Pacuvius (220-c. 130 B.C.E.) and Lucius Accius (170-c. 86 B.C.E.). Like their dramatic predecessors, none of these authors was from Latium, and all continued to produce adaptations of Greek originals or, more rarely, *fabulae praetextae*.

Drama in Rome was also important as a means of transmitting Greek culture to the plebeian class. While the other literary forms of the period were, for the most part, directed toward the educated, leisured classes, drama was intended for public performance, especially at religious and civic festivals, and hence introduced less educated Romans to the new, Hellenized Latin literature. The popular, oral literary forms also continued in this period. Although evidence is limited, these forms, too, probably became Hellenized, with Saturnian verse gradually giving way to Greek meters.

Another dramatist of the period warrants special mention here because of his prolific nondramatic output. Quintus Ennius (239-c. 169 B.C.E.) was from Calabria in southern Italy. In addition to at least twenty known tragedies (including one *fabula praetexta* titled *Rape of the Sabines*) and a few comedies, Ennius produced a major epic, *Annales* (first century B.C.E.; *Annals*, 1935), in eighteen books covering the history of Rome from Aeneas to Ennius's own day. Ennius's epic, which survives only in fragments, apparently owed much to the annalistic tradition in Rome, to the Greek epic genre, and to his precursor Naevius. One of Ennius's most significant contributions to the Latin epic was his use of dactylic hexameter, the traditional Greek epic meter, rather than Saturnian verse, which was never again used in a Latin epic. Besides the *Annals*, Ennius tried his hand at elegiac verse, as well as at several lost didactic works with philosophic themes: *Epicharmus*, a poem about the famous Sicilian Pythagorean, and *Euhemerus*, a work, perhaps in verse, on the well-known Greek rationalist. Ennius also wrote four books of satire. In the native Latin tradition of satiric medleys, these books were a miscellany of themes and meters.

Gaius Lucilius (c. 180-c. 102 B.C.E.), a Campanian and a member of the Scipionic circle, followed Ennius in writing thirty books of satires, also in mixed meters and themes, including political commentary and travel journals. Because the satires of Ennius and Lucilius represent a native Latin genre and inevitably influenced later writers such as Horace and Juvenal, their loss creates a most unfortunate lacuna in the history of Latin poetry.

The literature that arose in Rome in the mid-third century B.C.E. may have been stimulated primarily by outside influence, but it began a literary development which led directly to Vergil and Horace and which continued for more than fifteen hundred years. Rome's debt to Livius, Naevius, Ennius, and Lucilius is immeasurable.

LATE REPUBLICAN POETRY (100-31 B.C.E.)

The final decades of the Roman Republic were a tumultuous period politically and socially and an exciting period intellectually. It is indicative of the age that some of its most politically active figures, such as Caesar and Cicero, found the time to write, both in prose and in verse. While most of the surviving texts of the period are historical or political prose, the late Republic was not an age exclusively of politics or prose. There is evidence of a poetic movement, although most of the contemporary poetry has now been lost. It is generally impossible to separate the politics from the literature of the period, but such a blending of purposes was never really a literary flaw in Roman eyes. In the late Republic flourished some of Rome's most versatile authors, who were prominent politicians as well as writers skilled in both prose and verse. By the next generation, authors tended to limit their attention to either prose or poetry.

The period from 100 to 31 B.C.E. was a time of nearly constant warfare, both on the borders of the empire and, more seriously, within Italy itself. The political events of this period not only led to basic changes in Roman political and social structures but also became a subject for later Roman poetry (such as Lucan's *Bellum civile* (60-65 C.E.; *Pharsalia*, 1614). The basic problem was the inability of Republican institutions to satisfy the political ambitions of rival military men. The 80's

B.C.E. witnessed a bitter power struggle between two generals, Gaius Marius, a native of north Italy and victor of the Jurgurthan War, and Lucius Cornelius Sulla, a member of an old noble family and hero of the war against Mithradates in the East. The forces of both sides exercised such horrible reprisals against each other that the old noble families were severely decimated. After Marius's death in 85 B.C.E., the conservative Sulla ruled Rome as dictator from 82 to 79 B.C.E. and attempted to revive the Republican constitution by means of a program of aristocratic reforms, including restrictions on the powers of the tribunes and enlargement of the Senate by admission of individuals of equestrian rank and of Italian background.

Sulla's reforms were unsuccessful, however, and his confidence in the Republic was unwarranted. The political chaos of the 80's B.C.E. was only a foreshadowing of worse turmoil later in the century. Within a generation of Sulla's death, several ambitious generals once again were contending for power. Both Pompey the Great and Julius Caesar used their military careers—Pompey's in Spain and in the eastern Mediterranean, Caesar's in Gaul—to further their own political ambitions. By 49 B.C.E., Pompey and Caesar had thrown the Republic into a fatal civil war. Most of the old aristocratic families supported Pompey as champion of the Republic, but their cause was lost at the sea battle of Pharsalus in 48 B.C.E. Unlike Sulla, Caesar followed his victory with clemency toward his opponents, but his acceptance of an unprecedented dictatorship for life incited his assassination by desperate Republicans led by Cassius and Brutus in 44 B.C.E.

Caesar's death precipitated a period of even more violent unrest. Marcus Antonius, Caesar's trusted lieutenant, and Gaius Octaviaus (commonly known as Octavian), Caesar's grandnephew and adopted son, overcame mutual distrust only long enough to defeat Caesar's assassins, at Philippi in 42 B.C.E., before they turned on each other. The following decade was marked by another wave of proscriptions (including the death of the great orator Cicero), by confiscation of the property of political enemies, by civil war throughout the empire, and even by foreign incursions on the borders, especially by the feared Parthians in the East. The entire empire was in danger of disintegration.

For a time, it appeared that the empire would be divided between Octavian, who controlled the West, including Italy, and Antony, who ruled the East and had allied himself with Cleopatra, the Ptolemaic ruler of Egypt. Octavian's propaganda, however, making much of Antony's "orientalization" and of his liaison with Cleopatra, succeeded in swaying popular opinion, and in 31 B.C.E., Octavian defeated his rival in a sea battle at Actium.

Octavian's victory placed him in unquestioned control of the empire. For all practical purposes, the Republic was defunct, although Republican institutions, such as the Senate, were allowed to continue. Octavian, who took the name Caesar Augustus (the revered Caesar) after Actium, may have avoided *rex*, the Latin word for "king," and preferred the title *imperator* (general), but he was monarch in all but name. Augustus's political settlement introduced a period of peace and tranquillity which contrasted starkly with the terrors of the Republic's final decades.

By the first century B.C.E., the social changes caused by the expansion of the Roman Empire and Rome's contacts with the Greeks had become nearly complete. Rome, no longer the society of farmers with traditional values that she had been in the third century B.C.E., was wealthy and cosmopolitan. Roman society had also become more Italian in background and Greek in culture.

Indeed, probably the most significant social development in the first century B.C.E. was the social unification of Italy. Bound politically to Rome since the fourth century B.C.E., the Italian tribes were thoroughly Latinized by the first century B.C.E., when their demand for political enfranchisement, climaxed by the so-called "Italian Wars" of 91-83 B.C.E., was a vivid indication of their assimilation into Roman political society. Italians in this period came to play visible roles in Roman politics and letters. Sulla's reorganization of the Senate increased the number of Italian senators. Marius and Cicero both hailed from the same north Italian town. Sallust the historian was from Sabine country, and Catullus was a native of Verona, in what was then called Transpadane Gaul. It took the Italian Wars to force the Roman ruling class to recognize the fact, but by the first century B.C.E. the distinction between Roman and Italian was a fine one. In fact, Latin was,

by this time, rapidly replacing the local Italian dialects and was beginning to become the language of trade throughout the western Mediterranean.

At the same time, Greek language and literature had achieved a permanent place in Roman society and were considered an essential part of a good education. Indeed, it became fashionable for Romans to travel to Greece to complete their education. Both Cicero and Caesar, for example, studied rhetoric at Rhodes. The effect of Greek philosophic training on nearly every important figure of the period—including that of Stoicism on Cato the Younger and of Epicureanism on Caesar and Lucretius—is also evident.

Another important change in Roman life was the liberation of Roman women, who traditionally had no legal or political rights and were absolutely bound to a male guardian. About the time of the Punic Wars, the status of women began to change, and they won increasing freedom to own property, to become educated, and to move about in society. While women never gained the right of suffrage in Rome, they did manage a great amount of indirect political influence. For example, Cornelia, the daughter of Scipio Africanus and mother of the Gracchi brothers, was the leader of an intellectual salon in the mid-second century B.C.E., while in the first century B.C.E., Clodia, the sister of the politician Publius Clodius, became the powerful leader of a notorious social circle and was perhaps the inspiration for Catullus's Lesbia.

At the same time, marriages became a tool of political alliance, and women were divorced and married as the political wind changed. Pompey's marriage to Caesar's daughter Julia was originally a sign of *amicitia*, or "friendship," between the two leaders. Apparently, this marriage was an unexpected success, and Julia's untimely death is usually cited as a major cause of the rift between her father and her husband. Antony's divorce from Octavian's sister Octavia, in order to marry Cleopatra, led to the Battle of Actium. Nevertheless, while women obviously played significant roles in the political and social life of the first century B.C.E., it would be at least another generation before a first female voice entered Latin literature.

Wealth and education led to more sophisticated and ostentatious social intercourse. The wealthy nobility led lives of luxury, with fancy city residences and huge country villas. Their farms and wealth were overseen by others, and they could devote themselves to politics, partying, and literature. The uncertain political situation and the fear of confiscation or even proscription fostered a life-style of gay abandon and recklessness. Traditional Roman *gravitas* (seriousness) gave way to a sophisticated sense of *urbanitas* (urbanity) and *humanitas* (culture), evident in both the life and the literature of the period.

The succession of proscriptions and wars during the century meant the loss of nearly an entire generation of young Romans. That Roman letters flourished as much as they did during this period is a testament to the tenacity of the Roman people. One of the most pathetic images of this determination is that of the elderly scholar Marcus Terentius Varro (116-27 B.C.E.) pursuing his studies in Rome even though his villa and books had been confiscated by Antony.

The literature of the late Republic was directed almost exclusively toward the educated classes and is for the most part intensely political. It was an age of political and historical prose written by men intimately involved in the politics of the day. It was also an age of verse. While only the poetry of Lucretius (c. 98-55 B.C.E.) and of Catullus (c. 85-c. 54 B.C.E.) survives from this period, nearly all the contemporary prose authors, including Cicero (106-43 B.C.E.) and Julius Caesar (100-44 B.C.E.), also composed in verse.

By far the most famous prose writer of the period was Cicero, whose rhetorical talents early fostered political ambitions. Although he did attain the coveted consulship in 63 B.C.E., Cicero's career was generally overshadowed by the conflict between Pompey the Great and Caesar, and in his later years he was left to direct his energies toward philosophy and letters. Cicero's extant corpus is extensive and includes fifty-seven public speeches, several books of epistolary correspondence, and several treatises on politics, rhetoric, and philosophy. Cicero is particularly admired for his periodic prose and was a pioneer in adapting the Latin language to Greek philosophic concepts.

Cicero was also a poet in his own right. He translated several Hellenistic Greek poems into Latin, wrote a short poem in hexameters on the general Marius,

and even composed an autobiographical epic titled *De consulatu suo* (*On His Consulship*). While his poetic output survives only in fragments, Cicero did make a lasting imprint on Latin poetry as the probable editor of the poet Lucretius.

By contrast to Cicero's elaborate sentence structures, the prose of Caesar is concise and direct. His extant works are political commentaries, *Comentarii de bello Gallico* (52-51 B.C.E.) and *Comentarii de bello civili* (45 B.C.E.; collectively translated as *Commentaries*, 1609). He also wrote speeches, letters, treatises on grammar and astronomy, a tragedy, and even love poems, all of which have been lost. That the most significant and active statesman of his day found the time for such a diverse literary output is an indication of the high degree of culture which Roman society had achieved.

Other historical texts of the period also demonstrate the pervasiveness of contemporary politics in Roman letters. Sallust (86-35 B.C.E.) served Caesar in Africa during the Civil War and spent his remaining years enjoying a luxurious estate in Rome and writing history. Abandoning the annalistic method favored by earlier Latin historians, Sallust wrote several thematic histories, two of which are extant, *Bellum Catilinae* (c. 42 B.C.E.; *The Conspiracy of Catiline*, 1608) and *Bellum Jurgurthum* (c. 40 B.C.E.; *The War of Jugurtha*, 1608). In both works, Sallust demonstrates his Caesarian and anti-Republican biases. Another historian of the period, Cornelius Nepos (c. 100-c. 25 B.C.E.), wrote a universal history as well as a collection of Greek and Roman biographies, some of which survive. While Nepos appears to have avoided political bias by emphasizing Greek or noncontemporary subjects, even here politics intrudes with Nepos's juxtaposition of Cato the Younger to great generals of the past. Like Cicero and Caesar, Nepos composed some poetry and received the dedication of Catullus's book of poems.

The scholar Varro (116-27 B.C.E.) perhaps best shows the bond between prose and poetry in the first century B.C.E. A prolific writer and scholar in the Alexandrian tradition, Varro is known to have composed numerous antiquarian and technical works, including the extant *De lingua Latina* (n.d.; *On the Latin Language*, 1938) and *De re rustica* (35 B.C.E.; *On Agriculture*, 1912), and he is believed to have been an early editor of the plays of Plautus. As a poet, Varro was best known in antiquity for 150 books of *Saturae Menippeae* (Menippean satires). Unlike the early satires of Ennius and Lucilius, which were in verse, Varro's apparently were modeled on the philosophic dialogues of the third century B.C.E. Greek Cynic Menippus of Gadara and were a mixture of verse and prose. Varro thus introduced into Latin a special satiric form, the prose-poetry medley, which would be explored by Seneca and Petronius and eventually carried into the medieval Latin tradition.

Only two poetic works survive from the late Republic: Lucretius's epic poem *De rerum natura* (c. 60 B.C.E.; *On the Nature of Things*, 1682) and Catullus's *Carmina* (poems). Both works show strong Hellenistic influence. Lucretius composed his didactic epic based on the philosophy of the late fourth century B.C.E. Greek Epicurus, while Catullus wrote a collection of short, mostly erotic poems in mixed meters according to Alexandrian poetic standards. There were many other poets of the period whose works do not survive. Indeed, Catullus was part of a poetic movement in Rome calling itself the Neoterics or *novi poetae* (new poets), who modeled their works on the Alexandrian standards of brevity, obscurity, and skill. Besides Catullus, other known *novi poetae* included Varro of Atax, Gaius Helvius Cinna (commonly known as Cinna), and Gaius Licinius Calvus. Without the knowledge that these poets flourished in the first century B.C.E., one might be tempted to consider Lucretius and Catullus anomalies of their age.

In a sense, both Lucretius and Catullus sought escape from their intensely political and dangerous age through their poetry. Lucretius appears to have isolated himself from politics and to have absorbed himself in Epicureanism, a much misunderstood philosophy which taught that the true goal of life was a pleasure achieved through *ataraxia* (nondisturbedness). A true Epicurean would not lead a life of luxury and debauchery, but rather would sever himself from the hectic world and lead a life of simplicity in the country. Epicureanism did not always appeal to the Roman mentality as much as other Greek philosophies, such as Stoicism, but it did seem to offer some attraction in the chaotic first century B.C.E. Caesar had a reputation as an Epicurean, and Cicero is said to have edited Lucretius's *On the Nature of Things*.

Unlike Lucretius, Catullus apparently did not avoid a political career but attempted unsuccessfully to make his fortune as a member of the provincial staff of a governor named Memmius, who may have been the same person to whom Lucretius addressed his epic. Catullus responded to his age not by losing himself in philosophy but by abandoning himself to his art and to his love for a woman called "Lesbia" in his poems. His poetry is intensely personal, sometimes obscene, often containing bitter invective. While such contemporary figures as Caesar and Nepos are named in Catullus's poems, they are mentioned only in passing. Catullus's focus is not on the momentous events taking place in the outside world but on the intensely personal world of his own feelings. Like Lucretius, Catullus was an escapist, and it is sometimes difficult to remember that both Lucretius and Catullus were contemporaries of Cicero and Caesar. However, despite their differences, the poetry and prose of the first century B.C.E. complement each other and together paint a vivid picture of a very turbulent age.

AUGUSTAN AGE POETRY (31 B.C.E.-14 C.E.)

Latin literature was approaching maturity in the first century B.C.E. just as the Republic was collapsing. The reign of Augustus (27 B.C.E.-14 C.E.) introduced a period of prolonged peace, a new political order, and the cresting of Latin literature. During this short period flourished such outstanding Latin authors as Livy in history, Vergil in the epic, and Horace in satire and lyric poetry.

The new literature was a mirror of a new age. Relief after the horrors of civil war and pride in the reestablished Roman state under Augustus permeate the age and its literature. These feelings of relief and pride were justified: It is a tribute to Augustus's military, political, and administrative skills that Rome did not merely survive the chaos of the first century B.C.E. but entered the next century with relatively settled territorial boundaries and a revised system of government which worked, with minor modifications, for several hundred years.

A major principle of the new Augustan order was

continuity. Far from eliminating Republican institutions and practices, Augustus maintained and encouraged them. The population of the Senate, severely diminished by a generation of civil wars, was buttressed by an influx of members from Italy and from the equestrian rank. Augustus's own powers were consistently defined in Republican terms; he was, at different times, *imperator* (general), consul, tribune, and *pontifex maximus* (chief priest). Thus, he sought to establish the notion that the Republic had been restored, not destroyed, under his rule.

A second Augustan principle was security. Augustus's defeat of Antony at Actium introduced a period of unprecedented peace within the boundaries of the empire. It would be nearly one hundred years before this Pax Romana (Roman Peace) was broken by a serious internal conflict. The problem of control of the armies was temporarily solved by making Augustus commander in chief and by fostering military allegiance to the emperor alone. During Augustus's reign, the empire made major territorial additions, especially along its northern boundaries, which provided more secure and natural limits.

As a result of this sudden political security in the Mediterranean, the empire entered a period of unprecedented prosperity. Agriculture and commerce flourished, especially in the provinces, and foreign trade increased significantly. Roman traders were making contacts in areas as far away as Britain, Scandinavia, India, and Mongolia. Urban life expanded and improved not only in Rome itself but also in other centers of population and trade. It was not long before municipal centers, constructed upon the Roman model with forums, public baths, and theaters, could be found throughout the empire. For several centuries, the Roman Empire had expanded rapidly; Augustus ushered in a long-overdue period of assimilation.

Augustan policy included a program of social legislation. Deeply concerned about a population decline among old Roman families and committed to restoring ancient Roman virtues, Augustus enacted a series of marriage laws which discouraged celibacy, adultery, and childlessness. While not very effective in countering either the population decline or the lax morals and high living to which wealthy Romans had become accustomed, Augustus's marriage laws reflected an interest in the past and its virtues which can be seen also in the literature of the period, especially in Vergil and Livy.

Indeed, the relationship between literature and public policy was particularly close in the Augustan Age. Augustus was a master of propaganda, as his earlier conflict with Antony demonstrated, and he was vividly conscious of the power of literature to sway public opinion. As a result, he encouraged a system of literary patronage which was based on the ancient patron-client relationship and which had been applied to letters as early as the late Republic (as in the relationship of Memmius to Lucretius and, perhaps, Catullus) or even the early Republic (as in the links between Scipio and the poets Terence and Lucilius). Under the emperors, such a patronage system became a political and literary necessity. Augustus needed to control the literary output of Rome, and authors needed powerful patrons to protect them from official disfavor.

Augustus's circle included a number of patrons and clients. Marcus Valerius Messalla, one of Augustus's generals, was the patron of Albius Tibullus (c. 55-c. 19 B.C.E.). Another member of his circle was his niece, the poet Sulpicia (fl. late first century B.C.E.), the only feminine voice in ancient Latin literature. Gaius Asinius Pollio (76 B.C.E.-5 C.E.), a general, a historian, and a poet in his own right, "discovered" Vergil (70-19 B.C.E.), who later came under the influence of Gaius Maecenas, Augustus's wealthy adviser. Maecenas was also the patron of the poets Horace (65-8 B.C.E.) and Sextus Propertius (c. 57-48 to c. 16-2 B.C.E.), and probably did more than any other individual in the Augustan Age to encourage letters. The emperor himself also showed personal interest in the works of Vergil, Horace, and Livy.

On the other hand, the dangers for a poet in an absolute monarchy were very real, as was proved by the careers of two Augustan poets, Gallus (69-26 B.C.E.) and Ovid (43 B.C.E.-17 C.E.), both of whom suffered for their indiscretions against Augustus. Gallus, the probable inventor of the Latin love elegy, was a lieutenant of Augustus in Egypt but was forced to commit suicide because of his administrative incompetence and also, it was hinted, because of his scandalous poetry. Although the cause of Ovid's exile to Tomis in 8 C.E. is also uncertain, it is widely believed that he was banished for his poetry. His *Ars amatoria* (c. 2 B.C.E.; *Art of Love*, 1612) is sometimes cited as the decisive indiscretion, flaunting Augustus's program of moral restoration.

As in the late Republic, Augustan authors wrote primarily for a very limited circle of educated and cultured Romans. There is ample evidence of public recitations and performances, often in the presence of the emperor. Authors of the period thus knew their primary audience intimately. At the same time, however, these writers experienced immediate success and popularity outside the court circle. That lower-class Romans knew these writers and their works is evidenced by graffiti in the ill-fated city of Pompeii, destroyed by an eruption of Vesuvius in 79 C.E.; the walls of Pompeii show quotations from Vergil, Ovid, and even Tibullus. Apparently, the writings of the Augustan Age quickly became standard texts, read by all literate Romans.

The consequence of this patronage system was a curious mixture of censorship, freedom of expression, nationalistic themes, and sophisticated literature. Encouraged to express certain themes and avoid others, writers were permitted free rein within these limits. Both patron and writer agreed that the duty of art was both aesthetic and utilitarian. According to Horace's *Ars poetica* (c. 17 B.C.E.; *The Art of Poetry*, 1567), a poet had to express himself *utile et dulce*, "usefully and sweetly." If one were able to create a refined piece of literature that was also intensely nationalistic, this was seen to improve rather than to detract from its literary quality. As a result of such restrictions, the literature of the Augustan Age may lack some of the vibrancy and excitement of the Republican period, but it achieves instead a refinement and polish that blend poetic expression and nationalistic sentiment in perfect proportion. For example, the *Satires* (35 B.C.E., 30 B.C.E.; English translation, 1567) of Horace are devoid of the biting political commentaries which were apparently commonplace in Horace's predecessor Lucilius, but what Horace lacks in what the modern would call "satire," he compensates for with the polish and good humor that he applies to the traditional Roman concept of satire as a medley.

While the late Republic was an age of great prose and poetry, the Augustan Age was, with the brilliant exception of Livy, an age of only outstanding poetry. Certainly, the political climate was not conducive to great oratory such as Cicero's, and history, especially contemporary history, was a delicate subject. Pollio's history of the civil wars conspicuously ended with Philippi, and even the 142 volumes of *Ab urbe condita libri* (c. 26 B.C.E.-15 C.E.; *The History of Rome*, 1600), by Livy (59 B.C.E.-17 C.E.) were published serially over a span of forty years; Livy did not reach the dreaded civil wars until late in Augustus's reign. The only other major prose text to survive from the period is *De architectura* (on architecture), a practical treatise by Marcus Vitruvius Pollio (fl. first century B.C.E.).

As in the earlier periods of Latin literature, nearly all the writers of the Augustan Age, both in prose and in poetry, were of Italian background. In fact, Tibullus is one of the few Latin writers who was actually born in Latium. By the time of Augustus, Latin literature had become, without question, a literature not merely of Rome, its literary center, but of all Italy.

In addition to the well-known poets of this period, especially Vergil, Horace, and Ovid, there were a great many other contemporary authors whose works are mostly lost. Works by two minor poets of the period survive, the *Cynegetica* of Grattius, a didactic poem on hunting, and the *Astronomica* of Manilius, a similar work on the stars. Both of these poems are modeled on the *Georgics* (c. 37-29 B.C.E.; English translation, 1589) of Vergil and follow a didactic tradition that can be traced back to Alexandria.

Several characteristics dominate the poetry of the Augustan Age. High poetic standards and careful composition were carried to an extreme. Vergil was a particularly slow craftsman and was so cautious that he requested on his deathbed that the unfinished *Aeneid* (c. 29-19 B.C.E.; English translation, 1553) be burned. Horace, too, sought perfection of form, especially in his *Odes* (23 B.C.E., 13 B.C.E.; English translation, 1621).

A second important characteristic of the period was genre innovation. Poets showed a definite inclination toward genres which had not yet been perfected in Latin: Vergil's *Eclogues* (43-37 B.C.E.; English translation, 1575) imitated the bucolic *Idylls* of the Hellenistic

Greek poet Theocritus and represent the center of a great European pastoral tradition, while his *Georgics* combined the Hellenistic type of didactic poetry with Roman love of the countryside. Horace's *Epodes* (c. 30 B.C.E.; English translation, 1638) and *Odes* were conscious and successful attempts to introduce into Latin the many meters of Greek lyric. Horace's *Epistles* (c. 20-15 B.C.E.; (English translation, 1567) and Ovid's *Heroides* (before 8 C.E.; English translation, 1567) and *Epistulae ex Ponto* (after 8 C.E.; *Letters from Pontus*, 1639) were all poetic variations on the prose letter or sermon. Ovid was also innovative with his *Fasti* (c. 8 C.E.; English translation, 1859), a poetic calendar of Roman religious events, and his *Metamorphoses* (c. 8 C.E.; English translation, 1567), a thematic rather than heroic epic based upon tales in which there is a change of form or shape. Finally, poets of this period, especially Tibullus, Propertius, and Ovid, created a new poetic genre, the Latin love elegy, which applied the Greek elegiac couplet to the theme of love.

Epicureanism is a third characteristic of much Augustan poetry. Vergil was taught by an Epicurean named Siro, and this philosophy permeates his work, especially the *Georgics*. The goal of pleasure in a secluded villa is a constant Epicurean theme of Horace, and Tibullus linked the same Epicurean principle with passion for Delia, his mistress, to create an ideal existence, a golden age.

Finally, Augustan poetry is distinguished by a nationalism combining patriotic feeling for Rome's past and for Augustus's settlements with a love of the Italian countryside. This combination can be seen in the *Eclogues*, where Vergil's allusions to the confiscation of his own farm are contrasted with his relief in the new peace instituted by Augustus. The *Georgics*, too, are filled not only with love of Italy but also with praise of Augustus as the savior of the countryside from the ravages of war. The *Aeneid*, the great national epic of Rome, uses the story of the Trojan Aeneas, his mission to settle in Italy, and his love for the Carthaginian Dido to praise the old Roman virtues of duty and *pietas* and to herald Rome's future greatness. With the figure of Aeneas, a hero of Greek mythology who settles in Italy, Vergil not only praises the Roman past but also symbolically unites Greek with Roman culture. Vergil's conscious imitation of Homer's *Iliad* (c. 750 B.C.E.; English translation, 1611) and *Odyssey* (c. 725 B.C.E.; English translation, 1614) in the *Aeneid* heralds a pride in Latin poetry that had finally reached a level of equality with its Greek models.

Nationalism can also be seen in Horace, especially in the *Odes*, where Augustus is frequently praised, and in Ovid, whose *Metamorphoses* climaxes with the apotheosis of Julius Caesar. In general, nationalism is not a dominant theme in the love elegy, which tends to avoid the outside world of politics in favor of the internal world of love and poetry, although Propertius, especially in his last book of *Elegies* (after 16 B.C.E.; English translation, 1854), sought to transform the genre, abandoning the love theme in favor of etiological stories praising the ancient city of Rome.

Augustan poetry, then, was the perfect combination of all the best features of Latin literature: the native Latin genius and character, Hellenistic literature and thought, and careful craftsmanship. The literature of this period, together with that of the last decades of the Roman Republic, represents the greatest literary achievements in Latin, and, for this reason, the approximately eighty-year period lasting from the mid-70's B.C.E. until the death of Augustus in 14 C.E., from the poetry of Lucretius to the works of Ovid, is often justly called Rome's Golden Age of literature.

SILVER AGE POETRY (C.E. 14-138)

The period usually referred to as the Silver Age of Latin literature is bracketed by the accession of Tiberius in 14 C.E. and the death of Hadrian in 138 C.E., and covers the reigns of thirteen very different emperors. The feeling of security created during the reign of Augustus did not last long after his death, in large part because the problems of succession had not yet been satisfactorily solved. While Augustus's four immediate successors, Tiberius, Caligula, Claudius, and Nero, were all his descendants or those of his third wife, Livia, none of the Julio-Claudian emperors, as they are called, felt completely secure on the throne. Their reigns were marked by fear of political intrigue, widespread use of imperial informants, and summary executions, usually of men of senatorial rank. Two of the emperors themselves died violently.

The political nadir of the period was the year 69 C.E., the infamous Year of the Four Emperors, which witnessed a complete breakdown in imperial control and the violent deaths of three emperors in succession. The fourth, Vespasian, restored a measure of stability and established a new "Flavian" dynasty with his succession by his two sons. His second son, Domitian, however, abused his power and was assassinated in 96 C.E. The last emperors of this period, Nerva, Trajan, and Hadrian, all avoided succession difficulties by the ancient Roman custom of *adoptio* (adoption), whereby each ruler chose his successor on the basis not of heredity but of ability. This system of succession established a series of "five good emperors" which lasted nearly a century.

The government became more openly monarchical after Augustus's rule, and the nominal powers of the Senate were gradually eroded. Although the body continued to meet, it did so increasingly to listen to the emperor's decrees rather than to enact its own legislation. The "swan song" of senatorial power occurred with the death of Domitian, when the Senate freely selected Nerva as emperor. Similarly, plebeian powers became extinct. The popular assemblies last met under the reign of Nerva. Nostalgia for the Republic and its freedoms became a theme for some writers and leading men of the period, but sporadic plots to replace despots with more enlightened rulers, especially in the reigns of Nero and Domitian, were aborted. The imperial system was too well established by this time for true Republican government to be restored.

By the reign of Hadrian, the Roman Empire had reached its farthest extent, with the addition of Britain under Claudius and Dacia (modern-day Romania) and Armenia under Trajan. A noteworthy trend of the period was the expansion of the Roman franchise outside Italy, beginning with Spain under Vespasian. Indeed, Spain's complete assimilation into the empire is demonstrated by the fact that the province produced not only the first non-Italian emperor, Trajan, but also most of the major writers of the period, including the two Senecas, Lucan, Quintilian, and Martial.

In general, the first century C.E. was a time of peace and prosperity within the borders of the empire, of increasing urbanization throughout the provinces, and of a growing interest in education. The growth in the number of schools and libraries, both in Italy and in the provinces, was considerable during this period, and this educational trend was perhaps the distinguishing characteristic of the age.

To be sure, Roman society had always been interested in education. In its earliest period, Roman education focused primarily on domestic and agricultural concerns and on traditional values such as discipline. With the introduction of Greek culture on a large scale, during the Punic Wars, education by Greek masters became commonplace. Gradually, there developed a three-tiered system, similar to the grammar-high-school-university sequence, in which a Roman youth was first taught his letters and introduced to classical texts by a *litterator*; then advanced to a *grammaticus*, who taught more than mere grammar, emphasizing oral and written exercises designed to increase the student's logical and compositional skills; and finally worked under a *rhetor*, who prepared his pupils for public life by instruction in deliberative and forensic skills. The surviving *Controversiae* (English translation, 1900) and *Suasoriae* (*Declamations*, 1974) of Seneca the Elder (c. 55 B.C.E.-c. 39 C.E.), are good examples of the kind of rhetorical exercises such students would pursue. Even after the fall of the Republic, the study of law and especially of oratory was the goal of most Roman education. Both Ovid and Propertius were educated to be lawyers, and, although they eventually abandoned the law for poetry, the effect of rhetorical studies on their poetry is evident in their language and forms of expression.

This educational system was privately financed and administered until the second century C.E., when there was a noticeable growth of governmental involvement in education. Vespasian fixed an annual salary for rhetoricians; Trajan financed the public education of five thousand poor boys; Hadrian introduced retirement pay for teachers and founded schools throughout the provinces. By the reign of Antoninus Pius (138-161), there is evidence that every municipality in the empire had its own educational staff.

Men of letters no longer had to rely for a livelihood solely on the whim of rich patrons, on public recitals, or on wealthy students. A formalized system of education, well on its way to being established in the second century C.E., meant a more secure position for scholars and a very favorable literary climate. An example of this system at work is found in the career of Spaniard Quintilian (c. 35-c. 96 C.E.), whom Vespasian salaried as a professor of rhetoric and whose extant *Institutio oratoria* (c. 95 C.E.; *On the Education of an Orator*, 1856; better known as *Institutio oratoria*) is a valuable record, not only of contemporary rhetorical education but also of literary criticism.

Many writers of the Silver Age also held prominent political positions. Seneca the Younger was tutor and adviser to Nero between 49 and 62 C.E.; the poet Silius Italicus was an informer under Nero, the last Neronian consul in 65 C.E., and proconsul in Asia under Vespasian; Pliny the Younger served in various offices under Nero, Domitian, and Nerva, and as governor of the province of Bithynia under Trajan, with whom he maintained a correspondence which is still extant. The two great historians of the period, Tacitus and Suetonius, both held significant political offices under Trajan, the former as governor of Asia and the latter as master of imperial correspondence.

The Silver Age also held its dangers for writers. Seneca the Younger spent eight years of exile under Claudius, and both he and his nephew, the poet Lucan, were forced to commit suicide under Nero. Both men probably suffered more for their political positions, but their literary creations certainly did not help their causes. The satirist Juvenal is also said to have endured a period of banishment during the reign of Domitian, allegedly because of his lampoons.

The nationalistic themes of the Golden Age receded into the background in the Silver Age, which emphasized instead individualistic feelings. Writers such as Seneca and Pliny the Younger in prose and Persius, Juvenal, and Martial in poetry were generally more interested in presenting their personal views than in praising Rome. As a rule, poets forsook nationalistic themes for the safety of the distant past and mythology. Silius Italicus (c. 25-100 C.E.) wrote an epic, *Punica* (English translation, 1933), about the second Punic war, and Statius (between 40 and 45 to c. 96 C.E.) composed the *Thebais* (c. 90 C.E.; *Thebiad*, 1767), about the War of the Seven against Thebes. Gaius Valerius

Flaccus (fl. first century C.E.) wrote an *Argonautica* (English translation, 1863) on the adventures of Jason and the Argonauts. Only Lucan (39-65 C.E.) dared a riskier political epic in his *Pharsalia*, which took as its subject the defeat of Pompey by Caesar. The Republican sympathies that Lucan projected in this epic were undoubtedly a factor in the poet's forced suicide under Nero.

Stoicism also became a very important theme in the literature and thought of the period. The list of Stoic writers of the Silver Age is impressive: Persius, Lucan, and Juvenal in poetry; Seneca, the elder Pliny, and Tacitus in prose. It was not long after this period that the Stoic Marcus Aurelius became emperor.

The men who were emperors from 14 C.E. to 138 C.E. were, as a rule, well educated and often writers and poets themselves. Tiberius was a friend of Messalla, Tibullus's patron, and wrote some poetry of his own. Both Tiberius and Claudius are said to have composed memoirs, and Claudius's brother Germanicus (15 B.C.E.-19 C.E.) was a talented and prolific writer of Greek comedies, elegiac epigrams in both Latin and Greek, and astronomical didactic poems. The emperor Nero, Germanicus's grandson, also professed vainly to write poetry and produced a variety of short verse, tragic monologues, and an epic on the city of Troy. Vespasian was well educated in Greek literature, could quote Homer fluently, and wrote his own memoirs; both of his sons were poets. Domitian supported public poetic competitions and was a friend of the poet Statius. Trajan encouraged the important writers of his day, including Pliny and the Greek authors Dio Chrysostom and Plutarch, and founded the largest library in Rome, the Basilica Ulpia. Hadrian, a Hellenophile who also wrote some Latin verse, probably did more than any of his predecessors to encourage art and letters, and his reign coincided with a revival of Greek literature in the second century C.E., including such authors as Plutarch and Lucian.

The literature of the Silver Age, very much the product of this educated environment, displays a consciousness that Latin literature had already reached a pinnacle of literary expression in the Golden Age. The influence of rhetoric and of Augustan literature was very strong. Rhetorical training made the Silver Age author emphasize artificiality, cleverness, literary convention, and, to a certain extent, encyclopedic learning. At the same time, imitation of the classics of the Golden Age became a common feature. "Vergilianism" is strong in such Silver Age poets as Persius, Lucan, Silius, and Statius. Poetic expressions and vocabulary also invaded Silver Age prose; the poetic *senium*, for example, replaced the prose *senectum* as the word for "old age" in Seneca.

Two major prose authors of the period were also active in poetic fields. Besides extensive extant philosophical, epistolary, and dramatic writings, Seneca the Younger (c. 4 B.C.E.-65 C.E.) composed elegiac and lyric poems, some of which survive in the *Latin Anthology*. Also often attributed to Seneca is *Apocolocyntosis divi Claudii* (c. 54 C.E.; *The Deification of Claudius*, 1614), a biting satire on the deification of the late emperor. This work was written partly in prose and partly in verse, in the tradition of Menippean satire employed earlier by the Republican satirist Lucilius. Another example of the prose-poetry medley is the partly extant *Satyricon* (c. 60 C.E.; *The Satyricon*, 1694) of Petronius. Both the *Apocolocyntosis* and the *Satyricon* serve as a reminder that the modern divisions of prose and poetry were not always fixed in the ancient world.

Another major prose author of the Silver Age who also wrote poetry was Pliny the Younger (c. 61-c. 113 C.E.), whose uncle and adopted father, Pliny the Elder, was a natural historian. Pliny is known today mostly for his extensive correspondence in nine books, but he also composed elegiac, lyric, and epic poems, and even a Greek tragedy, all lost. Pliny was also part of an important literary circle that included the poets Silius Italicus and Martial and the prose authors Frontinus, Tacitus, and Suetonius.

The African historian and rhetorician Florus (fl. 100-130 C.E.) may also have been a poet, since several poems in a variety of meters survive under his name. Florus is best remembered for his extant *Epitome bellorum omnium annorum DCC* (n.d.; *Epitome of Roman History*, 1852), a summary of Livy's histories. He may also have been the author of the *Perviligium Veneris* (vigil of Venus), a short religious poem in trochaic tetrameter that is often considered one of the loveliest Latin poems.

The most popular poetic forms of the period were satire and epic. In addition to the Menippean satires of Seneca and Petronius noted above, the Silver Age produced two outstanding verse satirists: the Stoic Persius (34-62 C.E.) and Juvenal (c. 60-c. 130 C.E.). Like their great predecessor Horace, Persius and Juvenal wrote their satires in hexameters. While the poems of the severe Persius and the bitter Juvenal are quite different in tone, both project the strong moralistic message traditionally characteristic of Roman satire.

The Spanish epigrammatist Martial (c. 38-41 to c. 130 C.E.) may also be listed with the satirists Persius and Juvenal. Although technically he wrote not satires but epigrams, short poems in mixed meters, Martial presents in his poems a critical picture of Roman society which the modern world, at least, would call satiric. In his career, Martial may have intersected with the great figures of the Silver Age. Critics speculate that in his youth, he may have been a member of the literary circle of his fellow Spaniards Seneca and Lucan; in later life, he was a friend of Pliny and, perhaps, Juvenal. Martial's poetry not only shows the influence of the Roman satiric and Greek epigrammatic traditions but also owes a debt to earlier Roman poets, especially to Catullus and Ovid.

The epic poets of the Silver Age can be divided into two groups: those, such as Valerius Flaccus and Silius Italicus, who wrote only in this genre, and those such as Lucan and Statius, whose poetic output was more diverse. In addition to his extant *Pharsalia*, Lucan produced a variety of works now lost, including the following in verse: *Adlocutio ad Pollam* (address to Polla), *Iliacon* (Troy), *Catachthonion*, about a descent into the underworld, and *Silvae*, a collection of miscellaneous poems. Lucan's *Epistulae ex Campania* (letters from Campania), in prose, has also been lost. The Neapolitan poet Statius, a younger contemporary of Lucan, also produced a large collection of *Silvae*, in addition to his epics.

Two other poets are usually dated to the early Silver Age and further demonstrate the diverse poetic output of the period: Titus Calpurnius Siculus (fl. first century C.E.), whose eleven extant *Eclogues* modeled on the Vergilian type were probably written during the reign of Nero; and Phaedrus (c. 15 B.C.E.-c. 55 C.E.), a freed

Thracian slave from the imperial household who published verse fables in the Aesopian tradition during the reigns of Tiberius and Caligula.

Despite an often oppressive political environment, then, the poets of the Silver Age, generally well educated and well versed in earlier Latin literature, continued the prolific and polished output begun in the Golden Age of the late Republic and of Augustus. The traditional label Silver Age suggests an inferiority to the Golden Age of which even Silver Age poets themselves were aware, but, despite their conscious imitation of their great predecessors, there is much life, ingenuity, and originality in their poetry. Juvenal and Martial, for example, are usually ranked with Horace as Rome's greatest satirists, and Lucan and Statius display poetic skill that has been much admired and influential in later periods. The Latin poetry of the Silver Age, then, is an eloquent testimony to the vigor and intelligence of Roman life and letters in the first and early second centuries C.E.

LATE ANTIQUITY (138-476)

After the reign of Hadrian, Latin poetry came to a virtual standstill until the early fourth century C.E. Once again, the history of Latin literature was strongly influenced by developments in the field of Greek letters, for this long poetic silence in Latin can be attributed, at least in part, to a renaissance in Greek prose literature which was carried into Latin.

The revival of Greek letters that began under Hadrian continued to flourish through the third century C.E. and produced several important Greek prose works: the histories of Appian (c. 95-c. 165) and of Dio Cassius (c. 150-c. 235 C.E.); the essays of Aristides (117-c. 181); the satires of Lucian (c. 120-c. 180); the works of the Neoplatonic philosopher Plotinus (205-270), and even the Stoic writings of the emperor Marcus Aurelius (121-180). This Greek Second Sophistic movement, as it is called, developed a style emphasizing rhetorical features and imitation of Attic Greek texts from the fourth century B.C.E.

The Second Sophistic's counterpart in Latin was *elocutio novella* (new speech), inspired by the African *rhetor* Marcus Cornelius Fronto (c. 100-c. 166). One of Marcus Aurelius's tutors, and later an epistolary corre-

spondent with the emperor, Fronto wrote speeches and letters using vocabulary and expressions from early Republican writers and from contemporary spoken Latin. Where writers of the Silver Age had imitated those of the Golden, Fronto and his followers sought their stylistic models in the Latin of Plautus. Consequently, works employing the *elocutio novella* are often characterized by archaisms.

The *Metamorphoses* (c. 180-190; *The Golden Ass*, 1566), a prose novel by Lucius Apuleius (c. 125-after 170), exhibits a striking blend of archaisms, linguistic innovations, and rhetorical figures of speech. Apuleius was, like Fronto, a *rhetor* from north Africa and was a prolific writer. In addition to the extant *Metamorphoses*, Apuleius produced works in a variety of genres, including speeches, hymns, and miscellaneous light verse in a volume called "Ludicra," all lost. The antiquarian tendency of the age is also evident in the extant *Noctes Atticae* (c. 180 C.E.; *Attic Nights*, 1927) of Aulus Gellius (c. 125-after 180), a friend of Fronto. *Attic Nights* is a compilation of extracts from Greek and Latin writers and discusses matters of archaic language, literature, and history, among other things.

The emphasis of *elocutio novella* on colloquial Latin also points to significant linguistic trends in late antiquity: the gradual transformation of the Latin language from its classical, "Ciceronian" models into more colloquial forms, and the eventual dissolution of Latin into the several Romance languages. Developments in second century Latin prose thus reflected a permanent change in Latin forms of expression. Latin poetry, when revitalized in the fourth century, already showed the effects of these linguistic changes.

The only Latin poet to emerge between the Silver Age and the fourth century C.E. was Nemesianus (c. 253-after 283), a Carthaginian whose extant *Cynegetica* (c. 283; *The Chase*, 1934) is a didactic poem on hunting strongly influenced by Vergil and Calpurnius Siculus. Nemesianus also wrote two other didactic poems, "Halieutica," on fishing, and "Nautica," probably on fowling, which are now lost.

The chaotic political situation of the late second century and the third century was certainly another factor affecting poetic output in this period. The series of "five good emperors" chosen by adoption rather than heredity was unfortunately broken by the succession of Marcus Aurelius's incompetent son, Commodus (180-193), whose inevitable assassination led to four rival imperial candidates, a brief civil war (193-197), and the accession of the military man Lucius Septimius Severus (193-211).

A major development during the reign of the Severian family (193-235) was the final extension of Roman citizenship, first to the eastern provinces by Septimius Severus and then to all free men in the empire by his son Caracalla (211-217). After five hundred years of empire, all free Roman subjects were finally granted Roman citizenship, and there was no longer a distinction between Roman and non-Roman within the empire. By this period, emperors themselves also came from all over the empire: The second century had seen the Spanish emperors Trajan and Marcus Aurelius; the third century produced Septimius Severus from North Africa; and later centuries brought Aurelian (270-275), Diocletian (284-305), and Constantine (308-337) from Illyria (modern Yugoslavia). This "internationalism" was paralleled in Latin literature, which embraced several Spanish writers in the Silver Age, North Africans in the second and third centuries, and Gallic writers in the fourth and fifth centuries.

In general, the third century C.E. was a period of military anarchy. Not only were there the internal problems of disrupted succession, with twenty-five emperors in the one-hundred-year period between Commodus and Diocletian, but there were also critical problems on the frontiers. Incursions by fierce Germanic tribes, including the Goths, Allamanni, and Franks, led to the temporary loss of the Danube and Rhine frontiers and the invasions of Gaul and even northern Italy. In the east, the important province of Syria was lost for a time.

These military difficulties caused major social and economic difficulties. Travel became severely limited; commerce was disrupted; urban life deteriorated as city populations shrank, municipal governments decayed, and cities walled themselves against invasions. Society became more rustic, more oriented toward the farmland, as large landholders usurped political and legal authority on their *latifundia* and their workers, formerly free *coloni*, became bound serfs with no freedom of movement. The medieval feudal system was thus already developing in the fourth century.

Through the military and administrative abilities of several good emperors, such as Claudius Gothicus (260-270), Aurelian, Diocletian, and Constantine, the boundaries of the empire were restored in the late third century and were preserved essentially intact for another century. Diocletian, recognizing the difficulties of governing an immense area with increasingly insecure borders, divided the empire into two administrative halves, the Greek-speaking East and the Latin-speaking West. This division became permanent in the fourth century. Under Constantine, the East, by then more stable than the West, became the site of the empire's new capital city, Constantinople (modern Istanbul), where the successors of Constantine continued to rule their Byzantine Greek empire for another thousand years. This division of the empire also led to a diminishing influence of Greek letters on the Latin West.

By the late fourth century, the city of Rome was no longer the capital city of even the Western Empire, the ruler of which sat in Milan for military purposes. The Roman senate continued to meet, but as a mere town council with a *praefectus urbi* (city prefect) instead of a consul as presiding officer. It is indicative, however, of the resilience of Roman political institutions that Constantine established a senate and consuls in his new capital.

The Western Empire was not as long-lived as its eastern counterpart. The early fifth century witnessed the loss of Britain and the permanent occupation of Gaul, Spain, and North Africa by Germanic tribes. The city of Rome itself was sacked in 410 by Alaric the Goth, and in 476 the last Roman emperor in the West, Romulus Augustulus, was deposed by the German Odoacer.

The causes of the fall of the Roman Empire in the West are complex, but it is significant that in the midst of the great political and social changes that occurred from the third through the fifth century, Rome maintained her status as the intellectual and literary center of the Latin-speaking world. Nearly all the writers of late antiquity had some contact with this city, which remained a magnet for scholars. Roman education, both in Rome and in the provinces, also continued to display a high level of quality and accessibility. The educational advances begun in the Silver Age were upheld in late antiquity. Both Diocletian and Constantine, for example, retained the financial privileges conferred on teachers by their imperial predecessors. Several emperors, including Septimius Severus, Constantine, and Gratian (367-383), were well educated, and Severus's Syrian wife, Julia Domna, even sat at the head of the important literary salon which included the Greek philosopher Flavius Philostratus (c. 170-245). The African *rhetor* and Christian writer Caecilius Firmianus Lactantius (c. 240-c. 320) held a teaching post under Diocletian and was tutor to the emperor's son Crispus. A significant number of the poets of late antiquity were *rhetores* by profession.

Another important development of this period, with profound consequences for Latin letters, was the growth of Christianity, which began in the East in the first century, as a religion especially of the non-Latin-speaking lower classes. Christianity suffered several centuries of persecution before it was officially tolerated by Constantine in 313, and several more centuries passed before Christianity had completely displaced the ancient "pagan" religions.

A major problem for early Christian writers was the role in Christian life and letters of the Latin literary tradition in which they themselves had been educated. Some Christians wished to dismiss the entire tradition as morally and religiously unwholesome; others argued strongly for the value of the "pagan" Latin literature in a Christian education.

Fortunately, these Latin classics managed to survive until Christianity, no longer threatened by the pagan world, became the conservator of classical culture, especially through the scribal efforts of medieval monks. Preservation of classical texts began to be particularly critical in the fourth and fifth centuries, as papyrus, long used as a writing material, became less accessible and scribes began using parchment. This change in material also meant a change in text format, with the transition from the scroll to the quarto. Because of these changes, if an ancient text was not copied onto parchment in this period, it generally did not survive.

Christians in late antiquity not only helped preserve these ancient texts but also continued the Latin literary tradition with their own poetic and prose creations. The Latin literature of late antiquity reflects the initial tensions between the classical and Christian worlds as well as their eventual reconciliation. The literary transition from "pagan" to "Christian," however, was not sudden, and the criteria for calling a fifth or sixth century Latin author "ancient" or "medieval" are often arbitrary.

Symbolic of these changes in Latin literature on the threshold of the medieval period are two Christian works: the *Vulgate*, a Latin translation of the Bible by Saint Jerome (between 331 and 347-probably 420), and *De civitate Dei* (413-427; *The City of God*, 1610), by Saint Augustine (354-430). These two works had a profound effect on contemporary and later Latin literature and, in a sense, mark the end of a literary era, the transition from "pagan" to Christian Latin literature. Jerome's *Vulgate* included translations of Hebrew poetic passages, such as the Psalms and the Song of Solomon, which established basic vocabulary and forms of expression for later Latin poetry. Besides *The City of God*, Augustine wrote some verse, including *Psalmus contra partem Donati* (393-396; *Against the Donatists*). This work, also known as the *Abecedarium*, was the first Latin poem based upon rhythm rather than on the quantitative system derived from Greek, and was thus another harbinger of the changes Latin poetry would undergo in the medieval period.

Contemporary with the *Vulgate* and *The City of God* is the *Saturnalia* (c. 400; *The Saturnalia*, 1969) of Ambrosius Theodosius Macrobius (fl. late fourth to mid-fifth century), a work which demonstrates the tenacity of classical religion and culture. Named after a major Roman religious holiday and modeled on the Platonic symposium, *The Saturnalia* discusses a broad range of topics, mostly antiquarian. As participants in his *Saturnalia*, Macrobius chose several contemporary literary figures, the most important of which was Quintus Aurelius Symmachus (c. 340-402), a famous orator of his day, a staunch defender of pagan culture, and a significant figure in the preservation of Livy's *Histories*. Servius (fourth century), another character in the *Saturnalia*, was a commentator on Vergil. A third, Avianus, wrote a collection of animal fables in elegiac verse (c. 400), which were extracted from Phaedrus and became particularly influential in the medieval period.

Macrobius's literary circle was quite learned and was committed to the preservation of the literature of the past. Commentaries and epitomes of classical writers were common in this period. Macrobius himself, a Neoplatonist, wrote a commentary on Cicero's *Somnium Scipionis* (51; dream of Scipio). The great fourth century commentator Aelius Donatus, who worked on Terence, was also a teacher of Saint Jerome. There was even a versified epitome of Livy, now lost, by the fourth century author Festus Ruf(i)us Avienus, who also composed several epitomes of ancient geographical and astronomical poems, some of which are extant. In the field of history, Ammianus Marcellinus (c. 330-c. 391), a Greek from Antioch, wrote a history of the years 96-378, more than half of which survives. Marcellinus was also a member of the circle of Macrobius and Symmachus. That a Greek-speaker from the East would choose to write a history of Rome in Latin in the fourth century is an eloquent statement of the empire's persistent cosmopolitanism and of the continued vigor of Roman culture and letters in this period.

Nor was Marcellinus an anomaly of his age. The late fourth century also produced the poet Claudian (c. 370-c. 404), an Egyptian who may have originally written in Greek but who produced a diverse poetic corpus in Latin, including public panegyrics, marriage songs, invectives, historical epics in the Vergilian style, and the Ovidian epyllion *De raptu Proserpinae* (rape of Proserpina). Claudian's work, filled with contemporary allusions to the court of Honorius (393-423), demonstrates once again the Roman tendency to forge politics into poetry, a tendency that had been with Latin poetry from its inception. Also significant are Claudian's literary debts to a long list of ancient authors, including Vergil, Ovid, Catullus, Lucretius, and Juvenal. Though he was nominally Christian, Claudian's poetry is generally "pagan" in theme, as the mythic title *De raptu Proserpinae* suggests.

Another member of Symmachus's circle was Decimus Magnus Ausonius (c. 310-c. 395). A Christian *rhetor* from Bordeaux, Ausonius became tutor to the future emperor Gratian, under whom he held several important political posts. He wrote epistles, mostly in verse, including exchanges with Symmachus; epigrams, mostly elegiac, in both Greek and Latin; and several miscellaneous poems in hexameter. Christianity is not a prominent theme in Ausonius's poetry. In his most famous poem, *Mosella* (fourth century; *The Moselle*, 1915), a description of the German river Moselle, Ausonius exhibits a fondness for the countryside and for travel, a theme which is indigenously Latin and which had previously appeared in such earlier works as Lucilius's and Horace's travel satires.

Rutilius Claudius Namatianus (fl. c. 417), a pagan from Gaul who served under Honorius, followed Ausonius's example and produced an elegiac travel poem, *De reditu suo* (fifth century; *The Home-Coming*, 1907). This poem, the beginning of which survives, describes an actual journey by Rutilius Namatianus from Rome to his home in Gaul in about 417 and includes some striking praise of the former capital by a Gallic poet.

Ausonius also shared a correspondence with his student, Saint Paulinus of Nola (c. 352 or 353 to 431), another Gaul, who later became bishop of Nola in Italy. Paulinus of Nola was one of the earliest composers of Christian lyric poetry. His works include eulogies on the saints and martyrs, the first Christian wedding hymn, the first Christian consolation for the dead, and *Eucharisticon*, an autobiographical piece in hexameters.

The Spaniard Aurelius Clemens Prudentius (c. 348-after 405) was another composer of Christian poetry. In addition to twelve lyric poems or hymns called *Cathemerinon* (late third to early fourth century; *The Twelve Hymns*, 1898), Prudentius produced the first Christian allegorical poem, *Psychomachia* (late third to early fourth century; *The Psychomachia*, 1929), and several didactic Christian poems, including, *Contra Symmachum* (late third to early fourth century; *Against Symmachus*, 1926). An effort to transform classical, "pagan" literary forms into truly Christian poetic expressions is especially evident in Prudentius's works.

Two other Christians who attempted to use poetry for didactic purposes were Commodianus (fl. third or fourth century) and Gaius Vetteius Aquilinus Juvencus (fl. early fourth century). Commodianus, who may be the first recorded Christian poet, produced a work titled *Instructiones* (n.d.; *The Instructions in Favour of Christian Discipline*, 1870), eighty acrostic satires of pagan gods, drunkards, and so forth. Commodianus also wrote the *Carmen apologeticum* (poem of apologetics), which was intended as an explanation of Christianity for the unlearned. Juvencus, a Spaniard, wrote verse paraphrases of the Old and New Testaments and the *Evangeliorum librum* (c. 330; book of evangelists), an epic poem in hexameter on the New Testament, composed in Vergilian style.

An important poetic form that appears early in the Christian Latin tradition is the hymn. Saint Hilary of Poitiers (c. 315-c. 367), known primarily for his theological treatises, may have been the first author of Christian hymns. Saint Ambrose (339-397) was, like Hilary, a doctor of the Western Church and was also an early composer of religious hymns, in addition to his treatises and letters. These early hymns began an extensive tradition in the Middle Ages.

Other Christian writers followed Ausonius, producing poetry that was not intensively Christian. Sidonius Apollinaris (430 c. 487) was born in Lyons and was the son-in-law of the emperor Avitus (455-456). His extant poetry consists of twenty-four pieces on miscellaneous subjects and in various meters, including two epithalamia. All of Sidonius Apollinaris's poetry predates his accession to the episcopacy at Clermont, after which he wrote only epistles. Magnus Felix Ennodius (473-521), born in Arles and later bishop of Pavia, wrote extensively in both prose and verse but avoided Christian themes. In addition to letters and several rhetorical discourses in the fashion of the elder Seneca, Ennodius wrote numerous pieces in verse, including marriage poems, epigrams, travel poems, panegyrics, and hymns.

De nuptiis Mercurii et Philologiae (n.d.; *On the Marriage of Mercury and Philology*), by Martianus Capella (fl. fifth century) is a fitting climax to the Latin poetry of late antiquity, at once looking back to the classical age and forward to the medieval period. Written in the form of a Menippean satire in prose and verse, the work of the North African Capella shows the influence of the classical satirist Varro and also has many linguistic parallels to Apuleius. *On the Marriage of Mercury and Philology*, which makes no reference to Christianity, is an allegorical introduction to the seven liberal arts of a traditional Roman education and became very important in the medieval system of learning. Capella's book thus marks the final success of the ancient classical literary tradition in an increasingly Christian environment.

MEDIEVAL POETRY (476-1700)

The dissolution of the Roman Empire in the West did not mean the end either of Roman political and social institutions or of the Latin literary tradition. Roman emperors may have been replaced by Germanic kings, but the new rulers and their subjects continued to consider themselves the legitimate successors of the Romans. In 800, Charlemagne, king of the Franks, accepted the title Roman emperor and thus established the concept of a Holy Roman Empire, which continued into the nineteenth century. Roman law, especially through codifications in late antiquity by emperors Theodosius II (408-450) and Justinian (483-565), maintained a continuous influence in the West and became the basis both of ecclesiastical "canon law" and of the legal codes of most of modern Europe.

Despite the growth of vernacular languages, Latin continued to be used as a medium of communication in the Church, in the universities, and in educated circles through the eighteenth century. While 500 to 1000 is often called the European Dark Ages, Roman culture and learning never really ceased. While literacy did decrease drastically among the general population, old Latin texts continued to be read and copied and new texts composed, especially in the monasteries.

The works of several sixth century authors demonstrate that learning did not die with the Western Roman Empire. Boethius (c. 480-524), a highly educated member of an old Roman family, was one of the last in the West to know Greek until the Renaissance. From the death of Boethius in 524 until the fourteenth century, the Latin and Greek literary traditions maintained little contact. Boethius's most important work, *De consolatione philosophiae* (523; *The Consolation of Philosophy*, late ninth century), a Menippean satire in prose and mixed meters, was written in prison while Boethius awaited execution for treason under the

Ostrogothic king Theodoric (493-526). *The Consolation of Philosophy*, which discusses the problem of evil in a world governed by a just deity, had considerable influence upon the later medieval period. Menippean structure and philosophic content demonstrate the author's debts to the classical past. It was especially through the influence of Boethius, as well as through Capella's *On the Marriage of Mercury and Philology*, that the prose-verse medley became a major genre in later European literatures, especially in the Renaissance, and continued to be used, even in didactic and scientific works, as late as the seventeenth century.

While not a poet, Cassiodorus (c. 490-c. 585), another native Roman and a friend of Boethius, is significant as the founder of an early monastery with a *scriptorium* for the copying of texts. Cassiodorus, who served in several royal offices from 507 to 537, produced a variety of prose works, including *Variae epistolae* (537), his official correspondence; a history of the Goths; speeches; and religious works.

Venantius Fortunatus (c. 530-540 to c. 600), who was born at Trieste and eventually became bishop of Poitiers, wrote several prose works, eleven books of miscellaneous poetry, and a long hexameter work, *De virtutibus S. Martini* (sixth century; on the virtues of Saint Martin). The themes of Fortunatus's miscellaneous poems show the influence of the Latin poets of late antiquity and include marriage songs, travel poems, and hymns. His verse demonstrates a peculiar combination of religious fervor, epicurean tastes, and mythological allusions, in marked contrast to the unlettered asceticism with which the medieval period is often erroneously associated.

A revival of learning in the reign of Charlemagne (768-814) is further evidence of the continuity of learning in the medieval period. This Carolingian Revival, as it is usually called, witnessed a major innovation in paleography, the transition from magiscule to minuscule writing. The period also saw a rejuvenation of Latin poetry under such writers as the English prelate Alcuin (c. 735-804), who wrote occasional, nonreligious verse, as well as a long hexameter poem on the history of York, and the German theologian Gottschalk (died c. 804-c. 868), who wrote some verse in addition to the heretical religious writings for which he was im-

prisoned. Perhaps the most brilliant poet of the Carolingian period, however, was Walahfrid Strabo (809-849), abbot of Reichenau and tutor to Charlemagne's son, Charles the Bald. Besides the prose *Glossa ordinaria* (ninth century), which is a collection of scholarly notes on the Bible, Walahfrid Strabo wrote a collection of poems, including some impressive Sapphics about his abbey, and a didactic work in verse, *De cultura hortorum* (ninth century; *Hortulus*, 1924), with a famous dedicatory poem reminiscent of Catullus.

One of the earliest "wandering scholars" was Sedulius Scottus (fl. 848-874), who went from his native Ireland to Liège and wrote much miscellaneous verse, including *Carmen Paschale* (ninth century; *The Easter Song*, 1922). Such wandering scholars, later known as goliards, are responsible for a great anonymous tradition of medieval verse, religious, moralistic, satiric, and erotic in nature, of which the best example survives in a manuscript from Benediktbeuern in Germany. This collection of medieval secular verse, known as *Carmina burana*, is perhaps best known through the musical adaptation of Carl Orff (1895-1982).

The ninth or tenth century epic *Waltharius* (*Walter of Aquitaine*, 1930), by Ekkehard I, a monk of the monastery of Saint Gall in Switzerland, stands out, in its epic form, from the rest of medieval Latin poetry, which is generally didactic or miscellaneous in nature. This work is stylistically indebted to the epic tradition of Vergil and Ovid but is thematically original, since its hero lived in the time of the European invasions.

A few poets of the late medieval period warrant mention for their varied and learned compositions. Hrosvitha of Gandersheim (c. 930-935 to c. 1002), a German nun, was one of the few women poets of the Middle Ages. Besides several prose plays written in the style of Terence, Hrosvitha's corpus includes religious narrative poems about Christian legends and a verse chronicle, *Carmen de gestis Oddonis* (tenth century; *Song About the Deeds of Otto the Great*, 1936), a work in which the resurgence of nationalism in Latin poetry begins to appear. Alain de Lille (c. 1128-1202), wrote theological treatises and allegorical poetry. An example of Alain's didactic and moral verse is *Anticlaudianus, sive de officio viro boni et perfecti libri*

(c. 1180; *The Anticlaudian of Alain de Lille*, 1935), an allegory on creation and the perfection of the human soul by God. *Vita Merlini* (c. 1150), in hexameter, by Geoffrey of Monmouth (c. 1100-1154), was part of a mythic tradition that later greatly influenced the Arthurian legend.

RENAISSANCE

The last stage of a living Latin poetic tradition was the result of the Humanistic revival known as the Renaissance, which began in Italy in the mid-fourteenth century and spread to northern Europe in the fifteenth and sixteenth centuries. Renaissance writers, exhibiting a renewed interest in ancient culture and literature, sought to uncover and preserve as many Greco-Roman texts as possible, and to use these texts as literary models.

Much Renaissance literature was written in the vernacular languages, but a significant number of works were written in Latin. Desiderius Erasmus (1466?-1536), for example, wrote his great prose satire *Moriæ Encomium* (1511; *The Praise of Folly*, 1549) in Latin. The Latin poets of the Renaissance, often called neo-Latin writers, flourished from about 1350 until about 1700, producing an astonishing variety of poetic types based upon classical models. The most popular genres were epigrams, love poems, elegies, odes, didactic poetry, epithalamia, and eclogues.

The list of Italian neo-Latin poets is impressive. The Florentine Petrarch (1304-1374) wrote twelve *Eclogues* of a Vergilian type and an epic poem, *Africa* (1396; English translation, 1977), about Scipio Africanus, which Petrarch modeled on the *Aeneid* and considered more important than his famous vernacular sonnets. Petrarch's friend Giovanni Boccaccio (1313-1375), best known for the Italian *Decameron: O, Prencipe Galeotto* (1349-1351; *The Decameron*, 1620) in prose, later composed *Buccolicum carmen* (c. 1351-1366; *Boccaccio's Olympia*, 1913), which, like Petrarch's poems, was filled with allegories and contemporary allusions.

The Neapolitan Giovanni Giovano Pontano (1423-1503) wrote Latin poetry in a considerable range, from love poems to an astrological poem, *Urania* (fifteenth century). Pontano's colleague, Jacopo Sannazzaro

(1458-1530), known in Latin as Actius Ayncerus, wrote much religious pastoral verse, such as *De partu Virginis* (1526; on the birth of the Virgin), and some secular poetry, such as *Piscatoriae* (1526; *Piscatorial Eclogues*, 1958).

A later Florentine neo-Latinist, Poliziano (1454-1494), wrote not only in Latin but also in Italian and Greek. His Latin output consists of a few elegies, odes, and epigrams which became models for later epigrammatists.

Poliziano's interest in Greek reflected an important Renaissance trend. While the poetic literature of the Middle Ages was the direct offspring of Christianity and of the Latin poetic tradition, the Renaissance saw a rediscovery of Greek literature, encouraged by the exodus of Greek scholars and texts from the disintegrating Byzantine Empire. One such Greek expatriate was the poet Michael Tarchaniota Marullus (died 1500), whose Latin love lyrics and poems of exile were long admired and imitated in France and Germany.

Two German neo-Latin poets were Konradus Celtis (1459-1508), who composed odes, love poems, and epigrams, and Petrus Lotichius (1528-1560), who wrote love elegies in the fashion of Ovid and Catullus.

Neo-Latin output in France was early offset by a preference for the vernacular, represented by *La Défense et illustration de la langue française* (1549; *The Defence and Illustration of the French Language*, 1939), by Joachim du Bellay (c. 1522-1560), but most of the members of the Pléiade, du Bellay's literary group, including du Bellay himself, produced Latin verse. Du Bellay's *Poemata* (poems) of 1558 included epigrams and love poems. J. A. de Baïf (1532-1589) published a volume of Latin poems titled *Carmina* (songs) in 1577. Perhaps the most unusual Latin poem of the Pléiade is by Rémy Belleau (1528-1577), *Dictamen metrificum de bello huguenotico* (sixteenth century), a macaronic poem on the Huguenotic wars. Despite the swift dominance of the vernacular in French poetry, Latin poetry continued to be written by French poets as late as the mid-nineteenth century, notably by Charles Baudelaire.

There was also a significant group of British neo-Latin poets, the most outstanding of whom was a Scot, George Buchanan (1506-1582), tutor to Mary Queen of

Scots. Buchanan was closely associated in his youth with the Pléiade and produced a variety of poetic works in Latin, including an influential version of the Psalms, plays, *Sphaera . . . quinque libris descripta* (1585, unfinished; a defense of Ptolemy), and occasional verse, such as an epithalamium for Mary's marriage to the Dauphin in 1558. Several other British neo-Latin poets are the great English epic poet John Milton (1608-1674), the Welshman Henry Vaughan (1622-1695), the religious poet Richard Crashaw (c. 1612-1649), and the Metaphysical poet Abraham Cowley (1618-1667).

After 1700, the gradual displacement of Latin as the language of the educated and the rise of vernacular poetry meant the end of a living Latin poetic tradition. Where Latin poetry continues to be written in modern times, it is done more as a sophisticated exercise and display of skill than as a true poetic statement. The Latin poetic tradition is most important for its influence on the Western literary tradition. There is no field of modern poetry and virtually no poet untouched either directly or indirectly by Latin poetry.

No better expression exists of the debt of modern poetry to Latin literature than that of the great Italian poet Dante (1265-1321), who was positioned at the virtual beginning of the vernacular poetic tradition in the West. While Dante did write in Latin, including letters and the treatise *De monarchia* (c. 1313; English translation, 1890; better known as *On World Government*, 1957) in prose and *Eclogae* (1319; *Eclogues*, 1902) in verse, his major work, *La divina commedia* (c. 1320; *The Divine Comedy*, 1802), is in the vernacular. In the first part of this monumental epic, *Inferno*, modeled on Aeneas's descent to the underworld in book 6 of the *Aeneid*, Dante replaces Aeneas's prophetic guide, the Sibyl, with Vergil himself, and praises his classical guide with the following immortal tribute:

> Tu se, lo mio maestro e, 1 mio autore
> tu se' solo colui, da cu' io tolsi lo bello stile
> che m'he fatto onore.

> You are my master and my author.
> You alone are the one from whom I took
> the beautiful style which has rendered me honor.

Dante's debt to Vergil is the West's debt to the Latin poetic tradition.

BIBLIOGRAPHY

Adams, J. N., and R. G. Mayer, eds. *Aspects of the Language of Latin Poetry*. New York: Oxford University Press, 1999. Based on a symposium held in 1995, this volume was issued as number 93 in the Proceedings of the British Academy. Essays by various scholars on the development of Latin poetry, discussing such matters as word order, the use of pronouns, and the expansion of the poetic vocabulary by using elements drawn from fields such as law and medicine. Introduction by the editors. Bibliographical references.

Braund, Susanna Morton. *Latin Literature*. New York: Routledge, 2002. Contains chapters on the relationship between Greek and Latin literature, the issue of intertextuality, and Roman identity and culture. Illustrated. Time line, list of authors and texts, indexes, and two appendixes. A well-written, lively introduction to the subject.

Conte, Gian Biagio. *Latin Literature: A History*. Translated by Joseph B. Solodow. Revised by Don Fowler and Glenn W. Most. Baltimore: Johns Hopkins University Press, 1999. Covers the major Latin writers through the early Middle Ages. Conte's work remains the authoritative study of the subject and is an invaluable resource for any student. Bibliographical references and index.

Edmunds, Lowell. *Intertextuality and the Reading of Roman Poetry*. Baltimore: Johns Hopkins University Press, 2001. Explores a critical issue that has preoccupied scholars and readers of Roman poetry for several decades: the relationship between a primary text and another that is inserted as an allusion or a quotation. Noting the many ways that the secondary reference may function, for example, as a stylistic device or as a part of the thematic structure, the author supports his theories with passages from such writers as Catullus, Horace, Vergil, and Ovid. Works cited, an index of ancient citations, and a general index.

Gale, Monica R. *Virgil on the Nature of Things: "The Georgics," Lucretius, and the Didactic Tradition.*

New York: Cambridge University Press, 2000. Places *The Georgics* within a tradition that goes back as far as the Greek poet Hesiod, with particular attention to the influence of Lucretius's *On the Nature of Things* on Vergil's work, which the author believes necessitates a new interpretation of *The Georgics*. All Greek and Latin passages are translated. Bibliography, index of passages cited, and general index.

Green, Ellen, ed. *Women Poets in Ancient Greece and Rome*. Norman: University of Oklahoma Press, 2005. The first collection of essays to examine the poetry written by Greek and Roman women, based on surviving fragments and on relevant comments by their male contemporaries. Bibliography and index.

Harrison, Stephen, ed. *A Companion to Latin Literature*. Malden, Mass.: Blackwell, 2004. The twenty-eight essays that make up this volume are grouped by subject matter into three sections: historical periods, genres, and themes. The author's introductory essay, "Constructing Latin Literature," is a good starting point for any student of the subject. Bibliography and index.

King, Katherine Callen. *Ancient Epic*. Hoboken, N.J.: Wiley-Blackwell, 2009. An introduction to six ancient epics, including Homer's *Iliad* (c. 750 B.C.E.; English translation, 1611) and *Odyssey* (c. 725 B.C.E.; English translation, 1614). Includes chronologies, map, chart of Olympian gods, glossary, and index. A source that is both readable and reliable.

Lyne, R. O. *Collected Papers on Latin Poetry*. Edited by S. J. Harrison. New York: Oxford University Press, 2007. Introduction by Gregory Hutchinson. Nineteen articles and essays, dating from 1970 to 2005, by one of the most highly regarded specialists in Augustan Latin poetry. Includes a bibliography, references, an index locorum, and a general index.

Thomas J. Sienkewicz

Latino Poetry

In the 1960's and 1970's, poets and other writers of Mexican, Puerto Rican, and Cuban descent formed three discrete groups in literary response to various social, historical, and cultural impulses in the United States at that time. The Civil Rights movement inspired literary Chicanos and Puerto Ricans (especially the Nuyoricans, as Puerto Ricans in New York were known) to write about their experiences in their own voices, which frequently were excluded from mainstream publications. The Cuban American poets of this period wrote primarily in Spanish and in response to the historical circumstance of their exile from Cuba. Chicanos, Puerto Ricans, and Cuban Americans still are the largest groups of Latino poets in the United States, although the field has grown to include writers of other backgrounds.

Literary magazines and anthologies

The literary magazines and small press publications of the burgeoning Chicano, Nuyorican, and Cuban American literary culture are an essential source of information on the initial development of Latino poetry. Among the magazines of varying regional or national renown, significance, and circulation were the Chicano periodicals *De Colores* (Albuquerque, New Mexico), *El Grito* and *Grito del Sol* (Berkeley, California), and *Tejidos* (Austin, Texas); the Puerto Rican diaspora magazine *The Rican* (Chicago); and the Cuban American review *Areíto* (New York). Some of these small journals were edited by leading poets, such as *Maize* (San Diego), by Alurista, and *Mango* (San Jose), by Lorna Dee Cervantes. These and numerous other journals, whether interdisciplinary or purely literary in focus (and many of them highly ephemeral), provided a necessary publishing outlet for the alternative voices erupting throughout the United States during the 1960's and 1970's. These publications grew to afford a rich historical record of a momentous turning point in American literature.

No serious study of the origins and development of Latino literature of any genre can be undertaken without considering *Revista Chicano-Riqueña* (1973-

1985) and its continuation, *Americas Review* (1986-1999). A long-running literary magazine founded by the scholar Nicolás Kanellos, the journal focused on creative writing, with interviews, literary essays, scholarly articles, book reviews, and visual art complementing each issue. Beginning with the premier issue, the work of most of the major Chicano, Nuyorican, and, as coverage quickly expanded, other Latino poets appeared in the pages of these magazines, in many cases marking the first appearance of a writer on the literary radar. Tino Villanueva, Alurista, Cervantes, Victor Hernández Cruz, Gary Soto, Ricardo Sánchez, Tato Laviera, Sandra María Esteves, Jimmy Santiago Baca, and Pat Mora—to indicate only a few—figure among the Chicano and Nuyorican poets featured. In addition, the magazines published the poetry of writers better known for different genres, such as Rolando Hinojosa, Carlos Morton, Miguel Piñero, and Tomás Rivera. Many of these poets and other writers helped shape and influence the journal by doubling as contributing editors or editorial board members. Special or monographic issues focused on particular topics within U.S. Hispanic literature. The celebrated *Woman of Her Word: Hispanic Women Write*, edited by Chicana poet Evangelina Vigil (volume 11, nos. 3/4, 1983) anthologizes the finest Latina writing of that time. Several issues emphasize the Latino writers active in various regions of the United States, including Chicago (volume 5, no. 1, 1977), Wisconsin (volume 13, no. 2, 1985), Houston (volume 16, no. 1, 1988), and the Pacific Northwest (volume 23, nos. 3/4, 1995). The tenth and twentieth anniversary anthologies (1982 and 1992) provide a selection of the major poetical works published in the *Revista* and the *Review* during those decades. *Americas Review* ceased publication in 1999, but Kanellos's singular mission to promote and publish Hispanic literature of the United States would continue through the ongoing publications of Arte Público Press (founded in 1979) and the activities of the Recovering the U.S. Hispanic Literary Heritage project (established in 1992).

Bilingual Review/La Revista Bilingüe (founded in

1974) is another long-standing periodical fundamental to the study of Latino literature. Primarily an academic journal of scholarly articles, book reviews, and interviews relating to bilingualism and to U.S. Hispanic literature, *Bilingual Review* has not published the same volume of creative writing as did *Revista Chicano-Riqueña* and *Americas Review*, despite a stated focus as a literary magazine. Even so, poetry appears in almost every issue (Gustavo Pérez Firmat, Martín Espada, and Judith Ortiz Cofer are among the poets represented) and is the subject of some of the research and interviews. More significant to the study of Latino poetry is Bilingual Press/Editorial Bilingüe, the press established by the journal in 1976. The extensive poetry backlist includes not only Chicanos of early distinction (Alurista, Alma Luz Villanueva, Tino Villanueva, and Bernice Zamora), but also Latinos of later periods (Marjorie Agosín, Elías Miguel Muñoz, Virgil Suárez, and Gina Valdés, for example). Several anthologies published or distributed by the press, along with monographic issues of *Bilingual Review*, contain representative Latino poetry in a variety of specialized categories. These include poets in New York (*Los paraguas amarillos: Los poetas latinos en New York*, 1983), poetry for or about young adults (*Cool Salsa: Bilingual Poems on Growing Up Latino in the United States*, 1994), and women poets (*Floricanto Sí! A Collection of Latina Poetry*, 1998). Such collections afford easy and important access to the vast and ever-flourishing numbers of Hispanic poets who have not gained the national prominence of the proportionately few better-publicized writers.

Anthologies, like literary magazines, are an invaluable primary source of Chicano, Nuyorican, and Cuban American poetry. Early anthologies like Luis Valdez and Stan Steiner's *Aztlan: An Anthology of Mexican American Literature* (1972) and Alurista's *Festival de Flor y Canto: An Anthology of Chicano Literature* (1976) indicate that Chicano literature, including poetry, was already under critical consideration by the early 1970's. (Virginia Ramos Foster annotates more than twenty-five such compilations from that decade in the Mexican American literature chapter of *Sourcebook of Hispanic Culture in the United States*, 1982, edited by David William Foster.)

Several early anthologies of Puerto Rican and Nuyorican literature share the distinction of bringing together island and mainland writers, in seeming recognition of the ongoing aesthetic and literary historical connections between "the two islands," Puerto Rico and Manhattan. (This concern exists to the present day for some scholars and compilers.) These compilations include Alfredo Matilla and Iván Silén's *The Puerto Rican Poets/Los poetas puertorriqueños* (1972), María Teresa Babín and Stan Steiner's *Borinquen: An Anthology of Puerto Rican Literature* (1974), and Julio Marzán's *Inventing a Word: An Anthology of Twentieth-Century Puerto Rican Poetry* (1980). Roberto Santiago has taken the same composite approach to Puerto Rican literature in *Boricuas: Influential Puerto Rican Writers—An Anthology* (1995). On the other hand,

Virgil Suárez (©Silver Image)

Miguel Algarín and Miguel Piñero's landmark *Nuyorican Poetry: An Anthology of Puerto Rican Words and Feelings* (1975) documents exclusively the initial period of creativity and so is the best starting point for any retrospective study of Nuyorican poetry.

The first Cuban American literature anthologies also emphasize the connections between writing in the United States and the homeland, Cuba. For example, several poets who write in Spanish in exile appear in Orlando Rodríguez Sardiñas's *La última poesía cubana: Antología reunida, 1959-1973* (1973; the latest Cuban poetry: an anthology), and exile poets are the exclusive focus of Angel Aparicio Laurencio's *Cinco poetisas cubanas, 1935-1969* (1970; five Cuban women poets); both collections were published in the United States. By the same token, an early critical dictionary, *Bibliografía crítica de la poesía cubana (exilio: 1959-1971)* (1972; critical bibliography of Cuban exile poetry), by exile writer Matías Montes Huidobro with Yara González, confirms that virtually all the poetry books of the decade under discussion were written in Spanish. The poetry in Silvia Burunat and Ofelia García's *Veinte años de literatura cubanoamericana: Antología 1962-1982* (1988; twenty years of Cuban American literature: an anthology) illustrates the tendency throughout two decades of exile and immigration to explore issues of identity within the context of the nascent Cuban American experience (and, in the 1970's as in the preceding decade, in Spanish). Ultimately, the study of the Chicano, Nuyorican, or Cuban American poetry in the foregoing and similar anthologies affords a synopsis both of individual poets and of each discrete group, at specific moments as well as over time.

Early Chicano poetry

Many of the poets featured in the early Chicano anthologies or in other publications continued to publish or to appear in later anthologies, suggesting their ongoing significance in Chicano literary history even as others emerged. These include Alurista, Angela de Hoyos, José Montoya, Luis Omar Salinas, Raúl Salinas, and Tino Villanueva.

Rodolfo Gonzales

Rodolfo Gonzales's *I Am Joaquín/Yo soy Joaquín* (1967) and the poetry of Sánchez are especially representative of this early period. The bilingual *I Am Joaquín/Yo soy Joaquín*, by Denver-based activist and writer Gonzales, may be the single best-known Chicano poem of any period. It has been widely read, reproduced, and distributed by newspapers and magazines, students and teachers, performers, labor organizers, and Chicano organizations and organizers in every possible educational, cultural, political, and social milieu. *I Am Joaquín* is as much a historical commentary as a modern epic poem, and intentionally so. An early popular edition (Bantam Pathfinder, 1972) even supplemented the poem with paintings depicting historical events and a chronology of Mexican and Mexican American history. Also, as Gonzales himself states in the informative fact list that prefaces the poem, "*I Am Joaquín* was the first work of poetry to be published by Chicanos for Chicanos and is the forerunner of the Chicano cultural renaissance." Gonzales combines the poetic sensibilities of Walt Whitman's "Song of Myself" and Allen Ginsberg's "Howl" (1956) as Joaquín, a Chicano Everyman, explores himself and the history of the Chicano people—from the pre-Columbian and colonial periods, through independence and revolution up to the present day:

> I am Joaquín,
> lost in a world of confusion,
> .   .   .   .
> and destroyed by modern society.

Repetition, enumeration, and parallelism dominate the poem's short lines and long stanzas. The liberal use of displaced lines and capitalized words emphasizes key concepts, such as "MY OWN PEOPLE," "THE GROUND WAS MINE," and, in the prophetic and self-affirming final lines of the poem, "I SHALL ENDURE!/ I WILL ENDURE!"

Ricardo Sánchez

Ricardo Sánchez also began writing in social protest. The lines that frame "In Exile" (from Sánchez's first book, *Canto y grito mi liberación*, 1971; I sing and shout my liberation) exemplify several of the salient characteristics of his poetry: the typographic hodgepodge and free verse, the sensation of getting out as much as possible in a single breath, and the vociferous sense of both self and people.

it is by way of definition that i
now write this short introduction of myself,

.   .   .   .

and
i write of my people, LA RAZA!

Elsewhere in this collection as in all his subsequent books, Sánchez frequently writes in Spanish or a mixture of Spanish and English, he experiments with word formation ("soul/stream"; *piensasentimientos*, or "mindfeelings"; *mentealmacuerpo*, or "mindsoulbody"), he inserts expository or poetic prose texts, and he articulates his aesthetic and political visions. The enthusiasm and immediacy of his Beat-inflected voice readily draw the reader into the experience. Even the titles of Sánchez's books and poems emphasize this aesthetic of spontaneity: "This of Being the Soul/Voice for My Own Conscienceness Is Too Much (Petersburg, Virginny)," *Hechizospells: Poetry/Stories/Vignettes/Articles/Notes on the Human Condition of Chicanos and Pícaros, Words and Hopes Within Soulmind* (1976), and *Eagle-Visioned/Feathered Adobes: Manito Sojourns and Pachuco Ramblings October 4th to 24th, 1981* (1990). Sánchez's poetry has enjoyed wide circulation in both small and university presses, and has even been published in a private edition (*Amerikan Journeys = Jornadas americanas*, 1994, in Iowa City by publisher and longtime Sánchez associate Rob Lewis). The publication of *Chicano Timespace: The Poetry and Politics of Ricardo Sánchez* (2001), a scholarly monograph by Miguel R. López, establishes in no uncertain terms Sánchez's position in the canon of Chicano—and, by extension, Latino and American—poetry.

NUYORICAN POETRY: 1970'S

The beginnings of Nuyorican poetry were equally strident. The 1975 anthology edited by Algarín and Piñero, *Nuyorican Poetry*, introduced a wide audience to the poetry that was coming out of the experience of being Puerto Rican in New York City. Even the subtitle of the anthology—*An Anthology of Puerto Rican Words and Feelings*—captures the emotive lyricism that underlies the use of an ethnic-specific lexicon ("Puerto Rican words") to document a group experience ("Puerto Rican feelings") in poetry inspired by a

place. Several of the featured writers went on to distinguish themselves in poetry beyond the anthology, including Sandra María Esteves, José Angel Figueroa, Pedro Pietri, and the compilers themselves. (Two poets active in the early 1970's, Cruz and Laviera, are not in the Nuyorican anthology.)

The late Piñero, known more for the play *Short Eyes* (pr. 1974) than for his poetry, made a significant contribution nonetheless. The selections in the anthology exemplify his savage irreverence. In "The Book of Genesis According to Saint Miguelito," for instance, Piñero derides the God who created ghettos, slums, lead-based paint, hepatitis, capitalism, and overpopulation. A later work, the much-anthologized "A Lower East Side Poem" (*La Bodega Sold Dreams*, 1980), covers similar ground as the poet contemplates dying among the pimping, shooting, drug dealing, and other unsavory activities of the neighborhood. The perverse but catchy refrain "then scatter my ashes thru/ the Lower East Side" affirms both Piñero's allegiance to his barrio roots and the musical rhythms that inspire many Nuyorican poets.

While social reality is a thematic interest and protest a dominant tone throughout *Nuyorican Poetry*, Algarín and Piñero clearly were committed to promoting diverse voices. The "dusmic" poetry of the third and final section of the book, for example, proposes the possibility of finding love, positive energy, and balance. Esteves's "Blanket Weaver" exemplifies this impulse: "weave us a song of many threads/ that will dance with the colors of our people/ and cover us with the warmth of peace." (Some of Esteves's later poems, such as those in *Bluestown Mockingbird Mambo*, 1990, indicate a similarly broad array of preoccupations and interests; these include a touching elegy for the artist Jorge Soto, numerous love poems, and strong but poetic statements against brutal regimes in Guatemala and South Africa.) Also, Algarín's introduction to the anthology, "Nuyorican Language," constitutes an indispensable discussion of the poet and poetry in the Nuyorican context, in both theory and practice.

Algarín, in fact, is located squarely in the mainstream of contemporary poetry and poetics. He has translated into English the poetry of Pablo Neruda, he has written extensively on poetics, and he has taken

Miguel Algarín (AP/Wide World Photos)

his literature classes from Rutgers University to the Passaic River and Paterson Falls to enhance his students' study of William Carlos Williams's *Paterson* (1946-1958). The Nuyorican Poets Café, a cultural-arts venue Algarín founded in 1974, has broadened considerably the scope of its poetry and performance activities.

PUERTO RICAN OBITUARY

One of many remarkable books to come out of the Nuyorican movement is Pietri's *Puerto Rican Obituary* (1973), published by the progressive Monthly Review Press. In the title poem (which had achieved underground cult status long before its initial publication), the generic Puerto Ricans Juan, Miguel, Milagros, Olga, and Manuel trudge repeatedly through the daily routines in "Spanish Harlem" that only bring them closer to death and, ultimately, burial on Long Island. In the final analysis, only the afterlife and Puerto Rico offer respite from the poverty and discrimination suf-

fered in New York: "PUERTO RICO IS A BEAU-TIFUL PLACE/ PUERTORRIQUENOS ARE A BEAUTIFUL RACE." Pietri is at his best with the anti-establishment rhetoric with which he parodies religious and civic mainstays like the Lord's Prayer and the Pledge of Allegiance, as in "The Broken English Dream," in which he pledges allegiance "to the flag/ of the united states/ of installment plans." The contrast between New York and Puerto Rico—and between English and Spanish—underscores the irony of the political status of Puerto Ricans vis-à-vis the racial discrimination and linguistic choices awaiting them as they pursue the elusive American Dream.

CUBAN AMERICAN POETRY: 1960'S-1970'S

Spanish, not English, was the language of record for Cuban exile poets and Cuban American poets during the 1960's and 1970's, so language choice per se was not a conscious issue of either form or content, as it was for many Chicano and Nuyorican writers at that time. In fact, in contrast to the Nuyorican example, Cuban poetry in the United States of this early period often was seen as part of Cuban literature or Cuban exile literature elsewhere, not as a nascent branch of American ethnic literature. (Naomi Lindstrom analyzes this problem in the chapter on Cuban American and mainland Puerto Rican literature in *Sourcebook of Hispanic Culture in the United States*, 1982, edited by David William Foster.) Even so, a number of individual poems anthologized by Burunat and García in *Veinte años de literatura cubanoamerica* illustrate the tendency to explore issues of identity within the context of Cuban exile in the United States.

UVA CLAVIJO

Uva Clavijo often defines her exile, as she does here in "Declaración" (declaration), in highly specific spatiotemporal terms:

> I, Uva A. Clavijo,
>
> . . . .
>
> declare, today, the last Monday in September,
> that as soon as I can I will leave everything
> and return to Cuba.

The enumeration of what she is prepared to give up—a house in the suburbs, credit, a successful husband and beautiful family, perfect English (in short, all the trappings of the American Dream)—presents a striking contrast to the specificity and simplicity of this declaration. In "Al cumplir veinte años de exilio" (upon completing twenty years of exile), Clavijo commemorates that anniversary as any other, pondering the growth and development of a Spanish-speaking, Cuban self formed "before confronting/ an immigration official/ for the first time." By the same token, Clavijo frames "Miami 1980" with very precise markers that pinpoint her loneliness and isolation: "Here, Miami, nineteen/ eighty, and my loneliness. . . .// And my astonishing loneliness." The simplicity of Clavijo's expressive and emotional needs in these poems might explain why she favors relatively short lines. In the Miami poem, for example, three especially significant lines succinctly capture the essence of the poem and the poet: "and hatred," "in the distance," and "loneliness."

ALBERTO ROMERO

For some Cuban American poets, the confrontation with New York is not unlike that of the Nuyoricans. In "Caminando por las calles de Manhattan" (walking through the streets of Manhattan), Alberto Romero meets with drug addicts, prostitutes, go-go dancers, and other marginal characters who people the streets of New York. Nevertheless, a sense of order and belonging pervades his search for God amid this riffraff:

> in the Jews of Astoria, in the Italians
> of Flatbush . . .
> in the Dominicans of 110th Street, in the South
>   Americans
> of Queens, in the Cuban refugees.

LOURDES CASAL

Place influences identity for Lourdes Casal, too, who is "too much a Habanera to be a New Yorker,/ too much a New Yorker to be, . . ./ anything else" ("Para Ana Veldford"). Despite some suggestive parallels with the Puerto Rican and Chicano experiences, however, the early Cuban American poetry written in Spanish was inaccessible to a broad readership of Latino literature. Moreover, the language factor has precluded the inclusion of these poets in English-language college textbooks like *The Prentice Hall Anthology of Latino Literature* (2002), edited by Eduardo del Río.

THE 1980'S AND 1990'S

By the 1980's and 1990's, the diverse body of Latino literature by Chicano, Puerto Rican, and Cuban writers in the United States was receiving considerable critical, popular, and pedagogical attention. As compilers were quick to point out, Latino poets—including those trained in graduate writing programs—were being recognized more widely through national fellowships, prizes, and other honors and awards. They, like other American writers, were publishing in mainstream literary magazines such as *American Poetry Review*, *Kenyon Review*, *Parnassus*, and *Poetry*. Latino literature in English in the United States was being included in general anthologies of American literature and in American literature curricula in North American colleges and universities.

Soto, Cervantes, and Baca are some of the Chicano poets of broad acclaim and distribution at the beginning of the twenty-first century. Soto not only is one of the most prolific Latino poets but also is probably the best known outside the confines of Chicano and Latino poetry. His sense of humor, the accessibility of his poetic language, and his sensitive portrayal of youth also have contributed to his success as a writer for young adults and children. (For many years, Soto was virtually the only Chicano writing for the important young-adult market.)

Like Soto, Chicana writer Pat Mora is a prolific poet and children's author. She counts several books of poetry among her works in various genres, including *Chants* (1984), *Borders* (1986), *Communion* (1991), *Agua Santa/Holy Water* (1995), and *Aunt Carmen's Book of Practical Saints* (1997). From her perspective as a woman and a Latina, Mora writes eloquently about diverse topics, including marriage, family life, and children; traditional and modern Latino and Mexican Indian culture; the Catholic devotion of saints; women; and the southwestern desert. In "Curandera" (folk healer) from *Chants*, for example, Mora interweaves several of these interests. When the villagers go to the healer for treatment, "She listens to their stories, and she listens/ to the desert, always to the desert." In many other poems, Mora similarly portrays the nurturing qualities of the southwestern desert, as in "Mi Madre" (my mother), also from *Chants*, "I say teach me. . . ./ She: the desert/ She: strong mother." Like the traditional healer and the desert-other, the many women who populate Mora's poems (the grandmothers, mothers, daughters, and granddaughters, the famous and the humble alike) tend to be strong, wise, and nurturing. That is not to say these women are uncritical, though. Extending the desert-woman metaphor in "Desert Women" (in *Borders*), Mora writes: "Don't be deceived./ When we bloom, we stun."

The 1975 publication of Algarín and Piñero's anthology *Nuyorican Poetry* helped pave the way for a later compilation of Puerto Rican writing, Faythe Turner's *Puerto Rican Writers at Home in the U.S.A.: An Anthology* (1991). Turner includes poets of both generations and recognizes the significant expansion of the Puerto Rican literary diaspora outside of New York. The newer generation includes poets Espada, Ortiz Cofer, Rosario Morales, and Aurora Levins Morales. Espada's poetry is informed variously by his own Puerto Rican heritage, experiences in the Latino enclaves of the United States, and radical causes in the United States and Latin America. Ortiz Cofer's *The Latin Deli: Prose and Poetry* (1993) invites the reader to negotiate a challenging but engaging combination of stories, essays, and poems that "tell the lives of barrio women." Similarly experimental in composition is Morales and Levins Morales's *Getting Home Alive* (1986), a mother-daughter collaboration of mixed genre (including poetry, poetic prose, and memoir), further distinguished by the intermingling of texts written by either mother or daughter. Significantly, the last piece, "Ending Poem," is itself a collaborative product (as indicated by the distinct typefaces):

> I am what I am.
> *A child of the Americas.*
> A light-skinned mestiza of the Caribbean.
> *A child of many diaspora, born into this continent at a*
> *crossroads.*

These Caribbean women are not exclusively African or Taíno or European: "We are new . . ./ *And we are whole*." And their measured celebration of multiculturalism contrasts markedly with the earlier antipoetic angst of the Nuyorican experience.

Unlike their predecessors, the later Cuban American poets write in English and as part of American, not Cuban, literature. Dionisio D. Martínez, for example, appears in the 1996 edition of *The Norton Anthology of Poetry*. In *Little Havana Blues: A Cuban-American Literature Anthology* (1996), Delia Poey and Virgil Suárez have identified a corpus of sixteen poets, several of whom appear in many other groupings of canonical Latino or Cuban American poetry. Among these anthologized poets are Carolina Hospital, Ricardo Pau-Llosa, Pablo Medina, and Gustavo Pérez Firmat.

GUSTAVO PÉREZ FIRMAT

The poetry of scholar and writer Pérez Firmat offers a good example of the new Cuban American poetry. As he explains in his memoir, *Next Year in Cuba: A Cubano's Coming-of-Age in America* (1995): "Born in Cuba but made in the U.S.A., I can no longer imagine living outside American culture and the English language." Much of Pérez Firmat's English-language and bilingual poetry in *Carolina Cuban* (pb. in *Triple Crown: Chicano, Puerto Rican, and Cuban-American Poetry*, 1987) and *Bilingual Blues: Poems, 1981-1994* (1995) supports this notion. For example, he calls the Spanish-language preface to *Carolina Cuban* "Vo(I)ces," in deceptively simple recognition of an anglophone self (*I*) located in between Spanish (*voces*) and English (*voices*). In the verse dedication to the same collection he ponders the paradox of writing in a language to which he does not "belong," at the same time belonging "nowhere else,/ if not here/ in English." Pérez Firmat explores the equivalence of language and place further in "Home," in which home is as much a linguistic as a geographic construct: "[L]et him have a tongue,/ a story, a geography." Bilingual wordplay at the service of identity is Pérez Firmat's forte, as in "Son-Sequence": "Son as plural being./ Son as rumba beat./ Son as progeny." Suggestively, the confluence in this poem of language (*son*, "they are," from the Spanish verb of being *ser*), culture (the Cuban *son*, a musical form), and ancestry (the English *son* or offspring) acknowledges some of the time-honored preoccupations of many Latino poets.

BEGINNING OF THE TWENTY-FIRST CENTURY

The changing demographic patterns of Spanish-speaking immigrants have combined with an ever-increasing interest in multicultural literature in both the marketplace and the classroom to bring broader recognition for Latino literature. Anthologies with a pan-Latino approach not only have brought together Chicano, Puerto Rican, and Cuban American writers but also have introduced new writers from other Latino backgrounds.

JULIA ALVAREZ

Certainly Julia Alvarez, a Dominican born in New York City, is the most prominent of these writers (if for her fiction more than her poetry). As in her fiction, though, she has examined various problems of language and identity in her poetry: *The Other Side/El otro lado* (1995), *Homecoming: New and Collected Poems* (1996), and *Seven Trees* (1998). Of special interest in Alvarez's poetry and poetics is the interplay of identity, form, and the poetic tradition as she proposes new ways to approach set forms (the sonnet, the villanelle, and the sestina) that reflect her identity as a woman poet, a bilingual poet, and a Latina poet.

A BROADER REACH

The example of Alvarez underscores some significant developments in the field of Latino poetry since the publication of foundational works such as *I Am Joaquín* and *Puerto Rican Obituary*. Latina poets, of course, have come to receive more attention than before. In addition, however, Latinas are included in the context of women poets in general. Similarly, anthologies and research have brought together Latinos and other poets on the basis of broad multicultural considerations. Some Latino poets also write for a young adult or children's audience. Other configurations have incorporated Latino poetry into American diaspora literature, Jewish letters, border writing, or gay and lesbian literature. Perhaps the most sweeping trend is the approach championed by the research activities of the Recovering the U.S. Hispanic Literary Heritage project: the inclusion of all Hispanic literature written in the United States, of all periods and in Spanish as well as in English. The project's anthology, *Herencia: The Anthology of Hispanic Literature of the United States* (2002), edited by Nicolás Kanellos, reflects this objective. In fact, in this body of literature, Latino literature written in English is incorporated within the broader parameters of U.S. Hispanic literature.

BIBLIOGRAPHY

Aragón, Francisco, ed. *The Wind Shifts: New Latino Poetry*. Tucson: University of Arizona Press, 2007. A collection of poems by twenty-five Latino and Latina writers, none of whom had published more than one book when their work was selected for publication in the collection. The settings of these poems and their themes are as diverse as the forms in which they are cast, which range from traditional to avant-garde. The editor's introduction is helpful in providing a context for the poems.

Cruz, Victor Hernández, Leroy V. Quintana, and Virgil Suarez, eds. *Paper Dance: Fifty-five Latino Poets*. New York: Persea, 1995. Notable for the inclusion of bicultural poets from numerous backgrounds, primarily Chicano and Mexican, Dominican, Cuban, and Puerto Rican, but also Colombian, Ecuadorian, and Guatemalan.

Dick, Bruce Allen, ed. *A Poet's Truth: Conversations with Latino/Latina Poets*. Tucson: University of Arizona Press, 2003. Fifteen poets, among them Chicanos, Puerto Ricans, and Cubans, discuss their craft and comment on social and political issues that affect Latino communities. These interviews provide biographical details as well as revealing insights into the differences between the three major groups.

González, Ray, ed. *Touching the Fire: Fifteen Poets of Today's Latino Renaissance*. New York: Anchor Books/Doubleday, 1998. Contains ten poems by each of the fifteen poets included, who range from well-established writers such as Judith Ortiz Cofer and Victor Hernández Cruz to new and emerging poets. Excellent introduction by González.

Hernández, Carmen D., ed. *Puerto Rican Voices in English: Interviews with Writers*. Westport, Conn.: Praeger, 1997. Puerto Rican writers discuss their lives and their works. General introduction, as well as specific information about each interviewee.

Kanellos, Nicolás, ed. *Herencia: The Anthology of Hispanic Literature of the United States*. New York: Oxford University Press, 2002. This multigenre anthology, which begins with the Spanish American colonial period, has an indispensable introduction and biobibliographical synopses of each of the more than 150 authors. Reflects the status of the Recovering the U.S. Hispanic Literary Heritage project at the time of its publication and of Kanellos's own contributions to the field.

Lomelí, Francisco, ed. *Handbook of Hispanic Cultures in the United States: Literature and Art.* Houston: Arte Público Press, 1993. An essential source with discrete essays (and extensive bibliographies) by experts on Puerto Rican, Cuban American, and Chicano literature; Hispanic aesthetic concepts; Latina writers; literary language; and Hispanic exile in the United States. The first of a four-volume set; the other three cover history, sociology, and anthropology.

Milligan, Bryce, Mary Guerrero Milligan, and Angela de Hoyos, eds. *Floricanto Sí! A Collection of Latina Poetry.* New York: Penguin Books, 1998. Brings together forty-seven both established and previously unknown or emerging Latina poets, including a few who write primarily in Spanish. These San Antonio-based writer-publishers had featured some twenty-five of the same writers in a previous compilation, *Daughters of the Fifth Sun: A Collection of Latina Fiction and Poetry* (1995). The insightful introductions to both collections elucidate aesthetic, thematic, critical, and bibliographic issues of Latina poetry and poetics in the 1990's.

Poey, Delia, and Virgil Suárez, eds. *Little Havana Blues: A Cuban-American Literature Anthology.* Houston: Arte Público Press, 1996. Features sixteen poets (mainly second-generation Cuban Americans) writing principally in English and from within the boundaries of American literature, as distinct from their literary forebears. A brief but informative introduction to the multigenre anthology outlines historical, chronological, aesthetic, and thematic considerations.

Quintana, Alvina E. *Reading U.S. Latina Writers: Remapping American Literature.* New York: Palgrave Macmillan, 2005. Essays on major genres, movements, and writers, as well as on important historical events and critical issues, in a book whose purpose is to arouse new interest in Latina writers and ultimately to expand the canon of American literature. Bibliographical references.

Sandin, Lyn Di Iorio, ed. *Contemporary U.S. Latino/a Literary Criticism.* New York: Palgrave Macmillan, 2007. A collection of scholarly essays that demonstrate how critical methods can be applied to Cuban American, Dominican American, Mexican American, and Puerto Rican writers. It is significant that these essays avoid the usual narrow issues but focus instead on the insights offered by Latino/a writers about living in a complex and ever-changing world.

Catharine E. Wall (including original translations)